THE

BOOK OF THE HORSE
Classic Edition.

MAMBRINO. BRED BY LORD GROSVENOR. FROM THE PICTURE BY GEORGE STUBBS.

IN THE POSSESSION OF THE MARQUIS OF WESTMINSTER, AT EATON HALL.

THE

BOOK OF THE HORSE

Classic Edition.

BY

SAMUEL SIDNEY,

With a Section on Veterinary Information by

GEORGE FLEMING LL.D., F.R.C.V.S.

WITH A NEW FOREWORD BY
HERM DAVID.

ILLUSTRATED WITH FULL-PAGE PLATES AND NUMEROUS WOOD ENGRAVINGS.

BONANZA BOOKS
NEW YORK

Originally published in the 1880s as *The Book of the Horse: (Thoroughbred, Half-bred, Cart-bred), Saddle and Harness, British and Foreign.*

Copyright © 1985 by Crown Publishers, Inc.
All rights reserved.

Published 1985 by Bonanza Books, distributed by Crown Publishers, Inc., One Park Avenue, New York, New York 10016.

Printed and bound in the United States of America

Library of Congress Cataloging in Publication Data

Sidney, Samuel, 1813–1833.
The book of the horse.

"Originally published in the 1880s as The book of the horse: (thoroughbred, half-bred, cart-bred), saddle and harness, British and foreign" — T.p.verso.
Includes index.
1. Horses.   2. Horsemanship.   I. Fleming, George, 1833–1901.   II. Title.
SF285.S48   1985   636.1   85-10930

ISBN: 0-517-480085

h g f e d c b a

CAUTIONARY NOTICE

This book was originally published in the 1880s, and offers extensive suggestions for the handling and care of horses commonly accepted at that time. Although there is value and interest in the long, vivid descriptions, the veterinarian advice in the book can not be substituted for modern methods of veterinary medicine.

Furthermore, as it pertains to human medical needs —as in the case of tetanus and other diseases—the information is thoroughly outdated and potentially harmful. The reader should consult his or her physician or other modern medical authorities.

CONTENTS.

VETERINARY INFORMATION.

LIST OF ILLUSTRATIONS.

LIST OF PLATES.*

—◆—

*The plates appeared in color in the original edition, but here have been converted to black and white. Three plates that appeared in the original have been deleted from this edition: A Dongola Horse, A Pupil of La Haute Ecole, and Captain Percy Williams on a Favorite Irish Hunter.

FOREWORD

A TRIUMPH of the art of publishing when it appeared in the 1880's, *The Book of the Horse* is now considered a classic. This rare and valuable work is sought and consulted for the range, quality, and quantity of its woodcut illustrations, and for the integrity and scope of its text. Until now, only a few could enjoy and refer to this treasure from yesteryear which fully describes a multitude of breeds, gives the origin and history of the English horse, and thoroughly covers horsemanship, equipage, hunting, training, breeding, and care of the horse.

In the 110 years since its initial publication, generations of owners and print dealers have extracted the beautiful and instructive illustrations from this book for framing. Intact copies thus have become quite rare. Fortunately, what print collectors have torn asunder Bonanza Books has restored in this volume. Virtually every feature and word of the utimate third edition, including its illustrated and decorated binding, has been faithfully reproduced for the current generation of horse enthusiasts.

For a space-walking, electronic generation there is fascination in the contemplation of life styles that existed when *The Book of the Horse* was first published. It was a world dependent upon horses for its work, its wars, its pleasures, and much of its pride of ownership. Engines had just begun to replace horses. Coaching was still a sport, and a necessity between all the towns and villages not yet served by railroads. Only the most prosperous could afford steam power to turn their machinery: in the more remote parts of Great Britain, horses still spent their days walking toward infinity, on treadmills or in circles. Muscles far more powerful than his own were man's entree into today's world.

Genetics is a still developing, twentieth century science. In the 1880s and earlier, most of our breed of domestic animals were created by people who were seeking practical solutions to their needs. Their only tools were keen observation, experience, and intuition. Isolation was both a help and a handicap. Regional variations were developed, and later blended to the benefit of each breed. There were no horse trailers or vans, and certainly no flying stables or stored semen. With two exceptions, it was not realistic to attempt transporting animals across great distances for breeding purposes. Breeding animals, horses especially, were frequent prizes of war; those displaying attributes sought at home were treasured. And potentates of every civilization have always favored animals as gifts between themselves, and to honored travelers.

Whether landed nobleman or tenant farmer, tradesman, cavalryman, merchant, or hack driver, the nineteenth century man was expected to be horse-knowledgeable. His peers appraised both has acumen and his social status by the quality of his horse or horses.

The wealthiest man in town was expected to drive to church behind the finest of matched harness horses. The very richest had the finest stables and the most notable packs of Foxhounds. Winning Thoroughbreds were the ultimate material status symbol. Farmers proudly displayed their horses and other livestock at county fairs.

Women who could afford the leisure to do so learned to ride and to speak the language of horsemen. Those deficient in such attainments frequently found themselves left behind in sport and on journeys, and on the outer fringe of male conversations. The long skirts and voluminous costumes dictated that a woman ride on specially designed side saddles; consequently, a female rider had to be twice the rider a man was.

The decade from 1875 to 1884 was perfect for a horse book of towering magnitude. Publishing had reached the stage when steam-powered presses offered much improved reproductive quality, before the advent of photographic reproduction. Woodcut artists, soon to be made technologically obsolete by photo engraving, were at their zenith. The publishers of *The Book of the Horse* found, in Samuel Sidney (1813–1883), the ideal person to bring their project into being. He was more than the author-researcher-editor. He was the man who, over a period of years, had brought the finest and most knowledgeable of the horesmen of Great Britain and Europe together. Sidney, when he managed it, put new excitement into the prestigious Agricultural Hall Horse Show at Islington. He knew everyone, and he knew who was most authoritative on each facet of equine activity. In his brief autobiographical notes, on page five, Sidney credits "my circle of acquaintances" for "their assistance and advice in making this at once a handbook and an encyclopedia of reference for horse-owners of every degree."

Publication of the first two editions of *The Book of the Horse* was so major an undertaking that subscribers bought it for distribution in serial form, unbound, over periods of two years each. The third edition has been chosen for republication because it was the last from Sidney, who died before it went to press. At that time his publishers stated there was no need to attempt enhancement of Sidney's thorough revision. However, they did engage an outstanding veterinarian of the day, Dr. George Fleming, principal Veterinary Surgeon to the British Army, to enlarge and update the veterinary information, and excellent anatomical plates were added.

Two aspects of this book require some words of explanation.

First, modern readers will note that the Introduction claims British superiority in horse breeding (implying Irish superiority as well), but, although the Bristish achievements in this area were admirable, those statements reflects a degree of ethnocentrism. The book, however, remains a valid source; not only does it include horses from around the world, but also the British influence in the late nineteenth century was enormous—their flags flew all over the world, and they took their horses with them, influencing breeding patterns thereafter, wherever they went.

Secondly, readers may question why, in some of the plates, prepared after the style of several of the finest British sporting artists, the horses frequently appear a bit grotesque. We must attribute this to a misguided connoisseurs' delight. Sometime in the seventeenth century it became a fetish to breed for horses with small heads. It is likely that in class-conscious England, no true gentleman or would-be gentleman wished to be suspected of using his work horse for his pleasure excursions. Nor did he wish to be accused of attempting, out of necessity, to breed up from stock tainted by work. When a painting of a horse was commissioned, the artist knew he was expected to exaggerate the subject's quality by painting the head small, and he did not get paid until he had it small enough to satisfy his client. One celebrated artist commented that it was far easier to persuade a man to part with fifty guineas for a painting of his favorite mount than for a portrait of his wife.

The days of dependency on horses are gone for most peoples of the world. But breeding, selecting, training, riding, and driving, even grooming them continues to fascinate many. This is a book for all who find enjoyment in the innumerable facets—from the greatest to the minutia—of horse lore, care and love.

HERM DAVID

San Diego, 1985.

A COUNTRY RIDE.

THE BOOK OF THE HORSE.

INTRODUCTORY.

ENGLAND—in which geographical expression Ireland, Wales, and Scotland are, also, of course, included—is the breeding-ground, the original home, of the best horses in the world. Englishmen invented, if one may be permitted to use so mechanical a term, the thorough-bred horse, which combines with marvellously increased size, speed, and power, all the fire, courage, and quality of his Oriental ancestors—the Barb and the Arab. The English thorough-bred is universally recognised as the sole source of improvement for every variety of the horse tribe in Europe and America, save those used in the dull useful labour of heavy draught; and even the British draught-horse has been brought to perfection by the application of principles which were first employed, although recently neglected, in the breeding of the incomparable race-horse.

At the present moment there is in Continental Europe scarcely a State in which the character of the riding and light harness horse has not been materially ameliorated by crosses of English blood. The importations by private breeders and by the governing managers of Royal and National studs, which commenced soon after the close of the great war in 1815, have been carried on ever since with annually increasing care and vigour. The first experiments with English blood-sires were made, towards the middle of the eighteenth century, in those ancient breeding-grounds of mediæval war-horses, Mecklenburg and Hanover. In the long peace which followed Waterloo, the merits of the thorough-bred sire conquered the prejudices of nations inclined to detest everything English; and now in the State studs of France, of the several kingdoms and principalities which form the northern portion of the German Empire, in the German dominions of the Austrian Kaiser, as well as in his horse-loving kingdom of Hungary, in the newly-formed Royalty of united Italy, and under the Czar of all the Russias, the English blood-horse holds the first place. It may safely be assumed that at the great Continental reviews—where emperors and kings, reigning dukes and famous military commanders, appear on horse-back surrounded by their brilliant staffs—nine-tenths of the chargers ridden by the more distinguished personages have been bred in England, or are the immediate produce of English sires.

All the best horses in the United States are directly descended from English thorough-breds, with a slight intermixture of Barbs or Arabs. Experts belonging to the great Anglo-Saxon republic trace back the pedigrees of their best trotters—the speciality of American horse-breeding—to Messenger, an imported blood sire, the son of grey Mambrino, who was bred by Lord Grosvenor, and painted by the celebrated George Stubbs, about 1774.*

It has been reserved for our colonists in South Africa and Australia to prove that the English blood-horse, unpampered, and trained for the purpose, while far exceeding the Arab in size and general utility, can equal him in endurance and the power of completing great distances in journeys extending over many successive days.

"The reason why" of the extraordinary success of the English as breeders, as originators, almost manufacturers, of a new tribe of blood-horses, is to be found not only in a favourable soil and climate, but in the general partiality of the English people for a country life, and their universal passion for everything connected with horses.

In no other civilised country are so many men, women, and children, in proportion to its population, to be found fond of riding and driving. Our equestrians are not confined to a privileged class, a military caste, or a select few of the upper ten thousand votaries of fashion; riding and driving are essentially English national amusements. In making this wide assertion no comparison is intended to be made with the nomadic inhabitants of countries where a horse is as much a necessary of life as a pair of stilts in the French Landes or a pair of snow-shoes for winter use in the Canadian backwoods ; nor, again, with the inhabitants of the great cattle-feeding plains of South America—where the men are true Centaurs, and where a mere child may be seen mounted, driving cattle, carrying an infant before him on the pommel of the saddle as he gallops over the smooth, stoneless pampas—nor, lastly, with the semi-oriental families of herdsmen on the rolling pastures of Poland and Hungary, the nurseries of the world-famous Polish lancers and Hungarian hussars.

Still less is it my intention to assume that first-class horsemen or first-class coachmen are only to be found in England. That was the vulgar error of a departed generation, which rarely travelled, and knew no language but its own, with which every foreigner was a Frenchman, and which took its idea of a Johnny Crapaud from the caricatures of Gilray and Rowlandson.

In the Crimea our men learned to respect the Chasseurs d'Afrique, who charged the Russian batteries at Balaclava to save their English allies. The deeds of the German cavalry are still green in our memories. For my own part, I have seen Russians and Austrians, Hanoverians and Hungarians, ride across a stiff summer-baked country in a style and with a determination that would not have disgraced the best of our own officers at the Windsor or Rugby military steeple-chases. And it must be remembered that these gentlemen have not, as we have in our hunting-fields, a training ground perpetually open to them from their earliest years.

---

* A portrait of Mambrino, from Stubbs' painting in the possession of the Duke of Westminster, by his Grace's permission. is one of the illustrations of this work.

Again, English coachmen are very good at their business—neat, firm, quick, impassive, undemonstrative, and decided—quite characteristic of their nation. But the essence of good coachmanship is to drive with safety and dispatch over difficult country. Russians, Austrians, Hungarians, and North Germans can boast of a wonderful class of Jehus in their own style; while on the other side of the Atlantic, the drivers of tandems and six-horse teams, over half-made roads in California, have astonished our best whips by their daring and their pace.

It is the universality of the passion for horses and horse exercise in every form that is so remarkable a feature in English social life, and in such strong contrast to Continental usages, where the horse, if not earning money or employed for military purposes, is considered rather as a fashionable ornament, an opportunity of displaying wealth, than as an instrument for obtaining healthful exercise.

Even M. Taine, in his "Essays on England," the best and fairest that ever have been written by any foreigner, who thoroughly admires our horse-loving taste, and attributes to it all sorts of virtues we never claimed for it, such as the vigorous character of our idle classes, the chastity of our rich and handsome wives—even he cannot understand how a stout, middle-aged materfamilias can exhibit herself in the unbecoming costume of an Amazone; for he cannot help looking on horse exercise as a dramatic performance, reserved for strong men and elegant women. "Vers deux heures la grande allée est un manége; il y a dix fois plus d'hommes à cheval et vingt fois plus d'amazones qu'au Bois de Boulogne dans les grands jours; de toutes petites filles, des garçons de huit ans sont à côté de leurs pères, sur leurs ponies; j'ai vu trotter des matrones larges et dignes. C'est là un de leurs luxes; par exemple, dans une famille de trois personnes à qui je viens de faire visite il y a trois chevaux. La mère et la fille viennent tous les jours galoper au parc, souvent même elles font leurs visites à cheval; elles économisent sur d'autres points, sur le théâtre, par exemple. Ce grand mouvement paraît indispensable à la santé. Les jeunes filles, les dames viennent ici même par la pluie."*

The essential difference between foreign and English notions of family horsemanship will be found in a comparison of the group engaged in an afternoon canter that heads this introductory matter, and the picture of a French gentleman out for a country ride, copied from a standard French book by Count de Lastic St. Jal, a superior officer of the late Imperial *haras* or breeding-studs.

The first idea of a successful Englishman is either to mount on horseback, to give his wife a carriage, or to do both. It is not only the young, the strong, the members of noble families and ornaments of fashionable society, the officers of cavalry regiments, or the sons of millionaires, financiers, and bankers, who are to be found in the Row. There you may see aged judges and solemn bishops, with their daughters; bankers on priceless cobs, successful engineers, hard-worked Queen's Counsel, topping tradesmen, dashing stock-jobbers, corn merchants from Mark Lane, indigo brokers from Mincing Lane, and representatives of every class that can afford an hour's leisure and the ownership of at least one horse. In the

---

* "About two o'clock the broad ride is like a school of horsemanship. There are ten times as many men, and twenty times as many women, on horseback, as in the Bois de Boulogne on great days; very little girls, boys not more than eight years old, ride their ponies alongside their fathers; and I have even seen stout, imposing matrons trotting along. Riding is one of the luxuries of the English: for instance, a family of my acquaintance, consisting of a father, mother, and daughter, keep three horses. The mother and daughter ride in the park daily, and often make visits on horseback. To afford this expense they economise on other amusements, such as the theatre. This active exercise seems essential to their health. Even in rainy weather you may meet both young and married ladies riding in the park."

early morning children, professional men, and government officials, at mid-day ladies, form the majority of the civilian cavalry. In a word, horses for one use or another, quite apart from fashion, form an important part of the life of every well-to-do English family, and are often considered essential as the means of obtaining health and exercise, or superintending a rapidly-extending business by those who are by no means rich.

The *nouveau riche* wishes to have his stud and appointments perfect and complete; to a man of narrow means it is an object to maintain his stable and coach-house at the least possible expense. Both need ample, plain, practical advice and information. It is for these—an annually increasing number of my countrymen and countrywomen, who wish to ride or to drive, or to be driven—that this work, long in preparation, has been written, with

A FRENCH MASTER OF THE HORSE. (FROM COUNT DE LASTIC ST. JAL'S WORK.)

the assistance of very famous performers in the field and on the road—horsemen, coachmen, and breeders of the best class of horses—to whom every description of horse life is as "familiar in their mouths as household words."

With this end in view I have endeavoured to begin at the beginning, to take nothing for granted, but teach the A B C of every subject within my programme.

I shall have something—though not very much—to say to the fortunate ones who had the stable-door and the school-room door opened to them at the same moment; who have grown from infancy to boyhood, and from boyhood to manhood, with the choice of riding-horses of every degree of size and training, from the family pony to the thorough-bred hunter or park hack, with the services and instruction of grey-headed huntsmen, or Yorkshire-bred stud-grooms; who commenced their studies of the mysteries of the whip and rein under some veteran family coachman, and who have graduated in all the stages of driving lore, advancing from the pony-cart to the mail-phaeton and tandem, or even culminating in the lately revived glories of the four-horse drag. But I write more especially for the information of a different and more numerous class, those to whom town pursuits have brought fortune, with leisure and desire to enjoy, and allow their families to enjoy, the pleasures, the exercise, the healthy excitement, which horses and carriages, riding, driving, and hunting, so eminently afford.

It is quite true that no book can without practice teach the reader how to ride or drive, how to choose or breed horses, how they should be fed, trained, and treated in the stable, or how to buy carriages, saddlery, or harness. Practical arts can only be learned by practical experience. Nevertheless, books on fishing, poultry, gardening, and cookery, which record the collected experience of many fishermen, poultry-keepers, gardeners, and cooks—if the writers understand their subjects, and take the trouble to give minute details—are found to be of great value to ladies and gentlemen who desire to be not entirely dependent on their own tradesmen and servants; and who prefer, where they can, to master a principle instead of accepting a rule of thumb.

I have devoted the greater part of my work to the severely practical. The reader will in the following pages be treated as if he or she had everything to learn.*

* With respect to the qualifications I possess for my self-imposed task of collecting into one work information on those practical subjects connected with horse management, now only to be found, if found at all, in many volumes, I must say something, even at the risk of appearing somewhat egotistical.

From my childhood I have been passionately fond of horses, and can scarcely remember when I could not ride. In 1846 I wrote "Railways and Agriculture," at the suggestion of the late Earl of Yarborough, which he presented to his friends at the York Meeting, the year he was President of the Royal Agricultural Society, in which my first hunting sketches (of the Brocklesby Hounds and the scarlet-coated Wold farmers) appeared. In consequence of these sketches I became the hunting correspondent of the *Illustrated London News.* By Lord Yarborough I was introduced to my ever afterwards kind friend the late Captain Percy Williams, the Master, for nineteen years, of the famous Rufford Hounds.

In 1850, being one of Her Majesty's Assistant Commissioners for the great International Exhibition, I was able, by the kindness of divers county gentlemen, farmers, and horse-dealers—desirous of paying a compliment to my official position, helped also by introduction from Brocklesby Park and Rufford Kennels—to hunt my way from Bramham Moor, in Yorkshire, to the Four Boroughs, in Cornwall, and saw more or less sport with twelve celebrated packs of foxhounds, besides harriers.

In 1858, at the special request of Messrs. Richard and Edmund Tattersall, I became Treasurer and Secretary to the Rarey Horse-Taming Subscription, and edited the illustrated edition of "Rarey's Art of Horse-Taming," which has long been out of print.

In 1860 I assisted in establishing the Agricultural Hall Company at Islington.

In 1864, with the permission of my directors, I arranged and managed the horse show at the Agricultural Hall, Islington, on a plan which has since been followed by the managers of the Dublin, Birmingham, and other horse shows of minor importance—that is to say, the horses, instead of being simply led round the ring for exhibition in bridles or halters, as at the shows of the Royal Agricultural Society up to that date, were ridden, driven in harness, and leaped. The experience of fifteen years has proved that this system gives satisfaction to exhibitors and intending purchasers, as well as to the public.

It is scarcely necessary to state that my position as the Secretary and Manager of the Agricultural Hall Horse Show has largely increased my circle of acquaintances of all ranks interested as breeders, owners, and judges of horses. I have not failed to avail myself of the information within my reach. Several judges and exhibitors of high reputation as masters of hounds and as breeders of horses have kindly afforded me their assistance and advice in making this at once a handbook and an encyclopædia of reference for horse-owners of every degree.

CHAPTER I

ORIENTAL BLOOD-HORSES: ARABS, BARBS, PERSIANS, DONGOLAS, TURCOMANS.

Meaning of "Quality" and "Thorough-bred"—The Reality of Equine Aristocracy—Advantages of a Cross of Blood—The English Blood-horse a modern Creation—Assyrian Bas-reliefs represent the Blood-horse—Arabs of Reality and of Poetry—Sidonia's Arab—The Poet Rogers—George Borrow—Turkish Horses Imported after Crimean War—Captain Morant's Little Turkish Hunter—Turkish Arabs of the Last Century—Omar Pacha's Arab in Northamptonshire of no value as a Sire—Parker Gillmore's Description of Barbs—The Shah's Persian Horses—The "Flying Childe's" Grey Arabian Hunter—Purchases during Crimean War—Anazeh Tribe—Anazeh Stallion—Turcoman Horses—Bedouin Horse-dealing—Wahabee Horses, Pure Nejed Breed, Giffard Palgrave's Description of—Pasha Baker's Turcoman Horse—Cossacks—Arabs bred in Galicia—The Dongola Horse, Bruce's Travels—Mr. Knight's Experiment on Exmoor with Dongolas—Objections to Arabs by a Breeder—Spanish and Arab Crosses—Account of Two Choice Arabs; bad Hacks, no Hunters, no Racers—The Cross of English Blood horses with Spanish Mares—Result of Cross of Spanish Mares with a Son of Sheet-Anchor—Continental Arab Studs.

IN the following pages the terms "thorough-bred" and "quality" will frequently be used. It may be as well to explain their meaning, for the benefit of readers who are not familiar with the early history of the horse.

"Thorough-bred" means that a horse's pedigree can be traced for generations from sires and mares of English pure blood, or from Barbs, Arabs, or Persians, recorded in the English "Stud Book."

The blood-horse, whether English or Oriental, is the natural aristocrat of the equine race He possesses physical qualities in bone, in muscle, and in skin, which no mode of selection, no advantage of soil and climate, have produced out of cart-horse breeds within historical times. Climate and soil may raise or reduce the size of a tribe of horses, accident may create and perpetuate singularities of colour or form; but the signs of blood can only be produced by the prepotent power of crosses of blood-horses or mares; for all practical purposes the interesting speculations of naturalists on the origin of the horse are useless, their conclusions are in defiance of all historical evidence.

Aristocrat, in all the countries of Continental Europe where pedigrees are preserved and valued, is expressed by a term implying well-born, such as the blue blood (*sangre azul*) of Spain, *gnadiger* of Germany, *noble* of France under her kings.

In England, where more than in any other country attention has been paid to the pedigrees of horses, of hounds, of cattle, of sheep, of pigs, and for many years past even of the best strains of poultry and pigeons, the pedigrees of the human aristocracy have, curiously enough, never been treated as of pre-eminent importance. This is proved by the fact that our language has no synonym for the word *mésalliance*, which in French means the alliance of a noble with peasant or shop-keeping, or even legal blood. Before the great French Revolution, memoir writers distinguished between recent creations as "Nobility of the Sword" or "Nobility of the Robe"*

* The friends of Alexis de Tocqueville considered that he had degraded his family by becoming a barrister—"A man cf the robe! Your ancestors have always been men of the sword."—*Nassau Senior's Recollections.*

—that is of the law—a distinction utterly unknown in England, where military, naval, and legal eminence and fortunate marriages, have created our greatest houses. As a matter of fact, the aristocracy of men is much more a matter of education, and position, maintained through two or three generations, than of pedigree. It would be impossible in a mixed assembly of well-to-do Englishmen and Englishwomen, for instance, at a Buckingham Palace ball or an Oxford convocation, to pick out the representatives of the most ancient families by their personal appearance, or to distinguish them from others who had enjoyed for only one generation the advantages of education, freedom from petty cares, and good society. Indeed, it has been argued, with a considerable show of reason, that our aristocracy includes so many beautiful women and handsome manly men, because our nobility have been in the habit of selecting their wives without regard to pedigree.

With horses it is quite different. It will take many generations to get rid of one cart-horse

HUNTING THE LION. (FROM AN ASSYRIAN SCULPTURE.)

cross; the stain will suddenly reappear after many years, in the most unexpected manner. The produce of a sire and mare, both apparently of the purest blood, will show some sign of a remote ignoble alliance, in a vulgar head, coarse mane and tail, or shaggy fetlocks.

"Quality" means evidence of blood, in the form and expression of the head, the symmetry of the limbs, and the velvet-like softness of the skin.

The advantages of a large admixture of blood are not merely picturesque. Blood implies superior wind, energy, endurance, and muscular power, bones of more ivory-like texture, and tougher tendons and sinews. Our English blood-horse is, in the historical sense, a modern creation, not two hundred years old. His ancestors came from Africa and Asia. The most ancient historical blood-horses were Egyptian. The Assyrian bas-reliefs preserved in the British Museum, and copied in Layard's great work, present faithful delineations of the Oriental blood-horse, harnessed to chariots, in war and in the chase, and carrying spear-bearing horsemen on their conquests some thousands of years ago. Egyptian bas-reliefs still more ancient than the Assyrian are in existence; but in them the horse is depicted in a conventional manner, and not with the life-like fidelity which distinguishes the work of the Assyrian sculptors. Still, they are sufficiently accurate to show that the Egyptian was a blood-horse. An ancient Persian monument shows a cart-horse very distinctly.

For all ordinary purposes, the English thorough-bred is more useful in this country than his progenitors, Barbs and Arabs, and as a rule less expensive ; that is to say, an English thorough-bred horse or mare, under 15 hands high, equal to carrying eleven or twelve stone as a hack, may be purchased for less money than an Arab of the same strength and quality in India, Egypt, or Persia.

The Arabs of reality, as distinguished from the Arabs of poetry and romance, although very picturesque, admirable for their fire and endurance, and perfect as the war-horses of single combat, do not by any means realise the descriptions of famous novelists. No Arab has ever won a steeplechase in this country like that over the vale of Aylesbury, so picturesquely described by the author of *Coningsby* (who had travelled in Arab lands) ;* and only one thorough-bred Arab hunter, of which an authentic account will presently be given, has made "a notch" in the annals of Leicestershire. Certainly one would be very much astonished to hear of any county gentleman, like the hero of a popular lady novelist, who rode his "black Arab" over park palings, with a little girl on the pommel before him, for no other reason than to find a short cut home.

Samuel Rogers, banker and poet, would not allow that Job's description of the horse was poetry at all. He could not understand—

"Hast thou given the horse strength ? hast thou clothed his neck with thunder ? . . . The glory of his nostrils is terrible. He paweth in the valley, and rejoiceth in his strength : he goeth on to meet the armed men. He mocketh at fear, and is not affrighted ; neither turneth he back from the sword. The quiver rattleth against him, the glittering spear and the shield. He swalloweth the ground with fierceness and rage. . . . He saith among the trumpets, Ha, ha !"

But Samuel Rogers was no horseman. That he did not care to talk about horses is proved by his own story of the groom who gave him notice to quit "because he was such dull company in the tilbury."

"Who," says George Borrow—the inspirer of esteem in the Spanish gipsies by his horsemanship—"that has ever seen a blood stallion excited by the din of a fair or a battle, and heard him so distinctly neigh, 'Ha, ha !' can doubt that the author of Job painted an Oriental war-horse from life ?"

The popular notions of the Arab, amongst those that know nothing about horses, are chiefly derived from the poetical descriptions of the Arabs themselves, who, full of Oriental exaggeration, describe the animal exactly fitted for their purposes (single combat and parade) and from pictures. One of the most popular, which has been repeated a hundred times, in

---

* "'I long to see your mare again ; she seemed to me so beautiful,' said Coningsby.

"'She is not only of pure race, but of the highest and rarest breed in Arabia. Her name is "The Daughter of the Star.' She is a foal of the famous mare which belonged to the Prince of the Wahabees, to possess which was one of the principal causes of war between that tribe and the Pacha of Egypt, who gave her to me.'"

She is then described with "legs like an antelope and little ears," points which no British horseman would approve. In the steeplechase that followed there were fifteen starters ; in the first two miles several remarkably stiff fences. "They arrived at the brook—seventeen feet of water, between high strong banks." A masked battery of grape could not have achieved more terrible execution. A high and strong gate came next; the distance was above four miles. There were thirty leaps done under fifteen minutes ; and the Daughter of the Star won "pulling double." After reading this performance an old steeplechaser observed "that the field must have been very bad to be settled by seventeen feet of water, with sound banks ;" but his reading had been confined to the *Racing and Steeplechase Calendar.*

cheap forms, since it was first engraved in 1810 for Lawrence's "History of the Horse," is the beautiful grey stallion, called "The Wellesley Arabian," painted by Marshall—a horse which according to the high authority of the author and editor of the "Stud Book" was not an Arab at all, but some Persian cross, and "very like an English hunter."

After the Crimean war a great many Oriental horses, or rather ponies, were brought home by our officers. These Turkish ponies had endurance and fair pace—they would canter all day. Captain Morant, Master of the New Forest Hounds, had, in 1865, a little chestnut Turk, that had won him several races in the Crimea, and proved a very good hunter in the New Forest country; but a celebrated breeder of ponies, to whom I offered him as a stallion, would have nothing to say to him, because he was deficient in the points most needed in a sire of hacks. The majority of the Crimean ponies were very bad hacks, and seldom fetched more than £30 at the hammer; there is, however, reason to believe that the Turkish horses imported into this country between 1616 and 1700 were animals of a very superior class. During that time the Padishah was the acknowledged Sultan of the Mahomedans in Africa and Arabia; he twice besieged Vienna—the second time in 1686—and received, as "Protector of the Faith," tribute in horses of the choicest breeds, from the deserts of Arabia, where the Wahabees still and for a long time past, have defied the power of the Europeanised Sultan.

One of the most celebrated of the Crimean importations was Omar Pacha, a bay horse, belonging to the Turkish general of that name. This horse was said to have been ridden by the messenger that brought the news of the repulse of the Russians from Silistria to Varna, a distance of ninety miles, without drawing rein. The messenger died, but the horse was none the worse for the journey. He was presented by Omar Pacha to General Sir Richard Airey, who sold him to Earl Spencer. After standing some time at Althorpe as a stallion, he was given by his lordship to Mr. J. Noble Beasley, of Pitsford House, who is a breeder of the best class of hunters. He writes that "many Indian officers on seeing Omar Pacha (he stood over 15 hands high) declared that he was not an Arab at all, but a 'Waler' (an Australian horse). He had very superior action, was strong for his size, heavy in his crest, with fine shoulders, and good fore-legs. His stock are sound and enduring, but have never proved valuable as either hunters, hacks, or harness-horses."

The story of Omar Pacha's ride from Silistria to Varna may be quite true; it is a feat that has been equalled and exceeded by many English blood-horses.

The Barb, which has had more to do with our English thorough-bred than the Arab, although not so handsome, being frequently goose-rumped, is often a very good hack. The best I ever saw of this sort were two bay horses, a little under 15 hands, which the Duke of Beaufort imported after his visit to Gibraltar. He ran them at Goodwood, and they were nowhere; they then became the favourite hacks of the duchess. Her Grace exhibited them at the Agricultural Hall in 1864. They were so like English thorough-breds that only a judge of horses would have marked them as foreign bred.

Captain Parker Gillmore, writing in *Land and Water* under the name of "Ubique," traces the merit of the American trotters to Barb blood. He says: "During an experience in the East that extended over three years, where I saw every variety of Arab, from the pure bred Nejed to the Persian, I never knew one that was a good trotter, or gifted with knee-action. Their paces are principally walking, galloping, and cantering; their movements being too close to the ground to excel in the trot.

"The districts where the high-caste Arab is reared is undulating, sandy, and sparsely covered with vegetation; there the colt and mare can without danger lay well down to gallop.

"But Barbary is rough, rocky, and mountainous, intersected with ravines, and in many portions thickly covered with shrubs. On such ground it would be impossible for a horse to gallop with safety; at any great pace he would be sure to come to grief. To avoid this, he trots, keeping his legs well under him, able to turn on one side or the other with great facility. The nature of the ground causes him to raise his feet high at each step. Thus the different action of horses of Barbary and Arabia may be accounted for, assuming that they have a common origin."

In a review of the French army by the late Emperor of the French, at Boulogne-sur-Mer, soon after he assumed the imperial crown, the field officers of infantry regiments which had

BELOOCH CHIEF MOUNTED.

recently served in Africa were most of them mounted on Barb ponies, many of them not more than 13 hands high, with nothing to attract admiration except their astonishing manes and tails, some of which actually swept the ground. I found in M. Fould and other French gentlemen engaged in breeding-race-horses quite as great a dislike to the Arab cross as prevails amongst the English.

The Shah of Persia, when visiting England, brought with him two Persian horses, which, by the kindness of Colonel Maude, the Crown Equerry, I had an opportunity of closely examining.

The Shah's favourite riding horse was a dark chestnut stallion, about 14 hands high, on short legs, well crested, very powerful, and with the peculiar picturesque style of tail of the Arab, but in other respects not to be distinguished from an English thorough-bred; his head, although very blood-like, not having the Arab character—the wide flat forehead and comparatively small muzzle. The other, which was "The Shah's war-horse," was a stallion, about 15 hands 1 inch high, grey, or rather with a white body and flea-bitten neck, and a head of the true Arabian character, powerful limbs, showing work about the hocks, and a flag magnificently carried. The chestnut might have been a valuable sire for breeding ponies ; neither had good action, or any action at all according to our sense of the term. They were supposed to be each worth £1,000, or nearly four times the value of a blood English hack of the same quality and superior action.

Major Thomas Francis, who was formerly at the head of the Remount Department at Bombay, writes in reference to the very common-looking (Arab ?) animal which is engraved on the previous page, from an original picture in my possession by Zeitter, a German artist,

ARABIAN MARE AND FOAL.

who lived some time in British India : "The horse in your picture (of a Belooch chief) is a Persian with a lot of good Arab blood in him. The Persian is the best animal to be purchased in Bombay as a hack and carriage-horse. The Government used to buy as many as they could get, at 550 rupees each (£55), at Bombay, to mount the dragoons and artillery. They are from 14 hands 2 inches to 15 hands 2 inches high, and better roadsters and chargers, and stronger, than the ordinary run of Arabs. The best bred Arabs seldom exceed 14 hands 2 inches, and are more frequently under that height, although I have known a few to reach 15 hands 1 inch. A well-bred, well-shaped Arab was worth £200 in my time, and I believe they are now dearer. No breed of horses has such a hardy constitution as the Arab, and stands the alternations of temperature, heat, and rain so well ; but the Persian is nearly as hardy, and a far pleasanter hack to ride."

This picture of the Persian horse is very like a chestnut entire pony, under 14 hands, which was long well known with the Queen's Hounds as the "Little Wonder." He carried his fore-hand quite low, in the ugly style of the Persian; he was cat-hammed and goose-rumped; in fact, except his blood head and well-carried tail, very mean-looking; and yet he could gallop like a race-horse, jump wide places that would stop the best part of a field, and never tired in the longest day. On one occasion, carrying me, my walking weight 10 st. 4 lbs., in a field of four hundred, with the Queen's Hounds, in a run in which nine-tenths of the field were pumped out and squandered all over the country, he galloped up in the second flight when the deer was being taken; that is to say, five horsemen arrived, some on their second horses, first, and then a little clump of about fifteen led by one of the Yeomen Prickers. Little Wonder was the first to get his wind, and begin to crop the grass at the side of the pond where the deer was at bay, while good hunters were still sobbing, and shaking their tails.

This pony was reported to be out of a West Country pony by an Arab; but every Oriental horse, Turk, Barb, or Egyptian bred, is called an Arab in this country.

The late General Angerstein spent £10,000, and devoted many years, in trying to improve the English blood-horse by crosses of Arab blood, without ever succeeding in producing either a race-horse or a good hunter. I have seen several of his breed; they were graceful little weeds, fit for park hacks to carry eight or nine stone at the utmost. One, full-sized, was purchased at the sale after General Angerstein's death, and converted by Messrs. Sangers, the circus proprietors, into a remarkable performing manége horse.

The best Arabs I have had an opportunity of examining may be divided into two classes—those scarcely to be distinguished from English thorough-breds, of perfect symmetry and fine quality, but not up to weight; and those of equal quality, built like weight-carrying hacks.

In the first class I should place an Arab exhibited in 1869 by Lady Ann Spiers, in the class for stallions under 15 hands: "Farhan (Joyous), a bay, with black legs, 14 hands 3 inches high, seven years old," of the breed of the blood-horses of the Anazehs, "purchased through the British consul at Damascus, and valued at one thousand guineas, to which the first prize was awarded."

Farhan was a perfect specimen of a blood riding-horse, with none of the usual defects of conformation of the Arabs imported, and much resembling a compact English blood-horse, with very good action; he was very docile, and allowed the groom to mount him bare-backed. The late Earl of Zetland came to see him, and examined him very closely. He said that he was the best of the kind he had ever seen. This horse was afterwards purchased by a Mr. Dangan, and exported to New South Wales as a stallion. Since the demand in Australia is not for large harness horses, but for stout enduring saddle horses, it is probable the Arab and Turcoman stallions, with the points essential in a good riding horse, would be the proper foundations of a much needed improvement in the colonial breeds.

Major Adrian Hope exhibited in the same class a very handsome black Arab of much the same character, an inch less in height, with a pedigree traced "from a filly once ridden by the Prophet Mahomed," of which the latter said, "On her back is majesty, and in her womb a treasure." This Arab has up to the present time been regularly ridden as a charger by Major Hope with a regiment of the City of London rifle volunteers, in which he holds a commission.

Sir Henry Rawlinson, K.C.B., exhibited, in 1864, a bay Arab, ten years old, about 14 hands 3 inches high, bred by the Sheikh of the Wahabees, purchased when Sir Henry was Resident at Bagdad, and stated "to have a pedigree of four hundred years." A grey Arab, of about the same size, stamp, and pace, was exhibited at the same time by Mrs. Harriet Turnbull, whose riding-horse it had been in India, said to be of the purest Nejed breed. Both these horses showed the fine quality and Arab character, especially in their heads and set of their tails : yet were up to great weight—in a word, they were what would be called thorough-bred weight-carrying hacks. The bay was exceedingly docile, and a capital hack ; but Mrs. Turnbull's grey would allow no one but herself to mount him.

In 1872 Mr. J. M. Clayworth, of Birmingham, exhibited a grey Arab, "Magdala," 14 hands 3 inches ; a good hack, and little hunter in the Warwickshire county, which he had himself imported from Egypt. With the highest quality, Magdala had the back and loins of a weight-carrier, capital hack action, and was very much admired by two such judges of pony hacks as Lord Calthorpe and Mr. F. Winn Knight, M.P. A hundred guineas was offered for Magdala by me, and refused.

These were as unlike the ordinary run of weak actionless pretty-headed Arab ponies, imported at vast expense from the East, as the most celebrated thorough-bred steeplechase horses are unlike the daisy-cutting weeds that are kept to win or lose handicap races of five furlongs.

In considering the merits of the best Arabs—common ones are the most worthless brutes alive—it must always be remembered that every one in England who breeds for profit wishes to produce either a cart-horse, a race-horse, a hunter, or a carriage-horse ; and that he desires them all to be over rather than under 15 hands 2 inches high. For the purposes of breeding race-horses, hunters, and carriage-horses, we have within this kingdom all the quality and endurance we require if proper use is made of our best materials.

CHILDE'S GREY ARABIAN.

The following account of the one Arabian celebrated in the traditions of Leicestershire hunting was furnished by Mr. Frederick Winn Knight, M.P., grandson of the gentleman who sold the horse to Mr. Childe, who is celebrated as the originator of the modern system of riding straight to hounds—a system which has completely altered the character of the English hunter. The old system was to take timber with a standing jump, and all leaps with a care and deliberation quite unknown to those who now aspire to be in the first flight with foxhounds in flying countries.

"All sporting authors agree that Mr. Childe, of Kinlet Hall, in Shropshire, was the father of the present system of *straight* riding to hounds. He was familiarly known as ' Straight Childe' and the ' Flying Childe.' He was one of Mr. Meynell's earliest followers to Melton, and for many years was the undoubted leader of the Melton fields. He only left Leicestershire, and retired to the mastership of a pack of foxhounds in Shropshire, when later in life he found himself unable to keep his old place in front of Villiers, Cholmondeley, Forester, Germaine, and others, his pupils in the art of riding to hounds. But it is not so generally known that Mr. Childe's best horse, in the palmiest days of the Quorn under Old Meynell, was a thorough-bred Arab ; although the ' Druid,' usually well-informed in such matters, has described him as a half-bred Arab. The story runs thus :—

"Lord Pigott, of Patsull, in Shropshire, who died (in prison) governor of Madras, passed most of his life in India. He sent home from time to time a selection of the best Arab horses and mares he could procure in the East, and with them established a small breeding-stud at Patsull. At the time of his violent death in India there were a number of young Arabs of various ages running unbroken in Patsull Park.

"The whole stud was sold by Lord Pigott's executors, and the horse in question was purchased at the sale, as a four-year old, by Captain Speke, of East Lackington, near Taunton, a scion of the same family that has since produced the great African explorer. Captain Speke was then quartered at Kidderminster, and rode the young Arab for one season with the harriers of my grandfather, Mr. John Knight, of Wolverley. On his regiment being suddenly ordered to India in the spring, the horse was sold for him by Mr. Knight to his kinsman and neighbour, Mr. Childe, for the sum of £25.

"The little grey, as described by an old sportsman who knew him well, was hardly 15 hands high, with small bone below the knees, yet with large knees and hocks, and singularly powerful back and loins. He was a surprising jumper; yet his pre-eminence depended chiefly on his peculiar manner of galloping over deep ground without sinking into it. His owner named him 'Skim,' from this power of skimming over the surface while other horses were struggling along fetlock deep.

"Mr. Childe, who rode about twelve stone, at first declined to buy him, thinking him too small for a hunter, and afterwards bought him to ride in the Park. But when the horse came to Melton in the autumn, his superiority and lasting qualities soon became apparent, and for a series of years Childe's grey Arabian was the leading horse in most of the famous runs of that era, so celebrated in the annals of English fox-hunting."

SYRIAN ARABS.

"Where are the good horses? was my first question," says Mrs. Burton, "when I had been at Damascus a couple of days. Except those that have been taken from the Bedáwin, or by compulsion by Turkish officials, or accepted from them as bartīl, you will have a difficulty in seeing them. You will see, perhaps, a dozen or two of half-breds and three-quarter-breds; the rest are *kaddishes*—but many of these are good serviceable animals. The famous mares are kept in the desert and in seclusion from Turkish eyes."

"For travelling purposes the Rahwán is the best animal. He is generally a 12 hands Kurdish pony, and he ambles along like a carriage and pair. He is never tired, nor does he tire you. You have to learn to ride him. I found the pace a bore, and always returned to my own horses with pleasure; yet those are wiser than myself who travel thus, for they cover twice the usual distance without fatigue. On long journeys I use two horses, riding them on alternate days, the extra Rahwán and donkeys run loose like dogs. Half-bred Syrian horses have certain disadvantages for marching. They must have full or even extra rations when hard worked. They come out in the morning too hot to hold, and look as if they wanted to kill and eat one. You cannot ride near anybody. About the middle of the day they settle steadily to work and leave off play—by that time your back is well-nigh broken by their fantasias under a broiling sun. At night they rest till about twelve. When the camp is sound asleep, it is aroused by a noise as if Hades had broken loose, and you find that they have either bitten their ropes through, or, if the ground be sandy, uprooted their pegs—irons a foot and a half long—by pawing and pulling alternately. Then they scour the camp screaming, lashing out, and fighting, nor can any man with safety separate them. And it is a sight to see them. Their ears lie back on their necks, their extended nostrils snort steam as they rear on their hind legs, with fore legs almost embracing each other, and their teeth fastened into each other's necks, and the set-to either disables them or leaves ugly scars next day."

"No one can afford blood mares of the three great Arab races. Several men buy and have a share in one, like a railway company and they divide the profits of her offspring. The

Bedawin never ride their best mares on plundering expeditions. You might shake a handkerchief at them and make them run away, if riding their mares, but if you see them coming on camels—be frightened. The mare comes before wife and child; she means money and something of reputation. I do not say there are no cases of attachment, but I will say that in five cases out of seven the mare merely represents capital."*

During the Crimean war some officers were sent to Syria to buy horses. They were provided with firmans from the Turkish Government, interpreters, horse-dealers accustomed to the ways of the desert, and an ample supply of English gold, with which they paid on the completion of each transaction. They formed camps in different convenient stations, made their errand known, and had opportunities of seeing the best horse-produce of the Bedouin tribes in that part of Asia, such as no single person, however powerful, could possibly enjoy.†

The dealings were principally carried on with the Anazeh tribe, amongst whom, "although the chiefs and men of wealth ride with Turkish saddles and bits, the appointments of poorer men's horses consist of a coarse pad of ragged dirty cloth; a thin leather, slightly stuffed to form a seat, pommel, and cantle, girthed with a bit of coarse web, with sometimes a breastband, forms the saddle, without any stirrups. The bridle consists of a halter, with a noseband of rusty iron links, without anything in the shape of a bit. A single rope or thong attached to this acts as a rein, and also to tether the horse when required. These accoutrements were often perfectly free of ornament, but, on the other hand, were sometimes decorated with long black and white tassels, like old-fashioned bell-pulls, suspended by ropes which almost allowed them to sweep the ground, with red cloth and ostrich feathers stuck all over the head-stall, and more frequently with a little short frizzy black plume set between the ears.

"When armed for war the horseman carries a light lance, at least twelve feet in length. The Anazeh does not exist who does not possess a spear; but when riding unarmed, the Anazeh always carries a small short stick with a crook at the end, with which he appears to guide his horse.

"The horses are small, seldom rising above 14 hands 1 inch, but they are fine, and have great power and size for their height. They would not be much admired by a purely English horseman. Indeed, Arab horses imported to England at a fabulous cost are constantly passed over as 'ponies.' The English and the Arab horse look each absurd by turns, as the eye has grown accustomed to the other; but, to my eye, accustomed for some time to rest on nothing but the Eastern horse, they seem to exceed all that I have yet seen in point of beauty. Stallions used to be led into our camp looking like horses in a picture—the limbs flat, broad, and powerful; deep below the knee, small and fine about the fetlock, of a beauty and cleanness of outline, enough alone to stamp blood on their possessor; the neck light, yet arched; the flanks closely ribbed up; the tail carried out with a sweep like the curve of a palm-branch; and the small head terminating in large nostrils, always snorting and neighing.

"It was a beautiful sight to see one of them, when he got wind of another stallion, draw himself up, with his neck arched, his ears pointed, and his eyes almost starting out of his head; his rigid stillness contrasting curiously with his evident readiness to break out into furious action. Noble, knightly, heroic!—an incarnation of fiery energy; a steed that Saladin might have mounted, and that would have matched his master!

"Grey of various shades, bay, chestnut, and brown, are the ordinary colours of the Arab horse; the commonest of all is a dark uniform nutmeg grey. Light grey, verging upon white,

---

* Mrs. Burton's (wife of the celebrated traveller) "Inner Life in Syria."   † "Blackwood's Magazine," 1859

is not peculiar to old horses. Next in frequency to grey comes bay and chestnut, both fine and rich in quality, the latter so prized that Arabs have a saying that if you hear of a horse performing some remarkable feat, you will be sure, on inquiring, to find that he is a chestnut. In my register of horses bought from the Anazeh, I find one black, a colour so rare that if I had merely trusted to my recollection I should have said I never saw a black horse in the desert. I saw no other colours except a skewbald, and cannot say whether he was an Anazeh, or belonging to some of the tribes where the purity of the breed can less be depended on.

"Besides the Arabs, in our neighbourhood were found the wandering Turcomans, a nomadic people, whose forefathers came into Syria to help to resist the Crusaders; and to this day they speak not Arabic but Turkish. They possess camels, goats, cattle, and horses. The latter brutes, not taller than Arabs, are heavy and clumsy, with coarse heads, very drooping hind-quarters, legs long below the knee, and draggled, ill-carried tails. They are almost all geldings, shy, obstinate, and vicious; the mares are better-looking, but coarse and *Flemish*.

* * * * * * * * * *

"Our encampment soon assumed the appearance of a horse fair. In the background were the snow-streaked mountains of the Druses; to our front a grassy plain, dotted with flocks and herds; coming over a distant ridge a party of the monkey-like Anazehs, their long spears over their shoulders, their high-bred horses at a walk; near at hand a group of Turcomans, distinguished by greater size and less dirty clothing, held ugly mares and uglier geldings, accoutred with gaudily-coloured worsted head-stall, with mameluke bits, and saddles with high pommel and cantle, and shovel stirrup-irons.

"All the horses offered to us for sale by the Bedouins were stallions. I do not at this moment remember having seen a gelding in their possession; and although they frequently rode mares into our camp, they never offered them to us. The last circumstance, I believe, is owing to the estimation in which they hold their mares as a source of national wealth, and to the fact of 'public opinion' having set itself so strongly against letting the breed fall into other hands by selling them, that no individual ventures to do so. Sentimental or affectionate feeling, I should imagine, is very little concerned in the matter. I never saw the slightest trace of any feeling of dislike on the part of the Arab to parting with his horse, provided the price was good. Once let him see a satisfactory heap of gold, and he turns his beast over to you, and his whole faculties to seeing that you do not cheat him of the tenth part of a piastre on the bargain; and never, in all probability, casts a look on his horse again, unless with the object of instituting a squabble as to whether or not he is to carry off the halter.

"None of the people of these parts are easy to deal with; but the Anazeh are the most difficult of all. Suppose that you ask the price of a horse. If the owner condescends to put a price upon him, it is about three times what he means to take; frequently he refuses to do it at all, but tells you to make an offer. You do so; he receives it with contempt, and the word 'Béïd' ('Far off'), pronounced with a lengthened emphasis, 'Bé—ï—d,' that sets strongly before you the enormous inadequacy of your proposal. You raise your price, and a contention of bargaining ensues, which is terminated by the owner riding off with his horse as if he never meant to come back any more. After a time, greater or less—in an hour or two, to-morrow, or the day after—you find that he has come back. A fresh battle ensues, which (if it is not interrupted by a second riding off) ends in the price being fixed. All is settled; the owner seems quite content; you proceed to mark the horse, when lo! his late master, suddenly stung by the intolerable thought that he has perhaps got less than he possibly might, seizes and drags off his beast in a fury, mounts, and goes off again. Again he returns, and again, finding you inexorable, agrees for the same sum. Again you want to mark the horse; and now he raises a dreadful outcry to be paid first. You consent, and call him into the tent. In he comes, attended by one or two friends and counsellors, sages supposed to be learned in Frank coins, and wide-awake to the ring of a bad piece. All solemnly squat on the ground, and you proceed to count out the gold.

"The huffiness exhibited by Bedouins in their horse-dealing transactions, in a great measure the outburst of an insolent, overbearing nature, is seldom able to stand its ground permanently against the greater strength of their passion for money. Of a hundred Bedouins that ride off in a fury as resolved never to set eyes on you again, ninety-nine will come back again. Perhaps

THE MAMELUKE'S CHARGER.

the hundredth will not. A Bedouin brought a horse of extraordinary size for an Arab into the camp. I did not much admire the animal, but a sum equal to £100 was offered for him. The owner, a breechless savage, in a sort of dirty night-shirt, rode away in wrath, and we never saw him again.

"The sum total of horses bought by us in the desert was one hundred. Of these seventy-two were Anazeh, from the Wulad Ali and the Rowallas; the remainder from the tribes of Serhan and Beni Sakhr, and from men of doubtful tribe. The following statements refer to the Anazeh alone. The highest price paid was £71 17s. This was given for each of two horses bought by private hand, of which one was the finest that I saw in the desert. Putting these aside, the highest price was a little more than £50, and the average price about £34. The average height was 14 hands 1½ inches, and the commonest age four and five years; but this would be an over-estimate both of the height and age of the mass of Anazeh horses offered for sale, as we selected the biggest and the oldest. Many of the horses brought were two and three years old, and might have been bought at much lower prices. Of the different breeds, the Kahailan seemed to be the most numerous, the Soklawye the most esteemed.

"The Anazeh inflict a temporary disfigurement upon their young horses by cropping the hair of the tail quite short, after the cadgerly fashion creeping in amongst English hunters, but leave the tails of the full-grown animals to attain their natural length. They denied being in the habit of making, as they are commonly believed to do, fire-marks on their horses for purposes of distinction; and denied also all knowledge of grounds for a report which I have seen brought forward very lately, viz., that English horses had been used to improve the breed. The foals, they said, though dropped most frequently in spring, were yet produced all the year round, in consequence of which the age of their horses dated from the actual day of birth, and not from any particular season of the year.

"With the exception of one Anazeh vicious at his pickets, I remember no instance of an Arab horse showing vice towards mankind.

"We had an Italian horse-dealer with us, a great black-bearded man, one Angelo Peterlini. He was a good and useful man in his way; well acquainted with the dodges and mysteries of Bedouin horse-dealing; cunning in guessing the price that an Arab would take for his horse, and careful to offer him only the half, that he might work up the other half in process of bargaining; sharp-sighted in detecting the two or three 'unlucky' hairs which in Bedouin estimation might lower the value of a horse, and as pertinacious in making them tell upon the price as if he believed in them; in fact, altogether well acquainted with the Bedouins, and monstrously polite to them before their faces, but with, at heart, a horror of them unspeakable (by anybody of less gifts of eloquence than himself), and with the intensest aversion to anything of the nature of what he called a 'baruffa' with them. Dogs, thieves, hogs, *canaille*, people of the devil—I wish I could convey the magnificent and sonorous emphasis with which he rolled out these and other epithets upon them behind their backs, or the ingenuity with which he framed speeches setting forth their precise relationship with the Fiend, and the exact nature of a most curious connection with the hogs which he attributed to them.

"I must add a postscript. Do not let any man, because I have rated the average price of an Anazeh horse at £34, suppose that £34 is to buy him a striking specimen of the race; or, because I have described the Anazeh horses as fine, imagine that the very fine ones are anything but the exception to the rule. With the Arab horse, as with everything else in the world, the average is grievously removed from the ideal, and all that you want above it you must pay for. Finally, let any one who may be tempted to seek for an Arab horse in his native deserts remember that though we, buying horses by the hundred, could attract numbers of sellers to our camp, it does not follow that he, in search of a solitary animal, could do anything of the kind, or, indeed, that he could draw together a sufficient number to offer him a reasonable choice; and above all, if he wish to avoid tribulation, let him receive as great truths all Angelo Peterlini's remarks upon the Bedouins, and shape his course so as—if he will take *my* advice—to keep perfectly clear of them."

Having given an extract which conveys so unfavourable an idea of the moral qualities of the Bedouin, of whom we have been accustomed to read such picturesque and romantic accounts, it is right to add that the British cavalry officer's admiration for the Anazeh as a horseman is unbounded; and I give his description here, although the subject does not properly come within the contents of this chapter.

"His horsemanship, when he chooses to display it, is very striking and curious. He puts his horse to the gallop; leaning very much forward, and clinging with his naked legs and heels round the flanks, he comes past you at speed, his brown shanks bare up to the thigh, his stick brandished in his hand, and his ragged robes flying behind; then, checking the pace, he turns right and left at a canter, pulls up, increases or diminishes his speed, and, with his bitless halter, exhibits, if not the power of flinging his horse dead upon his haunches, possessed by the Turks and other bit-using Orientals, at all events, much more control over the animal than an English dragoon attains to with his heavy bit. On these occasions, it appeared to me that the halter served to check, and the stick to guide; but I have seen the same feats performed when the horseman was carrying the lance, and, consequently, was without his stick. Our purchases in the desert amounted to one hundred horses; amongst all I saw tried, I never saw one attempt to pull, or show the least want of docility.

"Most horsemen will admit that this is an extraordinary performance, and that none will allow it more readily than those who are acquainted with the Arab horse as he appears in our hands in India, where—so far as I may trust my own experience—he is hot, and inclined to pull. Why should he display this failing with us, and not with his original masters? My own impression is that the secret lies in the different temper of the English and the Bedouin horseman. The Bedouin (and every other race of Orientals that I am acquainted with seems to possess somewhat of the same quality) exhibits a patience towards his horse as remarkable as the impatience and roughness of the Englishman. I am not inclined to put it to his credit in a moral point of view; I do not believe that it results from affection for the animal, or from self-restraint; he is simply without the feeling of irritability which prompts the English horseman to acts of brutality. In his mental organisation some screw is tight which in the English mind is loose; he is sane on a point where the Englishman is slightly cracked; and he rides on serene and contented where the latter would go into a paroxysm of swearing and spurring. I have seen an Arab stallion, broken loose at a moment when our camp was thronged with horses brought for sale, turn the whole concern topsy-turvy, and reduce it to one tumult of pawing and snorting and belligerent screeching; and I never yet saw the captor, when he finally got hold of the halter, show the least trace of anger, or do otherwise than lead the animal back to his pickets with perfect calmness. Contrast this with the 'job' in the mouth, and the kick in the ribs, and the curse that the English groom would bestow under similar circumstances; and you have, in a great measure, the secret of the good temper of the Arab horse in Arab hands."

WAHABEE HORSES.

In 1856, Mr. William Giffard Palgrave, formerly an officer in the Indian army, published an account of a journey through Central and Eastern Arabia, and his stay, disguised as an Oriental, in the capital of the Wahabees, the most bigoted tribe of Mahomedans, from which the following account of the purest race of Arabs is extracted. He describes a type which has rarely if ever been seen in England :—

"During this time I got a sight of the royal stables, an event much desired and eagerly welcomed, for the Nejed horse is considered no less superior to all others of his kind in Arabia than is the Arabian breed collectively to the Persian, Cape of Good Hope, or Indian. In Nejed is the true birthplace of the Arab steed, the primal type, the authentic model—thus, at any rate, I heard, and thus, so far at least as my experience goes, it appears to me, although I am aware that distinguished authorities maintain another view; but, at any rate, among all the studs of Nejed, Feysul's was indisputably the first, and who sees that has seen the most consummate specimens of equine perfection in Arabia, perhaps in the world. It happened that a mare in the imperial stud had received a bite close behind the shoulder from some sportive comrade, and the wound, ill-dressed and ill-managed, had festered into a sore, puzzling the most practised Nejdean farriers. One morning, while Barakat and myself were sitting in Abdallah's *le-hawah*, a groom entered to give the prince the daily bulletin of his stables. Abdallah turned towards me, and inquired whether I would undertake the cure. Gladly I accepted the proposal of visiting the patient, though limiting my proffer of services to a simple inspection, and declining systematic interference with what properly belonged to a veterinary province. The prince gave his orders accordingly, and in the afternoon a groom, good-natured as grooms generally are, knocked at our door, and conducted me straight to the stables. These are situated some way out of the town to the north-east, a little to the left of the road which we had followed at our first arrival, and not far from the gardens of Abd-er-rahman the Wahabee. They cover a large square space, about 150 yards each way, and are open in the centre, with a long shed running round the inner walls; under this covering the horses, about three hundred in number when I saw them, are picketed during the night, in the day-time they may stretch their legs at pleasure within the central courtyard. The greater number were accordingly loose; a few, however, were tied up at their stall; some, but not many, had horse-cloths over them. The heavy dews which fall in Wad Haneefah do not permit their remaining with impunity in the open air; I was told also that a northerly wind will occasionally injure the animals here, no less then the land wind does now and then their brethren in India. About half the royal stud were present before me, the rest were out at grass. Feysul's entire muster is reckoned at six hundred, or rather more. No Arab dreams of tying up a horse by the neck; a tether replaces the halter, and one of the animal's hind-legs is encircled about the pastern by a light iron ring, furnished with a padlock, and connected with an iron chain of two feet or thereabouts in length, ending in a rope, which is fastened to the ground at some distance by an iron peg. Such is the customary method, but should the animal be restless and troublesome, a fore-leg is put under similar restraint. It is well known that in Arabia horses are much less frequently vicious or refractory than in Europe, and this is the reason why geldings are here so rare, though not unknown; no particular prejudice that I could discover exists against the operation itself, only it is seldom performed because not otherwise necessary, and tending of course to diminish the value of the animal. But to return to the horses now before us. Never had I seen or imagined so lovely a collection. Their stature was indeed somewhat low; I do not think that any came fully up to 15 hands, 14 hands seemed about their average, but they were so exquisitely well shaped that want of greater size seemed hardly a defect. Remarkably full in the haunches, with a shoulder of a slope so elegant as to make one, in the words of an Arab poet, 'go raving mad about it;' a little, a very little, saddle-backed, just the curve which indicates springiness, without any weakness; a head broad above and tapering down to a nose fine enough to verify the phrase of drinking from a pint pot, did pint pots exist in Nejed; a most intelligent, and yet a singularly gentle look; full eye; sharp, thorn-like, little ear; legs, fore and hind, that seemed as if made of hammered iron, so clean and yet so well twisted with sinew; a neat, round hoof, just the requisite for hard ground; the tail set on, or rather thrown out, at a perfect arch; coat smooth, shining, and light; the mane long, but not overgrown or heavy; and an air and step that seems to say, 'Look at me; am I not pretty?' Their appearance justified all reputation, all value, all poetry. The prevailing colours were chestnut or grey, a light bay, an iron colour; white or black were less common; full bay, flea-bitten, or piebald, none. But if asked what are, after all, the specially distinctive points of the Nejdee horse, I should reply—the slope of the shoulder, the extreme cleanness of the shank, and the full rounded haunch; though every other part too has a perfection and a harmony unwitnessed, at least by my eyes, anywhere else.

"Unnecessary to say that I had often met, and after a fashion studied, horses throughout this journey; but I purposely deferred saying much about them till this occasion. At Hazel, and in Djebel Shomer, I found very good examples of what is commonly called the Arab horse, a fine breed, and from among which purchases are made every now and then by Europeans—princes, peers, and commoners—often at astounding prices. These are for the most part the produce of a mare from Djebel Shomer or its neighbourhood and a Nejdean stallion, sometimes the reverse, but never, it would seem—although here I am, of course, open to correction

DERVISH, AN ARABIAN HORSE.

by the logic of facts—through Nejdee on both sides. With all their excellences, these horses are less systematically elegant, nor do I remember having ever seen one among them free from some one weak point—perhaps a little heaviness in the shoulder, perhaps a slight falling off in the rump, perhaps a shelly or a contracted hoof, or too small an eye. Their height, also, is much more varied; some of them attain sixteen hands, others are down to fourteen. Every one knows the customary division of their pedigrees—Manakee, Siklamee, Hamdanee, Tarypee, and so forth; I myself made a list of these names during a residence, some years previous, among the Sebaa and Ruala Bedouins, nor did I find any difference worth noting between what was then told me and the accounts usually given by travellers and authors on this topic; nor did the Bedouins fail to recite their oft-repeated legends about Salaman's stables &c.; but I am inclined to consider the greater part of these very pedigrees, and still more the antiquity of their origin, as comparatively recent inventions, and of small credit, got up for the market by Bedouins or townsmen; nor is a Kahlanee mare by any means a warrant for a Kahlanee stallion. Crossing the breed is an every-day occurrence, even in Shomar. Once arrived at this last district I heard no more of Siklamee, Delhamee, or any other like genealogies; nor were Salaman's stables better known to fame than those of Augeas in Nejed. I was distinctly assured that prolonged lists of pedigrees were never kept, and that all inquiries about race are limited to the assurance of a good father and a good mother; 'as for Salaman,' added the groom, 'he was much more likely to have taken the horses from us than we from him' —a remark which proved in him who made it a certain amount of historical criticism. In a word, to be a successful jockey in Nejed requires about the same degree of investigation and knowledge that it would in Yorkshire, and no more, perhaps less, considering the stud-books. The genuine Nejdean breed, so far as I have hitherto found, is to be met with only in Nejed itself. Nor are these animals common even there; none but chiefs or individuals of considerable wealth and rank possess them. Nor are they ever sold, at least so all declare; and when I asked how then one could be acquired, 'By war, by legacy, or free gift,' was the answer. In this last manner alone is there a possibility of an isolated specimen leaving Nejed, but even that is seldom; and when policy requires a present to Egypt, Persia, or Constantinople—a circumstance of which I witnessed two instances, and heard of other—mares are never sent; the poorest stallions, though deserving to pass elsewhere for real beauties, are picked out for the purpose.

"Abdallah, Sa-ood, and Mohammed, keep their horses in separate stables, each one containing a hundred or thereabouts. After much inquiry and remark, my companion and I came to the conclusion that the total Nejdean horse census would not sum up above five thousand, and probably fall short of that number. The fact that here the number of horsemen in an army is perfectly inconsiderable when compared to that of the camel riders, may be adduced in confirmation, especially since in Nejed horses are never used except for war or parade, while all work and other drudgery falls on camels, sometimes on asses.

"Pretty stories have been circulated about the familiarity existing between Arabs (Bedouins in particular) and their steeds—how the foal at its birth is caught in the hands of bystanders, not allowed to fall to the ground; how it plays with children of the house; eats and drinks with its master; how he tends it when indisposed, whilst it no doubt returns him a similar service when occasion requires. That the Arab horse is much gentler, and, in a general way, more intelligent than the close-stabled, blinkered, harnessed, condemned-cell prisoned animal of merry England I willingly admit. Matters, alas, cannot be otherwise. Brought up in close contact with men, and enjoying the comparatively free use of his senses and limbs, the Arab quadruped is in a fair way for developing to full advantage whatever feeling and instinct good blood brings with it; nor does this often fail to occur. If, however, we come to the particular incidents of Arab horse life just alluded to, they certainly form no general rule or etiquette in practice. Nor would any Arab be the worse thought of for rapping his mare over the nose if she thrust it into his porridge, or for leaving Nature to do the office of midwife when she is in an interesting condition. Still, I do not mean to say that the creditable anecdotes immortalised in so many books may not, perhaps, take place here and there; but, to quote an Arab poet, 'I never saw the like, nor ever heard.' For my own personal experience, it goes no farther than feeding Arab horses out of my hand, not dish, and prevailing on them, better than the spirits of the vasty deep, to come when I did call for them. The rest I cannot help classing, though reluctantly, with many other tales of the desert. After a delightful

GOLDIE, HIGH CLASS ARAB.

THE ARAB PONY CHARGER OF GENERAL SIR HOPE GRANT, G.C.B.
IN THE INDIAN MUTINY OF 1859, AND CHINESE CAMPAIGN OF 1860.

hour passed in walking up and down among these beautiful creatures, attended by grooms professionally sensible to all the excellences of horseflesh, I examined the iron-grey mare in question, saw another whose appetite was ailing, prescribed a treatment (which, if it did no good, could certainly do no harm), and left the stables with longing, lingering looks behind, whither, however, I subsequently paid not unfrequent visits befitting to a doctor.

"Farther on, when we cross the eastern and southern limits of Toweyk, we find the Arab breed rapidly losing in beauty and perfection, in size and strength. The specimens of indigenous race that I saw in Oman considerably resembled the 'tatties' of India; but in the eastern angle of Arabia the deficiency of horses is in a way made up for by the dromedaries of that land. Nejdee horses are especially esteemed for great speed, and endurance of fatigue; indeed, in this latter quality none come up to them. To pass twenty-four hours on the road without drink and without flagging is certainly something; but to keep up the same abstinence and labour conjoined, under the burning Arabian sky, for forty-eight hours at a stretch, is, I believe, peculiar to the animals of the breed. Besides, they have a delicacy, I cannot say of mouth, for it is common to ride them without bit or bridle, but of feeling, and obedience to the knee and thigh, to the slightest check of the halter and the voice of the rider, far surpassing whatever the most elaborate manége gives a European horse, though furnished with snaffle, curb, and all. I often mounted them at the invitation of their owners, and, without saddle, rein, or stirrup, set them off at full gallop, wheeled them round, brought them up in mid-career at a dead halt, and that without the least difficulty, or the smallest want of correspondence between the horse's movements and my own. The rider on their backs really feels himself the man-half of a centaur, not a distinct being. This is in great part owing to the Arab system of breaking-in, much preferable to the European in conferring pliancy and perfect tractability; nor is mere speed much valued in a horse, unless it be united with the above qualities, since, whether in the contest of an Arab race, or in the pursuit and flight of war, doubling is much more the rule than going ahead, at least for any distance. Much the same training is required for the sport of the *djereed*—that tournament of the East—and which, as I witnessed it in Nejed, differed in nothing from the exhibitions frequent in Syria and Egypt, except that the palm-stick or *djereed* itself is a little lighter. I should add that in the stony plateaus of Nejed horses are always shod, but the shoe is clumsy and heavy. The hoof is very slightly pared, and the number of nails put in is invariably six. Were not the horn excellent, Nejdean farriery would lame many a fine horse."

THE DONGOLA.

The Dongola is an Oriental blood-horse to which the term "pony" does not apply. Attention was first called to the Dongola by James Bruce, the traveller in Abyssinia. He described the first horse he purchased as a black Dongola horse, 16¼ hands high, fully equal to his weight with his heavy Turkish saddle and arms, this must have been some sixteen or seventeen stone (Bruce was over six feet high), with lofty action, but not remarkable for speed.

Some few years after the publication of Bruce's Travels, Mr. John Knight—who afterwards purchased Exmoor—being at the house of Sir Joseph Banks, the eminent naturalist and companion of Cook in his first voyage round the world (Lord Moreton, an enthusiast in horse-breeding, Lords Headley and Dundas being also of the party), the conversation turned on the book of the day, and Bruce's description of the big Nubian horse. It ended in their each writing a cheque for £250, and handing them over to Sir Joseph Banks on account of the expenses of bringing over some specimens of the Dongola.

The matter was placed in the hands of Mr. Salt, the British consul in Egypt. After a delay of some years, and an expense of several thousand pounds, eleven Dongolas—five stallions and six mares—arrived in England. Mr. Knight purchased Lord Headley's share, and became possessed of two stallions and three mares. They fully answered Bruce's description; were 16 hands high, with the quality of skin of a blood-horse; had rather long legs, with white stockings, and the action of a "school-horse" right up to the curb-chain. The Nubian groom who accompanied them used to perform a trick common amongst Oriental horsemen; gallop them at a wall in the riding-school, and stop them dead with the cruel Turkish curb.

Some of the produce of these Dongolas, out of well-bred English mares, turned out hunters of remarkable endurance and speed. General the Marquis of Anglesey admired them very much, but he was a fanatic on the subject of manége riding, which may account for his taste.

Lieutenant-Colonel Frederick Winn Knight has permitted me to copy, for one of the coloured illustrations of this work, a portrait of the Dongola stallion, executed for his father by the celebrated animal painter, James Ward, R.A., in 1828. He writes, on sending the picture, "With the black Dongola horse, Mahmoud, came a bay, which, like the black, stood over a good deal at the knees. He was castrated, and I hunted him for several years on Exmoor with the wild stag hounds. He went well, and never tired. The black was in Scotland with Lord Moreton before he came to us, and was an old horse then."

The picture of Mahmoud is, in Mr. Knight's opinion, very faithful—certainly it is not a flattering portrait; and such a stamp offers no temptation for a repetition of the experiment. Probably this horse, with his bright eye, burnished black coat, and fiery action, produced an effect which could not be translated on canvas. But the portrait is a curiosity, because it suggests the origin of a peculiar breed of horses which are still carefully preserved by several families of the Spanish nobility.

A friend who has recently travelled in Nubia states that the tall black-and-white prancing horses are by no means rare there, and might easily be procured if required.

ARAB SIRES TO CROSS THOROUGH-BRED MARES.

The question of making use of Arab sires or Arab mares to improve the British blood-horse has been repeatedly discussed for more than fifty years. It is an idea that seems to crop up vigorously from time to time, and then die out. In 1864 a Scotch correspondent of the defunct *Sporting Magazine*, who had recently imported two Arab mares by way of experiment, sent the following letter from Aleppo:—

"I have made five experiments in horses here (Aleppo). 1st. Out of thorough-bred English mares by Arabian stallions. 2nd. Out of the best Arab mares by thorough-bred English horses. 3rd. Rearing the best Arab blood on succulent forage, as in England. 4th. Rearing thorough-bred English stock in the desert on dry food. 5th. Buying colts and fillies superior to those usually sold by the Arabs.

"The first experiment has led to no great results; the produce being merely handsomer than English horses, without being faster than Arabs.

"The second experiment has succeeded occasionally; but out of four, three are leggy, weak, and unfit for racing.

"The third experiment is a complete failure, except in increasing the size. The produce has the defects of the English horse without having the merits of the Arab.

"The fourth experiment is perfectly successful; the stock, though smaller than their parents, being better able to stay a distance. The heat of the desert; the dryness; the constant galloping from their birth after their dams, and ridden by children from a year and a half); the she-camels' milk with which the Arabs feed their foals (and which they think imparts the camel's endurance); the oxygenation of the blood by being always in the open air; the kind treatment (preventing bad temper, which impedes development); have all a great combined effect in bringing out the good qualities of a horse. A cubic inch of the tibia of a horse so reared weighs twenty per cent. more than stabled stock. I have now a colt out of Test by Touchstone, dam Tarella by Emilius, got by Chilton by Cowl, which I offered a few days ago in the desert, as a present to any Arab who could catch him. They tried their best, but he ran right away from them. I must say, however, that there were none present of those very superior Arabs which formed my fifth experiment. This fifth experiment is, in my opinion, the surest card of all. One has a greater choice, and need buy nothing without speed and stoutness; whereas, breed what you like, more than half your young stock will never be racers. The fact is this, there is blood and stride in the desert which has never been seen out of it.

"The Indian market is supplied by the Aghel tribe, who go about the desert buying chiefly colts rather than fillies, never paying more than five thousand piastres (£40), and sell with a small profit to the great purchasers at Bagdad and Quaid, who pass them on after a year or two to the Bombay dealers. The Arabs will not give their best blood and figure for that price; in fact, as you will have found out by this time, it is difficult to get them to sell it at all. I am perhaps the only one who has ever succeeded. I help them in their business with the Turkish pachas, prevent oppression, enable them to trade in safety with English exporters of wool; and even after a deal of trouble on my part, I buy a first-class horse or mare from them as a great favour, and at a long price. I have just sold, for instance, two mares to the Emperor of Russia for £500. One of them was of this class, and cost me £300; she had great speed and stoutness. She belonged to the almost extinct breed of Seglawi Jedran. She would have made a fortune in India; such a stride—15 feet 1 inch. The Arabs say no one ever got such a mare from them before. I have another now in my stable which cost me £300. She is of equal breed (Maneghi Stedrudj), equal height, beauty, and lasting power; but, unfortunately, she has no great speed, otherwise I would propose to send her to you."

From internal evidence it may be assumed that this Scotch correspondent was John Johnstone, Esq., successor of Andrew Johnstone, of Heath Hall, Annandale, the breeder (amongst other turf notabilities) of the celebrated race-horse Charles XII. Mr. Johnstone kept in 1872, and had kept for many years, a racing-stud at Sheffield Lane Paddocks, Yorkshire. Before he returned to England he was a celebrity in the Calcutta Hunt Club, famed in songs celebrating the chase of the wild boar as "Josto, King of Speares," and very successful on the Indian turf. He bought a celebrated Calcutta Arab race-horse, Minuet, which "The Druid" relates carried his owner, weighing thirteen stone, in a famous run with Sir Watkin Wynn's hounds, and could screw through or jump anything. But a part of Sir Watkin's country is better suited to ponies than full-sized horses; indeed, before a Pytchley huntsman superseded a Welshman, the huntsman in the mountain country frequently rode a pony.

Minuet and other Arabs were put to the stud by Mr. Johnstone; but up to 1878 no racehorse and no remarkable hunter had resulted from experiments tried under very advantageous circumstances.

TURCOMAN HORSES.

The Turcoman horse had the reputation of being an ugly inferior brute until brought into notice by Baker Pacha in his interesting book, "Clouds in the East."

The Turcoman horses appear quite thorough-bred, yet often reach the height of 16 hands.

and on one occasion General Baker saw a perfectly thorough-bred dun horse full seventeen hands high. These horses always stand in the open air, carefully clothed in thick felt rugs and hoods, the latter so heavy that the manes are worn away and then hogged. In the spring they are fed on green food, afterwards on barley, chopped straw, and clover hay. "The horse I brought to England had no mane, but since his arrival it has grown freely."

A high-class Turcoman horse is always followed by a pony carrying his heavy clothing. The Turcoman is quite as gentle as the Arab, and generally more quiet and sedate in his ways, on the whole equally courageous.

"A very high Turcoman will often fetch from £400 to £500 sterling. Why this country produces such horses is indeed singular. Why on these deserts the Arab should have grown into an animal more like an English race-horse than any other horse in the world, with powers of endurance possesed by no other race, is beyond my comprehension."

Having become possessed of a fine specimen of them, which he named Merv, after a city important in the military history of the country, he had an opportunity of trying his powers in a race for life. "We came across a troop of fourteen gourka (wild asses) on the edge of a great plain. The men of our escort had been bragging how they constantly rode down the gourka. I was riding Imaum, G. was on the bay horse he bought at Meshed. The wild asses halted, and we got within a quarter of a mile, then they started at a great pace. We were gaining on them steadily although slowly, it was simply a question of which could stay the longest. At length we got within three hundred yards. The wild asses made for rough bushy ground near the stream, and in going over gained a slight advantage. On we went for more than half an hour; suddenly they crossed the *nullah*, which was deep; by the time I got over it was evident that Imaum was pumped, and that it would be useless to persevere. On looking back I saw that the whole of our escort was beaten off, G.'s horse nearly as much done as Imaum. We halted and dismounted.

* * * * * * * * * * *

"The horse-keeper at length came up with my *Dereguey* (Turcoman thorough-bred) horse. I mounted, and rode off unattended into the plains; after going about two miles I espied some gourka. Away I went in pursuit; my horse went like a steam-engine, as if he would never stop; after riding about three miles, and gaining on the wild asses hand over hand, I became aware of some men who were evidently stalking *me!* I was compelled to retrace my steps to avoid being cut off. I pulled up, and having given Dereguey his wind, sent him along at a rattling pace. The robbers followed for three or four miles, but, quite outpaced, gave up the pursuit."

A reference to Captain Burnaby's ride led a correspondent, under the initials of W. T. L. (? Lyall), who had passed most of his life in Asia, to address a letter to the *Field* in April, 1877, on "Asiatic Horses," from which the following interesting and comparatively unknown information is extracted :—

"The term ponies is correctly applied to every breed of horses in Asia, including Arabs, as judged by English standards, except Turcomans.

"The Turcoman animal is about the only one that comes up to our idea of a horse, averaging 15 hands, and being often nearer 16. He is a maneless, or next to maneless, horse, of racing build, and capable of doing immense distances on very little sustenance.

"He is, in fact, like all the best breeds in Asia, an animal developed by the practice of plundering, for which purpose great distances have to be traversed across deserts, often for several days in succession, with no feed except what the riders can carry with them.

"These horses will gallop for a week or eight days together, doing one hundred to one hundred and twenty, or even a hundred and fifty miles a day; being fed, or rather

" bolused," from time to time with balls of barley flour kneaded up with sheep-tail fat, which the riders carry in their saddle-bags. At other times they are picketed (always heavily clothed), and fed on barley and "samaun" or bruised straw (what is called "boosah" in the Punjab), several handfuls of the former being mixed carefully up in an immense nosebag, or "tobra," holding a bushel or so of the latter. In spring they are "soiled" for a fortnight or three weeks on green corn or green herbage, like Persian and Turkish horses, which their normal treatment resembles.

"Before making their 'atamans,' or forays, they are galloped eighteen miles a day for a fortnight, and the barley meal and mutton-fat boluses gradually substituted for the barley and chopped straw. They have large, coarse-looking heads, and often ewe necks; their other points are good. Their ears are peculiar, small, pointed, and turning inwards—a peculiarity noticeable in many Punjabee breeds, which I suspect they have inherited from the Turcoman; country-bred horses in India being, like the natives, often a *mélange* of different races.

"The Tartar or Kirghiz pony or horse is quite a different animal, being of a type approaching the Chargoshee, the Yabboo, the Yarkand pony, or Bootia pony of Thibet; all the Tartar breeds are closely related.

"Many of the Cossack animals are of this type. They have (excepting some of the better bred ones, which are rare) a large head well set on, a big barrel well ribbed up, short legs, and a dense mane and tail. They are weight-carriers, stand almost any roughing and hardship, and may be seen in the depth of winter, with the thermometer several degrees below zero, apparently enjoying the cold—rolling in the snow, or scraping it up with their feet to get a bite at the withered grass or stubble beneath.

"These are the animals that the Tartars of former times used to make their raids on during the Turkish invasions of Austria and Russia, when the Tartar Khans of the Crimea, feudatories of the Turks, had to supply a contingent of sixty or seventy thousand irregular horse. These, acting as an immense advanced guard to the main army, ravaged the country far and wide, burnt villages, carried off women and children, and performed the usual "atrocity" business inseparable from Mahomedan campaigning, often penetrating leagues beyond Vienna.

"In ordinary times they made raids on their own account into Poland, or campaigned against the Cossacks, who were kept up by the Russians as a check upon them. Being often pursued and hard pushed on these occasions, their animals were obliged to be "fit." The training the best of them often underwent as a preparation for the business was something appalling, and to any one unacquainted with the strength of constitution and iron hardness of the Tartar ponies would be completely incredible. Their method of training a horse, or rather the ordeal they made him pass through before he was considered suitable for the "war path"—which they admit used to kill two out of five who underwent it, and was, of course, only compatible with the possession of an unlimited number of animals costing nothing or next to nothing to keep, being grazed on the steppe all the summer, and half starved on a little dry fodder during winter—was in this wise :—

"After picking out a likely one, rising seven or eight—before which age no horse was allowed to be selected for raiding—they loaded him on the saddle with a sack of earth or sand, at first only the weight of the rider, but gradually increased for eight days, till the horse carried 20 stone or 22 stone. As the weight was increased, the horse's ration of food and water was diminished. He was trotted and walked six or seven miles daily.

"After the first eight days they gradually, for other eight days, decreased the load, still, however, decreasing the feed until the sack was empty; finally giving him for two or three days absolutely nothing at all, but merely tightening up the girths at intervals.

"About the nineteenth day they worked him hard until he sweated, when they unsaddled him, and poured buckets of ice-cold water over the animal from head to tail. He was then picketed, all wet, to a peg on the open steppe, allowed to graze, or fed sparingly, giving him every day a little more feed and more rope for seven or eight days more, after which he was turned loose to run with the herd as usual.

"A horse that had undergone this discipline was considered a valuable animal, and a sort of fortune to a man, being able to travel almost continuously for four or five days together, with only a handful of fodder once in eight or ten hours, and a drink of water once in the twenty-four.

"This training was, of course, a sort of epitome of what the animals often had to go through on an actual foray, when they had frequently to swim semi-frozen rivers, to carry great weights, to go for days almost without food, to be picketed on the steppes, perhaps sweating from a long journey, in snow and sleet, without any covering, &c.

"The Persian horse--which must not be confounded with the coarse showy animals much affected by wealthy natives of India, and there called "Persian" horses, but which come in reality from Khorassan—is another good Asiatic type, three-parts Arab, exceedingly enduring, fleet, and hardy; he, however, instead of being turned out into the snow to rough it, like his Tartar cousin, is taken a great deal of care of, warmly clothed with felts, carefully groomed and fed, and kept in warm stables, often underground.

"This treatment, however, does not by any means seem to produce softness or 'want of grit,' these animals doing a hundred miles cheerfully, and roughing it, on occasion, almost as well as the Tartars.

"An animal of this breed, or rather of the Karabâgh (formerly a Persian province, now under Russian rule), which is much the same, had a trick of rubbing off his blanket at night, when on a journey, which he would often do with the thermometer near zero, yet never appeared to suffer in the least from the cold, though his coat was as fine as an Arab's."

In fact, all the horses of Asia Minor, Central Asia, Tartary, &c., whether taken care of, groomed, fed, and clothed, in the Persian and Turkish fashion, or turned out to take their chance in snow-storms, over-worked and half-starved, like those of the Cossacks and Tartars, seem to possess an invincible hardness of constitution, chiefly, perhaps, owing to climate; but, I believe, in great measure also to a judicious system of breeding and working. They have great endurance, which, however, they lose in India; the nearer they approach the tropics, and the more they get within the range of the monsoon, the softer they become. There was a tolerable breed for India in the Deccan in the old Mahratta days; and there is now a very good breed, although impetuous, in Kattywar, but the climate of Kattywar approaches nearer to that of Arabia than any other part of India; however hot in summer, or cold in winter, it is dry. The question of climate has a deal to do with good breeds of horses. We see that our English breed, transported to Australia or the Cape, though often roughly treated in comparison with home animals, and badly fed, begin to display an endurance and stoutness in those dry climates rivalling the Asiatic races. *Per contra*, a Kirghiz pony, however good, if transported to England, cannot perform the feats, even if well fed and cared for, that he does in a half-starved state on his native steppe. He would miss the dry elastic air and familiar expanse, while his iron hoofs would begin to soften in our damp climate and on our muddy roads.

TARTARS OF THE KIRGHIZ STEPPES.

No horses are so hardy as the Tartars of the Kirghiz steppes, says Captain Fred Burnaby in his celebrated " Ride to Khiva." The feeble ones die of starvation in hard winters.

The Kirghis never clothe their horses in the coldest winters. They get snow instead of water. Early in the spring the animals gain flesh and strength, and are capable of performing immense marches, a ride of a hundred miles on end not being uncommon in Tartary.

The Tartar horses are not generally well shaped, they cannot gallop very fast ; but they can travel enormous distances without forage, water, or halting.

For very long journeys they employ two horses, one carries a little water, and from time to time they change horses.

In 1870, Count Borkh, a Russian general, made a forced march of 266 miles in six days over a most difficult country ; on some days they marched sixty miles through rocky defile and barren sandy wastes destitute of forage and water. The heat was excessive during the day, sometimes reaching 117° Fahrenheit, while the nights were cold and frosty. There were only twelve horses with sore backs, which had been ridden, not by Cossacks, but by riflemen, who had neglected to adjust their saddles properly before mounting.

Captain Burnaby, who weighed, with his cold-defying clothes, furs, and accoutrements, twenty-two stone, purchased for his journey a black horse about 14 hands high, with gaudy painted saddle and bridle, for £5.

" The guide and myself pushed forward at the slow ambling pace peculiar to horses of the steppes, which some of them can keep up for twenty-four hours on an emergency. Not so fast as the huntsman's joggle when returning with his pack to the kennel, but much more jolting.

"We galloped across the frozen surface of the Syr Daryon, and pulled up at Nurozoff's hostelry. We had ridden 371 miles in nine days and two hours, thus averaging more than forty miles a day, with an interval of only nine days rest, having previously carried me five hundred miles. With my twenty stone he had neither been sick or lame during the journey, and had galloped the last seventeen miles in one hour and twenty-five minutes."

Merv, brought to England by Baker Pacha, was stationed as a stallion at Newmarket, with a fee of eighty-five pounds ; but breeders of race-horses would have nothing to say to him. He was afterwards offered to owners of half-bred mares, but did not meet with any favour. A correspondent wrote me in 1877—" In looking for a horse to put my hunting brood-mare to, I came across Merv. He looked to me to stand about sixteen hands high, fine shoulders, good head and neck, fine skin, good wearing legs, bad feet, and leggy. I thought him unsuited to breed hunters : thought he would do to put to a Suffolk cart mare, or get hacks out of Norfolk cobs. The high fee (£85) put him out of the question. He looked to me about an eleven-stone horse, and not like going through dirt." In the end no mares were covered by Merv while at Newmarket ; and in 1877 he was sold to the Earl of Charlemont for his breeding stud in Ireland.

ARAB AND SPANISH CROSSES.

In the preceding pages are embodied the opinions of writers who are enthusiastic admirers of the Arab, who have been charmed by his endurance, his fire and courage, and not a little by his picturesqueness, if such a term may be applied to a horse. But in order to do justice to this subject I shall present the other side of the question, in the words of one who was, in all that concerns the horse, in the strictest sense of the word, an *expert*—one who had been engaged in dealing in the best class of horses all his life ; who has bred horses, trained them, ridden them, on the road, in the field, and over the steeplechase course; driven, bought, and sold them; who was as much at home in the horse world of Spain and France as of England—the late Mr. Thomas Rice, who, being educated as a veterinary surgeon, managed the late Lord Dalling's stud when he was our ambassador in Spain. These are his answers to a series of searching questions:—

"Do I like Arabs? No. In my opinion they have not one point to recommend them for use in England in which they are not excelled by our own thorough-breds. They are, with very rare exceptions, very bad hacks; they cannot walk without stumbling—in fact, they are always stumbling; they have no true action in either trot or canter; they are slow in their gallop, as compared with any well-bred English blood-horse. They are too small for hunting or for first-class harness, and cannot race with common English platers. All I ever saw were so formed, with the croup higher than the withers, that they rode *down-hill*.

"When I was living in Spain, the Emperor of the French, for whom I had procured some high-class Spanish parade-horses, presented me with two Arabs of the highest caste—purchased without limit as to price, in the neighbourhood of Damascus—a black and a grey. They were as handsome at first sight as any picture of Arabs that I ever saw; about 14 hands 3 inches high, very temperate to ride, with great power in their hind-quarters, but wanting that slope in the shoulders, and that proportionate length, breadth, and power in motion, which are essential to make first-class riding action.

"I had at that time English thorough-breds and half-breds, Spanish mares of the *carnero* or Don Carlos breed, half-breeds between the English blood-horse Kedger (by Sheet Anchor) and Spanish mares. These Arabs, which had cost, perhaps—not counting political influence—£1,000 apiece, were inferior in hack action and as hacks to English or Spanish horses of one-tenth the cost. I rode the grey with a pack of harriers I kept; he was an unpleasant hack, and no hunter. I trained them both, and they were distanced by horses bred out of Spanish mares by my English blood-horse; finally, I put them to the stud, and their produce out of some twenty of my best Spanish mares were inferior in size, early maturity, and market value, to the stock of my blood-horse.

"To sum up, Arabs are very bad hacks, they are too small for hunters, even where exceptionally they have hunting conformation; too small and too devoid of elegant action for harness, and too slow for race-horses; as sires, they are inferior to the English blood-horses of power and symmetry, which are to be purchased when too slow for racing at a less price than a high-caste Arab."

The one quality in which Arabs excel—endurance—and which they share with Australian horses and Indian mustangs, is not required in those civilised states where travelling is either performed by railways or by post-horses.

CONTINENTAL ARABS.

On the continent of Europe, and especially in Eastern Europe, Arab sires are much more esteemed than in England, where hunting and racing have made a tall blood-horse the more valuable animal.

The small, active, blood-like horses of one district of France (Tarbes) have not been effaced by the popularisation of the English race-horse, because the pasture is too poor to support a well-bred horse bigger than a pony. The native horses of Poland, Hungary, and Eastern Austria, are all of Eastern descent, and "hit" well with Arabs for the purposes of their owners; namely, for light cavalry, and long journeys over the rolling plains of Eastern Europe in harness. Between the eighth and the seventeenth centuries Europe was repeatedly invaded and partially subdued by the Saracens and Turks. The Saracens were defeated in the great cavalry battle of Poictiers, by Charles Martel, A.D. 732, in which their loss has been variously estimated at between half a million and one hundred thousand! At any rate, the survivors retired after the battle across the Pyrenees, and they must have left behind them enough Oriental horse blood to stock the country for centuries.

"Vieille Moustache," who has seen cavalry service in Spain, in India, and the Crimea, and who has had experience in breeding, in breaking, and training thorough-bred horses of the first class, in a correspondence in *The Field* does justice to the unquestionable merits of the Arab in his proper place :—

"The truth is, that great speed for a mile and a half or two miles is not the *forte* of Arabs. The flying two-year-old races in England, or, indeed, such contests as the Derby and Leger, would not suit them; they would be outpaced for such distances. Stoutness, endurance of hunger, thirst,

TARBES ARAB.

and fatigue, enormous power of carrying weight far above what their size would appear to warrant, fine temper and wonderful hardihood of constitution, enabling them to endure intense cold equally with great heat, and to do well on the food of any country—these are the characteristics which make the Arab horse so valuable. Their staying quality renders the admixture of their blood with that of Western-bred horses, in my opinion, most desirable, while their rare intelligence and sagacity must always win the true lover of the equine race.

"As regards the capability of the Arab to carry weight, it is difficult to convey to any man who has never ridden one any idea of their power in that way. When I first went to India I had an Arab horse given me to break. My eye was then only for the large horses bred in this county (Leicestershire), and my notion of a weight-carrier was intimately connected with 16 hands 3 inches or thereabouts. The horse I was about to ride in Bangalore was not over 14 hands 3 inches, but he certainly had both substance and quality, as well as length, which most Arabs are deficient in. Nevertheless, I did not for a moment believe the little animal could carry me. I was never so deceived in my life, for I was not five minutes on his back before I found he had the power of four ordinary horses. This very horse, I believe, is now at the stud of the Duke of Leichtenstein. He was a grey Kohlan, named Nobbler, and was owned by the Hon. Algernon Moreton, of the 15th Hussars. Mr. Moreton sold him to Captain Fletcher, of the 12th, who again disposed of him to Sir William Gordon in the Crimea. The latter officer sold him to General Laurenson; and when I last saw him, on Warwick race-course, five years ago, his legs were as fine as the day he was foaled. He was then twenty years old. I believe he is still to the fore, and getting stock in Germany. I know that the late Mr. Bamberger purchased him from General Laurenson at a long price for that purpose. This, I submit, carries out my assertion that the Arab horse possesses a constitution of rare hardihood. Still, for cavalry chargers you must cross them with something that produces weight as well as endurance and stoutness, in order to stand the crush of a heavy cavalry charge.

*   *   *   *   *   *

"In 1837 I rode in a charge of cavalry in Spain. I was mounted on a brown thorough-bred mare, than which to this day it is admitted that a better one of her inches never looked through a bridle. She was by Tramp out of Bartolozzi, was bred by the late General Grosvenor, perhaps a trifle too fiery for a charger, and was considerably heavier than most Arab horses. In the charge I speak of, with plenty of way on, I came in contact with a great lumbering Andalusian horse, mounted by dragoon to match. The Spaniard treated me to a thrust with his lance, but missed me, for the simple reason that his great black *destrier* knocked me end over tail, mare and all, into a shallow gravel-pit half full of mud and water. Perhaps I was not so hardly done by as some of my comrades, after all."

The *Times* correspondent, describing, in October, 1873, the Vienna Horse Show, says :—"By far the most remarkable in the whole show was a string of twenty-four pure-bred Arab brood mares, exhibited by Count Drieduszycki, of Galicia, who has for many years past devoted himself entirely to breeding Arabs. In 1845, after spending two years in Syria, and visiting the desert tribes, he brought with him to Austria four Arab mares and three stallions, to form the nucleus of a stud. He has since imported many Arab sires, and has kept his stock perfectly pure from any other strain. They are all, with one exception, flea-bitten greys, and the whole string, when walked out together, formed a sight well worth seeing, and are as high-caste a looking lot as one might expect to see issue from Aga Khan's stables in Bombay.

"This Vienna Show has brought prominently into notice the very great partiality felt by Austria, Hungary, Russia, and Germany for Arab blood ; in fact, it would almost appear as if these four nations had combined to bring their favourite strain to the notice of the world. The following facts are remarkable :—Germany shows thirty horses in all, and ten of them are stated to be pure or half-bred Arabs. Austria shows 258 horses, of which a great number are for heavy draught, but of the remainder no less than fifty-two claim to be pure Arabs or of Arab parentage. Hungary shows seventy-eight horses, of which twenty-four are full or half-bred Arabs. Russia shows forty-four horses, out of which eight are stated to be pure-bred Arabs, and a large proportion of the remainder claim Arab descent. To crown the triumph of the Arab horse, Egypt sends eight desert-born stallions, of great beauty and of priceless value, the property of Sefer Pasha and Arthur Bey. These are of the Nejed and Anazeh castes, and contrast very favourably, in the eye of a judge of Arabs, with eight mares which stand near them, belonging to a Russian, Prince Sanguszko, and which are stated to be thorough-bred Arabs, although some of them measure over 16 hands.

"From Hungary Count Julius Andrassy shows four thorough-bred English horses of his own breeding, and Count Alfred Andrassy a stallion of the Czyndery or Tartary breed. The greater part of the remainder are stallions and brood mares, selected for exhibition from the Government studs at Babolna, Mezohegyes, Kisber, and Debreczin. These are of English, Norman, Spanish, Lippizaner, and Arab origin; but on looking through the whole of the Hungarian horses, one cannot fail to remark the manifest preponderance of Arab blood."

"At Bolzna, in Hungary, a great royal stud is maintained for breeding nothing but Arabs, which formerly enjoyed a European reputation; but, whether from the poverty of the soil or other causes, this stud, which consists of over 600 horses, has very much deteriorated.

"The late King of Wurtemburg had a passion for Arab horses. Whilst Crown Prince he rode through the last campaign against Napoleon I. on an Arab charger, which he afterwards sent into a stud he had established in 1810 near Stuttgard; but it was not till he came to the throne, in 1817, that the stud attained the large proportions which it maintained till his death, in 1864. His Majesty took extraordinary pains to obtain all the best blood from the East. By his marriage with a Russian princess he was enabled to procure some very high-bred mares from the Caucasus; and he sent special commissioners to Hungary, Russia, Syria, Constantinople, and Egypt, for the purchase of horses.

"On the death of William IV., he bought, at Hampton Court, the black horse Sultan, said to have been the highest-caste Arab ever brought to this country, and which had been presented to the English monarch by the Imâm of Muscat. Altogether his Majesty succeeding in procuring for his stud no fewer than eighteen horses and thirty-six mares, all of pure Arab blood and birth; and in 1861 the stud contained over 100 brood mares, fifty-one of which were Arabs. It will thus be seen that during half a century and more, during which the stud was conducted with royal magnificence, every opportunity was afforded for trying the effect of Arab crossings. Freiherr von Hügel, who was chief of the stud, writing in the lifetime of the king, speaks most favourably of the results, so far as the breeding of pure Arabs was concerned. According to him, the produce became bigger and stronger than their parents. It is to be apprehended, however, that, as in India, where the breeding from pure Arabs was also for a long time attempted, although the young produce became much longer in the leg than Arab-born horses, what they gained in size they lost in symmetry and compactness. Abbas Pacha, late ruler of Egypt, made a shrewd remark to Von Hügel when he was describing the pure Arabs in the royal stables at Stuttgard: 'Even if you succeed in getting hold of genuine Arabs, you will never breed pure Arabs from them, for an Arab is no longer an Arab when he ceases to breathe the air of the desert.' With respect to half-bred stock, the crossing of Arabs with Wurtemburg mares failed signally, as it did with Russian and Polish mares, but it succeeded better with those from Persia and the Caucasus. With sixteen English hunting mares imported in 1816, and crossed with Emir, an Arab horse purchased at Damascus, an excellent strain of carriage-horses was produced. A similar importation of Yorkshire and Irish mares in 1822, which were crossed with another Arab, Mahmoud, laid the foundation of the present fine breed of carriage-horses which are to be seen drawing the royal carriages, averaging 17 hands in height. The king's favourite colours were black and grey. From the English mares and Mahmoud descend the greys, whilst the blacks owe their origin to mares procured from the Thakehnen stud, in Prussia." *

* One of the finest Arab crosses I ever saw was of the Wurtemburg breed. He was a charger, ridden, in 1844, by the landlord of the "Two Swans" at Frankfort, an officer in the mounted Burgher Guard of that city—a beautiful grey, over 15 hands 2 inches, with fine charger action, very docile, and full of courage. He was old, and had never been shod; his hoofs perfect. To be sure, he had never done anything beyond walking exercise, except on days of drill and parade.—S. S.

EGYPTIAN ARABS.

Another great breeder of Arabs, the greatest, according to Baron Hügel, since King Solomon, was Abbas Pacha. Himself a child of the desert, for he was brought up in Arabia, where his father was Governor of Mecca, he displayed throughout life the greatest love for the horse; and his stud was brought to the hammer at Cairo in 1860. At the time of the sale only 300 animals were left; for the successor of Abbas Pacha, a madcap youth of eighteen, had given them away right and left to every one who managed to approach him with a well-turned piece of flattery. Von Hügel attended the sale on the part of his royal master, and had to give exorbitant prices for the two stallions and three mares which he purchased, but which were of the highest caste. The sale lasted three weeks, and the bids were made in English guineas. On one day twenty-six horses fetched 5,000 guineas. Aged mares twenty years old were sold at from 180 to 250 guineas, colts and fillies from 300 to 700 guineas each.

*   *   *   *   *   *

According to Hammer Purgstall, the beauties of the Arab horse are celebrated by no less than eighty-six classical Arabic and Persian writers.

CHAPTER II.

THE ORIGIN OF THE MODERN BRITISH HORSE.

William the Conqueror's Roan Cavalry—Chaucer's Horses—The Earl of Northumberland's Stud, 1500—Henry VIII.'s Law Regulating Horse-breeding not Carried Out—Blundeville, *temp.* Queen Elizabeth—Shakespeare's Horse of Adonis —Gervase Markham, a Traveller and Sportsman, *temp.* James I.—Condition of English Horses in his Time—Hunting —High-school Riding—The Yeomanry rode often—Description of the true English Horse—The Courser of Naples— The Turkish Horse—The Barbarie Horse—The Genet of Spain—The High Almaine—The Fleming—The Friesland— The Irish Hobby—Michael Barrett's (1618) "Vineyard of Horsemanship"—Hunter of the Period—The Running-horse— The Stag-hunting of the Nobility—The Hare-hunting of the Yeomanry—The Traine Scent—The Wild-goose Chase— The Duke of Newcastle, 1658—Advice on Choice of Horses—His Pictures—Cart-horses with many Names—High-school Riding in 1865—Importation of Oriental Horses between 1618 and 1688—The Italian Notion of Horses same Date— Illustration of Italian Beau-idéal—Paduan Horse—King William III.'s Charger.

ALL the horses in this country, on the Continent of Europe, and of the English-speaking nations of America (except those employed in slow heavy draught), depend so much for their best qualities on large and repeated crosses of blood, that it is essential that any writer on the subject, however anxious to avoid unpractical disquisitions, should tell the story of the origin and gradual progress to perfection of the English blood-horse, and his effect on the races of other countries.

England, Scotland, and Ireland, have, from the remotest historical times, had useful breeds of horses, suited to the requirements of the age.

The climate that suits horse-breeding so well now was equally favourable in the time of the Roman Conquest. At the period of Cæsar's invasion ponies were bred on the hills and mountains, and larger horses on the richer lowlands; but it was not until the middle of the last century that the English blood-horses competed with Spanish and Oriental horses in the favour of Continental equestrians, and it was only under the reign of William III. that the heaviest draught horses were introduced from Holland with the engineers who drained the fens of Lincolnshire.

The followers of William the Conqueror imported the large Norman horses, so suitable to carry knights in complete armour. That celebrated work of art the Bayeux Tapestry represents the boats of the invading army full of red and blue horses (roan horses). Every knight had a small hack on which he rode without his armour, while his great war-horse was led by one of his squires. For this purpose the Crusaders brought back to England some of those Eastern steeds which were well known and esteemed in France and Germany, and are still esteemed in Spain, as "genets."

Chaucer gives us an idea of the various kinds of horses familiar to his countrymen in the fourteenth century. His Canterbury pilgrims were all on horseback. Of the Monk, whose ambling nag was "brown as any berry," he says—

> "Full many a dainty horse had he in stall;"

of the Old Knight— "His horse was good, albeit he was not gay;"

of the Young Squire— "Well could he sit his horse, and fairly ride;"

and of the Wife of Bath— "Upon an ambler easily she sat."

A good notion of the stables of a great nobleman in 1512 may be gathered from the regulations and establishment of Algernon Percy, fifth Earl of Northumberland.

"This is the ordre of the chequir roul of the nombre of all the horsys of my lorde's and my lady's that are appointed to be in the charge of the hous yerely, as to say, gentell hors, palfreys, hobys, naggis, clothsell hors, male hors.

"First, gentell hors, to stand in my lorde's stable, six.

"Item—Palfris for my ladis: to wit, oone for my lady, two for her gentlewomen, and one for her chamberer.

"Four hobys and nags for my lorde's oone saddell; viz., one for my lorde to ride, one led for my lorde, and one to stay at home for my lorde.

"Item—Chariot hors to stand in my lorde's stable yearly; seven great trottynge hors to draw in the chariot, and a nag for the chariot-man to ride—eight. Again, hors for Lord Percy, his lordship's son and heir; a great double trotting-hors, called a curtal, for his lordship to ride out of townes. Another trottynge gambaldyne hors for his lordship to ride when he comes into townes; a proper amblynge little nag, when he goeth hunting and hawking; a great amblynge gelding or trotting gelding, to carry his male."

Hobys were little hacks, described by early writers as commonly bred in Ireland.

The clothsell horse followed at the same rate as my lord; and when he had reached a town it was the custom for his lordship to change from his easy-trotting or ambling nag, and mount a parade horse, in order to make his entry in the form and state expected of great personages in those days. No doubt he put aside his rough travelling clothes, and attired himself in one of those magnificent costumes which are so picturesque in the portraits of the Tudor age, and must have been so impossible as a riding-dress on the roads of either North or South.

Writers on the history of the British horse have attributed a good deal of importance to an Act of Parliament, 32 Henry VIII., cap. 13, under which it is enacted, "That no person shall put in any forest, chase, moor, heath, common, or waste, any entire horse above the age of two years, not being 15 hands high, within the shires of Norfolk, Suffolk, Cambridge, Buckingham, Huntingdon, Essex, Kent, South Hants, Berks, North Wilts, Oxford, Worcester, Gloucester, Somerset, Wales, Bedford, Warwick, Nottingham, Lancaster, Salop, Leicester, Hereford, or Lincoln, nor under 14 hands in any other county." And it is enacted that any person may seize any horse so under size, "and, after having him measured by the keeper of the forest, or the constable of the next town, in the presence of three honest men, if found contrary to what is above expressed, to be turned to his own use." By the same statute, "all commons and other places shall, within fifteen days after Michaelmas, be driven by the owners and keepers, and if there be found in any of the said drifts any mare not able to bear foals of reasonable stature, or to do profitable labour, in the discretion of the majority of the drivers, they may kill and bury them." It was also ordered that the archbishops and all dukes should keep seven entire trotting-horses for the saddle, each of which was to be at least 14 hands high. Every clergyman possessing a living of the amount of £100 per annum, or any one whose wife should wear a bonnet of velvet, was to keep one trotting entire horse, under penalty of £20.

But it seems to be forgotten that although the imperious Henry could make any laws he chose to dictate to his Parliament, he had no such means of carrying out his decrees as have since been invented in the centralised governments of France and Prussia. According to historical evidence, the effect of these enactments was to diminish the number of horses;

for when, in 1588, in Elizabeth's reign, England was threatened by the Spanish Armada, there was a scarcity of horses. With all the enthusiasm that pervaded the nation, the queen was only able to muster 3,000 cavalry, which Blundeville, who wrote a book on horsemanship at that epoch, says were "very indifferent, strong, heavy, slow draught-horses, or light and weak."

Shakespeare had a very good notion of what a war-horse or weight-carrying roadster should be, but the animal he provides for Adonis was neither thorough-bred nor fit to carry a man in the first flight over Leicestershire. He might have borne the Earl of Essex grandly at a tournament, or satisfactorily in hunting a buck in a great park, but would have had no chance in a modern fox-hunt over on ox-feeding county, or in a Grand National Steeple-chase. As Shakespeare was never out of England, he must have seen the animal he describes.

> "Round-hoofed, short-jointed, fetlocks shag and long,
> Broad breast, full eyes, small head, and nostril wide,
> High crest, short ears, straight legs, and passing strong,
> Thin mane, thick tail, broad buttock, tender hide."*

Although the shaggy fetlocks show that Shakespeare's horse was half-bred, his "small head and nostril wide" and his "thin mane" prove that he had "quality," perhaps derived from some Spanish ancestor, some Barb sire introduced under the reign of Queen Mary by her Spanish husband, or some Syrian Arab, the prize of a Crusader.

Gervase Markham,† a very accomplished writer on several rural subjects, writing in the time of James I., described all the European horses of that period, and there is internal evidence that he had at any rate travelled in France and Spain.

The time of Gervase Markham may therefore be taken as a standpoint for summing up the condition of the English horse before the production of the thoroughbred race-horse, which was not effected until nearly a hundred years later. Ploughing and the heavy draught of agriculture were carried on chiefly by oxen. Goods and merchandise were conveyed from one part of the country to another almost entirely by pack-horses of an active breed, the use of which had not been entirely discontinued in the West of England at the commencement of this century. The Devonshire pack-horse was one of the boasts of that county within living memory. Carriages hung on rude springs were one of the luxuries of the wealthy; and hack carriages, to the disgust of Thames watermen, had been to some extent established

* "Venus and Adonis," Canto L.

† "Containing all the arts of horsemanship, as much as it is necessary for any man to understand, whether he be horse-breeder, horse-ryder, horse-hunter, horse-runner, horse-ambler, horse-farrier, horse-keeper, coachman, smith, or saddler. Together with the discovery of the subtil trade or mystery of horse-coursers, and an explanation of a horse's understanding, or how to teach them to do tricks like Bankes his curtall. Newly imprinted, corrected, and augmented, with many worthy secrets not known before."

The first book, and all the others, are dated 1617, but, curiously enough, the second is dated 1616. Each has the same title-page—a rude wood block, representing in five circles as many shapeless brutes, described as "The Neapolitan horse for service; the Barbarie running-horse; the English ambling gelding," all with long tails; and the "English hunting-horse," with his tail tied up. Each of the eight books has two separate dedications, the first being addressed, "The most high and mightie Charles Prince of Wales, Duke of Cornwall, York, Albanie, Rothsay, &c." In the second dedication, "to the three great columbes of this empire, the nobilite, the gentrie, and yeomanrie of Great Britaine," he says that it is an enlargement of "that small treatise on horsemanship which about sixteen years agone (when my experience was but youngly fructified) I brought forth into the world. A copie thereof being corruptly taken, and covetously offered to the printing without my knowledge, I thought as good to publish it myself with his natural wantes as to let it come abroad by others deformities."

in London.   Every knight was bound to keep horses in proportion to the military service due from him—every landed squire and squire's lady, every yeoman, kept one or more active riding-horses, and performed all journeys on horseback.   There were no public conveyances. Hunting the buck and the hare was much practised, as well as running-horse matches for wagers and for bells of honour.

The high-school or manége riding was an accomplishment confined to gentlemen of great landed estates and of the knightly class.   Manége horses in the time of James were just as much an expensive luxury as a stud of thoroughbred Leicestershire hunters at the present day.   There existed then, as the next reign proved, a large class of gentry and yeomanry possessing plenty of

THE MARQUIS OF NEWCASTLE : MANÉGE SEAT.

good horses, which they rode on the natural, as distinguished from the artificial seat of "the school," in pursuit of their ordinary business as well as for their pleasure, hunting and racing.   Their horsemanship differed as much from manége riding as dancing differs from running.

In the following passages from Gervase Markham, we learn whence came those horses on which Cromwell's Ironsides, a few years later, rode down the Cavaliers led by Prince Rupert at Grantham, at Gainsborough, at Marston Moor, and at Naseby, all battles decided by cavalry :—

"I do daily finde," says Markham, "in mine experience, that the vertue, goodness, boldness, swiftness, and endurance of our true-bred English horses is equal with any race of horses whatsoever.   Some former writers, whether out of want of experience, or to flatter novelties, have concluded that the English horse is a great strong jade, deep-ribbed, sid-belled, with strong legges and good hoofes, yet fitter for the cart than either saddle or any working employment. How false this is all English horsemen knowe.

"The true English horse, him I mean that is bred under a good clime, on firme ground, in a pure temperature, is of tall stature and large proportions; his head, though not so fine as either the Barbarie's or the Turke's, yet is lean, long, and well-fashioned; his crest is hie, only subject to thickness if he be stoned, but if he be gelded then it is firm and strong; his chyne is straight and broad; and all his limbs large, leane, flat, and excellently jointed. For their endurance I have seen them suffer and execute as much and more than ever I noted of any foraine creation.

NOBILISSIMO, COURSIER NAPOLITAIN (AFTER THE MARQUIS OF NEWCASTLE).

"I have heard it reported that at the Massacre of Paris (St. Bartholomew), Montgomerie, taking an English mare in the night, first swam over the river Seine, and after ran her so many leagues as I fear to nominate, lest misconstruction might tax me of too lavish a report.

"Again, for swiftness, what nation hath brought forth that horse which hath exceeded the English—when the best Barbaries that ever were in their prime, I saw them overrunne by a black hobbie at Salisbury; yet that hobbie was more overrunne by a horse called Valentine, which Valentine neither in hunting or running was ever equalled, yet was a plain-bred English horse both by syre and dam? Again, for infinite labour and long endurance, which is to be desired in our hunting matches, I have not seen any horse to compare with the English. He is of tolerable shape, strong, valiant, and durable."

This passage is important, because it is a popular notion that the goodness of English horses began with the race-horse in the time of Charles II., whilst there is much to be said in favour of the theory that our big blood-horse is the result of crosses of Oriental blood out of English mares, cultivated by careful selection and generous treatment.

Next to the English horse Markham places the "courser" of Naples, "a horse of a strong and comely fashion, loving disposition, and infinite courageousness. His limbs and general features are so strong and well knit together that he hath ever been reputed the only beast for the warres, being naturally free from fear or cowardice. His head is long, lean, and very slender; doth from eye to the nose bend like a hawke's beak. He hath a great full eye, a sharpe eare, and a straight legge, which, to an over-curious eye, might appear a little too slender; which is all the fault curiositie itself can find. They be naturally of a loftie pace, loving to their rider, most strong in their exercise, and to conclude, as good in all poynts that no forayne race has ever borne a tythe so much excellencie." The kingdom of Naples was, when Markham wrote, a viceroyalty of Spain.

Next to the Neapolitan he places the Turkish horse. All he had seen came from Constantinople, "which is part of Thrace," "not of monstrous greatness, but inclining to middle size; finely headed, almost as the Barbarie. They have excellent fore-hands, both for length, depth, and proportion. They are of great courage and swiftness, for I have seen them used at our English bell-courses. Naturally they desire to amble, and, which is most strange, their trot is full of pride and gracefulness."

Next to the Turk he places the Barbary. "They are swift beyond forayne horses, and to that use only we employ them in England."

Next to the Turk he names the genet, which he had seen in Spain. "The genet may passe a carriere (run a course in tilting), some twelve or twenty score, with great puissance and swiftness, but for running our English courses, which are commonly three or four miles, we have not seen such virtue in them." He describes them as with fine crests, naturally taking to ambling; their trot long and waving, and the animal himself not full-grown until six years old.

The High Almaine horse, "of great and high stature, having neither neatness nor fineness; some men esteem him for the shock (charge) or the manége. They are much used for warres, but, I think, like their countrymen, rather for a wall or defence than either for assault or action. They are great, slow, hard trotters."

The Fleming he describes as "resembling the Almaine. His place is the draught, in which he exceedeth all other horses."

And the Friesland horse, is, like the Fleming, "not so tall, of a more fiery and hot courage, but more fit for service; being able to pass a short carriere, beat a curvet, and such like," but vicious; his pace being a short hard trot.

Last he mentions the Irish hobby,* "having a fine head, strong neck, well-cast body, good limbs, sure of foot, nimble in dangerous places, lively courage, tough in travel, but much subject to frights and boggarts," due, Markham thinks, to the rude manner in which they were handled, which "these ruder people" know not how to amend.

That hunting had, long before public races for money, obtained the importance which created the race-horse, is confirmed by the writings of Michael Barrett, who, in 1618, wrote a fantastic book on horsemanship, full of sound precepts written in the pedantic language of the age, in which he speaks of Gervase Markham with great respect.†

Barrett's description of the hunting-horse of that age would not be amiss for the present day, except that he says not one word about leaping, although we know from Gervase Mark-

* "Hobby," from the French *hobbin*, meant "pony;" so, too, "hackney," from the French *haquinée*, Spanish, *haccanea, haca*.
† Michael Barrett, 1618. "The Vineyard of Horsemanship. Dedicated to Prince Charles, the Bishop of Peterborough, and the gentlemen of Nottingham and Lincolnshire."

ham's account of a "catte" now called a "drag hunt," and of a "wild-goose chase," that they rode over every obstacle; while his directions for choosing a racing-horse would have answered for selecting the half-bred or cocktail racers that were run against thoroughbreds even in the first quarter of this century.

After advising those that require deeper knowledge to consult "Maister Blundeville" and "Maister Markham," he proceeds to sum up the merits of the horses of the day in the following manner :—

"I hold that the Barbarian and the Turkey stallions are the best for all general uses, for service (that is, war), swiftness, and proud going, as well for pleasure pace as a gallant trot.

"Although the Spanish genet, the Irish hobby, and the Arabian courser, are held both by Maister Blundeville and Maister Markham to be the chief for pacing and neat action, there is the bastard stallion, begotten by one of them on our English mares, which doth exceed either of them in toughness—the English mares to be of good stature, somewhat large, but not very high, a small head, full eye, wide nostril, a pricke ear but somewhat long, a firm thin crest, with a long straight necke, well compact in the cragge at the setting-on of the head, a broad breast, deep-chested, a round backe, being barrell-ribbed, and the short ribs shot up somewhat close to the huckle bone, the buttocke somewhat long, so as it be proportionable, a flat legge and straight foote, and a hollow hoof."

THE HUNTER OF 1618.

"For the pleasure of hunting is so great that it exceedeth all others, that if it brought no other profit than the delight to follow a pack of good dogges (having a good horse), were enough to countervail the danger, for I esteem it above all earthly pleasures. It maintains the health, causeth an agil and apt body, increaseth knowledge how to correct his horse as occasion shall be offered, whereby if he should goe upon any martial service he will be ready to perform any desperate exploits with celerity and quickness. Beside the use of riding up and down high places and deep earths, so a hunting-horse may be made more servicable for war, through his toughness and speed."

The hunter was to be "about 16 hands* in height, his head of a mean bignesse, his chank thin and wide, his eare not too little, and if he be somewhat wide-eared, it is a sign of toughness, so they be sharp; his forehead broad, having a bunch standing out in the midst like a hare; his eye full and large, his nostrell wide, with a deep mouth; all his head leane, a long, straight neck; a firm thin crest, well reared; a wide throstle, a broad breast, deep-chested; his body large, his ribbes round and close, shut up to his huckle-bone; a good-filled, long buttocke, not very broad, well let down in the gaskins (gascoyne); his limmes clean, flat, straight, but not very bigge; his joints short, especially between the pasterne and the hoofe, having little haire on his fetlock, a straight foot, black hollow hoof, not over big." From which it seems that the points of a good riding-horse were perfectly understood in the reign of King James I.

The following description might stand for a modern steeplechaser :—

A RUNNING-HORSE, SAME DATE.

"For the shape of a running-horse there is not much difference betwixt the shape of him and the hunter as there is in their ends of training; for the hunting-horse must endure long

---

* *Let him be of a meane stature,* that is, *some sixteene hand of height* (sic).

and laboursome toyle, with heates and cold, but the running-horse must dispatch his business in a moment of time. Have as near in proportion as the former, only he may have a longer chine, so that his side be longer, he will take a larger stroke, especially on light earths; and if his limmes be more slender and his joints more loose, and not so short at the pastern, he may be very excellent and swift for a course."

These lean-headed, flat-limbed, fine-haired hunters and running-horses formed a class completely apart from the prancing *destriers* maintained for daily amusement in the riding-school which was attached to every great house. In these schools the young gentlemen of the period practised equestrian feats, some of which are still essential to a cavalry education, but the most difficult and useless are only to be seen in circus exhibitions of the *haute école*. They prepared themselves to make a gallant figure in riding at the ring, in processions and parades of ceremony, and to hold their own in duels on horseback, or in the single combats into which cavalry actions, as long as fire-arms played only a secondary part in war, resolved themselves. The trained war-horse was expected to take as much part as his rider—in every encounter striking with his fore and kicking with his hind legs—making *balotades, croupades*, and *caprioles*.

But while great noblemen indulged in the amusements of the manége, and had the exclusive right to hunt the stag, wild or parked, the English yeomanry and wealthy farmers—a class who existed at that time in no other European State—indulged in hunting the badger, the fox, and the hare, in matches, races, and in "wild-goose chases," for proving the speed and stoutness of their horses, with as much freedom and enthusiasm as their feudal superiors; so that the cultivation of good horses did not depend, as in other countries, on the patronage of kings and great noblemen, but was pursued by cultivators who were also owners of the soil, throughout the length and breadth of the land.

Almost all modern writers on the subject concentrate their narratives on what was done by kings and Acts of Parliament, and seem to overlook the steady improvement in the breed of riding-horses that took place generation after generation, through the passion of Englishmen of all ranks for hunting, and, to speak plainly, for gambling, in the way of wagers, on the speed and stoutness of their horses.

According to Markham, the fox, in the time of Elizabeth and James, was, as a beast of chase, put on the same low level as the badger, and pursued only in woods, "where a horse can neither conveniently make his way or tread without danger of stumbling." More highly esteemed was hunting the wild stag, which, however, as well as the parked deer, was nominally the exclusive privilege of kings and very great nobles. For park hunting rectangular rides were cut through the woods, up and down which the cavaliers and their dames cantered composedly, after the fashion practised in our own times in France and Germany—a fashion which was revived, with the costume and all the splendour of the days of Louis XIV., by the Emperor Napoleon III.

But hunting the wild stag or the moorland hare required a horse of a very different character from the ambling palfreys used within enclosed parks. Markham says, "When he (a stag) is at liberty he will break forth his chase four, five, and six miles; nay, I have myself followed a buck better than ten miles forthright, from the place of his rousing to the place of his death, beside all his turnings and windings and cross passages." Evidently old Gervase was a keen sportsman, and kept his horses in pretty good condition. He goes on to observe that as stag-hunting is in season between April and September, and as it is "most swift and violent" when the sun is hottest and the ground hard, it is not fit for training young horses, but for those of staid years and long practice. There was "a certain race of little horses in Scotland called Galway* nags, which he had seen hunt the buck exceedingly well, endured the chase with great courage, and the hard earth without lameness better than horses of greater puissance and strength." But the chase which he most recommends for training young horses was that of the hare, "not a privilege confined, like that of the buck, to great noblemen, but a sport easilie and equallie distributed, as well to the wealthie farmer as to the great gentleman." He also recommends "the chace of a traine scent," which was nothing else than the modern "drag" hunt of Oxford, Windsor, and garrison towns—"a scent drawn either across ploughed lands, or athwart green fields, leaping ditches, hedges, payles, rails, or fences, or running through a warren."

There was also "the wild-goose chase," the forerunner of the steeplechase (which within this century has been played at Irish horse fairs), where half a dozen mad riders tried which could set the others the most desperate or cramped and difficult leaps, and the rider who could within a certain time keep forty yards ahead won the wager.

In like manner, although racing had not assumed the importance of an art, as it did in the reign of King James's son, Charles II., yet matches were constantly made, and horses were trained to win private wagers all over the kingdom; the prize of the public racecourse was only a bell, but the wagering was heavy. The principles of training were the same as now, although less intelligently applied. The "runners," as they were called, were physicked (sometimes with very ridiculous drugs), exercised, clothed, and groomed with very great pains.

Cavendish, Marquis of Newcastle, published an edition of his celebrated work on "Horsemanship" in French, in 1658, at Antwerp, during the time that he was an exile and Cromwell was Protector; an English edition with the original copper-plate illustrations appeared in 1667, after the Restoration, dedicated to the king, who had created him Duke of Newcastle.

The few pages which he devotes to the general subject of the horse are most interesting, because they show that fifty years after Markham, although at least one Oriental sire destined to be famous in the records of the stud-book had been introduced, the English blood-horse had not been manufactured.

His master, Charles, had obtained a footing in Africa, Tangiers being part of the dowry of his Portuguese wife, and he had imported the celebrated "royal mares" of Barb, Arab, Persian, or Turkish blood, no one can positively say which. The duke, whose whole heart and soul was in the tricks of the manége, expresses himself very cautiously as to the value of the English breed. In the following passage he speaks as if the horses of the time were presented to him in mixed lots, like the droves that used to be seen at fairs, when fairs were a much more important institution than they are at present. "If," he says, "a horse is fit to go a travelling pace, let him do it; if he is naturally inclined to make curvets, he must be put to it; and so of the *demi-airs, passadoes, terre-à-terre, croupades, balotades, and caprioles.* If he be not fit for any of these, put him to run the ring; if he be not cut out for that, use him as a drudge, or to go of errands. If none of these suit him" (and here mark his contempt) "he will perhaps be good for running, hunting, or travelling, or for the portmanteau, or for the burdens, or for coach or cart; for really there is no horse but what is fit for some use or other." And he goes on to observe, with trenchant irony, considering the character of his king :—

"If princes were as industrious to know the capacities of men for different trusts they put

---

* In 1715 the Earl of Stair, ambassador at the Court of Louis XIV., "sometimes presented to persons of distinction a pair of Galloways; the pure breed of small Galloway horses being then nearly extinct, and highly valued."—*Memoirs of Earl of Stair.*

in them as good horsemen are to employ each horse in that which Nature designed him for, kings would be better served than they are, and we should not see confusion that passes Babel happen in States through the incapacity of persons entrusted. He that is qualified to be a bishop is not fit to command an army, &c. . . . . But leaving kings to choose their officers as they please, let us follow Nature in what concerns horses.

*   *   *   *   *   *

"'What nation produces the most beautiful horse?' To which I answered that I could not decide till I knew for what the horse was intended.

"I have heard Neapolitan horses commended, but these were ill-shaped, though strong and vigorous. I have seen Spanish horses, and have had them in my own possession, which were proper to be painted, or fit for a king to mount on a public occasion; for they are not so tender as the Barbs, nor so ill-shaped as the Neapolitans, but between both. Genets have a lofty, fine air, trot and gallop well, but are seldom strong, though when well chosen they bear a good character. The best breed of horses is in Andalusia, especially that of the King of Spain's, at Cordova.

SPECIMENS OF BRANDS OF ITALIAN BREEDERS OF HORSES.

"With regard to the Barbary horses, I freely confess they are my favourites, and I allow them the preference as to shape, strength, natural genteel air, and docility. I confess they have not so genteel a trot or gallop as the genets, but no horses in the world have a better movement in general, when they are well chosen and well instructed; though I have been informed in France, by an old officer of the army in Henry IV.'s time, that he had often seen a Barb beat down by the superior strength of a Flemish horse.* I have experienced this difference between the bone of the leg of a Barbary horse and one from Flanders, viz., that the cavity of the bone of the former shall scarcely admit a straw, whilst you may thrust your finger in that of the latter. The generality of Barbs are sinewy, strong, swift, and good-winded. Mountain Barbs are horses of the best courage; many of them bear the marks of wounds they have received from lions.

"With respect to the Northern horses, I have seen some beautiful in their kind, genteel in all sorts of paces, and which have excelled all others in leaping. Moreover, they have a peculiar excellency in the motion of their fore-legs, which is the principal grace in the action of a horse; but they sooner come to decay than a Barb, and you will always find among them more horses fit for the cart than the manége.

"The best stallion is a well-chosen Barb or a beautiful Spanish horse. Some people pretend that a Barb or genet produces too small a breed. There is no fear of having too small horses in England, since the moisture of the climate and the fatness of the land rather produce horses too large.

* See anecdote of a cavalry charge by "Vieille Moustache," page 32, chapter on Oriental Horses.

" In the choice of breeding mares, I would advise you to take either a well-shaped Spanish one, or a Neapolitan. When these are not easily obtained, then a beautiful English mare, of a good colour and well marked.

*   *   *   *   *   *   *   *   *   *

" I am no friend to astrological remarks in this case. The moon's aspect or that of any other celestial body are equally absurd in affairs of this kind ; it matters not whether the moon is increasing or decreasing, or whether any other planets are in conjunction or opposition, for horses are not begot by astronomy or by the almanack."

But although the Duke of Newcastle expresses himself thus impartially on the merits of all the breeds of horses known to him, it is a very curious circumstance that the forty-three elaborate copper-plates which illustrate his book all represent one style of horse—the Flemish war-horse, of large limbs, heavy crest, shaggy fetlocks, flowing mane and tail. The horses ridden by Charles I. in Vandyke's portraits of that monarch at Windsor and Warwick Castles and Blenheim Palace are fine specimens of the breed.

In the Winter Exhibition of the Royal Academy in 1877 Her Majesty contributed a portrait of Charles I. in armour, mounted on a dun-coloured horse, probably also a portrait of the Flemish breed, by Sir Anthony Vandyke. This is the sketch for the large picture at Blenheim.

There is not the slightest difference in the apparent breed of the following list of horses, which are drawn on a double folio page :—" *Paragon*, un Barbe ;" " *La Superbe*, Cheval d'Espagne ;" " *Mako-melia*, un Turque ;" " *Nobillissimo*, Coursier Napolitain ," " *Rubetan*, un Roussin (a thick stallion of moderate size). There are also two large plates, one representing mares and foals, and the other three-year-old colts, in an enclosed paddock, gambolling in various attitudes, making natural curvettes and caprioles, but all of the hairy-heeled sort, like the Norman horses that used to draw the French diligences thirty years ago, or the improved Suffolks. The Neapolitan war-horse only differs from the Barb in that he has a rather more drooping croup, and is branded on the rump with the mark of his breeder, as horses bred on Italian plains are to this day. Some of these old brand marks are represented on the preceding page. These plates illustrating the Marquis's book were all drawn by Abraham Diepenbeke, a Flemish artist, "under the Marquis's immediate direction." Several of them represent the Marquis on horseback, performing one of the feats of the *haute école*, or high-school of riding, and engraved conspicuously across them are the words, " *Monsieur le Marquis Donne une Leçon*." So that after commencing by saying that he prefers a Barb, this noble teacher of horsemanship depicts nothing but a series of lively cart-horses, rather heavier than that hearse-like animal, in an impossible attitude, on which Charles I. is mounted at Charing Cross, which Horace Walpole, who was no horseman, so much admired.

This anomaly occurred vividly to me in 1865, when present at the opening of a French Horse Show in the Palace of Industry in the Champs Elysées. A troop of the pupils of the cavalry school of Saumur appeared in the arena, dressed in the style of Louis XV., with small three-cornered hats with ostrich plumes, green and gold coats, white leather breeches, and black boots, mounted on well-bred horses. They commenced by drawing up in a line, and at foot pace *passaging* (moving sideways) in front of the Emperor's box, each man as he passed saluting by raising his plumed hat ; the horses keeping an exact line, every foot rising along the line at the same moment—a performance I had often seen attempted at professional hippodromes, but never with horses so fine or men so admirably trained. Other feats followed, the least successful of which was the leaping of low hurdles. After this very pretty exhibition, the troop retired, and presently returned mounted on fat Norman horses with buckskin demi-piqued saddles, without stirrups, their manes plaited with ribbons, their tails plaited and tied on one side; in a word, an exact reproduction of the horses and pupils of the Marquis of Newcastle. After saluting the Emperor, they proceeded to execute ballotades, caprioles,* and all the tricks delineated in the elaborate copper plates of Abraham Diepenbèke.

I dwell upon this curious and costly publication,† because it is so extraordinary that such an expense should have been incurred for engravings of horses, in none of which, out of more than forty plates, does one blood-horse, or even moderately well-bred horse, appear.

The author of "The Gentleman's Jockey," the ninth edition of which is dated 1704, "with additions," undertakes to explain how a horse may be prepared "for a running course in two

ITALIAN HORSE, 1688.

months." He says of the English horse that he "may be known by his strong knitting together;" as the Neapolitan by his hooked nose, and the Barbary by his fine head. Cox, writing in 1686 his "Gentleman's Recreations," gives exactly the same list of horses as the Duke of Newcastle, adding particular directions for obtaining and importing Spanish, Arab, Barbary, and Turkish horses.

William III. was passionately fond of horses and hunting. The condition of his stud formed the subject of many letters to his favourite, Bentinck. That he liked Italian horses we learn

---

* In a ballotade the horse jumps off the ground, bending both knees and houghs, and showing his hind shoes without kicking out. In the capriole the horse does the same, and kicks out with both hind legs.

† I have only been able to find three editions—the first, in French, which the title-page calls a translation from English, published at Antwerp during the Protectorate, in 1658; the second, in English, in London, in 1667, after the Restoration; and the third, a reprint, in 1743—but all with the same copper-plate engravings, with titles and descriptions in French.

from *Forbes's Journal*, 1688, where it is stated that " Sir James Dalrymple, being seventy years old, accompanied the Prince of Orange on his expedition to England in 1688. On landing at Torbay William sent to inquire concerning Sir James's health, and perceiving that horses were not come up for him ordered *a Neapolitan horse belonging to himself* to be assigned for his use."

A portrait of William III. by Gaspard Netscher, in the possession of the Earl of Radnor, represents him on a coarsely-bred chestnut horse with white legs, evidently a portrait.

During the period between 1618 and 1688 no doubt a constant importation of Eastern horses was taking place, which, crossed with the best native mares, and selected by racing men and hunting men for speed and stoutness, gradually and almost insensibly produced the English blood-horse, whose superiority to all other breeds of horses was incontestably proved early in the eighteenth century.

It is noteworthy that in a book* on the treatment of the Horse, published in. Rome with permission of the Pope in 1689, from which the illustration on page 46 is copied, no reference is made to English horses. The author claims that the native horses have been brought to perfection, have derived their pleasant temperament, from the influence of the air, robust constitutions from the nature of the country, beauty of form from the crossing of various breeds, and fine paces from the training of their excellent riders. Rome, the kingdom of Naples, and Tuscany, stand first for good breeds of horses.

ITALIAN HORSES.

The high reputation which the Italian breed enjoyed as war-horses in the sixteenth century has been traced with great industry by a student of Italian literature, who has allowed me to condense in a few paragraphs the result of his labours.†

In Italy for a thousand years every warlike invader had brought his horses.

"The shape of the Roman horse is well known—a strong brute without much quality; but in A.D. 568 the Lombards invaded Italy, and Alborino their king brought with him out of Pannonia a breed of horses which was evidently highly esteemed, for Paolo Diaconi (Paul the Deacon), a Lombard whose great-grandfather came into Italy with Alborino, relates that when Alborino created his nephew Gisulfo Duke of Friuli and that part of Italy which has since formed a portion of the Venetian States, the latter made it one of the conditions on which he would accept the duchy that when his uncle advanced farther into Italy he would leave some of the Pannonian horses.

Twenty thousand Saxons, we learn from the same author, joined Alborino in his invasion. Their northern horses no doubt brought another cross to the native race.

In the eighth century the Lombards, firmly seated in Italy, sent an army to assist the French to repel the Saracen invasion. This having been done successfully, no doubt the Lombard allies brought back some of the Oriental horses of the defeated Moslems as part of their spoil.

During four centuries the Crusaders and pilgrims from every part of Europe passed through the Venetian States on their way to the Holy Land. As all travelling was performed on horseback, they must have left many horses to swell and cross the equine breeds of those States.

Thus for nearly a thousand years there was a constant influx to the neighbourhood of Mantua of the best breeds of horses of Asia, Africa, and Europe. The result was the production of the Mantuan horses, which became famous as war-horses in the sixteenth century.

They were considered the *destriers* fit for kings. Bernard Tasso, writing A.D. 1525, from

* " La Perfettione del Cavallo di Francesco Liberati Romano. All'illustries el Eccellèntiss. Principe il Signor D. Gio. Battista Borghese, Principe di Sulmona. In Roma, per Michele Hercole, 1669. Con Licenza de Sup."

† Ralph N. James, Esq., F.R.II.S.

the French camp, just before the battle of Pavia, says that the king, Francis I., the most accomplished horseman of the day, was much delighted with the Mantuan horse which had been sent him as a present from the Marquis of Mantua, and that it was much admired by everybody." Charles V. also used in war a Mantuan charger. The poet Torquato Tasso, in his " Forna della Nobilla," observes that, " A horse-dealer seeing any stallion of the Mantuan breed, *branded with the sign of the sun,* is ready to pay a good sum for him, for rarely do we see bad horses produced from a good breed. A purchaser would not do the same if he had to buy a slave, and found that he was an African or a Turk."

Some idea may be gathered of the shape of Mantuan horses from such equestrian statues

MOUNTED ITALIAN WARRIOR (FIFTEENTH CENTURY), FROM A STATUE AT PADUA.

as that of Gallamelata by Donatello, the designs of Leonardo da Vinci, and the drawings of Giulio Romano.

It is more than probable that the latter artist, when adorning the palaces of the Duke of Mantua, would introduce portraits of the horses of which the Duke was so proud. Supposing that they were portraits, and not, like most of the horses of the most celebrated painters and sculptors, conventional animals, the Mantuan horses (circa 1525) were not handsome, or even shaped for carrying weight and galloping according to our modern English ideas.

Under sixteen hands, with slight limbs in proportion to their bodies, the neck short, the head long with small ears, rather like the modern Norman horse, the back unusually short, the hind-quarter round, the tail set singularly low, and so thin of hair as to be almost what we call rat; this last peculiarity alone strengthening the idea that the fine original was a portrait of a favourite parade horse of the Duke of Mantua.

At any rate, the pictures do not justify the reputation of the Mantuan breed.

The wars that took place after 1628 between the Empire and France, as to the succession of the Duchy of Mantua, were fatal to this breed of horses. It disappeared with the great family of Gonzaga that had fostered it for centuries with so much care.

It has usually been taken for granted that Peter Paul Rubens took the models of the war-horses on which he mounted his kings and military chiefs from Flemish models, such as may still be seen, yoked in pairs, ploughing the fat land of Flanders. But Rubens resided, in 1600 and for several following years, in Mantua. Amongst his pictures is one of a bison hunt. Now Paul the Deacon makes particular mention of the bisons of Pannonia, enormous beasts which the Lombards encountered in the Monte Reggio, by which the Lombards arrived in Italy.

Whether in the time of Rubens the Mantuan horses had improved in beauty since the days of Giulio Romano, or whether Rubens improved them to please his own artist eye, cannot be settled.

Virgil had a better notion of a good horse than the Italians of the seventeenth century, if we may judge from the following passage from the 3rd Georgics :—

VIRGIL.—GEORG. iii., 75—91.

"Continuo pecoris generosi pullus in arvis
Altius ingreditur, et mollia crura reponit ;
Primus et ire viam, et fluvios tentare minaces
Audet et ignoto sese committere ponti,
Nec vanos horret strepitus. Illi ardua cervix,
Argutumque caput, brevis alvus, obesaque terga,
Luxuriatque toris animosum pectus. Honesti
Spadices glaucique, color deterrimus albis,
Et gilvo. Tum, si qua sonum procul arma dedere,
Stare loco nescit ; micat auribus et tremit artus ;
Collectumque fremens volvit sub naribus ignem.
Densa juba, et dextro jactata recumbit in armo,
At duplex agitur per lumbos spina ; cavatque
Tellurem et solido graviter sonat ungula cornu.
Talis Amyclæi domitus Pollucis habenis
Cyllarus, et quorum Graii meminere poetæ,
Martis equi bijuges, et magni currus Achillis."

"The colt of a generous breed, from the very first, has a lofty tread, stepping daintily on his tender pasterns. He is the first that dares to lead the way, to ford a threatening stream, to trust himself on an unknown bridge. No empty noises frighten him. His neck is carried erect; his head is small; his belly short; his back broad. Brawny muscles swell upon his noble chest. A bright bay or a good grey is the best colour; the worst is white or dun. If from afar the clash of arms be heard, he knows not how to stand still; his ears prick up—his limbs quiver ; and, snorting, he rolls the collected fire under his nostrils ; and his mane is thick, and reposes tossed back on his right shoulder. A double spine runs along his loins. His hoof scoops out the ground, and sounds deep with solid horn. Such a steed was Cyllarus, tamed to the rein of Amyclean Pollux ; such were the two steeds of Mars, famous in Greek poetry ; such a team drew the chariot of Achilles."

CHAPTER III.

HISTORY OF THE ENGLISH BLOOD-HORSE.*

Mr. Weatherby's Stud Book—Oriental Ancestors of the British Race-horse—Early Races at Newmarket, 1720—A List of a Hundred well-bred Horses and Mares between 1711 and 1720—Berenger's History of Horsemanship, 1771—John Lawrence's Reminiscences, 1800—Contemporary Account of Godolphin Arabian—Darley Arabian—Flying Childers—Eclipse, Description of, from Lawrence's Personal Recollections—Pedigree of Eclipse—Pictures of him as a Race-horse and as a Stallion —His Value as a Sire—Improvement of Ordinary Horses between 1700 and 1800—Effect of Hunting field on Breeding— Act for Discouraging Pony Races, 1740—The Strong Race-horse Sampson; his Dimensions—His Grandson Mambrino— Portraits of Race-horses in Mr. Tattersall's Album—Admiral Rous a Sceptic as to Merits of Flying Childers and Eclipse, —His Evidence before Lords' Committee—The Earl of Stradbroke differs from his Brother—General Peel's Opinions— Gambling the Foundation of the English Blood-horse.

IN 1791 Mr. Weatherby—founder of the firm of that name which is the banker or stakeholder to owners of horses engaged in every race advertised throughout the three kingdoms, with the exception of a few insignificant meetings, and one of whose descendants is still secretary of the Jockey Club—published the first edition of his "Stud Book," which has since become the official register of the pedigrees of all the thoroughbred horses bred in this kingdom. In the preface to the fourth edition he gave, as the result of very laborious investigations, in which he had access to the best sources of information, the following list of the Barbs, Arabians, and Turks, which had more or less contributed to create the British race-horse :—

He commences by stating that King James I. bought, December 20, 1616, an Arabian of Mr. Markham, a merchant, for five hundred guineas, probably the first seen of his breed in England. And this statement has been repeated by successive writers on the same subject ever since. But after the issue of the first edition of the "BOOK OF THE HORSE," a correspondent of the *Times*, under signature of H., wrote on the 1st of September, 1875 :—

"In the records of the Exchequer, an office copy of which is now before me, it appears that King James never spent more than £900 on horses in one year, and that as to the Markham Arab there is the following particular entry :—

"'Item—December 20, 1616, paid to Master Markham for the Arabian horse, for His Majesty's own use, £154.

"'Item—The same day paid to a man that brought the same Arabian horse and kept him, £11.'"

The Duke of Newcastle says, in his treatise on "Horsemanship," that he had seen the above Arabian, and describes him as a small bay horse, and not of very excellent shape.

That Markham was the first seen of his breed is in the highest degree improbable, considering how many Oriental horses were brought to Europe by the Crusaders.

"The HELMSLEY TURK was the property of the Duke of Buckingham, and got Bustler, &c.

"PLACE'S WHITE TURK was the property of Mr. Place, stud-master to Oliver Cromwell, when

---

* The Honourable Francis Lawley, whose knowledge of everything connected with racing and racehorses is well known, has kindly revised these chapters, and corrected statements and figures as to dates and pedigrees not easily to be found in any printed documents.

Protector, and was sire of Wormwood, Commoner, and the great-grand-dams of Wyndham, Grey Ramsden, and Cartouche.

"King Charles II. sent abroad the Master of the Horse to procure a number of foreign horses and mares for breeding, and the mares brought over by him (as also many of their produce) have since been called royal mares.

"DODSWORTH, though foaled in England, was a natural Barb. His dam, a Barb mare, was imported in the time of Charles II., and was called a royal mare. She was sold by the stud-master, after the king's death, for forty guineas, at twenty years old, when in foal to the Helmsley Turk with Vixen, dam of the Old Child mare.

"The STRADDLING or LISTER TURK was brought into England by the Duke of Berwick, from the siege of Buda, in the reign of James II. He got Snake, the Duke of Kingston's Brisk and Piping Peg, Coneyskins, the dam of Hip, and the grand-dam of the Bolton Sweepstakes.

"The BYERLEY TURK was Captain Byerley's charger in Ireland in King William's wars (1689, &c.). He did not cover many thoroughbred mares, but was the sire of the Duke of Kingston's Sprite, who was thought nearly as good as Leedes; the Duke of Rutland's Black Hearty and Archer, the Duke of Devonshire's Basto, Lord Bristol's Grasshopper, and Lord Godolphin's Byerley Gelding, all in good forms; Halloway's Jigg, a middling horse; and Knightley's mare in a very good form.

"GREYHOUND. The cover for this foal was in Barbary, after which both his sire and dam were purchased and brought into England by Mr. Marshall. He was got by King William's white Barb Chillaby out of Slugey a natural Barb mare. Greyhound got the Duke of Wharton's Othello, said to have beat Chanter easily in a trial giving him a stone, but who, falling lame, ran only one match in public against a bad horse; he also got Panton's Whitefoot, a very good horse; Osmyn, a very fleet horse, and in good form for his size; the Duke of Wharton's Rake, a middling horse; Lord Halifax's Sampson, Goliath, and Favourite, pretty good twelve-stone plate horses, who ran in the North, where he was a common stallion, and covered many of the best mares.

"The D'ARCY WHITE TURK was the sire of Old Hautboy, Grey Royal, Cannon, &c.

"The D'ARCY YELLOW TURK was the sire of Spanker, Brimmer, and the great-grand-dam of Cartouche.

"The MARSHALL or SELLABY TURK was the property of Mr. Marshall's brother, stud-master to King William, Queen Anne, and King George I. He got the Curwen Old Spot, the dam of Windham, the dam of the Derby Ticklepitcher, and great-granddam of the Bolton Sloven and Fearnought.

"CURWEN'S BAY BARB was a present to Louis XIV. from Muley Ismael, King of Morocco, and was brought into England by Mr. Curwen, who being in France when Count Byram and Count Toulouse (two natural sons of Louis XIV.) were the former Master of the Horse and the latter an admiral, he procured of them two Barb horses, both of which proved excellent stallions, and are well known by the names of the Curwen Bay Barb and the Toulouse Barb. Curwen's Bay Barb got Mixbury and Tantivy, both very high-formed galloways (the first of them was only 13 hands 2 inches high, and yet there were not more than two horses of his time that could beat him at light weights); Brocklesby, Little George, Yellow Jack, Bay Jack, Monkey, Dangerfield, Hip, Peacock and Flatface (the first two in good forms, the rest middling); two Mixburys (full brothers to the first Mixbury middling galloway), Long Meg, Brocklesby, Betty, and Creeping Molly (extraordinarily high-formed mares); White Neck, Mistake, Sparkler, and Lightfoot (very good mares); and several middling galloways, who ran for plates in the North. He got two full sisters to Mixbury, one of which bred Partner, Little Scar, Sore Heels, and the dam of Crab ; the other was the dam of Quiet, Silver Eye, and Hazard.   He did not cover many mares except Mr. Curwen's and Mr. Pelham's.

"The TOULOUSE BARB afterwards became the property of Sir J. Parsons, and was the sire of Bagpiper, Blacklegs, Mr. Panton's Molly, and the dam of Cinnamon.

"DARLEY'S ARABIAN was brought over by a brother of Mr. Darley, of Yorkshire, who, being an agent in merchandise abroad, became member of a hunting club, by which means he acquired interest to procure this horse.   He was sire of Childers, and also got Almanzor, a very good horse; a white-legged horse of the Duke of Somerset's, full brother to Almanzor, and thought to be as good, but, meeting with an accident, he never ran in public ; Cupid and Brisk, good horses ; Dædalus, a very fleet horse ; Dart, Skipjack, Manica, and Aleppo, good plate horses, though out of bad mares ; Lord Lonsdale's mare, in very good form ; and Lord Tracey's mare, a good one for plates.   He covered very few mares except Mr. Darley's, who had a few well-bred besides Almanzor's dam.

"SIR J. WILLIAM'S TURK (more frequently called the Honeywood Arabian) got Mr. Honeywood's two True Blues.   The elder of them was the best plate horse in England for four or five years, the younger was in very high form, and got the Romford gelding and Lord Onslow's grey horse, middling horses, out of road mares.   It is not known that this Turk covered any mare except the dam of the two True Blues.

"The BELGRADE TURK was taken at the siege of Belgrade by General Merci, and sent by him to the Prince de Craon, from whom he was a present to the Prince of Lorraine.   He was afterwards purchased by Sir Marmaduke Wyvill, and died in his possession about 1740.

"Of BLOODY BUTTOCKS nothing further can be traced from the papers of the late Mr. Crofts than that he was a grey Arabian, with a red mark on his hip, whence he derived his name.

"CROFT'S BAY BARB was got by Chillaby, out of the Moonah Barb mare.

"The GODOLPHIN ARABIAN was a brown bay, about 15 hands high, with some white on the off heel behind.   There is a picture of him and his favourite cat in the library at Gog Magog in Cambridgeshire, at which place he died, in the possession of Lord Godolphin, in 1753, being then supposed to be in his twenty-ninth year.

"Whether he was an Arabian or a Barb is a point disputed (his portrait would lead to the latter supposition), but his excellence as a stallion is generally admitted.   In 1731, then the property of Mr. Coke, he was teaser to Hobgoblin, who refusing to cover Roxana, she was put to the Arabian, and from that cover produced Lath, the first of his get.   It is remarkable that there is not a superior horse now on the turf without a cross of the Godolphin Arabian, neither has there been for many years past.   There is an original portrait of this horse in Lord Cholmondeley's collection, at Houghton ; on comparing which with Mr. Stubbs' print of him, it will be seen that the disproportionately small limbs as represented in the latter do not accord with the painting."

From some one or more of these sires all the best race-horses of past and present times have descended ; so that down to the present day the Derby and St. Leger winners may be invariably traced to one of the Oriental sires of the seventeenth century recorded by Mr. Weatherby.

The prize of races in the time of James I. was a bell, which in the time of Charles II. was exchanged for a bowl, the original King's Plate.   In the time of George II. the silver bowl was replaced by a purse of one hundred guineas, which at this day is called the Queen's Plate, and bestowed on certain favoured localities in England, Scotland, and Ireland, to the extent of about three thousand six hundred guineas—ten of the English plates being paid for out of Her Majesty's

Privy Purse; the remainder and the Scotch Plates out of the Consolidated Fund; and the Irish Plates by annual votes in Parliament. But the encouragement to select, breed, and train horses to win races, and thus to improve the breed of British horses, was not in these early days so much the public prizes, bells, or bowls, as the rivalry between neighbours and counties, between the North and the South, supported by heavy wagers.

There were no sporting newspapers to report these races, but Racing Calendars have been collected by Mr. Weatherby that go much farther back than the "Stud Book," and present many names still familiar amongst our nobility and gentry as breeders of blood-horses.

In 1720 there were twenty-six matches run off at Newmarket, and for a hundred years previously races had been run at the king's favourite park of Theobalds at Enfield, at Croydon, and Epsom; while during Charles II.'s reign Newmarket became what it has been since, the head-quarters of the racing world. From the beginning of the eighteenth century racing became one of the institutions of Yorkshire, which has always been pre-eminent for its horses and horsemen.

Weatherby gives in the second part of his first "Stud Book" pedigrees of more than two hundred horses and mares of note between 1711 and 1759. These are, it will be observed, all closely allied to Oriental blood, the first English stallion appearing to be Basto (by the Byerley Turk); he died in 1723. Among the celebrities is Bald Galloway, by a Barb out of one of Charles II.'s royal mares, the sire of Cartouche, who came from Place's (Master of the Horse to Cromwell) White Turk. Cartouche, while in the possession of Sir William Morgan, of Tredegar, covered several seasons in Wales.

"Bonny Black, foaled in 1715, a very famous mare, by a son of the Byerley Turk, her dam by a Persian stallion; thus, probably, with at least two crosses of English blood."

"Jigg, the sire of Partner, a capital horse, of whom a portrait by Seymour is extant, was a common county stallion in Lincolnshire, till Partner was six years old; while Partner, foaled in 1718, covered most of the best mares in Yorkshire for four years. He was bred by Mr. Pelham," the ancestor of the present Earl of Yarborough, and breeder of several celebrated horses and mares, amongst others Brocklesby Betty, one of the early English racers.

It is therefore abundantly clear that, without any assistance from the State beyond the importation of Charles II.'s royal mares, and a trifling sum annually expended in King's Plates, the noblemen, county gentlemen, and yeomen of England, succeeded between the years 1618 and 1700 in founding on the stock of the best British mares, by the aid of Oriental sires— Barb, Turkish, Arab, Persian—and a few Oriental mares, a tribe of horses superior to either.

In 1724 the reputation of our blood-horses must have increased, for the giant Maurice Saxe, illegitimate son of the last king of Poland, who twenty-one years later was our conqueror, as Marshal Saxe, at the battle of Fontenoy, came to England to buy horses. He visited Newmarket races, and delighted his English friends by pitching an insolent scavenger into the midst of his mud-cart.

In 1771, "Richard Berenger, Gentleman of the Horse to His Majesty King George," published his "History and Art of Horsemanship," from which most writers on the horse since that date have drawn freely for the historical part of their subject. He is the first up to that period who makes any distinct allusion to the changed character of the British horse. He writes with the feeling of a manége or high-school rider, with little sympathy for either hunting or racing. He expresses regret that the royal prerogative of regulating bits and bridles by decree had passed away with the House of Stuart, and not descended to the House of Brunswick.

He says, "The finer and better sort of the more modern English horses are descended from Arabians and Barbs, and frequently resemble their sires in appearance, but differ from them considerably in size and in mould, being more furnished, stout, and lusty ; in general they are strong, nimble, and of good courage, capable of enduring excessive fatigue, and both in perseverance and speed surpass all the horses in the world." But from the following remarks, it is evident that in Berenger's time English blood steppers, the whole class of park hacks and light harness horses, with " up to the curb chain action," had not been produced ; for he adds · " It is objected to them that they are void of grace and that expression in their figure and carriage which is so conspicuous in foreign horses, and so beautiful and attractive as even to be essentially requisite on occasions of pomp and parade ; but, instead of displaying a dignity of motion, and a conscious air of cheerfulness and alacrity, as if they shared in the pleasure and pride of their riders, they appear in their actions cold, indifferent, and unanimated. The most heedless and ignorant spectator who should see them contrasted with the horses of action (Hanoverian, Spanish, Italian) would be struck with the difference, would be uninterested with the lame and lifeless behaviour of the one, and ravished with the sensibility and well-tempered fire of the other. . . . Besides this, the English horses are accused, and not un-justly, of being obstinate and uncomplying in their tempers, dogged and sullen ; of having stiff and inactive shoulders, and wanting suppleness in their limbs, which defects make their motions constrained, occasion them to go near the ground, and render them unfit for the manége."

A little farther on Mr. Berenger regrets that Charles I., who did by Order in Council command his people to discontinue the use of snaffle and adopt curb bridles, did not follow the recommendation of a memorial presented by Sir Edward Harwood, and enact that noblemen and gentlemen, instead of running races for bells, should breed stronger horses fit for war. In every age we find writers deploring the decline of our breed of horses, and imploring the interference of the State, either by restriction or artificial encouragements.

In 1826, George IV., according to Greville's Diary, made a little speech at a dinner he gave to the Jockey Club, recommending "that the exportation of horses should be forbidden."

My next authority in this sketch of the history of the English horse is John Lawrence,* whose book, in quarto, magnificently illustrated by copper-plates exquisitely engraved after pictures by George Stubbs, B. Marshall, and Gilpin, contains portraits of the Godolphin Arabian, Eclipse, Shakespeare, King Herod, Flying Childers, and other famous race-horses.

Lawrence's history of the British horse up to 1770 is chiefly compiled from Berenger's book ; but he is an authority on his own time, for he was an enthusiast and a gossip, and seems to have spared no pains to obtain authentic portraits of horses which were the foundation of the best qualities of the English blood-horse. In one place he tells his readers that he " has pried into, nay, devoured, every page and every line of Mr. Weatherby's then recently published 'Stud Book,'† with all the enthusiasm of an amateur ;" in another that " he would willingly have ridden a hundred miles to ride a celebrated race-horse a sweat." His remarks on the famous sires and race-horses mentioned by Weatherby in his miscellaneous list become most interesting, because he says that in 1778 he was " frequently in the habit of visiting old Eclipse, then at Epsom." Lawrence gives dates to the list of Oriental horses collected by Weatherby. He says, " I know of no pedigrees traceable beyond Place's White Turk " (Place was Master of the Horse to Oliver Cromwell) " and the Morocco Barb of the Lord General Fairfax." During the reigns of Charles II. and James II., the most famous blood sires were

* " History and Derivation of the Horse in all his Varieties." By John Lawrence. 1809.
† First volume, 1791.

the Walmsley Turk, Dodsworth (a Barb foaled in England, his dam a royal imported mare) the Taffolet Barb, the White-legged Lowther Barb, and the Straddling or Lister Turk, brought by the Duke of Berwick from the siege of Buda, in the reign of James II., at a time when the Sultan was a great European as well as Oriental power, and had, by conquest and by tribute, the finest Oriental horses in his armies. During William III.'s reign there were imported the Byerley Turk, sire of Sprite, Black Hearty, Basto, and Jigg; Greyhound, purchased a foal in Barbary by the King's stud-master Mr. Marshall, with his sire a white Barb, Chillaby his dam, Slugey, and the Moonah Barb mare; the D'Arcy White and Yellow Turks; and the Marshall or Sellaby Turk.

"In the reign of Queen Anne sportsmen bred from the Curwen Barb, the Toulouse Barb, a son of Chillaby, the famous Darley Arabian, Williams's Turk, also called the Honeywood White Arabian, the St. Vuter's Barb, Cole's Barb, and many others.

"About 1730, temp. George II., the following foreign covering stallions were kept in this country:—The Alcock Arabian, the Bloody-shouldered Arabian, the Belgrade Turk (taken at the siege of that place), Bethell's Arabian, Burlington's Barb, Croft's Egyptian horse, the Black Barb, Cyprus Arabian, Devonshire Arabian, Johnson's Turk, Godolphin Arabian, Litton's Chestnut Arabian, Matthew's Persian, Pigott's Turk, Lonsdale's Bay Arabian, and half a dozen others."

At the same time the following English thoroughbred horses (recorded in the Appendix to Weatherby's first volume of the "Stud Book") were covering:—Bay Bolton, the Bald Galloway (a pony), Aleppo, Almanzor, Basto, Bloody Buttocks, Bartlett's Childers, Bollan's Starling Arab, Cartouche, Flying Childers, Fox, Greyhound, Hartley's Blind Horse, Hampton Court Childers, Hutton's Grey Childers, Hobgoblin, Jigg, Manica, Lamprey, Partner, Sore Heels, Small's Childers, Tifler, Woodcock, Young Belgrade, and Young True Blue—names which are not barren, because every good race-horse for the last twenty or fifty years may be traced back to some of them, and through them to Oriental sires. Lawrence records the names of some dozen other Orientals imported between 1730 and his time, but as none have become famous it is not worth while to repeat them.

In an advertisement of the Damascus Arabian, it states that he was "of the purest Arabian breed, without any admixture of Turcoman or Barb," "which shows," says Lawrence, "the fashionable opinion in 1773."

After about 1750 no Oriental blood, Arab, Barb, or Turk, seems to have been used with success, although stakes for imported Arabians were run at Newmarket. All the most famous race-horses trace their pedigrees between 1730 and 1750, through English sires, to the Darley or Godolphin Arabians. "Our best horses for nearly a century past have been either deeply imbued with their blood or entirely derived from it."

According to Lawrence, "the Godolphin Arabian was in colour a brown bay, somewhat mottled on the buttocks and crest, but with no white excepting the off heel behind, about 15 hands high, with good bone and substance. His portrait, by Seymour, was in the library at Gog Magog, the seat of Lord Godolphin. It is presumed that the famous portrait by Stubbs (engraved in Lawrence's book), which sold at his sale for 246 guineas, was a copy of Seymour's. Artists say that the crest of the horse is quite out of nature. However, from all accounts and the various representations I have seen of this horse, his crest was exceedingly large and elevated, his neck elegantly curved, and his muzzle very fine. He had considerable length, his capacious shoulders and head the true sloping position, and every part materially contributed to action. According to tradition he was picked up in Paris, where he was drawing a cart." But William Osmer, who published "A Dissertation on Horses," in 1756, three years after the death of the

Godolphin Arabian, and had evidently seen him, says :—" Whoever has seen him must remember that his shoulders were deeper and lay farther into his back than any horse yet seen ; behind his shoulders there was but a small space ; before, the muscles of his loin rose excessively high, broad, and expanded, which were inserted into his quarters with greater strength and power than any horse ever yet seen of his dimensions. It is not to be wondered at that the excellence of this horse's shape was not in early times manifest to some men, considering the plainness of his head and ears, the position of his fore-legs, and his stunted growth, occasioned by want of food in the country where he was bred." " He was not used as a sire until 1731, when his first produce was Lath, out of Roxana, who was considered the best horse since Flying Childers. After Lath, until his death in 1753, being then twenty-nine years old, the Godolphin was the sire of a series of prodigies. That he was a Barb and not an Arabian I am convinced more and more every time I contemplate his portrait. The name or breed assigned to foreign horses by their importers is not of the smallest consequence. If a horse be purchased in Turkey he is styled a Turk. Amongst us all southern horses are called Arabians. The Compton Barb was more commonly called the Sedley Arabian, and Sir John William's Turk the Honeywood Arabian."

" The Darley Arabian got Flying Childers, and others less known to modern fame. He had not the variety of mares that annually poured in upon the Godolphin Arabian ; indeed, he covered very few excepting those belonging to the proprietor, Mr. Darley, but from these sprung the largest and speediest race-horses ever known—Flying Childers and Eclipse, the swiftest, beyond doubt, of all quadrupeds."

"Flying Childers was a chestnut horse, with white upon his nose, and whited all-fours upon his pasterns. He appears 15 hands high or upwards, and to have been of the short compact form, his immense stride being furnished by the length of his back and loins, the former appearing in every portrait of him of extraordinary length. He was foaled in 1715 ; got by the Darley Arabian out of Betty Leedes. He was bred considerably in-and-in with a number of Arabian and Barb blood. He never started but at Newmarket, and there beat all the best horses of his time."

The story of his running three miles six furlongs and ninety-three yards in six minutes and forty seconds, although often repeated, is now generally treated as a mistake.

ECLIPSE.*

" Eclipse was a chestnut horse, about 15½ hands high, foaled in 1764, by Marske, a great-grandson of the Darley Arabian." He was not trained until five years old. " When I first saw him," says Lawrence, " he appeared in high health, of a robust constitution. His shoulder was very thick, but extensive and well placed ; his hind-quarters appeared higher than his fore-hand ; and it was said that no horse in his gallop ever threw his haunches with greater effect, his agility and his stride being on a par. He stood over a deal of ground, and in that respect was the opposite of Flying Childers—a short-backed, compact horse, whose reach lay in his lower limbs. When viewed, fat as a stallion, there was a certain coarseness about him. Eclipse was never beaten ; never had a whip flourished over him, or felt the rubbing of a spur—out-footing, out-striding, and out-lasting every horse that started against him."

The late Mr. Percival, a distinguished veterinary surgeon, writing on the same horse, says

* There are doubts about the height of Eclipse. A contemporary broadside accompanying an etching of Eclipse in racing condition gives his height as 15 hands 2 inches, and equal to eighteen stone.

that "he was a big horse in every sense of the word, tall in stature, lengthy and capacious in body, and large in his limbs. For a big horse his head was small, and partook of the Arabian character; his neck was unusually long; his shoulder was strong, sufficiently oblique, and although not remarkable for, not deficient in depth, his chest was circular; he rose very little on his withers, being higher behind than before; his back was lengthy, and over the loins roached; his quarters were straight, square, and extended; his limbs were lengthy and broad, and his joints large, in particular his arms and thighs were long and muscular, and his knees and hocks broad and well-formed."

Mr. Percival came to these conclusions from the descriptions of contemporary writers like Lawrence, and from an examination of the skeleton, then preserved in the Museum of the Royal College of Surgeons. The skeleton is not now in the Museum of either the College of Surgeons or Physicians, and doubt exists as to the true height of Eclipse; sixteen hands and a half sounds like an error; but if the measurement is correct, the late Admiral Rous's statement that the height of race-horses had been increased five or six inches was evidently a mistake.

Of the pedigrees of celebrated race-horses, carried back to the commencement of the eighteenth century, one may safely say that nearly all go back to the Darley Arabian (1715), or the Godolphin Barb (1724), or to both. The following pedigree of Eclipse will sufficiently establish facts familiar to all students of turf literature :—

PEDIGREE OF ECLIPSE.

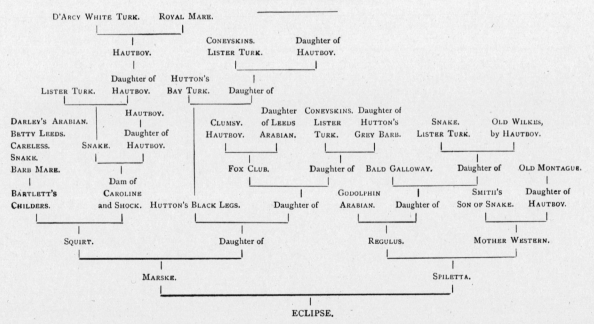

ECLIPSE.

The learned in thoroughbred pedigrees declare that there are two blanks in the pedigree of Eclipse, which would probably be filled up by two half-bred mares.

PICTURES OF ECLIPSE.

Mr. Edmund Tattersall has kindly allowed me to reproduce G. Townley Stubbs' engraving of Eclipse in racing condition, from his celebrated father's picture, and also to make a coloured fac-simile of an original portrait of Eclipse, after he was put to the stud. Both show an animal of high quality and great power.

The annals already quoted prove that while a few were engaged in breeding race-horses, a great many landed gentlemen, as far apart as Mr. Pelham, at Brocklesby Park, in Lincoln-shire, and Sir William Morgan, of Tredegar, in South Wales, were, between the years 1700 and 1800, improving the horses of their district by encouraging their tenants and neighbours to cross the horses of the district with sires of racing blood.

Fortunately the tastes of breeders when the British blood-horse was being manufactured were not entirely directed to speed. The hunting-field created a demand for well-bred horses, and for thoroughbred hunters equal to carry weight, a demand which has continued and increased ever since.

County races were often the offspring of county hunt clubs. The rivalry between different counties was keen, and the taste for the blood-horse spread from squires to yeomen and farmers, encouraged by the demand for swift roadsters and carriage-horses. Every provincial capital, like Exeter, Salisbury (one of the oldest), Leicester, Chester, and York, had, as well as its theatre, its assembly rooms, and its cock-pit, its racecourse. Yorkshire met Lincoln-shire. At Holywell the Cheshire met the Welsh squires, and at Chester their Lancashire rivals. There was rivalry between the Ridings of Yorkshire, and the keenest competition between the North of England and South.

Thus it was that hunting on horseback, following hounds over wild, rough, and enclosed country, a sport popularised in England when the farmers of other European countries were little better than serfs, contributed greatly, with racing, to distribute well-bred horses over the three kingdoms.

In 1740, the reign of George II., an Act had been passed for the suppression of public pony races, and the discouragement of small, weak horses; no prize for race-horses was to be of less value than £50. Every horse of five years old was to carry ten stone, of six years old, eleven, and seven years old, twelve stone. But there is no evidence that this Act, probably the child of some independent member of Parliament, was ever put in force.

Until the commencement, and well into the first quarter, of the present century, there was a great deal of racing of horses which were admittedly not thorough-bred, known on the turf as "H.B." (half-bred) or "cock-tails;" these when contending with thoroughbred horses, had allowances in weight. The system of allowing weight to H.B.'s was eventually abolished, in consequence of the opening it gave to fraud by substituting a thorough-bred foal for a half-bred of the same colour; but for a time it must have had the effect of encouraging farmers to put their mares to blood-horses for the chance of getting a racer, and if not a racer, a hunter.

"Through Childers and Blaze," says Lawrence, "descended Sampson, the strongest horse that ever raced before or since his time, entitled to equal pre-eminence if viewed as a hackney or hunter. Sampson was 15½ hands high, and his dimensions, as taken by his owner, the Marquis of Rockingham, as follow:—

	Inches.
From the hair of the hoof to the middle fetlock-joint . . .	4
From the fetlock-joint to the bend of the knee	11
From the bend of the knee to the elbow	19
Round his leg below the knee, narrowest part	8½
Round his hind-leg, narrowest part	9

The girth is unfortunately not given, or round the fore-arm; but these dimensions show a powerful and compact blood-horse, although of no great reputation as a race-horse.

These particulars are interesting, because Sampson was the grandsire of Mambrino, foaled in 1768, considered in his time a wonderfully fast trotter for a race-horse; and Mambrino, described by Weatherby as "a very moderate race-horse," was the sire of Messenger, who.

exported to America, became the root of a many-branched pedigree of the best trotting-horses of the United States.

Mambrino is quoted as one of the examples of "strength with quality" which the author of an anonymous work, published in 1836,* and illustrated with a series of rudely-executed lithographs, thought it the duty of the nation to cultivate. The weight of evidence would incline one to believe that the race-horse, as exhibited in the winners of the great annual races, viz., the Derby, the Oaks, and the St. Leger, was as perfect for all practical purposes in 1803 as at the present day; whether he was as fast for running purposes has long been a matter of dispute.

Gimcrack, a dark iron-grey horse, who was less than 15 hands in height, was bred in 1760 by Mr. Gideon Elliott, of Murrell Green, in Hampshire, and was got by Cripple, his dam being

ECLIPSE AS A RACER. (FROM THE PORTRAIT BY STUBBS.)

by Mr. Grisewood's Partner. Gimcrack during his racing career passed through many hands, having been successively the property of his breeder, of Mr. Green, Mr. Wildman, Lord Bolingbroke, Count Lauraguais, Sir C. Bunbury, and Lord Grosvenor. Gimcrack started for the first time at Epsom in 1764, and won seven races—all that he started for—during his first year. From 1764 to 1770 inclusive he ran in a vast number of races, most of them in heats, and over a distance of ground, and was beaten but ten times during his long and active career. He is the only English race-horse after whom a still existing association is named, and the Gimcrack Club at York, founded in 1766, attests his excellence and prowess. Gimcrack was always a prodigious favourite with Admiral Rous, who constantly referred to him in his turf anecdotes and public letters, and was very proud of the picture of the little grey, from an unknown brush, which he acquired by purchase at an advanced period of his own life, and bequeathed upon his death to the Jockey Club. Perhaps the most remarkable of Gimcrack's achievements was that

* "A Comparative View of the Form and Character of the English Racer and Saddle-horse during the last and present Centuries."

which, as the property of Count Lauraguais, he performed in France, when, in 1766, he ran twenty-two and a half miles within the hour, and netted a very large sum for his owner. His remarkable stamina was an additional confirmation of the truth of the maxim held by the late Sir Tatton Sykes, that little horses are the best stayers.

In looking over the album of portraits of race-horses, blood sires, and brood mares, from the earliest times, collected by the late Mr. Richard Tattersall, the first rude etchings represent a series of impossible animals—the very reverse of the illustrations of the English horses in the Duke of Newcastle's book, or the Italian horse of 1688, given in our last chapter—with scraggy bodies, needle-like legs, and the necks of camels. They seem to have been veritable

PORTRAIT OF GIMCRACK, WHOSE PICTURE WAS BEQUEATHED TO THE JOCKEY CLUB BY ADMIRAL ROUS.

weeds. Sir William Morgan's Coneyskins, a famous race-horse in 1726, is indeed a miserable wretch; while a little later, Marske, the sire of Eclipse, is represented as a thorough-bred weight-carrier all over. Whether the improvement was due to the horses or the artists there is no reliable evidence.

For useful purposes (whatever may be the requirements for a modern mile race) it would be difficult to find more satisfactory models than the Earl of Egremont's Gohanna, racing in 1790, to whose blood Irish hunters owe so much of their well-deserved reputation; or Eleanor, who won the Derby and Oaks for Sir Charles Bunbury in 1801, and looks fit to ride hunting; Truffle and Benedict, in 1808, Woeful and Whisker, in 1812, leave nothing to be desired in the way of strength and quality. To be sure, their short tails give them a compact look. At the present time the most popular race-horses are three-year-olds, which have not come to their full development; not "furnished," in dealers' phrase; and their portraits, to the unlearned in horse matters, convey a very false idea of our best thoroughbreds, considering them as horses, and not as racing machines.

The merits of Flying Childers, Eclipse, and other "Conscript Fathers" of the British race-horse, and the traditional accounts of their performances, are not accepted without dispute. Influential parties connected with the turf hold very opposite opinions; one that the British horse is very much deteriorated, the other that he is very much improved. Perhaps they are looking at different sides of the same shield; perhaps one is thinking only of the perfection to which the art of winning and losing money in one afternoon at Newmarket has arrived, and the other of the number of "terrible" high-bred sires perambulating the country to propagate every kind of hereditary unsoundness and malformation.

Before a Lords' Committee on Horse Supply in 1873 the question of deterioration was incidentally raised, and elicited evidence of a very contradictory character.

The late Admiral the Honourable Henry Rous, "who is sorry to say that for upwards of fifty years he has observed every thorough-bred horse of racing reputation, and for the last thirty years has noted down every night of his life the results of every race," as a preparation for "handicapping many thousand horses," has the greatest contempt for these racing gods of the old generation of Englishmen, and utterly disbelieves in the racing merit of Childers and Eclipse.

He told the Lords' Committee that "in 1700 the average size of the thorough-bred horse was 13 hands 3 inches, and that since that date it had been increasing an inch every twenty-five years." He must have meant the ordinary size, because in 1740 pony racing was declared illegal. Herod (1758), was 15 hands 3 inches; Eclipse (1764), over 15½ hands; Jupiter (1774), 15 hands 1 inch; and these were what may be called representative horses. It must not be forgotten, in discussing this historical question of height, that tall Turcoman horses may have been imported and used, and called Arabs.

"At present," said the admiral, "the average height of the race-horse is 15 hands 3 inches, and there are not less than twelve horses in training which are 17 hands high, a thing not known fifty years ago;" but as the admiral admitted that Prince Charlie, "the best horse in the world for *a mile*, and 17 hands high, was a roarer," and that "tall horses are more frequently roarers than small horses," it does not seem that the breed of English horses is likely to derive any more benefit from these equine giants than the Prussian nation did from King Frederick William I.'s Patagonian regiment of body guards.

The Earl of Stradbroke, the brother of the great handicapper * and oracle of the racing world, held (as will be seen in the following extract from his evidence before the same Committee) a totally different opinion; but then he is a zealous county gentleman, interested in providing the Suffolk breeders with sound and useful stallions.

"For more than sixty years I have had great experience in breeding all sorts of horses, and have taken great interest in their enduring qualities. At one time of my life I bred a great many thorough-bred horses. I believe that horses have deteriorated of late years.

"Queen's Plates were originally given for horses to carry heavy weights and run long distances. In the last century, and in the beginning of this century, there were a great many valuable horses that could run three or four miles without the slightest trouble or injury of any kind, but now that description of animal does not exist. My firm belief is that there are not four horses in England now that could run over the Beacon course (4 miles 1 furlong

---

* The art of handicapping consists in bringing horses of different ages and speed as nearly as possible together, by imposing graduated weight in proportion to their previous public performances.

and 138 yards) at Newmarket within eight minutes, which in my younger days I used to see constantly done.

"You can hardly persuade gentlemen to run four miles, because they can win large sums in running short races,* and their horses can come out oftener. I am afraid that it is more a question of winning money than it used to be eighty years ago, when there were a vast number of persons who took a great pride in breeding horses of a different stamp. I dare say that at Goodwood for the last ten years there have not been more than three horses entered for the Queen's Plates, and these have walked half the distance."

The evidence of General Peel,† which conforms neither to the opinion of Admiral Rous nor to the melancholy forebodings of the Earl of Stradbroke, perhaps presents the fairest picture of the present condition of the British blood-horse. General Peel had "had fifty years' experience as a breeder of horses, having, in conjunction with his brother, Mr. Edmund Peel, bred his first animal in 1821, a filly which ran second to the Earl of Jersey's Cobweb in the Oaks in 1824." He considered that "there are quite as good horses now as at any former period, but that there are more bad ones bred in proportion to the total number, in consequence of the whole system of breeding being altered.

"Formerly the proprietors of race-horses were the breeders of them. They had their own brood-mares, their own paddocks; they carefully selected the sire that would suit each mare, and they kept the produce entirely for their own racing. At that time it was very difficult to purchase yearlings, now nine-tenths of the horses are bred for sale. When, some years ago, very large prices were given (at sales by auction) for yearlings, the supply quickly followed the demand. Everybody took to breeding, and stud sales were organised all over the country. More horses are bred (there were nearly three thousand thorough-bred mares last season), and more bad ones, because breeders for sale put all their mares to the stallions they purchase or hire, whether the cross is most suitable or not.

"This opinion is sustained by the fact that although there are very few private as compared with public breeders, almost all great stakes are won by animals bred by private breeders."

But the object of this chapter is not to discuss racing and its drawbacks, moral and physical, which are as inevitable as other mental and bodily diseases of civilised life, but to sketch with a rapid hand how the love of country sports, how the love of riding, of hunting, of wagering on matches, and, finally, the concentration of the gambling spirit (in which in some form all civilised and semi-civilised nations indulge) on horse-racing has, in less than a century, laid the foundation of the finest breed of horses in the world. Without the race-course the English blood-horse would never have existed. We must take the good with the bad of that as of other truly English institutions. At any rate, it is quite certain that to revert to the old style of four-mile races at heavy weights is as impossible as to reproduce long whist in good society, or go back from iron steam-driven war-ships to the wooden sailing frigates which Admiral Rous so infinitely preferred, for the admiral was strictly conservative on every question except that on which his clients (in the Roman sense), the betting fraternity, thrive. Large vested interests have been created and are supported by the modern system of infant horses, short distances, and all the chances of stakes of thousands, and wagers of tens of thousands. Whether it promotes breeding sound and useful blood-horses is quite another question.

---

* £80,000 was won in bets on one race by one person in 1873.
† Evidence of General the Right Honourable Jonathan Peel before Select Committee on Supply of Horses.

CHAPTER IV.

THE MODERN BLOOD-HORSE.

Points of a Race-horse—Copperthwaite's Description—The Ugliest often the Best—Size and Substance—Large Head no Objection—Nor Large Lopping Ears—Great Length from Hip to Hock Essential—Note on—Broad Chest Objectionable—Anecdote of Sir Anthony Harbottle—Digby Collins hates Pony-headed Horses—His Notion of a Race-horse's Hind-quarters—The Arab Style of Quarters and Tail Bad—Mean Quarters of Blink Bonny and Caller Ou—Abd-el-Kader's Description of an Arab Horse—Comparative Difference of Steeplechaser and Hunter—Touchstone; his Son Motley worthless as a Race-horse, first-rate as Sire of Hunters—Colours of the English Blood-horse—Statistics of the Turf—Tables of Race-horses from 1797 to 1872—Table of Distances run—Number of Races in 1872—The Earl of Coventry's Letter—The Race-horse as a Stallion—Examples—Stockwell and West Australian—Anecdote of Earl Derby and Lord Palmerston—Their Favourites for the Derby—The Life of a Race-horse at Two Years, Three Years, and Four Years Old—Three-year-old Races at Fixed Weights—Weight for Age Races—Queen's Plates—Handicaps the Principal Prizes—Betting Men Classed—Gambling has changed its Form—Anecdotes of the Old Generation of Gamblers—Wilberforce—Charles Fox—William Pitt—Gambling Houses formerly Licensed—Gilray's Caricature of Ladies Buckinghamshire and Archer—Prince of Wales and Lord Chief Justice Kenyon, 1799—Betting Presents the "Potentiality of Wealth beyond the Dreams of Avarice"—Bookmaking Trade described—Anecdote of Palmer the Poisoner—The Customers of Bookmakers Analysed—Racing Frauds in 1844—Charles Greville's Diary—A Typical Betting Man—The Origin of the Derby and Oaks Races—Won in 1801 by Eleanor; in 1857 by Blink Bonny—Lord Melbourne's Description of the Blue Riband—Lord Glasgow's ill Luck—Lord Clifden's and Mr. Chaplin's great Luck—The Derby won by a Foreign Horse, Gladiateur—The Blood-horse as a Useful Sire—The Glasgow Stud—Blood Sires—Plan of Hiring Recommended—The Thorough-bred out of Training—Various Uses—Edmond—The Race-horse in America—Description of Races in Jerome Park, New York—The Race-horse in France: Excellence of—Race-horses in Germany.

THE following extracts from the works of two writers—one, Mr. Digby Collins, an educated man as well as an accomplished horseman; the other, Mr. Copperthwaite, a specimen of a person with no literary cultivation or pretensions, whose life was devoted to the turf—will perhaps give a fair idea of what racing-men like in a race-horse.

Mr. Copperthwaite begins by saying that "Some of the ugliest horses are best shaped when properly looked over. The worst shaped horses for running purposes are frequently the handsomest. It would hardly be going too far to add that they are almost invariably the very worst. The greatest failures are generally very handsome, and only fit for Rotten Row.

*　　*　　*　　*　　*　　*　　*

"Size and substance are indispensable; not a tall, narrow, 'clothes horse,' but rather thick-set than otherwise when in fat condition previous to going into training. Coarseness should be avoided, especially as regards the head, neck, and shoulders. The eye should be large, clear, and bright, with a sort of baldness, arising from the absence of coarse hairs around it, which is a sign of high breeding. The jaw-bones should taper gradually towards the nose; the forehead should be wide and flat between the eyes; but there are many exceptions to these descriptions, many first-class horses having large, bony kind of heads. The head should have a sensible look; the eye clear, full, and steady, which denotes good temper and enduring qualities; a fiery, anxious eye, with more white than usual, is generally found in flighty-tempered, speedy non-stayers. The ears, provided they are not of the long, upright form, like a donkey, stuck up on each side of the head, may be large.

Some of the best horses have had lopped ears coming down over their eyes like a rabbit. Horses with lopped ears are generally good-tempered. If when cantering a horse pricks his ears alternately, first one then the other, it is the sign of good temper, and such are generally long runners. The nostrils should be full and moving; the neck should be of a reasonable length, but muscular, without being coarse. A short neck generally accompanies round, heavy shoulders; shortness in other respects is the worst fault of a race-horse.

"But length does not mean a long back. We must judge of length by the ground an animal covers underneath.

"The body, or middle piece, of a true-made, weight-carrying race-horse, when in condition, should present depth of girth, a good back, muscular arched loins, but should not be coupled up too closely towards the hip. The longest runners and best weight-carriers, and most speedy, present the appearance of being light in the back ribs. The great point of all lies in the hind-quarters having *good length from the hip to hock*,* with good hocks and thighs; the shoulders, which should be well placed back, together with good length from hip to end of haunch-bone, supplying length where it is most needed. A slight drooping towards the tail is preferable to too level an appearance. Animals with a drooping shape are generally better turned under their haunches, and possess more propelling power. The arms should be muscular and reasonably long; from knee to fetlock shortish, clean, with good bone—not round or gummy; the fetlock-joints should not be upright, as they frequently are. Arched knees, provided the horse has done no work, are preferable to 'calve-knees,' which have the contrary appearance.

"Where race-horses are very close, and well-ribbed up, that is to say, where there is but a small space between the back-rib and hip, the latter being somewhat deep and round, there is freedom of action, propelling power, and fine stride. The height should be from 15 hands 2 inches to 16 hands.

"When the chest is broad, and the animal stands wide on the ground, you may pass him as 'no race-horse.'† A speedy and stout runner will be *deep*, yet narrow, between the fore-arms or the chest. Fisherman walked wide on the ground, but was narrow above. Some flat-ribbed animals, with an extraordinary appearance of weakness behind the saddle, stay well, and they have extraordinary propelling powers.

"I have seen few pony-headed horses of the first class. Teddington was the prettiest-headed horse I ever saw for a good one."‡

Mr. Digby Collins, who is an authority as a breeder, as a horseman, and steeplechase-rider, treats the subject of the form of the race-horse more elaborately and scientifically. As to size, after naming the little and tall race-horses that have won the great races, he concludes as follows: "Whatever the weight may be, there must be length and size somewhere, and the more size and length there are on short legs the better. I decidedly object to the small

---

* Much importance, says an anonymous writer, is assigned to great length between the hips and hocks. This form, carried to the extent it is amongst our race-horses, is wholly fallacious, and the pure result of long-continued selection for speed, as exhibited in the greyhound; it was formerly much less developed, and if we may judge of the older race-horses by their portraits, was unknown to them.—*On the Deterioration of the English Horse.* By a Cavalry Officer. 1854.

† Sir Charles Bunbury was discussing with Lovell Edgeworth, the father of Miss Edgeworth, after dinner at Newmarket, the reading of a passage in Cicero, when Sir Anthony Harbottle, a north-country squire of the Squire Western type, waking from a doze, caught the name of a horse in training, and roared out, "Cicero; what about Cicero? He's narrow behind, and broad before, and not worth my hat full of crab-apples."

‡ *The Turf.* By R. H. Copperthwaite.

Arab head, which denotes cunning and temper. I do not object to size, so long as it is not out of proportion to the general frame. Large long ears are a sign of gameness. A good neck means a strong, deep, broad neck, running right into the shoulders imperceptibly. I abhor either a thin, weak, fine neck, or a light, tapery-arched peacocky neck."

Passing over Mr. Collins's ideas on the shoulders, the chest, the fore-limbs, &c., as to ribs and back he says: "I do not at all dislike a rather hollow-backed horse; they are nice to sit on, and many race-horses have run well with this formation. Ragged square hips are frequently met with in hunters and steeplechase-horses that are great fencers, but very seldom in successful race-horses.

"From the hip-bone to the setting-on of the tail, the structure should never be level, or what jockeys call 'peacocky' and 'high-setting on of the tail' is a decided defect. Most of the first-class horses, both on the flat and across country, have their tails set on low, with long wide quarters, approaching what racing-men term 'mean-quartered.'

"Two mares—Blink Bonny, the Derby, Oaks, and St. Leger winner, and also Caller Ou—were remarkable instances of this extreme formation."

But with this elaborate description of what a good race-horse should be, Mr. Collins admits that many trainers consider that "fore-limbs have nothing to do with racing;" that "horses run in all forms," that "if they will have to run in flying handicaps of six, five, and even three furlongs, which pay as well as anything in these days, and are not expected to be good enough for the Derby, Oaks, St. Leger, or Doncaster, Goodwood, Chester, and Ascot Cups, *then mere formation must be thrown to the winds,* and the pedigree of the sire be carefully weighed."

It may be observed, in passing, that the public interested in useful horses have no concern with the winners of the great races, until they fail to beget winning horses, because their fees—of from thirty to one hundred guineas per mare—put them out of reach of the breeders of any kind of hunter or riding-horse intended for sale.

ARAB POINTS COMPARED WITH RACE-HORSES.

If one compares the *points* of the English race-horse with Abd-el-Kader's description of the Arab horse, the different requirements of a single-combat desert war-horse and of a horse destined to tremendous exertion for less than three minutes, may be seen at a glance.

"The horse of race has ears short and mobile; bones heavy and thin; the cheeks lean and unencumbered with flesh; the nostrils wide; the eyes fine, black, brilliant, prominent; the neck long; the chest prominent; the withers high; the loins well gathered up; the haunches strong; the fore-ribs long; the hind-ribs short; the belly sloping upwards; the croup rounded; the arms long, like an ostrich, with muscles like a camel; the hoof black.

"Four things broad—the forehead, the chest, the croup, the limbs.

"Four things long—the neck, the arms and thighs, the belly, the haunches.

"Four things short—the loins, the pasterns, the ears, the tail."

In a word, a race-horse is bred to be very like a greyhound; consequently hundreds are bred every year too slow for the racecourse, and unfit for any other useful purpose. Mr. Collins, in describing the difference between the formation of a race-horse, a steeplechase-horse, and a hunter, the latter being, in his best form, the most useful horse for every purpose except heavy draught, marks the needful variation between the living machine, which is to be wound up for intense exertion, over smooth turf, during a period rarely exceeding three minutes, and the steeplechaser or hunter, in a very few effective words :—

" 1. The withers of the steeplechase-horse should be higher, and the shoulders longer.

" 2. The girth deeper, and the back ribs shorter and lighter.

" 3. The hips should be wider, and the pelvis broader.

" In the gallop the steeplechaser should be a dashing, savage goer, bending his knees well. The race-horse should glide along with a straight reach, as smoothly as a cutter through water.

" The hunter should differ from the steeplechaser in one particular ; his back ribs should be deeper and more expanded, to enable him to go through many hours of severe labour without food."

A careful consideration of these " points," noted down by the two *practical men* already named, unembarrassed with the theories which often fetter public writers on the same subject, will show that a race-horse may be first-class in his trade—the trade of winning races at light weights and distances not over a mile—while wanting in the qualifications essential to make a good hunter or riding-horse of any kind. As for the outlines most admired in the modern Oriental horse, they are detested by English trainers.

They object to the very small head, and small pointed ears ; " to the high setting-on of tail," which gives so much character to the Arab. On the contrary, as stated in the preceding page, most first-class horses on the racecourse and across country (steeplechasers) have their tails set on low.

From time to time instances occur in which the type of the far distant Eastern blood is reproduced with curious fidelity. For example, Touchstone, winner of the great St. Leger in 1834, was a very famous sire of race-horses. From him, amongst others, are descended Orlando, to whom the Derby was awarded in 1844 under rather curious circumstances; Surplice, winner of the same race and of the St. Leger in 1848 ; and Newminster, winner of the St. Leger in 1851.

Touchstone's pedigree goes back through six sires to Eclipse, whose descent from Oriental stock is shown in the pedigree set out at page 57. Amongst the numerous sons of Touchstone was Motley, who never distinguished himself on the turf. When Motley was exhibited at Islington in 1865, being then fourteen years old, he received, on the express recommendation of Mr. Weatherby, of Old Burlington Street, an extra prize in consequence of his remarkable reproduction of the type of his remote Oriental and particularly Arab ancestors. His head was the head of a thorough-bred Arab ; his fault—withers lower than his croup—was an Arab fault, which he had in common with his ancestor Eclipse. It was apparently counteracted by his union with hunting half-bred mares with good riding shoulders. At any rate, as soon as his produce came into work, he attained a high reputation as a sire of hunters, which he enjoyed till his death, but he was never sire of a good race-horse.

Modern race-horses are no longer required to carry twelve stone in races for four or six miles, and in England the barbarity of heats has entirely disappeared. They were common in country racecourses in the middle of the present century, and are still continued in America and France.

THE COLOURS OF THOROUGH-BRED HORSES.

The modern thorough-bred horse is most commonly bay, frequently chestnut, less frequently brown, rarely black, and still more rarely roan, and scarcely ever grey. Cecil, an authority, writing in 1855, calculated that in the previous thirty years the Derby had been won by sixteen bays, seven chestnuts, and seven browns; the St. Leger by seventeen bays, eight browns, and five chestnuts. Since 1855 the proportionate number of bays has been maintained, the number of chestnuts has increased, the number of browns diminished, and no grey or roan has won either of these great stakes. Gustavus, a grey, won the Derby in 1821, and Frederick, another grey, won the same race in 1829; nothing of that colour since. There has been no grey horse of repute since Chanticleer, who, at four and five years old, in 1847 and 1848, won many Royal Plates, the Goodwood Stakes, and the Doncaster Cup. There were only two grey stallions

ORLANDO, WHO WON THE DERBY, RUNNING SECOND TO THE FOUR-YEAR-OLD RUNNING REIN.

named in the "Racing Calendar" of 1872—Master Bagot, an iron grey; and the Strathconan, a light grey, descended from Chanticleer, through his dam. Strathconan is credited with only nine foals, none of them grey; and Master Bagot with only one, a bay. Roans came into notice in 1864, when Rapid Rhone won the Claret Stakes at Newmarket for the Earl of Glasgow, beating the St. Leger winner, Lord Clifden. He was of the Physalis blood; and the earl bred many of the same tribe, amongst which in the stud bequeathed to General Peel were "Brother to Rapid Rhone," a roan horse, Beauvale, and others. A friend writes: "In a visit to Lord Glasgow's stud farm, in 1865, I saw a yearling filly, in colour a beautiful yellow dun, but as she never ran she was probably converted, like many other foals on the same farm, into cats'-meat; for such was the custom of a peer as eccentric as any ever described in a French romance." The roan thorough-bred sires have been chiefly employed in covering half-bred mares.

No thorough-bred piebald has appeared in public in the present century; but in a letter to the author from the Duke of Beaufort, his Grace mentions that a Physalis mare once bred him piebald twins.

Skewball, foaled in 1741 by the Godolphin Arabian, dam by Whitefoot out of the Leedes mare (the dam of Flying Childers) bred by the Earl of Godolphin, won a great number of plates and prizes in England, and one famous match in Ireland.

The breeders of pedigree farm stock, from bulls to prize poultry, are very particular about colour—a black-nosed Shorthorn, a foul feather in a Spanish bird, or blue legs in a game cock, are considered fatal defects—and foreigners object strongly to white marks in the sires they purchase, whether thorough-bred or trotting; but this objection is not entertained in England if the mark is not an ugly one.

An examination of the "Calendar" shows that very frequently race-horses do not perpetuate their own colours. For example, the "Calendar" of 1872 showed that out of the bay King Tom's nine foals, four were chestnuts and one brown; Lord Lyon had eight bays, five browns, and four chestnuts; Blair Athol had seventeen chestnuts, his own colour, fourteen bays, and one brown; Old Voltigeur in his decline got all bays or browns; Young Melbourne four browns, all the rest chestnuts; while Saunterer, who was black, was the sire of fourteen chestnuts, of ten bays, three browns, and only two blacks. It is the opinion of the training fraternity that there never was a good black mare on the turf, although traditions of the hunting-field name many not quite thorough-bred. Comparing the colour of the British thorough-breds with the Arabs of Syria and the Wahabee country, it will be observed that the chief difference is in the rarity of greys and presence of roans in the English breeds. Black is equally rare in both.

Many thorough-bred horses have grey hairs thinly distributed over a dark coat, a variation not objected to; but the prejudice against greys is very strong in training stables. When, some years ago, a grey son of Chanticleer was quoted in the betting for the great race at Epsom, the Honourable F—— L——, one of the highest authorities on racing pedigrees, wrote, "I can never believe that a grey horse can win the Derby." In November, 1878, three grey thorough-breds were sold by auction at Tattersall's—viz., Little Nell, grey mare by Blair Athol out of Ellen the Fair, by Chanticleer, a grey filly by Musket and a grey colt by Knight of the Garter, both out of Little Nell. It will be observed that none of these sires were grey, but the blood of Chanticleer was so prepotent as to colour that it outbalanced the chestnut of even Blair Athol; but these greys did not inherit his racing merits, and none of them fetched a hundred pounds.

French and German writers devote pages to a description of the different shades in the colours of horses, but it is a subject on which no accurate information could be conveyed without a lecture illustrated by living subjects, or plates more costly than the question is worth. It is difficult to describe where bay ceases and brown begins. A black horse in low condition often appears of a rusty brown. In England alone a black horse with tan muzzle and flanks is conventionally called a brown horse. Chestnuts have nearly as many shades as bays, between the light gold and the dark sorrel which is black in a gloomy stable. Roans may be black or red. The late Earl of Derby had, early in his racing career, a black roan race-horse called Parolles; Lord Glasgow's breed are red or yellow roans. Grey means any colour between steel grey and light mottled grey. Grey may be of a shade most fashionable or extremely vulgar.

The following tables and figures, collected from the "Racing Calendar" for 1872, epitomise the then history and condition of the British turf.

In 1872 there were registered as the sires and dams of thorough-bred foals :—

STALLIONS 387

Two or three of the most fashionable sires are credited with from twenty to over thirty foals, descending in the scale until several have only one recorded against their names ; but the "Calendar" does not notice the produce of the half-bred mares who are the customers of the less famous and less expensive sires.

BROOD MARES 2853

Accounted for as follows :—

Barren 661
Slipped foals 85
Not covered 155
Covered by half-bred horses 50
Died before foaling 108
Exported before foaling . . . . 53—1112

Produce—viz., Colts 875, Fillies 866 . . . 1741

In 1800 there were bred thorough-bred colts and fillies . 600 | In 1802 the number of race horses was . . . 536
In 1831 there were bred thorough-bred colts and fillies . 961 | In 1872 the number was 2310

The following table shows the number of horses of different ages that have run in the undermentioned years :—

YEARS.	Yearlings.	Two Years.	Three Years.	Four Years.	Five Years and Upwards.	TOTAL.
1797	...	48	161	122	262	593
1802	...	31	117	108	280	536
1807	...	33	230	148	280	691
1812	...	55	324	188	254	821
1817	...	78	309	174	239	800
1822	...	112	285	194	387	988
1827	...	142	361	210	453	1166
1832	...	200	395	237	407	1239
1837	...	215	326	210	462	1213
1843	...	213	384	236	456	1289
1849	...	264	419	254	378	1315
1859	9	576	496	240	324	1645
1860	...	608	521	302	286	1717
1861	...	661	550	214	342	1767
1862	...	626	528	291	381	1826
1863	...	643	510	291	393	1837
1864	...	664	548	298	438	1948
1865	...	659	572	359	449	2109
1866	...	729	572	364	447	2042
1867	...	752	661	408	637	2458
1868	...	844	631	418	617	2510
1869	...	842	673	402	617	2534
1870	...	807	709	442	611	2569
1871	...	732	740	450	561	2483
1872	...	699	627	382	390	2098

From this table it will be seen that for seven years, ending 1872, over 700 foals were required to supply the annual demand for two-year-olds. Of the remainder, a certain number are not run until three years old, or are used as stallions or brood-mares without being trained. The rest are drafted off as steeplechasers, or as hunters, riding-horses, barouche and team leaders. The inferior are distributed over the country, and become cheap hacks, or find their way down to cabs and tradesmen's spring-carts.

It will be observed that one-third of the two and three-year-olds disappeared from the four and five-year-old races, and only 380 four and 390 five-year-olds and upwards remain. The surplus (554) passed through the same sieve as the yearlings. Death and damaging accidents accounted for perhaps twenty per cent.; a few were transferred to the stud-farm, the rest were converted into horses of general utility. An elaborate calculation has shown that out of fifteen foals only two would remain worth training at three years old.

It is therefore plain that on the character of these drafts from the turf the character of the English pleasure-horse mainly depends.

The following table shows that the number of races run in the United Kingdom has diminished since 1869 by more than three hundred; but the stakes have been increased in far greater proportion, and the wagering has attained vastly more importance, although it was easier twenty years ago to win a larger sum upon three or four of the chief races run for each year than is now the case.

DISTANCE.	1867.	1868.	1869.	1870.	1871.	1872.
Half a mile and under	390	417	464	388	179	188
Over half mile, and under one mile	745	803	850	814	1020	1032
One mile	337	323	325	281	253	264
Over a mile, and under two	411	410	383	397	353	323
Two miles, and under three	225	181	190	173	158	96
Three miles, and under four	25	23	22	21	20	17
Four miles	7	5	4	4	4	3
Total	2140	2162	2238	2078	1987	1923

This table shows the following change in racing arrangements:—

In 1867 the races for a half mile and under were   390
For over half a mile and under a mile   745
In 1872 the competitors for the half mile and under were   188
Over half and under one mile   1032

Out of 1,923 races, only 116 were for two miles and upwards.

The number of races run for during 1875 was slightly in excess of the previous season, the exact figures being 1,909, as against 1,873. The increase was almost entirely in the short-distance races; for there were 261 of half a mile or under, or twenty-eight more than the previous year. More than half of the total number of races were run for on courses of more than half a mile and under a mile; 256 were mile races; 261 were over a mile and under two; 79 were over two miles and under three; 11 were over three miles and under four; and six were decided over a four-mile course.

The Earl of Coventry, as an owner and breeder of race-horses, a master of hounds, and acknowledged judge of the points and qualities of a useful horse, in a letter he addressed to

The Times, dated 5th of November, 1873, expresses himself very plainly on the evils of five and six furlong races :—

"The short races which now-a-days prevail have a far greater influence for evil, in my opinion, on the breed of horses than the mischievous practice of running two-year-olds early in the year. I brought forward a motion at a recent meeting of the Jockey Club to the effect that there should be no more races for three-year-olds and upwards of a shorter distance than one mile, but it was negatived by a large majority.

"The number of short races is increasing, for I find that in 1871, out of 1,253 races 646 were under the distance of one mile; in 1872, out of 1,269 races, 741 were under a mile. I have not included two-year-old races in this calculation, which I believe to be a correct one. We all agree that soundness of wind and limb is the most important element in the constitution of the horse. It is generally admitted that roaring is a hereditary disease, and it is an equally well-known fact that roarers can win over short courses; therefore, the scurry races, of which I complain, may be regarded as a premium for unsound horses. Admiral Rous, in a letter which he published a short time ago in *The Times*, said 'The breed of horses of which we are so proud will eventually be beaten by the French;' and states as his reason for thinking so that 'Frenchmen reject roarers and infirm legs.' Can that be a matter of surprise, when it is recollected that in France there are no races under a mile, and, in consequence, there is no occupation for roarers and cripples? At many of the horse shows I am in the habit of seeing stallions that I know to be roarers, but they have acquired—thanks to the short races—a reputation on the turf, and their services at the stud are sought by breeders.

"There is plenty of evidence to show that the disease of roaring has been more frequently met with of late years, and we find that the number of short races is increasing. Layers of odds and owners of bad horses are fond of short races; the general racing public dislike them: and I believe that if they were done away with altogether there would be a very perceptible decrease in the number of roarers bred in years to come."

Since Lord Coventry published this letter the evil has rather increased than decreased, because racing every year falls more and more under the control of professional bookmakers.

THE RACE-HORSE AS A STALLION.

The character of a thorough-bred stallion is as delicate a matter as the credit of a bank or the reputation of a woman; and, like a beauty's charms, it is constantly threatened by young rivals rising every season. It is, therefore, as well not to mention living celebrities, either to condemn or praise, especially the latter, as a few years have seen the idols of one year utterly discredited by the unfortunate racing results of their produce.

Such examples may be found in the careers of Stockwell and his rival (as a sire) West Australian, two of the most popular race-horses the English turf ever produced—both dead, the one at twenty and the other at twenty-one years of age.

Stockwell's pedigree may be traced not so directly from sire to son as Touchstone, who was the sire of Orlando and the grandsire of Teddington, but he was of the Eclipse blood, thus :—

Foaled 1849. By the Baron out of Pocahontas by Glencoe; out of Marpessa by Muley. out of Clare by Marmion, out of Harpalice by Johanna, out of Amazon by Driver, out of Fractious by Mercury, her dam by Woodpecker, out of Everlasting by Eclipse.

In 1852 Stockwell won the Two Thousand Guineas at Newmarket, was first favourite for the Epsom Derby, but was not placed (the winner being little Daniel O'Rourke); he won the St. Leger, and nine other races in the same year. The following year he was beaten by Teddington at Ascot for the Empress Cup, and his career on the turf closed at the end of his fourth year, having won during that period stakes of the value of rather less than ten thousand pounds.

But as the sire of winners of great races Stockwell has had no equal. For several years before his death his fee was one hundred guineas, and his subscription was always full. Amongst his stock were included St. Albans, Blair Athol, Lord Lyon, Achievement, Doncaster, winners of three Derbies and four St. Legers, with several running second and third for those races, whilst his winning grandsons and grand-daughters may be counted by scores.

FLYING DUTCHMAN, WINNER OF THE DERBY AND ST. LEGER, 1849.

West Australian in 1853 won the Two Thousand Guineas, the Epsom Derby, and the Doncaster St. Leger. At four years old he won three races, and was then put to the stud. The late Lord Londesborough, on setting up a racing stud, purchased him for £4,750. Put to a series of first-class mares he got nothing worth recording in turf annals. On the death of Lord Londesborough in 1860, he was sold by auction to the Comte, afterwards Duc, de Morny, for three thousand guineas. In France he was equally a failure. On the Duc de Morny's death the Emperor of the French purchased him for £1,500, but he died without being sire of one good horse of any kind. His French stock, whether race-horses or steeplechasers, all broke down in training. Yet he was one of the best runners ever seen, a far more promising colt than Stockwell.

THE FLYING DUTCHMAN AND VOLTIGEUR.

"The British turf has produced many a pair of famous animals which, like Bay Middleton and Elis, Charles the Twelfth and Euclid, Lord Lyon and Savernake, Kaiser and Gang Forward, invariably suggest thoughts and reminiscences of each other.   Such will always be the case when the names of the Flying Dutchman and Voltigeur are mentioned with pride; and although within the last dozen or fifteen years the 'classic races' have fallen almost without exception to the equine champions of the South, it will be long before two such noble representatives of the British thoroughbred will be stripped upon a racecourse as were sent by the North to do battle for Epsom's great race in 1849 and 1850. The Flying Dutchman, by Bay Middleton out of Barbette, by Sandbeck, was bred in 1846 by Mr. Vansittart, at Kirkleatham in Yorkshire, but his breeder, who died in 1848, was not spared to witness the Dutchman's triumphs as a three-year-old at Epsom and Doncaster. The colt passed immediately after his birth into the possession of the late Earl of Eglinton, who, after the victories as a two-year-old of the Flying Dutchman's half-brother, Van Tromp, entered into a convention with Mr. Vansittart, binding him to give one thousand guineas for every perfectly-formed foal thrown by Barbette.   From the moment when, as a yearling, the Flying Dutchman reached the stables, at Middleham, of Fobert his trainer, it was anticipated with confidence that he would gain the highest honours that it is in the power of the turf to bestow.   His fame preceded him to Newmarket, where he was stripped for the first time in public as a competitor for the July stakes, and such was the impression produced by his grand appearance, his faultless action, and by his easy victory upon that occasion, that he was at once backed at five to one for the Derby, and during the intervening eleven months between the July of 1848 and the May of 1849 his backers never for a single day had occasion to regret their spirited investments.   The Flying Dutchman was one of those exceptional animals which, at two and three years old, are never sick or sorry for an hour; and such was the perfection of his respiratory organs that Fobert used to pronounce it impossible to make him blow hard even after a four miles' gallop. He had the misfortune to run both for the Derby and St. Leger when the ground was deep and holding, but his action, which was that of a hunter, and his large feet, enabled him to hold his own in both races.   Hotspur ran him close for the Derby, but the St. Leger was never more easily won than when he 'romped home' in front of Nunnykirk and eight other starters.   As a four-year-old he made such an example of his field in the Ascot Cup that Mr. Greville proclaimed him to be the best animal that in his long experience he had ever seen.

" Nevertheless, it was destined that his colours should for once be lowered, and to the Earl of Zetland's Voltigeur was reserved the honour accorded to the Duke of Wellington by a French print, which was sold for a short time in Paris after the battle of Waterloo, and at the foot of which were printed the significant words, ' Il vaincu l'invincible.' Voltigeur, a dark brown horse, standing fifteen hands three inches high—the same colour and the same stature as the Dutchman's— first saw the light in the paddocks, at Hart, in Durham, of Mr. R. Stephenson—the same paddocks which subsequently produced Virago, perhaps the best mare of this century. Voltigeur, the son of Voltaire and Martha Lynn, only started once as a two-year-old, when he had little difficulty in winning the Wright Stakes, at Richmond in Yorkshire.   After this race he was purchased by the late Earl of Zetland for one thousand guineas, with the promise of five hundred more if he should win the Derby.   The Earl of Zetland thought him heavy-shouldered, but was persuaded to become his owner at the urgent instance of Mr. Williamson, the brother to Lady Zetland. It was a fortunate purchase, and the popular spots of the Lord of Aske—which have since been adopted and rendered famous at the Antipodes by Sir Hercules Robinson, late Governor of New South Wales—were never carried by a better animal. The first and only visit of Voltigeur to the South was upon the occasion of his gallant victory for the Derby of 1850. It was the opinion of many excellent judges that his dead heat with Russborough, for the St. Leger, was occasioned by the bad riding of his jockey, Job Marson, who was unnerved by the sudden and tremendous rush of Jim Robinson upon the Irish champion. Then followed that memorable race for the Doncaster Cup, which still lives in the recollection of those who witnessed it, and makes the equine struggles of to-day appear 'flat, stale, and unprofitable,' in comparison with the more exciting scenes of their youth. For the only time in the history of the turf the Doncaster Cup was a match between a couple of 'double firsts.' The odds, laid eagerly by the shrewdest judges, were six to one upon the Flying Dutchman, who jumped off with a long lead, and made running at a pace which seemed to make pursuit hopeless. He passed the stand, and dashed up the hill with a lead of a dozen lengths, and during the first two miles of the race, odds of ten to one were freely offered upon him. Then as he passed the Red House, Flatman upon Voltigeur began to draw up, and, inch by inch, to overtake the leader. At the distance the two horses were close together, and amidst a scene of such excitement as no Yorkshire racecourse had heretofore witnessed, Lord Zetland's gallant three-year-old passed the winning-post first by half a length. Pale, and with tears streaming down his cheeks, the Earl of Eglinton leaned for support against the wall of the Jockey Club stand,* but the story is still told that Marlow, over-confident in the powers of the matchless animal that he bestrode, disobeyed his orders, and made running when he had been told to wait. The Flying Dutchman, for the first time in his life, had been a little off his feed, and showed nervous fretfulness at the post. Fobert's injunctions were peremptory, that Marlow should ride a waiting race, and, had they been obeyed, it is probable that the Dutchman would have retired from the turf without having ever experienced the bitterness of defeat. In the match between him and Voltigeur at York in the following spring, the superiority of Lord Eglinton's horse was incontestably manifested; and great as is our respect for Voltigeur, we hold beyond all question that the Flying Dutchman was the better animal of the two.

"At the stud neither of these famous racehorses has added to his laurels. The only Derby winner sprung from the Dutchman's loins is Ellington, a moderate animal; and in the St. Leger, Oaks, Two Thousand and One Thousand Guineas, no son or daughter of his stands inscribed upon the roll of fame. Vidette is the only first-class performer with Voltigeur for his sire; and, although nothing is more certain than that in these days of extravagant prices the Flying Dutchman and Voltigeur would, in each case, fetch, upon retiring from the turf, as much as was given for Blair Athol and Doncaster, they can lay no claim, as sires, to such lustre as attaches, on the one hand, to Touchstone, to his sons Newminster and Orlando, and to his grandson, Lord Clifden; or, on the other, to Stockwell, and to his sons Blair Athol and St. Albans."

GLADIATEUR AND BLAIR ATHOL.

The career of Gladiateur, bred in France, by Monarque, a French sire, presents another sample of the uncertainties which attend breeding for the turf. He began by winning, in 1865,

---

* This account of the Dutchman and Voltigeur is contributed by a Yorkshireman who was present at the Dutchman's defeat and at the match where he recovered his honours.

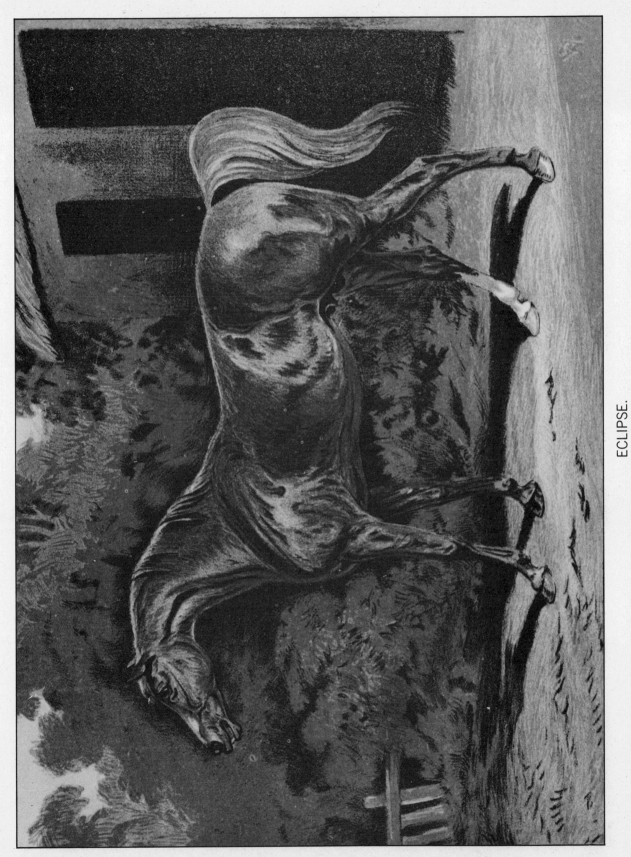

ECLIPSE.

FROM AN ORIGINAL PICTURE IN THE POSSESSION OF EDMUND TATTERSALL ESQ.

THOROUGHBRED SIRE BLAIR ATHOL.
WINNER OF THE DERBY & ST. LEGER 1864.

the Two Thousand, then the Epsom Derby. The Emperor of the French, on hearing the news, embraced Count Lagrange, the owner of Gladiateur, in public, declaring that "Waterloo was avenged!" Gladiateur next crossed the Channel, and won the Grand Prix de Paris, returned to England, and carried off a couple of small races at Goodwood, and wound up the year by winning the Doncaster St. Leger, where he beat the famous Regalia, winner of the Oaks. Gladiateur made another successful journey to Longchamp the same year, and returned in time to win the Newmarket Derby. When a four-year-old he won the Ascot Cup, beating Regalia and Breadalbane.

On the sale of Count Lagrange's stud during the Franco-German war Gladiateur was purchased by the late Mr. Blenkiron for stud purposes. On his decease, his stud, which included both Gladiateur and Blair Athol, came under Mr. Tattersall's hammer. Gladiateur fetched five thousand guineas, Blair Athol twelve thousand five hundred guineas.

Blair Athol is by Stockwell out of Blink Bonny, by Melbourne, her dam Queen Mary by Gladiator, grand-dam by Plenipotentiary out of Myrrha by Whalebone.

Blink Bonny in 1857 performed the rare feat of winning the Epsom Derby on the Wednesday, and the Oaks on the Friday. Blair Athol won the Derby in 1864, was beaten for the Grand Prix de Paris, won the St. Leger, and retired from the turf in 1865, when he was purchased by Mr. Jackson, a leviathan bookmaker who was founding a stud, for seven thousand guineas. On Jackson's death he was purchased at auction at Tattersall's by Mr. Blenkiron for five thousand guineas.

Gladiateur died without having begotten one famous winner, while the "Racing Calendar" year after year contains the names of winning colts and fillies by Blair Athol. Such are the lotteries of the turf.

The reputation and consequent annual income of a stallion (as far as thoroughbred mares are concerned) depends, in his first years, on the prowess of his running progeny. A winner of any of the great three-year-old races can always secure good mares at the commencement of his career. At the end of four or five years his custom depends on the success of his produce. His reputation may continue to improve until the period when his powers decline—an advanced age—or sink in four or five years to the value of a country travelling stallion. In the stallion list are many horses nineteen and twenty years old. There have been stallions, like Newminster, which have continued to maintain a high reputation as sires long after they were crippled by injured limbs or fevered feet, or partly blind; and some sires of famous pedigree, like Gladiator who ran second in Bay Middleton's Derby, and Young Melbourne, have, from the success of their produce on the turf, attracted a large annual income without having won a single race.

The fees vary, and are sometimes very high. In a recent "Racing Calendar" two stallions are advertised at one hundred guineas each, and Blair Athol in 1878 commanded a fee of two hundred guineas. The prices for horses of reputation, either from performance or blood, are commonly from twenty guineas to thirty-five guineas. In the list of stallions in the "Racing Calendar" at the head of the list of foals, many have not more than one, others only half a dozen, attached to their names. But as this would not pay for their keep, the probability is that these, where not old exhausted heroes, are engaged in serving half-bred mares at from two to five guineas each.

In 1859, when the fate of the Conservative Government was trembling in the balance, Lord Palmerston had Mainstone, and Lord Derby Cape Flyaway, in the coming Epsom Derby, both favourites named in the betting. The day after the Derby Cabinet had been beaten in the

House of Commons in a division on the Address, the rivals in politics and friends in society met at Tattersall's, in that paddock attached to the old "Corner" which the subscribers to the present sumptuous club-house regret so much. "Well, Palmerston," said the earl, "you don't expect to win the Derby? Two wins in one week are too much!" "I don't know," replied Lord Palmerston, interrogatively; "Mainstone's a good horse." But he was, his friends said, "got at;" and, like Cape Flyaway, Mainstone was nowhere, and finally descended to the useful and inglorious position of a farmer's stallion in Essex, for the benefit of Sir Thomas Lennard's friends and neighbours, with only one thoroughbred foal to his credit in the "Stud Book" in 1873.

THE LIFE OF A RACEHORSE.

The age of a racehorse, whenever foaled, dates from the 1st of January, it is therefore the object of breeders that foals should fall early in the year. If one falls in December, it is at once excluded from all the races confined to two-year-olds and three-year-olds, and, in fact, from all races where the weight follows the age, because at one year old it is counted two years old, and so on. On the other hand, a colt foaled in June would have, as a two-year-old and three-year-old, to compete with others nominally of the same age, but really several months older.

"A yearling," according to the evidence of General Peel—who "can show to a fraction what each horse in his stud costs"—"cannot be brought to face Mr. Tattersall's hammer under £100; but this," he adds, "would not meet the expense in cases where stallions cover mares at twenty guineas and upwards." The price of Stockwell, and of his son, Blair Athol, in 1873, was one hundred guineas. A nominal yearling, but frequently sixteen months old when put up to auction in June, will often, from the effects of nourishing food, cows' milk, if needed, and oats from the time he can be persuaded to nibble, reach the average size of a full-grown hunter.

In August or September the expensive education and training of the yearling racehorse commences. In the following year, in March, or, if discretion rules the stable, in July, the racing career begins in earnest. At Newmarket alone there are the chances of winning several stakes of from £1,000 to £3,000. Many capital horses have been and are annually used up in this part of their career.

In the second year—viz., at three years old nominally, really at three years and some months —the pick of a racing stable, if duly entered as yearlings twelve months in advance, are qualified for the great three-year-old stakes, in which a colt has to carry 8 stone 10 pounds, a filly 8 stone 5 pounds. These include, in April, the "Two Thousand Guineas" at Newmarket, worth over £4,000, and "One Thousand Guineas," for fillies, worth not much less than the Two Thousand; late in May or early in June, the Epsom Derby, which has been worth £7,000, open to fillies as well as colts; the Oaks, open to fillies only, value on an average over £4,000; a fortnight later, at Ascot, the Prince of Wales' Stakes, over £3,000, and the Coronation, over £1,000; and in September the great Doncaster St. Leger, value between £4,000 and £5,000.

At three years old the racehorse can compete in handicaps, which are more numerous and more popular than any other class of races, because they afford more room for betting operations, and because the public are interested in seeing the winners of the greatest events brought down to equality by weight. The Newmarket Cæsarewitch and the Cambridgeshire handicap races are both run in October, when a foal of January, nominally three years, will be really three years and six months old.* Racehorse breeders do not, however, approve of foals dropping so long before the mares can get into the grass paddocks.

At the end of the three-year-old season, the winners of the great events, if colts, are often put to the stud, and the severe weeding of second and third-class horses already alluded to takes place. After four years old very few horses of a high class remain on the turf; in fact, a very good horse is almost driven from the course at or after four years old by the penalties of weight, under the system of handicapping, which, abused and condemned by leading turf authorities, but tolerated as a necessity, is really the foundation of modern English racing.

The Queen's Plates are open to all horses of three years old and upwards, except geldings, weights being for three-year-olds from 7 stone to 8 stone 3 pounds; for four years old, 8 stone 7 pounds; five and six years old, from 9 stone 12 pounds to 10 stone 4 pounds.

The Royal Plates in England and Scotland are awarded on the theory of encouraging horses equal to long distances at heavy weights. In 1872 the distance run was in one instance more than three miles; in four instances three miles; in the rest about two miles. In three instances the winner walked over; in ten, two competed; in five, three competed; in eight, four competed; in two, five competed; in four, six competed; in one, seven competed. One horse won five plates, one four, and two horses each three; that is to say, four horses took fifteen plates, most of them winning with ridiculous ease—Corisande by fifty lengths.

The value of a mare at the stud who has won one of the great three-year-old races, when the time comes that age and heavy handicapping drive her from the turf, is infinitely less than that of a horse. In the first place, she can only produce one foal in a year; when twins occur they rarely turn out well. In the next place, experience has shown that mares, almost unconquered on the turf, have frequently been, by the effects of training or some other cause, so much exhausted as to be almost valueless for breeding purposes. Thus, Queen of Trumps, winner of the Oaks and St. Leger, never threw a racehorse. Fille de l'Air, who was only second as a racer to Blair Athol, was put to Gladiateur, their union produced one colt, called Eole, a wretched brute. That training has something to do with this is confirmed by the fact that a mare which has been in training for three years will rarely breed at all until a year has been passed in cooling her down on soft food. It will be observed from statistics at page 69 how large a per-centage of thoroughbred mares are barren.

A close parallel may be found between the careers of the *alumni* of our two great universities and of the thoroughbred foals training for the turf. A considerable number of undergraduates take no degree at all—a great many merely obtain a simple pass. Out of those who do go out in honours, the majority are only famous in university circles for a year. Out of the annual double-first-class men, senior wranglers, and Smith's prizemen, the majority subside into country clergymen or undistinguished members of the bar, members of Parliament who thin the House when they rise, or county magistrates who bore their less learned neighbours; a few become famous orators, Chancellors of Exchequer, Prime Ministers, Lord Chief Justices, and Bishops. Nevertheless, the undistinguished out of their own social circle help to leaven the mass, and give a tone to the education of the well-to-do classes of this country. So, too,

* In 1873, for the Cæsarewitch there were seventy-nine subscribers, and thirty came to the post, including Marie Stuart, winner of the Oaks and St. Leger of that year, a three-year-old, carrying 8 stone 5 pounds. The winner was King Lud, a four-year old, carrying 7 stone 5 pounds, against whom the odds laid a week before the race were 60 to 1, and on the day of the race 20 to 1—a fine example of the uncertainty of turf predictions. The distance was 2 miles 2 furlongs 28 yards. It was run in 4 minutes 10¼ seconds by Benson's chronograph.

the blood-horse, rejected or expelled from the turf, has leavened the whole mass of our riding and light draught-horses with an infusion of blood that makes them unequalled in every other country for quality and size.   Unfortunately, at the present day too many of these cast blood sires are affected with hereditary diseases.

THE SUPPORTS OF THE TURF.

In the preceding pages the object has been to describe the turf in its present state—an institution which has in fact created the blood-horse—not to dwell upon vain projects for reforming a mode of gambling which if it did not suit the national taste would not exist.   To pretend that modern race-meetings are held for the purpose of improving the breed of horses is rank hypocrisy.   They do indirectly improve the quality of horses; but races are held, and some £60,000 awarded in stakes in the seven Newmarket meetings alone, in reality to afford the world of betting men an opportunity of winning and losing immense sums.

Amongst the layers of wagers on horse-races perhaps the greatest contributors to the gains of the professional "bookmakers" are not confirmed gamblers.   The taste of the English for everything connected with horses leads thousands of many classes, from the peer and county gentleman down to the farmer, the tradesman, and that very sporting tribe the domestic servant, to risk a few shillings, or a few pounds, or a few hundreds, on the result of a national or local race, just as they would play whist, bezique, piquet, cribbage, or a round game for a trifling stake; without anything of the ardour and determination of those *habitués* of the London and Paris clubs, to whom every day seems long until they can sit down before a green cloth and cut the cards.   Although the stakes of these amateurs are individually insignificant, they form a considerable item in the winnings of the professional bookmaker.

Amongst the owners of race-horses are a few—at the present day four or five—who breed, train, and run them purely for sport, and never risk enough in bets to press upon the income of a month or a day.

Besides the mere amateurs who only bet on two or three races in the year, there are those who annually and systematically risk a portion of their income for the purpose of improving it—£10, £25 (technically a pony), or £100; such calculating bettors are to be found amongst the younger sons of good family and officers of the army.   The navy is not much given to the turf, although the great god of the silversmiths of that Ephesus, Albert Gate, was for many years an admiral.   Finally there is the never-ceasing, annually-recruited army of born gamblers, male and female, high and low, who have by the progress of legislation been gradually squeezed out of all the ways of risking their money which their grandfathers and great-grandfathers enjoyed, and driven into the betting-ring.   Lotteries, once a source of considerable revenue to the State, have been abolished within the memory of veterans of the turf. In the early years of George III. the royal family played faro on birthday nights, and all courtiers were expected to risk a few gold pieces.

When Mr. Wilberforce entered public life as a young, a rich, and unconverted man, at every club in St. James's hazard was played, and at the private houses of ladies of great fashion faro-banks were open every night of the season.   Of Charles James Fox it was said, pleasantly, and not as a reproach, that he could have made a fine income at whist and piquet, but he preferred to ruin himself at hazard, declaring that "next to the pleasure of winning at hazard, the greatest pleasure was losing."   Everybody played; many fine hereditary estates passed away from noble to obscure owners; those who objected to play were ridiculed as "Methodists."

General Scott—two of whose daughters married, one the statesman George Canning, and the other the Duke of Portland, father of Lord George Bentinck—more fortunate than his grandson, accumulated a fortune by his skill at cards without disgrace.

Lord Holland in his " Memoirs of the Whig Party," says, " Mr. Pitt was, I believe, a partner in the faro-bank at Goosetree's (St. James's). At that period many men of fashion did not scruple to belong to such associations, and to avow it. I mention the circumstance not to the discredit of Mr. Pitt, but to show by the example of so correct and decorous a man the character and habits of the times."*

Within the first quarter of this century gambling was openly carried on in tents on race-courses and rooms at every race-meeting. The stage-coachmen used to point out sheep marked " E.O." browsing on Bagshot Heath, whose owner had won the capital for stocking a farm at Ascot in an E.O. tent. A gentleman who tried to put down the hazard rooms opened during Doncaster races in 1827 was not only pelted in the streets, but the subject of a vote of censure at a public meeting of respectable inhabitants.

In St. James's Street, in 1825, it might literally be said—

> " The gates of hell stood open night and day ;
> Smooth the ascent, and easy was the way,"

to an exclusive set, privileged to ruin themselves if they chose at Crockford's ; and, if they did not, to enjoy the luxuriously-furnished club, with the great *chef* Ude's exquisite cookery, and wines purchased regardless of expense.

It is at Crockford's, on the eve of a Derby, that the Earl of Beaconsfield,† who was one of the members or constant visitors with Count d'Orsay (Mirabel), opens one of his novels with a life-like dialogue ; and the same club was always one of the most popular scenes in those rubbishy " fashionable novels " which Bulwer and Mrs. Gore (photographing from real lions) killed.

But Crockford, the proprietor, like the North American Indians, who clear a country of all game and then starve, consumed all the wealth of the " golden youth " (*jeunesse dorée*) of his

---

* Gambling-houses were regularly licensed, just as public-houses and music-halls are now. In 1799 the Lord Chief Justice Kenyon, in one of his charges, recommended the prosecution of fashionable (unlicensed) gambling-houses, saying, "If any of the guilty parties are convicted, whatever may be their rank or station, though they may be the first ladies in the land, they shall certainly exhibit themselves in the pillory." The next week Gilray had a caricature of Lady Buckinghamshire and Lady Archer in the pillory. About the same time another judicial charge on the same subject involved his Lordship in a correspondence with H.R.H. George Prince of Wales.

The magistrates of Middlesex had asked Lord Kenyon to strengthen their hands, and assist them in resisting an application for a license for a new gambling-house in Bond Street, St. James's, about to be opened, under the patronage of the Prince of Wales, by a Mr. Martindale, lately a bankrupt, and defendant, as it happened, in a case tried before Lord Kenyon, at Guildhall. The Chief Justice, on this person's name being mentioned, in an annuity case, said that "he remembered in a cause tried before him Mr. Martindale's certificate as a bankrupt was proved of no legal effect, because he had lost certain sums of money by gaming. He had heard it mentioned that spacious premises were preparing in which this personage was to keep a gaming-house, under the patronage of an illustrious person. That could not be done without a license. He trusted the magistrates would do their duty to the public—granting such a license would be contrary to their duty ; there were gaming-houses enough already." The Prince of Wales immediately addressed a letter by the hand of his Attorney-General, demanding a retractation and apology, which contains the following passage : "It is true I have assented to my name being placed amongst others as a member of a new club, to be under the management of a Mr. Martindale, merely for the purpose of social intercourse, of which I can never object to be a promoter, especially as it was represented to me that the object of this institution was to enable his trustees to render justice to various fair claimants. . . . Give me leave to tell you that you have totally mistaken my character and turn, for of all men universally known to have the least predilection to play, I am perhaps the very man in the world who stands the strongest and the most proverbially so upon that point " (*sic*). Lord Kenyon stuck to his guns ; the king was his private friend. In his reply, he said, "I have for years laboured to put an end to gaming. Many inferior offenders have been brought to justice, but no effectual prosecutions have commenced against the houses in the neighbourhood of St. James's, where examples are set to the lower orders which are a great scandal to the country."—*" Life of the First Lord Kenyon,"* by his Grandson. 1873.

† In the " Racing Calendar " of 1872 there is a colt named " Disraeli, by Prime Minister out of Mystery."

time, was obliged to take to horse-racing for want of victims; he only died just in time to save himself from the bitterness of the ruin on which, over a green table instead of green turf, he had battened and fattened. His horse Ratan, a great favourite for the Derby, was poisoned the night before the race, by the man shut up in the stable to guard him.

The law, assisted by the New Police, put down gambling-houses between 1843 and 1848. Hitherto legislation has not attempted to interfere with the betting transactions carried out in private subscription-rooms and in the betting-rings of public racecourses, by professional gamblers who strictly perform their engagements on pain of expulsion, and who are supposed to lay the odds to nothing less than a "fiver," *i.e.*, five pounds, and to owe the money until the regular settling day. Ready-money gambling is illegal, and sometimes checked by the police, but in 1878 it was carried on conspicuously at all the great race meetings.

The expenses of a racing stud are enormous. The winnings of a racehorse are insignificant, even when such prizes as the Two Thousand Guineas, the Derby, the Oaks, or the Doncaster St. Leger are landed, in comparison with the possible gains of betting on the scale in which that business is now carried on.

Betting presents—in the words of Dr. Johnson (speaking of Thrale's brewery)—to the sanguine man or boy a "potentiality of wealth beyond the dreams of avarice." In 1869 a horse, described by a sporting reporter as "a common ninety-guinea plater," won for his owner the Cambridgeshire handicap, worth £1,900 in stakes, and £12,000 in bets!

The losses are proportionate. A volume of Sir Bernard Burke's "Peerage," or of Mr. Walford's "County Families," annotated by one of those not quite ruined gentlemen who have made the turf the business of their lives, would trace the decay of many ancient and noble names and the dispersion of many grand estates to losses on the turf. The rise of the representatives of professional betting-men to the position of landowners would be equally marked and curious.

As the value of racing stakes and number of racehorses have increased, the trade of gambling in bets has been organised into a business, the professor of which regularly follows circuits of the most important race-meetings, prepared to bet against every horse. Those who were called "legs" or "black-legs" in the last generation, now bear the more genteel name of "bookmakers." They are on the turf what jobbers are on the Stock Exchange —always ready to do business by laying against every horse in every race. They include men of every degree of wealth and credit; one virtue only being required to secure a permanent place in the betting-ring and in the privileged subscription-rooms—*punctual payment.* Corsairs of the sporting world, they must be

"Linked with one virtue, and a thousand crimes."

The most shady antecedents,* the vilest habits, a language compounded of the slang of

* Long before Palmer had been arrested, convicted, and hanged, for poisoning his confederate—having, there is no doubt, previously poisoned his mother, his wife, and several others—the fatality that attended his friends had obtained for him among his betting associates the playful nickname of "The Doser." The year that Wild Dayrell was a favourite for the Derby the use of strychnine to make horses "safe" formed the subject of a facetious correspondence in a sporting paper edited by a turf oracle.

No saint, no martyr, ever showed greater calmness than this villain Palmer. Lord Chief Justice Cockburn, then Attorney-General, replied on the evidence against him in a speech of remarkable lucidity and power. When the verdict of "Guilty" was delivered, Palmer wrote something on a scrap of paper, and handed it to his counsel. These were the words : "It was the riding that did it." The ruling passion strong in death.

A proprietor of travelling waxwork, who thought of visiting a town where Palmer had many friends, was warned not to go if he had the poisoner in his "chamber of horrors." "For," said the adviser, "poor Palmer, though he was hung, was very much respected at ———; for whenever he had a good thing he always put us on."

thieves and the oaths of Lancashire miners, are compatible with a high position as a book-maker, if prepared to bet on the largest scale against everything, and pay on the fixed settling-day without quibbling evasions. The bookmaker on a great scale, attended by his secretaries (he is often perfectly illiterate), has more correspondence, receives and despatches more telegrams, exercises a great deal more influence, than an ordinary country banker.

Bookmakers find their customers in the persons already alluded to, familiarly known as "backers of horses"—a numerous tribe, who either "from information they have received," or from the love of gambling, or for an occasional fancy, desire to wager on a particular horse.

In every race of importance each horse of any reputation has a price quoted against its name in the morning and evening papers. As a rule odds are laid against any one horse winning, and as only one horse can win, the bookmaker makes his profit by laying against every horse in a race if he can find backers—an essential point. The great object of the bookmaker's trade is to find out horses that cannot possibly win—"dead 'uns" is the technical term—and, by laying against them, so far make sure of a profit. The successful bookmaker may and often does, know nothing about the proper shape of a racehorse; but he is well acquainted with its performances, and spares no pains or expense to learn the state of health of each favourite by means of spies, called, in racing phrase, "touts." The object of the owner of racehorses who makes a book, is to conceal all about his own horses and know all about his competitors' In a trial that took place some years ago, it came out that a nobleman with a stud of racehorses employed "touts" to report the progress of rival stables.

The ring is fed by a constantly-recruited crowd of persons, who back a horse for all manner of reasons: because they bred him; because a friend owns him; because—this is very common—they have dreamed a dream; because he was bred in their own parish or county; because they have read a favourable account of him in one of the sporting papers (whose business it is to follow the birth, report the education, training performances, and health of every race-horse until his or her final breakdown or retirement from the turf); because—this is the most dangerous of all reasons—they have been privately and con-fidentially informed of the results of a private trial, and that consequently a certain animal must win. They have been what is called "put up" or "put on" to "a good thing." In the crowds that assemble outside Tattersall's Subscription Rooms before any great betting race, amongst the persons not admitted to that paradise there are always a large per-centage of persons who have been reduced to beggary by putting their trust in "good things" and "backing horses," or attempting to make a book on imperfect resources.

It must be admitted, however, that the ring attracts a good many people of means and leisure, who bet a little and gossip a good deal, by way of passing time, and obtaining the relaxation of society—such as it is. Mrs. Guy Flouncey, whose rise, progress, and final triumph as a leader of fashionable society, are chronicled in "Coningsby" and "Tancred," made her husband go on the turf "for the sake of making acquaintances which she knew how to improve."

Harriet Lady Ashburton, no novelist's creation, but one of the cleverest and most charm-ing women of her generation, once said, according to Lord Houghton, "If I were to begin life again, I would go on the turf to get friends. They seem to me the only people who really hold close together. I don't know why; it may be that each knows something that might hang the other, but the effect is delightful and most peculiar."*

---

* Lord Houghton's "Monographs."

The theory of making a book so as to win in every event is extremely simple; but the practice depends on so many unforeseen circumstances that it is extremely difficult. For example, the profit rests on the assumption that every loser will pay; for if a man has so laid his bets that he has £800 to receive and £500 to pay, his balance of profit will be entirely upset if persons who owe him £400 prove defaulters. When Wild Dayrell won the Derby, in 1855, fourteen bookmakers who had laid against him defaulted, and, according to the mild phraseology of the *Sporting Gazette*, " ceased to be members of Tattersall's."

Paternal legislation, acting in the interest of shopkeepers with tills and householders with plate, has successively put down with a strong hand various ingenious establishments by which the chances of the turf were apparently brought within reach of the million; so that every man, woman, or child, who could beg, borrow, or steal half-a-crown, could back a favourite for any great race.

In 1850 and for several years afterwards *lists* of horses favourites for coming races were put up at sporting public-houses, with the odds that the owner of the list was daily prepared to lay against each, down to as low a figure as half-a-crown.

Some of these were held by professional bookmakers, who had earned a considerable position in the betting ring, and were the means of pouring a large amount of ready money into their hands. The rich and honest list-keepers paid when some favourite that every one was backing won, the dishonest levanted whenever fortune turned against them.

"During the few years that the lists were in their glory," says a writer of considerable authority on racing,* " and especially at one kept by a celebrated bookmaker, known as Leviathan Davies, at a little tavern called the ' Salisbury Arms,' leading out of the Strand, it was easy to take the odds to a couple of thousand pounds about a Derby favourite," or to a pound or even half-a-crown. Amongst the great wagers recorded is one in which Davies (who had been originally a journeyman carpenter) laid Mr. Greville forty thousand to two against Teddington in the winter of 1850-51. This bet was taken by Mr. Greville for Sir Joseph Hawley, and when Teddington came to 5 to 1, the Kentish baronet hedged by laying Davies 10,000 to 2,000 back, and thus stood £30,000 to nothing upon this three-year-old. The cherry jacket of Sir Joseph Hawley had hardly passed the winning-post first in the Derby, when Davies ran up to Mr. Greville with a cheque for £15,000, adding that the remaining half would be forthcoming at Tattersall's upon the following Monday. In 1852 Davies laid in two successive bets, £30,000 to £1,000 and £25,000 to £1,000 against Daniel O'Rourke within a week of the Derby, which he won. But, even apart from "the Leviathan," it was the easiest thing in the world for an owner to back his fancy before Christmas for the coming Derby to win from fifty to one hundred thousand pounds.

"In those days the betting on the Derby and Chester Cup was enormous during the winter which preceded the occurrence of these two races. It was confined to what were then known as ' sporting circles,' and the outside public had little to do with the game. There were no telegraphic wires, no training reports, no daily sporting papers, and few big handicaps. A favourite for the Derby might be lame for months without going back in the betting; and Lord George Bentinck used to chuckle over a story to the effect that he sent a noble friend of his down to his training quarters, where a chestnut colt was seen to gallop in first-rate form, which personated another chestnut colt quoted at a short price in the betting, but which, in reality, was hopelessly broken down."

" The first Derby winner that sensibly quickened and whetted the public appetite for betting on horse-races was the Earl of Zetland's Voltigeur, in 1850, whom all the men-servants and maid-servants at Aske, from the ladies'-maids down to the scullery-maids, had backed for all their savings and perquisites, the tip being followed by their numerous friends and acquaintances. The 'talent' backed other horses. The money went mainly into the pockets of the servants' halls and the outside public. Upon the morning after the race Davies paid £70,000 across the counter in little bets. In the years following Voltigeur's victory, the flow of sovereigns into the till of Davies was unchecked and prodigious. Then came a dismal tale of ruined butlers and grooms and clerks, who had robbed their employers in order to stake their money with Davies and B. Green. At the instance of Sir Richard Mayne the lists were suppressed by an Act of Parliament. The lists were an institution which directly tempted clerks and shopmen to embezzlement, but they were an immense convenience to owners of horses who wanted to back an animal in one sum for a big stake, without anything being known of the transaction. It is an accepted maxim that no owner of a stud of racehorses can pay his expenses without the gains of betting. In 1876 every existing owner of racehorses, except Lord Falmouth and Mr. Houldsworth, depended partly on betting for making a profitable balance at the end of the year. But it has become more difficult for an owner to take advantage of the goodness or badness of any of his stud. His 'commissioner' is watched and imitated."

" The public, who are vigilant and ceaseless readers of 'training reports,' are ever ready to jump in so soon as fifty or one hundred sovereigns have been invested for the stable. So correct and penetrating is indeed the information about every training stable which, by a dozen underground channels, now finds its way to little backers, that it is rare for the stable to get the first skim of the market. The result is that owners of small studs of horses, and especially those who train at Newmarket, are at their wits' end. Having kept a horse that can run for twelve, eighteen, or twenty-four months, the hapless owner finds that when he sends a commissioner to back the rod in pickle the public know as much as he does, and cannot be stalled off. So long as the *Sportsman* can be bought daily for one penny, there will be thousands of readers who know whether a horse is doing strong work or not, and how he galloped upon the previous morning. There is no possibility of having false favourites in these days. The betting lists have been put down by successive Acts of Parliament and the severity of the magistrates of the metropolis ; to a great extent they still exist like illicit stills. Ready-money betting has also been made illegal.

But the small fry of bookmakers, for the most part " welshers " (*i.e.*, people who never pay, except, like Pistol, on compulsion), are still numerous, and still pursue their wretched trade under difficulties, hunted from public-houses to the parks, from the parks to the waste lands of the City, from the waste lands to quiet lanes, and there continually made to " move on." They still swarm like locusts round the gates of authorised betting-rings, and reap a scanty silver harvest from a never-ceasing crop of fools at once credulous and greedy.

The Legislature has not thought fit and does not seem likely to interfere with the branch of the wagering profession which still flourishes in clubs and subscription-rooms to minister to the demands of the wealthy for this essentially British form of gambling. It is presumed that the members of Tattersall's and other clubs established on the same principle are able to take care of themselves. The late Richard Tattersall used to say that the bookmakers' club, the Victoria, was founded because the aristocracy who would bet would not "eat" with these professional gamblers.

In my first edition I tried to give those of my readers who were quite outside the turf operations some idea of an institution which occupies so prominent a part in public life of many eminent men, and particularly of our legislators in both Houses of Parliament. With that view I gave extracts from novels by authors familiar with the pleasures and the rogueries of racing.

In this edition I have cancelled fiction to substitute fact, and availed myself of the "Confessions," as frank as Rousseau's, contained in the journal of Mr. Charles Greville, who raced, and betted, and lived in intimate connection with the most aristocratic supporters of racing, for more than forty years.

Mr. Charles Cavendish Fulke Greville, whom I propose to treat as a typical representative of the turf in its best form, was "no vulgar boy," no needy adventurer, no ruined spendthrift soured by a series of disastrous racing speculations; on the contrary, it is believed that the result of his racing transactions rather added to the very sufficient income which he enjoyed from his earliest years, as Secretary of Jamaica (a sinecure) and Clerk of the Privy Council.

On his father's side he was descended from a cadet of the noble family of Warwick. His mother was a sister of the third Duke of Portland; he was, therefore, a first cousin of Lords George and Henry Bentinck, names famous in the annals of sport.

His official position brought him in contact with the more distinguished men of both parties in the State. He enjoyed the intimacy of the Duke of Wellington and Earl Grey. He was private secretary, before he was twenty, to Earl Bathurst, and he occupied for the last twenty years of his life a suite of rooms in Bruton Street, in the house of Earl Granville

Mr. Greville was a very accomplished man. He was familiar with English literature; he spoke and read French and Italian; had a cultivated taste in art, as his Italian diary shows; was a welcome guest at Holland House, and warmly appreciated the conversation of Mackintosh, Macaulay, Sydney Smith, and the galaxy of talent of every kind which was gathered together in the early part of this century by Lord and Lady Holland. He never seemed so satisfied with himself as when listening to highly intellectual conversation, or riding on horseback amongst sylvan scenes. Yet he was not like Lord Palmerston, who made breeding and racing two or three race-horses one of his relaxations from his great political labours; nor Lord Stanley, who enjoyed a race-meeting like a boy, yet never allowed gambling to debauch his wondrous mental powers. Charles Greville made racing-gambling the business of his life. When he died, the racing literary touts, of whom he had been at once the idol and the oracle, found with disgust that he hated and despised the craft and mysteries which he had practised for forty years.

Mr. Charles Greville was born with a taste and talent for the turf which he must have cultivated early, for in his twenty-sixth year he was selected to manage and re-form the racing establishment of the Duke of York. He began by weeding it of a useless lot of animals, and managed in his second year to win the Derby for the Duke, with Moses. The success of the Duke's stable did Mr. Greville credit up to the time it was brought to an end by a sale of the whole stud.

Mr. Greville for some short time assisted his uncle, the Duke of Portland, in his racing-stable, and afterwards became *confederate* with the young Earl of Chesterfield; then with his cousin, Lord George Bentinck, who, from his father's opposition, could not run his horses in his own name. As a matter of course the cousins quarrelled.

In 1834 Mr. Greville owned a good mare, Preserve, and with her won the Clearwell and Criterion, and in the following year won the One Thousand Guineas. In 1837 he won the St. Leger with Mango. Almost up to the last he had a few horses in training, and was a noted figure, "open-mouthed" on his pony at the Newmarket Meetings.

The following extracts from his diary speak the true voice of a man "who, to gamble, gave up what was meant for mankind."

"*June 29th*, 1828.—Dined with the King at St. James's—his Jockey Club dinner. After dinner, the Duke of Leeds, who sat at the head of the table, gave 'The King.' We all stood up, when His Majesty thanked us, and hoped this would be the first of annual meetings under his roof. He then ordered paper and pens, and they began making matches and stakes. The most perfect ease was established, just as much as if we had been dining with the Duke of York, and he seemed delighted. He made one or two little speeches, one recommending that a stop should be put to the exportation of horses. He twice gave 'The Turf.'

"*August 25th.*—Went to Windsor to-day for a Council. The King gave the Chancellor Lyndhurst a long audience, and another to Peel, probably to talk over Dawson's speech* and arrange politics. After the Council, the King called me, and talked to me about racehorses, which he cares more about than the welfare of Ireland or the peace of Europe.

"I might as well have put in what the King said to me, as it seems to have amused everybody. I was standing close to him at the Council when he put down his head and whispered, 'Which are you for, Cadland or the mare?' So I put down my head too, and said, 'the horse,' (meaning the match between Cadland and Bess of Bedlam), and then as we retired he said to the Duke of Wellington, 'A little bit of Newmarket.'

"*June 24th*, 1829.—Ascot races. The King was very anxious and disappointed. The King has bought seven horses successively, for which he has given 11,300 guineas, principally to win the Cup at Ascot, which he has never accomplished. He might have had Zinganee (which won) but would not, because he fancied the Colonel would beat him; but when that appeared doubtful, was very sorry not to have bought him, and complained that he was not offered to him.

"1830, *August 14th.*—Stayed at Goodwood till the 12th. Went to Brighton, riding over the Downs from Goodwood to Arundel. A delightful ride. *How much I prefer England to Italy!* There we have mountains and sky; here, vegetation and verdure, fine trees, soft turf; and, in the long run, the latter are the most enjoyable.

"I never come here (Goodwood) without fresh admiration of the beauty and delightfulness of the place, combining everything that is enjoyable in life—large, comfortable houses, spacious and beautiful parks, extensive views, dry soil, sea air, novels, rides over the Downs, and all the facilities of occupation and amusement. The Duke ＊ ＊ ＊ ＊ appears here to advantage, exercising a magnificent hospitality, and as a sportsman, a farmer, a magistrate, a good, simple, unaffected, country gentleman, with great personal influence.

"*May 27th*, 1833.—I went to the 'Oaks,' when Lord Stanley kept house for the first time. It is an agreeable sort of place. It has for forty years been the resort of our old jockeys, *and is now occupied by the sporting portion of our Government.* We had Lord Grey and his daughter, Duke and Duchess of Richmond, Lord and Lady Errol, Lord Althorp, Sir James Graham, Lord Uxbridge, the Duke of Grafton, the Earl of Litchfield. It passed off very well. Raining all the morning. An excellent dinner. Whist and blind hookey in the evening.

"It was curious to see Stanley (Lord). Who would believe they beheld the orator and statesman, only second to Peel in the House of Commons, on whom the destiny of the country

* George Dawson, M.P., was the brother-in-law of Sir Robert Peel, and up to that time the darling of his constituents, the Orangemen of Derry. In this speech he virtually avowed his conversion to Catholic Emancipation. The Duke, when it was reported to him, said, "Such a man is only fit for a strait-waistcoat." The indignation of the Ministerial press was hot and heavy. The next year the Duke and Peel "emancipated" the Roman Catholics.

perhaps depends? There was he as if he had no thoughts but for the turf, full of the horses of interest in the lottery, eager, blunt, noisy, good-humoured,

'Has meditans nugas et in illis.'

At night equally devoted to play, as if his fortune depended on it. *Thus can a man relax whose existence is devoted to great objects and serious thoughts!*

"1833.—I had considerable hopes of winning the Derby, but was beaten easily, my horse not being good. An odd circumstance occurred to me before the race: Payne (George) told me in strict confidence that a man, who could not appear on account of his debts, and who had been much connected with turf robberies, came to him and entreated him to take the odds for him to £1,000 about a horse for the Derby, and deposited a bank-note in his hand for the purpose. He told him half the horses *were made safe*, and that it was arranged this one was to win. After much delay, and having got his promise to lay out the money, he told him it was my horse. He did back the horse for the man for £700, but the same person told him if my horse could not win *Dangerous* would; and he backed the latter likewise for £100, by which his friend was saved, and won £800. He did not tell me his name, nor anything more, except that his object was, if he had won, to pay his creditors, and he had authorised Payne to retain the money, if he had won it, for that purpose.

"*June* 11*th*, 1833.—At a place called Buckhurst, for Ascot races. Racing all the morning, then eating, drinking, and play at night. I may say, with more truth than anybody, '*Video meliora proboque, deteriora sequor.*' He who wastes his early years in horse-racing, and all sorts of idleness, figuring away among the foolish, must be content to play an inferior part among the learned and wise.

"When I read such books as the 'Life of Mackintosh,' and see what other men have been, how they have read and thought, a sort of despair comes over me, a deep, bitter sensation of regret 'for time mis-spent, and talents misapplied,' not the less bitter from being coupled with a hopelessness of remedial industry, and of doing better things.

"Dined yesterday with Stanley, who gave me a commission to bet a hundred for him on Bentley, against Bubastes, for the Derby, and talked of racing with as much zest as if he were on the turf. Who, to see him and hear him thus, would take him for the greatest orator and statesman of the day!

"All last week at Epsom, and now, thank God, these races are over! I have had all the trouble and excitement and worry, and have neither won nor lost; nothing but the hope of gain would induce me to go through this demoralising drudgery, which I am conscious reduces me to the level of all that is most disreputable and despicable. My thoughts are eternally absorbed by it. Jockeys, trainers, and blacklegs are my companions, but it is like dram-drinking, having once entered upon it, I cannot leave it off, though I am disgusted with the occupation. Let no man who has no need, who is not in danger of losing all he has, and is not obliged to grasp at every chance, make a book on the Derby. While the fever it excites is raging and the odds are varying I can neither read, nor write, nor occupy myself with anything else.

"At the gaming-table all men are equal; no superiority of birth, accomplishments, or ability avail here—great noblemen, merchants, orators, jockeys, statesmen, and idlers, are thrown together in levelling degrading confusion. The only pre-eminence is that of success; the only superiority that of temper.

"Play is a detestable occupation, it absorbs all our thoughts, destroys the better feelings, it incapacitates us for study and application of every kind, makes us irritable and nervous; all our cheerfulness depends on the uncertain event of our nightly occupations."

The published diary closes in 1837, the diarist died in 1865, living the same life to the last.

LORD PALMERSTON'S RACING.

Lord Palmerston followed racing nearly all his life, but in quite a different spirit to Mr. Greville. "He commenced in his own county in 1815 at Winchester, with a filly called Mignonette.* He usually bred his animals himself, and named them after his farms. A visit to his paddocks at Broadlands made his favourite Sunday walk. He seldom betted.

In 1841 he won the Cæsarewitch with Iliona, or rather John Day his trainer won, to settle a rather long training-bill. At that time Lord Palmerston had invested so much capital in improving his Welsh estate at Portmadoc (a very fine investment), that he was short of ready money. The victory of Iliona (daughter of Priam) led to a very lively discussion on the pronunciation of her name, in which a racing poet, young Lord Maidstone ("John Davis" in sporting literature), took an active part.

In 1860, Mainstone, before mentioned, was third in the betting for the Derby, but tenth in the race.

Lord Palmerston rode down to Epsom to see, to his great disappointment, Thormanby win instead of Mainstone. Mr. Ashley, his biographer, says, "He was convinced that if his horse had been fairly dealt with it would at any rate have made a good show in front.

After the Mainstone disappointment he left his trainer "*honest*" John Day, and never again owned an animal of any merit except Baldwin, having transferred his horses to the stables of Henry Goater at Littleton.

In 1852 Lord Palmerston wrote to his brother at Naples, "I have only one horse in training this year, he is three years old, and I have won four races with him. He runs next week for the Goodwood Cup, but I do not expect he will win, as he has to meet some very good horses. He is by Venison, out of an Emilius mare I have had some time."

THE DERBY AND OAKS.

Historically the Derby and Oaks are more interesting to the *dilettanti* than any other races, although of late years the interest in both seems to have declined, perhaps since the course has been, to coin a word, so *mobilised* by the rival railways.

The founder or name-giver to both was the twelfth Earl of Derby, the sportsman, as distinguished from his son the naturalist, his grandson the orator, and his great-grandson the statesman. The earl had a pack of staghounds in Surrey, and a hunting-lodge called the Oaks, near Epsom. General Burgoyne, unfortunate as a general in the American war, named one of his comedies "The Oaks," and the same name was given to the race for three-year-old fillies at Epsom, founded in 1779. In the following year the Derby was established for three-year-old colts and fillies. In 1801, the distance being then a mile, and the two races being run on two following days, was won by Sir Charles Bunbury's Eleanor, a near descendant of Eclipse. The feat was not repeated until 1857, when Blink Bonny won the Derby on a Wednesday and the Oaks on a Friday—the distance having been for many years previously increased to a mile and a half.

The founder Earl won the Derby once with his famous strong horse, Sir Peter, in 1787, so called after Sir Peter Teazle in Sheridan's comedy *The School for Scandal*, which had recently

* "Life of Lord Palmerston," by the Honourable Evelyn Ashley.

taken the theatrical world by storm. Some years later, on the death of his first wife (a daughter of the Duke of Hamilton) he robbed the stage of its most charming actress, Miss Farren, the original Lady Teazle, by making her a countess. There is a tradition that to this lady, his step-grandmother, young Stanley owed his first lessons in elocution. As before observed, the Derby winner is the senior wrangler of his year; but the race has been the subject of many strokes of luck, has been carried off by horses that never afterwards distinguished themselves on turf or at the stud. Some men have made this victory the pursuit of their lives, without success; others, like Lord Clifden in 1848 with Surplice, and Mr. Chaplin with Hermit in 1867, who started at the odds of 66 to 1 against him, have triumphed in the earliest years of their turf ventures. Lord George Bentinck devoted the best part of an energetic life, the largest breeding establishment ever formed by one person, and several fortunes, to the pursuit, and sold the winner in 1846 with his stud to Lord Clifden, when he temporarily abandoned the turf to be still more unfortunate in his political aspirations.

In that political romance, the "Life of Lord George Bentinck," the author relates that when Lord George heard that Surplice, whom he had bred and sold, had won the Derby he gave a superb groan, whatever that may mean (Qy. the converse of a horse laugh?) and in answer to the attempted consolations of Mr. Disraeli, ejaculated, "You do not know what the Derby means!" "Yes, I do: *the Blue Riband of the Turf.*" By that name the Derby has been familiarly known ever since. That great master of phrases the Earl of Beaconsfield was never happier than when he improvised this synonym, for it was of the blue riband that Lord Melbourne once said: "What I like about the garter is that there's no d——d pretence of merit about it." Lord Melbourne was, like his contemporaries, an habitual employer of oaths, and the blue riband had *then* been usually given to royal personages and great noblemen, generally to dukes, not because they had done anything, but because they were great magnates.

The fifth Earl of Glasgow, with greater means than Lord George Bentinck and equal tenacity (for racing was his one pursuit), was not more fortunate than the brilliant fourteenth Earl of Derby; both ran second with horses that in ordinary years would have won. But there was this important difference between them—racing was one of the Earl of Derby's amusements, it was the Earl of Glasgow's daily occupation.

Twice has the Derby been won by a horse born abroad: in 1865 by Gladiateur, and in 1876 by Kisber. But for an accident, it is almost certain that Chamant, the easy winner of the Two Thousand Guineas in 1877, would have won a second Derby for Count Lagrange.

The Derby is memorable as the scene of a great fraud, the subject of a very interesting law-suit. In the good old times when highwaymen still stopped and robbed gentlemen returning from Newmarket Heath, a wretch named Dawson was hung for poisoning favourite racehorses. Much more humane methods of making dangerous horses *safe* are now adopted by those who bet against them—they buy them. But in 1844 there was a scheme for "ringing the changes" by exchanging a three-year-old entered for the Derby for Running Rein, an English four-year-old, and also for running a German-bred four-year-old. The race came off. The German horse, Leander, fell, broke his leg, and was buried the same night. The changeling, Running Rein, won, Colonel (afterwards General) Peel's Orlando being second. The secret of the swindle oozed out; payment of the stakes was refused, and an action was brought to recover them. It was tried before Judge Alderson. The evidence was of the usual contradictory character in horse cases; but the judge, with his characteristic acuteness, adjourned the trial for the production of the most important witness—Running Rein himself. When the second day of trial came he was not to be found, so a verdict went for the defendants, and the stakes were awarded to that famous horse, Orlando, sire of many good race-horses, hunters, and hacks, whose portrait we gave at page 67. Some curious people dug up the body of Leander, to look at his mouth, but found his lower jaw had been removed.

It was given in evidence before a committee of the House of Lords, in 1844, that besides Running Rein and Leander, a horse called Maccabæus—really Goneway, and a mare called Julia, all entered as three-year-olds, were four-year-olds, and a horse, called Bloodstone, entered as a two-year old, was a three-year-old. Since that date the marks of age shown by a horse's teeth have become familiar to every groom.

Every foreigner who visits England, and every Englishman, whether he cares for racing or not, should see the Derby once, and watch the sights and sounds of two hundred and fifty thousand people wrapped for a minute in intense excitement. That a quarter of a million, including all the ruffianism that London and every racecourse in the kingdom can produce, should assemble and disperse in so orderly a manner, with so little police restraint, is not the least curious part of the day, and a strong tribute to the law-abiding character of the population. In any other European country an army of infantry, cavalry, and artillery would be called out to keep the peace.

The picturesqueness of the "road" has departed with the advance of the railroad to the race-course, and a lady—at any rate, a young lady—can only see the Derby, removed from the disgusting scenes and language of the "hill," and with comfort to her friends, in one of the private boxes into which the grand stand has been divided, to the destruction of all that was sociable and pleasant about the Derby in 1848, when Surplice won.

Ascot Heath still preserves a share of its ancient glories, still retains its royal pageant, a procession of the Master of the Buckhounds, with the huntsman and yeoman prickers in full uniform, the arrival of the revived four-horse coaching clubs, and a display of rank and beauty in gorgeous array on the grand stand lawn which made an enthusiastic American, familiar with Paris, exclaim that it was alone worth the voyage across the Atlantic.

But to see racing divested of all its coarse and disgusting accessaries—the degraded mob, the blasphemous, greedy, obscene Bohemianism that riots on Epsom Downs—a visit must be paid to Goodwood Park, where the privileged enclosure and the police exclude nearly all that the most fastidious would desire to exclude; and affords on a golden afternoon of August, with its smooth turf, ancestral trees, and picturesque shrubberies, peopled with manly men and lovely women, scenes that Watteau never equalled in picturesqueness and colour. Nothing has been seen like it, even at the most elaborate fêtes of the Courts of Europe in their most magnificent days—not even at Fontainebleau, under the last Emperor of the French; for at Goodwood the races give a pleasing excitement to the scene; they are an accessary to a gorgeous picnic. You need not, unless you choose, even listen to the hoarse roar of the betting-ring beneath the grand stand.

The Doncaster St. Leger affords an opportunity of seeing a Yorkshire crowd, the very opposite of a Derby-day mob, for in Yorkshire every man, down to the humblest, is familiar with the pedigree and performances of all the favourites at least, and carries in his head a history of racing, and particularly of St. Legers, that would puzzle a Civil Service Examining Commissioner. In a word, the Doncaster St. Leger is run in the presence of a crowd of critical experts, amongst whom the racehorse is the object of as serious worship as the cat, the ox, or the crocodile, was to the ancient Egyptians.

Newmarket races are supposed to be conducted on severely practical principles. The mere pleasure-seeker has no business there; the regular frequenters mean business, and nothing else.

The excursionists brought by rail on the occasion of great races are a modern nuisance, and little provision is made for their accommodation or amusement. To spend a day at Newmarket with any profit you require a good hack, and a mentor, also mounted, familiar with all the celebrities of the racing world—the backers of horses and layers of odds of all ranks and both sexes.

THE BLOOD-HORSE AS A USEFUL SIRE.

Fortunately for the many, in every part of the civilised world, who are interested in the reproduction of "sound and useful horses" not required for winning races and wagers, it is possible to select out of the many hundreds bred for turf purposes every year a considerable number of sires and mares which combine with the fullest height desirable in any riding-horse, strength equal to great weight, symmetry, and beauty, with all the "quality," courage, and refined qualities of their diminutive Oriental ancestors.

The late Earl of Glasgow bequeathed his stud to General Peel and the late Mr. George Payne, on condition that the sires should never be sold. These sires were remarkable for their strength, and perhaps for this reason never achieved a Derby, an Oaks, or a St. Leger. As long as the Earl of Glasgow lived, he never sold, but in preference shot any produce he did not consider first-rate, and the services of his sires were obtained with difficulty, and only for thoroughbred mares. On obtaining the Glasgow stud, General Peel removed them to a farm at Enfield, and commenced a new system, which, if more widely adopted, would exercise a very advantageous influence on the horse-breeding of this country. The stallions were annually offered to be let by auction for the season, three or four being reserved for the use of the mares of the Glasgow stud. Fifteen were let in this manner, in 1872-3, and dispersed all over England and Ireland, the whole number being twenty-one, those that remained at Enfield being offered to the public at fees proportionate to their value. The fifteen averaged a rent of £125 each. They were taken away on the 1st of January, and returned at the end of the breeding season. "These stallions which, while Lord Glasgow lived, never covered a half-bred mare (except by special favour or accident), now cover about a thousand half-bred mares. Fifteen or twenty of these stallions are strong enough to carry me" (General Peel), and are stronger and better (for breeding hunters and riding-horses) than for racing purposes. Amongst this stud of sires was "the Drake, who measured ten inches below the knee." This evidence, with that of other witnesses not less competent, shows how easily and how surely the nation might get the benefit of many useful, sound, thoroughbred stallions out of the "Calendar" list of 360, which are, because they are strong and useful, too slow for racing purposes, if our Agricultural Societies introduced the system of hiring thorough-bred stallions, and ceased to give prizes to sires only accessible at fees beyond the reach of those who breed for the road and the hunting-field. On the death of Mr. George Payne the Enfield stud was broken up, and the horses disposed of on condition that they should be destroyed when no longer in breeding condition.

THE THOROUGHBRED OUT OF TRAINING.

The thoroughbred horse does not attain the perfection of his strength and beauty until he is at least six or seven years old. Under the modern system of racing both horses and mares are withdrawn from the turf at five years old, if not at four. If of superior reputation, a stallion becomes one of the aristocracy of the stud; if inferior, he may descend from the Stud Book Register to be a sire of hunters, or, lower still, to travel the country and cover mares of any breed at trifling fees.

THE DRAKE: A SPECIMEN OF A THOROUGHBRED HORSE EQUAL TO CARRYING SIXTEEN STONE TO HOUNDS.

R C WEST. SC

It is as a stallion that the blood-horse of mature age, and not over-fat, attains the highest poetic beauty. The blood-mare with a foal at her feet, stands next; in a park, sheltered by ancestral oaks, deer are not more graceful and interesting.

The racer found too slow for the flat will often be tried "across country," and if displaying superior leaping powers and the indispensable amount of courage, be converted into a steeplechaser. It is amongst steeplechasers that the strongest full-developed specimens of the blood-horse are to be found. Others, again, not quite up to racing speed, are castrated, and turned into hunters, with which, at least, every man must be provided who aspires to ride in the first flight over the country round Melton, Market Harborough, Rugby, and other ox-grazing pastures. Then, again, there are a limited number of thoroughbreds of extraordinary and even extravagant action, which become harness-horses, which fetch fabulous prices (such was Edmond), and riding-horses for Rotten Row.

It is amongst the full-aged steeplechasers, hunters, and other useful horses, that the thoroughbred is to be found in perfection of strength and quality, scarcely to be recognised as of the same breed as the long-legged lean animals, two or three year olds, when they are trained down to the last ounce for some great race.

It cannot be too strongly stated that for all the purposes of utility except where heavy draught requires weight, the blood-horse is the best (the most beautiful, the strongest, the most enduring, the most intelligent), when soundness and suitable action are combined with power. Unfortunately, like the British infantry, the numbers that come up to this description are few; strength not being a recommendation for modern racing, and symmetrical conformation not a necessity for flying handicaps. A considerable number of horses which would be most valuable as sires are disqualified without being put into training, because a weight-carrying thoroughbred horse is always in demand at a good price, whilst there is no organised system for making the services of the best class of sound, strong, slow (in a racing point of view), thoroughbred stallions available for useful as distinguished from gambling uses.

Emblem (of whom a coloured illustration is given) was a mare that made a brilliant success "across country," after an unsuccessful career on the flat. She was by Teddington out of Miss Batty, by the Hydra. She was purchased by Lord Coventry at five years old. She stood fully 15 hands 2 inches high, had magnificent shoulders, was remarkably deep through the heart, had good quarters but a light middle piece, and was not well ribbed up, and consequently looked weedy. She took to jumping naturally; in the winter of 1862 was hunted regularly with the Heythrop and Cotswold Hounds; and in the spring of 1863 won three steeplechases off the reel. She finally broke down at exercise, was put to the stud, but produced nothing of any value, and died in 1870. Emblem is an example of extraordinary jumping merit in a very weedy three-cornered looking animal. The following particulars were kindly furnished by the Earl of Coventry:—

"New Year's Day, 1874.

"Emblem died in December, 1870. She won the Birmingham, Derby, Liverpool, Doncaster, and Cheltenham Grand Annual Steeplechases in 1863, and the Leamington and Cheltenham Grand Annuals in 1865. She ought also to have won the Liverpool in that year, but she got the best of her jockey, and, indeed, ran away with him in the race. However, she turned the tables on Alcibiades (the winner in that year) at Warwick, where, with poor George Ede up, she completely ran away from him. I see it frequently stated that she was a jade, and would only accomplish short distances on the flat. That was not so. Although her form as a racehorse was only moderate, she could stay, as her performances show. She won her steeplechases at her fences; and I attribute her extraordinary quickness in jumping to her very excellent shoulders" (which are well shown in the portrait, engraved from a small oil-painting by Mr. H. Hall)

THE THOROUGHBRED ABROAD—AMERICA.

Thoroughbred horses were imported by the colonists of Maryland and Virginia as early as the reign of George II; the first pedigree horse, Spark, having, according to tradition, been presented to Governor Ogle, about 1750, by Lord Baltimore, who had received him as a present from the Prince of Wales, the father of George III. The work from which my information is obtained has a list of stallions and mares imported between 1750 and 1865, which fills one hundred and fifty imperial octavo pages,* and records with barbarous details matches run between rival States and between North and South, within the last half-century. The great insurrection of the Confederate States extinguished the wealth that supported expensive amusements in the South; and in the North a passion for trotting in harness superseded flat racing for a while.

In the spring of 1879 great sensation was created in the racing world by the first public appearance in England of M. Pierre Lorillard's six-year-old brown gelding, Parole, by Leamington, out of Maiden, who won the Newmarket Handicap, easily beating Mr. Gretton's Isonomy, when in receipt of eight pounds from the latter. Again, at the Epsom Spring Meeting, Parole was victorious in the City and Suburban and Metropolitan Handicaps, but was beaten at Chester in the Tradesman's Cup, although able upon the following day to win the Great Cheshire Handicap. At Ascot Parole failed to get a place in the Ascot Stakes; and thus having been beaten in two long races, he acquired the reputation of being a first-class animal over mile-and-a-quarter courses, although, like so many of his English rivals, unable to compass a longer distance.

Amongst the imported horses mentioned in Forester's book is Messenger, the son of Mambrino, who arrived in 1786, and was considered by a writer in 1856 to have been "the best horse, take him all in all, ever brought to America," both as the sire of racehorses and of roadsters. Messenger must have lived to an immense age, or the writer of the following passage must have been a centenarian. "Well do I remember him—his large bony head, rather short straight neck, with windpipe and nostrils nearly twice as large as ordinary, with his low withers, shoulders somewhat upright, but deep, close, and strong. Behind lay the perfection and power of the machine. His barrel, loin, hips, and quarters were incomparably superior to all others; his hocks and knees were unusually large; below them his limbs were of medium size, but flat, strong, and remarkably clean, and, either in standing or in action, their position was perfect."† This is interesting, because the best American trotting-horses, as already noted, trace their pedigree to Messenger, and also because the description so closely agrees with the engraving of Mambrino.

About the years 1835 and 1840, amongst the importations of English racehorses into the United States were Priam, winner of the Derby in 1830; Spaniel, winner of the Derby, 1831; Barefoot, winner of the St. Leger, 1823; St. Giles, winner of the Derby, 1832; and with a score of others, including Zinganee and Lord Jersey's Glencoe, of the best blood, though unsuccessful in the greatest English races, although Glencoe won the Two Thousand Guineas, and was the second three-year-old that ever won the Goodwood Cup. The edition of Frank Forester's "American Horse" of 1871 gives the name of no English racehorse later than 1865; it may therefore be presumed that the importations have not been of any turf importance.

Enough has been quoted to show that, like every other country, the United States rely

---

* "The American Horse," by Frank Forester.   † Correspondent of Frank Forester, 1856.

for obtaining speed and quality in their ordinary horses upon crosses of the English blood-horse. An American writer on breeding trotting-horses says, "When we find our stock want courage, we take a cross of the thoroughbred horse." The best racing stock in the country traces its descent from Sir C. Bunbury's Diomed, winner of the first English Derby, who was subsequently imported into Virginia, where he lived to a great age, and became the progenitor of many excellent sons and daughters.

The preference the Americans have for harness over riding-horses would, of course, influence their selection of stallions.

The following extracts from a letter addressed to the most literary of the sporting newspapers gives a picturesque and exact account of the racing of the day in New York, by a very competent observer and reporter:—

A VISIT TO JEROME PARK.

"A warm, sunny autumn morning was Saturday, the 15th of October. Carriages were pouring up Fifth Avenue and away through the Central Park for the races, and our drag was at the door of the Union Club, waiting for Mr. Lawrence Jerome to mount the box and tool us there also. A strange drive is this to Jerome Park—pleasant enough round the winding roads of the beautiful Central Park—but a little less pleasant, if more exciting, for the rest of the journey. The scene is like, yet very unlike, the road to Epsom on a Derby Day. The dust is there, and so are the carriages, but the motley mob, made up of costermongers and publicans, is not. In place of these characteristic representatives of London life are innumerable human beings mounted on fragile-looking vehicles running on two and four wheels, and dragged by one or two horses. These are the 'trottists,' and the drivers thereof are whirled through the air at the rate of seventeen miles an hour. Their minds are in an apparent state of painful tension, with eyes starting from their sockets, legs planted firmly and widely apart forward, a rein twisted round each hand; a frightened woman on the off seat clutching nervously at the iron rail, and in momentary fear for the fate of her waterfall and bonnet; and so the controller of this strange spectacle hurries on. He has a frantic ambition to pass everything that can be passed on the road, and if he succeeds in doing this, he has achieved something worth living and driving a 'trottist' for. This mode of moving about, when assigned to its proper place and time, is said to have fascinations not to be resisted after once it has been indulged in; but I imagine that it is not every Englishman who would care to make the acquaintance of this inexpressible charm. Fortunately, in the Central Park policemen are stationed to regulate the speed of all vehicles to seven miles an hour, and their duties are almost as light as the solitary one of those policemen who are stationed in Broadway to seize the arms of ladies and convey them safely over the crossings; for be it understood that no one attempts railway speed in the pleasant defiles of the park, and the driving there is as sedate as it is on the road by the side of Rotten Row on a June afternoon.

"Soon the piazza around the club-house is filled by one of the gayest throngs of beauty a race-going man ever gazed upon. I will not say that these American ladies are more beautiful, or more dressed, or that they talk better, than English ladies; but they are beautiful, their dress is such as would inspire the literary milliner of the *Court Tattler*, and their talk must be brilliant—it is listened to so devoutly. Jerome Park did not exactly accord with my English ideas of a park, neither did the Central Park; both are beautiful in their way, and each is certainly unique. The 'Central' may have the finest carriage-drive in the world, as the guide-book says it has, or even in the United States, or in New York, and may have cost ten millions of dollars; still it does not look like a park, any more than the parade at

Brighton or the Promenade des Anglais at Nice. Racecourses, we all know, differ all over the world; and if Jerome Park is unlike a park, it is certainly as much unlike an English race-course as anything I ever saw. Still, it is a racecourse, if an invention; races take place there; it is the temple of the American Jockey Club; and is one of the pleasantest resorts for a few hours' diversion a traveller could visit.

"The club-house is quite an institution; it has dining-rooms, drawing-rooms, bed-rooms, billiard-rooms, and a large ball-room, and, indeed, every luxury of a club and comfort of a private dwelling. Visitors to the races eat their breakfasts here and their lunches, and some stay to dine. After the racing is over, a 'German' is gone through in the ball-room, to the excellent music of a reed band; and when the festivity is over, the drive back to New York in the brightness of the harvest moon is found to be not the least pleasant part of the day's excitement. Some perhaps will stay the night, or return the next morning to breakfast; but no matter when they go or come, the club is always open.

"The racecourse consists of circuitous roads formed on a plateau beneath the club-house. These roads, or tracks, wind round in a way something like a figure 8, and their surface is like Rotten Row, though a little harder. One instantly asks why turf is not preferred to a hard road; and the answer readily given is that the loose earth road, hard as it is, is the more suitable for American horses. On the other side of these tracks—which, by the way, are all railed in—and facing the club-house, is a long row of stands, the centre one of which is reserved for members of the Jockey Club. The whole park, as it is termed, is closed in by hills, on whose sides are growing trees, and their leaves are just now turning to the rich crimson and golden hues of autumn. The first race is about to commence, and everybody, ladies and all, leaves the club-house and walks across the tracks for the Jockey Club Stand. The numbers of the horses about to start are hoisted, but we do not hear anything about 6 to 4 on the field, or 4 to 1 bar one. The air is as undisturbed as during the hush after the start for the Derby. But our mentor is at hand, and directs our wandering curiosity to an elderly gentleman leaning out of the window of an elevated box at one end of the stand; he is selling pools, and a pool is conducted in this way: Supposing three horses start; one chance may sell for 200 dollars, another for 100, and another for 50. The buyer of the chance that wins takes the whole 350 dollars, less 3 per cent. commission charged by the pool-seller. Posted in the betting, we turn our eyes to the racing. The horses are out, and galloping around the track in clothing. Presently one is pulled up outside our vantage-ground, and we stare as one, two, three heavy woollen cloths are taken off the panting animal. The thermometer is at 80 deg., and the coat of the horse is foaming wet. All are galloped in clothing, and stripped in this way; and then the race commenced. Away they go, all pulling hard, at a cracking pace and in a cloud of dust. Now they disappear, and where will they reappear?—will it be down the steps by the club-house? No; the track has taken a turn we had not noticed, and there they go in full view opposite the stand; another deep bend, a turn, and they are in the straight for home. We watch curiously for the finish; shouts are raised that something or other will win; the ladies stand up, and excitement is culminating. On they come, the two leaders leaving the other three concealed in a thick wall of dust, and everybody is wrong as to what is winning; a black boy, his two eyes looking like white rosettes on his ebony face, is 'coming;' he has got his saddle forward on his horse's withers, and his feet are apparently kicking at the horse's mouth; but no matter, his horse is a good one, has plenty left in him to finish with, and wins by half a dozen lengths. It was a good race, for all the horses as they straggled in were fairly ridden out.

" The conclusion an Englishman arrives at after witnessing such a scene is, that the American horses are trained to run their races very fast, and that they all apparently, until they are beaten, pull tremendously. A two-year-old race of one mile and a furlong run in 2min. 4sec., one of half a mile in 54sec., and another of three-quarters of a mile in 1min. 18sec., strike one as being fast, although I have no evidence at hand to decide whether it would be considered fast by American turfites. Of this, however, there is no denying, that, considering the few race-horses in America—there are not, I believe, more than two hundred in training—it is a matter of surprise that there should be so many that are seemingly good. A mile and a half was run at Long Branch in 2min. 37sec., which is at the rate of one mile in 1min. 45sec. Whether they succeed in obtaining greater speed and staying powers than English trainers and breeders could only be decisively proved by a series of trials; but it seemed to my not very practised eye that all the races, taken from start to finish, were run at a much greater speed than is usually seen at home, although the finishes were anything but brilliant, notwithstanding they are aided by a great deal of whip and spur. The extraordinary part of the business is, that such great speed should be attained with such wretched jockeyship. It would be difficult to say which ride the worst, the white or black boys, so bad are both. Anything like an artistic finish is seldom seen, saving when a couple of what are called the best jockeys get on pretty equal mounts. A lack of good horsemanship is peculiar to the country, and it would be gross adulation to simply say that an American looks ill at ease on horseback. There are of course exceptions; but riding is at least one thing which our Transatlantic friends do not do well, especially in the matter of jockeyship."

THE RACEHORSE IN FRANCE.

The racehorse is as completely an exotic in France as Italian Opera in England, although famous in the annals of the English turf are the triple victor Gladiateur, Fille de l'Air the Oaks winner in 1864, and Chamant the winner of the Two Thousand in 1877. In addition another French horse, Verneuil, performed the unparalleled feat of winning the three principal long distance races at Ascot, in 1878.

It will astonish those not familiar with the social history of the other side of the Channel to learn that there were in 1874 forty-eight regular training establishments in France, the greater number of which are also breeding-studs; and this in spite of the reductions caused by the fall of the Empire and the disasters of war.

The climate and soil of France have proved particularly favourable to the early maturity of the thoroughbred. The Government, as a matter of policy, gives very large prizes, on the principle of our Queen's Plates; that is, for horses not less than three years old, running not less than two miles : and the pick of the French stables have the advantage of being permitted to compete for the best English as well as the best French stakes.

It is, however, a curious circumstance, that although racehorses have been bred and trained in France for nearly half a century (of course, entirely of English blood), all the trainers, all their assistants, and, with one or two exceptions, all the jockeys, are English. A work by Le Baron d'Etreilles (" *Le Pur Sang en France*") gives the most ample details of the present condition of the French turf. Nothing approaching this book in completeness exists on the subject of the horses of England; nothing has been written on the equine history of Ireland, the horse-breeding country of Europe *par excellence*.

The Baron gives the name of each owner of racehorses, of his trainer, his jockey, and even of his "head lad," with portraits of all, which, to say the least, are not flattering. He also minutely describes some hundred stallions, mares, three-year-olds, and two-year-olds, in training in 1873.

The French Government under the Empire, when racing became a fashion, if not a passion, amongst the wealthy and noble, gave up breeding thoroughbred horses in the State studs, with the view of encouraging private enterprise.

At the present moment, says the Baron, "*le cheval de pur sang* (the thoroughbred) is more than ever ostracised, neglected by the official breeding establishments, obliged to be disguised by cutting its tail to be admitted into the ranks of the cavalry, or to get mixed up with the ordinary trade in riding-horses; only the two extremes of the *chevaline* hierarchy are open to it, the racecourse and the hackney-cab. The subventions to the turf have been diminished, prizes are no longer given for steeplechases, or premiums for thoroughbred brood-mares, and very little pecuniary encouragement is afforded to thoroughbred stallions." But it seems as if the same transformation of tastes to which we have already alluded, as having in England sent gamblers from the green cloth to the turf, had taken place in France. The wealthy and titled not caring for politics, and following the fashion of the country with which they are on the best terms, are taking to field sports instead of the amusements of cities. We find an example of this while turning over the pages of "*Le Pur Sang*," in a name which was that of one of the splendid runners at Newmarket in October, 1873, when, M. Le Comte de Juigné's Montargis, a rank outsider, ridden by a French jockey, Carratt, the Fordham of France, won the Cambridge-shire, beating the two favourites, King Lud and Walnut.

"Le Comte de Juigné began with a passion for driving. For several years he had a reputation for carriages and horses of the finest class for quality and action. Tired at last of the mill-horse round of steppers and four-in-hands, he sold everything off, bought a few good mares, and began to breed." As a matter of course (in France), he commenced by trying to produce that eternal half-bred trooper without a thoroughbred sire, although they are as closely allied as cause and effect.

"After a time, associated with Prince Aremberg, he commenced on the turf." In 1872 his stud consisted of nine two and three-year-olds.

That racing is quite foreign to the tastes of the French nation is shown in the following of several passages to the same effect:—"We cannot count on public opinion for encouragement in anything affecting horse-breeding in France as they can in England, where such questions are considered to be of national interest. Our political and social organisations render such a state of feeling impossible; such subjects will always remain the speciality of a class. As an example, when the question of horse supply was recently discussed in the British Parliament, the debate was adjourned because several members competent to speak on it were absent fox-hunting. Had such a delay been proposed in France, it would have been howled down. Yet the statesmen in England are not inferior to ours in questions of general interest, but the taste for sport is innate in the Englishman, and only exceptionally found in the Frenchman. For this reason, State aid is essential to support horse-breeding on sound principles in France."

Facts prove that there must be something extremely favourable to the production of the thoroughbred horses, either in the climate of France, or the selection of stock by French breeders; for the proportion of victories obtained by French-bred horses on the English turf, looking at the comparative number bred in each country, is very large.

In November, 1873, Mr. Digby Collins showed that the Earl of Stradbroke was wrong when he told the Lords Committee on Horse Supply that there were not three horses in

England that could "stay" over two miles, gave the names of forty horses, in four classes, that in his opinion contradicted this theory. Amongst this forty, ten were French, a very high per-centage.

THE THOROUGHBRED IN GERMANY.

Thoroughbred breeding-studs are maintained by the Emperor of Austria, who has a large establishment with an English trainer at its head. In his kingdom of Hungary the nobility and landed gentry largely cultivate the blood-horse for racing and riding purposes; while for driving they adhere rather to Arab crosses of native breeds. The Hungarian is as fond of a horse as an Irishman, and understands him as well as a Yorkshireman.

In Prussia, "The German stud-book describes eighteen private studs of thoroughbred horses." So far advanced is the pursuit that the landed nobility are asking to be relieved from the competition of the Government.

Russia, too, for more than half a century has steadily imported thoroughbred sires, more for improving her native races than for turf purposes.

In a word, the English thoroughbred has made his merits felt and acknowledged in every country in the world where size as well as quality is an object; for "blood," in the words of the French baron already quoted, gives "strength, agility, endurance, and energy."

CHAPTER V.

HALF-BRED HORSES.

HALF-BRED, designated in reports of races by the letters "H.B.," does not mean what the words would imply in their literal sense—the produce of thoroughbred on one side and cart blood on the other—but only that there is some stain in the traceable pedigree, which may indeed be so remote as not to be detected by any external sign.

For instance, Lottery, the famous steeplechase horse whose name thirty years ago was associated with the many triumphs of Jim Mason, the most elegant, if not the best, cross-country jockey of that day (they figure together in Herring's portrait picture of steeplechase cracks), was a racehorse to look at all over, but, in racing parlance, half-bred. To come to more recent times, the Colonel won the great handicap cross-country race, the Liverpool Grand National, in 1869, and again in 1870. The Colonel, foaled in 1863, was by Knight of Kars out of Boadicea, by Faugh-a-Ballagh—Boadicea by Baronet, out of Princess of Wales; Princess of Wales out of Modesty, by Pill-Garlic; Modesty, foaled in 1827, was a half-bred mare by Sancho. This slight stain (for Modesty was no doubt a good mare), in spite of the Colonel's splendid symmetry and admirable performances, disqualified him from being enrolled in the British *Libro d'Oro*, the "Stud Book," and from taking his place and fixing his price with thoroughbred stallions of inferior external form, and of inferior performances, but unblemished pedigree. Breeders for racing purposes always fear that the alloy will come out at a pinch; therefore, in this country, sires not thoroughbred in blood but thoroughbred in appearance never take a high rank.

The Colonel was sold a year before the Franco-German War to M. Cavaliero, for £2,600, and after running once more in England, passed into the stud of the Emperor of Germany.

On the Continent this class of sire, when showing much substance, is greatly esteemed. In answer to inquiries addressed by a commission appointed to investigate the condition of horse-breeding in the twenty five circles into which France is divided, more than half applied for English "hunter" stallions.

Fair Nell, the subject of one of the coloured illustrations, who never ran in England, but whose reputation became world-wide amongst horsemen for a few years after she beat the Pacha's best Arab, may have been thoroughbred, but as her pedigree was not enrolled, she would have been set down in England as half-bred. The following is her story:—Abbas Pacha, whose rare stud is mentioned at page 34, in the chapter on Arabs, somewhere about 1853 sent a challenge to the Jockey Club to run any number of English racehorses against his Arabs for any sum not less than £10,000. The Jockey Club owns no horses, but is in effect a little autocracy for settling the rules of racing generally, which exercises absolute control over the races run on Newmarket Heath, and fixes the weights and conditions of certain matches and handicaps run there. The challenge was therefore necessarily declined, and it was understood that the Pacha would not make a match with any private individual; at any rate, nothing came of it.

Haleem Pacha, the foolish boy who inherited Abbas Pacha's unequalled stud of Arabs—a stud which had cost his father nearly a million sterling to collect and breed—did condescend to make a match with some Cairo merchants to run eight miles for £400 a side. The Cairo merchants sent to England and purchased Fair Nell, an Irish mare without a pedigree, from Mr. Edmund Tattersall, who had used her as a park and covert hack.

The race came off within two weeks of her landing in Egypt; and in the eight miles she beat the Pacha's best Arab over a rough stony ground by a full mile, doing the distance in 18½ minutes, and pulling up fresh. In fact, Fair Nell won so easily that it was found impossible to make another match.

The portrait is from a picture in the possession of Mr. Tattersall, by the late Byron Webb. She was a bright bay, with black legs; stood 15 hands 1½ inches high, with such beautiful shoulders, with so much before you, and with such an elastic stride, that it was easy, even delightful, to sit on her, although her temper was hot, and at times she plunged violently. She pulled hard, but had a good mouth, and required light give-and-take hands. She often carried Mr. Tattersall, riding twelve stone, sixteen miles to covert, including stoppages, within the hour, to meet hounds, and seemed to be cantering all the time until you tried to trot alongside her. She was bred in Ireland, and was not in the "Stud Book," but was supposed to be by the celebrated Irish sire Freney. There is no doubt in the mind of the writer of this chapter, who frequently rode Fair Nell, that—half-bred or thoroughbred—she would have beaten any Arab in the world in a twenty-mile race, or would have equalled the most extraordinary feats ever recorded in long distances for several days in a *temperate* climate.

At one time real half-breds, the produce of a thoroughbred sire out of a cart mare, were cultivated with the view of producing weight-carrying hunters, on the recommendation of "Nimrod" (Mr. Apperley), who had found at Melton at least one extraordinary bit of the kind carrying Mr. Edge, an eighteen-stone yeoman, in the first flight in Leicestershire; but it was soon found that the prizes were rare and the blanks numerous. The more common result of such *mésalliances* is a monster, composed of two different kinds of horses badly joined in the middle. Sometimes when a blood-mare refuses to breed with sires of her own degree, she will take a cart-horse; and from such accidents here and there an extraordinary performer is obtained, with great power, and the courage of the nobler dam. In the winter of 1873 an American gentleman, a heavy weight, was riding a hunter of very plebeian appearance in the best runs in Leicestershire in a good place which was bred by Mr. John Bennett, of Husbands Bosworth, got by a cart-horse stallion out of his famous thoroughbred mare Lady Florence, dam of many good thoroughbred horses. When Lady Florence failed to breed with blood sires, she was put to a cart stallion.

But as a general rule in this country, when a breeder decides not to put a mare to a thorough-bred sire, he chooses a roadster trotter.

TROTTING STALLIONS.

The English trotting stallions, as far as can be ascertained by inquiries in the counties where they originally became famous, are of Dutch or Flemish origin. At any rate, they were first heard of about a hundred years ago, in the fen districts of Lincolnshire. Their merit lies in compactness, strength, and action; their pace, which so much astonished the last generation, has been completely thrown into the shade by the feats of the American trotters—a very different class of animals.

Although the origin of the roadster trotter is not very remote, it is as mysterious as every historical fact connected with the English horse.

John Laurence (1810) says: "It is a remarkable fact that no instance is recorded of a thoroughbred horse being a capital trotter"—this, according to American experience, is a mistake—"although some racers, for example Shark, Hammer by Herod, and, I believe Mambrino, had a short quick trot. Infidel, by Turk, trotted fifteen miles in one hour, carrying ten stone, on the road between Carlisle and Newcastle, about twenty-five years ago (1785). Old Shields, sire of Scott, was got by Blank out of a strong common-bred mare. The best trotters now to be found in Lincolnshire have proceeded from Old Shields (Shales?). They were distinguished in the first produce by the round buttock and wide bosom of the cart-bred sire. The stock was improved by crossing with racing blood. Pretender, a son of Cub, was out of a well-bred daughter of Lord Abingdon's Pretender, by Marske (sire of Eclipse). Pretender was said (I am not compelled to believe it) to have trotted a mile in two minutes and a half."

Marshland Shales, according to a memoir that accompanies his portrait, by Abraham Cooper, in the old *Sporting Magazine* of 1825, "was foaled in 1802. He stood 14 hands 3 inches high. In 1824 his crest was still very large; when he was young and in high condition it was immense. His hind-quarters were neat, and showed racing blood, but his head resembled the old Suffolk Punch. He was fully master of twenty stone, and was styled in Norfolk a 'thundering trotter.' Although he bent his knee well, he was not a remarkably high goer. He once trotted seventeen miles within the hour on the hard road, carrying 12st. 2lbs. What he would have done with a light weight on a soft trotting course may be imagined. He covered in Lincolnshire, the Fens, Norfolk, Cambridgeshire, Suffolk, and Essex." Lavengro* has described Marshland Shales in his own peculiar style:—"It came to pass that I stood upon this hill (Norwich Hill), observing a fair of horses. I had no horses to ride, but I took pleasure in looking at them, and I had already attended more than one of these fairs. The present was lively enough, indeed, horse fairs are seldom dull. There was shouting and whooping, neighing and braying, there was galloping and trotting; fellows with highlows and white stockings, and with many a string dangling from the knees of their tight breeches, were running desperately, holding horses by the halter, and in some cases dragging them along; there were long-tailed steeds and dock-tailed steeds of every degree and breed; there were droves of wild ponies, and long rows of sober cart-horses; there were donkeys, and even mules—the last rare things to be seen in damp misty England, *for the mule pines in mud and rain, and thrives best with a hot sun above and a burning sand below.* There were—oh, the gallant creatures! I hear their neigh upon the wind—there were (goodliest sight

* George Borrow.

of all) certain enormous quadrupeds, only seen to perfection in our native isle, led about by dapper grooms, their manes ribboned, and their tails curiously clubbed and balled. 'Ha, ha!' —how distinctly do they say, 'Ha, ha!' An old man draws nigh. He is mounted on a lean pony, and he leads by the bridle one of these animals; nothing very remarkable about that creature, unless in being smaller than the rest, and gentle, which they are not; he is almost dun, and over one eye a thick film has gathered. But, stay; there is something remarkable about that horse; there is something in his action in which he differs from all the rest. As he advances the clamour is hushed, all eyes are turned upon him. What looks of interest—of respect! And what is this? People are taking off their hats; surely, not to that steed? Yes, verily, men, especially old men, are taking off their hats to that one-eyed steed; and I hear more than one deep-drawn 'Ah!' 'What horse is that?' I said to a very old fellow, the counterpart of the old man on the pony, save that the last wore a faded suit of velveteen, and this one was dressed in a white frock. 'The best in mother England,' said the very old man, taking a knobbed stick from his mouth, and looking me in the face, at first carelessly, but presently with something like interest. 'He is old, like myself, but can still trot his twenty miles an hour. You won't live long, my swain—tall and overgrown ones like thee never does— yet if you should chance to reach my years, you may boast to thy great-grand-boys thou hast seen Marshland Shales.' I did for the horse what I would neither do for earl or baron—doffed my hat; yes, I doffed my hat to the wondrous horse, the fast trotter, the best in mother England. And I, too, drew a deep 'Ah!' and repeated the words of the old fellows around: 'Such a horse as this we shall never see again; a pity that he is so old!'"

Mr. Euren, of the *Norwich Mercury*, in the course of his investigations of the pedigrees of Norfolk trotters, has recently traced the pedigree of Marshland Shales up to Eclipse.

Market Weighton, in Yorkshire, was formerly celebrated for its trotters, but they seem to have come originally from Lincolnshire or Norfolk, or both, as they bear the familiar names of Performers, Merrylegs, Roan Phenomenons, Norfolk Phenomenons, Prickwillows, Fireaways— all names found on the cards of Norfolk sires.

The type of a Norfolk trotter is not over 15 hands 2 inches high, made like a refined edition of a Suffolk Punch or Clydesdale cart-horse, with extravagant action, which varies from the rate of fourteen miles to seventeen miles an hour for short distances. Their weight renders long distances at a great pace on hard roads impossible. Silver and red roan are favourite and hereditary colours. There are also bays, browns, and chestnuts, which are more valued by foreign purchasers if entirely without white. The prejudice against white marks in a chestnut or bay trotter sire is curious, because in thoroughbred horses, and even in Arabs, white marks are common, and neither as a rule transmit their colours like a pedigree bull, Shorthorn, or Alderney. Trotters are not a distinct breed at all, but the result of judicious crosses and careful selection, maintained by alternate crosses on the cart or the blood side, as occasion required. They are used with very well-bred not quite thoroughbred mares, when more strength is required than is often found in the thoroughbred stallions that cover at a farmer's price, and especially when harness-action is an object. Lord Calthorpe's celebrated hack, Don Carlos, which is the subject of a coloured illustration of this chapter, was the pro- duce of a Norfolk sire and a well-bred pony. The following is an extract from a letter addressed to the writer by a well-known Suffolk exhibitor and prize-winner with both trotting and thoroughbred sires :—

"I feel sure that the counties of York and Norfolk imported the first roadsters from Lincolnshire. The old roadster is reviving again in favour with our breeders; thanks to a very

FAIR NELL.

ENTIRE PONY HACK DON CARLOS.
PROPERTY OF LORD CALTHORPE.

decided foreign demand. They are not crossing them so much with blood. The foreigners do not object to a coarse head if they can get strength and action. For my own part, I always try for a pure roadster, one whose pedigree goes back to roadster sires for several generations; as they say in Yorkshire, 'I like brandy or water, and not brandy and water ready mixed.' The great fault now is, that people look too much to fore-leg action, and forget the more important hind-leg action.

"I remember well the old trotting roan Phenomenon of Mr. Lines. When in action coming toward you, all his four legs were up close to his belly; all you saw was a barrel rushing towards you like the boiler of a steam-engine, with a head and neck on it. Nowadays, they pick up their fore-legs prettily enough, but leave their hind-legs behind them. Foreigners are giving very large prices for Norfolk sires, so I think we may expect the breed to be more cultivated; they don't mind coarseness, or ugly heads, if they can get bone with action. I dare say you have remarked that the foreigners who come here to buy horses, whether French, Germans, or Italians, are remarkably good judges of every point of a horse, and know exactly what they want. As to size below the knee, I have never found one that fairly measured nine inches. Eight inches and a half is a good girth for a trotter. Legs are very deceiving to the eye, and tell different tales under the tape. Trainers do not like a very big leg in a thoroughbred horse (trainers want quick not hunter sort of horses). As a rule, the shoulders are the weak points in modern trotters, and will not bear comparison with the pictures of the old sort. In my opinion, the present show-horses are too high on the legs, rather more coach-horses than hackneys. The pure Yorkshire coach-horse we have not got in the Eastern Counties, and perhaps it is no loss.

"I prefer roan trotters to any other colour, because they are more likely to possess the old trotting blood; but many of the present roans are dreadfully coarse, only the leavings that the foreigner won't buy. In trying this year to buy two Norfolk trotters for New Zealand, I saw a good many, but quite failed to get what I wanted. They are too big or too small, with no sharpness of action; vulgar heads, and high rumps. The old roadsters had beautiful heads, like Arabs."*

At the present time, with the exception of a few coaching sires of great size travelling in Yorkshire, those who do not resort to thoroughbred stallions employ Norfolk trotters.

Roadster trotters were largely purchased by the agents of the French stud-farms under the Empire, to improve the Norman breed; and some of the best mares, kept for posting purposes in the Imperial stables, were the produce of trotting sires.

In a conversation with General Fleury, the Master of the Horse to the Emperor, when the writer expressed his admiration of the big, cobby, high-stepping, dark bay mares, with their tails *en queue*, their picturesque harness, breast-collars, and bells, of the Imperial posting establishment—exhibited at the Paris Horse Show—the General answered, "You have the same animals, but put them to a different purpose. Some of these are English."

The late Mr. Crisp, famous for his Suffolk cart-horses and Suffolk pigs, once exhibited at a Suffolk agricultural show a thoroughbred stallion by Fandango, out of a mare by Grey Momus, which he had purchased from Sir Tatton Sykes, and obtained a prize in a trotting class; but this was generally considered by the Suffolk breeders of trotters a mistake on the part of the judges, due to an extravagant preference for blood "at any price."

Trotting is not one of the amusements of the English gentleman. Those whose tastes lie

---

* Letter from Lieutenant-Colonel Barlow, of Husketon.

that way must study Woodruffe's "Trotting Horse of America," the country where the art has been carried to perfection. Just as Ireland may claim to be the birthplace and nursery of the steeplechaser, and England of the racehorse, so the United States has made the trotter her own.

At the meeting of the Yorkshire Agricultural Society, at Beverley, a few years ago, a prize was awarded to the American trotter Shepherd F. Knapp, whose action was as beautiful as anything ever seen in this country, his hind-legs following or pushing on his fore-quarters outside his fore-arms. For pace no English roadster could touch him. He was not a roadster sire according to Norfolk, Suffolk, or Yorkshire trotting authorities; in fact he was nearly

ROADSTER STALLION, THE PROPERTY OF MR. JOHN ABEL, OF NORWICH, 1871.

thoroughbred. Major Stapylton, of Myton Hall, Yorkshire, so well known some years ago as a breeder of high-class horses of every kind—racehorses, hunters, and harness-horses— in Yorkshire and in town, and for the stamp of horses he drove in his four-in-hand coach and other carriages,* writes about the Shepherd F. Knapp: "He is, according to the American pedigree, out of an Arab mare by Ethan Allen, by Morgan Black Hawk, by Sherman; Morgan Howard's mare by a son of Hambletonian; his dam said to be by imported Messenger, a thoroughbred horse by Mambrino. His produce out of thoroughbred mares in the course of four years showing more of the shape of the dams than the horse, with good size, have obtained the points so often wanting in so many of our hunters and trotting-horses—capital legs and shoulders, with action and constitution. With half-bred mares his power is still more

* A picture of the Major's celebrated horse Saladin, so admired in his four-in-hand team, for which he refused 700 guineas, appears in the chapter describing the mail phaeton.

shown. They have invariably followed the horse in shape and action, getting the Arab head and fine temper. As yearlings and two-year-olds they have fetched high prices."

The following extracts condensed from the evidence before the Earl of Rosebery's (" Lords ") Committee on Horse Supply in 1873 give authentic information on the true value of Norfolk trotters :—

Mr. Phillips, of Knightsbridge, who collected most of the unequalled stud formed by the late Emperor of the French, said : "Roadsters date back from Mr. Theobald's Champion, that cost a thousand guineas, and Mr. Bond's Phenomenon. Phenomenon was taken into Yorkshire by Robert Ramsdale, of Market Weighton—crossed with the Yorkshire mares, and a superior breed was produced. Roadsters are bred in Norfolk, Suffolk, and Cambridgeshire; but the Yorkshire breed from the Phenomenon cross are superior to the original Norfolk breed, and handsomer. Roadster stallions are much patronised by foreigners, not so much by the English. The last two horses I sold were both by roadster sires—one, a carriage-horse, for three hundred guineas; the other, a pure roadster mare, for two hundred and fifty guineas. The mare was 15 hands 2 inches high ; the carriage-horse, purchased by the Earl of Lonsdale, 16 hands 1 inch.

The Earl of Charlemont, the largest breeder of horses in Ireland, said "that he finds it pay better to breed harness-horses than any other, although all sorts pay except racehorses." He put most of his mares to a Norfolk horse called Broad Arrow, a carty-looking horse, with excellent action, of whose pedigree he has no notion. He stands 15 hands 3 inches, looks like a cart-horse, but has no hair on his legs; a very superior action, and a perfect temper. This horse covered sixty-one mares for the farmers and eleven for the earl—seventy-two altogether. " I never asked for his pedigree, because my theory in breeding is to judge by the stock that a horse produces."

Mr. William Shaw, "thirty-six years a horse-leader (stallions) in Yorkshire," who had travelled in the Holderness district—the East Riding of Yorkshire—for the previous seventeen years, said : "When I began the trade, it was the old-fashioned coach-horse that was in vogue—the Clevelands—big bay horses. In 1836 I began leading a big bay horse; at first he leaped one hundred and sixty mares in a season, but the fashion went down, until at the end of that time he got only fifty mares.

"There was a change in the trade ; a new fashion in horses came up. London gentlemen wanted a horse that stepped higher. Formerly it was a big coach-horse that was wanted ; now a horse of blood is wanted, with fine high-stepping action. The price for four-year Cleveland geldings fell from £120 apiece to £20. Then the railways came up; the farmers got frightened, and said, 'We have nothing for you, the railways will stop all horse trade.' For eleven years, after I gave up Clevelands, I led a roadster stallion. My price was thirty shillings ; my horse was in fashion, and although trade was bad, I made pretty good seasons. Then I took to a thoroughbred, and have stuck to thoroughbred ever since. I get two guineas for him.

"The gentleman who first brought roadster stallions in our country, Mr. Ramsdale, brought up some very good ones of the old Phenomenon and Wildfire breed, descended from a cross of carty and blood. Mr. Ramsdale went about amongst the farmers, and picked up where he could a colt a year old good enough for a stallion, and he got the farmers to keep the best uncastrated for the same purpose. Many of this sort were bred in East Yorkshire; the North was always for the coaching line, Clevelands, but these are all but extinct, because there is no demand for them.

"I think there are fewer roadster stallions bred now than there used to be. It is something like forty years since Mr. Ramsdale started breeding that sort of horse. We have kept on improving them ever since. We try to keep them as near as possible to the pure breed of roadsters, crossing them with the best blood we can get with a stepping horse. But now farmers prefer a thoroughbred if they have a good nag mare. A colt out of a nag mare, by a thoroughbred horse, at three years old will fetch sometimes £120."

TROTTING HORSE REGISTER.

In August, 1878, an attempt was made to establish a stud book for roadsters, cobs, ponies, and hackneys, under the editorship of Mr. H. F. Euren, of the *Norwich Mercury*. At a meeting called at Downham, over which Mr. Anthony Hammond, of Westacre, M.F.H., presided, it was stated that for the previous six years above a hundred roadster stallions had been exported every year. France, Germany, Austria, Italy, and America, as well as the Indian Government, were amongst the importers.

"Mr. Euren, of the *Norwich Mercury*, the promoter, explained that 'the first object of the register would be to put on record, in as complete a manner as possible, the pedigrees and all that was known about horses which had travelled in Norfolk, Yorkshire, and other counties, or had been exhibited at the local and Royal shows. This would establish pedigrees once and for all. The next thing it was desirable to have in the register was as complete a record as possible of really good hackney mares of known breeding.'" At this meeting Mr. Wallace of New York, editor of the American "Trotting Horse Register," which is supported by the American Association of Trotting Horse Breeders, stated that "in 1822 Mr. J. Boot of Boston imported Bellfounder, a Norfolk trotting horse, bred by a Mr. Farrar. It was part of his business in England to trace the pedigree of Bellfounder, as he was imported with an impossible and fictitious pedigree. Bellfounder's blood mingled kindly with old Messenger's blood, and that of the whole trotting family. The Hambletonians (a famous American breed) were out of a mare by Bellfounder. Bellfounder was just such a horse as he saw at Downham in the class for the roadster stallions under 15 hands 2 in. When he saw that class he thought he must be in New England, where they had a family of horses called Morgans, all trotters, with high action, stylish heads and tails, not so fast as the trotters of the Messenger blood, but they mingled kindly with it, and gave it substance and compactness. The Morgans were exceedingly gentle and kind."

The proposal received the support of:—The Duke of Hamilton and Brandon; the Marquis of Bristol; the Earl Spencer; the Earl Romney; the Lord Calthorpe; Sir Thomas Hare; Sir W. B. Ffolkes, Bart., Norfolk. Messrs. A. Hammond, Master West Norfolk Foxhounds; C. W. Wicksted, Master Ludlow Hunt; J. J. Colman, M.P., Norwich; E. Greene, M.P.; H. Aylmer, Westacre; H. Birkbeck, Stoke Holy Cross; W. D'Urban Blyth; C. Beart, Stow. And there was a reasonable prospect of success in December, 1878.

THE CONDITION OF THE HORSE SUPPLY IN 1874.

There has never been a period in the history of this country since books were written that there has not been a cry, a lamentation, over the decline and proximate fall of the British horse. De Blundeville in the time of Queen Elizabeth; the Duke of Newcastle in the time of Charles II.; De Berenger in the early years of George III.; and since De Berenger, a host of publications large and profusely illustrated quartos, pamphlets, and hecatombs of magazine articles, have been devoted to essays to the same text. There is nothing extraordinary in this. The oldest man, the most profound student of our history, cannot name the date when " the Church was not in danger : " the two services of the army and navy " going to the deuce ; " the whole agricultural interest on the brink of total ruin ; all domestic servants, and all young people of every class, inferior to their predecessors at some remote unnamed period. We cannot be expected to take a more cheerful view of our position than the contemporaries of Homer, who inform us that " Ajax threw a rock which not two men of our degenerate days could lift."

In the Session of 1873 the Earl of Rosebery made himself the organ of the numerous parties who despaired of the future of the British horse, and obtained a Committee, from which we have quoted more than once, which sat twelve days, and examined thirty-nine witnesses. The Committee did not venture, except incidentally and by an aside, to investigate the condition of the British turf, the cradle of the racehorse, who is the inevitable parent on one side or other of every useful riding-horse in the kingdom ; perhaps wisely, because no evidence and no report of any committee would or could have exercised any influence over the proceedings of the " master of the situation," the bookmaker.

The Committee collected facts and figures never before brought together by authority, and recorded very contradictory theories.

It is true that every dealer examined complained in almost acrid tones of the persistent avidity with which that (in every country) detestable person, *the foreigner*, bought up the best English mares ; just as the French, Belgian, and Dutch farmers complain of the 1,900 cart-horses we imported in 1862, swelled to 2,300 in 1870, and 12,000 in 1872.*

The cause of the temporary decline in the numbers of English and Irish horses has been explained in the clearest manner in the evidence of some of the horse-dealer witnesses. Englishmen are very fond of horses, so are Irishmen and Scotsmen too, although they are less given to field sports ; but they are all more fond of profit. It takes four years to bring a half-bred hunter or carriage-horse to market after putting the mare to the horse, and to restore the diminution of numbers produced by a long series of unprofitable sales was simply a question of time.

It must not be supposed that the horse supply had not preserved a due proportion to the increase of population. As long as there was a duty on horses, the number of duty-paying horses could be ascertained, and it is found that they more than doubled in thirty years ; but for a long series of years every riding, driving, and hunting horse, every pony and cob brought to market, was produced at a loss to the breeder. At the same time, facilities for conveyance by good roads, railroads, and steamboats, enabled a vast number of acres that formerly produced such locomotive live stock as colts and fillies to grow more grain, roots, mutton, beef, and pork, for sale in the markets of the metropolis or the great cities of the empire. When droves of well-bred two-year-old colts brought from Ireland to the Midland Counties would only fetch ten, fifteen, and at most twenty pounds apiece, the breeder had every temptation to turn his attention to growing pigs or bullocks.

Lord Rosebery's committee did good service by supplying facts and figures, thus helping to dissipate an unreasonable scare, and to put an end at once and for ever to the absurd idea of encouraging horse-breeding by forbidding exportation, and thus depriving our native breeders of their customers amongst the agents of foreign powers.

The returns of the number of horses charged to duty in Great Britain for every year from 1831 to 1872, published in the Appendix to Lord Rosebery's committee's report, proved that " the popular notion that there has been a steady decline in the number of our horses in the course of the present century is entirely without foundation, although from time to time a temporary diminution of breeding

---

* A few years ago John Bull was burned in effigy by the Flemish labourers, for raising the price of provisions by his imports.

and an increase of exportation have taken place. Thus, the returns of horses liable to duty show, between 1831 and 1841, when breeders thought that railroads were going to make horses a drug, there was a decline from 459,000 to 415,000, or about 44,000 horses. In 1854 this class of horses had increased to 475,000, in 1864 to 615,000, in 1872 to 860,000, or double the number paying duty in 1841."

It was certainly shown that horse-breeding fell off sensibly, or, rather, did not increase in proportion to the increase of the population between 1855 and 1868; that in 1870 came the Franco-German war, creating an unusually large exportation, and intensifying the home demand.

These were two causes which combined for a short time to check the trade of horse-breeding. In the first place, before the country was netted with railways, horses were bred on large tracts of land which are now occupied as stock farms; they consumed grass of little value at that time, and then carried themselves to market on their four legs. Secondly, for a long period, there was an average loss of twenty pounds on every nag horse bred on land fit to carry cattle or sheep.

Mr. Edmund Tattersall, the head of the greatest horse auction mart in the world, produced before the Earl of Rosebery's Committee a statement of the average price of the horses, leaving out thoroughbreds, sold in every year from 1863 to 1872. This statement was prepared by taking one day in every month in 1863 and the consecutive years, dividing the numbers sold on each day into two classes, one containing all the hunters and high-class horses, the other the miscellaneous lots, beginning at No. 1 in the catalogues. The price of each horse in each of the two classes being added together, and divided by the number of horses sold, an average was arrived at for every year.

The result showed that the average price of hunters and first-class horses, in 1863, was £40 19s., and of the second-class lots £21 11s. By gradual advances in 1867, the first class had advanced to an average of £57 5s., and the second class to £24 9s.; in 1870, first class to £80 14s., second class to £29 12s.; in 1872, the last year in which Mr. Tattersall struck an average, it was £90 for the first class, and £36 10s. for the second class.

This evidence was confirmed by another witness—William Shaw. He handed to the Committee a book in which he had entered every fee that he had earned in his trade for every year since 1835. It appeared that 1864 was his worst season, "his horse having only served eighty-two mares," on which he observed, "*I could easily make at this day £40 apiece for such horses as I was then selling for £15 and £18. Breeding is looking up in Yorkshire.*"

This witness traced the variations in the trade of horse-breeding very clearly. He began to lead a stallion in 1836. At that time "the demand was for a big coach-horse got out of a Cleveland mare, and a good colt at four years old would sell for £120 apiece; but the fashion of blood horses came up, and we could not make £50 of them; that knocked on the head the Cleveland breed; all the good mares were sold to foreigners. Then the railroads came up, and at every farm-house the farmer used to say when I came round, 'We have nothing at all for you this time; the railways will stop all trade;' and I only got one instead of five or six mares. Afterwards (1854), the Russian war came, and helped us a bit, for the Government bought all our horses; but soon afterwards the trade went down, and we were selling for £15 horses that ought to have brought (to pay) £50 or £60."

The same witness said, in answer to a question from the Duke of Cambridge, "Mares (brood) are not as good as they used to be, but I think if we continue as we have been going on we shall get them as good as ever. Not the old fashion (Cleveland bays); that fashion will not come up again, but a good class of hunting mares that have knocked off work."

The general conclusion of Lord Rosebery's committee's report was that as nothing real could be done, it was better to do nothing! To rely on the certain laws of supply and demand of the nation. The question of the quality of stallions they did not dare to touch. Ninety per cent. of the stallions used for getting half-bred horses of a high class are thoroughbred. These are supplied by the turf. To have entered into an inquiry on the effect of the modern racing system would have not only embarrassed the Committee much, but been useless. The turf is a great commercial interest ruled by the betting men and bookmakers.

To interfere with it would be hopeless. As Cromwell said of the lawyers, "The sons of Zeruriah were too much" for him, so the turf combinations of autocrats and democrats, backers of horses and bookmakers, can defy attempts at legislative reform, which could mean nothing if it did not mean destruction.

The first question to be answered is whether Lord Rosebery's Committee was right or wrong in reporting that high prices would stimulate horse-breeding.

Statistics show that the Committee were right.

It appears from the returns of tax-paying horses in 1873, that there was an increase in licensed horses and unbroken horses and mares of 24,000 over 1872, and 50,000 more than in 1870.

In 1874, the duty on this class of horse having been repealed, there was no return of their numbers, but the increase of unbroken horses and mares over 1873 was nearly 5,000; 1876 showed a further increase of 17,000, so that it is within reason to estimate our horse stock for 1877 at fully three and a half millions, with a steady increase, stimulated by a steady demand at double the prices of 1866. It must be noted that the increase of half a million in horses bred and imported has not materially diminished prices.

The General Omnibus Company of London, whose working horse stock—exactly the class required for artillery—numbers above 8,000, and requires an annual purchase of from 1,800 to 2,000, pays as much for each horse as it did in 1873, within, at most, ten shillings. In 1873 the average price was within a trifle of £40 apiece; in 1877 it averaged £39 10s.

But within that five years, although importation of foreign horses has nearly quadrupled, the Omnibus Company is able to provide its service with ninety per cent. of English horses instead of, as in 1873, with only forty per cent.

Their English horses come from Yorkshire, and from Wales; their foreign horses chiefly from Normandy.

Between 1861 and 1869 the average number of foreign horses imported did not exceed fifteen hundred. In 1870 the importation was three thousand four hundred; in 1871 three thousand five hundred, and in 1872 it had mounted to twelve thousand six hundred; in 1873 to seventeen thousand eight hundred; 1874, twelve thousand six hundred; in 1875, twenty-five thousand six hundred; and 1876, forty thousand seven hundred; and since that date it is supposed to have exceeded fifty thousand.

Our importations were originally confined to heavy draught horses from Holland, Belgium, and France; but since 1870 every horse-breeding country of Europe has been put under contribution. Lots of ponies used by tradesmen have been imported from Eastern Russia, from Poland, and even Finland; good riding and driving horses from Hanover and from Hungary, a superior class of riding and driving horses from the United States and Canada, and a very common class of small animals from Texas and South America; and as long as the prices keep up the cry will be " still they come."

DETERIORATION OF THE BRITISH HORSE.

But although only the remunerative prices created by a steady demand can increase the number of horses in this country, something practical may be done to improve their quality, and check the mischievous deteriorating influence of the unsound stallions yearly manufactured by our six-furlong races. The evil of unsound thoroughbred stallions is set out very plainly in the evidence of Mr. John Mannington, veterinary surgeon of Brighton, and of Mr. W. T. Stanley, veterinary surgeon of Leamington. Mr. Mannington said: "There are a lot of stallions travelling the country that poison the breed of horses. There are perhaps every year six or seven thoroughbred racehorses as good or better than they ever were, but the generality of thoroughbred racehorses are not so sound as when I first went into practice. There are diseases amongst them that we never heard of then. Lameness in the knees was a disease almost unknown before Wild Dayrell. Ever since his stock have been about the country we have lots of horses lame in the knee, bred from him and his descendants. There are more roarers than ever there were. Blair Athol gets an enormous number of roarers. If you get a superior racehorse that happens to be unsound, people send mares to him, irrespective of his unsoundness. Perhaps he gets some very good (winning) horses as two-year-olds or three-year-olds; then, although they are unsound, they are used as stallions," and the evil spreads.

Mr. Stanley, although not so plain-spoken about individual horses, was equally decided. He said: " The owners of half-bred mares cannot afford to put them to the best horses, which can command heavy fees," such as the horses that carry off the thoroughbred prizes at the meetings of agricultural societies. " So the farmers put their mares to any advertised brute that men take about the country with a long pedigree—brutes with spavins and ringbones, roarers, or whistlers—being led away by the long pedigree."

Lord Calthorpe, in 1874, addressed letters to the principal masters of foxhounds, inquiring how their districts were off for stallions. The replies were placed by his lordship at my disposal for publication in a pamphlet printed for private circulation. The following is the substance of the more important of those replies. They fully confirm the evidence of Messrs. Mannington and Stanley. The Earl of Macclesfield, Master of the South Oxfordshire Hounds, writes: " I am sorry to inform you that there are no sound well-bred stallions standing within the limits of my county."

Another M.F.H. writes: " I send the names of five thorough-bred stallions covering in my county. I do not think you could find in the lot one really sound, likely to get hunters. The best was good, but is now worn out." Another M.F.H. "presents his compliments to Lord Calthorpe, and begs to say, in reply to his letter, that, in his opinion, there is not one good stallion in his county."

Another writes: "Out of six thoroughbred stallions in one district (whose sires were respectively Kingston, Newminster, Lord Clifden, Ely, Rataplan, and Macaroni), four are unsound, two blind, three roarers, one has ringbone, two have spavins and ringbone! The stallion that travels the country serving mares at the lowest fee gets the most mares, quite irrespective of soundness, shape, and action."

The Earl of Coventry, whose reputation stands so high as a judge of horses, as an owner and breeder (formerly, of race-horses), and as a master of hounds, in a letter addressed to me on this question, says: "Short races (*i.e.*, under a mile) make people careless as to whether they breed from sound horses or not; *roarers get a short course as well as the soundest horses*, but they are generally useless as racehorses at any distance beyond six furlongs. Roaring is the most hereditary disease known among horses. And yet people breed from roarers, and will continue to do so as long as there is a preponderance of races which they can win with roarers."

The pressing question, then, for those interested in encouraging sound, useful, half-bred horses, is what practical remedy can be devised as an antidote to the poison of these unsound six-furlong stallions.

The remedy lies in bringing to the doors of breeders of horses sound thoroughbred stallions with riding, not racing, action.

At present, sires of the character of the late Earl of Glasgow's stud, sound, with size, power, and riding action, if not fast enough to win in their youth, and beget race-winners in their retirement, are either purchased by foreigners to improve the breed of half-bred horses, or castrated and sold as hunters, a weight-carrying thoroughbred hunter being the most salable animal in the horse market next to a race-winning stallion.

Thus, strange as it may seem, the popularity of the turf, and of the hunting-field, combines to diminish the number of the most valuable, and to encourage the use of the most unprofitable class of thoroughbred sires.

Lord Calthorpe proposed to raise, and maintain for five years, by private subscription, a fund of £10,000 a year, to be devoted to purchasing thoroughbred stallions of a class too costly for an investment by those who look to their remuneration from the fees paid by the owners of half-bred mares; that is to say, horses for which the managers of national studs in France, or the empires of Germany and Austria, are willing to pay from £1,000 to £2,000.

To send these stallions to centres in the breeding districts of Great Britain and Ireland, and to have them led from place to place, covering half-bred mares at fees of from two to five guineas, according to the circumstances of the breeders of each district.

This plan was sound as far as it went, but his lordship failed to find a hundred subscribers, although the list was headed H.R.H. the Prince of Wales.

Low fees are essential if a stallion is to serve farmers' horses, because average farmers prefer the horse at the lowest fee, irrespective of merit. But low fees are not enough to keep the best horse in full work. Farmers will often use a wretch brought to their doors in preference to a horse of the finest quality and action at the same fee but twelve miles off.

The Rawcliffe stud, near York, founded by a joint-stock company under excellent auspices, and admirably managed, proved a complete failure, and was wound up with heavy loss. Amongst their investments were a number of thoroughbred stallions of the very best class for covering half-bred mares. But farmers would not take the trouble to send to them. Many of them "did not earn enough to pay groom's wages." "Sir John Barleycorn just paid his way." "Underhand and Woolwich were good movers. They got big horses, 16 and 17 hands, although neither stood 15 hands 1 inch. They did not get enough mares to keep one of them." "Jordan, Windham, and Fortunio were not more patronised, although they covered at £5 5s., and later on at £3 3s." None of them standing at Rawcliffe could make a living, while Shaw, leading a stallion about in Holderness, could make a good profit out of the thoroughbred horses which he brought to the farmers' doors.

Before the Lords Committee, Mr. Thomas Parrington said (*Q.* 1512): "There is a great want of thoroughbred stallions suitable for farmers. Those that are sound cover at too high a price, or they do not travel the country; *farmers will not be at the trouble of sending to them*. Bad stallions travelling are plentiful. However good a stallion may be, he cannot establish himself until the people have seen his stock. His keep would be about £60 for the season. The charge would be £2 2s. each mare, and if he got one hundred mares it would pay well."

As to the number of mares a horse can serve. "I was part owner of a stallion named Perion, celebrated for getting half-breds. I have known him serve 150 mares, and have 120 foals dropped to him in a season."

On the same question, W. Shaw (*Q.* 1156) says: "A horse that travels will cover three times as many mares as one that stands at home. One horse I had leaped 192 mares in one season—you will find it set down in my book—and only had 22 barren mares. If you only take care of the horse, the more he travels the more foals he will get. If you take proper precautions, he will travel thirty miles a day, resting on Sundays."

From Shorthorns down to pigs and poultry, the whole farm stock of the kingdom has been improved by the selection of male animals, maintained not by Government but by private individuals, either for pleasure or profit, or both. There are instances where within a few years one parson with a taste for pedigree pigs has improved the swine for twenty miles round his church.

In order to multiply good thoroughbred sires let the members of local agricultural societies encourage the formation of horse improvement committees with a

STALLION HIRING FUND.

Let there be established in every district where there are any considerable number of persons inclined to breed horses a Stallion Hiring Fund; the money so raised would procure a direct result. The committee of each local society would hire one or more stallions for the season, which they would send round the district, and give the preference to subscribers. This plan would require much smaller subscriptions than the purchase of stallions, and would secure for the owners of mares in the district the services of horses at moderate fees that had been selected because *suitable* to that district. Kent and Devon might not require the class of stallion fancied in Holderness. The hiring system once introduced would spread, and the demand create a supply of stallions "to let." The subscribers would be recouped for their subscriptions by getting the use of superior animals at a reasonable fee. The sum required would not be large for each "stallion circle" or district. About £100 a year will hire a good thoroughbred stallion. To that sum must be added the cost of his keep and management for the season by a professional stallion leader, paid partly by salary and partly by fees.

Private associations have done everything great in England in agriculture, commerce, manufactures, and public works; and private enterprise can, if directed by our natural leaders, the country gentlemen, of England, improve the quality of thoroughbred hunter sires and their produce. This, I contend, will be more effectually done by the steady demand of annual hirings than the lottery of prizes, although there is no reason why both systems should not flourish side by side.

All that this plan requires to become universal is a few influential patrons and careful and energetic managers. It would spread as local agricultural and horticultural societies have spread, and create a market for slow (in a racing sense) sound stallions with useful action, that are now too often a drug on the market, because not related to some famous unsound racehorse, such as Oulston.*— *From a Pamphlet, dedicated to the Earl of Rosebery, "On the Deterioration of the British Horse."* (1878.)

---

* DEATH OF OULSTON.—This son of Melbourne and Alice Hawthorn was lately destroyed at the age of twenty-six years, he being quite worn out. Oulston was a good racehorse, although not quite amongst the first flight horses of his year; on two occasions the great Rataplan went down before him. As a sire Oulston was not a success, as, although a large number of winners claim paternity from him, the best of his get was Russley, *who, like his sire, was a roarer*, which affliction is said to have lost Oulston the St. Leger.—*Sporting Paper.*

CHAPTER VI.

FOREIGN AND COLONIAL HORSES.

French Breeds of Light Horses—Ardennes—Limousin—Tarbes—Descendants of Saracen Cavalry—Decline of the Limousin—Of Equitation in France—Louis XIV.'s Cavalry Mounted on Danes and Germans—Origin of French State Studs—State of Supply 1813-14—Serious Investigation, 1830—System Adopted Described—1,500 Official Stallions—Normans the Best French Riding-horse—Ancient Reputation—English Sires used 1774—Degradation of Norman—Result of Madame Du Barri's Fancy—Greatly improved under Napoleon III.—The Percheron—Origin of—Camargue—Lorraine—Breton Horses—Camargue Horses Trampling Out Grain—The Lorraine—The Breton a Welshman—His Horse—*Double-bidet*, a Cob—The Boulonnaise—The Mule-breeding Poitevin Mare—The Two Breeds—Reasons for the French System of State Studs and Stallions—The French bad Grooms—Anecdote of French Circus Rider—Frederick the Great's Cavalry—Prussian System of Depôts—The Best Horses from East Prussia—Great Improvement in Province of Posen—Westphalia prefers Hogs to Horses—The Royal Breeding Studs—Royal Carriage Horses—Austria—Horse-loving Hungary—Anecdote of Emperor as King of Hungary—Statistics of Horses in Austria and Hungary—The State Studs and Stallions—Hungarians fond of Hunting and Racing—Boner's Posting in Transylvania—Note, Description of Hungarian—Russia: its many Breeds of Horses—The Russian Country Gentleman resembles Old English Squires—The Orloff Breeds: their Origin—Orloff Trotters—Russian Mares may be worth Importing—Italian Horses—Account of Roman Horses before Roman Fox-hunt established—Lieut.-Colonel F. Winn Knight's Account of—Note, Virgil's Horse—Alfieri's First Horse—The Roman Horse, by a Master of Roman Fox-hounds—Norwegian Horses—American—No Aboriginal Horses in America or Australia—Frank Forester on the Horse of America—The Mustang, Colonel Dodge's Account of—Lord Southwell's Indian War-horse—Anthony Trollope's—Lady Duff Gordon and Lady Barkly on Cape Horses—Canadian Horses Useful and Tough—Colonel White's Opinion of them for Cavalry—The Americans have no Taste for Horsemanship—Trotters engross their Taste and Wealth—Australian Horses—Colonel Mundy on—A Mob of Horses—Exciting Scene—Tasmanian Horses—Description of Australian Horses, by a Tasmanian.

A FEW years ago all that would be likely to interest an English reader on the subject of French horses might have been comprised in two or three paragraphs—we imported no French horses; we exported every year a few of our own of the best blood and action. The exportation of high-class English horses appears to have commenced as early as 1608, in the reign of Henri IV., and has continued ever since, when not interrupted by wars. But this importation has generally been more important for quality than for number. Indeed, under the fashion set by the late Emperor of the French, higher prices were obtained in Paris than in London for "*steppares*," whether for harness or riding. For more than forty years the managers of the national studs of France have almost every year purchased a certain number of thoroughbred and half-bred English horses and mares for stud purposes; but the remount department of their army has only come to us when it has been necessary to put the cavalry and artillery on a war footing.

After 1872 the export of French horses to England assumed great commercial importance. So late as 1870 two Percheron stallions—saved from the roasting spit during the siege of Paris, which had received medals of honour wherever they had been exhibited in their own country—were passed over by the judges of the Agricultural Hall Horse Show as quite unworthy of notice; and it was only on further appeal that medals were awarded to them as a matter of hospitality, in the character of "distressed foreigners." Since that date we have been only too glad to get anything in the shape of a French omnibus horse to work our omnibuses, &c.

It is true that more than twenty years before the Franco-German war a few large cart-horses from the Continent were imported, chiefly by Mr. Henry Dodd, a great dust contractor, for the London trade, who went over to France and Holland on the suggestion of Mr. Shillibeer, the founder of the London omnibus system. But since 1871 the importation of French omnibus horses, and what may be called trotting draught-horses, has increased so rapidly, that in 1872 the London demands alone reached 12,000. In the following year the stables of the General Omnibus Company were almost entirely recruited from France and

FRENCH HALF-BRED GOVERNMENT STALLION.

Belgium; and nearly all the horses purchased for the Autumn Manœuvres were foreigners—Normans, Boulonnais, and Percherons.

The horse stock of France amounts to about three millions, and has for more than a century preserved the same proportion to the number of the population, except in time of war, when it has always been unequal to the demand, although the character of the horses bred has changed in a very remarkable manner, under the influence of changed institutions and altered systems of cultivation. The inclination of the modern French farmers, except in one or two restricted districts, is to breed a sort of cart-horse that can trot slowly; and of these, if peace prevails, they are likely to produce a plentiful supply; but there is, and always has been, a notable deficiency of saddle-horses, cavalry horses, and horses for light harness, in spite of extraordinary efforts made and extraordinary expenses incurred by successive Governments for the purpose of encouraging their production.

Previous to the wars of the first French Revolution, France possessed in Ardennes, in the *Midi* (we have no English synonym for this word), under the Pyrenees, on the plains of Limousin and of Tarbes, several tribes of well-bred horses, the descendants of the cavalry of the Saracens, who were defeated and dispersed A.D. 732 by Charles Martel. These were cultivated and improved by the blood of Oriental sires, imported by way of Marseilles, for the use and amusement of the French nobility before the centralising system of Louis XIV. had lured them from their country seats, sports, and duties, to hover round the court of *Le Grand Monarque* and his two successors.

The Limousin, according to the description of mediæval authors, was the finest gentleman's hack it is possible to imagine, bred in the parks and on the farms of the descendants of the Crusaders; but even in the time of Louis XV. it had begun to deteriorate, having ceased to receive infusions of the choicest Oriental blood. Attempts unskilfully conducted to cross it with Arab, English, and even Spanish blood, resulted in destroying the original character of the Limousin. The English blood-horse gave it size, the Spaniards action, but the two crosses did not hit. A large importation of Arabs in the reign of Louis XVI. was thought to have revived the character of the race, but the deluge of the Revolution of 1789 swept away, with ten thousand abuses, every attempt at agricultural improvement beyond the peasant's sweat and the peasant's spade. Napoleon tried to restore the ancient glories of the race by an importation of Egyptian stallions, but for some unknown reason their produce was small, weedy, and unfit for any useful purpose. "Formerly," writes a Limousin gentleman, "riding on horseback was one of the accomplishments of every French gentleman. We galloped in chase of the deer, the wild boar, and the wolf; France had only a few highways, other means of communication than riding were difficult, so that it was absolutely necessary for every country gentleman to keep a stud containing manége horses, hunting horses, pleasure hacks, and even horses for riding post. In the last fifty years (1832) all that has passed away. Equitation is no longer an art, there is very little hunting, and France is intersected with excellent roads; hence the reason why Limousin has almost ceased to be a horse-breeding country."

Forty years later than this writer, the Baron d'Etreilles complains that in France a taste for horses "is associated in the public mind with frivolity; and that the statesman, judge, barrister, physician, or attorney, who ventured to appear on a well-bred hack, or driving himself in a phaeton to the Legislative Assembly, the Courts of Law, or a place of business, would endanger his reputation as a practical man and serious character."

To this social discouragement must be added the drawback of the system of arable cultivation, which, in all but a few grazing districts, is universal in a country composed of peasant proprietors. Horses cannot be reared without pastures; and colts, as French Commissioners observe, reporting on the horses of Alsace, "never attain perfection if from a very early period they are shut up in stables."

The French farmer, if he breeds a horse, naturally prefers one which will be useful on the land at two years old, and he is encouraged by the improvement of the roads to substitute a heavy cart-horse for the pack-horse on which he formerly rode and carried his goods to market. In the Ardennes there was formerly, according to General Fleury, *Grand Ecuyer* of Napoleon III., a capital breed of horses, fit for the service of the artillery, but it had been almost extinguished by the ravages and requisitions of the wars of the first Napoleon.

The Government attempted to revive the breed by sending good coaching stallions into the circumscription (district), with the view of breeding artillery horses; but the peasant proprietors would have nothing to do with these sires, even at nominal fees. They found it more profitable to put their mares to Flemish wagon-horses. "Les rouleurs flamand ont été préféré à nos bons étalons carrossier."

It is, then, to fill the place occupied in this country by a resident country gentry and a horse-loving race of farmers, to encourage and assist a race of peasant cultivators, and to secure as far as possible for the use of the French army a class of horses for which the riding and hunting tastes of England afford an unlimited demand, that the French Government has been compelled for more than forty years to maintain a system of artificial encouragement on a very extensive scale.

The production of the class of horses required for the French cavalry, that is, carriage-horses and well-bred riding-horses—"*des chevaux à deux fins*" ("horses with two good ends," as London dealers say)—has never in France been equal to the demand even in time of peace. The deficiency between importation and exportation has been estimated at fifteen per cent. The deficiency has existed from the seventeenth century, that is, as soon as standing armies were established.

The first measures for improving the horse-supply of France were taken in the reign of Louis XIV. As a matter of course, in the spirit of the age, these attempts mainly consisted of a number of vexatious regulations, suggested by naturalist philosophers of the desk.

Under Louis XIV., his subjects in Lorraine and Alsace, amongst the few Frenchmen (they are in blood Germans), says M. Gayot, "who are really fond of a horse, and who took special pride in their teams, were so harassed and discouraged by the plunder of foreign and the requisitions of their own armies, that they, on system, took to breeding miserable brutes just able to draw a plough or cart, and not worth stealing.

At this time the household cavalry of the king were mounted entirely on black Danish or bay Mecklenburg horses.

The nobility of the Court imported well-bred English horses—that is, in the intervals of wars. Under Louis XV., Marshal Saxe came to England to buy chargers. Under Louis XVI. races were run in the English style on the plain of Sartory, and Philippe Egalité rode as a jockey. In 1798, under the Republic, the Council of Five Hundred decreed that stallions of pure races should be provided at the expense of the State, for the benefit of the breeders. Races and other modes of encouraging breeding were established.

The same system, with slight modifications, was adopted under the first Empire, when the series of wars made a severe run on the horse production of France, although all Continental Europe was requisitioned for mounting the Imperial cavalry. Stallions and mares were imported from the East; but, except for the short period of the Peace of Amiens, the English market was closed to French purchasers, official and private.

In 1813-14 requisitions for the cavalry had reduced the horse stock of France to its lowest condition, and very little was done to stimulate horse-breeding under the Governments of Louis XVIII. and Charles X.—the latter monarch having a prejudice against everything foreign and everything new worthy of English country squires in Pitt's time.

After the Revolution of July, 1830, a serious inquiry into the condition of horse-breeding led to the establishment of the very elaborate system, "de l'encouragement," which was adopted, enlarged, and improved by the late Emperor of the French, who employed a German gentleman to organise a system of stallion studs on the plan adopted in the kingdom of Prussia.

The main object of this system was to provide a sufficient number of stallions (fit for getting troopers) for the use of the farmers at low or nominal fees. By decrees framed on the report of extensive inquiries in 1856, all cavalry remounts were ordered to be purchased in France in time of peace. The price of the troop-horses was raised to a sum which the producers considered remunerative, without regard to their market value. The same number of horses, as nearly as possible, were purchased every year, so that the breeders could rely on the military demand.

Stallions which covered at low fees were distributed over the country. The old stud-farms of Pin and Pompadour were strengthened, and others established in favourable situations, for breeding various classes of stallions, and for making experiments in producing Anglo-Normans, Anglo-Arabs, pure Arabs, and English thoroughbreds. Races were established for blood-horses and for trotters. Prizes were given for mares, and for their produce as two and three year olds. To carry all these plans out, colleges of equine learning, composed of cavalry officers and veterinary professors, were established in different parts of the country, which, in a very few years, became as pedantic and absurdly theoretical as such institutions always do when not controlled by an intelligent public opinion.

Training-schools for the education of grooms were supported by the State, and very much approved by provincial councils.

In the systematic manner copied from Germany, France was divided, for horse-breeding purposes, into twenty-five circles, called in official language "*circumscriptions*," over which fifteen hundred official stallions, of the breeds considered most suitable by the central authorities, travelled or stood at depôts, covering at nominal fees. Beside the official stallions, those of private individuals, if approved, were exempted from heavy taxation, and received State subventions.

Ninety race-meetings were held in the course of the year, where racehorses, steeplechasers, and trotters, competed, supported by funds partly provided by the Government, and partly by municipal taxes, imposed by the official representatives of the Government. The result of this vast and costly machinery for encouraging the supply of saddle and cavalry horses is not a little curious.

The quality of the heavy draught trotting-horses, which composed the posting and diligence studs before railways absorbed the passenger traffic on all the great routes of France, was very much improved, although they were the class of horses that received the least encouragement.

The demands for the highest classes of riding and driving horses continued to be supplied from England.

The supply of cavalry horses remained insufficient, whenever the peace footing was disturbed.

All the attempts to revive the ancient breeds of French well-bred hackneys failed, because the farmers were not prepared to incur the expense of feeding the young stock before they were ready for sale, even if any considerable number of gentlemen had been ready to buy and ride them.

In spite of the most decided discouragement, the breeding of heavy cart-horses in the North, and of mules in the *Midi*, became a flourishing industry.

Official influence, backed by the authority of prefects, sub-prefects, commanding officers of gendarmerie, and all the rest of the army of Government's appointed agents, failed to induce the horse-breeding farmers to castrate colts until the latest moment for selling them to the remount department, while the draught-horses, to the great injury of breeding, were and are all retained entire.

The most decided success obtained by forty years of Government inspection, Government studs, Government stallions, and Government prizes, was in the ancient horse-breeding district of Normandy, a grazing and dairy country, where large farms still prevail, where the produce of English blood-horses out of Norman mares were supplied with the food and the care required for rearing vigorous full-sized stock.

Speaking in round numbers, for nearly forty years more than £50,000 a year have been expended by the French Government in prizes and premiums for the encouragement of French horse-breeding; to this must be added the cost of maintaining fifteen hundred State stallions and several breeding farms, and the extra prices paid for the troop-horses purchased for the cavalry—in all, at a reasonable estimate, not less than £250,000 sterling per annum.

There has been a decided increase in the number of horses bred in France—an obvious improvement, as already stated, in the quality of heavy draught, for which no money prizes were offered. But at no period since these efforts were made and expenses incurred has France been able to put her troops on a war footing without resorting to foreign importations; and it was found that the protective or artificial price fixed for cavalry horses almost entirely put an end to the home trade of horse-dealers, and drove them to make their purchases of nag and light harness-horses abroad; it has, therefore, been given up.

In 1878 the Minister of War estimated his requirements for the army and gendarmerie at 123,000. The breeders of light and medium horses formerly found a difficulty in selling them, because, as before observed, there is no demand for riding-horses, and very little demand for well-bred harness-horses out of the small, select, luxurious upper classes of Paris. But this difficulty has been removed by the steady demand that has been established since 1870 in England for horses "*with two good ends*" from any country. Admirable horses for saddle and harness are bred now in Normandy, which fetch very high prices on the spot. They have, however, the defect of being unsound when first taken into fast harness work. With care they recover.

In 1874, by a decree of the National Assembly, all the horses and mules six years old and upwards in France are to be registered and classified, with the view of making them available for public service in time of war. With this view the general commanding each military division is to visit every commune, and, in the presence of the mayor, muster all the animals. "This registration is a great nuisance. It sometimes lasts five days, and men wanted at home have to come five or ten miles with their horses. The examination only lasts a few minutes, but the delay is a grievance"—something like calling out our army reserve, who liked the pay very well for doing nothing, but (at least some of their friends) made it a grievance when the men were called to give the consideration for which they had been enjoying pay.

But the French system answers its purpose, for, according to a correspondent of *The Times*, the arrangements are so perfect that in the course of six days allowed for mobilisation all the corps would be supplied with the horses they required without any fuss. Compensation is to be settled by a committee of landowners (*proprietaires*).

It is stated that the Algerian bred horses that are quiet at pickets and drill in Africa become quite unmanageable on the different food and climate of France. There is only one Government breeding stud in France, at Pompadour, in Limousin, which has been re-established for the purpose of breeding Arab and Anglo-Arab thorough-bred stallions. It is to consist of sixty brood-mares. "The sires used in France are about 12,000 in number. Of these the State owns about 1,000. Those intended for getting saddle-horses are selected after a public trial. The blood-sires are tested at a gallop over a flat course; the half-breds over a two-and-a-half-mile course at a trot, in saddle or in harness, or at a gallop over a mile and a quarter with eight fences. At Caen recently, in the autumn, 600 horses rising four years old were put through these trials, and the Government bought 156.

As a test of the merit of stallions, nothing can be more fallacious than these trials; but they amuse and interest the Norman breeders, and that is a matter of some importance.

Besides the Government stallions, there are 700 in the hands of private individuals, which have been passed, and received a certificate from public officials. The stock of good sires is not considered sufficient, as the other few thousand in the hands of peasant farmers include every degree of ill-shape and unsoundness. On the whole, the efforts of successive French Governments to improve the native breeds of riding-horses have been fairly successful, considering that "outside the army no one rides in France," and therefore there is no school of critics or mass of critical purchasers. The best horse-shows out of Paris are held in Normandy, at Caen, Falaise, and Alençon, in the autumn. Brittany and Picardy stand next to Normandy as horse-breeding districts.*

NORMANS.

Normandy originally possessed two very distinct breeds or tribes of horses—both with a high reputation—the one most fit for harness, the other for the saddle. The horses most esteemed by French and English knights in the ages of heavy armour were Normans. "Nearly a hundred years ago (circa 1760), the Norman breed having very much deteriorated, some coarse-bred English stallions were imported, but without satisfactory effect. The Prince de Lambesc, *Grand Ecuyer* (Master of the Horse) to Louis XVI., imported for the use of the stud-farm of Pin (which is still in existence) twenty-four stallions, none thoroughbred, which produced a very decided improvement by an infusion of blood into the Normans. (We presume that these were stallions the produce of thoroughbred sires and well-bred hunter mares). These English stallions must be considered as the great-grandsires of the present race."

In 1790 the studs were suppressed, and England being closed by the long wars, a very inferior class of sires was used; at the fall of the first Empire the quality of the horses of Normandy was at its lowest ebb.

In 1830, when the improvement of the horse-supply of France was taken into serious consideration, the Norman horses were remarkable for huge, coffin-like, Roman-nosed heads, a legacy from Madame du Barri, the infamous mistress of Louis XV. That personage having received as a present from the Danish ambassador a pair of Danish horses, with monstrous heads, small pig eyes, and long flopping ears set close together, these hideous peculiarities became the fashion. In fact, according to M. Gayot's account, the Norman horse of 1830 was very like the worst example of our black mourning-coach stallions.

Since that date, and particularly during the reign of the Emperor Louis Napoleon, who was a consummate master of all the arts connected with horses, the Norman breed has been steadily improved by crosses of English thoroughbred and roadster trotter sires; and for some years past carriage-horses have been bred in Normandy which might have passed, and do sometimes pass, for the produce of Yorkshire.

The Percherons are another breed of light grey trotting cart-horses, which have in name a considerable reputation in England, as useful animals for slow trotting draught, although in form quite the reverse of what a judge of Clydesdales or Suffolks would select. But the greatest equine authorities of France altogether deny that the Percherons have any claim to be

---

* Abridged from Gibson's "Corn and Cattle of France."

a distinct breed or tribe, like our own Suffolks. The name was never mentioned in any work or record before the present century. " M. Devaux-Loresier," says Professor Moll, " a skilful breeder in La Perche, and an enthusiastic advocate of the Percheron, declares that it dates from the decree of 1806, establishing the stallion stud at Blois; that it was the expression of a want —the manufacture of man, not the result of soil and climate—and that he could breed Percheron horses anywhere, even in Limousin, with fenced pastures and plenty of bran." Others have described the Percheron as a grey trotting cart-horse, with clean limbs and a neat head. These Percherons, in their best form, were the post-horses of France. Some

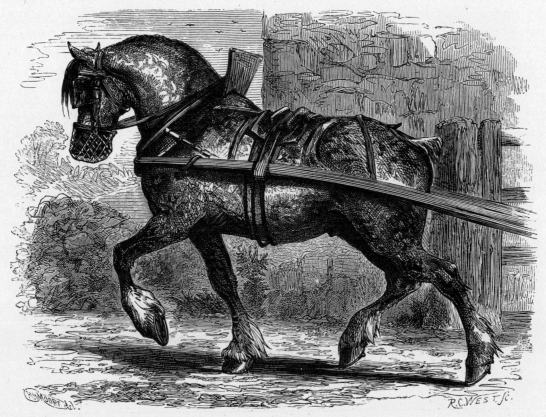

A PERCHERON CART STALLION.

persons consider that of late years they have deteriorated in quality—especially in the neatness of their heads—and become coarse; but, coarse or not, the mares are being imported into England by thousands. The Percheron, according to a writer in the *Revue Contemporaine*, was originally of a bay and sorrel colour, but was turned grey because the chief purchasers, the postmasters, gave a higher price for grey horses.

THE LIMOUSIN.

Of all the riding-horses of France, the Limousin, the descendant of Saracen ancestors, was, as already mentioned, the best—an active and enduring Barb—but in the palmy days of this race the district of Limousin consisted of open grassy plains, well suited for breeding horses. After the Revolution the grass was gradually converted into arable land; and when Mr. Nassau Senior visited Alexis de Tocqueville, in 1850, the breed was almost extinct, and all attempts to revive it, made at a very great expense by the Government, have failed. Probably the cessation of local demand for riding-horses had had a depressing effect. This was not always so. A friend of M. de Tocqueville's remembered a wedding amongst the *vieille noblesse* at which "many of the ladies arrived on horseback, followed by a servant leading a donkey which carried the ball-dresses in a band-box." In the coach-house of the De Tocquevilles was a horse-sedan, a *vis-à-vis*, with a pair of shafts behind and a pair before, to which two cart-horses used to be harnessed instead of men (in China mules are thus harnessed to litters), in order to pay visits where there was no road for wheeled carriages; and even at that date Mr. Senior found the peasantry carrying their harvests home in a sort of cradle on a horse's back, —six sheaves on each side—the lanes being just wide enough to admit a loaded horse.

Extinguish hunting in this country, extinguish a resident nobility and gentry who make riding on horseback a fashion, extinguish farmers who ride in favour of peasants who drive ox and cow carts, and the decline of the quality and numbers of riding and driving horses in England would be certain and rapid.

CAMARGUE, LORRAINE, AND BRETON HORSES.

Amongst the breeds of French horses which, like the Limousin and the Ardennes, have been superseded by modern style of cultivation and modern demands, it is impossible to pass over the Camargue, if it were only for the place it holds in a very interesting epoch of the history of France.

The river Rhone, before flowing into the Mediterranean, forms a vast delta, an island to which the name of Camargue has been given. On this for centuries flourished races of half-wild cattle and half-wild horses. According to tradition, the Camargue horse dates from the introduction of Numidian cavalry, when, in the year of Rome 629, Flavius Flaccus occupied Arles; and received further recruits of African blood from the colony of Julia, and from the two invasions of the Saracens, who occupied Provence about A.D. 730, and again at the epoch of the Crusades.

It was from Camargue that the Camisards—the Calvinists of Cevennes, whom the persecution of Louis XIV. and the pious Madame de Maintenon drove into rebellion—formed their cavalry.

At any rate, whatever be the origin of the Camargue horse, he is to this day characterised by a sort of Tartar air, peculiar to animals living in a wild state.

They were not esteemed for warlike or parade purposes in the twelfth, thirteenth, or fourteenth centuries, ages when every cavalier and every cavalier's horse was barded with steel; they were too small and light of bone.

There is reason to believe that at one period the resident gentry of Camargue took particular pains to keep up the quality of the breed, both by importations from Africa and by the castration of inferior colts; but with the Revolution of 1789 these special precautions disappeared.

They still run wild during winter, in herds of from twenty to one hundred each, under charge of mounted herdsmen, who use the lasso with considerable dexterity, either for catching horses or wild cattle.

One of these wild horsemen is the hero of a picturesque romance by Madame Georges Sand.

The wild horse of the Camargue, fed entirely on wild land, is little better than a pony, and generally of a light grey colour. A cross with a thorough-bred sire brings a very good animal, but the produce, like the Exmoor cross, requires better food in winter than the grass of the wild moorlands, and that does not suit the agricultural economy of the little farmers of the district, although the climate is most favourable to stock-breeding of every kind.

These semi-wild horses were in past time, and are still to some extent, employed in the primitive operation of treading out the corn, a labour of a most exhausting nature.

"At about four or five o'clock in the morning, the sheaves having been thrown in a huge heap, the horses are driven on them, and sinking in the straw until only their heads and backs are seen, are forced round struggling as if in a morass. This work is continued until nine o'clock, nearly five hours, when they are let out to drink, and rest for half an hour. Then they are again compelled

BRETON MARES BY A PERCHERON SIRE.

to mount the pile and trot round and round until two o'clock in the afternoon, when they rest an hour. At three they begin again, and are kept at a sharp trot until six or seven o'clock, when the straw is expected to be broken into lengths of about six inches. They get nothing to eat except what they can pick up under the sharp eye and whip of the driver. This operation is continued in the Camargue for nearly a month, of course not always with the same troop of horses. The work of treading-out done, the herds of horses are driven back to the marshes until the next harvest."

Such is, or rather was, the principal value of the Camargue pony, which under the modern system of agriculture is being superseded by the flail and the threshing-machine.

The modern Lorraine horse, which before the era of good roads, diligences, and carriers' wagons, showed strong traces of Eastern blood, now converted into a heavy harness-horse, still exhibits some of the quality of its ancestors, and trots freely.

The Lorraine farmers have given up riding on horseback, says Professor Moll, but they go long distances, always at a trot, in their *char-à-bancs* (the original of the wagonette), and you never meet a Lorrainer in an empty wagon walking his horses; indeed, he often trots with a load of hay or straw. It is amongst the horse stock of this class, improved by crosses of English sires, that we find the supplies which are becoming an important feature in the live-stock importations of England.

Brittany has an excellent race of small, active hacks, known by the terms *bidet* and *doubles-bidets* (pony and cob).

They are active and enduring, sometimes very good-looking, and would no doubt be brought to a high pitch of perfection if there were the same good understanding that usually exists between our country gentlemen and the surrounding farmers. The Brittany *double-bidet* has been appropriately called "the Cossack of France." They cross very successfully with small English thoroughbreds.

Unfortunately, the Bretons do not even speak French. One of the requests of the Council-General (which represented Brittany) to the French Commission on Horse Supply in 1863, was for a treatise on the breeding and treatment of horses, translated from French into "Breton."

But the Breton, like his brother Celt in Wales, and like the North Devon farmer, seldom walks to market if he can help it; the women never—indeed, they seem not to know how. "You meet them sitting astride on a linen bag stuffed with straw, with their feet pushed hard into rope stirrups, their knees as high as the pony's withers, with a cord-bridle in one hand and a long stick in the other, carrying on one arm a basket of butter covered with a clean white cloth, and with two baskets of chestnuts hanging down on each side of the straw-stuffed pad. Presently come men also mounted, driving before them droves of ponies as shaggy and wild as Welshmen."

The Boulonnaise breed includes to the English eye all the cart-trotters of France—the Picard, the Flamande—names and little else, distinctions without difference. In England, unless a railway van-horse is a chestnut, when he may be a Suffolk, buyers and sellers have until recently ceased to name carty-bred horses by the name of any district or county. From the frequent and easy intercourse between the *Pas de Calais* and England, and by the intelligent attention of landed proprietors connected with Boulogne, the horses of that country have been during the last thirty years wonderfully improved. The grey cart-stallions—there was not a cart-mare in the whole city—of Paris excited the admiration of our best farmers when, at the invitation of the late Emperor, that city was invaded by quite an army of eminent British breeders of every kind of live stock.

THE MULE-BREEDING POITEVIN MARE.

This sketch of the French native breeds of horses would be incomplete without an account of one which is maintained solely for the purpose of breeding mules, a pursuit which has grown in the course of a century, and attained a high degree of prosperity and importance, not only without the assistance so lavishly given to the breeding of troop-horses, but in spite of very decided discouragement. The ready sale at remunerative prices for mules has outweighed all the artificial encouragement and discouragement of the official studs.

Poitou has two breeds or tribes of horses—one crossed with English blood, called *Anglo-Poitevin*, which occasionally gives some fine carriage-horses; the other of very inferior appearance, the mares of which are exclusively employed in breeding mules, and called (the words are not translatable) *Poitevine mulassière*. None produce such good mules as the big heavy mare of the marshes of Poitou—a coarse stocky beast, with a large barrel, big bone, and hairy legs; heavy, slow, and fit for nothing but to drag a load. In fact, said Jacques Bujault, a celebrated breeder of mules, "imagine a big barrel, supported on four stout legs; that is the *mulassière*, the mother of mules." "Those who buy mares with two good ends, fit to sell for troopers or diligence work, if they should refuse to breed to the donkey sire, make a bad business, and are in a fair way of being ruined." The *Poitevine mulassière* was originally bred on the marshes of La Vendée (just the sort of land as that on which the nearly extinct black Lincolnshire dray-horse cultivated by Bakewell was bred), a vast tract of land, formerly constantly soaked, at present thoroughly drained, and only covered with water at the time of inundations after heavy winter rains. But this idea that good mules can only be bred from the coarse Poitou mares is a provincial delusion. Any good English, French, or American cart-mare will breed a strong mule by a strong ass sire, as has been proved in the United States.

The fillies being reserved for mule-breeding, the colts are sold at two years old to dealers;

A MULE OF THE MIDI.

so the horses of Berry, La Béauce, and La Perche are employed in agricultural work until they are five or six years old, and are then sold either for omnibus work or for heavy draught. Some very fine horses are purchased among the Poitevins by the Berry Remount Depôt, for the artillery.

FRENCH GOVERNMENT STUDS.

The system adopted by the successive Governments of France for increasing and improving the breeds of horses is based on principles followed by all the Continental Governments of Europe at more or less cost to the State.

Our island position relieves us from the necessity of placing cavalry on a war footing at short notice—a necessity which is and has long been a matter of paramount importance with France, Germany, and Austria. The inhabitants of democratic France and aristocratic Prussia and Austria have always been accustomed to rely on Government aid for the encouragement of everything connected with agriculture, public works, and a host of other institutions which Englishmen will not allow a Government to touch.   I have often found it difficult to explain to a foreigner the meaning of "The Royal Agricultural Society of England," to which the Government gives no assistance, and over which it exercises no control. France has no resident landed gentry, in our sense of the term—that is to say, men of wealth and position who perform gratuitously a number of official duties which are filled on the Continent by paid functionaries, and who take the lead, and are followed by their neighbours, whether it be in founding an agricultural society or building an hospital, improving the breed of cattle, or getting up a horse show.   In France, whether Royal, Imperial, or Republican, you might travel a whole day and not find one person above the rank of a peasant farmer not in pay of the Government, and certainly not one who dare take the initiative in a public enterprise without the sanction of the Prefect, or Sub-Prefect, the Maire, and the Commissaire de Police; and if a French gentleman, bitten by English ideas, did attempt to take the lead in a local improvement of any kind by forming an association, he would certainly be looked upon as an impertinent person by the officials, and with great suspicion by all the little farmers round him.

In fact, if the French Government had not taken up the business of offering prizes for mares and foals, and providing stallions, there was no other authority which had the power or the means.

In Prussia the same reasons existed. The Prussian landed gentry were poor, very poor, until improved means of communication by roads, railroads, and steamboats gave value to agricultural produce, and justified the cultivation of great crops by expensive means. When old Blucher astounded the Duke of Wellington by proposing to shoot the Emperor Napoleon, if he were caught after the battle of Waterloo, one of the reasons he gave was "that the Emperor had entirely ruined the Prussian nobility."   Besides, all Germans are accustomed from the earliest years to find Government regulating the affairs of their private life.

Neither the machinery for interference nor the reasons for interference with private enterprise exist in England.   In Ireland there is something of French feeling about Government help in more ways than one, perhaps because the landlords have been so long divided in feeling from their tenants.   To set up Government studs of stallions in England at reduced fees would be to compete with patriotic landlords and industrious horse-leaders.   In a word, Government interference and assistance are essential in France and Germany, because those countries do not possess the advantages we enjoy for promoting that particular object in resident gentry, horse-loving farmers, and an unlimited demand at rising prices for any number of horses fit for saddle or light harness.

There are in England alone, without counting Scotland and Ireland, irrespective of packs of harriers, more than 130 packs of fox-hounds, every one of which forms a "*circumscription*" for encouraging horse-breeding. All these hunting-fields are open to every one who owns a pony and cares to ride in them ; in nearly all every class of horse-owning society is represented. Was there not a sweep once "who allus 'unted with the Duke ?" The majority of a hundred packs of harriers are supported by farmers, and very small farmers too.

In France or Germany, where by-the-bye there is quite as good hunting as in Devonshire, the New Forest, Cumberland, or the mountainous parts of Wales, the native merchant or professional man, not being noble or invited, who joined a hunt, would be considered and treated as an impertinent intruder—the doctor would lose his patients, and the notary his clients; while in England and Wales the lawyer, the doctor, the brewer, the innkeeper, are leading personages in rural hunts.

The mistake the French Government have made in their arrangements for improving the lighter breeds of horses has not been in principles but in details; that is to say, in the choice of foreign stallions. They have been too fond of purchasing celebrated race-horses of great size, winners of great stakes, without regard to the uses for which they are required. In Austria they understand this business better. Moderate-sized thoroughbred horses, with plenty of bone and good action, that have never raced and never could race with success, would do more for the cobs of Brittany, the ponies of the Ardennes, the Barbs of Tarbes, and the wild horses of the Camargue, than the uncertain Anglo-Normans, the narrow, cat-hammed Arabs, or the West Australians and Flying Dutchmen, on which so much money has been wasted.

Besides the difficulty in want of natural pastures, and customers out of Paris, the French breeder and trainer of good horses labours under immense disadvantages from the want of good grooms. Out of Normandy it is difficult to find a man with knowledge of and pride in his horses. German grooms are often excellent. The Northern Italians are good; but a really competent French groom is a phœnix. So much is the want felt that not only were the *écoles de dressage* (schools for training grooms) established by the late Emperor well supported, but several private establishments were founded and assisted by a State subsidy. The French grooms have not the prevalent vice of English and Irish grooms—drunkenness—but they seldom take pains with or pride in their horses.

A celebrated French *equestrienne* complained to the English proprietor of a circus that her groom, a Lorrainer, was too ill to attend to her horses. "Been getting drunk, ma'm'selle, I suppose—ha!" "Oh dear no; he has been stuffing himself to death with hot pastry!" Now this man really was a good stableman, although he clattered about in wooden shoes and made himself sick with penny tarts.

PRUSSIA.

Prussia, as long as she has been a kingdom, has numbered amongst her German subjects a race of gentlemen, true knights, enthusiastically fond of the horse; and among her Polish subjects a nation of born horsemen—horsemen not only from taste, but from make and shape; lean, sinewy fellows, with no inclination to grow into the terribly fat sergeant-majors of England and France.

Frederick the Great had the finest cavalry of his day, and won some of his greatest victories with them—Kesseldorf, Rossbach, Zorndorf. He drew his light horses chiefly from Poland, and his heavy cavalry from North Germany. His cavalry sat as he did himself, on a natural seat, and rode well. It was not until the time of his ignoble successor, the accomplice and victim of the conqueror at Jena, that the ridiculous "tongs on the wall" seat was adopted; to be copied, after the Peace of 1815, by the royal commanding officers of other countries, who ought to have known better, along with the absurdities of tight uniforms.

Prussia has, like France, depôts for the purchase and training of cavalry horses; six in East Prussia, one in Brandenburgh, one in Posen, one in Hanover, one in the province of Saxony, two in Pomerania, and one in Grand Ducal Hesse. Each depôt consists of several farms, on which the greatest part of the forage is grown; and, what is very extraordinary in a Government establishment, these farms actually realise a profit—actually cover a large share of the yearly expense. The young horses, purchased at three years old, are stabled from the 1st of October to the 1st of May, and fed in meadows in the day-time during the rest of the year.

The Prussian-bred horse develops late, and is in his prime for military purposes at from seven to fourteen years old. A useful system has recently arisen, under which the richer private horse-breeders buy two-year-olds from their poorer neighbours, and feed them with corn, to be re-sold at three years or three years and a half. This arrangement, the result of German education, solves the difficulty which in France has deterred peasant proprietors from breeding a good class of animal. The imperial army of Germany requires more than eight thousand horses every year in time of peace.

The best horses come from East Prussia, which has been a horse-breeding country from time immemorial. This race shows a large infusion of Oriental blood, from which it originally descended during the Saracenic invasion of Europe. The Hanoverians and Mecklenburgers are bigger and more powerful than the East Prussians, but, as a matter of course, softer, and less enduring.

Unlike France, horse-breeding is an important part of rural industry in nearly all parts of the old Prussian monarchy, as well as in some of the provinces annexed after the war of 1866.

The provinces in which this branch of industry is new show extraordinary progress. Half a century ago (1820) in Posen the peasant was a slave bound to the soil. The greatest increase of horse-breeding has taken place in this province. In Westphalia (known chiefly in England for its hogs and hams) nothing has occurred to awaken the rural population from their adherence to the stupid customs of a past generation. "You can have no idea," said a German cavalry officer to the writer, "how difficult it is to teach a peasant, only accustomed to a cow, to groom a horse." In the eastern provinces foreign dealers make large purchases, not only of colts but of brood-mares, to an extent which has recently caused serious alarm. Indeed, in every country of Europe, except Russia, a sort of horse panic arose in 1872 from the same cause—the rivalry of sheep and cattle, and the conversion of grass into plough land.

As a matter of course, the best horses come from the provinces where there is the least arable agriculture, and the worst from the Rhine provinces, where the French law of inheritance prevails, where properties are divided into such little plots that open air grazing is next to impossible. Prussia obtained fine breeding-ground for powerful horses when she annexed Hanover and Schleswig-Holstein.

General Walker, our military *attaché* at the Court of Berlin, tormented himself very unnecessarily to account for the superior endurance of the Prussian troop-horses as compared with our own. A cavalry officer at the head of the imperial studs gave several reasons, one of which was sufficient—viz., the hardy way in which the foals were reared. In his first, "the nearer affinity to pure Arab blood," I have not the least faith. If that were so, the stud-bred horses of India ought to be the best in the world; the contrary is the fact. What is more enduring, what is so enduring, as a Welsh, Exmoor, or Dartmoor pony? You can never, in horse-dealers' phrase, "see the bottom of them." Why? Because, like the Prussian cavalry, they have been hardily reared. What is so enduring as a sound thoroughbred pony, that has never been raced, always well-fed, but roughly treated? Our horses, as a rule, are coddled from birth to death. The German cavalry-general justly observed as to our troopers in the pre-practical age—the system has changed of late : "Two drills a week, and an hour's watering order on other days, only tend to relax instead of to brace the constitution of troop-horses."

In 1867 the kingdom of Prussia, containing nearly 24,000,000 inhabitants, had rather more than, 2,300,000 horses. Of these, 1,600,000 were employed in agriculture. But in East Prussia, as in Ireland, there are very few horses of the cart-breed; the farm work is done with horses that can gallop when fed on corn.

The Prussian Government takes most elaborate means to encourage horse-breeding, but contrives to combine efficiency with economy in a manner which appears impossible with English, French, or American officials.

There are three breeding-studs which were originally founded to supply the royal stables with carriage and riding-horses, but now employed to breed covering stallions for country studs; twelve depôts for covering stallions.

Prizes (on a very moderate scale) are awarded to covering stallions kept by private persons approved by the official heads of depôts, and also to good brood-mares and foals.

Loans bearing no interest are granted to associations founded for the purchase of stallions.

The first stud was established at Trakehnau, in East Prussia, a province as horsy as Yorkshire, by Frederick William I., successor of Frederick the Great, in the year 1732, for the supply of the royal stables; and by this was established three tribes, we cannot call them breeds, of carriage-horses, distinguished from each other solely by their colours—black, bay, and chestnut.

Two other studs were established in 1788 and in 1815.

The eleven country depôts for covering stallions—a twelfth has recently been established in Pomerania—are recruited from the already-mentioned royal breeding-studs, and from purchases in Germany and in foreign countries, notably since 1870 in England. The number of stallions at the eleven depôts as reported in 1873 amounted to 1,750.

The director-general of each district stud, at the proper season, distributes the stallions over the country in small detachments of six or eight. He generally quarters the horses, under charge of servants of the stud establishment, on country proprietors who are interested in horse-breeding.

These arrangements are worthy of attention, should it be decided to give Government assistance in the way of stallions to Ireland. Beyond the maintenance of these studs, the expenses incurred by the Prussian Government in prizes and premiums are very insignificant.

The total number of horses required by the North German imperial army on a peace footing is little under 100,000, on a war footing it is nearly 300,000. After reading these figures, one is not surprised to learn that the German losses of horses by death and sickness in the Franco-German war exceeded a million, and are by some put as high as a million and a half. The original number were three times renewed, including all the horses of the French army taken prisoners at Sedan and at Metz.

Should peace be preserved, Prussia is one of the countries from which English prices may attract a supply of well-bred riding and harness-horses. Nowhere is horse-breeding carried out on more intelligent principles. The stock of mares in East Prussia and Galicia is of the right stamp, and English stallions are most judiciously selected and employed.

AUSTRIA AND HUNGARY.

Not in Yorkshire, not in Ireland, are the gentry and commonalty more fond of a horse than the subjects of Francis Joseph's kingdom of Hungary. As for the Hungarian cavalry officers, as horsemen, and learned in every kind of horse lore, they are second to none. The Emperor himself is, without flattering exaggeration, one of the finest horsemen in Europe. When he was crowned king of now loyal Hungary, part of the ceremony compelled him to ride a fiery horse to the top of a mound of sacred earth, there halt, and, while his charger curveted and reared, wave the sword of Hungary to the four points of the compass. When he performed this feat, an Englishman present—not unfamiliar with our cross-country riders, and no mean performer himself—exclaimed, in relating the incident, "I trembled for the king; I thought the horse would have rolled back on him."

Official reports made by our military *attaché* at the Court of Vienna give us the latest and most authentic information. The latest census gives for Hungary 2,160,000 horses, for the Austrian provinces 1,367,000.

The separate Ministries of Agriculture for Austria and Hungary each systematically encourage the breeding of horses, and for this purpose annually purchase carefully-selected thoroughbred stock in England.

There are two Government studs in Austria, three in Hungary, and a fourth is about to be established in the recently made accessible province of Transylvania—*Trans-sylva*, "beyond the forest"—a country of extraordinary and undeveloped wealth.

The business of these studs, which have been in existence since the latter part of the last century, is to breed mares for the service of the studs, and stallions sufficient in number to supply the wants of the country generally, which are distributed over depôts established for the purpose. At each stud stand stallions of different races—Arab, English thoroughbred and half-bred, Norman, and Lepiza, descended from the old Spanish stock bred in the imperial studs. It is impossible to imagine greater brutes than these, according to our English notions, unless it be our own cream-coloured State stallions.

The number of mares in each depôt varies from 200 to 400, a few being English thoroughbred; but the majority are half-bred English, Arab, or Norman mares, bred in the country on one side or other for generations.

These studs have suffered during the vicissitudes of the Austrian Empire. During the great Hungarian insurrection a number of valuable private studs, collected at vast expense, were dispersed or destroyed, requisitioned, or carried away as the spoils of war. At present the system is to keep the races distinct, and to send the kind of stallions to each district which they are found by experience to suit best.

The Hungarian Government owns nearly 1,800 stallions, the Austrian 1,600; and as these numbers were insufficient, in 1873 the Government was engaged in buying more. Annual horse shows are held in each district, where Government commissioners award money prizes and medals for the best mares with foals, for yearlings, two-year-olds, and three-year-olds. The Government also allows from £10 to £30 annually for each approved stallion in private hands.

At present the peasants are not sufficiently rich or intelligent to breed many good horses; but the rapid introduction of improved means of communication and improved agriculture, with consequent wealth to the farmers, is likely in a few years to produce a decided improvement especially in Hungary, where no man walks if he can ride. The Emperor, the Archduke, and the wealthy landowners of Bohemia, Galicia (Poland), and Hungary have studs for breeding good carriage and riding horses.

The Austrian "Stud Book," issued periodically, which notices every breed of horse, forms a large volume. The climate is a great drawback in Hungary, and seems likely to make breeding any great surplus stock for exportation unlikely. There are only three or four months of the year when horses of value can get pasture good enough to keep them in condition, and the hay made is generally very bad.

Races in Hungary are attended, unlike those of France, by enthusiastic crowds of peasantry.

Gentlemen riders of the first class are numerous. There are several packs of fox-hounds and harriers, kept up quite in the English, or rather the rough Welsh style, where the same pack will hunt everything that will run—from a hare to a polecat. Near Vienna a pack of stag-hounds for hunting carted red deer has been established.

The late Charles Boner,* whose charming book on Transylvania was written in 1864-5, before the happy reconciliation between Francis Joseph and his Hungarian subjects, gives a delightful picture of travelling in that horse-loving country, in the following passage:—

"We now changed horses for the last time, and with four little animals started off again. A merry youth drove them, and the delicious elasticity of the air seemed to have inspired and made him happy and buoyant. By Jove! how we whirled along with that young charioteer! Hark how he shouts to his horses, and they answer to his voice! Before the lash of his long whip flying through the air can touch the leaders, they spring forward as if in a race, and another team, panting for victory, were close behind them.

"Now the whip is caught up with a jerk, and the wheelers are double-thonged in the most approved style. Again a loud shout, the shout of youth and joy, and the little wiry animals spring forward at their utmost speed. How that boy enjoys his drive; and how I enjoy it too! For the whole distance he never ceased calling to his team; and thus, the bells merrily jingling, the whip whirling round his head, and with loud and noisy shouts, in we came to Karansebes as though we were an express with the intelligence that the whole frontier was up in arms, that the Servians had crossed the frontier, or some other equally momentous piece of news."

Mr. Boner found at Gernyeszeg an exceedingly well-bred stud belonging to Count Dominik Teleki. "His horses are the produce of thoroughbred sires and Transylvanian mares, are hardy, and bear cold without injury; are tall, good-looking, and fit for any gentleman to ride. The distances people travel with the same horses for days together are astonishing; they neither break down nor refuse their food. The foals stroll about the farm-yard the whole day in winter, with coats as shaggy as bears, and get little corn. Count Lazar has also a considerable stud. He has spent large sums for the best English blood, and the horses he has bred are very strong animals, but less fitted to stand wear and tear than those of Count Teleki."

Since this was written the Emperor Francis Joseph, to his immortal honour, has cast behind the prejudices in which he was nurtured, reconciled himself to his Hungarian subjects, and adopted over all his dominions those constitutional principles of government which the noble Hungarians cherished and died for, while all around them submitted to the stupid despotism organised by Metternich and blessed by successive Popes.

RUSSIA.

The Russian Empire, like the United States, is so vast that it extends over many climates, differing as much in temperature as Norway and Sicily. Russia also includes many races—German, Scandinavian, Sclavonic, Oriental, and semi-Oriental, Poles, Tartars, Lesghians—

* Boner's account of the Hungarian gipsies explains the principles on which the horses of thickly-populated countries like England become soft, while those reared on the sandy plains of East Prussia and Eastern Europe are hardy. The children of these gipsies go perfectly naked until they are ten years old. "They may be seen sliding down ice slopes on their seats." The consequence is the weak ones die; those who survive can live where a townsman would perish with cold and want of food.

amongst which are to be found horses of so great a variety that at an exhibition held in Moscow the horse show prize list was divided into not less than fourteen classes, viz. :—

1. Thoroughbreds, English and Arab.
2. Saddle-horses, half-bred.
3. Orloff trotters.
4. Carriage-horses.
5. Carabaghs — saddle-horses crossed from Arabs and Trouchmens.
6. Trouchmens — a fine breed from Central Asia, much resembling the Arab.
7. Horses from the Don—the well-known irregular cavalry horses of the Don Cossack.
8. Cart-horses.
9. Voitugs.
10. Finlanders.
11. Smouds.
12. Baschkines.
13. Ponies.
14. Horses from the Caucasus.

The landed proprietors of Russia proper include a great many country gentlemen, who live on their estates, large or small, much as our squires did in the days of the first Georges, when there was a distinction between the courtier, the citizen, and the well-acred squire (admirably painted by Macaulay), which has long totally disappeared in Great Britain. The Russian novelist Tourguénet, in his "Days of a Russian Sportsman," has also painted the Russian squire, neither courtier nor soldier ; proud of his horses, his Persian greyhounds, and big wolf-hounds, and devoted to field sports. Among this class horse-breeding is pursued with passion, and riding is one of their principal occupations in summer. In winter, sledge-driving presents the only means of conveyance for passengers or merchandise. For military exigencies, every Russian officer must know how to ride, and ride well ; but all over the empire harness-horses of pace and endurance are required to cover the long distances between country house and country house, and between towns and villages. Over a territory so vast and so barren, railroads can only be carried to unite important cities and ports ; and, if ever, centuries must elapse before sledges or horses cease to be the principal conveyances.

A hundred years ago the Russian nobility began to import English blood-horses to cross with their excellent mares, and judicious importations have continued ever since. Whenever the means of communication have been rendered less costly than at present, it is from Russia that we are most likely to obtain a supply of useful riding-horses, the produce of native mares by English sires ; for Russia has native breeds, with size, substance, and riding action, besides her tens of thousands of Cossack ponies and Oriental galloways. The pictures of the Russian sledge-horses show more blood than those of France or Northern Europe.

The Russian horses imported into England and France are always said to be of the Orloff breed, and are of two totally different tribes. The one is a leggy riding-horse with a great deal of quality of the Arab style. The others are Orloff trotters, which are large horses, generally brown, sometimes grey, fast according to European notions, but with a shooting action with the fore-legs which we do not admire in this country, but which may be well calculated for sledge-travelling. In an article attributed to Sir Erskine Perry,* he has traced the origin of these trotters, some of the finest specimens of which were exhibited at the Hamburg Agricultural Show in 1865.

Alexis Orloff (brother of Gregory), the lover of Catherine II. (Catherine the Great), to whom an imposing monument has just been erected in St. Petersburg, received from a Turkish pacha as a present a Barb, Smolenska, whose skeleton is preserved to this day in the Orloff Museum. The stud was commenced in 1700 with the following collection, according to the Russian horse-breeding records :—

	Stallions.	Mares.		Stallions.	Mares.
Arabs	12	10	Persian	3	2
Turkish	1	2	Danish	1	3
English	20	32	Mecklenburg	0	5
Dutch	1	8			

* Edinburgh Review.

"Smolenska, from a Danish mare, got Vulcan, who was the sire of Barss, out of a Dutch mare. Barss exhibited extraordinary trotting powers; and all the modern trotters of Russia trace their lineage up to him, and to daughters of Smolenska, out of English and Arab mares. Count Orloff also obtained from England two sons of Eclipse, two sons of Highflyer, and the winners of the St. Leger in 1798 and of the Derby in 1794, Tarta and Dædalus, besides many others. The race of trotters thus produced became a distinct type in about thirty years, and, curiously enough, since that period all attempts to improve the breed by fresh blood, whether Arab, English,

POSTING IN RUSSIA.

French, or Dutch, have failed. Count Alexis was most unwilling to sell any of his best sires, and at his death, in 1808, he provided by his will that none should be disposed of. In 1845 the prohibition was removed, when Government bought from his daughter and heiress the Krenothan stud; and now it is calculated that there are no fewer than 1,600 private studs in Russia, with nearly 6,000 stallions, and upwards of 50,000 mares, from whom the Orloff trotters are produced."

The Orloff trotters are not esteemed as they were formerly, because in harness-horses action is more required than pace, and even in pace they cannot approach American trotters. Besides the Orloff trotters, the Orloff nags or saddle-horses are celebrated. These also descend from

Smolenska and another Barb called Sultan, crossed with English and Anglo-Arab mares. According to Russian writers, they combine the good qualities of both their parents, and without equalling their English progenitors in speed, they exceed them in beauty, soundness, docility, and aptitude for all military purposes. Like the trotters, they preserve a distinct character, and every attempt to introduce fresh doses of English or Arab blood has failed signally.

The Duke of Sutherland brought a grey trotting stallion from Russia when he visited St. Petersburg, as Marquis of Stafford, with a distinguished party, on the occasion of the present Emperor's coronation, which he used to drive constantly in single harness in a Stanhope phaeton. This horse was certainly showy in action, with a great display of mane and tail, but coarse, and not of a sort we should care to perpetuate.

The best Russian park hack I ever saw was a grey, apparently thoroughbred, which was exhibited and took a prize at the Agricultural Hall—the property of Colonel (now Sir John) Dugdale Astley, Bart. The horse was not only beautiful and full of quality, but trained to passade, change legs, and other feats, about which circus equestrians make a great labour, on the imperceptible indication of the accomplished rider.

An eminent horse-dealer, in his evidence before the Lords Committee on Horse Supply, pronounced some Russian riding-horses imported into Hull the best he had seen—the best "foreigners" he had ever seen—but they were not cheap. If prices justified importation, Russian mares of fine constitution and high quality might be collected for breeding purposes. "Russian horses," says the correspondent of *The Times*, 1st February, 1874, "generally are, indeed, a wonderful race. Cossack cavalry will keep in good condition when they can get nothing to eat but the twigs of trees; and from what I have seen of them I should say that the St. Petersburg sleigh and carriage horses are the most marvellous breed in the world. Carriages are never sent home here, as in London, after they have taken their owners out to dinner or the theatre. They will stand for hours and hours in fifteen or twenty degrees of frost, after the horses have been heated by rapid driving. Neither do coachmen, so far as I have seen, walk their horses to and fro while they are waiting, but stand them still at the doorway, or get into their places on the rank and stop there. Yet the animals seem to take no harm, and you seldom see one with a cold." Frank Forester remarked the same quality of endurance in the most valuable American trotters.

ITALY.

The Government of United Italy is paying attention to improving the native breeds of Italy by the importation of English sires and mares. The climate is favourable, there is plenty of pasture in certain provinces, and tens of thousands of acres might be reclaimed from marsh and jungle if a settled condition of political affairs allowed the Government to carry out comprehensive plans of main drainage, assisted by windmills and steam pumps.

The mares of Tuscany and the Roman territory cross well with English blood sires, the produce making excellent troopers, with more hardy constitutions than the English race. Horses are not cheap. There are Government breeding studs, but they are insufficient to supply the army.

The tastes of Victor Emmanuel, the first king of Italy, in the way of horses were strictly military, and His Majesty required a weight-carrier in the broadest sense of the term. On his shooting excursions he invariably rode Sardinian ponies—little brutes, sure-footed as goats, with the fire and fine heads of their Barb ancestor, but very mean hind-quarters, the usual result of chance breeding.

His successor, King Humbert, is passionately fond of horses, a fine horseman, and has advisers about him who thoroughly understand how the native breeds should be improved. I have had the honour of selecting for His Royal Highness several chargers, all of the same stamp, about 16 hands high, well bred, up to weight; first-class Leicester hunters, in fact, but with rather more knee-action and more showy fore-hand than is required in English hunting.

The Roman Hunt, patronised by royalty, is breeding up a number of Italian gentlemen and nobleman to this the healthiest and most manly of all sports.

ROMAN HORSES.

"When I first knew Rome, in 1838, the only noticeable horses were the large blacks in the cardinals' carriages. They were slow, ill-bred animals, with very high, round action in their lugubrious trot. The best of these were bred by the family of Prince Chigi. The best large riding-horses were of the Santo Spirito breed. My brother Charles (for some years Master of the Roman Fox-hounds) bought a promising grey of this breed, and I rode him hunting for a season. But no horseman in the world could get one of this sort over the top bar of an *astaggionata* (timber bullock-fence of Campagna), although this grey was made to make his way through a good many fences of the kind, on the principle that the impetus is calculated by multiplying the weight into the velocity.

"The establishment of a pack of fox-hounds by the Earl of Chesterfield was followed by races and steeplechases, and these produced an immediate change in the quality of the horse bred on the Roman Campagna. The first races at Rome, under English auspices, were held about 1842. In that year several of the Roman princes clubbed together to buy an English thoroughbred stallion. Soon afterwards one of the large *mercante di campagna* (graziers), Signor Polverosi, called familiarly by the English 'Dusty Bob,' imported several English stallions, and began to breed thoroughbred horses. His example was imitated, and 'crossing with English blood-horses' became an established custom. One farmer told me that he was obliged to cross because all the others did. Signor Polverosi said that his horse-breeding investment paid; but first he speculated in some iron-works, and was unfortunate; then he meddled in politics, and was exiled. At present he holds an official appointment under the Government of the King of Italy, as the head of a horse-breeding establishment in one of the Roman provinces, having previously held one in the Neapolitan provinces.

"Early in the horse-breeding movement, Prince Borghese tried several Arab stallions in his stud.

"In 1838 I found a few niceish hacks in Rome, bred in Calabria, with a strong cross of Barb blood, but they had not strength or size enough for hunting. In Florence all the vehicles at that time were drawn by good-looking ponies, imported from Corsica and Sardinia."

This reminds one that the first horse of the Italian poet Alfieri, a passionate lover of horses, was a Sardinian. "My first horse," he says, "which I took with me into the country was a beautiful white Sardinian, of the most elegant form, especially his head, his neck, and his chest. I was madly fond of him; I could not sleep (Alfieri was then fifteen years old) or eat for thinking of him, if he was the least off his feed, which happened very often, for he was high-couraged and delicate. My affection for him did not, however, prevent me from ill-using him when I rode him, if he did not do exactly what I wished." (I am afraid there are a good many English boys not unlike the rich young Italian nobleman.) "The delicacy of this admirable animal afforded me an excuse for purchasing another saddle-horse, then two for my carriage, then one for my cabriolet, and then two more saddle-horses; so that in the course of the year I managed to have eight horses in my stable. My stingy guardian protested, and that was all the satisfaction he got." * This was in 1764.

In answer to inquiries by the writer about the present condition of Roman horses :—

"The old Roman coachman was no coachman at all, he could only whip, whip, and when that would not do he knew nothing more—the old Roman horse would stand it.

"The San Spirito had a cross of blood from a stallion brought into the country by the Fathers, and thus they became in one way the best breed.

"The Chigi breed was the best for high steppers—the two wheelers in the Pope's carriage used to be Chigis.

"The old Roman horse was not fast, but a good traveller, working day after day. Now all the breeds have been crossed with the English blood several times, and the best carriage-horses are large and nearly thoroughbred. The breeders give great prices for English stallions.

"All the cardinals' horses were of the old Roman breed ; but after the first English races at Rome all the breeders began to cross to get quicker animals.

"The Roman Campagna is a great place for breeding horses, but the English horses will not live if turned out there to run like the Roman breed. It is therefore necessary not to cross too fast, but to get them accustomed to the climate and the mode of treatment before following it up.

"The Roman horses are now fast improving. The crosses of English blood often go well over the stiff fences of the Campagna with the fox-hounds ; and in 1871 I saw between twenty and thirty perfectly well-appointed carriages, beautifully horsed, following a grand funeral.

"When I first went to Rome it was difficult to get a horse with hind and fore legs to correspond- The mediæval statues represent a breed of slow, lasting, high-stepping horses."†

THE ANDALUSIAN HORSE.

The Spaniards have been famous for their horses from the earliest historical times. The Andalusian horse was acknowledged to be the best in Europe until the English produced the thoroughbred. Spain still possesses breeds of horses remarkable for quality and for stately action ; but those which might appear likely to be of value crossed with the English blood-horse are in the hands of a few noble families, and only to be obtained at fabulous prices.

The *mares* of the Spanish genet breed (famous since the wars recorded by old Froissart) are kept and much valued as riding-horses for long distances by wealthy Spaniards. The genet, a light, slim, blood-like animal, is the evident descendant of the Barbs brought into the country by the Moors, when they conquered the greater part of Spain.

The horse of the country, familiarly known as the horse of the *contrabandista*, is a hardy, enduring, useful animal, which occupies much the same place as the Devonshire pack-horse did before roads spoiled his trade. He is probably the descendant of the horses on which Hannibal mounted his Spanish cavalry, when he fought the battle of Cannæ, and nearly conquered Italy. He is, in fact, an animal which a traveller would use in the country, but not often care to take out of it.

The third race is that of the ancient Spanish war-horse, the true *destrier*, whose form has been handed down to us in the equestrian portraits of Velasquez, and whose praises fill the pages of every writer on horsemanship up to the period when armour-wearing knights and high-school

* "Autobiography of Count Victor Alfieri."
† Extracts from letters from Lieut.-Colonel Frederick Winn Knight, M.P., of Exmoor, and his brother Charles, an ex-Master of the Roman Fox-hounds.

horsemanship disappeared, to be replaced by racing and hunting, and the value of blood, power, and size, as united in the English thoroughbred, became acknowledged throughout Europe.

Gervase Markham, the Duke of Newcastle, Cox, Barrett, and, lastly, Berenger (who wrote a book dedicated to George III. in 1771) all refer to the Spanish or Neapolitan horse as unrivalled for war and the manége, and the older writers even name him as a stallion to be employed for improving the breed of English horses.

For the following description of the modern Spanish war-horse—the horse on which the murdered General Prim appears mounted in the celebrated picture by the French artist Regnault—I am indebted to the late Mr. Thomas Rice, V.S., who took charge of the stud of the late Lord Dalling when British Minister in Spain :—

"The Spanish horse stands generally from 15 to 16 hands, with rather a large bony head, in shape like the face of a Merino sheep (thence called *el carnero*) with full eye, and large expanding nostrils, which denote his remarkable vigour and power, a shortish muscular neck, strong shoulders rather narrow in the back, but with magnificent quarters—thighs, hocks, and hind-legs placed well under them ; the arms, fore-legs, and feet are as good generally as can be, feet well formed, short cannon-bones, and back tendons strong and standing well out. All elasticity and action in walk, trot, canter—*faster than this they should not be asked to move, as at a forced pace they lose their beauty of motion, and appear to be disconcerted from the extravagance of their action.* In my opinion no horse is superior, either in the park or on parade, to a well-bred and broken Spanish horse of the best breed, such as that known as the Don Carlos, or those of the Duke de Berwick y Abba, at Carpui, near Cordova ; or those of the Marquis Alcanices, now the Duke de Sestos, a few miles from Madrid ; of the Dukes de Burrowers and Abrantes ; the Marquis de Perales ; and several other noblemen near Baelen and Cadiz. These families brand all the horses they breed on the rump. This disfigures them to an English eye. The constitution of this breed is stronger than that of any other foreign horses that I have met with ; roaring and whistling are unknown amongst them. They rarely fall, trip, or stumble ; they are generous and free, either in riding or driving, if properly used. Although entire, they are docile. They know the value of a good horse in Spain, and a first-class one will cost from 25,000 to 35,000 reals, or 250 to 350 guineas.

"The Spanish mares of this breed, as a rule, do not run so large as the horses. They are very seldom broken or used, but are simply kept for breeding purposes ; and are rarely fed as they should be in order to produce fine animals. In the spring and summer they have plenty, but in the winter they seldom get anything but straw. They run wild in herds, and can only be approached by the men that attend them. They are powerful animals, with the best-shaped legs and feet possible ; rather coarse heads, and inclined to be too low at the setting-on of the tail, or, in common English, goose-rumped. I crossed several of these mares with the Kedger. This horse had a beautiful small head, a strong straight back, with tail set on high, points which exactly counteracted what was unsightly in the Spanish mare. The produce at four years old were very good-looking, with action, power, size, and substance enough for almost any purpose. In fact, I don't think it possible to have a finer cross for general use than the English pure-bred horse and the Spanish mare. I have also bred from the Cleveland coaching and Yorkshire and Norfolk trotting stallion, also from the pure Arab. All the crosses seem to combine well with the Spanish mare except the Arab. To the latter they did not appear to 'nick;' I mean, they did not increase in power or height, or give the produce the beautiful head and straight quarters that distinguish the high-caste Arab. There is nothing like what we call cart-blood in Spain ; all heavy draught is done by mules. In my opinion, the Spanish mares only want the same treatment that a good brood-mare gets in this country to make the produce equal to our own. They are of all colours, many spotted and pied. One very beautiful colour, not uncommon, is Isabel or *café au lait*, with black bands down the back, thighs, and legs."

Colonel Henry Shakespeare, writing on "The Breeding and Rearing of Horses in India," mentions the Kattiwar breed, of the same Isabel colour as the Andalusian. "They stood high for an Eastern horse, 15 hands or more; the prevailing colour a dun, with a black stripe down the back, with black mane and tail; of great power and courage. I conclude that the native mare must have been improved by a cross with the high-caste Arab, for the Kattiwar horse had the beautiful eye, breadth of forehead, and endurance of the Arab."

It is worthy of remark that the big head, with the hooked or Roman nose,* which we so much condemn, but which Spanish horse-fanciers look upon as an essential point of distinction in the pure breed, not a little resembles the Roman-nosed Dongola, the only African horse that, reaching and exceeding 16 hands, has all the quality in skin and hair, and all the fire of the Oriental blood.

It may be that this *carnero* breed is the result of a remote cross with the Dongola, possessing, as he does, the size, power, and slow stately action well calculated to carry a knight in armour proudly, and bear him in a short course at a tournament or in a martial procession. A portrait by Velasquez of the Conde Duque Olivarez, represents that celebrated statesman in armour, mounted on a prancing grey horse, what we should call a dray horse with a back as broad as a prize Shorthorn.

The stallions of this breed are invariably used as riding-horses. Every great Spanish nobleman has or had several in his stables (before English horses came into fashion), trained to the nicest points of manége riding by *picadors*, that is, riding-masters, kept in every great establishment for that and no other purpose.

How they look in a procession has never been better described than in one of George Augustus Sala's letters, from Madrid.

"I was fortunate enough to reach the Fonda de Paris, Madrid, ten hours before the royal entry took place. Now, some loyal admirer at Valencia had presented to the royal youth the tallest, handsomest, and the wickedest white steed that eyes ever beheld. He was Bucephalus; he was Incitatus; he was a Pegasus without wings. He was bigger and more vicious than the terrible black *destrier* which poor little General Prim bestrides in M. Regnault's picture. Now, as the boy king came, bareheaded, with radiant joy in his face, and mounted on his great white horse, into the Puerto del Sol from the Calle de Alcalâ, there arose from the enormous multitude a *gritaria*—a shout not only of loyalty to the monarch, but of admiration for the superb horseman—*caballeresco en su caballerosidad*, as an enthusiastic Castilian by my side

* "The Asturian and Galician horses are described by Pliny to have been of a middling size (like the present genets), remarkable for the time and exactness with which they dealt their feet, and, so to say, regulated their motion as it were to count their steps. Martial, speaking of the Spanish horse, describes their distinct and bold action :—

'Hic brevis ad numerum rapidos qui colligit ungues
Venit ab auriferis gentibus, Aster equus.'
('This little horse that moves his feet in time,
Came from Asturia's gold-producing clime.')

Vegetius (A.D. 392), who lived at Constantinople, and compiled a book on the art of war, says that the African mixed with the Spanish blood produces most active and fleet horses, and the fittest for the saddle. . . Succeeding times have confirmed their character, and they stand now, as of old, most valued and most admired.—"*History and Art of Horsemanship,*" by *Richard Berenger, Gentleman of the Horse to His Majesty.* **1771.**

remarked. It was plain to all eyes that the wicked white horse had got his master in Don Alfonso de Bourbon, and that the Valencian 'Cruiser' knew it."

A Tasmanian traveller, Mr. Carr, who neither understood nor cared for mere parade horses, writes :—

"The Andalusian horse of the present day is healthy and vigorous, works hard on little food, and is up to great weight; but, according to our English notion, he is a brute.

"At a great show of saddle-horses at Seville, held in the Corrida de Toros, I was permitted to descend into the arena, and inspect the animals with the judges. The Spanish judges admire everything we dislike in a horse; they set no store on a lean fleshless head, with an open intelligent eye, and a light, active, firm walk.

"They like a short, high-crested, thick neck, if the horse is fifteen and a half to sixteen hands high, bay being the colour preferred, with a luxuriant mane and tail, short back, body rather round than deep, wide chest, with strong arm and gaskin, good sound feet, wide hips, and muscular couplings; if he performs the *paso* to their satisfaction, is fat as a hog, has a good coat, is placid in temper, but proud and fiery in his gait, he comes up to their idea of what a riding horse should be. His shoulder may be straight and heavy, his pastern straight, his bone round, his head coarse—something, in fact, like the sort of animal that a Suffolk mare might throw to a cart-horse—and he will not be disqualified for a prize.

"He is ridden with a strong heavy curb, his head is held high, and his chin is forced close to the lower part of his neck; then, with the spur in his side he does the *paso*—that is, he seems to walk on his hind legs, while he lifts his fore-feet very high with a dishing turn of each foot, throwing up mud and dust, then plants them with a blow very nearly on the spot from which he raised them. This is the much-esteemed *paso*, which could only be rivalled by our best black funeral stallions. In all the great inland cities of Andalusia you see the young cabellero take his daily ride in the national costume, reining back his steed with the long Eastern curb. The swarthy complexion of the rider, the stately head of the horse, his Moorish saddle and shovel stirrups, the gorgeous shawl that falls across his knees, the many-coloured housings, and huge tail tied up with ribands, recall, as he passes down the narrow cartless streets, the day of his Moorish predecessors."

PORTUGUESE HORSES.

Portuguese horses, or rather ponies, have no European reputation, but they have, according to Mr. Latouche, some of the merits of all Eastern breeds—endurance, showy heads and tails, and a sort of grace. In a country of such indifferent roads there is no such pleasant way of travelling as on horseback, for a man who speaks the language. A native proverb says, "A good man on a good horse is a servant to no man; the caballero stops when he pleases, and eats and lodges where and how he chooses." The Portuguese horses are moderately strong and active, but seldom exceed thirteen hands in height.

The horse brought by the Saracen conquerors was "an Arab pony—not the Barb"—which was, says Mr. Latouche, the produce of a cross between the pure Arab and an indigenous horse of the Barbary coast. High-actioned trotters show the Barbary horse.

In the early days of the Portuguese monarchy, a man, although not of noble blood, who kept a horse (for war purposes) at his own expense, was remitted the jugada—the tax levied on every man who kept a yoke of oxen.

Horse-dealing in the Iberian peninsula is carried on with a dignity and deliberation that is amazing and irritating to an inexperienced purchaser of English, Scotch, or Irish race. Mr.

Latouche, wanting a horse to ride a long journey, was returning from a search through Malaga, without finding one to his mind, when, in his own words, "I perceived a gentleman in high boots, with immense silver spurs, a well-used velveteen jacket, and a dirty red sash wound several times round his waist. He had so evident an expression, attitude, and bearing, of being connected with horse-flesh, that I instantly accosted him. After being shown a lot of miserable ponies, 'Sir,' said I, with solemnity requisite in horse-dealing in Spain, 'pray look well at me, and having done so, inform me on which of these animals you recommend me to confide my person for a journey of some three or four hundred miles.' The horse-dealer gravely and politely removed his hat for the purpose of the desired inspection, and having concluded it, he replied, 'Caballero, I perceive you are not to be imposed on. These animals are certainly not capable of carrying your distinguished person;' he ended by telling me that he possessed one horse of superlative excellence." Finally, after much bargaining, Mr. Latouche purchased a strong, serviceable Andalusian, which turned out well on a long journey, for £25.

NORWEGIAN HORSES.

A few years ago, before Norway had become one of the established playgrounds of English travellers, Norwegian ponies could be purchased in that country at very moderate prices, and a good many were imported. Some fine specimens of yellow duns, with black points, manes, and tails, were seen in very fashionable carriages in London. The best have fair knee-action, although not fast, eight miles an hour being their average pace. From their docility they make very suitable pairs for ladies' phaetons; but as their chief merit lies in their endurance on long journeys on scanty fare, and as the home demand has greatly increased, it is only by exception that a superior Norwegian pony can be picked up worth the cost and trouble of importation.

SERVIAN HORSES.

On the Morava Valley road, although we found no evidences of war, there was more traffic than we had seen between Belgrade and Semendria. Long strings of bullock carts were passed or met, drawn by white oxen with black muzzles, the doubles in all save ferocity of the Chillingham cattle. Equestrians there were in plenty, riding with short leg—à la Cossack—on the high ridge of a Turkish saddle, made higher still with housings and blankets, and with feet stuck in stirrups that served as slippers at the same time. They mostly were mounted on weedy, blood-looking ponies, with wild, vicious heads, ewe necks, high rumps, a great deal of tail and mane, and any quantity of daylight under them. I saw very few that would have been cheap at a five-pound note; but they make capital hacks, these greyhound-like animals, ambling along at a great pace under any quantity of Servian baggage, with head high in air and legs wobbling about in a curious intricate fashion that comes out all right in the end. Servia is a great horse-breeding country, and there trots alongside the traveller by waggon or on horseback the foal of the mare in the shafts or in the saddle. No doubt the horses are suited to the country.—*Correspondent of the Daily News.*

BULGARIAN HORSES.

"The account of our life in the Dobrudja," writes Mr. Barkley in his "Five years in Bulgaria," "would be incomplete without a short description of our two horses, Cole-ci and Kar-yardi (dun, and snow-streaked).

"Cole-ci was a beautiful mixture of dun, chestnut, and bay, with ashen on his coat it would have puzzled Rosa Bonheur to paint. He came from Central Asia, his sire a pure Arab, his dam of common breed, not quite well up to 14 stone, and as beautiful as a picture. He was a little swell, and a rollicking one too, but when pushed would go through the hardest work and put up with the poorest fare.

"Kar-yardi had no great beauty about him, and was not, like Cole-ci, of the swell type. He was a thorough-going workman. Like Cole-ci he had Arab blood in him, as all good horses in Turkey have, but he did not show it much. He had a long body, short legs, never carried much flesh, and had a raffish look all over. He was the best-tempered beast in the world in and out of the stable, and no vice; but his fixed idea was to pull at his rider's hands from morning till night; he would run away at a walk; and when once in a gallop there was no stopping him. I have ridden him thousands of miles, and can safely say that he was all the time running away with me; but he became the property of a lady, and with her never pulled an ounce; if she lent him to a man he bolted directly. He was nimble as a roe-deer; would jump a high gate with ease. Both horses became passionately fond of coursing."

AMERICAN HORSES.

There were no horses on the American continent until it was colonised by Europeans. The beast of burden of the Peruvians was the lama; the horses ridden by Cortes and his companions were taken by the Mexicans for a sort of centaur beast.

The horses of the United States and of Canada are the descendants of English breeds, crossed with a few imported Arabs. The Dutch settlers brought some of their cart-horses to New York.

In Virginia, Maryland, and other Southern States, the tastes of the English yeomanry were imported with the settlers. Blood hunters and race-horses were bred, and riding on horseback was one of the habits of the Southerners until the great rebellion brought their means to an end.

In the Northern States driving and trotting matches have been popular amusements for nearly a century.

An American paper, in September, 1878, after reporting that the famous *Rarus* had fairly trotted *two successive mile heats in two minutes thirteen and a half seconds*, the fastest time on record, quotes the following from the *Connecticut Journal* of June 19, 1806. "FAST TROTTING.—Yesterday afternoon the Haerlem racecourse of *one mile distance*, was trotted around in *two minutes* and *fifty-nine seconds* by a horse called Yankey, from New Haven a rate of speed, it is believed, never before excelled in this country, and fully equal to anything recorded in the English sporting calendars."—*N. Y. Spect.*

At that date some of the best thoroughbred blood of England had been imported into the United States. "Amongst those was Diomed, the winner of the first Epsom Derby, who covered for many years in America, and died at thirty-six years old, leaving hundreds of offspring to perpetuate his name. No State in America, and no province in Canada, is without sires and mares combining the blood of Lexington and of Yorkshire." According to the opinion of a recent traveller in the States, "the blue grass of Kentucky has produced a race of horses as good as any in the world for the production of English hunters."

During the struggle between France and Germany, when Europe seemed trembling on the verge of a universal war, attention was drawn to Canada as a country from which our War Office in emergency might draw a supply of troopers, so long as we maintained the command of the seas.

The Canadian horses of the present day are the produce of the French breeds already mentioned and crosses of English blood, introduced by British colonists, by military men quartered in the country, and by Canadian Agricultural Societies, and also of some of the approved sires raised in the United States. They are entirely employed in harness; riding on horseback, except in the capital towns, not being the custom of the country, or possible at all in the long winters.

Colonel White, who commanded a regiment of cavalry many years ago in Canada mounted on native horses, wrote several letters in favour of the idea of importation. He said they were hardy, active, docile, remarkably surefooted, and in every way suited for cavalry purposes. His views were confirmed by other known equine authorities, amongst others by Colonel Soame Jenyns, C.B., who told the Lords' Committee on Horse Supply that "Canadians made first-rate troop-horses, very fairly bred, capital hacks, a little straight in the shoulder, which is of course objectionable, but wonderfully good sound horses, and capital fencers—such as you get here for £60 or £70—admirable animals." Canadian horses are merely harness-horses, no one rides them; and they want a great deal of bitting. A large number are exported to the States. In answer to a question from H.R.H. the Prince of Wales, Colonel Jenyns said, "In general they are not so valuable as ours, but if judiciously picked they would be quite as valuable. I bought 180, and I do not think I ever had better troopers." This was in 1870.

Frank Forester, an English sportsman who settled in the United States, considered that all special breeds had been absorbed into one general American race, possessing a large admixture of thoroughbred, and that from these, most of them crossed with thoroughbred, the incomparable American trotters are selected and trained. He speaks with especial praise of the Vermont draught-horse, which must be something very different from the dreadful picture which illustrates that chapter of his book—a representation of a horse in the first stage of tetanus. "In 1837," he says, "during the Canadian rebellion, the 1st Dragoon Guards were magnificently horsed from Vermont, and the whole of the artillery from a heavier class of horses of the same district; and," he continues, "I heard a distinguished officer of rank say that the artillery had never been better horsed."

But the town residents of the United States are not given to horse exercise. There are few men of leisure; those engaged in business find it less trouble, less an interruption to business thoughts, to drive than to ride; besides—probably not a small consideration in a country where the men and women expend such vast sums on outward and visible signs of wealth—harness affords more room for display than any number of saddle-horses. The same rule prevails there which has been noted in one of the early chapters of this book. The first step of the wife of the new rich man towards making a stir in her world of fashion is to order a carriage in which she may display furs, feathers, velvet, and lace—a very pleasant and harmless kind of vanity.

The prices given for a pair of American trotters far exceed anything paid for the finest steppers in London or Paris.

But recently the fashion of European carriages, built for comfort and for show, not for speed, has made its way among the fashionable "upper ten" of New York, with whom our coachmakers are doing a good deal of business, and these must be horsed with something very different to the American trotter, so inimitable in its own particular way. They want more substance at some sacrifice of pace.

A Lincolnshire wolds farmer, a very hard rider with hounds, and fond of dealing in horses, who spent some time in the States, and who travelled from New York to San Francisco, told the writer that "the trotting-horses, for their particular work on the soft sandy roads of the country, were so superior that we have nothing to compare with them; but they cost from £500 to £1,000 each, and a racing trotter sire of reputation will fetch from £3,000 to £5,000. When a friend at San Francisco drove me out with a pair of four thousand dollar trotters, we generally walked all but half a mile out and half a mile back to town. Trotting in mail phaeton style, eight or ten miles an hour, in perfect form, is not understood at all; everything is sacrificed to pace. I never met an American gentleman who took a ride alone for pleasure. Amongst the stock-breeders of California I met some famous horsemen, but the majority ride in the old Spanish saddle, in which leaping is out of the question, for if your horse fell you would be impaled on the piques."

HUDSON'S BAY HORSES.

Major Butler, in his "Great Lone Land," gives the following account of the endurance of North American horses, which appears to rival that of the Tartar steppes:—

"It was the last day of October, almost the last day of the Indian summer; the horses trotted briskly on, under the care of an English half-breed named Daniel. My five horses were beginning to show the effect of their incessant work, but it was only in appearance, and we increased instead of diminished the distance travelled each day. We had neither hay nor oats to give them, there was nothing but the dry grass of the prairie, and no time to eat but the cold frosty night. We seldom travelled less than fifty miles a day, stopping one hour at mid-day, and going on again until dark.

"My horse was a wonderful animal; day by day I feared that his game little limbs were growing weary, and that soon he must give out. But not a bit of it; his black coat roughened, his flanks grew thinner, but still he went gamely on. When I dismounted, to save him, and let his companions go on before, he never rested until I mounted again, and then he trotted briskly on until he regained them. At the camping-place my first care was to remove saddle, saddle-cloth, and bridle, and hobble him with a bit of soft buffalo leather twisted round his fore-legs, and then poor Blackie hobbled away in the darkness to seek his provender. After a time we drove all the horses down to some lake, where Daniel would cut little drinking-holes in the ever-thickening ice. Then up would bubble the water, and down went the heads of the thirsty horses at the too often bitter spring, for half the lakes and pools between the Assiniboine and South Saskatchewan are harsh with salts and alkali. Sometimes night would come down upon us whilst still in the midst of a great treeless plain, without shelter, water, or grass. Then we pushed on in inky darkness, and Blackie stepped out briskly, as if he could never tire. On the 4th of November we rode over sixty miles, and when we camped in the lee of a little clump of bare willows, Blackie and his comrades went out to shiver through their supper on the cold, snow-covered prairie, the bleakest scene my eyes had ever looked upon."

So pathetic is the story Captain Butler tells of the end of poor Blackie that I cannot omit it, although not exactly within the scope of this chapter. The party had to cross a half-frozen river.

"Would the river bear? that was the question. We went out early, testing it with an axe and sharp-pointed poles. In places it was very thin, but in other parts it rang hard and solid to the blows. The dangerous part was in the very centre of the river. One light horse was passed safely over. Now came Blackie's turn. I was uncomfortable about it, and wanted to have his shoes off, but my experienced companion demurred, and I foolishly gave way. Blackie was led by a long line; I followed close behind him. He took the ice quite readily. We had got to the centre of the river, when the surface suddenly bent down, and to my horror my poor horse plunged into the deep, black, quick-running water. He was not three yards in front of me when the ice broke. The horse, although he plunged suddenly down, never let his head under water, but kept swimming stoutly round, trying all he could to get upon the ice. All his efforts were useless. A cruel wall of sharp ice cut his knees as he tried to lift them on the surface, and the current repeatedly carried him back underneath. I got almost to the edge of the hole, took hold of the line, but could give him no assistance in his struggles. Never shall I forget how the poor brute looked at me. If ever dumb animal spoke with unutterable eloquence that horse called to me in his agony; he turned to me as one from whom he had a right to expect assistance. 'Is there no help for him?' I cried to the other men. 'None,' was the reply; 'the ice was dangerous all round.' I rushed back to the camp where my rifle lay, and back to the spot where the poor beast still struggled with his fate. As I raised the rifle, he looked so imploring that my hand trembled; another moment and the ball crashed through his head. With one look, never to be forgotten, poor Blackie went down under the cold ice. I went back to camp, sat down in the snow, and cried like a child."

It is to the United States and Canada that this country must in future look for any considerable supply of full-sized, well-bred horses.

They have been, and are being, so largely imported, both of a cheap sort, for use in London tramway cars, and Liverpool cabs, and of a superior class by the trade, at large prices, for hunters, hacks, and carriage horses, that it would be superfluous to describe them—especially as, if the best Americans are mixed up with a number of English bred horses, it is difficult to distinguish the one from the other.

I closely examined a number of the American horses which were imported in 1878 for use in the North London tramcars. They were nearly all remarkable for quality and action, with neat heads and tails stylishly set on. They had courage, and were very good-tempered. The defect of the inferior sort was being too long in the leg, and too much split up behind. They are said to have remarkably good constitutions. Altogether, taking the number imported at one time, at necessarily low prices, they were far superior to the average of anything imported from the continent of Europe. There cannot be a doubt that when the American breeders fully understand the nature of our demand for riding-horses, they will be able with their vast tracts of grass lands and crops of maize, to supply it—"at a price!"

They are the only nation except ourselves that have sires with quality, size, and action. The American stallions are more sound and have better trotting action than average English blood-horses.

In preparing this second edition of the "Book of the Horse," I was fortunate enough to receive from Mr. J. Sharples, "A Horseman," who had spent twenty years in various parts of South America, the following practical description of the various breeds of South American horses.

HORSES OF THE RIVER PLATE STATES.

The horse was introduced in the southern continent of America in the sixteenth century, by the Spanish "Conquistadores." During the frequent commotions and "guerillas" which distracted their early settlements, some of their horses (both stallions and mares) escaped into the immense plains (pampas), and there formed themselves into herds, which were sub-divided by the natural instinct of the animals into families, called by the Spaniards "Manadas." These herds. being left in peaceful possession of the plains, multiplied in the course of time to such an extent that they now form an essential part of the national wealth of the Argentine Republic.

The number of horses pasturing on the plains of the Argentine Republic at the present day has been roughly computed at two and a half millions, not including the east coast of the river Uruguay, which probably contains an additional half-million. The annual *nett* increase may be set down as 300,000, the residue finding their way to the slaughter-houses (saladeros), or perishing in the long droughts from want of pasture and water.

The provinces of Buenos Ayres, Entre Rios, Santa Fé, Corrientes, and Cordova, are the cnief horse producers; the remaining provinces, indeed, are insignificant contributors towards the grand total.

The breed is undersized, averaging about 14.1 or 14.2 hands, and are of every conceivable colour. Piebalds and skewbalds, when curiously marked, were much sought after some twenty-five years ago, and brought more than average prices. A very beautiful colour, now, unfortunately, almost extinct, is the "plateado"—a white horse with black skin, magnificent prominent black eye, and bluish-black muzzle. There are also some beautiful shades of dun, with black stripe along the back and across the shoulders, and black bands on the legs. Horses of this colour are supposed by the natives to be descended indirectly from the donkey, probably on account of the black cross on the back. An exception as to size is to be found in the southern districts of Buenos Ayres, notably in the *Montes Grandes* (Great Thickets), where horses of 15 hands and 15 hands 2 inches are frequently to be met with. The difference in size is owing to the richness and abundance of the herbage, also to the shelter which the woods afford from the heats of summer and the cold of winter. On account of their size they command far above average prices in the city of Buenos Ayres, as hacks and carriage horses; but for work on a cattle farm, or for a long journey, they are quite inferior to their smaller brethren. Plenty of large, roomy mares might be selected from these districts for crossing with imported sires, and would give what is at present the great desideratum—size.

The breed of horses in the Argentine and Oriental republics is extremely hardy and enduring, and exempt from nearly every ailment that afflicts horseflesh. Hence I consider the breed as constituting a good foundation for the building up of a superior class of horses; and, to my mind, there is no doubt but that the liberal introduction of thoroughbreds from England and elsewhere, combined with a judicious selection of mares, will in a short time so improve the existing breed, that exportation from those countries will become an extensive branch of business.

During the last thirty years many attempts have been made in the right direction by the introduction of European sires, and with the best results, as far as the production of useful, shapely, and good-sized horses is concerned.

As far as I can learn, the first thoroughbred sire introduced into the province of Buenos Ayres since the conquest was in the year 1850,* and in the following year a second was sent out from this country.† Since then numbers of European stallions have been introduced; and, notably during the past year, scarcely a steamer leaves for the River Plate without having on board one or more thoroughbreds, or heavy cart-stallions.‡ The latter, however, is totally unfit

---

* Bonnie Dundee, by Bay Middeton, imported by Mr. Samuel Renshaw Phibbs.

† Elcho, by Harkaway, taken out from this country by Mr. James Sharples.

‡ During the past eight months I myself have sent out five thoroughbreds—viz., Lifeguard by Lancer, Climber by Westwick, Sir Joseph by Sir Garnet by Fortunio, Rupert the Brave by Rupert, Bernac by Fitz-Gladiator, also two cart and one roadstei stallions.

for the small South American mares.   After the thoroughbred, what is most required is an active, clean-legged, smart-looking horse, about 15.2 hands, such as I have often seen in tradesmen's goods carts in the streets of London.

Breeding horses in the River Plate States, so much favoured by pastures and climate, and with an unlimited quantity of mares from which to select, cannot but prove lucrative if carried on by men of intelligence, and with a fair knowledge of their business.   But they must be prepared to expend time and money in the introduction of thoroughbred stock, and be content to await the result.   The day will come when the southern continent will be a formidable rival of the northern in the exportation of horses, and it depends upon the exertions of the breeders whether that day be remote or otherwise.

HORSE-BREEDING IN THE RIVER PLATE STATES.

The common system of breeding in the settled districts at the present day differs very little from the natural system which the horse had established for himself on the open plains some 300 years ago.   The herds are divided into families called Manadas, which pasture all the year round in the open, exposed to all the vicissitudes of weather and seasons, and are, as occasion requires, driven up to the homesteads and enclosed in the "corral," for the branding of the foals, denuding the mares of their manes and tails for the sake of the hair, or for the domestication of the colts.   Newly-formed Manadas are frequently enclosed during the night as a precaution against straying; also when horse-stealers are about, and when mosquitoes are prevalent, the annoyance from these being such that horses will stray long distances up wind during the night.   Each of these Manadas has a stallion at its head, and consists usually of twenty or thirty mares, with a sprinkling of colts and fillies.   Over these the stallion keeps most jealous watch, pursuing and bringing back, in no gentle manner, any mare which attempts to wander.   By instinct, the stallion does not allow full-grown fillies, his own progeny, to remain in his harem, and he suffers them to be appropriated by his rivals without opposition. He will also appropriate any stray mare which may come his way, and occasionally he will make a raid on a neighbouring Manada, and attempt to steal away a mare or two, when right royal fights take place between the rival stallions, and the prize is carried off by the victor.   These fights are very frequent in the plains, and occasionally are to be witnessed between horse and stallion donkey, often ending in the victory of the latter; indeed, the horse as a rule does not seem to care much about attacking the donkey, having a wholesome dread of his teeth, which he uses in fight with the same tenacity which distinguishes the Bulldog.

The selection and occasional changing of stallions for their "Manadas" is the only improvement or modification of the system established by the horse himself at the time of the conquest, at least as far as concerns the great majority of native breeders; exceptions are to be met with in a few of the native and most of the foreign breeders.

The old class of "Domadores" (breakers)—a set of reckless centaurs—is now almost extinct; in fact, I only saw some half-dozen during the latter years of my residence in the Argentine Republic, 1865 to 1875.   That such is the case is, however, matter for small regret, for, though they were grand horsemen, and endowed with a courage which made light of perils calculated to dismay a foreigner, they were bad breakers, and so violent and rough in handling horses, that they ruined a vast number that passed through their hands.   About the year 1855 I employed one of this class to break some ten or twelve colts.   His daring and the way he stuck to a buck-jumper, was something wonderful to behold; no effort or manœuvre of the horse could unseat him, nor was he ever hurt by the horse throwing himself down or backwards. Yet he was, withal, a bad breaker; indeed, he did not know what a really well-broken horse was, and if he had known, I believe he would have preferred a plunger or a buck-jumper to a steady one. He invariably vaulted into the saddle, never using the stirrup, cared not how much they shied, nor how they went. The result was that out of the dozen colts which I gave into his hands, one half were unsafe as hacks, and the others were lamed in the process of breaking. The "Domador" of the present day is vastly inferior in pluck and horsemanship to him of the past, but horses come out of his hands much better broken and in sounder condition than formerly, so that a fair horseman may ride them with moderate safety, if not with pleasure.

There is a remarkable exemplification of instinct in horses, which may or may not be peculiar to horses bred in the Pampas, but which I have never seen in print. It is the wonderful manner in which horses, taken away from their birthplace, will return as soon as they regain their liberty. I have known horses return two or three hundred miles, swimming rivers, and overcoming every obstacle. It matters not if they be taken away at night, or by a circuitous route, they will find their way back—not indeed by the circuitous way they may have come, but in a direct line. It always appeared to me a marvellous instinct which could guide them so unerringly over such long distances, over immense open plains, with scarcely a landmark to assist them. This instinct, though common to all horses that are taken from one breeding-ground to another, is, however, much stronger in some than in others. For instance, horses reared on rich pasture have the instinct much stronger, or at least they retain it much longer, than those reared on poorer lands. Those bred in the districts of the Montes Grandes, where the grasses are especially luxuriant, scarcely ever lose this home-pining; and though they are the finest-looking horses in the Republic, they are of little value to farmers, as it is next to impossible to keep them from straying. As hacks, in the city of Buenos Ayres, they soon lose this instinct, probably owing to total change of diet and the comforts of a stable. A very marked exception to this instinct is to be found in the "Bagual"—strictly speaking the wild horse of the Pampas, as distinguished from his domesticated or semi-wild brethren of the settled districts. The "Bagual," when captured, tamed, and taken to the settled districts, seems to lose this instinct entirely. He has also another very singular peculiarity—the transformation from a wild to a domesticated state causes him to lose his gregarious habits. He will stray away here, there, and everywhere, but seldom will he associate with other horses, and never with the same for any length of time. This horse is popularly supposed never to become thoroughly confidential for riding, being it is said, apt to buck-jump and plunge when least expected. I, however, had one for five or six years. He was very quiet and steady, and a good useful horse for general purposes. He would not have the head-collar at any price, but would stand saddled loose all day long, with the reins put behind the stirrup leathers.

Horses of the Banda Oriental, or east coast of the river Uruguay, are much the same in general characteristics as those of the Argentine Republic. In size they are a trifle smaller than those bred in the southern districts of Buenos Ayres, but they stand almost unrivalled in powers of endurance, frequently compassing journeys of 100 miles in the day. Owing to civil wars, revolutions, and petty broils, few attempts have been made to improve the existing breed by the introduction of European sires.

Horses of the West Coast (Chili). The republic of Chili, on the west coast of the southern continent, produces a breed of horses superior in size, quality, and shapeliness to those of the

River Plate States. Bays, blacks, and browns, are the prevailing and most esteemed colours. The origin of this breed is identical with that of the Argentine horses, and their superiority may be traced to more careful selection and breeding. In height they vary from 14.3 to 15.2, but their chief superiority consists in their fine action and perfect education.

As far as my experience goes, no pleasanter or more perfect hack exists; for what better qualities are to be looked for in a hack than an exquisite mouth, easy paces, good up action that renders stumbling an almost impossibility, fine courage, high mettle, and extraordinary tractability. I speak here of the superior and not general class of horses in Chili. The Chilian horses have usually high action, but the trotting pace is twofold; some being trained to throw their feet outwards towards their arms; these are called "brazeadores," from "brazas," Anglicè "arms"; others have straight, high action (much preferable to the former), and are called "pisadores," steppers. Their high action is partly natural, inherent to the breed according to some, and the result, according to others, of the nature of the land on which they have been reared, which is stony, rugged, and intersected by numerous watercourses. Their natural high action is increased and improved during the process of breaking by means of *bolitos* (wooden balls about an inch and half in diameter, loosely beaded into a string, and tied round the pasterns of the fore-legs, which have the effect of causing them to throw their legs high). The high action towards the arms (*brazeadores*) is produced by tying strong strips of raw hide round the pastern, and which are allowed to trail on the ground to the length of six or seven inches. To avoid treading on them, the horse throws his legs outwards, and in process of time this becomes a second nature, and clings to him through life. A Chilian horsebreaker is a breaker in the best acceptation of the word; he is a perfect master of his art, and quite at the top of the tree as an educator. The Argentine, on the other hand, is a breaker in the worst meaning of the word, and the best among them cannot turn out a horse with perfect manners. The Chilian requires a much longer time to educate a horse, but the delay is amply compensated for by the accomplished manner in which he does his work.

I have ridden hacks by the score, both in England and South America, and the pleasantest one I ever crossed was a Chileno. He had extraordinary mettle, but was so gentle and tractable that a girl seven years of age has frequently ridden him; his mouth, paces, and manners were perfection, and I never remembered him to have committed a fault either in the stable or in the saddle. He would have been an invaluable horse for a timid lady to ride in the Row; I don't think he would have gone wrong in a crowd with the reins thrown loose over his neck.

The bit in use in Chili is, I believe, similar to the Moorish bit introduced by the Spaniards 300 years ago. It is very severe, and requires good hands, especially with young horses. My friend, Mr. Downes, rode a thoroughbred mare regularly in Hyde Park with a bit of this description, contrary to the advice of his friends, who said she would rear and fall backwards with such a thing in her mouth. He made her wonderfully handy in two or three weeks, and she was much admired; but her rider was one in a thousand as far as regards "hands."

For polo I consider the riding horses of Chili much superior to anything I have yet seen; but I must confess that my experience is limited, having only seen some dozen games. They are, however, much quicker on their legs, and can be brought up in a much smaller space than any of the polo ponies I have seen; and were I fond of the game I should not be long before I had one brought over.

The curiosity of the American horse tribes is the Mustang, or Indian pony, described in the following passages from the most recent authorities.

THE INDIAN MUSTANG.

When the red Indian of North America first began to ride on horseback there is no evidence to show; but Captain Butler, in his "Great Lone Land," states that the Indian word for horse also means "big dog."

Viscount Southwell exhibited a mustang at the Agricultural Hall in 1867, which he has thus described in the catalogue: "Ishto Plac, an Indian war-horse; dark chestnut; 13 hands high Bred by the Comanche Indians of North Texas, North America." This pony was sent without bridle, saddle, or any man to show him off, and was therefore exhibited at the greatest disadvantage. He was very docile, just of the stamp that you could buy at that time in a fair in South Wales for about £15. It is to be presumed that Lord Southwell would not have gone to the trouble of sending an inferior specimen to England.

The following account of these animals, on which, Tartar like, the Indians have for centuries carried out their border raids against Mexican, and recently against Texan settlers, is by Lieutenant.-Colonel Dodge, of the U.S. army, who commanded a force employed to keep them in check.* It must be taken with some allowance for the American taste for sensational statements.

The pony used by the red Indians of America is scarcely fourteen hands in height, rather light than heavy in build, with good legs, straight shoulders (like all uncultivated horses?), short strong back, full barrel; he has no appearance of "blood," except sharp, nervous ears, and bright, intelligent eyes; but his endurance is incredible. He is never stalled, nor washed, nor dressed, nor blanketed, nor shod, nor fed. When not under saddle he is picketed or turned loose to shift for himself.

In winter he is a terrible object—an animated skeleton. His pasture being buried beneath the snow, he would perish if the squaws did not cut branches of the cotton-wood tree for him to browse on. But when the spring brings out the tender grass he sheds his coat, scours his protuberant belly, and moves with head erect, ears and eyes full of intelligence. He will climb steep rocks like a mule, plunge down a perpendicular precipice like a buffalo; only the elk can more successfully cross swamps, and he will go at speed through sand-hills and ground perforated with holes, where an American horse would fall in the first fifty yards of a gallop. The work he can do is astonishing; no mercy is shown.

The Indian pony is the same animal as the mustang, or wild horse of Texas. He is sufficiently tractable to the rough-riding Indian, but when stabled, and fed on corn and oats, he becomes either a vicious, dangerous brute, or a fat, lazy cob.

An Indian will ride a horse from the back of which every particle of skin and much flesh has been torn by the ill-fitting saddle, ride him at speed until he drops, then force him to his feet, and ride him again.

There is a "plain" saying that a white will abandon a horse as broken down; a Mexican will then mount and ride him fifty miles further; an Indian will then mount and ride him for a week.

Riding is second nature to the Indian, strapped astride of a horse as soon as he can walk.

The bit is the Mexican bit; the bar bent in the centre, from two to four inches long, extends backwards to the horse's throat. To the upper end is attached an iron ring, which embraces the chin, and forms a curb. Long side levers are attached to the bar with reins of horse-hair or raw

* "Hunting Grounds of the Great West." 1877.

hide. The head-stall is of horse-hair, elaborately ornamented with silver or plated buckles. With his bridle the horse can be turned on its haunches with one turn of the wrist.

The saddle is a light frame of wood, the side pieces shaped to fit a horse's back. The seat is almost straight, and nearly forms a right angle with the pommel and cantle; these are about eight inches above the seat. The pommel ends with a knob. The cantle, rather wide at top and bottom, is cut away in the middle to fit the leg or heel of the rider, and form his support when he throws himself (out of sight) on one side of the horse, right or off-side, leaving the left hand free to grasp the reins, while the right grasps the mane or pommel. When riding under ordinary circumstances his seat and carriage are very ungraceful; the short stirrups force him to sit almost on the small of his back; his head pokes forwards as far as his neck will let him; his left hand holds the reins, his right is armed with a short stick with a lash of raw hide. With a light blow of this he marks every slip of his horse. He has no spurs, but his heels are constantly drumming his horse's ribs with a nervous motion. He scarcely ever turns his head, and when most watchful appears to see nothing. Looking stiff, constrained, uncomfortable on horseback, he yet will, with his horse at full speed, pick a small coin from the ground, and throw himself on the side of the horse in such a position that only a small portion of his leg or foot can be seen on the other side.

The ponies are as carefully trained as the riders. Colonel Dodge relates (but does not say that he was present) how a Comanche pony in Texas, "a miserable sheep of a pony, with legs like churns, three inches of rough hair all over the body, with a general expression of neglect and helplessness and patient suffering, which struck pity into the hearts of all beholders," ridden by a stalwart Comanche of one hundred and seventy pounds (12st. 2lbs.), armed with a club, first won a race of four hundred yards from the third best horse of the garrison by a neck.

Then another race against the second-best blood-horse. "The officers, thoroughly disgusted, proposed a third race, and brought to the ground a magnificent Kentucky mare of the true Lexington blood, which could beat the other two at least forty yards in four hundred. The Indians accepted the challenge, and not only doubled the bets, but piled everything they could raise on it. The riders mounted, the word was given. The Indian threw away his club, gave a whoop, and the sheep pony pricked his ears and went away two feet to the mare's one. The last fifty yards of the course was run with the rider sitting with his face to the tail of the pony, grimacing horribly, and beckoning the rider of the mare to come on!" (!!!)

The woodwork of the saddle is covered with green hide, which drying, binds all the parts together, and makes the saddle almost as strong as iron.

The girth is a broad band of plaited hair, terminating in iron rings, which are attached to the saddle on the principle of the Mexican cinche, by which a man of ordinary strength can almost crush a horse's ribs.

The stirrup is of thin wood, fastened to the saddle with raw hide. The skin of a wolf or calf, or a pair of old blankets, is used as padding between the horse and saddle. The stirrups are extremely short and of little use, except to mount or rest the feet.

PONIES IN MARYLAND.

"The little nag I bestrode was barely fourteen hands, and although I rode thirteen stone and a half, and had come twenty miles over very bad roads, she was just as fresh and anxious to push on as if she had just left the stable. All I saw would have been regarded as extraordinary little creatures for their inches. More lasting, more valuable, not so high but stouter, are the Beach ponies, brought from the island of Chincolique, a long, comparatively waste on the Atlantic sea-board, where they roam about in large herds, wild as the mustangs on the prairies of Northern Mexico. Since their capacity for work, high courage, and sure-footedness have become known they have become expensive. Ten of the Beach ponies which I saw at Baltimore reminded me much of the admirable ponies which are found in Morocco. The outline, topping shape of head, and setting on of both, were the same Their origin is unknown. Probably they are of Spanish breed, bred originally in Mexico."*

AUSTRALIAN HORSES.

The Australian colonies *had* horses equal to any in the world either for useful or ornamental purposes. (I said "have" in my first edition, but in this I correct my error.) The first settlers imported them chiefly from the Cape and from Valparaiso. These were crossed with the thoroughbred sires imported from the mother country.

The country was as favourable to the multiplication of horses as the plains of South America, and the breed came of a better stock than the Spanish. One of the principal pursuits of the colonists—rearing cattle—required good horsemen, and these, being Englishmen, lost no time in establishing horse-races; indeed, it has been asserted that in 1870 the stakes run for at the races of the Australian colonies exceeded in value those of all the governments of the Continent put together; without counting the catch-weight races which are held whenever a few stockmen—that is, cattle herdsmen—are gathered together.

As the colonists grew rich, they indulged, amongst other luxuries, in the importation of thoroughbred horses and mares, purchased in England at the highest prices of the day. The consequence is that the three colonies of New South Wales, Victoria, and South Australia are well provided with blood-horses of the purest pedigree; and Queensland, the great island of Tasmania, and New Zealand (the Britain of the South) have race-meetings conducted with all the English forms and ceremonies. The Australian bush horses are equal in powers of endurance to anything recorded in equine history, but in other respects, in consequence of the manner in which they have been treated, they have deteriorated, and are inferior in quality and symmetry to the small select stock of riding-horses raised when New South Wales and Tasmania were the only colonies in that region.

Of late years some very fine Arabs have been imported by Australian colonists, but not enough is known at present to state anything certain of the results. If anywhere, the desert Arab transplanted should find a congenial home in the hot plains of Australia.

There was a considerable trade in the export of Australian horses to India for military and racing purposes, where they are familiarly known as "Walers," an abbreviation of "New South Wales," but that trade has recently declined in importance.

The Australian horse has deservedly the reputation, both at home and in India, of being vicious, especially for a trick of spitefully plunging (colonially, "buck-jumping").

The explanation is simple enough. The breed has not the placid temperament of the Spanish horse, will not bear the brutal treatment under which the Spaniard cowers and trembles.

"Time and labour," said Colonel Mundy, in 1847, "are precious in these colonies. Each poor brute is broken by force in a few days. He is handled, lunged, backed, and turned out a 'made horse;' broken in spirit, or a 'buck-jumper' for life. The Australian buck-jumper, roaching his back, bounding into the air, and descending on four stiffened legs, with his nose between

* Parker Gilmore.

his knees, will not only unseat nine good horsemen out of ten, but at times actually force the saddle over his withers, if he does not succeed in bursting the girth.

"I was fortunate," says the colonel, "in possessing several excellent saddle and driving horses, amongst them a pair of carriage-horses of such figure and action as are not often out-done in Rotten Row.

"My faithful Merriman, who served me during the whole period of my stay in Australia, I doomed to a merciful death two days before I left the country, bringing away with me as a relic his splendid mane, attached to a strip of the skin. The hair is twenty-six inches long; and the 'rein,' *i.e.*, the space along the side of the neck from the spot where the mane springs on the wither to the root of the forelock, measures the uncommon length of four feet seven inches.

"His height was under 15 hands 3 inches; steady, yet spirited as a charger, gentle and safe as a lady's horse, honest at the wheel, fiery yet tractable as a leader, old Merriman was one in a thousand."

The deterioration of Australian horse stock is to be ascribed to the bad custom of permitting a herd of horses and mares to run loose together without any attempt at weeding or selection.

The great horse-breeders in California adopt a plan copied, we presume, from their Spanish predecessors. They pick out a stallion and about forty mares, *corral* them—that is, keep them in a pound for a certain number of days—and then turn them out to the open pasture plains. The mares then keep to the horse, and the horse permits no intrusion, at least not until he has been defeated in pitched battle by some rival sire.

Nice intelligent little boys are to be met with in France and Germany by travellers of paternal instincts, some extraordinary musicians and capital dancers; but we fancy that such precocity as described in the following contrast is peculiar to the Anglo-Saxon breed :—

"At the Marine Hotel the post of waiter was filled by a lad about twelve years old, the son of our landlord. He brought up our meals, waited at table, joined in conversation, drew and helped to drink the wine, knew everybody and everything about the place. He constituted himself my guide in our rides to see the lions of the neighbourhood; assuring me that his three-year-old filly, by Young Theorem out of a 'Scamp mare,' was nearly clean bred, that he had broken her himself, and that she was a pleasant hack."

"A highly-entertaining scene is the driving in from their pastures of a 'mob' of young horses. Two or three mounted stockmen had started by daybreak to hunt up the number required. About ten o'clock the sound of the stock-whip—an awful implement, having twelve or fourteen feet of heavy thong to two feet of handle, and crackable only by a practised hand—accompanied by loud shouts, and a rushing sound like the stampede of the South American pampas, announced the coming of the cavalry. They came sweeping round the garden fence at full speed, shrouded in a whirlwind of dust, and in a few minutes, snorting, kicking, and fighting, about 150 horses were driven within the stock-yard, surrounded by stout railings seven or eight feet high.

"The highest leaps I ever saw were taken on this occasion by some of the wild young colts; more than one heavy, perhaps ruinous, fall was the result."

Tasmania, formerly known as Van Diemen's Land, is the "Sleepy Hollow" of the Australian colonies. With a magnificent climate, warm yet temperate, without the drawback of the violent winds and snow-storms that affect New Zealand, it vegetates for want of elbow-room in pastures and the stimulus of mineral wealth.

"On the way to the racecourse," writes Colonel Mundy, "we were passed by a dog-cart or two driven by young farmers; by fast-trotting hacks ridden by rustic beaux in tops and cords, straw hats and hunting-whips.

"The running was absurdly bad, but there were some very nice horses on the course, and a few of a good old-fashioned stamp, such as is not common anywhere, and is unknown in New South Wales. Among the running horses was a mare worth going some distance to see, 'The Farmer's Daughter,' a splendid creature for size, shape, colour, and breeding; 16 hands high, jet-black without a speck, and of admirable symmetry. She would have made a sensation in Rotten Row mounted by one of the tall swells of the period, although far from first-class as a racehorse."

Such were the impressions of an English colonel thirty years ago. Twenty years later a Tasmanian colonist* lifted up his voice, or rather took up his pen, to point out the steady deterioration of the Australian horses which had taken place within his remembrance. He commences by saying that, "Circumstances have led me, during twenty years, to pass more time in the saddle than falls to the lot of most men. The journeys I have made of from 100 to 1,000 miles are innumerable. I have lived amongst people of similar occupations. I have had personal experience of the horses of England, Ireland, France, Spain, Turkey, Syria, Palestine, Egypt, Brazil, and New Zealand, as well as those of Australia and New Zealand."

In the early days of New South Wales considerable care was used in breeding saddle-horses. Sires were selected with some judgment, and fillies allowed to reach a fit age before they were bred from.

The first horse stock came from England; full-sized mares were imported from the Cape of Good Hope and from Valparaiso, pony mares from Lombock and Timor; a constant succession of thoroughbred sires were imported from England, most of them unfortunately racing weeds. Arab sires have also been introduced from the Cape and India, but not in sufficient numbers to have much effect on the native breed. But as colonists multiplied and spread over the country, and horses were bred in increasing numbers with little or no attention to the quality of the sires, or the age of the dams, the horse stock rapidly deteriorated.

The foundation of the colonies of South Australia and Victoria (Melbourne) opened a new market for the horses of New South Wales, and this is the Tasmanian's account of them in 1840:—"When I landed in Melbourne horses were coming slowly from the Sydney county—poor, stunted, miserable wretches, the produce of early breeding and haphazard sires; leggy, boneless abortions, with here and there an occasional 'Satellite' horse, one of the remnants of the original New South Wales stock, 'sinewy, of exquisite symmetry, with great power.' Worthless as the mares were, anything decent sold for £60; but before the flood of insolvency of 1843 ceased three of these £60 horses would barely fetch in the market of New South Wales the price of one saddle.

"Taken as a whole, the saddle-horses of Victoria, New South Wales, and Queensland—of which I speak from personal observation (I believe those of Adelaide offer no exception) are in height decidedly below those of England, inferior in figure, utterly wanting in quality. Year by year they have been settling down to a dead level of badness, and the bright exceptions that were frequent twenty years ago (1843) have all but totally disappeared. Amongst the scores that are sold by auction every day, scarcely one tolerably good colt could be picked up. The Australian horse, in comparison with the English horse, is ill-broken, his temper cross, his paces disagreeable, and, if compared with the horses of the Arabs, of southern

---

* "English, Arab, Andalusian, and Australian Breeds of Horses." By E. M. Curr. Melbourne.

Italy, Asia Minor, or Egypt, he is sluggish in temper, unsound in his legs, soft in hoof, and wanting in stamina. The one favourable feature in our Australian horses is their great capacity for work as compared to their figures. Thus, a hundred miles are frequently done in Australia by very miserable-looking wretches, in fifteen hours, without preparation, and off grass. Eighty miles for two days consecutively, and seventy miles for three or four days running, are constantly ridden in the routine of business. In a journey of 400 miles I have started with two fat horses, neither of which had been backed for a month previously, riding one, leading the other with a small pack on his back, changing the saddle occasionally from one to the other. The 400 miles were always accomplished without trouble in eight days, and after three days' rest the horses were ready to return at the same speed. Each night they were trotted out, usually on very scanty grass, and never tasted artificial food of any kind.

"My object in taking two horses—a practice which is common in New South Wales, and amongst the Boers at the Cape—was because, if obliged to camp out, two horses in company will generally stop well; whereas one, however tired, will often, even in hobbles, wander ten or fifteen miles, and not be found for a week. I rode thirteen stone in those days, and could have done the last hundred miles in fifteen hours had I desired it.

In overlanding with cattle—that is, driving from one colony where the cattle were bred, to South Australia or Victoria, in the early days of colonisation, the drivers are allowed two horses each—the work was done at the slowest possible walk, for the horses are under saddle twelve hours at a stretch, and are ridden and rested alternate days. The journey often lasted ten months. If the grass was plentiful the horses grew fat; if scarce they became skeletons.

"The English specific for the improvement of the horse races had not been neglected. Jockey Clubs in Sydney, Melbourne, and Adelaide, offered prizes for winners with no niggard hand. The betting rings were well attended, betting was brisk, black-legs became acclimatised and flourished. In fact, I know no country where racing has been carried on so extensively in proportion to its population as in New South Wales. In that district you cannot find a township where there are but half a dozen huts congregated together that does not boast its annual races—hardly a roadside bush public-house that has not its racecourse. I have seen races over stony ground, hilly ground, hard sun-baked plains rent with wide fissures, and over land heavily timbered."*

The plan recommended by Mr. Curr for the improvement of Australian horses was the destruction of the mass of wild horses, and the introduction of well-shaped Arab sires (a race of pure *saddle* horses) instead of English racing, greyhound-like stallions, bred to gallop five furlongs with a feather-weight.

Something has, I believe, been done in this direction in New South Wales. If the parliaments of these vigorous colonies come to consider the wild horse a commercial nuisance, he will be extinguished as wolves were in Great Britain, and by the same means.

Mr. Anthony Trollope, a horseman and sportsman, several of whose novels form a perfect text-book for the tyro in the hunting-field (for his portraits are equally true and unflattering), found the wild horses of Australia just as the Tasmanian colonist described them.

"The herds of wild cattle and wild horses which roam and wander at will over the pastures of distant squatters, afford perhaps the most remarkable evidence of Australian fecundity. It is by no means an uncommon thing for a squatter to drive in four or five hundred wild

* *Live Stock Journal*, 1879.

horses to yards prepared for the purpose, and there to slaughter them. If any of them be branded, thereby showing that they are not in truth wild, but are or have been the property of some individual, the brands are advertised and the horses pounded, so that the owner may recover them on paying the expense. This is at least what should be done. It is, I fancy, generally found easier to shoot them and to destroy the skin, so that no testimony may be left as to the brand. The skins and hair of those which are really wild are sold, and the carcases are destroyed. Now and again a wild horse may be found as to which it is decided that he shall be kept, and broken in, and used. The value of the animal, however, seldom pays for the trouble and cost. They are very pretty to look at as they are seen scouring over the plain or rushing into the thick scrub; they are sleek, and bright-eyed, well furnished with mane and tail, and they go with a free action, but they are not often well made or fit for use, having almost always poor shoulders, with straight limbs, and narrow chest. They are already becoming a pest to the squatter, destroying his fences, eating his grass, and enticing his own horses out of the horse paddock. The work of running them in is not bad sport; but they who do it must be well mounted, and the doing of it is utterly destructive to the horses ridden.

"A Victorian coach, with six or perhaps even seven or eight horses, in the darkness of the night, making its way through the timbered forest at the rate of nine miles an hour, with the horses frequently up to their bellies in mud, with the wheels running in and out of holes four or five feet deep, is a phenomenon which I should like to have shown to some of those very neat mail-coach drivers whom I used to know at home in the old days. I am sure that no description would make any of them believe that such feats of driving were possible. I feel that nothing short of seeing it would have made me believe it."

CAPE HORSES.

Cape horses acquired a high reputation amongst military men when we kept a number of regiments permanently to defend the colonists from Kaffir invasion at the expense of the Imperial Government, and when the Cape was the regular half-way station of all ships bound to India. The following extract of a letter addressed to the *Country Gentleman's Paper*, dated "King William's Town, 21st August, 1878," gives late information on a very important subject:—

"Having been in King William's Town, the headquarters of the army during most of the campaign which has now come to an end, I have had opportunities of seeing some thousands of horses sent down for remount purposes, for artillery, mounted infantry, and volunteers. The neighbourhood of King William's Town is not a horse-producing country, so most of the horses bought for remounts were purchased between Queenstown and the Orange Free State by men sent up by Government. The price allowed by Government for mounted infantry and volunteer horses was £25, but the average price given was about £21. The animals sent down were what in England would be called ponies, of from 13.2 to 14 hands, certainly capable of doing hard work with a small amount of food, and suffering hardships which would kill an English horse, as during the campaign they have had to stand out at night without blankets, sometimes in pouring rain, and at others with the thermometer under 30°. But this class of horse would be quite unfit to mount an English regiment of cavalry, as they could neither carry the weight of a man in marching order, nor move at the pace required.

"A horse of 15 hands is looked upon out here as quite a *rara avis*, so much so that when a field battery of artillery landed in the country in the beginning of this year, it was thought by most of the people in King William's Town impossible to get horses of sufficient size to draw the guns. However, Captain Smith, R.A., who was sent by the General to purchase for the battery, managed to get together a remarkably good-looking lot over 15 hands, at an average price of £25; but I believe he had to go over a very large tract of country before doing so. From all I can learn it would now be quite impossible to send from this country five or six hundred horses fit for artillery and cavalry purposes, as was done in the Indian mutiny time. This is the more remarkable, as no country is more suitable for horse breeding than this, almost every farmer having large tracts of grass land far in excess of what he requires for his stock, and well suited for horse rearing; but unfortunately those who do breed horses seem to give no thought either to the selection of mares or stallions. The consequence is that the breed of horses in this country is steadily degenerating year by year. There is no doubt the Cape horse stands the Indian climate much better than the Australian horse, being a hardier animal, and continuing fit for work to a much more advanced age. The Cape horses imported during the Indian mutiny are still spoken of by cavalry and artillery officers as the finest lot of horses ever imported for army purposes into India. Unless the subject is taken up either by the Colonial or Indian Governments, I think in a few years there will be scarcely a good horse in the country, as the colonists themselves rarely use horses for draught purposes, and seem to be quite satisfied if they can get an undersized pony at a small price to carry them twenty or thirty miles, after which they knee-halter and turn the poor brute out to grass without grooming or feeding, apparently not much caring whether it is alive or dead in the morning. For this reason a high-priced horse would be looked upon as rather a nuisance, requiring a certain amount of care which they seem unwilling to give."

HOTTENTOT DRIVERS.

"Eight or ten swift wiry little horses are harnessed to a wagon—a mere platform on wheels—in front stands a wild-looking Hottentot, all patches and feathers, and drives them best pace all 'in hand,' using a whip like a fishing-rod, with which he touches them, *not savagely*, but with a skill which would make an old coachman burst with envy.

"I watched the process of breaking a couple of colts, which were harnessed second and fourth in a team of ten. The colts tried to plunge, but were whisked along and couldn't; then they struck out all four feet and skidded along a bit, but the rhenoster bushes tripped them up (there are no roads), and presently they shook their heads and trotted along quite subdued. Colts here get no other breaking, and therefore have no pace or action to the eye.

"The wagon teams of wiry little thoroughbreds, half Arab, look very strange to our eyes, going at full tilt. There is no such thing as a cock-tail in the country.

"I could write a volume on Cape horses, such valiant little beasts and so composed in temper I never saw. They are nearly all bays, a few dark greys, very few white or light grey, I have seen no blacks, and one dark chestnut. They are not tall, and have no beauty, but one of these little brutes will carry a six-and-a-half-foot Dutchman sixty miles a day, day after day at a shuffling easy canter, six miles an hour; you let him drink all he can get, you off saddle every three hours and let him roll, his coat shines, his eye is bright, and unsoundness is rare, their temper is perfect. Every morning all the horses of the village are turned loose; a general gallop to the water tank takes place, where they drink and lounge a little, the young are fetched back by their niggers; the old stagers saunter home by themselves. Our groom at home would be astonished at offering a horse on a journey nothing to refresh himself but a roll in the dust!"*

"A very pleasing farmer put his own and his son's riding-horses in a cart and took us for a little drive. At a hard gallop (with the mildest and steadiest air and with perfect safety), he took us right across the country; over bushes, ditches (there were no fences), lumps of rock, watercourses, we jumped, flew, bounded, and up every hill we went at racing pace. I arrived at home much bewildered, but Mr. M——'s pleasant face was quite undisturbed, and I was assured that such was the way Cape farmers always drove." †

* Lady Barkley's Journal.　　　　　† Lady Duff Gordon's Letters from the Cape.

CHAPTER VII.

HEAVY DRAUGHT-HORSES.

The True Cart-horse—Natural Pace a Walk—Weight Essential—Size of Value—A Dray-horse the largest Type—The Opposite of the Blood-horse—The Cart-horse a Distinct Breed—Not to be Ridden—To Draw Great Loads at a slow pace—No Cart-horse will Breed a Blood-horse—No Blood-horse a Cart-horse—Present to Runjeet Singh—Dray-horses—Astonished the Sikhs—Origin of Cart-horse in Netherlands—Attained Perfection in England—Size and Pluck—The Light Cart-horse the War-horse of Rubens—Modern Cart-horses Divided—London Dray-horse—The Shire-horse—The Clydesdale—The Suffolk Punch—The Old Suffolk Punch of the Last Century—Mr. John Cullum on—Trials in Pulling Weights—Suffolk Mares Formerly Used to Breed Hunters—Lord Strathnairn's Recollections of Lord Jersey—Points of a Model Plough-horse—The Lincolnshire Black—Now Superseded—Scotch Origin of Clydesdale—The Speaker's Carriage Drawn by Pickford's Van-horses—Description of a Cart-horse—Age of Cart-horses—Commence at Two, Die at Twenty—New English Cart-horse Stud Book Society.

THE true cart-horse—the heavy animal whose natural pace is a walk, whose power consists in no small degree in his weight, whose temperament should be essentially placid, and who must to be of any value in the condition of life to which nature and art have called him, greatly exceed in stature and weight the most useful class of nag-horses, is found in his grandest form in the London dray-horse.

The illustration of this chapter is copied from a portrait of one of the finest of the teams of Messrs. Barclay, the great brewers, and represents at one end of the scale what the portrait of the blood-horse, the Drake, at page 91, does at the other.

The blood-horse and the dray-horse will breed together, and their produce will be fertile, but with the exception of that fact in natural history, their qualities differ as much as those of the horse and the poor man's friend, the much-enduring ass. The cart-horse requires courage, but not the sort of courage which blood bestows; he requires pluck to move and draw a heavy load, and to pull again and again if required until he stirs the inert mass; but the courage of the blood-horse would in him be quite out of place. The beauty of the cart-horse depends not only on quality and symmetry, but on a sort of elephantine ponderosity that bespeaks power in every muscle and every limb.

The true cart-horse is a distinct breed, which soil, climate, and food may decrease or diminish in size, or otherwise vary; but which no change, no selection, however careful, could convert within historical times into anything but a cart-horse, destined for drawing heavy loads.

In the same way, the blood-horse uncrossed may be as small as a Sardinian pony barb, or tall as the last roaring monster of the English turf; but no external changes can bring his bones, his muscles, or his blood to the condition of the draught-horse breed. In the East, the birthplace of the blood-horse, the cart breed is unknown.

When the East India Government wished to make a present to Runjeet Singh, the old "Lion of Lahore," they sent him a pair of London dray-horses, 18 hands high; these were perfectly useless in that country, where heavy work is much better done by elephants, but the objects of unbounded astonishment and admiration in a land where any horse over 15 hands is tall, and where the cart breed is unknown.

Many specimens of fairly good draught-horses may be found in Flanders and Northern Germany, whence we derived the progenitors of our carty breeds; in France, here and there very fine teams of small muscular cart-horses may be purchased, especially in Paris and the provinces bordering on Belgium. The *Percheron*, already described, is the most esteemed and useful breed in France. As you travel south you find the ox and the cow doing cart-horse work, until you pass the line, where, for road work the mule is preferred to either ox or horse. But it is in England that the cart-horse, like every other kind of live stock valuable in agriculture, has attained the greatest average perfection, because the principles of breeding have been more carefully considered by our farmers than in any other country, and also because it is the country where, as compared with the rest of Europe, the roads are good, the farmers are rich, and the hereditary landowners, as a matter of pride and duty, without regard to immediate profit, have led the way in this as in every other stock-breeding improvement.

The first heavy draught-horses of which we have any authentic record were bred in those fertile districts of Northern Europe where agriculture was in an advanced state while our rural condition was little better than barbarous.

When William III. took possession of the throne left vacant by James II., the Dutchmen who followed in his train, and set to work to drain the fens of our east coast, brought with them the heavy black horses of their country; and from somewhere about that time the black cart-horse became naturalised in England, and has since reached its highest development in the fen counties.

A somewhat lighter animal, with a good deal of the cart breed in him, had been in use from the eleventh century, as long as heavy armour was worn; for nothing less powerful than a Mecklenburg half-bred cart-horse would bear a knight encased in iron and steel. But these huge animals were not expected to move beyond a walk except for about a hundred yards in "a course" at a tournament, or on a battle-field. The knights did not ride these ponderous and picturesque brutes upon journeys, or for pleasure, or hunting. Their squires led the war-horse bearing the armour; while the knight, without it, mounted a good roadster hack or prancing genet.

The ideas of the general public on the subject of war-horses have been very much confused by the historical pictures of eminent artists, who, if they paid any attention to details of costume, generally drew the horses from some conventional model of decidedly cart-horse descent. The mane and tail being the most important points in an artistic point of view, modern painters have mounted Eastern princes—from Saladin to the last Shah of Persia—on Flemish destriers; and Boadicea harangues the Iceni from a Roman car drawn not by her own ragged hill ponies, but by steeds stout enough to be harnessed to Queen Victoria's state coach.

In modern England draught-horses have attained their present perfection because they are strictly bred to draw heavy weights, and not to carry heavy men.

According to agricultural writers, at the commencement of the present century there were distinct breeds of draught-horses in at least half a dozen English counties; at present nearly all such distinctions have been effaced, and until quite recently it was only by exception that the purchaser of a plough or wagon team made any inquiry as to breed or pedigree, unless it was of the chestnut Suffolk breed.

For all practical purposes the true draught-horses of England may be divided into the

R.C.WEST. Sc.

ENGLISH DRAY-HORSE, FROM THE STUD OF MESSRS. BARCLAY, PERKINS, AND CO.

London Dray, the Shire Horse, the Clydesdale, and the Suffolk Punch, the Cleveland Bay having become extinct, or nearly so. It is only within a few years that the Scotch have taken the lead in establishing a Stud Book for Clydesdales, and it was not until the year 1878 that the breeders of Suffolk English cart-horses followed the sound example.

THE DRAY-HORSE.

The London Dray-horse (and all the horses of the same size and character used in Liverpool and Manchester) is recruited from the largest specimens of the true Shire horse, slow, stately, ponderous, not less than 17 hands high, often 18 hands; he is in horses what a corporal major of Life Guards is to a private of Dragoons.

Weight in the brewers' horses is essential, because they have to move great weights for short distances, and the shaft-horse frequently has to hold up and back and turn with enormous loads; for although barrels do not look very large, when filled with beer their gravity is far in excess of the idea conveyed by their bulk. No doubt something is due to fashion and tradition, in the employment of these equine giants by the beer kings of London. First-class farmers, who plough the stiffest land deeply, who are not content with what Mr. Mechi called "the traditional three inches of agricultural pie-crust," consider that 16 hands high is high enough for the very best plough or cart team, although they do not object to an additional inch in an active, well-shaped animal.

Formerly the twelve great brewing firms, familiarly known as the "Beer Kings of London," used to be as particular about the colours and matchings of their dray-horses as of their own four-in-hands or the Court chariot pairs of their titled wives: one was celebrated for a black, the original dray-horse colour; another for a brown, a roan, a grey, or chestnut team. But at present such is the demand for horses of this class, that they are compelled to be content with any colour, and to moderate the old standard of height. The parade of teams belonging to Liverpool merchants, on the occasion of the annual show of the Royal Agricultural Society of England being held in the year 1877, was probably the finest gathering of dray-horses ever witnessed.

Following the plan adopted in preparing this work, of going to headquarters for special information, a set of queries were forwarded to Mr. James Moore, junr., the veterinary superintendent of Messrs. Barclay, Perkins, & Co.'s. stud of brewery dray-horses, to which he has, with the sanction of the firm, kindly returned the following pithy answers:—

"Heavy draught-horses suitable for dray work are English bred, and are generally from Wiltshire, Berkshire, Oxfordshire, Herefordshire, Lincolnshire, and Yorkshire; bred by farmers who in many instances are horse-dealers.

"They are bought at five to six years of age, and last about ten years.

"One horse here stood 18 hands high, and weighed nearly 18 cwt. He was a fine handsome red (or strawberry) roan horse, named 'Baly.' When Garibaldi visited the brewery, in 1864, he particularly noticed the horse, and he was ever afterwards known as Garibaldi. He was about seventeen years old when he died, in 1870.

"There are several horses at the present time in the brewery that stand 17½ hands high, and they are mostly of a roan colour.

"No mares are used in the brewery.

"Horses that are used for our country work travel from twenty-five to thirty miles on some days. It is rather difficult to say what distance the horses used for town work travel.

"The weight drawn in a two-wheeled dray is from 3 tons 16 cwt. to 4 tons ; two horses used, sometimes three.

"The weight drawn in a four-wheel van is from 6 tons to 6 tons 10 cwt. ; three horses are used, sometimes four.

"Their food consists of—

Oats, 13 lbs., beans, 6 lbs., maize, 3 lbs. = 22 lbs. per day per horse.
Clover chaff, about . . . . 15 „   „   „

15 „   „   „
—
37 „   „   „

Sometimes peas are given, then either beans or maize are stopped.

"From April to September about two thousand bundles of green tares are consumed amongst the sick and rest horses.

"From May to August three hundred bundles of green tares are given to all the horses every week for about fourteen or fifteen weeks ; one bundle is given to each horse on Saturday evening, and one on Sunday morning.   Carrots are occasionally given.

"The cost of feeding, including the above items, amounts to about three shillings per horse per day.

"Brewers' horses are not, as you suggest, kept for ornament, but for work.

"Shoeing costs about one shilling and eightpence per week, being about fifty-nine shoes per horse per year.   As a matter of course, some horses wear their shoes out sooner than others.

"The diseases to which brewers' dray-horses are subject are catarrh, influenza, bronchitis, congestion of the lungs (more in summer from violent exertion), nephritis, hepatitis, weed, cellulitis, colic (more cases of colic on commencing green food), sandcracks, treads, quittors, and wounds from picking up nails, stones, and other foreign agents in the streets.   We have had several cases of ruptured livers between 1867 and 1874, the livers in these cases weighing respectively 73 lbs., 89 lbs., 82 lbs., 61 lbs., and 101 lbs.

"Horses will drink beer if they can get it.   We generally give it when they are recovering from an illness, and with beneficial results.

"The vulgar idea which exists that brewers' horses are fed upon wet grains is incorrect.

"Dray-horses are not so heavy as they used to be ; they are shorter and stouter.   The animal known as a 'little big horse' is preferred ; a smaller horse is more active, and gets over the ground quicker ; this accounts for the great demand at the present time for the Clydesdale breed.

"I think the popular opinion that roans, red and blue, are more hardy than horses of other colours, is correct.

"We use neither bearing-reins, nor winkers on the bridles.

"In a few years' time the brewer's two-wheel drays will be a thing of the past.   They are a great weight upon the horses' backs.   I have known several instances where horses have been permanently injured through falling down, and a cask of beer, generally a puncheon, weighing over 8 cwt., rolling over their loins."

THE SHIRE OR ENGLISH CART-HORSE.

The Shire horse is the final result of the improvements of agricultural horses commenced early in the first half of this century.   He is found in the shires where the strongest class of plough-horses are required—a breed, if it is a breed, which has superseded the Lincolnshire black horse, which Bakewell of Ditchley, the first man who clearly laid down the principle of breeding live stock, thought he had brought to perfection. Bakewell had crossed the native Lincolnshires with Dutch stallions, and they held a prominent place in the works of every agricultural writer up to 1825. As late as 1840, Mr. Burke, who was one of the editors of the early volumes of the Transactions of the Royal Agricultural Society of England, wrote in a note on cart-horses: "A Lincolnshire black of the pure breed stands foremost in the rank of every cart race in the kingdom." But this opinion has not been maintained by the decisions of the judges at the shows of this Society, the balance of favour being decidedly towards well-shaped cart stallions, bay and brown being predominating colours, although blacks and greys have also taken honours. Honest Tom, supposed to be the best cart stallion ever shown in an agricultural ring, was a Shire horse of a bay colour. In the counties where the cultivation of a stiff retentive soil has been carried out on large farms, the name "Shire" has for several generations been the accepted term. But when an attempt was made to found a stud-book of agricultural horses not being Clydesdales or Suffolks, the name was objected to as being too narrow and special, and the indefinite title of the *English Cart-horse Society* was adopted. Nevertheless, the Shire horse is the only agricultural horse which has a pedigree to be traced for from seventy to even a hundred years.

The following description of this tribe is from the pen of a gentleman who has devoted many years to collecting and breeding specimens of first-class merit for use in his business and on his farm.

"In considering the more important points in an agricultural horse, I will place action first. Unless he can move true and well in the cart, horse pace-walking, his value is considerably lessened; if required to trot—and trotting in these fast days has for many purposes become a necessity—he should have the action of a Norfolk cob.

"The feet should be well proportioned, better too large than too small: depth of foot and width at heel being important elements, but wide flat feet are very objectionable, especially for road purposes.

"The fore-leg should be put on parallel at the shoulder and wide enough, so as to support weight. Too great width between the fore-legs is not often seen, but is possible; this is objectionable, as it generally impedes the action. The pasterns should not be long or straight. The leg-bones flat and short between fetlock and knee ; they should not measure less than 10 or 10½ inches below the knee. A stallion should not be less than 11 inches; a few reach 12 inches. The Earl of Ellesmere had one that measured nearly 13 inches. The hinder legs of a cart-horse are even more important than the fore-legs. A horse should not be "split up" too high behind, or be cow-hocked; he should have large, round thighs, large, flat, clean hocks, short pasterns, and the leg should measure between the hock and fetlock at least one inch more than the fore-leg. The legs should be well covered with long *silky* hair, this being regarded as a sign of constitution."

As to height, 16 hands 2 inches is high enough for work, but 17-hand horses sell well. Seven feet six inches is a good girth, but 8 feet is often reached. "The first thing," said an eminent War-wickshire grazier, "that I look at in a cart colt is 'his cupboard.' If this is not roomy he will not have the constitution to stand a day's work." The chest should be wide, shoulders well thrown back, head big without coarseness, back short, with wide muscular development of the loin, long quarters, and the tail set on well and high. To sum up: a good specimen of the Shire horse is a long, low, deep, wide, well-proportioned, and active animal. Geldings of this description are in great demand, and in their prime fetch from 100 to 140 guineas each.

The other points of a Shire cart-horse are those of every well-shaped harness-horse, considering always that most his business is all to be done at a walk; in towns at the present day a good deal of the work of cart-horses has to be done at a trot. "With double-furrow ploughs fast coming into use, horse-engines requiring speed, good size—not at the expense of activity and compactness—is essential."

The famous black horse no longer exists with sufficient distinctness to claim a class, like the Suffolks, but crops up from time to time in his native county, Lincolnshire. And colour is never an objection in any cart-horse otherwise well shaped, not being a Suffolk. Many breeders of Shire horses are steadily selecting browns or bays.

Mr. James Howard, of Clapham Park, Bedford, who, as a plough manufacturer (James and Frederick Howard), had so often, before steam cultivation was established, to compete in ploughing-matches with such famous horse-masters and plough-makers as Messrs. Ransome of Ipswich, and Hornsby of Grantham, gives the following idea of a very perfect

AGRICULTURAL CART-HORSE.

"Captain was one of a pair of cart-horses with which I took the first prize and gold medal at the Grand International Exhibition in Paris in 1867. He was a dark bay with black points (no white), as clean in the legs as a thoroughbred, height 16 hands and ½ in., weight, in good working (not show) condition, 14 cwt. He girthed 7 ft. 2 in., the circumference of his thighs was 21½ in., and that of his fore-arms 24½ in. The length of his fore-legs 31 in. The other horse was an excellent match. The pair showed immense power, accompanied with great elasticity and quickness of movement, always an indication of pluck.

"I prefer a cart-horse under than over 16½ hands. The three cardinal points are quality, symmetry, substance, and action—that is, a firm, quick, not too long and striding action. Some breeders say a draught-horse cannot well be too short on the legs. I differ from this opinion; if very short their pace is sure to be slow. Captain was not too short, for he could walk pretty well as fast as a man.

"The legs should be outside the animal, so that each bears its fair share of the weight of the carcase. You cannot well have too much bone; the thighs and fore-arms in particular should be large and muscular; the hocks big, clean, and well defined; the knees should be broad and large. I do not like much hair about the heels, although some breeders say it is a sign of constitution. Some of the strongest and best constitutioned horses I have had have been as clean as a blood horse.

"The body of a cart-horse should be cylindrical, or well arched in shape, broad across the loins, and deep in the girth. The back ribs should also be deep; a shallow-back-ribbed horse, in nine cases out of ten, has not endurance, and is seldom or never of a robust constitution. I never buy a narrow horse—breadth of frame is essential, and a horse split up far behind should be avoided; a good *posterior* is a very important consideration.

"The head should not be small or nag-like, but of fair size without coarseness; a long, fine ear, full eye, and intelligent expression. The neck if too short is a great hindrance to the animal grazing. I don't like shoulders made as a hunter's ought to be, but more upright, so as to take the collar at the proper angle; sloping shoulders are not good for moving much weight, neither are long joints. The foot of a horse is a very important point. A broad, flat foot is objectionable; such feet cannot stand the road, and on the land it is difficult to keep the shoes on.

"*As to quality*, it is a thing that is to be understood rather than expressed—it cannot be put upon paper.

"I have bred some very good horses by a Clydesdale stallion out of clean-legged, deep-made mares, bred in Essex. The great fault of most of the Clydesdale horses is their small barrels and want of breadth in the frame. These faults were corrected in the cross I have tried, while the activity of the Clydesdale was preserved."

THE CLYDESDALE.

The Clydesdale is of Scotch origin ; according to tradition, for which there is very little evidence, the result of a cross made by a Duke of Hamilton between the draught mares of the country and some Dutch stallions. It is a breed which was formerly seldom found in England, except on the fancy farms cultivated regardless of expense by great landed proprietors, and maintained as stallions for the benefit of tenants. The Clydesdale is certainly the most taking of the cart race, and only wants, with his handsome head and graceful forehand, a little fining down to figure as a charger in the picture of some imitator of Vandyke or Rubens.

Clydesdales are remarkable for fast action in the walk, and even in the trot. At a local show held some years ago on Clifton Downs, near Bristol, a Clydesdale stallion, exhibited by the Duke of Beaufort, "weighing nearly a ton," out-trotted all the hacks in the show in a course of a few hundred yards. The Clydesdale has more quality in head, hair, skin, and style, than any other cart breed. Bays and browns are the prevailing colours ; the faults are a light body, legs too long, and a hot temper at work. Sixteen hands to sixteen hands one inch is the usual height ; the finest specimens are taller. Of late years the light body has been corrected by judicious crosses.

At a plough trial at Versailles, which took place during the first Paris International Show, a pair of Clydesdale horses, as recorded in a French official report, beat easily several teams of three horses of the best French breeds—Percheron, Boulonnois, &c.

The late Prince Consort had some very fine Clydesdales of his own breeding at his model farm in Windsor Park. The coloured illustration to this chapter has been painted from the stallion Prince Albert, probably one of the best Clydesdales in the kingdom, the property of Colonel Loyd Lindsay, V.C., M.P., of Lockinge Park, Berkshire, who writes, "Prince Albert is 17 hands in height, 7 feet 6 inches in girth, 18 inches round the fore-arm, and 10½ inches below the knee." These dimensions are quite beyond the average.

The finest exhibition of Clydesdales is to be seen at the agricultural shows held at Glasgow and Edinburgh.

At a stallion show held at Glasgow in 1874, at which, besides the Glasgow, more than twenty other societies contributed, offering about £1,500 in prizes, twenty-five Clydesdale stallions of a high class were paraded before the judges. After the prizes had been awarded, the agents of various districts in Scotland and the North of England made arrangements for securing the services of the horses they fancied by paying a premium for their travelling in particular districts. These premiums, by way of retaining fees, varied from £100 to £160 for the season ; in the latter case for a guaranteed list of 160 mares. The colours premiumed at this great show were bay and brown, and one black.

In 1873 the representatives of two horse-breeding associations formed by the farmers of Cornwall each purchased Clydesdale stallions in Scotland at £300 apiece. But Cornishmen have always been famed for independence of character, and put their own shoulders to the wheel instead of whining to a Downing Street Jupiter. The present breed of Clydesdales is both compact and active. Messrs. Pickford and Co. for some years past have used nothing else in their railway vans, and engage the exclusive services of a dealer to buy them at all the horse fairs in Scotland. But, on the other hand, in 1876 a committee of English gentlemen attended the great Glasgow show of cart stallions, for the purpose of selecting and purchasing a young stallion; they found and eventually bought a horse that was left in the ring with nine other competitors for the champion cup, and this, in the home county of the Clydesdales, turned out to be the Shire horse described at page 160.

Both breeds now have stud-books of their own, and this will no doubt tend in future to keep their characters more distinct.

THE SUFFOLK, OR SUFFOLK PUNCH.

The Suffolk is another breed very much esteemed in its own district, and seldom found out of it, except on fancy farms; but there is a steady demand for Suffolk stallions of a good chestnut colour for exportation to the Continent.

According to popular notions, the Suffolk is always chestnut of one of five different shades. Mr. Longwood, who read a paper on this breed of horses before the Stowmarket Club in 1872, mentioned five different shades, viz., dark chestnut, dark red, bright chestnut, silver-beamed, and light chestnut. But, according to the same authority, there are in the county a good many teams of bay Suffolks. Those who breed for sale are particular about purity of colour, and preserve it by the well-known expedient of keeping nothing but chestnut horses on the breeding-farm, and taking care that the mare, when she takes the stallion, shall have a chestnut horse or pony before her eyes—an expedient as old as the time when Jacob served Laban.

The Suffolks are now bred large, and reach from 15 hands 3 inches to 16 hands. They were formerly a small, thick, stocky class of horse, hence called "Punches." The breed is of a remarkably docile and placid temperament, very true in the collar, and excellent for plough teams; but apt, according to agricultural authorities who do not live in Suffolk, to fall lame at road-work or drawing timber. A Mr. Cross, who took part in the discussion of the Stowmarket Club, said that some farmers were of opinion that cross-breds between Suffolk stallions and Cambridgeshire mares stood road-work better than pure-bred Suffolks, which were apt to be light of bone below the knee. But no description of cart-horse fetches higher prices than picked specimens of Suffolks. At a sale, before the dearth of horses raised their prices all over the kingdom, six mares were sold by the Earl of Stradbroke by auction for twelve hundred guineas.

The following is a description of the Suffolk Punch breed as they were before the development of agricultural show competition and comparison.

"They are generally about 15 hands high, of a remarkably short and compact make; thin legs, bony, and thin shoulders loaded with flesh. Their colour is often of a light sorrel, which is as much remarked in some distant parts of the kingdom as their form. They are not made to indulge the rapid impatience of this posting generation, but for draught they are perhaps as unrivalled as for their gentle and tractable temper; and, to exhibit proofs of their great power, drawing matches are sometimes made, and the proprietors are as anxious for the success of their respective horses as those can be whose racers aspire to the plates at Newmarket." *

The *Suffolk Mercury*, 22nd June, 1724, thus advertises the first match that took place:-

---

* "The History and Antiquities of Flamstead and Hardwick, in the County of Suffolk." By the Rev. Sir John Cullum. Bart., F.R.S., F.S.A.

"On Thursday, 9th July, 1724, there will be a drawing at Ixworth Pickarel, for a piece of plate of 45s. value; and they that will bring five horses or mares may put in for it : and they that draw twenty the best and fairest pulls, with their reins up, and then, they that can carry the greatest weight over the block, with fewest lifts and fewest pulls, shall have the said plate; by such judges as the masters of the team shall choose. You are to meet at twelve o'clock, and put in your names (or else to be debarred from drawing for it), and subscribe half-a-crown a-piece, to be paid to the second best team."

Sir Thomas Gery Cullum, in a note to the second edition of his brother Sir John's work, adds : " The trial is made with a wagon loaded with sand, the wheels sunk a little in the ground, with blocks of wood laid before them to increase the difficulty. The first efforts are made with the reins fastened as usual to the collars, but the animals cannot, when so confined, put out their full strength ; the reins are therefore afterwards thrown loose on their necks, when they can exert their utmost powers, which they usually do by falling on their knees, and drawing in that attitude. That they may not break their knees by this operation, the area on which they draw is strewn with soft sand."

In the " Suffolk Agricultural Report," 1794, page 41, allusion is made to these competitive trials of strength : " Amongst the great farmers in the Sandlings south of Woodbridge and Oxford, there was forty years ago a considerable spirit of breeding and drawing team against team for large sums of money. Mr. Mays, of Damsholt Dock, was said to have drawn fifteen horses for 1,500 guineas."

"An acre of our strong wheat land ploughed by a pair of them in one day," observes Sir John Cullum, "and that not an unusual task, is an achievement that bespeaks their worth, and which is scarcely credited in many other counties." "Though natives of a province varied with only the slightest inequalities of surface, yet," he adds, in his panegyric, "when carried into mountainous regions they seem born for that service. With wonder and gratitude have I seen them, with the most spirited exertions, unsolicited by the whip, and indignant as it were at the obstacles that opposed them, drawing my carriage up the rocky and precipitous roads of Denbigh and Carnarvonshire."

Suckling, in his work on the "History and Antiquities of the County of Suffolk," alludes to the Punches as a docile race, unrivalled at what is provincially called "a dead pull." In describing them, he says, " They are middle-sized, very short made, and though low in the fore-hand, are active in their paces, and on the lighter lands of the county will draw a plough at the rate of three miles an hour."

At one time Suffolk Punch mares were used to breed from, crossed with thoroughbred sires, with the view of producing hunters and carriage-horses. But the quality and pace required in the present time will not admit of any admixture of carty blood, although the Suffolk, which trots with empty carts from the hay-field, would occasionally afford some happy hits. General Lord Strathnairn mentioned to the Lords' Committee, of which he was a member, that the Earl of Jersey (the fifth), a very famous horseman and rider, hunting from Melton in its most palmy days, found one of his best hunters in the produce of a Suffolk Punch mare and an Arab sire. At present nothing less than a thoroughbred, clear in the pipes, can live in the first flight of Leicestershire.

The most memorable occasion in modern days of cart-bred horses taking rank with carriage-horses occurred when Her Majesty in solemn procession proceeded to return thanks at St. Paul's for the recovery of the Prince of Wales from an attack of typhoid fever, in 1872. For some unknown reason the Speaker's carriage was not, according to precedent, drawn by six horses, that is, four-in-hand and a pair conducted by a postillion, but by a pair of Messrs. Pickford's finest black wagon-horses, led by their accustomed attendants, clad in gorgeous liveries for that day only. They appeared to walk away with the ponderous coach, as weighty as the Lord Mayor's, at the rate of at least five miles an hour.

On light sandy land plough-teams of a light description may be used with advantage, of the same class as those magnificent animals that may be seen in single harness, in pairs, and unicorns, drawing the spring vans of warehousemen in the City of London. These were formerly bred between Cleveland stallions and cart mares; how they are bred now no one cares to inquire. On the light sandy lands of Bedfordshire and Norfolk, a pair of cast-off carriage-horses, or even hunters, would make a plough-team, but wherever the land is stiff there must be size and weight.

In spite of the rapid spread of steam cultivation, there is still a mass of work on every well-cultivated farm that can only be done by horses and by ploughs. "For this purpose," writes one of the most practical and advanced farmers of the day, "let me have plough pairs at least 16 hands high, as well-shaped as any carriage, girthing from 7 feet to 7 feet 6 inches, as active in walking as a good park hack, with stout limbs and plenty of hair about their feet, a weighty fore-hand to throw into the collar, a sensible but not too small a head, a courageous but docile temperament. Well fed and well tended, they will do twice the work of soft cross-made brutes."

THE BISHOP STORTFORD STALLION COMPANY.

Getting the use of cart stallions, big, sound, and with good action, has as yet been very difficult, because more than half the cart stallions that travel the country are either unsound or ill-shaped, and it has been no one's business to find fault with them. The Stud Books that have been recently established for registering the pedigrees of the Clydesdales, the English Cart-horse (that is really the *Shire Horse*), and the Suffolks, will no doubt do something to check the trade of inferior brutes by establishing a standard of comparison.

An experiment made two years ago at Bishop Stortford, a town in Hertfordshire 40 miles from London, has shown how easily, with little expense, a small committee of farmers may secure the benefit of first-class cart stallions. In January, 1877, a few gentlemen formed " The Bishop Stortford Agricultural Horse Company," with a capital of £2,000, on an entirely new plan.

The nominal capital was divided into 100 preference shares, of £10 each, and 20 promoter's shares, of £50 each. Of these, 60 preference and 20 promoter's were at once taken up. The preference shareholders were entitled to the first call on the entire horses, the property of the Company, and each preference shareholder was bound to send two mares, at a fee of £3 3s. (5s. for the groom), for each share he held, or to forfeit £3 3s. for each mare not sent. No payment of profits, interest, or return of capital, was to be made to any member until the final closing of the accounts, in the year 1879. In that year the Company is to be wound up, and, after the repayment of £10 per share to the preference shareholders, the balance remaining of the capital is to be divided *pro rata* amongst the holders of promoter's shares. Should any balance remain, it is to be divided *pro rata* amongst both classes of shareholders. The capital raised was 12 promoter's shares at £50, £600; 60 preference at £10, £600; sum total £1,200. Two stallions were purchased for less than £1,000; the surplus, which was over £200, was placed at interest, and the two years' earnings of the horses are being added to it. "The result," writes Mr. Walter Gilbey, the originator and most active promoter (on the 24th Nov.,

1878), "is up to date satisfactory; and when the horses are sold, in 1879, there is every reason to believe that the subscribers will get a full return with interest, and I doubt not also a bonus." They will also have had the advantage of the use of two very first-class horses.

The first horse purchased was Paragon—a pure-bred Shire stallion; whole-coloured dark bay, with black legs; stands 17 hands high; bred by Mr. Richard Porter, Sowerby, Yorkshire, in the year 1872. As a three-year-old (1875) he stood third at the open show at Glasgow, gained the Highland Society's silver medal at Kilmarnock show for the best stallion of any age; also a prize at the Highland Society's show at Glasgow. As a four-year-old (1876) he stood in the short leet of 5 out of 71 stallions for the Glasgow prize. As a five-year-old (1877) he was shown at the Glasgow Society's show, and he was selected from 93 competitors (horses of all ages not above ten years old), and left in the prize ring with four other horses to compete for the Society's premium of £100 and a silver medal. After which Mr. Gilbey bought him.

CHAPTER VIII.

ASSES AND MULES.

The Ass the Poor Man's Horse—Feeds like a Goat—Can ill Bear Snow Regions—No Asses in Norway or Sweden—The Abyssinian the Original of the European Ass—Collection of Various Ass Tribes at Regent's Park Zoological Gardens—The Hemione—The Onager, the Zebra, the Quagga—Ass Esteemed as a Hack in the East—A useful Drudge in England—Not worth Corn and Groom's Care—Not a Good Riding Animal—London Costermongers own the best—The best Asses Black or Dark Brown—Anecdote of Hunting—The Ass divided into Two Classes, Light and Heavy (see Illustrations of Cairo Donkey and of French *Baudet*)—Mistake to increase the Size of the British Ass—The Egyptian Donkey Boys—The French Stallion Ass for Mule-breeding—The Poitou Peasant's Ass and Mule-breeding *Cheptels*—Treatment of *Baudet*—Lives to a great Age—Value of Two-year-old Male *Baudet*—Wild Asses—The Syrian Wild Ass, or Hemione—The Indian Wild Ass, or Onager—Not a Donkey at All—Description of Chase and Capture—Story of—Mules and Mule-breeding—Mules used by the Ninevites—In France an Important Trade—Poitou Mules—How Prepared for Sale—The Mule Suited to coarse Herbage and no Roads—Not Found in Flanders, Normandy, or New York—Plentiful Round Avignon—Duke of Beaufort's Agent on Mule-breeding—Mr. Sutherland's advocacy of Mules against Horses—The Cyprus Ass—American Account of—The Henny, Cross between Male Horse and She Ass.

THIS work would not be complete without some notice of the ass—the "donkey" of English children, the "cuddy" of Scotch, the "moke" of the London costermonger, the "*baudet*" of France, the "*borrico*" of Spain, whence the finest breed is derived, and where he holds a place of the highest utility as a beast of burden.

The ass is the poor man's horse; with no groomings, with a rough stable, a sufficient supply of coarse herbage which every other domestic quadruped except the goat would reject, it will thrive, and work, at its own pace, for long hours, either drawing a vehicle or carrying burdens, as it did for Joseph's brethren, a task for which its conformation is particularly suited.

In one respect only is the ass more delicate than the horse—it cannot thrive or multiply in regions where the snow covers the ground for several months of the year. A horse will bear a severe degree of dry cold under which the ass would die. Asses are not known in Northern Russia; and an eccentric traveller who made a tour in Norway with three gipsies and a donkey, found the latter as much an object of curiosity as a tame bear in England.

About the origin of the domestic ass there is not quite so much mystery as about that of the horse. The Zoological Gardens, in 1874, had in its varied collection of the ass tribe a male Abyssinian wild ass, which in no way differs from the ordinary grey donkey of the streets; and if it really is a wild species, and not an importation from Egypt, there can be no question about the African ancestry of our useful drudge.

But the ass tribe has this essential difference from the horse. For breeding purposes there is only one race of horses—all, from the Norwegian to the Thibetan or Siamese, from the Cossack pony to the Sardinian, from the dray-horse to the Icelander, will intermingle freely, and their produce will be fertile—but of the ass tribe there are half a dozen varieties closely resembling each other in externals, which are as distinct as the horse and the zebra, and if brought together only produce mules. Nevertheless, eminent physiologists maintain that the horse, the ass, the zebra, all have one common origin; but the links that would prove that those who now breed a mule would breed a horse or an ass have not been detected in three thousand years.

CLYDESDALE STALLION & MARE.

THE PROPERTY OF COL. LOYD LINDSAY V.C.M.P. FROM A PICTURE BY SHELDON WILLIAMS ESQ.

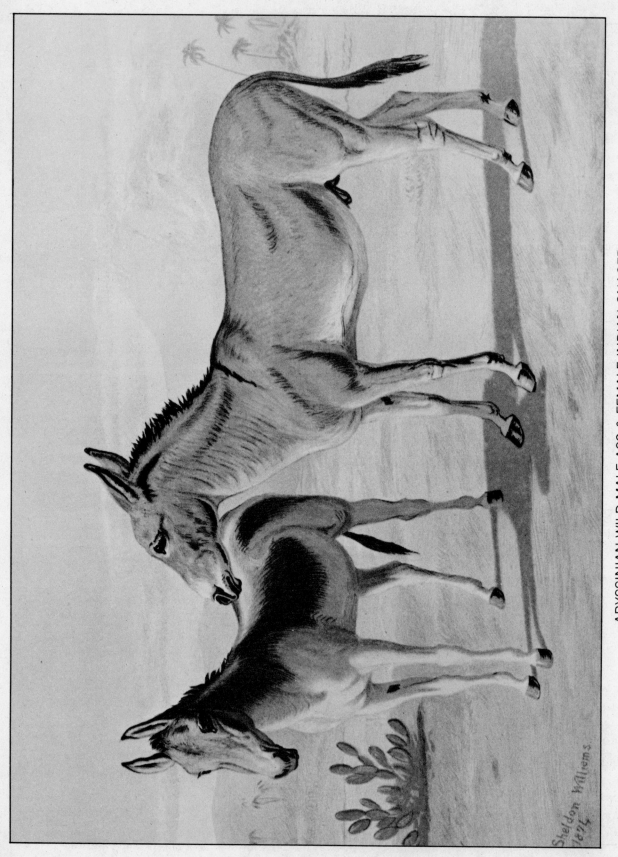

ABYSSINIAN WILD MALE ASS & FEMALE INDIAN ONAGER.

FROM THE RUNN OF KUTCH. FROM AN ORIGINAL PAINTING TAKEN IN THE ZOOLOGICAL GARDENS REGENTS PARK 1874.

BY SHELDON WILLIAMS ESQ.

The ass appears to have been subjected to the use of man long before the horse. The female was preferred for riding, in consequence of her superior docility, and as a dairy animal was of special value to nomadic tribes.

Even at the present day native Egyptians prefer the quiet ass—which neither rears, plunges, nor shies, and keeps a steady pace, quite fast enough under a tropical sun—to the more high-couraged horse, except on occasions of parade. In fact, in the East the horse is chiefly valued as a charger for war purposes; the ass is the hack for daily use where the much-enduring camel is not employed. A wealthy Copt will give as much as £200 for a white ass of good stature and easy paces.

In England a good donkey is invaluable for family use, to enable the young son of the house *to teach himself* to ride, to draw a clothes-basket carriage with a curate's too numerous family, to harness to a cart of appropriate size—in fact, as a humble servant of all work; not expensive to purchase or to feed, not requiring the services of an accomplished groom, and not liable to any worse vice than obstinacy. With a well-trained donkey you are safe from any of those sudden ebullitions of excitement which sometimes bring the soberest ponies to grief. The vicious New Forest horse-fly either spares the donkey, or fails to penetrate its thick hide with the poisonous sting which often drives well-behaved horses, if strangers to the county, to madness.

Except as a question of safety from accidents, the donkey is not a good steed for a boy to commence his career on as a horseman; it has not riding shoulders, and does not afford a proper seat for a saddle. The riders of donkey-races sit on the hind-quarters. Anatomically considered, the ass is essentially a beast for the pack-saddle. The ass has also a mouth so callous to the bit as to lead boy equestrians into very bad habits when they advance in dignity, and have to deal with the exquisitely tender mouths of horses. All donkey-riders not packed in Oriental saddles must hold on by the bridle, a habit fatal to good horsemanship.

As to what may be done with donkeys in harness, the best examples may be seen daily in the streets of London, amongst costermonger hawkers of fruit, fish, and vegetables. As a body the costers are by no means the brutes their appearance and language would convey—at least, in the treatment of their donkeys. The pace at which the costers' asses travel, the distances they complete in a day with a well-balanced load on their clever "go-carts," and the sleek appearance of the animals, prove that in the main they are well treated—often better treated than the costers' wives—and they must be well fed. The owner of a very fast donkey, on the Brighton road, in answer to an inquiry as to how he fed him, replied, "Like a race-hoss."

In all classes of society great affection for dogs, donkeys, and other lower animals is not unfrequently displayed by persons who are, to say the least, hard in their dealings with human beings.

The costermonger lives as familiarly with his donkey as the Arab of the tent with his horse; he lives in the same room with him, where the health authorities do not object. He gets his living out of him, and seldom ill-treats him in his sober moments. If you watch a costermonger in the streets, you often see the harnessed donkey following his master like a dog, which he would not do if he was afraid of him.

In England we do not pay much attention to the varieties of the ass, because we have a better breed of ponies than any other country; but there is one, generally of a dark colour, with finer limbs, more active and swift than the ordinary grey drudge, which is to be preferred for riding and light harness. I have seen the two small sons of a gentleman in the North of England following the hounds on their black donkeys, creeping through and over most difficult places, and even achieving very respectable leaps.

Some enthusiasts have recommended that family donkeys should be groomed and fed like horses; but this would be a waste of time and money, which would be much better bestowed on a pony if pace is required. The donkey should be well fed and kindly treated; but do what you will, the animal in this cold climate will after all be only an ass, which can be kept clean with a few strokes of the currycomb, and in sufficient condition for reasonable work with grass in summer, hay and roots in winter. Where long daily journeys are required, oats and beans will not be altogether wasted, but comfortable shelter in cold weather is a matter of importance.

POITOU BAUDET (THE SIRE OF DRAUGHT MULES).

For practical purposes the domestic ass may be divided into two classes: the one seen constantly at the watering-places of Europe, in the streets in light carts, and in rural districts in light carriages, which arrives at the greatest perfection in Eastern climates, where it is used as a beast for riding, as well as to carry burdens; the other is the dray-horse of the ass tribe, cultivated in Spain and in certain districts of France, chiefly for breeding mules.

The Arab and the dray-horse are scarcely more dissimilar than the Egyptian saddle-ass and the mule-begetting *baudet*, of which illustrations are given: the first from a photograph taken in Cairo; the other from a portrait by Mr. Sheldon Williams of the Poitou stallion ass exhibited at the Crystal Palace by Mr. Pease, at the suggestion of Mr. Sutherland, who has taken up the advocacy of mules as beasts for heavy draught with great zeal. Some enthusiasts have proposed to improve the character of the ordinary British donkey by crossing with the tall asses of Spain, Malta, and France. As far as the trade of the costermonger and travelling tinker is concerned, this would be a mistake. It is like a proposal for breeding moor ponies up to 15 hands high. An ass of average size requires a proportionate supply of food, and only a small shed in the back yard of the coster's lodging. A coster or tinker would no more accept a 14-hands Spanish ass as a gift than a dray-horse, if he were bound to keep him.

Since Egypt has been brought by steam and the enterprising Mr. Cook within reach of the million, every one knows the donkey of the country; but as few English travellers understand Arabic, they do not appreciate the familiar conversation of the donkey-boys, of which Mansfield Parkyns, the Nottinghamshire squire, who lived for years the life of a native Abyssinian, half naked and covered with butter, gives so amusing an account in a book which has been forgotten since the march to Magdala and death of King Theodore.

EGYPTIAN DONKEY-BOYS.

"The donkey-boys crowd round the wharf, and beleaguer the traveller, who with difficulty extricates himself from their clutches by desperately throwing himself, for no earthly reason, on to the nearest animal, and riding a distance of a hundred or two yards in a most uncomfortable manner. In saying uncomfortable, I mean only for new-comers; old residents find that the donkeys go wonderfully easy, are sure-footed, and get over the ground at a great pace. On my return to Cairo, after some years' residence in the upper country, I was astonished at this difference, and attributed it to my having become more of an 'asinestrian,' or to the breed having improved. I discovered, however, that it altogether depended on a peculiarly African cast of features and complexion that a long stay in the country gives to Europeans, distinguishing them from the new arrivals. I was enlightened on the subject by a donkey-boy of my acquaintance, who, at my particular request, made the ass I was riding change at once from a free-going, easy-paced animal to the most stubborn brute that ever was crossed. A very favourite trick of the boys is to give the ass a peculiar dig with the end of a stick on one side as if to make him accelerate his pace, whereas the only effect produced is a most disagreeable sideways wriggle of the hind-quarters, which generally half dislodges the novice; a second dig in another place produces a kick, which often completes his overthrow, to the great amusement of the boy, who, however, is always ready to howl, and thus attract for you the attention and ridicule of all who may be passing by, if you should make the slightest gesture indicative of an assault on his person. I am speaking now, perhaps, more of the young gentlemen of Cairo than those of Alexandria. I have, since my return, been gratified by seeing them described in tourists' books as active, lively, and amusing. Most truly are they so; for activity they cannot be surpassed, nor for their amusing talents either, though these are generally employed at the expense of the traveller, rather than for his benefit.

"I have often, while passing, been made to laugh at the *doubles entendres* contained in the remarks of some of these boys, and the very simple and self-satisfied answers of their green-veiled and parasoled employers. I have more than once rated them, and still more often joined in the mirth they caused at their patrons' expense; but I once thought it might afford me some amusement if I could, by shamming ignorance of the language, have a long ride and its accompanying conversation. After making several attempts at disguise, which failed in consequence of my truly African complexion and manner, at last I bethought me of the veil and umbrella dodge; and having equipped myself altogether *à l'Anglais* (that is, with shoes, a straw hat, and thick stick), I addressed a boy, beginning my conversation (as all Englishmen are supposed to do) with a strongish expletive, and continuing my inquiry in very bad English,

EGYPTIAN DONKEY AND BOY

as all Englishmen do, in the idea, I suppose, that because the natives speak a broken language, they will digest it better if broken up ready for their use. The bait took, as the boy's answer convinced me—'Here, master, *you* very good jackass.' We went a long ride down to Shoubra Gardens (I was then at Boulac), and the boy kept up, with the gravest possible face, a desultory conversation of the following nature. (N.B. The words in italics are supposed to be said in Arabic.) The donkey stumbles. 'You boy, your donkey not good at all!' 'Yes, master, him berry good ; *better than his rider.'* 'Go on fast.' 'Yes, master ; a—a—a' (with a dig, causing a wriggle)—[to ass]—'*Get on, Christian, son of a Christian, ridden by a Christian ; ass, son of an ass, ridden by an ass ;* kàfir (infidel), *son of a kàfir, ridden by a kàfir.'* And then, perhaps, he would amuse himself and the passers-by with a native roundelay :—

> 'Christian, blessed dog,
> Ate the sweet thing, and left me,
> Here he is, the Christian !'

'That's a very nice song ; what does it say ?' 'All 'bout master and donkey, berry good, me behind, with stick make'm go ; master give me shilling me sing him again !' Then he would, perhaps, give the donkey a spiteful dig under the tail, thereby eliciting a kick, while at the same time he would express a wish (in Arabic) that the stick in his hand were a *khasoug* (or impaling post), dedicated to the especial elevation of the ass and his rider. So we went on for a long time (the parts of conversation I have selected are the few which would bear printing in English), till at last, as Fortune would have it, I was recognised by a Turkish friend of mine, who addressed me in Arabic.

"I first got a good hold of my follower, which interrupted him in a most benevolent expression of the kind manner in which he would like to treat all the members of my family, enumerating each one in succession, from my great-grandfather and his respected lady downwards, and intermingling them in a most facetious manner with the ancestry of the animal I bestrode. 'You would, would you, you son of a dog ?' said I. 'And now that I have you in my power, what shall I do with you ?' To this, of course, were added one or two of the rather strong Turkish expressions which appear to be necessary to make his own language intelligible to an Arab of Egypt. The change in the boy's face was so amusing that I could scarcely forbear from laughing. My friend also came up and joined in the fun. The boy was all prayers and entreaties. I gave him a few kicks, and having taken off my veil, and giving him the umbrella to carry, we returned home.

"On the way back both donkey and driver behaved remarkably well. After paying the boy his just dues, and not a para more, which he received without a grumble, I administered a few more kicks, and then gave him a shilling for the amusement he had afforded me."

THE STALLION ASS FOR MULE BREEDING.

The French have a race of strong dray-horse-like asses, used for breeding mules, called *baudets*, which are supposed to have been originally imported from Spain, and to have been brought into Spain by the Moors from Africa ; although the asses commonly found in Northern Africa are small and light-limbed, while the *baudet*, perhaps so-named from the Spanish *borrico*, is the largest and strongest animal of its race. The *baudet* has a much larger head than the ordinary domestic ass ; teeth so hard that it is almost impossible to guess his age after he casts his milk teeth ; ears of extravagant length and size, garnished with a mass of long hair, called, in the language of Poitou, *cadenettes*. The neck and shoulders are much more muscular than those of the common ass, but exactly of the same shape. Length is considered a point of great importance in a *baudet* for begetting large mules. The breast is broad and the belly ample ; the muscles of the arms and thighs long and flat ; the joints as strong and large as those of a good cart-horse.

The following are the dimensions of the stallion ass of our illustration, as given by Mr. Sutherland, who calls him a good fair specimen of the Poitou ass, suitable for breeding heavy draught mules from cart-mares :—

Height, 14 hands 1 inch.	Greatest girth, 77 inches.
Fore-arm, 19½ inches.	Girth behind shoulder, 66 inches.
Knee, 15 inches.	Length of head, 25 inches.
Below knee, 8½ inches.	Length of ear, 15 inches.
Hock, 17½ inches.	Ears, tip to tip across, 32 inches.
Below hock, 12 inches.	

A coat of long, thick hair, especially about the legs and feet, is much esteemed ; and hoofs much larger than those of the common ass are an important point.

Their value greatly depends on their height, ranging from 12½ to 14½ hands.

The Poitou breeders always select black or brown donkey sires with white bellies, and will have nothing to say to greys. On the contrary, in Egypt, where the breed of asses is generally small, a good white ass for riding fetches as much money as a good park hack in London.

In consequence of a stupid prejudice on the part of the Poitou peasant breeders, the ass stallions are never brushed or dressed ; so the winter coat adheres to the summer coat, like the fleece of an unshorn sheep, year after year, until not unfrequently a disgusting cutaneous disease is produced. The ass with the roughest, longest coat is the most admired.

The period of gestation with the she-ass is twelve months. The Poitou breeders, amongst other ignorant practices, half starve their she-asses, under the impression that it promotes the health of the offspring. About a month before the time of foaling, the farmer or his son sleeps regularly in the dam's stable, to be ready in case of accident ; no stranger would be trusted with so important an office.

The starvation system inflicts many maladies on both dam and foal. The she-ass, under this treatment, rarely has enough milk for her foal, and the consequence is great and needless mortality. But the ignorance of the French peasant, living entirely amongst his own class, into which books, newspapers, or oral instruction rarely if ever penetrate, is something appalling. The only peasant-farmers of any intelligence are those who have served in the army.

For the first month the male foal, called a *fedon*, is overwhelmed with attention, and crammed with a gruel of milk and flour and other food, to make up for the shortcomings of his half-starved mother ; he is also clothed and watched day and night. After that period the owners content themselves with giving the dam more food. He is weaned at nine months old on farinaceous gruel (*panades*), or soaked bread, in the interval between passing from milk to grass and hay.

At thirty months old he commences his duties as a sire, and up to two years old he is fondled and caressed ; from that age he is doomed to solitary imprisonment in a dark loose box, which is seldom cleaned out, only let out when his services are required. In consequence of this treatment, at an early age he becomes fiercely savage, and coated with dirt and the matted accumulation of cast coats of successive years. Nothing can be more savage and repulsive looking than a five-year-old *baudet*. The stallion season commences in the middle of February, and finishes in August.

The *baudet* lives to a great age, and is of use as a stallion until he is thirty years old. Those who wish to purchase one of these male *baudets* must go to their owner's farm for the purpose, as they are never taken to fairs. When sold, the *baudet* is conveyed to the purchaser in a covered wagon. The best-bred male *baudets* are worth a hundred francs, say £4, for each month of their age. A male ass two years old, 14 hands high, and in other respects perfect, can rarely be purchased for £100.

WILD ASSES.

Mr. Waterhouse Hawkins, in his notes on his portraits of animals collected by the thirteenth Earl of Derby, grandfather of the present peer, in that very scarce work, "The Knowsley Menagerie," doubts if the breed of the domestic ass has ever been found in a wild state not being the descendant of some donkeys which had escaped from the care of man. The difference is important. The young of domesticated horses, cattle, and pigs, which have escaped and grown wild are easily reclaimed. This has been repeatedly proved in the case of foals and calves in Australia. In New Zealand the produce of tame pigs which have escaped into the bush assume the appearance and acquire the ferocity of the wild boar race; but Lady Barker relates, in her interesting "Station Life," that the young of a very savage wild sow which her husband killed became so tame as to be positively troublesome pets.

But repeated experiments have shown that the offspring of a truly wild race, like deer, buffaloes, aurochs, and swine, relapse to their original state the moment that daily personal care is relaxed.

The wild asses of Syria and of India are no more asses than the zebra or quagga, and are just as untamable; if they were not they would afford a fine field for the exertions of an acclimatisation society, as in beauty and in strength they are as superior to the domestic race as a thoroughbred horse is to the wild horses of Australia or Tartary, or as a red deer of the German forest to the fallow deer of English parks.

In the Regent's Park Zoological Gardens may be seen a Syrian wild ass, or hemione, which has bred with the domestic ass, and produced a mule. The colour is the yellow of an antelope, the ears rather smaller, but in every other respect—head, neck, legs, and tail—very like an ass. Another variety is the onager, from India, which, in the delicacy and strength of its limbs, differs from a common donkey so much that it might be called a thoroughbred, for it partakes of the character of a blood-horse. The first idea suggested by a sight of this very handsome animal is, what a fine cross it would make with an English, French, or Spanish ass; but, on inquiry, it appears that it will no more breed reproductively than an horse and an ass, or a pheasant and a game-fowl.

This Indian wild ass, or *Equus onager*, has excited great interest because it differs essentially from any other specimen in the collection, and more than realises the following description by Captain Nutt, who caught and presented it to the Gardens :—

"Having heard a good deal about the wild donkeys to be found on the Runn of Kutch, I took the opportunity when lately paying an official visit to the Mallia State—the extreme north-west corner of Kattywar—to try my luck at capturing a specimen. Mentioning the subject to the Mallia chief, I found that he took a lively interest in the matter; and as he tendered his personal services, as well as those of some thirty Meeanas, whom I knew to be well-mounted and practised riders, I at once closed with his offer, and began to make the requisite *bundobust*. I was joined by seven enthusiasts from the neighbouring State of Dhrangdra, and six from Mornee; so, with my own little detachment of six, the entire party, including myself, numbered fifty-one. My camp was at a place called Ghantéla, bordering on the Runn of Kutch. *Puggees* were sent out to obtain information; and in about three or four days time they came in with the news that there was a *tola* of eight—four big ones and four young ones—in a 'grass beer' known as the Kesmalla Beer, some eleven miles off. It appeared on inquiry that the animals when chased would in all probability make for a hill called the Murdoch Doongur, distant from Kesmalla Beer nine miles. This hill (a famous place of call for robbers and dacoits) was not of very great extent, and was surrounded on all sides by the Runn. It was then agreed that the best plan would be to send on a party of twenty to Murdoch Doongur, there to lie in wait so as to take up the running in case the beasts took that way; the other party of thirty-one waited till midnight, so timing its departure to Kesmalla as to arrive near the place before dawn. I sent on a fresh horse with the first party to Murdoch. At five A.M. we were close to Kesmalla Beer, but it was still quite dark. The cold was intense on the Runn at that early hour; we all had to keep very quiet, and of course were unable to light a fire.

"The party generally was well-mounted, all on Kattywar horses and mares. The animal I rode was a Katty galloway, that could do his half-mile under a minute at any time, and had plenty of honest endurance. Some of the Meeanas' nags were very blood-looking, and as fit as fiddles. At last it was time to tighten girths and mount. Moving quietly towards the Beer, which in the subdued light looked very dark and mysterious, we were met by other *puggees*, who had been watching ever since the *tola* was first discovered early the day before. Our party of thirty-one was then broken up into three divisions; and advancing direct from the centre, with our outer divisions spreading to the right and left flanks, we embraced the whole ground, and compelled the animals to break towards the Murdoch Doongur, which was dimly visible in the extreme distance. On surmounting the grass ridge I perceived some little dots, apparently a mile or so off on the Runn, and with the aid of glasses I found these dots were, as the *puggee* said, four big and four small animals—it was quite impossible to see whether they were donkeys or not. They were moving quietly on, and did not apparently see our party; so I thought it best to creep up as quickly as possible towards them without actually breaking into a gallop and beginning the chase. In this way we managed to get rather nearer; but very shortly after the alarm seemed to have been taken, as I saw them, after turning round two or three times, begin to canter away. No time was then to be lost, so I at once gave the word, and we all started off at a brisk pace in pursuit. I felt full of confidence, as my horse was in good spirits; and as we went bounding along, every moment getting nearer to the little band in front, visions of a speedy capture rose before me. My companions were wise; they allowed me to make all the running, whilst they themselves rode a waiting race, doubtless feeling sure that in due course of time the quarry would come back to them. After covering about five miles, and finding the donkeys still continuing the pace at which they started, I thought it high time to try the effect of a spurt, and, my horse answering bravely, I found myself riding within pistol-shot of the *tola*. I was then able to take a good look at them. Not having read Jerdon's description, I expected to find them white, and was surprised and delighted to find that their colour was most peculiar— to a certain extent like that of the ordinary jackass, but more defined—the belly very white, the flanks a reddish chocolate, and a broad dark brown stripe extending along the spine from apex of shoulder to tail, very marked; the legs very fine, like those of a deer; the tail furnished with long hairs at the extremity only; mane short and reddish brown; light brown bars on hocks and fore-arms; ears smaller than those of the domestic ass, and constantly pricked; eye of unusual brightness; about the size of ordinary mules. They seemed to be going well within themselves— in fact, from beginning to end of the chase I never noticed any of that extending or laying themselves out which is so generally observed in the action of a hunted animal when hard pressed; on the contrary, these donkeys did not seem to take the slightest trouble to hurry themselves but simply kept steadily on at a regulated pace. When close up I saw the older ones give a push every now and then to one of the younger ones; and I can quite believe the statement made to me some time before by an old *shikari*, that when put to it the bigger donkeys close in behind the young ones, and regularly push or butt them on with their foreheads.

"The effect of my riding at them in this way was to break up the *tola* into two divisions—one division consisting of two big ones and three young ones, and the other of two big ones and one young one. My first impulse was to follow the three young ones, especially as I noticed that they were smaller than the young one in the other division; but when I saw the bigger division heading straight up the Runn, whilst the smaller one was holding on in the direction of the Murdoch Doongur, where I knew my second horse and a fresh party were lying in wait, I considered it best to stick to the latter. Arrived at the hill, the animals took along the base, which was unpleasant going, being much cut up and very rocky. Some of the fresh party appeared and joined in, but my second horse was nowhere to be seen. In despair I urged on my already tired horse, and so continued for about five miles further, when my animal, completely exhausted, could go no longer. I then pulled up, turned his head to the wind, and loosened the girths. Whilst doing this, one of the pursuing party from Murdoch passed me, and to my joy announced that my second horse was coming. A few minutes later and I was on his back, and away, but I found I had lost ground terribly. The donkeys and the leading horsemen were nowhere to be seen; but in the distance, appearing like a dot upon the horizon, was the last man who had spoken to me, and who I knew was on the track. I galloped after him, and after a long chase managed to catch him up. It is very difficult to calculate distances upon the Runn; but when I got up to this man he pointed out some specks, which he said were the leading *sowars*, and they seemed to me some two or three miles off. By dint of riding I managed to get up close, and after going about ten miles I found myself gradually gaining on them. They were still, however, only indistinctly visible, as the mirage made everything look strange and distorted. The pugs of the donkeys were clear: there were the prints of the two bigger animals, and there were the sharper and smaller prints of the young one. The sight of these pugs cheered me on and filled me with hope. Presently I saw the dots in front all apparently commingling, and shortly afterwards I saw that they were stationary, and that I was gaining on them every stride. Another couple of miles and I was up, when I found the young ass effectually secured by two long ropes and held between a couple of grinning Meeanas of the Murdoch Doongur party; only myself of the first party which started from Kesmella Beer being up. The animal appeared much exhausted, and was bleeding from a wound in the quarter, which the Meeanas said was from a horse-bite, but which was really a spear-wound inflicted by one of them who lost his head in the heat of the moment; in fact, this was the way they stopped her.

"The little donkey—a female— stands 9 hands 2½ inches high (according to Jerdon, it will ultimately reach 12 hands), and appears to be about 6 months old. It soon got over its exhaustion and wound, and is now as lively as a kitten. I have offered it to the Zoological Society at home; so it is quite possible that its days, begun on the Kutch Runn, may terminate in the heart of London.

"It has been estimated that the total distance of the hunt, from Kesmella Beer to the place of capture, was forty miles. The chase commenced at 6.25 A.M., and terminated at 9.30 A.M., so that it lasted exactly three hours and five minutes. Considering the rate of going, I imagine this estimate to be correct; my first horse was ridden to a standstill, my second almost so. Men and cattle were all more or less done up. I rode 11st., my companions considerably lighter."

Mr. Fraser Hore* gives the following description of the young onager. See Baker Pasha's hunt, at page 26.

"Its age at the present time (Oct., 1873) is about one year; its colour is a mixture of white and fawn; the under part of the body, the neck and chest, nose and nasal region, back part of face, rump, channel, and inside of the legs, are white; the mane is short, stumpy, and dark brown. A dark dun streak of longish hair runs down the back, broadening towards the rump, and continuing down the tail to the end. The other parts of the body and head are of a fawn-colour, the entire coat being smooth and glossy; the tail has a small tuft of long dark brown hair at the end. The legs are beautifully clean and flat, the back sinews standing well out; and there is a black, shiny, horny ergot high up inside each fore-leg; the feet are beautifully formed, hard, and very small; pasterns very long on fore-legs, rather upright on hind-legs. Viewed from behind, her quarters and gaskins appear enormously large in proportion to the size of the animal. She is a wonderful jumper, and tried an eight-foot wall, but did not get over, having a log of wood tied to one of her hind-legs. The eyes are large, quite black, and very expressive. The muzzle is small and black, the nostrils large and open. The ears are long, outside light fawn-colour, inside covered with long white hair. Outside the knees and hocks there are faint traces of three brown bars. The animal shows no indication of the cross, or shoulder-stripe, found in other donkeys. She is at present over twelve hands high, but is not yet full grown.

" These animals have constantly been chivied on the Runn of Kutch for years past by parties of officers on horseback, with spears; but, with the solitary exception which I have above mentioned, when a man named Elliott speared a jenny on the point of foaling, no wild donkey has ever been run down until my friend Nutt got hold of this one.

" This donkey was exhibited at the horse show in Poona, in September, and was looked upon as the greatest curiosity and attraction there. She bites and kicks at every one that approaches her but her own *syce*. It took a whole day to get her to stand steady, in order to take the photographs I send you; and at one time she lashed out with her hind-legs, and kicked the photographer and his apparatus over. They say there is no possibility of ever taming her. You will doubtless see her before long, and I am sure you will say she is one of the most beautiful animals you have ever seen."

When I visited the Gardens, in March, 1874, after reading the preceding description, I found that the onager completely realised Captain Nutt's description; with fine, clean, flat, sinewy legs, and apparently as much strength and activity as a large antelope or red deer. After examining its limbs, it was easy to understand that such an animal would outpace many horses. The head, ears, neck, and tail, were those of a well-bred donkey in its summer coat, but of a colour quite unique. This pretty creature, petted by the sailors, became tame on the voyage. Mr. Bartlett, the Superintendent of the Gardens, received news of its arrival at Southampton, and expected to be informed of its despatch in time to meet it on the railroad; but about nine o'clock in the evening of the same day, the bell of the Superintendent's house was rung violently, and on going out a tall stout man was there, holding some animal. "What have you got there?" asked Mr. Bartlett. "Well, I thought it was a donkey, but it has turned out a dreadful wild beast." It seems that when it was taken out of the horse-box at Waterloo Station, it was so docile that it was thought to be a tame Indian donkey, and a man accustomed to leading thoroughbred colts and entire horses undertook to lead it to

* Communicated by Mr. Sutherland to *The Field.*

the Gardens. He was, although a very powerful man, thoroughly beaten and exhausted, and would never have succeeded had not an Indian officer he met accidentally recognised the wild ass, and volunteered his assistance.

In 1878 this onager had grown at least an inch, and "furnished" into a very powerful thoroughbred creature. It had bred a foal to the Syrian wild ass, but would give it no milk, and killed it with bites and kicks before it could be rescued.

MULES AND MULE-BREEDING.

Mules are invaluable as beasts of draught and beasts of burden in the south of Europe, and in certain parts of northern and southern America. They were known, and in common use, as appears from Assyrian bas-reliefs, in the earliest historical times. Layard's great folios of coloured illustrations of his work on Nineveh contain pictures of mules, both ridden and driven in chariots, and in one instance of a mule ridden by a woman.

In France mule-breeding has gradually grown into an important branch of rural industry, in spite of discouragement from the officials charged with improving the breeds of horses. There are two kinds of mules: a light kind used for light carriages, and in Spain and Africa for saddle, and a strong kind used for heavy draught; the character and quality depending on the selection of the donkey sire and the horse mare.

In 1870 there were eighty-six mule-breeding farms in the department of Deux-Sèvres, in Poitou, the real mule-breeding district of France, which maintained 432 of the largest kind of stallion asses *(baudet étalon espèce mulassière)*. The little male donkeys used in the *Midi* of France are for the most part imported from Lombardy and Sardinia; small and slight-limbed, their produce from the mares of the country are undersized and light of bone, and can in no way be compared with the powerful magnificent animals which dealers from Languedoc, Béarn, and Spain come annually to purchase in Poitou.

Africa breeds the best riding mules, and France the best for pack-saddle or heavy draught.

The male mule is stronger, has more bone than the female, and more courage, but is less docile. Nevertheless, the female is worth twenty-five per cent. more than the male, because in very hot climates she is not subject to several diseases which affect the male, and she does not require so much care.

Poitou breeds and the *Midi* rears the mule. About 12,000 are bred every year; two-thirds of which are sold at one year old, at from 90 to 180 francs each. As soon as brought home they are turned out on the mountains to graze, and remain there until the frosts set in. At the commencement of winter they are stabled for a couple of months. In the spring a good many are sold for exportation to Italy. The remainder are sold by the breeders at two, four, and five years old; never at three, few remain at six years.

Spain imports annually six or eight hundred saddle and carriage mules of the very finest class direct from Poitou. Spain also imports lighter mules from the *Midi*—the value altogether, with the Italian importations, amounting to upwards of £120,000 sterling annually. The total exportation from France in 1871 exceeded 17,000 head.

The mule begins to work at eighteen months or two years old. It is more hardy than the horse, but more delicate in its food than the ass. The mule-foal in Poitou is born much stronger than the horse-foal, and is said to be more difficult to rear; but this is not surprising, for the ignorant peasants will not allow them to suck freely the first milk, dose them with white wine and oil, and sometimes bleed them!

To prepare them for sale they are placed in separate stalls of low, hot, ill-ventilated stables, fed liberally on good hay, *baked* potatoes, wheat, oats, barley, and maize (cooked or crushed), and sometimes oilcake, in order to make them as fat as pigs—a point the dealers insist on.

Although mules very rarely breed, it is advisable to castrate the males, which otherwise become violent and vicious at certain seasons of the year.

I have given the preceding account of the Poitou *baudet* and the mule-breeding establishments of Poitou, of which he is the foundation (chiefly extracted from an elaborate work by M. Eugene Gayot), because the mule is a valuable animal in the West Indies and several English colonies and dependencies, and has long been bred and used successfully in the southern semitropical regions of the United States. It is essentially the animal for a country of bad or no roads, coarse and scanty herbage, uncertain supply of water, a mountainous or sandy country, and hot climate. Under certain circumstances the mule will endure privations that would kill a horse, but he requires management by people who understand his peculiarities. The mule is of little value without the mule-driver. Where he is wanted he takes his place naturally; his position is a question of geography. You do not find him regularly at work, superseding the horse and the ox, in Flanders, or in Normandy, or in New York, or Boston; but after you pass Avignon he becomes familiar, and rivals the horse on the Pyrenees; in Kentucky he is part of the stock of the farm, and in California mules are as plentiful as costermongers' donkeys in London.

The asses of Cyprus are much valued for their strength and docility; they are of a yellow colour. The mules are finest in the Levant; a large number were used in the Ashantee expedition.

Mules in England are accidents, or fancy stock on fancy farms. They have long been bred and used on the home farms of certain noblemen. The late Lord Leconfield had several teams of draught-mules full 16 hands high, and very strong. They were sold at Tattersall's on his death. They are still bred and used at Badminton; and four, ridden by postillions, used to draw the hound van. It is difficult to discontinue any usage on a great estate. The following letter from Mr. John Thompson, the agent to the Duke of Beaufort, in answer to inquiries addressed to him by the writer of this chapter, gives late and authentic information on the subject :—

"Mules were first introduced at Badminton about seventy years since. The first Spanish Jack was imported during the Peninsular War, and the first mules by him were out of a large active cart-mare. Three or four which she bred were upwards of 17½ hands high. Mule teams have been kept up ever since, chiefly home bred; and in consequence of the difficulty in procuring first-class Jacks, imported animals have latterly been introduced. We have bred them from both cart and half-bred mares, and find that the stock from these are more powerful than the imported animals, being larger in the bone, and of greater substance. We have had Jacks from Malta and Spain, but those from the latter country are generally superior. The mule foals are very hardy, there being no difficulty whatever in rearing them, and when grown up are less expensive to keep than horses. Ordinary carters drive the teams, which are composed of four mules each, driven double; and they will each with ease draw a load of 50 cwt., in addition to the wagon, at the rate of four miles per hour on a good road. They are especially useful in carrying hay or corn during harvest, being much quicker than horses with light loads. We have seventeen at work at present. They last longer than horses, a mule at thirty years old being about equal to a horse at twenty."

Mules and goats are generally found in the same climate, and under the same circumstances. But if any gentleman chooses to amuse himself with breeding mules, either in this country or in

Australia, he must procure the services of a good Spanish or French *baudet*, and select a strong active Suffolk Clydesdale or Shire mare of as good a temper as possible. The value of mules as draught animals is very fairly summed up in the following letter, addressed to *The Field* by a correspondent in Louisiana:—

"This southern country (Louisiana) is full of mules, and their size certainly cannot be objected to. Our drayman runs three mules, the smallest 15½ hands high, and considered to be a 'good little mule,' the largest 16½ hands high, and considered as being a 'good-sized mule' in common parlance. But the largest of these is nothing to the mules employed in the contractors' stables for hauling machinery and heavy articles. A neighbour of mine has twenty mules over 17 hands, and as powerful as any London brewer's horses to be found. Our wealthy coal merchants, Igar and Co., have mules that are perfect pictures, not one less than 16 hands, and they bring their ton of coals along as easily as any cart-horse in England. The forte of the mule lies in the cleanness and flatness of the legs, which are more like the thoroughbred horse than any quarterbred horse ever would be, and the foot is small and pointed. There is but one morsel of lumber about the mule of this country, and that only in those that are worked hard and are low in flesh, and then after feeding the belly is distended and unsightly. As for temper and sagacity, they beat the horse, but if not well broke are timid and a little 'skeary.' For work they are admirable, *but the pace tells on them a little more than on the horse of equal ability.* Slow work is their best point, and at that they will beat a horse 25 to 50 per cent., taking their longer life into consideration, and their exemption from disease. In the city railroad lines here there are over 1,000 mules, averaging about 15½ hands, used, and not more than twenty horses. They prefer the smaller mules for the city cars, as costing less, eating less, and being a little quicker on their feet. The difference in price here is very great. A horse and mule for the same general purpose would cost relatively $175 and $300.

"We bought lately for use of house a capital young horse, for $175. He has to take a four-wheeled buggy with two persons through country dirt roads, and is good enough to drive anywhere. *A mule at $300 would not answer so well, as the work would become occasionally too fast for him, and it blows them.* As for riding, there are exceptions, *but generally the shoulder is too low and the back too much arched to render them desirable mounts, and their paces are not good one time out of* 10,000. The mules used here are by donkeys of enormous size, principally from Spain and Malta, and one-fourth to three-fourths bred mare, of large roomy build. They are raised in Kentucky and Tennessee, where the climate, herbage, and trees, are so much like the middle English counties that there can be no objection to the climate of England in raising them easily and profitably. And another great point in their favour is their early maturity. At three years old they can be used advantageously for all light work, and will last till twenty or twenty-five years old with certainty, barring disease."

Mules are bred in South America for certain purposes. Mr. George Henry Beaumont, a correspondent of the *Live Stock Journal*, says of South American mules: "As a rule they give more trouble, kick, and bite harder than horses. They keep much healthier in hot climates than horses; they are handier in stony, rocky, and all mountainous countries. One mule in such places is worth more than two, if not three, horses, for any work. They are shorter and stronger in the back, and can carry heavier loads than horses of their own size; they eat much less, and are not so particular as to their food; they are much surer footed, owing to the formation of the hoof, pastern-joint, and shoulder; they can carry a load in places where a horse could not travel even without one; they can travel longer distances than a horse can, and keep in better condition during the journey. I will give an example of this: The journey from the Cordilleras to Buenos Ayres is always done by the 'Colleros' on mules, for the reasons I have just given. I have often asked them why they did not come on horses. They laugh, and tell you that they do not want to be left on foot—that is, horses would get sore-footed, and would not stand the fatigue of the journey. Mules have nearly always very dark hoofs; they are much tougher than those of the horse. I have helped to cut and trim a good many, and, if I may be allowed to make use of the comparison, there is about the same difference in cutting a horse's hoof and a mule's as there is in cutting a piece of birch-wood and a piece of elm. In the time of drought in the River Plate, when horses can with difficulty be found with sufficient strength to carry themselves, mules are still to be seen working in the 'diligencias' and carts; and fortunate is the proprietor of a 'diligencia' who has some teams of mules in these hard times. They are not generally used in Buenos Ayres or the Uruguay, for the reason that they are more difficult to tame than a colt, and are slower; and as pace is everything with these 'diligencias,' mules are not thought much of till the pastures are all scorched up, and nothing is left but thistle-stalks and roots to eat, upon which the mules keep in good hard condition, when the horses are nothing but skin and bone.

Mules are also used in Brazil. A macadamised road was made for one hundred miles to the north of Pheopolis in 1875. A coach, built after the English pattern, starts every day at 6 A.M. from opposite the Emperor's palace at Persepolis, and deposits passengers at 6 P.M. at the door of the hotel at Juiz da Fora. In this time is included not only the work of one hundred miles, but an hour for dinner and another hour for halts at other stations. The work is done by relays of elegant little mules, which seemed to enjoy the fun of going as fast as they could. I timed four over a ten-mile stage: they did it in fifty minutes; and a stage of six miles has been done in twenty minutes. They never seemed tired or hot. No horses could keep up such a pace in such a climate.*

To carry burdens or pack-saddles the mule is, no doubt, from his conformation, superior to the horse. In war, for drawing artillery, he has one disadvantage: it is not every man that will make a muleteer, but every one can lead a horse.

The Spaniards do not write books; but Mrs. Ramsay, who is familiar with all the post and travelling animals of Europe, says in her delightful book, "A Summer in Spain," published in 1874, after a visit to the royal stables at Madrid: "Until one has seen a Spanish mule one has no idea to what perfection the animal may be brought. They were not glossy, but their skins looked like black velvet. We were carefully warned that the majority were vicious." In another place Mrs. Ramsay mentions that it is the custom in Spain to have one horse ridden by a postillion as leader to the ten mules that draw the diligence, and it is the duty of this postillion never to leave his horse; nevertheless, on one occasion she awoke to see the postillion fast asleep beside the driver, and the whole team galloping free alongside frightful precipices.

The Earl of Mayo, in his "Sport in Abyssinia," says: "English hunting saddles did well for the mules we rode in Abyssinia." He adds at another place that they should have had cruppers. The Earl also used snaffle bridles, "which were a great deal better than the severe bits of the country."

"A good sheepskin *numbdah*, or one made of cotton cloth folded in many folds—the older, and therefore the softer, the better—is put under the Abyssinian saddle. On the march, when they halt for the day, they take off the saddle, *but leave* the numbdah on, tying up the mule in the shade until the animal is cool. They then remove the *numbdah* and lead the mule

* "Over the Sea," by T. W. Hinchcliff, M.A. 1876.

to roll in the dust. In Abyssinia there are regular rolling-places for mules and asses. After he has rolled they take him to water, hobble him, and let him go out to graze. The Abyssinian hobble is the best I have seen. The near fore-leg is tied with a leather thong, about three-quarters of an inch wide, to the off hind-leg, or *vice versa*, so that the mule can walk, but not go faster."

THE HINNEY.

The mule of commerce is, as before stated, the produce of a mare horse by an ass. The hinney, which is never intentionally bred, unless by some fanciful amateur, is the produce of an ass by a horse, and resembles its sire by having the tail, the mane, the legs and feet, and sometimes, but more rarely, the head of a horse. The hinney is rarely larger than a common ass, while a mule will generally be much taller than either of its parents.

CHAPTER IX.

ON THE PURCHASE OF HORSES.

Purchase from a Horse-dealer—From a Farmer—At a Fair—By Advertisements—Comparative Advantages—Anecdote of the Duke of Norfolk—Precautions required at Auctions—Tattersall's Rules—Copers and their Tricks—The Effect of Harness-work on Riding Horses—Stallions, Geldings, or Mares—To choose a Horse know what you Want—Useful Soundness and Warrantable Soundness—Judges of Form—Anecdote of Squire Foljambe—Points of Soundness Important—Eyesight—Wind—Whistling and Roaring—Degrees of Lameness—Vice and its Degrees—The Law of Warranty—Colours—Light Grey and Piebald objectionable in Hacks—Action—Its Varieties—Safe and Slow—Fast and Safe—Brilliant and Slow—Brilliant and Fast—Action of a Funeral Coach-horse—Of a Race-horse—Value of a Good Walker—Trotting—Slow and Fast—Value of Courage—Cutting and Brushing—Various Horse-boots Illustrated—Value of Aged Horses—Sights and Sounds—Shying from Ignorance—From Defective Eyesight—From Freshness—From Vice—A Patient Horse-breaker Required for a Colt—Examples—Pullers and Runaways—A Horse that Bridles well—Value of a suitable Bit—High Condition and Want of Exercise—Excitement—Vicious Habit—Use of a Martingale—Constitution and Temperament—Bad Feeders—Crib-biters—Value of a Placid Temperament—Violent Vice Hereditary—Effect of Cruelty—Bad Breaking—Slugs—The best Class of Horse courageous and placid—Exercise Essential for high-couraged Horses—Mares and Riding Hacks may be Driven in Harness.

THERE are several ways in which horses may be purchased, as, for instance, from a horse-dealer, from a farmer who breeds or who buys colts and breaks them, at an auction, at a fair, from persons who advertise in the newspapers, from a friend who happens to have to sell the sort of animal you want. There are advantages and disadvantages in all these methods.

If high-class and therefore expensive horses are required, and if—an important point—you know exactly what you want, there is no better plan, if you reside in London, than to go the round of the leading dealers on both sides of the water; then, if you cannot find anything to suit you. to place yourself in the hands of one of them, with or without a limit as to price, according to the state of your finances.

Respectable horse-dealers never buy an unsound horse if they know it; and when they take a horse that makes a little noise, or has some other defect, within the list of what makes a "useful screw," they generally send it to be sold as a screw, at screw price.

At a first-class dealer's, in town or country, you must expect, for obvious reasons, to pay a full price. The trade expenses of such dealers are very large; besides the rent, wages, and fodder, of an extensive establishment, there is the interest on the capital invested in horses purchased raw from the breeder, or at great prices at the sales of famous studs, and all the losses by death, sickness, and deterioration from—to use the veterinary surgeon's phrase—"diseases of the visual and respiratory organs."

"There's a horse," said a great dealer, "by which I shall lose two hundred pounds. I gave two hundred pounds for him as a four-year, and expected to make at least three hundred by him as a hunter. He had the influenza, and when I began to get him into condition he made a noise, so, as he was of no use for hunting, I ordered him to be broken to harness. The first time he was put in the break he threw himself down, blemished his hocks, and broke his tail; so now he's barely worth twenty pounds." Then long credit and bad debts form not a small item of loss or expense. The ideas on payment of certain distinguished members of the fashionable world used to be very curious; at the present day the tide of opinion is rather turning towards discount for cash payments. A late noble patron of the turf and everything that was expensive, owed a large sum to an eminent firm of horse auctioneers for the purchase of yearlings. When his lordship sold a large stud of hunters, under the hammer of the same firm, he was very much surprised that he did not receive a cheque for the sale-money, and was both astonished and indignant when reminded that, even after deducting the proceeds of the hunting stud, there was still a considerable balance on the wrong side against him.

The advantages of buying from a first-class dealer are considerable. In the first place there is the opportunity, worth at least ten per cent. of the purchase-money, of a full trial; then there is a warranty of soundness and freedom from vice; and, finally, the opportunity of changing if the animal does not suit, although this arrangement of course involves some additional cost. Consequently, it becomes rather expensive to people who "never are but always to be blest," who never know their own minds, or are constantly seeking an ideal and impossible horse—

"The faultless monster that the world ne'er saw."

The thirteenth Duke of Norfolk was showing his agent, a plain, blunt man, his last acquisition in hacks. "Very nice indeed, my lord, and he ought to be, for he cost your Grace a thousand pounds." "A thousand pounds!" the duke incredulously repeated. Upon which Mr. Y—— proceeded to prove how the original purchase at two hundred and fifty pounds had within twelve months grown by successive chops and changes to the four figures named.

There are also some disadvantages in purchasing from a dealer's stables, for which a novice must be prepared, amongst others, that nine horses out of ten never look so well anywhere as in dealers' condition in a dealer's yard, resplendent with bright red sand. The horses are so fat, round, and sleek; they are bedded up to their knees in beautiful clean straw; the grooms are so neat, silent, and attentive; the break-men or riding grooms such masters of their arts; the whole *mise en scène* so perfect, that the leading actor, the horse, never again appears to such advantage. Add to these attractions the astounding eloquence of the salesman, by which no one but a deaf man could be entirely unaffected.

But it must always be remembered that there are "horse-dealers and horse-dealers" of divers grades, including, the most dangerous of all, the gentleman who has seen better days, and the professional coper, whose trade it is to look out for unsound horses of splendid form and action, for the benefit of the large crop of conceited fools to be found every day in a great city; that while there are members of the trade whose word may be as safely taken as that of the bankers with whom they deal, there are many with very little capital, credit, or character, yet so clever that they only require honesty to make a permanent instead of a precarious livelihood.

Although London attracts, in harness-horses and finished park hacks, as in almost everything else, the best and most expensive, especially in harness, there are establishments in the country only second, if second, to the leading London firms. Every hunting county supports at least one local celebrity. Some dealers only purchase horses at least five years old which have been partly broken, others make a point of securing from the breeders every promising colt, and regularly fill their stables in the autumn with four-year-olds to be prepared for sale in the spring.

Men of established fortune and position have their horse-dealer just as they have their tailor and their bootmaker. This tradesman is always on the watch to secure the class of animals his patron requires. People of moderate means cannot afford so great a luxury. The man who wishes to possess harness-horses of extraordinary action must be prepared to secure them when-ever they come into the market, whether his stable be full or not, because the number in existence is limited. Of course the man who goes for the first time to buy a single horse cannot expect to be as well treated as the regular customer who purchases on a great scale. As a rule, those who require horses highly trained and broken (except hunters) are most likely to suit themselves in the stables of London dealers; those who like unfinished harness-horses or hacks, on the farms of country dealers.

The sales by auction, except where studs of great celebrity are submitted to the hammer, afford opportunities of purchasing at much lower prices than from a dealer, with the disadvantage of a very imperfect opportunity for examination, and no satisfactory trial. You must set the advantage in price against the risk, which you may well do when you want useful animals at a comparatively low price, if you have the assistance of a competent adviser, and can learn something of the biography of the nag you fancy. The difference between auction price and dealers' price generally affords a pretty good margin for insurance against mistakes in a series of purchases, but auctions are for the young and the strong. The timid and the aged must venture on no rash experiments in horses they require for their own riding.

To purchase with any safety at an auction you must be certain that it is honestly conducted, and not an affair got up between some unknown auctioneer with no reputation and the pro-prietors of a lot of screws made up for the occasion. Horses sold from a stud of reputation will fetch more by auction than they ever will again when sold singly. Even when the auction is conducted with the most perfect integrity, the intended purchaser must be on his guard against the contrivances not only of professional copers, but of "gentlemen" who send in a complete stud to get rid of two or three worn-out or vicious brutes. In fact, you want to know not only something about the horses, but about the owners. In this pursuit a few half-crowns judiciously administered to the attendant grooms may prove good investments. The lots most to be distrusted at an auction are the very good-looking ones, with no description.

A single horse generally sells for less money than one of a noted stud, and at Tattersall's a *single horse*, entered in the catalogue as quiet to ride, may be ridden by the rough-rider attached to the establishment for the purpose, at the request of an intending purchaser. Always have the animal trotted over the pavement passage alongside the boxes. If a horse is entered "quiet in harness" in the catalogue that is a warranty; but "has been regularly driven in harness" is no warranty. "Quiet to ride" is a warranty against vice, but "has been ridden by a lady or boy" is no warranty. "A good hack" has been held in a court of law to be a warranty against lameness. "A good hunter" must have perfect eyesight, and be clear in the wind. It is a doubtful point whether he need be able and willing to leap anything. In some parts of Hampshire, Devonshire, and Somersetshire, the hunters are never asked to leap. "Has been hunted" warrants nothing.

At Tattersall's horses purchased on a Monday must, if not answering the description, be returned on the Wednesday following, and will then be subject to the following conditions :— "Horses returned for not answering description shall be tried by the firm of Messrs. Tattersall or one of them, or some one appointed by them, in such manner and for such length of time as they or he shall think fit, and their or his decision shall be final and binding on both vendor and purchaser, and the loser of the trial shall pay the expenses; or Messrs. Tattersall, or one of them, or some one appointed by them, may, instead of making an actual trial of, or in addition to an actual trial of, such a horse, make their or his decision upon evidence of such nature and taken in such manner as they or he shall think fit. Reasonable notice of any such trial shall be given or sent to both vendor and purchaser; if after such notice either party or both parties shall be absent at the time fixed, Messrs. Tattersall, or one of them, or the said person appointed. may proceed to try and make a decision in his or their absence. No action shall be brought against Messrs. Tattersall or one of them, or the said person appointed, in consequence of any decision made in accordance with the above rules."

Farmers who hunt have often very good horses, made handy in summer as hacks and in winter as hunters. They are dealers, in fact, and ask as much money as dealers. They seldom have highly-finished harness-horses, and often lose a profit by not taking enough pains to complete the education of good-looking young hacks. A quarter of the value of a handsome riding-horse depends on his manners.

An inexperienced person who goes with his groom to a fair to pick up anything better than an unbroken pony, out of a Welsh or Irish drove, deserves the fate of Moses Primrose. Advertisements in the London daily and sporting newspapers offer opportunities of purchase from private individuals, who, in consequence of a death, or loss of fortune, or some other honest cause, desire to sell genuine horses; but there are a great many advertisements concocted and inserted day after day by organised gangs of swindlers. Whenever you find that the advertiser is "willing to allow a month's trial," you may take it for granted that he is a coper. When you read of "a pair of horses, quiet in harness, excellent hacks, and perfect hunters, the property of a gentleman deceased, price not so much an object as a good home," then you may be sure the thing is a swindle. There is, however, one test as infallible as Ithuriel's spear—propose an examination at the Royal Veterinary College.

The victims of coping advertisements are generally people who know nothing yet desire to secure wonderful bargains, or the very clever, conceited people who, knowing a little, fancy they know everything, and that nobody can take them in. A coper, in a moment of gin-and-water candour, confessed that his principal victims were the country clergymen and Indian officers.

There is one axiom which, whether true or not in literature, is strictly true in horse-dealing— "A little knowledge is a dangerous thing." If nature has given you a good eye for proportion, and a natural talent for observation, when you have successively bought a horse with every fault you will begin to be able to choose one for yourself.

If you know nothing when you commence, you must trust some one, and the great point is to trust one whose knowledge and experience deserve your confidence. Veterinary surgeons, like the medical attendants of human beings, are of all degrees of aptitude and experience. Natural aptitude, cultivated by constant practice, makes a veterinary surgeon a judge of soundness, action, temperament, and constitution. But as there are people whom no amount of instruction will ever make musical, so a man may pass his life amongst horses and not learn the difference between a good one and one good for nothing.

Assuming that your intended purchase is substantially sound—that is, "competent to do the ordinary work of an ordinary horse"—and that he is not vicious, and is broken to ride or drive, or both, there are several other important points to be taken into consideration before you are sure of "a good horse," which, unless you have a much longer trial than can usually be expected, must be taken on trust; for instance, temperament and constitution, and other faults that do not amount to actual vice or positive unsoundness.

RIDE AND DRIVE HORSES.

The opinion that harness-work destroyed the fine action of a riding-horse or hunter was quite true in days gone by, when all roads, in wet seasons, were at least fetlock deep in clay or mud, and when all the carriages were from one-half to one-third heavier than at the present time.   In the early part of the present century, "a devil's wagon" was the slang term for a kind of four-wheeled phaeton supposed to be in favour amongst the richer manufacturers of Spitalfields and Bethnal Green; for it was then considered impossible for one horse to draw a respectable four-wheeled carriage.

If a horse, in order to draw a family brougham or any other capacious vehicle, has to throw himself into the collar and haul away by his weight, he must lose that balance which is essential to pleasant riding action; the drudgery of such a load will soon destroy the courage or break the heart of a well-bred horse.   But if a single horse is put to a light carriage, with a proper height of wheels—a carriage that he can set in motion without effort, and which, having four wheels, casts no weight upon his shoulders—then, so far from a reasonable harness journey being a tax on his power, it may be a seasonable relief from weight under a saddle.   Still more is this the case where a pair of horses are put to a modern phaeton, wagonette, or light brougham—the exertion is child's play to them—and ten or fifteen miles at a reasonable pace healthy exercise.   Colonel Fitzwygram recommends driving in a light brougham as the best summer exercise for a couple of hunters; my experience quite agrees with his advice.   Of course this is taking for granted that the horses have not been worked in the winter so hard as to require entire rest in the summer.   The convenience of having horses which can be both ridden and driven, as well as the advantage of being able to exercise two horses in harness at once with or without one servant, are obvious.   The exercising of horses is always a great difficulty where the exercise-ground is not under the master's eye.

To secure this general utility it will frequently be found necessary to break riding-horses to harness, after they are six or seven years old, but as a rule aged horses submit to harness even better than colts.

There are of course exceptions—there are horses that the most skilful breaker, with the best tackle and the greatest patience, cannot persuade to harness satisfactorily.   I have put every horse I ever possessed in harness, and never met with but one mare that it was impossible to drive either in single or double harness.   Horses inclined to kick occasionally go best in single harness, furnished with a sufficiently strong and properly applied kicking-strap.   Horses inclined to jib—that is, stop suddenly and back—will frequently go satisfactorily in double harness.

There is one class of horse that should never "look through a collar"—that is, a lady's horse. Some ladies trot—not a very graceful action for them at the best, although a good change for the horse; but a horse in harness, except the leader of a team, should never canter.

There are horses which, perfectly quiet in harness, will not submit to be ridden; and there are more frequently horses too high-couraged for harness that become perfect under saddle.   A remarkable instance of this kind came under my notice lately.   A gentleman who keeps a complete stud of hacks, hunters, and carriage-horses, purchased for his barouche a most beautiful horse, which it was found impossible to match—without vice, he was so fast, high-couraged, and impatient, that he outpaced and outworked every horse put alongside him.   It struck the owner's son, an officer in a light dragoon regiment, that the horse, which had been bought as one of a pair, and had never been ridden, would make a charger.   Put into the military riding-school, he was trained without difficulty, was soon passed for service, and was noted as one of the handsomest and best chargers in the brigade during one of the early autumn manœuvres.   It is by no means uncommon to meet with advertisements of cavalry chargers which are also hunters and quiet in harness.

STALLIONS, GELDINGS, MARES.

Stallions are seldom used in this country for harness, hunting, or as hacks. Now and then a stallion of extraordinary beauty and gentleness is met with amongst parade chargers and park hacks; in nearly every hunt you will hear of some wonder of a stallion; but as a rule half-bred horses are castrated as yearlings, and thoroughbred horses as soon as they are thrown out of training and brought into ordinary use. It must be confessed that there is a grandeur, especially about the neck and fore-quarters of a full-aged stallion, a special character that is very picturesque. But in this country, whether from the higher system of feeding that prevails, or from the impatient character of our grooms, stallions are extremely troublesome; while in France, Spain, South Germany, and Russia, stallions are in almost universal use for light harness and saddle.

It would be difficult to decide whether we gain or lose more by our system of castration. On the one hand, we do prevent a great many useless, ill-shaped brutes from reproducing their defects; on the other, we reduce to sterility the whole class of magnificent animals which form the studs of the pasture counties. The French writers on breeding attribute the superiority of our horses in a large degree to our preference for geldings.

In Prussia the system of castration is carried still further. No one is allowed to keep or use a stallion that has not been approved, branded, and registered by a Government officer.

All things being equal, a gelding will fetch more money as a hunter, carriage-horse, or hack, than a stallion or mare. Indeed, a stallion, if aged, unless with a character as a hunter, or remarkable action, and warranted quiet, is very difficult to sell at all, unless thoroughbred or of the heavy draft breed. Railroad companies charge double or nearly double fare for a single stallion, and often compel you to take a whole box.

The common theory is that for saddle a gelding is worth at least £5 more than a mare equal in every other respect. For harness purposes some persons will not use a mare at all. High-priced pairs of full-sized carriage-horses are always geldings. Job-masters have scarcely anything else in their stables; but on turning to the advertisements of sales by auction at Albert Gate, or to the catalogues of horse shows, it will be found that a very large number of hacks not exceeding 15 hands 2 inches are described as quiet to drive as well as ride, and that a very large percentage of these are mares, which, when well bred, are usually handsomer than geldings, and have more character.

You find a great many mares worked in harness in light carriages—both single and double. In my time I have had more mares than geldings, always drove them in harness, and never met with a serious accident; but then my horses, although full-fed, were never idle, a condition which in horses as well as men is the root of all evil.

A good mare must not be rejected, although a gelding is decidedly to be preferred for harness purposes, for it can be shown, on undeniable evidence, that a number of very valuable harness-horses are mares, and equally good in harness and under saddle. Before the Franco-German War, a light-boned grey mare was the by-word for the most unprofitable, unsaleable article in horseflesh; but since that cavalry-consuming epoch there is a purchaser for a good horse of either sex or any colour.

To horse suitably is much more difficult than to buy a carriage, because horses cannot be made to order. The first point is to know what you want. But many people do not, and, more, cannot make up their minds without the eloquence of a salesman to assist them.

Suppose it is for a brougham, promised by the coach-builder to be ready in the course of two months. Your first brougham! Is the horse to be ornamental, or useful, or both? Does a lady only require it to take her into the park, on a round of visits every afternoon in the season, and through a course of shopping; or is it to be a family vehicle, to hold all the children, and crawl out on constitutionals as a sort of nursery on wheels? Or, again, is it intended for country use and long expeditions, to run morning and evening several miles to and from a railway station, or to convey a quartogenarian fox-hunter fifteen or sixteen miles to cover? Is it for a general practitioner going his mill-horse rounds in Peckham or Clapham, or the physician in whom duchess-mothers put their trust? Is it to draw a light phaeton, and be used on alternate days as a hack? When this point is settled, the choice can be made with more or less difficulty, in proportion to the degree of perfection required. Useful animals, strong, slow, and steady, with no pretensions to beauty, sufficiently sound for all practical purposes, and others active and fast, but without beauty, and that action which is in horses what "style" is in women, are comparatively plentiful, and to be purchased by those who know how to go to market at comparatively moderate prices. Before the Franco-German War my limit for such horses was £40, and I have purchased very useful blood ones at £25; but the war changed all that, and it is impossible to say when, if ever, the price of horses will fall. Between 1863 and 1873 the price of all horses, except the very best, was at least doubled.

A horse may be serviceable without being absolutely sound. A one-eyed horse may go very grandly, and a horse touched in the wind will not always make a noise in his trot; harness hides many blemishes and original defects. A pig-eyed coffin-head, or a rat tail and scanty mane, will seriously depress the price of an animal otherwise excellent. Where immediate hard work is not essential, it is cheaper to buy a horse thin and out of condition from hard work; for then, if constitutionally sound, he improves every day under the effects of regular exercise and sufficient hard food, while a horse fat from grass or in dealer's condition begins by melting away.

But before purchasing it is important to ascertain that the horse is sound enough for your use.

Perfectly sound horses that have been worked long enough to know their business are as rare as landed estates without a flaw in the title; and if an unwilling purchaser desired to cancel a bargain there are very few horses in which a clever veterinary surgeon could not detect some latent defect. On the other hand, a horse may be apparently sound, and yet have disease, or the germs of disease, which only a trained and experienced professional eye can detect. There is also a third contingency, when, from carelessness, or to conceal ignorance pure and simple, and be on the safe side, a veterinary surgeon rejects every horse presented to him with whose history he is not perfectly acquainted. I lay great stress on practical experience, because no amount of study in the library, the lecture and dissecting rooms, will make a man a good judge on a question of soundness, unless he has constant practice in examining horses, and the natural gift of correct observation and comparison.

Some people have this gift of comparison, or, as phrenologists call it, "form," so highly developed, that if they once get the proper conformation of a horse in their eye they become better judges than others who have owned horses from their earliest years.

I have particularly observed this faculty (in which I am myself extremely deficient) in eminent engineers and artists, who did not become owners of or interested in horses until they arrived at thirty or forty years of age.

There are persons whose sense of hearing is so accurate, that after listening to a horse trotting on hard ground they will discover without seeing on which leg he goes lame.

I once accompanied the late Mr. Foljambe, of Osberton, celebrated as a breeder of horses, hounds, and Leicester sheep, on a visit to the late Rawcliffe stud, for the purpose of choosing a stallion for his hunting mares. His observations from hearing alone (he became blind at about forty years of age) on the paces of the horses led out were most accurate. He had then been blind about twenty years.

There is truth in an old Yorkshire proverb, that "you must buy a horse with every fault before you are fit to buy in a fair."

If you are a novice, get a competent person to advise you; and the most competent is a veterinary surgeon who is daily engaged in examining horses. There are amateurs and grooms who are excellent judges, as far as form and soundness of limb are concerned. Where low-priced horses are in question, you may risk something, and you must always risk a great deal in buying by auction and at fairs. But where you want to purchase a high-class animal, at a proportionate price, it is well worth while, as in every other business transaction, to pay for competent professional advice.

Harnessed in brilliant carriages, and mounted by very fashionable personages, you may see every day in the London season horses with all sorts of defects—very old or very groggy, or touched in the wind, or defective in eyesight—but used because they possess some real or imaginary merit of action or form. Wonderful are the cripples which draw about the old-fashioned chariots of wealthy old maids and well-dowered dowagers who will not condescend to job their horses. The following are a few of the points to which attention should be directed:—

A hack should have two good eyes; so should a hunter, although in every hunting-field there is a tradition of some Cyclops an extraordinary performer. One of the best mares I ever rode hunting had been foaled blind of one eye. But a horse that has lost one eye from disease is very likely to lose the other at no distant date. A one-eyed horse, in other respects perfect, may do very well in double harness with the blind side to the pole; indeed, if economy is an object, and the roads in your district are good, you may put up with one totally blind horse in a pair, if his courage, form, and action make him look worth at least three figures; but it is as well to know of the defect, and get it allowed in the purchase-money.

In dealing, the only safe way is to peremptorily reject a horse with any weakness or defect to the eyesight, and listen to no excuse, unless you are prepared to buy a blind horse at a blind price. A certain class of persons always have a plausible excuse for every suspicious appearance, whether it be a blind eye or a pair of broken knees.

The "wind," to use a popular term, that is, the state of the lungs, windpipe, and throat, demands careful examination; any signs of past or present affection of the lungs is a fatal objection to any horse valued at more than £6. The defects of roaring or whistling are matters of degree and of price. A roarer may be for certain purposes a useful animal, but it does not pay to buy one without knowing the drawback.

Copers, who have made a trade of purchasing unsound horses of fine figure and action, have a way of temporarily subduing the signs of broken wind. A broken-winded horse may be compared to a man far gone in asthma. Broken wind is an incurable disease of the lungs; but there are many degrees between absolutely broken wind, and what is called "making a little noise."

Whistling and roaring are caused by thickening or some other defect or disease of the windpipe, and may exist with very good although not the highest rate of speed.

A horse turned out of a first-class hunting stable for whistling or roaring may be used for years as a slow hack, or for harness, without being heard. Very recently one of the sensation horses of the Park, ridden daily in the season by a lady of title—the two a perfect picture—was a rank roarer at any pace beyond eight miles an hour; but this beautiful mare's beautiful mistress was judicious, and knew when and how long to canter, and when to drop into a graceful walk.

There are, I believe, horses that are not stopped in their gallop by roaring, but it is difficult to understand how any one can have pleasure in riding them, however good. I once heard Charles Payne, huntsman of the Pytchley, cry out in cover, "I cannot hear the hounds for this roarer."

So, too, there are degrees in lameness, from the grogginess and dottiness of the old hunter—still good on soft ground—and the stiffness that goes off in harness-work and returns in the stable, to positive disease of the feet or the joints, or absolute breaking of the tendons. For instance, a horse of fine courage, good shoulders, and strong hocks, loins, and back—that is to say, with strong propelling powers, may go well as long as you do not ask him to gallop on hard ground or jump into hard roads. Amongst hired hack hunters there are many such game old cripples. It is on such well-bred, clever, but terribly groggy animals, that a good horseman of light weight in a soft winter will go along as well and better than millionaires mounted on hunters that cost more pounds than the screw did shillings.

Foot-lameness, where the cause is not obviously a thrush or a slight corn, and therefore curable, is a fatal objection, because there are no ways of patching up a foot, whilst a good deal may often be done with a leg. A horse will work a long time in double harness after he is not safe in a two-wheeled carriage.

Broken knees, when not grievously disfigured, are not a fatal objection to an otherwise useful horse; if he has good action and sound fore-feet you may believe that accident has caused the damage. Scores of hunters sell at three figures in spite of broken knees, but then they come to the hammer with established characters.

No one will knowingly buy a lame horse if he wants it for immediate use, but there are many who will speculate in a lame horse when it is supposed that the lameness is curable and the price justifies some risk. For instance, a horse may be lame from thrush in neglected frogs, from corns caused by bad shoeing, or other curable causes. But the man with a small stud, and especially the man who knows nothing about horses, had better have nothing to do with a lame one, however fascinating.

Herring-gutted "washy" horses are generally deficient in endurance. They will not last long days, but, if suitable in other respects, they may make very good hacks for gentle exercise. A narrow chest is considered liable to inflammation; an extravagantly broad chest may belong to a trotter, seldom to a pleasant or fast galloper.

It is one more illustration of the folly of human nature, that horses sell best when in the very worst condition for useful work, viz., "hog fat," although every one who buys a horse ought to know that the only use of fat on a horse is to conceal defects.

Age may be known up to seven by the teeth, and may be pretty nearly guessed by experts up to twenty. At six a horse has passed all infantine diseases. If a horse that has been fairly worked is sound and fresh on his legs and without vice at ten years old, he is far more valuable than a promising five-year to the person who keeps only one horse. A pair of barouche-horses, the property of Mr. East, the great job-master of Mayfair, which took a prize at the Agricultural Hall Horse Show in 1864, were both not far from twenty years old.

After unsoundness comes vice, which broadly means either "not quiet to ride or not quiet to drive," or dangerous in the stable, or quiet in double and not in single harness, or *vice versâ*. Vice again is a matter of degree. A timid person would call that vice, perhaps justly, which a bold horseman would treat as play.

These preliminary observations bring us to the important question of *warranty*. No

WALKING.

sensible person purchases an expensive horse by private contract without requiring a warranty, either general or special, of soundness and freedom from vice. I should never think of depending on the warranty of a low-priced horse; in fact, I should not ask for it, unless from a seller whose word was to be depended on, because it will not pay to go to law for a small sum of money.

The first value of a warranty depends on the way it is expressed, and the next on the solvency of the person who gives it. Professional horse-copers never hesitate to give the most unlimited warranties, just as they also offer a week or a month's trial to the purchaser who is foolish enough to part with his cheque without a veterinary examination.

A warranty, to be of the greatest practical value, should be in writing, because, although a verbal warranty is held good in law, it is extremely difficult to prove what has been said; therefore, a trial on a verbal warranty resolves itself into a contest of hard swearing.

A horse must be of considerable value, and the defendant must be rich enough to pay damages and costs to make it worth while to venture, as plaintiff, into the expensive annoyance of that worst of lotteries—a lawsuit. Sir James Stephens, a solicitor, wrote a book, with the title of "Caveat Emptor," at the beginning of this century—which made a great sensation, and has run through many editions—in which he gives the whole law of horse warranty, and paints so picturesquely the pitfalls open for purchasers, that it is almost a wonder how any novice can venture to buy a horse after reading it. But for the purposes of the present work I have nowhere found all that a purchaser should know so simply and plainly laid down as in an essay by A. T. Jebb, Esq., barrister-at-law,* from which the following extracts are abridged :—

"A representation that a horse about to be sold by auction is sound does not afford any warranty to the purchaser at auction. According to Maule I., the contract commenced when the horse was put up for sale, and ended when he was knocked down to the highest bidder. But if a person sell a horse for a particular purpose—as a hunter, as a hack, to carry a lady or a child—he could not fix on a purchaser a liability to pay for it unless it were a horse fit for the purpose for which it was required. Whether a hunter must jump well is a question for the jury ; but he must not be blind or wrong in the wind. In like manner, it has been decided that a horse sold as 'a good hack' must not be lame. The servant of a private owner entrusted with selling a horse, '*not at a sale or mart*,' cannot bind his master by giving a warranty. It remains a doubtful question whether a special agent, entrusted with the sale of a horse in a fair or other public mart, is or is not authorised to give a warranty. But where a horse-dealer or livery-stable keeper employs a servant to sell a horse, any statement made by him equal to a warranty will bind his master."

It must, however, be carefully borne in mind that the seller of a horse may tell a great many lies and use a great number of laudatory expressions that will not amount to a warranty. Hence the necessity of a written warranty.

"The rule as to unsoundness is that if at the time of sale the horse has any disease which either actually does diminish the natural usefulness of the animal, so as to make him less capable of work of any description, or which in its ordinary progress will diminish the natural usefulness of the animal—or if the horse has, either from disease (whether such disease be congenital, or arises subsequently to its birth) or from accident, undergone any alteration of structure that either actually does at the time, or in its ordinary effects will, diminish his natural usefulness—such a horse is unsound. The importance of the term 'natural usefulness' in this definition must be borne in mind, for 'one horse with a heavy fore-hand is liable to stumble, and is continually putting to hazard the neck of his rider ; another with an irritable constitution and a washy make loses his appetite, and begins to scour if a little extra work is exacted from him.' To this it may be added that such defects as cutting, speedy cut and overreach, which arise from imperfection of form, though impairing the usefulness of a horse, do not impair his natural usefulness, and therefore cannot be pronounced a breach of warranty of soundness. As long as he is uninjured he must be considered sound. Although it was otherwise held by Mr. Justice Eyre in one case, and by Mr. Justice Coleridge in another, it would appear to be now well established that a warranty of soundness is broken if a horse at the time of sale has any infirmity upon him which renders him less fit for present use and convenience ; and his subsequent recovery is no defence to an action on the warranty. In conformity with this principle, Lord Ellenborough laid it down many years ago that it was not necessary that the disorder should be permanent or incurable. 'While a horse has a cough,' he remarked, 'I say he is unsound, although that may be either temporary, or ultimately prove fatal.' And in a later case, Mr. Baron Parke, in summing up, said, 'I have always considered that a man who buys a horse warranted sound must be taken as buying for immediate use, and has a right to expect one capable of that use, and of being immediately put to any fair work the owner chooses.' Still more recently the judges in the Court of Exchequer, after a full previous consideration, arrived at a precisely similar conclusion."

The best form of warranty is—"Received from A B the sum of £   for a chestnut horse, warranted sound (quiet in harness or to ride), six years old, and free from vice."

Where a horse does not answer the warranty, the purchaser has no right to return it unless the power to do so was part of his bargain; his only course is an action for damages. "As soon as a breach of warranty is discovered, the purchaser should immediately tender the horse to the seller, and if he refuse to take him back, sell him as soon as possible for what he will fetch." The purchaser is also entitled to charge against the seller as damage the expenses incurred in keeping the horse for a reasonable time, until he can be properly disposed of. "I can conceive no case," observes Lord Denman, "where a purchaser returns a horse, in which the seller may not be answerable for some keep."

COLOURS.

The trite proverb that every good horse is of a good colour, like a good many other familiar quotations, is not true. There are colours that diminish the value of an otherwise excellent horse in a very annoying manner for the breeder. In England many object to ride a light-grey horse, although it is a favourite colour on the Continent, and one of the most common colours in the East.

On the other hand, foreigners object to English horses, when either bay, chestnut, or black, with white marks, which would be no detriment to their value in our markets, either as harness-horses or hunters, or even as hacks, if their action was satisfactory.

For harness all *distinct* colours are good, even piebalds, but bays, browns, and dark chestnuts are most in favour: greys are not fashionable, but those who fancy a pair of good greys, whether mottled or iron-grey, have to pay an extra price for them. In 1872 there were only two grey thoroughbred stallions advertised in the annual list. Where horses are to be ridden by men any extraordinary colour is objectionable. If a lady rides a piebald or a white horse it ought to be unexceptionable in form and action. Red or strawberry roan is a fashionable harness colour.

ACTION.

In horses, as Demosthenes said of Greek oratory (the maxim does not apply to English), action is the first qualification. Fine and appropriate action will counterbalance many defects in form. Harness action is of two kinds, safe and not too high, esteemed in roadsters and phaeton pairs, or dog-cart horses required for country use, and high "up to the curb-chain," esteemed for the Park, the parade, and in the Champs Elysées.

In fact, action may be safe and slow or safe and fast without any brilliancy, or it may be brilliant and slow or brilliant and fast. When a horse can do six miles and fourteen miles an hour with equal grandeur, moving all round, that is perfection.

A portrait of Mr. Charles Baynes's Columbine, which took the first prize in the single-harness class for horses not exceeding 15 hands 2 inches, at the Agricultural Hall in 1872, forms one of the coloured illustrations of this work. Columbine was a brown mare, 15 hands 1½ inches high, very fast—in fact, so fast that her owner was unable to match her—and very grand in her slow paces. The price put upon her was 400 guineas.

In making these observations, I am taking it for granted that a horse is required for pleasure. If you want nothing better than a mere drawing-machine, the cab-horse of a four-wheeler will serve your purpose.

The extremes of vile action may be found on the racecourse and in a funeral procession

TROTTING.

—in race-horses that extend their fore-legs as straight as crutches, and kick every pebble in their way when they walk; and in the solemn, much-maned, long-tailed, herring-gutted, black Hanoverians, that bend their knees up to the curb-chain, and flourish their feet while making the least possible progress in a slow funeral procession or rapid return from the grave.

A horse with really good action moves each of his four legs evenly, bringing the hind legs well under him at every movement; but this is a fine degree of machine movement long sought and seldom found. To say that a horse moves all round is to say a great deal in his favour. Hearse-horses to the eyes of a horseman are brutes, but they do their duty in the state to which they have been assigned to the perfect satisfaction of the people who use them. Racehorses, with the most wretched walking and trotting action, often gallop fast and win races, which is all their trade requires them to do. And there are hunters, too, the most generally useful class of horses, that cannot walk decently. Jack-a-Dandy, the best horse of that celebrated master of hounds and horsemen, Assheton Smith, was so bad a hack that he was always led to cover.

A horse of general utility should be able to walk in regular time—one, two, three, four. No riding-horse is worth his corn that cannot walk, for it is one of the principal paces of a

A GOOD HIND QUARTER.

hack in town or country—one of the greatest luxuries of a studious or hard-worked man. There are a great many gradations in walking. Four miles an hour done in harmonious cadence, without stumbling, dropping, shuffling, or breaking, for an hour at a stretch, is a very good pace, although every good walker is said to do five miles an hour. The style is the first consideration; after four miles an hour is reached and exceeded, to do five miles an hour in good form is a very rare performance. I have had hacks that would do five miles an hour, nodding their heads, and carrying them in the right place, without tripping or shy-ing, *when going home*, or when competing with another horse; but the most famous Piccadilly dealer once said to me, "I will go a long way to see a horse that will begin and walk at the rate of five miles an hour alone on *leaving* his stable." Hacks walk well in Rotten Row, when it is crowded; they are full of emulation, and there is no better place for teach-ing them to walk without breaking. A heavy man should find out if the hack offered him for purchase can *stand still under him*, and walk down hill without a trip or drop. Begin, therefore, when selecting a horse for generally useful purposes, by finding out whether he can walk, first led with a loose rein and then with a rider on him. A good walker is a treasure not to be expected, if the animal is also good-looking, for a low price. If you want to ride for pleasure have nothing to do with a bad walker at any price.

The faults of walkers are dropping, tripping, brushing, and cutting. Dropping is a very unpleasant defect, it gives a sensation as if the horse were about to fall on his knees; if he never has fallen perhaps he never will, but it is generally the sign of overwork or old age, or both, and if of old age incurable. A horse may be useful and go in very pleasant style in harness which is not at all fit to ride. At the same time, after a change from a heavy man to a light one, horses will sometimes cease to drop. *If a horse trips while fresh, look to his shoeing;* bad shoeing will make the very best horses stumble, and the very best horses will stumble and trip when they are tired. A horse not in condition is very soon tired, then stumbles, trips, brushes, cuts, and perhaps knuckles over with hind or fore-legs.

It is a common phrase that a horse that walks well can do every other pace well. No maxim can be more fallacious. A broad-chested horse may walk magnificently, but he is likely to be slow, and will probably roll in his gallop. A horse may walk well and not be able to trot any pace; finally, a magnificent walker may be a perfect slug. Amongst the horses ridden by the police patrol are to be found examples of fine walkers that can by no persuasion of whip or spur be made to do more than six miles an hour. The best hack I ever possessed, with no pedigree, but supposed to have a cross of thoroughbred and Barb blood, could walk five and trot sixteen miles an hour with a loose rein. This mare rolled in cantering in a most ridiculous manner, and could not gallop faster than she trotted; she never broke in trotting, however pressed. She continued sound until fourteen or fifteen years old, and then died from the effects of an accident. I also had a thoroughbred hack, by Voltigeur, afterwards the favourite of an earl's daughter, that walked admirably and cantered perfectly, but could not trot six miles an hour.

A hack that can carry weight, and do nothing else but walk really well, stepping "briskly out of the ground," "carrying his own head," is worth money, provided always that he has "character" and "good manners." The customers who most value such an animal are heavy, no longer young, and rich. They do not want to gallop at all, and a very slow smooth trot or canter is enough for them.

The trot is the all-important pace in harness, and the favourite pace of Englishmen riding. It may be fast or slow, or both, but to be perfect it should be performed with the most mechanical precision by all the four legs. Under saddle, a good trotter can do six miles an hour in good form, and increase the pace up to eight, ten, or twelve miles an hour; beyond twelve miles an hour with most horses, except in harness, it is better to turn to a hand-gallop. For park work, or on the stones, eight miles is quite fast enough in either saddle or harness. In harness a horse ought to be able to do ten or twelve with ease. Mail-phaeton horses and the wheelers of a four-horse coach are not perfect unless they can do what the Americans call a "square trot" of fourteen miles an hour. Beyond fourteen miles an hour it becomes racing pace, only expected from sporting publicans or American millionaires displaying their really wonderful carriages and trotters. The class of young gentlemen who in England would indulge in a well-appointed mail-phaeton or four-in-hand would in the United States have one or more 2.40 horses, that is, horses that can trot a mile in two minutes and forty seconds.

Pace is not the principal point in a gentleman's horse except it may be in a cover hack or railway station trapper. A horse or pony that can trot eight miles an hour in good form, bending his knees, and carrying himself like "a gentlemen," will fetch more money than a vulgar brute with no other merit than extraordinary speed.

Pages might be employed, without giving any distinct ideas, in trying to describe what good trotting should be; but it is a subject that, after all, must be studied from the live animal. The trotting action that is admirable in harness, combining a fast pace with a sprightly or a grand style, may be perfectly detestable under saddle; a degree of high, even rough, extravagant action, may be accepted and much admired in harness, which under saddle would wear the rider to death and make him look ridiculous. So, too, a large number of horses perform with perfect safety, and even brilliantly, in harness, which could not carry even a boy in saddle; because all horses intended for riding as well as driving must not only have riding "shoulders" with good legs and feet, but the proper riding action, which, as before observed, will soon be spoiled if put to draw heavy weights; and they should bridle well, which no horse can do which has not a head joined to his neck in the proper way.

A horse may have extravagant knee-action, and yet not be safe to ride. Safety depends not only in lifting each fore-foot fairly up, but in the way it is put down. It is because it is comparatively more easy to accustom young horses to a "square trot" in harness than in saddle, that light harness-work unquestionably improves them as hacks.

It is, however, much easier to find an ordinary useful harness-horse than an ordinary useful and safe riding-horse, for one important reason, amongst several, *i.e.*, good shoulders are rare in all horses, and still more in ponies. Without good sloping shoulders, no horse can be perfectly safe in saddle, but one with rather straight shoulders, low withers, and ribs so framed that a crupper is indispensable if the saddle is to be kept in its place, may run well, look well, and never tumble while properly driven in harness.

There is, however, one quality common to all good horses, which is much more essential in harness than in saddle, that is courage—the courage that will keep him trotting all day long up to the bit and into the collar without whipping. A harness-horse that requires really whipping is only fit for a four-wheeled cab or a hired fly. A horseman can make a saddle-horse go up to the bit, and increase his pace without any visible demonstration, by a squeeze of the legs, or a more or less sharp touch with the spur; a really good horseman can, as it were, mesmerise the animal he is riding. Some of the very best hacks are inclined to be lazy at starting on the road; besides, a hack has alternations of walking, trotting, and cantering. A harness-horse has to trot for hour after hour. High courage and fine action will atone for a multitude of shortcomings and defects in harness; but it must never be forgotten that a horse to draw a heavy carriage must have weight and power, good back and loins, and powerful hocks and thighs.

It takes at least six months to break an average pair of well-bred horses, or a single brougham-horse, fresh from the country, to town use, although many go well in six weeks. A horse that has once kicked or lain down in harness is never safe. Some horses will only

go double, some will only go single, and some will never go safely in harness at all. A
harness-horse should stand stock still, and yet be always ready to trot and trot on the driver
saying "Come along," and gently pulling at the bit, without ever requiring the whip. The
slug is even more dangerous in the streets than the hard puller. As a rule, horses regularly
worked in town become quiet, probably from being occupied by a multiplicity of sights and
sounds.

Those to whom horses are a necessity, and economy is an object, may purchase good-
looking, useful animals, with unimportant defects, at a reduced price at the end of the London
season.

Amongst the defects to which fast-trotting horses, and particularly young harness-horses,
are subject, are cutting and brushing.

Brushing is striking one ankle against the other ; cutting is striking the foot or shoe
against the other leg. A horse that cuts or brushes with the fore-legs is a very dangerous
animal under saddle. Almost all green horses, fresh from grass or recently broken, cut or
brush with their hind-legs when put first in harness.

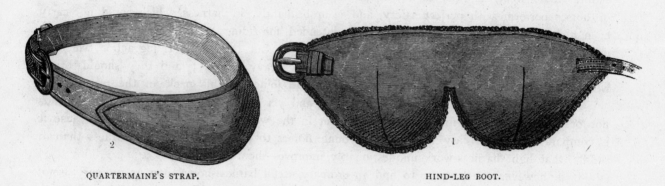

QUARTERMAINE'S STRAP.   HIND-LEG BOOT.

The first step with horses which are from any cause weak is to protect the part wounded,
and the next to get them into hard condition. The defect will often entirely disappear with
age and condition.

In breaking colts into harness there is no better precaution than the Yorkshire boot, a
piece of thick woollen cloth tied with a string so as to fall double round the fetlocks. But
if a horse cuts or brushes, it is better to resort to a proper boot or other protection before
a raw is regularly established and a permanent blemish created. Boots are sold of leather
and of india-rubber, fastened with one or more buckles. This contrivance has often a mischievous effect. The buckle is drawn tighter and tighter to prevent the boot from turning,
thus first inflammation and then an enlargement is created. The best boot for a fore-leg to
guard against cutting is made of leather lined with cloth, laced, not buckled, outside the leg.

A very good boot for the fetlock-joint of the hind-legs is made of leather in the shape of
a pear split open, united at the back and buckled at the front of the fetlock. From its exact
fit, this boot is not likely to turn from the stroke of the opposite leg, or to require tight
buckling. (See woodcut No. 1.)

For guarding against a particular way of cutting common to fast trotters, a very good contrivance was invented by the late Mr. Quartermaine, the Piccadilly dealer, for a famous fast
harness-trotter. It consisted of a a strap padded to the thickness of a forefinger, and buckled
between hair and hoof of the hind-leg. (See woodcut No. 2.) There is an objection to horse

boots entirely made of india-rubber, the material contracts with cold and expands with heat. A hunter with india-rubber boots on his fore-legs has been observed to be quite crippled after standing for some time at covert side, fetlock deep in mud, on a cold day.

These faults of cutting and brushing are much aggravated by forcing young raw horses beyond their pace. When first noticed the shoes should be carefully examined and altered by an intelligent smith. The great point is to stop the defect before it becomes a habit. If, however, a horse in trotting or galloping strikes the inside of one fore-leg with the shoe of the other—in technical phrase, "speedy cuts"—have nothing to say to him for saddle or for harness in a two-wheeled carriage, for he may come down at any moment as if shot. It is a fault which, if not incurable, is too dangerous for experiments by amateurs.

AGE.

Aged horses, if sound in legs and wind, are the best for harness, because they are seasoned, and safe from a variety of ailments and diseases incident to juvenile horseflesh. An organised system of tampering with the teeth, in the breeding counties, make three year olds seem four, and four seem five. An honest seven, or nine, or ten, with good legs and wind, is cheaper than a dishonest five. Few veterinary surgeons can detect the deception.

SIGHTS AND SOUNDS.

Shying, when it amounts to a full stop or a complete turn round, is vice, and most dangerous; but there are many intermediate stages. Shying arises either from ignorance, or defective eyesight, or freshness, or a confirmed vicious habit. Colts shy from ignorance, because they are afraid of almost everything they meet, and continue to shy at various objects, until, by practice and gentle treatment, they have learned that nothing is going to hurt them. With pains and patience, almost any horse may be trained to meet without flinching railway trains, military parades, elephants, camels, and other most alarming objects. But it is not only colts that are ignorant; aged horses, if brought from the country to the town, or brought in contact with troops in scarlet uniforms, omnibuses, windmills, or road locomotives, will generally turn round, and often try to run away.

If, as is not uncommonly the case, a horse shies because his eyesight is defective, either from a sort of short-sightedness or from the commencement of blindness, the fault is incurable, and the only resource is to put him in harness with very close winkers I once had a mare of an extremely placid temperament that always started and shied violently at the sight of anything white—a white horse, a cow, a hen, or dog, in the road threw her into mortal terror, although nothing else seemed to disturb her. This was no doubt the result of some defect in her eyesight.

Some horses will shy when they are very fresh, just as they will kick up their heels on coming out of the stable, and after an hour or two's work take no notice of the objects which at first seemed to alarm them. If, then, a horse shies, take means to ascertain whether there is any defect in his eyes. If he shies at objects on one side only, the probability is that the eye on that side is affected. Dark stables have a tendency to make horses shy. I once observed that all the hunters of a hard-riding farmer shied, and found on inquiry that he kept them in loose boxes in a dark barn. A horse that has been some time in use, and shies at everything he meets, especially if it is coming towards him, has most probably defective eyesight. A good horseman may continue to use him in the country, but it is madness to ride such an animal in a town, because a bound of a yard or even of a few inches may bring horse and rider on the pole or the wheels of a carriage. Supposing the eyesight all right, there are few cases of shying—that is, alarm—that may not be cured; but it must be done by some good-tempered, patient person, who will give up days to the task.

There is nothing at which horses are more fearfully alarmed than at camels. The proprietor of a circus informed me that he found that all horses, even thoroughbred stallions in high condition, after being shut up in a stable within sight of camels for a few days, paid no more attention to a hideous double-humped dromedary than to a horse. Railway trains at first alarm horses very much, not only from the strange sight of a big black object rushing along belching out white steam, but from the shrieking sound; but if a horse is quietly led and firmly held in a field or road running parallel to a railway train, but with his head *away from it* as it passes him, after a very short time he will treat the train, the smoke, the fire, the steam-whistles, and the steam-cloud, with perfect indifference. A hansom cab horse, that could be with difficulty held by half a dozen men the first time he saw and heard a train at the Great Eastern station, having been treated as above described for a few days stood on the rank facing the arrival trains and never flinched. It cannot be too strongly stated that whipping, spurring, forcing a horse to face the object that excites terror, or any violence, may do a great deal of harm, and cannot do any good. A cavalry officer informs me that in his experience he only knew one horse out of hundreds that could not be broken to stand regimental sights and sounds.

Few gentlemen have the time or the patience required for breaking a colt or a full-aged horse of his terrors. It is much better to confide the task to a man whose business it is, and whose system discards the use of whip and spur. The best horseman may not only be dismounted by a shying horse wheeling round when least expected, but find himself under the wheels of a butcher's cart, driven at butcher's pace. A fine-tempered, but high-couraged hack, when ridden in London for the first time, found so many sights and sounds alarming that it was a work of danger to get him from Kensington to Westminster. In a short time, by quiet firm treatment, he became accustomed to meet, pass, and be passed by omnibuses, pleasure-vans, and all the ordinary vehicles of the street; but with the time at my disposal I was less successful in accustoming him to three particular objects of his aversion—a fizzing railway train passing under a bridge he had constantly to cross, a line of guardsmen on the march, and the drum and pipes of Punch. On one occasion, cantering up the slope of a bridge just as an engine passed blowing off its steam, he stopped and reared round so suddenly that he tore off a hind shoe. I sent him to an anti-whip-and-spur horse-breaker; and, after a fortnight of daily practice, he met locomotives, drums, firearms, and scarlet banners, as calmly as the oldest trooper in the life-guards. When very fresh he would curvet a little, but never attempted to turn round. Previous to this breaking he would try to run away at the sight of soldiers in line or on the march.

Well-bred horses, properly broken, are more courageous than coarsely-bred horses. Indian sportsmen say that only a high-bred Arab can be depended on in spearing a fierce boar or leopard. Therefore, although thoroughbred horses resist violently, they are easily taught when once put in such a position that they cannot resist.

I had a thoroughbred mare, full of fire and courage, that no train, sight, or sound, seemed to alarm. She would face the foot-guards, marching with their band, as if she enjoyed the sight, and was perfectly steady, although excited; but when taken into the hunting-field for the first time, being then at least ten years old, as soon as she heard the hounds give tongue in cover, she plunged violently, and was in a few minutes covered with sweat and foam. When the hounds broke cover she became perfectly frantic. On the other hand, I have known an old hunter, of the quietest temperament, become perfectly unmanageable at a review, when the forces advanced in line with bayonets at the charge.

These examples are mentioned to show how great a mistake it is to be angry with a horse that is frightened at any unaccustomed sight or sound. Twenty years ago I wrote, "a perfect horseman knows neither fear nor anger."

A nervous horse, which cannot be accustomed to strange sights and sounds, is as dangerous as a really vicious horse; but a young or very fresh horse should not be condemned because he starts at sounds, and shies, on first leaving the stable.

PULLERS AND RUNAWAYS.

A horse that "bridles well," that is, one that neither knocks out your teeth with his poll nor pokes his head like a pig, but one that bends his neck, and champs the bit with a good natural mouth, has been really well broken, can easily be soothed and restrained when boiling over with high spirits from want of exercise, or excited by a gallop over grass fields. But there are a great many intermediate stages between the best mouth and a bull-headed brute.

If a horse from his shape cannot or has not been taught to bend his neck at the will of the rider, there is very little pleasure in riding him, however good he may be in other respects.

With a new horse, the first thing is to find out what bridle suits him and you. An accomplished steeplechaser may ride a horse and make him do what he likes with a racing snaffle or even a halter; another less perfect horseman may get on very well with a plain double bridle; a lady, or a man deficient in strength, may require a very powerful bit—a Chifney, a Hanoverian, or even an Iron Duke. A horse may go perfectly well on five days of the week; but in high spirits, or frightened by something, or differing with his rider on the sixth day on the propriety of taking a ditch in cold blood, he will try to bolt. If he succeeds, or if he has been in the habit of succeeding, and if he has a mouth at all, you must get a bit that will hold him, acting on the maxim of "ride on the snaffle, but have plenty of bit in his mouth."

In the course of my journeys as Assistant Commissioner to the Great Exhibition of 1851 and also on agricultural tours, I frequently hunted a dozen different horses in the course of a month. I always carried with me, for making an ordinary bit more powerful, a bit of whipcord, with which I could make a nose-band in five minutes and so keep a pulling horse's mouth shut.

If you find that with no bit can you comfortably hold a horse, get off him, and get rid of him. A horse that cannot be controlled and stopped is dangerous, not only to the rider, but to every living being he comes across. But a really good horse should not be given up without a fair trial with different bits and bridles. Let a horse once feel that you can master him, and in nine cases out of ten he will not try to rebel, or will give up the attempt at the first hint from the curb-rein.

Some horses become positively mad with fright or the mere excitement of galloping; they will rush without hesitation at iron bars or a brick wall. Others, scarcely less dangerous, are cunning, and will thread their way through forest trees, to the infinite danger of the rider's brains and knees. Other horses gallop off merely because they are fresh and if it is on the way to cover, with a clear country road, you may go on at the rate of fifteen or sixteen miles an hour without pulling, persuading them that they are going your pace.

A good horseman, when he knows the country, and that his pulling hunter really knows his business, will take the opportunity of a sharp run to ride across a line of his own at least fifty yards wide of the hounds, and alongside them, and never let the animal know that he is running away. The very best horses pull when they are fresh, and require daily exercise. Some of the most perfect harness-horses cannot be left two consecutive days in the stable without showing that "they are above themselves." When you are young and strong, and a tolerable horseman, you will not find fault if your saddle-horse plunges and pulls a little when he leaves the stable; but a horse in harness, driven in town, that cannot be stopped, is a most dangerous animal.

If a harness-horse carries his nose in the air, as some very fine steppers do, to hold him you must put a standing martingale on him, fastened to his nose-band, or buckled to the rings of a snaffle, as the case may be. A light-mouthed horse of this kind will often go best with a ring-snaffle and martingale. A severe bit on a high-couraged horse, driven in harness, soon entirely spoils his mouth. For such cases Blackwell's patent reins are to be recommended, especially for coachmen with heavy hands. A coachman must be able to turn quickly and stop short. He can do neither if he cannot hold his horse.

After making due allowance for the effects of idleness, that is freshness, if a horse is found bull-necked, with a leather mouth, get rid of him for the benefit of some hansom cab. A runaway horse in harness may cost you not only life or limb but hundreds of pounds of damages in a few minutes.

A horseman can manage a puller that is not also a rogue in the country but not in town. In a field he may ride him in a circle until he gives way to the bridle; on downs or sands he may ride him until he slackens his pace. In a word, when a new purchase, in other respects to your mind, pulls hard, and would run away if he could, try the effects of regular exercise, and find a bit that will make him bend to your hand; try every kind until you find what suits him, but have nothing to do with a mad or vicious runaway brute at any price.

The very fine horses occasionally found in hansom cabs, "steppers," without a blemish, are generally vicious horses that nothing but daily hard work can keep in decent order.

CONSTITUTION AND TEMPERAMENT.

No horse can be placed on the list of *useful* that has not a good constitution. He may be sound, good in all his paces, handsome to look at, pleasant to ride and drive, quiet in the stable; but if he is always sick, easily tired, or incapable of a long day's journey, he is out of place except in the long stud of a rich man. There he may be a luxury—admirable for park and parade purposes—just able to do a little gentle exercise, and then rest, after being fed by the ounce; but to the man of moderate means he is useless.

The greatest defect in this line is bad feeding, in fact, bad digestion; and, consequently, bad appetite. You may meet with a horse that will bound from the door the picture of health and strength at a rare pace, and so continue for a short time, then flag, drop to a slow jog-trot, and require the whip to keep up a decent pace—this occurring when in full hard condition. Another form of the same defect is where the horse goes bravely all day, but on returning, after a reasonable day's work, say twenty miles with a bait, refuses his provender, and hangs his head the picture of misery. If you can give him a day's rest, perhaps he will come again for a short turn, quite fresh; but if you work him from day to day he loses flesh, his coat stares; in fact, he starves in the midst of plenty.

I have known a hunter that would perform in the most brilliant manner with staghounds for a burst of twenty-five minutes, galloping in the first flight, and clearing every kind of fence including water and lofty bullfinches in grand style; at the end of that time she would tumble over a sheep-hurdle, or roll helpless into a ditch without an effort.

This weakness must not be confounded with the failure of horses fresh from grass, or in dealer's condition; in both those cases it requires time, slow exercise, and proper food, to get them "fit" for hard or fast work. But where, after a fair day's work in harness or saddle, a horse that is not sickening with any malady will not eat heartily, get rid of him, unless you have a place for him as a fashionable luxury.

There are also horses, especially crib-biters and wind-suckers, which are subject to attacks of colic. This is probably unsoundness, but it may be difficult to prove it. A gentleman of our acquaintance had a capital hunter that was attacked with colic after every hard day with hounds. So regular were the attacks, that the groom was always provided with a colic draught. At length he sold him at the hammer, out of condition. He was bought by a small trades-man fond of hunting, for a small price. Meeting him, or rather recognising the horse one day in the field, I asked how he got on with the colic. "Very well indeed, he has never had but one attack. I feed him myself, am never out more than three hours, and in that time give him two stale rolls I carry for the purpose." He was a sporting baker.

Another dangerous defect of constitution is a tendency to inflammation of the lungs, or the membranes of the lungs (pneumonia), which often accompanies a narrow chest. Your veterinary adviser should protect you against purchasing a horse with any outward and visible signs of tendency to such maladies, but if a horse of any value is attacked and cured, sell him as soon as possible; in the case of a low-priced horse with an acute attack, I am convinced that the cheaper plan is to have him killed at once. He will be three months on the sick-list; the surgeon's bill, night-work included, will be ten or twelve pounds; and if he comes out a roarer, as he probably will, he will not be worth that sum unless he is big enough and strong enough for a plough or harrow horse.

"I understand, sir, perfectly; you want a good hack with a placid temperament." These words were addressed in our hearing by George D——, the celebrated steeplechaser, and then horse-dealer at Kensington, as much noted for his picturesque horse-language as his astounding pluck, to one of his customers famous in days of health as a fine horseman; a hard man in the hardest riding counties, then reduced by rheumatism and gout to hobbling feebly on foot with the help of a stout cane, or riding in a low park phaeton.

The phrase, given after George's manner with a most insinuating accent, set me thinking often since how much the comfort of a rider or driver is dependent on his horse's temperament —a temperament suited to his age, his health, spirits, and occupation. The horse in which a lieutenant of light cavalry or a hunting undergraduate would delight would be mounted misery to a Queen's Counsel for his morning exercise, to an invalid taking his first ride after months on a bed of sickness, or to a middle-aged Master hunting his own hounds, however consummate a horseman. And just the same rule will apply to driving-horses. With twenty miles of clear highway before a pair of mail-phaeton horses, you can, if an experienced coach-man, with undamaged nerves, put up with an amount of impetuosity, especially if your carriage is strong and your seat high, that would be absurd and dangerous for a pleasure drive in a crowded city.

Age, hard work, anxiety, sickness, tell on the finest and the most finished horseman; the first alone brought, at last, that brilliant cavalry leader, Field-Marshal Lord Combermere, to a thirteen-hand pony of placid habits. That being the case, in spite of the exceptional and extraordinary horsemen of threescore and ten and fourscore years, it is much more necessary to consider temperament when selecting horses for men who never have been famous for their skill in equestrian arts, and for ladies whose courage is so often greater than their experience.

No one will willingly select a vicious horse for pleasure purposes. I mean a horse that from hereditary disposition, or imperfect breaking in early life, or cruel treatment, has become incurably spiteful: seeking opportunities to bite or kick those who approach it; kicking persistently in harness; rearing, kicking, plunging, and bolting, when mounted, not from excess of high spirits, but with the deliberate intention of dismounting the rider.

There are persons who, confident in their strength and skill, will tackle such brutes when they possess extraordinary qualities as hunters or trappers, and with success, when the horses are not confirmed in vice by age, and are treated by persons who have patience and time to spare, as well as strength and skill. This was the practice of a very famous master of the Pytchley and Atherstone hounds. But such accomplished equestrians want no advice from me.

I know no social offence more unpardonable than that of the man who takes a horse known to be a kicker amongst other horsemen. Next to a really vicious horse a nervous horse is the most dangerous, because he is uncontrollable when once he takes fright, and will in an instant spring into a chalk-pit, or dash against the vehicles of a crowded street. Nervousness may be much mitigated by care and kindness; but where it is hereditary—and this is not unfrequently the case with very beautiful high-bred animals—they are not fit for town use. Nervousness is sometimes the result of cruelty. Certain Irish dealers, who bring over strings of superior horses to English fairs, make a practice before bringing one out for a customer of putting the unfortunate animal against a wall, and flogging it for several minutes; then only, after a considerable application of "ginger," is the horse considered fit to be shown.*

The reverse of a high-couraged animal is a slug. Slugs suit a certain class of customers very well—dowagers, and their fat, sleepy, autocratic coachmen; single ladies, who make pets of their ponies, and pass most of their drives at the walk; and the middle-aged stout men who ride, not for pleasure, but on medical advice. There are also naturally sensible horses, that seem to understand what they are wanted to do with a very little showing; and others so stupid that they are only fit for a mill-horse round.

The best class of horse unites the greatest willingness to go at a walk, trot, canter, or gallop, when called upon, with immediate obedience when starting, stopping, or turning, is required, and perfect indifference to strange sights and sounds. With such horses you may thread your way, driving off a racecourse, yet make an excellent pace when you reach a clear road. With such a hack you may walk up the most crowded streets of London in the height of the season; steadily he will proceed, noticing nothing, and obeying the slightest indication of your hands or legs.

The spirit or courage of a horse is a good deal affected by his breed, age, food, and work. Coarse-bred horses, if inclined to be restive, are generally stupid and stubborn; high-bred horses are more sensible, and, if violent at all, more violent. The most sensible, tractable, and yet high-couraged horses, are to be found amongst blood-horses, English or Oriental. But many horses have their tempers destroyed by the tricks of stable-boys.

Young horses, as a rule, require more exercise to keep them "within themselves" as

* Mr. Grout, the dealer, of Woodbridge, Suffolk, who is my authority for this statement, tells that, on the last day of a York fair, he requested an Irish dealer to show a particular horse without flogging or ginger. "Faith!" was the Irishman's reply, "the divil's mine, and as long as he is mine I shall do as I like; when he is yours you can show him as you like."

distinguished from "above themselves," but we have known horses fourteen years old which, although perfectly docile with regular exercise, required "a man on them" after a few days' idleness on corn and beans.

This question of natural temperament is of the greatest possible importance in selecting horses for those who are not practised horsemen or finished coachmen, who have not nerve, strength, and practice. When you are young, bold, confident, experienced, in "fit" condition, nothing is more delightful than to mount and master violence, whether arising from high spirits and high courage, or naturally bad temper.

The great sporting novelist of our day has admirably described the two opposite temperaments in two thoroughbred hunters of the highest steeplechasing class. A young dragoon goes to an Irish farmer to see an untried mare: and here is a scene drawn by a master hand —a first flight man in Northamptonshire and many other countries :—

"Over the rough paved yard, through the stone gap by the peat stack, not the little cropped jackass himself could have behaved more soberly; but where the spring flowers were peeping in the turf enclosure beyond, and the upright bank blazed in its golden glory of gorse bloom, the devilry of many ancestors seem to pass with the keen mountain air into the filly's mettle. Her first plunge of hilarity and insubordination would have unseated half the rough-riders that ever mis-handled a charger in the school. Once, twice, she reached forward with long powerful plunges, shaking her ears and dashing wildly at her bridle, till she got rein enough to stick her nose in the air, and break away at speed. A snaffle, with or without a nose-band, is scarcely the instrument by which a violent animal can be brought on its haunches at short notice. But Daisy was a consummate horseman, firm of seat and cool of temper, with a head that never failed him, even when debarred from the proper use of his hands.

"He could guide the mare, though incapable of controlling her, so he sent her at the highest place in the fence before him; and, fast as she was going, the active filly changed her stride on the bank with the accuracy of a goat, landing lightly beyond, to scour away once more like a frightened deer. 'You can jump,' said he, as she threw up the head that had been in its right place hardly an instant, while she steadied herself for the leap, 'and I believe you're a flyer; but, by Jove, you're a rum one to steer!'

"She was quite out of his hand again, and laid herself down to her work with the vigour of a steam-engine; the turf fleeted like falling water beneath those smooth, sweeping strides. They were careering over an open, upland country, always slightly on the rise, till it grew to a bleak, brown mountain, far away under the western sky. The enclosures were small; but notwithstanding the many formidable banks and ditches with which it was intersected, the whole landscape wore that appearance of space and freedom so peculiar to Irish scenery, so pleasing to the sportsman's eye. It looked like galloping, as they say; though no horse, without great jumping powers, could have gone two fields. It took a long Irish mile, at racing pace, to bring the mare to her bridle; and nothing but her unusual activity saved the rider from half a dozen rattling falls during his perilous experiment. She bent her neck at last, and gave to her bit in a potato ground, and they arrived at that mutual understanding which links together so mysteriously the intelligences of the horse and its rider."

In the contrasting scene the hero's wife is in the first flight of a desperate stag-hunt in the Vale of Aylesbury, and determined to keep it.

"Norah roused Boneen; that good little horse, bred and trained in Ireland, seemed to combine the activity of a cat with the sagacious instinct of a dog. Like all of his blood, *he only* left off feeling lazy when his companions began *to feel tired.* 'I could lead the hunt now

Daisy, if you'd let me,' cried Norah. 'Little Boneen's as pleased as Punch ; *he'd like* to pull hard, *only he's such a good boy he does not know how.'* "*

Thus Satanella was the pet of a wild subaltern of light cavalry; but little Boneen, who could go as fast and jump as far, was the horse for a lady.

There are, however, in reference to temperament, two conditions that are always to be taken into consideration. A horse never shows his real temperament until he is in high condition. The racehorse or the hunter that can scarcely be kicked into a trot at the end of a hard season may require a very good man with a powerful bit to hold him, after rest, gentle exercise, and proper food have had their usual effect ; and the same may be said of harness horses.

Again, a horse with fine shoulders, with a good place for the saddle, where the rider has plenty before him, a barrel that affords a good grip for the thighs and legs, and a mouth which, without being morbidly tender, yields to the bit, may be violently high-couraged, plunge, do everything but fall backwards in rearing, and still with "ample verge and room enough," be brought to reason.

In harness, unless a horse has the vile trick of carrying his nose in the air, a tender mouth is not a serious objection. You may drive with reins held as if they were a worsted thread. Moderate horsemen, and horsewomen, too, are puzzled by the delicate mouths which masters of the arts of horsemanship would play upon as Arabella Goddard or the Abbé Liszt play on the piano.

Average riders hold on a great deal by the bridle—that is, when any unusual start or bound takes place. Most men like a hunter that "takes a good hold" at his leaps ; so that while nothing is so dangerous as a horse that can neither be turned or stopped, a horse that can only be ridden with a worsted thread is "caviare to the multitude." There is an important difference between the horse that when fresh must be ridden a mile or so to calm him down, and the brute that, increasing his pace from a walk to a trot, and from a trot to a wild gallop, goes where he likes, if he does not set his mind—by plunging, kicking, bucking, and starting— to get rid of his rider.

MARES—RIDING AND DRIVING THE SAME HORSES.

I have said something in another page about a common prejudice against riding and driving the same animal in harness, and traced the origin of the objection back to the time when carriages were at least one-third heavier than they are at present. I have also noted the objection to mares for harness.

In the course of an examination of the catalogues of the Agricultural Hall horse shows, we have collected the following not uninteresting evidence bearing on both these questions :—

It was not until 1868 that classes were made for any harness animals except ponies, so that the catalogues previous to that date do not afford much information on the important questions which this chapter is an endeavour to elucidate. But in 1867 the chestnut mare Beauty, 15 hands high, entered in the name of Mr. Banks, of Gray's Inn Lane (but well known as the property of Mr. Purday a great amateur of steppers), took a first prize in hacks. In the following year the same mare took the first prize in single harness. This mare was sold more than once at over £300.

In 1868, in a class " for horses of the best shape with park action, exhibited in single harness," out of nineteen entries eight were also entered in riding-classes at prices of from one hundred and twenty to two hundred guineas, and eight of the entries in this harness class were mares. The same proportion of mares was found in the two harness classes for ponies.

In the following year the same proportion of mares and riding and driving entries prevailed. Amongst those entered as hacks and for single harness was a most beautiful horse, the property of Captain Robert Campbell (Campbell of Monzie). In 1870, Mr. Frisby, of the Stock Exchange, well known as the owner of horses with extraordinary action, took with his mare Daisy the first prize in the cover hack class and the first prize in a single harness class. He also took the first prize in single harness for horses not over 14 hands 2 inches, with Dunstan, who was also entered in a riding class; while Colonel Burnaby, of the Guards, carried off the prize for phaeton pairs with the mares Empress and Queen, and Queen was also entered in a class for park hacks.

BROUGHAM-HORSE.

The late Captain Spiers, of the Guards, took the prize for harness pairs in 1867 with a pair of harness mares for which six hundred guineas was refused. In the following year Mr. Walter Gilbey's Lily and Lilac took the first prize for phaeton pairs, and Lily was highly commended in a class for park hacks. For this pair of mares the sum of eight hundred guineas was refused; six hundred being offered for Lily alone—perhaps the finest stepper in both slow and fast paces ever exhibited at any show; indeed, it was found impossible to match her in her fast paces. The second prize in the single harness class, in which Lily took the prize, was a piebald, which also competed in a hack class.

It is not necessary to pursue the subject further. These examples are sufficient to show that in horses between 14 hands and 15 hands 2 inches, of remarkable action, and of the greatest value, a large per-centage are mares, and a large per-centage fit both to ride and to drive. In horses of less value, the proportion of mares useful for the two purposes is still greater. Since the date quoted, the high price of good horses has brought mares more into use for harness; even job-masters buy them for the smaller class of carriages.

CHAPTER X.

USEFUL HORSES AND PONIES.

A MAN who has risen from the ranks generally opens his stable with one horse, and, if married, with a strong animal capable of drawing a family brougham or landau, or other covered carriage. Some begin at once with everything in the most correct style—carriage, horse, harness, coachman—others work up by degrees, and are contented to commence with the simply useful. Perhaps it will be better to take it for granted that the best is required, and describe the brougham-horse as he should be where a lady is to be pleased and economy is not an object.

A BROUGHAM-HORSE.

A first-class brougham-horse (according to a great authority at Knightsbridge, who long had the exclusive selection of the late Emperor Napoleon's harness-stud) should be long and low, full-barrelled, and from 15 hands to 15 hands 3 inches high, according to the size and weight of the carriage. Nothing looks worse than a horse too small or too tall. In the one case he seems buried in the shafts and harness; in the other he is constantly pulling up the wheels, and by his size dwarfs the brougham. He should have a broad chest, a lofty crest, a broad back (if rather hollow it is no objection), a flowing mane, a full tail, well carried, presenting a combination of breeding and power. His action should be grand, stately, machine-like, forward action all round, each foot keeping time as truly as Sir Michael Costa's bâton. Champing his bit, arching his neck, and bending his knees, he should trot eight miles an hour, and be able to do twelve; for although the brougham is not intended, when drawn by one horse, to be rattled along like a hansom cab, there are times when you are really hurried—late for an appointment with a lady, or a Secretary of State—then it is very provoking to have your coachman whipping, and your two-hundred-guinea purchase see-sawing like a rocking-horse, "all action and no go."

There is no mistake greater than selecting horses too large for single harness—15 hands 3 inches is high enough for any brougham; above that height they may do for parade purposes, but they wear themselves out with their own weight on anything like a journey, say from Kensington to Highgate.

There is another point that ladies who admire a sensational horse should remember. In harness, as in many other conditions of life, ornament and hard work do not agree well. That rare and costly quality, high action, requires as much care as a tenor singer's voice or a tea-taster's palate. To develop it in perfection the coachman must be a genius in his way, with fingers as delicate and sympathetic as the fashionable violinist of the hour; so that whilst the high-couraged horses rush forward at each step, he, as it were, sustains them in the air, After having, then, retained the artist—the coachman—the instruments must be always in tune, stuffed with corn and beans above their work, with just enough exercise to keep down fever.

A very short season of steady, regular day-by-day morning concerts, afternoon visits, and park drives will bring five-hundred-guinea action down to a hundred, or even forty. This is a fact it is very difficult to make ladies understand.

Prince (then Count) Esterhazy was once famous in London for the magnificence of his equipages, and particularly for the beauty and action of his harness-horses. His secret lay not only in buying horses of splendid action—that many of greater wealth could do—but in always having his pairs *above their work*. For that end he had six horses to do the work of three. The pair that excited murmurs of admiration in the Park, or at a Sion House or Chiswick fête, one day, rested the next, with one hour's slow exercise in a brake; and if any one horse showed the least symptoms of flagging, he was at once sent for a holiday in a loose box at the farm of his Mentor, Mr. Phillips of Willesden.

If, however, the question turns from the ornamental to the useful, there is no doubt that more pleasure-horses are ruined by too much and irregular rest, too many oats and beans, stables too hot, and very little exercise, than by hard work and hardships.

As a matter of course, no one who enjoys riding would think of riding a regular brougham-horse or any other horse that drew a heavy vehicle. The moment a horse begins to bend and throw his weight into the collar, he loses that elasticity that makes the pleasure and the safety of a good hack.

There is, however, no reason why the single horse driven in a stanhope phaeton or other carriage equally light, should not also be used in saddle. Still more suitable are pairs driven in any light carriages—broughams, victorias, wagonettes, mail phaetons—if selected for the double purpose of riding and driving.

PONIES.

Next to or before the brougham-horse in general utility comes the pony, which is a sort of equine servant-of-all-work, the *souffre douleur*—the whipping-block on which the boys and girls learn to ride, and the ready resource in any emergency, when the boy-page or groom has to hurry off with a letter or telegram, or to fetch some forgotten article for the cook.

The late Sir Robert Peel did not ask a more difficult question when he invited the House of Commons to tell him "what is a pound" than the man who, in a company of horsey men collected from the four points of the compass, inquires, "What is a pony?" In Yorkshire, Leicestershire, and Northamptonshire, anything under 15 hands 2 inches is called a pony. The famous steeplechaser, the Lamb, which twice won the Liverpool Steeplechase, and stood 15 hands 2 inches high, was called "The Pony" by the professional reporters of his struggles and his triumphs. In Suffolk, which is well known as a great horse-breeding county, the height of a pony is settled at 13 hands 3 inches.

In Nottinghamshire, as will be seen from a letter of great authority presently quoted, the height is considered to be anything under 14 hands 2 inches; whilst in Devonshire and Somersetshire "the oldest inhabitants" consider any pony more than 12 hands high as the degenerate result of some foreign cross of the ancient Exmoor breed

Strictly speaking, a pony is one of a tribe reared for generations untold on mountains and moorlands, without shelter and without other food than the natural herbage. The true pony is bred because nothing of a greater size can be reared under the circumstances of soil and climate. The smallest size for any useful purpose is about 9 hands (*i.e.*, 36 inches); well-shaped ponies under that height are only fit for pets or for the establishment of a showman. Two very perfect pairs of ponies 9 hands high, of totally different styles, have come under my notice within the last few years. The first, a pair of brown stallions respectively named Jack and Jill, were exhibited by the Countess of Hopetoun at the Islington Horse Show in 1871, in a curiously ugly wagonette; one took a prize in the small stallion class. In form they were admirable Norfolk trotters. The other two were a perfect tandem, the property of Mr. Myring, of Walsall, exhibited in 1872, and were miniature hunters of perfect shape, and that is the shape of every good riding pony.

THE SHETLAND PONY.

Where a pony under 12 hands is required the Shetland breed is rarely excelled. In the Shetland Islands the soil and the climate make it impossible to breed a large animal of any kind, whether ox, sheep, or horse. There—as also in Devonshire and in Clydesdale—is a tradition that the native breeds were improved by stallions which escaped from the wrecks of the Spanish Armada. But there is not the slightest historical evidence of this cross, and it is much more likely that the Shetland is the descendant of the Norwegian pony, considering that the islands were long part of the Scandinavian kingdom. In districts and countries bordered by lands which will rear a full-sized horse, there is a constant temptation to the breeder to put his mares to large-sized sires. In the Shetlands there is not, and never has been, any such temptation; and, therefore, symmetry has not been neglected in favour of size. The breeds, however, have been very much influenced by the demands of the export trade. Lord Ashley's Acts, which came into operation about the year 1840, and forbade the use of boys as beasts of draught, created a demand for ponies small enough to draw coal-trucks on underground tramways. For the last thirty years they have been bred for that purpose rather than for riding or drawing pleasure-carriages. The "Druid"* visited the Shetland Islands for the express purpose of adding a description of the ponies to his agricultural notes. He says: "Every one uses the ponies of the country. The Norwegian colours—dun, with black mane and tail, and a black stripe down the back—are in request; bays and blacks are most common, greys and chestnuts scarce. Piebalds are to be found but are not in favour with many native buyers, from an opinion that they partake of an Iceland cross, and are softer and slower than the true native Shetlander. The Icelanders average two hands higher than the Shetlanders. They are often imported in great numbers at Granton and Aberdeen. The best Shetlanders come from Unst. They are bred on a thin soil, studded with large red stones and kinds of rocks, amongst which one sees scores of ponies picking the green grass which the light of heaven and the breath of the Gulf Stream force up from a barren-looking bed. Unst may be regarded as the heart of Shetland—a sunny, genial-looking spot when other parts of the country are dismal enough in the late spring. If well kept, the ponies reach 44 inches (11 hands), but the average is 38 to 42 inches. Each cottar has generally a few ponies on the hill, which they catch, and offer to the dealers for sale in May and October. When the trade in ponies for the coal-pits was at its height five hundred were

* "Fold and Fern," North

taken every year (not thirty mares amongst them), and about two hundred for general use, of all ages, from two to twelve years. These heavy sales, continued for some years, drained the Shetlands of aged ponies. Of late the dealers' purchases have fallen off. In 1867 a good horse pony was worth £7; a mare, unless a wonder, £2 less. The chief demand of mine-owners is in January and February.

"In the Durham collieries Welsh ponies outnumber the Shetland. The Scotch have the lead in Northumberland, where larger ponies are required. The Scotch ponies, bred chiefly in Argyllshire, Mull, and Skye, and the western part of Ross-shire, average 12 hands 2 inches, the Iceland 12, the Welsh 11, and the Shetland 10.

"Some of the ponies have not seen the light for fifteen years. In well-regulated pits they are kept in as good condition as hunters, with green food in summer, and a full allowance of oats, beans, and peas, crushed and mixed with hay, chaff, and bran. They suffer most from indigestion—viz., greedy feeding when hungry—scarcely ever from diseases of the lungs or eyes. The average work is twenty miles a day, half with empty tubs. Accidents of broken legs and backs are frequent."

The Orkneys had once a galloway or garron, now pretty well extinct; it would have been better if they had been quite extinct, so that some better animal might have been found than the half-broken, out-of-condition brutes which the "Druid" shipped at Kirkwall and rode to Kensington, an expedition which no doubt shortened his industrious life. Some of the best Shetlands are bred on the Balfour estate, in Orkney.

"The Druid (a stallion) headed the Shetland pony contingent. His mares are duns, browns, mealy-bay, and a piebald. Colonel Balfour, the grandfather of the present proprietor, began pony-breeding at the beginning of the century. He improved the form. Where the colours did not come as the natives expected, they laid the blame on the black Orcadian water-kelpie, 'Sprunky,' who was, they say, the sire of the finest original or aboriginal ponies of the island. Three celebrated piebald sires and a grey are mentioned by the Druid. The stock are shifted from island to island as the grass suits. They require careful drafting to keep them down to 9 hands" (36 inches).

THE EXMOOR.

Exmoors are another famous breed of ponies, on which very careful and costly experiments, with the view of improvement, have been tried by one family for a long series of years. The following account of them, written by me many years ago for the *Illustrated London News*, has been brought down to the present day by information recently gathered on Exmoor itself. The Exmoors are interesting in an historical point of view, because they so clearly show how sparse feed will dwarf and good feed increase the size of horse stock.

"Exmoor, afforested by William Rufus, continued up to 1818 to be the property of the Crown. It was leased to Sir Thomas Dyke Acland, who has an estate of a similar character close adjoining. He used its wild pasture (at that time it was without roads) for breeding ponies and summering the flocks of Exmoor sheep bred in the surrounding parishes. There are no traces of any population having existed in this forest since the time of William Rufus. The Romans are believed to have worked iron mines on the moor, which have recently been re-opened. Exmoor consists of 20,000 acres, at an elevation varying from 1,000 to 1,500 feet above the sea, of undulating table-land divided by valleys, or 'combes,' through which the river Exe, which rises in one of its valleys, with its tributary the Barle, forces a devious way in the form of pleasant trout streams, rattling over and among huge stones and creeping through deep pools—a very angler's paradise. Like many similar districts in the Scotch Highlands, it has from primeval times been the resort of the red deer. It is still called a forest, although the trees with which its valleys were once filled have long disappeared.

"The sides of the steep valleys, of which some include an acre and others extend for miles, are usually covered with coarse benty herbage, here and there with heather and bilberry plants, springing from a deep black or red soil. At certain spots a greener hue marks the site of the bogs which impede but are never deep enough to engulf the incautious horseman.

"Exmoor may be nothing strange to those accustomed to wild barren scenery. To one who has known country scenes only in the best cultivated regions of England, and who has but recently quitted the perpetual roar of London, there is something strangely solemn and impressive in the deep silence of a ride across the forest. Horses bred on the moors, if left to themselves, rapidly pick their way through pools and bogs, and canter smoothly over dry flats of natural meadow, creep safely down the precipitous descents, and climb with scarcely a puff of distress these steep ascents, splash through fords in the trout streams swelled by rain without a moment's hesitation, and trot along sheep paths bestrewed with loose stones without a stumble; so that you are perfectly at liberty to enjoy the luxury of excitement, and follow out the winding valleys, and study the rich green and purple herbage.

"A sight scarcely less interesting than the deer was afforded by a white pony mare, with her young stock, consisting of a foal still sucking, a yearling, and a two-year-old, which we met in the valley of the Barle. The two-year-old had strayed away feeding, until alarmed by the cracking of our whips and the neighing of its dam, when it came galloping down a steep combe, neighing loudly, at headlong speed. It is thus these ponies learn their action and surefootedness.

"It was a tract of hill land such as we have traversed, entirely wild, without enclosures or roads or fences, that came into the hands of the father of the present proprietor, Mr. Frederick Winn Knight, M.P. He built a fence of forty miles around it; made roads, enclosed farms for his own use near Simon's Bath, introduced a large breeding-stock of Highland cattle on the moor, and set up a considerable stud for rearing full-sized horses, to which the pony stock formed only a secondary consideration.

"The Simon's Bath stud consisted of thoroughbred sires, and about thirty large well-bred Yorkshire mares, together with several thoroughbred ones. It contained, among others, two entire horses and three mares of the Dongola breed (of which more hereafter), and a very few ponies. The result was the production of many valuable hunters, hacks, and harness horses.

"For many years, when the staghounds or foxhounds of this wild district faced the open hills, the Exmoor-bred horses soon went ahead, and in a long moor run were not unfrequently the only horses left with the hounds at the finish. Twenty-eight horses of the Simon's Bath stud were at one time going as the best hunters with the various packs of the neighbouring counties, besides those selected by the owner for his own hunting stables.

"The Exmoor stud was sold at the demise of Mr. Knight, sen., in 1850, by his executors, and the Simon's Bath farm lands were let.

"The efforts of the late Mr. Knight for the improvement of Exmoor did not meet with the success they deserved. He persisted for many years in following the four-course system of cultivation, under which he had seen, in his own time, a larger tract of sandy and far more barren heaths in the north of Worcestershite converted into excellent turnip and barley land. His numerous ox-teams and large corn-fields were not suited to the elevation and climate of

Exmoor; his mode of cultivation rather opposed than encouraged the production of improved permanent grass land, for which the soil and climate of these hills have since been proved to be so well adapted. The great increase in the prices of sheep, cattle, and dairy produce, and the improved facilities afforded by railways for reaching the Bristol and London markets, are now rapidly augmenting the value of the grass lands of North Devon.

"Coming, as we did, from a part of the country where ponies are the perquisites of old ladies and little children, and where the nearer a well-shaped horse can be got to 16 hands the better, the first feeling on mounting a rough, little, unkempt brute, fresh from the moor, barely 12 hands (48 inches) in height, was intensely ridiculous. It seemed as if the slighest mistake would send the rider clean over the animal's head. But we learned soon that the indigenous pony, in certain useful qualities, is not to be surpassed by animals of greater size and pretensions. We crossed the stream, not by the narrow bridge, but by the ford, and passing through the straggling stone village of Simon's Bath, arrived in sight of the field where the Tattersall of the West was to sell the wild and tame horse-stock bred on the moors. It was a field of some ten acres and a half, forming a very steep slope, with the upper part comparatively flat, the sloping side broken by a stone quarry, and dotted over with huge blocks of quartz. At its base flowed an arm of the stream we had found margining our route. A substantial, but, as the event proved, not sufficiently high stone fence bounded the whole field. On the upper part a sort of double pound, united by a narrow neck, with a gate at each end, had been constructed of rails upwards of five feet in height. Into the first of these pounds, by ingenious management, all the sale ponies, wild and tame, had been driven. When the sale commenced, it was the duty of the herdsman to separate two at a time, and drive them through the narrow neck into the pound before the auctioneer. Around a crowd of spectators of every degree were clustered —squires and clergymen, horse-dealers and farmers from Northamptonshire and Lincolnshire as well as South Devon and the immediate neighbourhood.

"These ponies were the result of crosses made years ago with Dongola and thoroughbred stallions on the indigenous race of Exmoors, since carefully culled from year to year, for the purpose of securing the utmost amount of perfection among the stallions and mares reserved for breeding purposes.

"The modern Exmoor seldom exceeds 13 hands; has a well-shaped head, with very small ears. The body is round, compact, and well ribbed, with good quarters and powerful hocks; legs straight, flat, and clean, the muscles well developed by early racing up and down steep mountain sides while following their dams. In about forty lots the prevailing colours were bay, brown, and grey; chestnuts and blacks were less frequent, although black was one of the colours of the original breed.

"The sale was great fun. Perched on convenient rails, we had the whole scene before us— the auctioneer, rather hoarse and quite matter-of-fact; the ponies, wildly rushing about the first enclosure, were with difficulty separated into pairs to be driven in the sale portion. When fairly hemmed in through the open gate, they dashed, and made a sort of circus circuit, with mane and tail erect, in a style that would draw great applause at Astley's. Then there was the difficulty of deciding whether the figures marked in white on the animal's hind-quarters were 8, or 3, or 5. Instead of the regular trot up and down of Tattersall's, a whisk of the cap was sufficient to produce a tremendous caper. A very pretty exhibition was made by a little mare with a late foal about the size of a setter dog.

"The sale over, an amusing scene ensued. Every man who had bought a pony wanted to catch it. In order to clear the way, each lot as sold, as wild and nearly as active as deer, had been turned into the field. A joint-stock company of pony-catchers, headed by the champion wrestler of the district—a hawk-nosed, fresh-complexioned, rustic Don Juan—stood ready to be hired, at the moderate rate of sixpence per pony, caught and delivered. One carried a bundle of new halters; the others, warmed by a liberal distribution of beer, seemed to stand

'Like greyhounds on the slip,'

as much inspired by the fun as the sixpence. When the word was given, the first step was to drive a herd into the lowest corner of the field, in as compact a mass as possible. The bay, grey, or chestnut, from that hour doomed to perpetual slavery and exile from his native hills, was pointed out by the nervous, anxious purchaser. Three wiry fellows crept catlike among the mob, sheltering behind some tame cart-horses. On a mutual signal they rushed on the devoted animal; two, one bearing a halter, strove to fling each one arm round its neck, and with one hand to grasp its nostrils, while the insidious third, clinging to the flowing tail, tried to throw the poor quadruped off its balance. Often they were baffled in the first effort, for with one wild spring the pony would clear the whole lot, and flying with streaming mane and tail across the brook up the field, leave the whole work to be recommenced. Sometimes, when the feat was cleverly performed, pony and pony-catchers were to be seen all rolling on the ground together, the pony yelling, snorting, and fighting with his fore-feet, the men clinging on like the Lapithæ and Centaurs, and how escaping crushed ribs or broken legs it is impossible to imagine. On one occasion a fine brown stallion dashed away, with two plucky fellows hanging on to his mane. Rearing, plunging, fighting with his fore-feet, away he bounded down a declivity among the huge rocks, amid the encouraging cheers of the spectators. For a moment the contest was doubtful, so tough were the sinews and so determined the grip of Davy, the champion wrestler; but the steep bank of the brook, down which the brown stallion recklessly plunged, was too much for human efforts. In a moment they all went together into the brook, but the pony up first, leaped the opposite bank, and galloped away, whinnying in short-lived triumph.

"After a series of such contests, well worth the study of artists not content with pale copies from marbles or casts, the difficulty of haltering these snorting steeds, equal in spirit and probably in size to those which drew the car of Boadicea, was diminished by all those uncaught being driven back to the pound, and there, not without furious battles, one by one enslaved.

"Yet even when haltered the conquest was by no means concluded. Some refused to stir, others started off at such a pace as speedily brought the holder of the halter on his nose. One respectable old gentleman, in grey stockings and knee-breeches, lost his animal in much less time than it took him to extract the sixpence from his knotted purse.

"Yet in all these fights there was little display of vice; it was pure fright on the part of the ponies that made them struggle so. A few days' confinement in a shed, a few carrots, with a little salt, and gentle treatment, reduces the wildest of the three-year-olds to docility. When older they are more difficult to manage. It was a pretty sight to view them led away, splashing through the brook—conquered, but not yet subdued.

"In the course of the evening a little chestnut stallion, 12 hands (or 4 feet) in height, jumped, at a standing jump, over the bars out of a pound upwards of five feet from the ground, only just touching the top rail with his hind feet."

Simon's Bath was too far from the rail to continue long to be the site of these sales. They were removed to Bampton, where the ponies were sold by auction in the fair—Bampton Fair being *par excellence* the pony fair of the West of England. Later on a little more breaking was bestowed on the ponies, and for several years the sale lots were sent by rail to Reading to meet the buyers.

But the Cheviot ewe, offering a lamb and fleece for sale every summer, found its way to the Exmoor pastures, and entered into competition with the pony, which required three or four winters before he came to the hammer. The black cattle have given way to the Cheviots, and the ponies are reduced to a decreasing herd of about forty head, which, instead of finding themselves as of yore, masters of the position, eke out a grudged existence among increasing thousands of Scotch sheep tended by Border shepherds.

In 1860* the tenant of an Exmoor farm tried to breed Galloways between 13 hands 2 inches

BORACK.

and 14 hands. With this view he employed as a sire a son of Old Port, the diminutive progeny of Sir Hercules and Beeswing, and afterwards the celebrated pony sire Bobby, who was descended through two degrees on his dam's side from Borack, an Arab of celebrity on the Madras racecourse, the sire of some of the best ponies sold at the sales of Mr. Milward of Thurgarton Priory. But the experiment was not a success, for the foals required to be wintered in paddocks and fed with hay as two-year-olds, and, being necessarily reared on the improved lands, cost as much to breed as would have produced larger and more valuable animals.

The true original Exmoor ponies, which were foaled and fed on the moor without any other food than they could pick up in winter on the moors after the Exmoor sheep had been removed to their winter quarters in the surrounding parishes, and which in hard winters sometimes perished of starvation, belonged to Sir Thomas Acland, who for many years rented the forest from the Crown. They are still bred uncrossed by the present Sir Thomas Acland, but without much improvement either in size or value, at Winsford Hill.

In 1864, when the Exmoor ponies were sold at Reading, three unbroken geldings averaged

* "Scott and Sebright."

forty guineas each; a blood bay filly, 12½ hands high, four years old—a perfect model of what a hack pony should be—was sold unbroken for thirty guineas. These were, however, the rare exceptions, and an average of £12 to £15 was a poor return for a lot of good-looking and useful ponies of from three to five years old. A cross between the mares of this breed and a thoroughbred horse produces the blood-like animal of 14 hands high so much sought for London use. But the unimproved Exmoor hills will not produce that half-bred pony, and on the improved land sheep-stock pay better.

The mares live on the hills all the winter, and seek certain favourite spots known to the herdsmen, who build up stacks of rough hay well protected by stout rails, from which in very hard winters they give out supplies to the snowed-out ponies.

The weaned foals are now all sold from their dams at the Bampton fair in October; none are kept except two or three for use on the estate, so that the picturesque sight of a mare with the progeny of three years is no longer to be seen. The sire in 1878 and for several previous years was a tan-muzzle black of fine riding form and action, nearly, but not quite, thoroughbred, and about 15 hands high. The progress of sheep-farming, assisted by growing root and rape crops, has, while reducing the number, enabled Mr. Knight to improve the size of his ponies, which have two great merits for family use—sure-footedness and hardy constitution. Exmoors are sometimes grey, occasionally chestnut with white marks, after a remote ancestor, the speedy Velocipede—but bay with mealy muzzle is the favourite Exmoor colour—rarely black, and never piebald, although piebald Exmoors are constantly advertised in the London papers.

Exmoor ponies, both of Sir Thomas Acland's and Mr. Knight's breed, are to be found in October at Bampton fair in reduced numbers, in fair competition with the other ponies of the south-west.

WELSH PONIES.

With respect to Welsh ponies, both north and south, it is very difficult to say where the districts to which they originally belonged begin and end. So many industries have been established in Wales, so many mines and manufactories opened, so many watering-places raised into importance, such numbers of settlers and summer travellers have been drawn thither by the facilities created by good roads and railroads, that the Principality is no longer isolated, and nearly all its live stock has been crossed by lowland breeds. Welsh ponies early in this century were largely crossed by thoroughbred stock, with the usual result, fine individual specimens, which were quite incapable of enduring the hardships of the native mountain breeds. The best are bred in districts like that near Wynnstay, where farmers have the use of Sir Watkin Wynne's blood sires.

NEW FOREST PONIES.

In the New Forest, which is Crown property, the wildest absence of all attempts at breeding by rule has always prevailed. Three hundred persons enjoy rights of pasturage, under which for the greater part of the year they turn their horses and ponies to graze in the forest. Amongst these have always been stallions of all breeds, sizes, and ages, with every kind of defect to which horseflesh is heir. These, enjoying promiscuous intercourse with the mares, have raised up just such a mongrel race as might be expected from what Horace Walpole described as the "daughter of nobody by the son of anybody."

The Commissioners of Woods and Forests have been repeatedly pressed to exercise control over the New Forest sires, with the view of excluding those likely to propagate offspring either ill-shaped or diseased; but the work seems to have been at once too practical and too troublesome for these often over-zealous servants of the Crown.

OTHER PONIES.

Those who require ponies should pay not the slightest attention to the tales as to "from whom descended and by whom begot"—tales which are probably not true, and if true, of no consequence—but confine their investigations to the merits of the animal presented to them.

In addition to the real ponies of Wales, Exmoor, Dartmoor, the New Forest, and the Shetland Islands, and all the ponies sold under the time-honoured names of these places, there are a certain number bred by farmers and gentlemen out of good animals, which, from their symmetry and price, are quite removed from the category of cheap family ponies; on the contrary, they are amongst the luxuries of the stable. Anxious for information on this class, I applied to the late Mr. Richard Milward of Thurgarton Priory, Notts, an active member of the Council of the Royal Agricultural Society, a Nottinghamshire squire who for many years made breeding and buying ponies a profitable hobby—I lay stress on profitable, because raising superior live stock of any kind without profit does nothing for its permanent improvement.

Mr. Milward wrote to me (April, 1873):—"About twenty-five years ago it was very difficult to find any ponies with good shoulders. After the success of my sales became known, ponies were offered me by farmers on all sides. Nine out of ten were under-bred, bad-shouldered brutes. I was always a buyer of anything really good, so I showed them their defects, explained what was and what was not worth buying at any sale in my neighbourhood (Nottinghamshire), and they began to breed a better sort of animal. And now, although I send about twenty ponies every year to Tattersall's between 13 hands 3 inches and 14 hands 2 inches high, they have nearly all good shoulders, and most of them are considered to be without a fault as regards symmetry.

"There are two modes of breeding ponies (I call everything a pony under 14 hands 2 inches): either from a small thoroughbred mare foal put to a Yorkshire (Norfolk?) trotter—this was how Don Carlos, Lord Calthorpe's celebrated stallion hack, was bred*—or, more commonly, by a small thoroughbred sire out of a Welsh, Irish, or other pony. I hold that to produce anything worth rearing, either sire or dam must be thoroughbred. I have had a few good Norfolk ponies, but they had not first-rate shoulders. Two Thousand (sold at my sale to Lord Hastings for 120 guineas), Dunstan and Crisis (with which Mr. Frisby carried off several prizes at the Agricultural Hall shows), Rarity (which was sold at the hammer for 160 guineas), had all fine harness-action, but none of them quite good shoulders.

"My best ponies have been bred in Shropshire and Cheshire, the sires thoroughbreds belonging to Lord Combermere and Sir Watkin Wynne. A very celebrated pony stallion was at one time in this country—Bobby. Bobby was bred by Mr. Ramsay of Barnton; his sire Robin, a son of Dr. Syntax and a Cotton mare dam by Borack, an Arab (see page 217). Brunnette, which was purchased at my sale for 110 guineas by Lord Stamford, and ridden hack by him for a dozen years, was by Bobby; and also a piebald which fetched the same price, and was driven for years by Lady Caroline Kerrison. Most of my ponies for this year's

* See Coloured Plate I.

sale (1873) have, at least, two crosses of blood. They are by Fingall, Park-keeper, Porto Rico, Chit-chat, Antwerp, Medas, Mr. Sykes, Dublin, Hercules, and Alchemist.

"You ask what is a cob? I hate the term, and never use it. I think pony covers every horse under 14 hands 2 inches, and hack all riding-horses above that size not being hunters. My object is to get ponies from 13 hands 3 inches to 14 hands 2 inches, as much like good hunters as possible; and I flatter myself, if I may believe the best judges, I have often succeeded."

It will be seen from this that Mr. Milward claims nearly all Arabs as ponies, for an Arab over 14 hands 2 inches is an exception.

London is the best mart for the purchase of a well-broken pony of any kind; and, next to London, some of the great manufacturing towns of the north, such as Manchester, where the great patron of a good pony, the sporting publican, abounds. I say this advisedly, because the Royal Agricultural Society and the Bath and West of England Society have more than once offered prizes for ponies at Southampton, in the New Forest district; at Plymouth and Exeter, near the Exmoor and Dartmoor districts; at Chester and at Cardiff, for North and South Wales; but the entries in these places have been limited in number, and never remarkable for quality, whilst at all the Agricultural Hall shows, where the entry fee is more than four times that of agricultural societies, the great trouble of the manager has been to keep the entries of ponies within fifty, and the excellence of the harness-pony classes has repeatedly called forth the admiration of the judges. In 1872, when the judges were the Earl of Shannon, Lord Calthorpe, and Colonel Maude, C.B., the Crown Equerry, the whole class for ponies not exceeding 13 hands 3 inches was "highly commended;" and again in 1873, when Sir George Wombwell acted with Colonel Maude.

Those who are willing to speculate in unbroken ponies may suit themselves at English fairs where droves of Welsh and Irish colts are regularly sent, as well as at local horse fairs in Wales and in Devonshire. As a rule the best ponies are bred on mountain regions, where short sweet herbage abounds, where keen winters carry off the cripples and the narrow-chested, and where they learn activity and the full use of their limbs while running beside their dams. A mountain-bred pony never falls unless over-weighted or over-tired, and it is very difficult to tire one.

Ponies bred on wild rough land are certainly not so subject to the numerous diseases of an inflammatory character that are the curse of studs, where horses of the finest pedigree are bred and reared with as much care and more expense than is bestowed on the most aristocratic babies. Like Red Indians, only those of stout constitution survive the hardships of infancy or foalhood; ponies that have reached maturity and been broken to harness or saddle are more likely to be sound than full-sized horses, because only the best are worth sending for sale out of their native localities.

PANNIER PONY.

The pony that is to carry panniers balanced by two babies should be good-looking, because such an arrangement is essentially a luxury. A good-tempered donkey is a safer conveyance, although not so aristocratic. Therefore the pannier pony should have a nice round barrel and broad back, "two good ends"—viz., a pretty head and well-carried tail—should walk well and freely, and above all be perfectly quiet, insensible to the strangest sights and sounds, and incapable of an excess of freshness.

By a good walker is meant an easy, willing, elastic walker—one that glides smoothly along, and does not by its harsh, rough movement put its infant burdens to torture. It is painful to witness the heads of young children rolling as if they were Mandarin toys.

A pannier pony should be as well trained to walk in hand as a Norfolk trotter. This may easily be done by a system of rewards and mild discipline, scarcely punishment, with touches from a gig-whip held in the left hand of the person who leads the pony, and applied behind his back to the hind-quarters of the animal. When the pony runs up from the whip he should be caressed, and encouraged with a carrot, apple, or lump of sugar.

A very good way of leading a pony or any horse is with a bamboo stick fitted with a swivel snap-hook; this keeps his head straight. I first saw this contrivance in Nottinghamshire, where a mounted groom thus led the blind Squire of Osberton to meet his friends at covert-side.

A pannier pony may also be driven with light cord reins carried through terrets fixed on to the panniers, where used by a mamma fond of long country walks.

The harness of a pannier pony should be complete, and consist of a snaffle bridle with large loops, the bit also attached to the flaps of the saddle by flap-reins. The pack-saddle must fit well, and be furnished with a crupper and a breastplate. The girths should be broad, on what is called the Melton pattern. The children should not sit back to back, but with their faces towards the horse's head. They should be well balanced by weights, if one child happens to be heavier than the other, or great mischief may be done. In a word, the whole arrangement needs the watchful eye of a mother or a kind intelligent nurse, who understands the ways of ponies as well as of children.

Pony panniers became more popular after a very pretty photograph had appeared of H.R.H. the Princess of Wales holding the rein of a long-maned, cream-coloured cob, which carried in panniers two young princes.

The pannier pony may also be made useful in harness to draw a four-wheeled carriage of suitable weight. Indeed, the very first step in the education of any pony too small to carry a man should be to break him to harness. As to size, the pannier pony should not be so tall that the children cannot be easily placed in and taken out of the seat by their ordinary attendant.

HARNESS PONIES.

For hard work in harness, day after day, there is nothing in the equine line so enduring, so safe, and where required within trotting limits, so fast as a pony. Straight thick shoulders are the common defects of ponies, and of horses bred in a state of nature, and withers so low that there is no good place for the saddle. This arises, according to the opinion of an experienced West of England pony-breeder, from the habit of grazing transmitted for generations; and he considered that the fine, sloping shoulders, which are so essential a part of a well-shaped horse, are partly the result of careful artificial selection, and that the well-carried head may have something to do with food provided in racks and mangers; but this is a theory rather thrown out for discussion than as a grave assertion. At any rate, there are thousands of ponies that may be made useful and even ornamental in harness which no one would care to ride for pleasure.

In this country size gives value to every average horse; therefore, all things being equal, you can purchase ponies for less money than full-sized horses. There are a great variety of carriages, from the lightest pony-trap up to expensive hooded phaetons for a pair or four which may be "horsed" with ponies of 12 hands high and upwards, quite as satisfactorily as by large and more expensive horses, if there is no grown man in the family who desires to ride.

For many years an absurd system of taxation, or rather of exemption, existed which gave a premium for the employment of ponies under 13 hands high; but all those exemptions having been first abolished, and then the tax itself sacrificed to conciliate farmers and country gentlemen, there is no advantage in looking out for ponies under 13 hands high. Thirteen hands and a half is an excellent height for all family purposes.

A considerable economy will thus be effected in first price, in keep, and in wear and tear; for ponies last longer at work than most full-sized horses, and can travel at least as far, generally farther, and quite as fast as any reasonable person desires. Indeed, it is scarcely possible to tire out a pair of good mountain or moor-bred ponies.

These observations particularly apply to ponies of average step, action, and quality. Anything of extraordinary merit will always fetch a fancy price. A pony under 11 hands high, which was afterwards presented to the late ex-Emperor of the French for the Prince Imperial, was sold at auction for sixty-five guineas; and a hundred pounds was refused for an extraordinary leaping pony of the same size. Since polo came into fashion the latter has become an ordinary price where pace is found along with beauty.

The modern school of coach-builders, with their light carriages and high wheels, under the four-hundredweight low licence duty, have done a great deal to encourage the employment of ponies for pleasure purposes.

BREAKING PONIES TO RIDE OR DRIVE.

When a pony has to be broken to ride and is not strong enough to carry a man, and a competent good-tempered boy is not to be found in the parish, the best plan is to break it to harness; indeed, it is doubtful whether all horses for useful purposes should not be broken to double harness before they are ridden. The usual brake and brake-horse will be too tall and ponderous for the purpose. After the preliminary lessons in horse education, when the pony has lost all fear of man, sights, and sounds, and has walked about in harness, and turns to right and left, as the driver, following on foot, pulls either rein run through the terrets of the dumb jockey, get a strong two-wheeled carriage of suitable size, fasten a splinter-bar to it by way of outrigger—you may see the arrangement during London winters, when, after a heavy snow-storm, four-wheeled one-horse cabs are turned into pairs—attach a steady, perfectly-broken old pony to the outrigger, if it is a riding pony, with a boy riding postillion, and put the unbroken pony into the shafts. With the harness and kicking-straps you have the young one under perfect control; with patience and daily lessons a good driver will not only teach him all his duty, but prepare him for the saddle. Boys are so cruel and thoughtless, that they can rarely be trusted with the task of teaching a colt without the supervision of some older hand.

RIDING PONIES.

"Of all the sights of London in the month of June there are few prettier than Rotten Row at that hour in the morning when grave judges, merchants of mighty name in the City, and the hard-worked of Her Majesty's Cabinet and Her Majesty's Opposition begin to ride away to their daily, never-ending duties; while the Park is alive with little mobs of boys and girls galloping, trotting, and walking as little as possible, with papa, mamma, or sister Anne, or mostly with some stout and faithful Ruggles, panting and toiling after his precious charges How bright they look, how happy with innocent excitement glowing on their rosy faces! No thought of heavy acceptances or of doubtful parliamentary contests, or of ungrateful Ministers of State, checks their ringing laughter, or their cheerful and childish talk. And then what pluck the little creatures have; and how gravely they imitate their seniors, in handling ponies a little bigger than Southdown rams!

"In those admirably-planned and picturesquely-arranged rides in the wood provided by the Emperor of the French for the inhabitants of his capital, the magnificence of the equipages on a great fête-day—a Gladiateur day—leaves nothing to be desired. Our Ladies' Mile is left in the shade by the splendour of a series of four-horse postillioned barouches, with liveries of every brilliant shade of velvet and satin, from the brightest canary to the richest ruby, beside hosts of grand steppers in broughams, and other triumphs of carriage-building art well copied from the London style. Horsemen are there, too, in very fair numbers, to whom a critical eye would most probably object that the horses are too good for their work, and that the men ride too well, too correctly, too seriously for pleasure—that they are perfectly taught, but are not to the manner born. Yes, the wealth of modern Paris rivals London in everything that is gorgeous for grown-up people. But when it comes to the little people and ponies Paris is a blank.

"Pony-boy-ship, not horse-man-ship, is the crowning glory of these equestrian islands. The word pony is feebly represented in other languages by two words implying little horse or dwarf horse; and the French have been obliged to borrow the term without being able to borrow the thing. In a brilliant horse show at Paris in 1866 there was only one real pony. There are small horses in many countries, but it is only in this among civilised nations that the let-alone system of education allows the family pony to develop into an institution. Good horses and horsemen are not confined to England. There are foreign artists who know well how to draw the single Arab, the war-horse of Job, or a whole charge of cavalry, but it is only in England that John Leech could have found his immortal boys on pony-back; above all, that genuine Master George on his Shetlander, his soul on fire speaking in his eyes, and eager for the hunt streaming away on the other side of the brook, answering the piteous 'Hold hard' of the much-enduring Ruggles, 'it's too wide and very deep!' with the happiest self-confidence, 'All right, we can both swim.' Master George did not mean to be saucy to the old coachman, or to be witty like those royal and imperial boys who make such wonderful *bon mots;* he only meant, in the language of the ring, 'business'—that there was a brook to be done and, dry or wet, Master George meant to do it.

"The family pony, ridden at all hours, with and without saddle, along bridle-roads, over the moors, in the hayfield, and through the wood, up hill and down dale, teaches the boy to go alone, to defend himself, to tumble cleverly, and to get up again without making a noise at a bump or two. As far as teaching the art of horsemanship goes, perhaps the completest plan with boys, as well as girls, is to allow no riding until they are eight or nine years old, and then to commence with first principles. Still, habits of independence are of more importance than perfect horsemanship; therefore, fathers living in the country, with a stable as well as a library, if wise, will not neglect the pony branch of education, but will let the boy, as soon as he likes, go wandering about the park, the farm, the village, learning how to take care of himself and his steed. With girls it is different. A girl can no more learn to ride gracefully than to dance gracefully without being carefully taught from the first lessons to the last."

These words were written in 1866, before France had passed under the "Caudine forks" of victorious Germany, and when Charles Dickens, in whose *All the Year Round* they were published, seemed built to reach at least fourscore years; but in the main they are true still. At any rate, it is not from the need of physical energy that the decline and fall of England, prophesied any time this fifty years by envious foreigners, will take place. We ride, young and old, and both sexes, harder than ever, and as wealth grows so grows the number of the equestrian race.

A pony to carry a little girl should have room for the side-saddle, and carry its head and neck in the proper place, not like a donkey or a pig. A crupper will generally be required. Cruppers are out of fashion for riding-horses, except those of the military and the police ; but those ponies which can carry a saddle safely without them are the exception. In choosing a pony on which your boys are to learn to ride, take one as much like a good hack in shape, and as little like a donkey as possible.

In a woodcut by John Leech, "The First Meet of the Season," which appeared many years ago in the *Illustrated London News*, there is a serious drawing, not a caricature, of a

A MOUNTAIN PONY.

blood-pony arching his neck proudly, and champing his bit, which gives a good idea of what the fore-hand of a riding-pony should be. A donkey is a very useful animal, but the worst possible tutor for future horsemen, because he has no shoulders, a straight neck, and a mouth of leather which never objects to the deadest pull. A boy's pony should be narrow, so that his little legs may have some real grasp. The fat round barrel of a family cob may do for panniers or a side-saddle pad, but a boy as soon as he begins to ride—say nine years old—should sit in as good form as when in later years he bestrides a full-sized hunter. The numbers who can afford to purchase perfection are limited in every mart, but it is well to have the eyes accustomed to correct forms.

GALLOWAYS AND COBS.

The moment we turn our backs on ponies we reach a mob of animals, including everything up to the full-sized horse (the proper height of which, in England, may be taken at 15 hands 2 inches), amongst which are the most useful, the cheapest, and the most expensive, as well as all sorts of inferior nags. The word "Galloway" has gone out of use, yet it was a convenient word to express what was too big for a pony, too small for a Yorkshireman or Leicestershireman's idea of a horse, and more active, more slim of limb, than the "stocky, weight-carrying cob."

The famous Dumpling that carried Julia Mannering's lover over the Cumberland hills behind the immortal Dandie Dinmont, was without doubt a galloway of the very best sort.

Old books on the British horse described a number of local breeds not thoroughbred, which were supposed to be peculiar to various districts of England. The Irish alone still often bear a national character. All these distinctions except Norfolk trotters have long since disappeared under the perpetual use of thoroughbred sires. Nearly all who go into horse-breeding for profit endeavour to produce a big animal, because it is always easier to sell a good big horse than a good little one. A good, big, well-bred horse may turn out a hunter; if not a hunter a barouche-horse; and if not handsome enough for that, a trotting van-horse; and so on, descending in the scale. It is only gentlemen breeding for amusement, and trying to perpetuate favourites, the produce of favourite mares, who seriously set about breeding cobs or small horses of any kind.

As a matter of course the size of horses to be found in any particular district is, to a certain extent, affected by the size of the county. In hilly regions, and counties where small enclosures prevail, the average size of the horses used for riding as well as driving will be regulated by the size of the mares in common farm use, and by the size of the hunters in use, and will therefore be small; while in counties where fields of fifty acres and upwards are common, tall horses will be the rule. Putting hunting in flying counties out of the question, and carriages used for fashionable purposes, there is no doubt that more general utility will be found between the heights of 14 hands and 15 hands 2 inches than any other size of horse.

On the question of size—an important point—the following reliable statistics are taken from the entries of ten horse shows held at the Agricultural Hall, London. The prize lists were altered from year to year for seven years, so as to obtain as full entries as possible for each class above 14 hands and under 15 hands 2 inches. The following is a summary of the entries in various classes in the year 1872. As the expenses of exhibiting each horse, including a £2 2s. entry, on an average rather exceed £10, it may be presumed that the majority of these horses are good of their size. In "the class not exceeding 14 hands 2 inches high, to be exhibited in harness," twenty-six were described as good hacks. In the class for "Park Cobs, High Steppers," there were twenty-one. Of these fourteen were described as quiet in harness, and many more were on sale as broken to harness. Of class "Park Hacks and Ladies' Horses, not exceeding 15 hands 1 inch," there were thirty-two, more than forty entries being rejected for want of room. There were also twenty-one entries of park hacks not exceeding 15 hands 2 inches. Of these two classes many were described as quiet in harness, and several were also entered as hunters. In the two cob classes, one for saddle and the other for single harness, the majority were well-bred little horses, but certainly not what is conveyed by the idea of a cob; that is to say, a hack to carry a heavy bishop or banker. Many of the cob classes were described as hunters. These figures justify purchasers in looking for the most generally useful horses, fit to ride, fit to hunt in a country where the fields are not too big; fit to trot in harness, single or double, in a carriage weighing not more than four or five hundredweight for each horse, without injury to their riding action, and in much heavier carriages when not required for riding purposes amongst small horses and cobs.

The cob proper of modern England is of two kinds—the priceless animal of grand symmetrical form, short legs, a round barrel, well ribbed up, a well-bred, intelligent head and a neck beautifully set on and carried, a tail to match; in a word, the strength of a dray-horse, the quality of a race-horse, the manners of a perfect gentleman, and at least two good paces, both easy—a square walk over four miles an hour, and a square trot of eight miles an hour— or a very perfect slow canter, performed quite on the haunches.   With these merits, a cob of proper sober colour is worth at least two hundred guineas to a dealer—and to the dealer when a heavy-weight millionaire comes to him in despair any price he chooses to ask.   I have known £400 given for a perfect cob, to carry a timid seventeen-stone man.   But such cobs are the few and far between exceptions—more difficult to find than even a heavy-weight hunter, because they are only bred by chance.

The vulgar idea of a cob is a diminutive cart-horse, and such, even without action, if very fat and not absolutely hideous, are constantly sold to ignorant people with plenty of money in their pockets at double their worth, because they fancy that thick legs (perhaps carefully shaved) and a fat body imply strength.   One of the safest tests of a weight-carrying cob is to try if he can walk down a steep hill with weight on his back and a loose rein.

The other, the ordinary cob, which may be worth anything between £50 and £100, if it is sound, has substance, can carry fourteen stone, move at a fair pace, with useful not showy action, and nine times out of ten will go well in harness.   It is in consequence of their bone and girth that cobs are of the generally useful class, as distinguished from light blood hacks, their weight enables them to pull a loaded carriage.   Those riders who are fastidious will not, if they know it, buy a cob that has ever been in a collar; but as such animals are, in nine cases out of ten, bred by chance, and work their way by degrees into good society, after graduating in country bakers' or butchers' carts, the odds are in favour of their being accustomed to the collar, even if they do not bear its blemishing mark.

The already-quoted statistics of the Agricultural Hall shows prove that harness " is the badge of all their tribe."

In 1872 a cob 14 hands 3 inches high, five years old, rather plain than otherwise, which won a leaping prize, was purchased by a heavy-weight financier at eighty guineas, for use as a constitutional park hack; he was disfigured by a collar blemish, yet was sold a year later at a profit.

This sort of cob decidedly comes within the list of useful family horses.   He may carry any of the family, including the girls, except the small, short-legged boys; he may run in single harness; two cobs will afford more riding and driving than any other class of animal. He may be used by the servants or the master; his size, his strength, his constitution, make him fit for anything or anybody's use.   Placid, not to say stolid, and in the worst form stubborn temperaments, are more frequently found amongst weight-carrying cobs than amongst light-weight blood hacks.

A hunter, or a covert hack, and many kinds of harness horses may not be able to walk well; but a cob that cannot walk at a good pace and in good form is not worth feeding with oats.   To describe what a cob ought to be would be only to confuse the readers who do not know—a live original is the best guide, and next to the real thing a good picture.   The engraving at page 231 represents what may be called a blood cob, very old when he was painted.   In his own county (Hertfordshire) he was a good hunter and hack; and he looks fit for every useful purpose, his one fault being his colour—grey—but some people do not dislike it. That eminent lawyer the late Judge Park always rode a grey cob, followed by his groom on another.

Nothing is more difficult to get together than a number of well-shaped, weight-carrying cobs, with the safe and pleasant action which is the combined result of a large cross of blood and fine symmetry.

THE COUNTRY HACK, OR ROADSTER.

The roadster hack of our grandfathers is almost a thing of the past. For want of demand the supply has ceased. The memory of them is contained in many novels, from Fielding's " Joseph Andrews " to G. P. R. James's perpetual "two horsemen."

"In the shady silence of Mayfair, over a corner public-house, is exhibited a signboard in a more elaborate style of art than is usual in modern public-houses, where the art is generally alive and behind the bar. A sprightly youth, in the costume of the "pampered" of the time of George II., with a long pole in his hand, is stepping away at the rate of some six miles an hour—not fair heel and toe be it understood, but an easy trot.

"The sign represents an ornamental luxury that died with the last famous or infamous Duke of Queensbury, who figures as Lord March in Thackeray's novel, "The Virginians," and whose later life at his mansion in Piccadilly is told in one of Lord Brougham's volumes of biographical sketches. The running footman, when he was really of any use, ran before and alongside the fat Flemish mares which drew the coaches of the Sir Charles Grandison period, warned innkeepers of the coming illustrious guest, and helped with their long staves the caravan-like vehicle out of the numerous ruts and sloughs that intersected the northern and western roads. Good roads substituted post for the family horses, and killed the profession of running footmen, leaving nothing but the costume and the long staff, which, turned into a gilded cane, is still the symbol of the gorgeous creatures who hang behind Court chariots, the coaches of Lord Mayors, and do ornamental duty in the vestibules of great houses."

With the decline of the running footman, and, from the same cause—the improvement in posting and stage coaches—began the decay of the famous British hackney or roadster. We may be sure the roads were very bad, and that travelling on wheels was very expensive, when the feeble deformed poet, Alexander Pope, rode to Oxford through Windsor Forest on a horse borrowed of the Earl of Burlington, and met on his road the bookseller Bernhard Lintot, also riding a horse borrowed of his publisher, "what he had of Mr. Oldmixon for a debt."

Those roadster hacks had qualifications rarely found, because not required in these days of Macadam and iron roads. But the qualities are latent and exist, for they are found in horses of British breed in our Australian colonies, as proved in many an overland cattle-driving expedition, in which the wonderful tales of the endurance of Arab horses have been at least rivalled.

They were seldom much over 15 hands high. A tall horse is not often so enduring in long days, or so hardy in every way. When the dashing Peninsular general Sir Thomas Picton ordered his infantry chargers for the Spanish campaign, he fixed on 15 hands as the proper height. These roadsters were strong, for they had to carry, besides the horseman in his heavy jack-boots, leather breeches, and broad-skirted coat, a horseman's cloak, saddle-bags, and holster pistols. They were tolerably swift, for the rider might have to owe his safety to his nag's pace. They had good shoulders and plenty before the pommel, capital legs and feet, and action more sure than showy, neither daisy trot, yet with the knee-action which is essential for admiration in the fine charger or the park-hack. They were hardy in constitution, or they could not have borne long days of rough weather, coarse fodder, and indifferent stables. They were required to carry their riders not for an hour or two occasionally, for the sake of constitutional exercise or fashion, but from day to day, for two or three hundred miles, and that with an easy even walk, trot, or canter.

Boswell, writing in 1766 to his friend Temple of a journey to Glasgow, says, "I shall chaise it all the way—thanks to the man who invented that comfortable method of journeying! Had it not been for that, I dare say both you and I would have circumscribed our travels within a very few miles. For my own part, I think to dress myself in a great-coat and boots, and get astride a horse's back, and be jolted through mire, perhaps through wind and rain, is a punishment too severe for all the offences I can charge myself with." This praise of the post-chaise reminds us that Dr. Samuel Johnson, the demi-god of Bozzy's idolatry, considered riding in a post-chaise with a pretty woman one of the greatest luxuries of life. Yet even the ponderous Doctor, as little like a horseman as any literary man, ancient or modern, provided himself with a pair of silver spurs, and rode post-horses—the only mode of conveyance during his journey through Scotland and the Hebrides.

After half a century of stage coaches had tempted most travellers on to wheels, came railroads, and destroyed the roadside inns, where the horseman used to find a warm welcome after a long, hard day. On the great north road, where twenty years ago the crack of the postillion's whip and the blast of the guard's horn, the rattling of hoofs and the jingling of pole-chains, resounded night and day, you cannot now make sure of a dry bed, a decent meal, or even a feed of corn. As for ostlers, the race is extinct; if you choose to ride or drive, you must bring your groom, or groom your horse yourself.

This decay of inns renders impossible feats performed by men of our own time, though of the last generation. Old Dick Tattersall, the uncle of the present head of that famous firm, had a relay of hacks on the road between London and Grantham. He used to mount, after a hard day's work in the auction pulpit at the abolished Corner, ride down one hundred and eight miles before morning, hunt the next day with the Belvoir hounds, and return by the same means to his duties. Sir Tatton Sykes of Sledmere, the last of the real squires, who was satisfied to spend a large income at home on hospitality, field sports, agriculture, and breeding Leicester sheep, and horses to win the Derby, without troubling either the world of politics or the world of fashion, or the world of betting men either, had a way of travelling (with as little baggage as Sir Charles Napier) to Epsom to see the Derby run, or to an equal distance to ride a race, that would now be impossible. Wherever he slept the first night he borrowed next morning a clean shirt from the landlord, and left his own to be washed ready for his return. He repeated the operation at each resting-place on the road, returning by instalments each borrowed garment, until he arrived back at Sledmere in his own shirt. A small valise carried the satin breeches and silk stockings that replaced his leathers and long boots in the evening. The operation was ingenious, primitive, and clean; but at the present hour the landlords with frilled shirts have followed the way of satin breeches, and are known no more.

Enduring hacks of the old sort are now only to be found in the hands of active farmers, who look over hundreds of acres before breakfast, of country surgeons human and veterinary, of maltsters, and a few other callings which take their followers out of the main tracks on to short cuts and bridle-roads. In pasture countries the young farmer fond of hunting usually prefers something better than a roadster—one that will grow into money. But the majority of modern farmers prefer wheels, or are generally satisfied with anything useful that will do their day's work. Changed indeed are habits and tastes since the time when a good roadster hackney was worth as much as, and was more carefully chosen than, the modern brougham horse.

Before railroads had ceased to be considered an unclean thing by the landed gentry, and when only a few main trunk lines had intersected the country, the tour on horseback was still to be enjoyed in perfection by a young horseman whose years, health, and spirits, could defy the damp days, muddy roads, dark nights, and uncertain inns, for the sake of independence, adventure, and the abstract pleasure there is in riding a good horse.

"The sage opinion passed on Colonel Mannering, 'that a gentleman may be known by his horse,' was shared by many of the ostlers who received him into their patronising hands. Well mounted, the young adventurer was not tied by a mile or two or an hour or two, and was not afraid of getting a little wrong in trying a short cut, or investigating a promising scene, a green range of hills, or ancient manor buried in a park of ancestral oaks. Country folk were wonderfully kind and cheery to such a traveller; stout farmers returning from market were hospitably pressing (in the northern counties); and squires, once assured the stranger was only travelling for pleasure, wonderfully kind on face of introduction of a well-bred nag and an inquiring face innocent of beard. Not unfrequently the adventure of Squire Western on his road to London was repeated—a chance run with hounds, and a dinner with a stranger to follow. All through the counties where, at war prices, moor land had been enclosed, there were long slips of greensward on either side of the highway, inviting a canter in the morning, and affording pleasant walking ground for the last tired mile or two. Then there were many delightful short cuts through bridle-roads, across fords too deep for wheels, and—by sufferance of lodge-keepers open to the blandishments of a smile, a pleasant word and a shilling—through parks rich in turf, water, woodland, game and deer. Oh, those were delightful days, when, young and full of life, and hope, and romance, with a good horse, a sufficiently well-filled purse, and more than one friend on the road, the youth who thought himself a man set out, not afraid of rheumatism, to travel some two or three hundred miles with a definite point to reach, but no particular day, or hour, or route!"

The rider of a really good hack can leave him to himself on the very worst roads with perfect confidence that he will pick his way and put every foot down on the best place The fore-feet of a good hack, be the pace fast or slow, are always well forward, and fall flat on the ground; the action in the trot such that the fore-legs work from the shoulders, and are bent so that the rider, sitting upright, can just see the knees as they rise, but not by any means "up to the curb-chain." Machine-like regularity and ease characterise all the good hack's paces—that is, the paces of a really good one—but it is astonishing how many queer animals fumble at a great rate along a good road without getting a fall. "A useful riding-horse may not have perfect shoulders," says a cavalry officer, who was a great authority in Rotten Row forty years ago; "but they must be strong, and the fore-feet not so far back as to make a horse stand over like a cart-horse, or many a useful brougham-horse." No horse can carry a heavy weight with too long a back, or without muscular loins and wide hips.

Above all things, for country use and long rides, the so-called cobs, that owe their apparent strength to a close connection with cart-horse blood, are to be avoided. Almost as a matter of course, they have straight shoulders, and their fore-feet are too far under them. For want of blood they soon tire; after a couple of miles trotting they begin to step short, then trip, and unless soon pulled up fall like logs, without an effort to save themselves.

Good shoulders do not mean, at any rate in a young horse, their being thin ("knify") at the withers; on the contrary, they can scarcely be too thick at five years old, provided they are not thick at the lower ends, while inclining their tops well back, leaving as great a space as possible between the end of the mane and the pommel of the saddle.

"There is a certain cross bone which connects the lower end of the shoulder-blades with the animal's fore-legs, which, when it is too long, throws the fore-legs back, and makes the horse stand over."

To get good fore-leg action is a great point—it secures safety to the rider—but to make a complete hack, the hind-leg action must also be good. The hock joints must when moving, whether slowly or fast, be bent well, and bring the hind-legs well forward, and under him; indeed, it cannot be too far as long as he does not strike the fore-legs. Racing trotters carry their hind-feet far before and outside the fore-legs. It is this power and regularity of hind-leg action that makes a horse easy in his slow paces. A horse with good shoulder action before, propelled by far-reaching hind-legs, whether walking, or trotting, or galloping, seems to be, as dealers say, "always riding up hill."

The chest of a speedy galloper should be protuberant and deep, but not broad; the ribs before the girths long, and behind the girths short. When the ribs are short before the girth, it is impossible to keep a saddle in the proper place without a crupper, though cruppers have been discarded for many years by the owners of hacks, hunters, and riding-horses of every kind; but at the time when George III. began his reign, as Squire Warburton sings—

"Each horse wore a crupper, each man a pig-tail."

The horse just described is the sort of animal required for country use, which may for business or pleasure be ridden twenty, forty, or even sixty miles, with comfort to the rider and without distress to the animal. The same sort makes an excellent railway station trapper, or one of a wagonette pair, without losing his saddle qualities. He has not the brilliant qualities of the park hack, but he is essentially useful.

THE COVERT HACK.

The covert hack is the nearest representative of the roadster hack of our grandfathers, and in his best form is a pony hunter. But the improvement of roads, the consequent facilities for using wheels, and the extension of railroads, have had the effect of greatly reducing the number of a class of animal that up to 1836 formed an indispensable part of every hunting-stud with any pretensions to completeness. Even in the pasture counties, where everything that is most expensive in the way of sporting appliances is the most esteemed, you do not see one-tenth of the number of genuine covert hacks come rattling up to covert-side from all points of the compass just as hounds are moving away, that you did when William IV. was king, when those model hunting squires Sir Charles Knightley and Sir Tatton Sykes were still first flight men in Yorkshire and Northamptonshire. Deduct those who come in one of the many varieties of dog-cart, mail-phaeton, and park wagonette, four-in-hand drag, and pair-horse brougham (these last are generally the middle-aged, and not least sensible), those who make the hunter do hack's work at all meets within from five to ten miles, or make one hunter a hack for the day and ride another when the serious work begins, not counting the sporting medicos and curates, the combined vet and dealer, and the many of the class who use a nondescript general utility animal, or those who, in quite another direction, make their London luxury, the fine park-hack, do covert-hack duty in the country (I have seen the late Mr.

Green of Rolleston, a Master of the Quorn in his day, cantering along bridle-roads to meet the hounds on his favourite park hack, a white Arab-like pony), and the residuum of real covert hacks will be found very small indeed.

The undergraduate's idea of a covert hack used to be a thoroughbred weed, that plunged and kicked for the first five minutes and then ran away, or galloped at any rate at top speed, for the next hour.

A perfect covert hack must do all his paces smoothly, with comfort to the rider. He should not be over 15 hands, should walk freely, and either trot thirteen miles an hour or canter fifteen miles an hour with a heavy weight on his haunches, and gallop twenty miles without making it a trouble, blowing, or shaking his tail, at the end of the journey. This sort of animal, which could not do the work if he had not sound lungs and capital legs and feet, is just the horse for any one who lives and rides in the country, although he never sees or

A USEFUL SORT.

wants to see a hound. It may be a vulgar-looking animal, and too nervous to ride over stones amidst the sights and sounds of a city. Pace is of course essential, but easy elastic action, which is only to be found in well-shaped, well-bred animals, is equally essential; otherwise you may arrive at the end of your journey as much beaten as if you had driven in a springless cart.

For a trap for country use any horse with pace may find a place in harness; but for saddle, whether it be a pony or a full-sized hack, hack action is essential. With good action you may overlook a coarse head, a rat tail, a goose rump, ragged hips, and any defects of shape that do not affect the ease of your travelling.

In the year 1873—as there had been any time for the last fifty years—a grievous outcry arose on the decline of the English riding-horse from the form and stoutness of those on which our cavalry were mounted in the Peninsular war. Horses, like every other article of agricultural produce, are subject to the laws of supply and demand. Horses for long distances are not required, and are therefore not specially bred. The whole gambling spirit of the nation, which formerly had many vents, is now concentrated on the racecourse. As the greater number of races are for a distance of six furlongs, with weights not exceeding and generally under eight stone ten pounds, as a racehorse is old ("the old horse") at six years, and as the many sporting newspapers proclaim far and wide the temporary triumph of animals which have snatched a handicap race of six furlongs, carrying six stone, it is not astonishing that many sires get custom which are anything but calculated to get "sound and useful horses." A man purchases the son, the grandson, or the cousin five times removed, of one of these wretched handicap winners, for a low price, prints a card of his pedigree more or less true, travels him at two to three guineas a mare, and gets plenty of custom—first because the fee is low, and next because the customers are smitten with a superstitious and ignorant admiration for the triumphs of the turf. They desire to breed a horse that can walk and trot; nevertheless, they select a sire that, if he can do anything, can only gallop, with perhaps imperfect wind, bad feet, straight ankles, low withers, and a vicious temper.

Lavengro describes the Irish cob on which he took his first ride "as barely 15 hands high, but he had the girth of a metropolitan dray-horse; his head was small in comparison with his immense neck, which curved down nobly to his wide back; his chest was broad and fine, his shoulders models of symmetry and strength; he stood well and powerfully upon his legs, which were somewhat short—in a word, a gallant specimen of the genuine Irish cob, a species at one time not uncommon, but at present nearly extinct." "There," said the groom, "with sixteen stone on his back he will trot fourteen miles in one hour, and clear a six-foot wall at the end of it."

But although riding-horses of great endurance are scarce, this country possesses the breed, which only requires careful selection and cultivation in those colonies and countries where the road and railroad luxuries of England are not to be had, to be reproduced in their pristine excellence. This has repeatedly been proved in Australia and South Africa, and in the crosses of the English with Continental horses in Germany and Italy.

CHAPTER XI.

PARK HACKS—PHAETON STEPPERS—CARRIAGE HORSES.

The Park Hack—The Many Sorts in Rotten Row—Morning Rides—The Chief Justice—The Queen's Counsel—The Greek Merchant—Baron Bullion—The Engineer—The Physician—The Park Hack Proper—Form, Action, Mouth, Manners—Description of Form—Must Behave like a Gentleman—The Bad Rider spoils the Good Hack—The Horse suitable to the Rider's Size, Age, Weight, and Character—Reminiscences of Rotten Row—Lord Althorpe and Top-boots—Lord Melbourne—Susannah and the Elders—Count D'Orsay, Earl of Chesterfield, Lord Sefton, the Last of the Dandies—Military Horsemen: Lord Anglesea, Field Marshal Lord Combermere, The Marquis of Londonderry—High School—The Duke of Wellington; his Horses—Lord Palmerston's Roadsters—Jacob Omnium—Earl Russell on his Pony—Anecdote—Modern Ministers on Horseback—Proposal for Cabinet Hacks—Polo Ponies' Fashion and Origin—Mail Phaeton Pair Steppers—State Coach, Chariot, and Barouche Horses—Phaeton Pair Steppers scarce—Require Lofty True Action, Beauty, Good Mouths, Courage, Fine Temper—Always Easy to Sell—Colours and Matches—Must Settle your Size—Must be Symmetrical—Grooms, Neat, Active, not too Big—Steppers must be Shown not Used—Ornamental Knee-action must be Protected—Coach, Chariot, and Barouche Horses of Great Size—Demand for Town Use—Court—Full-dress Entertainments—Park Parades—England the Last Country adopting Pleasure Carriages—Beckman's Account of Neapolitan Caretta, Thirteenth Century—Early Picture of a Charette—Taylor the Water Poet's Protest—Flemish—The Fine, Fashionable Carriage Horses—Cromwell's Coach Upset—Queen Anne—Sir Charles Grandison—The Coach-horses of George II. same as of Roman Cardinals, 1848—Her Majesty's State Cream Stallions—Black and White Hanoverians Discontinued—Anecdote of William IV. and Plaiting Manes of State-horses—The Cleveland superseded Flemish—The Blood-horse extinguished Cleveland—Blood Carriage-horse reached Perfection in the Time of George Prince Regent—The Horse of the Period what the Period Requires—The Modern Carriage-horse for Pleasure, not for Journeys—Must look well Standing—Bearing Reins, Advantage and Disadvantage of—Grand Action—Eight Miles an Hour Fast Enough—Colours—Barouche-horses more Blood than Coach-horses—The Large Horses almost entirely in Hands of Jobmasters—Experiment with German Coach-horses a Failure—Evidence of Colonel Maude, C.B.—Joshua East—Edmund Tattersall before a Committee of the House of Lords—Principles of Selecting Coach-horses, from Gervase Markham.

THE park hack is essentially an ornamental animal. He may be an extraordinary weight-carrier, strong as an elephant; but to deserve the prefix of "park." he must have style, if not elegance. He may be strong, he must not be coarse.

It is quite true that people who ought to know better ride horses in Rotten Row in the height of the season which are as much out of place in that scene of equestrian luxury as a coalheaver, in the costume of his trade, in the stalls of the opera. Some ride coach-horses of camel-like proportions; some ride brutes that would be useful in a carrier's cart, and call them cobs; some ride weeds with every sort of defect, and no merit except a head and tail derived from an illustrious and remote ancestor; tall men are to be seen on ponies, and short men on giraffes; country gentlemen appear on old hunters, valuable animals in the field, no doubt, very safe conveyances over a cramped country, but showing, in round stiff joints, a poking neck, and many scars, anything but the action and appearance of an old gentleman's hack; ladies who have declined to go into a weighing machine, in spite of the tempting invitations at every metropolitan railway station, are to be seen risking their lives on screws two stone under their weight; but, perhaps the very worst class of horse will be bestridden by some rich man, who tells you, with all the fond pride of a parent, that he "bred it himself."

These remarks only apply to Rotten Row at the hours in the season when everything most correct in style and costume is to be found there or thereabouts, on foot and on horseback. Nothing need be said to those unpretending people who frequent the Park at early hours simply for exercise, not merely to see and be seen, and learn the gossip of the hour.

Anything useful and safe—the latter quality is most important—will do for exercise, because the matutinal promenaders are not presumed to be sacrificing to appearance. But no sight can be more ridiculous than that of a well-dressed man or woman parading, with an intense air of self-satisfaction, on a hideous or broken-down nag at mid-day, in the height of the season; dirty gloves and unblacked boots are quite as excusable in such a place.

In the morning rides one Chief Justice prefers a Leicestershire hunter, another learned brother a fat pony; a Queen's Counsel, the terror of prevaricating witnesses, seems to have a fancy for the cast-off weeds of a racing stable. The young Greek merchant, at whatever hour, is always to be seen on a *steppare* valued at three good figures; and when Greek joins Greek to the number of half a dozen, they will "step" along in a row, a wonderful sight, with nearly £2,000 worth of horseflesh, in a line.

Baron Bullion generally prepares for the city on a creditable weight-carrying cob. Engineers are, as a rule, well-mounted, according to their weight, because they are a class who, if they appear above the ruck of respectable at all, endeavour to get the best article in the market, and they take a first-class dealer into their confidence; but fashionable physicians, when they do ride abroad, seem very often to resort to livery, and not to get the best hacks.

The following sketch is from the pen of a famous Piccadilly dealer, well known as a finished horseman and fine coachman in London and Paris. Need I name the Mr. Sago who sold Digby Grand his first cabriolet horse?

"The park hack should have, with perfection of graceful form, graceful action, an exquisite mouth, and perfect manners. He must be intelligent—amongst horses senseless brutes are legion—for without intelligence, even with fine form and action, he never can be pleasant to ride. Thoroughbred is to be preferred; and if not quite, as nearly thoroughbred as possible, of any colour except mealy or foul-marked. White marks often much improve, sometimes quite disfigure a horse.

"The head should be of the finest Oriental type; the neck well arched, cut not too long; the shoulders light at the points, long, and grown well into the back. The loins should be accurately arched, and the quarters level and nicely rounded, not drooping abruptly towards the tail (like many capital hunters, famous racehorses, and useful road hacks). The mane and tail should be full, straight, without the least suspicion of a curl, and every hair as soft as silk; four clean, well-shaped, well-placed legs, the fetlocks rather longer than would be chosen for a hunter—from such a form action pleasant to the rider may be confidently expected, and paces agreeable for even the commonest observer to follow.

"The walk of a park hack should be perfection—fast, springy; the legs moving as it were independently of the body, without apparent exertion, with all the certainty of machinery, the head carried in its right place, the neck gracefully curved, and the tail displaying a full flag gracefully keeping time with the foot-falls. From the walk he should be able to bound into any pace, in perfectly balanced action, that the rider may require."

A slight defect in the wind will not be noticed if the rider knows when to drop from too sharp a canter to a walk; as for age, there are horses, the daily admiration of the Row, so beautiful and so gay that they might be taken for colts, although they have nearly reached man's majority. Perfect symmetry with perfect temper, the high courage that no sight or sound alarms, perfect temper, luxurious paces, and, as a crowning glory, perfect manners both as regards his rider and other horses, will command a fabulous price in spite of the defects above described.

When a great man, celebrated for his park hacks, departs this country, or this world, there will be nearly as many competitors for them as for his pedigree pictures, his old Dresden dinner service, or his own-imported cigars.

Manners are, above all, important—indeed essential—for a first-class park hack. He must conduct himself like a gentleman,* not only to his rider but to other horses—a degree of liveliness (not to put too fine a point upon it) that may be all very well in a deer park, is quite out of place in Hyde Park. Good manners are founded on a naturally good disposition, cultivated by a professor of the art of horsemanship, one who has taken at least a "double first," with a perfect seat, fine hands, and impassive temper; this education maintained by constant practice. A heavy-handed, ill-tempered, or idle, careless groom, will soon spoil the mouth and manners of the finest hack; therefore, once found, no pains should be spared to keep this instrument of pleasure in the finest tune. For, as I venture to repeat from a sketch written many years ago, "The army of pleasure-seekers who work in England hard at amusement— the gatherers and distributors of wealth—find in a perfect park hack a luxury, a rest, a healthy excitement, a pleasant fatigue, a medium for grave or serious converse, for light lively gossip, for making love, for making friends, for patching up quarrels, for selling bargains, or arranging political combinations, which the old-fashioned squire, the provincial manufacturer, and the man who never rides but looks on horses as mere machines for betting on, cannot understand, and therefore despise. Character as well as manners are indispensable in the park hack. A hunter may have a plain head and a rat tail, may be a stumbling slug on the road, or a hard puller in the field, but if he fence brilliantly, can gallop, and live through a first-class run in a first-class country, he will command a long price, because all minor faults are forgiven in consideration of his perfection in his trade."

The hack of every man or woman who aspires to fashionable distinction, or who from any cause has become a public character, should be handsome, if ridden by the young; and have "character" if the rider be neither young nor of a good horseback figure.

The horse should be as suitable to the rider as his clothes. The pink cravat that may become a young officer of the Guards in mufti would look absurd on a country banker; the hack that suits a slim and perfectly-dressed figure may be quite out of character with a horseman whose waist is dumpy and whose legs are short.

There are horses which, without any pretensions to elegance, have a well-proportioned compact-ness and a regular perfection of action suitable to middle-aged riders of serious pursuits.

Under ordinary circumstances a town hack should not exceed 15 hands in height, because horses of that size are the most handy and safe in turning corners and walking over slippery pavement. Indeed, it may be laid down as a rule that every inch after about 15 hands adds in geometrical proportion to the difficulty of getting a perfect horse. But tall men of position require tall horses; a man of six feet wants a horse 16 hands high to look well when mounted.

Before the year 1873 I should have said that a park hack might be of any height from 14½ hands to 16 hands, but the game of polo brought ponies into fashion. Formerly, a number

---

* "The late Duke of N—— mentioned, as an instance of the ill-luck that had pursued him through life, that at the grand review of the Volunteers held by the Queen, he, who was a good horseman, was the only Lord-Lieutenant who was thrown. 'But why,' he was asked, 'did you stick to the bridle, and allow yourself to be dragged about in a ridiculous manner?' 'Because my beautiful horse was such a vicious beast that he would have flown at and attacked the horses of the royal suite.' Why, then, was the natural question, did he ride such a vicious beast?" [A horse without manners.—Ed.]—*Hayward's Essays.*

of very fine horses, both cob-like and blood-like, were ridden into the city.   In the last century a lively competition in fast trotting hacks existed amongst the younger representatives of banking and brewing firms; but at the present time the horsemen of financial position who pass farther than Westminster Bridge may be counted on the fingers of one hand, although the embankment affords a tempting ride, free from stones, through both parks to Blackfriars Bridge; and this route has recently been adopted by equestrians of the Temple and Printing House Square, who previously tempted Providence in the crowded ways and slippery roads of Fleet Street and the Strand.

The tall men to whom personal appearance is a matter of importance require tall park horses, which are, in fact, of the same stamp as those "first chargers" which the commanding officer of a crack cavalry regiment expects his officers to reserve sacredly for parade and review purposes, at any rate not to use as so many chargers are used, for hunting and for harness.

ROTTEN ROW.

Rotten Row in Hyde Park has long been exclusively devoted to the use of horsemen and horsewomen, and still continues to be the part of the Park where the finest specimens of Park hacks are to be seen, although in recent improvements soft rides round nearly the whole of the Park have been constructed for the benefit of equestrians.   The "*Ring*," so often referred to by several writers in the time of Queen Anne had disappeared before my time.   It was marked by trees behind the corner where the statue of Achilles stands.   The Ladies' Mile exists still on the north side of the Serpentine, but is no longer "the Mile," as it was even twenty years ago when ladies there only displayed the finest equipages.   Amidst every improvement of Hyde Park, and they are many, "the Row" retains its favour for early morning, mid-day (a comparatively modern fashion), and afternoon rides.   Royalty only is permitted to traverse Rotten Row on wheels.

George IV. rode on horseback a great deal in his younger days, talked of riding, and bought horses and boots, and wore breeches, a few years before his death, when his height and health made such exercise seem impossible to every one but himself.   He was an excellent judge of every kind of horse, and kept, after he came to the throne, such a stud as has never been collected since in our royal stables.   The king had a preference for grey hollow-back horses which partly concealed the size of his limbs.

A scarce mezzotint represents him in his teens, in a hussar uniform, sitting on his horse— an impossible, prancing, Flemish horse—with the long stirrup and straight leg of the Prussian school of the last century.   It is related in the life of Sir Fowell Buxton, the slave emancipator, that the king was particularly struck by a very powerful blood-horse ridden by the baronet, which, in the midst of a mob howling and hissing as the king passed in his carriage, stood, like some fine statue, with head erect, ears pricked, and nostrils breathing hard with excitement, perfectly still.   The reply of Sir Fowell to a request—king's requests are generally considered commands—to "name his price" was, "John Bull is not for sale."   This was not the only refusal the king sustained in the matter of horses.   Matt Milton, a celebrated dealer, went to Edinburgh to purchase for His Majesty a celebrated trotting hack belonging to the Duke of Hamilton (known as "The Proud Duke").   Milton began by offering a thousand guineas for the trotter.   The reply was "Tell the man I can afford a thousand-guinea horse as well as the king can."

Until the death of William IV., one of the most familiar and remarkable equestrian figures was his brother the Duke of Cumberland, afterwards King of Hanover, attended by his double and equerry General Quentin—handsome, stern, forbidding countenances, with heavy moustaches, then uncommon—perfect specimens of the stiff Hanoverian style of military horsemanship.

William IV. never rode after he came to the throne, although he did constantly when living at Bushey Park; but Charles Greville relates the sensation he made a few days after succeeding to the throne, by appearing in a full general's uniform with spurs!

Her Majesty Queen Victoria succeeded in 1837, and according to Raikes' Diary sent for the Earl of Albemarle, her Master of the Horse, and said, "My Lord, I wish you to immediately provide me with six chargers to review my troops." The young queen had evidently in her mind Queen Elizabeth at Tilbury Fort.

R. B. Davis, brother of the celebrated huntsman of the Royal Buckhounds, and son of the huntsman of George III.'s Harriers, became an artist of horse subjects under the special patronage of that sovereign. He painted a picture of the girl Queen Victoria, riding in the Windsor Park attended by her Prime Minister, her Foreign Secretary of State, and others of less note in England's history. The engraving of this picture had considerable temporary popularity, and from it the caricaturist of the day, "H. B." (the father of Richard Doyle, who delights the present generation in a very different style), produced "Susannah and the Elders" —Her Majesty riding between Lord Melbourne and Lord Palmerston. It was very funny, but did not hit off the essential difference in character between the horses of the Premier and Lord Palmerston.

Lord Palmerston rode tall blood-horses; if they were up to weight, with the best possible road action, could trot ten miles an hour, and gallop, he did not ask for manners, airs, or graces. Lord Melbourne rode a style of horse seen in another picture, painted by the late Sir Francis Grant, in 1840. The Queen is mounted on a dappled dun or grey horse with black mane, tail, and legs, of Hanoverian breed, accompanied by Lord Melbourne riding an old-fashioned bay hunter, with a white blaze down his face, a portrait evidently, while the Marquis of Conynghame, a model courtier on a model brown hack, with his hat in his hand, balances the picture and makes a striking contrast to the calm repose of the Premier and his horse.

Lord Melbourne rode often in the Row with his brother Ministers, always on powerful, useful easy-paced horses, such as might have been expected from his character—luxurious, and indifferent to appearances. He also rode constantly in the streets, but the streets were not so crowded as they now are; omnibuses were scarcely established and hansoms were not in existence.

On my first arrival from the country about the year 1835, and visit to the Park—then a very rough, ill-kept, swampy place, fed over by deer and the Ranger's cows—I saw at the end of the Row, facing Apsley House, a ponderous man about fifty years of age, with a round, red, good-humoured face, and black hair under his broad-brimmed hat, beginning to get grey, dressed in white cord breeches and top-boots, with silk stockings seen between them. I took him for some rich grazier from Lincolnshire, and was not far wrong. This was Lord Althorpe, celebrated as a breeder of Shorthorns and Master of the Pytchley, one of the best packs of hounds in the kingdom; the "Honest Jack" of his friends—he had no enemies; the Chancellor of the Exchequer and leader of the House of Commons in Earl Grey's Administration, in which duty, although one of the worst speakers that ever held a seat in that fastidious assembly, he exercised as great or greater influence than any of the brilliant orators who preceded and succeeded him. The Shorthorns were his hobby, and the Smithfield Club Show his delight. When a phrenologist had given him a serious political character, he said that "to see sporting dogs hunt gives me the greatest pleasure in the world." From his earliest to his latest days he never went on wheels when the saddle would serve him.

In 1806, being then only 24 years of age and a Lord of the Treasury, he used to have hacks posted on the road from London to Althorpe (78 miles), at about ten miles apart; he built a rough stable where there was no roadside inn. As soon as the House of Commons rose, he mounted and rode down, all night if needful, to hunt with the Pytchley the next morning. Thirty years later his tastes were still the same; the American Charles Sumner, met him at Wentworth House, Earl Fitzwilliam's, and was surprised to find him on a rainy day in boots and breeches at breakfast preparing to ride twenty-five miles before dinner to see a gaol at Mansfield.

Lord Althorpe was not the only gentleman of high degree who wore top-boots and breeches in London in 1834. Sir Francis Burdett, Sir Charles Knightley, and other landed squires of ancient pedigree, still adhered to the costume which was the height of fashion in the days when the Prince of Wales, Charles James Fox, and Brinsley Sheridan, were friends and allies, and which was the costume which county M.P's. were accustomed to wear when they took up any special county address to King George III.

While county gentlemen still adhered to top-boots and cord or leather breeches, there used to gather every afternoon of the season (noonday rides had not been established, and the City had not conquered and colonised Tyburnia) a group of horsemen under the shadow of the Achilles—a group of a tribe long since extinguished by real wars and the taste for athletic sports, the successors of Beau Brummell, an affected school of dandies, curled, perfumed, silked, and satined.

Three were remarkable, caught the eye and dwelt in the memory of every "young man from the country" who had read "Pelham," and saw them for the first time. The Antinous, Count D'Orsay, the Count Mirabel of Lord Beaconsfield's novel, the Alcibiades of that age, resplendent in a costume which Maclise has handed down to posterity in his portrait of young Charles Dickens (a costume absurd to modern swells), which Charles Sheridan has celebrated in his "Chaunt of Achilles"—

"Patting the crest of his well-managed steed,
A coat of chocolate, a vest of snow,
Well brushed his whiskers and his boots below;
A short-napped beaver prodigal of brim,
With trowsers tightened to a well-turned limb."

Alongside him was his copy, white-cuffed, primrose-gloved, save that the profuse curls were golden instead of raven-black, his features anything but Grecian, and his horse a flea-bitten grey. From time to time, in reply to the salutes of many pretty hands, he raised a hat of a shape now consigned to perfumers and dancing-masters with a grace his ancestor, Earl Chesterfield (of the "Letters"), would have approved and admired. The third of the party was Lord Sefton, almost old enough to be the father of the other two, almost humpbacked, the "cod's head and shoulders" of the caricaturist, perfectly dressed, admirably mounted on a stolid hack—the Ulysses of the Whig party and the world of fashion, famed for his political zeal, his mordant tongue, his skill as a coachman, his dinners, and the sumptuous example he had set when Master of the Quorn hounds.*

* Charles Greville, describing Lord Sefton's cheer when the majority on the third reading of the first Irish Reform Bill was announced breaks unconsciously into verse—

"And Sefton's yell was heard amidst the din."

Lord Chesterfield survived these, and almost all the gay companions of his youth. Sharing neither the accomplishments, nor the wit, nor the wisdom of D'Orsay and Sefton, he retained to the last, when "time had thinned his flowing locks," a style of grand and graceful courtesy which reminded one of the grand seigneurs of the Court of Louis Quatorze.

The Earl of Chesterfield has one claim to be remembered in every history of the modern horse. He established the first pack of foxhounds at Rome, and gave the Italian nobility a taste for horses that could gallop and jump. The improvement—it may be said the transformation —of the dull Roman and Neapolitan parade-horse into a creature of life and courage dates from Lord Chesterfield's winter in Rome.

I describe these three men, "the admired of all admirers" in that day, because they were types of a class utterly extinct and impossible in this generation.

Contemporary with the top-booted squires and the dandies tittuping up and down the Row, the toes of their varnished boots (a new invention) just touching their stirrups, were to be seen distinguished soldiers, survivors of the great Continental wars—the Marquis of Anglesea, Field Marshal Lord Combermere, who at seventy years rode still like a young man (he lived to be ninety) and the Marquis of Londonderry—all distinguished cavalry generals, and living examples of the almost forgotten, if not lost, as far as England is concerned, *haute école*, the high school of horsemanship. Of the three, the Marquis of Anglesea, a tall, thin, elegant man, on his celebrated thoroughbred charger Pearl, presented in spite of his cork leg, the finest example of the "balanced seat," horse and horseman both perfect, a very triumph of art. All three generals, as they rode along, *passaging* and *piaffing*, evidently demanded the admiration they deserved. No British general officer of the present day, however accomplished, would venture on such exhibitions of horsemanship, out of a riding school. It is related that the Marquis of Anglesea once cantered his horse nineteen times round the corner from Piccadilly to Albemarle Street, and was not satisfied with his horse's performance until the nineteenth time.

The Duke of Wellington, although educated at the military school of Angers in France, which was noted for its fine *manége*, never shared the taste of his companions-in-arms for parade chargers and high-school horsemanship. The thoroughbred chestnut Copenhagen, which carried him so stoutly at Waterloo, was, according to Lord Francis Egerton, "a very pretty horse," without any parade action—it was only 15 hands high. The horse the Duke preferred during the last twenty years of his life was a hunter class of animal, a good walker, ridden in a snaffle-bridle, like a huntsman's horse, without a thought of showing off the animal's paces. Before age had bent him his seat was remarkably upright ; lost in thought, he passed along, mechanically acknowledging with his upraised forefinger the many hats raised to salute the Great Duke. The Duke, with the Marquis of Anglesea, were the two who accompanied the Champion as Esquires at the coronation of George IV.

As he grew old and infirm, instead of bending forward like most old men, he leant back, literally hung on by the bridle, generally going down St. James's Park to the Horse Guards at a huntsman's shog-trot.

The duke could not bear to be helped to do anything he thought he could do himself. Haydon, the artist, who visited him at Walmer Castle to paint his portrait, says in his Journal— "The Duke told me he brushed his own coat, and would like to black his own boots." In the same spirit, the Duke's groom had a very difficult task in assisting him to mount when he grew very feeble without his Grace finding him out.

Amongst the statesmen of the departed generation, Sir Robert Peel was certainly, if not the very worst, the most awkward horseman that ever rode in Rotten Row. Bending over his horse's ears, he appeared to have no pleasure in the exercise, and performed his ride as a matter of duty, for the sake of health, and companionship with his several more or less illustrious colleagues. Sir Robert was killed by a shying hack purchased for him by an excellent judge of horses, the late Lord Ossington, at Tattersall's, ridden in defiance of the warning of his old coachman. But the best judge in the world cannot tell whether a horse shies or not without trying him. The moral to be derived from the lamentable event which deprived this country of a great statesman is that when a man immersed in deep affairs requires a horse for exercise, he should not go to an auction, but place himself in the hands of a first-class dealer. Lord Palmerston wrote to his brother at Naples, after Peel's death, July, 1849:— "Peel was a very bad horseman and an awkward rider. His horse might have been sat by any better equestrian, but he seems somehow to have been entangled in the bridle, and to have forced the horse to step or kneel upon him. Sir Robert Peel died much richer than people expected, and no wonder, for just before he bought the brute that killed him he refused to buy a perfect hack, called the 'Premier,' after a full trial, because he could not believe that any one ever gave £400 for a hack."

The last representative of high-school riding in Rotten Row disappeared with Lord Cardigan, "the last of the Cardigans;" and he, although highly accomplished in the *manége* style was but a pale copy of the Waterloo Marquis, still the talk of the sexagenarians in Dublin, who remember the time of the Anglesea viceroyalty—for no man with two sound legs ever made a finer display in the artificial style of horsemanship than the cavalry general who had left one leg at Waterloo, unless it be Mr. Mackenzie Greaves, domiciled in Paris, but an occasional visitor in the London season.

We do not seem to have any one capable of producing equestrian caricatures after the fashion of those published by Maclean, which gave the politicians of the time of Lord Melbourne, Sir Robert Peel, and the Duke of Wellington, so much amusement. The two ages of man were admirably expressed in the Earl of Westmoreland, father of the musical earl, bending over his horse's ears in the old jockey style, trotting a big hunter fourteen miles an hour, as "Old Rapid;" and Lord Castlereagh, son of the statesman, sitting back galloping his pony with a loose rein, as " Young Rapid."

> " Turn we a different genius to survey
> When Joseph (Hume) homeward plods his weary way ;
> Blind to the throng, for appetite he rides,
> And kicks with spurless heel his lumbering hackney's sides." *

I do not remember ever seeing or hearing of Thomas Babington Macaulay in Rotten Row, although we have his own evidence that he could ride, and that should be an encouragement to the most ungainly figures. The great historian writes in the diary of the "Journey through Ireland, 1848," quoted in Mr. Trevelyan's admirable and delightful life:—"I went twelve miles on horseback. I had not crossed a horse since I rode with Captain Smith, 'a quiet Arab,' through the mango gardens of Arcot in 1834. I was pleased to find that I had good seat ; my guide professed himself quite an admirer of the way in which I trotted and cantered ! *His flattery pleased more than many fine compliments which had been paid to my History.*"

For many years Thomas Carlyle took exercise on a bay hunter-like horse every evening

---

* "The Chaunt of Achilles."

in the Park, but always after the gay throng had disappeared. Earl Russell, of all men in the world, has described (in 1836) the Row and the Town out of season, in lines beginning :—

> "Remote, unfriended, melancholy, slow,
> A single horseman faces Rotten Row ;
> In Brooks's sits one quidnunc, to peruse
> The broad dull sheet which tells the lack of news ;
> At White's a lonely Brummel lifts his glass
> To see two empty hackney coaches pass."

PARK HARNESS HORSES—MAIL PHAETON PAIRS—STEPPERS.

The mail phaeton of the pre-railway generation required a pair of powerful horses, nearly if not quite 16 hands high. The modern phaetons, which have taken the place of that ponderous carriage so useful and pleasant in its way, intended either for country use or park parades, are so much lighter that full-sized horses are quite out of place in them. A phaeton of suitable size may be perfectly well horsed in every respect by horses of from 14 hands 3 inches to 15 hands 1 inch. When a pair of horses are used for several purposes—to draw a full-sized brougham or landau, as well as a mail phaeton—15 hands 2 inches may be found a more useful size. Beyond that height, unless exceedingly well-bred, it is difficult to find horses which are pleasant for a gentleman to drive.

Harness horses to be used in the Park ought to be, above all, ornamental; if simple utility for country use is all that is required, it is easy to get horses which, without being by any means exactly matched in size or character—they must be matched in pace—will go together pleasantly enough for all ordinary purposes; but if you aspire to make a good appearance, not to say sensation, in the fashionable circles of London or Paris, then you have a task before you which requires a good deal of knowledge on your own side or on the part of the man you trust to buy for you, not a little trouble, and plenty of money.

Sensation horses—that is, steppers in the Park meaning of the phrase—are very scarce. One of the notabilities of London as the owner and driver of this particular class of horses—a gentleman who has won prizes year after year at every show where classes were opened for harness-horses—to whom I applied for information, answered, " I always purchase a really good stepper of the size I use when I meet one, whether I want it or not, if he (or she) is fairly sound, and seems to have a good-wearing constitution, because this class of horse is so scarce. I do not meet with a superior stepper, of which I have not heard before, once in a year. They are scarce, because, in order to be of the first class they require such an extraordinary combination of qualities—that is to say, high true action, beauty when harnessed, good mouths, courage, and fine temper. The last quality is essential, because horses that are to be driven, and driven slowly, in crowds, must know how to behave themselves in the society of other ' gentlemanly ' horses.

" A superior stepper, if he does not die, is not an expensive horse in one point of view, because, if fairly bought, you can always sell a horse with a reputation at a profit ; and this rule still more applies when you have succeeded in matching a pair. There are always persons willing to pay an extraordinary price for harness-horses, if they are unquestionably the best article of the kind. A nonpareil phaeton pair is much easier to sell at 400, 500, and 600 guineas, than a pair of ordinary useful ones that have cost £80 each. And a pair of horses that match perfectly in size, character, pace, action, and style of going, will be worth four hundred and five hundred together that may not be worth more than half that sum separately."

A match in colour is excellent, but if you delight in steppers you must never hesitate to purchase a match in all other respects, of whatever colour. There are certain colours that go very well together by contrast, as chestnut and well-mottled grey, a skewbald or piebald and a chestnut or a grey; but even where the colours do not harmonise there is always the chance of matching one of the two. You must also make up your mind to the size you mean to drive, because the carriage must fit the horses and the horses the carriage for Park purposes; 15 hands 2 inches in a phaeton meant for 14 hands 2 or 3 inches looks as much out of character as a tall man in a little man's clothes. In this class of equipage everything must be in keeping, everything the best of its kind, as far as they can be bought for money. If the owner cannot drive well he must learn, if he would not look ridiculous. The grooms must be neat, active, not too big, and know their business. In a word, the phaeton with a stepping pair cannot be done economically; expense must not stop the owner from obtaining the best of everything. He invites attention and criticism by his horses' action, and is bound to present something complete and perfect, "as far as money will supply it."

At the present day there are two popular styles of phaeton horses. Either may be selected, but whichever is chosen should be adhered to in the whole stud. They may be light and blood-like, or cobby, but they must have symmetry and character. Two pairs are the least with which a man can appear daily behind *steppers*.

One all-important point remains to be noticed as regard Park steppers. Having purchased them you must not use them, you must only show them. There is an old story which perfectly applies to this case. An English lady went to a celebrated Paris artist for a pair of shoes. In a few days she called, and complained that one shoe had split. The *cordonnier* looked at the triumph of his skill with an injured air, and exclaimed, "Why, madame has been walking!" So you may drive your steppers generally very slowly, and a little fast if they shine in a fast trot, for two hours or so every day; but if you want to drive to Brighton, or even to go ten miles out of town and back, you must fall back on a useful pair or hire post-horses.

There are exceptions, but as a rule, brilliant knee-action is ornamental, and to be used, guarded, and preserved like any other costly ornament.

COACH, CHARIOT, AND BAROUCHE HORSES.

For no class of horses is there a more regular and increasing demand than for large, sufficiently well-bred animals, not under 15 hands 3 inches, averaging full 16 hands, exclusively required as harness pairs for heavy and expensive carriages, like coaches, chariots, barouches, and landaus, which are chiefly used in great cities like London and Paris. One of the coloured illustrations of this book is a portrait, painted by special permission, of a state carriage-horse the property of His Royal Highness the Prince of Wales, fully 17 hands high, with superb action.*

During the last twenty years a steady change has taken place in the direction of using smaller and lighter horses for all country and many town carriages. Full-sized harness pairs are valuable in proportion as they combine with size and power the style of beauty and of

---

* A horse like this is worth from 400 to 500 guineas; but they are so scarce that no money would buy a team without some months of search.

action esteemed for state occasions and fashionable parades. They are to be seen in perfection in the equipages of royal personages. They are one of the principal parts of the show on the days of drawing-rooms and levées. They catch the eye on their way to state dinners, to garden parties at Chiswick or Sion House, and the suburban villas of the leaders of fashion and the pillars of finance—the harness, like the liveries of the coachmen and footmen, gorgeous ; the carriages brilliant, and fitted to the horses. They are also one of the sights of London, in less magnificent trappings, but not less proudly stepping, in the height of the season in the daily parades of the Park, when cotton stockings replace the silk of the much-calved footmen and coachmen on Court days. As a matter of course, in the several thousand pairs at work in London alone, every degree of merit down to simple utility is to be found.

Specimens of this class of horse ascend as well as descend in the same scale; sometimes they rise from drawing one of the huge spring vans of a city warehouseman to be one of a pair in the Court chariot of a duchess or the barouche of a millionaire ; more frequently they fall, after losing their action, to drawing fly-broughams.

The type of the coach-horse of the time of Queen Anne and the greater part of the reign of the first two Georges was the same as that which was lately found in the coaches of the cardinals at Rome—of great size, as fat as prize oxen, proud and prancing at starting, "all action and no go." This type is still preserved in the royal stables, in the shape of the cream-coloured Hanoverian stallions, which were once invariably employed to draw the royal coach when the British Sovereign proceeded in full state to open or close the Houses of Parliament, or any other ceremony of equal importance.

Since the death of the Prince Consort the state coach and its team of eight gigantic cream stallions has never been used, but the breed is still carefully preserved at the royal breeding paddocks, Hampton Court. During the reigns of the four Georges and until the death of William IV.—when the kingdom of Hanover passed, by the operation of the Salic Law, to Her Britannic Majesty's uncle the Duke of Cumberland—the royal stables always contained, beside the creams, two other sets of Hanoverian state horses, one black, the other white (albinoes) the last being the representatives of the white horse of Hanover. These were regularly imported from the king's stud farms in Hanover. Since the Prussian conquest and the incorporation of the kingdom of Hanover with the German Empire, the breeding-stud has disappeared, and when inquiries were made in Germany in 1870, with the view of purchasing a team of white horses for a circus, not a single specimen could be found. There is a picture at Windsor Castle, by the late R. B. Davis, of the procession of King William and Queen Adelaide to their coronation, in which the carriages with six black stallions, six white stallions, and several sixes of Yorkshire bay geldings, precede the state coach containing the king and queen, drawn by eight creams.

By the kindness of Colonel Maude, C.B., the Crown Equerry, three of the original oil sketches for that picture have been engraved for this work. The manes of the creams are plaited with purple ribbons, the whites, blacks, and bays with crimson. This ribbon-plaiting, a most elaborate and almost artistic operation, takes a great deal of time. In 1831 it assumed the importance of a political incident. When Earl Grey and Lord Brougham waited upon the Sailor King, to request him to dissolve the Parliament which had all but rejected the first Reform Bill, at the last moment, when all the king's scruples had been overcome, the Earl of Albemarle, the Whig Master of the Horse, protested that there was not time to plait the manes of the state carriage-horses. The answer of the king, that he "would go down in a hackney coach," was soon spread through the country, and for the time he was the most popular of European monarchs. The cream-coloured horses, not having been exercised as usual, or else imbued with Hanoverian prejudices, were above themselves on that important day. "As the carriage containing the King and his Master of the Horse was passing the guard of honour the ensign in charge of the colours lowered them to the sovereign according to the established formula. The usually impassive 'cream-colours' took umbrage at this act of homage, swerved and broke into an undignified trot. Mr. Roberts, the coachman, whose mind and body were alike thrown off their balance by the unwonted hurry of the morning, and by the insubordination of his steeds, proceeded, in utter forgetfulness of the royal presence, loudly to anathematise the guard of honour generally, and the standard-bearer in particular. Before the procession had reached the Horse Guards the opprobrious epithets had winged their flight to the officials

ROYAL HANOVERIAN COACH-HORSE.

within the building. The consequence was that Mr. Roberts, who had played so important a part in the morning pageant, was compelled to make a public apology to the offended guard of honour before it was marched off to its private parade."*

The Cleveland bay superseded the German coach-horse when the highways, improved for mail-coach use, increased the pace of travellers, whether with their own or with post-horses. Yorkshire horses, as far as can be ascertained, have always been large. The Cleveland was probably the result of a cross between the large native horse referred to by Gervase Markham and the blood-horses that early took root in that horse-loving country. According to pictures, the old Cleveland bay was very much like the coarser specimens of the Yorkshire coach-horse stallion, of which a few specimens still travel the northern counties; but according to the latest authorities, the real Cleveland bay, partly by repeated crosses of blood-horses, and partly by the large exportation of mares between the years 1830 and 1860, has been almost improved out of existence, and is only now rarely to be found except in Her Majesty's stables.

* "Recollections of the Sixth Earl of Albemarle."

The English coach-horse arrived at perfection as a powerful well-bred animal, with really fine moving action, early in the present century, under two influences—the high roads constructed for the mail-coaches, and the wide distribution of thoroughbred sires, which it was part of the dignity of every local magnate to keep and to breed, in order to be represented at county races. A portrait of a carriage-horse, by Benjamin Marshall, the property of Henry Villebois, Esq., engraved in " Laurence's Delineations of the Horse, 1810," is as fine a specimen of a powerful blood wheeler as could be found in any modern coach, although disfigured by cropped ears and a tail closely docked.

Before stage-coach travelling and posting were brought to the perfection which was extinguished with the coaches and the horses by the railway system, every great landed gentleman, peer, or squire, kept a large stud of coach-horses, and performed all journeys within

A WHITE HANOVERIAN LEADER.

a hundred miles, certainly all within fifty, with his own horses. Great noblemen travelled from Northumberland, Yorkshire, Lancashire, and Cheshire, with their own horses, by easy stages. A squire of two or three thousand a year, in the midland or northern counties, did not consider his stable furnished without five or six full-sized, well-bred coach-horses. Noblemen counted this part of their studs by the score. The heads of the noble families—like the Duke of Northumberland, Earl Fitzwilliam, Lord Darlington, the Earl of Derby, Earl Grosvenor, and the Duke of Portland—seldom rode out in their carriages with less than four horses and as many outriders. If they visited the local race-course, six horses were attached to the family coach. These horses were in greater part bred by themselves. The favourite race-horses of these great noblemen, when removed to the stud, covered the half-bred mares of their tenants and neighbours at nominal fees.

Thus in 1780 one of the most famous horses of the day was the Earl of Derby's Sir Peter Teazle, of which Sir Charles Bunbury wrote, when he first arrived a colt at Newmarket, " Lord Derby has sent a coach-horse here;" shortly afterwards, "The coach-horse can gallop;" a little later, "The coach-horse is the best horse here." The tradition of breeding coach-horses as well as race-horses was maintained at Knowsley up to the time of the lately-deceased earl, Edward Geoffrey Stanley, the great orator. At the present day, and for many years past, a horse as famous as Sir Peter, when placed in the stud, would only be permitted to serve a limited number of thoroughbred mares at fees of from fifty to one hundred guineas; and however admirable as a sire, would do nothing for increasing the number and quality of any except race-horses. But the Earl of Derby, as a kind of county potentate, patronised his neighbours, and allowed them the use of Sir Peter. For many years afterwards every gentleman in Lancashire who prided himself on his coach-horses had or claimed to have at least one brown Sir Peter in his stable; Lord Grosvenor did the like service for his tenants and neighbours in Cheshire and in Shropshire, which was long famous for its hunters. The same system was at work in every horse-breeding and racing county in England and Wales, before roads and railroads centralised horse-racing and effaced county dignities and distinctions. Thus there was at the same time a demand for large harness-horses with good travelling action which are not now required, and facilities which do not now exist for obtaining the services of superior thoroughbred sires.

The horse of the period is always what the period requires. The carriage-horse of the present day is essentially a horse more for pleasure than for use. Ten miles in and as many out again, with a rest between, is considered a long day's journey for carriage-horses. Nine pair of carriage-horses out of ten, or more probably ninety out of a hundred, are not required to leave the limits between Hyde Park and Richmond Hill once a year, or to extend their trot in Paris beyond the *Bois*.

What, therefore, is required in a carriage-horse is an animal that will look well in harness, although he may be rather mean out of it. He need not be able to walk, but he must be able to stand after being properly borne up by the bearing-reins, like a statue. There are very useful riding and driving horses, and very brilliant hunters and race-horses that "stand over" with the fore-feet approaching the hind-feet in a very ugly manner—like a goat. Such a form is out of the question for a carriage-horse of high price. On the contrary, standing with the fore-legs projecting as far as a line drawn from the nose, in a sort of statuesque position, is a habit natural to a few and taught to a great many carriage-horses. The neck may be much too long for a riding-horse, and the whole fore-hand what is called "peacocky," a very expressive term; but the neck must be able to bend, either naturally or by artificial means. The mane should be plentiful, and fall well.

The shoulders may be anything but riding shoulders, if they are so shaped as to be consistent with imposing action, which may be so rough that it would be unbearable in a riding-horse. The back may be hollow—indeed, a hollow back, if the loins and quarters are strong enough to stop a heavy carriage, is considered rather a point of beauty in harness—but every pair of horses intended for heavy carriages, which must be stopped quickly and turned sharply, must have strong loins, thighs, and hocks. It is of importance that a state carriage-horse should have a full, not too long, tail, and carry it well. As for pace, eight miles an hour, looking like twelve, is quite sufficient for ornamental purposes.

The best colours for full-sized carriage pairs are bay with black legs, brown with tan muzzle (a very fashionable colour), and dark chestnut. Greys were worth £10 each more than any other colour during the time that the Prince Regent led the fashion. Grey stallions of a high class were maintained in the royal stud. It is at present difficult to get greys sufficiently well-bred. The Duke of Sutherland has discarded iron-greys in favour of browns. The late Duke of Beaufort used to horse his barouche in the country with four piebalds *à la Daumont*, but that was quite an exception. True blacks are rarely met with in great stables, for the same reason perhaps as greys—there are very few black thoroughbred sires. The Earl of Harrington, who married the great actress Miss Foote, was the last nobleman who drove the old black long-tailed coach-horses in his unique equipages—his chariot, or extinct *vis-à-vis*. Amongst Arabs black is the rarest colour, while grey is the most common. Lord Aveland, true to Lincolnshire fen traditions, drives roans, a very difficult colour to match in large horses.

This class of harness-horse, in addition to the varying gradations of excellence which exist between the simple utility which satisfies those who never look at their horses and only consider them as machines, and the perfection required either by the taste and ambition or the social position of others, may be divided into coach-horses proper and barouche-horses.

Barouche-horses are expected to show more blood and quality, to be better travellers, and would be selected for a suburban visit rather than grand elephantine-stepping coach-horses; indeed, the best barouche-horses are very like the best hunters.

The system of jobbing large carriage-horses, which has been in existence for more than half a century, has within the last twenty years assumed extraordinary proportions.

In the first place, as already explained, the same class of horse is not required in town as in the country; in the next, space has become so valuable in the metropolis that very few establishments can obtain the stabling necessary for horsing the carriages required daily in season for morning concerts, garden parties, shopping, dinner parties, operas, and a succession of balls and receptions. Less than four horses, probably six, would not do the season's work of a family with daughters which lives in the full swing of a London season. But besides the carriage-horses, there are three or four riding-horses, perhaps a pair of high-priced mail phaeton or park phaeton horses, which require room. A stable to accommodate half a dozen horses is pretty large. In town stalls for a dozen could only be provided at extravagant expense, not counting the outlay of the horses not required for daily use, but which must be provided to take the place of one lame or sick, if the head of the family decides to drive nothing but his own horses.

In this dilemma the job-master appears as the *deus ex machina*, and provides for a fixed sum per pair not only one or more pairs of horses, but undertakes to replace any one disabled, at any hour of the day or night. For £100 a year, or £20 a month in the season, a pair of first-class horses are provided; and for thirty-five shillings a week in addition they may be fed, foddered, and shod. The conveniences of the system have caused its adoption by many noble families who a few years ago would disdain the idea of hiring horses. Under the jobbing system, in the height of the season, one pair of stalls will hold in turn all the horses that can be used in one carriage.

In the "Post-Office Directory" for 1873, the names of one hundred and forty persons calling themselves job-masters appear. Some of them, no doubt, are in a very small way of business, but there are two who each job five hundred pairs of horses, besides single brougham and victoria horses; there are others who job over one hundred each. The stables of these are open to supply the sudden demands of their customers all night during the season.

Formerly the great job-masters never dreamed of purchasing any horse under 15 hands 3 inches, the preference being for at least 16 hands; but now the popularity of light single broughams and victorias, many of them hired from the coach-builders for the season, compels them to purchase suitable animals, even as small as 14 hands 3 inches, of the right style and action.

About the year 1860 the great job-masters of London thought that they had discovered a mine of wealth in purchasing the largest class of carriage-horses in Holstein, Mecklenburg, Hanover, and North Germany generally; all countries whose war-horses were famous in the sixteenth and seventeenth centuries. These carriage-horses were for the most part the produce of crosses between English sires and German mares. They had imposing fore-hands and high action, and they were twenty-five per cent. cheaper than English geldings of the same size. One of the greatest job-masters, in the course of a tour made for the purpose, purchased several hundred pairs. After a trial extending over more than ten years, the result is pro-

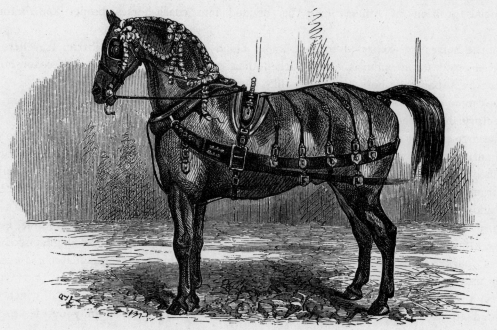

CLEVELAND BAY STATE CARRIAGE-HORSE.

nounced not satisfactory. The majority of these German horses showed the defects that Gervase Markham pointed out two hundred and fifty years ago—they were soft. They flourished about very superbly from shop to shop, from street to street, or up and down the drive in Hyde Park; but if they were wanted to go to Richmond, for instance, the chances were that they could scarcely crawl back again; "and if they fell sick of influenza, or anything of that kind, they were sure to waste to nothing or die." A dealer and job-master who had had a great many of them through his hands, attributed their softness to the want of corn when between three and four years old, and added, "Most of them, like hearse-horses, have neither arms nor thighs;" that is to say, are conspicuously deficient in the most important muscles of the motive limbs. Since 1877 a new supply has been opened to job-masters in the horses imported from the United States and Canada.

The evidence before the Earl of Rosebery's select committee of the House of Lords on the supply of horses, issued in August, 1873, while these pages were passing through the press, contains a mass of valuable information, from which the following passages, bearing especially on this subject, have been condensed.

COLONEL G. A. MAUDE, C.B., CROWN EQUERRY.

In answer to a question from H.R.H. the Prince of Wales, Colonel Maude said, " Formerly all the (royal) work was done by coaches and chariots, now there are broughams and clarences ; for these we buy smaller horses. We have nothing under 16 hands in the town carriages. The smaller horses are much more durable ; in fact, if it were not for the look of the thing, they would draw the big coaches much better than the bigger Clevelands. The smaller horses are more fashionable, more are bred, and therefore they are more easily obtained ; they are much less likely to become roarers than larger horses. We hardly ever had an instance of a harness-horse not over 15 hands 3 inches becoming a roarer, whereas almost all our big bay horses end by being so. We never buy foreign horses for the Queen's stables if we know it, but we do sometimes. They are as harness-horses very inferior. I have seen some as nice Prussian saddle-horses as any bred in this kingdom, but the Mecklenburg harness-horse which is sometimes imported is a very bad animal. . . . Since Hanover has been inde-pendent of England we breed our cream-colours in England. We have imported no stallions, and breed in-and-in ; but, extraordinary to say, they are getting larger. We keep four breeding-mares ; the produce never has a bit of white. We never sell any."

William Shaw, another witness before the same committee, who has been for "thirty-six years an entire horse leader in certain districts of Yorkshire," and for the last seventeen years in the East Riding, said, "There has been a great change since I began. It was the old-fashioned coach-horses that were in vogue at that day—the old-fashioned Clevelands. At the end of five years, beginning from 1836, my custom fell off by more than two-thirds ; there was a change in the trade, a new fashion in horses came up. The London gentlemen then wanted a first-class fashionable horse, that stepped up higher. Formerly a big coach-horse, now a blood-horse, is wanted, with high-stepping action. Seventeen years ago I began to lead a roadster, and continued for eleven years, then I took a blood-horse. A blood-horse is all the go to-day, and I would have nothing else."

MR. JOSHUA EAST.

" We have over a thousand carriage-horses (all geldings) at work on jobs. We are obliged to purchase about three hundred horses a year to keep our stock up. We sell about that number by auction at St. Martin's Lane, without reserve. We do not lose above two and a half per cent. by deaths. . . . Seeing that the best Yorkshire mares had gone to Germany, on the persuasion of my German friends, I went after them. They were nice handy horses to buy ; they were broken, which ours were not. The German horse was more ornamental than ours, and £10 to £15 cheaper. He had good action, and was capital to sell, but he was like Peter Pindar's Jew's razors—he was worth nothing to use. If you got him to Brentford you would never get him farther. . . . They were the worst brutes I ever saw, and I should soon have lost all my customers if I had stuck to them, so I got rid of them all. . . . At this moment we have three hundred horses lying by not earning a shilling, that we may have them ready when we want them in next May or June. Our horses vary in size, from 15 hands 2 inches to 16 hands 2 inches. We like them bred from a thorough-bred horse and a half-bred mare."

GERVASE MARKHAM.

While writing on harness-horses it will not be out of place to give a quotation from Gervase Markham, a very accomplished gentleman and experienced horseman, who flourished in the reign of James I., and who was, considering the limited advantages which the age afforded, one of the most acute and shrewd writers on the subject. The principles he laid down in that remote period are just as applicable now as then. We have better roads and streets, lighter carriages, more highly-bred horses; but his advice is still sound.

"The use of coaches hath not beene of any long continuance in this kingdome, especially in that general fashion they are now used; for if formerly they were in the hands and for the ease of particular great persons, yet now they are grown as common as hackneyes, and are in the hands of as many as either esteem reputation or are numbered in the catalogue of rich persons. . . . Neither is it my profession to meddle with the shapes of hunters, nor will I speak of the several customs or fashions of Italy and France, because, as far as I can judge, whatsoever we practice in this art of coach governing is but an imitation of the shapes and chaunges of those kingdomes. Therefore, for my own part, I mean only to handle some few notes, touching the charge of coach-horses, their keeping and appareling.

"First, then, to speak of the charge of coach-horses. Some are of opinion that your Flemish horse is the best for that purpose, because he is of strong limbes, hath a full breast, a good chyne, and is naturally trained up more to draught than burthen; others doe preferre before these horses Flemish mares (and I am of that opinion also), both because of their more temperate and coole spirits, their quiet socialleness in company, and their bringing up, which only is the wagon, by which means, travelling with more patience, they are ever of more strength and endurance. Yet both these horses and mares have their faults ever coupled to their virtues; as first their paces are ever short trots which contain much labour in little ground, and so bring on fastness of spirit in little journeys, whereas a coach-horse should stretch forth his feet, and the smoother and longer he strides the more may he be ridden. and the sooner comes to his journey's end without tyring. Next, their limbs from the knees and camtrells downward are so rough and hayrie, and the horses themselves so subject to sault and fretting humours in those parts that neither can the coachman keep them from the paines, scratches, mallendars, sollandars, and such like diseases, nor the farrier ofttimes with his best skill cure them when they are diseased. Lastly, they are for the most part of resty* and hot spirits, so that although they shall be excellent and forward in the draught, yet in our English nation, amongst our deepe clays and myrie trailes, they are not able to continue, but grow fainte and weary of their labour; and it is ever a rule amongst them, that after they have been once tired there is no means to restore them to their metall or spirits.

"Now to tell you mine opinion which is the best coach-horse either for streetes of cities or journeying upon the high waies, I hold not any horse comparable, either for strength courage, or labour, with the large-shaped English gelding, for he is as milde and sociable as the Flemish mare, more able to endure travell, better shaped, and long continued in service. Next to him is the Flemish mare, and the last is the Flemish horse.

"The Pollander (Polish) is exceedingly good, but he is somewhat too little and too fierce. a nature; but for tiring, that he will seldom or never do with any indifferent order.

"When you have determined touching the breed or race of your coach-horses, you shall

* Our country people still talk of a horse rusting—*i.e.*, refusing—"He rusts at the lane corner."

then look to their shapes and colours. Observe that your coach-horses be all of one colour, without diversitie, and that their marks be also alike; thus, for example, if one have white starre-bald face, white foot, or be of pide (pied) colour, that then the other have like also.

"For their shapes you shall chose a lean-proportioned head, a strong firm neck, a full, broad, and round breast, a limbe flat, short-jointed, lean and well hayred, a good bending ribbe, a strong backe, and a round buttocke. Generally they should be of broad strong making and of the tallest stature; for such are most serviceable for the draught, and best able to endure the toyle of deepe travell.

"Now for the properties. They must be as nearly alyed in nature and disposition as in colour, shape, and height; for if one be free and the other dull, then the free horse taking all the labour must necessarily over-toyle himself, and soon destroy both his life and courage; so they must be of like spirit and metall. Also you must have special regard that their paces be alike, and that the one neither trot faster than the other nor take longer strides than the other, for if their feet do not rise from the ground together, there can be no equality in their draught, but one must over-toyle the other; whereas they ought to be of such equall strength, pace, and spirits, that, as if they were one body, their labour should be divided equally amongst them.

"They ought also, as neare as you can, to be of a loving, tractable, and mild disposition.

"They should also have good and tender mouths, and ought to have their heads well settled upon the bit before they come into the coach, being learnt to turn readily upon either hand without discontentment or rebellion, to stoppe close and firm, and to retyre back freely with good spirit and courage—which are lessons fully sufficient to make a good coach-horse.

"I advise all that are desirous to better their judgment in such knowledge, to repair to the stables of great princes, where commonly are the bell-men of this art, and there behold how everything in his true proportion is ordered, and thence draw unto himself rules for his own instruction.

"This slight precept I will bestow upon him—that he have a constant sweete hand upon his horse's mouth, by no means losing the feeling thereof, but observing that the horse does rest upon his bit and carry his head and rein in a good and comely fashion; for to goe with his head loose, or to have no feeling of the bit, is both uncomely to the eye and takes from the horse all delight in his labour."

The English coach-horse's tail has been subjected to curious changes of fashion since the time of Gervase Markham. He then wore a long tail flowing down to the ground, and cut square, like King Charles's charger at Charing Cross. It was adorned with ribbons on gala days, and strapped up in a leather case in winter weather; thus a certain harmony was preserved between the wig of the master and the tails of his horses. By the time of George II. a short wig and a pig-tail had taken the place of the flowing curls in which the Cavaliers of Charles I. and the rakes of Charles II.'s court delighted. The brilliant idea occurred to Lord Cadogan, a cavalry officer of that period, of reducing the tails of his dragoon horses to a short dock—whether this was with the view of saving his soldiers the trouble of cleaning those long tails, and avoiding the nuisance of the splashes uniforms and accoutrements must have received from such hair streamers, or whether the debased taste of the age made him really think the appearance of his regiment improved by bobtails, history does not relate—the next step was to turn bobtails into plug-tails, by cutting all the hair for the last two or three inches of the dock. Having thus succeeded in disfiguring the hind-quarters of dragoon horses to the utmost, some monster devised the additional barbarity of cropping their ears. The operation became fashionable, like many hideous and barbarous fashions which are supposed to improve and adorn the heads of women in 1873.

It will be observed that the fine coach-horse engraved after Marshall on this page is both cropped and docked. The practice of cropping the ears has now entirely disappeared, although it was not uncommon to find even hunters thus tortured and disfigured as late as 1840; while to a much later date the stupid fashion of depriving cart-horses of their fly-flappers was usual in several counties. Mr. Villebois' coach-horse is a specimen of a fine blood animal spoiled by the fashion of the day. By intermediate stages the tails of coach-horses were lengthened until the whole dock was preserved, and the hair squared off to a racing tail. In 1873 the tails are cut according to the character of the horse and the style of the carriage. Since that date the vile fashion of short docks has again come into fashion and in imitation of polo ponies, even well-bred full-sized horses are turned into caricatures by hogging the flowing mane, one of the most picturesque points of a blood horse.

A COACH-HORSE, A.D. 1780, DOCKED AND CROPPED.

CHAPTER XII.

HORSEMANSHIP, OR THE ART OF "EQUITATION."

Horsemanship came with Horses from the East—Affected still by Military Traditions—Horse-mounting on Left Side—Oriental Horsemanship Wonderful—Do not understand Flying Leaps—Historical Modifications of English Horsemanship—The High School of Horsemanship—Modified by the Hunting-field in the Time of James I.—English Military Horsemanship Improved since 1850—The Fashionable Style of 1835—Count D'Orsay—The Earl of Chesterfield—Equestrian Portraits of—Steeplechase Riders the Reformers of English Horsemanship—Alken's and Herring's Horsemen compared—Horsemanship may be Self-taught, with Aptitude and Nerve—Good Models for Imitation Essential—England has the Best and the Worst Equestrians—Fine Horsemanship, that is, Military Horsemanship, out of England—Indian Irregulars—Circassian Cossacks—To Learn to Ride, Clear your Mind of Conceit—Horsemanship for Adults—Prescribed by Physicians—Advice Easy to Give, Difficult to Follow—Sailors Learn Easily, and all Gymnasts—Difficulties of Ordinary Riding Schools—With Courage, Industry, and Perseverance, a full-grown Man may learn to Ride—Preliminary Preparation, that is, "Condition," Important—A Proper Horse—A Proper Saddle and Bridle—Proper School—Proper Teacher—The Horse may have Faults Mentioned—Must be Placid in Disposition, Safe and Pleasant in Action—Free, but not Violent or Skittish—Not too Light a Mouth—Head and Neck like Illustration—Up to the Weight of the Rider—An Old Screw may be Valuable—Good Looks Desirable, not Essential—Exercise Essential—Idleness the Root of all Evil—Anecdote of a Brighton Hack—The Bridle Double—Snaffle Reins to Hold—Curb for Emergencies—Holding on by the Bridle Legitimate for Old Men and Raw Horsemen—The Ordinary Park Saddle Unsuitable—Illustration of Gervase Markham's Saddle—Plain Hunting Saddle—Colonial Saddle—The Somerset Saddle—How to Mount—From a Horse Block—Charles Simmonds' Contrivance—Illustration—Length of Stirrups—Management of Reins—First Acquire Seat—Constant Practice and Short Lessons Essential—Riding Dress Important—Thick Trousers, well-made, strapped-down—Thin-soled Wellington Boots—Equitation for Children, a Word to Mothers—Pannier Ponies—Danger of Pannier Riding—Illustration of Proper Bridle—Leading-Stick—Proper Rein—Infant's Pony Saddle, Illustration—The Best Pony for a Boy—the Best Form of Pad—Stirrups—The *Pro* and *Con*—First Lessons—No Bridle—The Circus System Practised with Children—The Proper Management of the Reins—Colonel Greenwood's Maxims—The Walk—The Canter—Children Imitative Animals—Summary of Essentials for Child Equestrians—Irish Anecdote—Lavengro's First Ride.

THERE is no purely English term which expresses the art of riding on horseback by both sexes like the French "*Equitation.*" Horsemanship applied to the instruction of women sounds something like a "bull;" and curiously enough in England, where horsewomen are more numerous and more skilful than in any other country in Europe, there is no such convenient word as *Amazone* for describing a lady who rides—a word so descriptive and compact, that it may certainly be used in the pages devoted to an explanation of the equestrian art without subjecting the writer to the charge of affectation. It is also curious that the French Academy dictionary condemns as obsolete the verb *chevaucher*, which our statesman William Pitt used in a letter to Lady Hester Stanhope, to express riding on horseback, while the lady rode in a post-chaise.

Horsemanship came with the horses from the East; the first horsemen were soldiers. The cavalry of Alexander the Great were of little account until he invaded and conquered Persia, and embodied Persian horses and horsemen into his army.

The art of horsemanship is to this day affected by military traditions. We are all taught to mount and dismount exclusively on the left or "near side" of the horse, because the military horsemen, whether Oriental or European, requires to mount and dismount with his sword or spear in his hand ready for attack or defence. Before the introduction of firearms cavalry engagements were, soon after they commenced, resolved into a series of single combats; and it was essential that the legs of the soldier's horse should move at his will, like the legs of a boxer or a swordsman; speed was a secondary consideration, as compared with docility and agility in turning on the pivot of the hind-legs.

Orientals perform feats of horsemanship of a most astonishing character to those who are only acquainted with the English style, and excite the admiration of such judges as Mr. Palgrave and the cavalry officer quoted in Chapter I.; at the same time the art of riding across country and taking leaps at a gallop was, and still is, unknown to many nations of warlike horsemen, the Circassians, for instance.

MARQUIS OF LONDONDERRY (HAUTE ECOLE, 1835).

In England the art of horsemanship has passed through successive modifications, influenced by the habits of the time. The knights, clothed in heavy armour, and packed into saddles which supported them before and behind, were compelled to ride entirely by balance, with stirrups stretched to the full length of their straight legs, as may be seen in mediæval statues of St. George; grip they could have none; once toppled on either side, the weight of their armour brought them to the ground—generally helpless.

On the experience of the knights of armour the "High School of Horsemanship" was founded, and carried to fantastic perfection in England and on the Continent during the period when the armour had been reduced to the weight of a breast-plate and back-plate. What this high school seat was like, and how far removed from the best modern style, may be seen at a glance in the illustration taken from the Duke of Newcastle's great book. The long-limbed cavalier seated on his fork may make an imposing appearance, but can only go through his performances on a perfectly-trained, coarsely-bred charger. But alongside the Duke of Newcastle's school of horsemanship there grew up—amongst the yeomanry and gentry of England, engaged in hunting hare and buck—another and more natural style, to which

Gervase Markham obscurely alludes, after giving a picture of "a perfect saddle," in which no one could safely ride across an enclosed country. The traditions of the high school system still flourish on the Continent; and they have only recently, speaking historically, become extinct in England, under the influence of the modern hunting-field and steeplechase course.

Our soldiers since 1850 have been taught to ride in a manner which enables them "to do anything and go anywhere" that a horseman should; but before the Crimean War there were regiments in which extravagantly long stirrups and "*the balance seat,*" *without clinging,* were the rule. To go still further back, soon after the Peace of 1815 a Prussian riding-master was employed, under the patronage of the Prince Regent, to drill our cavalry to ride with nearly as straight a leg as the Duke of Newcastle in 1658, on their forks, instead of on their seats. My informant, the late R. B. Davis, the animal painter, frequently witnessed this barbarous performance in the fields where Belgrave Square now stands; it was not discontinued until a large per-centage of the troopers had been disabled by ruptures.

Under Frederick the Great the Prussian cavalry, which gained his most important victories, rode well on a natural seat, if an opinion may be formed from a curious equestrian portrait of old Fritz himself, upon a black Holstein charger.

As late as 1835 it was the fashion for the swells or dandies of the period—Count d'Orsay, the Earl of Chesterfield, and their imitators—to tittup along the streets and in the Park with their toes just touching the stirrups, which hung three inches lower than in the hunting-field. But about the same time arose a school of professional steeplechase riders, founded on the soundest principles of "the school, the field, and the turf," which had followers and pupils amongst the highest aristocracy; and this school eventually extinguished the affectations of the fribble school and the pretensions of the high school, and established a style at once practical, manly, and elegant, which has since been emulated by all the best horsemen on the Continent.*

At the beginning of this century, as may be seen from hunting pictures (in which the admirable pencil drawings of Alken are disfigured in coarse coloured lithographs), the style of horsemanship was decidedly bad and vulgar—a sort of imitation of the jockeys of the turf, who have a sound reason for bending forward over their horses' withers in a gallop of a few minutes. Compare these prints of Alken's or Sir John Dean Paul's with the pictures of the elder Herring —as for example, that of "Steeplechase Cracks," and take for an example of the proper form of a born horseman the portrait of Jem Mason, on Lottery (whose only fault was to sit too far back on the saddle), and the difference between the Georgian and the modern style of horsemanship is seen at a glance more clearly than could be explained in a dozen pages. This style, formed by the professional steeplechasers, and soon adopted in the fashionable hunting shires, was in every respect the very reverse of the fribble style of the Park and of the single-handed, snaffle-bridle, pig-tailed squires of the previous century, who hated everything foreign, and with whom everything foreign was French; and this natural style in which the maxim "*ars celare artem,*" so congenial to English tastes, was strictly followed, soon made its way to the road and the Park from the steeplechase course and the hunting-field.

The best instruction in equestrian arts is that obtained by word of mouth from a competent instructor, with living examples to illustrate each precept; but it is not in the power of every one to obtain the services of a really competent riding-master, either on the road or in

* Particularly by the subjects—Hungarian and German—of the Emperor of Austria, and by the steeplechase sportsmen of the French school.

a riding-school; and written rules, illustrated with engravings, can teach any one willing to learn at least how to avoid many bad habits and awkward tricks.

Riding on horseback is an art which those who have natural aptitude of form and nerve may teach themselves by practice and imitating the best models; but it is also an art that, by judicious instruction, especially if the pupil is taught young, may be acquired by those whose shape and temperament would never permit them to shine as jockeys or horsebreakers. Any one with the courage of a bull-dog and the indifference to bruises of a lizard may ride badly and boldly; but very often the courage of ignorance disappears with the first serious accident.

To give a youth or girl the best chance, not to say of excellence, but of avoiding awkward habits hard to cure, the early lessons of horse-life should be given with good models for imitation.

There are certainly more accomplished horsemen and horsewomen at the present time than at any other period of the history of England; and there are also more bad ones, especially in Rotten Row, because it is the fashion for those who aspire to fashionable society to exhibit themselves in that delightful lane of gossip and display, "with or without twelve lessons" from a corporal of dragoons, or after learning everything that ought to be avoided from some most respectable family coachman.

It should clearly be understood that there is very fine horsemanship (that is, military horsemanship), which is totally unlike our style, out of England—horsemanship suited to the country and the habits of the horsemen, those, for instance, of India, who sit cross-legged and not on chairs. In their way, the corps of irregular cavalry of India—native gentlemen riding their own horses, in their own Oriental style, commanded by British officers—are second to none; not the least famous of these was commanded by Colonel (now General) Sir Dighton Probyn, K.C.S.I., Equerry to His Royal Highness the Prince of Wales. When General Sir Arthur Conynghame, K.C.B., who has seen service in all the wars of this generation, visited the Caucasus, the feats of the Lesghians astonished him, familiar as he was with all that our Indian horsemen can do with sword, lance, and firelock. Now these horsemen ride buried in a stuffed leathern pillow, with long stirrups, a straight knee, and a snaffle bridle.

Dr. Johnson, one of the honestest of men, once said to a young friend, "Above all, clear your mind of cant." So it may be said to the pupil in horsemanship, "Clear your mind of conceit;" dismiss the idea that you or your countrymen excel every one. Practice on sound principles makes perfect, but practice on false principles only confirms mischievous habits.

HORSEMANSHIP FOR ADULTS.

"Horse exercise" is a common prescription of a fashionable physician addressed to a patient whose general derangement of stomach, liver, and skin, not to mention brain, has been brought about either by indolence and excesses of the table, or by sedentary and mental exhaustive pursuits—intellectual or financial.* Perhaps the patient has never been on a horse in his life, in which case it sounds something like advising a man who cannot swim to plunge into deep water; or perhaps he has ridden in the days of his youth, distant a quarter of a century, when he also climbed trees, and danced reels or even hornpipes. At any rate, to follow the prescription seems at first sight almost as difficult as for a banker's clerk, married, with a family, and a nervous disorder, "to live well, and drink good sound claret."

* John Locke, the great philosopher, wrote—"The properest recreation of studious sedentary persons, whose labour is thought, is bodily exercise," and he practised what he preached, for he kept two riding-horses.

According to rule, if you want to learn German you engage a German tutor; if you want to learn to dance, you subscribe to Mr. Turveydrop's dancing academy; but if you want to learn to ride, you generally find a Procrustean system in force which is the same whether you are a boy, or a full-grown man, or recruit who has enlisted in a cavalry regiment to escape a wife or spite a sweetheart.

Any one clever at other athletic sports may be thirty years old, and yet easily acquire the essential parts of horsemanship; but it is not to men of well-exercised muscles, in hard condition,

COUNT D'ORSAY (AFTER AN OIL SKETCH BY SIR FRANCIS GRANT, IN SIR RICHARD WALLACE'S COLLECTION, ABOUT 1830.)

that these lines are addressed. They are meant for the student who has lived in his books until type melts before his eyes in one confusing haze; for members of the learned profession who have worked so hard in climbing to the top of the tree that they feel no longer able either to balance themselves there or hold on by the branches; to money-making geniuses, who have been so successful that they are no longer able to enjoy anything that money can buy.

As a matter of course, the simplest plan for carrying out Dr. M.D.'s advice, "horse exercise," is to subscribe to a riding-school. Advertisements appear daily in the London papers offering to teach riding in twelve lessons for two guineas. Those who accept the invitation have no reason to complain even if they do not feel themselves competent to undertake a ride on a strange horse in the quietest of by-lanes at the end of a fortnight. Three shillings and sixpence for an hour's exercise on a trained horse in a school is cheap enough at the present rate of the expenses of those establishments; but, as a rule, their arrangements are not made to suit the class of nervous and somewhat inactive persons for whose benefit this chapter has been specially composed.

The full-grown pupil is shown how to mount in the approved military manner, and, when mounted on a slippery saddle, is instructed how to sit, how to hold a pair of double reins in one hand and a whip in the other, how to guide his horse, how to hollow his back, how to keep his heels down, his elbows and his arms close to his sides, all at once. The result is a feeling of idiotic confusion. The grown man becomes again a little schoolboy in the hands of a terrible pedagogue.

But if the patient has courage, industry, and perseverance, and is prepared to begin with the alphabet of the art, there is no reason that he should despair of becoming a very fair horseman, able, on a well-broken horse, to enjoy rides in green lanes with friends, to take constitutionals early in the morning in the Park, and even to be present at the meets of hounds in company with that large constituency, to be found at all meets of hounds near great towns who gallop boldly, but never on any provocation take a leap.

The first and most important point before the full-aged man takes his first riding-lesson is to be in proper condition, or, in a sporting and expressive phrase, "fit." As to who is full-aged, that has very little to do with years after the teens are past. Some men feel younger at forty than others do at twenty-five. The next point is a proper horse, the third a proper saddle and bridle, the fourth a proper place to ride in, and the fifth a safe companion or teacher. The case of a fat flabby man requires care and consideration. Such men are dangerous subjects for a fall, and, it is useless to disguise it, those who ride must sooner or later expect a fall, although every possible pains should be taken to avoid a catastrophe which, laughable in a boy, may be serious in a heavy man.

Boys learn to ride anywhere, on any sort of animal; and tumble off without any serious accident until they learn to stick on, but bystanders who are not brutes shudder when they see a heavy, over-bold, middle-aged student of equitation come to the ground on the hard high road, with a frightened face and fearful flop.

To get into moderate condition before commencing riding-lessons, the usual treatment must be adopted. Walking will generally be out of the question, because the middle-aged convalescent who can take constitutional walks need not ride—unless it be on a bicycle. If the patient is stout, and troubled with the corporate honours that made Mr. Banting famous, a diet of lean meat and poultry, with sound claret, may be advisable; to be followed or accompanied by a mild course of drill in the extension motions, with the view of bringing the muscles of the limbs generally into play. The Turkish bath, and the packing-sheet process of the hydropathic establishments, are both very effective in improving the respiratory powers of the sedentary, and preparing them for horse exercise; for when riding is taken up not merely as an amusement, but as part of a course of physical and mental treatment for restoring an exhausted body and a wearied mind, unnecessary pain and fatigue are to be as much as possible avoided. A little preparatory training, carefully conducted, will do much towards rendering the first riding-lessons easy. Muscular, active people, who can run and jump, may exercise their muscles, and tire themselves by long hours of unaccustomed exercise, without fear of any feverish action. A mild course of gymnastics, coupled with the Turkish bath, is the best kind of preliminary exercise.

The horse on which a grown man should commence his lessons may have faults and defects which would reduce his money value in the open market to a very low figure, but he must have certain qualifications of form and temperament. He may be nine or ten years old, or more, if he has not, from over-work, lost that elasticity of motion which makes horse exercise wholesome and pleasant. He may be a whistler, or, in horsey phrase, "make a noise," whenever pushed beyond a very moderate pace. If he can walk well, evenly, and willingly, four miles an hour, and trot or canter six miles an hour safely and pleasantly, that is quite fast enough to begin with. There are very noble and distinguished statesmen who have never ridden faster in their lives.

He may be such a delicate feeder, badly ribbed up, or, to speak in grooms' vernacular, so "herring-gutted" and "washy," that two hours' exercise are as much as he can stand. He may be severely fired for spavin, and rather stiff in his hind-legs on leaving the stable, although not positively lame. He may be plain in his quarters, with a rat tail; indeed, he may be an ugly brute all over, with a great coffin head, so long as he has not the evil eye of a vicious horse. Two eyes are by no means essential, so long as the remaining organ is thoroughly sound.

But he must be of a placid and sensible temperament. He must have good fore-legs and feet; and neither stumble, drop, nor shy. He must be a free mover, ready to walk on at a word, not requiring whip or spur, and yet not inclined, when regularly exercised, to increase a walk to a trot and a trot to a wild gallop. He must have a good but not too light a mouth—a mouth that will bear the hauling of a heavy hand on a smooth snaffle. His head and neck should be properly set on, so as to require neither martingale nor manipulation to bring both to the right angle; in sporting phrase, he must bridle well. His sloping shoulders and well-arched neck must give the timid rider the feeling of "plenty before him." There are first-class hunters who never seem to raise their heads except when they go at a fence, and valuable cobs with necks nearly as straight as a donkey's, but the invalid's horse must bear himself well, and carry head and neck like the coloured portrait of the Earl of Pembroke's chestnut, ridden by Mrs. Reynolds. A star-gazing or ewe-necked brute is as objectionable as the horse who carries his head in the form of a costermonger's "moke." As a matter of course, he must have a back and withers formed to carry a saddle in its proper place without a crupper, even if the girths become rather slack; and he should have, whatever be his deficiencies of tail, enough mane to hold on by on the occasion of any crisis. With these qualifications, he should be well up to the lumpy weight of a raw rider.

Thus it will be seen that for a special purpose what all dealers and most horsemen would call "an old screw" may be a very valuable animal.

As a matter of course, a suitable animal is much to be preferred if he can be described like the charger of a volunteer lieut.-colonel—"He is a screw and a roarer, but he can walk five miles an hour, trot seven, stands fire like a rock, and looks like a gentleman!" There are many people who could not be happy riding a really ugly horse, however excellent in temper and paces; but the invalid adult commencing horse exercise must make utility and fitness the first; beauty of form, the neat head, the flowing mane, the good colour, the second consideration.

It must also be remembered that horses have a wonderful instinctive knowledge of their rider's qualifications, and that an animal that would be perfectly quiet with a real horseman will very soon begin to play tricks with a nervous or awkward rider.

In nine cases out of ten the adult invalid would do best by purchasing a school-horse that he has found to suit him, at about double its market value ; but he must take care that he is not saddled with an animal so inferior in feet and legs that it cannot move anywhere except on a bed of soft tan and sawdust.

There is at least one firm which sells horses on commission, and declares the peculiar infirmities and defects, if any, of each occupant of their stalls in the most candid manner. The head of the firm will say, "This cob has been carrying Mr. Bullionist for five years. He makes a little noise, and he is as slow as a top ; but he is a capital walker, and as quiet as a sheep." Such a recommendation may be depended on. At any rate, the adult invalid should have nothing to do with any animal recommended by a polite recently-introduced stranger at a dinner party, unless he can get as satisfactory a character with the nag for discreet behaviour as he would require from a butler who was to have charge of a closet full of plate ; he will act most wisely in selecting a respectable dealer, and trusting to his judgment.

After having purchased a safe and pleasant equine conveyance, it requires care to keep it in proper condition for a novice who is at first not able to "sit down" on an over-frisky horse and "ride" him into sobriety. If the owner does not like the hack to be ridden by a groom, let it be lunged at a slow pace for an hour before being dressed.

The best-tempered horse in the world may be spoiled, rendered dangerous, even vicious, if not regularly exercised. "Idleness," with horses as with men, is "the root of all evil." A great personage in finance, who had risen from the ranks, and knew a great deal more of the arts by which money is made than of the art of horsemanship, was so much pleased with a hack that he had hired and ridden every "lawful" day during a month at Brighton, that he purchased it and sent it to join company with a very miscellaneous stud at his country house. There "Brighton," while his master stayed in town, grew fat on regular feeds of corn and the irregular exercise of a badly-managed establishment.

At length, one day the master arrived for a holiday, and ordered Brighton to be saddled for a morning ride over the farm. As soon as he attempted to put his foot in the stirrup the seaside model hack, with a cow-kick forward, sent his master head over heels. The groom, as peremptorily ordered, not without difficulty reached the saddle, to be immediately kicked over the brute's head. Brighton, who had cost a pretty stiff price considering his appearance, was sent to the next market town, and sold for a song to a little tradesman. Within a few weeks he was to be seen sometimes carrying a boy with a letter-bag, sometimes drawing a baker's cart at a fair pace, quiet as a sheep.

BRIDLE AND SADDLE.

The ordinary double bridle with well-fitted standing martingale is the best for a beginner. The reins of the snaffle should reach no further than the cantle of the saddle when the horse's neck is fully extended, and the reins of the curb, which are only to be used on an emergency, should be short enough to hang on the horse's neck. This is best done by an arrangement of two buckles, like those on a bearing-rein. The rein of the snaffle is the one on which the rider will rely to guide his steed and to steady his seat. A pupil whose great object is constitutional exercise has quite enough to do in keeping his seat and directing his horse, without attempting to solve the mystery of managing the reins of a double bridle. This snaffle rein should be broad, soft, and the bit smooth and thick.

Three or four tabs sewn on the snaffle rein at such distances as will bring the hands into the right place, that is, just in front of the pommel, while the elbows touch the hips, will be found useful. The use of this snaffle bridle is twofold, yet simple. First, to guide the hack. For this purpose it is held in both hands; when the rider wants to go to the left he is to pull the left rein, and when to the right the right rein, in open defiance of the rules of the school, where he is presumed to be always carrying a sword in his right hand. The other use of the snaffle rein, with a properly selected horse, is—hear it with horror, riding-school rulers—to hold on by; an expedient entirely opposed to the theory of good horsemanship, although

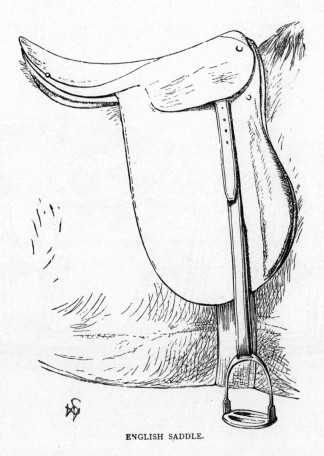

ENGLISH SADDLE.

largely practised by great men and even great horsemen in their declining years. For ten years before his death the great Duke of Wellington always held on by the bridle, and sometimes by the pommel as well. It is a practice not to be commended, but it is better than falling off; just as crutches are better than not walking at all. The boy who attempts to support himself by leaning on the bridle or catching hold of the pommel (except when a horse is rearing and plunging) deserves a sharp cut from the teacher's whip; but where the subject is a valetudinarian of forty years, he must be taught to stick on by holding on; without he feels safe he will derive no benefit from his first equestrian constitutionals. Indeed, it was the maxim of a most accomplished horseman that it was better to hold on by the pommel and the cantle too than to tumble off.

When a grown man, after the time when his bones are set and his muscles assume new duties with difficulty, takes to horsemanship, either as an heroic remedy for indisposition of body or mind, or as an accomplishment which his position in life compels him to acquire, his vanity should not prevent him from availing himself of the saddle which makes it most easy for a novice to retain his seat under difficulties. This, in its best English form, is the "Somerset saddle," invented for the use of one of that noble family of hereditary horsemen which claims the Duke of Beaufort as its chief, after losing a leg in the military service of his country, to enable him to continue to perform his duties as commanding officer of infantry. This saddle is much used by even practised horsemen at the time of life when the muscles are less strong and the nerves less steady than "once upon a time."

Indeed, for town use a Somerset saddle is essential, if an adult invalid is in his first years of horse exercise; in the country, where appearances are of less consequence, a plain saddle

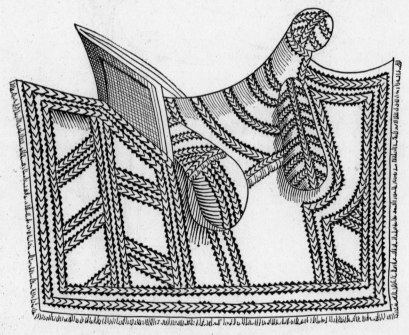

GERVASE MARKHAM'S PERFECT SADDLE.

may be converted into a patent safety by very cheap contrivances—such as a covered pad of brown Bedford cord.

To be thoroughly comfortable and safe, it is as necessary that the pupil should be measured for a Somerset saddle as for a pair of trousers or breeches. The seat must be large enough, the ridge under the thighs fit in well, and the pads in front of the knees be arranged to a nicety. A celebrated tragic actress, who had been in training to perform Joan of Arc on a very common saddle, described the change to a well-stuffed well-fitted Somerset as "all the difference between abject terror and perfect confidence."

The slipperiness of an ordinary saddle may be avoided in a Somerset either by expensive quilting or by using buckskin, which does not wear well in wet weather, or by the less common plan of employing the rough instead of the polished side of the leather. Nothing is more likely to cause a fall than a smooth saddle. All new saddles are slippery.

The stirrups should be large and heavy. The best stirrup-leathers for ordinary use are the old civilian (not military) pattern; but for the adult pupil there is a kind of stirrup-leather, invented by White,* which is more convenient to alter, although it only allows a variation of three holes, and wears out fast when used for hunting.

Having the horse, the bridle, and the saddle, next comes the operation of mounting. How this should be done, according to the best examples, will presently be explained with several illustrations, but the adult need not trouble himself with the niceties of the art, so long as he takes care to stand near enough to his nag's shoulder not to get kicked. In reality, one side is as good as the other for mounting, often better, although according to military school rule the left, or " near," is the right side, and the right or " off " the wrong side. To avoid all unnecessary exertion, let the pupil use a horse-block, if there is such a thing left in his county. They were universal when demi-pique saddles were the rule, and when the wives of farmers and doctors rode to market or visiting on pillions; but of late years they have

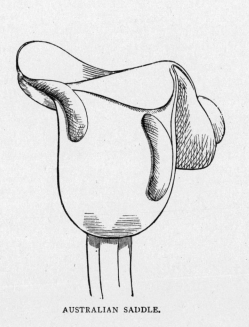

AUSTRALIAN SADDLE.

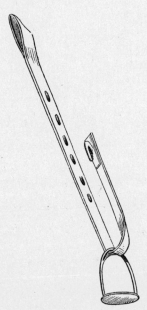

WHITE'S STIRRUP-LEATHER.

generally been pulled down, and used for building piggeries or dog-kennels. If the hack selected is not more than fourteen hands high, the pupil will be able to mount from the ground; but if some artificial aid is required, and if there is no place for the purpose—no bucket without a handle—the Charles Simmonds horse-step is the best; any carpenter's apprentice can make it in half an hour. It consists of a square box, to which is attached the handle of a hay-rake. It is light, and may be moved anywhere at a moment's notice.†

The best place for an adult to take his first ride in is a riding-school; and the best instructor is a riding master, if that master has the common sense to know that such a pupil is not to be treated like a raw cavalry recruit. The great point is that the adult pupil should be made as comfortable as possible under the circumstances. The idea of tormenting him in order that he may at once acquire the regulation seat of, say a sergeant of police in training previous to promotion to an inspectorship, must be dismissed.

The length of the stirrups can be settled by no fixed rule, they should be adjusted to that length that will give the pupil the most confidence, and that will vary according to the

---

* Sold by White and Coleman, Bishopsgate Street.   † In use at the stables of Mr. Charles Simmonds, Holywell, Oxford.

conformation of his extremities; and the size of the barrel of the horse, the round, plump, thick-thighed subject cannot fit himself to the saddle like an incipient Don Quixote. The point is to get into the middle of the saddle comfortably, sitting upright, but not stiffly upright, with the shoulders well thrown back, and this will be done by turning the toes out in a natural way, not turning them in like a trooper, nor yet too much out. If a man has acquired round shoulders and a stoop over the desk, it will generally be found rather too late in the day to drill him into a better form, and the best must be made of his scholastic attitude. If he does habitually poke his nose forward, he should be advised to avoid damage by keeping his head on one side or other of his horse's neck, and take care not to ride one of the many capital horses that always throw up their heads when they are fresh without a standing martingale. If there is no riding-school to be had conveniently, an empty barn will afford a very efficient substitute; and if there is no barn, then some empty fold-yard or other enclosure, where there is nothing to distract the attention of the pupil or his steed.

In the first instance, it is quite sufficient for the adult pupil to acquire the mystery or knack of "seat," without troubling himself about the niceties of holding the reins. They are, however, as already observed, to be held the one in the right and the other in the left hand; not only because this is the common-sense method of guiding a horse not intended for battle, but because with a rein in each hand the rider is most likely to sit *quite square*, a very important point.

Holding the reins too short is a very common fault, and fatal to a good seat. The arms from the shoulders to the elbows should hang loosely in a line with the hips, and the hands should scarcely extend beyond the pommel of the saddle; at the same time giving and taking with the play of a free walker's head, not held rigidly, but always returning to the right attitude. You can never go into the Park without seeing a great many boys and some men holding the reins short in one hand, and that hand half way between the pommel and the horse's ears, with an almost straight arm—a vile and dangerous habit; yet, curiously enough, some very famous artists have drawn horsemen with one arm at full length holding the reins, and leaping a gate. Having arrived thus far, if the adult pupil cannot subscribe to a riding-school, where everything is done in regular routine, let him put his pride in his pocket, and selecting some quiet lane or solitary common for early morning or late evening exercise, submit to be led at a walking pace

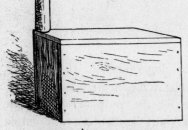

SIMMONDS' HORSE BLOCK.

either by an attendant on foot or on horseback, until he feels and finds that he can turn round and look behind him, stoop down and adjust his stirrups on either side, and perform other simple motions without losing his balance or his nerve. Practice makes perfect. The first practice should be in a straight line, then in a small circle, changing from right to left. It is far better for the first dozen lessons that the pupil's horse should be led, and that he should not be troubled with attempts to guide it.

The lessons should be short; with a person in delicate health, and therefore easily fatigued, half an hour's walking and softly trotting exercise is enough for the first dozen lessons—in no case should the lesson exceed an hour. This warning is important, because men of pluck, slightly excited by successful first attempts, are apt to do too much at one time. But if the lessons or exercises are short, they should, if possible, be continued from day to day; six half-hour rides on six successive days will do infinitely more towards moulding the muscles to the equestrian form than three lessons of two hours each with an interval of a day between.

When the services of a competent teacher cannot be had, the next best aid is that of a good model to imitate: not a soldier, although some of the very finest horsemen are found amongst cavalry officers, because a soldier has to follow rules which do not affect a civilian; not a huntsman, because to the best huntsman the horse is only a machine, and one hand is always occupied with the horn or the whip; but from watching a clever colt-breaker or accomplished professional steeplechase rider very useful lessons may be learned.

It may safely be assumed that any man of forty, not disqualified by physical defects or oppressed with excessive corpulence, may, with patience, perseverance, and pluck without rashness, learn how to ride and how to enjoy riding any well-broken horse, without looking ridiculous, after from fifty to sixty well-arranged rides, within the space of three months. But it is a sort of exercise that cannot be taken up and abandoned for a long interval with impunity. Even practised horsemen suffer severely after a certain time of life, if, after a long cessation from horse exercise, they attempt the feats of their youth; feverishness, indigestion, a fluttering heart, a disordered liver, remind them that for long days the man requires preparation as much as the horse.

A great deal of the comfort of riding depends on proper garments for the lower limbs. Theoretically, there is no riding-dress so comfortable as well-made breeches and boots, either of the modern cavalry or the plain "butcher" pattern. The next best substitute is a pair of leather overalls, fastened at the sides by buttons, not with springs. But those whose age and position would make boots for riding in a town objectionable must pay attention to their trousers. The material for riding-trousers should be thick woollen, and may be dark—there are some very nice partly-elastic materials in dark colours—they must be constructed by a real trouser-maker, who will make you sit down when he measures you, and they must be worn with straps, whether straps are in fashion or not. Wellington boots are the best with trousers; shoes are quite out of the question. Trousers without straps, slipping up the leg of a timid horseman, are an acute form of unnecessary misery, which was the fashion for many years up to 1877, when straps again appeared on the trousers of the more correct riders in Rotten Row.

EQUITATION FOR CHILDREN: ADDRESSED TO MOTHERS.

Irreparable injury has been done to young children of both sexes by the ignorance of parents nurses, and grooms in attendance on babies riding in panniers. Children should not be put into panniers (except in a reclining position, supported by pillows as in a bed) until they have attained a certain degree of strength. To a thoughtful person there is something frightful in seeing a couple of infants bobbing their heads with every step of a pony or donkey, like a porcelain mandarin, and so continued until the period fixed for the constitutional ride is completed; for these poor little things, if they have the sense, have not the strength to complain after half an hour's jolting. Children in panniers look very pretty, and if they are strong, and at least five years old, the air and exercise may prove useful; but weak children and infants of tender years are much more liable to suffer in brain and in spine than to derive any benefit from the shaking they are sure to endure.

In all cases the panniers should be of the modern shape, that is, constructed so that the children, well balanced, sit with their faces in the direction that the pony moves. The back of the pannier should be high, and stuffed like the back of a carriage, to support the backs and heads of the children, when tired, in an easy position.

If a pony is used for carrying panniers, in all cases flap-reins (see illustration next page) should be fitted to the bridle; and so buckled as to restrain it from increasing its pace beyond a walk, or from the effects of a sudden ebullition of high spirits. Donkeys do not require such precautions.

For instructions as to leading-stick and reins, page 221 may be consulted. Neat leading-reins

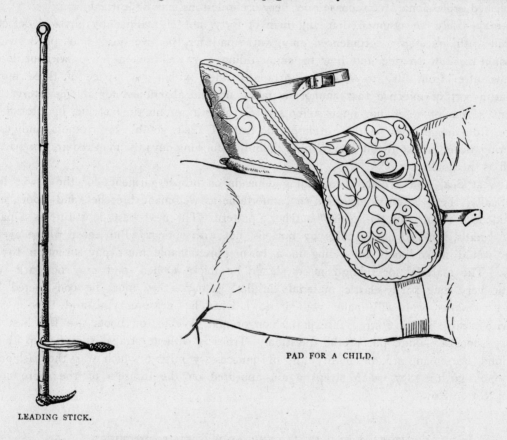

LEADING STICK.

PAD FOR A CHILD.

for pannier ponies may be made from the white cords sometimes used for pillar-reins. The Dutch make some extremely neat black hemp driving-reins, so rounded as to be convenient for the soft hands of women.

PONY RIDING.

There are boys on farms and in mansions where the stable is always full and the stable door always open, who from their earliest years cannot be kept from riding, or trying to ride, every four-footed creature they come across. They mount the big house-dog, and get many falls in experiments on the docility of pigs, calves, and goats. They make friends with the grooms, and while still in short petticoats are lost by the nursemaid, and found sitting on the back or rather neck of some steady old nag in his stall, while Robert the strapper hisses away at polishing harness or boots. A little later they ride one of the plough teams as they slouch slowly home, and take unlawful possession of that useful slave the family donkey.

These sort of boys seldom come to any serious grief. As to trying to restrain the equestrian propensities—inherited perhaps from some very distant ancestor, which sorely vex the hearts of pious and pedestrian parents, whose greatest daring has stopped at a chariot and pair of fat hay-fed coach-horses—that is always a waste of time.

But where there is no such violent taste, nine or ten years old is quite soon enough to commence the horse education of either boy or girl. Many boys of tender years have been ruptured, or otherwise seriously injured, by premature attempts at making them ride astride broad-backed, rough-trotting ponies, or donkeys of uncomfortable paces ; and many young girls owe a twisted spine or high shoulder to premature pony exercise on an improper saddle.

The pony for a boy should be shaped like a good hack, with a head and neck that bends and bridles well, and so narrow across the back that his little legs can easily grip it. The best saddle for commencing is a pad without a tree, made of some soft rough substance (felt is as good as anything), with bolsters in front to keep the child's knees back, fastened with one girth, and secured by a surcingle, without which a pad will rarely keep its place. But where a child is to ride without stirrups, which he ought not to do at a faster pace than a walk until he has learned to trot and canter with stirrups, a woollen rug folded to the right size, and secured by a girth with a buckle and tongue, is better than any pad. Better still is a pillow, stuffed not too tightly with hair or flock, covered with soft leather, and secured on the pony's back by a broad girth, so that the child sinks securely into his seat. This is an Oriental plan, and makes a most comfortable seat for a boy. Any one with a sewing machine can make the pillow. Stirrups may be attached to the girth if required.

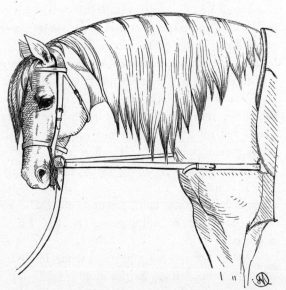

PONY WITH FLAP-REINS.

A good form of pad, which may be used for either a boy or for a girl with pommels added, is given in the preceding page. A strap buckled in front of a young child makes it assume the right position, and acquire the habit of sitting up straight. But it must be distinctly understood that the strap of this pad saddle is only to be used when the pony is led, or when loose in a school or barn. It might be dangerous if the pony got away with a child fastened to the saddle. The advantage of thus being strapped in is that a timid child acquires confidence, and the proper form of upright seat, and does not begin by hanging on the bridle. At an early date the strap must be discontinued, and soon afterwards a pad without the back should replace this chair form. With respect to stirrups, it is a disputed question amongst authorities of equal value whether boys should commence their lessons with stirrups or not. My own opinion is decidedly in favour of using stirrups for the first lessons to boys, because the seat and grip acquired by riders without stirrups are essentially different from the seat of a horseman on a saddle. Riding on a smooth saddle without stirrups is equally absurd and dangerous.

On the principle of starting as one means to go on, it is better that the boy should commence by learning to depend on the three legitimate aids to the seat of a civilised European, viz., "balance, grip, and stirrups."   After he has acquired the first principles of equitation, he may ride hunting on a pillow or pad, or folded blanket, without stirrups, if he is long and strong for his age.   Major Dwyer, in his very able work on "Seats," now out of print, recommends that stirrup-leathers should be fixed nearly, not quite, in the middle instead of on the front of the saddle; and this would seem a sensible plan, at any rate in pad saddles for boys.   The stirrups should be of the modern shape of the ladies' patent stirrup, of a size proportioned to the rider's feet, with a padding to protect the child's instep.   The length of the stirrup-leathers should be carefully adjusted to suit the child's shape, seat, and comfort.

In the first lessons the boy or girl should not be allowed to take hold of the bridle at all. A good example in this respect is presented by the practice of professional circus riders. Their children, boys and girls, commence their serious equestrian education at about ten years of age, under the instruction of a strict, sometimes of a very severe, teacher.   I have had the advantage at the Agricultural Hall of watching from day to day the whole course of instruction of the children of professional circus riders, from the first elementary lesson to the finishing touches of *la haute école*.   The circus children are of course taught to ride entirely by balance.   The lessons are given in the circus ring, on a pony trained to canter at an even pace.   Sometimes a soft pad is used, sometimes the animal is bare-backed; but in either case, until the pupils are far advanced, they are not allowed any bridle.   The pony is fastened down with flap-reins, the inner rein, that is, the rein nearer to the inside of the circle, being buckled shorter than the outer rein, so that it can only canter slowly; while the teacher restrains the pony with a lunging-rein, and urges it when necessary with a driving whip.   The child, whether boy or girl, commences by riding astride, is taught to sit in an upright easy position, just like the Greek equestrian statues in the Greek Court at the Crystal Palace, with the shoulders well thrown back, each hand resting on each knee, or with the arms crossed over the breast. Thus no trick of holding on by the bridle or leaning forward over the pommel can be acquired.

When a firm seat and confidence have been gained, the child may be trusted with a pair of single reins.   But whether in an enclosed place or on the road, the flap-reins should be used, so as to avoid any necessity for the young rider pulling at the horse's mouth; pulling to the right or to the left at the word of command, without any particular method of holding the reins, being quite sufficient for all practical purposes.

"When," says the late Colonel Greenwood of the Life Guards—a most accomplished horseman in the *manége* school, the hunting field, and the Park, and a very good rider of races on the flat—"you wish to turn to the right, pull the right rein stronger than the left.   This is common sense.   The common error is, when you wish to turn to the right to pass the hand to the right; by this the right rein is slackened, and the left rein is tightened across the horse's neck—a monstrous and perpetual source of bad riding and bad usage to good animals. When double bridles are used, one rein should lie loose or knotted upon the horse's neck."

It is far better that the child should from time to time hold on and steady itself by a pull at the mane of the pony or the pommel of the saddle, than ever learn to depend on the bridle as a means of keeping its seat.   The hard plucky boy only needs good models for his imitation, and he will teach himself while laughing at his own tumbles.

When the child pupil can sit at ease at a brisk walk, buckle a long rein to a cavesson, and slowly canter a well-trained pony or a horse if narrow enough for a boy, in a circle alternately to the right and to the left.   There is no advantage in using a pony less than 14 hands, unless to get a narrow seat.   Small horses are generally better broken than small ponies.

After mastering the canter, you may proceed to the more difficult pace of trotting. Where a riding-school is not to be had for the first lessons, a quiet paddock or a disused chalk or gravel pit may be made to serve the purpose. A soft ground, and the absence of everything that is likely to distract the pupil's attention, are the main points. After putting the stirrups at the right length, it is important to measure and mark the soft snaffle reins exactly at the length at which the child should hold them in both its hands when sitting in the right position. One-handed riding in the early stages of horsemanship should never be permitted, because one-handed riding means riding on one side. When Colonel Greenwood published the first edition of his " Hints," in 1839, the only style of riding taught was the *manége,* or military one-handed, sword-handed style; but these, with other social matters, have been altered for the better since, and the best teachers only admit the use of one hand in advanced pupils. But as we seldom forget what we learn when very young, it is most important that the habit of sitting upright in the middle of the saddle, with a rein in each hand, should be acquired at that period—for "as the twig's inclined the tree is bent." Children are imitative animals, so if they are taught at all they should be taught on sound principles from the first. If a boy has taught himself to ride boldly and badly, his bad habits should be eradicated without mercy by an imperious master.

One of the best teachers of boys and girls, as well as of men and women, this generation has seen, was Dan Seffert, who commenced his equestrian education in the first years of this century in the *haute école* under his father, Master of the Horse to the celebrated Countess of Craven, Margravine of Anspach, and became in 1830 one of the new school of professional steeplechase riders. He won the St. Albans Chase somewhere about that time, on Moonraker. He gave his children-pupils of both sexes a style, seat, and hands that could never be acquired on the military one-handed plan.

Seffert's plan was to teach one thing at a time, and he began with the seat. When his pupil could turn, twist, and bend in every direction on the saddle, he began the bridle lessons. Without a firm seat, he used to say, the rider will be too much frightened to use the hands effectively when most wanted. There are at least some schools in London where riding is taught on these sound principles.

To sum up, children must have well-trained ponies, if boys—girls may ride light-stepping horses—not over 15 hands, with suitable saddles and bridles. They must not attempt too much, and commence by learning to sit without touching the bridle. They should never be allowed to run the risk of a fall; but should a fall occur without serious damage, they should be made to mount again immediately, with as little fuss as possible. The first lessons should be in a school or enclosure; no awkward habits should be permitted. Stirrup-leathers must not be too long or too short; the reins must not be too short.

The whole principles of good horsemanship are summed up in an old Irish huntsman's answer to the widow of his lord :—

" Don't you think, Mick, it's almost time that Master Ulick learned to ride?"

"My lady, get him a nice little horse, with some divil in him, of the Chit-chat shape; let him keep his legs to the pony's sides and his arms to his own. Tell him to keep his hands down and his heart and his head up; and very soon, I go bail, he'll ride as well as the masther, Heaven rest his soul!"

What a strong lad of thirteen or fourteen may do in learning to ride in one long lesson at a walking pace, has never been better described than in the autobiography of Lavengro, when his father's groom sent him off by himself, on a sensible cob, for a ride round a mountain in Ireland. But Lavengro* was tall and thin, with the instincts as well as the shape of a born horseman. The gipsies, whose language George Borrow early acquired, always believed that he was one of their race; and the undebased gipsy is a born horseman and horse jockey or coper. The word "jockey" is derived from a Romany word which means a whip.

LAVENGRO'S FIRST RIDE.

"How easy is riding, after the first timidity is got over, to supple and youthful limbs! and there is no second fear. Oh, that ride! that first ride! most truly it was an epoch in my existence; I still look back on it with feelings of longing and regret. People may talk of first

NOT THE SORT FOR ROTTEN ROW.

love, but give me the flush, the triumph and glorious sweat of a first ride, like mine on the mighty cob. My whole frame was shaken, it is true; and during one long week I could hardly move foot or hand; but what of that? By that one trial I had become free, as I may say, of the whole equine species. No more fatigue, no more stiffness of joints after that first ride round the Devil's Hill on the cob. Oh, that cob! that Irish cob!—may the sod lie lightly over the bones of the strongest, speediest, and most gallant of its kind! Oh, the days when, issuing from the barrack-gate of Templemore, we commenced our hurry-scurry just as inclination led, now across the fields, direct over stone walls and running brooks—mere pastime for the cob—sometimes along the road to Thurles and Holy Cross, even to distant Cahir! What was the distance to the cob?

"It was thus that the passion for the equine race was first awakened within me, a passion which up to the present time has been rather on the increase than diminishing. It is no

* George Borrow, author of "The Bible in Spain."

blind passion, the horse being a noble and generous creature, intended by the All-Wise to be the helper and friend of man, to whom he stands next in the order of creation. On many occasions of my life I have been much indebted to the horse, and have found in him a friend and coadjutor, when human help and sympathy were not to be obtained. It is therefore natural enough that I should love the horse.

"I cannot help thinking that it was fortunate for myself, who am to a certain extent a philologist, that with me the pursuit of languages has been always modified by the love of horses; for scarcely had I turned my mind to the former, when I also mounted the wild cob, and hurried forth in the direction of Devil's Hill, scattering dust and flint stones on every side. That ride, amongst other things, taught me that a lad with thews and sinews was intended by Nature for something better than mere word-culling; and if I have accomplished anything in after life worthy of mentioning, I believe it may partly be attributed to the ideas which that ride, by setting my blood in a glow, infused into my brain. I might otherwise have become a mere philologist, one of those beings who toil night and day in culling useless words for some *opus magnum* which Murray will never publish, and nobody ever read; beings without enthusiasm, who never having mounted a generous steed, cannot detect a good point in Pegasus himself; like a certain philologist, who, though acquainted with the exact value of every word in the Greek and Latin languages, could observe no particular beauty in one of the most glorious of Homer's rhapsodies. What knew he of Pegasus? He had never mounted a generous steed; the merest jockey, had the strain been interpreted to him, would have called it a brave song!"

CHAPTER XIII.

A LESSON ON HORSEMANSHIP.*

A Real Horseman able to Control any Controllable Horse—The Essentials—The Right Shape—Sound Instruction—Practice—Courage—Temper—For Military Horsemanship Military Master Indispensable—The First Lesson in Riding, a Firm Seat—The Next to Use the Reins—Drill and Gymnastics the Best Preparation for Horse Exercise—Impatience and Conceit the Great Obstacles to Improvement—The Horseman's Lower Limbs to be Attached to the Horse like a Centaur—The Trunk Balanced and Flexible—The Place on the Horse over the Fourteenth Dorsal Vertebra—For Proper Seat see Diagram of Skeleton—Anatomical Description of—Seat Dependent on Shape of Thighs—Turning out the Toes often Essential—Archbishop Harcourt and Canon Sydney Smith—The First Lesson on a Rough Saddle—The Trussed Chicken Lesson—Stirrups or no Stirrups, that is the Question—The Length of Stirrup-leathers—The Length of Reins—Reins in Both Hands—The Lesson on Guiding—By Hand and by Leg—Walking a Horse—The Head to be felt, but free—Three Indications: Restraining, Urging, Guiding—The Hands Restrain and Guide—The Legs Guide and Urge—The Importance of Collecting a Horse before he Moves—Walking an Important Pace—How to Walk Fastest—How with Most Action—Trotting an English Pace—The Military—The English Style—The Canter a Luxury with Sound Horses—A Resource with Screws—The Gallop—Requires Practice for Horse and Man—When to Stand Up—When to Sit Down—How to Turn—How to Stop—How to make a Horse Back.

IN the preceding pages an attempt has been made to assist grown men desirous or compelled, when no longer flexible and young, to learn to ride on horseback, by a series of suggestions in the nature of makeshifts. It has throughout been assumed that the adult pupil would be provided with a well-broken, docile animal, and that the pupil himself will take the shortest and quickest road to horsemanship, by sacrificing nothing to the conventional elegance of the riding-school, and adopting any and every means that will secure him safe conveyance.

In the paragraphs devoted to the pony-riding of children of tender years, the main object has been to warn parents, governesses, and nurses, against the dangers of ill-considered attempts to make children ride, either when they are too young for the exercise, or when neither the animals or fittings are suitable for the purpose. In this chapter it is proposed to collect and arrange as many useful hints as possible, for the benefit of those who aspire to be horsemen in the best sense of the term—able to train and control any horse that a civilised man should ride, with as much grace and elegance as the rider's shape and make will permit. It is scarcely necessary to repeat that the most docile and intelligent pupil can no more learn the art of horsemanship from a book than the art of playing the violin; but the young man who learns nothing from the collected experience of the finest horsemen of the present and past generations must be a very poor or a very conceited creature.

To acquire the highest excellence in horsemanship requires well-shaped, well-proportioned limbs, education on sound principles, constant practice, calm courage, and an even temper. No man can correct his shape, many cannot enjoy the practice required for very fine horsemanship; but all may start on sound principles, all may control their temper in dealing with an unreasoning animal, and all who begin to ride when young may acquire the courage of average skill. Between

* In this chapter I had the assistance of Mr. D. Seffert, Messrs. George and Thomas Rice, and Mr. Frederick Allen, of the Seymour Street Riding-school.

the perfect horseman, who is prepared and able to train and subdue any horse, however high-couraged, if not irreclaimably and obstinately vicious, and the horseman who can fairly take his own part on any horse of average training and average temper, there are many degrees of skill. It is to the latter class that this chapter is specially addressed.

Where the pupil-student desires to acquire military horsemanship—as, for instance, in the case of a subaltern of volunteers preparing for promotion—there is only one course open to him. He must place himself in the hands of a military riding-master, whether he has learned to ride before or not. To military horsemanship the writer of this chapter has nothing to say, although the precepts it contains have been approved by brilliant cavalry officers who have also graduated as masters of fox-hounds.

The first thing a rider has to learn is how to sit his horse in that form which will make his seat most secure, and consequently give him the greatest command over his horse; but a "horseman," in the best sense of the term, should not only be able to stick to his horse under difficulties, but be able to control and direct him; make him walk, trot, canter, gallop, leap, stand, and move on at his will; should know "how to quiet and subdue the hot-tempered, and put life and action into the sluggish."

All this is easy to say, to do is quite a different thing. It shall be assumed that the pupil is a youth arrived at the age when he may be expected not only to imitate like a child the examples set before him, but to be able and anxious to understand the reason why of every axiom laid down by his instructor. It shall further be assumed that he is strong enough, and has pluck enough, to go through the fatiguing process of adopting his limbs and muscles to an entirely new set of motions. As in the case of young children, military drill or gymnastic exercises are the best preparation for lessons in horsemanship. The youths who go through the exercises on the horizontal bars, and other performances of a graduate of the *Turnverein*, will not find any of the attitudes and motions prescribed by the riding-master difficult.

The principles laid down by Madame Brenner, in her excellent treatise on calisthenic and gymnastic exercises,* apply equally to first lessons on horsemanship for both sexes and all ages. "Two grand rules," she writes, "must be constantly observed—first, the avoidance of fatigue; secondly, the recognition of amusement in connection with the lessons. The exercises or lessons must be conducted according to the physical capabilities and requirements of the individual."

The greatest difficulty in carrying out a system of gymnastics (or horsemanship) is "impatience." The story of a lady who declared, after seeing the first exercise, that she could do it in five minutes, but who afterwards admitted that it required five days, might be matched by every serious teacher of horsemanship. Another golden rule is, that "no exercise should ever be carried on until the pupil is tired out."

The first lessons of gymnastics in the book from which these quotations are made, are directed towards "the vigorous healthy action of the muscles connected with the chest, arms, and shoulders"—"to strengthen the lower limbs, and induce suppleness and pliability."

Again, "the swinging dumb-bell exercise—the dumb-bells not being too heavy—is one of best aids towards the development of the chest, *from its compulsory detail of a firm position* of the lower half of the body, while the upper half is actively employed."

Now that is exactly what is needful for a horseman—that his lower limbs should be attached to the horse like a centaur, and his trunk should be well-balanced and flexible.

* "Gymnastics for Ladies," by Madame Brenner, Bruton Street. 1870.

There are young men in such fine condition as to need no preparation for commencing any athletic exercise, however foreign to their previous habits. To such these hints on preparation and training do not apply.

In the hundreds of elaborate treatises that have been written on the art of horsemanship, from the time of Xenophon to the thirtieth year of the reign of Queen Victoria, none have explained the principles on which a horse should be saddled and a rider should sit on his saddle so logically as Major Dwyer,* to whose scientific essay on the most important points of good horsemanship the writer is much indebted, although the practices have been followed by all fine horsemen of all nations, unwittingly, just as Molière's *Bourgeois Gentilhomme* talked prose without knowing it.

Major Dwyer commences by describing the skeleton of an average horse standing in a natural position; that is, with its head stretched forward, and its hind-legs, instead of being perfectly perpendicular from the hocks downwards, brought forward to assist in maintaining its equilibrium.

"The animal is at rest, but a greater share of weight rests on the fore-legs than on the hind, because the head and neck in that position are heavier than the tail.

"It will be observed of the framework of the back—the spinal column—on which the rider's weight is to be placed, that whilst the under line of the vertebræ inclines slightly downwards towards the fore-hand, the spinal process of the first thirteen vertebræ of the back, reckoning from the point where the neck is attached, incline backwards; whereas those of the fifteenth, sixteenth, seventeenth, and eighteenth dorsal and the six lumbar vertebræ incline forwards; the *fourteenth dorsal vertebra* with its process, standing perfectly upright, and forming as it were the keystone of the arch, so that, in fact, the fourteenth dorsal vertebra is the centre of motion of the horse's body. This is further shown by the distribution and points of attachment of the muscles of the back and adjacent parts of the fore and hind-quarters." The conclusion, then, from an examination of the skeleton and the bones clothed with muscles, assisted by Major Dwyer's commentary, is that the seat of convenience on the horse and of comfort for the rider is just over the fourteenth vertebra, the keystone of the arch, the centre of the balance—the saddle in the middle of the horse's back, the rider in the centre of the saddle. It is from want of knowledge of this anatomical fact that strong bold horsemen, sitting with a firm grasp too far back, have broken their horses' backs in taking leaps, especially down jumps, requiring more than ordinary exertion.

From the study of the anatomy of the horse, we learn that "the fore-legs are essentially bearers; and the hind-legs, although chiefly propellers, also to a certain extent bearers."

Those who wish to pursue the scientific deduction from this state of facts still further are referred to the first pages of Major Dwyer's book. The plain conclusion is, that to obtain the full use of both hind and fore legs, the rider must endeavour to preserve a just equilibrium. "Judicious handling and riding are nothing else than finding a proper balance of forces for the well-built horse and the horse defective in symmetry."

The first lesson, then, the pupil has to learn is how to sit in the middle of the saddle and keep there. In fact, to deserve the highest praise that can be bestowed on a steeplechase rider, "he never moves in his saddle."

The proper seat is neither on the fork, like the Duke of Newcastle's, nor on the *Os coccygis* —the tip of the spine—where the tail would be if man had one, but on three bones, viz., two

* "Seats and Saddles." By Francis Dwyer, late Major of Hussars in the Austrian Service. Blackwood.

which form the junction of the pelvis with the thighs, which are parallel with the hip-bones and the tail-bone.

This seat has been more successfully described in the following extract from a letter from my friend Dr. John Reeve, of Great Marlborough Street, Regent Street :—

THE SEAT ON HORSEBACK ANATOMICALLY CONSIDERED.

"What is a man to sit on ? Well, he has two bones in his pelvis* (the sitting bones)— each one is anatomically described as the *Os ischium*, or *sedentarem*—and a third in the posterior portion of the pelvis, called the *Os sacrum* (or sacred bone). The *Os coccygis* is a small bone at the end of the *sacrum*, and is said to resemble in shape and size the cuckoo's bill; it is the rudimentary tail bone,† and is highly developed in tailed animals.

"The two sitting bones in front, with the *sacrum* behind, form a sort of triangular base for the human seat on horseback.

"If the rider sits in his proper place, he will mainly rest on the two sitting bones, and partially at times on his *sacrum*. He may thus be said to rest on a triangular basis, a seat affording the greatest degree of comfort.

"If, however, the rider throws his thigh and leg forward too much towards the horse's shoulder, the *sacrum*, which forms the posterior portion of the bony triangle, will come in too much contact with the back of the saddle.

"Finally, if the rider throws his thigh and leg too much back towards the horse's tail, he must then necessarily sit on the front part of his sitting bone (the *perineum*), a position of discomfort and even danger."

"The only firm and steady seat is on this triangle." The Monboddo bone (the tail bone) must neither be over-weighted nor made too conspicuous. "No good rider sits on his fork, but on his seat."

How this seat is to be obtained depends on the conformation of the man. The round,

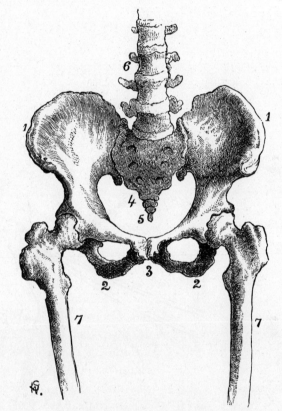

DIAGRAM SHOWING FRONT VIEW OF THE PELVIS (IN A STANDING POSITION).

1. The *Os ilium* (hip or haunch bone). 2. The *Os ischium*, or *Os sedentarium* (sitting bone). 3. The *Os pubis*. 4. The *Os sacrum*, or sacred bone. 5. The *Os coccygis* (huckle or tail-bone, the extremity of the spine). 6. The lumbar vertebræ, forming the base of the spinal column. 7. The thigh bones.

short-thighed man will have more difficulty in fitting himself to his saddle and settling the length of his stirrup-leathers than the born horsemen who win steeplechases. For this purpose

---

* See diagram of part of skeleton.

† Hudibras, boasting to his lady-love, says :—

> "I am no horse,
> That I can argue and discourse ;
> Have but two legs, and *ne'er a tail.*"—Part ii., Canto i.

the toes should never be turned in, as the old teachers of the *haute école* required, or out, like a splay-footed opera-dancer; but just enough to increase the hollow of the thighs. The round-thighed man may have "to get up a hollow curve by turning out his toes a little in excess," says Major Dwyer.

DIAGRAM OF A MAN ON HORSEBACK, EXHIBITING SIDE VIEW OF THE PELVIS.

The pelvis is a strong, basin-like, bony cavity, situated at the base of the spinal column, and above the inferior extremities. The bones composing it are :—1. The *Os ilium* (hip or haunch bone). 2. The *Os ischium*, or *Os sedentarium* (the bony seat, is a rough, thick, strong protuberance). 3. The *Os pubis*. 4. The *Os sacrum*, or sacred bone. 5. The *Os coccygis*, or huckle bone, is a continuation and termination of the *Os sacrum* or sacred bone and vertebral column. 6. Base of the spinal column.

Archbishop Vernon Harcourt, who was a very fine horseman, and, before he was promoted to the bench, always in the first flight when fox-hounds were running, once said to the wisest wit of the last generation, "I understand, Mr. Sydney Smith, you object to clergymen riding on horseback." " Not," was the reply, " when they ride very badly, and turn out their toes." For Sydney Smith took the *haute école* view of horsemanship.

The old *haute école* plan of giving a seat and carriage of the body in the earlier lessons was very good ; at any rate, it was a plan on which such horsemen as Mr. D. Seffert and Mr. George Rice took their first lessons. The pupil was mounted on a school-horse, on a buck-skin-covered not a slippery saddle, with well-stuffed bolsters before his knees, but without stirrups, a snaffle rein in each hand, and his elbows kept back by a stick thrust through them behind his back, like a trussed chicken.

This plan may have a tendency to make the action of the arms rather stiff, if persevered in too long, but it will certainly stamp in the habit of keeping the hands down and the elbows close. Habits, especially in the young, are wonderfully tenacious, whether they are good or bad. This may be seen in discharged soldiers, who for years after leaving the army show an inclination to salute an officer, and always walk not as civilian mechanics walk.

It is a question worth experiment whether an elastic band or ring of india-rubber—a Ranelagh, in fact—would not be a more satisfactory instrument for confining the elbows than the trussing-stick.

On the question of commencing riding with or without stirrups, different opinions are held. I am inclined to believe that it is better to begin with stirrups, because " the pupil first acquires one seat without stirrups, and then another, which he is to use permanently, with stirrups ;" so that it is plainly more in accordance with common sense to begin as you mean to go on. " The most difficult thing to acquire is balance ; stirrups were invented to assist in maintaining balance. To add stirrups to a saddle after the pupil has acquired balance, is like giving a boy an air-collar after he has commenced to swim." If it is decided to dispense with stirrups, then, as already observed, not a hard, smooth saddle, but a soft pad without pommel or cantle should be employed.

My friend the late Captain Percy Williams, who served in the 9th Lancers before he became famous as a master of hounds, was considered one of the best men of his day as a gentle-man jockey and a rider to hounds. When quartered at Hounslow, in his frequent visits to London, Major Whyte Melville states that it was his practice as soon as he left or before he came to the stones, to throw the stirrups over the pommel, and ride his fast-trotting hack by grip and balance alone—to this practice he attributed his marvellous seat, and Percy Williams was a first-class horseman.

The one instance in which I should be inclined to dispense with stirrups is when a young boy or girl with a very clever miniature pony is in the habit of following the hounds ; because their being dragged by the stirrups may be more dangerous than any fall. I have known one instance of a fatal accident from a boy's foot being hung in the stirrup after a fall at a leap. Boys' stirrups are usually too small ; they should be in the modern form of ladies' stirrups.

After a certain amount of skill has been attained in grip, the stirrups may be taken away in a school lesson, to perfect the balance and grip.

The length of the stirrup-leathers should be regulated by the length of the legs and thighs, when they are hanging in a proper position. There is no fixed rule by which this length may be calculated within an inch, because it will vary with the shape of the man's limbs and the horse's barrel. On changing the saddle to a different horse, it constantly happens that you find it necessary, in consequence of one girthing several inches more or less than the other, to take up or let down a hole. The rough-and-ready measure is by the length of the arm; but very often this is found too long or too short, as arms do not bear an invariable proportion to legs. The only way to arrive at the best length for the stirrups is for the rider to mount, sit down in the middle of the saddle, and adjust the stirrup-leathers so that he feels firm in them and able to get his heels down a good inch; not so short that his legs are cramped, and that he is forced back in the saddle into a position which makes it most easy for a kicker to send him over his head. For this reason an adult pupil should take pains to purchase a horse of the size that will suit his length and shape of his limbs.

As to the position of the lower limbs, "the nearer the whole of the leg is brought to the horse's side the better, so long as the foot is not bent below the ankle-joint." *

So soon as the pupil begins to feels confidence in walking, trotting, and cantering slowly in a school, before he enters on the mysteries of managing his horse—a delusion in early lessons, for the school-horse knows his business, and the pupil does not—it is well to commence practice in the motions which involve the body below the hips being firmly attached to the horse, the body above the hips flexibly moving; learning, while still riding first slowly and then fast, to touch the croup of the horse with the shoulders, to bend down and put on and take off either stirrup, and in fact to go through the exercises which are taught by the best modern military riding-masters.

The whole aim of teaching horsemanship is expressed in the few words which I have heard Mr. George Darby, of Rugby, ex-steeplechaser, repeat hour after hour while teaching his young children (girls as well as boys riding astride) in his school in Kensington— "Shoulders back." "Waist slack." "Heels down." "Hands down." "Walk. Trot. Canter. Gallop!"

Until the back-bone ceases to be rigid, and the waist becomes hollow without effort, you cannot have a horseman's seat.

MOUNTING.

In a previous chapter I advised middle-aged pupils to mount as best they could from a chair or a bucket, if a horse-block was not to be had. The correct way of mounting is delineated in the following drawings of the four actions of a man able to bend his knee, standing near to the shoulder of an averaged-sized English horse. Some men could no more assume the attitude of Mr. George Rice in these pictures than they could walk along the tight-rope. They are obliged to stand back in order to get their toe into the stirrup.

But the first thing is to make the horse stand still, a lesson every good hack ought to learn; but even when learned, not always repeated by a fresh and excited animal.

If there is any difficulty, shorten the off or right-hand rein, until the horse's nose points towards his right shoulder; in that position he cannot move, and if possible put his head against a wall or gate. Mr. G. Nevile recommends that young horses should always be mounted in the stable-yard with their heads against the stable door, until they learn to stand still without being held.

If the horse is too tall for a short rider, and no convenient eminence near, the stirrup-leather may be let down two or three holes, and taken up again when the rider is mounted; but if this expedient is likely to be required, the holes of the leathers should be punched large enough for the buckles to pass through easily, and punched not as usually on the outer, but the inner side of the leather. The "White" stirrup-leather is very convenient for short men.

* Nolan.

According to military directions, the horseman, before mounting, is to twist a lock of the horse's mane round one finger of his left hand. This may do with trained troop-horses, but adopted with a high-spirited fresh hack or hunter might end in an unpleasant drag, and a broken finger or dislocated wrist. A grasp of the mane with the reins will usually be found sufficient.

The following successive motions seem very long and tedious in detail, but so would detailed instructions to a savage king on the use of a knife and fork :—

The first position of the accompanying sketch is more easy and relaxed than military rules would allow. The reins hang loose, it being supposed that the horse has either learned to stand still or is held by a groom ; if not, it will usually be found safer to have the curb rein drawn through the fingers, so as to feel the mouth and render it easy to stop the horse if he move during the operation.

In No. 2, the rider balancing lightly on his right toe springs to position No. 3. With a fourth movement he throws himself into the saddle, appears as in No. 4, and takes up the reins in one hand.

The sketch on this page shows the square seat, the upright carriage, the fall of the legs, and position of the toes, which a well-made man ought to assume on horseback.

In hunting most men thrust the foot home. A man must be very strong to retain his foot half way in the stirrup in a very bustling run, with a variety of up, down, and wide leaps ; yet I have seen an Irish horse-dealer's feet swing in the stirrups while his horse cleared six feet.

THE REINS.

A firm seat having been attained by continuous practice and close attention to the style of such horsemen as the one delineated in the preceding illustrations, the pupil has arrived at the stage where he may learn to guide his horse.

Until a pupil has acquired that firm attachment to the saddle which is the combined result of grip and balance, only obtained by patient practice, he does not guide his horse ; on the contrary, if any difference of opinion arises, his horse guides him.

Horses are managed by the use of the reins, the legs, and the voice—the voice to soothe, to encourage, and sometimes to threaten.

Military and *haute école* instructors have written very elaborate descriptions of the modes of holding the reins in one hand and regulating the motions of the horse with the little finger. No doubt, those who have thus written can do what they attempt to explain ; but pupils can no more learn these extraordinary feats from written rules than to play like Hallé or Arabella Goddard.

A neat way of holding double reins in one hand is shown in the illustration, page 283.

A DOUBLE BRIDLE IN ONE HAND.

The bridoon or snaffle rein is divided by the third finger, the bridoon rein being upper-most ; and thus you may ride a perfectly-trained horse who has learned that he is to turn to the right when the left rein is pulled, and to the left when the right is pulled, as well as possible by a turn of the wrist and a pressure of the leg. But as even a colt, whether he obeys or not, can understand that when the left rein is pulled he is intended to go to the left, a pupil is saved a great deal of unnecessary trouble by commencing in the style of colt-breakers and of common sense, and taking the reins in both hands.

SECOND POSITION.

FIRST POSITION, MOUNTING.

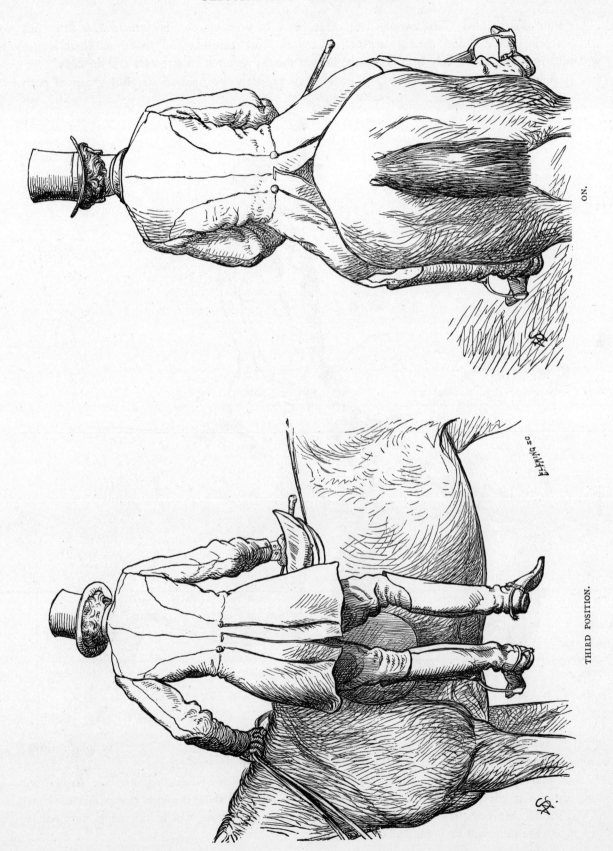

ON.

THIRD POSITION.

"But," says Colonel Greenwood, "he must be a very uncommon horseman who attempts, without long practice and careful instruction, to use both bridles; and to adjust their length without disturbing the double bearing on the horse's mouth requires infinite tact and delicacy."

A single rein with a fresh or pulling horse may properly be held in the full grasp of both

MODEL SEAT.

hands.   When for any reason it is necessary to ride with one hand, it is better to place three fingers of the left hand, viz., second, third, and fourth, between the single reins.

To shorten reins held in both hands, having first taken care that they are not made too long by the saddler, extend your arms, allowing the reins to slide through the palms of your closed hands, then bring them together, and by that simple motion, which can be performed at full speed, the reins will be found suffic'ently short.

After all, the exact mode of holding the reins is not important, so long as they are held smoothly and flatly, with the hands, arms, and elbows in the right position.

The very finest horsemen seem to regulate all paces from the motion of the wrists and fingers only.

Novices in the art of horsemanship should always have their bridles fitted with a standing martingale, because if a horse does not throw up his head it does not harm; if, when fresh, he does try to fling his ears into your mouth, as the best horses will do at times, the martingale gives you complete command over him.

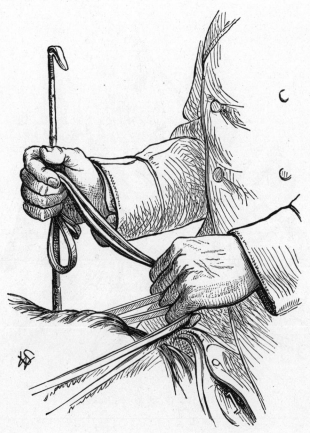

DOUBLE REINS IN ONE HAND.

The principles of horsemanship require that the horse should instantaneously obey the indications of the legs and the hands of the rider; but to describe in an intelligible manner how these indications, except the very simplest, are to be given is a task beyond the limits of written description.

The best teachers make their lessons lectures, illustrated by the examples of a mounted horseman or horsewoman; and I am convinced that a great deal of useful preliminary education may be given to pupils seated in the gallery of a riding-school while a teacher with the gift of picturesque description illustrates himself, or by some one mounted for the purpose, each rule of instruction.

Colonel Greenwood, who was the first to substitute the plain English word "indication" for the, in this case foolish, French military term "*aid*," puts the question tersely when he says, "There are three sorts of 'indications,' viz., retaining, urging, and guiding." The hands retain or restrain and guide, the legs guide and urge. If a horse is mounted, and allowed to stand still for any considerable time, he will most likely sprawl and extend himself in an attitude which is not only ugly, but which requires a decided change of position before he can either walk, trot, or canter in the form he should. If a horse is ridden with a loose rein and careless legs, he can turn round or to one side before he can be stopped; and if he is very much tired is very likely to overbalance himself and fall. All men who perform great feats in walking and running have a balanced pace. Although perfectly-trained horses of admirable symmetry do stand and go alone, a good horseman is always in a position to instantaneously control his horse.

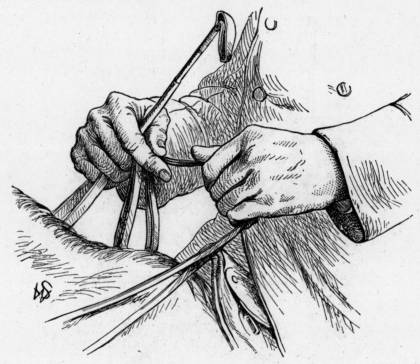

DOUBLE REINS IN BOTH HANDS.

For this reason—although in the hunting-field you often gallop off the moment you are mounted—after dismounting at a locked gate or after a fall, without being settled in your seat and with the reins held anyhow, because you are in a hurry and have confidence in yourself and your horse, that is the exception to a sound rule of horsemanship—viz., that a horse should be collected before he is asked to move at any pace, that he should be slightly retained by the bridle, and slightly pressed by the legs. This makes, or should make him, if he knows his business, stand square, ready to lead off with either leg as desired, and to walk, trot, or canter with mechanical precision. The grooms' phrase of "pulled together," for "collected," is very expressive.

Once in motion the legs of a good horseman on a well-trained horse, however high-spirited, will imperceptibly guide and regulate his paces almost as much as the reins, when after a longer or shorter acquaintance, rider and horseman have learned to understand and trust each other.

WALKING, COLLECTING, REINING BACK.

Walking is one of the most important paces of a hack, especially of a town hack, and it is a pace that can be very much improved by practice when the animal has any natural aptitude for it. It may safely be asserted that every horse that is fit for a hack can be made to walk well, that is, when gentle exercise has taken off the freshness of a young, well-bred, high-couraged horse. Every riding-horse should be made not only to stand still, but to start at a walk.

The prettiest walk is when the nag, quietly settled down, and taught by long experience with a firm rider that he must not break, steps in true time smoothly along, with loose reins, nodding his head. But these are exceptions. There are very few horses which it is safe to leave entirely to themselves when they are fresh, without the silent monition of a rein lightly but so firmly held that the least deviation from the paths of propriety brings the bit to bear on the mouth.

METHOD OF SHORTENING REINS.
(See page 282.)

To walk at the fastest pace an animal is capable of the snaffle rein only must be used, or the double bridle with the curb rein held so as merely to indicate its presence. But in the street and the Park, where the best appearance is to be made by the horse, good horsemen ride on the curb, so as to obtain the utmost action at some sacrifice of pace. It is in this simple operation that the first experience is found of the meaning of light hands, a quality of the same character as "touch" in a pianist, which is important in every pace, from the slowest to the fastest, which is seldom found amongst bruising, brutal riders, and never amongst those who have not attained a secure seat. Light hands mean the power of restraining a horse with the least possible exertion of force, and indicating, by the faintest and most elastic touches of the fingers, what the horseman desires to convey to his horse through the action of the reins and bit, or bits.

To make a horse walk there is nothing more stupid than ill-temper, the use of a whip, or the abuse of the spur. "A good horseman," I said in my first book about horses, "knows neither fear nor anger."

If a horse is very fresh from want of exercise, the first step is to "sit down and ride him" at a sharp pace until he is settled, and this may be done if there is a clean and soft road or a field convenient for a hand-gallop, without in the least fatiguing your nag. Then, if he is a young horse, be content with the slowest pace of walking, as long as he does not "jog," or "shog," as some call it. At every break he must be stopped firmly and patiently, and made to begin again. In the meantime, if the rider is a novice, he must carefully study the walking attitudes of those who ride well, and seek to obtain an easy not slovenly style. It may be positively dangerous to try to hold a fresh high-couraged horse down to a walk on starting, although he may settle down soon afterwards, and walk with a loose rein; be satisfied if he can be kept to a fast trot over the stones until you reach an open ground. If you lose your temper, and tug at the reins, hit with the whip, or dig in the spurs, the high spirit of the horse may very speedily be turned into vice. He will begin to plunge or kick, and if he does not succeed in dismounting his rider, will perhaps slip down, or do himself some permanent injury.

The best way of improving the pace of a young horse is to keep to a walk when travelling towards the stable, to which your horse is eagerly looking for his corn.   Although a perfect hack may be trusted to walk with a loose rein, this is a practice which cannot be safely followed with a tired horse.   He must be held so that he will be compelled to move his legs alternately and evenly.   No man in the world can hold a horse up, at any rate as long as he sits on his back; all that he can do is, by a judicious, smooth, steady feel of the reins, particularly the curb rein, to draw the horse's head downward and toward his chest, and thus incline him to bring his hind-legs under him, in regular time, in support of the fore-legs.

Walking over deeply-ridged ploughed fields, and fields where turnips are grown on ridges, is capital practice for young riders and young horses.   Thoroughbred horses, recently drafted from the turf into hack or hunter stables, and a fine class of park and ladies' horses, which have been bred and trained on the smooth turf of counties where hills are unknown, may be very much improved by being daily trotted and cantered over rough, undulating, and hilly ground.

Young riders are apt to despise the walking pace, and to be not unnaturally impatient to press on the smart trot or the luxurious canter; but they may depend on it that a close observer will learn a great deal that must be learned to become a real horseman in walking exercise, by studying a finished horseman and his horse when walking.

Practised horsemen often appear very careless in their seat, and in the way they handle their reins; they have, not without reason, confidence in themselves.   But young students must not copy the carelessness of accomplished cavaliers, until that confidence is justified by the essential habit of never being taken by surprise whatever the horse may do.   And it should always be remembered that every well-bred horse will, now and then, at the most unexpected moments, take a fit of staring, starting, and plunging.   I remember one very hot summer's day kicking a thoroughbred mare along (who, though brilliant in the field, was a slug on the road) past Apsley House, when suddenly I found myself standing on my feet at her head, with the reins in my hand, having performed an involuntary somersault, for which I received the undeserved compliments of the Irish crossing-sweeper, anxious to earn sixpence.

"A horse should never be turned without being made to collect himself, without being retained by the hands, urged by the legs, and guided by both.   In turning to the right both hands should retain him, the right the strongest; both legs press him, the left the strongest, the rider leaning to the right; the shorter the turn and the quicker the pace, the more the horse's hind-legs should be brought under him, and the more both horse and rider should lean to the right;" but the right rein must *indicate*, not haul.   The practice of good polo players illustrates this.   A bad heavy horseman turning sharply to the right, and not leaning in the same direction, but clasping his pony hard with his long muscular legs, will often bring him over.

In reining a horse back, the rider and also a driver must remember that he cannot move if pulled back, so hard and suddenly as to get both hind-legs under him; therefore, the horse must be collected every time he resists, brought square on his four legs, and then reined back.   Brutal, ignorant carters may be seen beating a horse for not backing a loaded cart, while the poor animal is in such a position that he cannot move his extended hind-legs.

The pupil horseman must remember that there is to be no jerking of the reins, no hauling, but a constant feel of the horse's mouth, so that when the animal is in movement there should be a constant touch, or feeling, or play, or bearing between mouth and the rider's hands.   "It is," says Colonel Greenwood, "impossible to bestow too much pains and attention on the acquirement of this touch. It is the index of the horse's actions, temper, and intentions. It forewarns the rider of what he is about to do; by it the rider feels muscularly, without mental attention, whether his horse requires more liberty or more collecting."

It is this sensitiveness of mouth which makes the horse so superior for riding and driving purposes to the ass. The fault of the ass is a deficiency of delicacy. You can guide a good horse as accurately as a sailing-boat; with an inch to spare, you can turn in and out of a throng of vehicles with perfect confidence. The ass, when willing to go at either his slow or fast pace, bores along incapable of receiving delicate indications.

The best horsemen guide their trained horses with their legs as much as by their reins, often without using them. It is because women ride on one side instead of astride that they can never equal first-rate horsemen in the management of raw colts and obstinate horses.

The importance of the preceding directions may not at first seem evident to pupils. They may not see why they should walk their horses in small circles when they would like to canter straight forward. They do not see why they should attempt to collect a horse that collects himself. But this " collecting, urging, and retaining " are the foundations of the obedience it is the object of horsemanship to enforce.

By collecting, the horse is kept well upon his haunches, is guarded from crossing his legs, and has, all the time, as the phrase goes, "a spare leg" to depend on. The horse's head, in turning a corner, should not be pulled farther round than to allow the rider to see his eye.

On broken ground intersected by ruts or holes, let the horse choose his ground, keeping him alive by pressure of the legs if lazy or tired, without flurrying him.

TROTTING.

The trot is essentially an English pace; that is, Englishmen invented the practice of rising in the stirrups, by which the trot can be performed with the greatest ease to the horse and the rider. Never begin to trot until you are quite at home in the walk, and feel that you can do nearly all in the saddle that you could sitting in a chair. Begin trotting on horses easy in their action and obedient to the reins, without being too light-mouthed. There are exceptional horses with so smooth and even a pace that it is not necessary to rise in their trot, or at any rate perceptibly.

The best trotters move audibly on hard roads in the time of 1, 2, 3, 4, perhaps most horses do; but there are certainly many which seem to trot 1 2, and it takes practice to "rise" in time with them. The picture at page 289 illustrates the distinct square trot of a roadster rather than a park hack.

The Continental and military practice is not to rise in the stirrups, but to try to sit close to the saddle, relieved a little by the support of the knees and stirrups. No doubt there must be good reasons for this practice of bumping (which was universal with all European horsemen, civilian as well as military, until steeplechasing with English horses and riders was introduced into France and Germany), because it is retained in the British cavalry in which the most distinguished officers have been and are hunting men, who adopt the English style of riding when they appear in plain clothes or hunting coats.

The military horseman uses the curb rein in trotting, although he receives his first lessons on a snaffle bridle without stirrups.

Trotting and rising in the stirrups should be performed with the snaffle rein only: the feet so placed in the stirrups that the heel can be kept well down without strain, the leg from the knee downwards falling straight, and moving as little as possible; the rise and fall to escape bumping just as little as the action of the horse will allow. Some horses, and particularly English horses, are much more *impressive* in their trot than others. The elbows should be close without clinging to the sides of the rider, and the snaffle rein should be held firmly, at the proper length, in each hand, and not be allowed to slip a hair's-breadth as long as the trotting continues; in this respect differing from the mode of regulating the reins in the canter or gallop. In the trot the rider appears to support the horse on the snaffle bit; of course he does not do so, but the well-trained horse relies on the rider to hold him to that pace. Horses may be trained to trot with a loose rein (the fastest trotter I ever possessed did this), and also to slacken their pace and halt as soon as the rider with a soothing word sits down and loosens the reins.

Perhaps more vulgarity is displayed in trotting than in any other pace by hard riders of the sporting publican class, their admirers and imitators. It is a pace in which, with a free goer, it is very easy to acquire bad habits.

On a really good trotter it is, *for a man*, one of the most pleasant and healthy forms of exercise. So thought Lord Palmerston, who might often be met, in his seventieth year, going down the Green Park from Constitution Hill, or by Birdcage Walk, to the House of Commons, on a hot summer's day, trotting at the rate of twelve miles an hour. "Twice in 1864, Lord Palmerston, being then in his eightieth year, rode over from Broadlands to the training stables at Littleton, to see his horses gallop on Winchester race-course—starting at nine o'clock in the morning and not getting back until two o'clock. It was his maxim that 'no other abstinence would make up for abstinence from exercise.' No member ever trotted harder with his own hand, and his rule was daily horse exercise." If George Grote, the historian of Greece, had not given up the horse exercise which for a long period was his favourite out-door amusement, his life and valuable literary labours might have been prolonged many years.

The young rider should bear in mind that there is a limit to the speed of a hack's trot— it may be at the rate of eight miles, ten miles, twelve miles, or fourteen miles an hour, within the limits of that pace he will travel farther, more safely, and with less fatigue to his horse, than at a canter; but pressed up to or beyond the limits of your horse's trotting powers, it becomes most exhausting, as any one may learn by trying to keep up a fair toe-and-heel walk with a pedestrian who is two miles an hour better than himself. The man who could walk all day at about three miles an hour would be very soon pumped out in trying to walk six miles in one hour. It is also dangerous, because, at full stretch, the horse on making a mistake has little chance of recovering his balance. Tightly and firmly held, at about eight or ten miles an hour, or whatever be the pace of the slowest of the party's horse on a fair road, trotting is a very conversational pace. Nothing is in such bad taste as for the owner of the fastest walker or trotter to be continually in front of a riding party.

Neither should horses be allowed to break from one pace to another; but a considerate horseman returning home or going to cover will do well to break now and then into a hand-gallop rather than strain his horse's sinews and joints, and vex his temper, in a vain attempt to keep up with some one who prides himself on a trotter of exceptional powers.

Such a wild goer as the one in the illustration at page 270 may be confided to a groom, ready to ride anything, but certainly is not in his place as a gentleman's hack or in the Park; although, perhaps, with patience and good handling, he may in a few months, be brought to more regular and less fatiguing paces.

Between the walk and trot is what is called the jog or shog trot. No trick can be more vile in a pleasure, park, or lady's horse, but it is a valuable pace for a tired hunter or roadster; easier to them than walking evenly or regularly trotting. There is no long road travelling in this country now, but the shog trot is practised on the way home by every huntsman, every whip, and every hunting man, after a long day, if he has any consideration for his horse.

Trotting and walking are the paces which, if attained at all in great perfection, are improved as the animal grows older, as long as he retains full possession of his powers. In America, where they understand trotting as well as we do flat racing, steeplechasing, and hunting, they do not consider that a horse gets his best pace as a trotter until he is at least nine years old.

RIDING TO COVER.

It is rare that a horse is equally pleasant in both trotting and cantering, especially if the trot reaches more than nine miles within the hour, that is, less than half the rate of American racing trotters. The pupil should practise trotting assiduously to attain a good style, watching the manner of the best masters of the art, and taking an occasional glance at his own performance in the reflection of plate-glass windows. In that pace particularly it is important to attain the peculiar graces of the modern English style—the *ars celare artem*—correct, without being rigid; easy, without being slovenly; upright, not poking toward the horse's ears in the old English style; legs, feet, hands, all in their proper places; rising to ease your horse in the trot not from the stirrups but the knees, not to show your seat, but to ease yourself and the horse with the least possible daylight between your seat-bones and the saddle.

A horse trotting fast should be stopped slowly, by gradually shortening the reins, sitting down and speaking softly the language the horse so soon learns to understand.

THE ACTION OF WALKING AND TROTTING.

The action of trotting squarely is distinctly diagonal, the off fore and the off hind foot following each other. It has always, and correctly, been taken for granted that the action of walking is the same, and is thus illustrated in the portrait of a very fine walker at page 193.

On consideration, every horseman will remember that the actions of the two paces, walking and trotting, glide so naturally from one into the other, without that distinct change which takes place when a horse either rises from a walk into a canter or subsides from a canter to a walk, that feeling and hearing alone suffice to settle the question, without the use of eyesight. Major Dwyer treats the question with his usual mathematical exactness in the following passages, in which he discusses it in reference to another question, viz., the effect of the rider's weight on the equilibrium of a horse at different paces.

"In walking and trotting, the horse moves its diagonal legs simultaneously—that is, the off fore and the near hind leg move together, and alternate in this action with the near fore and off hind ones; so that while one pair is being moved forward the other sustains the weight of the animal.

"In cantering and galloping (slowly), the two legs *at the same side* are advanced simultaneously, the other two remaining behind. But the two diagonal legs of every pair are not set down simultaneously. One hears distinctly four beats in the case of walking and trotting, and two, three, or four in cantering or galloping, according as the horse's weight is adjusted to the latter movement. Of the two legs acting in concert, the fore one is lifted and set down somewhat sooner than the hind one; were not this the case, a horse could never tread in his own hoof-marks, as he usually does in the trot.

"In very rapid trotting, the animal is off the ground with all four legs for an instant.

"The veterinary surgeon of the famous Austrian stud at Trakenen has observed that the near hind-leg and the off fore-leg of most horses are stronger than the other two, and he attributes to this cause the fact that horses naturally prefer to lead with the near leg in cantering and galloping, the weight being then supported by the two strongest limbs, the near hind and off fore leg. For the same reason he asserts that spavin occurs more frequently on the off than the near side; and that horses in wheeling through restiveness always do so to the left, on the near hind-leg."

These explanations show why trotting is the safest pace for a sound-footed horse trotting within his powers, for then he is always supported diagonally on two legs, and two legs are alternately coming to his support. For the same reason, trotting is a dangerous fast pace when one leg or foot is painfully unsound; so, too, walking is dangerous when a young or tired horse is permitted to take a long, lounging, slovenly stride.

THE CANTER.

The canter proper is the first stage before galloping, which is performed with the same action, except at the utmost rate of speed. Then a well-bred horse seems in his gallop to cover the ground by a series of bounds.

The canter is performed on the haunches, the fore-legs seeming to act chiefly as props, and to take very little share in the work of propulsion, if so grand a phrase may be pardoned.

A fine cantering hack moves forward in a series of graceful curves, in the form illustrated by the woodcut of the Marquis of Londonderry at page 259 (copied from a series of equestrian portraits published between 1830 and 1840). The canter of Count D'Orsay's fierce hack, which seems to be standing on one leg (page 257), is rather in the style of display than of the luxury of the middle-aged dandy marquis. A view of the Achilles monument would have been more suggestive of the man and the horse than the wild mountain scenery which forms the background.

To canter properly the park hack must be collected, brought almost to a standstill and on his haunches with the curb rein, touched with the heel or whip on the side meant to lead, and drawn by the rein on the opposite side until the rider can see his horse's eye. Once started, the curb reins only must be used, with a slight give-and-take feeling, the rider balancing himself to the time of the horse's movement. But the hand on the hip would scarcely be considered "good form" at any time since manliness superseded the effeminate affectation of the dandies of King William IV.'s time.

It is difficult to find a horse that can canter pleasantly and slowly in a grand and graceful style, because strength is required in the loins, hocks, and thighs, to perform a pace which throws so much strain on those muscles and tendons; and the combination of strength with soft action is rare.

Ladies' horses are always required to lead with the off fore-leg, and this undue strain on one pair of limbs generally produces lameness or ossification in the joints of the near hind-leg. Indeed, there are few horses that have been constantly cantered by ladies that are not in some degree damaged in the overworked sinews and joints.

Sound horses are easily taught to lead with either fore-leg. But if a horse otherwise docile obstinately declines to lead with either fore-leg, it will generally be found that the leg or foot he objects to use is unsound.

Cantering is the pace for park or country use on soft ground. No park hack is worthy of the name that will not, on slight indication, canter at the rate of six miles an hour (any well-bred screw can gallop), springing into the canter from a walk at the rider's first indication.

To canter straightforward at a moderate pace is the easiest of all horse exercise for a novice. The best practice for a pupil is to canter in small circles to the right and to the left, and in a figure of eight on a horse trained to change his leg from right to left, and *vice versa*, without indication from the rider.

In England cantering is considered an effeminate pace, only to be used occasionally; but the best horsemen in performing long distances alternately walk, trot, and canter, thus resting all the legs of their hack, and cover very great distances without distressing him.

It is not needful to dilate at any great length on a pace so familiar, but the young horseman should particularly bear in mind that the slow or collected canter in which a handsome hack makes the greatest display is a pace that tries a horse much more than a trot or hand-gallop at the rate of eight or nine miles an hour, for the collected canter is a strictly artificial pace, produced by gentle "urging" against the delicate restraint of the curb; the more collected, that is, slow, the greater the weight thrown on the horse's hind-quarters. Ladies, with the cruelty of ignorance, often abuse pets which would suffer less from a daily "terrific" gallop over sound turf, than from a couple of hour's slow cantering up and down Rotten Row.

For the same reason, although a fresh horse should not be allowed to break and shift from a trot to a canter and from a canter to a trot, it is absolutely cruel to hold a horse down to the same fast pace on a long journey. A horse, if ridden by a heavy man, or by one who does not "rise in good time," will break into a canter in order to relieve the strain on the fore-legs unduly jolted by the rider's weight, and shows his good sense in thus silently rebuking his rider.

Besides the true collected canter there is the "screw canter," affected by horses unsound in two or three legs, or all four, a combination of running and cantering, in an effort to ease their poor feet.

It was at a screw canter that Tennyson's Northern Farmer returned from market, hearing at every step the welcome sound of "Proputty, proputty, proputty"—a sound which the little vulgar street boys impertinently translate into "Three-halfpence and twopence," much to the annoyance of many a Sunday horseman rejoicing in an outing on a hired steed.

THE HAND-GALLOP.

A slight additional urging, a little more liberty of rein, and the pupil advances to the "hand-gallop," the fastest pace permitted in the Park, and, on suitable ground, perhaps the most exhilarating for the rider and the horse. At the hand-gallop conversation is still not only possible but pleasant, and the horse, if high-spirited, is relieved from a restraint that is sure to fret him if the scene is not Rotten Row, but some manorial park or wide-spreading undulating downs. When the pupil can confidently take part in the hand-gallop, and start and stop his horse when he pleases, he has made a great step in advance.

This pace cannot be defined in miles. Some thoroughbred horses will be cantering within themselves, and appearing to be only doing eight or nine miles an hour, when they are really stepping over twelve; while your fat cob will, as French romancers say, be "burning the pavement," and yet scarcely get through seven miles an hour.

The hand-gallop is play, the pace of pleasure parties not hurried, of hunting-men going to cover with a half-hour to spare. Galloping is a serious business; it taxes the best efforts of the horse, and requires all the attention of the horseman.

THE GALLOP.

To gallop, the pupil must sit firmly down in the saddle, and take hold of his horse with a rein in each hand, holding him together with the snaffle, and making him just know that the curb is there, ready to be used at a moment's notice, and to be used if the horse endeavours to get beyond the pace required. How to so hold a horse it is impossible to explain by written directions. But the object of holding a horse together in galloping, instead of playing with him as in the canter, is to keep him to a measured pace, to make him stride evenly, and prevent his increasing his rate of going at his own will and pleasure. This requires in the pupil horseman both strength and attention. Jockeys stand up in their stirrups, lean over their horse's withers for the five furlongs, or mile, or mile and a half they have to traverse, until the "supreme moment," when they sit down to finish a close-run race. In this way, for the few minutes occupied in covering a short distance, they relieve the propelling limbs from weight, and give them more power to force forward the horse's fore-hand. But although the practice of standing up and leaning forward over the withers is sound as regards racing, it is both absurd and awkward in riders either on the road or in the hunting-field. Whyte Melville says on galloping: "Riding thus two-handed, if he bends to you in the canter you may safely push him to a gallop, taking care that he does not extend himself too much. As long as his haunches are under him you can command him; when he goes on his shoulder he commands you."

A hundred years ago all fox-hunters stood up in their stirrups; in the first quarter of this century the English horseman who did not adopt the *haute école* style rode on the road and in the field in a stupid imitation of the jockey style. It was in reference to these mistaken souls that "Nimrod," the great reformer of the hunting world, said about galloping, "Sit down in your saddle; don't stand up and stick out your hind-quarters as if they did not belong to you." You still see a good many men, some fair horsemen, lean unnecessarily forward, but that is not the style of Seffert, or Rice, or Frederick Allen, or the Darbys of Rugby, father and son, or of the most famous Master of the Rufford (see coloured plate), or his brother officer in the 9th Lancers and sometime Master of the Pytchley; or, to hark farther back again, of that most finished horseman, for twenty years Huntsman of the Royal Buckhounds, Charles Davis, whose portrait is given in the chapter on Hunting.

With the shoulders well back, the double reins held in both hands, or, if the horse can be trusted, the snaffle reins only, and the curb reins, knotted or buckled, not too short, hanging loosely on his neck ready for any emergency, the rider gives and takes with every stride; holding his hands low, and making his elbow-joints hinges, he avoids the rigid pull which deadens a horse's mouth. Thus he swings along in a sort of delicious dream, fully occupied with his horse, the pace too good for conversation.

The points to be aimed at are a firm seat, as motionless as possible below, while the trunk above gently gives to the horse's motion, and hands so holding the reins as to be able to perfectly control and rapidly to arrest the pace. These essential points can only be attained by practice on high-couraged horses in open fields or downs.

Without practice, the pupil who has acquired all the arts that can be taught within the walls of a school—and they are many and valuable—would find himself perfectly helpless if called upon to gallop on the best-trained Leicestershire hunter; for it is not enough to be able to stick on—the pupil must learn to guide, to turn, and to stop an excited horse.

The first lessons in galloping should always be given on horses with good mouths, and capable of being pulled up without difficulty.

It has already been observed that some most docile road hacks become almost delirious with excitement when galloping in company with other horses over elastic turf. Indeed, the first change from macadam to grass seems to have a champagne-like effect on young well-bred horses.

Over ridge and furrow it is not a bad plan to stand up in the stirrups, and so avoid repeated shocks; but this feat must not be attempted until the rider can stand upright without relying on the snaffle reins for support, without, as the saying is, "riding on his horse's head."

A fine firm feeling of the horse's mouth is as important in galloping, if not more important, than in other paces, in order to provide for unexpected obstacles or breaks in the ground. The best pace cannot be got out of a horse without holding him together. Victor Hugo's description of a charge of cavalry at Waterloo, "the horses first deprived of their curb-chains," is simple nonsense; and so is the poetical phrase of "loose reins and spur in flank"—he who looses his reins and spurs his steed will very soon come to grief.

When a pupil can gallop with confidence over flat ground, he should practise riding down hill, which, with a horse whose fore-hand is properly set on, is much safer than it looks; as long as the horse is kept straight he cannot be too lightly held. If not held straight he is likely to cross his legs, and then a terrific fall is certain. But on holding ground horses gallop safely down hill, because, if they have courage, they get their hind-legs well under them.

Here I come to the end of my hints—they are nothing more than hints—on the various paces to be practised successively by those who would be horsemen—walking, trotting, cantering, and galloping. I have done all I expected if I have succeeded in impressing on my reader the importance of mastering the details of each pace.

There can be no doubt that if a novice has found out what it is necessary for him to learn before he becomes a finished horseman, he will learn more from watching a skilful and illiterate colt-breaker than from any number of printed lessons. He will thus learn the how, although the colt-breaker may not be able to tell him the why.

A great deal has been written, and might be written, on the management of the reins and the sort of bridle to be used for fast paces; but I think that everything useful may be summed up in this axiom: "Always have a bit that will stop your horse; but, as long as you can, keep to the snaffle."

RUNAWAYS.

It is much easier to say what will not, than what will, stop a runaway horse, horses run away from so many different causes. Some from mere temporary excitement gallop off with a feeble rider, and, if wildly handled, make a regular bolt of what a skilled horseman would have reduced to a measured canter in a few minutes; others will try to run away when asked to do something they do not like, as, for instance, to jump a trifling fence. I have seen a horse in the hands of an accomplished horseman walk out of a yard, in spite of all his efforts, on being shown a leaping-bar—this walk would have been exchanged for a trot, and the trot for a gallop, in the hands of a less skilful horseman.

Other horses will, on slight provocation, run away if ridden with a snaffle bridle, when they would not attempt anything of the kind with the common double bridle of curb and bridoon, although the curb-reins hung loosely without being used. Such horses have felt the effect of the chain on the chin, and its pressure has what is sometimes called a "moral influence."

Some horses will be perfectly docile until alarmed by the sight of a few scarlet-coated soldiers, or the sound of artillery, of thunder, or of a pack of hounds, and then become absolutely mad and unmanageable; but nearly all such horses may be subdued by patient, gentle treatment, judicious training, and the application of proper bits. But for the moment a nervous horse in a fright is as dangerous in a crowded city as a real "rogue runaway"—indeed, more dangerous, for the rogue will generally take care of himself, although ready to dash under or through anything, at the sacrifice of his rider's head or limbs.

The horse that has once acquired the habit of running away will bolt on the first opportunity. If you suspect his intention, the best plan is to check it the moment he begins to move, taking hold *of one rein with both hands*, and giving it one or two such violent jerks that the rogue must pause or turn round. Then stop him, and, if you doubt your being able to hold him, get off. Perhaps a too vigorous "plug" may make him cross his legs and fall—not a pleasant contingency, but anything is better than being run away with in a street.

In open country you may compel the runaway to gallop with a loose rein until he is tired, or to move in a constantly-narrowing circle until he is glad to halt. A ten-acre field is big enough for this expedient. But the great point is to stop a runaway before he gets into his stride; after he is once away few bits will stop a real runaway—a steady pull is a waste of exertion on the rider's part. Some horses may be stopped by sawing the mouth with the snaffle, but nothing will check an old hand. Another expedient is to hold the reins very lightly, and on the first favourable opportunity, as a rising hill, for instance, to try a succession of jerks. But the cunning, practised runaway is not to be so much feared as the mad, frightened horse. The mad horse will dash against a brick wall, or jump at spiked railings of impossible height. I once saw a runaway horse, after getting rid of his rider, charge and burst open his locked stable door.

On the other hand, I have known horses that never attempted to bolt as long as they were ridden with a sufficiently powerful bit, who started from the stable-door the moment they found that they were trusted in a simple watering bridle.

TO MAKE A HORSE STAND TO BE MOUNTED.

Horses in high condition, not sufficiently exercised, are very impatient, and often will not stand still to be mounted, even with a groom at their head. To active young men, who like their horses to be full of fire and ardour—"above themselves," in stable phrase—this is not of much consequence: work will bring the thorough-bred hack to decorous docility; but sometimes this fidgetiness amounts to a vicious trick, and a horse, quiet enough when mounted, will do all he can to prevent his rider from getting into the saddle.

Young horses should always be made to stand still when the rider is about to mount. With patience and time, there are very few that cannot be taught that they have no business to move until mounted, and that then they are to start at a walk.

Baucher, the great authority in France on all questions of equitation, says that a horse may be taught to stand to be mounted in two lessons of half an hour each; but I very much doubt whether a high-bred, corn-fed horse would submit to half of one of his lessons. "Go up to the four-year-old gently, as you should with every horse; soothe him with your hand and voice. Then take hold of both the curb reins, a few inches from the cheeks, with your left hand; in the right hand hold your whip with the point down. Tap him gently on the chest, he will retreat; tap him again, slowly, without anger, and speaking to him caressingly all the time. The horse, tired of running back, will try to avoid the whip by rushing forward. Then stop him, and make much of him. This repeated a few times will teach him that to stand still is to avoid punishment." Mr. G. Nevile's plan is simpler and better: to mount a young horse with his head to the stable door.

At any rate, it is worth while to spend a great deal of time in teaching a riding-horse to stand to be mounted without a groom at his head.

Few grooms know how to hold a horse while being mounted by a man, so as to hold the stirrup at the same time. They catch hold of the reins so as either to pinch the jaw or to bring the curb into action. The proper mode is to take hold of the bridle cheek above the bit, or of the nose-band, with the right hand, while holding the stirrup with the left; but if the horse is very fresh, then he should be held by *one* snaffle rein close to the cheek. When a lady mounts, of course the groom stands in front of the horse, holding the snaffle reins in both hands.

As the most spirited carriage-horses are taught to stand still when harnessed, there is no reason why riding-horses should not acquire the same lesson; indeed, unless a real hack stands still to be mounted he is not quiet to ride.

Horses sometimes acquire a dangerous trick of running back while being mounted. On investigation, it will generally be found the cause lies in too severe a bit, roughly held by a heavy-handed groom. The substitution of a light bit will, according to my experience, often cure this vice after severe measures have failed.

Occasionally a horse is met with which, although quite quiet when once mounted, will plunge and kick violently when the rider is in the act of mounting or dismounting. Probably some accident, such as the saddle turning round, has frightened the animal, and shown it how to get rid of its rider.

I once took in exchange from a horse-dealer in a small way—for a hunter that did not suit me—a Prime Minister hack that I had often admired ridden on the road. When the deal was completed, the groom, in return for my fee (not the first he had received at my hands), whispered, "She's a capital bit of stuff, but you must not try to get on her or off her without having her head held by a man." He laid stress on the word "man!"

A few further inquiries the following day brought out the fact that the little mare had more than once thrown a very good horseman over head by plunging before he was fixed in the saddle; but that once firmly mounted, all vice disappeared until the time came for dismounting, when the same tricks were repeated, unless she was tired out by a long day's work. Severity had failed to cure this most unpleasant vice, so I determined to try a milder plan.

I took the mare into a riding-school, put on a pair of knee-caps, strapped up her near fore-leg, coaxed her into hopping about on three legs—very gently and very slowly—for a quarter of an hour, in order to teach her that if she attempted to move violently she would fall. No sane horse will willingly fall; a mad horse fears nothing.

When I had fully satisfied her on this point, I threw the rein of a single snaffle bridle loosely on her neck, and, without any one standing near her head, proceeded to mount and dismount many times. Then, unstrapping the near, I strapped up the off fore-leg, and again mounted and dismounted on the off side until I was tired. This lesson was repeated for about half an hour on five or six days, after which she would permit me to mount and dismount anywhere—in the street, on a racecourse, in the hunting-field—standing like a rock. Once only, in a country lane, she showed signs of her old complaint. I tied up her leg with my pocket-handkerchief, mounted, dismounted, untied her, and mounted again, without the least signs of reaction.

A more obstinate or vicious animal might have required more lessons to subdue, but the principle of making a horse incapable of resisting is the foundation of all sensible horse-breaking.

In the same way many a horse that has felt the effect of a strong kicking-strap in single harness will travel quietly as long as he feels the strap there, but will very often recommence his old tricks as soon as he finds that it has been omitted in harnessing.

When the soft tan-and-sawdust floor of a riding-school is not to be had, a cattle-yard well filled with straw and muck may be used, or any other quiet place where a horse can fall without damaging his knees.

A distinction must be drawn between a really vicious horse—one intent on getting rid of and damaging a rider at any cost: one that not only kicks you off, but kicks at you when you are down—and a horse which from some accident has fallen into a single bad habit, such as the one just described with its cure.

WHIPS AND SPURS.

A whip in the hand of a horseman not riding a race or breaking a young horse is carried more for ornament, or as a mild indicator, than for punishment. A lady's whip is supposed to supply, on certain occasions, the squeeze or the kick of a man's right leg.

No one who can help it will ride a hack that requires a whip to urge him along; a slug is much more conveniently excited by a pair of spurs. The grand rule for using a whip is never to apply it in anger.

It is an even greater mistake to quarrel with an unreasoning brute than for a schoolmaster to fall into a passion with a stupid pupil; and it is the greatest mistake of all to flog either in a passion.

The best whip for punishing purposes is in the form of a jockey's, which, tapering from the butt, is not too flexible; and if horses are whipped at all it should be effectually. The most assailable spot of a restive horse is the shoulder. I remember a clever breaker who used to bring his right arm across his breast and left shoulder, making the point of the whip play on a stubborn colt's croup in a way that subdued him when other applications had failed to obtain obedience. Make a practice of starting a horse by touching him with whip or stick behind the saddle, and the same to make him go faster. Reserve a cut down the shoulder to punish vice; but a horse ought to be started by pressure of the legs.

As a general rule, you should not strike a horse about the head; but there are occasions in fighting with a truly vicious kicker or plunger, when a few calm, deliberate strokes with the pointed end of a jockey whip across the ears or over the muzzle will bring the brute to reason. Brutal men, in a passion, use the butt-end of a whip on a horse's head, hitting here and there, and perhaps destroying an eye.

Spurs, properly employed, are essential for making the best of most horses; but they should not be worn until the rider can stick to his horse without involuntarily spurring—an accident that happens at times to the very best horsemen in hunting. There are a few, delicately thin-skinned, nervous horses which cannot be ridden with spurs at all; there are a great many that ride much more pleasantly with spurs, although there may never be any need to use them. Such horses are conscious of their presence, and obey the indications of a slight pressure of the legs which they would not notice if they found that the rider's heels were unarmed.

Almost every good hack and hunter has been broken with spurs, and obeys a pressure of the legs or a kick of the heel, because he has been made to move forward or to either side by the prick of the spur. Although the best horsemen seldom ride without spurs, they use them rarely, and only for some real reason. But when they mount a strange horse, they generally commence by letting him know that they have spurs on, so that he may be prepared for punishment if inclined to be disobedient.

With well-broken horses there is not the least reason for the rowels of the spurs being sharp; on the contrary, they are just as useful in giving a needful indication to move from too close vicinity to a cart-wheel if ground down to perfect bluntness. It is in riding in crowded streets that the use of spurs is most essential, and of a whip the most useless; the reins in both hands, and spurs on both heels, you are in a position to restrain and urge simultaneously, and with the utmost rapidity thrust through the smallest possible opening. It may truly be said that, in a crowd of carriages, the "horseman who hesitates is lost."

Spurs are essential for forcing a horse at slow paces "up to his bit," so that you can guide him with the greatest certainty; they are also essential for enlivening a slug, and for keeping a tired horse on his legs, but they must be employed with a clear meaning and with discretion. The horsemen who are most able to dispense with spurs are endowed with long, muscular legs, with which they can give a resisting or lazy animal a vice-like squeeze.

For road-riding two kinds of spurs are in use—the box spur, which is fixed into the heels of the boots, and the trouser spur, which is attached to the boot with straps. The best shape of box spur for walking is the swan-necked, which has the advantage of allowing the trousers to fall nearly to the bottom of the heel. Trouser spurs with straps are less expensive than box spurs, and avoid the necessity of fixing boxes in all your boots.

THE TROUSER SPUR, WITH STRAP
COMBINATION.

In the original form the horseman who wore trouser spurs was troubled with two sets of straps—one for the spurs, the other for keeping down his trousers; a simple improvement has overcome this difficulty: by sewing an inch and a half of trouser strap to the sole strap of the spur, one strap does double duty. When you have buckled on your spurs, you have only to button the inside button of your trousers to the button-hole of the additional strap.

For hack purposes, it is better that the necks of the spurs should be very short. At any rate, inexperienced horsemen, if obliged to wear spurs for a sluggish horse, diminish the chances of unwitting spurrings by selecting spurs with short necks, and taking all the points off the rowels. Spur buckles may be dispensed with by employing india-rubber instep straps, buttoned where the buckle usually hangs.

TO MAKE A HORSE LEAD PLEASANTLY.

It is a great convenience that a hack should lead and follow pleasantly when you have occasion to dismount and walk any distance on foot. The best examples of horses following, accompanying, and going before a man with a leading-rein are to be seen in the displays of roadster trotters at fairs and horse-shows. Their free going and obedience to the voice and rein are delightful to witness. It is an acquirement very easily imparted. The needful instructions were very clearly given by the famous American, Rarey, in his original pamphlet.

"Provide yourself with a common gig-whip and three or four carrots cut in slices. Lead the horse out in either a halter or a common watering-bridle. A closed barn or riding-school is the best place for all instruction, because there is then nothing to distract your horse's attention; but a quiet lane will do as well. Begin by fondling your horse, talking to him in horse language, and giving him one or two bits of carrot, for which, if he has not been fed recently, he will be eager, and begin to push his nose into your hand for more; then commence by leading him backwards and forwards with one hand, holding the gig-whip trailing behind you with the other, calling to him by name, if he has one, all the time, as thus:—'Come——come along, come along, old fellow,' touching him up gently, or sharply, as the case may be, on his hind-quarters with the point of the gig-lash to drive him forward, and fondling and rewarding him as he comes up to your hand. He will soon learn to press forward to avoid the flick of the whip behind, and to come to your shoulder to be caressed and rewarded. Instead of flying from you he will learn to seek safety by your side, and follow you anywhere."

When you wish a horse to follow you who has not been thus trained, the best plan is to walk on before him, holding the reins at full length, without looking at him.

Time and patience are well bestowed in teaching a horse such things as to stand still to be mounted, to start at a walk, to walk his best pace whether ridden or led, and to follow his owner in perfect confidence wherever he may lead.

LEAPING.

Every one, man, woman, or child, who learns to ride should learn to leap, whether intending to hunt or not; because no one can be said to have a secure seat who has not practised the balance required when a horse bounds in the air from high spirits, or when called upon to pass over some unexpected obstacle in a country ride—a newly-made ditch, or a sheep-hurdle set up to stop a gap.

When a horse leaps, he throws the untaught or unprepared rider forward. The object of instruction and practice are to teach and accustom the rider to resist, or rather to neutralise, by his position in the saddle, the impetus forward created by the horse's bound.

With this object in view the young horseman must sit firmly in the middle of the saddle, with the snaffle reins held in both hands, and both hands held low over the horse's withers, and look straight between his horse's ears. As the horse approaches the leap, he should bend his body back from the hips upwards over the cantle of the saddle, while keeping his "seat" firmly in its place by the grip of his legs and thighs; and, as a great horseman used to express it, in less anatomical language, "curling his sitting-bones (rear) under him." The degree of leaning back depends on the extent of the leap and the action of the horse; at a great down jump, the best horsemen almost touch the horse's croup. Some make the mistake of sitting back *on* the saddle, and thus exposing themselves to the action of the loin-muscles; whereas it is not their seat, but their shoulders, that should flexibly fall back, and return to the upright position when the horse is landed.

According to military instructions, "the body is to be inclined forward as the horse rises, and backwards as he alights;" but that is a feat which only a long-practised horseman can accurately perform. The chances are that the pupil who attempts it, if he does not get a black eye or bruised nose from the horse's neck, will find himself jumped out of the saddle from not having timed his change to the backward motion accurately.

The art of leaping with an easy-leaping horse is easily acquired if the pupil is properly taught. But some horses, from their powerful hind-quarter action, are very difficult to sit; and some men who have been hunting and riding hard all their lives present examples of every kind of habit that ought to be avoided—notably the foolish practice of throwing up the right hand, instead of keeping it almost level with the pommel, parallel with the left hand; and the awkward practice of pushing the legs straightforward like crutches over the horse's shoulders, instead of keeping them close to his sides, with the knees fairly bent.

More will be said on this subject in the "Hunting" chapters.

The mode of learning to leap is to commence on a perfectly quiet, free-and-easy leaper—one that in clearing a three-foot bar makes scarcely more exertion than in dashing into a gallop and with a slight obstacle to cover. If a leaping-bar is not at hand, the trunk of a tree is still better.

In the open country little ditches present as useful practice as bars or hurdles. After two or three preliminary lessons, the pupil will do well to follow a good horseman over easy places, such as gaps in hedges, with ditches on the taking off side. The pupil should on no account wear spurs in the preliminary stages of instruction.

In one of the elder Herring's hunting pictures, in which the hounds are in full cry, an odd-looking man, in a tall hat, is craning forward just as his brown horse is in the air clearing a solid oak fence with a brook on the far side.

Several masters of fox-hounds in flying counties, after examining this picture, have made the same remark: "If that horse makes the slightest mistake on landing, with that seat the rider must come over his head." This figure is said to have been a representation, but may not have been a correct one, of Assheton Smith's seat, although that hard bruising rider was celebrated for the number of his falls.

In reference to this picture, a West of England squire, one of the hardest riders of his day across the Vale of Aylesbury, told me that although he had ridden to hounds up and down the hills of Exmoor from his childhood, he discovered when he first came to London and observed the form of Middlesex steeplechase horsemen, who then made the hunters of Anderson, Elmore, and Tilbury,* that he was all wrong, and from that time completely changed his style of riding at big fences, and leaned well back over the cantle.

The best example I ever saw of the advantage of lying back at a big leap was exhibited by a son of George Darby, then a child about ten years old, riding a wonderful pony, which (only 10 hands high) would jump a hurdle in a riding-school four feet two inches high, that is, ten inches higher than itself.

The pony used to be led to the far end of the school, and when let go, galloped as hard as he could up to the hurdle, and bounded over it like a deer. The boy sat from the first leaning back over the cantle, but as the pony rose he seemed to be lying on his croup; as he landed he rose up as easily as one of those Chinese figures seated in a globe of porcelain.

You will frequently see in the hunting-field men take hold of the cantle of the saddle to hold on. This is nearly as bad as throwing up the right arm. But if a horse is very light-mouthed, a pupil may be permitted to hold on by the breastplate in order to learn to lean back.

Most men in leaping depend a little on the snaffle bridle; you hear them say they "like a horse to take hold of them." This being the case, it is most important that the reins should be held long enough to give the horse power to fully extend his neck. Nothing is more common than to see half-taught riders pulled out of the saddle at a leap by the extension of the horse's neck; and many a horse makes a mistake or refusal from being thus held hard when his mouth should be *felt*, not restrained.

Above all, the pupil should bear in mind that his aim should be to keep his hands as still as possible, and that he should not attempt to move the reins when the horse is rising or about to rise at the leap.

Practice over small natural fences, on a well-trained horse or pony, is better for a boy or young man than in a riding-school; with ladies, for several reasons, the first leaping lessons should be in a school.

VICES.

No sensible man or woman will keep a really vicious horse—that is, a horse that, not from exuberance of spirits, but from malignant spite, seeks to unhorse his rider or injure his groom. But the very best horses, well fed and not sufficiently exercised, will start, shy, plunge, rear, or kick.

A horse not absolutely vicious will seldom both rear and kick, but will follow one of those two vices in preference. Horses that have a backward look and show much white of the eye are almost invariably vicious.

Horses generally give warning by setting back their ears, or by a curious wriggle of the body, when they meditate some vicious trick.

* Will. Bean, D. Seffert, G. Rice, J. Mason, W. and A. Macdonough, &c.

KICKING.

A kicker seldom rears. However excellent in other respects, a kicker is unfit for park or town use. The risk of being dismounted is sufficiently unpleasant, without the further chance of maiming some other horseman or horse. The power of thoroughbred horses in kicking is something amazing; they will kick in a sharp gallop, and, as grooms say, "high enough to kick your hat off."

A kicker must be ridden in a severe bit; at the first symptom his head must be pulled high up and bent round until he is compelled to turn. His first effort will be to get his head between his knees. As long as you keep his head up, turning him round and round, he cannot kick. Apply the whip from time to time sharply across his shoulders and ears, and spur on the opposite side to that on which you are turning him.

When the kicking is merely an ebullition of high spirits, and an open country is before you, get fast hold of his head, stand up in your stirrups jockey-fashion, and send him along until you have taken the raw edge of his pluck out of him.

Mares are more given to kicking than geldings. If you are not quite sure you can get the best of a kicker or rearer, the better plan is to dismount. Young kickers may sometimes be cured by strapping up a fore-leg, and leading them about on soft ground, and mounting them while thus made helpless; but aged horses are quite incurable.

REARING.

Rearing, as long as a horse is cunning enough not to fall backwards, is a less annoying vice than kicking. If you are aware of the character of the vice, take care to ride on the snaffle reins only; and catch hold of the mane with one hand, while you pull the horse with one snaffle rein, so as to make him change his leg. Some horsemen drop the reins, and put one arm round the rearer's neck. You may spur but not whip a horse while rearing.

Most horses can be restrained from rearing by a rearing-bit attached to a standing martingale, which jags his mouth when he attempts to rise; but a confirmed rearer is only fit for a Hansom cab.

Fresh horses often plunge without meaning any harm. In such cases keep fast hold of the head; sit back, and urge into a gallop. If not a confirmed "buck-jumper," he will settle down in a few minutes. If he is a real rogue, get off him, if you can, and let some one else have the benefit of his peculiarity. The only instrument for stopping a fierce plunger is a bit that will not let him get his head down.

Very often horses over-fed and not properly exercised begin to rear, kick, and plunge in play, manage to dismount their riders, and thus become from a first fault irreclaimably vicious.

But he is a very poor horseman who cannot take good-temperedly the "lightheartedness" of a fine horse when he first leaves the stable after a long holiday.

SHYING.

When a horse shies and turns half round, it is useless to try to force him back, because he always turns on his strongest side; but quick as thought turn round in a complete circle, and if he still hesitates to go forward, circle him again and again, because in this motion he cannot resist.

If a horse shies without turning round, always pull him from the object of his alarm. If he tries to rub you against a wall or tree, pull his head towards it. If a horse is really and justifiably alarmed, as, for instance, at a threshing machine or bicycle, dismount, soothe, and lead him past.

A FEW RULES.

Make it your habit to fondle your horse before mounting, so as to accustom him to your voice.

Always approach his head first.

Do not touch your horse's side with your toe in mounting. In dismounting have only the toe in the stirrup, if you are tall enough to touch the ground with the other foot. If you are not, throw both feet out of the stirrups at the same time, and dismount holding the reins and mane in one hand, the cantle of the saddle in the other.

Do not trot until you have learned to walk, or gallop until you are at home in the trot.

The bridle-hand is the left hand, but both hands ought to be equally the bridle-hands of a civilian.

The whip-hand is the right hand.

The near side is the left side, as you sit and face the horse's ears. The off side is the right hand.

All horses have a strong side; you must turn a restive horse on his weak side.

A horse with fine shoulders and flexible action is easier to sit, even when plunging, than a more placid horse that carries his saddle badly.

Never begin to fight with a horse unless you have breath and strength enough to win.

POLO.

The game of polo has, since this book was commenced, attained such importance among the class of horsemen to whom the price of a few ponies more or less is of no consequence, that I need make no excuse for adding a few lines on this latest development of good horsemanship; for although only ponies are employed, polo players to excel must learn to gallop, stop, and turn at speed with a precision not required at any other horse exercise, unless it be a bout with single-sticks, instead of sabres, as practised by the cavalry officers in the great riding-schools at Vienna and Pesth.

Polo demands skill as well as strength, indeed, more skill than strength, although a man must be in first-rate condition to go through a well-contested game without distress. Polo, since 1873, has become a familiar game in every cavalry regiment in the kingdom; good polo ponies fetch fabulous prices. The London clubs included, in 1874, civilians as well as soldiers, scions of the highest aristocracy and sons of the "newest rich men"—to use a French phrase—who not only played every week of the season at Lillie Bridge, but introduced this new form of "jousting," as a rival amusement to the "Tournament of Doves," within the exclusive precincts of Hurlingham. Yet this game, new to England, has been played in the East for at least a thousand years. In the "Arabian Nights" we read that a king, afflicted with leprosy, was cured by playing at "Mall" (that is, polo) with a stick, in the handle of which some subtle medicine had been concealed, which penetrated into the king's hands when he was heated and perspiring with the game.

It is not a slight recommendation of polo, as an exercise of the horseman's art, that a very hard, bruising rider across country, one of those thrusting fellows who are equally ready to risk their own and their horse's necks and limbs if they can only be first, would find a great deal to learn beyond blind pluck before they could make even a decent appearance at polo.

A MORNING CANTER IN THE PARK.

CHAPTER XIV.

SADDLES, BRIDLES, BITS, MARTINGALES.

THE ordinary saddle in use in England either for road riding or hunting affords (unlike Gervase Markham's perfect saddle) the rider no support beyond the stirrups. It is a purely English, and probably Yorkshire invention, the outcome of the taste for riding across country in pursuit of hare, stag, or fox.

Before hunting habits put high-school precepts out of fashion our ancestors rode either upon the high piqued saddles used by knights in armour, or on a demi-pique something like the modern military. On the Continent, until when late in this century the English style of riding became naturalised in France and Germany, the gentry used nothing but semi-military saddles, high behind and before, in which the rider was securely packed with the help of a sheepskin or something of the kind. No doubt the excellence of English horsemanship is largely due to our ancestors having more than a generation back dismissed most of the arm-chair-like aids on horseback, and been content to rely for keeping their seats on balance, grip, and stirrups.

There are, besides the Somerset saddle already recommended for an adult pupil at p. 262, three kinds of saddles in common use in England :—

The plain flapped saddle used by huntsmen and most masters of hounds, which is the cheapest saddle made, and also the most slippery. This saddle is seldom used in London or other great cities ; it answers well anywhere for good horsemen except in very hilly countries. You really do require a roll of leather to keep back your knees when descending declivities nearly as steep as the roof of a house, for that reason in the mountains of California the Spanish saddle is universally used.

The saddle more in favour for both park and road riding, as well as in hunting, has the flaps stuffed, they therefore yield comfortably to the pressure of the knees. The small roll in front of his knees supports the rider a little, if the stirrup leathers are so suspended that he can touch them without disturbing his seat.

The third kind of saddle is quilted all over, and affords a softer seat, and the flaps are less slippery. The quilted saddle is in favour with horsemen who have little grip, and with those who don't feel as young and as strong as they did thirty years earlier.

For the Australian bushmen our wholesale saddlers supply a cheaper form of saddle, but after the pattern of the Somerset.

In order to meet the peculiar tricks of the half-broken vicious-tempered bush horses (referred to at p. 149 in the description of Australian horses), the thick pad before the knees supplemented by "the kid," a blanket rolled in a cylinder (like the cloak of a horse patrol) affords a sort of fulcrum to resist the dislodging effects of a "bush jumper."

A practical horseman says on the question of saddles: "Formerly pommels and cantles were made of much greater height than in more modern saddles; even now they might be improved by being made much flatter than they are. Half-cut pommels look as if half the pommel had been cut off, and are commonly made; but whole-cut pommels are rarely seen, and are the best of all."

"They will fit any horse without hurting his withers because the part of the tree which generally comes down on the withers in these (without pommel) saddles falls not across the withers but across the broad part of the back."*

"You are not so likely to be hurt by being thrown forward, as the best horsemen sometimes are, on a saddle without a pommel as on a saddle with one. The cantle ought to be flat, like a lady's modern saddle, and the inside of the saddle ought to press on the horse's back from end to end, so that the weight is distributed over a large surface."†

Stirrups for country use should be large, not too high, and of a size proportioned to the foot. The spring bars which attach the stirrup leathers to the saddle should always be open. The stirrup-leathers of a man who rides daily, whether he hunts or not, should be either renewed or shortened every year by cutting off the buckle and sewing it on again, thus shifting the spot where the iron loop of the stirrup wears into the leather.

The holes of the stirrup-leathers should be not more than *half an inch* apart, and punched on the inside of the leather where the tongue of the buckle enters, instead of the outside; stirrup-leathers so arranged will enable a horseman to alter the length with one hand and while in motion; the holes are usually made too small and too far apart.

The position of the spring bar to which the stirrup-leathers are attached is a subject on which very first-rate horsemen differ. Probably for military and parade purposes the centre of the saddle is the best place; hunting men with short legs and round thighs will find it convenient to have the bars fixed an inch nearer the centre than in the hunting saddles of the best makers; some men with long flat legs like them placed still further forward, almost parallel under the pommel. I have tried both kinds of saddles, and, being one of the short ones, find myself firmer when galloping a well-bred full-sized horse over a rough country if the stirrup-leathers fall *just in front of my knees* when I am sitting as I desire in the middle of the saddle, then I am not obliged to push my foot far beyond my knee to catch hold of the stirrup. A man who can afford it will do well, if he is not one who can ride on anything, to be measured for two or three saddles.

The best kind of woollen girth is that called the "Melton," consisting of one broad girth with two buckles, and a narrow one drawn over it.

Of late colonial girths, made of raw hide plaited or stamped into net-work, have been used and praised by hunting men. They never slip, may be drawn less tight than a woollen girth, and require no washing.

On this question Squire Froude Bellew, Master of the Dulverton Hounds, writes: "As to girths, I prefer and use the open stamped leather girths, a great improvement on non-ventilating woollen girths. Instead of felt or other saddle-cloths, I use a plain light leather pannel well saturated with tallow, which keeps the horse's back cool, fastened on the horse's back with a surcingle, and put the saddle over it. I never have sore backs in my stable, either with our horses or Mrs. Bellew's, and you know what a rough country I hunt and what long days I have."

* "Horse-Riding." By George Nevile, M.A.   † Saddles without pommels, made by Messrs. Urch, Long Acre.

"In my opinion there is no greater mistake than the military nummah, which, soaked with sweat, keeps the horse's back in a perpetual poultice, and is the direct cause of tender skins and sore backs."

When, from the formation of a horse's barrel or from his being over-fat, the saddle slips forward, it will be found a good plan to put on the girths crosswise, each being buckled to the strap not opposite, the point strap to the strap near the cantle, and *vice versâ*. But as a rule the proper plan for fixing the girths is in the middle of the saddle. But no mode of girthing will keep a saddle in its place that does not fit the horse.

Over-tight girthing has ruined the temper of many good horses, and killed many men— horses should be girthed by degrees—first in the stable, then before the owner mounts, finally, if necessary, when the horse has emptied himself after travelling a few miles.

Never let a groom show his strength and temper by over-girthing a horse.

A steel spring that would give and contract as the horse's belly shrinks, would be a useful addition to girths, especially for ladies' horses.

The saddle in the centre of the horse's back, the girths and the rider in the centre of the saddle, are sound maxims.

Saddles for country use or on journeys, as well as hunting, should have breast-plates; with a breast-plate it is not necessary to draw the girths so tight. All side-saddles should have breast-plates. The most expensive are of two pieces of leather sewn double; those made of a single strap look quite as well if broad enough, if not better, and are less costly.

Cruppers are not now used except for cavalry and police saddles, but those who propose to travel in foreign countries, where the horses are small and badly shouldered, should have their saddles furnished with cruppers as well as breast-plates.

BRIDLES AND BITS.

The bridle is the instrument for guiding, restraining, and stopping a horse.

The most important part of the bridle is the bit. A bit, whether for riding or driving, should be of such a shape and dimensions, and fitted on in such a manner as to control a horse with the least possible effort of the rider or driver. These essentials may be obtained in the highest degree without irritating the animal. Unfortunately, from sheer carelessness and ignorance, a great deal of cruelty is daily practised on the horses of the higher and richer classes, in the way of ill-proportioned, ill-shaped, extravagantly large, heavy, and misfitting bits, which, drawn tight by bearing-reins on the gag principle, convert them into instruments of torture, cultivate vice and create unsoundness.

The names of bits are legion, but they are constructed either on the principle of the snaffle or the curb, or on a combination of both.

The collection of bits and bridles at page 307 and page 309 represent nearly all the patterns in common use for riding.

THE SNAFFLE OR BRIDOON BIT

Is the simplest and oldest form of bit, and was probably originally, as it is still with the North American Indians, only a bit of wood.

The ordinary snaffle for use without any other bit is jointed with two cheeks like No. 4. It is the exception when a riding-horse goes comfortably, and carries himself properly as a hack in a single snaffle-bridle.

In some few instances horses will not bear anything more powerful than a snaffle.

There are two modes by which the snaffle can be made a very powerful instrument for stopping a horse: one when it is provided with two rings in which the bit plays loosely (see Figure No. 5 of accompanying illustration). This is seldom used except in harness, but I have

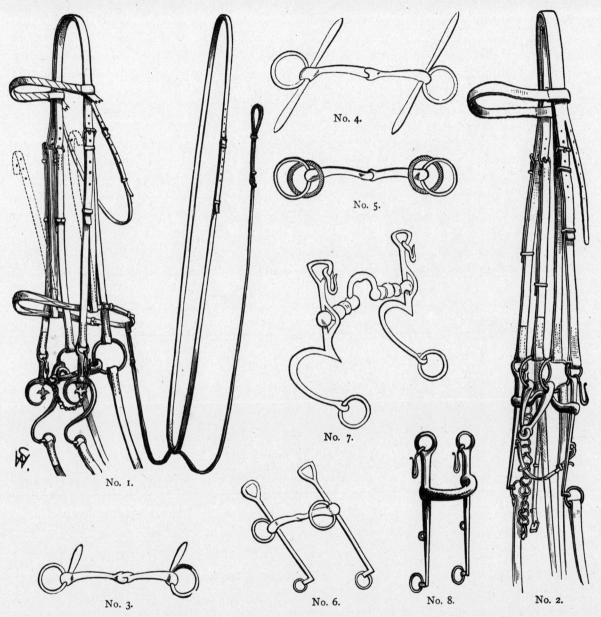

No. 1. Park Double Bridle, with Detached Noseband and Standing Martingale.   No. 2. Hunting Double Bridle.   No. 3. Half-horn Snaffle, best for Hunting Bridle.   No. 4. Plain Snaffle.   No. 5. Ring Snaffle.   No. 6. Plain-jointed Pelham.   No. 7. Hanoverian Pelham.   No. 8. Variation of Curb Bit.

seen it on young horses ridden by Irish gentlemen in the hunting fields. It is a good form for use in exercising horses that a plain snaffle will not hold, because a heavy-handed groom cannot spoil a horse's mouth so much with any kind of snaffle as with a curb-bit. The other form is the gag-bit, which is used particularly in hunting with horses that bore and snatch at the bit. It slides on a round cheek rein, and would pull a horse's mouth, if he resisted long enough (up to his eyes as they say). It is always used with another plain snaffle, forming a double bridle, and is of value in the early training of young horses.

The better the horseman the less dependent he is on the shape of his bits.

THE CURB-BIT.

The ordinary form of curb-bit consists of two cheeks and a mouthpiece, with a curve in the centre called the *port*, and a chain—the curb-chain—attached to the cheeks in such a manner that when the curb reins are pulled it acts and presses the chin of the horse. See below.

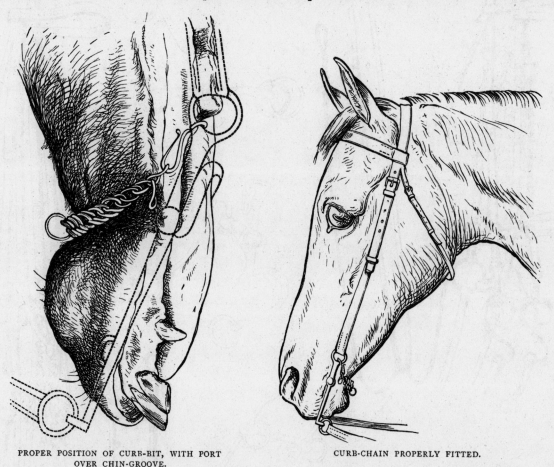

PROPER POSITION OF CURB-BIT, WITH PORT
OVER CHIN-GROOVE.

CURB-CHAIN PROPERLY FITTED.

There are a variety of shapes for curb-bits, the Chifney being the most powerful, and requiring delicate hands not to misuse; the Hanoverian, which has several joints in the mouthpiece; the *bit à pompe*, most commonly fitted to harness bridles, but not necessarily, in which there are no ports, but, to give room and play for the tongue, the mouthpiece rises and falls on the cheeks.

The very high ports of bits intended to hold a pulling horse are abominations; a port should only be used to give room for the tongue, and for no other purpose. The best double bridle for ordinary use is composed of a curb-bit of the Dwyer pattern (see next page), and a snaffle bit like No. 1 and No. 2. But I prefer the snaffle used in hunting to have half horns like No. 3, so that in a flurry there is less chance of the bit and snaffle being drawn through the horse's mouth. In all the curb bits on p. 307 the cheeks copied from common bits are too long.

Riders of park hacks of perfect manners often use only a single curb-bit, called a "hard and sharp;" others a Pelham in which one bit with cheeks and two sets of reins is supposed to combine the advantages of a double bridle.

The Pelham may either be in the shape of No. 6 or of No. 7, with curb-chain attached, and although it is difficult to see how a mouthpiece *with a joint* can press a horse's chin and act as a curb, in practice it is found that light-mouthed horses do bend to the pulling of the curb-rein after being ridden on the snaffle. As to the value of the Pelham, which I myself only use to horses with good snaffle-bridle mouths,

"Who shall decide when doctors disagree,
And soundest casuists doubt, like you and me."

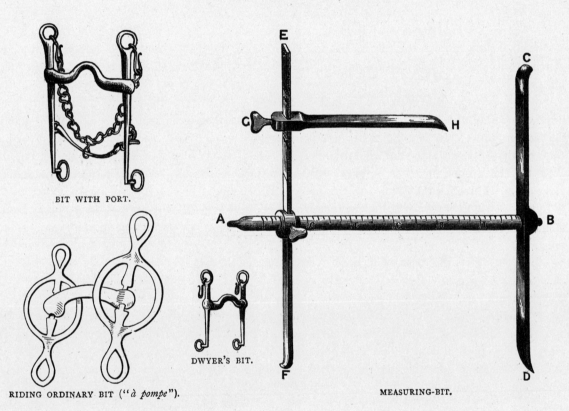

BIT WITH PORT.

RIDING ORDINARY BIT ("*à pompe*").

DWYER'S BIT.

MEASURING-BIT.

Major Whyte-Melville recommends the Pelham, which is much used in Irish hunting fields; Mr. George Nevile utterly condemns it.

ON BITTING A HORSE.

One of the most common expressions in speaking of horses is to say that such a one has a hard mouth. It is true that the mouths of some horses are rendered callous on one or both sides from the improper use of the halter, used as a bridle when colts, or the abuse of a bit while being broken, or after being broken; but what is called a hard mouth is as often as not the result of an improper application of a bit that does not fit the horse, a difficulty which may be removed by changing it.

The whole question of mouths, bits, and bridles, has been the subject of serious scientific investigation, accompanied by experiments on thousands of horses by several distinguished cavalry officers of the Austrian army. The result of their investigations has been rendered into

English in the small book already quoted, by Major Dwyer. The following passages abridged or paraphrased from the Major's work equally apply to the bridles of riding or driving horses:—

"On looking into a horse's mouth it will be seen that the lower jaw consists of two flat, irregularly-triangular cheek-bones, whose anterior branches form the channel in which the tongue lies, enclosed towards the root, between the two rows of molar (grinder) teeth, further by those portions of the jaw or gums that lie between the point where the grinder teeth cease, and the incisors (cutting teeth) commence, which is known generally as *the bars*, that is, the gums; on the lower portion of *the bars* the *tusks* are to be found in male animals.

"It is of the utmost importance that the curb-bit should be laid on the proper point of the *bars*, where alone it can have the most effect, and do no harm. (See illustration at page 308.)

"There is a military rule of thumb for placing the *bit* (as distinguished from the snaffle) at a certain height above the tusks, but as mares have no tusks this is an imperfect rule, not worth attending to, when Nature has provided an infallible mark for showing where the curb-bit should be placed."

"The lower surface of the lower jaw is covered with a very thick skin, underneath which lie the roots of the beard, fat, and membrane. This structure is continued up into a certain depression under the chin, called by the Germans the *curb-groove*: the bone beneath the thick skin of the *chin-groove* is flat, and rounded off in all directions." A flat curb-chain, not too wide for the groove, may be applied, by the action of the bit, with a sufficient amount of pressure to control, without hurting the horse. If the bit is placed in the mouth exactly over or opposite the chin-groove, and a curb-chain is linked to it at a proper length, the instrument will infallibly fit into its proper place, to be acted on by the action of the hands on the reins.

But to make the best of a horse's mouth, it is absolutely necessary that a point should be attended to which is almost universally overlooked in this country—*i.e.*, the bit should fit the horse's mouth.

"There are three dimensions of the interior of a horse's mouth, which should be accurately ascertained before attempting to fit him with a proper bit, in addition to the size of the tongue, if a port is used. The first and most important is *the width of the mouth* from side to side, measured opposite the chin-groove, including the thickness of the lips. *If that is too narrow*, the lips are liable to injury, or to be squeezed up so as to cover the bars, and thus neutralise the action of the instrument. If too wide, the bit slips from side to side, displaces *the port* from its proper position, and renders it impossible to accurately fix the length of the curb-chain."

"The *port* is the arched portion of a curb-bit, intended to make the pressure rest on the bars instead of partly on the tongue.

"The second measurement is of the *width of the channel in which the tongue lies*, in order to settle the proper width of the port, the remainder having to be reserved for the bars.

"The third dimension is *the height of the bars*, that is, the distance between the surface of the bars, naked gums, and the undermost point of the chin-groove."

All this sounds at first very complicated, and these measurements are only necessary when a valuable horse presents difficulties in the way of fitting him with a bit; but the principal of these measurements have been brought to the following averages by the experiments of Colonel Von Weyrother with a simple instrument (see the illustration on p. 309, half the original size), by which the operation of measuring is easily performed.

This "mouth-gauge"* is made of steel, and consists of a bar, A B (about six inches long will suffice), fitted on one side, at right angles, with a fixed cheekpiece, C D, of the form shown by the figure, and having on the other side a sliding cheekpiece, E F, of the same shape and dimensions (six inches long), fitted with a screw for fixing it where required. This bar A B is made oval in the transverse section, with the greater axis about one inch, in order to displace the lips nearly as the mouthpiece does, and is usually graduated throughout; but it will evidently suffice to do this with the fourth and fifth inches.

If this gauge be placed in the horse's mouth like a bit, with the bar A B at exactly the proper point (opposite the chin-groove), the fixed cheekpiece C D being then held gently up to the off side of the mouth (the operator facing the horse's forehead), the sliding one, E F, may be shoved up just close enough to the cheek, at the near side, not to displace the lips; and then fixing it with the screw, and removing the gauge, we can read off the dimensions of the width of our mouthpiece from the scale engraved on A B.

The figure shows further a rod, G H, fitted to slide up and down the movable cheekpiece, E F, which is graduated into inches and eighths or tenths on its lower limb. This contrivance enables us to measure the height of the bar of the mouth, which is done in the following manner :—The instrument, adjusted to the proper width of the horse's mouth, is placed as before, with the bar, *a b*, opposite the chin-groove, but *underneath the tongue*, and is then wheeled round on its own axis till the upper limbs of the cheekpieces stand nearly perpendicular to the general line of the horse's nose. This, of course, brings its lower limbs in the opposite direction towards the neck, and the rod G H is then gently shoved up till it presses lightly into the chin-groove, taking care that the gauge stands square, and that the mouthpiece lies equally on both bars of the mouth. The rod G H is then screwed fast, whilst the screw of the cheekpiece, E F, is loosened altogether, so that the latter may be removed without disturbing the rod G H. We then read off the height of the bar on the lower limb of E F, and have all the necessary dimensions.

"*The average height of the bars of a horse's mouth is* 1¾ *inches ; the upper cheek of horses under* 18 *hands, need not be longer. This gives* 3½ *inches for the lower one, and a total of* 5¼, *measured from where the curb-hook rests in the upper ring to where the lower ring plays in its socket.*

"For ponies these dimensions must be reduced to 1½ inches upper cheek, 3 inches lower cheek. The curb-chain and two hooks must be once and a half the width of the horse's mouth.

"One-quarter or even an eighth of an inch higher or lower in the mouth makes all the difference between right and wrong ; therefore the headstall or cheekpieces must be provided with the needful buckles, if the bridle is to be used for more than one horse with a curb-bit.

"The first grand rule is, that in all cases the mouthpiece must be exactly so wide that when placed in the mouth it fits close to the outer surface of the lips, without either pressing on them or being subject to be displaced laterally.

"*An extensive examination has shown that the width of the mouths of horses from* 15.1 *to* 15.3 *averages four inches, a few very large ones went up to four inches and a half, while very small light horses did not exceed three inches and three quarters. The maximum width of the port of a bit should be about one and one-third inches, an important matter, because if the mouthpiece is*

---

* This, and all Major Dwyer's tackle, have, at my request, been taken up by Messrs. White and Coleman, of Bishopsgate Street, London.

of the right width, and the port is wider than the channel in which the tongue lies, its corners will come on the bars of the horse's mouth, and cause intolerable pain; if a bit with a port is too wide, every pull of the reins will bring its angles into painful contact with the bars of the mouth.

"*Light bits, accurately fitted*, are more to be relied on than the most atrocious instruments of torture ever invented.

"It is a great fault when a curb-bit comes out in a straight line with the reins; it is then not so useful as a plain snaffle. It may arise from the curb-chain being too long, or the upper cheek too short, or the lower cheek, proportionately to the upper cheek, too long. The result is that the lever action is lost. The curb-chain does not pinch the horse's chin, or press the bit against the bars of the mouth.

"The next greatest fault is when the bit stands stiff in the horse's mouth, which will arise from the curb being too tight, for then the slightest pull of the curb-rein puts the horse in pain, or the upper bar too long—the latter always produces a third fault—the rising of the curb-chain out of the chin-groove; hence sore chins and restive horses.

"Horses, from bad bitting, sometimes acquire the habit of getting their tongues over the mouthpiece, a trick which renders the whole action of the curb-bit uncertain. Old horses are generally incurable; with young horses the best plan is to ride or drive them for some time with the snaffle, and then carefully fit them with a bit.

"The cheek may be curved and shaped into any fashion that pleases the eye, so long as it is of the proper length. The lower portion of the cheek should never exceed in length exactly the double of the upper portion. Even when the reins are habitually fastened into a ring below the cheek, still the weight of the projecting arm must affect the leverage of the whole instrument."

But the experience of very competent observers in this country has shown that these Dwyer bits, with maximum cheeks of five inches, are not sufficiently powerful to control English horses which have already acquired bad habits as runaways or violent pullers, that they are the bits with which colts should be trained to the use of the curb there can be no doubt, and for average horses they are, when accurately fitted, superior to the ordinary curb-bits.

But when a horse cannot be driven in a snaffle, or controlled by a curb-bit of something like the dimensions of the "Dwyer," the better plan is to adopt a Chifney bit. The lower arm of the cheek of a Chifney is separate from the upper arm, and is not therefore affected by its length. When the curb-chain is properly fitted, it is perfectly easy until the horse pulls, then the leverage is so powerful that if a knife were substituted for a chain it would cut clean through the lower jaw. But for this very reason a Chifney curb in a double bridle must only be used with a delicate hand on emergencies to let a horse know that you are his master.

THE CURB-CHAIN.

The best-fitting bit, even when placed in its proper place, will not work unless the curb is of the proper make and length. The curb, whether single or double, should work quite flat when twisted up to its fullest extent without overtwisting. It should be as broad as it can be made without being too broad for the chin groove, which it must not quite fill. If it is too broad, there is always danger of the upper edge rubbing against the bone of the chin. The hooks for attaching it should be the same on both sides of the bit.

It cannot be too often repeated that good bitting gives control without pain. A bit that gives pain should never be used ; or rather, one that produces pain which the horse cannot cause to cease by dropping his head to the right position and yielding. A tight curb-chain and powerful bit make the horse poke out his chin ; and then an ignorant person pulls harder, tightens the curb, and resorts to a bit still more severe.

TO BRIDLE A HORSE.

"To put a bridle on a new horse :—First, fit the head-stall to the horse's head, taking care that neither the forehead-band nor throat-band is too tight ; then, by the buckles, fit the snaffle-rein so that it falls a quarter of an inch below the angle of the mouth ; then fit the curb-bit, so that the mouth-piece shall rest on the bars of the mouth, exactly opposite the chin-groove ; if some irregular disposition of the tusks should render this impossible, it must be moved only just so much higher up as is absolutely necessary to clear the obstacle. The curb may then be hooked, first at the off side, leaving one reserve link, and then at the near side, where it should be long enough to leave two links, taking care that it lies flat on the chin-groove, without the slightest tendency to mount upwards when the reins are drawn.

"There should always be room for the first and second fingers (of an average-sized hand) to pass flat between the chain and the chin ; if, on gently pulling the reins with the left hand whilst the two fingers are so placed, a pinching action takes place, the chain is too tight."

NOSE-BANDS AND MARTINGALES.

Nose-bands form part of bridles either for use or ornament ; as to the latter they diminish the apparent length of a horse's head. They should always be attached to separate cheeks and not to the cheeks of the curb when used with a double bridle (see No. 1, p. 307). If a horse opens his mouth a snaffle has very little power over him. In such cases a nose-band buckled just where the bone of the head ceases and the fleshy muzzle commences will have a considerable effect.

A very ingenious nose-band, an improvement on the Bucephalus for stopping violent pullers, has been perfected by Mr. Souter, saddler, of the Haymarket, on the suggestion of Mr. Edmund Tattersall. Mr. Souter was a hard rider to hounds, and therefore a practical man. But as the Bucephalus acts by compressing the nostrils, and therefore diminishing the breathing powers of a galloping and perhaps half-mad horse, it is a very dangerous instrument except in the hands of first-class horsemen.

A nose-band is also required in order to use a cavesson or standing martingale. There are a host of theoretical reasons against the use of a cavesson or martingale of any kind. A well-shaped, well-broken horse of perfectly placid temper, never disturbed even by too many beans and not enough exercise, needs no martingale. But how about those capital horses that get "above themselves," after a very little idleness, or those capital movers and jumpers with slack ewe necks and the head put on the wrong way?

Sir Tatton Sykes said once when he replaced a complicated bridle and martingale with a simple snaffle on a horse he was about to ride in a race, "my hands are my martingale." But then Sir Tatton was as a horseman one in a thousand, six feet high, all bone and muscle, and always on horseback.

But few horsemen are like Sir Tatton in either skill, experience, or training, and horses are not all well shaped or perfectly broken, therefore I entirely agree with the maxim of a horseman, "that when you have a martingale on you are master of your horse, but when you have not (if he chooses) he is master of you," "and for this reason I should always ride a young horse or a strange horse with a martingale until I know that he will go without one."

A REARING BIT.

The cavesson standing martingale must be very carefully fitted; if too loose it is useless; if too tight it will needlessly impede the action, and even throw a good horse down.

Where a horse, especially a lady's, is inclined to bounce about and even rear when fresh, instead of the nose-band the cavesson rein may be attached to a round ring bit, to which, substituting it for curb or snaffle, reins may be attached. In this way using the rearing bit as a curb bit I rode with safety and pleasure a thoroughbred mare that had previously given me more than once a black eye and a swelled nose by suddenly throwing up her neck and head while standing still, without any provocation.

The martingale in ordinary use for hunting and road riding has two reins with rings at each end, which are attached when used either to the snaffle or curb reins. This martingale must not be used without the precaution of either having the rings so small that they can by no possibility pass over the reins of the bit (and in this case the riding reins must be sewed, not buckled on), or stops must be used, leather being the best, of a pattern familiar to all saddlers.

Let me repeat that it is of the utmost importance that every man or woman, boy or girl, beginning to ride, should learn, down to the minutest detail, how a horse is to be properly saddled and bridled.

CHAPTER XV.

HINTS TO "AMAZONES."

Horse Exercise for Women Invaluable—Women as a rule ride badly—Why?—Not Sufficient Practice or Instruction Seldom Hear the Truth—Some Never Learn How to Sit; or How to Guide—Some Sit Fast and Inelegantly—Qualifications Essential—Physically Fit—In Active Condition—Wear a Suitable Dress—Have a Proper Saddle—A Trained Horse—A Competent Teacher—Preparatory Physical Training Sketched—Dress Described in Detail—Boots—Chemise—Trousers—Corset—Head-dress—How to Hold the Habit—The Side-saddle, with Illustration—Dimensions of Side-saddle—Description of Third Pommel—Stirrup-leather, both Patterns—Princess of Wales's Pattern of Side-Saddle, Illustration—Girths Important—Crupper, when Useful—The Horse—Important Points of—Height to be in Proportion to that of Rider—Paces—Queen Victoria's Opinion of a Lady's Horse—Temperament—Age—Mounting: First Position, Illustration; Second Position; Third Position; Fourth Position, and Descriptions—Common Errors—Fifth (Bad) Position—Riding Boldly and Badly—Reins, Management of—Requires Manual and Verbal Explanations—Illustration, Reins in Both Hands; see also Coloured Picture for Seat and Reins—Trotting, Illustration—Cantering—Galloping—Necessary—How to—Proper Preparation—Leaping—Every *Amazone* should Learn How—"Vieille Moustache's" Instruction for Water-Jump—Importance of Exercise for a Lady's Horse—A Lady's Hunter, Illustration—Etiquette of Gentleman Riding with Lady—Anecdote of the Duke of Wellington—Improved Leading-rein, with Illustration—Other Hints—Treat your Horse as a Friend—Observe if he is uncomfortable—How to Mount without Assistance.

HORSE exercise, for women who are fit for it, is a healthy, innocent, and social amusement; when performed in perfection it is also an outward and unmistakable sign of wealth if not of position. It is not, therefore, necessary to write a long chapter to recommend the equestrian art to the attention of the mothers and daughters of England. Whatever prejudices may have existed against equestrianism for women in the minds of the manufacturing middle class before 1830—that year of social as well as political revolution—have long since disappeared.

In Hyde Park a hundred riding-habits are to be seen where there was not one before the date of Earl Russell's Reform Bill—so Lord Vivian, a very competent witness, told a Committee of the House of Lords. At every English watering-place the mob of *amazones*, ill-dressed and well, moderately and execrably horsed, is quite appalling to the observer who does not enjoy the ignorance which is bliss.

"Not to put too fine a point upon it," the majority of horsewomen—or, to adopt the more convenient word, *amazones*—ride abominably; so badly that it must be presumed, looking at the rarity of accidents, that they enjoy the benefit of the special providence said to preside over the lives of idiots and drunkards. Perhaps the secret of their immunity is to be found in the hard-worked character of the horses they generally ride, or the watchful care of attendant grooms or friends.

The reason why women ride so badly is not far to seek. A man may learn to ride by tumbling off until he learns how to hold on, and by imitating the good horsemen he meets in his rides, friends or strangers; because a man's is a natural seat; elegance is not indispensable; and last, though not least, he has ten times the opportunity of practice that any woman living in a civilised country can possibly enjoy. A young man can ride any horse, in any dress, with or without a saddle, in town or country; without losing social position, he may make friends with all the grooms and horse-jockeys of the neighbourhood; in fact, he "may range the roads, the farms, the fields." Without being guilty of eccentricity, he can risk his bones on any horse that others have ridden, and be his own groom if no assistance is to be had.

If the raw man-rider makes himself particularly ridiculous, he is sure to receive candid criticism from passing strangers; whilst those of his friends and acquaintances who are versed in the art he is acquiring, either out of good-fellowship or to display their superior knowledge, are only too glad to give him the benefit of serious advice or sarcastic chaff.

With women, commencing to ride is a serious business, requiring a competent teacher, a special dress, a special saddle, and, for safety and symmetry, a horse specially trained for the purpose.

The time and fuss required to set a riding party in motion when only two or three ladies have to be fitted to strange horses and strange saddles, even if they are all practised horse-women, is terribly exhaustive of the patience of those who are past the age of indiscriminate admiration; and when any of the fair equestrians are only half taught and timid, each will require, if particularly pretty and coquettish, the assistance of two grooms and at least two gentlemen during the operation of mounting.

Few riding-masters who have their bread to earn, and still fewer gentlemen, care to ruffle the plumes of a charming novice, unaccustomed to contradiction of any kind, by once, twice, or thrice telling her that she does not understand or does not follow the rules requisite to form a real horse-woman. A severely truthful tutor runs the risk of being considered impertinent if a paid teacher, and a "tiresome bore" if an admirer.

The consequence is that you see amongst the fair would-be *amazones*, who have the power of acquiring every accomplishment money can buy, frightful examples of some one of every kind of inelegant or dangerous habit. A maker of side-saddles, whose high reputation enables him to speak the truth, informs me that he has offended many fair heavy-weight customers by saying plainly, "Your horse's sore back has nothing to do with the fit of my saddle; he will always have a sore back as long as you sit on one side and hang on the pommels."

Some ladies never take the trouble to learn how to guide a horse. For years they ride daily, but they ride placid steeds, accompanied by some mounted man, who looks after them just as a nurse looks after a child when it begins to run alone. Rotten Row in the season is full of horsewomen who would not ride a strange horse alone over a strange road for any consideration.

Others acquire a really strong seat, ride hard to hounds, handle the reins with more or less skill, but present an appearance painful to contemplate. Amongst such may be counted the daughters of hard-riding hunter-breeding farmers, as well as ladies of fortune who never hear the jokes of their flatterers or see the caricatures that are handed round when they have left the room.

Every one flatters the latter, and the former too if they are good-looking; so they continue to ride at and over everything, until a severe fall or serious domestic duties put an end to exhibitions equally absurd and alarming to those who really know how, when, and where women ought to ride.

The best horsewomen are found amongst professional *amazones*, who have gone through a regular course of instruction under teachers who as likely as not enforced their precepts with an occasional flick of a riding-whip; and amongst ladies of high position, in whose families saddle-horses of every kind in the stable are as much a matter of course as silver forks on the dining-table, whose natural taste for equestrianism has been cultivated as regularly and carefully as all the other accomplishments of a wealthy and well-born dame, who has in a tribe of sisters, aunts, and cousins, relations and friends, models of excellence and elegance. A few years ago two wives of earls and three daughters of an earl—some of them mothers of families and welter weights, some of them young and feather weights—were equally remarkable for their grace in the Park and their skill in the hunting-field. To mention their names would be an impertinence, and contrary to the plan of this book.

Therefore young ladies who cherish the in every respect praiseworthy desire to enjoy the delicious and healthy excitement of horse exercise, and thus to be able to take part in one of the pleasures of their fathers, brothers, lovers, husbands, and friends, will do well to master the following essentials for safe and elegant equestrianism:—

First, they must be physically fit for the exercise, as to lungs, heart, and, above all nerves.

The girl who is afraid of the common objects of the farm and field, who screams on the slightest possible excuse, who flies from a peaceful milch cow, and trembles at a mouse, is not fit to mount a horse, that is, if her terrors are real. They may be either a foolish imitation of other silly women, or one of several small expedients for exciting interest in the male breast. In the former case, a course of cold bathing and a few timely words from a sensible and good-natured woman would probably effect a cure.

A month of hydropathy, at one of those great establishments which the majority of patients frequent rather for amusement than to cure any serious disease, is not a bad preparation for equestrian lessons.

Secondly, the intending pupils should be in fair condition—able to dance all night, and play at all games from battledore to lawn tennis, without inordinate fatigue—that is, unless they are prepared to be content, as invalids must be, with walking exercise on a softly-stepping little horse.

Thirdly, they must wear a suitable attire, from the chemise to the riding-habit.

Fourthly, they must be fitted with a saddle.

Fifthly, they must have a horse perfectly trained for a lady's use, and suitable in size, quality, and temperament, to the work and the rider.

Sixthly, when provided with the horse and appliances, the pupil aspiring to become a capable and elegant horsewoman can do nothing without a competent teacher—one who will insist on attention to details apparently insignificant: on that steady practice of walking before cantering, cantering in many forms before trotting, and trotting with ease and certainty before galloping, which are the successive steps of the equestrian art.

The born and skilled horsewoman has, it must be admitted, two advantages over men. She relies for ruling her horses on skill rather than on brute strength; and possesses a mysterious influence over very high-couraged animals, as if, in mesmeric *argot*, she had the power of placing herself *en rapport* with steeds that obstinately resist the strength and skill of the coarser sex.

As to the age at which women should commence to ride, it is by no means necessary, in order to acquire the highest skill, with natural aptitude for equestrianism, that they should commence practice in their childhood; although, if judiciously taught, a well-grown girl may advantageously take her first lesson at ten years old. Some of the finest professional horse-women, well known in Rotten Row and the hunting shires in 1860, did not take their first lessons until they were over eighteen years of age; and our Indian Empire affords many

THE PARK CANTER.

examples of strong and graceful horsewomen whose first lessons were taken at the cavalry stations of the Indian army after marriage.

In dealing one by one with these six conditions for training a young *amazone*, it may be assumed that a girl who is constitutionally timid and nervous when in an average state of health should never be permitted to mount on horseback at all.

As to the preparatory physical training which is required for those young ladies who have not had the advantage of the athletic out-door exercises which are open to their sex, their best preparation will be found in the gymnastics referred to at page 273 as likely to be of use to adult men pupils.

The recommendation of preparatory exercises for male applies with tenfold force to female pupils. In Madame Brenner's book, already quoted, a series of exercises are described, fitted to the physical capacities of mere infants and of full-grown girls, which it is not necessary to repeat in detail; but the following extracts, giving a good idea of the principles on which this physical training is conducted, are due to the importance of the subject :—

"The first exercise is with the elastic india-rubber chest-expander.

"The movements in connection with the chest-expander are always necessary. They may be likened to the scale practice of the pianoforte. They should never be neglected, but should stand at the beginning of each morning's work.

"No pupil can with comfort or success engage in exercises more elaborate and more complicated, *until the body and limbs, by being progressively warmed and relaxed, are rendered pliable.*"

The length of time during which this exercise should be practised must depend on the constitution of the pupil. "Ten minutes is the extreme limit; but no exercise should be carried on to the point of fatigue. At first the chest-expander exercise should be only used once a week; in the second or third week, twice a week; and so on increasingly, until limbs and joints gain the suppleness desired, which enables the pupil to perform this and other exercises not only without fatigue, but with freedom and pleasure." "I watch," says Madame Brenner, "the faces of those I instruct, and whenever I notice an expression of weariness in the features, I direct the pupil to desist."

This is a bit of sound advice, which teachers of equestrianism, professional or amateur, would do well to bear in mind. Too often the pupil or the pupil's parent is inclined to insist on the full hour's lesson for which she has paid.

In treating of another series of exercises, the same writer lays down, in the following passage, *the principles* which it is the aim of an equestrian teacher to impart, and which can evidently be best imparted by preparing delicate girls for horse exercise by suitable gymnastic exercises :—

"The special advantage of the wand exercise is found in the vigorous and healthy *action of the muscles connected with the chest, arms, and shoulders;* there comes from it that compelled steadiness of the lower limbs which is so important a feature in the physical education of women."

In the same line, exercises with dumb-bells, "weighing not more than from five ounces to twenty-one ounces the pair," *strengthen the muscles of the back as well as of the arms. Throwing the whole of the upper frame into healthy and exhilarating movement, it is one of the best aids to round the arms and develop the chest.* "From its compulsory detail of a firm position of the lower half of the body while the upper half is actively employed, this exercise compels, in a remarkable degree, that steadiness and equal balance of frame which it is the business of gymnastics (read horse exercise) to induce."

The special use of certain of these exercises is summarised as follows :—

"1st. Steadiness of body in certain difficult positions, under the muscular exertions of both sets of limbs. 2nd. Graceful movements. Gymnastics (read horse exercise) should play into the hands of health. Exercise should be no fatigue, for fatigue is more or less a strain on the constitution. The every-day movements of life in the case of the gymnastic (trained) pupil require less exertion than those of the unskilled and untrained. There is plenty of vigour to spare. Thus prepared, the pupils of the riding-school will advance by easy steps ; and such ejaculations and expressions as 'Oh dear, I am tired to death !' 'I am so stiff I cannot move !' 'That ride has killed me !' will not be heard."

It must be borne in mind that gymnastics bring into play muscles not actively employed in walking, and horse exercise muscles not called into action in either walking or gymnastics ; hence the necessity for short and frequent lessons.

HOW TO DRESS THE "AMAZONE."

If expense is a matter of no consequence, the easiest way of obtaining a suitable costume for horse exercise is to go to the best and most expensive tradesmen. But ladies have to ride who do not live in London or Paris, and to whom economy is an object ; hence the following notes, directed rather to the principles than the details of dress :—

When a young lady undertakes to ride in earnest, she must discard every article of her previous attire, except her stockings, and re-clothe herself from head to foot.

The ordinary fashionable boot, with its narrow waist and high heel, will not do at all. The foot she puts into the stirrup must feel the stirrup, and be capable when she is mounted of comfortably supporting her whole weight. The sole of the boot must, therefore, be perfectly flat, as broad as the foot, long enough not to cramp the toes, but not extravagantly long. The heel must not be more than half an inch thick, and long enough to cover the natural heel, so as to catch and keep the stirrup in its proper place.

Riding-boots must be by no means tight, unless the lady prefers cold feet in winter. It is pretty well understood now that a well-proportioned boot will make a foot look much smaller than a tight one.

The most comfortable style of boot for riding long distances is the Wellington, or cavalry boot, which protects the calf of the leg from friction against the saddle. The upper-leather of the feet should be of kid, the leg of morocco or buckskin. The drawback of this kind of boot is that it hides the symmetry of the ankle, and that, if not made to fit easily, it necessitates the dreadful picture of a lady with a pair of boot-hooks struggling into a pair of tight boots, and out of them with a boot-jack after a long ride.

The best form for ladies' use, under all circumstances, is that of the boot which came into fashion for a short time, with short costumes and long walking-sticks, at Biarritz. This boot comes up to the middle of the calf of the leg, and should be laced up in front, not buttoned. Buttons do not answer at all for riding, and elastic sides have many disadvantages. It is made with the leg of either cloth or leather ; if cloth, the colour to match the riding habit, the foot of kid or patent leather, the sole flat, exactly like the sole of a man's hunting boot with the same long low heel. But if a lady determines to adhere to a short *bottine* for mere park exercise, she must give up the fashionable, narrow-waisted, peg-heeled shape, and adopt a boot that will allow her to place her foot flat in the stirrup.

The advantage of the "Magyar," or, as some call it, from the name of the dance, the

"Cracovienne" boot, is that, while it protects the leg and affords a sensible support to the ankle, it is put on and taken off by unlacing, without an ungraceful struggle.

Cold feet are one of the acute miseries of long winter rides. The first condition for securing warm feet is to have them warm from exercise or friction before starting; the next, to wear warm hose. Canadian experience has proved that one pair of silk socks, supplemented by a pair of woollen stockings, preserve more warmth than any one pair of stockings, however thick. Tight gartering will produce cold, as well as tight boots. If socks could be worn with tight silk or woollen drawers, according to the season, garters could be dispensed with; but this suggestion pries almost too closely into the mysteries of female attire.

The feminine chemise (old as old Egypt), flowing to the ground, with short sleeves, must be dismissed in favour of a garment fashioned on the principles of the masculine shirt—that is, with a collar round the neck, long sleeves with cuffs descending over the wrists, a front that may be displayed when the jacket is unbuttoned, and skirts or tails so short as not to make unsightly lumps or inconvenient wrinkles on the drawers.

Drawers should be elastic and tight; in fact, very like those men wear.

Trousers are, as a rule, fastened by a belt to the waist, and strapped under the boots, if Wellingtons are worn; but if long-laced boots are worn a sort of full-flowing knickerbockers or breeches going into the boot would be more sensible. If the habit is of a dark colour, the trousers may be of black chamois leather, strapped with cloth below the knee; but if the habit is made of light tweed, or any shade of linen or other summer material, then the trousers should be as nearly as possible of the same material and shade of colour. White trousers or petticoats are altogether inadmissible under a riding-habit of any colour, except one of white linen, which, braided with coloured worsted, is sometimes worn in summers of tropical heat.

To argue with those infatuated females who superstitiously believe that men's eyes are charmed and that men's hearts are won by a waist resembling as nearly as possible the form of a wasp or an hour-glass, would be a waste of time. No number of surgical cases would convince them that to compress the stomach, the bowels, the heart, the lungs, the liver, within the limits of a corset several sizes too small is, sooner or later, equally fatal to health and to beauty. But of one fact in regard to equestrianism they may easily convince themselves—namely, that as the elegance of a woman on horseback depends entirely on the flexibility of her figure, no woman can ever ride well enough to be worth looking at off a walk, unless she is contented with a corset that will support the body without compressing the vital internal organs. If she cannot lace her own boots and put up her back hair, she may give up the idea of becoming a horsewoman, or anything better than a stuffed doll on horseback. A woman who means to ride well can neither afford to cramp her muscles nor to impede the circulation of her blood.

Modern staymakers thoroughly understand the proper proportions of riding-corsets, which, like many other articles of dress, have been immensely improved in the direction of elasticity and comfort since the days of our grandmothers. The one golden rule to be adhered to is, that the wearer—mounting, mounted, or dismounted—must feel thoroughly comfortable, that is, with the full use of every limb and of every muscle. The French proverb, "*Il faut souffrir pour être beaux*," a favourite excuse with bootmakers and staymakers, must be reversed. The *amazone* cannot be elegant if she "suffers." In consequence of the peculiar position of the body on a side-saddle, tight-lacing invariably produces pain on the right sides, and pain and stiffness just where there ought to be "willow-like flexibility." "In dressing for a ride," said that accomplished horsewoman, Mrs. Stirling Clarke, "everything should be avoided that may cause uneasiness. Pins should not be used; every article should fit neither too tightly nor too loosely;

and all details should be seen to, so as not to require repairs and delay when the horses are at the door—no buttons wanting, no hooks or eyes to be sewed on."

In commencing to learn to ride it is not at all necessary to begin with an expensive habit or complete costume. Any sort of dark skirt, with one of the numerous patterns of yachting jackets, buttoning loosely round the figure, and any quiet-shaped straw or felt hat that will not fall off, will do for early practice. When the pupil has reached the stage for riding in public, then a complete and a correct costume, according to the fashion of the time, may be ordered. But from the first day of the first lesson, suitable boots and underclothing made on correct principles, are indispensable.

"The body of the habit," says Mrs. Stirling Clarke, "should be carefully made to fit the breast, ample room being always allowed across the chest, which expands in riding. It should be carefully cut, so as to be wide enough at the back of the neck, thus avoiding the disagreeable tightness which is a common fault in ill-made habits. The waist must not be too long, in fact; if not shorter than the bodies of most dresses it will wrinkle." The sleeves must nowhere be tight, for both arms are required to be actively used.

Youthful and slim figures look well in plain jackets fitting like a skin. Ladies who are fully developed, not to say stout, will look better in a loose jacket coming down to the saddle, cut to the shape, but not adhering to the figure.

The grand principle in ordering the jacket is to have it so easy that the wearer could in it with comfort play at any outdoor game in which ladies take part.

For winter, a riding-jacket is sometimes made exactly like a man's, with a waistcoat. An overcoat trimmed with fur, like a hussar's pelisse, is a comfortable addition in cold weather, besides having the advantage of displaying the rider's taste and luxury in one of the most genuine of female decorations—expensive fur.

As to the skirt, a lady, an authority on the subject, says, "Unless the cloth be full broadcloth width, it must have two breadths and a half in the skirt to afford an easy and graceful flow of drapery for use in riding in or near a town; a hunting skirt is a special garment."

To have the skirt too long, even for park display, is a mistake. It is always dangerous, as likely to catch the horse's feet; and in muddy weather becomes an unsightly, uncomfortable drag. For country rides, a habit need only be long enough to hang gracefully over the feet, but leather linings should be carefully avoided. In the season of 1878 the Park riders, who had almost swept the Row with their absurdly long habits, rushed into the other extreme and wore skirts so short that very often the boots were discovered. But fashions are so eccentric that I leave the paragraph against long skirts, written in 1870.

Economy is often important to a father with a number of daughters able and willing to ride; but it is no economy to go to a man not accustomed to make ladies' habits or ladies' riding-boots—these are specialities, especially the former.

As to the head-dress, there are only two rules that can be safely laid down, looking at the constant changes of fashion, from the hideous to the elegant, and from the beautiful back to the frightful, within the twenty-five years ending in 1874.

First, it should fit so as neither to fall out of place nor fall off; for a horsewoman to have to hold on her hat under any circumstances is absurd, and may be dangerous. Next, it should become the face. The chimney-pot suits some faces admirably, others not at all. The many variations of the Spanish hat, the deerstalker, &c., have the advantage of being properly completed by a plume or rosette of brilliant and appropriate colour.

Formerly something ought to have been said about dressing the hair; but as the damsels

of these days for the most part buy their tresses ready made, it would not be wise to interfere with the special province of the *coiffeur.* Good thick kid or calf-skin gloves are more
suitable for riding than dog-skin; the reins can be felt through them. Dog-skin are too hard
and too soon dirty. In winter, mits of silk or woollen, long in the wrist, with a hole for the
thumb and no fingers, go well over kid gloves; but in wet weather woollen gloves are more
comfortable than leather, and a pair should always be carried in the pocket of the side saddle
in wet weather or hunting.

Attention should be paid and some pains devoted to holding the habit gracefully when
walking. "To hold the habit properly, the skirt should first be taken at each side, as far
down as the arms will reach without stooping, drawn out evenly to its full extent, and
gathered up until sufficiently short for walking. The hands should then be brought forward,
with one rather higher than the other, so as not to appear stiff or formal. If the skirt is
made in two breadths, it should be gathered up from the seam at each side, otherwise it will
drag on the ground behind. When a lady is accompanied by a gentleman, she should hold
the habit on the side on which he is walking, so far down only as to enable her to take
his arm and clear the skirt from the ground, turning a bit of it over her thumb, to prevent its
slipping from the hand." These actions should be practised at home, and before a glass.

The following extracts from letters which appeared in *The Times* and in *The Field*, in
consequence of a letter from Captain Lovell describing how his daughter was hung by her
habit and stirrup, give very useful hints :—

"*One who hunts, and is accustomed to ride over a rough country, where one must often get
falls,*" says : "I am quite sure that the shorter and tighter ladies' habit skirts are the safer they
are ; also there should be two straps of elastic—one for the right foot and the other to go on the
heel of the left foot. By these means, if the habit be well cut, there is no possibility of the skirt
getting caught on the leaping-head. Another safety is to have the leaping-head quite close up
to the pommel round which the right leg is put. Saddle-makers are very fond of putting it low
down and making it long and curved, which prevents ladies being kicked or bucked off, but
which keeps them fixed like a vice, so that if their horse comes down they cannot get away
from him. If the pommel is small, high up, and close to the other, it ought to be quite sufficient
for a good rider, and at the same time if the horse falls it leaves you free to get away from him."

Another lady writes me : "A loop on the heel of the left foot is dangerous in hunting ; it
prevents the lady from getting her foot out of the stirrup if she has a fall."

Another lady writes :—"I think I may venture to speak with some authority on the
subject, as my sister and I have been hunting for some years in a country in which falls must
necessarily be somewhat frequent, even with the best-trained hunters. Yet I cannot recall any
instance of our ever having been, even momentarily, suspended in the manner your correspondent
describes. We attribute our escape to the following simple precautions : 1. Our habits are made
of thick cloth—thin material being sure to catch round the pommels ; the skirts are short, and
very narrow at the back, which prevents them clinging round the leaping-head. A skirt without
hem, as suggested by your correspondent, would soon be pulled out of shape, and go to pieces
with hard wear. 2. We use a man's plain stirrup, as large as is possible. There is no danger of
the foot slipping through. We ride with as long a leather as can be ; thus the foot usually
jerks out at the first shake of the horse falling, and it is very easily replaced if the animal
eventually recovers himself."

[A lady's seat has less use for the stirrup than a man's.]

"By the use of a stirrup either with a simple joint on each side, or with that of Mr. Davis which comes completely apart when the foot hangs, no accident can possibly occur. The jointed stirrup was in use by men some fifty years ago, and was discarded on account of its clumsy appearance; but, being scarcely visible under the habit, no such objection applies to its adoption by ladies."—ED. *Field*.

THE SIDE-SADDLE.

Whatever economy may be needed in other directions of the *amazone's* equipment the side-saddle must be the best of its kind; it may be perfectly plain—without a stitch of

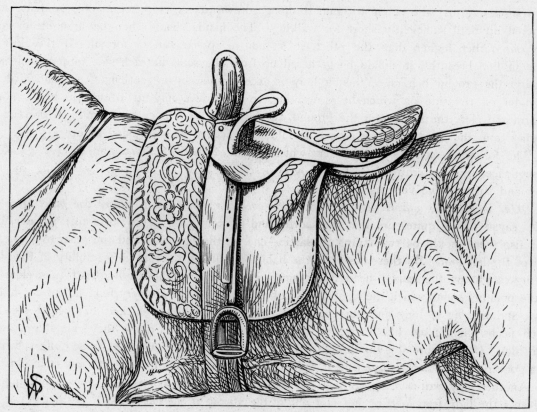

STUFFED BUCKSKIN SEAT.

ornament, but it must be of the best materials and workmanship and from a saddler who has studied the needs of the sex; above all, it must fit the horsewoman, otherwise she can never ride in comfort or security.

The legs of a moderately good horseman are as good as an additional pair of girths, astride on a man's saddle, but the security of a side-saddle must depend on fit and the girths alone, which will often have to resist very unequal strains, especially from a bad horsewoman.

Again, a man, by lengthening or shortening his stirrup-leathers, can accommodate himself to any average saddle; but a woman, if the saddle is too short, rides in constant misery, and, if the two pommels on which she depends for her grip do not suit the length and size of her limbs, she rides in constant danger.

Formerly women rode entirely by balance, deriving slight support from two pommels, one on each side, between which the right thigh was packed. Somewhere about 1830 the hunting-horn pommel was added. This addition eventually led to the reduction of the right-hand pommel by the best makers to a mere indication. This improvement gave women as strong, indeed a stronger seat than most men obtain sitting astride. It was invented by Mr. Fitzhardinge Oldacre, to enable a gentleman to ride a match for a wager on a side-saddle.

The woman's right leg grasps the upright pommel, while the knee of the left leg presses upwards against the hunting-horn. In this position, on a well-fitting saddle, it is impossible for a woman to be thrown as long as she retains her nerves.

But to obtain this advantage the saddle must be fitted to the length and dimensions of the horsewoman's limbs. The same saddle will not fit two ladies of the same height if the limbs of one be thin and the other full and round ; indeed, it is more necessary that a lady should be measured for her saddle than for her boots. Nothing can be more absurd than buying a second-hand side-saddle without seeing it, and yet ladies buy and ride on second-hand saddles, who would never dream of buying boots not made to measure. Side-saddles are generally made too short. The following is a useful table of dimensions :—

MEASUREMENT FOR A SIDE-SADDLE.

For a lady 5 feet 0 inches high. 17 inches long.	For a lady 5 feet 6 inches high, 19½ inches long.
,, , 5 ,, 2 ,, ,, 18 ,, ,,	,, ,, 5 ,, 8 ,, ,, 20 ,, ,,
,, ,, 5 ,, 4 ,, ,, 19 ,, ,,	,, ,, 5 ,, 10 ,, ,, 20½ ,, ,,

According to the latest pattern patronised by fox-hunting *amazones*, the side-saddle is built nearly flat from the front to the cantle. Buckskin seats are more expensive than plain pigskin, but are well worth the extra expense for beginners. It is easy to cover a pig-skin side-saddle with a shifting case of felt or buck-skin.

Some persons have recommended the retention of the right-hand pommel, in order that the timid horsewoman may have something to lay hold of in a moment of danger from a fresh bouncing horse ; a much better plan is to attach a sort of leather handle on the off side of the saddle, just where the hand would fall naturally when sitting upright—this may be fastened to two buckles, and removed when not required.

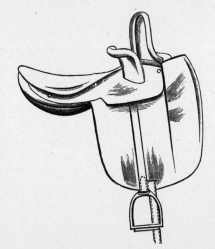

The advantage of this addition is that if a horse begins to flirt and bounce, a lady, without losing her right rein or disturbing her proper seat, can catch hold of the leather handle, and regain nerve and confidence. This *safety strap* may be made longer or shorter, according to the taste of the rider. The same buckles, when not employed for the strap, may be used to attach a waterproof coat or a sandwich case.

The hunting-horn pommel is made in two shapes—the one short, stumpy-looking ; the other curved into a large segment of a circle, and of a more elegant appearance on the saddler's stand—but, as the letter already quoted states, accomplished horsewomen agree that the latter form is no improvement, that it seriously interferes with a lady's rise in

THE PRINCESS OF WALES' PATTERN.

trotting, and would pin the rider down if a horse fell. As this pommel is not seen when a lady is mounted, its shape is of no consequence. It should be padded, so as to be as soft and elastic as possible.

"*Vieille Moustache*" (whose book * should be in the hands of every young riding-master) observes about the third pommel, it "should never be removed, as is too frequently done when the saddle is cleaned." This removing wears out the screw, and the crutch will not remain in its proper position, wobbling about to the great discomfort of the rider. "Some men say that in putting a lady on horseback it is necessary to turn the third crutch round; but for my own part I could never find any difficulty in clearing a lady's skirt when lifting her into the saddle."

On the other hand, a lady of great authority on the subject has all her saddles, which are made by one of the first houses in London, with three different holes for the hunting-horn crutch.

At any rate, whatever be the shape of the hunting-horn, let every young lady, as soon as she has completed her elementary lessons with a master, who has saddles of all dimensions, go to a competent side-saddle maker, and be as carefully measured as a man would be for a set of leather breeches.

One of the latest improvements in the hunting-horn crutch is to reverse the thread of the screw, making it turn from left to right, instead of in the usual fashion of screws from right to left. The effect of this alteration is that the pressure of the left knee fixes instead of unfixes the screw.

The seat of a side-saddle should be ample, not only for the convenience of the rider, but for the comfort of the horse. The larger the surface the greater the adherence, and the less the strain upon the girths.

The average weight of a side-saddle for a full-sized woman and horse is eighteen pounds; nothing is gained by diminishing this weight to compensate for the increased risk of that curse of the lady's horse, "a sore back." Although eight pounds are an all-important consideration in riding a race, they would not have an appreciable effect on the powers of a lady's horse in a whole day's work. Besides, there is no rule more absolute than that a lady's horse should always be equal to a stone above her weight.

The stirrup-leather of a side-saddle is attached to the saddle by an iron ring; without that spring-bar attachment which is intended to release the stirrup-leather of a man's saddle if the rider's foot should stick fast in the stirrup.

The ladies' stirrup-leather sometimes forms a girth, to which, in ignorance of mechanical principles, absurd retaining powers have been attributed.

In the latest and simplest form (patronised by a royal lady), the stirrup is sewed to a single strap, which, passing through the ring-bar, descends until it comes out within a couple of inches of the bottom of the flap, and passing round the belly of the horse, is buckled a single tongue on the other side, thus keeping both flaps of the saddle close, and dispensing with the old leather girth. By this arrangement the horsewoman can shorten or lengthen her stirrup from the right side without assistance, and without disturbing the stirrup-leg. In the course of a long ride the stirrup-leather becomes almost imperceptibly longer, in consequence of the girth of the horse diminishing as he gets rid of his food, for he is an animal of quick digestion; therefore, the lady or her attendant should remember to take up the stirrup-leather a hole after an hour or two's ride.

A stirrup-leather an inch too long often brings on a sore back for the horse; not to speak of a fall for the rider deprived of accustomed support. The quietest horses will now and then give an unexpected start, especially while returning home in the dark.

* "The Barb and the Bridle."

By way of precaution, the stirrup-leather should have three or four numbers deeply punched—in the way already described for men—into it, say the figures 1, 2, 3, an inch apart, the first number at the point which the lady considers her proper length; she will then at any halt be able to learn by feeling with the finger whether the stirrup-leather has stretched, and, if needful, can take it up a hole. If a lady rides a great deal, the leather should be cut off at the joining with the stirrup and re-sewn at the beginning of every hunting season.

Colonel Greenwood, as far back as 1839, made the following suggestion for improving ladies' stirrup-leathers, but I cannot find that any side-saddle makers have experimented on his ideas. Yet he was a great authority amongst the officers of the household cavalry and their wives and daughters.

He says: "The saddle should be kept in its place by elastic webbing girths. The leather surcingle is used to prevent the small flap on the off side from turning up, and the large flap

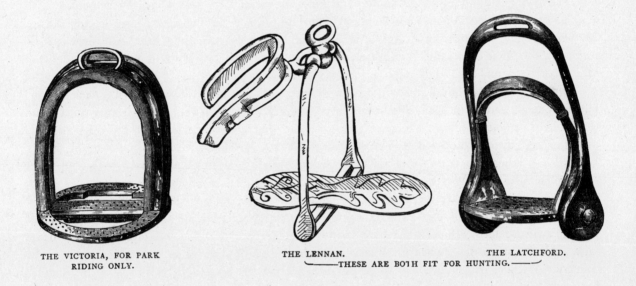

THE VICTORIA, FOR PARK RIDING ONLY.　　　THE LENNAN.　　　THE LATCHFORD.
————THESE ARE BOTH FIT FOR HUNTING.————

on the off side from being blown about with the wind, and it should only be drawn tight enough for these purposes. But the strap on the near side should not be attached to the small flap, as is customary, but to the lower part of the large flap on the near side. This will leave the small flap on the near side loose, as in a man's saddle, and will allow liberty for the use of the spring-bar. It will also lessen the friction, by rendering the side of the saddle perfectly smooth except the stirrup-leather.

"To lessen the friction, I recommend a single thin strap, as broad as the stirrup-leather of a man. It may have a buckle, for lengthening or shortening, just above the stirrup-iron; or the strap may take on and off the iron by a slip-loop, and passing over the spring-bar as usual, be fastened by a loose buckle, only attached to the strap by the tongue. For hunting, I [the Colonel] always use a single strap, sewn to the iron with a **D** above the knee, and with a double strap and buckle between the **D** and the spring-bar."

The slipper-stirrup for side-saddles has been entirely discarded since the hunting-horn crutch was adopted. Three other forms of stirrup are in common use:—First, the ordinary pattern of a man's stirrup, with the inside of the ankle protected by padding. Secondly, the invention of Mr. Latchford, the celebrated London loriner, which is a stirrup within a stirrup, and releases the foot instantaneously in case of a fall. Thirdly, the invention of Mr Lennan, of Dublin, which effects the same object in a different way (see illustrations on p. 327).

Mr. Lennan's patent is most patronised in Ireland, Liverpool, Manchester, and Cheshire; Mr. Latchford's in London and the hunting shires. It has been objected to the latter that the second stirrup works loose after a time, and is apt to be lost in the hunting-field. This might be obviated by connecting it with the fixed stirrup by a cord strong enough to hold the inner stirrup, but not strong enough to resist the rider's weight. An eminent saddler has approved of this suggestion. No lady should venture into the hunting-field without a Latchford or Lennan stirrup.

Every side-saddle should be provided with leather pannels like that recommended by Mr. Froude Bellew, used with such perfect success by one of the most brilliant horsewomen hunting in the West of England. She also uses the raw-hide girths. I hear that girths made of plaited horsehair are still more useful for side saddles.

The girths of a side-saddle and the girthing are most important points; because with a side-seat everything depends on the saddle not shifting or turning under any circumstances. If there is any difficulty in fixing a side-saddle—which is sometimes the case when it is necessary to use felt or saddle-cloths to make one fit a horse for which it was not made—the safer plan is to make all tight with a jockey's surcingle.

A man who is a fair horseman, on a well-shaped horse, may ride miles with slack girths; but a woman's saddle in such circumstances is almost sure to turn round. It is easy to assume that a lady's horse will have a perfect shape for carrying a saddle, and that the side-saddle is manufactured by one of those who make side-saddles a speciality; but, as a matter of fact, a great many ladies who ride in this country, in India, and in the Colonies, have to put up with such horses as they can get, and in such cases fashion must be sacrificed to safety.

Cruppers are completely out of fashion and out of use, except for the horses of cavalry and policemen. It is assumed that every horse that requires a crupper to keep his saddle in its place will be forthwith transferred to harness. A crupper is ugly, and often makes a horse kick. At the same time, when a horse which is required to carry a lady long journeys in the country, or India, or the Colonies, is suitable in every respect, except the form of his saddle-back and ribs under his shoulders, it may be wiser to have a crupper fitted to the side-saddle than to get rid of an animal whose paces and temper are unexceptionable.

For the same reason, the breast-plate, which is universally employed in the hunting-field, will be found a proper addition to the side-saddle of a lightly-ribbed horse in a hilly country.

Some young ladies, and many children, under medical advice, ride on the off or right-hand side. Some hard-riding hunting ladies habitually use two saddles on alternate days, one for the right and one for the left side, on the ground that it saves their hunter's legs, and makes them more certainly straight at their fences. The idea seems theoretically correct, but the examples, probably from the expense, are rare.

Her Royal Highness the Princess of Wales rides habitually on the off side, on a saddle without any ornament (p. 325) made by Messrs. Wilkinson and Kidd. Messrs. Langdon, of Duke Street, Manchester Square, have made side-saddles a speciality; and Messrs. Bligh, of Park, have a great reputation. Excellent side-saddles are made by Mr. Lennan, of Dublin, and no doubt by many provincial makers in hunting counties.

Little girls may take their first lessons on a pad like that shown at page 266, provided with shifting pommels adapted for either side.

THE BRIDLE.

A lady riding in parade form, like the illustration at page 318, in the "Row" or the "Bois," is supposed to always ride like a cavalry soldier, with one hand on the curb alone. That will assume that she only rides for display, and always rides a perfectly-broken horse. But as a matter of fact, in England, ladies, fortunately for domestic life, health, and society, do not confine their equestrian exercises to places of public resort; they ride a great deal in the country, making horse exercise a pleasure and a swift mode of conveyance on a round of social visits, "assist," as the French say, in the inspection of farms, trot along country roads, and gallop over open downs. Many ladies who do not hunt ride to cover, and in India and the Colonies no precaution should be neglected for making the most of the rough horses which they are frequently compelled to ride.

For these reasons the ordinary bridle of a lady should be a double bridle of snaffle and curb, which will enable her to use either or both reins, according to her inclination and skill. These reins should be of the length that she can shorten them by extending both arms at full length, and allow the reins to run through her hands.

THE WHIP.

A lady's whip is generally a highly-ornamented toy; but if the horse is not so broken as to act entirely independently of right-hand indications, the whip, however elegant in shape and adornments, should be of a substantial character; for it is meant to supply the place of a man's right leg, and should be fit to give, if needful, an unmistakable "indication."

A properly-made whip may be light, elegant, and yet capable of inflicting a severe cut. It should be furnished with metal loops, for reeving a silken cord, by which it may be suspended from the owner's wrist, if she has occasion to take the reins in the full grasp of a small hand.

A LADY'S HORSE.

Horses cannot be manufactured, like side-saddles. Even those prepared to pay the highest market price may have to go far and wait long before they can obtain their ideal. Average purchasers must be content to take the best article their finances and ideas of expenditure will afford, out of the limited number presented to them for choice.

In Chapter XI. will be found a description of a park hack, which might be applied to a lady's horse without altering a syllable. But such perfection is very scarce, and, when found, very expensive.

The following are points which should be carefully considered in selecting a lady's horse :—

A gelding is to be preferred to a mare, all other qualities being equal, because most mares are restive at certain seasons.

It should be well up to the weight of the intending horsewoman, allowing from eighteen to twenty-four pounds for the saddle and habit. Young ladies, if at all inclined to a luxuriant shape, are as mysterious about their weight as elderly maidens are about their age. They should be put in the scale with their riding-dress before a horse is finally decided on. At any rate, a lady's horse should be a good fourteen pounds above its rider's weight, when her habit is neither muddy nor soaked with rain.

The height of the horse should bear due proportion to the height of the rider. A lady

5 feet 8 inches high should select a horse of not less than 15 hands 3 inches, and of suitable character as to strength and substance. Although a narrow thoroughbred horse may be able to carry a lady of fourteen stone, a broad figure looks still broader mounted on a narrow horse. In the opposite direction, nothing looks worse than a short, delicate figure, mounted on a sixteen-hands weight-carrier. Weight-carrying cobs are out of place under any lady riding in London parks, unless she is very large, and riding strictly for constitutional exercise. Lord Chief Justice Denman, writing to his son-in-law after a visit to Windsor Castle, soon after

A LADY'S HUNTER.

Her Majesty came to the throne, says, "The Queen wants a horse; it must have quality; to quote Her Majesty's words, 'None of your cobs.'" Yet for country use, a blood cob with a suitable saddle is more get-at-able than a hack horse, and more handy in galloping over a farm or park.

A lady's horse must be long enough in the back to carry a side-saddle comfortably and look well. A short-backed horse, however useful under a man, never can look well in a side-saddle.

Low withers, and a neck carried like a racehorse, are altogether inadmissible either for comfort or appearance. Good shoulders, and head and neck that will bridle well, are points of the first importance. The special paces of the lady's horse are walking and cantering; if it can also trot smoothly eight miles an hour or more, the owner is fortunate.

The importance of walking well in a lady's horse cannot be exaggerated. A horse that will jog and cannot walk fast and in good form may be a useful conveyance, but is not a lady's horse. Some years ago one of the sensations of Rotten Row was a very handsome actress, past the first bloom of youth, a fine figure, a welter weight—say well on the other side of thirteen stone, for she was tall—who rode a magnificent sorrel chestnut of perfect manners. This horse and lady never within the memory of the oldest frequenter of the Row went off a walk. But what a walk!—stately, stepping out of the ground as if he were carrying an empress!

Of the canter enough has been said in a previous chapter on horsemanship. The lady's horse must trot in perfect time, with that shoulder-action that scarcely stirs the rider from the saddle. The most accomplished *amazone* on a harsh, high-trotting horse presents a repulsive figure; equally offensive is a girl jogging along beside her unmindful parent on a little shambling cob.

Temperament of the right degree—free, apparently fiery, but without a particle of violence —is an essential quality in the perfect lady's horse. A slug, requiring constant application of the whip, is detestable; equally detestable and alarming is a hot-tempered brute, always struggling, sidling, prancing, snorting for a gallop, trotting when it should canter, cantering when it should trot, never at rest for a moment. The golden mean will be found in high courage, tempered by the docility obtained by careful breaking and good sense, kept in perfect tune by regular exercise.

Men may put up with and ride down a considerable excess of high spirits and of tricks which uncorrected would grow into vice; but although a fine horsewoman subduing and settling down a rearing, kicking, plunging four-year-old, fresh from the stable, is a fine sight once in a way, that should no more be the daily duty of a lady than riding a steeplechaser or driving a tandem. A professional horsewoman is quite in her place on such an animal.

In the same direction, it is essential that a lady's horse should be free from the slightest suspicion of the unsoundness in feet and fore-legs, or those tricks of stumbling, that lead to falls. Although there are horses that go stumbling and dropping for years without falling, they are not the sort one would like to see under one's sweetheart, wife, sister, or daughter.

To summarise: The lady's horse must be elastic and easy in paces, free from all vice, a willing mover, carrying its own head, and as handsome as can be had for the limit of price.

As to age, an animal not less than six years old is to be preferred, when coltish tricks have passed away; and if still sound, springy, elastic, and high-couraged, not to be rejected, but rather to be preferred, at nine or ten years old. There are first-rate ladies' horses which number not much less than twenty years. The legs, feet, and temperament, not the teeth, are the points to be most considered in choosing a lady's horse.

But when a young horse can be found apparently possessing all the qualifications for a lady's use, either unbroken or as yet unaccustomed to the hands and the habit of a woman, it is well worth while to go to the trouble and expense of having it broken by a competent riding-master—the best of whom are to be found, *out* of London, at cavalry barracks. Three months is not an unreasonable time for the full course of instruction of a well-bred colt intended to carry a lady.

MOUNTING.

Mounting for the man, or rather the male who is not going to be a soldier, is not an important matter. The details may be deferred until substantial skill in the management of a horse has been attained; but with a woman, whose seat is purely artificial, it is of great importance that the first step should be the right step. It is literally "*le premier pas que coûte.*"

Men and boys are presumed to know something about horses in stables and the field,

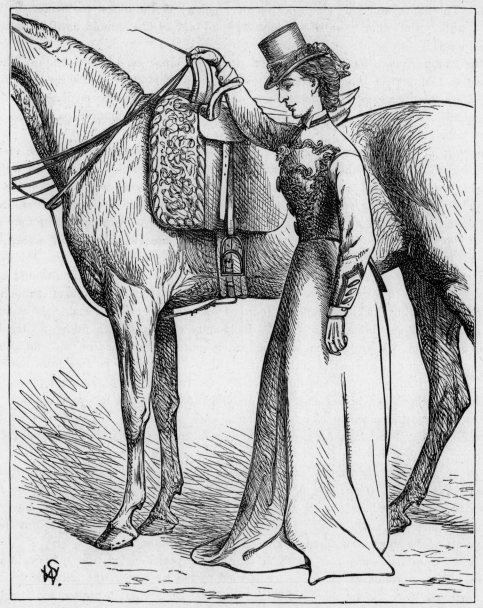

MOUNTING—FIRST POSITION.

even if they have never ridden one; but it is often decided that young girls shall learn to ride who have no more personal familiarity with the equine race than with the tame beasts of the Zoological Gardens. Hence they are not unnaturally very much alarmed when first, without previous introduction, put on the back of a great and powerful beast, whose good-tempered snorts and sneezes carry terror into their souls.

It is, therefore, to be recommended that young ladies who have not had the advantage of a preliminary "stable" education should be familiarised with horses as pets before commencing riding lessons.

SECOND POSITION.

Any jacket, and any skirt, not too long, will suffice for the first lesson; a whip is a superfluity; but the boots must be sensible boots as to soles and heels.

The illustration at page 332 represents the lady in the first act of mounting. "The right hand placed on the second pommel, with the reins placed under the hand, and drawn sufficiently tight to prevent the animal from moving forward should there be nobody holding his head;

the lady's body in a line with the saddle, and about four inches from it ; the left shoulder thrown slightly back.

"The pupil should then raise the skirt on the left side, in a line from the hip, to about the length of a walking dress, to enable her to place her left foot in the hand of the master.

THIRD POSITION.

She should bend the left knee slightly, in order to give the cue, at the same time leaning well upon the pommel with the right hand to assist the spring."

"There should be complete unity of action between pupil and master, but much depends upon the *position* of both, especially the latter. Standing well forward, he should be in a line with the lady's left hip, and bending down, should close both hands to receive the lady's left foot. The moment that he receives the cue—for example, the word 'now'—moving in exact accord with the pupil, he will, as he raises himself up to a standing position, easily place her on the saddle (see Second Position). He should then with his left hand raise the skirt above the right knee; this will prevent the skirt from dragging, and give ease and freedom to the rider.

"The lady should sit well down in the saddle, in an easy position, placing the left foot in

FINAL POSITION.

the stirrup (not home, as is generally done), with the stirrup under the ball of the foot, in the form adopted in the military style, or by a gentleman when riding a hack (see illustration above).

"The heel should be well pressed down, the toe raised from the instep, the left knee close to the saddle, and in a line with the ground. Ladies frequently draw back their heels—a dangerous trick, as it unconsciously imitates the action of spurring, and irritates a high-couraged animal; even the best behaved and broken horse is likely to mistake the motion for an indication to increase his pace. By bending the knee, dropping the toe, and raising the heel, a lady riding displays the sole of her foot to those riding in rear of her—an equestrian blunder of a grave character. This faulty position of the leg and foot also prevents the rider from sitting straight in the saddle, and unduly throws her weight to the right side. Another very common fault, although not so dangerous, is equally defective as to the straight position of the lady on her horse—that is, when the heel is pressed down while the knee is straightened. This makes the saddle slip to the left side, causing pain, and frequently giving the horse a sore back and withers.

"No lady can have a straight and elegant seat unless she so places her knee and foot that her knee is in line with the ground, and the leg from the knee to the foot perpendicular to the knee.

"In order to ensure a straight seat, when the lady alights on the saddle she should look straight between the horse's ears. This will make the saddle sit fair and square upon the horse's back, and give a proper and even bearing to the girths."

The lady is now on her saddle, in a position from which, as long as her limbs retain their ordinary muscular force and the horse keeps on his legs, she cannot be displaced. It is, as already mentioned, a seat much stronger than a man's astride, with the double disadvantage of being entirely dependent on the girths for safety and of not being able to urge the horse on more than one side.

The picture at page 335, the first of the kind ever published, must be carefully studied by every one who really desires to become a horsewoman, because it is on an implicit imitation of this seat as regards the position of the two legs that a good seat depends. More than half the ladies riding in public poke out the right toe and draw back the left heel.

It is in consequence of the importance of strictly observing the details of the seat that, in my humble opinion, all lady pupils above the age of mere children should receive their *primary* education—to adopt a School Board phrase—from women. Men, in nine cases out of ten, are much more capable teachers of all the niceties of horsemanship than even the finest horsewomen; but where it is necessary to put feet and legs in their proper places, the duty is more properly placed in the hands of a woman.

In the same direction, it may be observed that a skirt which conceals all defects is not the proper dress for preliminary lessons. At all gymnastic institutions the pupils wear a costume which consists of a tunic and a loose pair of trousers buttoned at the ankle. In that easy dress all the ladies who frequent a celebrated Liverpool gymnasium appear, and it is also the costume at Madame Brenner's institution.

In order to show as plainly as possible the proper angles of a lady's seat as regards the pommels, the trousers in the preceding picture have been made tight, but that is not essential. Ladies who swim wear a bathing costume, not a loose gown; it is quite time that a similar reform in the direction of common sense should be introduced into the riding-school.

The pupil properly seated should appear on her horse like the right-hand figure at page 338; but the average horsewoman, afraid of falling over on the off side, or with a stirrup-leather an inch too long, unconsciously, and perhaps perfectly well satisfied with herself, appears, especially if trotting, like the other figure on the same page, all one side!

Once properly placed in the saddle, the next point is for the pupil to attain a "seat," which, amongst other things, means a confident feeling that no ordinary accident will unhorse her. To complete this important part of a lady's equestrian education the following suggestions will be found useful. She ought not to be troubled with the management of the reins, much less with a whip, which she can have no idea of properly employing; her whole attention should be concentrated on learning the proper grip of the pommels and the proper balance on the saddle.

Lady Mildred H——, herself the daughter of a noble lady who was second to none in the hunting-field, never permitted her daughter to touch the reins until she could confidently walk, trot, and canter a school horse in a figure of 8, as well as perform all the other school exercises.

Where a perfectly-trained school horse is not to be had, it is advisable to confine the head of the horse used with flap-reins, buckled to a snaffle bit and to the flaps of the saddle—a simple expedient, which, combined with a head-stall martingale, ought to be adopted by those timid riders who will insist on prematurely appearing in fashionable parades. A horse cannot bolt if thus restrained.

The lady who has mastered the first lessons in the equestrian art, and can sit her horse properly at a walk or show-school canter, is then in a position to decide whether she will learn to rule her horse, or whether she is content to pass through life dependent for her comfort on the temper of her steed or the close, nurse-like attention of some groom or gentleman. The horsewoman should sit so that the weight of the body falls exactly in the centre of the saddle, without heavily bearing on the stirrup; able to grasp the upright pommel with the right knee, and press against the "hunting-horn" with her left knee, yet not exerting any muscular action for that purpose. For this end the stirrup-leather must be neither too long nor too short.

The ideal of a fine horsewoman is to be erect without being rigid, square to the front, and, until quite at home in the saddle, looking religiously between her horse's ears. The shoulders must therefore be square, but thrown back a little, so as to expand the chest and make a hollow waist, "such as is observed in waltzing," but always flexible. On the flexibility of the person above the waist, and on the firmness below, all the grace of equestrianism—all the safety depends. Nervousness makes both men and women poke their heads forward—a stupid trick in a man, unpardonable in a woman.

A lady should bend like a willow in a storm, always returning to an easy yet nearly upright position. This seat should be acquired while the lady's horse is led, first by hand, then with a leading-stick (see page 266), and finally with a lunging-rein, which will give room for cantering in circles. But where a pupil is encumbered with reins, a whip, and directions for guiding her horse, she may be excused for forgetting all about her seat or her position. The arms down to the elbows should hang loosely near but not fixed to the sides, and the hands, in the absence of reins, may rest in front of the waist.

Common errors are either to sit too much over to the right, and then, in attempting to balance, to lean the shoulders to the left, while the head is inelegantly twisted to the right —this is when the stirrup-leather is too short; or when the stirrup is too long, and the lady ignorantly timid, sitting too much to the left, bearing hard on the stirrup—a hideous position, suggestive of an early sore back for the horse.

The error of hanging on by the pommels is carefully to be avoided. The great object is to acquire a firm, well-balanced seat, without unduly depending on pommels or stirrups. "Let the pupil," says an accomplished horsewoman, "practise riding in circles to the right, sitting upright, but bending a little to the horse's motion, following his nose with her eye; beginning with a walk, proceed to a slow trot, increasing the action as she gains firmness in the saddle." When, in a smart trot in a circle to the right, the pupil can, leaning as she should to the right, see the feet of the horse on the right side, it may be assumed that she has arrived at a firm seat.

Nothing but practice, frequent but not too long continued, can establish the all-important balance. Practice and practice only enables the rider to instinctively bear to the proper side, or lean back, as a horse turns, bounds, or leaps.

"The movements of the rider should ever harmonise with those of the horse. Thus, when the horse is standing still, at liberty and disunited, the rider in like manner sits at her ease,

QUITE WRONG.   QUITE RIGHT.

and may be said to be also disunited; as she begins to collect and unite her horse, so she collects and unites herself. When the rider is pressing her horse to the union, and drawing from him his proudest and most animated action, then must her own bearing be the extreme of elegance, and her animation in proportion to that of her horse."

Perhaps it may be thought that in the preceding directions too much stress has been laid on "grace" as an important consideration in the equestrian art; but, as a matter of fact, the principles that secure elegance in a graceful figure are also those that ensure safety.

There are many charming women to whom, in the direction of elegance, Nature has not been bountiful—"dumpy"—or large, stout figures, to whom horse exercise is not only a pleasure, but a necessity of health. These, if they "know themselves," will not deny themselves the pleasures of horse exercise, but will be content to avoid conspicuous display in dress, in the colour or the action of their steed, or in attempts "to witch the world with noble horsemanship."

A lady should no more be deterred from riding, if that is her inclination, because she is not of the tall and slight figure which alone is perfection on horseback, than from walking or dancing because she has a large foot or a thick ankle.

What is truly ridiculous is a lady riding boldly in an awkward way, with crooked, confident seat, or riding in evident terror, her eyes constantly fixed, not on her horse's ears, but on her attendant horseman; because she has never had the patience, the humility, or the common sense, to engage a proper instructor, and attend to her or his instructions.

If a lady, young or middle-aged, cannot trust herself on horseback without a groom alongside her, there must be some great fault in her nervous constitution, her equestrian education, or in the character of her horse. In either case she ought to seek some retired place for her constitutional *promenades à cheval*, and not display her incompetent

CIRCUS PRACTISING DRESS.

timidity at fashionable hours in fashionable resorts, when an old coachman close to his lady's bridle-rein looks absurd, and a young handsome groom often scandalous.

For all these reasons, ladies who mean to ride should leave whips and reins alone until they have acquired a firm square seat at a walk, a slow canter, and a slow trot. To acquire this seat it is absolutely necessary that they should place themselves under the tuition of some one able and willing to cure them of their faults.

The accomplishments of an *amazone* cannot be learned in a day, a week, or a month; although a strong, courageous girl may learn in a few hours how to stick on and look ridiculous.

THE LADY'S REINS.

When a lady has acquired a *seat* in the saddle, she may properly commence her instruction in the art of guiding the horse by the bridle. On this most important part of the subject the instructions will be the same as those addressed to men in Chapter XIII.; but as the conventional mode of holding the reins in one hand is quite useless except where the horse is perfectly obedient under all circumstances, no matter how excited, repetition may be excused.

The finished horsewoman on the finished horse rides like the figure at page 341, but a long course of study has to be pursued before "a double first-class degree" of excellence is attained.

The ladies should use double bridles, with curb, snaffle, and a Cavesson martingale, except when they propose to leap, when the martingale must either be taken off or lengthened. In the case of a lady pupil, the curb rein should be shortened, either by knotting or an arrangement of buckles, so that it will lie on the neck or over the right-hand pommel. One rein is enough to commence with, and that the snaffle; because a frightened beginner is very apt to make dangerous use of the curb rein, especially if the horse is what he ought to be —high-couraged.

Lessons on equitation given on dull slugs are like lessons in dancing without music.

The snaffle reins must be held in both hands at equal lengths. This is more important in teaching women than in teaching men, because it is an additional inducement to sit square.

In using one pair of reins it is not of much consequence how they are held, so long as the arms are kept near the side, the wrists turned rather in, the left hand as low as the knee will admit without resting on it, and the right hand about on a level with the third pommel.

The pupil is to be taught—contrary to cavalry practice and "The Book of Aids"—that when she wants her horse to go to the right she must pull the right rein, when she wants to go to the left the left rein; but these actions must be performed smoothly, moving the arms as little as possible, with the wrists—only in fast paces are the fore-arms to move from the elbows, "giving and taking."

When both reins are used, the object is to guide and hold the horse with the snaffle bit, the reins of that bit being the tighter of the two; the curb reins being used to collect and restrain, except on parade occasions, when the curb only is used. To explain the exact arrangement of these two reins would take up a great many words, even with explanatory woodcuts, while the whole mystery of placing them relatively between the fingers may be learned in a few minutes from personal instruction. It is the object of this chapter rather to lay down general principles than minute details. For an example of a fine seat, the reins held in both hands, the curb the lightest (the horse being on parade action), nothing can be finer than the portrait of Mrs. Reynolds on the Earl of Pembroke's horse, given in the coloured plate, the same horse on which the same artist painted the Empress of the French in a similar attitude.

The manipulation of the reins, when once explained, may be practised at home by attaching reins to an elastic band, fastened to something about the height of a horse's head. In the same way, mounting may be practised on a convenient chest of drawers.

Mrs. Stirling Clarke gives the following five positions of the reins as held in both hands.

TROTTING AWAY.

I do not consider them clear enough to be of much value, but quote them as the advice of a very accomplished *equestrienne :*—

"In the first position, with a rein in each hand, the hands are held about three inches from the body, about four inches apart, in line with each other, with the thumbs uppermost, and the little fingers on a line with the elbows.

"The second consists of a slight yielding of the hands, by which the horse is enabled to advance.

"The third shortens the right rein by turning the little finger of the right hand upwards towards the waist, and inclines the horse to the right.

"The fourth shortens the left rein by turning the little finger of the left hand upwards towards the waist, and inclines the horse to the left.

"The fifth shortens both reins by turning the little fingers up at the same moment, and stops the horse, while by bending the hand inwards towards the body, this position compels him to go forward."

All which may be quite true and easy to professors of the *haute école*, but little fingers of such extraordinary power are rare; and a little experience will teach riders, male or female, to effect their object in a less complicated manner. The point to be aimed at is a delicate yet firm touch, a constant feeling of the horse's mouth, with not more restraint on either or both reins than is required to make the steed turn either way, stop, or back.

Slack reins, or reins jerked instead of pulled smoothly, are equally errors of equestrianism.

Light hands give and take, and always return to the right position. A fresh horse may be allowed to draw the reins through the rider's fingers; but they must always be shortened again, so that the rider has command of the mouth, just as the steersman of a row-boat never allows the lines to become slack. The body must act with the hands. When a horse stumbles, or starts suddenly into a gallop, or plunges in high spirits, the body inclining backward gives weight to the grasp of the reins in the hands.

On walking enough has been said in a previous chapter. A horse at fast paces should always be stopped by degrees; the rider bending back her shoulders as she presses the bit evenly on the horse's mouth.

TROTTING.

Ladies must learn to trot for several reasons. As already explained, a change of pace is a great relief to a horse in a ride of more than an hour. Almost all horses trot a little when stopped from a hand-gallop. Sometimes the choice is between riding a horse that will trot well and will not canter, and not riding at all. Besides, a lady cannot have a perfect seat without being able to trot.

Short women look better trotting than tall women, unless the horse trots so smoothly that a perfectly upright carriage can be maintained. To see a lady leaning forward over her horse's ears on the trot is very offensive.

"*Vieille Moustache*" recommends that a pupil should prepare for trotting by practising rising and falling without a stirrup, the horse standing still; and that the first lessons in motion, with the foot in the stirrup, should be performed with the assistance of the master riding alongside, with his left hand under her right elbow.

"There should be no twist from the waist; the shoulders perfectly square, every movement in exact harmony with the horse's motion."

As a rule, the appearance of ladies trotting is vile, for want of proper instruction, and sometimes from their having adopted a masculine style. Under any circumstances, trotting lessons should be very short.

The same experienced instructor recommends that pupils should (in a school) trot without reins, "the hands behind the waist, the right hand grasping the left elbow." This was George Darby's system of teaching before he gave up the riding-school to his brothers for the Rugby dealing establishment.

CANTERING.

The canter is essentially the ladies' pace; and on a good horse it is so easy to balance that it deceives many pupils into believing they are adepts when they have only learnt the A B C of the art. In the canter the lady's whip, if needful, urges the horse as a man's right leg and spur would. The instructions for cantering are the same for a lady as those given for a man. A horse must not be permitted to break from a trot to a canter, but reined up and made to begin again.

Some horses trained to lead with either leg go as pleasantly with the one as the other. This capability of changing saves a horse very much. When a lady rides on the off side, she requires her horse to lead with the near leg.

GALLOPING.

To gallop, a lady must invariably take her reins in both hands, feeling the horse's mouth firmly with the snaffle and lightly with the curb. A writer, already quoted, who holds to the theory of a woman riding with one hand, like a cavalry soldier (which was exactly the reverse of Dan Seffert's early lessons), permits division of the reins between both hands when galloping, and directs that the lady "places her right hand outside her right knee, and her left hand outside the near side upper crutch, the hands not more than six or eight inches from the body, the knuckles upwards, elbows slightly bent," the hands, firmly holding the reins, resting against the saddle.

When she desires to decrease her speed she leans back gradually, draws her hands towards her waist, and with her fingers brings the curb reins into action, thus reducing the gallop to a canter, and the canter to a walk.

But for a gallop the pupil must have been prepared by long preliminary walks, trots, and canters, and be in the healthy condition of a gymnast in full practice. No woman is a horse-woman, or fit to be trusted without a leading-rein, until she can gallop and stop her horse.

LEAPING.

Every lady who learns to ride should learn to sit a leap; not only on the principle that if a thing is worth doing at all it is worth doing well, but because no lady who rides can ever be sure that on some occasion her horse—stung by a fly or excited by a thunderstorm—will not make a series of bounds quite equal to any probable leap in the hunting-field.

Of course, if a lady has made up her mind that she will never leave the promenades of fashionable resort, that is a different thing; on the same principle she may decline to receive any lessons except walking and slow cantering, because she has made up her mind never to go beyond those paces. But to make quite sure, she must be certain no horse she may mount will ever insist on a fierce trot or a wild gallop.

When a lady has attained the whole art of equestrianism she is prepared for every kind

THE COUNTESS MONTIJO (AFTERWARDS EMPRESS OF THE FRENCH) AS A CONTRABANDISTA.

of adventure at home or abroad; she can put up with a hunter not educated to carry a lady, and she can make her way on horseback if her lot takes her to any of the wild countries of Europe, the back settlements of America, or those essentially horse colonies, Australia and New Zealand.

The first lessons in leaping should, if possible, be given in a school, and on a full-sized horse—one that perfectly understands the business and enjoys it. A sheep-hurdle is quite high enough, and the trunk of a tree is quite wide enough, for the first steps in leaping. Balance, grip of the pommels, and support of the stirrup, must be combined; the seat as near the centre of the horse's back as the pommels will permit; the figure erect, not rigid, with the shoulders back, ready to bend gently backwards as the horse rises in the air—not leaning forward, twisted over on the near side, like a popular, spirited, and absurd picture ("First at the Fence"), which really shows "how not to do it;" the snaffle reins held in both hands, at a length that will enable the horse fully to extend himself, and the rider to bear on his mouth as she bends back over his croup when he is landing. All the time her eyes should be looking between the horse's ears, so as to keep perfectly square in the saddle.

In the first lessons the pupil should not attempt anything but to retain her balance, without requiring or attempting to urge her horse. All the lessons not done at standing leaps should be done at a slow pace; for it is not the business of a lady to ride at fences like a steeplechase-rider or a lunatic, unless water or something else of an equally exceptional character has to be covered in the hunting field. As a rule, the worst and most nervous riders, male and female, are most apt to gallop wildly at their fences.

"*Vieille Moustache*" says:—

"She should take a firm hold of the upper crutch of the saddle with her right knee, sit well into the saddle —not the back of it, because the farther back the greater the concussion when the horse alights—put her left foot well home in the stirrup, and press her leg—(he must mean thigh)—firmly against the third crutch, while keeping the left knee flexible and the left foot well forward, lean slightly forward, *avoid stiffening her waist in order to throw the upper part of her figure backward at the right moment in order to preserve her balance.* The hands must not move except with the body; and, above all, no attempt to enliven the horse by jagging his mouth as he is about to rise—a pernicious habit, practised by riders of both sexes who ought to know better. The horse on which a lady leaps should not require violent urging, and only needs to be properly collected before starting. Reins too short, head too forward, and pace too hurried, are the ordinary faults of beginners. Women have on their saddles a firmer seat for leaping than men."

In this branch of equestrianism practice and sound instruction are the essentials. The occasions when a lady has to gallop at full speed at a wide jump of water or a doubled fence are rare, but to complete the subject the following instructions are quoted from the eminent riding-master already named:—

"*Her elbows should be drawn back until they are three inches or thereabouts behind her waist; her hands below her elbows, six inches apart, grasping the reins divided with the least possible feeling of the curb; the fingers turned inwards and upwards, touching the waist.* As the horse is galloping up on the point of springing, the body from the waist should be thrown back, the hands shot forward, held low, thus giving the horse his head as he springs, but supporting him as he lands."

But after all, words will do very little towards cultivating this very useful and pleasing accomplishment.

Ponies are much more difficult to ride at leaps than full-sized horses, and well-bred horses are more elastic and pleasant than the cleverest coarse-bred cobs.

A lady's horse should be carefully exercised on the days she does not ride. Many serious accidents have arisen from ladies objecting to any one riding their pets except themselves ; the very best horses acquire vicious tricks from idleness in the stable.

Not many years ago a lady, a fine horsewoman, the mother of a family, who would not allow any one except herself to mount her thoroughbred horse, was run away with in Rotten Row. The horse rushed madly out of the Park at the Kensington gate, against the wall where the fountain stands, and was killed with his rider—a horrid spectacle.

All highly-bred, highly-fed horses, that do not get some hours' real work for five days of the week, should have at least two hours' exercise before they are ridden in town by ladies.

When Her Majesty rode on horseback regularly, it was the duty of a lady attached to the Master of the Horse's establishment to ride and sweat the royal horse, in the school at Buckingham Palace or at Windsor, early enough in the day to allow him time to be cooled and dressed before Her Majesty rode out.

All stud-grooms who understand their business take the same precaution without consulting their "young ladies." *A bucket of water, judiciously administered before proceeding to the Park*, will produce a soothing effect on a fiery horse ; but then there must be no galloping, or serious internal injuries may follow.

The highly elegant creature referred to as the perfect lady's horse and park hack, page 318, is often too delicate and too ornamental for country use. For general utility in the country, the stamp of horse for a lady's hunter is the best. The illustration at page 330 is taken from a lady's hunter in Lord Calthorpe's Leicestershire stud, one good at walking, good at trotting, pleasant at a hand-gallop, able and willing to leap anything a lady should leap.

When a gentleman rides in the Park or other public place, etiquette requires that he should approach a lady on the off or right side ; and that in either meeting or passing, if she be alone, he should slacken his pace to a walk. In a visit which Lord Chief Justice Denman paid to Walmer Castle, three years before the Duke of Wellington's death, in a conversation about riding, the Duke said : "When I meet a lady on horseback I always stop, and if her horse seems troublesome, offer to ride alongside her in the Row until it is quiet. The other day I met a lady on a fresh, violent horse, so I took off my hat, and said, 'Shall I ride with you? my horse is perfectly quiet.' She knew me, for she replied, 'No, your Grace ; I think I can get on very well.' After she was gone, I felt sure that it was Jenny Lind." "We all agreed," adds Lord Denman, "that the great singer should have accepted the services of the great Duke, whether she wanted them or not."*

When a gentleman accompanies a lady on horseback, he should ride on the right side, holding his own bridle and whip in his right hand, that he may be prepared to assist her with his left hand if needful. When it is necessary for a horseman to secure a lady's horse with a leading rein, it *may* be attached to the snaffle bit with spring hooks, in the following manner : —The hooks to be hooked to the rings of the snaffle ; the rein, which should be thin and round, fastened to a ring in the centre of the leather band which unites the hooks. The rein should  then be passed through two rings, one of them close to the front flap of the saddle, the other farther on, beyond the right-hand pommel. By this contrivance, if it be necessary to use

* "Life of Lord Chief Justice Denman," by Sir Joseph Arnould.

the rein, the head of the lady's horse will not be drawn on one side in the usual awkward manner; and the horseman, holding the rein in his left hand as he rides alongside, will have perfect command without attracting attention to the safety bridle. After a time, if the lady gains confidence, the leading rein may be fastened to a **D** under the cantle of her saddle, so as to be easily laid hold of in a gallop, if required, without disturbing her own hold of the reins.

Nothing is so rude as for a gentleman to gallop past a lady on horseback. A gentleman should never ride between two ladies unless at their request.

Those ladies who ride perpetually on the curb should examine the chain before mounting, to see that it is neither too tight nor too loose. The disadvantage of riding on the road on the curb is,

GOOD SHOULDERS, BRIDLES WELL.

that if a horse stumbles and is checked by it, the pain throws his head up, and then he is pretty sure to come down very hard.

All hacks, but particularly those ridden by ladies, should be started at a walk, and walked for some distance before being allowed to go fast. The only exception is when a fresh, excited horse—such as a lady ought not to mount under ordinary circumstances—requires a preliminary trot or hand-gallop to settle him down, and this cannot be done in a town.

If two or more ladies are about to ride together, as soon as one is placed in the saddle let her move forward out of the way, *and stand still*, so that her horse may not make the other horses restless while being mounted. Never ride on a side-saddle that is not long enough from the pommel to the cantle. Always settle the length of the stirrup-leather comfortably before starting.

Treat your horse as a friend about whose health and comfort you are interested—not like a mere machine. If a horse usually free and gay appears dull, droops his head, or coughs harshly (not the cough grooms call blowing his nose), or if his coat stares, the rider may fairly suspect that he is sickening for an influenza or some other ailment; return him to the stable, consult some proper person, and *do not* let the groom give him "a something"—"a ball" or "a draught"—or poison his drinking water with nitre. With horses the "stitch in time" maxim is all important.

If a horse is found going on one side, with an uncomfortable gait, with an occasional attempt at a cow kick, the chances are that the side-saddle is wringing his back; if further examination confirms this notion, dismount, and have the saddle removed and re-adjusted. The back of a lady's horse is so liable to be chafed that it should be carefully examined with the hand after every ride, and especially after using a new or strange saddle. Rest is the only sure cure for a really sore back.

A lady, not being professional, should never enter into a pitched battle with her horse if he suddenly turns restless, and refuses to go down a particular street or to pass some strange object, as she cannot squeeze him between her legs like a man armed with a pair of spurs, and as her sex and position make a contest undignified. At the first symptom of resistance, let her groom or some bystander take hold of the snaffle rein, and lead the horse a few yards.

If a groom attends on ladies, in order to be of any use in an emergency he must ride a horse twice as fast as those he follows. A groom on a cob following a thoroughbred may be ornamental, but is not useful.

All ladies who ride in the country should learn to mount without assistance. A lady's horse ought to stand like a rock; but if at all fidgety put him against a gate or bank, with some one at his head. Then let down the stirrup to an easy height, and mount by taking hold of the upright pommel. If necessary, one rein may be drawn tight round the upright pommel until mounting is completed. When mounted, if the stirrup is fastened on the off-side, as in illustration at page 318, or if White's stirrup leather be used, there will be no difficulty in lengthening or shortening it. In crossing a ford in hot weather, nevet let a horse drink, as he will be apt to lie down and roll; push him across as fast as possible, not sparing a cut with the whip over the shoulder.

A horse, however gentle in temperament and pleasant in paces, is not fit for a lady to ride unless he will face military and street music, waving banners and plumes, a marching regiment, or a society of Odd Fellows, and every queer noisy movement. The training needful will not impair the spirit of the highest-couraged horse. A really nervous horse can never be trained for the work of a lady.

Speak always when approaching your horse; pat and caress him when leaving him.

Learn how the saddle and bridle ought to be put on.

A LADY'S HORSE—THE PROPERTY OF THE LATE EARL OF PEMBROKE.
FROM AN ORIGINAL PAINTING BY MONPEZAT.

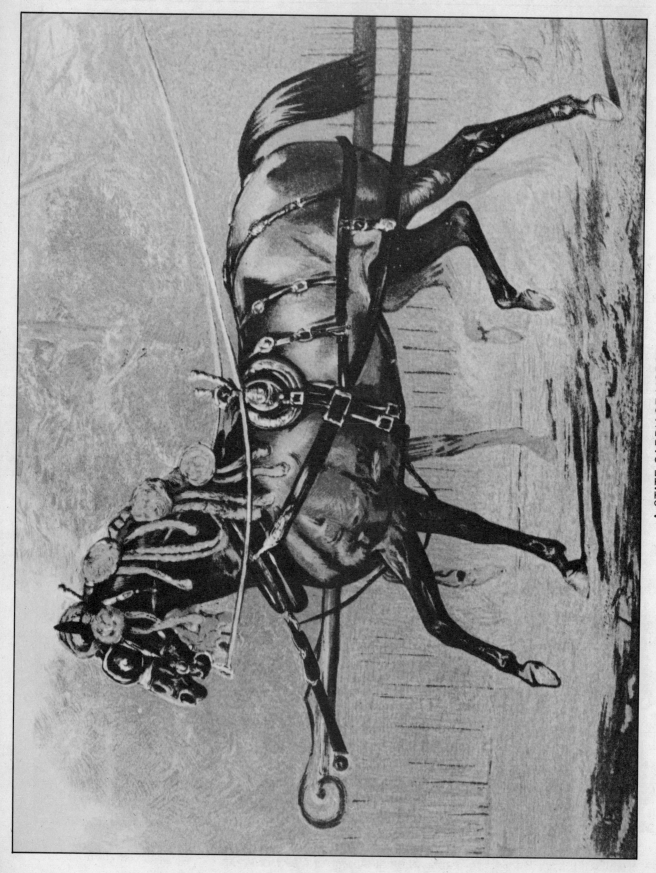

A STATE CARRIAGE HORSE.

THE PROPERTY OF HIS ROYAL HIGHNESS, THE PRINCE OF WALES.

CHAPTER XVI.

HARNESS.

DRIVING one, a pair, or even four well-bred, well-broken, high-couraged horses, in good form, is an accomplishment which may be acquired by many to whom horse exercise is impossible, if only they will take the trouble to be taught from the first, and have sufficient courage to practise what they have learned.

Next to horse exercise there is no more healthy, pleasantly-exciting way of taking the air than driving a pair of good horses in an open carriage. There is something very exciting in the tramp of their hoofs, the rumble of the wheels, and the gentle swing of a well-built carriage.

But to drive really well, the driver, whether man or woman, and particularly a woman, must from the first be taught by a really good coachman.

It is even easier to drive boldly and badly than to ride, and quite as difficult to abandon vicious habits once acquired. Little or no exertion is required to retain the seat, however awkwardly occupied. The indications of the reins are in a great degree regulated by rings (technically, the terrets) of the harness through which they pass, and a well-broken horse, or pair of horses, in regular work, will submit to a great deal of ignorant coachmanship.

It must, however, be noted that accidents on wheels are generally more serious than in saddle. A bad horseman often tumbles off at an early stage of a difference with his horse and escapes with a bruise or two, but when a horse in harness runs away, or sets to work to kick in earnest, the occupants of the vehicle are lucky if they escape with only broken bones.

It is not enough that a lady or gentleman, who can afford to keep horses with breeding and fashion, should be able to drive swiftly and safely; to do credit to their equipage they should be able to drive slowly and steadily at a measured pace, and in the "best form."

For powerful, skilful rattling along crowded streets, twisting round sharp corners, and backing into narrow gateways, the youths who drive unicorn spring railway vans of London would be very bad to beat, and for reckless pace in single harness who can excel the butcher-boys and drivers of mail carts? But none of them have the style a gentleman would like to see in his four-in-hand coachman or mail phaeton groom, still less in his wife or daughter.

There is no more legitimate luxury for a young lady of fortune, whose tastes lie that way, than a well-appointed phaeton and pair; none which excites more legitimate admiration when driven in the manner which shows perfect command over the horses; none which excites more pity, if not contempt, than a nervous, awkward, or bold awkward driver of a pair of ill-matched, ill-groomed, ill-harnessed horses.

Given the sort of horses a lady should drive, and the nerve that most healthy young ladies possess, nothing more is needed than a few weeks' instruction from a really good coachman, and a few months' practice in quiet streets or lanes under the eyes of a steady groom on the back seat, who may be a very good, without being a skilful and elegant driver.

There are two accepted styles of driving:—The English, which is the only style that ladies—for whom this chapter is particularly written—can adopt, and the Russian, which is also the American.

The English coachman drives with his elbows near his hips and his hands near his body. The Russian and American extend their arms to their full length, and when trotting often make the horses almost draw by the reins instead of the traces.

With American drivers speed is the great object, and to pace everything is sacrificed; with the English the object is a good style. In fact, pace with an English horse in a gentleman's gig or mail phaeton ends when an American begins to trot in earnest.

Fourteen miles an hour is quite the outside pace of an English pair in a private carriage of any kind, and ninety per cent. of the best appointed harness teams in and out of London never exceed ten miles an hour.

If the wheelers in the thousand-guinea team of a four-in-hand drag can trot fourteen miles an hour, returning from an expedition into the country, from races, a garden party, or pic-nic, they do all that is likely to be required of them in the way of pace.

But no young gentleman in the United States of horsey tastes is satisfied with a trotter not able to do his "2.40"—that is, a mile in two minutes and forty seconds, or at the rate of twenty-two miles an hour. His ordinary pace in driving out of town, with other friends competing, will be about seventeen miles an hour.

In the following pages, noted down from the lips of some of the most accomplished coachmen of the day, an attempt will be made to teach as much as can be taught in writing on a purely practical art, with the view of enabling an aspirant to a first, second, or third class degree in coachmanship to profit as much as possible from the *vivâ voce* lectures of a professional instructor.

No amount of instruction will stand in the stead of courage, of "nerve," as it is popularly called, but many of those who are very nervous on first taking the reins in hand will, if they have any natural aptitude, acquire confidence after a reasonable amount of practice, in the same way that experienced drivers, who have lost their nerve from illness and long absence from the road, soon re-acquire it when once fairly settled behind a team of good horses.

It is assumed, for the purposes of this chapter, that the pupils are in a position to obtain well-broken, free-moving horses, suitable carriages, harness, and well-trained servants.

To drive one or a pair of the sort of horses a lady should drive, or even four perfectly-bitted ponies, does not require strength. But for driving a full-sized team of four horses in hand with comfort and confidence, a certain degree of strength is indispensable.

No one should attempt to drive high-couraged horses (any one can drive a cab-horse in a four-wheeler) without before, or while learning to drive, becoming familiarly acquainted with the use of every part of harness, and the way of putting it on the horse. This knowledge is quite as necessary for women as for men. Without it they cannot tell whether a roadside ostler or a muzzy groom has harnessed their ponies, or put on their bridles after a bait properly or not. Half the accidents in harness happen from there being something wrong in the fit of the leathers.

SINGLE HARNESS.

Harness for one horse in the heaviest kind of English four-wheeled carriage consists of—

> Collar with traces.
> Pad or saddle, to which are attached
> Tugs, for supporting the shafts.
> Crupper, for keeping the pad in its place.
> Breeching, to assist in backing or holding back a heavy carriage in descending hills.
> A kicking-strap where required.

These are the parts of the harness that make the horse part of the locomotive machine. To guide the horse there is the—

> Bridle, composed of the
> Headstall.
> Bit or bits.
> Reins for driving ; and, if required,
> Bearing-reins.

In a light four-wheeled carriage the breeching is frequently omitted for town use, and also for country use if the district is flat or the carriage is provided with a patent drag. Light two-wheeled carriages are generally driven without breeching, with a kicking-strap, and without bearing-reins.

THE COLLAR AND TRACES.

The collar is the first part of the harness to be put on a horse in harnessing. It is composed of two parts—a leather collar and a pair of metal *hames* to which the traces are attached, and to which also a pair of rings *(terrets)* are fixed, through which the reins pass. The terrets are sometimes fixed solidly, and sometimes are loose rings.

The fitting of the collar is a matter of the greatest importance ; when it does not fit, pain, wounds, blemishes which often permanently disfigure the horse, and not unfrequently rearing and gibbing, are the result. On the proper fitting of the collar, and attachment of the traces to the *hames* at the proper point, the comfort and power of draught of the horse greatly depend. It is a matter on which temporary grooms are so often careless and indifferent that it should always be attended to by the owner.

The subject of harness has been treated in a more practical and scientific manner by an author already quoted* than by any of the many writers whose works I consulted, after talking over my own experience with harness-makers and coachmen ; I have therefore freely extracted and condensed a number of passages from his somewhat abstruse essay :—

"A collar too small chokes a horse. In certain positions it will actually stop one by

---

* "Bits and Bridles, Draught and Harness." By Major Francis Dwyer. Blackwood & Sons.

pressing on the windpipe—a case not unfrequently seen with cart-horses starting heavy loads. But a collar too large is even more likely to create a sore, or "raw," than one too small.

"The collar should be so made that, when pulling, the weight attached to the trace should be distributed over the whole surface of the shoulders, instead of being concentrated on one point, or, what is quite as bad, rubbing up and down.

DRIVING A PAIR.

"A draught on one end of the collar will make it gape away from the horse's neck at the other end, and consequently cause it to grind up or down in a manner which is pretty sure to establish a raw.

"The great mistake made by harness-makers working by rule of thumb is, that even when their total dimensions are correct, they think too much of producing a symmetrical oval figure, and not enough or not at all of the natural lines of a horse's neck and shoulders. The under part of the collar is frequently made narrow, whereas it should be from one inch to one and a half inches wider at its base than anywhere else. A front view of a horse's shoulders in the picture of a pair which illustrates this chapter shows what the shape of the collar should be, and that it should never come lower than *the dotted line*.

"When fitting a collar, it is not enough to adjust it to the horse's neck and shoulders when standing still; he should be put into draught at a good pace, because the shape and dimensions of the neck and shoulders, especially those of high-crested horses, are wonderfully altered when they come to trot. A collar that appears quite long enough for a horse standing at ease will frequently prove two or three inches too short when he is put to a trot."

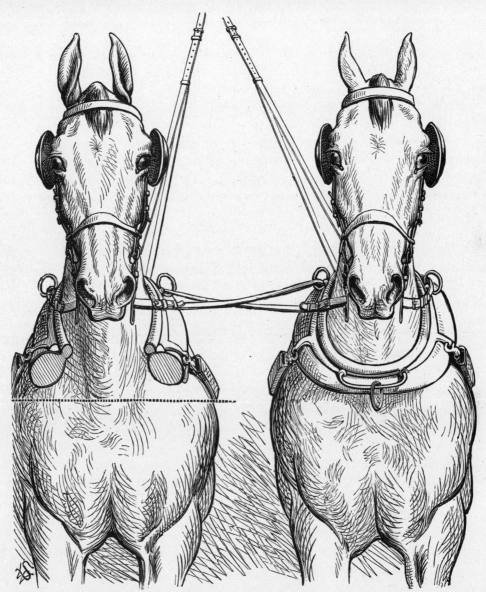

PROPER POSITION OF COLLAR.

The point of attachment, technically *the draught* of the traces to the hames, is a matter of great importance. Sometimes the attachment is so low down that the *pull* is opposite the *articulation of the shoulder-blade with the arm-bone*, so that at every step the trace presses the movable articulation of the point of the shoulder; while if a horse is to exert his full strength the trace must be attached opposite the *immovable* point of the shoulder-blade.

Collar-makers who understand their business understand the conformation of horses' necks and shoulders, and know where to attach the traces to the hames. Where they do not, even when the collar fits, if the traces are attached too low they will draw the collar away from the upper part of the shoulders. When this is found to be the case, the obvious remedy is to shift the point of "*draught*" until an even bearing is obtained. Ignorant people "adopt two remedies, one of which partly conceals, whilst the other aggravates instead of curing the error. The first is to curve the upper part of the collar backwards; this, if not carried to excess, is harmless. The other is to lead a strap back from near the top of the collar to the trace buckle, which practically converts the front end of the trace into a fork whose points are attached to the hames, opposite to the two movable ends of the shoulder-blades, so that in fact *the play of this bone is effectually checked at both ends alternately.* The trace, as before observed, should be attached as nearly as possible opposite to the immovable part of the shoulder-blade—that is, to the centre of the shoulder-blade, which is about an inch higher than the hame-hooks of the majority of wholesale-made collars."

The best modern collars and hames are constructed in this manner. When, from any peculiarity in a horse's make, there is a difficulty in fitting him with a collar that will not gall him, resort may be had to what is known in the trade as the "Bencraft" hames, by which the point of traction ("*draught*") can be shifted to suit the shoulders of the horse or the height of carriage wheels.

But this contrivance has such an awkward appearance that it is by no means generally adopted, although it has been before the public many years. Indeed, there is no more conservative trade than that of harness-makers, perhaps because all the metal parts of this work are made every year in Staffordshire, by tens of thousands, from fixed patterns.

Various modes are adopted of attaching the traces to the hames, as may be seen in any harness-maker's shop. One of the best is a French invention, little known in England. A hammer-head is fixed to each side of the hames; at the end of each trace is a metal loop or *slot*, of a shape which will pass over the hammer-head sideways, and be retained safely when pulled straight.

The advantages of this plan are considerable: amongst others, the trace plays easily; the collar, with the hames loosely strapped to it, can be passed over the horse's head without the encumbrance of the traces; one of a hot pair of horses may be loosed from his traces by one person without leaving his head.

All young horses new to harness, and all fat horses that have not been in harness for some time, are liable to chafe under the collar. This must be attended to at once; they must be rested, if stuffing the collar or altering the draught of the traces will not remove unequal pressure, and the galled parts bathed with cold salt and water or some astringent lotion. If this is neglected, a permanent blemish may be created in a few hours. If for some reason it is absolutely necessary to keep the horse at work, where the carriage is light, a breast collar may be used, although that contrivance, from its passing directly over the "movable articulation of the point of the shoulder," is the very worst for drawing heavy weights.

In a stable where young or green horses are being trained to harness, the better plan is to have a number of the cheap straw collars of different sizes, so that there may be no need of using a leather one that does not fit. Many a valuable horse has been spoiled to save the cost of a new leather collar. The collar that fits a horse fat from grass will become loose and gall him as he fines down into condition.

The traces of the harness for private carriages are generally encumbered with a huge buckle for shortening and lengthening them. This buckle, in single harness, is often inconveniently near the shafts, where it can with difficulty be unbuckled in case any alteration is requisite;

indecd, in hard-worked establishments it is often not unbuckled from one year's end to another. In single-horse phæton or gig harness, fashion permits the buckle to be placed within a few inches of the splinter-bar, where it can be more easily got at; but fashion does not permit this sensible arrangement in brougham or double harness.

The buckle is of little real use; it is considered an ornament, otherwise it would have been discontinued long since in private carriages, as it has in public cabs. A substitute, introduced more than twenty years ago, is a peg and slide patented by the late Mr. White, of Tewkesbury, first exhibited at the International Exhibition of 1851. It lies flat, and allows the length of a trace to be easily shifted. It has not made the way that might have been expected, because the cost is somewhat greater than that of the old buckles, and saddlers have no incitement to use or advertise a rival's invention; but of its superiority to the buckle for traces there is no question. For pair and leader harness, this flat White tug is particularly neat. It does not

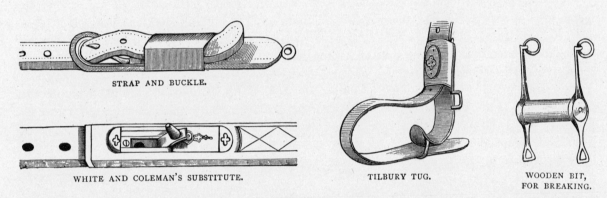

STRAP AND BUCKLE.

WHITE AND COLEMAN'S SUBSTITUTE.

TILBURY TUG.

WOODEN BIT, FOR BREAKING.

answer well for the pad-tugs or cruppers of single harness. Messrs. Lennan and Son, of Dublin, have patented a simplification of White's invention, which certainly is an improvement as far as cruppers and pad-tugs are concerned, but it is very doubtful whether, applied to traces, the iron peg will retain its place under the strain of a hard pull. If it will stand, there is no reason why harness made on the Lennan plan should not be as cheap or cheaper than with the old buckle, which can only be opened by tremendous exertion.

The first step in harnessing is to put on the collar. To put a collar over a horse's head, the hames ought either to be removed or to be strapped on very loosely. The collar must then be taken upside down in both hands, and after being stretched on the knee to the utmost limits, pulled as wide as possible at the moment that it is passed over the eyes.

Many horses with broad foreheads have had their eyelids torn and their eyes cruelly injured by efforts to force over their heads a tight collar, or a collar on which the hames have been buckled tight to save the groom trouble. If the groom's common sense and humanity are not to be trusted, he should be peremptorily forbidden to put on a collar without removing the hames, and a two-foot rule should be employed to ascertain that the collar can pass over the head without injury.

When the collar is on, the hames must be tightly buckled at the top with a sound strap, for everything depends on their holding fast, whether in single or double harness.

For breaking in young horses a collar that opens at the top will be found useful; it spares them one cause of fright.

Collars have been the subject of innumerable patents, but, with the exceptions already mentioned, the old form, probably of Norman origin, retains its superiority. When a horse has to draw a heavy weight, the collar must be thick and heavy; where, as in so many modern carriages, the weight is nominal, it may be made according to taste, as light as the American patterns, or it may be dispensed with altogether in favour of a breastplate for country use, which fits every horse, and can be put on in one minute in the dark.

THE PAD—TUGS—CRUPPER—KICKING-STRAP—BREECHING.

The pad, or saddle, of a four-wheeled carriage has no weight to sustain beyond the shafts, and no strain, except when a horse is descending a hill without breeching or drag on the wheels. The size is therefore quite a matter of taste—modern taste is in the direction of lightness—but a pad of good breadth need not be so tightly girthed as a smaller one, and looks better with a ponderous carriage and horse.

The shaft-tugs attached to it may be either simple loops, retained in their place by the metal stops of the shafts and the traces—and these are the best for dog-carts and other two-wheeled vehicles, which require the horse to be loose in the shafts—or they may be hooks on which the shafts in harnessing are made to fall, retained in their places by a girth passed round the shafts as well as the belly of the horse, which so binds them that the shafts become in fact traces. These are called "Tilbury tugs" (see illustration), after the name of the inventor. It is of importance that the shaft-tugs should be of the right length, so as to suspend the shafts at exactly the right height—that is, the middle of the swell of the pad-flaps, both perpendicularly and horizontally, unless the shafts are much bent, when the tugs must be shorter. The proper horizontal position of the shaft-tugs can only be maintained by the traces being of the proper length; if they are too short, the tugs and pad, when the horse is moving, are forced forward, and the crupper is thus drawn so tight as to provoke kicking. If the traces are too long, the horse draws the carriage by the tugs instead of by the traces—an absurd arrangement. In either case, a horse of a naturally placid temperament is uncomfortable, and not unfrequently becomes restive, to the astonishment of an ignorant driver.

Tugs too long, and the shafts in consequence too low, are a mistake in harness common with country grooms; but traces too long and too short may be seen every day in the fly-broughams and even private carriages of London.

The crupper, discarded from civilian saddlers, seems indispensable to keep the pad in its place in single and double harness, and to allow the attachment of a kicking-strap in the latter.

The late Honourable Sydney Pierrepoint—a great coachman in the palmy days of road and private four-in-hand coaches—used to drive a pair of horses with unlined straps, instead of pads, to support the traces and carry the terret rings, and no cruppers; the leaders of some fast coaches were driven without cruppers, as one learns from the song of the Tantivy Trot. But these are eccentricities, and the use of the crupper may be said to be universal, yet it is a prolific source of kicking, and should not be used in the first breaking of very high-couraged horses to harness. A crupper should be very thick, and stuffed with linseed. A thick crupper is less likely to gall than a thin one.

There is an invention called the "Nichol's Crupper," in which a sort of shelf is provided for making horses who carry their tails badly hold them out. Whether it can be used without galling the tail is a disputed point; but if it does not it may be useful for the harness of carriages where the splashboard is low and the tails of the horses are long—a conjunction which sometimes leads to the rein getting under a horse's tail, upon which he tucks it in close and often runs away kicking, while the driver is powerless. With the " Nichol's Crupper " the horse could not put down his tail to hold the rein.

Breeching is only required where a carriage is heavy, to assist in backing it. It may be short, as shown in picture of state coach, and is then most effective, but if a kicking-strap is used, then long breeching (see single harness illustration), of which it forms part, ought to be adopted.

With a horse, and more particularly a mare, in single harness, traced up close until the tail almost touches the splashboard, a kicking-strap is often ind'spensable, but it is useless unless properly put on.

It must be only just loose enough to allow the horse to trot without his back being chafed by it, and it must be fastened to the shafts *full two inches behind the hip bones,* that is, the place where a loin strap, if used, would pass. An over-tight or over-loose kicking-strap, or one passing in a direct line from shaft to shaft, is worse than useless—it may be irritating.

The pad, and the parts attached to it, must always be put on the horse *after the collar,* and before the bridle.

After purchasing a harness-horse, it is important to fit it with the bits in which it will travel most pleasantly ; for average harness horses the best is a Buxton bit, in which a port to receive the tongue is not required, because it moves on the cheeks. For single harness some horses go better in a Liverpool bit (*à pompe*). Others, again, that naturally carry their heads well and have light mouths, travel best with a ring or other harness snaffle. If driven with a curb or Buxton bit, experience will prove whether the reins must be buckled to the cheek or the bars. It is of the utmost importance that the mouthpiece should fit the horse's mouth. For instruction on this point see Chapter XIV., in which the subject of bits and bitting is treated exhaustively, with extracts from Dwyer's book.

HARNESS, BITS, AND BEARING-REINS.

Harness horses, from bad bitting, sometimes acquire the habit of getting their tongues over the mouthpiece, a trick which renders the whole action of the curb-bit uncertain. Old horses are generally incurable ; with young horses the best plan is to ride or drive them for some time with the snaffle, and then carefully fit them with a bit.

"The unsightly trick of lolling out the tongue, common in carriage horses and circus horses, is the direct consequence of tight bearing-reins and severe bits. The first step is to remove the bearing-reins, and substitute a rational bit. If that fails, a fringe of leather or hempen nose-bag may be attached to the noseband. The tickling sensation sometimes induces the horse to draw back his tongue, but there is no certain cure.

"Every horse goes best in a well-fitting bit. Enormous bits are constantly used in harness, with cheeks nearly a foot long, weighing from two pounds and a half to two pounds fourteen ounces, which are both cruel and mischievous, and are the result of a depraved, ignorant taste. Large carriage horses frequently have large heads, but it is doubtful whether five per cent. of the horses used in harness require bits of greater dimensions than $1\frac{3}{4}$ inches for the upper and $3\frac{1}{2}$ inches for the lower cheek.

"The cheeks may be curved and shaped into any fashion that pleases the eye, so long as they are of the proper length. The lower portion of the cheek should never exceed in length exactly the double of the upper portion. Even when the reins are habitually fastened into a ring below the cheek, still the weight of the projecting arm must affect the leverage of the whole instrument."

The bottom bar of a driving curb-bit is dangerous if used without a bearing rein, because horses are apt, when their heads are free, to hook it on a shaft in single, and on the pole in double harness.

But when a horse cannot be driven in a snaffle, or controlled by a curb-bit of something like the dimensions of the "Dwyer," the better plan is to adopt a Chifney bit, with Blackwell's india-rubber reins. When the curb-chain is properly fitted it is perfectly easy. Unless the coachman has firm and delicate hands, he must drive on the cheek or snaffle, and rely on the india-rubber reins when a strong pull is required.

It is an objection to this invaluable contrivance that the reins have rather a clumsy look, but this is easily amended. Instead of buckling them on the flat leather reins, a neater and more convenient plan is to buckle them to a *billet* (tongue strap) sewn on to round reins, the india-rubber being also round.

In dealing with horses that have an inclination to run away, it is necessary to take care that they do not get hold of the cheek of the bit—a very common trick with runaways. This is partly guarded against in riding-horses by the use of the lip-strap, and also by making the cheeks of an S, or the shape of the Hanoverian bit. Messrs. Wimbush, the job-masters, have for full fifty years broken all their harness-horses in with a bit with the cheeks bent back at an acute angle (see woodcut), which makes it impossible to lay hold of them. This prevented their young horses from ever acquiring the dangerous habit, *a habit much cultivated by the system of having bits broader than the horses' mouths.*

A gentleman, an owner of racehorses, applied to the saddler whose name has just been quoted for bits to stop a pair of thoroughbred horses that had more than once bolted with his coachman and himself. It was found that they had the trick of simultaneously laying hold each of one cheek of the Chifney bits with which they were tried. Finally they were fitted with bits of the Wimbush pattern, and to the astonishment of the owner, from the moment they found they could not lay hold of the cheeks, they submitted, and became perfectly docile. This was the moral as distinguished from a physical effect.

It cannot be too often repeated that good bitting gives control without pain. A bit that gives pain, or rather, that produces pain that the horse cannot cause to cease by dropping his head to the right position and yielding, is inexcusable. A tight curb-chain and powerful bit make the horse poke out his chin; and then an ignorant person pulls harder, tightens the curb, and resorts to a bit still more severe.

BLINKERS.

Blinkers, or winkers, sometimes called blinds, are almost universally used on the bridles of pleasure carriages in England, and generally on cart harness. In America, harness bridles are generally without blinkers.

Whether they are more useful or mischievous has been a subject of dispute for many years, but up to the present time, the more expensive the horses and harness the more certain are blinkers to be attached. The horses of the job-masters of London—more than a thousand pair—are all driven in blinkers, and I do not think any state carriage has ever been driven to Court without them.

The objections urged against them are, that if a horse can see behind he is less likely to be alarmed, run away, or set to kicking if he can see what is the matter; that blinkers in summer weather heat the eyes in an injurious manner; and finally, that they hide the most beautiful features of a horse's head—the eyes.

The first objection would be sound if every driver trained his own horses, and could be sure that every horse he purchased had been regularly driven without blinkers. It does not make a horse restive to put on a bridle with blinkers, but one accustomed to a naked bridle probably would become so.

After giving the subject—ever since the American Rarey published his arguments against the use of blinkers—a good deal of consideration, I have come to the following conclusions:

That it is a good plan to break in horses to harness without blinkers, because, when gradually introduced to the weight and noise of a carriage, they are much less likely to be frightened if they can see what is going on, if you have plenty of time, and break them in a light single carriage, without blinkers; if you are hurried, you must use a break-horse and blinkers.

That there is no objection to driving a single horse without blinkers in the country or in town, if it be one of those bold or placid animals that are not afraid of anything, especially of the waving whips of drivers met and passed, and that if he has a really handsome head it cannot be bridled too nakedly. But the average harness-horses are very much afraid of whips, and have large heads, which blinker-bridles improve by apparently diminishing their size.

That the objection to driving a pair of horses, as well as many single horses, is, that they are always looking back, watching the driver, starting the moment he mounts his seat, and flinching whenever he lays hold of the whip, so that he cannot touch the *slug* without exciting the *free-goer*.

That the advantage of blinkers, especially with high-bred, high-couraged fresh horses, full of corn and beans, is, that they help to concentrate their attention on the road straight before them, to render them in crowded streets less liable to shy to one side or the other on any sudden display of any alarming objects. In an American pattern of harness introduced with American horses by one of the tramway companies the blinkers are made to stand out. This looks strange and ugly, but it has the advantage of hiding the movements of the whip and not heating the horse's eyes; he can see all before him, but not behind.

That the eyesight of horses varies very much. Some fine goers, but timid shiers, are obliged to be driven with a band of leather connecting both blinkers, thus only allowing them to look down on their toes. There are racehorses of no mean merit that are run in blinkers, and even with front shades. It is certainly an advantage, where horses used in harness are also regularly ridden, that they should always wear the same kind of bridles—that is, without blinkers.

That where horses—for instance, those of a medical man in full practice—are driven fast and hard every day, they become such steady machines that they may safely be driven in almost any bridle or bits. But where they are objects of luxury and show they must be endowed with a placid, sensible temperament, and have careful training, if they are to face the crowds of the parks and streets of London in the season without blinkers.

Messrs. Barclay and Perkins the great brewers, as well as the owners of most of the trotting railway vans of London, have given up blinkers; and many sets of plough and cart-harness are to be found without them. But some persons urge as a reason for retaining them the necessity of protecting the eyes of cart-horses from the whips of their own drivers.

Any one who proposes to drive one horse, or a pair-horse phaeton, without blinkers, will find a very obstinate opposition in the harness-makers, who are naturally opposed to every change in the direction of that naked simplicity which is to be seen daily in the accoutrements

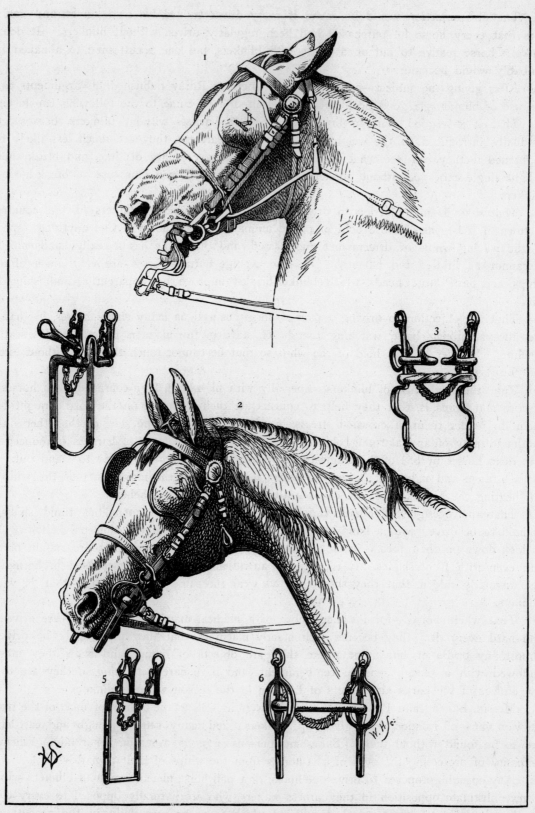

1. Horse in Torture.　2. Horse at Ease.　3. Instrument of Torture.　4. Exaggerated Chifney.　5. Wimbush Bit too long in Cheek.　6. Liverpool Bit.

of the tramway-car horses—*i.e.*, nothing more than a collar and traces, and bridles with their reins, without blinkers.

After all, it is, no doubt, much a matter of taste. It has been suggested that American trotting horses are driven without "blinds," that they may see when their rivals are overtaking them.

BEARING-REINS : THEIR USE AND ABUSE.

The bearing-reins are buckled either to a separate snaffle when a double bridle is used, or to the cheek of a Pelham bit, then passed through rings suspended from the head-stall, and hooked on a metal peg or hook provided for the purpose in the harness-pad.

This is the proper form, if a bearing-rein is to be used at all; but the fashionable bearing-rein consists of a round rein passing from a point of the head-stall at the joining of the frontlet, through a swivel attached to a snaffle-bit, through another ring, and then drawn to any degree of tightness a coachman may fancy over the pad-hook. This is the gag bearing-rein.

The object of a bearing-rein properly applied is to divide the weight upon the driver's hands; so that whenever the horse droops his head below a certain point, his mouth will come upon the bit of the bearing-rein, instead of leaning on the driver's hands. It causes a horse to bring his haunches better under him, prevents him from having too much liberty of head and neck, and removes the temptation of a horse full of beans to set to or run off with his driver.

It is also intended to prevent horses when standing still from dropping their heads in a very inelegant manner, rubbing them against each other or against the pole, to which, if there is a crossbar to the bit, they are likely to get fixed, when a frightful accident would be almost inevitable.

There are some horses that it is difficult for a strong man, and quite dangerous for a lady, to drive without bearing-reins—that is, with their heads free; and there are times when naturally docile horses are so fresh that it is advisable to put on bearing-reins, and this even with horses that carry their heads naturally in the beautiful form which it is vainly attempted to imitate with gag-reins.

The proper and only way in which bearing-reins should be allowed is when two conditions are observed : first, the snaffle-bit, instead of being drawn up into the cheeks, wrinkling and almost tearing them, should hang full *a quarter of an inch from the corners of the mouth*, next, the bearing-rein should be of such a length that the moment the horse raises his head to move into a trot it should become amply slack. A horse that habitually carries his head and neck like a pig is not fit for a pleasure carriage; but there are many intermediate stages between the grand style of head and neck at p. 347, which needs no bearing rein, and many a very good harness-horse.

Fitted as above directed, the bearing-reins will do no harm, and will prevent a pair of fresh horses in the hands of a fair driver from getting their heads first down, then up and away at the pace of destruction.

But this is not the sort of "fit" that satisfies your London coachman of the highest fashion. He begins by drawing up the gag-bit until he has enlarged the horse's mouth by at least a couple of inches. He then adds a curb-bit of an inch too wide and four inches too long, quite regardless of the size of the horse's mouth, and having curbed this up tight, takes up the reins, climbs on his box, and makes, whether moving or standing at a door, a display very satisfactory to the distinguished owners, who have not the least idea that their horses are enduring agonies for hours.

The result is shown by degrees in foaming, bleeding mouths, lolling tongues, roaring, spavins, restiveness—results to which less attention is paid because the greater number of the finest carriage-horses are jobbed, and job-masters are at the mercy of the "bad coachman."

Mr. Edward Flower, of Hyde Park Gardens, well known when he lived at Stratford-on-Avon as one of the hard-riding heavy weights of the Warwickshire Hunt, has agitated this question for some time, with that exaggerated enthusiasm which is essential if any deep-seated grievance is to be reformed. No great reform, from the time of Martin Luther to Clarkson and Wilberforce, has ever been effected by cautious advocates and soft suggestions.

Mr. Flower has particularly directed his attention to the iniquities of the gag bearing-rein, which may daily be seen in torturing operation in the best carriages in the height of the season, even in the carriages of the noble vice-presidents, patrons, and patronesses of the Royal Society for the Prevention of Cruelty to Animals.

There is not the least doubt that a bit of moderate proportions is, with a properly-fitted curb-chain, sufficient to restrain and drive, in the best form, any average horse. But as an ounce of fact is admitted to have more weight than a pound of rhetoric, I will quote the following example of Mr. Flower's experience:—"I bought," he says, writing in 1874, "some years ago, a magnificent horse at the hammer for a mere song, with the character of being a *roarer*, a *gibber*, and a *rearer*. He had been driven with a gag bearing-rein drawn up as tight as flesh would bear, and a bit weighing one pound fourteen ounces, eleven inches long in the cheek, and six inches long in the mouth. I took away the bearing-rein altogether—he naturally carried his head and neck magnificently—and substituted for the instrument of torture a simple 'Liverpool bit.' The roaring ceased soon after the bearing-rein was taken away; the bit and harness having been made easy, he ceased to pull, became docile, and grand in all his paces, and I might easily have had a profit of £150 on my purchase. I now drive him in my phaeton with a young horse broken on my own plan. I drive them in town and country, and they both obey the slightest touch of the reins."

It is necessary, however, to add that very good and humane coachmen object to the Liverpool bit for horses driven in pairs, because the action of the inside reins is likely to drive the upper part of the steel check into the horse's cheek when hard held.

In relation to the abuse of the bearing-rein, drivers should be reminded that although with the great majority of horses the conformation of the jaws opposes no obstacle to the head assuming the most desirable position, this is not always the case; if the space contained between the two jaws is narrowed so as to prevent the neck fitting in, as it will in a perfectly well-shaped head, he cannot bend his head into the curve we require to obtain the more perfect control over, and the best appearance in, a riding or carriage horse. In such cases, to try to make a horse bend his neck by the action of a bearing-rein is something like trying to straighten a limb with a stiff joint.

Again, there are certain glands which lie just under the angles of the two jaws, and run up in the direction of the ear. They are the seat of the affection, to which all young animals are subject, called strangles. Sometimes these glands are naturally very large; sometimes they become large as the result of disease; sometimes they become inflamed and enlarged from a driver attempting to obtain an impossible curve of the neck by bearing-reins and severe bits.

The agony of the animal under such pressure is excruciating; to get rid of the intolerable pain it will lie down, rear, kick, run away, and the ignorant brute on the coach-box knows no better remedy than "to flog the sulk out of him," whereas the whole restiveness is the result of bad bitting and bridling. Many young horses have lost their eyesight from undue pressure on these glands.

PAIR-HORSE HARNESS.

In pair-horse harness the pads may be as light as is consistent with the character of the vehicle, for they have not to sustain the weight of shafts or to assist in backing ; the latter is done by aid of the pole. In America, the pole of light trotting-wagons is sometimes fastened by a hinge, so as to fall on the ground when the horses are unharnessed, and is fastened to the pads for support as well as to the collars by a sort of splinter-bar arrangement, but this system has not found favour in this country.

Breeching is only used in the double harness of state carriages of great weight, and sometimes in stage-coaches, to divide the strain on the collars when travelling down hill ; but have been less used since patent breaks—which can be instantaneously put in action by the right hand of the coachman—have been brought to such perfection.

To put a pair of horses into double harness, each one should be taken up to the pole and attached to it by buckling the pole-pieces (the leather straps that are attached to each side of the pole), or hooking on the pole chains, which are used instead of leather in mail and Stanhope phaetons, as loosely as possible. Then buckle on the reins to the outer side of each, hanging the hand-pieces of the reins, knotted up, over the pad of one of the horses ; then, if there is only one man to harness, pass the traces over the roller-bolts—if there are two, these operations are performed simultaneously—and, finally, draw up the pole-pieces to the length required to make the traces draw evenly and squarely. For country work the collars should be attached to the pole, with ample play, so as to leave the horses with as much liberty as possible. In fashionable town carriages it is, on the contrary, the custom to draw the horses very closely to the pole, so as to make them as much as possible a part of the machine, and enable them to turn more rapidly within short spaces.

This tight harnessing is not so pleasant for the horses, and very much spoils the action of riding-horses, if driven in harness. It is quite unnecessary for useful work, but it is a matter of course in state and park parades.

The action of the reins in pair-horse harness is essentially different from that of single-harness reins, which act on each side of the horse's mouth.

In pair-horse harness, the part held in the hands, as to the outside reins, runs up to and is buckled to the outside ring of each horse's bit, but the inside reins (called coupling-reins), which are made with buckles movable up or down the outside reins, each pass through the terrets of the pads and of the collars, the right-hand rein through the inside terrets of the right-hand or off horse, the left-hand rein through the inside terrets of the left-hand or near horse ; but after passing through the collar's terrets they are crossed and buckled to opposite horses, so that when you pull the reins of the right-hand or off-side horse, you also pull off the rein of the near-side horse, and *vice versâ.*

The arrangement of these coupling-reins is a matter of great importance, for if one horse is more lively and faster in pace than the other, the whole comfort of driving depends on being able to bring them both to the same pace. To do this, the coupling-rein of the fresher or faster horse must be shortened by the buckle being brought nearer the driver's hands, so that a pull will act on him before it restrains the placid or dull horse. You may have to hold in the fresh horse while you apply the whip to the slug.

This is one of the prime arts of the good coachman, and is referred to in the song in the lines—

> " Here's to the wagoner, skilled in the art
> Of coupling the cattle together."

In order that the buckles of the coupling-reins may be adjusted more easily, their length has of late years been increased by about two feet, so as to bring them within not less than six inches of the hands of the driver. This variation has another advantage: it enables him to stop a pair of violent horses if they show any inclination to run away. By laying hold of the two inside and dropping the outside reins, he will bring their heads and legs so close together that they must almost inevitably stop or fall down. If a young or newly-purchased horse insists on cantering in harness, put on, in addition to the pair-horse reins, a pair of single-harness reins, as with these he can more easily be held down to the trot.

A good driver looks all over his horses' harness before taking his seat, sees that the curb and snaffle bits are properly adjusted in his horses' mouths, that the coupling-reins are buckled at the right length, as well as the pole-pieces or chains; if the latter are used, that the hooks are placed downwards and not upwards, so as not to catch in the bits or collars; then he deliberately takes his seat.

In taking horses out of harness, begin by unloosing, but not unfastening, the pole-pieces; then unbuckle the coupling-reins; then unloose the traces, rolling them up compactly to the pads; then unbuckle the pole-pieces, leading the horses clear away from the carriage, without allowing any part of the harness to dangle about them. Two halters should be ready to substitute for the harness bridles, which should be removed from their heads at once, and a hand-block put to stop the carriage-wheels from moving while unharnessing is going on.

Where the services of two or more grooms are available, the successive stages of harnessing and unharnessing may be performed almost simultaneously; but the occasions are frequent when the owner has to harness or unharness his own horses, with or without the assistance of some perfectly-ignorant yokel or street arab; and it is therefore important to know the due order for each successive operation.

Where bearing-reins are used, they should not be drawn over the pad hooks until the horses stand in their places beside the pole, and they should be unhooked before they are led away, after unharnessing.

TANDEM HARNESS.

Tandem, once the most fashionable style of driving, is very little seen now in great towns. A few years ago there was a tandem club amongst the officers quartered at Woolwich. In Australia it is much in vogue, probably because the roads are bad, and a traveller has an extra horse for use at a pinch. The tandem is one plan for keeping a riding-horse—the leader—in condition in the summer.

The latest improvement in tandem harness consists in the adaptation of three bars fastened to the shafts, which often prevent a leader from stepping over his traces. The tandem leader must have the natural courage that will keep him always up to the bit and in the collar; he must have no "shy" about him.

The tandem driver's safety and comfort depend entirely on the steadiness and power of his wheeler.

BREAKING TO HARNESS.

The easiest way of breaking a horse to harness is to put him into the hands of a professional breaksman, who has a break, an old break-horse who understands every word he says, and all the necessary apparatus.

These men, when they are sober, good-tempered, and not in too great a hurry to pronounce their pupils "quiet in harness," do wonders. The last is the greatest fault. Nine horses out of ten submit to everything the breaker requires, and with the help of an old break-horse, as sagacious as a tame elephant, may be returned, fit for the use of gentlemen, in three weeks, or even a fortnight; but the tenth, and perhaps a better animal than either of the other nine, objects to the bit, the collar, and the blinkers, refuses to go, stands still, or stops suddenly (technically, jibs), when forced up to start takes to kicking, and finally becomes so intolerably vicious as to be only fit for a Hansom cab, the final destination of a number of horses of the finest shape and action, who are not to be trusted in any less commanding vehicle, or spared from daily work.

There are, however, many instances in which the services of a breaker and break-horse are not to be had. The latter want is serious, because a break-horse at first does all the work, and the raw horse has only to run alongside the pole, and learn by degrees how to share the work. The driver of a break, seated high, and assisted by his intelligent quadruped partner, has such complete command, that only horses of immense power and determined vice dare resist him.

Horses that have been constantly ridden for a year or two—especially hunters accustomed to all sorts of blows, buffets, scratches, and squeezes in coverts and gateways—are, with rare exceptions, easily and quickly broken to harness, and, with the help of such things as are to be found on every farm, without any professional assistance.

The foundation of the art of breaking horses, whether to ride or drive, whether colts or practised hunters, is the same—viz., to accustom them by degrees to everything likely to alarm them; to avoid anything that may needlessly irritate them; and, finally, to keep them in such positions that they shall never have the least possible chance of successfully resisting the wishes or operations of the breaker.

That is not the ordinary course in ignorant stables: the animal is pulled out of his stall, where he may have been idly eating corn for a day or two, first alarmed by having a round collar forced over his head and eyes, then irritated by having his tail thrust through a crupper, still more irritated and alarmed by a bridle, with a pair of blinkers, and a huge bit, with no attention to fit, forced into his mouth. He is allowed very little time to get accustomed to all these trappings, even if pains are taken to prevent the traces and straps of the breeching from flapping about in an unpleasant manner.

The sensible plan is to have a collar that opens at the top; if he is going into single harness, a crupper that unbuckles, and may be slipped under instead of drawing the tail through it. Breeching is needless as a commencement. The bridle should fit. The bit a snaffle, unless there is reason to fear that he may bolt, when a pair of india-rubber reins may be buckled, as before described, to the lower bar of a Wimbush pattern bit.

Vieille Moustache, a high authority, the correspondent of *The Field* and *The Queen*, is in favour of blinkers for breaking; but I say no, let the horse or colt see what you are doing. This opinion is borne out by an experiment of the American Rarey.

The commanding officer of one of the regiments of household cavalry placed in his hands a cream-coloured stallion from Her Majesty's stud, that had resisted every effort of the rough-riders of the regiment to make it carry the kettledrums.

The horse was in the riding-school. Rarey took one of the drums, placed it before the horse's nose, and by degrees got him to smell it; then gave it a slight tap with his fingers, on which the horse started, but smelt it again. Repeating this operation again and again louder, and each time with a drumstick, after a series of starts and smells, the horse began to find out that the drum did him no harm. The drum was then placed against his side, and the tapping process repeated; finally, within certainly less than an hour, Rarey mounted his pupil and marched him round the school, beating the drum loudly. From that time forward the cream

EDMOND, BY ORVILLE, THOROUGHBRED HORSE, IN HARNESS.*

stallion bore the gorgeously-attired drummer, beating the silver kettledrums, pacing proudly at the head of the regiment.

Many horses cannot be broken, especially to harness, without a certain degree of force and punishment, but it should be the aim to create no unnecessary alarm.

With the harness on, let the horse be led about, and finally driven about, by a man on foot, until he becomes thoroughly accustomed to it. Some persons recommend having two men to hang on the traces, to teach the horse the feel of the collar; but this takes up the time of three men, which is not always convenient.

Where a large empty barn or other covered place, or an empty fold-yard, is available for these preliminaries, and also for putting in harness and driving in a carriage the first time,

* Was first hunted. In harness could trot sixteen miles an hour. Shot when twenty-four years old, after an accident.

it is better than an open road or field, because everything likely to excite or distract the attention of the equine pupil should be avoided. It is also advisable not to put harness on a well-bred hunter or riding-horse until he has had two hours of regular exercise, at such a pace as without exhausting, will take away all that superfluous energy which leads an animal to bounce and start at the slightest provocation, or if a young unbroken colt, by laying carefully. It may be advisable to break tight-bound three-year-olds to harness before they can be ridden safely by any one but a boy, and then laying is a valuable preparation.

The next question is, to what vehicle shall the horse be harnessed?

The circus people generally employ a log, with a splinter-bar to keep the traces, which should be very long, apart. This answers very well in a school, but in a field a light bush harrow, made of hurdles and the cuttings of hedges, would answer even better. In this way a horse is taught by degrees to pull a weight, and if he stops suddenly, the log or bush harrow does not run on him as a vehicle on wheels would.

The Americans, who make a study of harness-horses, generally break their trotters in one of their light four-wheeled wagons, which is not a wagon at all in our sense in England, but a very light phaeton. In this country a high two-wheeled vehicle of the dog-cart class is generally preferred.

There are two modes of using it. In one, and the less common, but suitable for training hunters, is to put a steady harness-horse in the shafts and attach the hunter, saddled and mounted, by traces to an outrigger pole with a splinter-bar, and have him ridden alongside the shaft horse. By this expedient a well-broken riding-horse in hard condition has been trained to harness in a single day. Another plan, especially adapted for horses inclined to kick, is to put the unbroken one in the shafts, where he is made fast by a strong kicking-strap, and accompanying him with a steady, well-broken horse harnessed to an outrigger, who will do all the work until he takes to the collar. Kicking can be kept down more effectually in shafts than in pair-horse harness.

The orthodox style of putting a new horse into single or double harness is fully described in the following paragraphs from the writings of a contributor to the *Old Sporting Magazine* who, in the course of his life and misfortunes, acquired great practical experience in every part of a coachman's art :—

" The horse should be harnessed in the stable, where he is least likely to be alarmed. A collar, opening at the top, should be put on. A crupper that unbuckles on both sides should be placed under the tail, which should be let down very gently on it. Everything should be done as quietly as possible. He should then be turned round in his stall, the bridle put on and buckled to the reins. He thus gets accustomed to winkers, which make every object come suddenly before him (this is my objection to breaking-in with winkers). After standing some time (Query, some hours), he should be led out to feel his new trappings, walked, and trotted.

"When he moves without being alarmed at these, the break, with the break-horse ready harnessed, should be placed where there is ample room for a plunge or two. The breaksman must find what sort of a mouth he has, and buckle the reins to the cheek or bars accordingly. The outside driving rein should be on him when he is led up, so that there is only the coupling rein to be fastened when he is put to. In forty-nine cases out of fifty the reins should be buckled to the cheek, but with a horse inclined to kick to the lowest bar.

" He must be taken up carefully, so as not to touch the pole suddenly. The breaksman stands at the head of the horses to give orders, one man is to be ready to pole-piece him loosely up, while at the same moment another man joints on the *outside* trace. He is now secure, and the inside trace can be fastened from behind the tame old break-horse. One of the men now takes the breaksman's place, caressing the pupil; if he is very restless he lays hold of his ear. The breaksman jumps up, and, unless with a very refractory customer, the old horse goes off gently. A man runs alongside the young one to encourage him, and keep his shoulder against him if he hangs too much out of harness. He should be allowed to trot along, without feeling either pole-piece or trace, until of his own accord he is willing to go forward. He should not be driven more than a mile, especially if in soft condition, lest his shoulders should be scalded, which would stop a daily lesson, and make him dread the collar. The greatest care should be taken not to alarm him in taking him out of harness. The coupling rein and inside trace must be first undone, then the pole-piece and outside trace, and care taken that he does not touch the break in going off."

To put a horse in single harness for the first time also requires three men, one at the horse's head—all the preliminary precautions having been observed—and two to quietly draw up the gig (a dog-cart with a seat behind, where a man can stand with his face to the horse, being the best for the purpose) and drop it into the open tugs. At the same moment the traces must be hooked on and the kicking-strap buckled to the proper length, which should be previously ascertained.

In this first lesson I think a bearing-rein, teaching the horse to be at ease on his haunches, almost essential. "The horse being in the break, and the driver in his seat, one man with a limp halter (which should be put on before the bridle) in his hand, the other with one hand on the shaft or the slip-iron, the first leads the horse, the other moves the cart gently on. No sound, no whip must be used. If the horse hesitates, let him stand still till he is inclined to move. When he does go, let him walk away, the man at his side keeping hold of the halter. After a time coax him to trot, the same man still running by his side. When he goes quiet, let this man fasten the halter to the 'D' of the hame, leave the horse's side, and step lightly up alongside the driver. Should the horse stop, let him stand. He will shortly want to go somewhere; let him take any road he likes, no matter which way, so long as he draws the break after him. *Of all things avoid a fight with a horse till the last extremity.* After a half an hour's drive at the outside take him out of harness with great precaution, lifting the shafts from him without allowing them to touch his flanks or rump."

CHAPTER XVII.

DRIVING.

The style of calm indifference which particularly distinguishes English coachmen, whether gentlemen or servants, has been very happily sketched by a French author, describing the court carriages at a Drawing Room in 1836, before the glories of dress coaches and chariots had been spoiled by such economical expedients as landaus and broughams, with their coach-boxes instead of hammer-cloths:—

"It is truly delightful to mark the fiery, almost fierce action of the horses, restrained without an apparent effort by an impassible coachman, seated on his hammer-cloth, like a throne; his left hand controlling the long white reins, with his whip, almost upright, resting on his right thigh.

"Napoleon, in giving instructions to David for his equestrian portrait, ordered that he should be represented calm, on a fiery horse—thus to characterise 'the power of mind over brute force.' On this principle every English coachman, seated on his box, has the air of a conqueror."

This calmness is as much the result of the national temperament (which has been described by another Frenchman as "the calmness of ferocity") as of the confidence of practised skill.

THE SEAT.

Every one who orders a carriage which he intends to drive himself should be measured for his seat, if he means to drive horses that require any driving at all. It must be of a height proportioned to the length of his legs, not too low, not too high, but easy and comfortable, just high enough to give the fullest power of hands and leverage of back and legs.

The upright position, almost standing against the sloping cushion of a four-in-hand drag or mail phaeton, much affected by the "golden youth" of the day, is a mistake. It leaves no strength in reserve; the driver can neither give nor take. If his horses pull, bolt, or fall down, he has no power to resist or assist them. As likely as not in a desperate case he may be pulled off his box. Nothing looks worse than to see a driver obliged to throw his head back if he pulls up suddenly. For this reason when a carriage is ordered the seat should be low rather than high, because a low seat can be raised.

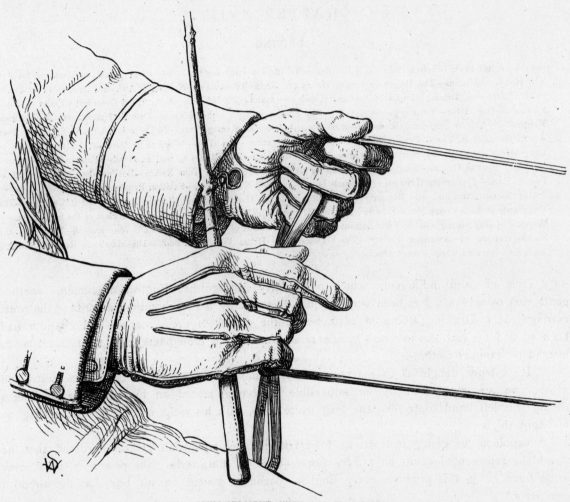

GOING STRAIGHT, WITH ONE OR A PAIR.

THE HANDS AND REINS.

The above woodcut (drawn from life) shows how the reins should be held, with one or a pair, going straight. (*The left hands in all the woodcuts are drawn rather too forward.*) The elbows should hang easily, be close to but not touching the hips, the wrists and hands slightly bent round in front of but not far from the body. This gives the fullest command over the horses, and should enable the driver to stop them without moving his body. No habit is more fatal to good driving than that of allowing the arm or hands to be dragged out by the pull of the horses until the elbows are away from the hips, and the hands approaching the splashboard, yet nothing is more common amongst amateurs of both sexes, who drive very expensive equipages. Raising the hands to the eyes when obliged to pull up suddenly, instead of shortening the reins by passing the right hand before the left, is the very worst form of driving. Equally offensive and equally frequent is the vile trick of bending the body and poking out the nose towards the horse's ears, instead of sitting squarely, not stiffly upright, in an easy commanding position. Every day in the London season you may see as many well-dressed persons of both sexes making pitiable exhibitions of their driving capabilities as you do of

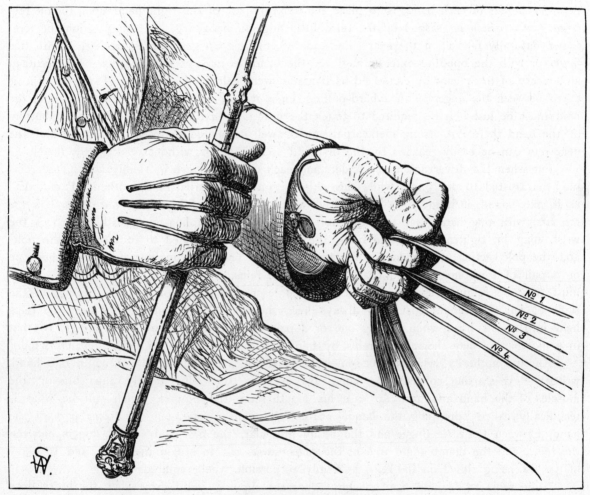

FOUR-IN-HAND, GOING EASY.

No. 1, Near-side Leader; No. 2, Off-side Leader; No. 3, Near-side Wheeler; No 4, Off-side Wheeler.

crippled screws, lapped in gorgeous-crested harness, driven by richly-liveried servants in carriages conspicuously emblazoned not unfrequently with coronets.

"The *rationale* of driving may be compared to steering a boat. There must be no pulling and hauling first on one side and then the other; the slightest movement will be felt (on a well-broken, well-bitted horse) and anticipated: just as much pressure as is needful to keep the head straight; this pressure on either rein is, or should be, very slight.

"Steady old stagers jog along in single harness without any particular guidance, except when pulled out of the way of something, and free horses press forward naturally in a straight line ; but a horse that has the slightest inclination to turn to either side cannot be guided with one hand. Yet driving horses in single harness with one hand is considered the correct thing, and practised by many self-taught drivers.

"With the reins in one hand in single harness you may at any moment be left perfectly helpless—the precious moment lost before you can get up the other hand. The slightest movement of the horse turns the shafts, and as the reins run parallel to the shafts, there is the least possible guiding power in the hand. The best way of using the second hand, if you do not take a rein in each hand, is to place the exterior part of the right hand upon the off rein (*right hand*), which is grasped by the third little finger if necessary. In this position the forefinger naturally falls upon the near rein, and by exercising a gentle pressure, either with this finger or with the opposite exterior angle of the hand, as may be required, as much accuracy and nicety of force may be employed as if a rein were held in each hand. If the off rein is taken between the fingers with a hard-pulling horse, it will soon cut and tire them, and the hold must be lost if it be required to touch the near (*left hand*) rein ; whereas, at the bottom of the hand there is a strong metacarpal muscle well calculated to resist the strain, and the near rein can be easily reached by the first and second fingers without relaxing the hold."

But when the driver and horse understand each other, and are in steady action, the reins may be trusted to one hand, while the whip is gracefully carried in the other. Paradoxical as it may sound, it is much easier to drive and turn a pair of horses, *if they go well up to the bits*, with one hand than a single horse, because the coupling-reins, with a turn of the wrist, may be tightened so as to bring the outside horse intended to turn toward the pole, and the pole, acting as a rudder, turns the carriage. Therefore, in starting with either one or a pair of fresh horses, good coachmen take the reins in both hands ; and in both hands must they be retained as long as there is the least probability of a horse turning to the right or left. A careful coachman always keeps his right hand conveniently near the reins held in the left hand when driving one or a pair of animals of blood and courage, so that in a moment he may shorten the reins by taking hold an inch or two before his left hand.

Another authority, who objects somewhat to the idea of holding the reins in one hand, writes :—"At starting collect your horse by grasping the reins tightly, thus bracing the muscles of the hand and arm ; to ease his mouth relax the muscles, which will be what is technically called 'dropping the hand.' Hold the reins gripped in the lower part of the hand, between the little finger and the fleshy muscular, the first and second fingers between the reins, and the thumb quite free of the reins, so as not to stiffen the hand, and to allow of the fist being closed on the reins as firmly as possible when required.

"The reins to be held firm enough to prevent slipping, yet lightly when the horse does not pull.

"The right hand holds the whip (which is held upright, slightly leaning to the left); when on the reins the exterior part of the hand rests upon the off rein, which is grasped by the little finger, if necessary, to steady the hand.

"In this position the forefinger easily falls upon the near rein, and by exercising a gentle pressure with this finger on the near rein, or with the opposite exterior angle of the hand on either rein, as may be required, as much accuracy and nicety of force may be employed as is necessary.

"The hands and arms to be kept quite steady (muscles relaxed), the hand with a steady even feeling on the horse's mouth. The reins always taut, but held as if afraid of breaking them ; the horse giving a little tug at each move. If the horse tries to bear on or take

Sheldon-Williams.

R. E. Nast Sc.

TAKING UP YOUR PARTY.

liberties with the hand the muscles of the hand and arms to be instantly braced, and then relaxed : this relaxing of the muscles forming, in horsey language, *the drop of the hand*.

"By closing and opening the hand the horse is kept collected and lively; if more collection is required the whip will be necessary.

"In fine driving for ladies, and with thoroughly well-broken horses, the off rein may be between the third and fourth finger of the right hand, instead of in the full of the hand, thus admitting of an easier change of hands and shortening of reins."

STARTING.

Having walked round to see that the harness is properly adjusted—nothing omitted, nothing too tight or too loose—the driver should, after taking his seat, begin by pulling his horses together, stopping them, as it were. Harness-horses, however high-couraged, should be taught to stand until the driver is quite ready, and to start at some familiar word, such as "*Come now !*" or "*Go along now, pretty boys !*" and not until it is given, and constantly stimulated to go up to the bit by the voice, instead of relying on that essential instrument the too-much-abused whip.

The horses must be always kept up to the bit, and the reins must always be held so that the driver can feel his horses' mouths, and at such a length, with the hand or hands in such a position, that they can be pulled up at any moment without any apparent exertion. A driver should be able to shorten his reins and stop a pair of well-bitted, well-broken horses with a turn of his wrist. But, at any rate, his right hand should be laid so handy to the left that he can place it two inches before it.

Accustom your horses to start slowly. When fairly under weigh, if driving a distance, choose a pace that suits the slower of the pair, and keep to it for any reasonable distance, taking advantage of the nature of the road, to save and ease them by averaging the miles per hour—making play over level and down moderate declivities, going slowly up hill—and only allowing them to walk if the road is very rough, in very hot weather, or up very steep hills.

In passing other vehicles, and rounding corners, always take plenty of room ; leaving "shaving to half an inch" to Hansom cabmen, van-drivers, and coachmen of *accoucheur* physicians.

In driving in town and in a crowd, horses must be kept on their haunches as well as up to the bit, so as to stop or turn instantaneously ; and the driver before pulling up must look well ahead, so as to select a clear space. In a mob of carriages, sluggish are even more dangerous than fiery horses ; but nervous horses, however beautiful and well-broken, are quite unfit for the use of ladies or timid drivers. To look well in town a pair of horses must step in time, like soldiers; style being more important than pace. "To step and go together " is perfection.

Ladies have much more need of a driving tutor than gentlemen. They must bear in mind that many family coachmen—safe, steady men—are ignorant of the first principles of their business.

In going down-hill with a pair of horses, the pace should be regulated by the steepness. The drag should not be put on unnecessarily : that is to say, only where the carriage would without it be likely to run on to the horse's hind-quarters. If it is necessary to go fast, the horses should, as it were, run alongside the pole with slack traces. If the carriage is to be held hard back by the pole-chains, a slow pace is essential. A bad coachman either wears his horses out with holding back, or by going too fast down-hill loses all command.

The whip is a part of driving apparatus that can rarely be dispensed with, yet which should be used as little as possible. Good horses who know their driver rarely require more than a slight indication. But if a horse declines to go into the collar and up to a bit that fits, and is not too sharp for him, the whip must be used freely, but without temper, until he gives way. But before resort is had to this *ultima ratio* of charioteers, the driver should

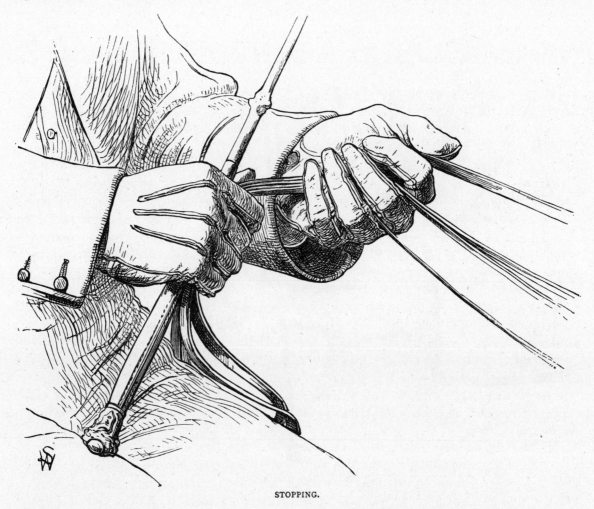

STOPPING.

be quite sure that all the harness fits, and that the bridle suits the mouth and temper of the animal.

A lady's whip should be very long, and as she generally sits low, she should be carefully taught never to hit horses behind the pad, and, if possible, on the forearm or shoulder.

Horses should work clear of the pole, but parallel with it. This may be helped by occasionally slightly touching the shoulders near the pole with the point of the whip. Whether they will work in the form they should will depend on their being properly coupled: that is, that the reins when crossed draw evenly, according to the shape and temper of each horse. An observant coachman will alter his coupling-reins half a dozen times in half an hour the first time he puts a new pair of horses in harness.

Horses strapped too close to the pole are sure to throw out their hind-quarters when suddenly stopped; they cannot help it, and yet they are often flogged for an ungraceful position produced by the mode of harnessing.

In every kind of harnessing the driver must remember to use his brains as well as his hands. When driving in streets he should look at least twenty yards ahead, and when on a country road as far as he can see, so that he may be prepared for any obstacle or anything

TURNING TO THE RIGHT.

that may make his leaders shy, and not be compelled to pull up unexpectedly, and of course start again with a jerk.

No matter whether it is the most unpretending single pony carriage or the most costly pair, the driver who desires to be safe, not to say elegant, in driving, should start on correct principles, listen to those competent to instruct, and study the best examples; for, to repeat a simile already quoted, the most elaborate instructions will not teach any one half as well how to use a wheelbarrow as to see a navvy wheel one.

DRIVING FOUR-IN-HAND.

The fashion, recently revived after a long interval, of driving four horses in hand is not a century old, although when every country gentleman was obliged by the state of the roads to drive at least four horses in his coach, the master must often have been obliged to take hold of the reins when his servant was absent or incapable from the too profuse hospitality of those days. The Earl of Albermarle, in his delightful " Reminiscences," says :—" In 1808, the year of my admission to Westminster, the famous Four-in-hand Club was established. It soon became the height of fashion to acquire not only the skill of coachmen, but to ape their dress, their manners, and their slang.

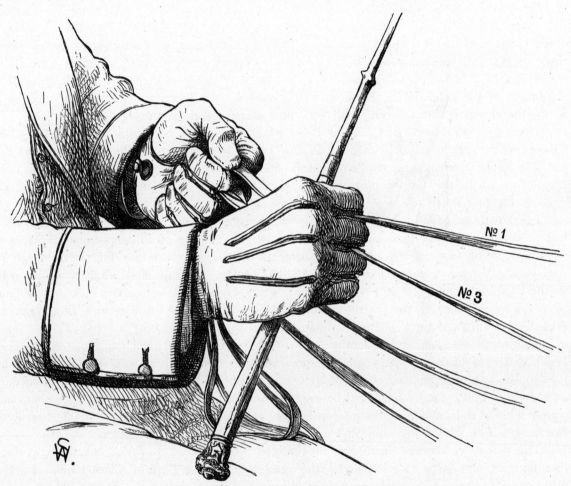

TURNING TO THE LEFT.

" We Westminster boys, of course, followed the fashion as far as we could. We drove hackney coaches whenever we could get the chance.

" One Sunday seven of us met by agreement at the top of St. James Street ; each engaged a hackney coach ; and having deposited our jarvies inside, we mounted our respective boxes and raced down to Westminster, the north end of Dean's Yard being our winning-post. Over such roads, with such sorry cattle, the wonder is that we all reached goal.

" When I became big enough to manage a team, I frequently had the honour of driving the London and Norwich mail."

George Prince of Wales patronised the new fashion, and made four-horse coaches one of the attractions of his residence at Brighton. Not that the Prince drove four-in-hand himself ;

for either as a point of distinction, or, as Charles Greville cynically hints, to make the task easier, the team of his barouche consisted of six horses, four of them in hand. The leaders were conducted by a postillion, an arrangement still perpetuated in the Lord Mayor's state coach.

"In those days," says Tom Raikes, "the Prince made Brighton and Lewes races the gayest scene of the year in England. The Pavilion was full of guests; the Steyne was crowded with all the rank and fashion from London, and the racecourse was crowded with the handsomest equipages. About half an hour before the signal of departure for the hill the Prince himself would make his appearance to the crowd. I think I see him now in a green jacket, a white hat, tight nankeen pantaloons, and shoes (!) distinguished by his high-bred manner and handsome person. The Prince's German wagon [so barouches were then called] and six bay horses—the coachman on the box being replaced by Sir John Lade—issued out of the gates of the Pavilion, and, gliding up the green ascent, was stationed close to the grand stand, where it remained the centre of attraction for the day."

When the "Tantivy" and "Tally ho's" were running on our main roads, broken-down dandies took to the coach-box, as they do now to the betting-ring and horse market, and did not disdain to receive the extra half-crowns middle-class passengers of horsey tastes were only happy to bestow for the pleasure of sitting alongside a scion of aristocracy, a *ci-devant* swell of the first water.

Besides those who were compelled by their necessities to do for a living what they had previously done for their amusement, there were a number of country squires, noblemen, and persons of less degree, who took shares in horsing fast coaches for the privilege of occasionally driving. Some, like the celebrated Captain Barclay of Ury, as may be read in the pages of "Nimrod" and "The Druid," went seriously into coaching speculations, not to make money, but for the fun of the thing. The captain once drove from Edinburgh to Aberdeen for a wager, and, after a hot bath, offered to drive back!

The result of coaching competition and the alliance of gentlemen, as a matter of sport and a matter of business, was a great improvement in every department—in the roads, the harness, the coachmen, and also the formation of a school of coachmen amongst the aristocracy and gentry, whose four-in-hand coaches and barouches were turned out in a number, and driven with a skill of which this generation had very little idea, until the sudden revival of the taste, which, after many failures, burst out suddenly about the year 1870.

The galaxy of dandies mentioned in the sketch of Rotten Row, of course, went into four-in-hands, and joined a club under the presidency of the Earl of Chesterfield, and the instructions, for those who condescended to be taught, of that good whip, Lord Sefton.*

In 1839, the year of the queen's coronation, the performances of this driving club are sketched in anything but flattering terms by the satiric laureate of Hyde Park, whose verses have already been quoted in Chapter XI.

> "Following his track [Lord Chesterfield's] succeeds a numerous band,
> Who vainly strive to work their fours-in-hand,
> For Richmond bound. I view them passing by,
> Their whips unsteady and their reins awry.
> Some chip their panels, some their horses' knees ;
> Beaufort and Payne, I class you not with these,

---

* I have a capital coloured caricature of Lord Sefton, entitled "A Good Whip," by Gilray.

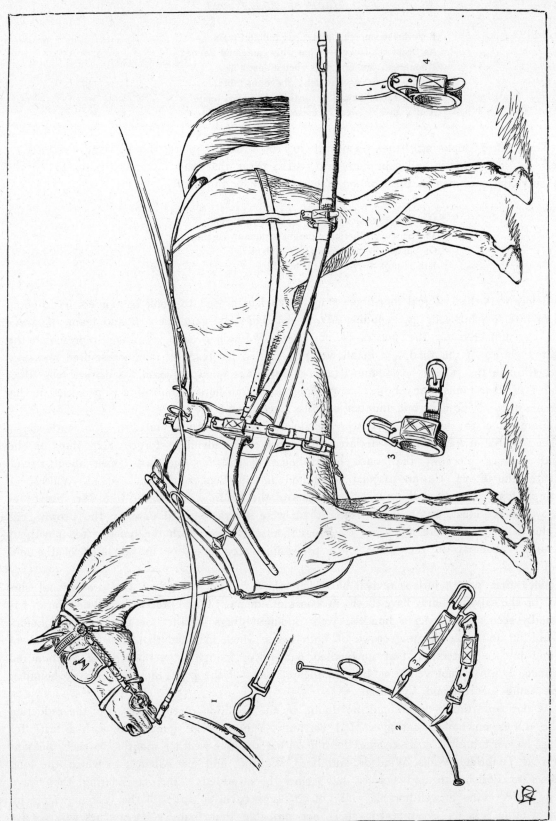

HORSE IN SINGLE HARNESS.

1. French Hammer-headed Hames.
2. Bancroft's Patent.
3. Shaft-tug, with Buckle for Long Breeching.
4. Kicking-strap Tug.

> For who so smoothly glides o'er hill and plain
> As Beaufort's Duke?—What whip can equal Payne?
> No matter; dinner comes when all are able
> To drive their coaches well; above the table,
> Ricardo [John Lewis] then can driving feats relate,
> And Bathyany swear he cleared the gate."

Then, after deploring "the season gliding by," he refers to the carriage destined to supersede alike curricles and cabriolets, and to the team that was for many years to be the only surviving specimen of the London coaches killed by railroads.

> " Haply there rattles through the evening gloom
> The one-horse chariot of the inconstant Brougham;
> Or Butcher Savage shows his coach of red,
> His harness dirty and his team ill-bred."

Before 1845 the last real four-horse stage-coach had ceased to book passengers in London. The private four-horse drags, including Mr. Henry Peyton's yellow coach and team of greys could be numbered on the fingers of one hand. "Butcher Savage" alone represented the departed glories of the road, and in all weathers rattled his team of four coarse-bred iron-grey horses through the suburbs—condemned, according to the gossip of omnibus drivers (who then included in their ranks many broken-down knights of four-horse fame), under penalties in his father's will, to drive a certain number of miles every day!

From time to time attempts were made to revive driving clubs, but, an authority— the head waiter at "Limmer's"—declared that most of the members forgot their whips on the second season's meet at that once noted house of call for the fast "men about town." In 1870, the F. H. C., an association limited in numbers, and exclusive as White's or Boodle's, alone maintained the ancient traditions of the road. And if the late Mr. Morritt of Rokeby, its president, was to be believed. there were several entitled to wear the brown coat and club button who were not willing to trust themselves even with the quietest team without "a nurse" at hand, in the shape of a professional coachman or an amateur of the old school.

Since that date a furious revival has taken place. The services of the professional survivors of the coaching era have been in constant demand; and recently Hyde Park has repeatedly seen as many as a hundred well-appointed drags paraded on the same day before an admiring and discriminating crowd of both sexes, which included the *crème de la crème* of the mid-day frequenters of that unequalled out-of-door lounge; the majority of the hundred coachmen, however, not venturing beyond the precincts of the park and the territory bounded by St. James's Street and Tyburnia.

At the same time—encouraged, no doubt, by the abolition of turnpikes, and the reduction of the duties on horses, carriages, and servants—a number of gentlemen, with a taste for driving, have established stage-coaches to run during the fine-weather months, to such pleasant resorts as Tunbridge Wells, Windsor, Guildford, Watford, and St. Albans; to which the long journeys to Portsmouth and Oxford have since been added. But considering the heavy expense of working a well-horsed, well got-up stage-coach, in spite of the best management, the inevitable loss on every season, it is not probable that many stage-coaches will survive the fashion of the present generation.

ELEMENTARY HINTS.*

"A man may learn many things in riding and driving by observation and practice, but no man can learn how to put four horses together, and drive them in the best English style, without going to school under a really good coachman, strictly imitating his example, and following his instructions.

"A first-rate 'wagoner' should have courage, decision, good eyesight, a flexible hand, and strength in the arms and back.

"It is assumed that the pupil knows how to drive a pair of horses. If he has only been accustomed to drive a light modern mail phaeton, he must commence his first lessons by driving a full-sized pair of horses with a heavy coach behind them, and he must practise with a coach and pair, until he has it under complete command, before he has the leaders hooked on.

"The mere exertion of holding four horses going freely for an hour is so great, that a pupil who has not been in the habit of using the muscles of his left arm by sculling, practising with dumb-bells or Indian clubs, or other gymnastic exercises, will find himself disabled before he has taken a lesson of a quarter of an hour. This preparatory training of the muscles of the left arm and side is particularly important in the case of slight, light men, who in this art are at a disadvantage as compared with tall, muscular, or heavy men.

"Indeed, the premature welter weight, who finds great difficulty in obtaining hunters up to his weight, may find himself quite in his place on the coach-box.

"The position of the coachman on the box is of more importance on a four-horse drag than on any other kind of carriage. It is essential that he should be able, in the event of a horse falling or the team attempting to bolt, to exert his utmost strength and weight at a moment's notice.

"This he cannot do if he is standing bolt upright against a sloping cushion, according to a modern mistaken fashion.

"The use of the whip may be learned in a great degree without the horses, sitting on any sufficiently high place, and practising how to wield it in a workmanlike manner.

"There is a proper position for the stick, and for every part of it down to the point, and the proper way of using it at full length, double thonged for rousing the wheelers, or curled round the shaft ready for immediate use either way.

"You are not a coachman until you are so familiar with its use that you carry it as it should be carried without thinking of it at all, and can use it, hold it, and curl it up as it should be used and held. At the same time, a common fault of young coachmen is to devote too much attention to the whip, endeavouring to employ it in a showy manner, curl and uncurl it, touching leaders that want no touching, double-thonging steady working wheelers, or letting the leaders get out of hand, do too much, wear themselves out, or at a sharp turn snap off the end of the pole or bring the whole drag to grief.

"The first few lessons will be well employed in sitting alongside the teacher, without taking hold of the reins, and watching his every movement, and learning by heart his instructions. Young men, especially young men of fortune, surrounded by humble toadies, are often too conceited to listen, and too impatient to begin the second lesson before they have learned the first.

---

* These hints have been taken down from the mouth of —— Carter, best known as "Tim Carter" (the consulting counsel of the younger members of the Driving Clubs) ; have been revised by the late Mr. Thomas Rice, of Kinnerton Street, and by some distinguished members of the "Road Club." The drawings have been made from life, Mr. Rice having *posed* for the purpose.

"The pupil, when he first takes hold of the reins, should not, out of natural pride, hold them after his arm is tired; there is not nearly so much to be learned by persevering in pain as by a series of short lessons.

"In a four-in-hand coach the wheelers should start it, and turn it round, without the leaders ever feeling their traces; and of course they must stop it with the traces of the leaders slack.

"Having carefully satisfied yourself that every horse is properly harnessed and bitted, mount the box deliberately, your grooms being at the horses' heads, and mind that they stand still until you give the word to start.

"This is an essential part of the breaking of a gentleman's team (often neglected), and should be insisted on.   Take your seat, adjust your apron and the reins, taking care to have the leaders so in hand that when they do move they will be *out of the collars and clear of the splinter-bars*.

"I repeat that it is essential for the comfort of the driver that a team, however high-couraged, should wait until he tells them to go.

"On starting, the reins must be placed, and throughout the drive retained, at such a length, and the right hand in such place, that you can pull up your team at any moment.

"Unless you can do this you cannot have proper control of your horses.   If I get alongside a young gentleman who has great conceit of his own driving, the first thing I ask him to do is to stop, and that suddenly, when he least expects such a request."

The first lessons should be devoted to learning how to start, how to stop, and how to turn on either hand.   Day after day should be devoted to this practice for successive weeks, until the pupil performs the requisite motions instantaneously and mechanically.   Practice may fairly be commenced with an old team, that have learned to obey the slightest indication and do half the driver's work for him; but a man is not *a coachman* until he can hold, turn, and stop fresh, fiery horses, not all of the same temperament.

All the first lessons should be on level ground, in roads clear of traffic, and not until the pupil has thoroughly mastered the elementary lessons should he be trusted in crowded streets or market-places.   As people generally get out of the way of a four-horse coach, he may delude himself into the idea that he is driving when he is only clearing the road.

When starting, going straight on level ground, turning right and left, and stopping have been performed in a satisfactory manner, then descending steep hills may be carefully practised, remembering to always go slowly over the tops of hills, whether big or small.

All this sounds easy enough; but how the wheelers are to do their work, when to run down without, when to put on the patent drags, how regulate the pace—these are material points which can only be acquired by long practice under judicious instruction.

Great care must be taken not to acquire slovenly habits, as nothing is so difficult to cure as a bad style.

FOUR-IN-HAND HORSES AND CARRIAGES.

The character of the horses for a four-in-hand will depend on the kind of carriage used and the purse of the owner.

As before observed, all the real work is done by the wheelers; therefore, if the carriage is heavy the wheelers must be able to start it up-hill and hold it down-hill.   As to pace: If the team is meant for work and distance, the wheelers should be able to trot at the rate of fourteen miles an hour, which will allow the leaders to gallop.   To try such horses, singly or as a pair, see if they can trot a mile in four minutes; if they can do that without making a fuss or a trouble of it, they are fast enough for anything in England.

Then set the pair to trot up a steepish hill, say to the "Star and Garter" at Richmond, at about eight miles an hour. If they will do that freely, without the whip, you may be satisfied that you have something quite above the average.

Formerly there were teams merely intended for the park and parade, but the present taste (1875-8) is for horses that can go down to Epsom from London, or some such distance, at a fair pace, with a full load, and return in the evening in good style. A well-matched team that combines brilliant action with pace is worth at least a thousand pounds. Extraordinary beauty is not to be expected in wheelers that have both pace and action, but if intended for ornamental purposes they should have "character." The leaders should have plenty of courage, carry themselves well, with, as the dealers say, "two good ends," and be both free and docile. The coachman, with a heavy coach behind him, has great command over his wheelers, but he has to trust a good deal to the honour of his leaders.

For utility in the country a team may be made up with a pair of barouche horses as wheelers, and a couple of hunters, or other riding-horses, as leaders.

The leaders are often an inch lower than the wheelers; although some contend that they should be taller, and others that all four should match in height. The most expensive teams match in height, action, character, colour, and age. But such are quite the exception. Most four-in-hand amateurs are glad to get two good pairs of horses, about the right size and character, with really good action, viz., two real machines as wheelers, two blood ones as leaders. As to colour, where the action is above average and the character right, there are often two, sometimes three, colours, and occasionally four shades of colour in the four. Brilliant step and go action cover a multitude of defects. As to age, some of the best horses in London teams are perfect patriarchs, but then they have never done any real work.

In the country for driving to cover, to races, to picnics, &c., scratch teams are made up anyhow, utility and pace being the principal considerations. In such cases a real coachman is required, if safety, not to say despatch, is an object.

There is one condition essential for driving four-in-hand pleasantly, and that is that the driver should have a high seat, overlooking and commanding his horses. Four ponies driven in hand from a low phaeton may be an amusement to the wagoner, and may be useful over very bad roads, but they always look like a draggle-tailed, make-shift affair, and they would be much better harnessed in the Russian or Hungarian style, three or four abreast

The Queen of the Belgians, who is a capital whip, used to drive four ponies in hand from a low *char-à-banc* on the sands at Ostend, but there the sands are so soft and deep that four ponies are really wanted to go into the collar all at once to get along even at a moderate pace.

There are at least three different kinds of carriages in common use for four-in-hand teams in this country.

First, the old-fashioned coach, which will stand a great deal of work and carry a great load—passengers and luggage. This is the pattern much affected by regiments, which make it, in their marches from station to station, amusing, useful, and ornamental. Secondly, what may be called the park drag, which is not meant to carry any luggage heavier than a ladder for the ladies to ascend and descend, an ice safe, and other materials for a picnic. Invention has been exhausted by such firms as Messrs. Peters, Barker, Hooper, Holland, and Shanks, in adding to the comforts and luxuries of the park drag. But it has one drawback: it only affords four good seats, all outside, in addition to the driver's, viz., his companion's and the three favoured mortals who sit behind him, although seats are sometimes improvised in returning from picnics, races, or other social meetings on the roof, as well as those facing and alongside the groom; yet it is not an arrangement to be commended.

Thirdly, the old-fashioned break, formerly chiefly used for exercising the stud and bringing fodder from the farm, which has been converted into a very luxurious open carriage—as a wagonette—with a high driving seat, holding two on the box and six or more inside, with places for two grooms, in two spoon-like seats outside, below the level of the company. Fourthly, borrowed and improved from the Continent, the *char-à-banc*, with a high driving seat, which divides the guests inside into rows across, instead of their sitting opposite as in a wagonette.

One advantage of the two last described carriages is that they can be built of a size and weight to suit any size of blood ponies and horses, from twelve to sixteen hands high, and the wagonette can be converted into an omnibus.

H.R.H. the Princess of Wales, when at Sandringham, drives from a high seat a very neat *char-à-banc*, four brown ponies, about twelve hands high, in hand. This carriage holds four inside, with two grooms sitting back, as on a dog-cart.

MAXIMS FOR YOUNG COACHMEN.

1. Look over horses, harness, and coach, before starting.
2. Make the team stand while you take your seat deliberately.
3. Start slowly, with the leaders out of the bars, but the traces slack.
4. With an eye to your leaders, look well ahead.
5. Don't shave close what you pass; take plenty of room round a corner.
6. Go slowly over the crown of all hills, great or small.
7. Look to the condition of each horse when you halt after driving a distance.

THE EXPENSES OF ROAD COACHING.

The following figures are not estimates, but the actual expenses which were divided between two gentlemen who worked thirty miles one of the pleasantest routes out of London in first-rate style:—

25 horses, at £60 each	£1,500
6 sets of harness, at £7 10s.	45
Other expenditure, say	255
Capital required	£1,800

Weekly Expenses.

Hire of coach, 2½d. a mile	£3 0s.
Coachman's wages	3 3s.
Guard	1 5s.
Horse-keepers	6 5s.
Forage	26 5s.
Shoeing	3 15s.
Standing of coach at both ends of journey	2 10s.
	£45 18s.

The capital would be partly returned on the sale of the horses, &c.

The expenses were £50 a week, and the return from passengers and parcels about £35 a week.

Another partnership of two gentlemen estimate the balance of loss on fifty miles of road for nineteen weeks at £1,000, or £500 apiece.

An offer has recently been made by a horse-dealer to supply horses and fodder for working the fifty miles for nineteen weeks for £1,000!

ANOTHER ESTIMATE.*

Horses cannot be purchased for less than fifty pounds apiece (the horses of the Guildford and Dorking averaged sixty). The contract in the country for feed is 17s. 6d. per horse per week. But it is a far better plan to have the chaff cut and the corn mixed at one depôt and deliver to the stablemen each week sacks enough for the stud for the week; it diminishes the temptation to steal, or feed pigs or fowls.

As to stabling, a farm-house is more desirable than a public-house, if it can be got The stages must not be more than eight miles apart: less if galloping is to be done.

The coach is usually miled at a price agreed on with the builder.

Colour is a matter of taste. White and red of the under carriage of the Tunbridge Wells, primrose and red of that famous whip the late Mr. William Cooper's coach, and the old mail red of the Windsor, are all good.

Modern coaches are too heavy (soft Wolverhampton steel instead of iron ought to be used). No passenger coach should weigh more than 20½ cwts. Each coach should be provided with two sets of wheels, and should be overhauled carefully at the end of each journey; wheels sometimes catch fire.

A dirty coach is not a nice thing to start with; a second coach is convenient, if not, the coach must be washed.

The appearance of a coach is improved by seating only the guard and two passengers on the hind seat.

Under no circumstances should passengers be allowed on the roof when it is intended for luggage; the less the better, if you want your stage-coach to run as light as possible.

Harness may sometimes be bought by auction at the end of the season very cheap, the property of young gentlemen who started with everything purchased on credit, regardless of price.

Following the example of the London General Omnibus Company, there should be a double set of harness at each stage, so that the man in charge can clean the dirty one and be ready with the clean one. Chain ends to the traces have one advantage: they tell in the dark if a wheeler is shirking his work.

Shoeing should be contracted for. Let the professional coachman examine each horse's feet at every convenient opportunity, and see how the work is done.

Helpers.—Pay them each £1 a week, and 5s. a week to be paid at the end of the season, if they stay and behave properly.

Stable utensils and headstalls are best purchased in London from the wholesale men. Stokes, Little Moorfields, is ready to contract for these and also for harness.

A corn chest with lock is required if corn is given unmixed, but a locked-up shed for the sacks of mixed provender is better.

Fares.—Threepence a mile should be the standard.

* Condensed from *Baily's Magazine*, June, 1878.

I cannot help thinking that on roads of not more than thirty miles, worked as they are now only in the summer season, the stage-coach pattern is not advisable, for outside places are more in demand than inside on short journeys. A good kind of *char-à-banc*, purchased by Sir Talbot Constable, was built by Bennett of Ipswich; something of the sort, with all outside seats and the luggage in a well, would probably prove a great success if introduced by a man of fashion.

AMERICAN TROTTING.

In England the most costly horse is a race-horse, for the simple reason that a race-horse can win more money in a shorter period than any other kind of horse while on the turf, and earn more as a stallion, if successful, on retiring from the turf. Race-horses in England are maintained as a trade by the many, and as an amusement by the few. A gentleman by birth and education, who would think himself degraded by keeping a shop or a public-house, has no hesitation in embarking in the financial and financing business of owning and betting on race-horses, associating with blacklegs, employing "touts" (*i.e.*, spies) to report on his rivals' horses, and agents to bet against his own.

Other pleasure horses, whether hunters, harness, or hacks, are not valued so much for mere speed as for other qualities. The park hack of great price may be even slow. The priceless harness-horses of the stately barouche, or even the fast mail phaeton, would seem to stand still alongside a third-class American trotter. The perfect, thorough-bred hunter, the pride of a Leicestershire stable, may have been, or would be hopelessly distanced in a cup race at Ascot or Goodwood. It is his fencing, his figure, and his gentlemanly manners, that raise his price to three large figures.

In a word—anything like hurry and bustle, except in the case of a good start from cover-side in a pasture country, are distasteful and foreign to the ideal of noble and fashionable English life. As for trotting for money, it is only pursued and patronised by a class of gamblers of the very lowest order. Why, it is difficult to decide, because there is nothing more disreputable in cheating in a trot than cheating in a gallop; but so it is. No lady is ever seen at the trotting-matches which take place near London, and, unless by rare exception, no gentleman. If one or two are tempted by curiosity to witness this very exciting amusement, if wise, they leave their watches and purses at home.

In the United States the roads near great cities, usually of soft sand, are suited to the amusement. On the hard English macadamised roads a trotter would be worn out in a few weeks.

America produces hickory and other woods tougher and lighter than any grown in other countries; and of these American mechanics produce marvellous specimens of ingenuity in strength and lightness, in two-wheeled and four-wheeled vehicles.

As drivers of trotting races the Americans cannot be excelled, if equalled; but the professional style which is copied by young gentlemen driving out to display their five hundred and thousand pound harness-horses is to English eyes hideous, presenting the maximum of discomfort and muscular exertion. The horse or horses pull their hardest against the driver, while he, leaning back, with his legs planted firmly against an iron bar, with the reins wrapped round each hand, does the work which with us is performed by the roller-bolts or splinter-bars. It is true that the author of "The Trotting Horse of America"* condemns "*holding*

---

* Hiram Woodruff's "American Trotting Horse," edited by Charles Foster, of Wilkes' *Spirit of the Times*, and dedicated to Mr. Robert Bonner; a most amusing book.

on like grim death to a dead darkey ;" but as few in America are able to follow Woodruff's precepts in driving as in England to ride and win a Grand National Steeplechase.

The last edition of Herbert's "Horse of America" contains a number of engravings of the most celebrated trotters at full speed. In this work, and Woodruff's, the fullest information on American trotting will be found.* But the following extracts from the recent travels of a lady who seems familiar with English road trotters, of a speed above the average, will afford a better picture of this favourite American "institution," as seen in the light of British eyes† :—

"The Central Park of New York ranks immediately after the *Bois* and Hyde Park in point of fashionable attendance, of handsome equipages, of pretty women, *chic* toilettes, and general gaiety. In point of natural scenery it far surpasses both.

"The real object of the extremely light structure of American carriages and harness seems to be to obtain speed ; everything is sacrificed to that one purpose. If a man can prove that his horse can trot his mile half a second less than his neighbour's he is happy, and all the country papers herald the fact, to his infinite delight and pride.

"But as it is necessary to have a track (of sand) specially prepared, an uncomfortable seat like the body of a long-legged spider, no end of training, strength of muscle, and yelling, to obtain a 'dash' of speed of a mile or two, give me in preference an honest English trotter who will take me over a fair country road at sixteen miles an hour (! *sic*), who draws with his traces and not with the reins, and whom I can pull up within half a mile !

"The American horses are well broken, their intelligence is developed, and it is rare that you see any indication of the viciousness or nervousness so common in our blood horses. An American thorough-bred is taught to obey every inflection of the driver's voice, and to stand still when wanted. The Kentucky breed make capital saddle-horses, and after a generation's training would, no doubt, equal our hunters.

"The Americans who have had a military education at West Point ride very well ; but of the equitation of those who have not been trained at that military school, nor practised during the Civil War, the less said the better. American ladies, as a rule, know nothing about riding, and very little of how to dress when they show their graceful figures and lovely faces on a side-saddle. White underskirts and unsuitable variation destroy the effect of one of the most effective of costumes. Even if they sit their horse gracefully, a want of firmness is apparent. They have no intimate knowledge of, and consequently are never *en rapport* with, the noble creature who does so much to enhance the beauty of his fair rider.

"While at New York, I was taken to see Mr. Bonner's horses (to whom Woodruff's book is dedicated), the possessor of Dexter, Pocahontas, and several other of the swiftest trotters. He commenced life in the lower ranks of the social ladder ; he is now rich, and his great hobby is to own the fastest trotters that money can buy, solely for amusement, for once in his stable they cease to be entered for races. When I visited Mr. Bonner there were ten horses, each occupying a roomy loose box in stables which were marvels of comfort, cleanliness, and method. One colt, about eighteen months old, had been bought, on the strength of the fleetness of his pedigree, for £3,000. He was expected some day to accomplish some such wonderful feat as trotting a mile in a minute and nine seconds (!). I should have thought five shillings nearer the value of the goose-rumped, heavy-headed little quadruped. I went to see little Dexter (who trotted one mile and twenty-seven yards in two

* "The Horse of America," by Frank Forester (Henry Herbert). A new edition by S. and B. Bruce, 1871.

† "Our American Cousins at Home," by Vera. Sampson Low. 1873. Vera appears to have visited America in President Grant's first term.

minutes seventeen and a quarter seconds, in 1867) and Pocahontas shod. They are both handsome horses for trotters, and, though small, with extraordinary development of muscle in their fore-arms and hind-quarters. Mr. Bonner, whose pleasure-horses have cost him £40,000 (not dollars), always superintends the shoeing. He told me that we knew nothing about that art in England, an assertion I did not attempt to contradict."

When there are such purchasers as Mr. Bonner and his followers to compete for the possession of American trotting sires, great as are their merits in the important qualities of action and constitution—qualities in which our horses, under the influence of short races and light weights, are becoming so deficient—no private individual in England can venture to run the risk of importing American sires; and, if imported, it would be impossible to obtain remunerative fees. The speculation, if ever undertaken, must be performed by stallion subscription associations.

American trotters are of all sizes. The Dutchman, the favourite idol of Woodruff, was sixteen hands high. Flora Temple, who was victorious on every course for a series of years, was only fourteen hands two inches.

Dexter, if he was the same horse whose feats are recorded in "The Horse of America," stood fifteen hands one inch high; and the wonderful mare Pocahontas was sixteen hands high; both were by thorough-bred horses out of very well-bred mares.

As to American coachmen, St. Kames, no mean authority, wrote from Kansas:— "Talk about coaching! There, indeed, it may be seen to what an almost incredible perfection this art may be brought—where an eye like an eagle, and a hand light as a feather but firm as steel, will steer six horses and a heavy coach along a road in some places a mere ledge on the sheer face of a rocky precipice, with only a few feet between the passenger and certain death; but horses and men are brought up to the business, and one never hears of a fatal accident happening to those under charge of these daring drivers. Once, however, I remember, on my way to Georgetown, we had an unusually heavy load—I think twenty passengers—the full complement inside and out. On arriving at the crest of Guy's Hill, a fearful declivity two miles long, 'Hank,' the driver, pulled up his team, and, getting quietly down, picked up a fragment of rock, and began hammering at something in connection with the running gear. Of course one or two of the more timid of the passengers—rendered more so at the sight of the steep decline in front of them—asked if anything was wrong, and if the coachman 'thought we should get down all right;' to which 'Hank' answered, 'Yes, he thought so, if his brake leathers hung together,' and he tapped away at them again. First one passenger thought he would walk to the bottom of the hill 'to stretch his legs,' and then another, till the whole lot were walking down-hill at their best pace, followed by 'Hank' and his team, the knowing driver winking at me, and chuckling to himself at the neat way in which he had got rid of his load down the hill. At first I thought of getting down too, but concluded that if 'Hank' could stand it I could, and so I kept my seat on the box. The coaches are made like our English four-in-hand drag in shape, only hung on crane-necked springs, and much larger in the body."

American trotters are not considered to arrive at their full speed until nine years old, and Woodruff names several celebrities that won great races at eighteen and nineteen years old.

The following extract from a newspaper in 1877 gives an idea of the trotting pace at which our American cousins have arrived:—"There are about six or seven trotters in the country (the United States) which can do their mile in two minutes and twenty seconds, or less, and each of them is worth a king's ransom. In the United States, in 1876, there were 'seven circuit congresses.' These 'congresses' are nothing else than race meetings for trotters, held at seven places—to wit, Cleveland, Buffalo, Rochester, Utica, Poughkeepsie, Hartford, and Springfield. During last summer there were seven animals which graduated in the first class. Their names and order of merit were as follows—Goldsmith Maid, Smuggler, Lula, Cozette, Great Eastern, Amy B., and Albemarle. Their averages range between 2.17, which is that of Goldsmith Maid and Smuggler, down to 2.20, which is that of Amy B. and Albemarle. The fastest heat or 'best record' made during the 'septilateral circuit' was that of Goldsmith Maid, who did her mile in 2.15, and that of Smuggler, who has 2.15½ appended to his name."

Woodruff is never tired of dilating on the merits of the descendants of imported Messenger (the son of Lord Grosvenor's grey Mambrino), who covered in the United States for nearly twenty seasons. Mambrino was a very moderate racehorse.

Besides matches and races in single harness, and pairs against pairs, the Americans some-times put a fast trotter in a four-wheeled racing wagon, "with a mate;" the mate galloping and drawing the vehicle; the trotter, relieved of the weight and stimulated by the com-panionship, trotting alongside faster than his best pace alone in single harness.

As coachmen over a rough country the Americans are not to be excelled, if equalled.

"I have," says Major Sir Rose Price, "had a good deal of coaching during my life in Ireland and Wales before railroad days, and in many foreign lands, but I never saw men handle the ribands like the Californian drivers.

"Their teams, nearly always consisting of six horses, are as well turned out, with regard to size, pace, and condition, as any four-in-hand one sees in the Park during the London season. Of course I do not allude to the appointments and harness, which are rough and homely enough, or even the grooming.

"The roads are simply frightful, often hanging over the edge of a precipice, constantly crossing at this time of the year the dried-up bed of a river paved with boulders, or going down a declivity many fellows would funk at out hunting.

"They have no guard or any one to assist them, but make the brake themselves, and go full spin round corners sharp enough to hide the leaders, avoid bad ruts in the most extra-ordinary manner, have less accidents, and get more out of their horses, keeping them at the same time in perfect condition, than any men in the world. These men I consider the finest whips in the world, and it is worth coming all the way to California if only to learn what coaching really is.

"A team of five horses, leaders harnessed, three abreast, with brake hard on at full trot over such ground, a man should have a nerve of iron, a hand of steel, and the eye of a hawk."*

DRIVING THREE ABREAST.

Driving three abreast is common in Russia and Hungary, but seldom practised in this country except in omnibuses. Where the roads are wide enough it is, as already observed, a capital plan for breaking in a high-spirited and timid horse, either by placing him in the centre in shafts between two old stagers attached to the outriggers of a two-wheeled carriage, or as one of the outside horses, with no weight to pull, of a four-wheeled carriage. Oc-casional examples are met with of park phaetons driven with three ponies abreast.

The best English coachman would find himself quite helpless with three fiery Russian

* "The Two Americas." By Sir Rose Price, Bart.

steeds at full pace, if he had not been previously instructed in the customs of the country. The late Hon. Frederick St. John, who was a first-rate four-in-hand coachman in the first quarter of this century, the most palmy days of that coaching age, relates, in his recollections of Continental adventures, the following anecdote :—" One day I accompanied the prince in his drosky to make a call. He drove *à la mode du pays*—three horses abreast—a very fast Orloff trotter in the shafts, with two outriggers called *furieux;* the near side horse galloping with his right leg foremost and his head inclining to the left, the off side in the contrary manner. On my friend entering the house he placed the bunch of reins in my hand. I was puzzled, but arranged them as well as I could and started the trap. As long as I was in the village they went very quietly, but when I thought I knew all about it, and encouraged them to a better pace, they started at score. The more I pulled the faster they went, and soon reached the open plain. Well, I thought, Russia is large and there is plenty of room. I managed to make them describe a circle, and, sitting astride on the centre bench of the drosky, kept my seat while the carriage cleared various little watercourses. Finally, I was able to turn their heads towards the village, and meeting my friend, he used some Russian word, and the horses stopped. After he had had his laugh out, he showed me that with fiery Russian horses you must hold half the reins in each hand, and to stop them easily pull with the two fists close together ; whereas I had pulled with my hands quite apart. *But more is to be done with these horses by the voice than any other means.*"

CANTERING IN HARNESS.

When one of a pair of horses insists on cantering in harness—a most annoying trick —the best plan is to buckle an additional rein to the inside of the bit, and pass it through the terrets to your hand. Thus you have the same power over your canterer as if he were in single harness, and can pull at him without worrying the other horse

CHAPTER XVIII.

HUNTING.

The Meltonian's Dream—Definition of Hunting—Hunter—Huntsman—Master—"The Field"—Hunting, Aristocratic and Democratic—The Prince of Wales's Speech—Extracts from "*Souvenirs*" of a French Sportsman—Hunting Fields Suited to all Ages and Purses—Sports in Different Counties—Information for those who have never Hunted—Example of Assheton Smith—Miscellaneous Character of "The Field"—Anecdote of Bishop Wilberforce—Hunting Districts for Young or Old—Masters of Hounds who Never Jump—Division—Fox-Hunting—Stag-Hunting—Hare-Hunting—Number of Packs Hunting in England and Wales, Scotland and Ireland—The Due Precedence of Fox, Stag, or Hare Hounds—Stag-Hunting Hard Riding, no Sport—Fox-Hunting both Sport and Hard Riding—Hare-Hunting, much Sport, little Riding—Shakespeare's Notions of Hunting—Gervase Markham on "The Music of the Pack"—Ancient Packs of Foxhounds—The Berkeley—The Brocklesby—Transformation of Barren Warrens to Turnip Fields—Somerville's Chase—Nicholas Wood's Hunting Horse, 1686—The Tarporley Club, by Warburton of Arley—Extracts from Rules and Minutes—Costume—Change of—Fines—Drinking Habits—Taste in Art—The Club not Literary—Improved Agriculture Flourished with Fox-Hunting—Mr. Pusey and Lord Yarborough's Tenants—How Found—Mrs. Beecher Stowe on Hunting—Washington Irving of a Different Opinion.

> "Select is the circle in which we are moving,
>   Yet open and free the admission to all;
> Still, still more select is that company proving,
>   Weeded out by the funker and thinned by the fall.
> Yes, here all are equal—no clan legislation,
>   No privilege hinders, no family pride;
> In the 'image of war' show the pluck of the nation,
>   Ride young patrician, democracy ride."*

"HUNTING," in the language of the modern English sportsman, is riding after hounds in pursuit of fox, stag, or hare; the "hunter" generally means the horse, not the man. In French, the word "*chasse*" means pursuing anything, from a lark to a wild boar, with a gun, net, or hounds. The word had once nearly as wide a signification in English. The huntsman means the artist who manages the hounds while hunting; there is no word to designate the man who rides after them for sport. Sportsman includes the fisherman and the shooting man. The word "Field" means the followers of the hounds as distinguished from "the Master," "the Huntsman" who is sometimes the same person, and "the whips."

Fox-hunting is an important institution in the rural life of England: at once democratic and aristocratic. It is supported by the wealthy and noble; it is followed by enthusiasts of every rank and of very humble means. In the hunting-field all distinctions are levelled. The moment the hounds begin to run, he goes first and keeps first who can; and no one is expected to give precedence to any one, however noble or rich, except the Huntsman and the Master of the Hounds.

This peculiarly English character of our sport was never more happily hit off than in a speech of the Prince of Wales, at a dinner given in 1874 to the farmers over whose fields the Royal Buckhounds hunt. His Royal Highness said:—"Amongst the many dinners I

* "The Meltonian's Dream."

have to attend during the year, there is not one that gives me more sincere satisfaction than that at which we are present this evening. I have a feeling that I am not here among strangers; on the contrary, among friends. Many of the faces I see around me to-night I have known from my earliest childhood. During the time my father kept the harriers at Windsor, I used as a boy to hunt with them. After my father's death I kept them for a certain time. I have since had the pleasure of frequently hunting with the stag-hounds. I hope to meet you in the hunting-field for many years to come. Hunting brings all classes together; everybody in the hunting-field feels upon an equality. I hope that hunting—whether fox-hunting, stag-hunting, or hare-hunting—may long continue to flourish in this country. I trust that for many years to come we shall ride together over the same fields and the same fences; that if we now and then have the same falls, it will only be to get up again and follow the sport with, if possible, greater zest than ever. I may take this occasion to say that the Princess of Wales is as keen a sportswoman as I am a sportsman."

Not so are the customs of the stag-hunts, fox-hunts, and boar-hunts of France and Germany, where the sport shown is often excellent, but where a stranger would no more think of intruding, however profound his knowledge of the sport, however admirable his horse and equipments, than into a pheasant-shooting battue in Norfolk or Suffolk.

The aristocratic quality of fox-hunting is shown by the position conceded to the master of a county pack, which socially is only second to the Lord Lieutenant.

But in this country there are hunts and hunting-fields suited to all purses and all ages. Packs, consisting of a few couples of merry harriers or beagles for hunting hares or Welsh foxes, are frequently kept up by the farmers and professional men of a rural district, at an expense not exceeding the cost of one horse for one season in Leicestershire or Northamptonshire. In the Midlands the man who cares about appearances, and desires to rank, if not to ride, with the first flight, must have at least six or eight well-bred, full-sized horses of high class, with grooms, and carriages, and other expenses in proportion, although he may never be seen out of a lane or bridle road after the hounds have commenced running in earnest; whilst in a country of small enclosures and frequent coverts, with a two or three day a week pack of fox-hounds, half the number of horses, of a fourth the value, will do all that a reasonable man can require. In the New Forest, the pheasant coverts of Kent and Sussex, or the high banks and deep valleys of Devonshire, a clever cob will afford more sport than a sixteen-hand blood Yorkshire hunter. As for the horses required with harriers and beagles in England and Wales, the majority of the field are generally mounted on their ordinary hacks and roadsters. In hunting the pleasure is by no means in proportion to the cost; and it is probable that as regards sport—not hard riding—the enthusiastic Welshman or Devonian on his pony has more enjoyment than many owners of perfect studs in flying countries.

As a matter of course, the man who makes hunting the occupation of his life, who means to hunt every day that hounds can run and horses stand on their feet, will, if he is young, strong, and brave, and can afford it, prefer a grass country, big fields, big fences, big horses, a great deal of galloping, and as little cold hunting as possible; and he may have all this far from the fashionable mobs of the Midlands or mobs of any kind. But the class to whom these pages are particularly addressed are those who never have hunted, and only think of hunting because, having at least one horse and being able to ride, they find themselves near a pack of hounds of some kind, with leisure enough to enjoy the sport once or several times a week.

Hard riding is a matter of health and age as well as means. Not unfrequently the fox-hunter who in his golden youth was one of the bright particular stars of the Quorn, the Belvoir, or the Cottesmere, is found at fifty settled within reach of a provincial pack, in a district where arable fields and frequent woodlands make brilliant bursts impossible, pursuing his old sport with as much pleasure as ever, with a stud of two or three useful animals, whose necks for nine months of the year are not unacquainted with the harness collar.

Besides the sportsman pure and simple, to whom hunting is the principal business of the winter season, and the chief subject of conversation and preparation for the year, there are (and this is peculiar to this country) a vast number of born sportsmen whose occupations and whose means only allow them to hunt at intervals—one day a week or three days a month—with the nearest pack, be it fox-hounds, harriers, or stag-hounds. In truly rural districts these include farmers on their market horses or on young hunters learning their business; military and naval officers retired to the economic dulness of the country; a few parsons* (their number and wholesome influence on the hunting-field is rapidly diminishing); a doctor or two, who persuade themselves, with more or less reason, that they make patients in the field; lawyers, with the same excuse and with more success; veterinary surgeons with young horses to sell; and, particularly in Wales, the thriving, hard-riding shopkeeper, the capitalist of the village. If it is in Devonshire, Somersetshire, or the hilly districts of Wales, the blacksmith, the miller, every small farmer, and, in fact, every one who owns a pony and can spare an hour, follows the hounds.

In the neighbourhood of great manufacturing or seaport towns, "The Field," as the assembly is technically termed, is still more miscellaneous. At many a gateway the old county squire is obliged to rub knees on one side with a cotton-spinner and on the other with a fishmonger, while scores of young fellows, well horsed and correctly equipped, whose fathers worked for weekly wages, are to be found in the first flight. In the neighbourhood of London, the retail tradesmen who hunt in the most expensive form are sufficient in number to fill a special train and form a sort of club.

English hunting is divided into—

> Fox-hunting,
> Stag-hunting,
> Hare-hunting.

"The Field Rural Almanack" for 1878 gave the particulars of one hundred and thirty-seven packs of fox-hounds in England and Wales, of thirteen packs of stag-hounds, and of ninety-two packs of hare-hounds; eight packs of fox-hounds in Scotland; in Ireland eighteen packs of fox-hounds, four packs of stag-hounds, and forty-four packs of harriers.

Out of the forty counties into which England is divided—or rather, forty-three, if the three Ridings of Yorkshire are counted as three counties—there are only three in which there are no recognised packs of fox-hounds—that is to say, in Westmoreland, Middlesex, and Lancashire. Middlesex has the benefit of the Royal Buckhounds.

---

* The late Bishop Wilberforce objected to hunting—which is not an ecclesiastical offence. Soon after he was appointed to the diocese of Oxford he observed, in a reproachful tone, to a hard-riding rector, "You hunt a good deal, I believe, Mr. B——; do you think it quite a clerical pursuit?" "Well, my lord, I don't think it worse than going to balls." "Ah!" replied the bishop, "you allude to my being at Lady Jersey's ball; but I beg to assure you that I never was in the ball-room." "My lord," answered the parson, "that's just my case; I go out with the hounds certainly, but when they are running I am never in the same field with them." The parson hunted to the day of his death, and was even chairman of the hunt committee. He was an excellent parish priest, and a popular magistrate with the labouring classes.

Some twenty years ago Norfolk, which was so famous as a fox-hunting county in the great days of the Holkham sheep-shearings, had no fox-hounds. But since that date two packs have been established, and carried on with as much vigour as when corn was twelve shillings a bushel, and Mr. Coke* encouraged his tenants to hunt in scarlet; although Norfolk is too arable and too much infested by pheasants to take even second rank as a fox-hunting county.

A judge, quoted by William Cobbett in his "Rural Rides," used to say, "All wine is good; the best is port, and at least two bottles of it."

THE HUNTSMAN'S HORSE.

In the same way, one may safely assert that all hunting is good. The best is where there is a real find, a real run, short checks, and a decisive finish, all which can only be combined in fox-hunting.

But in hunting, as in every other amusement of a busy people, the majority of its followers cannot choose their place and time; if they are determined to hunt, they must be satisfied with the hounds—fox, stag, or hare—within reach.

Stag-hunting, as carried out with the Royal Buckhounds, Baron Rothschild's, the Surrey, and some other advertised packs, affords the maximum of hard riding and the minimum of sport, unless drag-hounds be considered to show any kind of sport.

Stag-hounds exist for the benefit of two classes: those whose occupations are political,

* Mr. Coke, of Holkham (born 1754), told Benjamin Haydon the artist that he remembered a fox being killed in the fields where Cavendish Square stands, and when Berkeley Square was a capital place for snipe.

financial, or commercial, who desire to hunt after reading their morning letters, and to be home in time for the evening post or Parliamentary division, and for those unhappily-constituted minds to whom sport is nothing, hard zealous riding everything—a class not altogether unknown to and heartily detested by the masters of fox-hounds in the best hunting counties of England.

Fox-hunting in a suitable country provides, in the course of a season, with plenty of scientific sport, enough hard riding to satisfy the greatest glutton; and even in a country which is unsuitable for hard riding, if it holds a good scent, it is capable of affording exquisite pleasure to real sportsmen.

Hare-hunting in a good country affords the maximum of sport with (in a Midland county sense) the minimum of hard riding.

Englishmen have been hunters as far back as history records, and continue to hunt in every country they colonise, if they can find a horse to ride and a wild animal that hounds will pursue.

The Norman hunter of deer, guided by the music of the hounds, lay in wait or galloped to points in order to bring down the game with bow or spear, in the style still practised with the rifle in the woods of Virginia and other States where farms are divided by forests.

Those who now hunt in North Devon or in any mountainous and wooded county, enjoy their sport as Shakespeare did more than three centuries ago. Nothing less than personal experience could have inspired the noble lines of Theseus and Hippolyta in "A Midsummer Night's Dream."*

Gervase Markham, writing not quite a hundred years after Shakespeare, declares that "of all the field pleasures wherewith old time and man's invention hath blest the houres of our recreation, there is none to excelle the delight of hunting, being compounded, like an harmonious consort (concert), of all the best parts of more refined pleasures—as music, dancing, running, riding, hawking, and such-like."

England's great philosopher, John Locke, who kept two riding nags until his infirmities compelled him to set up a carriage, wrote in 1660:†—"It is man's proper business to seek happiness and avoid misery. Hunting and other innocent diversions delight me, and I make use of them to refresh my health, restore the vigour of my mind, and increase my pleasure; but if I spend all or the greatest part of my time in them they hinder my improvement in knowledge and useful arts, and give me up to a state of ignorance in which I cannot but be unhappy."

Fox-hunting is, speaking historically, the most modern of British chases. The Norman gentry hunted the deer, the boar, and the wolf. The yeomanry, who had become an important constituency in the time of Queen Elizabeth, hunted the hare, the martin-cat, the pole-cat, and the badger. The fox did not rise to his present eminence as a beast of chase—sacred as the Egyptian apis, except before hounds—until millions of acres of woods, moors, and marshes had been converted, if not into farms, into valuable pastures and sheep-walks.

The "*riding to hounds*," so essential a part of the pleasure in "the shires," is an art not a hundred years old, which can only be practised in perfection where the grazing system requires large grass fields and big strong fences, and practised at all where farms are enclosed.

We read in Macaulay's "History" (Vol. I., p. 311) that in the drawings of English landscapes

* Act iv., Scene i.   † Fox Bourne's "Life of John Locke."

made in the seventeenth century for the Grand Duke Cosmo scarce a hedgerow is to be seen, and numerous tracts now rich with cultivation were then barren as Salisbury Plain.

Between Biggleswade and Lincoln there was scarcely an enclosure; nor from Abingdon to Gloucester (forty or fifty miles).

John Ogilby, the Cosmographer Royal, in *Itinerarium Anglia*, 1675, describes great part of the land as wood, fen, heath, and marsh. In some of his maps the roads through enclosed districts are marked by lines, and through unenclosed by dots; the proportion of unenclosed country (which, if cultivated must have been wretchedly cultivated), seems to have been very great.

In 1685 the arable and pasture were supposed to amount to little more than half the area of the kingdom; the rest was believed to consist of moor, forest, and fen. And yet the value of the produce of the soil far exceeded that of the other fruits of industry.

At Enfield was a region twenty-five miles in circumference, which contained only three houses and scarcely any enclosed fields. Deer wandered there in thousands, free as in an American forest.

The red deer were then as common in Gloucestershire and Hants as they are now among the Grampian Hills. On one occasion Queen Anne, on her way to Portsmouth, saw a herd of no less than 500.

Hedges must have greatly altered the aspect of this country at the time when they came into general use—with the introduction of the Flemish husbandry in Norfolk at the end of the seventeenth century. Until the time of George I. almost every part of the country was composed of four kinds of scenery:—1, the houses and parks of proprietors and the villages adjoining, where their farmers and labourers resided; 2, the common fields under the plough; 3, the common pasture or waste; 4, the woods and forests.

King James I., his grandsons Charles and James, were keen sportsmen, but they hunted the deer only—sometimes in parks like Greenwich, sometimes at Enfield, where the crafty Sir John Reresby, as he relates in his curious autobiography, made the acquaintance of Charles II. and his brother, in consequence of having an excellent horse. Queen Anne hunted deer in Windsor Park, driving herself in a one-horse carriage—furiously, as Dean Swift writes Stella, like Jehu, and one day drove forty-five miles.

The fox's day of worshipful dignity as the premier animal of the British chase is not more than a hundred years old; it had not yet come under the Stuarts.

In a speech of Oliver St. John against Strafford, quoted by Macaulay, he said:—"Strafford was to be regarded not as a stag or hare, but as a fox, who was to be snared by any means, and knocked on the head without pity."

Nicholas Wood, whose third edition of "The Gentleman's Recreations," with the addition of "The Hunting Horse," was published in 1686, names "five beasts of venery, also called beasts of the forest (that is, only to be hunted by the privileged feudal superiors)—the hart (which hath his season in summer), the hinde (which begins when the hart's is over), the hare, the boar, and the wolf. There are also five beasts of chase—the buck, the doe, the fox, the martin, and the roe." Fox-hunting was evidently considered inferior to hare-hunting; he divides it into hunting underground with terriers, and above ground. On the latter he says:—"To this purpose you must draw with your hounds about groves, thickets, and bushes near villages, for a fox will lurk in such places to prey on young pigs and poultry. But it will be necessary to stop up his earths, if you can find them, the night before you intend to hunt. At first only cast off your sure finders; as the drag mends so add more as you dare trust them. Let the hounds kill the fox themselves. Fox-hunting is very pleasant, for by reason of his strong scent he maketh an excellent cry."

Messrs. Dickenson's "Exhibition of Pictures illustrative of Two Centuries of Hunting" contained a hunting-horn, lent by Reginald Corbet, Esq., which bore the following inscription:— "Thomas Boothby, Esq., Tooley Park, Leices. With this Horn he hunted the *first pack* of Fox Hounds then in England, 55 years. Born 1677, died 1752. Now the property of Thos. d'Avenant, Esq., county Salop, his grandson."

On seeing this statement, Lord Arundel of Wardour wrote to the editor of the *Field*, "that his ancestors kept a pack of fox-hounds hunting Wiltshire and Hampshire from the year 1696 to 1782, as proved by documents in his possession."

Pope, in a letter to Addison, November 19th, 1712, referred to "Mr. Roper as having the reputation of keeping the best pack of fox-hounds in the kingdom."[*] Further inquiries showed that Mr. Roper was a Kentish gentleman who hunted a pack of hounds in Charlton Forest for the amusement of his patron, the Duke of Monmouth. He fought for the Duke at Sedgemoor, escaped after that terrible defeat to France, where his skill in venery made him friends and gave him the privilege of hunting in the Royal Forest of Chantilly. He returned to England, when that good horseman and keen sportsman, William of Orange, had chased away the bigot James, and became, with the Duke of Bolton, the Master of the Charlton Hounds—very famous in their day. Goodwood Park was formed out of a slice of Charlton Forest. Mr. Roper died in 1715, and some time afterwards the hounds passed from the Duke of Bolton to the Duke of Richmond, who built Goodwood House, and adorned it with paintings commemorative of the Charlton Hunt. For this hunt the Earl of Burlington designed a banqueting hall, where they feasted with their ladies (the Duchess of Bolton, daughter of Monmouth, was one) after a day's sport. There is a tradition in the county of the Marquis of Hartington's riding down Seven Down, and leaping a gate at the bottom. On the fourth Duke of Richmond going to Ireland a Lord-Lieutenant, he presented the hounds to the Prince Regent in 1813; and in 1819, on symptoms of hydrophobia appearing, they were all destroyed.[†]

The oldest pack of fox-hounds by *name* is the Old Berkeley, which in ancient days had its kennels at Wormwood Scrubs, and hunted all the way through Hertfordshire to Gloucestershire; but the continuity has long been broken, and, after having been re-established, by the advice of his physician, by the second Earl of Lonsdale, is now chiefly a subscription pack, supported by residents of the West End of London. The Berkeley Hounds, kept at the castle of that name by the Fitzhardinge family, are a comparatively modern creation. The Old Berkeley Hunt has its kennels at Watford, in Herts, and dresses its huntsman and whips in the orange-tawny plush livery of the Berkeley family.

The Brocklesby pack has been maintained in the family of the Pelhams, Earls of Yarborough, more than 150 years, and a written pedigree of the pack has been kept for upwards of 120 years; it is therefore the oldest pack in the kingdom. In 1850, by the kindness of the second Earl of Yarborough, I was permitted to examine all the papers connected with his hounds. Among them is a memorandum, dated April 20, 1713, by which "it is agreed

---

[*] "Papers of a Critic," edited by Sir Charles Dilke, Bart.

[†] Somerville, who describes himself as "a well-born squire of Warwickshire, and six feet high," in his poem of "The Chase," devotes separate cantos to stag-hunting, hare-hunting, and fox-hunting; the first Lord Fitzhardinge, of Berkeley Castle, used to declare that he learned all he knew of scent from that poem. This was a joke, for it tells nothing!

between Sir John Tyrwhitt, Charles Pelham, Esq., and Robert Vyner, Esq.,* that the fox-hounds now kept by the said Sir John Tyrwhitt and Mr. Pelham shall be joyned in one pack, and the three have a joint interest in the said hounds for five years, each for one third of the year" [therefore they must have hunted all the year round]; "that the establishment shall consist of sixteen couple of hounds, three horses, and a boy." The united pack soon passed into the hands of Mr. Pelham, and down to this day the hounds are branded with a "P."

I also examined at Brocklesby rough memoranda of the kennel from 1710 to 1746. From 1746 the stud book has been kept up without a break. From 1797 the first Earl of Yarborough kept journals of the pedigree of the hounds in his own handwriting; since that time, up to the date of my visit, they had been kept by three generations of huntsmen of the name of Smith. The last Smith was killed hunting a few years afterwards, a very unusual death for a huntsman. In the time of the first Lord Yarborough, 1794, his country extended over the whole of the South Wold country part of the Burton Hunt, which is now hunted from Lincoln; and he used to go down into these districts for a month at a time to hunt the woodlands. He told his grandson that when he began hunting, about 1750, there were only three or four fences in the thirty miles between Horncastle and Brigg. Turnips had not then conquered heath-land and rabbit warrens. Hugo Meynell, the father of modern fox-hunting, and the founder of the Quorn Hunt, formed his pack chiefly of drafts from the Brocklesby kennels.

A good picture of the manners and customs of fox-hunting men of the last century may be gathered from the "Annals of the Tarporley Club," by Mr. Rowland Egerton Warburton, of Arley Hall, which forms the introduction to the last edition of his hunting songs. Mr. Warburton was long not only one of the most brilliant horsemen, but the poet-laureate of that famous hunting club.

THE TARPORLEY HUNT CLUB.

The Tarporley Hunt was established for hare-hunting, on a very primitive plan, in 1762. Those who kept harriers brought out their packs in turn. If no member of the Society kept hounds, it is ordered by Rule VIII. that "a pack be borrowed and kept at the expense of the Society."

The country was then, as now, a dairy district, but very little fenced in, until the discovery of the value of bone-dust in fertilising pastures and the profits of potato-growing made farmers insist on dividing their improved fields from waste lands with which the country was intersected. After 1798 war stimulated and made universal enclosures and reclamation.

The founders, ten in number, included the names of John Crewe, Booth Grey (a son of the fourth Earl of Stamford), Sir Harry Mainwaring, two Wilbrahams, a Cotton of Combermere, and a lady patroness (Miss Townshend), all names still prominent amongst the local aristocracy of Cheshire.

By the rules of the club they agreed—

"'To meet twice every year, the meeting for hunting to be held the second Monday in November.' They assembled, it seems, at the club room, at the Swan Hotel, Tarporley, over night. 'Each meeting to last seven days. The harriers never to wait for any member after eight o'clock in the morning.'

* Ancestor of the Author of "Notitia Venatica," and formerly Master of the Worcestershire Hounds.

"'Every member must have a blue frock, with plain yellow metal buttons, scarlet velvet cape, double-breasted scarlet flannel waistcoat, the coat sleeve to be cut and turned up.'

"The following year it was voted that 'the metal buttons be changed for basket mohair ones; and that every member provides himself with a scarlet saddle-cloth, bound with blue.'

"In 1764 it was voted that 'if any member does not appear in the strict uniform of the Hunt (as before described), he shall forfeit one guinea for every such offence.' Two years afterwards Mr. Crewe was fined for having his bridle lapt with red and blue; Mr. Barry for not taking the binding off the button-holes of his coat; Mr. Whitworth for having his saddle-cloth bound with purple; Lord Grosvenor for riding to cover with a white saddle-cloth, and likewise for having his bridle lapt with white; also for having quitted the Hunt without leave on Tuesday, he was fined five guineas.

"In 1770, the club having then become a fox-hunting club, it was voted 'that the Hunt should change their uniform to a red coat unbound, with a small frock sleeve, a grass-green velvet cape, and green waistcoat, and that the sleeve has no buttons, the red saddle-cloth to be bound with green instead of blue, the points of bridles same as before.'*

"Leather breeches were the universal wear in the morning, as well as when hunting, amongst country gentlemen of that day. By the 16th rule of the club, 'If any member of the Society should marry, he is to present each member of the Hunt with a pair of buckskin breeches.' In 1764 this was altered into one guinea for each member of the club, to be paid into the hands of the Secretary, to be spent in leather breeches. Two years later it was voted that 'any member of the Hunt that marries a second time shall give two pairs of leather breeches to each member of the Hunt.'"

Drinking, in accordance with the spirit of the age, when all or nearly all our most eminent statesmen drank hard,† was an important business at the Tarporley meetings, and is the subject of a series of rules. It will be observed from the following extracts that, unlike the Yorkshire and Devonshire squires, claret, not port, was the favourite liquor.

"At the first meeting of the Tarporley Hunt, 7th November, 1762, it was ordered that Mr. Booth Grey (the Secretary) procures for the use of this Society two collar glasses and two admittance glasses of a larger size. The 9th rule being 'that three collar bumpers be drank after dinner, and the same after supper; after they are drank, every member may do as he pleases in regard to drinking.'

"In 1769 a change was made in the direction of temperance; the club having been enlarged to twenty-five members, 'never to exceed the same,' it was agreed that, 'instead of three collar glasses, only one shall be drunk after dinner, except a fox is killed above ground,‡ and then, after the Lady Patroness, another collar glass shall be drunk to Fox-hunting.'

"In 1772, 'Lord Kilmorie's mild and pleasant administration was approved,' not only by his second election, but by his health being drunk in three goblets. The next year it was voted 'that every member introducing a stranger pays for the second night of his staying one gallon of claret; for the fourth night two gallons; and if he stays three hunting days, one dozen.'

"In 1778 it was ordered that the part of the order containing these words, 'that the claret never be admitted into the house bill,' be rescinded, and that the deficiency of the claret after what is paid for strangers be inserted in the bill. Claret must have been cheap in those days, for the Secretary's accounts were settled and allowed, being 'on claret account £15 5s. 6d., and on house account £2 2s.' Voted 'that each member of this Hunt deposit 29s. in the Secretary's hands for a fund to purchase claret, and that Mr. Roger Wilbraham be requested to order it down.' In 1779 it was 'agreed to allow the landlord fifteenpence a bottle and the bottles for drinking our own claret.'"

In 1782 the superiority of fox-hunting was fully established, for

"Offley Crewe and Sir Peter Warburton were found guilty of a most heinous offence, in having crossed a hare's scut with a fox's brush, and fined one gallon of claret each: a very light fine for such an offence.

"In 1806 it was unanimously agreed that the members should subscribe the sum of £3 3s. next year for silver forks."

---

* The present uniform of the Cheshire, like the Surrey Hunt, is scarlet with a green collar.

† In the memoir of Gilbert Elliot, first Earl of Minto, he writes that he left Fox and Grey (the proud, decorous Grey) at the "Crown and Anchor," "very far gone."

‡ As it was impossible to stop all the earths in a wild country, this "killing above ground" was a rare event.

Mr. Warburton adds—

"I am assured by a lady now living, that so late as 1809, in one of the most hospitable houses in the county, a silver fork was never seen on the dining-table."

In the same year it appears that Mr. Smith Barry was the first master of a pack of fox-hounds in Cheshire, supported entirely at his own expense. Mr. Smith Barry's name is celebrated in the annals of fox-hunting as the owner of two hounds, Blue Cap and Wanton, which, in October, 1762, ran a match for five hundred guineas, over the Beacon Course (about four miles) at Newmarket, with a couple of hounds the property of the still more celebrated Hugo Meynell, and beat them. Mr. Barry's hounds were trained in Essex, on Tiptree Heath (since made famous in a different line by Mr. Mechi), "over ten miles of turf." "Blue Cap came in first, Wanton very close to Blue Cap; Hugo Meynell's Richmond was beat by upwards of a hundred yards; the bitch never ran at all. Sixty horses started with the hounds; only twelve were up at the finish. The first up, ridden by Mr. Barry's huntsman, was rode quite blind; and a King's Plate horse, called Rib, was twelfth. The distance was done by the hounds under eight minutes." Mr. Meynell's hounds, it was said were fed on legs of mutton during the time of training.

In 1773, at the request of the Club, Mr. Smith Barry sat for his portrait to a local artist, Crank of Warrington, "one of whose pictures was sold for a large sum recently as a Gainsborough." But evidently in those days portrait painters were not much more valued in Cheshire and Lancashire than house painters, for "the picture is a full length; at his master's feet sits Blue Cap, the winner at Newmarket; the portrait of the master is excellent," yet the Club paid only £21 for it, and £9 16s. for the frame!

The Cheshire County Subscription Hounds originated in a pack established by Sir Peter Warburton (an ancestor of Egerton Warburton) and others, after the Hunt Club had quarrelled in 1798 with Mr. Smith Barry and warned him off their covers.

So much for hunting-clubs, which flourished in every hunting county at the time when a distinct line divided country gentlemen from courtiers and wealthy citizens.

Hare-hunting was in the highest favour in England when the country was intersected with hundreds of thousands of acres of waste lands and poor pasture, employed in feeding rabbits or miserable sheep; which turnips, fed off by improved breeds of sheep, between 1730 and 1814, turned into carefully-fenced grain-growing farms.

Resident landlords, improved agriculture, and fox-hunting, have flourished together; and if the scent is not so good and the runs not so long as when wild foxes were hunted over a wild country, there are more packs of hounds and more followers of the chase by many fold than in the days when amongst the educated class a fox-hunter passed for, if not a fool, a clown.

"Three generations of Pelhams turned thousands of acres of wastes of Lincolnshire heath and wolds into rich farm-land. The fourth (the late earl) did his part by giving the same districts railways and seaport accommodation. 'Brocklesby Kennels' and the 'Pelham Pillar' may be called as witnesses to the common-sense of English field-sports. It was the love of hunting that led the Pelham family to settle in a remote county of wild heath, and to colonise a waste with farmers of the first class."*

* When the late Mr. Pusey, in a speech at a tenants' dinner at Brocklesby Park, said, "What astonishes me is where Lord Yarborough gets his tenants," a stout farmer answered at once, "I'll tell you, sir; his lordship breeds 'em." In the Midland Counties it is considered an impertinence for a tenant farmer to wear scarlet; but the Brocklesby Hunt was composed chiefly of tenants, who wore scarlet, with the button of the Hunt.

American gentlemen have frequently distinguished themselves as hard riders to hounds in our best hunting counties, as they generally do whenever they take up any pursuit that requires pluck and decision; but Mrs. Beecher Stowe, like some English literary critics, could not understand fox-hunting at all. She relates in her "Sunny Memories" that, dining with Earl Russell, the conversation turned on hunting, and that when she expressed her astonishment "that in the height of English civilisation this vestige of the savage state should remain," they only laughed, and told stories about hunting.

It must be admitted that Mrs. Stowe's observations were very natural in a woman who had never been under the influence of hunting associations. She was probably not aware that the hunting-field, judiciously used, is not only an exciting, healthy amusement, but one of the roads to the anxious desire of so many—good society. Washington Irving, who was a man with sympathies for every class and every pleasant pursuit, took a different view of the rural sports that have created our resident gentry out of the rude squires and vulgar citizens of the days of Pope and Addison. He says, in his charming "Sketch Book":—"The fondness for rural life among the higher classes of the English has had a great and salutary effect upon the national character. I do not know a finer race of men than the English gentlemen. Instead of the softness and effeminacy which characterises the men of rank of most countries, they exhibit a union of elegance and strength, of robustness of frame and freshness of complexion, which I am inclined to attribute to their living so much in the open air, pursuing so largely the invigorating sports of the field."

CHAPTER XIX.

HARE-HUNTING—FOX-HUNTING—STAG-HUNTING.

Hare-hunting—The Best Introduction to Fox-hunting—What it Teaches the Young Sportsman—The Arts of the Sports-
man—And of the Horseman—An Excellent Apprenticeship for the Young—And for the Old—Anecdote of an Old
Baronet—Peter Beckford's "Thoughts on Hunting"—Analysis of Ninety-eight Packs—Hallamshire Heavy Harriers—
Trencher Fed—Welsh Hounds—Devon Hare-hounds—Three Different Kinds of Country—The Horse for Hare-Hunting
—A Parson's Celebrated Pack—Fox-Hunting—Song, "The Galloping Squire"—Charles Fox's Pleasures—The Hunting
Map of England—Its Extent—Its Variety—Hugo Meynell, the Founder of the Quorn Hunt—The "Flying Childe"
Hard Riding—George Morland's Hunting Pictures—"Each Nag Wore a Crupper, each Squire a Pigtail"—Ralph
Lambton—A Refined Country Gentleman—Lord Sefton, an Epicurean, Introduced the Second Horse System—The
Paradise of Fox-hunters—A Ride Round Melton—Other Counties—The Rule for the Learner in Fox-Hunting—Stag-
Hunting—In Feudal Times—Temp. George III.—The Present Royal Buck-hounds—Date from 1813—Pure Fox-hounds
—Of Large Size—The Royal Huntsman, Charles Davis—Earl Granville's Opinion of—Royal Deer—How Bred—Trained
—Caught—Carted to Meets—The Earl of Derby's Stag-hounds—Their Successes—The Surrey—Baron Rothschild's and
the Vale of Aylesbury—Whyte Melville's "Lord of the Valley"—The Petre Stag-hounds, Essex—The late Charles
Buxton—His Stag-hunting Ballad, "Forrard Away"—The Black St. Hubert Blood-hounds—Lord Wolverton—
Mr. Roden—Wild Stag-Hunting in the West—Sketch of, by a Q.C.—Note on Octogenarian Parson Sportsman—The
Drag Hunt.

DIFFERING from very high authorities, I consider that the young horseman, not bred to
field sports, not familiar with the etiquette of the hunting-field (which in its way is quite
as important for success in society as the etiquette of the drawing and dining room), after
he has mastered the management of his horse, will do best by commencing his career as
a sportsman with hare-hounds. He will learn, amongst other useful lessons, to understand
the important part that the pack plays in the performance; that hare-hounds are expected
to do their own work, without the assistance of "views" from the field; that they are
never on any excuse to be overridden. He will also learn the autocratic position of the
huntsman, the importance of silence, and the impertinence of any interference with the hounds.

With fox-hounds in a flying country, a plucky young fellow, ignorant of the first
rudiments of the art of hunting, following the bad example of men who ought to know
better, may, with a good start and a good horse, make and keep a place in the very
first flight, with half the pack behind him, on his very first appearance on the hunting-
field, and from that time forward consider himself to have taken a first-class degree in a
science which requires a good deal of experience, at least to pursue it like a sportsman
and a gentleman.

In hare-hunting the hare goes first, the hounds always next, then the huntsman, and
lastly the Field.

There is another advantage in hare-hunting as a preliminary education for the nobler
pursuit. As a general rule the chase is deliberate; the competition for a place in the front
being less keen, the novice has time to watch the example and to listen to the sage
precepts of the mentors of the hunt, amongst whom, if it is an established pack, some fine

sportsmen will certainly be found, not unfrequently veterans who have been hard riders to fox and stag in "their hot youth."

Now the arts of the sportsman are as well worth acquiring as those of the horseman. Hare-hunting is not only an excellent apprenticeship for the young fox-hunter, but a safe recreation for those who have taken to horsemanship late in life, because they can take just as much of it as suits their constitution, and leave off when they please.

The hare, unlike the fox, runs in circles. You have therefore your choice either to follow the hounds, or to ride the segment of a circle, saving the devious turns; or, indeed, you may stand still and, if the country is open and undulating, watch the chase while waiting for the return of the hare and the pack.

Amongst my earliest hunting recollections is one of an old Somersetshire baronet, who used to take his post on a fat cob in the middle of a hundred acres of grass almost surrounded by coverts, and spend the morning in listening to and watching a pack of queerly-bred beagles chasing hares out of and into the coverts. On rainy days the groom who stood at the cob's head completed the picture by holding a huge gig-umbrella over Sir Edward's head.

This was in a part of the county never visited by fox-hounds; and when one day the pack got upon an outlying fox and raced him, followed only by one very young whip and a stranger youth, for thirty minutes, great was the sensation; nothing but very humble flattery on the youth's part saved the whip's place.

Down hares are stouter than the hares found in arable districts, and frequently run nearly as straight as a fox. In Ireland it is said that the hares in the grass-feeding, stone-wall-divided districts afford quite as good sport as foxes in our second-class counties.

Peter Beckford had, he relates in his "Thoughts on Hunting," a very perfect pack of hare-hounds, in what he describes as "a very bad county for the purpose," that is, closely enclosed and too plentifully provided with coverts and hares. He sums up the advantages of the sport in a very few words: "Hare-hunting is a good diversion in a good country. You are always certain of sport, *and if you really love to see* (and hear) *your hounds hunt, the hare when properly hunted will show you more of it than any other animal.*" "It should be taken as a ride after breakfast, to get an appetite for dinner. If you make a business of it you spoil it."

The packs of hare-hounds enumerated in the summary of the tables of the "Rural Almanack" differ more in breed, size, and quality than any of the established packs of fox-hounds. They are variously described as harriers, fox-hounds, beagles, and cross-breeds of those three breeds—a very favourite cross being between the harrier and the fox-beagle, which was the blood of which Beckford's pack was composed. Many packs consisted of purely-bred dwarf fox-hounds. They varied in height from beagles of fifteen inches to pure harriers and pure fox-hounds of twenty-two inches; the intermediate size of nineteen inches for cross-bred harriers appearing to be most popular. The number of couples varied from ten to twenty, fifteen being about a fair average. A dozen packs of beagles not exceeding fifteen inches in height were generally hunted on foot.

The countries hunted over by hare-hounds differ as much as the packs. Thus the Earl of Pembroke's, which hunt the country round Salisbury, including Salisbury Plain, and which acquired their reputation during a quarter of a century under the mastership of Mr. Walter Flower, were pure harriers; an equally celebrated pack, the Brookside, hunting Rottingdean, on the Brighton Downs, were from a cross of fox-hound and harrier. Sir Robert Harvey's, hunting round Slough, in Buckinghamshire—formerly Prince Albert's—were pure harriers; a pack hunting near Dartford, in Kent, with a great reputation for showing sport in an enclosed country without ditches, were half-bred fox-hounds, and nineteen inches high. Admiral Lord Phillips hunted near Haverfordwest, Pembrokeshire, with a pack of very small harriers; Sir Francis Winnington, in Worcestershire, with dwarf fox-hounds; at Torquay the pack was composed of harriers.

Amongst the curiosities of former days were the Hallamshire "heavy harriers," which were trencher-fed, have never had kennels, and are assembled at the sound of a horn blown

LIGHT-WEIGHT HUNTER.

on a hill, and hunted for the amusement of the Sheffield journeymen cutlers. Several Welsh, Westmoreland, and Cumberland packs have been kept in the same manner from time immemorial.

The Welsh, Devonshire, and other mountain packs, frequently hunt everything, from a foumart to a fox, from hare to an outlying deer.

Devonshire probably supports more packs of hare-hounds than any county in the kingdom.

In the first quarter of the present century, it is in the recollection of a sexagenarian squire, who himself hunted his father's scratch pack of fox-hounds, that nearly every rector in North Devon kept a pack of hounds for the amusement and with the help of his parishioners, and that there were at that time not less than forty packs of one kind or another north of the river Exe. Amongst these parsons were the Rev. Mr. Froude, who, with his ferocious pack of fox-beagles, hunting deer, hare, fox, and human beings indifferently, has been the subject of one of Mr. Blackmore's sensational novels. Another parson, Barter, of a milder type, had a pack of beagles which he hunted himself, whipped in by the parish clerk, a cripple, who was unable to ride astride, but lay across his moor-pony like a sack of wool, and in this position galloped and holloaed, and cracked his whip with infinite zeal and skill.

Hare-hunting countries may broadly be divided into three descriptions :—Enclosed fields, like Berkshire and Kent, where in short bursts there is plenty of fencing for those who like it, while those who do not are pretty sure that if they do not ride up to the pack the pack will come back to them. Hilly countries, like Devonshire and Somersetshire, Westmoreland, Cumberland, and Wales, North and South, where riding to hounds is generally impossible if once they leave the open moors for fields enclosed by high banks. In these counties every little farmer is a sportsman, knows every hound by sight and voice, understands the meaning of every note, knows the habits of hare or fox familiarly, and hunts with all his soul—if old and heavy, from the top of a hill. Jumping is quite out of his line ; a select few may rush down the steep hills, and curiously climb, partly on foot, the steep sides of valleys, and by exception leap a gate or stile—but that is quite the exception. The third class of hunting country is over open undulating downs, like Salisbury Plain and the South Downs of Sussex, home of the best mutton in the world, and of very stout hares, which have been known to run clean away from the hounds.

The horse for hare-hunting need not, in an enclosed country, be fast, but should be clever at cramped places. A very good sort of horse for hunting hare or fox in a county of small fields is shown at page 231. No horse, however quiet on the road, should be trusted by an unpractised horseman or horsewoman with hounds, even if only to see the find, without any intention of following them, because some of the most placid of mature years become dangerously frantic when the pack lift up their voices in melodious chorus. In hilly countries and on downs, the hare-hunting horse or pony must be well-bred, or he will soon come to a standstill. Indeed, if up to the weight of the rider, there is nothing so good as a well-bred pony for galloping up and down steep hills or over long rolling downs. A tall pasture-county hunter is quite out of place.

Lancashire, which has no fox-hounds, had five packs of hare-hounds mentioned in the " Rural Almanack," and has probably many more. Lady Duff Gordon, one of the most accomplished women and genial travellers of this century, was an enthusiastic huntress. In a letter quoted in her " Life " she says : " The Princes (of Orleans) always sent to tell us of the meets of their harriers. We had famous runs in the cramped country about Esher, small fields, big fences, and large water-jumps in the low-lying flats near the river."

FOX-HUNTING.

" Come, I'll show you a country that none can surpass,
 For a flyer to cross like a bird on the wing :
We have acres of woodland and oceans of grass,
 We have game in the autumn and cubs in the spring.
We have scores of good fellows hang out in the shire,
But the best of them all is the Galloping Squire.

" One wave of his arm, to the covert they throng ;
 ' Yoi ! wind him ! and rouse him ! By Jove, he 's away !
Through a gap in the oaks see them speeding along
 Over the open like pigeons—they *mean* it to-day !
You may jump till you're sick—you may spur till you tire !
For it 's catch 'em who can !' says the Galloping Squire.

"Then he takes the old horse by the head, and he sails
        In the wake of his darlings, all ear and all eye,
    As they come in his line, o'er banks, fences, and rails,
        The cramped ones to creep and the fair ones to fly.
    It 's a *very* queer place that will put in the mire
    Such a rare one to ride as the Galloping Squire.

" So forty fair minutes they run and they race—
        'Tis a heaven to some, 'tis a lifetime to all—
    Though the horses we ride are such gluttons for pace,
        There are stout ones that stop, there are safe ones that fall.
    But the names of the vanquished need never transpire,
    For they 're all in the rear of the Galloping Squire."   J. WHYTE MELVILLE.

Charles James Fox once said there was no pleasure so great as winning at hazard, and the next greatest pleasure was losing at hazard. Those who have the sporting instinct, a combination of the tastes of the hunter and the horseman, will agree that the finest sport in the world is fox-hunting in a country like that of the Galloping Squire; and the next best sport, fox-hunting in a country bad for riding but good for hunting.

An examination of a hunting map of England will show the large place that fox-hunting has in our agricultural economy. It begins in Northumberland, a county of hills, dales, and downs, or of great woods that you can ride through, which is bounded by the best hunting counties of Scotland—Roxburghshire and Dumfries—it ends in Cornwall; it extends from North Wales and Cheshire on one side to Norfolk on the other. It flourishes in the greatest perfection in the counties like Leicestershire, Northamptonshire, and Herefordshire, where rich grass pastures feed fat oxen, where the fields range from twenty to fifty acres, and big fences and broad streams demand blood, courage, and condition, if the riders mean to be in the first flight. But it is also pursued with enthusiasm by resident sportsmen far from "the madding crowd" of fashion, over the great arable fields and wide ditches of the "roothings" of Essex, over the flint-covered plough-lands and rolling downs, scarcely relieved by a jumpable fence, of Hampshire, over the small fields and heavy banks of Suffolk and Sussex, and amidst the hop-gardens of Kent. The grassy vales and sheep-feeding stone-wall-divided districts of Gloucestershire and Oxfordshire are second to none for affording sport; while in North Devon and the adjoining hills of Somersetshire, although riding to hounds in the way men ride over the Vale of Aylesbury and the other feeding not breeding counties is impossible, every little farmer understands the "noble science," and takes the deepest interest in the performances of miscellaneous packs, often kennelled in barns, hunted by parsons, and whipped into by ploughboys. Indeed, it may safely be said—for horsemen you must go to Yorkshire, Leicestershire, Northamptonshire, Gloucestershire, or other pasture counties; but for sportsmen learned in the working of a pack, familiar with every note, to Devonshire and Somersetshire, Cumberland, Westmoreland, and Wales.

Hugo Meynell, the founder of the Quorn Hunt (before his time fox-hunting was assumed to be the amusement of uncultivated squires) first made it fashionable. He established the Quorn somewhere about 1750, and retained the mastership until 1795. He discontinued the old plan of commencing hunting at daybreak or even by starlight, in order to come on the scent of the fox on his midnight marauding expeditions, and "drag" up to his lair in the thickets where his kennel had been previously closed by the midnight earth-stopper.

It was under Mr. Meynell's dynasty, greatly to that mighty hunter's disgust, that Mr.

Childe, of Kinlet, Shropshire (the "Flying Childe"), introduced what is called the Leicestershire style of riding up to the hounds, and flying the fences as they came. This system was at once adopted in the adjoining hunts of the Belvoir, the Cottesmore, the Pytchley, and thence spread through every hunting district of England, Wales, Ireland, and Scotland, where the fields were level and large enough to gallop in, and the fences jumpable and required to be jumped.

George Morland's hunting pictures give a very good idea of the old style, for he was essentially a realist.

> " Ere Blue Cap and Wanton taught fox-hounds to skurry,
> With music in plenty. Oh, where was the hurry—
> When each nag wore a crupper, each squire a pig-tail;
> When our toast, 'The Brown Forest,' was drunk in brown ale?"

With demi-pique saddles, the old school galloped standing up in their stirrups, holding on with a single snaffle bridle, and made their half-bred nags take, after first pulling up, stiles that could not be avoided and gates that could not be opened.

Ralph Lambton, uncle of the first Earl of Durham, of a family which had lived on their estates from Saxon times, member for his county, a most refined gentleman, was one of Mr. Meynell's earliest and best pupils. He carried the manners and customs of the great fox-hunting reformer into the North, and was long master of one of the best packs of fox-hounds in England. Durham had not then been honeycombed with coal-pits and gridironed with railways. He used to cheer his hounds with, "Hi haro! Forrard! Hi haro!" a Norman hunting cry, not known since in England, but which is still heard in France when representatives of the old nobility in Bretagne are hunting boar or wolf, or leading a charge with bayonets, as at Inkermann.

In Durham flourished one of the first of the hard-thrusting riders, the Earl of Darlington, Master of the Raby Hounds, celebrated in a song the heroes of which are forgotten, and nothing interesting to the present generation remains except the Irish chorus—

> " Lately passing o'er Barnsdale, I happened to spy
> A fox stealing on with the hounds in full cry;
> 'Tis Darlington, sure, for his voice I well know,
> Crying, 'Forward, hark forward!' for Skelbrook below.
> With my Ballymoonora, the hounds of old Raby for me!"

Of the local heroes described in this and many once celebrated hunting-songs like the Billesden Coplow, the Cheshire, and other ballads, one may say with Sir Walter Scott's harper—

> " Their bones are dust, their spurs are rust,
> Their souls are with the saints, we trust."

Of three packs of hounds still hunted under difficulties in Durham, the Raby country is alone worthy of Durham's ancient reputation.

Lord Sefton succeeded Mr. Meynell in the Mastership of the Quorn. He was more of a *bon vivant*, a politician, and a man of fashion, than a sportsman, but he, too, was a reformer of the hunting-field. He improved Mr. Childe's flying style of riding by introducing a second hunter, to be ridden judiciously by a light weight as near the line of hounds but with as little jumping as possible, so as to afford him a relay the moment the hounds checked, if, as was usually the case with his twenty-stone weight, his first horse was pumped out; this luxury in the direction of humanity has since become universal in all "flying" as distinguished from "creeping" counties, with those who can afford the expense. For those who hunt every day in a galloping county it is an economy, as a horse relieved of a heavy rider's weight at the end of the first sharp run will be ready to come out again sooner than if compelled to toil on all day.

The Duc de St. Simon relates in his "Memoirs" that his father obtained the favour of Louis by a method of changing horses in hunting without dismounting which might be followed in fox-hunting. St. Simon rode up and along the off side of the king's horse, with the second

GOOD FOR ANY HOUNDS.

horse's head to the head of the tired horse. The king having passed his left leg over his own horse's neck, and, sitting sideways, was able to mount the second horse without a minute's pause.

The paradise of the fox-hunter is certainly comprised in the circle on which fashion, not without reason, has set its seal, of which Melton and Market Harborough are supposed to be the head-quarters, although railways have made Oakham, Leamington, Rugby, and Northampton, equally accessible. As regards sport, Yorkshire has some dozen packs of hounds, supported by a numerous local aristocracy. Holderness, its best pasture district, is not second to Leicestershire. Lincolnshire wolds and heath have long been famous as the training-ground of the best class of hunters. Nottinghamshire, with the enormous woodlands of the "dukeries," open and intersected with green rides circling round Sherborne Forest, and with a quantity of light land not good for scent, stands high in the annals of fox-hunting as the home of such famous masters of hounds and huntsmen as the late Chaworth Musters, Percy Williams, and Squire Foljambe. The Rufford and the Grove are very far from first-class, but picturesque, romantic, and rare for cub-hunting. Buckinghamshire, Oxfordshire, and Gloucestershire, in which two noblemen maintain hereditary packs, Wiltshire, with its Vale of the White Horse, all afford flying countries and grand sport. In North Devon all the niceties of ancient woodcraft come into play; riding hard is impossible, but an earl, representative of a long line of sportsmen, kills his full share of foxes *secundum artem*, with the assistance of a field of farmers and parsons on different hills, hollaing every time they view the chase. Many of these are competent to hunt a pack of hounds in Devonshire.

In Surrey and the greater part of Hampshire jumping is optional. Surrey has several packs of hounds, some of which afford sport in the woodlands and others on the hills. The latter would be pretty good if two-thirds of the coverts were destroyed, and the flints removed from the fields. A beginner in London cannot do better than become a subscriber and try his 'prentice hand with the Surrey Fox-hounds, or with one of the Kentish packs. Near Ashford there is an extraordinary bit of "Leicestershire" grass. The Old Berkeley, in Hertfordshire, has long been sadly deficient in foxes, which have been eaten up by pheasants, but it is easily reached from London within less than two hours.

But after all there is only one good rule for the learner. Take the nearest hounds, as long as you do not take a fashionable pack where the field is counted by hundreds—with such there is nothing to be learned. If there is a choice, bad scenting countries and countries scarce of foxes are to be avoided. Better to hunt a good hare than a bad fox. Ten times more is to be learned on the Lincolnshire wolds, with the small fields of country gentlemen and farmers, or in Nottinghamshire, or with such packs as the Fitzwilliam (The Milton), near Peterborough, one of the best in the kingdom, and one of the best countries of grass, than in the mobs that take possession of the fashionable counties.

It should be clearly understood that some of the very best packs of hounds hunt very unfashionable counties, because the character of a pack depends not on the country, but on the intelligence and zeal of master and huntsman. Breeding a pack of hounds is a rare and difficult art. No money can improvise a good pack of hounds. The best huntsman is lost with a new pack in a new country.

"GO HARK!"

"Yon sound 's neither sheep bell nor bark;
They 're running, they 're running, Go Hark!
The sport may be lost by a moment's delay,
So whip up the puppies and scurry away.
Dash down through the cover by dingle and dell,
There 's a gate at the bottom, I know it full well;
And they 're running, they 're running, Go Hark!

"They 're running, they 're running, Go Hark!
One fence and we 're out at the park.
Sit down in your saddles, and race at the brook,
Then smash at the bullfinch; no time for a look.
Leave cravens and skirters to dangle behind,
He 's away for the moors in the teeth of the wind,
And they 're running, they 're running, Go Hark!

"They're running, they're running, Go Hark!
Let them run and run on till it's dark!
Well with them we are, and well with them we'll be
While there's wind in our horses and daylight to see:
Then shog along homeward, chat over the fight,
And hear in our dreams the sweet music all night,
Of—they're running, they're running. Go Hark!" CHARLES KINGSLEY.

STAG-HUNTING.

Stag-hunting in feudal times was the exclusive privilege of royalty and of nobility. Wild deer abounded in the forests and woods that have long since been disforested to make way for corn and grazing farms. The hounds used were slow and deep-mouthed; they were set on in relays, in likely places for the deer to pass, by foresters learned in woodcraft.

"The hart," says Nicholas Cox, "hath his season in summer, and when the hinde's begins the chase of the hart is over; that is to say, the hart fifteen days after midsummer till Holy Rood day, when the chase of the hinde beginneth, and lasteth till Candlemas." But this is not the modern practice—the season of the Devon and Somerset Stag-hounds commences about the 15th August, and ends on the 18th October, after which hind-hunting commences.

The fallow deer was also hunted in enclosed parks, across which rides were cut for the hunters, such as may still be seen in the forests of France and Germany. The game when driven to bay was slain by a stroke of the hunting-knife, or a shot from the hand of the most noble person present.

In 1748 the Duke of Cumberland (of Culloden fame) was Ranger of Windsor Park, and lived at Cranbourne Lodge when not on active service. He was a constant attendant on the Royal stag-hounds, which hunted on Tuesdays and Saturdays from Holy Rood Day (September 25) till Easter week. The herd of red deer in Windsor Forest amounted at that time to about twelve hundred head, which were replenished occasionally with deer taken from the New Forest in Hampshire. It was the duty of the yeomen prickers, in liveries of scarlet and gold, with French horns slung round them, to single out from the herd the quarry for the day's diversion. As soon as he had been separated from his companions the hounds were laid on—powerful animals of the old stag-hound breed, not fox-hounds entered to deer, but the true yellow pie, very sonorous in note, and having the character of the blood-hound in shape. The country was then an immense tract of open heaths, growing nothing but broom and gorse, with here and there impassable bogs and sheets of water, dirty and deep, and at all times a most distressing country for horses. When the deer was pulled down and killed, those persons who intended to run their horses for the king's guineas at Ascot had to apply to the huntsman for qualification tickets that they were well up with the hounds at the kill. At the close of the season 1751-52 his royal highness ran his chestnut gelding Button for the plate at Ascot, for horses that had been up at the death of a leash of stags in Windsor Forest during the previous season. But it was little likely that a horse fitted to carry the Duke's great weight to the end of a long, jading run should shine as a racer, and, of six competitors in the race, Button was the last.*

"I was at Ascot Heath in King George the Third's time, from 1810 to 1813, under Wetherall, at Chivey Down Lodge, (Tommy Coleman of St. Albans). At that time the

* *Baily's Magazine*, May, 1876.

JEM MORGAN—HUNTSMAN OF THE BERKELEY HUNT.
TEMP. EARL OF LONSDALE.

MR. CHARLES DAVIS—HUNTSMAN OF THE ROYAL BUCKHOUNDS.
FROM AN OIL SKETCH BY SIR FRANCIS GRANT, P.R.A.

king gave a hundred-guinea plate to be run for by horses belonging to his yeomen prickers who rode after him with the stag-hounds, and he gave another hundred-guinea plate at Ascot for horses that had been in at the taking of ten stags. I have had many a hard ride and long day to get a ticket, as the runs were usually severe, and you must have been at the take to claim a ticket, which the huntsman gave you; and it was absolutely necessary to have the number to qualify, and they were particular as to your going right to the end of the day. The king's yeoman prickers carried large French horns slung over their shoulders, which could be heard at a great distance off, and wore scarlet coats trimmed with broad gold lace down their backs. There were ten of them in number. Lord Cornwallis was Master of the Buck-hounds, and lived at Swinley Park,* and the deer were kept in the paddocks there, great red deer as big as donkeys; they'd frequently go fifteen or twenty miles, and they thought nothing of crossing the River Thames."

George III.'s hunting seems to have been a compromise between the old and new style; the stags were known by name, and not killed if it could be helped. But they were not as carefully prepared as at the present day. The hounds, forty couple, were of the breed depicted in Bewick's "Quadrupeds," twenty-four to twenty-six inches high, with big head, immense ears, and voices deep as the tolling bell of St. Paul's Cathedral. Unlike the fox-hounds now used, they flagged after the first burst, and did not run into a sinking deer; indeed, like blood-hounds, they scarcely lifted their noses from the ground until the stag was driven to bay.

George III. rode nearly nineteen stone, his horses were under-bred, the hounds were constantly stopped to allow his majesty to get up, and altogether it was a dreary affair, often prolonged into late in the evening, as may be gathered from the doleful lamentation of the king's attendants, recorded in the diary of Madame d'Arblay then Miss Fanny Burney.

During the long illness of the king the stag-hound pack was sold to go abroad. In 1813 the Prince Regent accepted the already mentioned pack of fox-hounds for stag-hunting from the Duke of Richmond, and from that time to the present the Royal Buck-hounds have been pure fox-hounds. Early in the present century another pack of true stag-hounds which hunted the wild deer in Devon and Somerset was sold to go to Germany; and when wild stag-hunting was re-established in the West, another pack was formed of the tallest hounds that could be obtained by drafts from fox-hound breeding kennels. Since that period all stag-hunting in England has been carried on by fox-hounds, except two packs of blood-hounds of very recent date, one of which was dispersed on the death of Mr. Thomas Nevile of Chilland.

The Royal Buck-hounds attained their highest reputation under the late Mr. Charles Davis, whose father had been Hare-huntsman of the royal kennels. He joined the Royal Buck-hounds as first yeoman pricker, when stag-hunting recommenced with the Goodwood Fox-hounds; and was appointed huntsman of them in 1822, a post he held for more than forty years, to the satisfaction and admiration of all who met him in the field.

Mr. Davis was tall, and walked very little over ten stone; in his gold-embroidered hunting coat he forms the subject of one of the coloured illustrations of this work, engraved from an oil sketch by Sir Francis Grant, P.R.A., kindly lent by Mr. Charles Phillips, of The Cedars, Mortlake.

The royal deer selected to be hunted are kept at Swinley paddocks, where once stood the official residence of the Master of the Buck-hounds. They are bred in the parks of

* The residence since pulled down, and an allowance made to Master of the Buck-hounds instead.

Windsor and Richmond; the stock is from time to time crossed with stags of vigorous character from other parks.

Stags with their horns cut were at one time used; but, confirming the dicta of Nicholas Cox, it was found difficult to make them run well. Therefore, between October and Christmas, hinds and haviers (castrated harts) have been preferred, and form the majority of what may be called the deer stud. Calves castrated never throw up any horns at all, while those operated on as yearlings throw up one set of short horns, which are never renewed.*

About a score, chosen for their vigour, are turned into a series of paddocks. During the hunting season they are fed on good hay, old beans, and carrots; they keep themselves in condition by playing about. The deer-cart, very like a race-horse van, holds two deer. The day before hunting a dog trained for the purpose is set to separate a selected pair from the herd, and drive them into a shed just big enough to hold them. As they are often fierce, when the deer-keeper has to go into the shed he protects himself with a large wooden shield. On the morning of the hunt the deer-cart is backed close against a movable door, and the first deer is driven into the cart—after one or two days' experience they willingly go in of themselves—a slide partition is then introduced; the first deer being shut in with his head to the door, the reserve deer is sent in with his head to the horses.

After one season the deer generally learn that the cart is a harbour of refuge, and when it is brought up after the chase leap into it of their own free will.

The average work of each deer does not exceed three runs in a season. They have been known to last five and even six seasons; one, which had been hunted four times a season for five years, had not a bite on him when he was killed, in consequence of an accident in the barn where he was shut up after a tremendous run.

The following extract from "The Hunting Diary" of a French nobleman gives an idea of the impression produced on an intelligent foreign sportsman by our Royal Hunt:—

"Un jour j'assistais à une chasse à courre avec la meute royale dans les environs de Windsor.

"J'étais arrivé au rendezvous tout plein de mes impressions des chasses de Compiègne et de Rambouillet, et, bien que je m'attendisse à voir quelque chose de différent, j'espérais rencontrer un style, une grandeur quelconque.

"Cette illusion fut de courte durée.

"Je m'apperçus bientôt que l'étiquette était bannie pour faire place au sans façon le plus complet, il me semblait que quiconque possèdant un cheval était venu se joindre aux piqueurs pour jouir d'un temps de galop.

"Neanmoins, ces apparences me semblant en quelque sorte subversives je résolus de les approfondir, et m'adressant à mon compagnon, charmant garçon Capitaine aux Gardes, je lui demandai si réellement ces messieurs en habits écarlates et ces brillantes amazones, appartenaient tous à l'aristocratie. 'Pas le moins du monde,' me repondit il en souriant, 'la plupart sont ce que vous appelez en France, des épiciers.'

"'Ils appartiennent au commerce et à la bourgeoisie; je puis vous montrer ici, trois marchands de vin, deux tailleurs, un notaire, deux commissaires priseurs, et un restaurateur; cependant, je puis vous désigner aussi, le Ministre des Affairs Etrangères et un ex-Lord Chancelier.

"'Quant aux dames, cette grosse brune est une marchande de modes, plus loin cette blonde qui a sans doute perdu son peigne pour montrer que ses magnifiques cheveux sont à elle, est sans profession, enfin cette mignonne créature à votre droite est un professeur d'equitation pour dames et autres dit on.'

"N'ayant aucune raison de douter de la veracité de mon ami, je ne pus m'empécher de souhaiter qu'en France nous puissions nous enorgueillir d'une telle bourgeoisie car tous les chasseurs étaient admirablement montés et la plupart m'ont paru être excellents écuyers."—"Souvenirs de Chasse," par le Baron de Sauviac.

The twelfth Earl of Derby kept a pack of hounds for hunting carted deer near Croydon at the commencement of this century, which have been fully described in one of "Nimrod's"

---

* The deer tribe, unlike the antelope and sheep, change their horns annually.

earliest "Hunting Tours." On his death they were discontinued; they were renewed as a subscription pack more than twenty years ago, and have been kept up ever since.

The Surrey Hounds have a fine wild sheep-feeding country, in spite of the encroachments of the villa-creating railroad stations on the Brighton line. Road-riding is not possible over the barren hills and downs of Surrey, when the hounds run straight. A second stag-hound pack has recently been established near Dorking.

Ever since 1839 the Rothschild family have kept up a pack of hounds for hunting deer over the Vale of Aylesbury, one of the finest countries in England; indeed, the Vale is nearly all grass, with fences, and a good deal of water to jump. There are, however, roads through this rich vale; and in his later years the late Baron Meyer, a welter weight, frequently showed that, with a sharp groom in attendance, it was possible to keep very close to hounds without taking a single leap.

Major Whyte Melville has admirably sketched the incidents of a carted-deer hunt over the Vale of Aylesbury, a country second to none in the following verses.

The last stanzas of the original have been omitted, for even Major Melville's enthusiasm could make nothing of "a finish" with a tame deer.

* * * * *   * * * * *
* * * * *   * * * * *

"Fresh from his carriage, as bridegroom on marriage,
   The Lord of the Valley leaps gallantly out.

"Then in a second, his course having reckoned—
   Line that all Leicestershire cannot surpass—
Fleet as the swallow, when summer winds follow,
   The Lord of the Valley skims over the grass.

"Yonder a steed is rolled up with his master,
   Here in a double another lies cast;
Faster and faster come grief and disaster;
   All but the good ones are weeded at last.

"Beat, but still going, a countryman sowing
   Has sighted the Lord of the Valley ahead.

"There in the bottom, see, sluggish and idle,
   Steals the dark stream where the willow tree grows;
Harden your heart, and catch hold of the bridle,
   Steady him! rouse him! and over he goes.

"Look, in a minute a dozen are in it;
   But forward! hark forward! for draggled and blown,
A check though desiring, with courage untiring,
   The Lord of the Valley is holding his own."

At Berkhampstead, in Hertfordshire, where there is a limited but fine tract of pasture, divided by ditches and quickset hedges, with open hills, a subscription pack of stag-hounds was established and has been hunted ever since 1874, instead of a pack of harriers which were kept by a late Earl of Brownlow; it has been supported, the farmers of the district (and this is worth noting) objecting to hare-hunting as much more destructive to their fences than a deer which goes straight away.

In Essex, in addition to four packs of fox-hounds and several packs of harriers, a very celebrated pack of stag-hounds, which were originally founded by a Lord Petre, has been kept up by subscription for many years.

The Essex country requires a fast and very clever hunter, for a mistake will not unfrequently involve not only a fall, but the need of a plough-horse and ropes to get your hunter out of a deep ditch.

This was the favourite country of the late Charles Buxton, M.P., a hereditary philanthropist, essentially a student, a serious politician of advanced views, an accomplished amateur artist, in fact, the very last kind of man that philosophers of the library and the desk would expect to find in the hunting-field. He was so fond of the Essex country that he used to travel from his seat in the heart of Surrey to join Lord Petre's hounds. He, too, tried his hand at a stag-hunting song, and a very good song it is, but it fails at the same place as Whyte Melville's, because there can be nothing poetical in putting a hart or hind back again into a van.

Wild deer in the West once in four or five years give a straight run of an hour, or even two, over the moors, but a run of ten and fifteen miles over an enclosed country with stag-hounds and a trained deer is an ordinary occurrence in the Vale of Aylesbury, in the Roothings of Essex, and in the best part of Surrey.

"FORRARD AWAY."*

" Forrard away, forrard away!
Cheerily, ye beauties, forrard away!
They flash like a gleam o'er the upland brow,
They flash like a gleam on the russet plough,
O'er the green wheat-land far to see,
Over the pasture, over the lea.
Forrard away, forrard away!
Cheerily, ye beauties, forrard away!

" A stiff ox-fence, with its oaken rail—
' Rap, rap ' go the hoofs, like a peasant's flail—
A five-foot drop ; see the rushing brook,
Send him at it, don't stop to look ;
Dash through the quickset into the lane,
Out on the other side, forrard again.
Forrard away, forrard away!
Cheerily, ye beauties, forrard away!

" A moment's check, one cast around,
'Tis forrard again, with a furious bound ;

Mellow and sweet their voices sound.
Steady, my pet, at the five-barred gate ;
Lightly over, with heart elate :
Up with the elbow, down with the head ;
Crash through the bullfinch like shots of lead.
Forrard away, forrard away!
Cheerily, ye beauties, forrard away!

" Look at the hounds, their muzzles high,
A sheet would cover them, on they fly,
'Tis music, now, not a whimpering cry ;
Neck or nothing, we'll do or die.
Swinging along at a slashing pace,
With souls on fire each risk to face.
Forrard away, forrard away!
Cheerily, ye beauties, forrard away!"

" Thread the hazels, over the stile,
'Tis forty-five minutes, each five a mile.
Cheerily, ye beauties, forrard away!"

HUNTING WITH BLOOD-HOUNDS.

Lord Wolverton, who established a pack of blood-hounds for stag-hunting in Dorset, in 1871, favoured me with the following letter, dated September, 1874 :—

"I began in 1871 by buying six couple of hounds from Captain Roden, of Kells, county Meath, which were excellent, but perhaps not quite the pure blood-hound ; they had a (fox) hound cross in them. I have bought and bred a good many pure blood-hounds, with sixteen couple of which I hunt red deer. These hounds are 26 to 27 inches high ; black-and-tan, with fine noses. They run very fast, getting over the ground with a long stride. *They will stand no lifting ;* and only lose a scent when they are pressed by horses, or taken off to attempt a cast, like fox-hounds.

"I find them handy to voice, but any 'whipping-in' makes them sulky. Their notes are very deep, and when running a cold scent the music is extremely fine. They race fairly together, and do not tail more than the ordinary stag-hounds. They do not dash for a scent like fox-hounds, but they *drive* in good style. I have hardly enough yet to draft, or

* " Posthumous Memoirs of Charles Buxton, M.P."

I could get them as level and to run as well together as fox-hounds. The puppies are very difficult to rear."

In reference to these blood-hounds, Captain Roden said, in a letter to *The Field*:—

"The hounds now in the possession of Lord Wolverton were bred by me—at least, eight couple were. I saw them last summer at his place. I obtained the breed from the late Mr. Jennings, in Yorkshire, and Mr. Conan, of Bladun Burn, near Newcastle. I then began my pack by keeping them as low as I could, but not less than twenty-six inches. Their weight at two years old should be about seventy to eighty pounds. They do not come to maturity until three years. They are very delicate until they are eight or ten months old, and require unskimmed milk and lots of room; in fact, should be at large for hours in the day *without* a man, for this reason—they have great intelligence, and are not mere machines, like fox-hounds; they soon learn by themselves what to avoid, and will act accordingly. I always hunted mine with a 'drag,' a small piece of *raw* meat, the fresher the better, about one pound weight. A man took it on foot, and I gave from two hours' to four hours' start if for horsemen, two hours if for mere exercise, of which they require a great deal—four hours, sometimes six hours. The man should go about five miles, and put the drag in a tree. Nothing is to be put in the meat on any account. They will not be driven or stand cracking a whip—get sulky or cross—they must be let alone, and the slower they go the more beautiful the hunting. In breeding I found that the narrower the head, a high point in show-dogs, the worse hind-quarters—no second thighs, and consequently they were unable to last for quick work. That and flat feet are the drawbacks. The sooner they are let hunt the better; at three months old I used to begin. They never seem to care so much for any scent as what they were first entered at. They require a large kennel, as when they fight there is much harm done, and they do not cool down for some time. One which had been petted by Lady W. was put back into the kennels, when the others killed him at once; but they are in general quiet. I don't think they are to be always left to servants; they can pick up bad habits like other animals, but to a master they are delightful —so affectionate and obedient. They must have a gallop of some kind thrice a week, or they get puffy, for you must not let them get low or shorten their food. They should be above themselves or they get tired; plenty of flesh, often given, raw, and large lumps at a time. The chewing promotes digestion. In work they do not cast like other hounds—each hound goes alone—and never watch for another dog; in fact, they never take their noses off the ground, and only one deer was killed by them in Dorsetshire. Even when in the same field they never get a view; so all deer have been saved without difficulty. A pack of ten couple is as many as should go out, as they all give lots of music. Fifteen couple should be kept, so many accidents occur. They eat more than other hounds, and won't stand short commons and have it made up with whip cord."

The great point in favour of carted stag-hunting with busy, hard-riding men is, that the fox chooses his time of breaking and his point across country; while the carted deer is led out at an appointed hour, with a fine open country before him that he must cross if he runs straight.

IRISH STAG-HOUNDS.

Ireland has one very celebrated pack of stag-hounds, the "Ward." They hunt close to Dublin, in one of the best countries in the world. Of these Whyte Melville sings—

"Not a moment to lose if you'd share in the fun;
  Of a gate, or a gap, not a sign to be seen!
Ere the dancers are ready the music's begun,
  To the tune, if you like it, of 'Wearing the Green.'*
For a horse may be grassed and his rider be floored
In a couple of shakes, when they start with the 'Ward.'"

WILD STAG HUNTING.

"On the hills and moors of Devonshire and Somersetshire, bounded by the Bristol Channel on one side, and on the other by the enclosed and cultivated farms, a limited stock of 'red-deer retain a doubtful hold upon Exmoor, and the hills, wastes, and modern plantations around it,' preserved by the exertions and at the expense of Earls Fortescue, Carnarvon, and Lovelace, Sir Thomas Ackland, Colonel Knight, M.P. (the owner of 21,000 acres of Exmoor), and other land-owners, and by the hearty assistance of the hill farmers, with whom to kill a wild deer, except before the hounds, would be as great a crime as to shoot a fox on Lincolnshire Wolds.

"Exmoor was afforested by William Rufus, and in those old days the red-deer, the chosen game of Norman kings, roamed in large herds over this remote and thinly inhabited district, attracted by (what still remains) the excellence of the summer pasture and the wildness of valleys no longer oak-clad. When Exmoor was disforested by Act of Parliament in 1818, it comprised, with the unenclosed lands lying open, 60,000 acres without a fence. Over these wastes there were no roads for the track of pack-horses; no enclosures, no cultivation, no dwellings, no population except the herdsmen who attended in summer to the feeding of live stock from the valleys, and the smugglers who made temporary depôts in the moors on their way from creeks of the coast convenient for their free trade." †

Since that date at least two-thirds have been enclosed and turned into arable, dairy, or sheep farms.

Long before Exmoor was disforested the red-deer had been reduced almost to extinction by miscellaneous shooting, and the barbarous practice of hunting and killing hinds heavy in calf. The primæval oak-forests had disappeared, and the stags and hinds now hunted are harboured in plantations not forty years old. In fact, although they have a wider range of wild country to roam over, they owe their existence as much to careful preservation as the herds of Windsor Park.

The enclosures of the moor country which are regularly hunted are generally of great extent, from fifty to two hundred acres. Red-deer, unlike fallow-deer, cannot bear any kind of enclosure, so when a few more thousand acres are converted by steam ploughing and liming from peat and heath to sheep pastures, it will become difficult to maintain even the present number, said to not much exceed two hundred, all told.

HUNTING ON EXMOOR.

"All who are fond of riding, not to say hunting, will find, at a time of the year when no other hounds are running, at least at a reasonable hour after breakfast, a climate round Exmoor as delightful and restoring as Switzerland, picturesque scenery of the most varied character, and every temptation and facility for the outdoor amusements of a family who like bathing, sketching, fern collecting, and hunting. They will also find great civility and hospitality to

---

* "Wearing the Green," a rebel song.   † Exmoor Reclamation : *Journal of the Royal Agricultural Society of England*, 1878.

strangers. With the Devon and Somerset stag-hounds no one hunting pays the slightest attention to the costume question. A select few, whom I could name and number on the fingers of my two hands, are dressed fit for covert side in the midlands. Half that number of ladies are dressed as well as they ride, which is saying a great deal ; but the multitude—male and female, children and adults, yeomen, farmers, and vacation visitors—wear clothes that may do for botanising, fishing, picnicing—in fact, anything handy. Best of all, they don't look odd by contrast ; the whole style of the district is amusement or sport, or both, not dress and admiration.

Then as to the horses. The best blood-hunters, if accustomed to gallop over a rough country and to take care of themselves going fast down-hill are not out of place, and, indeed, may find a very good preparation for hard work in November. A few of such are to be found at covert side on Exmoor in August and September ; but, for a family party, the sort of ponies that run in butchers' and bakers' carts, taken straight from hard work, will afford an ample allowance of sport, do all that can be reasonably required of them, and look quite in character with the majority of the field. For choice, I would sooner ride a blood horse, not over fifteen hands high, with the Devon and Somerset, although I have been perfectly carried by a hunter of 16½ hands ; but I have observed that the ponies are generally there, or thereabouts, at a check or kill. Lots of the farmers ride rough three-year-olds. I can speak with confidence on this point, having been on every occasion mounted by the squire of Exmoor on a blood hunter bred on the moors ; yet, whenever galloping ceased (it never lasted very long), I found the long-striding hunter had very little advantage in pace over the rough ponies ridden by natives of the district. This arises from the nature of the country and the absence of fencing.

In the first place—and this is all in the favour of a family party—there is no such thing as jumping with the Devon and Somerset staghounds ; some of the very best local men have never in their lives taken a leap three feet high while hunting ; and for a very good reason—ninety per cent. of the fences on the moors are impracticable, stone walls on turf banks with a wire at top, or else turf banks with a perfect fortification of growing beech-trees at the top. The hunting grounds of the Devon and Somerset may be divided into two parts—the first and best the moors, which are either quite unfenced or separated into fields of not less than sixty acres, with open or easily-opened gates. These moors are intersected by narrow valleys, along which trout streams flow ; and these the deer traverse by preference, while the horsemen are continually travelling along both sides of the valley. The other country is cut up into small enclosures by banks like fortifications ; and if the riding is not along the deep lanes or the beds of the streams—which you sometimes follow under arching trees for miles—it is pursued under difficulties through the gates of miniature fields. There are also on the open moors boggy places, which although never dangerous, are deep enough to take a stranger's horse up to his belly. For all these reasons the Paterfamilias with his brood is never likely to be left hopelessly behind, as he would be on a good day in any hunt where fencing is the principal part of the business.

To try to "keep with the hounds," to "sit down in the saddle, and put his head straight," is simply impossible. Perhaps once in three or four seasons there is a straight run, in which the deer gallops clean away from the hounds, and the hounds from the field ; but, as a rule, the deer don't run straight, checks are frequent. The people who know the country, and the habits of the deer, are seldom far out at the kill or the finish if they can keep up an average pace of ten miles an hour. At this pace they see a great deal as easily as they could with the harriers on the Southdowns, but with a much more beautiful country of streams, and woods, and moors. That an ounce of fact is worth a pound of theory is an accepted axiom. On a day which has been described in print, when, after two hours' hunting on the moors, the deer turned into the close enclosed country, and running up the bed of the river Exe, was killed at a place called, I think, Winsford, the veteran parson of the hunt, the Rev. Jack Russell, presented the slot to a child in a scarlet jacket, ten years old, who, led with a rein by her father, a naval officer and a stranger, and accompanied by a brother and sister three or four years older, all mounted on the roughest of ponies, had ridden from the find to the kill; often left behind by the well mounted, but always turning up again at the right moment. Let this anecdote encourage other fathers of horsey families to "go and do likewise."

HOW TO GET THERE, AND WHERE TO GO.

The hunting district is environed by two lines of railway, both starting from Taunton The one takes a coast-line passing Dulverton and Dunster, until it terminates at Minehead, where one of the kennels of the Devon and Somerset stag-hounds is situated. The other, more inland, conveys the traveller to Barnstaple, passing through the South Molton Station, the nearest to the centre of Exmoor. It may roughly be stated that all the best meets of the stag-hounds lie on the moors between Dunster and South Molton. Castle Hill, the seat of the Earl of Fortescue, is close to South Molton, and his lordship and family hunt with the deer regularly.

The best stations for hunting are Minehead, Dunster, Dulverton, Porlock—the last situated in a very deep valley—Lynton, Simon's Bath, and Exford. The kennels are at Minehead and Exford. The best way of getting about is in a light, strong, open carriage with a patent break, and pair of horses that can also be ridden. An Oliver or Perth dog-cart is a good model.

Dunster is perhaps the best on that side of the country; and from Dunster you may for a change go down into the steep gorge where Porlock lies. The descent will tax your break and your horses' hind-quarters. Then go on to Exford, where the other kennels of the stag-hounds are situated. There is a comfortable old-fashioned tavern at Exford. Thence you may proceed to Simon's Bath, in the centre of the Exmoor, where there is an inn frequented by hunting-men; lodgings and good stabling may also be had at a farm-house, but no beer or spirits are sold in the whole village. On the other hand, the milk, cream, and butter, are excellent. Trout, small but sweet, abound in the Barle and Exe, and any quantity of mushrooms may be had for the trouble of pulling.

THE CHARM OF THE WEST.

The charm lies in the strange wild rocky scenery, intersected by many streams, the luxuriant plantations, the far-rolling brown moors, the exhilarating softness of the air "as refreshing as Switzerland," the long gallops over turf without a fence, the expectation of seeing the antlered deer; and, not least, the extreme enthusiasm and hearty ways of the rural sportsmen. The drawbacks are the long distances to cover, the frequent rain, and the many blank days, or days when a deer will not leave cover.

Hard riding there is none, but of excitement of the best kind for a whole family of hunters in embryo there is plenty.

It must be remembered that the hounds only meet twice a week, and every meet is not within reach or worth reaching, therefore a family party require some other resources.

THE ORDER OF THE HUNT.

In going to the meet obtain if possible some experienced sportsman or mounted shepherd to guide you. Then, instead of sticking to the roads, which are generally good if steep, you may enjoy short cuts across moors, sheep walks, and dells. On arriving at the meet (the usual hour is eleven), the harbourer has first to make his report to the huntsman. The harbourer is a more important person than the earth-stopper to fox-hunters. It is his business to track a stag (*slotted* is the term) to a covert convenient for the meet, and learn whether he has stayed there. For this purpose, where the paths would receive no mark of foot, he places wisps of straw or brambles in any gaps out of the wood.

If the report is satisfactory, the huntsman proceeds to shut up the body of the pack in some outhouse or barn, having first drawn out two, three, or, at most, five couple of old sagacious hounds, to act as tufters—that is, to find and drive the game out. The coverts are generally plantations of no great age, but of great extent, situated in valleys or dells; sometimes a deer is found on the open moor, but that is a great stroke of luck, a hunting day to be marked with a white stone.

The field of horsemen spreads over the hills that command a view of the covert, into which the huntsman and one of his whips only enter. *To* follow him would be a gross breach of etiquette. The distance from the hounds is often great, they don't give tongue in a very resounding manner, nothing like what I have heard with fox-hounds when hunting with the Rufford in Nottinghamshire. From time to time a few white spots may cross an open space, a faint sound of a hound giving tongue rises to the top of the hill, and the occasional cheer of the huntsman, these are the only signs that anything is going on. This delay may last an hour, two hours, three hours, for it is not enough to drive *a* deer out of cover, it must be *the deer* the Master decides to hunt, so there may be two or three moments of agreeable excitement when out bursts a hind, or unwarrantable deer, not considered fit to be hunted on that day. In truth, it is often dull work, for blank days or days without a run are not uncommon.

At length the joyful moment arrives, a grand dun antlered fellow, nearly as big as a Jersey bull, bounds up the side of the combe (Devonian for gorge), and gallops away for the moors— that is, if it is a lucky day. If it is not, he takes to the enclosed country, with its deep lanes, and, until he is killed, you see neither deer nor hounds, nothing but the tail of the pony ridden by your pilot.

Now comes an awful pause, most trying to those not accustomed to the sport. Only the tufters follow the stag, and these are stopped as soon as possible. You don't take hold of your horse, sit down and ride—at least, you only ride to the top of the hill, and "mark the course the antlered monarch takes." Arthur gallops off to the barn, where the pack are impatiently baying, and you must wait for them exactly as in the Vale of Aylesbury you have to wait until the hounds are laid on the "carted calf." They come at last, are laid on the line, give tongue to the scent if there is any, and away they go in a long straggling line, eager but comparatively silent, going too fast, it is said, to make much music, quite unlike the sonorous staghounds heard in French and German forests, and not nearly so exciting. In a season you may get one gallop right across the moors for five or even ten miles on end; and if you are well enough mounted, and can get a pilot who will keep you clear of bogs, you will find the field squandered in two miles. But this is quite the exception. The general character of the best moor country is that of long green undulating table-lands, intersected continually by long steep gorges provincially called combes, down and up which the horses of the country scramble, slowly but safely; at the bottom of most of these is a stream rattling over a pebbly bottom, except where an accidental dam has formed a bog. These combes run into each other, and the deer and the hounds alternately descend and ascend the steep sides, while the native sportsmen ride along the ridges as long as they can, and know when it is absolutely necessary to descend the steep sides and climb the opposite precipitous banks.

The horn sounded and the hounds away, if the moor is open, away go the well-mounted horsemen, as if they were going to leave all the ponies behind. But the stranger on a cob need not despair; as a rule, checks are frequent; the deer takes every chance of resting himself in water for a few minutes, and if the pony riders can only manage to keep on at about ten miles an hour, in the wake of some farmer, and if they will only harden their hearts, sit back to ride down hill (I never saw a horse fall going down hill) and take hold of the mane or breastplate, not the bridle, to climb up, and not try an independent gallop, stick to the ruck of native sportsmen, they will be pretty certain to catch up the fast young fellows on real hunters. They will have, most likely, a series of ten or twelve short bursts of five or ten minutes; they will not only cross streams, but ride along the beds of bubbling brooks, through over-arching green woods, and finally see the stag at bay in the pool of some brook; see him killed, if they like to see that butchering operation, and hear the *morte* sounded on the huntsman's horn. Even if a great run takes place, it is seldom quite straight. The wonderful knowledge the farmers have of the run of the deer and the geography of the country, enable the pony-riding stag-hunter nine times out of ten to reach the hill before it is all over.

Although the hunting commences in the middle of August, the hard runs with the stag do not commence until September, when he has recovered from the exertion of growing his new antlers, so the stranger has August to prepare himself and his horses for a real moor run, if lucky enough and horsed well enough to see one. Towards the middle of October stags go out of season, and at that time the hinds are hunted, and often show better runs than stags. In the middle of September packs of fox-hounds in that part of the country begin their early morning routing of the cubs, and have very good runs. A wandering moor fox very often shows rare sport.

When the stag is killed or lost, and the hunt is over, the strangers will often find themselves a very long way from their temporary home. The first thing is to refresh from absolutely the necessary flask of cold tea or whiskey, or wine-and-water, and the indispensable sand-wich-case, for in these regions Publics are very few and far between; at dairy farms milk may be obtained for a few civil words.

Young men who defy rheumatism may ride home in their cold or damp clothes, but ladies and men who object to rheumatism should be provided with a Cardigan or warm jacket, strapped to the saddle. The farmers will be found most kind in showing the way as far as they go. But my advice is not to follow their advice and try short cuts when they leave you, but stick to the roads which are, if steep and long, good. A compass may be of use in crossing a moor, although I never tried to use one. A resident in the country would easily mark out the cross roads, which are not shown on the old ordnance map. A pair of field-glasses are a decided acquisition, and much used in stag-hunting.

The following is a list of the meets where there is the most chance of a gallop. I believe they are marked on Mr. Sandford's map, copied from and corrected by a Devonshire stag-hunter :—Cloutsham, Dunkerry Hill Gate, Hawkcombe Head, Brendon, Two Gates, Larkborough, Mouncey Hill Gate, Tar Steps, Yard Down, Marsh Bridge, Hele Bridge.

DRAG-HUNTING.

This chapter would not be complete without a few words about the drag hunts in which a scratch pack of hounds is set to hunt a train scent or drag, taken by a man across a country intersected by fences more or less difficult, according to the tastes of the managers.

It is not sport in the hunting sense of the word, but it is a very exciting amusement for men and horses, and capital practice for those who wish to learn how to ride fast and straight across a flying country.

In a drag-hunt the young horseman learns to "harden his heart," to "take hold of his horse by the head," and decide at full gallop where and how he will get out of a field the moment he has jumped into it. He can also get himself into condition before serious hunting commences. At Oxford the drag-hounds were formerly kept by the principal "tuft," *i.e.*, nobleman, of Christchurch College ; but this laudable custom may have recently been discontinued in deference to the seriousness of the age.

A drag-hunt, not ridden too fast, is an excellent method of preparing young horses for the hunting field, by exercising them to leap and accustoming them to the cry of hounds. But it requires a very cool old head not to do too much with a four-year-old if you have a good place.

Drag-hounds may be of any breed, and the wilder the better. Fox-hounds are the best where great pace is required, but great fun may be had out of heavy harriers or even beagles.

A scratch pack of drag-hounds might be introduced in many parts of the Continent, where the prejudices of the landed proprietors and the foreign laws of trespass would not permit real hunting.

The drag is generally made with woollen rags dipped in aniseed fastened to the feet of a man who runs the course prescribed, or a fox's bush ; but a very good one is a ferret's nest wrapped in a cabbage net.

CHAPTER XX.

HUNTERS.

The Hunter—Poetical Description—The Five Essentials in Prose—Height of According to Country—Extraordinarily Small Horses—Exceptions—"The Unknown"—Analysis of Size of Hunters at Islington Show—Height of Horse partly Depends on Height of Rider—The Points of a Hunter of any Size—Hunter's Action—Bad Shoulders Dangerous—Welter Weights —Their Preference for Five-Year-Olds—Celebrated Old Horses—Iris—Rainbow—Faults of Old Hunters—A Hunter should Jump in Cold Blood—Hunters Trained by Farmers the Best—Curious Habits—Anecdote of Irish Hunter—The Sort for a Big Country—For a Closely-Enclosed Country—Advantage of a Horse Leading Well—Charles Buxton on Choosing Hunters—A Master of Fox-hounds' Plan—To Job or to Buy—By Auction—Hack Hunters of Oxford—Cambridge—Cheltenham—Windsor—To Turn a Hack into a Hunter—Walking Lessons.

> " A HEAD like a snake, and a skin like a mouse,
>   An eye like a woman, bright, gentle, and brown,
> With loins and a back that would carry a house,
>   And quarters to lift him smack over a town.
>
> " When the country is deepest, I give you my word,
>   'Tis a pride and a pleasure to put him along ;
> O'er fallow and pasture he sweeps like a bird,
>   And there's nothing too wide, nor too high, nor too strong.
>
> " Last Monday we ran for an hour in the Vale ;
>   Not a bullfinch was trimmed, of a gap not a sign ;
> All the ditches were double, each fence had a rail ;
>   And the farmers locked every gate in the line.
>
> " I'd a lead of them all when we came to the brook,
>   A big one—a bumper—and up to your chin ;
> As he threw it behind him, I turned for a look ;
>   There were eight of us had it, and seven got in !" *

The essentials of a hunter of any size may be very shortly stated without any veterinary technicalities.

1. The hunter must have at least one good eye, for a hunter must see his way.

2. He must have lungs good enough to gallop without distress. There are horses that roar, to the great annoyance of every one within hearing, without any apparent effect on their speed or endurance. It certainly requires great courage in a gentleman to ride such nuisances.

3. He must have a back equal to the weight he has to carry ; quarters, hocks, and thighs

---

* From " The Clipper that Stands at the Top of the Stall," dedicated to Colonel the Hon. Charles White, M.P., by Major J. Whyte Melville.

with propelling power to carry him over any reasonable fence. There are beautiful park hacks and showy harness-horses that have not power to jump over a rail three feet high or a ditch a yard wide.

4. He must have such shoulders, and legs so fitted to his feet, that he can land without tumbling on his head, and gallop without tripping over a molehill, a rut, or a clay furrow.

5. All these qualifications are useless unless the hunter has endurance enough to carry him through a day which frequently begins at nine o'clock in the morning, and ends at dark, ten or fifteen miles from home.

If, in addition, he has with high courage a fine temper, will allow his rider to open a gate and mount again after a mutual fall; if he really likes his trade, cries " Ha, ha!" at the sound of a huntsman's horn; if he goes at his fences with his ears pricked forward, delighted, and picks his places with sense, has a "fifth leg" always to spare in a scramble; if he has a good constitution, drinks his gruel freely after the last run of the day is over, and eats his feed and lies down after he gets home; if he will stand three good days in a fortnight, and two ordinary days in a week, he is a treasure, although he may have an ugly head, a rat tail, an unfashionable colour, contracted feet, corns at times, and many skin-deep blemishes. If, in addition, he is a good hack, can after a hard day alternately walk and shog for ten or twelve miles at about five miles an hour, he is an invaluable animal, especially to the man whose love of hunting is great and means for enjoying it limited.

One of the best modern authorities on hunting and steeplechasing, in both of which pursuits he has often been first, and generally among the first,* lays it down that "in a big flying country the height of a hunter is of little consequence so long as it is over 15 hands 1 inch." The "Unknown" was only 14 hands 3¼ inches; he was ridden with the Quorn and the Pytchley for several years, without ever giving Mr. John Bennett, his owner, who rode thirteen stone, a fall. At timber he was extraordinary; indeed, the late Sir Richard Sutton, Master of the Quorn, said he was one of the best hunters he ever saw cross Leicestershire. The "Unknown" was a plain but sensible-looking animal, and, like the steeplechase mare Emblem, an exception to all rules. (See portrait at the end of this chapter.) The list of little horses that have distinguished themselves in Leicestershire might be extended to pages; but the solid fact remains, that the men who habitually hunt the Melton circle prefer big blood-horses, and will rarely look at anything under 15 hands 3 inches high.

That tall horses are the most saleable is proved by the Catalogue of the Islington Horse Show in 1874, when out of about 100 hunters, nearly all for sale at prices varying from 120 to 400 guineas, thirty-five were over 16 hands, and not a dozen were under 15 hands 3 inches.

The annals of steeplechasing prove that a horse 15 hands 2 inches high can fly across the biggest country, and probably there are more perfect hunters of that than of over that height; but tall horses make tall fences look less, and that is a point of importance to many keen sportsmen. To carry great weight, a horse, whatever his height, must be very broad and not too long. Of course a symmetrical sixteen-hand horse is better than one of not superior shape and courage two inches less. The heavier the man, the greater the breadth and the less the length required. Shape, however, is useless, without true action. There are plenty of hunters exhibited, which, although very powerful to the superficial eye, are really not able to carry their own weight across a country.

* Digby Collins.

In a district of hills, banks, and dales, a full-blooded cob, from 14 hands 2 inches to 15 hands 1 inch, of the right shape, will go up, down, and over, with more ease to himself than the lengthy flyer in flat countries. Wherever hills have to be hunted over at any pace, blood is essential, the nearer thoroughbred the better. In those countries where the fields are small, where you have to pull up at nearly every fence in order to hop on a bank so as to clear a double ditch, blood is less important than exceeding cleverness, because your horse gets his wind between every fence, and tall horses have no advantage whatever. Men

A GOOD START.

under five feet six inches should, in preference, select hunters not exceeding 15 hands 2 inches, because horses exceeding that height are very inconvenient for them to mount in a hurry, or remount after falls that are inevitable for any who attempt to ride straight.

All hunters, whether 13 hands 3 inches or 16 hands 3 inches high (with certain packs of harriers and even fox-hounds, a pony carries a sportsman of the right height and weight as well as any Northamptonshire giant), must, to excel, have the following points well developed :—"The withers high and the shoulders long, in order to enable him to rise well at his fences, as well as to clear the obstacles that may come across him, in the shape of ridge and furrow, drains, hillocks, &c.; the hips and pelvis should be broad, with light back ribs and a loose flank, in order that he may be able to dash his haunches under him at a big jump.' I have seen these 'points' intensely developed in a pony 10 hands high."

"It is a good sign when a hunter gets his hind-legs well under him in walking, lifting them rather high, and appearing to almost balance himself on them."

The hunter's actions must not, like many a fashionable town hack's, be knee action; it must be shoulder action—"without correct shoulder action the best hind-leg action will be useless, because it is the business of the shoulders in leaping to throw the weight back to the hind limbs." It will be observed that Lord Coventry, in his letter to me (page 92), attributes Emblem's extraordinary quickness in jumping to her excellent shoulders. This is what is meant when a hunter is said to bend himself, "which he could not do without breaking his back in two pieces if he had bad shoulders."

A hunter with bad shoulders (there are plenty for sale) will lean against instead of rising at his fences; in country phrase, he will "pitch" at his jumps. If he is gay and good-looking, ridden by a lively young farmer's or dealer's clever boy, he may go scrambling along in countries where timber-jumping is never attempted, until, falling into the hands of some victim, he will tumble headlong over a stile in the middle of a run, and certainly fall at any heavy down jump.

A hunter, like all other horses except race-horses, is considered to be in his prime at six years old, and so he is for selling purposes, if he has previously been in the hands of a man who has thoroughly taught him his business. The welter weights who do ride hard in flying countries often choose a "a raw five-year-old," preferring the courage of youth to the cautiousness of age. On the other hand, there are hunters whose reputation is maintained in the market through a full decade, as, for instance, Captain Anstruther Thomson's Iris, on which he is painted by Sir Francis Grant in the presentation picture of the Pytchley Hunt; and Rainbow, which shared with other horses in the honours of the famous Waterloo Run. Iris was sold for 500 guineas, and Rainbow at little less when over ten years old.

I saw at Cheltenham, in 1851, a white Irish hunter that went in the first flight over the stone-wall country, and was said to be twenty years old. His teeth, long and curved, showed a great age. Hunting farmers, with horses to sell, ride them pretty hard at four years old. The Duke of Rutland was well carried one season by a horse which was purchased as a four-year-old; it turned out to be three, and was spoiled. A very straight-riding farmer declared that he was never better carried than by a thorough-bred three-year-old, and he rode thirteen stone some pounds; but having put this filly by, expecting her to grow up a wonder, she was never worth a farthing afterwards.

The fault of old hunters is that they are too clever. They calculate distances *too accurately*. My advice to beginners is to purchase finished hunters, which are chiefly to be found without mark of mouth, because of the two performers one ought to have experience. If the eyesight be good, the lungs sound, and the legs in good galloping condition, age is no consequence, neither are the blemishes of bangs, blows, and thorns.

There is a great difference in the performance of even clever hunters. Some are foaled natural jumpers, and seem to know how to take off and how to land the very first time they are shown a fence; they appear to enjoy the sport. These when well bred are treasures. Other hunters, and not the worst, leap with such a "spang" that even good horsemen, if not forewarned, have been dismounted at the first fence. Others have the unpleasant trick of pausing and then bucking over, giving the rider a horrid jar. For these reasons it is well worth the while of young sportsmen to pay handsomely for a trial in the field, where sometimes, the temperate are hot and the hot temperate. A friend of mine purchased a big, well-bred horse, after seeing him leap every kind of fence in cold blood in the finest form; but this horse although by no means hard-mouthed, was so excited in the field that he was only fit to ride a straight run with stag-hounds. Such instances are common. At the same time, it must be remembered that many horses, both hacks and hunters, that are apparently hot and pullers while new and strange to the rider, settle down comfortably after a short mutual experience. But the horse must have a reasonably good mouth, and bridle well. A horse that will be delightful to a young straight rider will be a perfect nuisance to a middle-aged man who only wants to potter about; a horse accustomed to go and not allowed to go is sure to pull. Except a kicker, no horse is so dangerous in the hunting-field as one the rider cannot hold; he is not only capable of rushing at and through impracticable fences, but of killing hounds, knocking over that sacred person, "The Master," and dashing into a gap where a man and horse are scrambling. And when a hard puller overpowers his rider, he is very apt to refuse his fences.

One of the best hunters I ever rode was most annoyingly fidgety on the way to cover, seeming more fit for a procession in a circus than the hunting field; but the moment the hounds found, she calmly settled down to business, and took her fences with the most delightful alacrity and precision.

The greatest fault a hunter can have is to refuse his fences—reasonable fences—either with hounds or in cold blood. It is a sure proof that either he is in a bad temper, or has weak legs, or tender fore-feet, or, which is quite as bad, that he has been badly ridden by a timid craning man.

You sometimes hear people say, "Oh, he is a very good horse with hounds, but he won't jump in cold blood." Then he is not a perfect hunter. Look at the ordinary case of riding to cover alone, with no horse to give you a lead over a fence. You see the hounds hunting slowly along a hill a mile off. You propose cutting off a long angle by taking the ditch and hedge out of the road. Your horse declines; rears, kicks, plunges, tries to bolt down the road, and makes you not only look like a fool, but perhaps lose "the run of the season."

For pleasant riding no hunters are equal to those broken to hounds by horse-dealing straight-riding farmers. These horses are ridden one or two summers about the farm, taught to stand to be mounted, to help to open a gate, to creep up, down, and through gaps. They are ridden not too hard until thoroughly trained; and then, as the rider knows every yard in the county, the taking off and landing of every fence, they are ridden straight but coolly and temperately with hounds over timber, stone walls, hedges, double ditches, or whatever comes in the country, and have no idea of refusing until they fall into the hands of some one whose heart fails him at the critical moment. A perfect hunter tries, at any rate, to do any leap his rider really wishes him to take.

In some counties there are very few ditches; in others, no water and no stone walls; in others, doubles are unknown; while, as before observed, there are hunts where you may ride all day close to the hounds without being obliged to take a fence. A horse sold by auction as a hunter must be sound in wind and eyesight—that is the only warranty in the word hunter; he need not be willing to jump a fence two feet high, although some juries have taken a different view. Of all fences, it is most necessary that a hunter should be willing and able to jump timber accurately and in cold blood. Hedges have gaps, ditches may be scrambled through, stone walls may be pulled down; but a stile, a new post and rail, or a locked gate, must be negotiated or tumbled over, if you do not consent to be shut out of "the run of the season." Now, tumbling over stiff timber is one of the most dangerous accidents of the hunting field. Every horse that has the propelling power in back, hocks, and thighs, and the courage essential for a hunter, can be taught to jump timber in good form, if not too old to be cured of bad habits. Some horses which have been badly ridden or steeplechased rush furiously at timber, and it is more dangerous to interfere with them than to let them have their own way. It takes a very fine strong horseman, with great patience and time, to cure this way, the very worst, of taking timber. Others, bad-tempered or practised too much at weak hurdles, will rush through without rising.

Unless you are young, strong, and very confident in your skill, not pluck, it is better to

A WEIGHT CARRIER—VERY CLEVER.

commit your hunter for improvement to some first-class professional horseman, who will keep him in one field all day sooner than let him refuse or rush his fences.

The perfect hunter will trot or canter up to his fence slowly as a matter of course; but on an intimation from his rider by legs and voice that powder is required, will regularly mend his pace until he comes with a rush and clears the bullfinch, wide bank and ditch, or brook, at a stride.

Horses leap in two ways, some with their hind-legs tucked up closely under their bellies others with their hind-legs streaming behind them; the former is the best form, stronger and safer. The horse then alights on his hind-legs, and is ready to repeat the spring or continue the gallop without a moment's loss of time. Some, at water, actually land sideways, the tail level with the head.

I once hunted a thorough-bred Irish horse by Burgundy that ran away if ridden in a snaffle, and if with a powerful curb galloped with his nose nearly on the ground until he came to his fences, when he raised his head exactly to the right position, leaped with the greatest accuracy, and then resumed his investigation of molehills. It was very unpleasant until you got accustomed to it, but he went over the worst ground, even through recently-stubbed plantations, with perfect safety. Far more dangerous are hot, ewe-necked, star-gazing, and peacocky horses, with weak necks and light mouths, which, when pulled, throw up their heads and drop short, or run into their fences. Nothing less than the practised hands of a steeplechase jockey can make anything of these misshapen brutes, some of which, however, might be perfectly in place in harness, or even as park-hacks, with a proper martingale. Novices should have nothing to do with light-mouthed horses, often praised as snaffle-bridle hunters. A great sportsman said truly not one horse in five hundred is fit to ride through a run with a snaffle-bridle; and not one man in ten thousand is fit to ride hunting on the curb. It is much easier and pleasanter to ride a horse that goes up to the bit and "takes hold of you." Light-mouthed, snaffle-bridle hunters are for horsemen with a close seat and fine hands, or for old gentlemen who ride to hunt but not straight up to the hounds.

Nothing makes you feel more helpless in a fast run than a light-mouthed horse that will not go up to the bit, stands still and kicks in the middle of a big field, if he or she —they are generally mares—is asked to turn from the ruck, to take a short cut, or in any other way differ from the rider. The perfect hunter for most tastes eagerly pulls at the rider, but can be easily stopped by a touch of the curb. But there are good horses and horsemen in both ways. About the time of the first Reform Bill there were in Suffolk two hunting parsons famed in that district of small enclosures as sportsmen and horsemen. One always took firm hold of his horses by the snaffle-rein, and to use a slang phrase, almost rode on their heads; the other rode with a perfectly slack rein, and guided his hunters entirely with his voice and a little crooked stick. It was a question in that county which of the two brothers was the better man across country.

The hunter *par excellence* is one fit to go on the best days in the counties of big fields and big fences with fox-hounds and stag-hounds. On such days, in such country, nothing but blood and high condition can keep on respectable terms with the pack; but, as already stated, there are more than twice as many packs of harriers as fox-hounds, which may be perfectly enjoyed with horses of less size, breeding, and, consequently, value, than are required to cut a respectable figure in the fashionable pasture counties. A handy horse, under 15 hands high, that can jump, and canter ten miles an hour, will answer every purpose in a closely-enclosed country with harriers, and indeed with fox-hounds. A sixteen-hands hunter of Yorkshire and Leicestershire stamp may be judiciously ridden to harriers at four or five years old for practice; but a corky blood cob will get to the end of ninety-nine runs out of a hundred just as well. In down and hill-pasture countries, where the hares are stouter and run straighter than in arable countries, where, without much travelling, they can feed fat on corn or roots, you must have blood, especially if you have to gallop and climb hills, For stag-hunting over the Vale of Aylesbury you want a tall, thorough-bred horse that will either fly or do doubles. No horse is a perfect hunter that cannot be turned in a very small circle.

In more than half the hunting districts it is at times necessary to dismount and lead your horse, either to ease him in ascending steep hills, or to get through a cramped place, or to relieve him of your weight in returning home on a cold night after a fatiguing day. It is therefore wise to teach your horses to follow you freely on either right or left hand, neither dragging back nor rushing at you over a fence. This is an accomplishment easily taught, and best taught by the young sportsman himself, with a pocketful of short carrots, a gig-whip, and a leading-rein, according to Rarey's plan. A few summer evenings spent in pushing through gaps leading over ditches, and even low stiles, is time well spent; but for perfection the hunter must learn to know and love his master's voice.

Abraham Cawston, a heavy farmer, a first-rate sportsman, who used to hunt the South Essex hounds, a clay country intersected by ditches and hedges, had a pony which always went first over cramped places, the farmer hanging on by the tail!

After the enumeration of the various perfections of a hunter, it is right to add that in every hunting-field there are to be found odd and apparently ill-shaped brutes steered by bold, practised, determined riders, who keep pace with, and sometimes out-pace, hunters of perfect form and priceless value; but these waifs and strays of sport, however coarse they may appear in head and heels, are always, if the truth were known, well-bred.

Tom Edge, the silent humble companion of Mr. Assheton Smith, who never spoke unless Mr. Smith spoke to him, never rode less than eighteen stone. In a very good thing, thirteen miles without a check, there were only four up, Assheton Smith and Tom Edge being two of the four. Minutes elapsed before any of the field got up; yet the horse Edge rode, Gayman, was "a queer-looking creature, thin neck, large head, raw hips, and a rat tail, for all the world like a seventeen-hands dog-horse. You couldn't get your hand between his front legs, they were so close; he always had to wear boots" ("Silk and Scarlet"). The murdered Earl of Mayo, also a crushing weight, rode just such an animal in the first flight in Northamptonshire.

"When I was young," wrote Charles Buxton, "I bought horses by their looks. I was careful to see whether they had good shoulders, were well ribbed up, and so on. Now I am old [he was then forty-five], what I want to know is how he goes; if he can go well I am sure he is made well."

A comparatively slow horse, if an extraordinary and resolute jumper, will often get the best of much faster horses in a five-and-twenty minutes' burst, if a few very stiff and awkward fences intersect the first half-dozen fields. A harum-scarum youth on a horse not worth thirty pounds will often clear stiff timber, or trot up to a double hog-backed stile, and, dropping like a cat into a rough lane, leave a dozen two-hundred guinea nags pounded.

The man who cannot afford expensive horses should have them clever and in first-rate condition.

There is a piece of sound sense in the following lines, dedicated by Mark King to Lady Florence Dixie, whom few men can beat in a sharp run.

THE BEST OF A MODERATE LOT. *

How a dealer would turn up his nose,
  How he'd sneer at that curious trot,
If I sought, for his coin, to exchange
  The best of my moderate lot.

* *Sporting Gazette,* July, 1877.

As a hack, I admit, he is vile ;
　　His temper's uncertain and hot.
But I don't keep for road promenades
　　The best of my moderate lot.

Would he pass a V. S.?　Not a bit !
　　Yet their theories clearly are " rot,"
For three days in each fortnight I ride
　　The best of my moderate lot.

No use, save with hounds, do you say ;
　　For that fact I care not a jot.
At his one game he's not to be beat,
　　This best of my moderate lot.

When the country rides up to the girths.
　　If you wish to be well "on the spot,"
Lay odds that he tires not nor blows !
　　This best of a moderate lot.

When the fence is repulsive or big,
　　An " oxer," blind ditch, or what not,
I put all my trust in his skill—
　　This best of a moderate lot.

In forming a stud of even not more than four hunters, it is desirable to fix on and keep to one stamp of horse. This involves some trouble and some expense ; but, always supposing that the stamp is suited to the country, it has the same sort of correctness as well-fitting clothes, and does credit to the taste of the owner. There are some very good sportsmen who pay no attention to stamp, seldom have two horses of the same sort ; ride a slashing thorough-bred one day, a cob the next, and a thick, old-fashioned hunter on the third day. There are others who could not enjoy looking over their stable if so incongruously filled. A master who hunted his own hounds for nearly twenty years, celebrated for the completeness and excellence of a hunting establishment maintained on moderate means, and whose horses, except as to colour, were always matches good enough for a team, writes to me on this point : " My practice was, being light (about eleven stone), to buy good-looking blood animals, not over four years old, *whether I wanted them or not*, if the price was anything like reasonable ; and I always drafted them at twelve years old, if they happened to last so long."

When a young or rather intending sportsman desires to form a stud of hunters, it is much easier to tell him what not to do than what to do.

If he begins in summer he may venture on horses made up for sale, that is, fat, a condition which every one knows to be foolish, but which no dealer dare neglect if he wishes to satisfy the majority, that is, the most ignorant of his customers.

The better plan for a young beginner, if he cannot buy horses after riding and seeing them ridden in the field, is to job three or four hunters from one of the hunter dealers who lay themselves out for that branch of the trade. He can then select them on the dealer's farm, find out if they suit his style of riding, and form some idea of their mode of fencing. If his engagements will not allow this, it is better to give the dealer an account of his weight, height, and ideas about riding, and leave the responsibility to him.

Jobbing is expensive, but you know the limit of the expense. You can change the

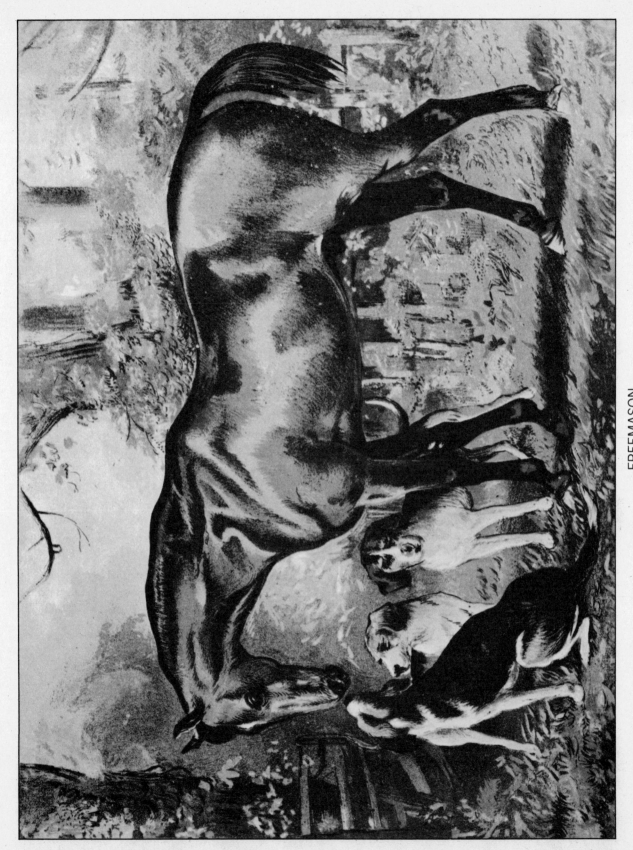

FREEMASON.

FAVORITE HUNTER OF THE LATE HUGO MEYNELL INGRAM ESQ.

Sheldon Williams
1874

STILTON, A HUNTER.

THE PROPERTY OF COL. LOYD LINDSAY V.C.M.P. A WINNER OF THE PUNCHESTOWN (IRELAND) STEEPLECHASE.

FROM A PAINTING BY SHELDON WILLIAMS ESQ.

horses that you do not like until you get suited, and you can arrange to buy any of the horses jobbed, at a price settled beforehand. It is not pleasant to be paying for the hire of three or four horses during a frost, but it is also unpleasant to have a stable full of horses of your own under the same circumstances.

Good hunters may be jobbed from well-known dealers in London, Oxford, Cheltenham, Wansford near Peterborough, and, in fact, in every hunting district. Oxford, Cheltenham, and Windsor **are** the best places I know for hack hunters for men not over eleven stone. When, after a trial, one of these has been found to suit, it is best to secure it at once for the month or the season. At Barnstaple horses may be hired for hunting on Exmoor.

Oxford and Cambridge will both be found desirable hunting quarters for novices during the winter vacation, because there are plenty of clever horses to be hired at these Universities, and in vacation time there is no one to ride them. Oxford is within reach of at least five packs of fox-hounds, which leave nothing to be desired by any reasonable man.

When a celebrated stud of hunters is sold by auction, they generally fetch more than they ever do again if sold singly. Such sales afford opportunities of buying horses known to be good hunters; but in a long stud there are always a certain number of screws and brutes, which fall to those trusting souls who buy blindfold. Only strong, practised horsemen buy hunters without either a trial or a character. Although the most satisfactory way of choosing a hunter is out of the hunting-field after a stiff run; so much depends on the rider, that it by no means follows that the horse that carried Farmer Thruster in the first flight will even go at all with a novice. Some men have the knack of making every horse that can gallop, gallop where, when, and as they please.

Finally, if you have no friend on whom you can rely to choose your first stud of hunters, the better plan is either to job or to place yourself in the hands of a dealer, with a limit as to price. In any case, the beginner should buy only hunters who perfectly understand their trade, and defer trusting himself on four-year-olds and unbroken hunters until he has had a little experience; for no extent of instruction, and no amount of pluck, will compensate for want of experience in the hunting-field.

There are, however, useful well-bred but not thoroughbred horses to be purchased at times, four, five, six, and seven years old, which are capable of being made hunters if put into proper hands. This is especially the case with half-bred horses not much over 15 hands high, which have not fallen into the hands of owners with hunting tastes. Such animals may receive an important preparation for the hunting-field at the hands of any young horseman in the course of ordinary country rides, before being placed in the hands of the "hunter horse-breaker."

As before observed, the first business of a hunter is to gallop over rough ground with a leg always to spare; but there are capital horses, especially thoroughbreds, of defective education, who would be in danger if a molehill of extra size came in their way, yet with practice these often become first-rate, as I have found more than once.

Whether a horse has come from a training stable, or has been passing his time in town work, if he has the right shape and temper he may be made a hunter for some country or other. The first stage is to teach him to walk—not on fine turf or Rotten Row, but where there are all the varieties of texture of a country where the condition of sport is excellent and of agriculture deplorable. Richmond Park is not a bad place for teaching a horse how to walk.

Begin by riding him daily and carefully, with a double bridle, for an hour at the most, at a walk over a ploughed ridge-and-furrow field, or a field of turnips set on the ridge, if it is your own, or the farmer does not object. Just feel his mouth enough to collect him, otherwise leave his head as loose as you can. After two or three days' practice, extend the time to two hours, and trot him for half the time. Do not spur or bully him if he makes mistakes, only collect him. Then walk him home. Then take him to some meadow full of hidden grips and watercourses, or some woodland plantations, and walk him with a loose rein for a week or two. At the end of that time, if his shoulder action is naturally correct and his legs are properly inserted into his feet, he will have learned to pick his way under difficulties—a lesson which a mountain or moorland foal learns at his dam's side. When he can walk safely over uneven ground he may be trotted sharply, and finally galloped. Afterwards, if there are any suitable steep hills, let him learn to descend them, first slowly then quickly. All this is practice for the young horseman as well as the young horse, and prepares both for the hunting-field. When the Prince of Wales hunted on Exmoor, half a dozen fine hunters fell over drains not much deeper or wider than a hat, hidden by grass, over which those bred in the country skimmed at full speed.

When the time for leaping lessons arrives, the novice should secure the services of some wiry old professional, of sober habits and even temper.

Formerly there were certain counties in which sportsmen looked for hunters, and Ireland was and is famous for both breeding and training horses fit for every style of hunting. But railroads, penny post, and telegraphs, have placed the whole kingdom on a level, and it is very rare that a man can buy a single horse more cheaply from the breeder than from a dealer. A great deal has generally to be paid for the "great expectations" that hang on a first-class four-year-old. The man who will be content with a second-class horse will generally be able to buy it, plus a very useful education, at seven or eight years old, for the price it was sold for at four.

One-half of the goodness of a hunter depends on the way in which it has been ridden, and the way in which it has been fed, since it was taken from its dam.

THE DREAM OF AN OLD MELTONIAN.*

I.

I am old, I am old, and my eyes are grown weaker,
   My beard is as white as the foam on the sea,
Yet pass me the bottle, and fill me a beaker,
   A bright brimming toast in a bumper for me!
Back, back through long vistas of years I am wafted,
   But the glow at my heart 's undiminished in force ;
Deep, deep in that heart has fond memory engrafted
   Those quick thirty minutes from Ranksboro' Gorse.

III.

He 's away ! I can hear the identical holloa !
   I can feel my young thoroughbred strain down the ride,
I can hear the dull thunder of hundreds that follow,
   I can see my old comrades in life by my side.

* By W. Davenport Bromley, M.P. The writer falls asleep in the House of Commons in the middle of the speech of Mr. Bore'm, and dreams of a famous run in Leicestershire.

Do I dream? all around me I see the dead riding,
    And voices long silent re-echo with glee;
I can hear the far wail of the Master's vain chiding,
    As vain as the Norseman's reproof to the sea.

IV.

Vain indeed! for the bitches are racing before us—
    Not a nose to the earth—not a stern in the air;
And we know by the notes of that modified chorus
    How straight we must ride if we wish to be there!
With a crash o'er the turnpike, and onward I'm sailing.
    Released from the throes of the blundering mass,
Which dispersed right and left as I topped the high railing,
    And shape my own course o'er the billowy grass.

V.

Oh, gently, my young one; the fence we are nearing
    Is leaning towards us—'tis hairy and black,
The binders are strong, and necessitate clearing,
    Or the wide ditch beyond will find room for your back.
Well saved! we are over! now far down the pastures
    Of Ashwell the willows betoken the line
Of the dull-flowing stream of historic disasters;
    We must face, my bold young one, the dread Whissendine.

VI.

No shallow-dug pan with a hurdle to screen it,
    That cock-tail imposture the steeplechase brook;
But the steep broken banks tell us plain, if we mean it,
    The less we shall like it the longer we look.
Then steady, my young one, my place I've selected,
    Above the dwarf willow 'tis sound I'll be bail,
With your muscular quarters beneath you collected,
    Prepare for a rush like the 'limited mail.'

VII.

Oh! now let me know the full worth of your breeding,
    Brave son of Belzoni, be true to your sires,
Sustain old traditions—remember you're leading
    The cream of the cream in the shire of the shires!
With a quick shortened stride as the distance you measure,
    With a crack of the nostril and cock of the ear,
And a rocketing bound, and we're over, my treasure,
    Twice nine feet of water, and landed all clear!

VIII.

What! four of us only? are these the survivors
    Of all that rode gaily from Ransboro' ridge?
I hear the faint splash of a few hardy divers,
    The rest are in hopeless research of a bridge;
Væ victis! the way of the world and the winners!
    Do we ne'er ride away from a friend in distress?
Alas! we are anti-Samaritan sinners,
    And streaming past Stapleford, onward we press.

IX.

Ah! don't they mean mischief, the merciless ladies!
    What fox can escape such implacable foes?
Of the sex cruel slaughter for ever the trade is,
    Whether human or animal—YONDER HE GOES!
Never more for the woodland! his purpose has failed him,
    Though to gain the old shelter he gallantly tries;
In vain the last double, for Jezebel's nailed him;
    WHOOHOOP! in the open the veteran dies!

THE UNKNOWN. (*See p.* 423.)

CHAPTER XXI.

TRAINING FOR HUNTING—RIDING TO COVER—RIDING WITH HOUNDS.

Necessity of Preparation by Training for Violent Exercise—The Author's Experience—How to get Exercise in a Town—Baths: their Use—Cub-hunting the Best Preparation—Going to Cover—Behaviour—First Lesson—Your Own Insignificance—Silence is Gold at Cover-side—The Way to Cover—Riding your Hunter of the Day, or a Hunter for Exercise, or a Real Hack—Advantages of Wheels: Dog-cart, Phaeton-drag, Tandem, Wagonette—The Light-weight Groom—Railway Conveyances: The Latest Luxury a Pullman's Car—Riding to Hounds—"A Word Ere we Start"—Requisites for First-flight Men—Audacity in Flying Countries—Ruffian often First—The "Leading Article"—The "Following Article"—The Sort to be Studied—Gate-opening a Useful Art—"Do not Speak to the Man at the Wheel"—Advice when Hounds are Drawing—Ready, not too Ready—The Find—The Rush—Tally Ho, Away!—Keep your Eye on Leading Hounds—Egerton Warburton's Ballad—The Field of a Run Analysed—Small Percentage of Straight Riders—Sketch of Pytchley Country by a Native—Poetical Advice—Importance of Blood—Condition in Man and Horse—Of Decision—To Ride or Not to Ride, that is the Question—Small Enclosures Easier Hunting—Hunter for the First Season must Creep and Fly—Timber-jumping—Its Importance—Dick Christian on Riding in the "Shires"—Falls to be Avoided in Training a Hunter—Sir James Musgrave and Tom Heycock—The Honourable Grantley Berkeley's Hints—Leaping in Cold Blood and Larking Spoil Hunters—Water-jumping—Big Waters Stops the Field: Why, and Why Dangerous—Anecdote of Brook-jumping with Stag-hounds—Another of a Cob with Harriers and Hind—A Stereograph of a Water-jump from the "Brooks of Bridlemere"—Lady Julia's Slang—Falling an Art and an Instinct—Old Horses Fall worse than Young Ones—Pleasures of Memory after a Run—Beware of Boasting—Captain Anstruther Thompson as M. F. H.—Poetical Sketch of—Ladies Hunting—How—First Class, Second Class, Third Class—The Old Marchioness of Salisbury—Increase of Hunting Ladies—Three Hunting, Hard-riding Countesses—A Clever Hunter Essential for a Lady—The Hunting Side-saddle—Hunting-bridle—The Pilot—The Honourable Mrs. Jack V.'s Pilot: his Fee—The Young Ladies who are a Nuisance—Ladies' Hunting Costume Requirements.

No man engaged in sedentary summer and autumn pursuits can enjoy a fast or a long day with hounds without a certain degree of preparation. Without preliminary training, a fast five-and-twenty minutes, with a fair share of "fencing" on the first day of his season, will tax, in a very painful manner, the action of the heart and lungs of a man who has been using his head and not exercising his body; and if, in addition, when the hounds leave off, there are fifteen or twenty miles to ride home, the unaccustomed sportsman will be stiff and sore from head to foot for a fortnight. *Experto crede.* I never endured more agony in my life than in the last ten minutes of a fast thirty minutes, ridden on a perfect thorough-bred hunter, with a good start, with the Milton hounds over a grass country. My summer had been occupied day and night with Parliamentary committees and literary work; my rides had been limited to Hansom cabs; my labours had been sustained by strong coffee, champagne luncheons, and the sort of dinners which successful railway promoters gave in the days when George Hudson was a king. With such preparation I was not half an hour in the saddle before I was doing my best to keep in sight one of the best packs of hounds in England, running with scent "breast-high." By instinct, good luck, a horse that never swerved a line from his fences, and a despairing grip of the breast-plate, I kept my seat over the last fence of the field when the hounds ran into their enemy in the open, but I was speechless, black in the face, my heart going like the engine of an express train, and

I was only saved from fainting, or worse, by the friendly care of a tall farmer, who lifted me off my horse, like an infant, laid me on the grass, and applied his flask to my parched lips. I rode home under the pleasant excitement, without complaining, but could eat nothing, lay awake all night in a burning fever, and did not recover my usual tone for a week, during which time putting on a coat or a pair of boots was a work of painful labour. Young men can survive such rash experiments, but at a certain time of life they become positively dangerous.

Where horse exercise in the non-hunting months is impossible, the requisite condition may be retained or obtained by any out-door or in-door athletic exercise that produces perspiration, and calls the muscles of the limbs and back into action. Violent exercise in the morning does not suit men engaged in serious mental pursuits; it is not a good preparation for brain work; but a great deal may be done by gentle exercise at convenient times after the labours of the day are over, whether it be with dumb-bells, Indian clubs, or rowing, or riding upon a bicycle. Lord Palmerston wrote to his brother, then ambassador at Naples, that when he went to live in Piccadilly, as he found the distance from Cambridge House to Downing Street not sufficient for exercise, he made a point of riding at least once round the Park between his hours of greatest leisure—eleven and one o'clock.* This probably brought one o'clock Rotten Row rides into fashion. In another letter, when his labours against the despots of Europe were unceasing, he says, "I have been hunting a little lately, and although over Hampshire (a very bad country), it always does me good."

Diet is of as much importance as regular exercise, and that every one can regulate for himself.

A few Turkish baths *after exercise* on foot or horseback followed by cold douches will do wonders towards reducing the superfluous fat, and giving tone to the nerves of a frame exhausted by mental and sedentary occupations, if there is no organic derangement; but exercise of any kind—gymnastics, lawn-tennis, rackets—is good if it brings into action muscles not ordinarily employed, while galloping and leaping put an extra strain on all the muscles.

Mere muscular fatigue, if not accompanied by want of sleep and fever, is not a serious consequence, but it is pain that may as well be avoided.

The particular kind of preparation by which a man should train himself so as to derive no harm and as much pleasure as possible from the exercise of the hunting-field must depend on his age, habits, and hours of leisure; but those who cannot find time to ride may train, by a gradual course of gymnastic exercise, either at home or in the hall of a *turnverein;* those whom the river does not suit may find an hour in daylight for the racket-court, or in the dusk for a bicycle ride. Volunteers who keep up their drill are always in fair condition; but it is no matter how it is done so long as in some way or other the heart and lungs are prepared for extra exertions, and the muscles suppled and strengthened by preparatory practice. Even professional steeplechasers who, being within the weight they had to ride, have indulged too much in the luxuries of the table, have been known to fail for want of condition in the final squeeze of a closely-contested race.

To sum up, a young man exposes himself to pain and ridicule, a middle-aged man endangers his health, by attempting hard riding after months of absolute repose.

Fortunately, at no period of the history of this country were there so many forms and degrees of athletic exercise within reach of the urban sedentary population.

---

* "Life of Lord Palmerston," by Lord Dalling, vol. iii.

The best preparation for fox-hunting, and the best introduction to "the noble science," is cub-hunting, which begins very early in the mornings of September with every hunt that has woodland covers. At cub-hunting, riding a clever cob or even pony, the novice has an opportunity of acquiring a vast deal of useful knowledge, by studying the refinements of fox-hunting before breakfast. While getting himself into condition, he can learn from the enthusiasts, who only are to be met with at that hour, much that must be overlooked in a knot of fashionable "thrusters." The huntsman is out to teach his young hounds, from the example of his old ones, their duty. There is no competition for the start, riding is a secondary consideration. Woodlands have to be threaded at some expense of rents and tears in the old shooting-jacket. Blind gaps have to be slowly negotiated and stiles jumped standing. If by exception there is a burst of ten minutes after an "old customer" or precocious cub, there is no one to record or observe feats of horsemanship. It is quite a case of *Fox et præterea nihil.* Therefore, I solemnly adjure young fellows anxious to become real fox-hunters not to neglect their cub-hunting. If conveniently near Exmoor with stag-hounds and fox-hounds it is a way of getting into condition not to be neglected, although not worth travelling a long distance with horses to get there.

GOING TO COVER.

The first lesson to be impressed upon the young sportsman about to meet the hounds for the first time is that what he wears, what he rides, and what he does in the hunting-field is not a matter of the slightest consequence to any one except himself. In a meet of fox-hounds in a fashionable country he will be as much lost in the crowd as any stranger in Rotten Row at one o'clock in the height of the season.

In one of Lord Palmerston's letters, he says, referring to the preparations of special ambassadors sent over to attend the coronation of Queen Victoria, " They will most of them be disappointed, for fine coaches, fine horses, and fine liveries, excite the attention of no one in London except coachmen, grooms, and coach-builders."

It is the same in the hunting-field. A young man turned out regardless of expense, and in the best taste, will at the utmost extort a few compliments from chambermaids, boots, and the red-coated, barefooted gate-openers attached to the hunt, dependent on casual half-crowns. The majority of a Leicestershire field take "correctness" as a matter of course ; while those who do think anything at all of coats and boots are too much occupied with their own get-up to notice that of " a young stranger."

In county hunts, where a few local squires and farmers form the field, anything unusual on the side of "swelldom" in dress excites prejudice against the wearer, unless he shows himself able to hold his own in the first real run.

The advice given to the groom who had married a lady, to "wear a black coat and hold your tongue," is not bad for the young sportsman in his first season—the silence applying to idle questions or wild "tally-ho-ing," not implying that sulky silence when addressed by strangers which some cantankerous fools take for dignity.

There are several ways of going to meet hounds, all good in their way and in their turn. Where the horseman's weight is not over eleven stone, and the distance is not over ten miles, a hunter will be rather benefited than otherwise by being ridden to the meet at an alternate brisk walk and slow trot. This is the practice of some of the very best sportsmen, who, with less than half a dozen hunters decline to keep any horses that are, at any rate, if not first-rate hacks, safe on the road. But the plan will not do for unpunctual languid lie-a-beds, like

Whyte Melville's Honourable Frederick Crasher. On the question of getting up early, Charles Buxton wrote very wisely, "Getting up early is a good thing if it comes of itself—that is from going to bed early; but if you don't allow nature her quantum of sleep, you burn the candle at both ends, and the time you steal from sleep you lose in vigour; in fact you shorten your life." Wealthy men can afford to buy hunting-machines, able to gallop and jump magnificently on soft ground, positively dangerous on the hard high-road. Such was Assheton Smith's crooked-legged Jack o' Lantern. But the real spirit of sport burns in many breasts not provided with incomes which make stud expenses a secondary consideration.

The hack, in an economically-managed stud, is one of the hunters, who gets his exercise and makes himself useful at the same time; or it is a four-year-old not yet taken into work, but exercised, accustomed to the sight and sound of hounds, and ridden by a steady groom (who has brought on the hunter of the day), a little way after hounds have found. In dry weather there is no pleasanter way of getting to cover than on a good galloping or smooth-trotting little hack, especially when a good part of ten miles or more may be done by short cuts over bridle roads, through field gates, with here and there a gap to be jumped. It forms a harmonious overture to the fox-hunting opera, and makes an enthusiast feel extremely eager for the hottest fun of the day, if fun there should be.

When the distance is long or the roads muddy, with rain threatening, wheels, whether they be attached to mail phaeton, ladies' phaeton, wagonette with a party, or any of the numerous forms of dog-cart, have the advantage of conveying the fox-hunter clean and dry to the cover side—

> " Fresh from his carriage as bridegroom on marriage."

If there are ladies of the party, who are not horsewomen, they may see more or less of a run, and dispense much appreciated hospitality, in the blank intervals of a long day, in a well-horsed, long-bodied wagonette, driven by a groom who knows the country.

A four-in-hand drag, or *char-à-banc*, is never more in its place than when conveying a party to cover-side; a tandem has almost an appearance of being of real use, harnessed to a well-loaded two-wheeled dog-cart, in a hilly country, and may be employed to get or keep a hunter, as leader, in condition; while to descend to the most economical level, a fast pony, in a Battlesden car, is a very perfect conveyance for two sportsmen and a boy-groom. But there is one condition essential for any enjoyment in going on wheels to cover—the horse or horses must be fast. To crawl along sticky lanes at the rate of seven miles an hour, behind a wheezy cob, is purgatory in an acute form. The last mode of getting to a meet by rail is familiar to those who hunt with stag-hounds from the metropolis, and with fox-hounds from Oxford. Their once familiar charge of "a tandem" or "hack on" has almost disappeared from the bills of Symonds and Tollett.

In a complete stud there is always at least one light-weight groom, a steady lad, whose business it is to take the hunter to cover-side, at such a pace as to bring him there as fresh as possible; but the young fox-hunter must take care how, under the idea of saving his horse, he trusts him to a scratch groom, hired for the job. He may find that halts at public-houses, and gallops to make up for lost time, have taken a good deal more out of his favourite than if he had ridden the whole distance himself.

Heavy weights must send on to cover, and save their hunter by dismounting and walking at every convenient opportunity, if they wish to make the best of the few extraordinary runs that fall to one man's share in one season.

There is no more luxurious conveyance than a railway carriage. Hunting-season tickets have long been an established system; and even Market Harborough may be reached by rail from London in time to meet the hounds. I once met a contractor who was in the habit of taking a special train to get to fox-hounds; but, as he failed for half a million, and paid an insignificant dividend, his is not an example to be recommended to men who, using ordinary conveyances, ought to be punctual.

The railway directors of the best hunting lines run specials, and put on *drop* carriages to express trains, for the accommodation of hunting-men. A party of from half a dozen to a dozen can engage a saloon carriage, provided with a dressing-room and even cooking arrangements. The finishing-stroke has been put to the luxuries of hunting by the addition of American sleeping-cars—dressing-rooms by day, bed-rooms by night—so that you may breakfast going down, dine, or take tea, and sleep or play whist returning. The Midland and London and North-Western Companies have found it worth while to make direct extensions for the accommodation of hunting-men; and all over the kingdom the locomotive has become a hunting machine.

HOW TO RIDE TO HOUNDS.

Boys, to the hunting-field! Though 'tis November
    The wind 's in the south ;—but a word ere we start :
However excited, you'll please to remember
    That hunting 's a science, and riding an art.
The fox takes precedence of all from the cover ;
    The hunter 's an animal purposely bred,
After the pack to be ridden, not *over;*
    Fox-hounds are not reared to be knocked on the head.
                 Warburton's " Words Ere we Start."

To ride to fox-hounds in a satisfactory, not to say the best manner, requires a knowledge of the sport, a knowledge of the geography of the country to be ridden over, the horsemanship which enables a man to make the best of his horse without using him up before the run is over, and that sort of courage which is expressed by " a warm heart and a cool head."

There are butcher-boys who have never seen a hound, and sailors who have scarcely ever crossed a horse, who, astride a perfect hunter, with a good start, a burning scent and flying leaps to skim, would in a single burst head and cut down a good many older and better sportsmen. In fact, when it comes to mere hard riding, the recklessness of youth will generally get the better of the experience of age in any country where spurs tell more than hands—where a bold, not a clever horse is required.

There is an enormous difference between the brilliant horseman—the mellow veteran who has made hunting for more than a quarter of a century the business of his life, still in the prime of equestrian vigour, mounted on one of a stud selected with first-rate judgment, the man and horse perfectly acquainted with each other, sailing over a country of sound turf and big fences, with every yard of which he is as familiar as with the fences of his private training-ground—and the politician, the Queen's Counsel, or the journalist, who snatches one month out of the year to ride strange horses in a strange country.

" Any one who keeps well up with hounds is a hard rider; but the man who always takes a line of his own, and leads, is one in a hundred. It is unlucky that as a rule the men who do lead are ruffians."* This harsh opinion is borne out, not only by the biographies of

---

* "Notes of Thought," by the late Charles Buxton, M.P.

several bruising horsemen, in which they are treated as demi-gods of the turf and chase, but by the autobiography of at least one hard rider, who has taken as much pains to write himself a brute as Dogberry did to have himself written down "an ass!"

The difference between the "leading article" and the "following article" in the hunting-field is so enormous that the two seem scarcely to belong to the same class of mankind. The man who never attempts to rush to the front may be an excellent sportsman; those only are contemptible who are always trying, and never succeed in holding a place in the first flight, or those who are never seen in front in the field, yet are always heard loud on their performances over the dinner-table.

Amongst the prominent horsemen in the hunting-field may be named those who have made hunting the business of their lives, and always have been seen in front. These are always born horsemen—wiry and long-limbed, and hard at the age when most men thicken in the girth, and grow obese. Few fat men are seen often in front after forty. There are those who ride to sell their horses—these include some of the very finest horsemen; those who ride to be seen and admired—none ride harder if they think ladies or the reporters of a sporting periodical are looking at them; those who ride, like undergraduates, for fun— ready to break their own necks, or their horse's, out of pure exuberance of animal spirits, these often settle down into capital sportsmen. Finally, besides those who hunt because it is the fashion, or because they have nothing else to do, or for their health, there are also those who ride to hunt—who never take an unnecessary fence, and never decline anything practicable when hounds are running in earnest. These last are the class whom the young sportsman should study and imitate.

Always, on arriving at a hunt, salute the master of the hounds, but do it in passing, as you would royalty, and not as if you expected him to stop and shake hands.

On board passenger-ships "Do not speak to the man at the wheel" is often written up conspicuously. The same rule may be applied to the huntsman. Strangers should not ask him questions. He is often obliged to reply to some perhaps important perhaps frivolous questions asked by an influential member of the hunt when he is deep in thought. He would much sooner be let off with a simple salutation.

Opening a gate cleverly, and holding it open, when going from cover to cover, while ladies and the grave and reverend seigniors of the hunt pass through, gains useful good opinions for the apprentice sportsman. To describe how a gate should be opened would fill a page, which then might not be understood. The theory is to ride your horses *at* the post; arriving there, to put him alongside the gate, then you are master of it. The young horse-man should practise so as to be able to catch hold with either hand, in the summer; the horse also must have practice. Nothing is more irritating to a crowd than a man fumbling at a gate which his horse will not approach, or which he does not know how to open. Few men get less gratitude than those who dismount to open a gate that has baffled them mounted. In a sharp run it is not expected that he who gets first at a gate shall do more than swing it wide, except for the huntsman or the "master."

When the hounds move off, keep them in sight or within hearing—if you can! In a woodland cover you will keep best within hearing by riding "down wind," so that the wind will bring you their voices if they give cry. Old hands who know the country and the run of the foxes may neglect these precautions, but even the cleverest sometimes lose a good run when the pack comes upon an outlying fox in a hedgerow or a turnip-field, or finds a wild one in a wood where the native foxes have been accustomed to hang a long time. Some say, always go where the hounds go; but that advice is rather too hard to be strictly followed by a stranger. It is sound if some experienced member of the hunt shows the way; but there are covers into which no one is expected to follow the huntsman, and a novice might make himself ridiculous, with scratched face and torn clothes, from pushing through thorns and brambles, when there was a sure point outside, to which all the experienced hands resorted. *A huntsman always dislikes to have any one near him in cover, still more to be asked any questions.*

While waiting at cover-side watching for the fox to break; on no account holloa when you first view him, or you will make him turn "back." Let him get well away, and then put your hat on your whip and give one scream, if you know how—"Tally—ho—a-way!!!" You put up your hat that the huntsman may know who saw him, as ten to one every one near will repeat "tally-ho!"—like children seeing a balloon. Do not presume to leave your post until the huntsman, with the body of the pack, comes up to the place where the fox went away, in order to get a start with two or three couples of hounds. Be ready to tell him in the fewest possible words exactly the line the fox took; it is still better if you can show him and only speak two words. The man who intentionally or unintentionally "heads"—that is, turns back a fox—is sure to be the object of some very strong language.

One of the greatest crimes a young sportsman can commit is to ride over a hound, and the next greatest is to have a horse that kicks at either hounds or horses. Many young horses will kick until accustomed to the hunting-field; such should have dogs always in their stable.

Until a man knows the country he will do well to take some experienced, well-mounted member of the hunt—a farmer in a black coat for choice—as leader, but with one precaution to be most strictly observed—to ride a few yards either to the right or left, as well as a few yards behind the pilot, or if it is a country where the practicable places are few, and you are obliged to take the same line as your pilot, then be very careful not to put your horse at the fence until he is clear away. To select a man as pilot without his consent, and then jump on him, is a piece of cowardly stupidity; it is no excuse that "you could not hold your horse." If your horse is such a rusher that when you show him a fence he will have it whether you mean it or not, it is your business to go first, or to go home.

As soon as you reach cover-side take stock of the nature of the fences and the country, and, as far as possible, make up your mind on your first two or three leaps. If there is one gate through which a whole crowd of horsemen must crush, ride carelessly along the hedge-row. Sometimes you may discover an unsuspected place in a thick bullfinch through which a determined horse will push, or a clever one bore his way, and by one jump get a fair start.

However anxious for a good start, the young stranger should take particular care not to make any mistake, and, by being too eager and forward, incur the just wrath of the huntsman.

The swelldom of Leicestershire, "fierce as eagles, jealous as girls," often outride the hounds, and overrun the fox; but these lines are not written for the benefit of swelldom, but of young horsemen, who will not be spared coarse epithets when they spoil sport. For the same reason, while riding as hard as you can, don't distract your mind with the performances of the rest of the field; attend to your own horse, and keep your eye on the hounds—that is, the *leading hounds*—so as to turn as they turn, and pull up the moment they check. Be sure to ride at least twenty yards, fifty is better, on one side or other of the line the hounds are going. The nearer you are to the pack the further you should keep to the right or left of them. If, by good riding or by a fluke, you are in the first flight, you will do yourself more credit by pulling up short, standing still, and noticing exactly where the check occurred, than by the most desperate leap. Never forget that your sport depends on the hounds first and the huntsman next.

Two of the best Masters who ever hunted their own fox-hounds never swore themselves, nor permitted their servants to swear, in the field ; but even strong adjectives are excusable in an old M.F.H. when a lot of jealous riders rush up and over-ride the scent at a check.

Generally speaking, it is an afternoon fox, that has completely digested the feast of the night, which affords the best sport—or a dog-fox in the clicketing season, who has travelled far out of his district to visit some distant seraglio.

If there were two hundred horsemen when the fox broke away, there would be hardly more than ten up in the field where he was run into, if the pace was a real gallop all the way and the time full twenty-five minutes over a strongly-fenced country ; perhaps twice as many more—including those clever old customers who rode to points instead of running the line, and knew every convenient gap, gate, and bridle-run in the country by heart—got up before the last vestige of the fox had disappeared, and the huntsman mounted and moved away. The rest, except those who kept strictly to a convenient road, if there was one, would be scattered in all directions, reduced to the slowest of trots, or obliged to walk, in consequence of the loss of shoes that no one ever was able to find. Much depends on the fences. In an open country like Cheshire, for instance, twenty abreast may take the fences. But the thinning-out is much more fearful in a real run from one of the crack Wednesday meets of the Pytchley bitch pack, as described by a resident—"All grass, chiefly strong (cattle) feeding-land ; the fences 'oxers,' cut and plashed with stubs as thick as your arm and as sharp as a palisade, or left as bullfinches, a ditch on one side, and a single rail to catch your horse's knees, if he is clumsy or tired, on the other ; fearful crushes at the gates ; nearly as bad at the gaps, in which there is room for about ten to get in front ; and although there may be fifty eager ones at the start, there is generally plenty of room at the end of a quick five-and-twenty minutes."

It is in such countries that blood, condition, and determined horsemanship tell ; and you may follow the advice of Egerton Warburton to the letter :—

> "If your horse be well bred, and in blooming condition,
>   Both up to the country and up to your weight,
>   Oh then give the reins to your youthful ambition,
>   Sit down in the saddle, and keep his head straight !"

But, first, you must be sure of yourself, and, next, of your horse.

Paraphrasing the lines attributed to Walter Raleigh and Queen Elizabeth, our only answer to those who, if they spoke truly, would say—

> "Fain would I *ride* but that I fear to fall."

is—

> "If you're afraid, then do not ride at all."

It is all very well to say—

> "Oh give me the man to whom nought comes amiss—
>   One horse or another, that country or this—
>   Through falls and bad starts, who undauntedly still
>   Rides up to this motto—'Be with 'em I will !'"

No doubt that is the spirit with which the young fox-hunter should go into the field; but it would be about as sensible to back a one-legged man against a champion pedestrian as to try to ride the line of a straight-necked fox over an ox-feeding country on a literally half-bred or half-conditioned or half-broken horse, or to cut your own work out with wild stag-hounds in the Exmoor country.

But because the horseman and the horse, or one of them, is not fit to contend in the first flight over the Midlands, that is no reason why the novice should condemn himself to mere road-riding. One thing he must do: he must gallop, and gallop best pace, up and down hill, over rough ground, without the slightest hesitation; keep his horse sufficiently in hand not to allow him to sprawl; be quick at turning; avoid as much as possible deep, sticky ground, going round along headlands rather than pump him out across the middle of a ploughed field; never hesitate at a practicable leap; and have eyes and ears alert to keep on terms with the hounds. It is by following these hints that so many heavy men, especially hunter-making farmers, turn up the moment the hounds throw up their heads, and are seldom far out when the fox is killed. The theory of these well-mounted fine horsemen, to ride the straight "string" instead of "round the bow," is not always practicable. To ride round on sound ground is not such a fine thing as being with the hounds "every yard," but much better than being out-ridden, out-jumped, left hopelessly in the rear, either in a ditch or on a gate, waiting for some yokel to bring back an escaped steed.

In a country of small fields and cramped fences which must be all negotiated at a very slow trot or a stand, and where a real splitting gallop is impossible, there is none of the feverish hurry of a good scenting day in the grass countries.

To get through crushes at gates and gaps where no jump is practicable, it is well to be as quick as possible—put on extra steam to get first. If in a crowd, the Warwickshire maxim is to "hold him and spur him," so as to be ready to bound into full speed the moment you get through the mob. If your horse is really clever in landing, it is always better to take a very big jump than trust a young hunter in a crowded gateway.

The hunter on which a young horseman should take his first experience in the field should be perfect in two ways of crossing fences: he should temperately and sensibly creep through gaps, step over moderate ditches, climb and descend banks, and also have the courage to dash over and clear a big fence when called upon, or trot up to and leap high timber.

If a horse will jump timber, and creep over and through hedge and ditch, he is perfect for most countries. A safe timber-jumper—that is to say, one that can be depended on after a good deal of galloping to clear and land safely over a full-sized gate or stile, is a treasure, because timber—rail, gate, or stile—is often the one way out of a field, a road, or across a railway. Of all accidents those over timber are the worst.

Any—one might almost say every—well-shaped, well-bred, hunter can be made to jump timber, if put in the hands of a competent trainer. Dick Christian said he only met with two horses in his long experience that he could not make jump, and they were both weak in the back. But there are scores of horses hunting that, from being badly trained, are not to be trusted at anything stronger than a sheep-hurdle.

The most annoying and dangerous tricks are swerving, refusing, and not rising sufficiently at or rushing through fences.

"If a rider has not knowledge or physical strength enough to collect and pull his horse on to his hind legs, so as to shorten his stride, before reaching his fence the animal is likely to refuse, because he feels he cannot leap the fence, or must take off too soon or too late."

Very fine steeplechasers say that they always fix with their eye the place from which they mean their horses to take off. I confess that, although after I learned the importance of the rule I always tried to collect my horse however fast he was going, I was obliged to leave the choice of the exact fulcrum to my hunter's honour. It is quite plain that if you have to cover fifteen feet, and your horse rises ten feet too soon, he will then have to cover twenty-five feet. Jem Hill, a late celebrated huntsman of the Heythrop Hounds, used to gallop across fields fenced in with stone walls at full gallop, and when he came very near the wall, pull his horse all together, and hop over four or five feet with unerring certainty. But many who tried to imitate him, with less correct hands, came to grief.

For a bold rider there is no fence so safe as a stone wall, because the landing is certain; for timid riders none looks so formidable. The horrid trick of rushing through fences without rising—I have seen a horse dash through a gate—can only be cured by having the animal ridden constantly at timber, not too high, that will not break. But this is not the proper duty of any gentleman, unless he be perfectly idle, and unencumbered with duties of any kind.

If a horse gets out of hand, and feels that he is going faster than you desire, he is very likely to refuse, although a perfect performer in the hands of a stronger horseman. I have repeatedly found that a horse which bolted and refused with the rider in a plain Pelham bridle, when held and collected in a sufficiently powerful double bridle, never attempted to swerve, although I held the curb loose as I came up to the fences, and only made him feel it when racing across big fields.

The habit of swerving, and perhaps jumping the wrong place, or absolutely refusing, is "frequently created by *the hateful practice of holding the reins in one hand as the horse is rising at his fence, and throwing up the other for the purpose of balancing the body.* This necessarily inclines the horse to swerve to the left, and allows him to run into the fence just as he pleases; indeed, swerving, refusing, not rising, and rushing, are all engendered by this most ungainly practice. Until men learn that horses have two sides to their mouths—require equal pressure to keep them straight, and an unequal pressure to make them turn—there will always be refusers and rushers." *

Another great practical authority, Dick Christian,† who was premier horse and hunter breaker for the "Leicestershire swells" in the first quarter of this century, whose sayings were Boswellised by "The Druid," has perhaps condensed in his "Lectures" nearly all the instructions that can be imparted in mere words. "As a steeplechaser," said Dick, "I always steadied my horse on his hind legs twenty yards from his fence, and I was always over and away again before the rushers. A man should get his horse collected. The front legs of a hunter should be higher than his hind ones when he comes down, but he must not buck [that is, jump from all four legs at once, like a deer.] Lots of young riders force their horses at fences too much; they'd never get hurt if they'd collect their horses.

"If you don't feel your horse's mouth you can tell nothing about him. If you hold him

---

* "The Sportsman's Guide," by Digby Collins.

† Dick Christian, on Mr. Coke's mare Marigold, charged a thick cut hedge, 4 feet 6 inches high, the mare alighting on a bank about a yard wide, with all her four feet together. "When I was in the air I saw my danger, so pulled as she touched the bank, and shot her legs right under her." Immediately below this bank was a steep declivity into an old stone quarry. The mare bounded to the bottom of the quarry in three springs, and alighted safely on her legs. The first leap over the hedge in a straight line—the height of the hedge not included—was 18 feet 8 inches; second leap, 10 feet 6 inches; third, 10 feet; fourth, 14 feet 9 inches—total, 53 feet 11 inches.—"*Post and Paddock.*"

he can make a second effort. If you drop him he can't. Horses have a bad mouth on the near side because they're always ridden with one hand.

"A horse wants a deal of handling at high timber. If we did not get their fore legs high enough, their knees 'ud get below it, and over they goes. Their tails often came clean bang into my face.

"A quick, safe jumper always goes from hind legs to hind legs. If a horse can't 'light on his hind legs he soon beats himself. Good rumps and good hind legs, them's the sort!

"In the Low Hills country it's most of it plough—the fields not more than ten acres, with a single fence with a ditch, and some with a ditch on both sides, *not very wide, but wide enough to throw a horse down.* The slower you ride at them the better. They want a handy horse—a perfect hunter, not a flying horse. In this country the horses can't stand above half an hour if the hounds keep straight on without a check.

"In the Vale [of Belvoir] the fences are tremendous when you come at them—staked and bound, wide ditches, timber very big. I once heard a reverend gent say he fairly trembled before a Vale fence, 'to think how he could get over.' And there's thirty miles, right on end, of grass all the way to Harborough.

*   *   *   *   *   *   *   *

"When I wanted to teach a horse to leap, I took him to a very low-fixed bar, or the trunk of a tree—not more than knee-high—and held him there until I got him on his hind legs, then let him go. As likely as not he dropped on the bar; I was patient, took him to it again and again; if he turned nervous, I soothed, and waited until he had calmed down. When he went readily at a stand from his hind legs I started him at a trot or canter, and made him slowly fly the body of a tree—so as to spread himself—or four feet of water. When I began on natural fences, I began with small places—first walked and then trotted at them—and soon was able to go over them at any pace I liked.

"The thing is to give your horse *confidence;* then you may take liberties with him; but do it calmly and in good temper, and keep him in the same. At *stitchers* [wide hedges and ditches] don't go too fast, so that he cannot measure his stride, or too slow, or he may stop; many horses have been spoiled by both mistakes. Give your young horse time to get his hind legs under him. If you're too slow, or have him too hard on the curb, he bucks, does not spread himself, jumps short into a far ditch, and then down you both go.

"When you set a horse going at his jumps hold him steadily by the head, not pulling him hard; the longer you hold him steady the further he'll go. A horse does not jump furthest by going over-fast at his fences, or even at water; he wants to be able to measure his strides up to where he takes off. He can't last long in a fast run if he's not kept collected, especially over deep ground, and ridge and furrow."

Brutal horsemen have not patience for such considerate methods of making horses leap. They tumble them about until they either learn to rise or are completely cowed. Sometimes the rude method which Assheton Smith practised succeeds. I have a well-authenticated account of a horse that, after falling twenty-eight times in going across a stiffly-enclosed country, finished by jumping, clean and clever, a new high, spiked gate, and never refused afterwards. But in nine cases out of ten, in a like experiment, if the rider had not been killed the horse would have been a coward for life.

"If," said Dick Christian, "a horse gets a bad fall it frightens him, and he does not enjoy fencing like one that has never had a fall. Let a young one scramble a bit in a ditch sitting quite still on him, but not so as to get cast."

And then he gives the following conversation between two notabilities of the past generation—a hard-riding farmer and a hard-riding baronet :—

" ' How do you like your new horse, Sir James ?'

" ' Pretty well ; only he makes me nervous, he hits his timber so hard.'

" ' I'll tell you what to do,' says Heycock, 'take him out by himself, quite private, and give him two or three heavy falls over timber. I always do it.'

" ' God bless me, Mr. Heycock ! you make my hair stand on end.' Them was Sir James's very words ; and he was a precious hard 'un too, was Sir James Musgrave.

*   *   *   *   *   *   *   *

" As to water, when I begin with a young horse I walk him to it (not too wide). I don't let him go away, I never lick or spur him, and, bless you ! he soon takes a delight in it."

Mr. Grantley Berkeley says :—" Do all you can to make your hunter *steady*, and if he makes a stumble by no means strike or spur him. If you do, the next time he makes a mistake, instead of coolly trying to save himself, he is likely to make wild scrambles to avoid your whip.

*   *   *   *   *   *   *   *

" Hunters should be taught to do small places—blind ditches, and the like—deliberately, for it is in rushing wildly at such places that the worst falls take place. The horse leaps too soon, puts his fore feet he knows not where, and crashes on his head. As to the pace for riding at fences there is no rule.

" You may pull your horse into a fall by nervous hesitation just as he is about to take off, or you may gallop him wildly into a fall by causing him to take off too soon, and therefore jump either not high enough or not far enough.

" The really first-class hunter flies smoothly beneath his rider, as if his joints were fed with oil. He stretches his splendid stride as if he felt no weight upon his back, and had at the same time each leg at command, his brain and eyes both serving him ; timing each step so as to safely span every grip, drain, or furrow that suddenly succeed each other, and with a few strides of *lessened* velocity bringing his fore feet *close* up to the fence, be it hedge, ditch, or brook, so as to compass it accurately—largely, if needful.

" The perfect hunter is prepared to exert his greatest power, if needful, yet never wastes his strength unnecessarily over low or narrow fences.

" The bad horseman spurs and rushes his horse at every fence, instead of reserving sharp urging for great obstacles.

" He swallows his fences as he would a nauseous dose of physic. Kicking with his armed heels, shutting his eyes, he disturbs the calculations of a really sensible hunter—feels a maddened rush, hears a crash, and is indebted to undeserved good luck if he does not find his horse in the middle of the fence, or on his back in the next field.

" The worst thing a man can do is to take his horse's attention from the work he has before him, by striking him with the whip, jagging at his mouth, or needlessly applying the spur. A hunter needs to have his mind at ease and his senses about him. If you flourish your whip or cram in your spurs when the poor dear is timing his stride so as not to take off too soon, looking whereabouts to land his feet on the outside of the fence in front, ten to one he takes off too soon, or rushes through the fence without rising at all."

At the same time Mr. Berkeley truly adds : " Men ride and go well over country in all forms. Some of the most uncouth and awkward-looking are hard to unseat, very hard to pound, and almost impossible to beat."

There are several points about timber-jumping which it is important the horseman in his first season should bear in mind.

It does not follow at all that because a horse will clear six feet when fresh from his stable he will do five or even four feet cleverly at the end or in the middle of a really good run. Coarse-bred cobs may be found that will do extraordinary things in the way of high jumps in a riding-school, at a horse-show, or in a slow run with harriers, yet would shut up after galloping half a dozen fields at full speed in a stone-wall country, or over a long line of stiles and locked gates, such as may be found in Gloucestershire or Warwickshire. If a young horse will jump four feet six inches freely, and in good form, it is not wise to torment him, by trying how high he can jump until he refuses or falls. Reserve the experience until the time comes when you must, with hounds running, and you and your horse, hot with excitement, either fly park palings, or high locked gates, or be left in the lurch.

If, like many capital old hunters, a horse which is a very big jumper is tender on his fore feet, he should not be taken out when the ground is very hard. There are horses that will gallop in dirt over their fetlocks, and fly their fences in the most delightful manner, that will tremble, sweat, and refuse sheep-hurdles, when the ground has been dried hard by March winds.

It is a very pernicious practice to leap a horse backward and forward over the same place—alone, in cold blood. If he is sensible, he feels that you are making a fool of him ; if he is inclined to be sulky, it is a sure receipt for increasing the fault.

Larking—that is, jumping real hunters without having hounds before them, merely to show what they can do, or to show off before ladies—spoils many capital horses, causing them finally to refuse. It is, if not advisable, excusable, when it assumes the form of a sort of race over a short cut home after a dull or blank day ; then the horses, being in company, get excited, and perhaps even believe that they are hunting. But very good horses are spoiled by racing, because it teaches them to rush at, instead of measuring their fences. There is not one steeplechase horse in a hundred that is worth a farthing as a hunter, because the business of a steeplechaser is to get over the ground without a pause ; while the best hunters and best hunting men make full use of "deliberation's artful aid"—although they do not appear to dwell either in taking off or after landing—and only come with a rush when a thick black bullfinch or a wide water-jump bars the way. Now, if a steeplechaser dwells one second unnecessarily at thirty fences, that makes half a minute—nothing in hunting, everything in a race.

As high, stiff timber is the most dangerous to horsemen, so wide water is most fatal to horses ; and yet, theoretically, water is the safest and easiest of all leaps if—there is great virtue in "if"—the landing and taking off are sound.

Blood horses that really like water scarcely increase their natural stride to cover any ordinary brook. But few horses like water. If a horse has tumbled over a rail he may jump higher at the next ; but if a horse, by his own or his rider's fault, jumps short, and gets into deep water, it is very difficult to get him to face a brook again ; and when a horse sees the water, and gradually refuses—"shuts up" is the professional phrase—no horseman in the world can get him over a wide place—unless in a boat.

There is no way in which hunters break their backs so often as in jumping at a brook. If they fail to land with their hind legs, the weight of the rider breaks or fatally strains the spine.

The reason that brooks of even moderate width—say fifteen or sixteen feet (a distance which any well-bred galloway can cover in his stride) stop fox-hunters is that both horses and riders are afraid—the horse of falling, the rider of getting wet and rheumatism. If the brook is full to the brim the shining surface alone will stop most horses at fifty yards' distance; if, on the other hand, it runs between steep banks, the horsemen of a prudent age, even if they ride at it, begin to think how they are to get out if they get in, and their horses find out their "weak knees." There is no saying more true than the way to get over a fence is to "throw your heart over it, and the horse will follow if he can."

Many horses jump short when put at wide water because they rise in the air, instead of skimming, as perfect water-jumpers do. In most cases the taking off at water is bad: if level, marshy, and cut up by cattle drinking; if high, rotten with the burrows of water-rats and the eating away of winter floods.

With firm turf to gallop on and take off from, a bold horseman and horse have repeatedly cleared thirty feet, but twelve feet of a brimming brook will stop the best part of a large field.

I remember once, with the Surrey Stag-hounds, when hunting slowly, leaping into a field of some fifty acres, at the bottom of which ran a brook certainly not fifteen feet wide, brimful, and shining bright as silver under an April sun. "Drive down as hard as you can," said a steeplechasing friend; "you'll never get over if you give any one time to refuse." As soon done as said, my thorough-bred scrambling a little on the landing side. Looking back, I beheld the extraordinary spectacle of some three hundred horses refusing, like a mob of irregular cavalry startled at a shell bursting, all over the field. Some prudent gentlemen had ridden down to look; their horses refused, and a cohort including many undeniable hunters followed suit. The great difficulty of water is that you have to negotiate it without having time to choose your taking off, on which, in a very big jump, everything depends. It is in such cases that local knowledge comes in, and enables the experienced man to choose the one solid spot for "having it," while strangers on better horses are beaten by the ground before they make the supreme effort.

The whole theory of riding at water is summed up in the lines.

> "Harden your heart and catch hold of the bridle—
> Steady him! rouse him! over he goes!"

The fact is, that if a horse has blood, stride, condition, and courage; if he be willing to jump ten feet of water (which he can do standing), and you are willing, he will surely clear five-and-twenty, *if he can get fairly at it*. But a really willing, clever horse, without blood or stride, cannot get over wide water. In nine cases out of ten he is beaten before he gets to it; for wide water which must be jumped is rarely met at the commencement of a run with fox-hounds.

Many years ago, when I rode under eleven stone, a friend invited me to join a breakfast-party on the last day of the season, with a pack of harriers, when a hind was to be turned out, and promised to "put me up on a snaffle-bridle cob that never had refused a fence." This turned out to be a very intelligent-looking galloway, which had gained a great reputation that season while "hunting of the hare."

As a matter of course we started at score, over a well-selected country, with a good many low stiles and high banks. Over stiles the cob, at first, hopped like a kangaroo, and climbed steep banks "like a fly on a wall;" but after a time the unaccustomed pace began to tell, and he blundered over a set of sheep-hurdles (with the snaffle I was quite unable to collect my game but out-paced little animal), and I was very grateful for a check at a thick plantation. Out of the plantation we galloped down a fifty-acre field, towards a brimful, sluggish, not very wide brook. I had a capital start, and as it was a very steep incline—I had been accustomed to hills—away I went, as hard as I could. Before me was only one horseman, a jockey-looking personage on a racehorse-looking animal. When we got within twenty yards of the brook it was over fetlock-deep in stiff clay. The blood horse galloped on, and without an effort took the water in his stride. With spurs in, determined "to do or drown," I pressed on, the cob declining at every yard, until at the brink he dwelt for a

A WATER JUMP.

second, and then plunged into the middle. Fortunately the impetus sent us close up to the opposite bank, on which, wet to the waist, I climbed, while the exhausted cob laid his head on a bank of rushes, and there rested, until, apparently refreshed by his cold bath, he answered the pulls of the reins and flicks of the hunting-whip, and struggled out with a great effort. All the field, except the steeplechaser, a farmer with a horse to sell, and myself, had crossed by a cattle-bridge not ten yards out of the line, although out of sight. I rode back, for the day was hopelessly lost, a damper and wiser man, and never afterwards attempted water or stag-hunting on a coarse-bred one, however clever.

Nothing can convey a better idea of how a big water-jump is cleared by a fine horseman on a fine horse than the following extract from Whyte Melville's "Brooks of Bridlesmere." The speakers are an earl, "whose familiarity with the country now stood him in good stead, though *the fine horsemanship and unshaken nerve of twenty years ago were gone never to return,*" and his daughter, a "girl of the period," the warm-hearted and slangy Lady Julia.

"These two [the Duke M. F. H. and Walter] seemed the only two inclined to face the water. Lady Julia and her father exchanged looks of intelligence. The young lady spoke first—

"'He means to have it! Papa, I knew he would. Look! he has set him a-going. How well he rides him! I wish I had a thousand (in gloves) on the event!'

"'No hunter in England can jump that water, Ju.,' answered the earl; he'll break his horse's back, and then he'll be sorry he did not come with us to the ford.'

"Walter had leaped Fugleman over *an awkward place, under a tree, in order to obtain a fair, sound headland, with a fall in his favour leading straight away to the water's edge.* It was the masterly manner in which he increased his horse's pace down the incline that elicited Lady Julia's enthusiasm. Fugleman's ears were pointed, his head was up; he had no more thought of refusing than his rider; at the pace they were going it must be in or over.

"'It's even betting! It's five to two! It's a guinea to a shilling!' exclaimed her ladyship, as Fugleman's quick, determined strokes bore him stride by stride towards his effort.

"'I tell you it's impossible,' answered her father. 'Ju., *don't* be so slangy.'

"'It's a monkey to a mousetrap!' added the girl, looking demurely into his face. 'Papa, the mousetrap's mine!'

"As she spoke Fugleman landed safely on the further bank, made a false step, a short stride, recovered himself, and was away once more after the hounds at his long, easy gallop."

FALLING.

When a man says that he never has a fall, you may take it for granted, if it be true, that he never rides hard except where he perfectly knows the country and the geography of both sides of every fence he puts his horse at; that he never comes across an unexpected grip or blind ditch—in a word, that he and his horse never make a mistake. If a man has very perfect horses, is never in a hurry, always picks his places, and always leaves off the moment his horse is tired, he may ride many seasons without a fall. But a man must be both very rich and a very good judge to find horses that never make a mistake, either galloping or leaping, and must enjoy a prudence of character that would rob youth of all its enthusiasm and half its pleasure.

At the same time, while falls are to be avoided if possible, they are to be taken as coolly as possible when they come. Those who are not afraid, and therefore not flurried, are the least likely to be hurt, and still less likely if they keep to the golden rule of never letting the bridle (and the horse) go.

Some—these are the finest horsemen—never leave the saddle in a fall, and are ready to recover their horse at the first opportunity; such have the horseman's structure—light, muscular, long limbs. Others—very good men in the hunting-field, but quite unfit to ride steeple-chases or races—short, thick-thighed, with "wash ball" seats, are pretty sure to roll off the instant their horse tumbles on his head. It is a disputed point which meet with the fewer accidents.

In one year—alluded to in the note to page 5—I must have ridden more than thirty strange horses, in strange countries, and that as hard as I knew how. I had many falls—

that is, the horses frequently fell—sometimes inevitably, sometimes from want of knowledge of the country, or of the horse, or simply from bad riding. A single link more or less in a curb-chain will often make the difference between a hunter going pleasantly or pulling and rushing. In that year I was several times severely bruised and shaken, but never broke any bones or was disabled from my daily responsible duties. This is not said by way of self-praise, but simply as encouragement to young horsemen in their first season.

Rules for falling there are never likely to be of any use. Dick Christian, whose trade was to manufacture hunters at steam-pace out of rare blood-horses, says:—

"When a horse made his start to jump I always knew if he was going to fall. I prepared myself: I could clap my hands on his withers, get clear of him, and keep my reins too." It is quite a point of honour with hunting-men to keep fast hold of the reins in a fall if possible.

Dick Christian was never displaced except when a horse fell; therefore he held opinions suited to a young horseman who had not acquired the instinct of sticking to the saddle under the most difficult circumstances. He says:—

"Gentlemen gets falls very bad; you see, they generally ride old horses, and old ones fall like a clod. If they get into difficulties they won't try to get out. They are like that when they get ten years old; they haven't the animation of a young horse. The young ones will still try to struggle themselves right, and will not touch you if they can help it. I'll be bound to be safer riding twenty young horses than one old one."

Observations in which there is a fund of truth, but which should not encourage an inexperienced horseman to experiment on any horse not really and truly a hunter.

One of the best points about hunting is that a day's sport, whether good or bad, affords a sportsman much room for afterthought. A man second in his literary and artistic accomplishments to few members of the House of Commons wrote: "Thinking over a good run well ridden is as good or better than riding it. Even a dashing rider is apt to feel some anxiety (not alarm, but anxiety) as each big fence (the landing a mystery) rises before him; but in chewing the cud afterwards, how he slashes over them, knowing then what the landing is to be!"*

To this candid bit of self-confession must be added a word of much-needed advice. The battle of the hunt should be fought over again in silence, or to your wife, sister, sweetheart, or confidant; at table let others talk, or talk of others. Old men, especially if they are very rich, are apt to grow into egotistical bores; but a young man who dwells on the performances of himself and his horse is not only an ass, but an ass of a very offensive kind. Perhaps one of the most absurd scenes for a calm bystander is a party of undergraduates after a good day's hunting; all have ridden as hard as they could, and all are talking at once of the irrepressible *ego*.

Not Cæsar was more picturesquely brief than the huntsman who summed up a rare run with—"The hounds ran like h——, and the old mare carried me like ile!"

The following description of a first-class horseman, by the laureate of Northamptonshire, was, it is no secret, meant for Colonel Anstruther Thompson, when he hunted the Pytchley hounds, who was a master of hounds while still a cornet in the 9th Lancers. He stood, and stands, over six feet two, had not a superfluous ounce of flesh on his bones, and with his own or some other hounds hunted every day of the week in the season, from November to May, in the woodlands, besides cub-hunting in August, September, and October.

* Charles Buxton's "Notes of Thought."

BETWEEN BOTH HANDS: READY FOR THE FIELD.

"A RUM ONE TO FOLLOW, A BAD ONE TO BEAT.

" Come, I'll give you the health of a man we all know,
  A man we all swear by, a friend of our own ;
With the hounds running hardest, he 's safest to go,
  And he's often in front, and he's often alone —
A rider unequalled, a sportsman complete,
A rum one to follow, a bad one to beat.

" As he sits on the saddle, a baby could tell
  He can hustle a sticker, a flyer can spare ;
He has science and nerve, and decision as well ;
  He knows where he's going, and means to be there.

" We threw off at the Castle, we found in the holt ;
  Like wildfire the beauties went streaming away,
From the rest of the field he came out like a bolt,
  And he tackled to work like a schoolboy at play.

" 'Twas a caution, I vow, but to see the man ride !
  O'er the rough and the smooth he went sailing along,
And what Providence sent him he took in his stride,
  Though the ditches were deep and the fences were strong,

" Ere they'd run for a mile there was room in the front,
  Such a scatter and squander you never did see !
And I honestly own I'd been out of the hunt
  But the broad of his back was the beacon for me ;
So I kept him in sight, and was proud of the feat—
This rum one to follow, this bad one to beat !
*   *   *   *   *
" For a place I liked better I hastened to seek,
  But the place I liked better I sought for in vain ;
And I honestly own, if the truth I must speak,
  That I never caught sight of my leader again."

TO LADIES HUNTING.

Whether the hunting-field is a proper place for ladies is a question not worth arguing, because it is one in which mere argument is not likely to alter convictions or control tastes. Although many ladies have been persuaded to attend the meets, and ride more or less hard with hounds, by the arguments of lovers or husbands, by the example of friends, or by the incalculable force of propinquity, the instances are very rare in which a lady who had really enjoyed hunting, who continued to reside in a hunting country, and been able to afford to keep hunters and ride them, has given up the sport on the ground of its being unfeminine or improper. Sometimes loss of health, sometimes diminished income, sometimes the cares of an increasing family, rob the hunting-field of its brightest ornaments. Sometimes ladies who have been the gayest of the gay, and even the fastest of the fast, renounce hunting, with other worldly amusements, in favour of some ascetic form of devotion ; but they do not expunge hunting alone from relaxation ; they give it up with dancing, theatres, novel-reading, because they are pleasant amusements, and because they have arrived at the conclusion that everything that is pleasant is wrong. Women, like men, who feel at home on horseback, hunt because they enjoy it, and give it up when they cease to enjoy it, without any profound arguments either way.

The habit of making excuses for indulgences that are pleasant was never better satirised than by Quin, the actor, who, entering a tavern, in the days when gentlemen frequented taverns, and hearing one fop drawl out, " Waiter ! give me a glass of brandy-and-water, because I am so hot !" and another of the same tribe, " Waiter ! give me a glass, because I am so cold," roared out in his gruffest tones, " Waiter ! give me a glass, because I like it." Right or wrong, the tastes of ladies for the hunting-field extends amongst us with the annual increase of wealth and luxury. The number of women who really can ride up to hounds will always remain limited, being most probably in tolerably near proportion to the percentage of first-flight men out of a Quorn or Pytchley field.

In the last, and beginning of the present century, before the third pommel of the side-saddle was invented, very few ladies rode to hounds. One of the most distinguished was the Marchioness of Salisbury, grandmother of the Cabinet Minister of 1874, who was burned to death in Hatfield House on the 13th of November, 1833, in her eighty-fifth year.

"Old Lady Salisbury," says Tom Raikes, "was one of the leaders of *ton* in the fashionable world. She was a half-sister of the late Marquis of Downshire" [misprinted "Devonshire" in the Diary];* "was one of the beauties of the day, famed for her equestrian exploits. In early life she hunted with Mr. Meynell's hounds at Quorn, in Leicestershire. Till a late period she constantly hunted with the Hatfield Hounds, in a sky-blue habit, with black-velvet collar and a jockey cap, riding as hard as any sportsman in the field. Her Sunday (card) parties and suppers in Arlington Street continued for nearly half a century to attract all the most distinguished society of London. She was the last remnant of what may be called the 'old school' in England, who for many years gave the *ton* to society. Remarkable for her fine figure, with the high-bred manners of a *grande dame*, Lady Salisbury scrupulously adhered to the state of former days. She always went to Court in a sedan-chair, with splendid liveries; she drove out in a low phaeton, with four black ponies, postillions, and outriders. At night (after the introduction of gas) her carriage was known by the flambeaux of her footmen."

The *grandes dames* are all gone. A peeress who attempted Sunday card-parties visible to beholders walking in the Green Park would be likely to have her windows smashed. There is not one sedan-chair in London. The only relic of flambeaux is to be found in the iron extinguishers still remaining over the doors of a few town mansions; while ponies, postillions, and outriders, are rarely seen, except on the carriages of royalty; but hunting flourishes more than ever, and the manners and customs of the hunting-field are softened by the presence of numerous noble matrons and virgins. Unfortunately, on the other hand, the multiplication of pheasant preserves has reduced the fox-hunting merits of Herts to a low scale; and the two last noble owners of Hatfield have not been fox-hunters.

In order to encourage the enriched mothers of the middle class, I venture making an exception from the rule of this book, and name, amongst the noble mothers of families who have been distinguished as accomplished horsewomen in the hunting-field—the Countess of Macclesfield, from whom, during his residence at Oxford, the Prince of Wales received his first lessons in the art of fox-hunting; the Countess of Coventry, seldom second when she rode with her husband's hounds; the Countess of Yarborough, whom the scarlet-coated wold-men of Lincolnshire swear by. A list might be compiled which would fill a page of other mothers and daughters of high position and stainless character.

When a lady hunts it is absolutely essential for the peace of mind of her friends that she should be properly equipped, provided with a horse she can control—"up to her weight," "up to the country"—and clever enough to leap any reasonable obstacle. Courage is important in the lady's hunter for her comfort, but docility is essential for her safety.

A young horseman is not fit for a second season of the hunting-field if he has not pluck and enthusiasm enough to take his chance on any horse that looks like a hunter, leaving the perfectly-finished animal for the aged, the cripple, the nervous.

It is youth's business—

> "To tame the wild young one, inspirit the old;
> The restive, the runaway, handle and hold,"

but that is not the part or the place of a lady. It is quite sufficient, if she has hands, seat, and courage enough, on a perfectly-made hunter, to follow the lead of a judicious pilot.

---

* "Diary and Reminiscences of Social Life, from 1831 to 1847, by Thomas Raikes, Esq."

The hunter for a lady who really means "to ride to hounds" must have a combination of blood and power; and he must also have courageous placidity of temper and a finished education. Be well up to the fair rider's weight. To make sure of this she must, however unwilling, go into the scales, and a full allowance be made for the saddle, which will be nearer eighteen pounds than fourteen. A light saddle for hunting is a mistake. The lady about to hunt must be referred back to Chapter XV. for information as to habit and saddle.

The pocket of a hunting side-saddle should be large, and arranged so as not to catch against anything. Although it is assumed that some one will always be in attendance on a lady hunting, gentlemen get overpowered by the enthusiasm of the chase, grooms get thrown out, and the flask of wine and water and sandwich-case, which ought to be attached to the saddle, may be urgently needed and not at hand.

The best form of hunting-bridle for a lady is that formerly made by Messrs. Whippy for Captain Percy Williams, the curb-rein of which can be shortened or lengthened as required, and either lie on the neck of the horse or be taken up in the full grasp of a small hand.

The hunting habit should be as short as possible, it is generally kept down by a loop over one foot, an expedient all hunting-tailors understand; but some experienced ladies object to the loop as dangerous. It should never on any consideration be lined with leather, or any material that will not tear and give liberty, in case of its catching in a fence.

A lady, unless she has a perfectly competent and devoted male friend, should always be accompanied by a real hunting-groom, mounted on at least as fast and clever a horse as her own. Without going so far as Anthony Trollope's Miss Carbuncle,* and saying that "gentlemen cannot open gates," it is far better to have a professional gate-opener than see the admirer, who was all pleasant attentions in the morning, getting bored and wearied towards the close of a chequered day—a change that is very likely to take place if politeness has lost him a good start in a good run.

Ladies should never attempt to go first—to "cut out the work" as the phrase is—in a strange country, because, while falls now and then are a matter of course with a forward horseman, a fall with a lady is a very serious thing, not to be contemplated. She cannot get away from her horse so easily as a man; she may be disfigured, if she is not seriously injured; or she may cut a very ridiculous figure in her trousers without a skirt—an incident which really happened to the daughter of a distinguished master of hounds, and was immortalised by John Leech.

Therefore, if ladies are competent and determined to really ride, they should always have a pilot. Young admirers and young farmers may generally be found ready to accept an office which requires quite as much discretion as courage, and a minute knowledge of the country. The task becomes more difficult when there are two or more ladies anxious to be in the first flight, and, like Lady Eustace, to outride some female friend.

Great ladies have been known to pay pilots—certainly an admirable plan if expense is not an objection. Professionals always excel amateurs where orders have to be obeyed, and dry work has to be done.

So far I have been treating of the select few—hard as pin-wire, fierce as goshawks, jealous as *soprani*—but so few that they might generally be conveyed to cover-side in one family brougham; and I have been leaving out of consideration the professional ladies who pursue and improve their business as horsebreakers in the hunting-field with extraordinary skill and

* "The Eustace Diamonds."

nerve—a very useful class. These perfectly well know how to take care of themselves Young ladies may derive many useful hints by noting, in silence, their performances. But there are a very considerable number of ladies who like, or would like, hunting, but who are, not unwisely, unprepared to expose themselves to "serious accidents by flood and field;" who, when hounds are running, prefer galloping round to a bridge, at the risk of losing a run, to the chance of a ducking; who decline to have anything to say to gates that cannot be burst open, or the bullfinches which are taking toll in rags of scarlet coats. As observed in a previous chapter, a lady who can gallop without losing her breath or her nerve, who can sit her horse in comfort over the average leaps, will, even in a flying country, with the assistance of the numerous hand-gates that are put up in all fashionable counties, and the many gaps that are established by the advanced guard of men, see a great deal of sport, and have quite as much riding as is good for most women, without doing anything to be talked about.

Ladies of this, which I will call second class, who are really well mounted, and who really possess the courage which proceeds from skill and fairly good nerves—not the audacity which is the result of ignorance and vanity—are a delightful addition to the pleasures of the hunting-field. They are happy, and they look graceful and contented. They do not alarm you by attempting feats which, unless perfectly well mounted, are much better left to men· They do not shock your taste by familiarity with persons who, though very well in their saddles, are not fit familiar companions for a lady—at least, a young lady. A middle-aged woman of fortune can do anything she likes without exciting the anxious sympathies of lookers-on, whether she is ducked in a brook or rides home in a fly *tête à tête* with a horse-breaker.

The young ladies who really are a nuisance in the field are those who, with neither seat nor hands, or mounted on coarsely-bred, under-conditioned brutes, with "lovely heads and flowing tails," will, in the hopes of exciting admiration, thrust themselves into positions in which they are as much out of place as in a Grand National Steeplechase. If their galloway jumps at all, they are continually asking some victim for a lead. They help to crowd into a gateway when hounds are getting away, although they have no more chance of riding straight through three fields than of jumping a twenty-foot brook; and they are as loud in calling attention to merits, beauties, and performances of an animal that would be dear at twenty pounds, as if it were one of the beauties of the Brocklesby stud. The fault of these young ladies—they are generally young, and often very charming on foot—is that they do not accept their proper position, which is in the third class of the hunting-field, with the old squires who have lost their nerves, the fat farmers on fat green colts, and the numerous tribe who love hunting, but honestly admit to themselves that they have not the least idea of keeping up with the hounds if the pace much exceeds ten miles an hour, or the leaps are beyond the powers of a sporting donkey.

Guided by local knowledge, these old hands rattle away along bridle-roads, by short and crafty cuts through woods, farmsteads, dells, and dingles, and continually turn up in the most unexpected places, close to the pack, to the infinite disgust of the young gentlemen who, having honestly ridden every yard, feel themselves robbed of half the credit of their performances.

"If your horse is not up to your weight or to the country," or if your nerve is not equal to the work of the day, the fault of having attempted and made a ridiculous failure is multiplied tenfold by pretending afterwards that you did or could, but for some accident that never happened, ride in a place to which neither you nor your horse was ever equal. This rule applies to both sexes in the hunting-field, but ladies should particularly avoid placing themselves in positions where, in spite of all manner of charms, they are considered, to say the least, very troublesome. On the other hand, there are not a few examples of ladies bred in town, and transplanted under favourable auspices to the country, who have commenced by riding the lanes on a pony, advanced to a slow, steady old hunter, and finished, well mounted, by taking up a position in good runs as advanced as their warmest admirers could desire. Given the natural strength, nerve, and taste for sport, the rest is merely a matter of experience and expense—the last being an essential ingredient in the hunting of ladies. The hunter of a lady who really means "to ride" in a good county must be *perfect*, and *perfection* is always costly. As a rule, if otherwise suitable, a lady's hunter should not be less than 15 hands 2 inches high, a height which is a happy medium for a hunter and a lady's hack.

The subject of the dress of *Amazones* has been very fully treated in Chapter XV.; but it is important to add that ladies returning from hunting by rail should be well provided with cloaks and rugs, because, after the exhaustion of a good day, the inevitable draughts of a railway-carriage are apt to give severe colds. If circumstances do not admit of a complete change of clothing on dismounting, before travelling home by road or rail, it is very desirable that the boots and stockings should be exchanged for warm, dry pairs, which may easily be rolled in a waterproof overcoat carried by a groom.

BOYS AND GIRLS HUNTING.

As soon as children who have ponies of their own can ride, there is no reason that they should not hunt, if hounds of any kind meet conveniently near, and many reasons why they should. A useful art cannot be learned too early in life. Riding to hounds, like dancing, is one of the accomplishments much better learned at the age when mankind most easily submit to reproof, and are strongly influenced by example. Boys and girls alike, if of tender years, should ride their ponies without stirrups or with the ladies' patent stirrup. Several fatal accidents have occurred within my recollection from children falling and being dragged by the stupid irons attached to their saddles. If girls have the third pommel they can ride perfectly well without a stirrup—boys should have quilted pads carefully filled and stuffed at the points where the knees without stirrups naturally press. If nothing better is at hand a flock pillow fastened with a surcingle will make a very good shift.

Little girls "to the manner born" perform extraordinary feats in the hunting-field on ponies; but these little wonders are always mountain-bred, and however small, have the true hunting shape. Therefore, ponies required to carry children with hounds should be selected with more care as to their symmetry and courage than if merely wanted for the road.

TAKING STAINS OUT OF A SCARLET COAT.

Three parts of pure nitric acid at 30° B., one part muriatic acid at 17° Shake gently, avoiding the corrosive vapours. Put a loose stopper in the mouth. Put into this mixture one-eighth of its weight of pure tin, in small bits at a time. When all is dissolved and settled, decant it into bottles, and close with ground stoppers. It should be diluted only when used. This is a recipe for *eau écarlate* that costs a guinea a bottle.

CHAPTER XXII.

HOUNDS AND MASTERS OF HOUNDS.

Division of Packs of Fox-hounds—Private—Subscription—Breeding Packs—Names of—County Packs—Masters of Hounds—Of Ancient and of Modern Families—Names of Sportsmen Born, not Made—Amount of Subscription—Cost of Hunting Fox-hounds—Of Harriers—The Difficulties of a Master of Hounds—Different Kinds of Masters—The Master who Hunts for Sport—The Master who Hunts for Position—Advice to Huntsmen—A Superior Class of Servants—The Qualifications Required—Knowledge of Hounds—Of Foxes—Of Country—Decision of Character—Horsemanship—The Old Idea of Drunken Huntsmen False—Tom Moody not a Huntsman—Two Model Huntsmen—Scent—A Mystery—Evidence from Huntsmen in Many Countries—The Belvoir County—The Dorsetshire—The Herts—The Essex—The Brocklesby—The Berkeley—THE FOX-HOUND—How Brought to Perfection—By Careful Selection—For Certain Qualities—Importance of Even Size—Average Sizes of Dogs and Bitches—Music of Hounds—Diminished by Pace—Canon Kingsley's Description of a Fox-hound—Of a Hunt in Hampshire—The Fox—A Picture from Life—The Hunting Men—*Note*—An American's Ride with the Milton Hounds—A Day in Sherwood Forest, by the Author—Hunting Lessons—A Farmer's Grievance in Queen Anne's Time—George III. the Farmer's Friend—The Hunting Club—Boodle's—Hunting Terms, List of.

THE attempt to give an historical and practical idea of modern fox-hunting, for the benefit of aspirants, would not be complete without some reference to Masters of hounds, huntsmen, and hunting-fields.

Out of 137 packs of fox-hounds in England and Scotland, recorded in the "Rural Almanack" of 1874, the following were maintained without subscription:—The Belvoir, by the Duke of Rutland; the Brocklesby, by the Earl of Yarborough; the Badminton, by the Duke of Beaufort (formerly hunted by the duke himself, and in that year by the Marquis of Worcester); the Berkeley, by Lord Fitzhardinge; the Duke of Grafton's; the Earl of Fitzwilliam's in Yorkshire, formerly in Northamptonshire; the Earl of Coventry's (hunted by himself) in Worcester-shire; the Cottesmore was taken up by the third Earl of Lonsdale on his accession to his title, and since by his son the fourth earl (for many years it was a subscription pack, but it was founded by one of his ancestors about a hundred years ago); the Lord Leconfield's in Sussex; the Earl of Portsmouth's in North Devon; Lord Tredegar in South Wales; Sir Watkin William Wynn in North Wales. In Scotland the Duke of Buccleuch maintained the pack of fox-hounds established by himself in his minority, and the Earl of Eglintoun the pack of hounds established by his father, of Eglintoun tournament memory. In Ireland, the Marquis of Waterford kept up the famous Curraghmore Hounds. There may be other packs less known to fame, maintained at their own expense by private gentlemen; but of the rest, by far the greater number are supported by subscription—in some cases limited to the members of a county club, in others open to any man willing to pay the fixed minimum contribution, and behave with common decency in the field. With respect to county clubs, a man buying and residing on an estate in the county would be looked on coldly if he did not subscribe; while in some instances—for instance with the Cheshire—"donations" are accepted from the hunting men of Liverpool and Manchester, but subscriptions with the right to wear the club uniform are declined.

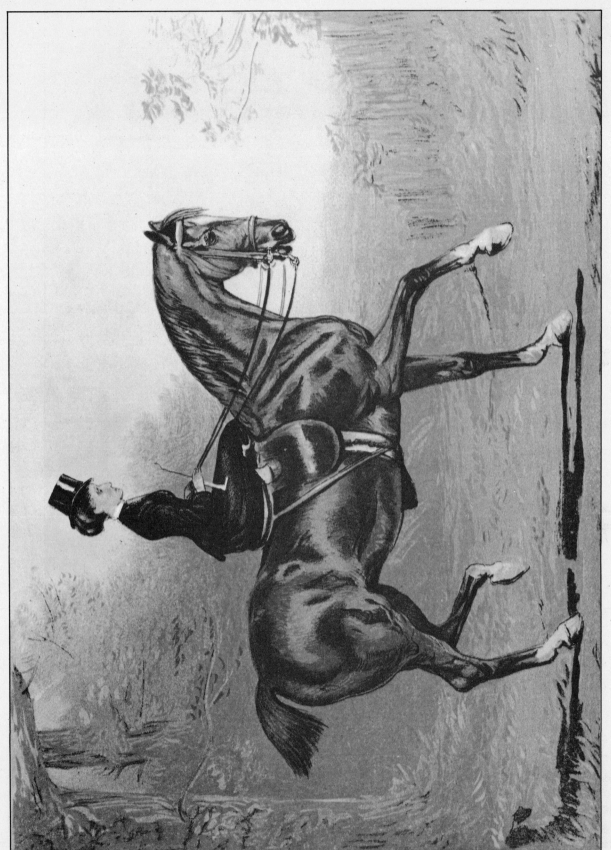

GOING TO COVER—A PORTRAIT.
BY THE LATE ALFRED CORBOULD ESQ.

"FULL CRY."

TOM CLARKE, HUNTSMAN OF THE OLD BERKSHIRE.

Some subscription packs have been maintained under one management for a long series of years. Such is the Bramham Moor, in Yorkshire, with which the name of the Lane Fox family is indelibly connected; while the Holderness had one Master in the late Mr. Hall, a banker, for nearly forty years. As nearly all the excellence of a pack of fox-hounds depends on breeding on fixed principles for a long series of years, it is a great disadvantage when a pack is broken up and for a new Master to commence to hunt the county with hounds collected from east and west, north and south. Such has been the fate of the Quorn more than once. Master has succeeded Master at short intervals; some managing without and some with a subscription. On each occasion the whole establishment of hounds, servants, and horses, has been dispersed; while subscription packs of merely provincial reputation have been maintained without interruption for generations.

The tesselated condition of English society—in which the choicest honours are open to the successful, no matter how born or bred—is faithfully reproduced in rank of Masters of fox-hounds. For example, in 1874, two peers were Masters of and personally hunted two subscription packs of fox-hounds in Oxfordshire; in Essex a Master was a real tenant-farmer; in Holderness the Master was a banker; in Suffolk, a few years ago, a father and son, brewers—the father an M.P.—managed at the same time two packs; in Surrey, a pack of fox-hounds, maintained on a very modest scale by local subscriptions, was not only managed but hunted by a genuine London banker—not a retired sleeping partner, but the working representative of one of the oldest City banking firms.

In the same direction it may be noted that the most celebrated Masters of hounds and sportsmen have been by no means exclusively enlisted from the ranks of noblemen or long-descended landed squires. The late Sir Tatton Sykes—the Sir Roger de Coverley of Yorkshire—passed some years of his youth in a solicitor's office in Lincoln's Inn Square, and was the grandson of a Hull merchant. Squire Farquharson, who hunted Dorsetshire for half a century, and looked the character of the leather-breeched, top-booted, country gentleman as much as his contemporary the Norman-descended Sir Charles Knightley—was the son of a nabob; Captain Percy Williams was son of an East India director. The late Captain John White, who was known, when Master of the Cheshire Hounds, as "Leicestershire White," and was considered the *beau idéal* of a sportsman in Melton's most palmy days, was the son of a Manchester physician. Out of living Masters of hounds hunting important countries a dozen examples might be quoted of men whose claim to the position rests on love of sport, and not the least on pedigree. The lineal descendants of that illustrious barber, Sir Richard Arkwright, the founder of the cotton manufacture, which enabled England to bear the cost of the wars following the French Revolution, supplied Masters of the fox-hounds in Essex, in Bedfordshire, and Warwickshire, in a father and two sons; and in 1874 three Arkwrights hunted a Bedfordshire, a Herefordshire, and an Essex pack. In the same year the Master of the celebrated Heythrop Hounds was a son of Mr. Thomas Brassey, the millionnaire railway contractor, one of his predecessors in the office having been Lord Redesdale, the paid chairman of the Private Bill Committee of the House of Lords.

The subscription to an established pack of fox-hounds is seldom less than twenty-five pounds, but there are landed proprietors who give five hundred pounds without attending a meet twice in a season.

The guaranteed subscription in 1874, to one of the best packs in a metropolitan county for three days a week, and an occasional by-day, was two thousand pounds a year; but in the same county very good sport was shown with a scratch pack of hounds by a *professional Master* for less than a thousand a year.

On the other hand, a pack of harriers may be kept up in really good style for about five hundred a year, and a pack of stag-hounds at about one thousand a year. Every gentleman who appears regularly at the meets of a subscription (not being a county pack) is expected to subscribe, and with the packs that meet within fifty miles of London, a stranger will probably receive a hint to that effect after the third or fourth visit. The farmers whose holdings are within easy reach of a metropolitan railway would naturally object to any hunting at all if the "fields" were not strictly limited. With harriers, a collection called "a cap" is generally made before the hounds throw off, of from two-and-sixpence to five shillings, from each non-subscriber.

For a new man, in the sense of the French term *nouveau riche*, to obtain admission into a county hunting club is almost as difficult as to be balloted into the most exclusive clubs of London, say White's or the Travellers', and can only be effected by the same means—good introductions. Money alone is not a passport, although with tact it will do a good deal.

The position of the Master of a subscription pack of fox-hounds involves, if properly performed, grave responsibilities, much time and labour, and a host of rural troubles. Varied considerations induce men to accept, and even to seek, the doubtful honour. In the first rank stand those who take upon themselves a government almost as difficult as that of Spain or France, because they are born sportsmen; because the subscription, added to their own means, enables them to enjoy more hunting than they could otherwise afford; because they are never so happy as when hunting their hounds in the season, and in attending to all the details of breeding, exercising, and training them out of season. Such men are content to shog along grass lanes with the pack at their heels for hour after hour in summer, and to spend afternoons in playing with them in some quiet nook of a park. The hounds, the kennel huntsman, and a few chosen friends deep in hound pedigree, content them for society during the best part of the year. Such men, although independent in circumstances, with moderate incomes, and no expensive tastes beyond the hunting-field, are generally popular with all the farmers of the district, and their wives! They make fair words go as far—or further—than money; they exercise infinite tact and temper in settling the inevitable difficulties of damages to fences and poultry, the still more difficult discussions with pheasant preservers and their gamekeepers, and of late years the costly negotiations for the removal of wire fences in the hunting season. When such men are also good horsemen, who, riding in front, can look the *thrusting* swells in the face when it is necessary to cry, "Hold hard!" they have less difficulty in keeping eager "fields" in order than those often capital M.F.H.'s, of mature years and heavy weight, who are obliged to trust to opened gates and easy gaps. But there are some countries where the armies of high-bred sportsmen can only be prevented from spoiling their own sport by the authority of one who combines high rank with hard-riding qualifications.

But even when everything is well managed in the kennel, the stable, and the field, when the farmers are friendly, wire-traps are removed, and foxes fairly preserved, there remain too often bitter drops at the bottom of the goblet of sport, in the shape of a meddlesome committee—of subscriptions insufficient or ill-paid—and of cantankerous supporters who persistently exercise the easy task of finding fault with the hounds, the horses, the huntsman, the style of hunting, and everything else.

Fox-hunting sport is dependent on scent—scent is the most uncertain thing in the world.

Without scent the most perfect pack cannot kill, cannot even hunt, and in the course of a few weeks will seem to lose all confidence in the most skilful huntsman. In a bad scenting season the life of a Master of hounds is one of misery at home and abroad. If he is new to the county, he and his establishment are set down as "duffers." Even if he is an old friend, some energetic new arrival in the county—some young peer or squire, fresh from the university, "who knows not Joseph"—gives the signal of discontent, which those who are always tired of "Aristides the Just" echo. The Master is "too old, too slow; he does not lift the hounds," &c. &c.; or, "is too fast and impatient." But this rising discontent will often be nipped in the bud by a change in the wind and a rapid succession of good runs and kills.

Quite different is the man who takes the management for the sake of position, and finds all or a large share of the subscriptions. The probability is that, even if he understands how to keep a respectable place with hounds, he knows little or nothing about hunting, or the equally important subject of kennel management, and maintaining the reputation of a pack by judicious breeding.

He is fortunate if his social position, style, and manner enable him to keep his "*field*" in order; still more fortunate if he obtains the services of a huntsman who thoroughly understands his business, and yet on the strength of his superior knowledge does not forget that he is the servant of the gentleman who employs him, and not of the young bloods who tip and flatter him.

Therefore, if a newly-enriched man—the son of some fortunate trader, solicitor, or contractor—determines on taking the responsibilities and honours of a M.F.H., he has one of two courses to pursue: either to qualify himself for the post by careful and assiduous study, or to confine himself to the financial and diplomatic department, leaving the practical part to his professional assistant—the huntsman.

There are two sorts of M.F.H.'s who are equally contemptible: the one who, knowing little or nothing of hunting, is continually blowing his horn and interfering with his huntsman, in order to show his authority; and the other, who, not interfering at all, allows himself to be the *butt* and the dupe of the great and imperious gentlemen for whose amusement he pays heavily and works hard.

Fox-hunting is seen under its most agreeable aspect either when the pack is the hereditary property or under the management of a gentleman "to the manner born," or where in truly rural districts it is maintained by a small body of subscribers, who are enthusiastic sportsmen, who all know each other, and to use a familiar phrase, "mean business," and nothing else.

Huntsmen, as a body, are an intelligent, sober, thoughtful class; servants not the least like the drunken reprobates who figure in the stories of the orgies of the last generation—the Tom Moodys, whose deathbeds and funerals were the occasion of scenes which sound blasphemous to a soberer generation. Tom Moody, by-the-by, was not a huntsman, but a whip; although a very great rider, he had no hunting talent to justify the hero-worship which song-writers and painters have accorded him. "He was a little eight-stone man, decidedly dirty; he would wear his boots without taking them off from Monday to Saturday. His whole existence centred in hunting; he could not read a word; his spare time in summer was spent in fishing for eels."

It is no exaggeration to say that the qualities which make a first-rate huntsman in the field are those which would also make a first-rate commander of cavalry. He must carry the geography of the country in his head, have an instinctive knowledge of the habits of the fox, a familiar acquaintance with the capabilities of every one of his hounds, and the faculty of being able to make up his mind in an instant. With these capabilities, he must be a bold, determined horseman, understand the art of bringing his pack at the commencement of each season into the highest possible condition, and know how to so select bitches and sires, and so draft the puppies of every year, as to bring them to the size and hunting qualities suited to the country, and in other respects, as near as possible to perfection in strength, speed, and hunting qualities.

Those who desire to know what a first-class huntsman at the head of a first-class establishment may be like, should read the sketches, almost photographs, of Will Goodall, huntsman of the Duke of Rutland's Belvoir Hounds, and Tom Sebright, forty years in the service of the Fitzwilliam family at Melton, by their enthusiastic biographer, "The Druid."*

SCENT.

Nothing is more mysterious than the "scent" on which fox-hunters are dependent for their sport. After a century, in which the experience of the most earnest observers has been recorded, no theory of any value has been framed.

The favourite idea of "a southerly wind and a cloudy sky," which has been embalmed in a popular hunting-song, is often found a deception and a snare. The famous poem recording the events of the great run from Billedon Caplow commences, "With the wind at north-east fordiddingly keen." Hounds have been known to run tremendously in snow-storms, rain-storms, and the coldest winds, and sometimes under a hot May sun, although that is more rare. As a rule, the best scent is found on grass, and the worst on ploughed land; and where hounds run from grass to plough, it is often found that they decline from racing breast-high to cold hunting; but there are many exceptions to this theory. For example, the Roothings of Essex are a district as flat as a billiard-table, all plough, very little under the influence of the modern system of deep draining, intersected by wide, deep, neglected ditches. There is no county in England that holds such a good scent *after* the ground is saturated with rain.

"The Druid," who never rode hunting in his life, and had the advantage of not starting with theory, has most industriously collected the opinions of a number of huntsmen and Masters of hounds. Thus, Will Goodall wrote: "I can't say I have observed any very great peculiarity of scent in any part of the country. With a north-east wind and a rising glass hounds will run over any part of it, and catch their fox; but with a *west* wind, which it has been nearly all the season, we have never had a week's good scenting." The late Squire Farquharson, who hunted Dorsetshire for nearly half a century, said: "I have known a burning scent when, according to accepted rules, there should be none; and I have known a great lack of it under the most propitious prospects; and I have seen hounds fly in a strong westerly wind, which is supposed to be most unpropitious for scent—in fact, I have seen them run in all winds and weathers. At the same time, I am inclined to think that when the quicksilver is low the atmosphere is disturbed, and scent is so fluctuating and *catching* that it varies momentarily; and that, on the contrary, when the quicksilver is steady and settled the scent is good. Dorsetshire (a dairy and hill county) cannot be called a good scenting county in a moist season; but then the *hills* and woodlands hold a good scent."

"The Puckeridge (Herts), nearly all plough, does not carry a good scent, and they like

---

* "Scott and Sebright," by "The Druid."

to force the foxes into Essex. The Puckeridge was the pack John Leech frequented, and from which he took most of his comical sketches.

"In the High Wold, Brocklesby country (a country of corn, root, and sheep farms, and a light soil, originally reclaimed from heath and rabbit-warrens), when the country is dry the scent fails. The more rain the better we go; best up to our knees and hocks in mud. In the Berkeley county (grass dairy farms) dry weather is most favourable to sport. The Cotswold Hills hold a better scent than the vale. The Beaufort county is richer land than Heythrop (Oxfordshire), has more grass, and it holds a better scent. The Duke of Grafton's county (Northamptonshire) has much grass land, and is first-rate, and so is the Pytchley, except the northern part adjoining Bedfordshire, which is notoriously the worst scenting county in the hunt."

"In Shropshire, whenever there is scent on the Haughmond Hill there is none in the valley, and the reverse holds good. The Old Berkshire shows most sport in a dry season. When scent had been bad on an October day the fog rose, and the hounds killed their fox in twenty minutes."

THE FOX-HOUND.

In no branch of breeding has the art been carried to such perfection as in the fox-hound. With definite objects, successive generations of huntsmen have selected and bred without any regard to cost, and with all the advantages of recorded pedigree which are enjoyed by the breeders of thoroughbred horses. But the breeders of racehorses constantly breed without regard to form, to soundness, or to constitution, if the blood of sire or dam promise speed. No matter what the defects of a sire that has won great races, his services will be in great demand. Not so with the fox-hound; as he is simply an instrument of pleasure, as his qualities do not win money, the breeder of the most obscure as well as of the most fashionable pack aims at the same perfections. The fox-hound must have the symmetry which insures speed and endurance, a vigorous body and limbs, with no superfluous flesh, and a full development of the chest and breathing powers. He must be keen-scented, and musical in the degree required in the country he hunts.

To all these, and other points too numerous to mention, the Masters of hounds and huntsmen of England, in continual communication with each other, have devoted their attention for more than a century, and have in that time got rid of the "crooked legs," the "dewlaps" of old English and Continental hounds, in some instances sacrificing scent and hunting qualities to speed, but always combining in a high degree hunting and racing qualities.

It is in the success with which a huntsman unites the best qualities of a hound, corrects the faults of a good bitch by putting to a stallion excellent in the qualities where she is deficient, or *vice versâ*, that the kennel excellence of a huntsman is shown.

In a pack of reputation it is important that all the dogs and bitches should be as nearly of a size as possible, whatever be the standard of the pack; dogs at the present day ranging from twenty-two inches to twenty-five inches, bitches from twenty-one to twenty-three inches. In some countries the dogs and bitches are hunted in separate packs, "ladies" being considered the fastest; in other countries, equally famous for sport, they are mixed, and then twenty-three inches is the more popular size.

Some Masters of hounds are as particular about colour as about size; others are satisfied if the pack will only hunt and race.

As to size, in the present civilised state of English agriculture the size of a fox-hound is much a matter of fancy; but where fences have to be run through small hounds are preferred, where great ditches are to be leaped a certain size is essential; little bitches get lost.

It is the mark of a high-couraged fox-hound that he flies his fences in full cry, instead of halting to look for a hole.

As to music, for which the old English and German hounds were so famous, it has been to a considerable extent diminished by the demands of pace. Certain packs of very high reputation, such as the Brocklesby and the Belvoir, having a very open country to hunt, are much more mute than those that hunt through wild and woodland countries. In Nottingham-shire, Essex, or Devonshire, a huntsman would soon be lost without the music of his hounds.

Intelligent a fox-hound must be, but not too intelligent, for such are "skirters," trying to hit off the scent right or left of the pack. Such might make capital pot-hunters in the woods of Virginia. Docility is essential, but not at the sacrifice of courage. It is not the best hounds who submit to the lash without a growl.

To a stranger to hunting there is no more extraordinary sight than that of a pack of hungry hounds crowded at a door in sight of their feeding trough, and not one venturing to come forward until called by name.

All great huntsmen are beloved by their hounds, although they could not rule them without severe discipline.

That earnest poet, Canon Kingsley, who was a daring horseman and a true sportsman, although "he never owned a horse worth fifty pounds in his life," describes "the fox-hound as the result of nature, not limited, but developed by high civilisation. Next to an old Greek statue there are few such combinations of grace and strength as in a fine fox-hound. The old savage ideal of beauty—type of mere massive force—was the lion; of grace, the fawn. Breeding and selecting, through long centuries, have created the fox-hound, which combines both types. . . . . Look at the old hound, who stands doubtful, looking up at his master for advice. Mark the severity, delicacy, lightness of every curve: his head fine as a deer's, his hind-legs as terse as steel springs, his fore-legs straight as arrows; and see the depth of his chest, the sweep of his loin, the mass of arm and thigh, the breadth of paw; and, if you have an eye for form, note the absolute majesty of his attitude. Majesty is the only word; for, if he were ten feet high, instead of twenty-three inches, with what animal on earth could you contrast him? It is a joy to see such perfection alive!"

There are other passages in the same paper, "A Concert in a Pine-wood"—the description of a hunt in Hampshire—so unlike the usual sensational pictures of life in Leicestershire, that I cannot resist the temptation of quoting them. It must be understood that the parson is riding on his old hunter through a pine-wood, to administer spiritual consolation to a poor parishioner.

"Stay! there was a sound at last—a light footfall—a hare races towards us through the ferns, her great bright eyes full of terror, her ears aloft to catch some sound behind. She sees us, turns short, and vanishes into the gloom. The mare pricks up her ears too, listens, and looks: but not the way the hare has gone. There is something more coming. Besides, that hare was not travelling in search of food. She was not 'loafing' along, looking around her right and left, but galloping steadily. She has been frightened; she has been put up; but what has put her up? And there, far away among the fir-stems, rings the shriek of a startled blackbird. What has put him rife?

"'Stand still, old mare! Do you think still, after fifteen winters, that you can catch a fox?'

"A fox it is indeed; a great dog-fox, as red as the fir-stems between which he glides. And yet his legs are black with fresh peat stains. He is a hunted fox, but he has not been up long.

"The mare stands like a statue, but I can feel her trembling between my knees. Positively he does not see us. He sits down in the middle of a ride, turns his great ears right and left, and then scratches one of them with his hind foot, seemingly to make it hear the better. Now he is up again, and on.

"Beneath yon fir, some hundred yards away, standeth, or rather lieth, for it is on dead, flat ground, the famous castle of Malepartius. I know it well; a patch of sand-heaps, mingled with great holes, amid the twining fir-roots; ancient home of the last wild beasts. Full-blown in self-satisfaction, he trots, lifting his toes delicately, and carrying his brush aloft, full of cunning and conceit.

"Suddenly he halts at the great gate of Malepartius; examines it with his nose; goes on to a postern, examines that also, and then another and another. 'Ah, Reineke! fallen is thy conceit, and fallen thy tail therewith. Man has been beforehand with thee, and the earths are stopped!'

"One moment he sits down to meditate, and scratches those trusty counsellors, his ears, as if he would tear them off, 'revolving swift thoughts in a crafty mind.' He has settled it now. He is up and off, and at what a pace, and with what a grace besides!

"Shall I notify? Shall I waken the echoes? Shall I break the grand silence by that scream which the vulgar *view halloo* call? It is needless; for louder every moment swells up a sound at which my heart leaps into my mouth, and my mare into the air.

"And now appear, dim at first and distant, but brightening and nearing fast, many a right good fellow, and many a right good horse.

"There is music, again, if you listen, in the soft tread of those hundred horse-hoofs upon the springy, vegetable soil. They are trotting now in 'common time.' You may hear the whole Croats' March (the finest trotting-march in the world) played by those iron heels; the time, as it does in the Croats' March, breaking now and then, plunging, jingling, struggling through heavy ground, bursting for a moment into a jubilant canter as it reaches a sound spot.

"The hounds feather a moment round Malepartius, puzzled by the winding of Reineke's footsteps. I can hear the flap and snort of the dogs' nostrils as they canter round me; and I like it—it is exciting; but why!—who can tell?

"I cap them on to the spot at which Reineke disappeared.

"Old Virginal's stern flourishes; instantly her pace quickens; one whimper, and she is away, full-mouthed, through the wood, and the pack after her: but not I. I am not going with them. My hunting days are over. Let it suffice that I have, in the days of my vanity, drunk delight of battle with my peers far on the ringing plains of many a country, grass and forest, down and vale.

"And hounds and huntsmen are already far ahead—are racing up the Roman road. Racing, indeed; for as Reineke gallops up the narrow heather-fringed pathway, *he brushes off his scent upon the twigs at every stride, and the hounds race after him*, showing no head, indeed, and keeping, for convenience, in one long line upon the track; but going, *heads up, sterns down*, at a pace which no horse can follow. I only hope they may not overrun the scent.

"They have overrun it; they halt, and put their heads down a moment. But with one swift cast, in full gallop, they have hit it off again, fifty yards away in the heather, long ere the horsemen are up to them; for those hounds can hunt a fox, because they are not hunted themselves, and so have learnt to trust themselves, and act for themselves, as boys should learn at school, even at the risk of a mistake or two. Now they are showing head, indeed, down a half-cleared valley, and over a few ineffectual turnips, withering in the heart of the wilderness, and then over the brook, while I turn slowly away, through a green wilderness of self-sown firs.

"Hark! a faint, dreary hallo off the moor above. And then another and another. My friends may trust it, for the clod of these parts delights in the chase like any bare-legged Paddy, and casts away flail and fork wildly to run, shout, assist, and interfere in all possible ways, out of pure love!"

The following candid account of a bad bold horseman's first experience of hunting and leaping will appropriately complete this part of my subject:—

"I am at Milton," writes Charles Sumner, the American statesman (so unfavourably known to this generation of Englishmen), "passing my Christmas week with Lord Fitzwilliam. Here I have been enjoying fox-hunting to the imminent danger of my limbs and neck. That they still remain intact is a miracle. I think I have never participated in anything more exciting than this exercise. After my arrival, I mounted at half-past nine o'clock a beautiful hunter, and rode with Lord Milton about six miles to the place of meeting. There were the hounds, and huntsmen, and whippers-in, and about eighty horsemen—the noblemen and gentry, and clergy of the neighbourhood, all beautifully mounted, and the greater part in red coats, leather breeches, and white top-boots. The hounds were sent into the cover, and it was a grand sight to see so many handsome dogs all of a size, and all washed before coming out, rushing into the underwood to start the fox. We did not get a scent immediately, and rode from cover to cover; but soon the cry was raised, 'Tally-ho'—the horn was blown, the dogs barked, the horsemen rallied, the hounds scented their way through the cover on the trail of the fox, and then started in full run. I had originally intended only to ride to cover to see them throw off, and then make my way home believing myself unequal to the probable run; but the chase commenced, and I was in the midst of it, and, being excellently mounted, nearly at the head of it. Never did I see such a scamper, and never did it enter into my head that horses could be pushed to such speed in such places. We dashed through and over bushes, leaping broad ditches, splashing in brooks and mud, and passing over fences as so many imaginary lines. My first fence I shall not readily forget. I was near Lord Milton, who was mounted on a thoroughbred horse. He cleared a fence before him. My horse pawed the ground and neighed. I gave him the rein and he cleared the fence. As I was up in the air for one moment, how I was startled to look down and see that there was not only a fence, but a *ditch!* He cleared the ditch too. I have said it was my first experiment. I lost my balance, was thrown to the very ears of the horse, but in some way or other contrived to work myself back to the saddle without touching the ground. How I got back I cannot tell, but I did regain my seat, and my horse was at a run in a moment. All this, you will understand, passed in less time by far than it will take to read this account. One moment we were in a scamper through a ploughed field, another over a beautiful pasture, and another winding through the devious paths of a wood. I have said that I mounted at nine and a half o'clock. It wanted twenty minutes to five when I finally dismounted, not having been out of the saddle more than thirty seconds during all this time, and then only to change my horse, taking a fresh one from a groom who was in attendance. During much of this time we were on a full run.

"The next day had its incidents. The place of meeting for the hounds was about fourteen miles from the house. Our horses were previously led thither by grooms, and we rode there in a carriage and four with outriders, and took our horses fresh. This day I met with a fall. The country was very rough, and the fences often quite stiff and high. I rode among the foremost, and on going over a fence and a brook together, came to the ground. My horse cleared them both; and I cleared him, for I went directly over his head. Of course he started off, but was soon caught by Lord Milton and a parson who had already made the leap successfully. The best and hardest rider in this part of the country is reputed to be a clergyman, and there was not a day that I was out that I did not see three or four persons rejoicing in the style of 'Reverend,' and distinguishable from the rest of the *habitués* by wearing a black instead of a red coat. They were among the foremost in every field. Once we came to a very stiff rail fence; the hounds were not in full cry; there was a general stop to see how the different horses and riders would take it. Many were afraid, and several horses refused it. Soon, however, the Rev. Mr. Nash, a clergyman of some fifty years, came across the field, and the cry was raised, 'Hurrah for Nash! Now for Nash!' I need not say that he went over it easily. It was the Rev. Mr. Nash who caught my horse. None of the clergymen who were out were young men, they were all more than forty-five, if not fifty.

"Dinner was early, because the sportsmen return fatigued, and without having tasted a morsel of food since an early breakfast. So after our return we only had time to dress, and at five and a half o'clock assembled in the library, from which we went into dinner. You have in proper succession soup, fish, venison, and the large English dishes, besides a profusion of French *entrées*, with ice-cream, and an ample dessert—Madeira, sherry, claret, port, and champagne. We do not sit long at table, but return to the library, which opens into two or three drawing-rooms, and is itself used as the principal one, where we find the ladies already at their embroidery and also coffee. Conversation goes on languidly. The boys are sleepy, and Lord Fitzwilliam is serious and melancholy, and very soon I am glad to kill off an hour or so by a game at cards. About eleven o'clock I am glad to retire to my chamber, which is a very large apartment with two large oriel windows, looking out upon the lawn where the deer are feeding. There I find a glowing fire, and in one of the various easy-chairs sit and muse while the fire burns, or resort to the pen, ink, and paper, which are carefully placed on the table near me."—*From Memorials of Charles Sumner.*

THE HUNTING SEASON.

The hunting season commences with the wild deer of Exmoor in the middle of August; in September the hare is hunted in those districts of moorland and down-land where there are no crops to be damaged by the sport. Fox-hunting properly commences in November, cub hunting as soon as the corn crops are harvested, and the season finishes, in most counties, about the last week of March, although in purely grass and woodland counties a May-fox is often killed if the season is favourable to scent.

From Norman times to the reign of George III. hunting was pursued all the year round. The "Spectator" arrived on a visit to Sir Roger de Coverley on the last day of June, and writes, "Sir Roger is so keen at this sport (hunting with *stop*-hounds, a sort of slow beagles) that he has been out almost every day since I came here."

Throughout Queen Anne's reign the farmers complained piteously of the losses they suffered of hounds and horses galloping through standing corn. Pamphlets were written, and every sort of appeal resorted to, in vain. "The Queen herself followed the hounds in a chaise with one horse, 'which,' says Swift, 'she drives herself, and drives furiously, like Jehu; and is a mighty hunter, like Nimrod.' She was, if Stella's journalist did not exaggerate, quite equal to runs even longer than those performed by the Coverley hounds; for on the 7th August, 1711, she drove before dinner five-and-forty miles after a stag."

It was not until George III., the "farmer's friend," came to the throne, and exercised a personal influence over legislation, that the abuse was abolished, and an Act passed by which the sport was limited to those months in autumn and winter which the old Saxon Chronicle had originally fixed as the "hunters' months."

The keen young sportsman, with time and money at command, may thus commence in Somersetshire in August, and if in September cub-hunting does not satisfy him, may hunt hares on Salisbury Plains, on the downs of the south coast, and the moorlands north, until November, when the best sport will be found in counties where there are no ditches, like the hill stonewall countries of Oxfordshire and Worcestershire. When winter frosts and rains have cleared leaves from hedges, and the rank growth of weeds from the ditches, then sport in the flying countries can be enjoyed in the utmost perfection with the least danger. In a damp spring, fine sport is to be had even up to the second week of May, in a country of pastures and woodlands. But not only crops have to be considered, but lands. Drainage is supposed to be hostile to scent, but it makes fields rideable that previously brought the best horses to a walk. "In that fifty-acre field," said the late Lord Berners at Keythorpe, to the writer, "I have seen five hundred horsemen brought to a standstill. Now you may gallop over it." Wire-fencing and the increase of sheep-feeding are the greatest obstacles to fox-hunting. More than forty years ago, at Wentworth House, the American Sumner "sat at dinner with Earl Spencer. We talked about hunting, which is now just beginning. He said he used to keep a pack of hounds formerly, and that the relations into which it brought him with his neighbours and the county had taught him more of human nature than he had learnt in any other way. *The whole affair of fox-hunting, he added, with all its trespasses upon property, could not be maintained if the whole neighbourhood did not take as great an interest in it as the owner of the hounds."*

THE FOX-HUNTERS' CLUB.

Boodle's, in St. James' Street, was until 1880 the fox-hunters' club *par excellence.* A dingy-looking establishment outside and in, as little like such modern clubs as the Travellers' or the Carleton, as the Cock in Fleet Street is like the Criterion in Piccadilly. Boodle's was established about a hundred years ago as a resort for country gentlemen who liked better dinners than the taverns of that day supplied. All Masters of established packs of fox-hounds belonged to it. They had an annual dinner, at which present and past M.F.H.'s exchanged notes on kennel questions, and fought the hunting-battles o'er again.

Disputes on questions of the unwritten law of fox-hunting, as to the limits of districts and the right to covers, were referred to the arbitration of the " Fox-hunting committee of Boodle's." But in 1880 the members had reason to find fault with rules the proprietor insisted on imposing on the members. The hunting men retired in a body, and Boodle's seems likely to lose all that made it distinguished.

HUNTING TERMS.

Hunting has its special vocabulary terms, a knowledge of which is essential for comprehending hunting conversation and reports. The proper pronunciation can only be acquired from *vivâ voce* instruction. My list has been partly compiled from the work of a great practical authority, Tom Smith—"Gentleman Smith," as he was called, to distinguish him from the wealthy hard rider, Assheton Smith. Gentleman Smith had but a very moderate private fortune, and was some fifty years ago what may be called a professional Master of hounds. He hunted the Hursley pack as far back as 1828, and boasted that with his own hounds, in that bad-scenting country, he had killed ninety foxes in ninety-one days' hunting. When he published the third edition of his "Diary of a Huntsman" in 1852, he was Master of the "Pychely" (*sic*) Hounds.*

Cover or *Covert* (spelt both ways).—Any wood, furze, gorse, rushes, heath, or sedge that will hold a fox. Artificial covers are sometimes manufactured of bundles of faggots.

Cover Hoick.—The huntsman's cry to encourage hounds on "throwing off" to rush into cover.

Eloo in, Yoi over, Edawick, Eadawick, Yoi wind him, Yoi rouse him, my boys, are similar encouragements, especially used in very large covers where the pack are out of sight.

Hoick, Hector, means Hark to Hector, a hound who may be depended on, and who has challenged, and may be continued with.

Have at him, old fellow.

Hoick together, Hoick.—To encourage when several hounds are heard, and are getting together.

Taaleo.—When a fox is viewed in cover by the huntsman.

Tally-o-back.—When the fox comes out and heads back again.

Tally-o-over.—When a fox has crossed a ride in a wood.

Ta-a-le-o.—When one of the field sees a fox clear away, to call the attention of the huntsman.

Hooi (after Tally-ho, away).—A shout to call hounds, if at a distance, on viewing a fox.

Gone away.—The huntsman's cry.

Elope, forrard, away.—Ditto.

Yo hote, yo hote, there.—Huntsman to make hounds hunt when at a check.

Forrard, forrard, hoick.—When some hounds have hit off the scent, to call on the rest.

Yo geote.—To call back hounds.

Hoick halloo, Hoick halloo.—When a halloo is heard from some one who has viewed the fox at a distance.

Burst.—The first part of a run, if quick.

Burst him.—A term used when a fox is killed without a chance of a check.

Burning Scent.—When hounds run almost mute, owing to the goodness of the scent.

Breast-high.—When the scent is so hot that the hounds have no need to stoop their heads to the ground to catch it, but can go at a racing pace.

Carry a good Head.—When the scent is good and spread out, so that it extends wide enough for the whole pack to feel it, and run well together. More frequently the scent is only good on the line, for one hound to get it, so that the rest follow and depend upon him. Hence

Line Hunters.—Hounds that will not go a yard beyond the scent, and keep the pack right; invaluable hounds.

* I have heard that Tom Smith was one of three brothers, all remarkable in their way : he for the sport he showed on a very small income and subscription ; the Rev. Samuel Smith, author of the Lois Weedon system of growing good crops of wheat year after year without manure ; and William Smith of Woolston, who was the first to produce a steam tackle that could be profitably used by tenants of small farms with small fields.

Crash.—When every hound in cover is throwing his tongue.

Cold Hunting.—When hounds can scarcely feel a scent, and pick it out with difficulty. "After a burst of ten minutes we came on the plough, and fell to *cold hunting.*"

Dwelling.—When hounds do not run up to a huntsman's holloa, perhaps feeling a cold scent, will not stir until moved by the whipper-in, or perhaps having lost confidence in the huntsman after a series of bad days. A slow huntsman is apt to dwell.

Full Cry.—When the whole pack are running hard and throwing their tongues.

Holding Scent.—Exactly the reverse. When the scent is quite good enough for hounds to hunt a fox a fair pace, but not enough to satisfy those who only come out to gallop and jump.

Lifting.—When hounds have checked and lost scent, or are scarcely able to over it across bad scenting ground, the huntsman, either because he hears a holloa forward from some one who has seen the travelling fox, or on calculation, *lifts* them forward, for the chance of getting on terms with the fox. This is contrary to the theory and feelings of the best sportsmen, who like to see the hounds do their own work; for, if hounds are continually lifted, they will always be looking to the huntsman, and will not hunt. On the other hand, there would be no sport if hounds were never lifted, either where the county is intersected by tracts of ground that hold no scent, or where, as in the fashionable counties, horsemen in hundreds so press on the pack that they cannot get room to hunt until the *mob* has been stalled off by a quick gallop over severe fencing.

Metal.—When hounds are very fresh and fly without scent, that is called metal.

Moving scent.—When hounds get on the scent of a fox disturbed in travelling; a scent fresher than a drag.

Mute.—Hounds run mute when the scent is so good that they gallop at such a pace that they cannot throw their tongues. A hound that runs mute, even if in every other respect the best hound in the pack, is a nuisance.

Riot.—When hounds hunt anything besides the fox, the call is "Ware riot! ware hare!'' Good hounds have been known to hunt cur dogs, and even a galloping donkey.

Heel.—When hounds, instead of following the fox, run back over the scent the way they came.

Sinking.—When a fox is nearly beaten.

Sinking the wind.—When men go down wind to catch the cry of the hounds.

Streaming.—When hounds go across an open county like a flock of pigeons, it is called "streaming away."

Tailing.—When hounds in a chase run in a line and not abreast—generally owing to a bad scent or the pack not being equal in pace—a common fault in "scratch" packs.

Scratch pack.—A pack composed of hounds begged or purchased, of any size or sort, anywhere, under an emergency, or for the sake of making up a cheap pack in a hurry.

CHAPTER XXIII.

PREPARATION OF THE HUNTER FOR—TREATMENT DURING AND AFTER—HUNTING.

Importance of Condition in a Hunter—Results of Ignorance Fifty Years Ago—A Brutal Age—Anecdote of Sir Harry Vane Tempest—"Nimrod" (Apperley)—The Reformer in Treating Hunters—Hunters Rarely Die of Over-Exertion now—Winter Condition to be Preserved through the Summer—Horses in Daily Use in Summer stand Hunting Best in Winter—Equally Important for Cobs or Ponies—Condition Explained by a Correspondent of *The Field*—How to Train a Stud of Hunters—Where Expense is not an Object—Value of Oats and Beans—How to Sweat a Hunter—Exercise—Flannel Bandages—Water—Must be Pure—Colonel Fitzwygram's Plan—A Summer's Run for Hunters in a Carriage—Dick Christian's Plan of Training—Use of Sawdust instead of Straw—How to Treat Hunters during a Frost or Snow-storm—Importance of Mashes—How to Make them—Value of Water in the Hunting-field—After Hunting Hard, Rest—At First Shelter—Gruel, how Made—How to Treat and Feed a Tired Horse—Importance of Fresh Air and Warm Clothing—Tired Horses to be Gruelled before they are Groomed—Mud Fever—A Great Pest—Three Letters on—Hot Water and Bandages—Cold Water and Bandages—No Water and Bandages—No Bandages, no Water—Clipping and Singeing—Origin of—Both Plans Described—Necessity no longer Disputed—New Clipping Machine Superseded Scissors—How to Clip Legs—Leave Nose, Eyes, and Ears Alone—Hunting Dress—To be Studied for Comfort—Great Improvement in this Generation—George the Fourthian Style Described—The Principles of Modern Hunting Coat—Colours—Scarlet for Choice—Waistcoat with Warm Back—Flap-Pockets—Breeches—Decline, Fall, and Rise again of Leather Breeches—Breeches-cutting a Fine Art—Boots, Varieties of Tops—Napoleons—Butchers—History and Description—Gloves—Buckskins no longer Worn—Whips—Spurs—The Hunting-Box—Principles of Construction—Warmth—Ventilation—Supplies of Water, Hot and Cold—Aim Maximum of Comfort, Minimum of Servants—Hunting Cottage for Six Bachelors Described—Or One Married Man—Ground-floor Dressing-room—How Furnished—Baths, Variety of—Drying-room for Cloths—Kitchen, its Hot Water Boilers—Doors, a New Style—Covered Passage to Stables—Lamps, Use of—Sportsmen's Fare—Principles of—Quickly Cooked—Appetising—Digestible, Nourishing—No Dishes that require Punctuality—How to Arrange a Series, from Soup to Cheese, and Nothing Spoiled—Breakfasts—Various Tastes—The Fox-Hunting Sandwich-Case—A Hunting-Meet Breakfast—How to Give.

To make the best of a hunter he must be properly trained, before the hunting season commences, into the condition required for extraordinary exertions in galloping and leaping; he must be treated with due consideration during the hours of hunting, judiciously cared for on his way home and after he reaches home.

Fifty years ago it was quite common to hear, after a very severe run in a fashionable county, of numbers of horses disabled for the season, and some killed in the field. In a brutal, bull-fighting, dog-fighting, man-fighting age,* it seems, from the accounts of great runs, to have been considered almost a sign of spirit in a sportsman to have ridden his horse to death.

You seldom hear of any accident of the kind now, for several reasons: condition is better understood, it is no longer the practice to bleed exhausted horses, and brutality is not now considered a sign of spirit.

English fox-hunters owe a deep debt of gratitude to "Nimrod" (Apperley) for his "Letters on the Condition of Hunters," published in the first quarter of the present century. His arguments

---

* Sir Harry Vane Tempest, the maternal grandfather of the present Marquis of Londonderry, who died, aged forty, in 1813, was one of the handsomest men of his time, and good-natured; yet he made a bet with Harvey Aston that he would knock down the first man that came into the stand at Newmarket, and won it. The turf, hunting, boxing, cockfighting, and drinking—the last killed him—were his pursuits; he did not gamble. He caused some sensation in 1799 by winning the Doncaster St. Leger with "Cockfighter," and riding him in the Park on Sunday, ten days afterwards—the Park being then crowded by the fashionable world. From Sir Harry the Marquis of Londonderry inherits the Durham Winyard property.—*Raikes' Journal.*

were not always as sound as his conclusions. Before "Nimrod" revolutionised the system of training hunters it was the custom, at the end of the hunting season, to turn a stud, the sound as well as the sick, out to grass on the richest pastures that could be got. Thus, every autumn, before the hunting season commenced, all the hard muscular condition of the previous season having been lost, it became necessary to spend valuable time in getting rid of the grass-fat of those hunters that did not come up broken-winded, or otherwise unsound, from the effects of their summer run, to the serious detriment of their legs and feet, before commencing their training for fast work.

Condition means the highest degree of health combined with the utmost muscular and respiratory powers.

The two extremes of *condition* are presented by a horse quite fat after six months on the grass of a rich pasture, and a racehorse trained until he is all bone and muscle, raced until he can with difficulty be kicked along a road, and can only be made to gallop by the instinct of the racecourse, and the hands and spurs of the jockey. There are, of course, many sub-varieties of bad condition; as, for instance, the mean man's hunter, with half the proper allowance of oats, hunted twice a week; or the ignorant, rich man's stud, whose horses, stuffed with corn and beans for the benefit of the corn-dealer, stay idle in the stable to save the groom's trouble.

Stated roundly, "Nimrod's" theory—now generally accepted—was that when once a hunter was in hard condition he should never be allowed to fall out of it until he was invalided; that he should be fed with a proportion of oats in summer, be kept in gentle exercise, and should only be entirely rested and fed on grass or soft food when really sick, or suffering from over-work in his feet or legs.

The common sense of "Nimrod's" theory was very soon made clear to hunting-men. Prize-fighting was one of the fashions of the day, and it was noted that Cribb, Belcher, and other fighting celebrities, were more easily trained for the prize-ring when fresh from hard work than when they had led the life of publicans; and that, in the same way, horses always fed on dry, compact food--good hay and oats—and exercised, not tired out, were ready to go through a hard run, or a long, dragging day in November, without ill effects; while those which had been fed on grass all the summer were not "fit" before Christmas, when they did not die of inflammation after a brilliant performance. Even at the present day, when every stud-groom understands the value of condition, cavalry officers on their second chargers, and men who ride horses that have had "a summer's run" as leaders in a drag, or as phaeton pairs, will generally be found in the best places in long, hard runs, on the autumn side of Christmas.

Condition is as essential for a cob or pony intended to hunt as for a blood hunter, because in the excitement of the chase every one is apt to forget the limits of equine endurance.

There is no fall so dangerous as that of a pumped-out half-conditioned animal, for he not only tumbles over a sheep-hurdle three feet high, or a ditch four feet wide, but lies on you after he has tumbled.

In studs of horses of moderate extent, where all except cripples are made useful all the year round, either under saddle or in harness, as long as they are in health, if they have a copious mash at least once a week—if on very high feed, and are rested twice a week— they will require no physic.

This mash should be composed of a quartern of oats for each horse, and a pint of linseed boiled at least three hours, then thrown into one or more glazed red pottery-pans, mixed with as much bran as will bring it to the proper damp condition of a mash, covered with a cloth, and left until it is quite or nearly cold, according as each horse prefers it. The object of adding the oats is to give it an appetising flavour which will tempt many horses that refuse a plain bran mash. A little salt, or for a sick horse treacle sugar, may be added with advantage.

In the last generation the practice of bleeding and physicking man and beast on the slightest or without any excuse was universal. The purging mania still prevails in some stables, as well as that of giving mysterious balls, condition balls, urine balls, and putting nitre and other nasty messes in the horses' water.

Nothing of the kind should ever be permitted, except on competent medical advice. Scores of horses are still killed every year through the quackery of grooms and uneducated farriers.

On the point of forbidding bleeding and physicking the master should be peremptory, whether he himself understands anything about horses or not.

"If a hunter doing five hours' exercise daily cannot eat five quarterns of mixed oats and beans, with a mash every Wednesday and Saturday, he should be turned out of the hunting to the hack or harness stable. The horse that cannot eat cannot work without becoming weak, and a weak hunter is useless.

"Of water there should be no limit. A large consumption of water is a sign of health." Water should be pure, in clean receptacles, not too cold, and not, on the other hand, allowed to stand in the stable to attract its impurities. A handful of hay, or a little bran or meal, will take the chill off water better than anything else. Warm water disgusts most horses; others will empty the pail of nearly hot water brought to wash them. The groom's panacea of nitre in water, and all farrier's messes, are to be sternly rejected. "If a horse roars he wants more, not less water. He should have water always by him, and a little drink whenever there is a chance in the hunting-field." This is exactly the reverse of the ordinary ignorant practice.

Colonel Fitzwygram* recommends that hunters should be driven as pairs in light carriages during the summer. Leaders in four-in-hands would do as well, as leaders do none of the serious work of stopping, backing, and starting a coach. Some persons summer hunters on tan, in boxes, with cut green food, and never have them dressed, but this must be a great mistake.

Dick Christian's ideas on the subject, as compressed in the following extracts, were those of a practical man, but they applied to young horses in their first season :—

"Begin with plenty of walking exercise, three or four hours every day, divided into at least two rides, and never make him sweat. The hay must be last year's, the very best, but with a horse fresh from grass you may begin with mow-hay, *i.e.*, hay of that summer ; gradually increase the quantity of oats, beginning with one peck a day. The best exercise-ground is up-hill for improving the wind, and over ridge and furrow for action. Without action the best-looking horse is like a pump without a handle. After the first week the walk may be exchanged every hour for a quarter of an hour's slow trotting, which may be gradually increased to half an hour—but not too much of it. The less you gallop hunters the better, if they are in hard condition and fresh on their legs ; with racehorses it is quite a different thing. No hunters should be galloped so hard as to find out their best paces until they are put to the test in the hunting-field. Many good horses are spoiled by such tricks."

* "Lectures on Stable Management," by Colonel Fitzwygram.

Atwood Bignall, of Croydon, who used to have a hundred hunters in his "Derby stables," belonging to subscribers hunting from London—many of them with those flyers the Surrey Stag-hounds- -used to say, "I leave my gentlemen to get the flesh off their horses;" but this was hard flesh, for nothing but first-rate condition could carry a stag-hunter up and down the Surrey Hills; and no Melton stud-groom ever turned out hunters more fit.

Digby Collins' recommendation of five feeds a day does not meet with universal acceptance; four feeds a day are the rule in very good stables. But there is one indisputable rule—a horse should never have more than he will finish at one time; he must always leave a clean manger. For this reason delicate feeders must have little and often; but delicate feeders have no business in the stable of a man whose horses are expected to be useful servants, not mere luxuries.

The horse of the fox-hunter will frequently be twelve hours under saddle without any food, except what he may get at a roadside inn. In fashionable counties, on the days that the hounds are out, every public-house with a stable prepares gruel, and gets ready for the custom of stray sportsmen; but in wild countries you may travel mile after mile, since coaching and posting disappeared, without meeting any better accommodation than a cow-house.

Under these circumstances the question is, whether hunters would or would not bear fasting better if they were not fed so frequently. There is a good deal to be said on both sides of the question—so much that I shall not venture to give my own opinion, but content myself with quoting the following letter, signed "Q.C.," which appeared in *The Field*.

"For many years I have accustomed my hunters to only three feeds per day—viz., first at 6 a.m., second at noon (only a small piece of hay), and the third at 6 p.m., so that on hunting-days my horses only miss the small feed in the middle of the day. Since I have adopted only three feeds per day, my hunters not only look fit to go, but after a hard day come home cheerily, and feed well. They are frequently out of their stable twelve hours, having usually long distances to covert." If the feeds are three, the horses must have the same quantity of corn and beans as if their feeds were divided into four.

Where hunters stand in loose boxes, as they should if possible, they are, if gross feeders, apt to eat part of their straw litter in the night, if they are not, like racehorses, muzzled. There are objections to the muzzle, and the difficulty may be got over by substituting a deep layer of sawdust or spent tan for straw. The hunter should have his usual supply of water to sip with his food on the night before hunting.

When hunters are wound up to high condition, if their daily exercise is stopped by a heavy fall of snow, or any other cause, they must be immediately put on bran mashes, most of their corn and all their beans stopped, otherwise the effect of large feeds of stimulating food is almost sure to produce attacks of inflammation, ending in roaring, ophthalmia, fever of the feet, and a host of diseases which will be still more dangerous if, to keep their coats sleek and shining, the stables are deprived of supplies of fresh air, and turned into the groom's paradise—a sort of hothouse.

If a hunter has to walk for an hour to cover-side, a bucket of water an hour before he starts will do him more good than harm. On the way to cover, after walking about half an hour, he should be taken into a stable to tempt him to stale. If this is not done, when he gets to cover-side he is likely to get erected, and not able to stale. This applies more to geldings than to mares. It also applies to horses doing a long journey in harness. In the field, in the intervals which are constantly occurring between hounds finding and running, he should be allowed to slake his thirst, without overloading his stomach, at any clean water. The man who would, after violent exercise, be seriously injured by drinking a quart of cold water, would be wonderfully refreshed by drinking the contents of a wine-glass. It is necessary to avoid loading the stomach of or chilling a horse, but that is quite a different thing from keeping him in a state of thirst, which will soon become fever. On the way home, after a severe run, on a long, dragging day, with ten or more miles to complete before reaching your own stable, the first opportunity should be taken of riding your horse through a shallow pond or ford, in order to wash the dirt off his legs and belly. This is said to be one means of preventing mud-fever. A halt should be made at the first place where shelter and gruel, or some substitute, can be obtained.

Gruel is best made of oatmeal, mixed with about a gallon of water, brought to the boil, and then turned into a bucket, to be filled up with cold water; but when oatmeal is not at hand wheat-meal or barley-meal may be substituted. If neither is to be obtained, a stale loaf, cut up and soaked in water, makes a very useful horse-soup, to which a few pinches of salt may be added. A carrot or two sliced up will tempt a feverish horse; and if he hesitates to drink his gruel let him commence with a couple of quarts of cold water.

It is not advisable to give an over-tired horse, or any horse on a journey, a quantity of hay, or even oats. The concentrated fodder recently invented by Mr. Goode is so portable that two cakes can be carried in the hunting-coat pockets. Horses greedily eat it, and digest it well.*

When a horse is thoroughly exhausted, a bottle of beer, strengthened with a glass of spirits, may be given with advantage. On no account should he be bled, except under the advice of a competent veterinary surgeon. All farriers like to bleed; it shows practice. It is not a bad plan to teach hunters at home to like beer; then the trouble of drenching, on an emergency, may be saved.

An exhausted horse, halted on his way home, needs *warmth and fresh air*. The warmth must be obtained by putting him out of draughts, bandaging his legs in flannel, and covering his loins with blankets or coats, if horse-rugs are not to be had. But fresh air to breathe is essential. How often do half a dozen well-meaning, thoughtless young fellows, excited by a capital run, leave their tired animals to the hands of some ignorant ostler, who crams them pell-mell into a close stable or cow-house, closes every chink where air could get in, and puts before them an ample supply of hay and oats! Presently, while the sportsmen are thoroughly enjoying themselves over a good fire, refreshments, and gossip, the ostler disturbs them with, "Please, gents, the chestnut horse is took very bad." Very likely foul air and unfit food will have disabled a good hunter for the season. If there's a cow-doctor near, and he, to stop the fearful action of the heart, bleeds the poor chestnut, he is pretty sure to be dead before morning.

In wild hunting countries a hard rider will do well to carry a set of flannel bandages in his overcoat case, to help to quicken the circulation of a tired horse.

It is not a good plan to torment an exhausted horse with elaborate grooming. Bandage his legs in their dirt, never wash his legs, dry his legs with sawdust and his ears by pulling them, put a cloth over his loins, get him to take some drink, and if he is much covered with dry sweat and mud, be content with slightly brushing him over with a damp brush until he gets into his own stable, where his own groom will know how to treat him. A bucket of linseed tea is a good thing for a hunter's first drink in his own box.

* Goode, Blackett Steam Mills, Bow, London.

The rider likes to be met in his dressing-room, before he takes off his boots, with a breakfast-cup of good *consommé*, or of tea, to support him under the exertion of undressing and dressing ; and so, too, the good horse should have something to cheer him before undergoing the salutary "shampooing," which is the true word for first-class grooming.

It has been assumed throughout in these instructions to the young fox-hunter that either his horses, being thoroughbred, carry a fine coat through the winter in spite of living in a healthy, cool stable, or that they have been duly clipped or singed, a practice once as much disputed as that of summering hunters in stables instead of in grass land, and now just as completely settled in favour of the artificial system. The man who insists on riding a hunter in a long rough coat should confine himself to a maximum pace of eight miles an hour. The man who keeps his stables hot in order that his hunters' coats may shine is only to be compared to the Chinaman who burned down his house to roast a pig.

MUD-FEVER.

Mud-fever is an irritation of the legs and belly, which often breaks out in wet seasons so acutely as to stop horses in their work; it has usually been supposed to be caused by want of care in washing and drying the hunter's legs after returning home; but balance of evidence is against washing.

"Some years ago," wrote Mr. Oliver to *The Field*, in 1874, "I asked an acquaintance, a very hard rider with stag-hounds, how he managed with his horses, as he often left off long distances from home, would make for the nearest railway station, give his horse a feed, put him into a train without clothing, seldom reaching home before ten or eleven o'clock. Did not his horses get cold or mud-fever? 'No,' he said; 'mine never do, because I won't have a spark of mud touched until next morning!' Now, I had been used to insist on my horses being groomed after hunting till they would not 'soil a white glove;' but, in spite of all the care taken of them, they were unfortunate, while my acquaintance's horses, more roughly treated, always looked well, and one thing was patent to those who hunted with him—he was bad to beat.

"I've tried both ways, and now neither in summer nor winter will I allow a horse's legs to be washed or bandaged. My hunters are clipped, legs and all; as they come in from hunting, so they stay till next morning, not a spark of mud is removed, and they escape mud-fever."

CLIPPING AND SINGEING.

Horses change or moult their hair, except the mane and tail, twice a year—in the autumn and in the spring. In the autumn they cast the fine silky glossy coat of summer, and by degrees put on a coarser hair, thick in proportion to the quality of the animal, and the cold he has to endure. Shetland and Highland ponies carry a fleece as thick and as long as Lincoln sheep, while thorough-bred horses in training, which are always under cover, when not at exercise, heavily clothed, and carefully groomed, are generally as sleek in winter as in summer.

There is no doubt that a great many horses are every winter oppressed by the growth of a natural great coat, which might be reduced materially, in weight and coarseness, by extra care and work on the part of the grooms who have charge of them. But such efforts take time. Time is money, and the whole tendency of the nineteenth century has been to save time and money whenever possible by mechanical means.

More than fifty years ago it was the common practice in the south of France and the north of Spain to clip mules in the spring with a pair of sheep-shears. The idea of clipping horses was first introduced into this country by officers of our army, who had seen it practised during the Peninsular War in Spain. At any rate, the practice was discussed as a novelty by "Nimrod," in the old *Sporting Magazine*, in 1825, and it was still under discussion in 1840, when Stewart published the last edition of his capital book on "Stable Economy."

After clipping came singeing, and one or other is in use every autumn in almost every stable of horses used for fast work, either in saddle or harness.

Here and there one may meet with some gentleman, or professor of the old school, who protests against depriving the horse of his native protection against winter cold, as a base concession to the laziness of grooms, but the world of horse-owners does not stop to argue with them, but goes on clipping or singeing every autumn, greatly to the relief of both horses and servants.

It may safely be taken for granted that there must be substantial merit in any practice, process, or nutriment that is adopted after violent opposition. According to some enthusiasts, the world is being slowly poisoned by the continued use of tea, coffee, and tobacco, while others trace "all the ills that flesh is heir to" to the consumption of salt. But no one listens to them, because daily experience contradicts their theories and their facts.

If you have a horse with a naturally fine coat, and if you can secure his getting the amount of grooming that will keep his coat silky through the winter season, by all means keep away the clipping machine and the singeing-iron. But this is rarely the case. Fine coats on unclipped horses are usually maintained by keeping the stable like a hothouse, to the danger of the eyes and lungs of the inmates. Besides, a horse that has once been singed or clipped, will require an annual repetition of the process.

Mr. J. Froude Bellew, Master of the Dulverton Hounds, North Devon, which he hunts himself, and who "has been a hard-riding horse-master ever since he was fourteen years old," wrote me in March, 1878, as to his treatment of hunters :—

"A couple of cloths on each horse, windows and ventilators always open according to the direction of the wind, and my horses look better in their skins now (10th March) than they did at midsummer, and why? because clipping and singeing was stopped in the middle of November. Clip or singe as early and as often as you please, but stop on the 12th of November.

"After work no leg-washing; if wet, they are quickly dried with sawdust.

"Instead of felt or other saddle-cloth, I use a light plain leather pannel well saturated with tallow, which keeps the horse's back cool. Fasten it firmly with a surcingle to the horse's back, then put saddle over it. There is no greater mistake than the military *nummah*, which, soaked with sweat, keeps the horse's back in a perpetual poultice, and is a direct cause of sore and soft backs. As to girths, I prefer and use the open stamped leather girth; a great improvement on the non-ventilating web. As a matter of course, I take it for granted the horses intended to have fine coats after singeing or clipping are properly *strapped*. Elbow-grease must not be spared if you want your horses to look well. My horses never want a V.S.; no one of the profession has been seen in my stables for the last sixteen years. In the hunting season they have plenty of old beans (half a peck a day) and oats, no bran, no powders, but a liberal allowance of linseed oil and turpentine once, and often twice a week."

Every one who has ever clipped a horse, after watching him for a few weeks in his long winter coat, has seen how the animal's appetite, spirits, and power of endurance improve in the most rapid and wonderful manner. The clipped or singed horse is dried and cleaned in one-fourth of the time of one with a long coat, if, indeed, the latter is dried at all. When a horse has a short coat, a groom has no excuse for not dressing him thoroughly; when he has a long one, it will not unfrequently happen that on arriving late at night, he will be turned into his stall to shiver in his clammy coat all night. Grooms are but men. We all like as little trouble as possible, and the best results for the least trouble. A long-coated unclipped horse never does justice to the groom's labours, let him work as hard as he will.

As to the chances of catching cold, they would be experienced, if anywhere, in the most famous hunting counties, where at cover-side at least four-fifths of the long-priced hunters are clipped or singed. But then these much-exposed horses are well fed and admirably groomed.

The practice of shaving horses is quite obsolete. Singeing, which was first and is still sometimes performed by a spirit-lamp, has become much more common since the use of gas has been so much extended. The gas-singeing apparatuses are very perfect.

Horses with very thick coats are better clipped than singed. Greys and light roans seldom singe well. Some horses absolutely refuse to allow a flame to approach them, and these, unless they can be "*Rareyfied*," must be clipped. To make a good job of singeing, the process must be commenced early in the autumn, and repeated little by little every fortnight, until the coat is reduced quite close. If this is skilfully done, accompanied by good grooming, exercise, and sufficient corn, the horse will carry a bloomy, glossy coat throughout the winter, and will change from the singed to the natural summer coat almost imperceptibly; but if poor and out of condition, he will look mangy all the summer. Any intelligent groom can learn to use either a clipping machine or a gas-singeing lamp. Singeing should be done on dry days; in damp weather the hair does not burn well.

If a young groom does not understand singeing, he should be taught—that is, if he be worth teaching anything. Singeing a horse's head is a very nice operation. On no account should the whiskers, eyelashes, or inside hair of the ears of a horse be touched. Grooms, like the barbers before beards came in, like to clear all before them. But the whiskers are the horse's feelers; to remove them is equally stupid and barbarous; while to cut the hair from the inside of a horse's ears is to remove an important protection, and make room for deafness and catarrh.

Scissors were formerly employed for clipping. It was a very laborious operation, requiring a good deal of practice and skill, but now the hand-clipping machine has been brought to such perfection that any ordinary groom can use one; and, consequently, it has to a great degree superseded singeing. To make a horse look well after singeing it must be commenced as early as October, and repeated several times before the hunting season commences. Clipping may be deferred until the whole of the winter coat has appeared, and then the job can be done once for all the season. In really skilful hands scissors make a better job than a machine, but the skilful hands are rare, and the operation, as we have said, is long and laborious. There are many good clipping tools, English, French, and American. I use Clarke's of Oxford Street, London, and find that it answers perfectly.

"It is a common practice to leave the saddle-place unclipped, with the idea of rendering the hair less liable to saddle-galls. I can only say that I have found the practice productive of the very evil it was supposed to prevent. Indeed, it stands to common sense that it should be so; for in proportion as the skin is saturated with sweat, so will it be liable to irritation." (D.C.)

Of course it is taken for granted that hunting saddles are carefully dried every day, and examined to see that they do not require re-stuffing.

The hair must be very carefully removed from the hunter's legs, in order that cuts, bruises, and thorns may be noticed when the legs are examined after hunting, *except the long lock of hair at the point of the fetlock joint; if this is cut off the symmetry of the fore-leg is destroyed.* Removing the hairs of the leg about the fetlock requires judgment and skill; superfluous hairs must be pulled out of the tuft. I have never seen the legs of a hunter so well trimmed as by a child under ten years old, the son of a horsebreaker.

After clipping or singeing, it is a sound practice to give the horse a sweating exercise, then to wash him all over with soap and water, dry him thoroughly by a good strapping and give him an extra blanket; then he will be much less liable to take cold than in his long coat.

A special drawer should be reserved for the clipping and singeing tools—both are required to finish a horse—that they may be packed away properly, and be ready in good order when wanted the following year. India-rubber tubes are less liable to get out of order than the more expensive gutta-percha.

Horses that have once been clipped or singed must have the operation repeated every year, or they will look worse than ever. In the spring of the year, when horses are moulting, especially if they have been clipped or singed, they require some extra food. I have found that a pound of linseed-cake to each horse, in addition to the regular allowance of corn, and five or six pounds of carrots daily, greatly promote the change of coat in the spring. Horses which are well fed get rid of their winter hair a month sooner than those kept on a short allowance of corn.

But, although the short coat obtained by clipping or singeing saves a groom a great deal of work, it is never in a well-regulated stable allowed to be the substitute for regular strapping.

Singeing must never be trusted to any one not thoroughly proficient, as if, through carelessness or clumsiness, the skin is scorched, it will look rough for a long time.

"A horse with a long coat, if soaked with rain in going to cover, remains wet until dried by a sharp gallop. He then sweats, remains wet, cold, miserable for the rest of the day, and ten to one is not three-parts dry the next morning, and has been wasting from evaporation all night."

"I once," says Mr. Digby Collins, "was persuaded to ride a horse, hunting, with the long shaggy coat he brought from the green field, and sacrificed a very hardy excellent horse to the experiment. He always got beat after going well over about a dozen fields, and finally turned roarer, and went blind."

HUNTING-DRESS, HUNTING-BOX, AND HUNTING-DINNERS.

To be well *and suitably* dressed, according to the country and the season, is a very important matter in the battle of hunting life.

Our great-grandfathers dressed for the chase in a sensible, if not an elegant style according to our modern notions, in large roomy horsemen's coats, long-deep-flapped waistcoats, stout and capacious buckskin breeches, and serviceable if somewhat clumsy boots, which came well over the breeches.

The quotations from the journals of the Tarporley Club, given in Chapter XVII., record the date at which fox-hunters finally adopted scarlet, as distinguished from the green or blue of the hare-hunting clubs.

When George Prince of Wales' consulting counsel, Beau Brummel, ruled the roast of fashion, elegance was sought in tightness; comfort and convenience were cast on one side as vulgar, like vegetables and other wholesome things. Doeskins fitting like a skin were the usual morning and hunting-dress of the period.

Once the Prince, ever on the look-out for some costly extravagance, astonished his world with a pair of white kidskin breeches; but the attempt was a failure. The British leather-dressers of those days were not then able to produce an article sufficiently stout for the purpose, and foreign aid was prohibited. Leathers continued in vogue for morning and hunting-dress until the Peace of 1814, when trousers of extraordinary shape were imported from Russia. Some time afterwards doeskin breeches were voted slow, and white corduroys became the only possible wear for a man of fashion in the hunting-field. There was a good wear-and-tear appearance about the hunting-dress in the first fifty years of George III., which was superseded by the Regent's style, as may be seen in George Morland's hunting pictures. The gold lace of George II.'s time had been for the most part discarded. The coat was single-breasted, and not scanty; the brown tops of the boots, tied with many ribands to the leather breeches, were long. The manufacture of a decent article in blacking had not made much progress; and the cravat above the largely frilled or laced shirt was more like a pudding-bag than anything else. But the men, in spite of their pigtails, looked like workmen; and it was in this stamp of costume that Beau Brummel made his rare appearances in the hunting-field, when he was the favoured guest of the Duke of Rutland at Belvoir.

But the Prince and the Beau quarrelled. The latter, ruined, carried his wardrobe, his insolence, and his talent for begging-letter writing to Calais, leaving, as a legacy to his numerous pupils, the white starched cravat, an absurdity which was indispensable in society until the Crimean War and the introduction of arms of precision abolished the soldiers' stock, and gave a degree of freedom to the necks of all Her Majesty's subjects, which had previously only been enjoyed by sailors, artists, and poets of Byronic proclivities.

Leathers are such delightful wear in dry weather that they never entirely passed out of use amongst the provincial hunting public, but at the period recorded by "Nimrod's" tours in Leicestershire, and etched by George Cruikshank's needle, the hunting-dress, in fashionable counties, had reached the lowest depths of vulgarity and inconvenience. A bell-crowned hat, which could not be kept on the head in windy weather, superseded the velvet cap; a high-starched cravat imprisoned the sportsman's neck. The roomy garment of his fathers was replaced by a dress-coat as tight as a tailor could make it, with a very short waist, a high collar rising to the ears, and swallow-tailed lappels, affording the least possible protection against rain and cold weather; while baggy white corduroy breeches, cut long at the knees, superseded orange or cream-coloured doeskins, to meet short pale pink tops, which were prepared, according to rumour, with champagne. Such was the correct costume of the swells of the period, faithfully depicted in George Cruikshank's illustrations of "Tom and Jerry."

Since those days a series of changes have taken place in hunting costume. Hats were superseded in 1840 by velvet caps, which were worn in nearly all the best hunts in the kingdom. Since the Prince of Wales joined the hunting-field, hats have once more taken the place of caps. Mr. Charles Greville records that when George IV. died, amongst his collection of some hundreds of garments (the first gentleman in Europe (?) never gave anything away), were *twelve pairs of corduroy breeches*, made, but never used, for His Majesty to hunt with Dom Miguel. But corduroys are now as much out of date as pigtails. The last Master of hounds I ever saw wear them was Sir Richard Sutton. They were of a dingy blue colour, and very baggy. Cotton cord has been superseded by Bedford cord, a woollen material which is not manufactured at Bedford, and by a variety of elastic woollen fabrics, some manufactured in Gloucestershire, some in Scotland, and others at that well-known fox-hunting centre, Chipping Norton. Woollen breeches are commonly used in rainy seasons instead of buckskins. The rage for tight garments, so tight that the man who used to help you on with your great coat after a dinner party *really earned his sixpence*, has passed away, and the dandy described in Lord Lytton's "England and the English," who could not sit down at a wedding breakfast because he had his stand-up trousers on, is known no more.

I do not know when the revolution commenced, but the first time I ever saw a pair of loose doeskin breeches and patent leather Napoleon boots was in 1843. They were worn by the Duke of Beaufort of that day, a first-rate sportsman, a most courteous Master of hounds, and of a figure that made every costume in fashion look well when worn by him. The duke was one of Brummel's youngest pupils and latest victims.

From that time there has been a gradual advance towards comfort and convenience in hunting-dress.

It took time to convert tailors and wearers to principles of common sense in the construction of hunting-coats. The first variation from the dress-coats already mentioned was a single-breasted straight-cut coat, which barely fastened with one button at the neck, or was united with a trinket long out of use, a coat-link, made with a fox's-tooth, or fashioned like a snaffle-bit, as may be read in sporting novels of the Jorrocks era.

Napoleon boots, butcher boots, and all the black variations from the legitimate top-boot, were long looked upon with great disfavour by the gentlemen of the old school, but when the fashion was taken up by the Badminton Hunt there was no more to be said against a boot that did not require an artist valet to clean it. The modern short cavalry boot only superseded trousers after the Franco-German War.

The Prince Consort used to hunt with his harriers in jack-boots, of the Life Guard cut, and had his imitators, but in the end the neat-fitting Napoleon carried the day. Boots, like coats and breeches, have benefited by the improvements in material which have taken place since all duties on the raw materials and manufactured articles of clothing have been abolished.

Brown and green coats, once universal with harehounds and common with foxhounds, where pink was not adopted, up to the first half of this century, have been superseded by the universal black. Scarlet is the uniform of every established fox-hunting club in the kingdom, except one—the Badminton—an hereditary pack in the family of the Duke of Beaufort through four generations, since, in the time of the fifth duke, a pack of fine staghounds was converted into foxhounds. Curiously enough, although the Somersets were among the stoutest friends of the first Charles and the last James, and have since the Georgian era been distinguished for the stiffness of their Tory politics,* the uniform of their hunt has always been the blue and buff of Charles James Fox, of his Whig followers, and of their organ, the *Edinburgh Review*.

---

* The sixth Duke of Beaufort, on his death-bed, in 1833, entreated his son, the Marquis of Worcester, to so educate the Earl of Glamorgan, the present duke, that in the event of the expected revolution depriving him of his property, he would be able to earn his own livelihood.—*T. Raikes' Diary*.

The best thing that can be said about it is that, made double-breasted, it is a very becoming riding-habit when worn by the ladies of the hunt.

Early in the present century a Lord Vernon had a pack of foxhounds in Derbyshire, and the uniform of the hunt was orange-plush; but it did not take. The sky-blue uniform of the Hatfield Hunt had been replaced by pink before the death of its greatest ornament, the Marchioness of Salisbury. Forty years ago parsons compromised by wearing purple instead of pink. Warburton, after referring to "Henry, our purple-clad vicar," continues in his Cheshire Song with—

> " If my life were at stake on the wager,
>   I know not which brother I'd back ;
> The parson, the squire, or the major,
>   The purple, the pink, or the black."

In the fox-hunting fields of the present day there is no choice in cloth coats between black and scarlet.

The majority of established fox-hunting clubs are satisfied with the distinction of a button bearing the crest of the Master, with an appropriate monogram or motto; but several have from the dawn of fox-hunting adopted a collar of a different colour from the coat. Thus, the scarlet coat of the Quorn has a white collar; the Berkeley, a black velvet collar, with a fox's head embroidered in gold and silver; the Cheshire and the old Surrey Clubs both wear a green collar.

An attempt has lately been reported from the fashionable hunting counties to bring black coats into fashion, instead of the accepted pinks, "which have become too common and vulgar." It is quite safe to prophesy that this bit of exclusive affectation will not survive many seasons. The advantages of pink are many : it can be seen far off; it is a good letter of introduction at every inn and turnpike-gate, for the man otherwise well appointed; most men look well in it; properly treated it wears longer than black. Formerly it was considered the correct thing to wear a scarlet coat much stained. Even artificial means were used to produce the desired effect; but of late the custom has been the other way, and hunting valets have discovered some means of making two or three hunting-coats look new every day of the season.

A man had better defer putting on a scarlet coat until he feels at home in the hunting-field. The simpler his attire—as long as his lower limbs are clothed in well-made fitting boots and breeches—the better. A velveteen or tweed jacket may prepare the way for a black coat, to be in its turn superseded by a correct pink ; and a pair of long black buttoned gaiters, worn with brown Bedford cords, are a sensible preamble to boots. Although one may lay down the principles on which a hunting-coat should be "built," it would be absurd to enter into details which may be changed by the force of fashion any day. When the late Lord Lytton—then plain Edward Bulwer—astonished the world with the first edition of "Pelham," he devoted a chapter to describing how coats should be cut; but in a very few years the fashions had so much changed, that directions which had cost the dandy author no small pains had to be omitted.

A hunting-coat should be a real thing, made to suit the sort of weather to be expected in November, December, January, and February—not a conventional sham—made not only to look well in the ladies' eyes at cover-side, but to protect the wearer as much as possible from cutting winds and heavy rain, when returning slowly home on a tired horse after a famous run, or jogging from cover to cover on a bad-scenting or blank day.

The coats to be worn as spring advances, or hunting the wild stag of the West in a dry September, may be of lighter material, and without the flannel linings which make modern winter coats so comfortable.

According to sporting novelists and sporting journalists, there are only two or three tailors in the world equal to building a correct scarlet coat; but that is nonsense, although the best reputed names have carried their art to great perfection, and made important improvements. Good workmen are to be found in every hunting centre. Imitation from a good pattern is easy, and it certainly is not necessary to send to London for a hunting costume from York, Bristol, Cheltenham, Chester, Northampton, or even Manchester.

At the same time it must be noted that no pretence is more contemptible than a badly-fitting scarlet coat of inferior materials.

A hunting-coat should have at least four pockets, besides a ticket or small-change pocket —that is to say, one outside the breast, for the handkerchief, one inside for the purse, and two in the flaps. Fashion has sometimes placed the pockets of a hunting-coat behind, like that of a frock, instead of on the hips. The flaps may somewhat detract from the elegance of the waist, but pockets so cut are easily accessible for either hand, even when half-frozen, to extract the many useful things a hunting-coat-pocket may contain. I remember, when the Earl of Hopetoun had the Pytchley Hounds, seeing one of the whips painfully trying to grope his way with a fox's pad into the pocket of his tight frock. Nothing could have a more absurd effect. Tailors of the first class perfectly understand how to combine elegance of cut with ease and liberty for every limb.

The best rule is to go to some tailor in town or country who makes hunting-coats a specialty. A hunting-coat of any colour should leave the horseman the most perfect liberty to use his arms, and be so made that the collar will turn up and button over the throat, as well as nearly down to the bottom of the waistcoat. Every man who prefers his comfort to his figure will have pockets at the sides. The waistcoat of a winter hunting-coat should be made like a jacket—that is, the same material, whether cloth, velvet, or fur, should continue all round the back, and not be eked out like ordinary waistcoats with calico or silk. The hollow part of the back is the place where one is most apt to catch cold, after getting into a violent perspiration. Hunting-waistcoat pockets should have flaps, to keep the small change from rolling out when you and your horse are rolling and struggling in a ditch. A recent useful invention is the "*beaver*-tailed waistcoat," made all of wool, with a flap falling over the loins.

The Crimean War universalised one of the greatest comforts of the hunting man—the flannel shirt. Many of our ancestors must have been sacrificed to the chill of linen worn before cotton became respectable. With the flannel shirt came another friend in cold weather—elastic woollen drawers, which superseded the horribly irritating Welsh flannel drawers; and, by abolishing stockings and garters, facilitated the fit of boots and breeches.

"The Cardigan"—the elastic sleeved woollen jacket, to be worn under the coat and over the waistcoat—is another Crimean result much to be commended. It may be white, grey, or black, the grey for choice—be worn open at chest until slow paces succeed the run, or strapped with an overcoat to the saddle. A very good sportsman, in a very wild and rainy country, once showed me a compact roll, consisting of a hand-knitted Cardigan jacket and a woollen comforter, wrapped in a mackintosh riding apron, occupying very little room when strapped close to the cantle of his saddle. With these he had frequently ridden home, after a long day with the hounds, wet, but warm and comfortable, five-and-twenty miles.

Cardigans are also made in silk net, with plain silk sleeves. They are not so warm as wool, or so generally useful, and they are very expensive.

The cutter-out of hunting-breeches should be an artist, and an artist whose natural genius has been cultivated by practice on most fastidious customers. The difference between well and ill-fitting breeches is the difference between comfort and misery, neatness and vulgarity. It is not always worth while to buy the most expensive garment of its kind; as, for instance, summer suits, which are to be cast aside for ever after a few weeks' wear; but every article worn in hunting should be of the very best material for hard wear, and the best cut for comfort. Doeskins, with reasonable wear and slight repairs, will last a very long time.

Leather breeches must be cleaned, and unless the young sportsman has a groom-valet up to cleaning them, sending them to a professional cleaner—not always to be found in country towns—means not only expense but delay, inconvenient to men who are on a hunting visit, and hunting five or six days a week. For this reason it is well to have a certain number of pairs of the various woollen materials, plain and corded, white for fashionable counties and fine weather, brown Bedford cord for Clayshire and persistent rain.

Where Napoleon, Hussar, or any of the modern varieties of black boots are worn, pantaloons buttoning at the ankle answer the purpose better than breeches, and are less a work of fine art, if made of elastic material.

A well-made man (for a top-boot) can button a pair of properly cut breeches, and draw them on over his calves to their proper place.

To put on and wear a pair of breeches properly, lessons from a fox-hunting expert are essential—from a tailor, for instance, who has been in the habit of hunting in the Midlands.

It should be noted that to ride a run in an absolutely waterproof coat, and then get cold by standing at cover-side or riding slowly home, is a fine preparation for rheumatic fever. Wet does not hurt any one in fair health, as long as warmth can be kept up, and this is best done by putting a dry garment over a wet one. The best and simplest protection for the stomach and thighs is a mackintosh riding-apron, already mentioned, which can be put on without dismounting.

Boots—that is, top-boots—are even more difficult to obtain in the best, that is, the most comfortable and correct style—than breeches. The late Mr. Bartley (who, amongst other equestrian feats, once rode a horse in a race for the Epsom Derby) had an immense reputation for the *tops* of his boots. It is he who is shown in one of Leech's sketches measuring John himself, and saying, as he took in hand a leg like a walking-stick, "Capital leg for a top-boot, sir; none of your dancing calves!" A profound hunting-boot truth, for no man with a pair of fat calves can ever look well in a top-boot.

Northampton, which is in the centre of one of the finest hunting counties in the kingdom, manufactures capital patent leather black hunting-boots, but whether the art of tops has reached perfection in the capital of "sutors," I am not informed. In London the best trade is in very few hands.

Hunting-boots should be large enough for thick woollen stockings; a tight boot means cold feet. A thin-soled boot that enables the rider to feel the stirrup is most agreeable, but a thin-soled boot does not answer in a clay country and rainy weather; for the greatest horsemen must walk sometimes.

The colour of top-boots is the subject of fashion more changeable than even ladies' hair was, *temp.* the Empress Eugénie. They have been worn of all shades, from deep mahogany to pale pink, of all lengths and all ways, from quite smooth to much wrinkled.

Colouring the tops of boots is one of the most difficult tasks of a servant, with a master who cares about such trifles. "Not quite the shade, more like the colour of a North Wiltshire cheese; you had better buy one for a pattern," says one of Whyte Melville's military hunting heroes. The soldier-servant on retiring confides to a friend that "them tops are the torment of my life, I shall be druv to drink by 'em."

Before railways cosmopolitanised all England there were provincial hunting-districts, showing first-rate sport, where, if a stranger appeared in boots not of the hunt colour, and breeches not of the county cut, he was set down at once as a Jacobin, and perhaps an atheist, and treated accordingly.

Boot-tops require a special apparatus for restoration after a day's hunting. Therefore, when a young sportsman goes on a visit to a great house not accompanied by his own servant, it will add very much to his peace of mind if he provides himself with two pair of patent leather Hussars or Napoleons. He will thus be spared the agony of seeing his fellow-guests ready to mount while he is shivering in his stockings, waiting for a pair of tops which my lord's fine gentlemen have forgotten. Patent leather does not easily get wet, and can be cleaned over a bucket with a sponge in five minutes, and although Napoleons are not perhaps so workmanlike as well-built, well-cleaned tops, they are much more easy to buy and keep in order.

Hot tin bottles, glass bottles, hot hay, are all used to dry boots which have been soaked through or filled after a drop into a brook. A couple of india-rubber bottles of the right size are easily carried, and useful for other purposes besides drying boots.

The head-dress for hunting must be that in use, unless the owner is so small or so great a personage that he can set fashion at defiance. The old high-crowned hat was the most absurd hunting head-dress ever invented; it took one hand to hold it on just when you wanted two for your reins. Many men have heads of shape on which no hat will stick over a big jump or in a high wind, unless tied under the chin. For convenience there is nothing like the shape of the hunting-cap which all huntsmen and whips wear, whether for keeping on or for riding through brushwood and briars. But no young man can set custom at defiance and be eccentric in dress. Within my time hats were all but universal in the hunting-field; at that time it took an hour to get into a pair of new leathers. Then caps became the correct style, and were worn by every one who mounted a pink and professed to ride. When the Prince of Wales took to fox-hunting he set the fashion of hats; and caps are (A.D. 1878) only worn by a few of the old school, and horse-dealing farmers in black coats, which do not go well with velvet caps.

But in the meantime an immense improvement has been made in hats. For hunting, felt hats have superseded both silk and the beaver of gentility, which was the only correct head-dress until Sir Robert Peel changed his mind on the subject of fiscal finance, and took off the duties on silk and wool. Once a silk hat was the sign of a cad; then, under the competition of improved silk, beaver passed so completely out of use that beaver-skins became a drug, and an animal in danger of extinction multiplied exceedingly in the wild North land. Felt hats, in their turn, have all but superseded silk in the hunting-field.

A multitude of felt "Jim Crows," "Pot Hats," "Deer-stalkers," "Meltons," "Pytchleys," "Market Harboroughs," "Oxonians," fitting quite as closely as the velvet cap, at one-third the price, and thrice the durability, are offered for the fox-hunter's choice. A low-crowned broad-brimmed felt hat is in favour with several modern Masters of crack packs of fox-hounds. But it is very probable that if the Duke of Connaught should take to hunting "with passion," and wear a velvet cap, all the rising fox-hunters of England would follow his example.

Hunting-gloves were formerly universally of buckskin. They are scarcely to be had of that material now for money. Calfskin has almost superseded dogskin. Stout kid selected for the purpose may be purchased in Fleet Street, opposite St. Dunstan's Church, at five shillings a pair. The fox-hunter should always have in his pocket, with a spare silk handkerchief, a pair of worsted gloves, through which the reins do not slip in wet weather, and in which the hands are not so cold as in wet leather.

A strong single or two-bladed knife, with a foot-picker in the handle, to cut a stick or a cord, or scrape mud off your boots after a run in ploughed fields, is often useful; but the knives containing an armoury of tools are only fit for schoolboys. Some old hard riders in thinly populated countries carry a case containing a knife, a pair of scissors, and a pair of V.S. tweezers for extracting thorns. A wood or steel paper-knife, to scrape the sweat off a horse at a check, is used by some hard riders, and takes little room.

The hunting man's whip should be of a length proportionate to his height. It should have a short thong, and a spike in the butt to hold back a gate. A heavy whip is a mistake, except in the hands of a "whip" or huntsman, who has to hammer at locks and hinges. Spurs should be of the huntsman's pattern, with short necks, and rowels rubbed to bluntness.

When a man goes out hunting he wants money, of course!—enough, and not too much. A hunting parson—a man of the world—always carried a bank-note in a pocket-book in his inner waistcoat pocket, a sovereign in his left-hand outside waistcoat pocket, a handful of half-crowns in his right-hand waistcoat pocket, and in his right-hand breeches pocket a handful of sixpences and fourpences. Thus he was prepared for all eventualities, from a turnpike toll to paying handsel on a horse purchase.

In a celebrated hunting county a story used to be told of a nobleman, now long deceased, equally noted for his wealth and his carefulness, that on one occasion his horse fell with him in the course of a run, and got away. His lordship sat on a gate, surrounded, as a lord always is on such occasions, by a circle of commiserating friends. His servant presently rode up with the fugitive steed, and immediately cried out, in a loud voice, "My lord, a joskin (countryman) caught him, and I gave him a shilling." "Hadn't you such a thing as a sixpence about you?" was the reply of the economical nobleman. Some profane ones laughed aloud, but remembered the hint, and provided themselves with small change. On the other side, a very vulgar millionnaire demoralised the labourers in a provincial hunt by giving every man who opened a gate for him half-a-sovereign.

In harrier-fields it is usual to make a collection, "a cap," before or after hunting, of half-a-crown or five shillings from each stranger. It may be clever, but it does not look nice, when some gentleman of imposing appearance asks for change of a fifty-pound note, and so saves his five shillings; yet such things do happen, even in a Royal Windsor hunting-field.

THE HUNTING-BOX AND ITS COMFORTS.

The principal requirements of a hunting-box, next to good stabling—of which anon—are warmth in the sitting-rooms and bed-rooms, with good ventilation, plenty of warm water, and such a distribution of domestic work as will afford good service with the smallest number of servants.

A closed porch, making a double entrance to the hall, divided from it by a glass door, is the first essential for making a house snug, for no amount of heating-power will keep a house warm if every time the entrance-door is opened a current of cold air is allowed to rush in.

The rooms required on the ground-floor may (according to the opinion of two eminent Masters of hounds, one of them noted for his simple yet excellent hunting dinners) be limited to—

1. A drawing-room, which will also be the library.
2. A dining-room, which will also be the breakfast-room.
3. A third room, which may be a billiard-room, a smoking-room, or anything else.

On one side of the hall should be fitted or built a dressing or rather undressing-room, in which the house-party and their friends can take off their boots, and, in wet weather, all their garments, before ascending to their bed-rooms, repose, and to dress for dinner. This arrangement will save servants an immense amount of time and labour. This room should be provided with a cocoa-nut, cork, or other carpet that dirty boots will not spoil, half a dozen sensible boot-jacks (see Engraving, p. 493), enough rails and hooks for hanging up coats, a long table for hats, whips, and gloves, a few *low* chairs and a long ottoman for seats when pulling on boots, and half a dozen good-sized basins, fixed in frames, with at least one tap of hot water. One intelligent boy—half page, half groom—will make the arrangements of this preliminary dressing-room complete.

BATHS.

If cash and accommodation can be found for making a bath-room next to the general dressing-room, that will be a wholesome luxury. This room should be provided with several hot and cold water taps, with a *douche*, if a fall of water can be obtained. To have full-sized hot baths for half a dozen persons is simply impossible, but with a simple arrangement of portable screens half a dozen persons can take sponge baths—hot, cold, or tepid—according to taste, at the same time.

An easier plan is to provide a hot-air bath, which can be built in most situations for a hundred pounds. To sit from a quarter to half an hour after hunting in a temperature of 120° Fahrenheit, then to use a sponge bath, with a *douche* to follow (the shampooing is not essential), will be found extremely refreshing, and less trouble to servants than as many hot-water baths.

The advantage of having a hot-air bath on the premises is that the same air may be utilised for drying the clothes and boots of men and the saddles and cloths of horses.

Such small and simple hot-air baths are very common round Rugby. As to morning ablutions in the dressing-room, it is not every one who can bear, without ill-effects, a cold tubbing in winter. To such the sitting-bath, warmed to 70° Fahrenheit, may be recommended as a morning restorer and refresher, taken with or without a cup of *café au lait* and a pipe. The sitting-bath is also very comforting after long hours on a wet saddle.

Another most valuable bath for the worn-out or much-bruised fox-hunter—as, for instance, after a roll under a horse in a ploughed field—is the sheet bath, which has the advantage of requiring no other apparatus than a couple of sheets, a big tub—say a pig-scalding tub—and three buckets, the first filled with water as hot as can be borne by the hand, the second heated to about 80° or 90°, and the third to 60°.

The patient must be seated in the tub, in a warm room, covered with one sheet, and another must be ready-heated before the fire. The first bucket is to be slowly poured over his shoulders, then the second, then the third and coldest; he is to be rubbed as much as his bruises will bear, dried with the hot sheet, and put to bed between blankets, with a hot india-rubber or stone bottle to his feet, and refreshed with a hot drink of some kind. A sportsman not bruised, but only tired, may dispense with the bed and the bottle.

I have known extraordinary benefit derived from this treatment applied at a little roadside tavern to a horseman, after a heavy fall.

Another invaluable hydropathic remedy is the packing-bath, which acts like a warm poultice on the whole body.

Water-bottles of india-rubber have in a great degree superseded warming-pans. They are one of the most useful portable adaptations of that invaluable material for the use of either man or horse, with either hot or cold water.

Of course, there are young and old fellows who require no comforts, can eat anything, sleep anywhere, despise under-garments, defy wet and cold, sit in damp clothes, and laugh at the milksops for whom these hints have been compressed, until they get rheumatism, neuralgia, or toothache!

In an old house the best plan for both comfort and economy in fuel is to replace every old grate with Mechi's Parson's stove, which is cheap and cheerful. The saving in coals will pay the whole cost in one season.

A kitchen-range may be obtained from any respectable manufacturer, which will cook and keep a first-rate dinner for a dozen, supply the whole house up to the first-floor with hot water, and, when required, warm the whole house through hot-water pipes.

If the vestibule and all the passages of a house are warmed with hot-water pipes in severe weather, and if all the rooms are provided with ventilating valves, moderate fires will keep the living-rooms at a pleasant temperature—neither close nor stuffy.

The kitchen apparatus should be on the kitchener rather than the open fire system, because fox-hunters often keep dinner waiting, and the close fireplaces are best adapted for cooking the dishes that are not spoiled by waiting. Douglas's, made by the Coventry Company, is very good, and economical in the consumption of coal. Of course there must be good arrangement for a broil. Wherever, then, there are half a dozen horses in the stable, and a cow or two kept for cream, it will pay to have a two-horse steam engine. This will cost about £100. The boilers of the engine will at the same time warm the house, the saddle-room, the drying-room, and, if required, a conservatory, and also afford supplies of hot water to the upper floors.

A drying-room, in which coats, breeches, and boots may be placed on suitable frames and slowly dried, as well as saddles, wet girths, and horse-cloths, is not only a comfort, but an important economy in a hunting-box. A centrifugal dryer has come into use at town hotels that do their washing in the attics. The steam engine whose boilers are thus utilised may be set in motion to pump water from a well, and to a cistern in the top of the house or the stables, to cut chaff, pulp roots, saw wood, or chop meat for hounds. These small fixed engines have been brought to such perfection, are so easy to work, and cost so little, that no country house of any pretensions should be without one.

Near the dining-room should be a wine-closet or cupboard, holding at least a week's consumption, because it is not pleasant to have at the last moment to send to the cellar. Of course, in mansions where butlers in solemn black preside, and *chefs* of the first order organise the dinners, no hints are needed.

There are several kinds of stoves suitable for the bed-rooms of a cottage the principal inhabitants of which are absent most of the hunting-day : for example, those American stoves in which coke only is burned, which combine the advantage of close and open fires. In these the fire may be laid, and a fine blazing heat obtained ten minutes after a match has been applied, when the doors may be thrown open. They are also capital for keeping a kettle boiling.

Mr. Walter Raleigh Trevelyan, writing from the Royal Institution, in December, 1874, to a contemporary, observes :—" For seven years I have found that if you can successfully heat the lungs of your house—your halls and passages—you may defy the open door to make you shiver. Every house has its kitchen fire summer and winter; let every kitchen have its stove-boiler, whence let hot water be conveyed to a 'coil' of 4-inch pipes in your hall, and thence let it pass, by a small 2-inch pipe, to a cistern for hot water at the top of the house, and you will have a well-warmed, well-ventilated, and comfortable house. All this can be obtained with a small additional expense of say £25 for a fair-sized house, and we shall be able to retain our 'cheerful open grate' and do without the 'close stove.'"

If the stable is close to the house, the same apparatus may warm and dry the saddle-room and supply hot water from a tap; but if the stable is at an inconvenient distance, a separate apparatus must be provided. It is a very great mistake to permit the grooms to be dependent on the cook for supplies of hot water.

It is important that there should be convenient independent access to the stables from the cottage in all weathers. If it does not exist, it should be made, in the shape of a dry and, if possible, covered passage.

The hand-lamps used in the stable should be fitted with flat hooks, so as to hang either on the walls or on the stall-posts. A hand-lamp with a powerful reflector, such as is used by railway policemen, is a very useful article in a country house if always kept trimmed and in order. A good lamp hoisted on a pole at the lodge-gate, about the time that the sports-men are expected home, is a comfortable beacon to the weary. Lamps burning mineral oils have of late years been brought to such perfection, and are sold at such low prices, that it is ridiculous to use even out of doors the old tallow-dip and horn lantern.

All the above suggestions may be carried out, if planned as a whole, at a very trifling addition to the inevitable expenses of a hunting-box. A cold house, smoky chimneys, a dearth of water, hot and cold, ill-ventilated draughty rooms, will make a party, otherwise prepared to be merry, silent, sulky, and quarrelsome. And this is particularly true as regards bed-rooms, where the old-fashioned grates burn a great deal of coal, give very little warmth, and create a fearful draught of cold air when the fire goes out. Roberts's portable terra-cotta slow combustion stove should be in the bed-rooms of every hunting-box.

In the same way, rooms amply warmed become stuffy and provocative of headaches when ventilation is neglected. Tobin's ventilating tubes cost little, and give fresh air without draught.

The doors of old-fashioned country houses seldom shut well. An amateur carpenter can for a few shillings make a most comfortable double door with a deal frame first covered with canvas, and then with one of the many patterns of leather paper.

Presuming that the wet and weary sportsman will be received into a well-warmed, well-ventilated house, with simple conveniences for getting rid of his wet garments, and per-forming his preliminary ablution with the least possible tax on the services of a limited number of servants,—that, on returning from the general undressing and bath-rooms to his bed-room, he finds a small brisk fire, an arm-chair or sofa, on which, wrapped in his travelling rugs, he may, if he chooses, repose until summoned to dress by the gong; a plain table, furnished with all the conveniences for writing, and a new magazine, newspaper, or book. All the furniture may be of the most inexpensive description: plain deal, or the oldest-fashioned mahogany, an iron bedstead with a good French flock mattress, and cotton, not linen, sheets—he will be more at ease than within chambers furnished regardless of expense, where everything seems too fine to use, and the couch and writing-table have been omitted. On this subject the following quotation from *The Lancet*, is very much to the purpose:—"Amongst certain persons—and the class is rather a numerous one—that which is comfortable is unconsciously considered to be wrong, and object-less self-mortification assumes the character of a virtue. Such persons never wear a top-coat, never have a fire in their bed-room, always shave with cold water, break the ice in their tub of a morning in order to bathe. They are apt to boast of these feats, and to look down upon their weaker fellow-creatures who do not imitate them. In the matter of the morning tub alone the absurdity is well shown. Now, granted that the cold-water bath is a good thing, it must be remembered that whereas in summer they immerse them-selves in water about 20° or 30° cooler than their blood, in winter the difference of temperature may amount, as it does sometimes, to no less than 50° or 60° Fahrenheit. To be consistent, they should raise the temperature of the bath in winter to that which it has in summer. As they are inconsistent, they suffer very often from muscular rheumatism. When it can be obtained, there is no way of promoting warmth so beneficially as by exercise; but business people, and those with sedentary occupations, are of course debarred to a certain extent from this, and are compelled to resort to artificial heat. It should never be forgotten that it is of the utmost importance to keep the extremities warm; and the feet should be especially cared for, more illness being caused by foolish neglect of them, and by allowing them to remain cold or damp, than people are generally aware of. The best way of keeping feet warm is to wear thick socks, and large, easy-fitting boots.

"There are some who would object to wearing 'great clumsy' boots, but although they should be roomy and not paper-soled, they need not be clumsy, and if not quite so neat and pleasing to the eye as the cold, tight-fitting, miserable things worn by dandies, they are at least more conducive to comfort. One word of caution, however, to those who may be inclined to act on the other extreme from the 'cold comfort' men:—Never allow yourselves to go to sleep with so many blankets covering you as to produce perspiration, nothing being more weakening or debilitating; and any excess of either cold or heat, being equally injurious, should be carefully guarded against."

The next grand point to make the hunting-box complete are daily, well-ordered, well-cooked repasts.

SPORTSMAN'S FARE.

How often is a good day's sport spoiled by a dinner of excellent but unsuitable viands—spoiled by the cook's relying on a degree of punctuality which, where fox-hunters are concerned, is simply impossible!

Fox-hunter's fare should be appetising, digestible, and nourishing. If the party is large, and composed partly of strangers to the host or hostess, it should include dishes which will satisfy a fine young healthy appetite, as well as dishes that will tempt those who feel a little feverish after their fatigue.

The nominal dinner-hour may be fixed at seven or eight o'clock, not earlier than six, but the whole *menu* should be capable of being set on the table in due rotation within thirty minutes after the hunters are heard tramping into the yard to the accompaniment of a deep-sounding table-bell.

To carry out this theory of fox-hunters' dinners, it is evident that large dishes of such boiled fish as cod, salmon, or turbot, or large joints of meat, that require a quarter of an hour to the pound weight to roast, are quite unsuitable. The unfortunate cook who has prepared a turbot and Dutch sauce, with a fine haunch of mutton to follow, for a seven o'clock dinner, will find these *pièces de résistance*, with their vegetables, completely spoiled at eight o'clock, and the same fate would await ill-chosen *entrées*.

It may be taken for granted, that however late the hungry hunters arrive, half an hour is the very least time in which they can exchange their hunting for their dining clothes. So short a time as thirty minutes will only be made to suffice where a very long ride and arrival home long after the nominal hour of dinner has made the manipulation of hair-brushes and the tying of cravats a secondary consideration. But whatever the time allowed between the arrival of the sportsmen and putting the first dish on the table, the bill of fare should be fitted to it.

I have assumed that, even where the party consists entirely of men, the wholesome rule is insisted on that at the least no one shall sit down in his hunting-dress.

At the celebrated hunting hotel, the Haycock, Wansford, in the good old times, it used to be the rule that every one should dress for dinner, so that there should be no room for the eccentricities of the lazy and slovenly ; and it proved to be a very good rule.

The first course should be soup—a clear soup—because a *potage* is more easily digested than a *purée*, which is thickened with flour of some kind.

Formerly it might have been necessary to swell these pages with bills of fare ; but, in the present day any lady who is her own housekeeper, and any housekeeper who is fit to take charge of a bachelor's hunting-box, ought to be able to construct *menus* for every hunting day that no amount of unpunctuality will spoil.

There are, no doubt, very good sportsmen who are perfectly content with a soup principally composed of hot water, grease, pepper, and wine ; fried fat chops from long-woolled sheep, following a cod-fish boiled to rags. There are others who do not object to a perpetual course of steak-and-kidney pudding or Irish stew, or who can satisfy the sacred pangs of hunger on a cold joint, accompanied with potatoes boiled to starch ; but these lines are addressed to those who like to *dine*, as distinguished from mere eating, once a day, and are not content, like schoolboys and ploughboys, with anything, so long as there is plenty of it.

English cooks do not, as a rule, understand making soup with flavour and without grease. For sportsmen there is nothing better than the French *pot au feu*, which is always at the side of the fire simmering day and night. But if the cook is not strong in this department, the Aberdeen tinned soups leave little to be desired by any reasonable person.

The fish to follow the soup must be either fried, or stewed, or broiled. Frying soles, or any other suitable fish, cut into small pieces, is only a matter of minutes, which may be done while the soup and glass of dry sherry are being discussed. The *entrées* (one should be enough) must be selected from the list of those which may be prepared all ready and cooked within twenty minutes. This list includes cutlets, larks, and *rissoles* of various kinds. A small braised joint of beef or mutton will stand stewing for an unlimited period, and form the *pièce de résistance*, or, in plain English, the cut-and come-again joint. If the party is small, a *poulet à la Marengo* is quickly cooked, and easy of digestion. Game, snipe, and plover can all be cooked within the limited time allowed for the dinner, say an hour. There is nothing easier of digestion or more succulent than a steak of red deer venison broiled.

It is not my object to write a cookery chapter, but to indicate the lines, by simmering, braising, frying, broiling, and *sautéing*, on which an intelligent cook may construct little dinners, which will be prepared between the arrival of the guests and the time when the sweets should be put on the table.

A nobleman, now deceased, who used to fill his country house in the hunting season with a fair proportion of hunters and non-hunters, never varied his dinner-hour; but, in settling every morning the *menu* with his *chef* (one of the most serious of his occupations), always decided on a series of dishes which would not be spoiled by delay. If we arrived at anything like near the dinner-hour we silently slipped into places, and, by omitting a course or so, by degrees got on good terms with the more punctual starters; but if we were absolutely late, a neat dinner, especially cooked for us, was laid out in the bachelors' breakfast-room.

Good cookery is not dearer than bad; but to obtain it, some one in the house must understand its first principles—if not the lady of the house, the housekeeper.

Immediately on arriving—before undressing—fox-hunters require something, when the day has been long and the weather inclement, as support during the time that must elapse before dinner is on the table. Some take tea; some brandy, rum, or gin-and-milk; others prefer a glass of dry sherry. I prefer a breakfast-cup of good clear soup.

In France, after a ball, in the small hours of the morning, at all good houses, every lady is offered a cup of appetising *consommé*, a clear soup, which is, they say, *calmant et digestif*, and, in my opinion, much more refreshing than tea after hunting.

Hunting breakfasts are proverbially substantial. For my own part I have never been able to understand how a man could ride hard after a hot cutlet, a couple of eggs, a plateful of cold meat, washed down with two cups of tea, a glass of curaçoa, and, with some, a pint of ale. Those who can digest all this before the hounds find their fox are very fortunate. According to the maxims of training, drink is hostile to the condition of a running or a rowing man. I think it the same with riding, and that a fox-hunter will go best through a severe day who eats only nourishing compact food, and drinks only enough to wash it down. A lean chump chop broiled, a hunch of stale bread, and a small cup of tea, or a tumbler of claret-and-water, support without stupefying. But there are no fixed rules for the sustenance of man—they vary with age, health, and dimensions.

The men who cannot find appetite and digestion for a solid, substantial breakfast must take care to furnish their sandwich-cases properly. Sandwiches are generally dry and thirst-provoking; very few cooks know how to cut them, even if they have the materials for making them. Cold fowl or game, not over roasted, make the best provant for the hunting-field. Here again the editors of cookery books might add a new chapter with advantage for the benefit of sportsmen and travellers.

The hunting-flask is presumed to be filled either for refreshment or for a "pick me up." The latter ought only to be required after a heavy fall. According to modern practice, instead of bleeding a patient who has been rolled over or otherwise knocked out of time, a nip of brandy or whiskey is administered as soon as he has sense enough to swallow. As no one expects to fall, although as a matter of fact every straight rider gets at least one fall in a season, the supply of neat spirits may be left to the good nature of the "field." On the occasion of an accident in any of the established hunting counties there are always at least half a dozen flasks at the disposal of the sufferer.

Some persons are never thirsty, and after the hardest run over the stiffest country require no fillip. These are usually young men in the highest condition, who have confined their dinner potations to a few glasses of sound claret. After late hours, with uncounted cigars and B. & S.'s, a hurried breakfast with no appetite, the drinking-flask is likely to be drawn on even before the hounds have found.

Flasks are filled with all sorts of drinks, from cold tea, claret, sherry-and-water, to brandy, whiskey, or gin. Two of the best Masters of fox-hounds this country ever saw filled their long horn flasks with gin-and-water, and seldom tasted them until they turned their horses' heads towards home. And I knew a very hard man who never carried anything in his flask but cold tea. Cold tea should be an infusion made with cold water.

The worst flasks are of metal, silver, or plated pewter, which cannot be properly cleansed. The best are of glass covered with leather if worn in the pocket, and with wicker if fitted into a hunting horn-case attached to the pommel of the saddle. There can be no doubt that the less a man drinks in the field the better for his riding. As for those poor wretches who require Dutch courage, in the shape of drams, to brace their nerves before riding a run, they are much fewer in number than when "Nimrod" wrote his "Life of Jack Mytton," and very much to be pitied.

It is quite certain that no man can retain his riding nerve who, after sitting up late to drink or smoke, is obliged to get up early to hunt.

On the way home, if it becomes necessary to take any refreshment at roadside taverns, brandy and wine are to be avoided, as the chances are in favour of their being, if not of British, of Hamburgh manufacture. Milk can generally be obtained; this, with a dash of the truly English liquor gin, will be found a wholesome restorative to an empty, exhausted stomach. In Scotland or Ireland whiskey would naturally take the place of "Old Tom."

The arts of "making shift" have been carried to such perfection of late years for the benefit of yachtsmen, boat pic-nickers and canoeists, that young sportsmen, encamping in an old-fashioned farm-house for the benefit of hunting, need no longer be dependent on the limited resources of a farm-house furniture and kitchen. The well of an ordinary dog-cart will carry enough to make any room of four bare walls comfortable, if not luxurious, while the preserved soups and meats and fish of Aberdeen and America will amply make up for the deficiencies of a rural larder.

I have not anywhere heard, except in the pages of a novel, of the resources of the private telegraph system being utilised in a country mansion. One can imagine an arrangement by which the return of a hunting-party might be notified to the stud-groom and *chef de cuisine* the moment they passed a telegraph station within ten miles, and again when the lodge-gates of a park are anything like a mile from the house.

"Nimrod" relates that the first Duke of Cleveland,

"Darlington's peer, with his chin sticking out and his cap on one ear,"

had suits of dress clothes deposited at several farm-houses within a certain distance round Raby Castle. To one of these stations he used to ride when the hunting day was finished, and dress while his pad groom went for a post-chaise. As the duke entered the lodge-gates, a mile from the castle, a cannon was fired, and as he drove up to the door the dinner was served. What became of his lordship's guest who had not dressing-room and dress suits at hand the chronicler does not mention. A simpler and cheaper plan than telegraph wires would be the cultivating of the homing pigeons which Mr. Tegetmeier has made so popular. A few deposited at farm-houses in a circle embracing the probable hunt might be loosed by

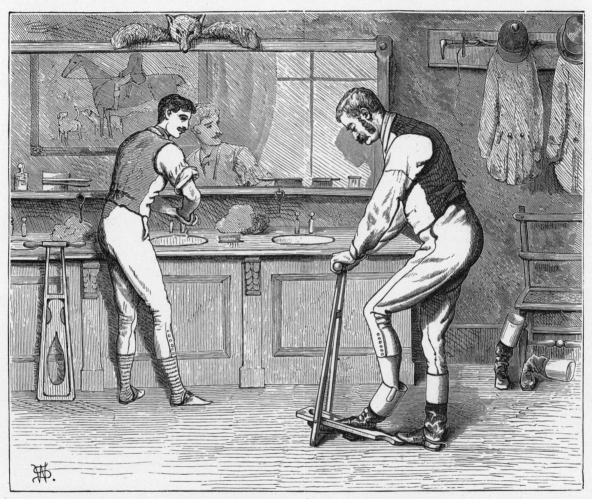

THE FOX-HUNTER'S BOOT-JACK.

a second horseman, with a cypher message for the cook or butler, when the master turned his horse's head homewards.

George III. did not manage his hunting so luxuriously as Lord Darlington, for he told the Duke of Gloucester that, "when we hunt together, neither my brother (the Duke of Cumberland) nor my son (the Prince of Wales) will speak to me; and one day lately, when the chase ended at a little village where there was only one post-chaise, my son and brother got into it and drove away to London, leaving me to ride to Windsor in a cart, if I could get one."*

* "Memoirs of Charles James Fox," by Lord John Russell.

HUNTING (MEET) BREAKFASTS.

It is a time-honoured custom that, when hounds meet to draw certain coverts, the resident at the nearest house should give a breakfast to the Master of the hounds and all comers, without invitation.   The persons who practise a kind of open-house hospitality, unknown in any other part of the world, vary in degree from plain farmers to great noblemen.   The ordinary character of these "free feeds" has been immortalised in John Leech's illustrations of the "Adventures of Mr. Soapy Sponge," the hard-riding horse "coper," and Mr. Jorrocks. grocer and Master of the Handley Cross Hounds.

When a rich migrant from town to country life, with all his way to make in the county, settles down in a mansion to which a famous fox-covert is annexed, where it has been usual from time immemorial to precede the drawing by a breakfast-meet ; or when, as is sometimes the case, the new squire makes a bid for the good word of the old squirearchy by establishing a fox-covert on his newly-purchased estate, the arrangement of the entertainment becomes a matter of serious consideration.

If it be done at all it should be done well, but not too well.   On this point some "grave and reverend seignior"—some acknowledged go-between—of the hunt, the sporting doctor or parson, should be consulted.   There is nothing county families resist more than being outblazed by mere money.   The object should be to give as good a breakfast as has ever been given, but not remarkable for any startling innovations.

Unless the rooms and hall are very large, and plenty of servants available, a stand-up breakfast, where people may freely help themselves, is the best.   The dishes should be selected on the plan of requiring the least possible amount of carving.

When the meet runs up to and over a hundred horsemen, no one but a millionnaire should attempt hot dishes.   The late Duke of Portland did once give to Lord Galway's hunt, at Welbeck Abbey, a hot breakfast as complete as ever was served up to a wedding party in Belgrave Square ; but there the underground kitchen communicated by a tramway and a lift with the (on all other days of the year for ten years) deserted banqueting-hall. This duke was more eccentric than the most eccentric English peer of a French romance. The breakfast is mentioned as a curiosity, not as an example.

The liquors are a matter of prime importance, and are too often neglected, that is, two qualities are provided, one for the Master of the hounds and his party, the other for the *oi polloi* —a very great mistake.   Sherry, brandy-and-water, with bitter ale, all good, are variety enough.   Six dozen of really good sherry at a hunt breakfast have been known to establish the reputation of a new resident, and £10 would probably represent the difference between a superior and a common article.   The brandy should be old ; the ale the cleanest tap that Burton or Stratford-on-Avon can produce, supplied from barrels if the "field" is very large, each barrel under the charge of an obliging servant.   In a fine ancient or modern baronial hall, quarter casks of sherry, with silver taps, may be set up with good effect ; the main object being to make the "Hunt" feel that they are welcome to come in and eat and drink without ceremony.

If it is the custom of the county to give champagne, not otherwise, it should be of a brand safe from headaches.

In very cold weather mulled claret, not poisoned with curaçoa or cognac or other messes, but simply warmed with sugar and a little spice, will be gratefully accepted by many who do not care to leave their horses.

Handing round glasses of cherry brandy is one of the superstitions of British hunting breakfasts, an excellent liquor for producing a headache in its ordinary home-made form. If, in deference to old established custom, it is considered necessary to give it in addition to dry sherry, old cognac, mulled claret, and sound bitter ale, the wiser plan is to purchase cherry brandy of Copenhagen manufacture.

The success of a breakfast meet is very much enhanced if the giver engages a large number of countrymen to hold the horses of the guests. Fifty men at a shilling apiece will take charge of a hundred horses, and then their riders will have no excuse for not availing themselves of the hospitality of the giver of the feast.

Some persons treat the Master of the hounds—especially if he be a peer—like royalty, and entertain him and his set in an inner apartment on superior fare. But it is certainly not "good form," and would not please such Masters of hounds as the Earl Spencer, the Earl of Coventry, or of Portsmouth.

Well-planned and well-executed, a hunt breakfast may be found a not unimportant step towards county society.

THE LITERATURE OF HUNTING.

Young people of both sexes who have not been bred in a hunting county or surrounded from their earliest years by fox-hunting society, yet in whom love of the chase has cropped up strongly, as it often does in the most unexpected places and families, naturally desire to know what to read in the days and in the evenings when they cannot be, whatever their means or their leisure, hunting or on horseback.

My answer when this question is put to me is:—"Invest in the railway-station novels of Whyte Melville and Anthony Trollope, and particularly, as to the latter, in 'Phineas Finn,' the 'Eustace Diamonds,' and the 'American Senator.'" No one can describe a good run with hounds like Whyte Melville; but for an unlucky day with a refusing horse, for all the drawbacks and commonplaces of hunting, including a blank day, commend me to Anthony Trollope. His "Masters of Hounds" and his "Members of a Provincial Hunt" are like perfect photographs from life.

The author of "The Handley Cross Hounds" and the "Adventures of Mr. Soapy Sponge" was thoroughly versed in the arts of the hunting-field and the ways of hunting men. In one or two characters—for instance, Mr. Jorrocks's north country huntsman, James Pigge—he fairly rivalled the immortal Sam Weller; but he was a writer of a diseased mind, and only delighted in describing what was mean, low, and disgusting; all his prominent characters—they cannot be called heroes—are coarse, vulgar ruffians, whether lords or tea-dealers. There are too many sporting writers who follow this line without Mr. Surtees' talents.

DISTRIBUTION OF THE DEAD FOX.

A fox killed by hounds belongs to the master of those hounds. 1. The head, or mask, is carried home, tied to the coupling-buckle, on the saddle of the first whip, to be nailed on the kennel door. 2. The brush, after a straight-away chase, is commonly claimed by "the first man up;" and this claim is always, by courtesy, acknowledged by the master. It is an act of courtesy on his part, and a general custom, but not an absolute right on the part of the man "first up." 3. The pads are the perquisite of the huntsman and whips. The second Earl of Lonsdale gave Hugo Meynell for his authority.

CHAPTER XXIV.

EXPENSES OF A CARRIAGE AND HORSES—STABLES AND COACH-HOUSES.

Jobbing, when Advantageous—Detailed Cost—Idleness the Bane of Pleasure Horses—Stables—A Dry Foundation—An Impervious Floor—Ventilation Without Draught—Stalls, Boxes—Washing-house—Sheltered Yard—Saddle-room—Lofts and Fodder Stores—Foundation and Drains Described—Best Material for Walls—Mangers—Partitions, Elm-wood—Corn Stores, Metal-lined—Water in Iron Buckets—A Tower Reservoir—A Force of Water Valuable—Economical Stables Described—Luxurious Stables—Value of Heating Apparatus and Warm Water Supply—Saddle and Harness Room must be dry—Drawers and Closets for—Modern Contrivances for Stable Use—Model Stables.

THE expenses of setting up a carriage may be divided as follows :—

1. The purchase of a carriage.   2. Purchase of a horse or horses, and occasional losses by death or sickness.   3. Cost of provender, shoeing, and veterinary attendance.   4. The cost and wear and tear of stable-fittings and tools.   5. The rent of stable and coach-house.   6. The wages and expenses of one or more servants.

Some of these expenses cannot be estimated.   A brougham horse will cost fifty guineas to one hundred guineas, according to the work required.   Any sum beyond one hundred guineas is paid for superior beauty and action.   A one-horse landau requires a tall, powerful horse of proportionate price.   A miniature brougham may be worked with a horse only fifteen hands high.   A brougham or landau will cost from £120 to £190.   A harness horse can be hired for £40 to £50 a year, and replaced immediately if sick or lame.

A first-class coachmaker will let you a new brougham of any colour you prefer, the panels bearing your own monogram or crest; he will keep it in perfect order, saving accidents—such as tearing off a door by opening it just as you pass a lamp-post—for £40 a year, paid annually in advance.   If the engagement is for five years certain, will give you a new carriage at the end of that time.

In London jobbing is decidedly cheaper than buying any expensive four-wheeled carriage, which is intended to be continually used.   But if it is only to be kept for show on a few days of the year, then it is cheaper to buy.   Dog-carts, T-carts, and waggonettes should be purchased out and out.

It may be taken as an unanswerable maxim in carriage keeping, that it is not the work a pleasure carriage horse does that wears him out, or makes him sick and sorry, but standing about, unnecessarily waiting for hours in draughts, in fog, rain, and snow, and, most of all, being confined to hot stables for day after day without exercise, to save the coachman trouble, "I have often," says Mrs. Burton,* a perfect "Mistress of the Horse" in every capacity, "felt amused in English country houses, where the host has sixteen or twenty horses, to hear the hostess say almost timidly to her fat powdered coachman—'Barker, do you think that I might have the carriage to-day?'   Barker (very crisply)—'No, my lady, you can't.'   Lady (timidly)—

* "Inner Life of Syria."

,Oh, never mind, Barker; I didn't know.' Know what? The sacred mysteries of an English stud. That the horses are choking with food till it bursts out in disease. That their chests and consequently their fore-legs are so affected by being pampered that they cannot do the slightest work with impunity. That the stables are kept so hot that it costs a fatal cough to take the beast outside it."

JOBBING.

In London, at any rate, ladies will find it more economical, and saving an immense amount of trouble, to get everything except the livery or box-coat of the coachman.

The following figures were furnished in reply to inquiries put to one of the most respectable firms in Belgravia, and there are competent job-masters to be found in every quarter of London who are also prepared, when the season is over, to find horses for country use at a considerable reduction on these prices.

A pair of horses, with shoeing and forage, by the year	190 guineas
Without forage	100 „
By the month, in the season ditto ditto	28 „
Without forage	20 „
A pair of horses, harness, brougham, forage, shoeing, and a London coach-man, by the year	315 „
A single horse, with forage, shoeing, &c., by the year	100 „
Without forage, &c.	50 „
A horse, harness, brougham, coachman, forage, shoeing, &c., by the year	210 „

Everything to look like a private equipage, with monogram or crest if desired; hirer to find livery.

Job-masters undertake to supply the place of a sick or lame horse with another: that is to say, where *you deal with a man who has a large stud* you are always sure of not being without a horse longer than is required to make the exchange.

The drawbacks of the jobbing system are that you cannot absolutely secure the class of horse, the colour of horse, or the sort of action you prefer; you must take what the job-master has got, and cannot expect, if you use only one or one pair of horses, to be as well served as if you took several pair for the season.

Job-masters make it a point to understand their customers' habits. They send much better horses to those who use them for two or three hours' steady slow exercise only than to those who keep them out late at night and early in the morning, or who insist on fast driving, and taking excursions to the very limit of the contract—in London, usually seven miles from Charing Cross.

On the other side, if you are fortunate enough to possess one or a pair of sound seasoned horses of your own, that are never, in dealer's phrase, "sick or sorry," they may last you three, five, or ten years. Even then, if full-sized, and somewhat stale, but not actually lame, they will sell or let for something considerable. A celebrated job-master in Mayfair had, a few years ago, a pair of blood barouche horses of the finest action, which were respectively nineteen and twenty years old, let in the season at the highest price.

Thus, the horse that cost you £80 to buy would cost you to job about £150 in three years. It is, in fact, a case between insuring and taking the risk on yourself. The lower the price of the horses you are contented to use, the more the calculation is in favour of purchasing against jobbing. But ladies who are obliged to trust entirely to servants should always job, if within five miles of a job-master.

A professional man (not a doctor) adopted the plan of always having one horse of his own and a jobbing one. Thus for his daily drive to Westminster he always had a horse at his service; his wife had a fashionable stepper for her afternoon calls; and when a distance was to be done, the two were harnessed as a pair. This is an ingenious arrangement, which combines the advantages of the two systems.

In the country, or wherever the nearest job-master lives a distance of a day's journey, or where a horse of a useful character and moderate price will do all that is required, and especially where you have a positive pleasure in admiring and petting your horse, you must purchase; but be prepared for a certain per-centage of loss on the average of a series of years, by death, sickness, lameness, and wearing out.

STABLES.

Nearly two hundred years ago De Grey wrote : " Your stable ought not to have any unsavoury gutter, channel, or sewer near it. The windows must be fitted with handsome casements and shuts, as well to keep out cold and wind as to let in cool fresh air."* These rules are as sound in the nineteenth as in the seventeenth century, but are often grossly neglected.

There are certain points that must be attended to, whether the stud consists of one or thirty ; whether the stables have to be built or are already built, and fitted with all the luxurious appliances that have been invented to meet the demands of modern wealth by the competition of the great stable-fitting trade.

A stable must, if the horses it accommodates are to retain their health, stand on a dry foundation. If it stand on a cold, retentive soil, the stud, however liberally fed and sumptuously clothed, will never be without cases of influenza and acute inflammation until the whole area occupied by the stables and yard has been thoroughly drained and dried.

This operation, placed in the hands of a competent agricultural drainer, can generally be performed at a moderate expense ; but, whatever be the cost, it will be cheaper than losing one horse by death, and the services of others for week after week. A deep drain of porous tiles, run round, or in some cases through and under the stable, and carried to a proper outfall, is the only resource on clay soils.

If a stable is to be built from the ground, unless the foundation is chalk or deep self-drained gravel, the better plan is to excavate, put in drains, and fill up the area to be occupied with concrete. These drains have no reference to those required for the surface drainage of the stable, but they may be connected with them.

Ventilation (that is, fresh air) is of as much importance as drainage (that is, dry ground) for keeping horses in the highest degree of health. Many a stud which has been neither sick nor sorry while standing in old-fashioned buildings that let the wind by the roof, the doors, and the windows, have pined and sickened when removed to a building erected regardless of cost.

A damp stable must be unhealthy, but a stable that is both damp and hot is a pest-house— a seed-bed of diseases of the feet, the lungs, and the eyes.

Horses that are out all day and every day can resist malarious influences which will surely affect horses highly fed and little exercised.

When the late Mr. Henry Hope built the mansion opposite the Green Park which is now occupied by a club, he also erected a magnificent set of stables on the first floor over his coach-houses, and carefully drained them into the street sewers. The result was that he lost nearly all

* "The Compleat Horseman" (1680).

his stud by a sort of sewer or typhoid fever; while stables in the neighbourhood without any surface-drains, but carefully cleaned out, were perfectly healthy.

On the other hand, when the Earl of Stamford sold his numerous stud by auction on resigning the Mastership of the Quorn Hounds, it was generally admitted that never had so many horses been brought to the hammer in such fine condition; yet they were lodged in stables not better than those of cart-horses on a large farm of the old style, before model farms were invented.

After the foundation, the floor is a matter of prime importance; it should be durable, quite impervious to wet, *and not slippery.*

If it is provided with surface-drains for carrying off the urine and washing of the horses, they should be constructed in such a manner that they can be cleaned out from day to day. Gratings and traps, however ingeniously devised, seldom prevent the drains being choked; and cast-iron traps, even if not lifted by the grooms, are pretty sure to be broken.

But if the horses are bountifully supplied with bedding of straw or sawdust, the damp portions of which are regularly removed every morning and evening, it is by no means essential that there should be surface-drains at all. A mere open channel leading to the *outside* of the stable is the best arrangement.

They are not used, according to Colonel Fitzwygram, in cavalry barracks. There were none in the Pytchley stables when Mr. Anstruther Thompson was Master, and there are thousands of hard-working horses standing on sawdust in London, without a drain.

An impervious floor is a great advantage: it can be washed and dried easily. Asphalte made rough is the best, but it is costly. A concrete foundation made up with gas-tar, four inches thick, on which stable clinkers are set and bedded, and grouted in with Portland cement, makes a very perfect floor.

The materials of the walls may be wood, stone, or brick. The bricks glazed on the inside are the best, as they hold no dirt. If stone, wood, or soft bricks be used, the walls facing the horses' heads should be lined with slate or tiles. For the convenience of manufacture the posts and ramps of the most expensive stables are usually made of iron. Oak posts answer quite as well, are warmer, and not so liable to cause capped hocks as iron. The divisions of stalls and boxes, if not of brick, should be of elm, beech, or oak, not less than two inches thick, but dents when a hoof shod with iron rattles against it. At Rugby, the stables of a dealer—"The Man of the Age," they call him—erected regardless of expense, are built entirely of brick—even the mangers are of brick, and each horse has a one-roomed cottage entirely to himself.

When the owner is only a tenant, it may answer to erect stables of wood, fixed on a properly prepared foundation, and constructed in such a manner that they can be taken to pieces and removed without much expense to another place. Such buildings may be procured from Sweden at a comparatively cheap rate, constructed from the owner's own plan, and fitted together like a toy-house.

Mangers may be of iron, slate, or hard wood, the edges lined with iron, or some impervious material that can be kept clean. A moderately long manger is to be preferred, because horses generally begin by spreading their corn about, and if the manger is too small, they waste a good deal by driving it over the edges. A circle of wood or metal, into which a full-sized galvanised iron bucket, with lips on each side, and without a handle, can be dropped, answers every purpose as well as the most costly contrivances. It has this great advantage over a permanent water-hole: that the bucket can be emptied every time before the horse is re-watered. There are very strong objections to a water-trough which cannot be emptied without giving the groom trouble.

The best plan of supplying hay is by an iron rack, fixed at just the height that a horse can feed without the hay-seed dropping into his eyes. Where the rack is placed level with the manger, the bars should be of strong wrought-iron, close together. Instances have occurred of colts and stallions injuring themselves severely by rearing and dropping their feet into a low rack.

The question of whether stalls or boxes may be here answered with, Both! Boxes are invaluable for a tired horse, a sick horse, for a young horse in course of breaking, or for a horse that must stand idle occasionally for several days. A horse which can change his position at will in a loose box, and thus ease his muscles, will last longer than one tied in a stall. If the stable is only for two horses, there should be one box, and so on in proportion.

A box should be, if possible, twelve feet by fourteen; but any box where a horse can turn round is better, as a change, than constant imprisonment in a stall. A box of brick should be lined throughout with wood, and the wood, wherever the horse's teeth can be used, lined with zinc plates. There should be no projections of any kind, as horses kick and roll in boxes more than in stalls, if fresh; and, where horses are very valuable, the feeding apparatus should be so contrived that they can be fed without entering the box. This may easily be done by a modification of Torr's pig troughs, manufactured by Crosskill, of Beverley, or by Professor Varnell's patent apparatus, sold by the St. Pancras Iron Works Company. Where space is limited, the end stall of a stable may be converted into a box by having a gate that can be hung on the stall post and fastened against the wall. A box is best closed by a screen hung on rollers from a top bar. No horse can open this, and it can never be out of order.

It is a disputed point whether horses do best alone, or within hearing of each other, in boxes. At the Rugby stables the horses are in solitary confinement, and can hear and smell nothing; and it is claimed for this plan that they are much quieter than on the old system. Certainly it is a better plan for mares and stallions.

The best windows for the smallest as well as the largest stables are *well-constructed sash-windows*, reaching to the ceiling, if not more than twelve feet high, and sliding both above and below, fitted with cords and pulleys of the best description. Iron sashes, opening in various ways, are often recommended, but they are inferior to wooden sash-windows for stable purposes, because they do not so easily lend themselves to ventilation. Sash-windows can be opened an inch at the top or the bottom, or the full width of one sash; and the draught thus created may be directed to the ceiling by a screen, or mitigated by a wire blind, or by many other contrivances. Except the cords, there is no machinery to get out of order in a sash-window. Any man or boy ought to be able to open or shut them.

They should be glazed with rough plate, which subdues the light and is strong enough to bear a thrust from a horse's nose. The master in a small establishment should see that the windows are opened daily, and consequently in good working order.

Where there is no ceiled loft, and the stable is open to the roof, the modes available for ventilation are too numerous to mention, but they are generally useless. Grooms, who usually prefer hot stables to elbow-grease for getting a silky coat on their horses, find ways of stopping them up. "The troop horses of my regiment," said the colonel of the 2nd Life Guards, "live in stables where the windows are open winter and summer. My hunters my stud-groom insists on keeping in a sort of hothouse. The troopers scarcely ever have colds; the hunters are constantly sick." Some persons use a deodoriser—the best deodorisers are cleanliness and fresh air. If a stable is properly paved, well ventilated, and the litter removed every day into the yard, the atmosphere would stand in no need of a deodoriser; while, if cleanliness and ventilation are neglected, the improvement effected by the best deodoriser will be very partial, and leave the root of the mischief unattacked.

Windows should be provided with inside or outside shutters or louvres, to keep out the light, heat, and flies in summer.

Stable doors should be not less than seven feet by four feet; eight feet by five are better dimensions, as they allow a horseman to ride out after mounting in the stable. Doors should be divided into two sections, so that the upper may be opened in hot weather, and its place, if needful, supplied by a lattice door. The fastening of the door should never project. Many a valuable horse has been blemished by a projecting key carelessly left in the lock.

The question of stalls or boxes is like that of the gold and silver shields—both, properly constructed, are good. To have the whole of a large stud in boxes is simply impossible; but however small the stud, the owner should contrive to have a certain number of boxes. An idle horse gets exercise, and a tired horse gets a degree of rest in boxes for every leg, that cannot be enjoyed in stalls.

Stalls for full-sized horses should be full wide. A set designed by Lord Combermere are all six feet six inches wide, but six feet is generally ample. Stalls should not be less than nine feet six inches long; ten feet is better. Horses constantly get kicked in short stalls.

Small horses not exceeding fifteen hands may be accommodated in narrower stalls. In London, where stable-rent is very high, large horses are constantly packed into such narrow stalls that it is a wonder how they can lie down.

Many cases of fractured hip-bone and dislocated spine have arisen from horses lying down in stalls too narrow for them. The divisions should always be so high that the occupants will not be tempted to try to bite or kick each other. Where well-bred mares are rails are objectionable; the division should be solid to the top. If the hinder part is not as high as the roof, it is better that it should be not more than four feet two inches, without a projecting pillar. Many a horse turning quickly in his stall at the call of an impatient groom has injured an eye by striking it against a high ornamental pillar or ball crowning the stall-posts. In the stalls of valuable horses coarse hempen mats should be hung at the end of each side of the stall.

It is not necessary to describe the details of a well-fitted stable, because they may be seen at the establishments of any stable-fitting manufacturer. In London the St. Pancras Company has a show-room a hundred feet long, fitted with every variety of stable establishment, from the cheapest to the most expensive.

Where it is decided to have lofts over stables, the best floor of the loft is of brick, arched, or of concrete; if of wood, the space between the floor and the ceiling should be filled up with old mortar, chalk, or other non-inflammable material, in order to exclude vermin and deaden all sound.

If the stable-yard is not covered with a roof, a convenient room, with a paved or asphalte floor, should be provided, for washing, singeing, and clipping horses. If gas is not available staples should be provided for fixing lamps, so as to obtain a first-rate light at night. It is an advantage if this washing-room adjoins the stables, and communicates with them by a wide door.

It is disadvantageous to have the coach-house and saddle-room communicating with the stable, because the fumes are sure to tarnish metal and glazed leather.

The harness and saddle room should be well provided with stands for saddles and harness, hanging-hooks for cleaning bridles, and with cases with glazed doors, which are for hanging up sets of harness, bridles, and bits, so that what is not used may be *seen* daily and not left to rust or become mouldy. There must also be presses for putting away horse-clothing, stocks of bandages, sponges, leathers, and all the reserve tools required by a groom. The saddle-room should be provided with a good stove (the pattern invented by Captain Galton, in use at Woolwich and in many barracks, is one of the best), taps with hot and cold water, and a sink. This will often be the coachman and groom's dressing-room, and when that is the case time will be saved and cleanliness ensured by good, plain lavatory arrangements. The hot-water pipes, as before observed, in the chapter on the hunting-box, should be utilised to keep the saddle-room dry; but to dry wet horse furniture of any kind, and the men's clothes, after hunting, a hot closet or drying-room should be expressly provided. Horses suffer greatly from being covered with damp clothing.

The money expended in making the saddle-room a comfortable living-room for the grooms is not wasted; it will save many an hour's work that would be wasted elsewhere, if

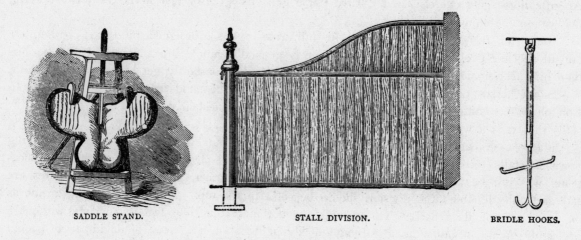

SADDLE STAND.   STALL DIVISION.   BRIDLE HOOKS.

it were dark, cold, and draughty. Dark holes and obscure corners are answerable for a great deal of waste of material and time in stables.

In large establishments oats are best stored in a proper corn-loft over some part of the stable buildings prepared for the purpose by floors and sides partly lined with lead or zinc, and communicating with a corn-chest, of iron, by a spout, all under lock and key in charge of the head groom.

In town stables, where space is valuable and ventilation important, stables are ingeniously planned so as to be open to the roof, but with galleries on each wall for the storage of fodder. But in every great town it is easy to find examples of well-planned, well-managed stables. The great point is to attend to the arrangements which secure plenty of light, dry, fresh air, and the detailed contrivances for securing neatness.

Coach-house arrangements are much more neglected than those of stables. A carriage requires as much care as a sofa, and is often treated like a wheelbarrow, thrust after use into a damp shed, to encourage the decay of the silk, velvet, or leather linings, and cause violent colds to the ladies who sit in it without the slightest precaution, when within doors they carefully dry and warm everything, from a pair of stockings to a pocket-handkerchief. The coach-house in small establishments is often also the harness-room. It should have a well-laid wooden floor—wood block pavement is the best—the walls carefully plastered or lined with match-boarding, and, if possible, be artificially warmed. Ventilation should be secured by shafts or windows; the doors should close and open easily.

At a mansion in Bedfordshire I saw wooden rolling shutters, like the steel shutters of shops, used for coach-house doors.

Every coach-house should be provided with a "pent," overhanging six or eight feet, under which a carriage can be cleaned in wet weather.

It is a great advantage to be able to apply a force of water, either to horses or carriages. A strong douche is a wonderful remedy for strained sinews of the legs or muscles of the back, as well as for washing a very muddy horse. A powerful jet directed on a dirty carriage, instead of a brush, will make paint and varnish last many years beyond average, and enable a man to get through his cleaning duty rapidly and effectually without the use of that mischievous thing, a spoke-brush; directed against the strained sinews of a horse's fore-legs, it will often supersede the use of blisters or irons.

For this reason a tower, to hold a water-cistern, to be filled by steam, horse, wind, or hand power, is a useful as well as picturesque addition to a complete set of stabling. It may also hold a clock.

The single row stables at Tattersall's afford a good example of stalls well fitted up, without any extravagant expense. Every horse there has a slate or glazed surface facing him—a very important point; but, except the mangers and glazed headstalls, all the other fittings may be of wood, if in the situation where the stables are constructed wood is cheaper than iron. Near great towns a contract with a manufacturer of stable-fittings will generally be found the better plan; a dry foundation, thoroughly drained, having been first secured.

The best set of stables I have seen near London are at Cricklewood, built by Newman and Stansley. Nothing is wanting for the comfort of horses in health or sickness except a Turkish bath, a most valuable remedy for influenza or exhaustion.*

CLOTHING.

Popular lecturers have compared the stomach of a warm-blooded animal to a furnace which must be fed with food instead of fuel. On this theory, when cavalry horses are picketed out in the open air, in cold weather, the best way of keeping up their condition is to give them an additional feed of beans and oats. Horses at liberty can bear a very low degree of cold, if they are not also exposed to wet. Exposed to cold they become rough as bears and sluggish as donkeys, but not incapable of work. Clothing assists, and is indeed indispensable, for obtaining a bright smooth coat, and for protecting horses from chill when they return to their stables after violent exertions.

The Turcoman robbers keep their thoroughbred horses they use on their plundering expeditions in the open air, heavily clothed with camel-hair felt.

In addition to the warm clothing required in the cold months of the year, summer clothing of light kersey, with a quarter-cloth of brown-holland, neatly bound with coloured tape, is often provided, adorned with the crest, or monogram, or initials of the owner—the last being a useful precaution in strange stables, where unmarked clothing and other portable articles are as likely to be lost or exchanged as hats and umbrellas in a coffee-room.

These day suits, complete, cost, without the supplemental blankets, from £5 to £6 each. Night suits, without hoods, of less expensive material, are also required to save the day clothing.

* Mr. Joseph Constantine, 23, Oxford Street, Manchester, manufactures a "Convoluted Stove," which is economical and easily managed, for heating a Turkish bath on a small scale.

But, except for travelling by railway or by sea, or in cases of sickness, it is very doubtful whether for horses in ordinary use hoods and breast-cloths are of any real advantage. At any rate, they are dispensed with in the stables of many first-class country horse-dealers, and only put on when a horse is dressed out for show or prepared for travelling.

It is very important to have enough clothing, of however plain and simple a character, to keep horses required to be in galloping condition thoroughly warm in cold weather.

For ordinary use, two suits—viz., a day suit and a night suit—will answer every purpose. The day suit may consist of a common rug cut out to fit, and fastened over the chest with a strap and buckle, and one or two additional blankets for colder weather, secured with a surcingle or stable-girth, sometimes called a roller, which is generally made of coloured webbing, with a stuffed pad, but wear better and are cleanest if all of leather, like those used by Mr. Rice of Piccadilly. Surcingles should have a bit of elastic inserted in the leather girth or a steel spring inserted in them so as to protect from the serious evil of tight girthing. Tom Colman, of St. Albans, invented, years ago, an elastic roller, which is, I think, sold by Mr. Blackwell. On most horses a breast-strap must be used to prevent the clothing from slipping and avoid an excuse for the mischievous practice of tight girthing. Well-fitting sets of knee-caps, of the best make, should be kept on hand in every stable, and always put on when horses are sent out to exercise. Hoods are, perhaps, wise precautions when sending horses long journeys by rail in cold weather. But several persons, who have been in the habit of sending their horses down and bringing them back, after hunting with the Royal Buck-hounds, without any clothing, declare that they have never known any ill effects to arise from a practice I should hesitate to imitate or recommend.

Whatever be the day suit, it is well to have a night suit, which may partly consist of an old patched day suit, with or without an additional blanket, according to the season of the year. Horse-clothing made of blankets, instead of the usual felted cloth, answers better for the night clothing, because it is sure to get dirty with the horses lying down at night, and blankets wash and dry much better than cloth.

When the night suit is removed, previous to the morning dressing, it should be brushed and sponged over to remove stains, and hung out of doors, or in a draught under cover, to dry.

If, from false economy, the same clothing be worn by a horse day and night, he will constantly be wearing it not only dirty but damp, to the injury of his health and appearance, and would be much better without any clothing at all.

A groom, like a sailor, should be able to use a tailor's needle and a saddler's awl. The best are the most willing to be generally useful in their own departments.

The best blankets for the purpose are coloured brown or blue, similar to those manufactured for the use of the army and navy. The groom should be able to cut the quarter-cloth out to the proper shape, and any village saddler can attach the strap and buckle.

All the horse-cloths, if properly taken care of, on the principle that a stitch in time saves nine, will last for years. The night clothing, which is more liable to be torn, should be carefully examined and repaired every day when it is taken off and hung up to dry.

In a show stable, where the owner is in the habit of bringing his friends to admire his stud and smoke a cigar, the luxuries of fine-coloured quarter-cloths, beautifully emblazoned with his crest, will of course be indulged in, and then they had better be obtained from a first-class saddler. But a horse may be kept quite as warm as is desirable, at half the cost, by using the cheaper material.

Two blankets are warmer than one heavy cloth.

There should always be a sufficient number of sets of bandages of both flannel and linen.

Flannel Bandages save time in drying wet legs, and are partly a substitution for hand-rubbing; by their warmth they act as a mild fomentation, reducing inflammation and swelling. But many very practical men object to their use after the legs have become dry, unless the horse is ill.

When they have been rolled on wet legs they should be removed as soon as dry, or they will cause injurious heat.

Linen Bandages, wet, and kept wet, are useful in cases of bruises or inflammation from other causes. Unless a groom's time can be punctually given to keep them wet they will do harm. An india-rubber water bottle, with a narrow tube, may be so arranged as to drop water on bandages for a whole day, if the horse is made fast to pillar reins.

Bandages should only be put on tight when it is necessary to reduce windgalls or other soft swellings.

Those bandages only meant for warmth, or to protect a young horse against thorns and bangs in the cub-hunting season, should be rolled on just tight enough to prevent their slipping down, and no more. It should be impressed on grooms, who generally put bandages on too tightly "that each succeeding fold increases the pressure of those below." The art of putting on bandages properly should be carefully learned by every young groom. Bandages are expensive to purchase in sets. Where they are much used, the cheaper plan is to purchase a large piece of the material, have it cut up into sets, and sewn by one of the grooms' wives or in the village girls' school. The saving will be in proportion of something like sixpence to two shillings. Two sets of bandages at least are required for each horse bandaged, because one should always be dry, and there should be some sets in reserve in the horse-clothing drawer for emergencies.

When a horse returns, wet and weary, after a severe day's work of any kind, clothing warmly and bandaging his chilled extremities, after gentle dressing, with appropriate food, a loose box, fresh air, and a soft bed, are the most important means of restoration.

Grooms should be made to understand that although draughts are injurious, horses will be poisoned in a hothouse-like stable, and may be kept in capital condition in the coldest dry stable if they are warmly clothed. The average temperature should be between 45° and 50° of Fahrenheit, or a little warmer in winter than the outside air. If it smells hot, it is too hot. A registering thermometer hung up in a stable of valuable horses will be a useful silent witness for the horse owner.

Headstalls and Ties.—The accompanying wood engraving is a good pattern for one, and will keep in its place, and cannot be easily rubbed off, although some "*rogues*" will pull anything over their heads, except a collar. Care should be taken that the headstall fits, especially that the frontlet or forehead band is not too short, and does not chafe the roots of the ears.

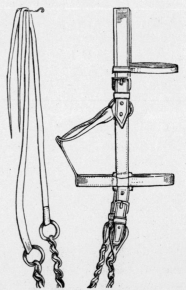

HEADSTALL AND TIE.

A horse should wear a headstall in a loose box, or even if turned out to graze for a few hours in a paddock, because it presents an easy way of holding him when needful. The "tie," as it is called, may be either of rope, leather, or chain. In the woodcut there are two ties next to the horse's head, of chain, so that he may not be tempted to bite it; the rest is of leather. The proper length of a tie should be such that the log will only just reach the ground when the horse is standing over his manger. If longer than this the horse may get his leg over it, and a serious accident follow. If shorter, he cannot lie down comfortably. Chains have the advantage over leather straps or ropes, that their weight prevents the liability to become slack between the ring and the horse's head. Their drawback is the noise they make.

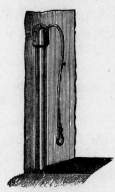

PATENT TIE.

When the stalls are very wide, two ties, as in the woodcut, are used, to prevent the horse turning his tail to the manger. But one is quite as commonly employed. It should be attached to the headstall by a spring swivel catch, which can be detached in an instant. Some very ingenious arrangements have been invented for receiving the tie in a tube (see illustration), so as to protect a horse from entangling a leg in a "slack tie."

In every stall or box there must be a rack-chain, to fasten up the horse's head while he is eating his corn, and when he is being dressed, if he is dressed in his stall, a practice to be avoided if there is convenience for the operation out of the stable. It is important that there should be no hook on this chain on which a horse could catch his eyelids or mouth.

The posts of each stall must be provided with a pair of iron or brass rings, screwed at about the proper height of a horse's head; to these rings are attached the pillar reins, for fastening a horse when saddled or harnessed. White cords, provided with brass spring swivel hooks, are a very neat substitute for chains, if kept perfectly clean. But old girths make very good pillar reins.

In the washing-house a sort of gallows, with pillar reins, to which horses may be fastened, when either dressed, singed, or clipped, is a useful piece of furniture. If a horse is inclined to kick, care should be taken that he is not put on pillar reins where the insufficient length of the divisions of the stalls would allow him to injure himself. Capped hocks are frequently produced in this way.

STABLE TOOLS.

In addition to horse-clothing, head-collars, and rack-chains, the following articles are required in the stable where even one horse and carriage is kept:—Stable forks, shovels, and brooms; pails, corn sieve, and measure; brushes, viz., heel brush, harness brush, plate brush, spoke brush, lining brush, body brush, dandy brush, currycomb; sponges, wash-leathers, scraper, foot-pick, scissors, and comb; iron setter for washing carriage; garden hydrant for ditto; singeing lamp or clipping machine; exercise saddle and watering bridle; buckets; a registering thermometer. See appendix for a priced list of these and other articles sold by saddlers. These articles, when delivered to the groom by the saddler or storekeeper, should be entered in a book, with the date of delivery, so as to check unreasonable consumption; and, if a saddler supplies everything, the book system common with butchers or grocers should be adopted, if economy is a matter of any importance.

The washing buckets should be of wood, the drinking buckets of galvanised iron. The drinking buckets ought never to be used for any other purpose, on any pretext. Fomenting buckets, which are essential in every hunting stable, are of wood or gutta-percha, made expressly for the purpose—narrow cylinders, in fact, as high as a horse's knees. A powerful garden syringe with and without a rose is a useful appliance in a hunting stable.

The prongs of stable forks are of steel; but, in consequence of several horses being severely pricked at the Agricultural Horse Show, I imported wooden forks from France, and they have given general satisfaction. A rack in which every set of forks, brooms, or floor brushes has to be placed, is a necessary fitting for every stable or "mess" of six horses.

For cleaning the stone or asphalte floor of a stable with water, the india-rubber "squeege," used to clean the foot-pavements and asphalte roadways of the City of London, may be used with advantage, in addition to the ordinary stable brooms and whalebone brushes.

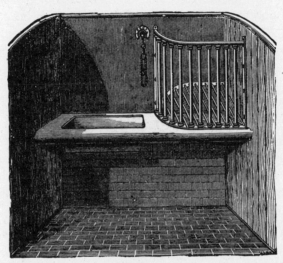

STALL FITTED UP.

Where three or more horses are kept, the better plan is to have a regular store, and lay in a stock of everything from each manufacturer—*i.e.*, brushes from the brushmaker, forks and iron buckets from the ironmonger, and so on. This will make a saving of from fifteen to twenty-five per cent. in articles of the best quality. Sponges may be bought by the pound, or by the hundred-weight, according to the consumption.

GROOMING.

Horses may and do work slowly with little or no grooming; but the best cannot be made of them, either for work or appearance, without perfect cleaning, accompanied by a good deal of friction.

"The outer skin of the horse is continually being renewed by the secretion of cells from the true skin below, and its outer scales are continually in their turn being cast off in the form of the scurf, which is found in the currycomb on which the groom has cleaned his brush. In the skin, having their origin a little below the true skin, are two sets of glands, viz., the sweat and the oil glands. The sweat glands secrete perspiration, and terminate by long-necked tubes on the surface of the skin. The oil glands secrete an oily substance. Each hair tube has one or more oil glands opening into it. It is the oil secreted by these glands which gives gloss to a well-groomed coat even in cold weather.* The oil glands are

* Lieut.-Colonel Fitzwygram's "Lectures on Stable Management.'

most numerous **and** complex at the heels, the bend of the knees, and **the** groin ; hence want of cleanliness and wet readily produce such local diseases as grease.

"It is said that the amount of perspiration given off by a horse in twenty-four hours is equal in weight to that given off as dung."

These explanations show why good grooming is essential to bring a horse to the highest condition, because good grooming removes the accumulation of sweat, scurf, and dirt, which otherwise clog the skin. In the absence of good grooming, the scurf collects at the surface of the skin and about the hair, fills up the pores and produces irritation, the sweat glands cease to act properly, and excretions which ought to be thrown off in sweating remain in the skin, and produce many diseases.

The best instrument for grooming is a good bristle brush, laid on briskly, steadily, and regularly, with a will, not merely rubbed over the surface to smooth the hair down. By this friction not only are all the dried substances, dandriff, and clotted sweat removed, but the blood is brought to the surface, and the glands and pores are brought into healthy action. To perfect the process, exercise should precede grooming, and the brush should follow the exercise, without allowing time for the sweat to cake on the skin and obstruct the pores.

Grooms often commence their work by "strapping" a horse with a damp wisp of hay. This is all very well as far as it goes. When vigorously done it has partly the effect of shampooing, by bringing the blood to the surface; but it must be clearly understood that no horse can be thoroughly cleaned by the application of a wisp, for it only plasters the dirt into him. Nothing less than a good bristle brush, skilfully and vigorously applied, will bring a horse's coat into proper condition.

When a horse returns from work or exercise, then is the time for drying and cleaning him. If he is very hot and exhausted he should be walked about until he is cool, and his pulse has resumed its usual action. The operation should not be deferred, as is often the case, until the polished parts of saddlery or harness have been cleaned. Bits, stirrups, &c., may, if needful, be rubbed with an oil rag to prevent rust ; but the owner should insist that the horses are cleaned first. But when a horse is exhausted from hunting, or long hours of continuous work, it may be better to simply sponge him over, clothe him, give him a drink and a mash, before proceeding to dress him thoroughly.

A horse's feet must always be washed, so that the groom may have no excuse for not seeing that the soles and hoofs have received no injury, and that the shoes are in good order.

Warm water is generally used to wash horses' legs in winter. This is really not for the benefit of the horse, but for the comfort of the groom's hands. This fact is an additional reason for constructing in every stable of importance a powerful *douche*. If the legs are washed, they must be carefully dried, but the bandages must be removed as soon as they have absorbed all the moisture in the hair. A horse's legs should never be washed until dry.

There is a carbolic soap expressly manufactured for stable use which is said to have valuable qualities. I have used it to wash young horses fresh from grass, and I think with advantage. It is better at any rate than the common soft soap.

Formerly it was considered essential to stop up horses' feet after work with a composition of clay, salt, and cow-dung, but since the introduction of the Charlier shoe, and since many who do not adopt the Charlier have taken to cultivating the frog, and using a shoe that lets it touch the ground, stopping has gone out of favour. With the Charlier shoe there is no room to stop. Altogether the balance of opinion is at present against stopping, as more likely to injure than improve sound feet. It is usual, for the sake of appearance, to rub a mixture of oil and lampblack over the hoofs before a horse goes out of the stable harnessed or saddled. It does no harm. Various unguents are advertised for increasing the growth of the horn. As the hoof is covered with a hard varnish like the human nail, it is difficult to believe that any ointment can soak into it or do it any good.

THE ORDER OF DRESSING.

The following is the order of dressing a horse after work, according to one of the best authorities :—

"If very hot, leave the saddle on, or throw a rug loosely over his back and quarters; pull his ears to dry them. In fine weather tie him up in the yard or washing-house; in cold weather he must be dressed in his stall.

"Wash and pick out any dirt from his feet, then rub off the loose dirt from his legs and belly with a straw wisp, or, still better, with sawdust. If there be any white about the legs, soft soap and washing blue must be used the next morning. If the horse's belly and legs are washed—a bad system where mud fever is feared—rub all the wet parts with dry woollen cloths, and roll bandages on all four legs, from the coronets to the knees or hocks.

"Remove the rug, and wisp the horse from head to foot until quite dry; then briskly apply a brush until all sweat and dirt is removed; follow up with a damp hay wisp to lay the coat smooth, laid on with a will; finish with a chamois leather, or, if luxurious, with a hair glove. The clothing should now be laid on, and secured with a surcingle, which, if the horse is light and herring-gutted, should be fastened with a wet girth across the breast, so as not to slip back, for a surcingle *should never be tight*.

"The next step is to sponge and wipe the horse's eyes, mouth, nose, and other delicate parts not covered with hair, and to carefully brush the mane and tail. A comb should never be used, as nothing so soon breaks and spoils horsehair. This dressing will take at least an hour and a half for each horse. Before shutting up for the night, remove the damp bandages, and, if needed, replace them with dry ones."

MANES AND TAILS.

It is impossible to put a money value on a well-grown and well-kept mane and tail, because, although neither will make a good horse into a bad one, the deficiency of either, and especially of the tail, will frequently make all the difference between selling and having to keep on hand a very high-class horse. Both manes and tails are too much neglected by farmers who breed "nag horses."

There have been famous hunters with rat tails, and famous men have ridden capital hacks with hideous docks; but no carriage-horse, no park-horse of any kind, can be ranked first-class without a noble flag. Nature must lay the foundation, but art can do a great deal. On the other hand, the very finest tails and manes may be utterly destroyed, and the horse rendered unsaleable, by neglect during a few days.

When a horse of any kind is taken up for grass, or purchased out of an Irish drove, no time should be lost in thoroughly washing his mane and tail with hot water and carbolic, or other vermin-killing soap. Indeed, the washing may be advantageously extended to the whole body. If the mane is too thick, it must be thinned with a steel comb which is made for the purpose. If it does not lie well on the side desired, it must first be bathed in very hot water applied with a brush, and then plaited with lead. If that does not answer, a canvas hood, plaited with sheets of lead, must be put on the head and neck, after the mane has been thoroughly wetted, and the wetting repeated from time to time, while the horse is either on the rack-chain or the pillar reins. This neck hood must be removed at night. The mane should never on any account be touched with scissors, and after it has been once reduced to a proper thickness, neither it nor the tail should ever be combed, but frequently brushed with a damp brush kept expressly for the purpose As a rule, the manes and tails of blood horses are rather inclined to be too thin than too thick. It is astonishing what improvement may be produced in these natural ornaments by constant attention. There are some good brushes with wire instead of bristle.

Docking.—Formerly horses were universally docked, sometimes very short, under the idea that it improved the appearance of their quarters. Of late the fashion of docking the tails and hogging manes has been revived by polo players. Even hunters have been thus disfigured; but, like crinolines and chignons, it is a beastly fashion that cannot last for ever. In this year (1878) a number of mares, which it was the fancy of an Essex baronet to collect for sale, were positively disfigured—I should say indecently—by the shortness of their docks. It is, however, often advisable to shorten the dock of horses used in single harness, or in pair-horse carriages where the splashboard is low. A long bang or switch tail splashes the dirt in the driver's face, is very apt to flap over one of the reins, and to set the animal kicking.

It is a popular opinion that a horse whose tail is not naturally well set on may be made to carry it better if early in colthood it is relieved from the weight of hair by shortening the dock. The Irish have a particular taste for such operations as docking and firing. You constantly meet with Irish mares, which should always have a full tail, spoiled by being too closely docked. As docking is a veterinary operation, it is not necessary to describe it. It is as well, however, to observe, that it is very easy to take two or three joints off a horse's tail, but impossible to put them on again. As harness horses and chargers wear cruppers, it is possible to supply them with false tails if a bald or rat tail destroys the otherwise grand appearance of a fine horse; but such an addition will be ridiculous if not manufactured and fitted by a real artist.

Horses fresh from grass, or standing idle in the stable, are apt to rub their tails, and if not attended to will soon seriously injure and even permanently destroy the hair.

The first step is to carefully wash the tail, and discover the cause of irritation. It may be caused by a skin affection of the dock or of the rump, or by the presence of worms in the rectum. In the latter and more common case, advice will be found in the chapter on "Veterinary Information."

Very little benefit is gained by the administration of the ordinary medicine for worms when the Oxyuris is present. A dose of physic may cause the expulsion of a few worms, but no marked relief from the annoyance which they cause is gained by this treatment.

If the irritation is in the dock alone, and application of water does not allay it, apply a lotion to the tail composed of chloride of lime, two and a half drachms in half a pint of water, and between the applications glycerine and oil with a feather. A wet woollen bandage may be rolled on at night.

There is one thing that will spoil a horse's temper without curing the habit of rubbing his tail, and that is beating him, as many stupid grooms do, even lying in wait for the purpose. Horses travelling long distances by sea or rail should have their tails carefully swathed in bandages, and sewn in leather cases.

WATER.

Horses should be watered in the morning before they are fed, and then water left beside them for an hour or so. To water horses after they are fed is a sure way of producing indigestion, if not inflammation.

When the water is collected in a cistern, it should be provided with a self-acting filter.

When a horse has water beside him when feeding, he may be observed taking a mouthful of oats and hay, and then a slight drink of water alternately. With this arrangement horses never drink too much, except when returning from exercise. But the water should not be left all day in a stable, to imbibe the fumes of ammonia.

Horses have been killed by drinking water from a deep cold well when heated; but warm or tepid water is as offensive to them as to us. It should be allowed to obtain a proper temperature by being placed under cover—in the saddle-room or washing-room, for instance— or by adding a little meal or linseed tea—not in the stables, to absorb the exhalations of the litter and of the horses.

Where horses scour after drinking, it is advisable to add just enough warm water to take the chill off, or a little wheaten flour, which has a slightly astringent effect.

BED LITTER.

An important item in maintaining the condition of a hard-worked horse is a good bed when he comes in tired. When he is not worked in the daytime he is much better standing on a hard flat surface than on soft litter, which produces half the diseases of the feet. Bog-earth, sand, fireclay, are all used for litter. The material is of no consequence so long as it is dry and soft for the horses to lie down. The ordinary material is straw; but in many instances sawdust is to be preferred. Where horses stand idle in loose boxes, it does not clog and heat the feet like straw impregnated with urine and dung. The droppings are removed from sawdust with ease, and without waste. Horses inclined to eat straw—even foul straw—will not touch sawdust.

Where the trusses of straw are long, it is a good plan to cut them in two with a knife fixed on a hinge and block made for the purpose.

The first duty of a groom in the morning, after watering his horses, is to sort out and remove the wet straw and dung, and take out the better part, which can be used again, to be dried in some convenient place, while the horse, racked up, is eating his first feed.

In some stables all the straw is removed until a fresh bed is made at night, and until that time the rack-chain prevents the horse from lying down. In any case, *the bedding should never be heaped up under the manger, under the horse's nose.* Indeed, it is well to fill up the space underneath the manger with boarding, so as to leave no space either for straw or the horse's head.

Fresh straw bedding should be placed in the rear of the stall, so as not to get the horse into the bad habit of eating his litter. But as no such precaution can be adopted in loose boxes, that is an additional reason for using sawdust in them.

Where the stud is large, it may be worth while to provide a shed for drying the litter, which may also be used as an exercising school in inclement weather.

It may be doubted whether horses can lie as warmly, although they may lie quite as softly, on sawdust as on straw.

FODDER.

Hay should be hard, sweet-smelling, rather green than brown, with plenty of leaves or flowers of grass, and, if possible, of the previous year. It should be heavy, and make a crackling noise when stirred; this shows that it has been well gathered. Ill-made musty hay is the source of a host of disorders; coarse sedgy hay contains little nutriment. The soft hay suited for cows is quite unfit for horses in hard work.

Oats should have a sweet taste and a sweet flowery smell, and thin smooth skins that slip smoothly through the fingers. Short plump oats are generally better than large long oats; size and colour are of no consequence, but those with beards are objectionable. The weight should be from thirty-eight to forty-two pounds per bushel. Light oats are composed of more skin than flour. Oats badly saved, mouldy, sprouting, or otherwise damaged, will cause disease in the best horses. Every horse-owner should make himself practically acquainted with the quality of oats, beans, and hay.

Beans should be one year old. New beans produce colic, and do not give strength. They should be hard, dry, sweet, plump, sound, and weigh from sixty to sixty-four pounds to the bushel. They must be split, otherwise they will pass through *the intestines* whole and undigested.

Modern ingenuity has produced a variety of machines for splitting beans, crushing, cutting chaff, and otherwise preparing horse food, which may be seen and studied in the galleries of the Smithfield Club Show and the tents of the Royal Agricultural Society.

Maize answers perfectly well for harness horses and hacks in constant, steady work. It is generally from fifteen to twenty per cent. cheaper than oats, because weighing about sixty pounds per bushel, but it must be cracked.

The following extract from the *Live Stock Journal* covers the whole question of the feeding value of oats, beans, maize, and bran :—

No men understand better or so well how to get blood horses into galloping condition as English grooms, they do not, and few of their masters do, know the reason why oats and beans are the best food for putting muscular flesh on a horse. The agricultural chemist steps in here, and shows that if you want lever-like pace, Indian corn, although nominally cheaper, is not cheap at all.

It was a common saying in Leicestershire, before deep-draining, clean-cut fences, and increased sheep-feeding had improved agriculture at the expense of fox-hunting, after one of those five-and-forty minute runs at best pace that are now so rare—"it found out the horse that ate old beans and best oats."

In fact, they made experiments they did not understand, which it was left for the modern chemist to explain.

When we feed a bullock, a sheep, or a pig for sale, after it has passed the store stage, we want to make it fat as quickly and as cheaply as possible; but with a horse for work the object is, give him muscle—in common language, hard flesh.

There are times when it is profitable to make a horse fat, as, for instance, when he is going up for sale, after a severe hunting season.

For this purpose an addition of about a pound and a half of oil-cake to his ordinary food has a good effect.

It is especially useful when a horse that has been closely clipped or singed is in low condition. It helps on the change to the new coat by making him fat.

A horse in low condition changes his coat very slowly.

When from any cause there is difficulty in getting a supply of the best oats, an excellent mixture may be made of crushed maize and beans, in the proportion of two-thirds of maize and one of beans, which exactly afford the proportions of flesh-forming and fat-forming food.

Bran is a very valuable food in a stable for reducing the inflammatory effect of oats and beans. Made into mashes it has a cooling and laxative effect, but used in excess, especially in a dry state, it is apt to form stony secretions in the bowels of the horse. Stones produced from the excessive use of bran have been taken out of horses after death weighing many pounds. When sawn through they appear to be composed of a hard crystalline mass, deposited in regular annular rings, resembling in appearance the concentric yearly rings of wood ; they prove to be composed of phosphate of magnesia and ammonia. Millers' horses are particularly subject to this malady.

The best way to guard against it is to add half a pint to a pint of linseed, boiled until quite soft, to the mash of each horse.

Green Forage and Roots.—Some persons make a point of giving their working horses green forage in spring, and if it is fresh, and given in moderate quantities, there is no objection; it may serve instead of mashes. Lucern is the best green forage, and vetches the worst. Good grass mixed with hay or oats does very well. Vetches are most commonly sold for the purpose near great towns.

Mangel-wurzel.—A very hard rider on the road as well as the field used and recommended mangel for riding horses not required for hunting. It is also, if pulped and mixed with chaff alone, or chaff and oats, good food for mares with foals, colts during breeding, and any horses in slow summer work.

All green food and roots are best mixed with a moderate portion of cut hay, where there is convenience for the operation.

Rye-grass grown with sewage irrigation has of late years come into use, especially for slow draught horses. It is best cut up with hay or straw into chaff. Old vetches are heating, and stale green forage of any kind is likely to produce dangerous derangement of the stomach and bowels.

Carrots are excellent horse food, which should be kept in store for use in winter and spring. They are particularly valuable for getting a horse into condition after sickness. Perhaps parsnips would answer equally well. Either may be given whole, or sliced in a turnip-cutter with oats and beans, or if oats are scarce, with beans and bran.

Bran.—A stable should never be without a supply of fresh bran. Bran, fresh ground and wetted, is a laxative. It acts mechanically on the lining membrane of the intestines, causing a slight amount of irritation, which increases the secretions and quickens the passage of the contents. Dry bran has an astringent effect.

Linseed.—A few bushels of linseed are as necessary in the corn-loft of a stud as bran. Linseed, unlike bran, will not spoil by keeping. It is, as already mentioned in a previous chapter, one of the best ingredients of a mash, hot or cold, and it is the foundation of a very wholesome drink.

Potatoes.—Nothing will make a horse fatter for sale than boiled potatoes mixed with hay chaff.

Salt is supposed to assist in keeping horses in health ; at any rate, they like it, and a lump of rock-salt may as well be kept either in the hay-rack or the manger.

Sugar makes fat, and may be given with advantage to horses in low condition in moderate quantities, either in mashes or mixed with corn. Formerly molasses were used in mashes, but as long as good moist sugar can be purchased at twopence a pound, it will be found a more convenient and cleanly saccharine article mixed with boiled oats.

Oil-cake of the very best quality, given, as already mentioned, when a horse is changing his coat, seems to have a very good effect. There are large quantities of inferior adulterated oil-cake sold.

Chaff composed of meadow hay, cut up with a machine, with each feed of corn, is of value to make a horse masticate his food, and is the most economical way of feeding with hay, but where horses come very hungry they should have a little long hay to occupy them. Chaff bolted by a hungry horse produces colic. There is no advantage in turning straw into chaff to mix with hay unless it is at least as cheap. Clover hay does not suit horses in fast work. Green oat straw cut from the owner's fields is very good chaff.

Mashes, if properly prepared and given at least once a week, will supersede the use of green forage, and render the administration of laxative physic unnecessary.

Where horses are being fattened for sale, some people boil beans in the mash as well as oats.

Thorley, Hope, and others, advertise condiments for getting horses into condition. These are of use in special circumstances, with delicate feeders, and with horses recovering from influenza or fever, as stimulants; but no horse can be got into condition for fast work who cannot eat his regular meals of oats and hay, with or without beans, according to age and constitution. These advertised condiments take the place occupied by pickles and "pick-me-ups" in the food of human bipeds. Goode's loaves answer very well when fresh, but they must not be kept more than a week, and that in a dry place. His concentrated food advantageously takes the place of beans, and is more digestible. It is made up in seven-ounce cakes, and costs 11s. 6d. for a case of 144 pounds. Delicate feeders eat it greedily. I have used it with good results on a hard-working brougham horse. Two to three cakes with or without oats every day.

The purchase of fodder is one of those matters that a horse-owner should not leave to the uncontrolled management of the groom, unless he be a servant (I have known many such) who may thoroughly be depended on. The fees a groom may receive from the horsedealer, the coachmaker, and the saddler, are only a tax on your purse. But inferior fodder, hay, and oats, that give a minimum of nutriment, even if not absolutely musty and poisonous, affect the health and condition of your horses insensibly. Corndealers and fodder contractors hold out extraordinary inducements to grooms and coachmen to pass whatever they choose to send in. They themselves are sometimes deceived in a rick of hay or a cargo of oats. As a matter of course they distribute the bad bargains where the master is careless and the groom needy. Prevention is better than cure. Such tricks will not be played on the master who is in the habit of handling the oats and smelling the hay. If the horse-owner's occupations are so onerous that he cannot personally attend to any of the details of a great stable, even for an hour now and then, he must choose his head groom well, making it worth his while to be honest, and making him understand that if *from any cause* the majority of the stud do not keep in good condition, he, the responsible person, will lose his place.

LIVERY STABLES.

The estimated consumption in one of the best livery stables in London per horse per week is about two bushels of oats, two bushels of chaff, one truss of hay, and two trusses of straw.

Job horses, full 15 hands 3 inches high, which it is the interest of the proprietor to keep in the best possible condition, are supplied with, per fortnight, eight to ten bushels of oats (or oats with beans if old horses), two sacks of good chaff of hay and clover, three trusses of hay, and four to six trusses of straw.

CAVALRY HORSES.

The regulated allowance per day is, of oats ten pounds, of hay twelve pounds, or about a quarter of a truss; but when horses have to camp out in wet weather officers should give their chargers an extra quartern of beans daily.

OMNIBUS HORSES.

The daily allowance of the London Omnibus Company's horses is to each seventeen pounds of corn, chiefly maize, with ten pounds of meadow hay and clover cut into chaff— the proportion of maize depending on its relative cheapness as compared with oats.

HUNTERS.

Twelve full-sized (seldom under and often over sixteen hands), hunters in Leicestershire, each in first-class condition, will not consume more than twelve pounds of oats, two pounds of beans, and six to eight pounds of the best hay daily.

The bedding of a horse in a stable may be well done with two to three trusses of straw per week.

STABLE MEASURES AND WEIGHTS.

Taking a bushel of oats to weigh 40 lbs. (They vary 36 to 42 lbs.)

A quartern weighs	2½ lbs.
Four quarterns (not quarts) make a peck	10 lbs.
Four pecks make a bushel	40 lbs.
Four bushels make a sack (in Norfolk and Suffolk a coomb) ...	160 lbs.
Eight bushels make a quarter	320 lbs.

Beans and maize average 60 lbs. a quarter.

HAY AND STRAW.

A load of old hay contains 36 trusses, each of 56 lbs., and weighs about 18 cwt.
A load of straw contains 36 trusses, each of 36 lbs., and weighs about 11 cwt. 6 lbs.

EXERCISE.

The best stables, the best food, and the best grooming, will not secure condition—that is, the highest degree of horse-health—without sufficient and regular exercise. The degree will depend on how long the horse has been in use. An animal fresh from grass must be brought gently into work. Colonel Fitzwygram's rules for training four-year-olds, often nearer three and a half years old, intended for troopers, fresh from the fields, give a good idea of the principles of exercise :—" For the first month half an hour's walking exercise is sufficient; for the next month an hour, during which he may be longed, and taught to carry a saddle. In the third month he may be ridden slowly for half an hour, and trotted another half hour. From the fourth to the sixth one hour and a half ordinary work in the riding-school will not be too much, and by the end of six months he will be fit for the regular work of a troop horse."

Horses five years old and upwards, used for riding or driving only (not hunting), should, on the days they are not used, have not less than two hours' exercise for six days of the week commencing about six o'clock in the morning, doing, if in a harness break, about twelve miles, and if under saddle about ten miles; walking and trotting at not more than six miles an hour.

The horses of ladies, and old or timid gentlemen, should be exercised soon after daybreak in winter, and at six o'clock in summer, for at least one hour every day.

Regular exercise is so important, that a shed or barn to be used for that purpose in inclement weather should always be erected or reserved for it; and in town advantage should be taken of subscription to a neighbouring riding-school. Grooms are but men; they do not like more trouble than they can help in cleaning up a muddy, sweating horse, and they are impatient for their breakfast, so they may be expected to seize on any possible excuse for not going out at all, or for cutting two hours down to one. A sportsman who was very particular about the condition of his horses always made one of the stable lads ring a bell that communicated with his bedroom when they started and when they returned. This continued as long as he was a bachelor; but on getting married the lady objected to this kind of matins, and it was observed that the hunters from Bullfinch Park lost their former reputation for high condition at the commencement of the hunting season.

The best fields for summer exercise are those that have been mown, because the ground has been partly protected from the sun. Grain stubbles, where fields have been laid flat for thorough drainage and deep cultivation, also afford good exercise ground. For winter, during frosts, a ride should be made of litter, tan, sawdust, or whatever soft material is cheapest.

A gentleman of moderate fortune, whose principal expense was his stud of six hunters, adopted the following plan to secure two hours' exercise :—At six o'clock the grooms went to the stable and gave each horse his water and less than half a feed of oats. While they were eating this, a bowl of milk or cocoa and a hunch of bread was consumed by each groom. This allayed the sharp pangs of hunger; exercise followed until half-past eight, when the regular breakfast for men and horses was ready for them. For he used to say, "It is a mistake to fight against nature."

Old beans, strong strapping, slow exercise, and plenty of all three, are the road to hunting condition.

Finally, galloping exercise will only do harm to a horse not already made hard by degrees. Condition once secured, it should be maintained, as long as a horse has health and sound legs, by regular exercise.

SUMMERING AND WINTERING HORSES.

When a horse becomes stale he must be rested; the question is whether to rest him in a loose box or in a paddock. The old plan of turning horses out to grass is never practised with sound horses by those who wish to have them in hard condition in November. Horses are more likely to be rendered unsound by galloping about rich pastures, and lying down on hot days in ponds, than by regular summer exercise or light harness work.

One plan is to keep the horses in small paddocks—too small to gallop in—giving them corn twice a day, and taking them up at night. If they are kept in loose boxes all the summer, and supplied with green fodder as well as corn, they ought to be regularly dressed. To leave them, as some great people do, in dirt, is to destroy more than half the advantage of rest.

If a lame horse is wintered in an open yard it ought not, as is so commonly the case, to be hock deep in muck.

The advantage of a run in a small paddock, or a winter yard, lies no doubt in the effect of fresh air on the constitution; it is impossible to believe that an artificial animal like a valuable horse can be benefited by living in a box ungroomed—*in fact, in dirt*. If any exact returns were made of the number of horses which return from a summer's run on grass kicked, roarers, and blind, as well as those that die of colic and inflammation of the lungs, people who have stables and money enough to pay for corn would hesitate before turning horses in hard condition out to grass from motives of economy. But even if corn be not given, the horse sheltered from flies in summer and fed with good green food will be in better condition than one turned out to grass.

Amongst the symptoms of staleness are—a rough, staring coat, in spite of sedulous grooming ; a falling-off of the crest ; the heels cracked ; the excrement hard, dry, and voided with difficulty ; a hard, hacking cough ; the legs swelled ; the ears cold and damp after work ; and a general dulness of spirits. Whenever any of these symptoms are observed, the horse, whatever the time of year, should be thrown out of work, unless the owner is prepared to see temporary ailments settled into chronic disease. Even a fortnight's work, "just to finish the season," may do an injury to the constitution which will require four or five months of absolute rest to cure, when six weeks' rest in good time would have proved amply sufficient.

As soon as the bad symptoms appear, the animal should be placed in a large loose box, sufficiently clothed, well supplied with fresh air, and fed on the mashes already described, and with some sound soft cow hay. Carrots, sliced mangel, or swedes, pulped with chaff, bran, and a reduced allowance of crushed oats, will prepare the way for grass when it comes into season. If the appetite is very bad, sugar, or one of the cattle condiments, may be added to the mashes. Hardwood sawdust, or spent tan from lead works, make the best bed. The shoes should be removed and replaced with tips, to preserve the hoofs from splitting. The horse should be gently groomed every day, and his mane and tail not neglected.

After six weeks' rest, with a daily allowance of soft food, if the horse is not ill or lame, he will be much benefited by an hour's walking exercise early every morning on damp grass, and a fair supply of grass, with two or three feeds of oats daily, according to his constitution, until the 1st September, when his regular preparation for the hunting-field must recommence.

If after three weeks' or a month's rest the bad symptoms continue, and the veterinary surgeon has not already been consulted, he should be called in ; but on no account should the groom be allowed to quack the equine patient with "balls" of any kind, still less should the farrier, or any one else, be allowed to bleed him.

If the horse is to be turned out to grass he must be gradually cooled down, his clothing removed by degrees, and his food more and more mixed with green fodder.

While at grass his feet, shod with tips only, should be examined at least once a fortnight.

If it is necessary to turn a horse out to grass in summer, it should be at night, and he should have a dark box in the day—dark, to keep out the flies. But summer is a bad time for even a lame horse of any value to be turned out to grass.

COACHMEN—GROOMS—STRAPPERS—PAD-GROOMS—STABLE-BOYS.

These may roughly be divided into stable servants, driving servants, and riding servants. In small establishments of riding and driving horses it is the object of the master to obtain one groom at least able and willing to dress, ride, and drive a horse. Where studs are large and incomes ample the horse duties are usually divided into departments, with one autocrat coachman or stud-groom at the head.

The most expensive class of servants are the head coachman of a lady of fashion and the stud-groom of a hunting stable. The business of a head, or, as commonly called, a "body" coachman is to drive his master or mistress, and superintend everything connected with the carriages, harness, and horses ; to see that everything is done that ought to be done, without ever touching anything with his hands in the way of work, except his reins and whip.

In addition to his wages, he often expects to pay the accounts of the corndealer, the saddler, the coachbuilder, the horsedealer, and the tailor who supplies his liveries, or at any rate to be remembered at paying time by these tradesmen. If they neglect him they seldom give satisfaction to his master. His first duty is to drive well, and this is a delicate and difficult task. The art of starting, rushing along and round the corners of London streets at great speed, and stopping suddenly at a succession of houses or shops, without jolting or jerking or discomposing the nerves of an hysterical lady or gouty lord, is very difficult to acquire, and when acquired worth high wages. But if one of these autocrats of the coachbox does happen to lose his place and his character he falls very low indeed. He is essentially an article of luxury and ornament.

If, in addition to the art of town driving, he adds that of superior stable management, and turns out "his" horses and carriages fed, groomed, dressed, and cleaned in the very best manner, at not too extravagant a cost for a rich man's purse, then he is in his proper place in an establishment where the best of everything is expected to be provided, and cost is a matter of little importance.

Indeed, the wages of a coachman or stud-groom in a large establishment are quite a secondary consideration, if for these wages he makes every man under him do his duty, and keeps the stable expenses down to honest prices.

Strappers—mere machines who work well under a master's eye—are always to be had for the average wages of the district ; but first-rate stud-grooms, like good managers, good foremen of any kind, who will see that every department of a great establishment is kept in the best possible order without waste or robbery, are always scarce, and always valuable in proportion, whether it be in the management of a warehouse or a stable.

In every stable of any importance there must be one person who understands how to get and keep horses in blooming condition, and if he is not a good coachman or a good horseman, it is better to hire another person to perform either of those duties than to have the all-important point of condition neglected. It is high praise of a servant to say, "He is a capital stableman; his horses always look well and go well."

The head of the stable must have the power of engaging and discharging the grooms under him, subject of course to the nominal approval of the master before an engagement or discharge. Without this power no head man can preserve the needful discipline. If it is found that, from bad temper or an insolent overbearing disposition, which is too often the failing of half-educated persons promoted to a position of authority, your stable premier is not to be trusted, your only remedy is to discharge him. No remonstrances have any effect on a really ill-tempered man, and, although discipline is essential, the despotism of a cantankerous temper is as mischievous in a stable as in a regiment.

Although a head servant to be fully useful must have confidence reposed in him, and a certain degree of patronage allowed him, the master is sure to suffer who allows a head groom to become *his* master.

When a coachman continually has a horse "lame," "sick," or "off his feed," or needing shoeing, when he is wanted for either day or night work, or when he is always grumbling at the horses supplied by the job-master, without having any specific complaint to make, the proper plan is to get rid of the coachman. The same rule applies to the management of hunters, or other riding horses: if they are not fit, the groom is not fit. Therefore, in engaging a head man, it is as well to tell him that his place depends not only on sobriety, honesty, and punctuality, but on the horses always being fit to be seen, and fit for real work, or ornamental work, as the case may be.

In the town servant appearance has its value ; in the country general utility is more to be considered.

As a rule the most expensive servants do the least work, but then they are ornamental.

One of the best all-round grooms I ever saw, turned out, with the assistance of a rough country lad and a little boy, six hunters in first-rate condition every winter, having broken and harnessed one or two of them in the course of the summer; and when the hunting season was over, took the management of a kitchen garden and farm of ten acres, having his master, an ex-M. F. H., as a docile assistant under his orders.

Where mere utility is required, one good man, with the assistance of an agricultural labourer, will do wonders in turning out two or three horses for country use. This may be seen in the stables of small country dealers and of hunting farmers; but then there is the

ASSYRIAN CHARIOT (FROM A BAS-RELIEF).

inestimable advantage of the eye of a master who knows how stable work should be done, how horses should be fed, and what quantity they can reasonably eat.

In circuses the horses travel twenty miles or more a day, only resting on Sundays. One man has to look after five of these horses, many of which are worth from one hundred to three hundred pounds each. Of course he does not groom them, he simply washes them in cold water, and they are seldom sick except with some epidemic. In the great cab stables of London one man has to dress six horses every morning, six every afternoon, and clean their harness; for this he is paid about forty shillings a week.

But no man can properly attend to more than two hunters, and if they are both hunted on the same day he must have assistance.

A coachman in a family with no pretensions to fashion, and not keeping late hours, may manage to turn out a carriage and pair of horses in decent condition most days of the week, if he has two sets of harness, one of them with as little metal ornament as possible; but if the equipage is to be turned out in first-rate style every day, the coachman must have a strapper to assist him. With a strapper three horses may be kept in first-rate condition.

A strong willing boy is often better than a man under a groom or coachman. Some of the best grooms are made out of boys thirteen or fourteen years old, fresh from a parish school, who know nothing about stable business, but are fond of horses and not afraid of them, under the discipline of a really good stableman glad of an assistant to save his back and joints. An intelligent boy, fond of animals, and accustomed at school from infancy to obey the slightest wish of a master, will learn nearly as much in six months as an uneducated clown in six years. Boys are mischievous certainly, and apt to be idle if not looked after, but they are observant, imitative, zealous, afraid of punishment, fond of praise, easily rewarded, able to bend and twist in all forms without trouble, and less tempted to intemperance and petty pilfering than the ordinary run of full-grown strappers. A boy gets on all the better if he has no bad habits to cure, as he might have if he has commenced his stable education by "fettling" a butcher's or baker's pony. But a groom boy with no master to teach and look after him is not an arrangement to be commended to any one who can afford anything better.

On the subject of wages, no rate can be stated and no rule laid down, except that a good servant's wages should be raised until he feels that he will not "better" himself by seeking a new place. Always make a present twice a year to a groom who does his duty, quite irrespective of his wages. It is a solid hint that you appreciate his zeal.

An experienced horseman will recognise a good or bad stableman the moment he takes hold of a horse to dress him. The real groom has a familiar trick in every movement, just as a first-class nurse has when she takes hold of "the very latest thing in babies." The trained groom always begins by pulling and drying the ears of a tired horse.

A boy cannot strap a horse thoroughly—that wants height and strength—but he can wash one, clean the mane and tail, hand-rub the legs (a most important operation), put on bandages, and clear away the superfluous hairs of the legs, better than a man.

A man of the middle class commencing to keep horses should prefer grooms from the stables of the masters of subscription packs of fox-hounds to those from the stables of great noblemen where a scale of hereditary lavishness has prevailed; but this maxim chiefly applies to small stables and ordinary grooms. If a coachman has only to drive, and the wages are no objection, there is no reason why the wife of a lately-become-rich mine-owner or contractor should not engage the ex-coachman of a duchess, or the son of a new-rich-man the stud-groom of an aristocratic *habitué* of Melton, except that he would probably not be able to use any one of his dozen hunters without his stud-groom's permission.

Poor men's horses are often worn out with too much work and not enough oats and beans, while rich men's horses become diseased from the effects of hot stables, over-clothing, over-feeding, and insufficient and irregular exercise.

LIVERIES.

Before a horse-owner decides to put his servants in any more distinctive livery than a great-coat bearing his initials on the buttons, he should make up his mind to the expense of having it changed often enough to appear always fresh. Nothing is more common, and nothing has a more shabby appearance than an ill-fitting, faded, threadbare livery. The gayer the colour the more frequently must the clothes be renewed. With ordinary wear and tear, two sets of liveries of sober colours should look well on a coachman or driving-groom for a year. If they are to be his own at the end of the year, he will have an additional inducement for keeping them in good condition. The modern white mackintosh overcoat preserves a coachman's suit through a wet season very usefully, and is a fine conspicuous object lighted up by the carriage-lamps at night.

Liveries should always be obtained from tailors who make them the subject of a special department. It is not every tailor who knows how to cut servants' breeches as they should be cut, or how to harmonise the coat and waistcoat of a new colour or pattern.

The following are the correct costumes for the daily wear (not court dress) of carriage servants :—

" The coachman's great-coat and frock-coat must have flaps at the sides ; the waistcoat may be of a bright colour, or a stripe, or the same colour as the coat ; the breeches of drab kersey, finished with top-boots. Where cotton or silk stockings display the coachman's calves, the breeches may be blue, brimstone, scarlet, or any other fancy colour.

"The footman's great-coat has long skirts almost touching the ground ; under it, or without it, he wears a coatee ; waistcoat same as coat, or of the same colour as the coachman's.

"By a modern innovation in undress black or Oxford mixture trousers are permitted to replace the invariable shorts of the footmen of our grandfathers.

"The groom's costume is exactly like the coachman's, except that the coats are more frequently Oxford mixture than any gay colour, and that neither great-coat nor frock-coat has flaps at the side." But both grooms and coachmen may wear trousers now, when not in full dress.

STABLE VICES.

Crib-biting and wind-sucking are most annoying habits, as they generally prevent a horse from getting into condition, and often cause indigestion. There are a host of mechanical contrivances recommended as remedies, some of which are more dangerous than the disease. Mr. Blackwell has a collection of straps, muzzles, forks, and bits, that those who can journey to Oxford Street, London, may examine with profit. Crib-biters can seldom be got into condition, and are quite unfit for a small stud, as they are likely to be ill when most wanted.

Kickers.—Some horses, particularly mares, will kick all night, and kick down any partition not of stout material and workmanship. Such animals generally have capped hocks and other blemishes, the signs of their amusement.

Straps, chains, and clogs, attached to the hind-legs, often fail to check this vice ; violent punishment has no effect. In the day time an experiment might be tried of carrying a strap from the hind-legs to a bit ; it might answer, from the severe punishment each kick occasioned, with a young horse. A very good anti-kicking strap has been invented and advertised by Messrs. Wilkinson and Kidd.

But although patience and perseverance may do a great deal with young animals, especially when the vice has been created by ill-usage, nothing will cure an aged and confirmed kicker who may generally be known by marks on his hind-legs.

Vicious in Cleaning.—Many horses resist and try to kick and bite the groom when cleaned in consequence of being very fine-skinned. If the brush hurts them they flinch and kick, and are tied up close, beaten, and brushed harder, until grooming them becomes a dangerous fight.

When a horse shows viciousness of this character, the better plan is to take him to some school, fold-yard, or other place where he cannot hurt himself if he throws himself down. Put a headstall on him with a huge wooden bit, which will not only make biting impossible, but occupy his attention. Strap up one fore-leg, and leave his head loose. Begin by wiping him all over with a wet sponge, washing him, in fact; then shift the strap to the other fore-leg, and dress him with a wet wisp of hay. Caress him; take out the bit, reward him with a few slices of carrot, and take him back to his feed. After a few lessons of this kind dress him with a soft brush, and, if not incurably vicious, when he finds you do not hurt him he will not try to hurt you. Dinneford, of New Bond Street, sells a horse glove, for dressing thin-skinned animals, which requires no special art to use.

Horses difficult to shoe must be treated on the same principles.

Twitches applied to the nose and ears may subdue a horse, but they give so much pain that they are sure to aggravate viciousness.

WILKINSON AND KIDD'S ANTI-
KICKING STRAP.

WOODEN BIT, FOR DRESSING
A HORSE THAT BITES.

CHAPTER XXV.

CARRIAGES.

Four-wheeled Carriages: The Brougham—Its Advantages—History of—Best kind of Wheels and Shafts—Its Drawbacks—Requisites of a Brougham Horse—Brougham Harness—Driver of Brougham—The Sociable Landau—Changes in Carriages owing to Macadam and Railroads—The Wagonette—Its Advantages—Necessary Size of Seats and Backs—The Coach—The Chariot—Anecdote—The Barouche—The Victoria—Carriages to be Driven by Owner—The Mail Phaeton, a Man's Carriage—The Park Phaeton, a Ladies' Carriage—Good Horses Required—The Stanhope Phaeton—The Four-wheeled *vis-à-vis* Pony Phaeton—Changes in Carriage Taxes, and Adoption of Light Four-wheeled Carriages—Four-wheeled Dog Carts. *Two-wheeled Carriages:* Ancient Use of—The Curricle—Expense and Disappearance of—The Cabriolet—The Gig—Care Required in Construction of—Effect of Mr. Lowe's Reduction of Carriage Duty on Two-wheeled Vehicles—The Private Hansom—The Sledge—Public Carriages—Taxes on Carriages—Hints on Preserving Carriages—Miscellaneous Notes.

EXCELLENT carriages are built in the north, south, and east of London, as well as in Long Acre and the west, and builders of well-deserved local reputation are to be found in Scotland, in Ireland, and in almost every county of England, but, it may be laid down as a safe rule, whether in town or country, that it is best to go to a man for what he is most in the habit of building. A coachmaker may turn out an excellent dog-cart, T-cart, wagonette, or any other sort of gentleman's driving carriage, who does not keep the workmen or the models for making a really satisfactory brougham, landau, or barouche, and *vice versâ*. As a rule, not without exceptions, the town builder best understands the requirements of town; the countryman is the best judge of the article for long distances and rough roads.

There are four essentially family carriages, although three of them may also be all that is most fashionable—the brougham, the sociable landau, the wagonette, and the four-inside four-wheeled pony phaeton. There are three essentially fashionable carriages, very expensive when purchased new, almost unsaleable when offered second-hand, even if all but new. These are the C-springed coach, in which the many-daughtered duchess proceeds to Court; the chariot, now scarcely used except at levees and drawing-rooms, by the sheriffs of the City of London, and a few physicians who affect the old style; and the barouche, the most aristocratic and stately of all carriages, when complete with a pair of gigantic steppers, splendid in plate and patent leather, and a coachman and footman of appropriate size, in gorgeous uniforms; or appointed in the style used by royalty, called by the French *à la Daumont*, with four horses and two postillions.

FOUR-WHEELED CARRIAGES: THE BROUGHAM.

For the owner of a carriage who does not make driving a pleasure, for a family, a single lady, or a bachelor, whether for town or country use, the brougham—which, speaking historically, is one of the most modern of close carriages—occupies the first place. It is the only close carriage that looks well with one horse and one man. It looks equally well with a pair, if their size harmonises with the carriage. It may be light and single for the

Park, or capacious and double for the happy pair with a full quiver. It is the warmest carriage in winter, and is cool, with all the windows open, in summer. It requires no second man-servant, although there is room beside the driving-groom for a page. It is equally useful for shopping on the stones; or, fitted with a luggage basket, as a conveyance in the country, or to and from the railway station. In the Park, and at other assemblies of the fashionable, the windows of a brougham are so "hung on the line" as to present a fair face at the very best point of view for admiration and for conversation. For these reasons it is worth while to make the chapter on the brougham the text for a brief sketch of the rise and progress to perfection of English pleasure-carriages.

The brougham, invented by the great and eccentric genius Lord Chancellor Brougham, whose name it bears, was the consequence of his finding his coachman and footman not

BROUGHAM.

ready one day with a chariot and pair, after a series of nights of waiting for the poli-tician, orator, author, and man of fashion. He asked his coachmaker for a close carriage, which one man could manage and one horse could draw, not so ponderous as the pill-box, the one-horse chariot of apothecaries, which was a standing subject for the jokes of wits of the time of George III. The first attempts were very heavy affairs, more of the present street-cab style than anything else; but, when taken up by the fathers of the West-end trade, they soon became, in spite of much ridicule, the rage.

The brougham killed the cabriolet, just as the stanhope gig and the cabriolet killed the curricle. The social results of this one-horse "carriage of gentility" have been immense. It has become alike the carriage of the family party and of the solitary "swell," of the hard-working professional man and of the "girl of the period." All conditions of men and women avail themselves of it as a thing of utility and elegance. The brougham is the parent of the four-wheeled cab, which, with all its faults, is an immense improvement in comfort, convenience, cleanliness, and economy, upon the straw-littered Jarvey. The history of the brougham—its origin, rise, progress, and triumph over fashionable prejudices—has not yet been written. In the work on pleasure-carriages published in 1837, by Mr. Brydges Adams, then a coachbuilder, he makes no reference to anything like it.

Broughams were at first built to hold two persons only. They were afterwards extended to accommodate four persons, and have finally settled into the two shapes, single and double. They rapidly came into use in the highest circles, when the fairest of the fair discovered that the windows presented charming portraits, and that, low hung on wheels, they had all the advantages of the curricle or cabriolet, with none of their dangers and difficulties. It was found that the magnificent class of horse previously appropriated to the cabriolet looked twice as well in a brougham, could travel twice as far, and, with a weight off his fore legs, last twice as long. Besides, if it were necessary to make a long journey instead of a succession of flashes through street or park, then, by exchanging the sixteen-hands stepper for a pair of small light blood-horses, the brougham became the most agreeable conveyance, where the beauties of nature were not the object of the journey. In the early days of broughams an attempt was made by the late Lord Lytton (then Mr. Lytton Bulwer) to reproduce the chariots with hammercloth and knifeboard for the footmen; but these were soon found to be mistakes.

The first broughams, as before observed, were very heavy; some fashionable builders, with whose customers the cost of horseflesh is no object, still build them up to great weights. These are the most comfortable, although the most expensive carriage; but the majority of brougham-builders nowadays confine the weight to from about six hundredweight for a single, to eight hundredweight for a double brougham. The ladies' broughams, called miniatures, drawn by a blood-horse under 15 hands 2 inches high, seemed only able to hold *one* in crinoline days. The single brougham has superseded not only the cabriolet but the *vis-à-vis*, which also held two only; and with coachman, hammercloth seat, and knifeboard, was a Court carriage. For town use, one horse of sufficient weight and courage is the most convenient, and particularly for night use, especially for those who do not keep a number of men-servants. For show, or for long distances in the country, a pair of small horses between 14 hands and 15 hands 2 inches, either cobs or highly bred, are better.

Broughams vary in price from £100 (country built) to £180. A very good carriage may be had for £150, with shafts, pole, and bars. It is one of the carriages in which the certainty of good materials, good workmanship, and a good price, if sold again, are worth something extra, even by way of insurance.

Broughams, it must be admitted, are not so easy in long journeys as a well-hung chariot, and they afford no view of picturesque scenery. They have little room for luggage; indeed, the latest forms of broughams are cut and carved so closely to make them light and elegant, that they barely afford a place for the travelling-bag of more than one passenger.

Broughams for invalids and London physicians have been built with C springs, but they are cumbrous, expensive, almost unsaleable second-hand, and absolutely require a pair of horses, the swing of the body adding a sensible increase to the absolute weight when still.

For country use, broughams may be provided with a basket fitted at the top, on which any reasonable number of trunks and portmanteaus can be secured without danger to the roof.

Broughams are usually lined with either leather or cloth, or a combination of cloth and morocco leather—the latter being a convenient and economical arrangement, as the cushions are used with the leather side uppermost in hot, and the cloth in cold weather Satin, in brilliant colours—blue, pink, rose, and even white—has occasionally been employed by those with whom expense was "no object." But such extravagances are confined to the few.

A number of convenient details have been added to modern close carriages, such as a speaking-tube for communicating with the coachman, a lamp for reading at night, a footstool to be filled with warm water in winter, a mirror craftily concealed, in which a lady may give a final touch to her head before arriving at a country house after a long drive, and door-locks that open and shut like those of a drawing-room.

All the latest inventions of the kind, whether useful or merely new and expensive, may be studied in a visit to the show-rooms of our most fashionable builders, or to the carriage bazaars of Belgravia or Baker Street, where sometimes at the close of the season very handsome equipages, purchased on credit, are to be sold at a "frightful sacrifice for cash."

Although, by occasional flashes of fashion, broughams are painted in bright and even gay colours, where only one is kept it is better to adhere to sombre shades. Bright colours suit only bright days. What would be suitable to the season in Paris would look as much out of place for nine months out of twelve in England as a summer paletôt in winter. Where taste or fashion is an object, the colour of the carriage and livery (if any) of the coachman should harmonise. Gaiety may be given to the more sombre hues by harness rich in metal ornament, by gay-coloured saddle-cloths, and rosettes.

THE BROUGHAM HORSE.

Every sort of horse may be seen in broughams: heavy brutes just fit for Pickford's vans; light weeds, more suited to a butcher's flying cart; prancing giraffes, that, if black, would be in place in a mourning coach; plodding cobs, travelling with necks poked out like a harnessed pig. Fortunately, many people are content with anything that will draw them, and no more think of looking at the form of a horse than at that of a locomotive steam-engine.

But the brougham-horse proper, although he may have many defects, should have certain qualities. He may carry such an exaggerated forehead as to make riding him out of the question; but he should stand well, in a noble attitude, and should move with a certain grandeur of action, the very opposite of the quick sharp pace of a mail-phaeton pair. He may have an ugly head, which can be concealed in a very elaborate bridle, and a shabby tail, which can be supplied by a false one, but he must carry both well. In a full-sized brougham, weight is indispensable; in a light, single, or miniature brougham, a blood-horse is more appropriate. In either case the size of the horse should be in harmony with the size of the carriage. It is as great an error in taste to use a large beast like a camel, almost lifting the fore-wheels off the ground if he make an extra stride, as to have a horse so small, and working with his neck so low, that he is lost in the shafts. If full of courage he will very soon be worn-out by over-weight.

A brougham intended to carry at least four persons inside should have a horse able to trot away with it easily at the rate of eight miles an hour, which is pace enough on the stones for any family party. There is nothing in worse taste, although it is often seen in the more fashionable quarters of London, than a small brougham, a massive coachman and a gigantic footman in full liveries, and a pair of sixteen-hands barouche horses before them.

The broughams which require a single horse from 15 hands 2½ inches to 15 hands 3 inches will be properly horsed by a pair of well-bred, well-crested horses of from 14½ to 15 hands. Always supposing that a horse has power enough for the weight behind him, his appearance depends more on the way he carries his head and neck than on his height at the shoulder.

As to colour, the purchaser of a brougham horse has much more range than the purchaser of a pair. If the sight and action are right, any colour will do, but the more extraordinary the colour, the more necessity for fine action. As a rule, the owner of only one horse should not choose a piebald or skewbald; nor, if he keep only one man, a light grey, for a light grey requires half a man more to clean than any other colour. But where a carriage is much used at night, white is a good colour for the coachman to find in a long rank, and a good colour to drive through dark lanes, as it reflects the light of the lamps, and leaves no excuse for the drivers of carts returning from market.

BROUGHAM HARNESS.

Brougham single harness should have a rather solid style, a full-sized pad, traces fairly broad, and where a kicking-strap is used—as it always should be with a mare—long breeching. Where breeching is really required to hold up a carriage, the short is considered the most effective; but the general introduction of the patent brake has rendered breeching necessary only for backing. A tall horse in a full-sized brougham does not, as a rule, look well "naked of leather;" his stately proportions seem to harmonise with a good deal of harness. In a miniature brougham the horse may be small if he carries his head well, and the harness light.

The metal-work may be silver, brass, or covered. Brass, to look well and wear well, must be of the best quaiity, and solid. It requires more work to keep clean and bright than silver. Brass harness is in England the royal and truly aristocratic style. Where there is only one man in the stable, the less metal-work he has to clean the better. Metal-work covered with leather, except where there is friction, or japanned black, may be relieved from any funereal suspicions by a gay saddle-cloth, coloured rosettes, and frontispiece to the bridle.

THE DRIVER OF A BROUGHAM.

The brougham, besides saving at least £100 on original cost, as compared with a chariot, dispensed with one horse and a footman, reduced the rank of driver, and rendered it possible even in families of high social condition to employ a much less important personage in a less expensive costume. The driver of a brougham wears a round hat (no wig) top-boots or gaiters, or, quite as often, trousers. The last is a modern innovation which cannot be sanctioned in the coachman of a chariot, barouche, or coach.

A brougham may be driven by a youth; and, if not too short, a lad of eighteen who really can drive looks a great deal better on the box of a single miniature brougham than his respectable welter-weight parent. But this presumes that the stable-work is done by a man of full age, and size, and strength. It takes a strong man in hard condition to put the best polish on a regularly-worked harness-horse. One man may manage a carriage and pair of horses, but only on condition that appearance is sacrificed to utility, and that the equipage is rarely required two days running. The varnish of a carriage soon suffers if not cleaned as soon as returned to the coach-house, at however late an hour; and one man cannot do that. Horses of good constitution will feed and do well with very little grooming; but they can never look so blooming as those to which one stout strapper gives his undivided attention twice a day.

In towns where stable-rent is very high, and only one horse and carriage are kept, it is more economical to put them to livery, taking care to reward the foreman of the yard whenever, by late hours or otherwise, you give extra trouble. This arrangement is made more perfect by employing a house-servant to drive, in addition to his other duties. Where that can be managed, the combined coachman and footman has only to change his coat, is always neat, is always at hand, and does not smell of the stable.

I am quite aware that there are weak persons who pretend to despise all small economies in horseflesh, and weaker authors who write as if no stable were worth consideration when not attached to an establishment of many thousands a year. Such is the tone of the toadies to be found round the table of a sporting Dives, ready to sponge on any one who endures their flattery, or to borrow from any one who cares for their spoken or written admiration.

SOCIABLE LANDAU.

THE LANDAU.

The modern sociable landau is one example of the many improvements in wheeled carriages, in the direction of lightness, cheapness, and general utility, which have been achieved since 1851 for the benefit of the middle, and freely accepted by the wealthiest classes.

"Since 1851 horses of a smaller breed have been used,* and a demand has arisen for smaller and lighter carriages. It is probable that the carriages exhibited in the British department in 1862 are one-fourth lighter than in 1851."

The ponderous coach, still maintained as an object of hereditary state in a few noble families, is built much on the same lines, although not of the same weight, as in the days of "Good Queen Anne," when a team of "long-tailed Flanders mares" were required to make the equipage complete. The Flanders mares were succeeded by the Yorkshire or Cleveland bay coach-horse. When roads improved and carriages became less ponderous, by repeated

* Report of Messrs. Holland, Hooper, and Peters, of London, Mr. Holmes, of Derby, on Carriage Department of International Exhibition, 1862.

crosses with blood-horses the Cleveland bay was improved into the modern blood barouche-horse. These changes in the direction of less expensive carriages have taken place for the benefit of classes who have risen to undreamed-of comfort and luxury with the progress of the manufactures and trade of the country.

But Macadam was the great reformer of the trade. Before his time paved mail-coach roads and highways had all but abolished the six horses attended by a bevy of running footmen, and occasionally supplemented by a team of oxen, which were required in the reigns of the two first Georges to draw a coach through muddy roads axle deep. Arthur Young devotes pages of his "Agricultural Tours at the Close of the Eighteenth Century," to protests against the abominable condition of the roads, and relates how, when journeying to Preston, he had to hire two men to support his gig. Macadam, by the even surface with which he replaced jolting stone pavement and miles of deep ruts, rendered it possible to dispense with the ton weight of wood and iron previously required to resist the shocks of a journey along the main roads of the country.

Macadam's works were followed by railways, which reduced stage-coaches, just as they had reached perfection, to the value of old materials; destroyed the professors of four-in-hand, and finally abolished those luxurious posting chariots, without which, before the days of the iron horse, no country gentleman's coach-house was complete.

The last coaches drawn by six horses, four being in hand, the leading pair conducted by a postillion, preceded and followed by a pair of outriders with harness-bridles on their horses, which were supposed to be there ready to take the place if any of the team were disabled, all the mounted servants wearing on one arm armorial badges, were to be seen on the racecourses of Doncaster, York, and Chester, about the time the Liverpool and Manchester Railway was opened, while racing was still a county institution.

The sociable landau is the latest outcome of the advances towards smooth roads and light vehicles. The design is very old, and, in a ponderous shape, was in use at least at the commencement of the present century—a double-seated coach, calculated to hold from four to six inside, and so contrived as to be converted, not without a good deal of trouble, into an open carriage. When of the chariot shape, it was called a landaulet.

By abolishing the heavy under-carriage with the perch, by the ingenious use of japanned leather of a size, softness, and quality unknown before the repeal of the excise and customs duties on leather, a carriage has been produced with as much internal accommodation as the old-fashioned coach, at about half the cost, of about half the weight, and with such improvements in mechanical arrangements of the top that it can be opened or closed with very great facility.

These sociable landaus are made in several sizes, up to the demands of the most numerous families, and fitted, if required, with a dicky behind, for the use, in the country, of the valet and lady's maid. They are also cut down to the weight of one horse; but they do not look so well, are not so neat as a brougham, and are much less durable. With a pair of horses less expensive than a heavier carriage requires, the sociable landau is a convenient and agreeable vehicle for town or country, for winter or summer. The fittings of the movable head requires the hands of a good mechanic, and should be of the very best materials.

These carriages are made sufficiently near the ground, with an automatic step apparatus, to dispense with a second servant, if desired; but they are more complete with a page or footman. They require more careful cleaning and attention than a brougham.

THE WAGONETTE.

The wagonette is quite a modern invention, and did not come into general use until some years after the International Exhibition of 1851, although, according to the Report on the Carriage Department of the Exhibition of 1862, "the first wagonette was built in 1846, under the personal direction of the late Prince Consort." It is a combination of all the best parts of the Irish inside car, the French sportsman's *char à banc*, the English brake, and the modern stanhope phaeton; it may be constructed so as to suit one pony or one full-sized horse, a pair of cobs, or a four-in-hand. It may be driven by a groom or a gentleman, to convey, besides the driver and his companion on the box, either two, four, or six, sitting face to face in pleasant converse, with two grooms hanging on spoon-like receptacles outside the

WAGONETTE.

door. It may be what is called "reversible," and converted into a stanhope phaeton; or, by letting down hinged seats, into a *fourgon* for luggage, or a wagon to bring home fodder from a home farm. With the addition of a sort of cover, which may hang suspended from a pulley in the coach-house, it may be turned into a comfortable omnibus. It may afford ample space for the lockers for wine, ice, and all the provisions of a picnic, or to stow away the tackle of a shooting or a fishing party. With the box-seat raised to the proper height, it forms a most agreeable summer four-in-hand drag, in which none of the party are banished to seats with their backs to the horses and their faces to the grooms; and thus it is an excellent vehicle for exercising old and practising young horses. Not least, it has the advantage of being accessible to women, children, and lame or feeble men, without the necessity for any special arrangement of steps or gymnastic feat in going in or going out over the wheels Indeed, it is one of the most accessible of vehicles, while, with its well-proportioned wheels and complete lock under, it is one of the easiest for horses to draw and to turn round.

The wagonette is, in fact, the perfection of a family country carriage; and, although capable of being made very tasteful and expensive through the perfection of a variety of details, it may also be built in a plain utilitarian style, at a moderate cost.

Wagonettes when first brought into use were uncomfortable; because, to make them light, the seats were made too narrow and the backs too low. For comfort, the seats should not be less than 18 inches wide and the backs 14 inches high, with plenty of breadth for the knees; finishing at either end with a graceful curve, which will afford four circular corner seats. A brake is almost indispensable in hilly countries, it lightens the harness by rendering breeching unnecessary, and saves horses much labour in going down hill.

THE COACH.

The royal family and a few very noble houses still retain the capacious coach, which is

STATE-COACH.

not complete without at least a pair of horses nearly, if not quite, 17 hands high, with superb action, a portly coachman, and two gigantic footmen. The late Emperor of the French had in his stud, to draw his bullet-proof coach, several pairs of English horses, approaching 18 hands in height. The cost of these vehicles is something fabulous, their duration equal to several generations, but their market value—when by chance the contents of the coach-house of some many-acred, long-descended deceased peer comes under the hammer—something under the original cost of the plate-glass windows and horsehair-stuffed cushions, the wood and iron are so firmly put together, that the expense of breaking up such a coach, like a man-of-war, is almost more than the value of the material.

In the beginning of the present century these vast, costly, unwieldy vehicles were to be met at races, on nomination days of county elections, assizes, and every gathering of country magnates in every county, drawn by six horses, at present they are scarcely to be found out of London; and, for ordinary use, royalty seems to prefer, when the weather permits, something less ponderous and gorgeous—a barouche, a laudau, or a brougham; but high sheriffs of counties are expected to provide a coach, as well as a trumpeter and javelin men, to receive the judges of assize. A firm in Long Acre makes it a business to job coaches and four-horse harness to these splendid annuals.

Lord Campbell, in his "Lives of the Chief Justices," tells that (in 1734) Mr. Attorney-General Ryder always rode from his house in Chancery Lane to his villa at Streatham in his coach and six. After his death in 1756 as Lord Chief Justice, just as the patent for his peerage was being prepared, his family had a quarrel with Lord Mansfield about the transfer of the dead judge's state coach at a valuation. Lord Campbell adds, "The Lord Chancellor's state coach is still transferred to his successors."

THE CHARIOT.

The full dress chariot is so brilliant a part of a Court presentation and the Court dress of a lady, that it is likely long to survive, not only in great families, where the use descends with the liveries and coat of arms, but with their imitators, the *nouveaux riches* of to-day, who will possibly be in the "upper ten" of to-morrow. The posting chariot, that exquisite triumph of the coachmaker's mechanical art, is almost as much out of date as a sedan chair. A few survive in the possession of maiden ladies of wealth and unchangeable opinions. With the posting chariot departed a host of minor and major posting vehicles—the britzska, the drosky, &c. Charles Dickens, writing to Mr. John Forster, in 1843, when preparing for his first journey to Italy, describes how he found, in an obscure corner of the pantechnicon, "a poor old shabby devil of a coach," which he finally bought for £45. "As for comfort, it is about the size of your library, with night-lamps and day-lamps, and pockets and imperials, and leather cellars, and the most extraordinary contrivances. When you see it you will roar at it, and then proclaim it 'perfectly brilliant, my dear fellow!'" When in Switzerland he met the late Lord Vernon, "travelling about in an extraordinary carriage, where you touch a spring, and a bed appears; another spring, and a chair flies out; another spring discovers a pantry and a closet of pickles." Such also was the travelling-carriage of Dr. Darwin, the friend of Priestley, poet, philosopher, and prophet of steamboats and locomotives. The post-carriage of the Emperor Napoleon I. has long been one of the trophies of Madame Tussaud's Exhibition.

THE BAROUCHE.

The barouche is a fashionable carriage for the summer season. Of late years it has been to a great extent superseded by the modern laudau, which is as a rule lighter, more comprehensive, and can be used at all seasons of the year. The driving seat is intended for a coachman and footman to sit together, as the footman if behind would be unpleasantly placed, looking down on and listening to the conversation of the sitters within. The barouche, when the head is thrown back and the knee-flap elevated, will hold four or six persons inside; but in wet weather, when it is closed, only two or three can be accommodated. The most fashionable barouches are on C springs, but they are also made with elliptic springs. Whether large or small, they always require a pair of horses.

The barouche is eminently suited for park display, with two great blood-horses in rich harness, stepping right up to their curb-chains, an imposing coachman and footman on the box, and a lady reclining almost at full length, displaying a costume light and diaphanous, or velvet and fur, according to the season. On visits to Ascot Heath or Doncaster town moor, or in the country anywhere, the barouche may be properly drawn by four horses, with private postillions—what the French call *à la Daumont.*

CREAM STATE CARRIAGE HORSE. (OF HER MAJESTY'S STUD.)

FROM AN ORIGINAL PORTRAIT BY ALFRED CORBOULD ESQ.

SINGLE HARNESS PHAETON HORSE COLUMBINE. PROPERTY OF CHARLES BAYNES ESQ.
1ST PRIZE FOR ACTION & PACE AT THE AGRICULTURAL HALL HORSE SHOW 1872.

In London the great job-masters reserve their very finest bred and high-actioned pairs for the barouches of noble and wealthy customers. A barouche horse means something with more blood than the finest coach-horse.

Barouches are built in all sizes, down to that suitable for a pair of fourteen-hand cobs; but for such a purpose, where only one carriage is kept, the sociable landau is more useful, and generally preferred.

For persons much in society a barouche alone is not a suitable carriage. In winter or for night-work it must be supplemented by a coach, a sociable, or a brougham. A full-sized barouche is quite out of place except where there is a complete establishment of horses and servants.

<h2 style="text-align:center">THE VICTORIA.</h2>

The victoria is a comparatively modern invention, or, rather, it is an adaptation of the old cabriolet phaeton, and as a fashionable carriage is a creation of the French Empire; it was in common use as a hack carriage in Paris long before it obtained a name in England.

The victoria has the advantage of being as easy for a lady to take her seat in or descend from, without letting down a seat, or the chance of soiling her robes on the wheels, as a brougham. It also displays better than any other carriage the toilette of the occupant, literally from the crown of her head to the sole of her foot. Certainly, if it is worth while to expend a fortune on clothes, it is still more worth while to show them at full length, and under the most advantageous arrangements. What the brougham is for the face of a beauty, the victoria is for the robes—a frame for the one, a pedestal for the other.

It has also the not small advantage to a certain class of involving, if desired, the utmost possible expense for the accommodation of the smallest number of persons—a pair of horses of great price, a coachman and footman of high class, in costly liveries; an expensive carriage to convey two persons—a carriage only available for ornamental purposes, for it cannot be used at night, or in dirty weather, or in the country, or anywhere except for the Park, for a little shopping and a little visiting. In cold, dry, frosty weather, the victoria has another merit—it may be employed as a vehicle for displaying a vast breadth and length of costly furs.

A light victoria may be drawn by one small blood-horse, but that one should have very fine action. The footman may be dispensed with, when not required to leave cards and make inquiries, as the victoria has no door to open, or steps to let down.

<h2 style="text-align:center">THE MAIL PHAETON.</h2>

Next come the leading types of four-wheeled carriages which it is presumed that the owner selects because he likes driving himself, in which in no case is a coachman, in the strict sense of the term (that is, a ponderous artist in a gorgeous uniform, shorts, and silk stockings), employed, except by accident, and under protest on his part. The proper servant for carriages driven by the owner is a top-booted groom, dressed in a black or Oxford mixture or dark-coloured livery coat. The oldest of this class still in use is the mail phaeton, of which, in its original shape, size, and weight, very few specimens remain.

By degrees, as our roads improved, and long journeys by the highways were discontinued in favour of the rail, all travelling-carriages, and notably the mail phaeton, which has always been both a town and fashionable carriage, were made lighter. The heavy mail-coach under-spring apparatus having disappeared, the word mail has lost its original significance. At present it only means a high-seated, hooded, pair-horse driving-carriage, to carry the driver and one other person besides the groom or grooms, which can be made sufficiently strong for every purpose, and not too heavy for a pair of light blood-horses, equally available for country use and the town, for the bachelor and the married man.

For the convenience of ladies steps have been contrived, which, fitting under the driving-seat, can be drawn out and returned with great facility.

For the driver and a companion, in the prime of life, with one or two grooms behind, there is no pair-horse driving-carriage that excels the mail phaeton in pleasure and comfort. It affords sufficient room to stow away any amount of men's—and even a reasonable wife's—

MAIL PHAETON.

luggage, not forgetting, in these days of dismal roadside inns, corn for the horses. The front seat is not only sufficiently high for fully commanding your horses, but for enjoying the scenery of the country through which you pass. It is well suited in town for displaying the points of the most extravagant steppers, if your fancy lies that way; while your wife or sister may, with the approbation of the most prudish maiden aunt, appear at your side. In the country, whether going to cover side, a dinner party, or even a ball, no vehicle is better calculated for conveying two over rough roads with "safety and dispatch" at as high speed as your horses can conveniently compass.

The very finest horses of the most brilliant action, "stepping and going," look their best in a mail phaeton; but if your taste and means incline you rather for utility than for ornament, for long distances rather than the solemn yet sociable parades of the Park or the Champs Elysées, a pair of low-priced *screws*, as your richer friends will term them, if with "character" and breeding, in first-class condition and workmanlike harness, will do very well.

It should never be forgotten that no one takes any particular notice of a family brougham—a sort of nursery on wheels—or any general practitioner's carriage, or in fact any carriage specially selected for economy, utility, and capacity; but a victoria, a mail phaeton, or a park phaeton, are all carriages with "pretensions"—what the French call *voitures de luxe* —and look contemptible when you see them, as you sometimes do, with varnish dull, harness rusty, and a man in shabby livery coat, with a cockade in his weather-beaten hat.

The process of getting into the hind seat of a phaeton has been reduced to quite a neat gymnastic feat by first-class grooms. Running after the phaeton to the near-side steps at No. 1, he springs with his *left* foot on the step, and stands straight on it; at No. 2 he brings his right leg out at right angles with his hip, and passes over the back rail on to the seat; and at No. 3 he elevates his left leg at right angles with his hip, and passes it over the wheel, and takes his seat as regularly as a soldier presenting arms at the word of command. The off-side groom of course begins with the right foot. I noted the operation as it was performed by the grooms of an officer of the Life Guards, an active member of two four-horse clubs.

I cannot give a more striking proof of the progress of the coachmaker's art than by two of the woodcuts which illustrate this chapter. The one is a modern driving or mail phaeton, copied from a picture by Mr. Alfred Corbould, painted for Major Stapylton, a Yorkshire gentleman famous for the completeness of an extensive stud of hacks, hunters, harness, and thorough-bred horses; the other the favourite carriage of the Prince Regent, "the high-perch phaeton." It was in a high-perch phaeton that Mr. Sampson Hanbury, the great brewer, used to start from his mansion at Ware at five o'clock in the morning, drive his pair of blood-horses to Spitalfields, there transact the business of his great brewery, and then, with a fresh pair of nags, drive back to Ware in time to hunt the Puckeridge Hounds, of which he was master.

And yet Mr. Felton, from whose curious "treatise on carriages, comprehending coaches chariots, phaetons, curricles, gigs, whiskeys," the picture of this hideous, dangerous, unmechanical vehicle is copied, says in his introduction, dated 1790: "The art of coachmaking within this last century has arrived at a very high degree of perfection, with respect both to the beauty, strength, and elegance of the machine. The consequence has been an increasing demand for that comfortable conveyance, which, besides its common utility, has now become a distinguishing mark of the taste and rank of the proprietor." Mr. Felton candidly warns his readers that the "high-perch phaeton" is apt, unless carefully driven, "to turn over in going round corners."

THE PARK PHAETON.

The park phaeton is essentially a lady's carriage, and one of the most elegant, whether constructed for ponies or horses, of all the intermediate heights up to 15 hands 2 inches, a height which should never be exceeded. The park phaeton is a carriage for town and country, and may be seen in perfection, including the fair drivers, at cover side in the pasture counties. It has a hood, which completely protects the fair driver and her one companion from everything except a shower directly in front, but it carries no lamps. It looks light, but runs heavy; it has no room for luggage of any kind, and must be attended on by a single groom sitting on the rumble behind, who may be a very neat lad or an equally neat slim old man, but must be in a very correct costume, or on state occasions by two grooms. In former times great ladies, like royalty, were attended by outriders, mounted on ponies with harness bridles of the same colour and stamp as the pair in harness; but the custom is so nearly extinct that when it occurs it creates a sensation.

The park phaeton is one of the most expensive carriages in use, not excepting the pair-horse victoria, as well as one of the most delightful; because, although a groom replaces the gorgeous coachman and the attendant Jeames, the horses or ponies must be of the most expensive character. Of whatever size, they must have quality, action, a proud carriage, irreproachable heads, necks, and tails; in a word, the symmetry of the ideal Arab, with the true action that "steps and goes." They must be a perfect match in colour, height,

PARK PHAETON.

and action; admirably broken, yet full of courage. In a word, they must have the appearance of fiery dragons, with the docility of trained chargers, and, while they step freely up to the bit, over the ground, shaking their long manes, must not pull an ounce. The long parasol-whip should be borne, like a flag, aloft, for ornament, not for use. It is difficult to say which is more detestable, to see a lady obliged to flog her horses along, or pulled out of that graceful seat, which is part of the show, by a pair of tearing brutes, very fit perhaps for a man's sporting phaeton, but quite out of place in a lady's hands.

For country use, a park phaeton may, without any material sacrifice of elegance, be built more capaciously, so as to hold something on a railway-station journey, with higher wheels, and fitted with a pair of good lamps. Although ponies are very well in Hyde Park, in country lanes a pair of fifteen-hand horses have a more imposing appearance, which has something to do with safety on a road where market carts and traps are liable to be met in the dark. Park phaetons grew out of the pretty pony phaeton invented for George IV. in his declining years, when he lived at the cottage by Virginia Water.

THE STANHOPE PHAETON.

The stanhope phaeton, which was originally contrived by placing the body of a stanhope gig on four wheels, with a boot behind for a servant, is an improvement on the old heavy cabriolet phaeton, being lighter, and easily drawn by one small blood-horse. It has also the advantage of being cheap. For those who like to drive themselves it is a pleasant carriage, although it does not give so commanding a seat as the mail phaeton, or so much accommodation as the wagonette. It is adapted for either one or a pair of light horses, and is easily made to come within the four-hundredweight limit of the Chancellor of the Exchequer's 1870 Budget. The stanhope has been varied in two directions; in its original shape it was an open carriage, like the gig. In the first instance it was increased in weight by the addition of a fixed or movable head, and sometimes by being enlarged in width, without the perch or heavy under-carriage, to the dimensions of the pair-horse double-groomed mail phaeton. In the other and later direction it has been cut down in size, the hind seat narrowed so as only to hold one person, hence called from its shape a T-cart—a name adopted by the Guardsman who invented it; an example of that "pride that apes humility."

THE FOUR-WHEELED VIS-À-VIS PONY PHAETON.

One more four-wheeled type of carriage, equally in demand in town and country—an essentially family carriage—is the pony phaeton, in which perhaps as much amusement and happiness is packed as in the most costly and gorgeous vehicles (not excepting the Court chariot of a lady who has so risen in the world as to be presented at Court, to the envy and amazement of the manufacturing town from which her husband sprung; or the City sheriff or provincial mayor on his way to receive—the result of a fortunate fluke—the honour of knighthood, and return Sir Peter or Sir John), whether of clothes-basket shape, of wicker or of iron wire, or of unpainted wood, low to the ground, drawn by a small, cheap, docile animal, for the express benefit of mamma, or the nursery governess, or the nurse and half a dozen children, either with or without the assistance of the gardener or the gardener's boy as driver.

The first light pony phaetons, invented at Croydon, were of wicker-work—or, as it is sometimes called, "osier"—which had the advantage of being very light and very low-priced, if not cheap. For a time they were quite the fashion; but of late years a number of materials have been used for low-priced carriages which are more durable, and more easy to clean and keep clean, than osier. There is a large and legitimate demand for low-priced carriages by classes who either like an occasional change of form and fashion, or who are indifferent to fine finish, for country use. The most numerous of these want a handy conveyance, and find that it suits their income better to pay £25 than £50. To supply this want during the twenty years that followed the International Exhibition of 1851 there sprung up in the metropolis, and in almost every market-town of England, a host of builders prepared to meet every variety of taste in cheap family and sporting vehicles. Fine flatted paint and varnish were superseded by plain paint, or wood merely varnished over it natural colour; iron wire superseded costly and little durable cane-work, and even wicker-work, was imitated. For morocco leather lining American cloth was substituted; and stained wooden splashboards took the place of patent leather. In a word, supply followed, and to this hour continues to follow, demand.

Amongst the various forms of family pony phaetons, boat or clothes-basket shaped, or wagonette, or *vis-à-vis*, fit for a cob, a twelve-hand pony, or even a donkey, all tastes and nearly all incomes could be suited. With the very plainest harness, with a breast-plate instead of a collar, and a pony, plucky and free, perfectly steady, but without a particle of shy in him, even if rather shaky on his fore-legs, you have something that will do for the daily exercise of the children, and for use as a market or luggage cart, or to take any one to the station at five minutes' notice; accessible, without a let-down step, to the feeble and fat. The first cost is trifling, the tax nominal; the cost of the pony, a truss of hay a week and an occasional feed of oats. In no description of vehicle is there more choice in any part of the country, of any material, from the more costly and highly-finished to the simplest demands of utility, new or second-hand, at all prices, from £5 upwards.

BASKET PONY PHAETON.

SPORTING, RURAL, AND MISCELLANEOUS FOUR-WHEELED CARRIAGES.

The names of the four-wheeled carriages intended solely for country use, which go under the name of dog-carts—although many of them have barely room to stow away a full-sized tom-cat—which have been invented since 1852 would alone fill many pages. There is the dog-cart proper, on high wheels, which carries four persons—two facing the horse or horses, and their backs to their two fellow-passengers; with room beneath for dogs, if needful, or a great quantity of baggage of any kind. This is a compact class of vehicle that follows well, having the fore and hind pairs of wheels near together; the body so constructed that fairly high fore-wheels will lock completely under. In a word, it is a very good *man's* carriage, although it may be used at a push by ladies. It is a carriage in which severe utility should be the rule, and no money wasted on mere ornament. Of this class of vehicle, where great capacity is an object, and one full-sized or a pair of small horses can be used, the style known as the Perth dog-cart is one of the best. In its largest form it holds six, and one or two more may be packed in for a short journey. Its luggage-holding powers are enormous; and instances have been recorded where a very good sleeping apartment for a couple of tired sportsmen has been arranged in a four-wheeled Perth cart.

There are also a considerable number of dog-cart variations of the American type, with the improvement of a complete lock-under, built expressly for lightness, strength, and high speed. The best type of these was constructed for Captain Oliver, a Northamptonshire sportsman, who after an accident, which prevented him from riding for a season, took to hunting on wheels; he did not confine himself to high roads or parish roads, but occasionally turned into "the open," and is even accused of having successfully charged more than one gap in a hedge with a ditch on the taking off side.

It is scarcely necessary to observe that the machines for effecting such feats must be constructed with the very best materials and workmanship.

Amongst the eccentricities of sporting carriages, the "boat carriage," invented for the use of luxurious Highland and island sportsmen, must not be omitted. Mounted on four wheels, it may be used as an ordinary driving carriage, or with post horses to reach some remote loch or firth; then the body launched is a stout gig—nautical, not equestrian—fully equipped with oars and sails.

TWO-WHEELED CARRIAGES.

The oldest carriages of which we have any historical or pictoral record were on two wheels. Egyptian and Assyrian sculptures, the chronicles of the Old Testament, and the poems of Homer, all prove that the use of chariots preceded that of cavalry in war. Egyptian and Assyrian kings are represented in bas-reliefs preserved in the British Museum, and copied in the Crystal Palace, doing battle, hunting wild beasts, and taking part in processions in two-wheeled chariots.

THE CURRICLE.

At the period when the heroes of Miss Austen and Miss Fanny Burney paid their state visits in "chariots and six," the most fashionable town-carriage was the curricle. Amongst the other extravagances reported of the nabobs of the period was an order in Long Acre of "a few curricles for the spring." Mr. Felton, in the book already quoted, describes and gives pictures of no less than four curricles and gig curricles, with contrivances for occasionally using one horse only, or on very narrow roads shafts, and a leader ridden by a postillion, and not one four-wheeled one-horse phaeton fit for modern use.

The curricle—with a body something like that of its successor the cabriolet—hung on C springs, on two wheels, drawn by a pair of horses perfectly matched in size, colour, quality, and step; the harness profusely decorated with silver ornaments, united by a silver bar, which supported a silver-mounted pole; preceded or followed by two grooms, mounted on another pair of horses equally well matched with the first, secured the driver and his companion—frequently a lady—a superb effect, which combined the maximum of expense with the minimum of convenience. Four horses and two grooms to carry two persons! After a time economical reasons prevailed, and, at some sacrifice of contour and elegance, the horses of the two grooms were dispensed with, and they were provided for in a sort of rumble behind the curricle, which was not without use in balancing the pole and taking the weight from the backs of the horses.

The mail phaeton as improved, and the cabriolet as perfected, killed the curricle. These, while nearly as expensive, were much less difficult to produce in perfection, and infinitely less dangerous.

The most original curricle of the last century, built at the order of that caricature of a dandy, Romeo Coates, was of copper, in the shape of a nautilus shell.

The first carriage set up by Charles Dickens, after he awoke one morning and found himself famous, was a curricle. It was in a curricle that he drove to pay his first visit to the young and rising artist, the painter of "Dolly Varden," since a Royal Academician, W. P. Frith. A curricle is one of the "properties" in the story of "Nicholas Nickleby."

Count d'Orsay was the last dandy who drove a curricle in the Park, and sent this costly, magnificent carriage out of fashion, when he took up the cabriolet, as Whyte Melville says, "with his whiskers and his cabriolet horse, he took the town by storm."

THE CURRICLE.

It was somewhere about 1846 that I saw the great Duke of Wellington driving himself in a sulphur-yellow curricle, with silver harness and bar, over old Westminster Bridge, to take part in a review at Woolwich; the late bridge was very steep, and he walked his horses up the ascent from Westminster.

THE CABRIOLET.

The cabriolet—which is still a favourite with a select few rich Guardsmen, fast stock-jobbers, and the survivors of the last generation of men about town, solely for Park use, and was the height of fashion in the early days of Queen Victoria's reign—is a curricle with a pair of shafts, and without the groom's rumble. Mrs. Gore, in one of her novels, makes it the carriage of a married couple of rank and limited fortune. That was before the invention of the one-horse brougham. It took the place for men not only of the curricle and the stanhope gig, but of the chariot and the *vis-à-vis*, for every use except Court drawing-rooms. Palace Yard was full of cabriolets on the night of 1835, when Lord John Russell carried the "Irish Church Appropriation Clause," when Sir Robert Peel was defeated, and the clause was buried, not to be dug up again until Mr. Gladstone succeeded to the place of his early mentor, "grave Sir Robert." Macaulay writes in 1831 :—"Lord John Russell drove me back to town from Holland House in his cabriolet." "Nimrod" about the same time speaks of this new carriage with the greatest contempt, as "only fit for a Frenchman afraid of the wind and the rain."

It was in a cabriolet that Theodore Hook used to drive home in the morning, after spending the night at Crockford's, when his physician ordered him "not to be out in the night air." Planché, in his memoirs, relates that Sam Beasley, the architect, "who never had five shillings, but could always find five pounds for a friend," once drove him home from a Greenwich dinner, and on his remarking on the convenience of a private carriage, answered, "Yes, I am rather a curious fellow. I have a carriage and a cabriolet and three horses, and a coachman and a footman and a large house, and three maid-servants, and half-a-crown!" Thackeray gives an idea of the general effect when, at Bungay's great dinner, he describes the arrival of the Honourable Percy Popjoy :—"As they talked, a magnificent vision of an enormous grey cab-horse appeared, and neared rapidly. A pair of white reins, held by small white gloves, were visible behind a face pale but decorated with a chin tuft, the head of an exiguous groom bobbing over the cab-head. These bright things were revealed to the delighted Mr. Bungay." But luxury has advanced since those days. Mrs. B—— would not now "disport in a one-horse vehicle ;" she would have her brougham.

The cabriolet required one horse only, but a horse of great size and beauty, with good legs and feet, and superlative action in his slow paces; and one groom hanging on behind, so small as to be of little use for any other purpose than display.

It was a very pleasant bachelor's carriage when perfectly appointed, as well as very imposing ; magnificent for short slow parades, and especially as an easy pedestal for gossip under the shadow of Achilles Wellington. The grand horse, the miniature groom at his head, the languid, well-gloved, dandy driver, formed a favourite picture with the novelists of the period, from "Pelham," "Coningsby," and "Pendennis," to "Digby Grand."

THE STANHOPE GIG AND DOG-CART.

Before the cabriolet came in, the gig, improved from the original "whiskey" shape depicted by Gilray in "Dr. Syntax's Tour," had made its way to the front against the curricle, and become a carriage in which ladies of fashion condescended to appear in the Park, at Ascot, and Brighthelmstone. Different coachmakers brought out the tilbury, the dennett (invented by Bennett, a coachmaker in Finsbury, whose B was changed at the West End to D), and the stanhope shape. This last was invented by Fitzroy Stanhope, a brother of Lord Petersham, afterwards the Earl of Harrington, who married Miss Foote. He had previously invented the tilbury; and Mr. Tilbury, the coach-builder, insisted that the last should bear the designer's name. Mr. Musters, Byron's successful rival with Miss Chaworth, was driving a lady in a gig in Hyde Park when the quarrel occurred which led to his duel with a colonel, and several other curious passages in the fashionable history of that time, recorded in a punning caricature. Gentlemen have now ceased to fight duels, and ladies of fashion no longer take drives in Hyde Park in gigs or any kind of two-wheeled vehicle. A writer in the old *Sporting Magazine*, in 1817, mentions that, "under the patronage of the Prince Regent, the gig had in a great measure superseded the curricle and tandem as a fashionable carriage."

Of the different shapes of gigs, the stanhope is the only one that survives as a town carriage. It is still built in the most expensive manner, by coachmakers of high repute; and is patronised by young gentlemen of fashion fond of a quick high-stepping blood-horse, for it is a kind of vehicle which shows off that class of horse in great perfection. For many years between the decline of the cabriolet and the rise of the brougham, a town-built stanhope was rarely seen on the stones; but since 1870 there has been a revival, chiefly due to the officers of the Guards and their numerous imitators.

At the time of Thurtell's trial for the murder of Weare, a witness gave "keeping a gig" as a proof of respectability, and the words have since been crystallised into one of Mr. Carlyle's favourite epithets descriptive of his favourite aversion, the British Philistine. But the

THE DOG-CART.

general diffusion of carriage-keeping on two and four wheels since 1852 has quite deprived the joke of its point. The class who once drove gigs now ride in broughams or in dog-carts, which last are not in any way a sign of gentility.

A gig, like all two-wheeled carriages of its class, requires careful construction to avoid the very disagreeable motion called technically "knee-action"—an irritating jogging motion, arising from the spring of the shafts. A number of inventions have been patented to cure this disagreeable motion, and some of them are very successful. At the commencement of the century, Fuller, of Bath, made a reputation by an invention of this kind; but now every builder of a dog-cart has his remedy, at the cost of two or three extra sovereigns. The man who cares for his neck, and rides on two wheels, should look to his shafts. They should be of lancewood. The late Mr. Allen Ransome recommended that they should be divided, lined with a steel plate, and cramped together. A shaft should never have a bolt through it.

An exemption from taxes made in 1843 (since abolished) not only introduced a two-wheeled carriage into families who were previously too proud to drive a market cart, but raised a number of ingenious country wheelwrights to the rank of coach-builders, at a time when none of the great men of Long Acre would condescend to build anything that was not finished and varnished like a piece of cabinet work, lined and stuffed like a drawing-room couch, strong enough and heavy enough to last for a generation, at a cost of at least seventy guineas, in its simplest stanhope gig form. Although the exemption has long been repealed, the result remains in a number of low-priced, two-wheeled vehicles, equally convenient for domestic and sporting purposes, for carrying children, small parcels, or luggage, to the station. "I will send the dog-cart to meet you," is the common postscript of a letter from either a mansion or a farm-house. The term has been naturalised in France as the "To-cart."

The sporting character of the original dog-cart has been attenuated to nothing, and the wheels, assisted by modern ingenuity in the management of axle-trees, are made of the best height for draught, while the body is kept low enough for safety and convenience. The family or private two-wheeled carriage may be classed in three types:—

1. To hold two only.
2. To hold four, *dos-à-dos.*
3. To carry four inside, on the old Irish inside car pattern.

The sporting types are the original Oxford dog-cart, admirably calculated for tandem driving; and the old Whitechapel, more favourably known since the Prince of Wales made Sandringham his country seat as "the Norfolk shooting-cart," the most capacious of all two-wheeled sporting and family carriages; which may be built plain enough to take pigs to market, and handsome enough to convey a party of cavalry subalterns to the meet of a crack pack, or with dogs and guns to a shooting party at the "Duke's." To ride safely in a high two-wheeled carriage you require a horse with good trotting action and sound feet. A game but groggy horse can safely pull a four-wheeler.

THE PRIVATE HANSOM.

In this list of English pleasure-carriages, which might be extended, in the shape of a catalogue, to volumes, the private hansom, so called after the original ingenious and unfortunate inventor, Mr. Hansom, architect of the Birmingham town-hall, must not be omitted. It is essentially a man's carriage for town use, in favour amongst surgeons in such practice that they can also afford to keep a brougham for inclement weather, surveyors, contractors, and others, who require to hurry about on business and get in and out frequently. The hansom has the advantage of air, and affords a very healthy pleasant sort of exercise. Although built to hold two, it suits one with very little luggage better, and is quite out of place where the ground to be traversed presents many steep hills. Ladies like a ride in a hansom, by way of a change, but for constant use prefer a single or miniature brougham, which is more generally useful, and on the whole not more expensive. A private hansom requires a better horse than a brougham, if not so fashionable, because, in spite of the very best balancing, there must be some weight in going down hills; and he should also be fast, equal to at least twelve miles an hour when required—fourteen are better. Pace and ease of motion are the features of this vehicle, which is a very useful addition to a well-furnished coach-house at a mansion where no severe rise intervenes on the road to a railway station to and from which the head of the establishment has frequent occasion to travel. The hansom should be provided with one or two brilliant lamps. The horse should be driven with a simple or ring-snaffle, according to his mouth. A curb-bit is altogether inadmissible, in consequence of the weight of the long reins.

INDIA-RUBBER TIRES.

India-rubber tires are a great luxury; they give to a wheeled carriage the smoothness of a sledge on hard snow, and subdue nearly all the rattle and noise of wheels. But they are usually made on a wrong principle. If india-rubber is stretched, every cut continually widens, and the tire is speedily destroyed. Tires made on a directly opposite plan will endure for an unlimited period; that is, a thick hollow tube of india-rubber shrunk on an iron core shorter than the rubber, and coiled round a wheel grooved to receive it. This kind of india-rubber has been used for many years on two carriages by the late Mr. Allen Ransome, the agricultural implement maker, of Ipswich.

THE IRISH CAR.

I hope I may not be considered to have added one more to the grievances of Ireland by declining to treat the Irish car so famed in song, "the low-backed car," as a vehicle worth transplanting from its native soil. With one horse and two wheels the Irish car has one merit—a capacity almost as unbounded as the corricolo of Naples—it will hold as many passengers and as much luggage as the horse can draw. It has another—it is almost impossible to upset it. But as the latter advantage is shared with numerous types of village carts, and the former cannot be favoured by any "merciful man," the Irish outside car remains a convenient vehicle for pic-nics and fishing excursions—less expensive, but not more sociable than a wagonette. The driver either sits sideways, with the least possible control over his horse, or on a seat in front, which unduly throws weight on the horse's shoulders.

THE SLEDGE.

One of the most delightful carriages for a winter in a country house, in any county where the snow lies long enough and deep enough, is a sledge holding two or four, besides a groom perched out of earshot behind, and driven with a single horse, a pair, or a tandem. Sledges are generally imported from Canada or the United States. They are in universal use in Russia, Scandinavia, Poland, Hungary, and Austria, in the winter months. They cost a great deal to fit up in proper style, with furs and bells; but the mere sledge may be made by any village wheelwright or carpenter, at very little expense. The body should be very light—it does not require the strength of a wheeled carriage of European make—so that it may be handled with ease. A Canadian sledge to hold four *vis-à-vis* which I purchased one summer for £5 only weighed 300 lbs. There are many occasions when you have to handle a sledge like a wheelbarrow; for instance, when you upset it. The harness may be of the simplest character, breast-plates instead of collars; sash-line rope traces will do very well, as they will be nearly sixteen feet long; it is scarcely worth while to provide leather traces for a vehicle that can only be used for a few days each time at intervals of two or three years. The only safe plan for enjoying sledging in England is to have the carriage, harness, and all the paraphernalia stowed away ready for use at a moment's notice. To begin to build or repair a sledge when the first snow-storm appears is to manufacture disappointment. Bells in driving on dark nights are necessary, for the sledge makes no sound; but sheep-bells, for want of better, will make the needful noise. As the horse is so far from the carriage, a tandem whip is requisite. Coloured blankets may fill the place of those splendid bear or buffalo robes which are so essential a part of the display in sledge-driving countries; there are very few seasons in England when it is worth while for persons of moderate means to prepare for a sledge drive as a matter of fashion, and furs laid by are very apt to get moth-eaten. On the other hand, at an insignificant expense, a vehicle with harness may be got up and put by in a country house which will afford a great deal of social fun when a heavy fall of snow has stopped skating, after a frost has stopped hunting. If there is in the family a mighty hunter from tropical or hyperborean regions, all his spoils of the chase may be utilised with excellent effect, whether of tiger, deer, bear, or buffalo. You may either drive one horse, or a pair to a pole, or in the Russian fashion, with one in shafts, united by a wooden arch painted bright blue or red, and hung with bells, and the other galloping alongside him harnessed to an outrigger.

Tandem is a favourite style in Canada, but it must require an exceedingly steady and staunch leader and a clever whip; he sits very low if he sits alongside the lady, and he is not very high if he stands behind and drives over the heads of two.

LAMPS.

Carriage-lamps are at the present day almost universally fitted for burning wax or composition candles, the manufacture of which last kind has been carried to great perfection since all customs and excise duties affecting them have been removed. The use of oil-lamps in private carriages is almost confined to four-horse drags and hansoms.

When candles are used, the owner should insist that in winter the lamps be always supplied with new candles whenever they are used, and that the springs on which the candles rest be regularly examined; otherwise he may find that lights are wanting when most urgently required. The value of lamps is not so much to show the coachman the road as to prevent careless drivers from running into him on a dark or foggy night.

AXLES.

Although Collinge's axles, which will travel without fresh oiling for three months, are the best for civilised countries, a simpler plan—the old mail-coach axle—will be found more suitable for the colonies, or in the wild out-of-the-way tracts of Europe, where the niceties of mechanical construction are unknown.

SHAFTS.

In describing the manufacture of a brougham, tubular iron shafts were recommended. It is, however, right to mention that there is one objection to their use—viz., if by any means strained or twisted, they cannot be returned to their original shape in the coachmaker's shop, as tough wood can, but must be sent back to the manufacturer for that purpose under any circumstances. It is a good plan to keep a pair of spare shafts in the coach-house. The latest improvement in shafts of four-wheeled carriages is a combination of wood and iron. Lancewood are the best for a two-wheeled carriage.

POLE.

The pole for a pair of horses should be made of the best ash—hickory has been used, but it is the opinion of eminent coach-builders that hickory poles do not wear so well in this as in the American climate. The breaking of a pole is a very dangerous affair; it is therefore of very great importance that it should consist of a sound, well-seasoned spar. The greatest strength is secured by a perfectly straight pole, which will bend, if required, like a fishing-rod. In many carriages, in order to obtain the necessary rise from low fore-wheels, the butt-end of the pole must be bent. In such instances extra precautions are required by the pole-maker.

It should always be remembered that the strength of a carriage, and consequently the size of a pole, should be proportioned to the size and weight of the horses. This is well explained in the following passage from the report by Mr. George N. Hooper, on the Dublin exhibition of carriages. After observing that the results will not be satisfactory unless carriages are properly horsed, the reporter proceeds to say: "Not unfrequently a carriage is ordered for one horse only. When it is partly made, or perhaps finished, fittings are ordered for two horses; and it sometimes happens that the two horses put to the light one-horse carriage are coach-horses, between 16 and 17 hands in height. Such horses, although well adapted to a heavy family carriage, are quite out of their proper place attached to a light one. Although they can draw it at a good pace, and over almost any obstacle in the road, and do their journey without fatigue, the carriage suffers sooner or later. The lounging of such horses against a light pole, the strain thrown on the pole in case of a horse tripping, the certain breakage that must occur in case of a fall, and the risk of over-turning the carriage, should all be considered before putting a very light carriage behind very large horses. It also sometimes happens that miniature broughams, and other very small carriages, built as light and as slight as safety will allow, are afterwards used with a pair of horses. In such cases, even if accidents do not occur through the great strain of a long pole acting as a lever on a very light mechanism, the parts become strained, do not work as they were intended to do, and necessitate constant repair from not being adapted for the work put upon them. Carriage-owners should, in their own interest, have their carriages and horses suited to what they ought and can undergo, bearing in mind that there are advantages and disadvantages both with heavy and light carriages. The former are easier and more comfortable to ride in; they are safer for horses, drivers, and riders; and the necessary repairs are less frequently required. The lighter carriages follow the horses more easily, and can therefore do a longer day's journey; and although the necessary repairs may come more frequently, the saving of the horses may be an advantage that many persons will consider of the utmost importance. Such light carriages should, however, be made of the choicest materials and workmanship, that they may do the work required of them."

DRAG OR BRAKE.

When breeching is not used—and blood-horses well ribbed up, with good quarters, look better without breeching or hip-straps—a drag of some kind must be used in the country, and a lever drag in town. The old-fashioned drag consists of an iron slipper attached to a chain. It is applied and removed by hand, and may be seen in daily use on London omnibuses descending Ludgate or Pentonville Hills. Since breeching went out of fashion brakes have been simplified and improved by English mechanics. The most general application is by a lever placed at the right hand of the driver, but it is in some instances arranged so as to be moved by his foot. Tramway cars are always stopped by a strong screw-brake, and never by the horses

Persons who have not paid any attention to the subject may object to the extra expense of a lever-brake. What is the result? In descending a hill all the pressure is thrown on the horses' necks and fore-legs. If the horses trot steadily, and the pole bears the extra pressure without breaking, all goes well. But the safest, steadiest horse sometimes trips, or shies, or bolts, startled by some unaccustomed sight or sound, or stung by an insect— he gives a sudden snatch at the pole, and at the critical moment the timber snaps. With a lever-brake the pressure on the neck, when a good coachman is driving, is entirely removed, the horses run loose beside the pole, with pole-chains nearly loose, and, in case of an accident, the carriage can be stopped with exceeding ease. But a stupid driver will wear out a lever-brake by using it on the slightest declivity.

HINTS FOR THE PRESERVATION OF A CARRIAGE.

A carriage should be kept in an airy, dry coach-house, with a moderate amount of light, otherwise the colours will be destroyed. There should be no communication between the stables and the coach-house. The manure-heap or pit should also be kept as far away as possible, as the ammonia exhaled from it cracks varnish, and makes the colours both of painting and lining fade.

Whenever it has to stand for days together, a carriage should always have on it a large linen cover, sufficiently strong to keep off the dust without excluding the light. Dust, when allowed to settle on a carriage, eats into the varnish. (N.B. Care should be taken to keep the cover *aired.*)

When a carriage is new or newly painted, it is better for it to stand a few weeks before being used. It will, however, even then be liable to stain or spot, unless care be taken to remove the mud before it dries on, or as soon afterwards as possible.

A carriage should never under any circumstances be put away *dirty.*

In *washing a carriage* keep out of the sun, and have the lever end of the setts covered with leather. *Use plenty of water*, which apply (where practicable) with a hose or syringe, taking great care that the water is not driven into the body, to the injury of the lining. When forced water is not obtainable, use for the body a large soft sponge. This, when saturated, squeeze over the panels, and by the flow down of the water the dirt will soften and harmlessly run off, then finish with a soft chamois leather and an old silk handkerchief.

The same remarks apply to the under work and wheels, except that when the mud is well soaked, a soft mop, free from any hard substance in the head, may be used. Never use a spoke-brush, which, in conjunction with the grit from the road, acts like sand-paper on the varnish, scratching it, and of course effectually removing all gloss. If persisted in it will rub off the varnish and paint, down to the wood. Never allow water to dry itself on a carriage, as it invariably leaves stains.

To remove spots or stains, a few drops of furniture polish, reviver, or even linseed oil, on a dab made of woollen rags (using as little of the fluid as possible), will generally suffice. If the panels are very bad, nothing but a regular flatting down and hand polishing, or even revarnishing, will be effectual.

Patent leather may be easily revived in the same way.

Enamelled leather heads and aprons should be washed with soap and water, and then very lightly rubbed with linseed oil. The enamelled heads of landaus, barouches, and phaetons should always be kept up at full stretch in the coach-house; and aprons of every kind should be frequently unfolded, or they will soon spoil.

In cleaning brass or silver, no acid, or mercury, or grit should be used; the polish should be obtained solely by friction.

To prevent or destroy moths in woollen linings use turpentine and camphor. In a close carriage the evaporation from this mixture, when placed in a saucer, and the glasses up, is a certain cure.

Be careful to *grease the bearings* of the fore-carriage, so as to allow it to turn freely. If it turns with difficulty the shafts or pole will probably strain or break.

Examine a carriage occasionally, and whenever a bolt or clip appears to be getting loose tighten it up with a wrench; and always have little repairs done *at once;* should the tires of the wheels get at all slack, so that the joints of the felloes are seen, have them immediately contracted, or the wheels will be permanently injured—"A stitch in time saves nine."

MR. *Sampson Hanbury's* HIGH-PERCH PHAETON. (*See page* 535.)

Collinge's patent axles, in regular work, will run about three months without being cleaned and oiled, and about six months without new washers. With the Mail Patent it is better to have a cleaning every two months, using neat's-foot oil. A little of this may be supplied to the caps more frequently, care being taken not to cross the threads or strain them when being replaced, as in that case they will be liable to drop off on the road.

Keep a small bottle of black japan and a brush always handy to paint the *treads and steps* when worn by the feet; nothing tends to keep up the tidy appearance of a carriage more than this. Lay it on as thin as possible.

Never draw out or back a carriage into a coach-house with the horses attached, as more accidents occur from this than any other cause.

As a general rule, a carriage with gentle work retains its freshness better than if standing for long periods in a coach-house. If the latter is necessary, draw it out occasionally to air.

See that the coach-house doors can be so fastened as not to blow to by the wind.

A good carriage kept as here recommended will always be a credit to every one concerned.

COACH-BUILDING TERMS.

AXLE-TREE ARM	The part of the axle-tree which passes through the centre of the wheel, on which it turns.
AXLE-TREE BOXES	Metal tubes fitted to the arms of the axle-tree, fixed firm in the wheel-stock, to contain oil or grease.
AXLE-TREE WASHER . . .	An iron collar or shoulder, fitted to the large end of the axle-tree against which the wheel wears, for the purpose of keeping in the grease ; a washer of leather is also used in all pleasure-carriages.
DASHING OR SPLASHING LEATHER.	An iron frame covered with leather, to prevent mud from splashing passengers or panels. Sometimes, for cheapness, made of wood.
FELLY OR FELLOE	A wooden section of the outside circle of a wheel round which the tire is fixed.
FORE-CARRIAGE	The under-part of a four-wheeled carriage, to which the fore-wheels are attached.
FUTCHELLS	The timbers or iron of the fore-carriage, to which the pole is fixed.
HAMMERCLOTH	An ornamental covering of the coachman's seat, only used now for Court and full-dress carriages, when footmen always stand behind.
NAVE	The centre or stock of a wheel, in which all the spokes are fixed, and through which the axle-arm goes. In the United States it is called the "hub."
PERCH	A long pole of timber or rod of iron which unites fore-wheels and hind-wheels of certain four-wheeled carriages ; notably all which have C springs.
POLE	The lever by which a four-wheeled carriage or a curricle is conducted.
POLE PIN	A round iron pin which passes through the futchell-ends and pole, to keep it in its place.
POLE PIECES	Of leather, or pole chains, which fasten the horses to the pole.
SPLINTER-BAR	The fore-bar attached to the fore-carriage, to which a pair of horses are fastened by passing the looped ends of their traces over the ROLLER BOLTS—viz., strong bolts, with flat heads. Three splinter bars are also hung to the end of the pole, for four horses in hand, which have hooks instead of bolts for the traces. The Americans call the splinter-bar "whipple-trees."
SPOKES	The sticks which support the rim of the wheel from the centre.
TIRE	The iron which forms the rim of the wooden fellces on wheel.

CHAPTER XXVI.

BREEDING, BREAKING, AND TRAINING.

BREEDING horses is a pretty amusement for those who can afford the luxury and reside on property suited for the purpose. The grass fields or park round a mansion must be fed over by something, and well-bred mares with their foals are almost as picturesque and more interesting than a herd of fallow-deer or of Alderneys. There is no reason why all three should not feed over the same pastures, assisted by a flock of sheep of the best mutton-making breeds—say blackfaced Highlanders, or Welsh longtails, or horned Dorset. Highland bullocks look well in a park, and pay their expenses, but will not always live in peace and amity with brood mares, and as a Highland bullock can gallop, and has horns if irritated, he is not always a safe companion for a valuable foal.

Mares and sires selected for breeding should be sound in wind, in eyesight, with no hereditary limb disease, such as spavin or ringbone, with naturally good feet, and good constitution. It is a waste of time and money to breed from a straight-shouldered, light-framed, washy mare, however great a favourite and however excellent in her place. As a rule, like begets like, although there are astounding exceptions.

If a mare has a decided defect in form, pains should be taken to put her to a horse excellent in that particular in which she fails.

More than twenty years ago (1854) Mr. Orton, of Sunderland, read a paper on "The Physiology of Breeding" before the Newcastle-upon-Tyne Farmers' Club, which has been the foundation of most of the papers on the same subject read before similar societies since that date. Breeding what is called "pedigree stock" is more certain in its results than cross-bred, but not absolutely certain ; it may, however, be assumed as ascertained that the more pure the pedigree the more "prepotent" will be the power of either horse or mare.

Mr. Orton supported the theory, long maintained, that the male animal gives the external and the female the internal structures—the male the skin and form of head, the female the size and quality. The breeding between the horse and ass is taken as an illustration of a theory that presents many exceptions.

The mule is the produce of a mare covered by an ass, and has the mane, tail, and hoofs of an ass, and the skin, ears, and colour of a horse somewhat modified. The hinney is the produce of a horse covering an ass, and has the mane, tail, hoofs, skin, and colour of a horse, the head sometimes resembling the dam and sometimes the sire, but generally the sire.

Mr. Orton came to the conclusion that in horses the sire gives the locomotive and the female the vital organs, that is, the constitution. For this reason no stallion should ever be used that has not good action for the purpose required; the action that wins races not being the action for a hunter, and the action of a hunter is not often the action of a park harness horse.

As the readers of this book will most probably be breeders for amusement and not for profit, it will be enough for them to be convinced that nothing satisfactory can be expected from an unsound animal on either side, and that the mare especially should have room to carry a foal, a deep chest, and, in fact, a good constitution.

For breeding high-class riding and driving horses thoroughbred sires are to be preferred to half-bred sires, not only because quality is essential, but because their pedigree can be traced, and any palpable defect or unsoundness will be found recorded. The produce of a line of American trotters have the same advantage, because the performances of their progenitors, like those of our race-horses, have been reported in the periodicals devoted to sport. An American trotter with an undoubted trotting pedigree is the animal to get horses with park action.

The form and action of the sire are of more importance than his height, if the mare is of the right size.

Where the breeder is anxious to produce a pair of horses of the same colour he must rely on the sire as well as the dam, and therefore ascertain what have been the usual colours of his produce. But the female generally gives the colour, and he must bear in mind that female animals, since the days of Jacob, are liable to transmit to their offspring the colours presented to their eyes during generation. The late Mr. M'Combie, a breeder of black Aberdeenshire polled cattle, found it necessary to exclude all red-and-white oxen from his breeding farms, and had all his woodwork painted black. I have a well-authenticated case in which a chestnut mare put to a chestnut thoroughbred horse, at Earl Spencer's seat, in the presence of a piebald pony, produced a fac-simile of the pony's colour. The piebald twins bred at Badminton, out of a thoroughbred Physalis mare, were no doubt the reflection of the piebald team which the late Duke of Beaufort was in the habit of using in his hunting carriage.

The expenses of breeding half-bred horses may be considerably diminished by employing the mares in harness in the light labours of a farm. They may be so employed for at least six months from the time they have taken the horse, not only without damage, but with advantage to their health, as long as the weights they draw, in pairs or in line, are moved without any straining or violent rushing into the collar.

The best horses are bred on dry uplands and well-turfed hills, whilst rich pastures on damp soil, like the Lincolnshire marshes, seem to produce large dray horses.

Young mares are to be preferred to old ones. They can adapt themselves better to change of food and temperature. In this climate the changes from heat to cold, combined with a damp atmosphere, are so great, that moderately good living is indispensable for the mare's health. Most of the dangers during the process of foaling are due to the feeble action of debilitated organs, not to mention a host of cutaneous diseases which may be traced to the same causes. Nevertheless, at certain seasons of the year, when the grass is too luxuriant, caution must be observed. Mares are apt (in the autumn when the foal has been weaned, and the udder still secretes milk) to eat too much, fatten, and become subject to plethora and inflammation of the bladder. At this period a poor pasture, with plenty of clean water at hand, should be preferred. Moor-land is very useful for running breeding animals on in the autumn of the year.

A mare cannot be kept too cool, either internally or externally. Anything that tends to increase excitement of the general system lessens the chances of generation.

On the other hand, to half-starve a mare and expose her to inclement seasons, without shelter, would be to run into another extreme, and, by causing debility, may occasion the loss of both mare and foal, or at any rate permanently impair the constitution of the latter.

A mixture of food which will be nourishing and wholesome without heating or fattening too much, consists of good sweet hay, carrots or mangel, oats, peas, or beans, with plenty of bran. For mares exposed to the changes of the atmosphere two quarterns of peas or beans, with a quartern of hay per day, is sufficient from the 1st November to the 1st May. Ample shelter will be afforded by a shed open only to the south (the entrance wide and the door-jambs round, and turning on pivots); the floor should be of hard concrete. Lime, gravel, and gas-tar make a cheap and excellent floor.

Each mare must be tied up to feed morning and evening (inside or outside the shed, according to the weather), otherwise some will fare well at the expense of others. Mr. Digby Collins, from whose work these instructions are abridged, calculates that a good mare may be kept liberally for £13 18s., exclusive of cost of attendance, which must be divided amongst the whole number; and that a foal will cost the same per year until taken up for breeding. The following are his figures, which may at any time be corrected by the selling price off a farm of hay and beans:—

	£	s.	d.
24 bushels of beans, at 5s.	6	0	0
4 cwt. of bran	1	8	0
2 acres of grass, at 30s.	3	0	0
Hay and chaff, half a ton, at £4 10s....	2	5	0
Straw, half a ton, at £2 10s....	1	5	0
	£13	18	0

N.B.—Crushed maize may be partly substituted for beans, if found to be cheaper.

To this must be added the wages of the man attending on the mares, divided by their number. Whether it be poultry, pigs, bullocks, or brood mares, live stock never thrive so well as when they have the undivided attention of one person.

Mares and foals, two-year-olds and three-year-olds, may be kept in good health and condition, when not intended for racing stock, on sliced or pulped mangel, or swedes, with an ample mixture of hay, or hay and straw cut into chaff. If intended for hunters, half a peck of a mixture of oats, beans, peas, or crushed maize, should be added in daily feeds to the roots and chaff. The latter should be cut long. Carrots are to be preferred when the soil is favourable for getting good crops, but where it is not mangel will be a valuable addition to the dry food to any unbroken horse stock, as well as of lean horses in slow work. When roots are given it must be remembered that they are composed of twenty per cent. of water, and must be mixed with a proportionate quantity of long chaff.

The above information embodies the experience of breeders with whom it has been an object to go to work in the most economical manner. In the following letter, addressed by Mr. William Blenkiron, of Middle Park Stud Farm, Kent, to Mr. Jenkins, the Secretary of the Royal Agricultural Society of England, is described the system of that once celebrated race-horse breeding establishment.

"A thorough-bred mare and her offspring require during the year the use and 'cream' of at least three acres of good grass land, from which no hay could be made, but on which, from what they would never eat on account of its becoming a little coarse, a couple of polled Scottish heifers might be fattened. During the twelve months the mare would consume about a ton and a half of good hay, about 10 qrs. good oats, say 1 cwt. of bran, 2 cwt. of carrots, about a gallon of linseed. The foal, presumably weaned the end of July, will take, to end of year, 7 qrs. best oats, 11 cwt. of first-class hay, 2 tons of carrots, 270 lbs. of split beans, ½ cwt. linseed, 5 cwt. bran. I have not included straw in the above, but the quantity required would be between five and six loads for the two." That is to say, between £40 and £50 worth of food, besides the value of the grass. To this must be added the expense of one or more cows, in proportion to the number of mares, to supply the foals with the milk which these highly-bred dames are frequently unable to supply.

Stallions at fees of from 25 guineas to 100 guineas, and mares purchased at from 500 to 1,200 guineas each, form an annual charge on the trade expenses of modern thoroughbred breeding establishments. It is not, therefore, extraordinary that nearly all the undertakings on a great scale (except the original Middle Park Stud) have proved eminently unprofitable. The Rawcliffe and the Cobham Companies are lamentable examples of failures.

But to turn to more modest undertakings, the following calculations, made by Mr. Edward Flower, of Stratford-on-Avon, when, many years ago, he contemplated and abandoned the idea of a hunter-breeding stud, will show at what expense a country gentleman, residing on his own estate and cultivating a home farm, may indulge his fancy.

It must be noted, however, that since 1850 the prices of inferior half-bred horses, which sold in that year at four years old for from £18 to £20, have more than doubled, and that dealers are now willing to purchase all the promising *three-year-olds* they can lay their hands on at liberal prices.

COST OF A WELL-BRED FIVE-YEAR-OLD, OUT OF A MARE COSTING £30.

	£	s.	d.	£	s.	d.
One year's interest on mare . .	1	10	0			
Ditto, insurance . . .	1	10	0			
Diminished value . . .	3	0	0			
Stallion's fee	3	0	0			
One-fourth of mares not standing	1	0	0			
Keep of mare six winter months, at 4s. per week	5	4	0			
Cost of foal at Michaelmas				20	8	0
Keep of foal first winter . .	5	4	0			
Six months' interest . . .	0	10	0			
Ditto, insurance . .	0	10	0			
Cost of yearling . .				26	12	0
One year's keep, at 4s. per week .	10	8	0			
Ditto, interest	1	6	0			
Ditto, insurance . . .	1	6	0			
Cost of two-year-old . .				39	12	0

	£	s.	d.	£	s.	d.
One year's keep, at 4s. 6d. per week	11	14	0			
Ditto, interest . . .	2	0	0			
Ditto, insurance . .	2	0	0			
Cost of three-year-old .				55	6	0
One year's keep, at 4s. 6d. .	11	14	0			
Ditto, interest . . .	2	15	0			
Ditto, insurance . .	2	15	0			
Cost of four-year-old . .				72	10	0
One year's keep, at 6s. .	15	12	0			
Ditto, interest . . .	3	12	0			
Ditto, insurance . .	3	12	0			
Ditto, groom, at 4s. per week .	10	8	0			
Ditto, blacksmith . .	2	0	0			
Breaking, docking, and veterinary	2	10	0			
Cost of the five-year-old .				£110	4	0

I do not charge for the keep of mare the first six months, as that expense would either be chargeable on previous foal, or, as a mare worth £30, she would be of some use till Michaelmas.

There is a method of economising the cost of breeding riding and high-class harness horses which is not sufficiently practised, perhaps because in the days when young horses were almost a drug in the hands of the breeders, dealers would not look at a mare that had had a foal, or, as they call her, a widow. The prejudice still prevails in some quarters, but on the other hand one of the greatest dealers in London confirmed my own opinion that a filly's appearance is improved by having a foal.

Let the owner of a filly of the make suitable for breeding from put her to the horse at three years old. Let her be previously "broken, made quiet to ride on the road, and taught to jump any kind of fence by being led over them with a long rein, *without* a rider on her back," or, as the case may be, broken to double harness, she will, at four years old, have produced a foal which may be weaned the October of the year of foaling; the dam will then be ready to go into work. Thus, the cost of idle brood mares, which has ruined every joint-stock horse-breeding company, will be saved. The process may be repeated with every filly bred. Foals will thus be obtained from fresh mares not injured by the effects of hard work.

Mr. Nevile, who makes the suggestion in his book, says: "I have ridden mares so bred for hunting, and never could trace any disadvantage from it." And I can myself confirm Mr. Nevile's evidence, having been well carried with the Devon and Somerset Stag-hounds by two mares that had been bred from as fillies. Mares that have had a foal are and look bigger in their middle piece, which is no real disadvantage. Of course the appearance of the teats tells the tale of the mare's early use. But times are very much changed since the man who bought a merely useful grey mare at Tattersall's had to make up his mind to keep her for life or give her away.

In rearing a first-class hunter the same quantity of corn as for a race-horse must be allowed during the first twelve months, if you desire to obtain bone and size. This is exemplified in breeding poultry. The modern gigantic prize Dorkings, which are twice the weight of ordinary barn-door Dorkings, are produced by feeding the chickens on the most nourishing food every hour of the day for the first three months. But ordinary foals may be well kept on pastures with grass chaff, pressed roots, and very little corn, until they are taken up for breaking.

"February is the best time to put the mare to the horse. If in hard condition she should have a dose of physic and cooling diet, and then if she shows no signs of being stinted, a few quarts of blood may be taken. But it is a much better plan to reduce the mare to a soft condition by degrees, with soft food and slow light work at drilling or harrowing, if she is not turned out to grass. *She should on no account be allowed to see the horse again under three weeks.* Many mares are rendered barren from allowing them to see the stallion frequently, to ascertain whether they are really stinted."

The food should be cooling, especially if the mare is in hard galloping condition (plenty of roots, with bran and linseed mashes). From this point the sooner the mare is put to grass the better. Of all things it is desirable to avoid cooping mares up in sheds and yards in the day-time. Exercise is always necessary for the proper working of digestion. Nothing renders animals so liable to mange, dropsy, water farcy, worms, &c., as want of sufficient space for exercise; the secretions of the whole system become morbid.

If any symptoms of the kind become apparent, rub the body with a mixture of sulphur and oil of turpentine, and give internally linseed gruel with half a drachm of iodide of potassium daily. Continue this for a week. Do not put more than six mares together in one field of at least ten acres.

The mare cannot be left too much to herself when foaling; taking care that no dangerous place is at hand, such as a deep ditch, pit, or the like, for to such places mares immediately turn when their labours commence.

Immediately after foaling the mare should be removed, with the foal, to a well-littered box, and have moist mash of bran and beans, with a large supply of water at hand, and all other liberal, but not heating, diet. If she should ·be very weak, there is no better food than bean-flour, linseed gruel, and old ale, given warm (Query, port wine). If she prove an indifferent milker, the best new milk should be given after the foal has dried its dam. A soda-water bottle is a convenient feeder (no doubt the india-rubber apparatus used for babies could be adapted to a receptacle of appropriate size).

WEANING AND CASTRATING.

Colts should be weaned early in October (if half-bred, and the mare not required for work, they may run with her until two years old), and, after weaning, turned into a piece of rich pasture (Mr. D. Collins recommends fat clover, but many foals have been killed by eating clover heads, which produce constipation) for six or eight days, at the expiration of which they will have gained flesh, and be ready for a feed morning and evening of finely crushed beans (Query, oats), bran, and hay chaff, in home paddocks, with a good bite of grass.

Colts should be separated from the fillies at this period, unless they are castrated, and, by precaution, the condition of both will be materially improved.

Colts should be castrated in April, or at the end of May, after which operation they should have one hour's walking exercise every day, to prevent swelling and inflammation, and no heating food given them—bran mashes and hay will be best—and as soon as they are all right they may be put to grass again. Colts castrated in the cold season of the year are likely to have permanently a rough coat. If it is worth while to breed it is worth while to keep the produce in fleshy, healthy condition until the time comes for breaking.

Hunting colts should be kept in roomy dry straw-yards during the winter, with a plentiful supply of clean water always at hand. They should all be tied up to feed, or they will rob each other of their corn. During the winter that a colt turns three years old, before putting him into the breaker's hands, he should be regularly dressed and handled every morning by the man who feeds him. His feet should be attended to from the first; the toes pared into shape, and, if needful, provided with tips to protect them from splintering on the hard ground. Colts thus early handled by a good-tempered, light-handed man are seldom difficult to dress or to shoe.

The education of a horse, like the education of a man, is most easily perfected if the pupil is placed in the teacher's hands young, and receives progressive lessons without serious interruption until his professional training is completed, and he is fit to carry a lady or a statesman, to do credit to a fashionable carriage, or form one of the young ones in a hunting-stud. But as it is the exception where the breeder follows the fortunes of his well-bred colt up to the time he attains his majority, say five years old, consideration must be given to those cases where the equine pupil has never looked through a bridle until turned four years, or where a thorough-bred, dismissed from racing stables at three or four years old, has to be taught to abandon the daisy-cutting action permitted on smooth turf, and has to learn to move as befits a park hack, a charger, or a hunter.

The amount of teaching and time required to make a first-class pleasure horse of any kind will vary according to its natural spirit and intelligence, but the principles of the art of breaking are always the same. To apply these principles in the best manner requires the services of an artist, a born horseman, with courage, temper, patience, and constant practice from his youth upwards. This equestrian schoolmaster may not be able to read or write, but he must have been a thoughtful student of that page of nature which it is his business to read.

On the South American pampas, where the horses are naturally of a very docile temperament, and where for hundreds of miles no barrier, no hill, scarcely a stone, interrupts the horseman's gallop, the Gauchos lasso a wild horse, throw him down, cover his head with a cloak, girth a heavy demi-piqued saddle on him, thrust into his mouth a huge Spanish curb-bit, capable of breaking a jaw at one effort, mount him with a pair of spurs with rowels as large as a cheese-plate, and gallop him until he sinks exhausted. But horses so tamed, if not vicious, are generally thoroughly cowed, and lose nearly all the sympathetic spirit that makes riding a pleasure. And when these same Gauchos tried their plan on high-bred Australian horses, they failed miserably.

In Australia the majority of the horses are vicious, and given to the trick of buck-jumping, that is, a succession of leaps from all four to all four legs. This is chiefly due to defective breaking, which, practised year after year, has created and cultivated hereditary vice. Labour is dear, the breakers are bold horsemen, and quite ignorant of the art of gradually breaking, if they cared to spare the time. In addition, the object of many Australian horsemen, when they take a young horse in hand, is not to pacify but to irritate him, to make him do his worst, and show that they can sit out his most violent buck-jumps. "There are no people in the world who can sit a vicious horse like the Australian-born Englishmen of the bush districts of New South Wales. They are, as a rule, tall, slight, with long wiry arms and legs. They are a muscular, active, and a decidedly sober race." "Ask one of them to ride a horse that has just thrown you—he examines the girths, crupper, and bridle, without a sign of emotion. If the tackle is right, he lifts his hat, lets the string fall under his chin as he replaces it, carelessly gathers up the reins, and mounts. If he knew French he would say, *J'y suis, je reste.* He enjoys the row in his own quiet way, resists the most violent buck-jumping, and dismounts as calmly as he mounted. Snaffle-bridles are the rule, curbs are rarely seen. A crupper is indispensable; without one either the saddle is forced on the neck, or the girths are burst in the horse's struggles to get rid of his rider. The Australian crupper is not fastened to a D as in English military saddles. That, in the ordinary struggles, would be broken. It is passed between the saddle-stuffing and the saddle-tree, and comes out on each side of the pommel, then is passed two or three times round a stick, about twenty inches long, as thick as the wrist, called the *kid*, and then buckled. The kid is strapped to two iron D's fixed behind the pommel. This kid comes across the horseman about six inches above the knees, and helps to keep him in the saddle."

It may be assumed, for the purpose of this chapter, that breeders of horses and the buyers of unbroken three-year-olds have the means and the time for giving them a regular education. To set down every step to be followed in breaking a young horse would occupy more space than can be spared, even if it were possible to learn the niceties of such an art from printed instructions; I shall therefore be content with laying down the broad principles of horsebreaking (no one detests principles like your practical man), and adding a few hints on what should, and still more important, should not be done.

The principles of horsebreaking are nowhere more clearly and concisely stated than in the original pamphlet by Mr. Rarey, of which I edited an illustrated edition in 1858. Mr. Rarey created a sensation by taming vicious horses, but his higher merit was in showing that horse-breaking was not a mere rule-of-thumb business, but rested, like every other art, on certain fixed principles, which could not be neglected with impunity.

The ordinary idea of horsebreaking, before so many distinguished horsemen became Rarey's pupils, was to tire out a high-tempered colt that resisted the breaker's first approaches by longeing, by withholding food and water, and by the free use of whip, spur, and painful bits. This was not the system of a born horseman like Dick Christian (p. 426), but in too many instances a colt was punished by ignorant drunken breakers for being frightened at what he had never seen before, or for not obeying instructions that he did not in the least understand.

Rarey maintained—1st, That any young horse can be taught to do anything that a horse can do if taught in a proper manner. 2nd, That no horse is conscious of his strength until he has resisted and conquered a man; therefore that the colt should always be handled in such a manner that he shall not find out his strength. 3rd, That as *seeing, smelling, feeling,* and *hearing* are the senses by which the horse examines every strange object, we may, by allowing him to exercise these senses, reconcile him to any object or sound that does not hurt him.

To punish a horse with whip, spur, or by a vicious jag at the bridle because he is frightened at the first feel of a saddle or harness, the sight of a flag, a riding-skirt, or a marching regiment, or the sound of wheels, drums, or firearms, is an ordinary form of ignorant stupidity.

The key-note of the common sense of horsebreaking is to be found in the opening sentence of Rarey's first lecture—" As a horse judges everything by seeing, smelling, and feeling, it should be the business of those who undertake to train colts that they shall see, smell, and feel everything that they are to wear or bear before it is laid upon them."

The first stage of breaking teaches the colt to submit to a bridle being put on, to being led about at the will of a man, and to meeting without fright the ordinary sights and sounds of country roads and city streets. The second stage accustoms him to bear a saddle and allow himself to be mounted. The third to understand the indications of the bit and reins. The fourth to acquire the paces and manners of the trade—hack, lady's horse, hunter, or harness horse—for which he is intended.

THE FIRST LESSONS FOR A WILD UNBROKEN COLT.

" If the colt has been running wild until taken in hand by the breaker, the first step," says Rarey, " is to get him into a barn or open stable. Enter alone, with a long whip in your right hand held pointing behind you. When you enter the stable, stand still, and let the horse look at you a minute. As soon as he is settled in one place, approach him slowly, with the right hand hanging by your side, and the whip trailing on the ground, the left bent, and the elbow projecting. Move towards him behind his shoulder, stepping right or left, to head or croup very quietly, so as to keep him in one place. When you are within reach of his head, pause a few seconds—he will probably turn his neck and smell your hand. As soon as he touches it caress him, and gently stroke his nose and neck, with some soothing words or sounds.

" If he lays back his ears as you approach, and turns his heels to kick you give him two or three sharp cuts on the inside of his legs close to his body, deliberately, not for the pleasure of hurting him, but to frighten the stubbornness out of him. Do it quickly, sharply, with a good deal of fire, *but always without anger.* Never go into a pitched battle with a horse;

never whip one until he is angry and ready to fight you—it would be better not to touch him. As soon as you have frightened him, so that he will stand up and pay attention to you, approach him again, and caress until he forgets that you whipped him.

"When you have established a certain degree of familiarity, which, according to the disposition of the colt, may take minutes or hours, approach him, taking in your hand a good leather halter. (See illustration of cavesson, p. 563.)   Never use a hemp halter and running noose for this purpose, as it will hurt the colt's nose, and create an additional difficulty. Stand at the left side pretty well back, and with both hands slip the halter over his head and buckle it. This operation may require a good deal of patience and temper on the part of the man. As soon as the halter is on, fasten to it a rope or strap long enough to let him go the length of the barn without your being obliged to let go the rope, for if you only let him feel the weight of your hand on the halter, and give him rope when he runs from you, he will not be inclined to rear, pull, or throw himself down. Thus you will be holding him and teaching him the first lesson of restraint without allowing him to find out his strength; as he soon would in a game of 'pull devil, pull baker.'

"Shorten the cord by degrees. As soon as he will allow you to hold him by a tolerably short strap, and to go alongside him without flying back, you can begin to give him a lesson in leading. With this view do not attempt to pull him after you, but pull him quietly in a half circle; he must bend his neck and shift his foot. Caress him, reward him with some food, a carrot or a few oats; repeat the operation again and again to the right and to the left, until that, having lost all fear of you, he will think that he is compelled to follow the indication of the halter when you pull it. After a few lessons of this kind, under cover, he will look to you for food, and come up to you wherever he is. After fully practising in the stable, lead him out into a quiet yard or paddock, taking care that there is nothing to frighten him. Walk out through the door, which should be wide, holding the halter with the left hand close to his jaw and the right hand holding to his mane. Do not let any one come near you when you first lead him out.

"When the colt will lead freely and obey the halter, the next step is to gradually accustom him to all sights and sounds, by leading him about and never forcing him up anything he is afraid of, but always encouraging him to smell it and touch it.

"A colt bred on an owner's farm ought, by the time he is three years old, to have gone through all the preliminary education to which colts that have been running wild up to that age must pass, and should have worn a headstall from six months old, and been taught to lead and to face all ordinary sights."

LONGEING.

Longeing properly employed teaches a horse obedience, but as it is very easy to make a horse run round a circle urged by a whip, and as it looks like business, it is a way of tiring a high-spirited horse, which is very much abused.

The cavesson must be fitted to the colt's head very carefully. If the noseband is too high it has no power; if it is too low, resting on the soft cartilages of the nose, it will impede respiration, and if jerked cause an acute pain, likely to cause rearing, and to create spavins, curbs, and strains of the hind-legs. It must also fit the colt's head so as not to turn round when the rein is drawn tight. The eyelids of colts have been seriously injured by a longeing rein in the hands of an ignorant man.

"It is absurd to believe, as colt-breakers tell you, that longeing will supple an animal that is already as supple as a wild deer, but after teaching a colt to be held by the head and to be led, it is the easiest act of obedience you can require.* In good hands it will never stiffen him; it is a certain mode of reducing a horse to submission, of getting him to go freely forward at your order. In bad hands, it is the fruitful source of spavins, curbs, and thorough-pins; far from suppling, it annually stiffens and breaks down thousands of horses, because the guiding and urging instructions are both on the same side of the horse. In the hands of a stupid man, the colt's head and shoulders are forcibly hauled into the circle by the cord, while his haunches are driven out by the whip."

"A horse should only be longed at a walk till he circles without force. He should never be compelled to canter in the longe, though he may be permitted to do it of himself. He must not be stopped by pulling the cord, which would pull him across, but by meeting him or running his head towards a hedge, so that he stops straight. A skilful person will single-handed longe a horse in many figures, and by heading him with the whip change him without stopping, and longe him in a figure of 8. When the colt goes without force, he should be longed on the snaffle instead of the cavesson. It will facilitate his being guided, and held by the mouth when mounted.

"In the longe he may be accustomed to feel the stirrups against his sides, and to carry the dumb jockey cross with a great-coat on it. The reins buckled to the cross should be long at first and shortened afterwards by degrees. It is better to fix the straps from the cross to the cavesson than to the bit, when a colt is to be left some time in that position, for colts left with a bit tightly buckled lean on the bit and even go to sleep. The lips become first raw, and then callous. A wooden bit of good size is the best.

"It is a good practice to clean a colt on an easy-mouthing bit, with the horse's head *towards the manger.*"

It will be observed, that the Rarey principle consists in teaching the colt as much as possible without putting him in any pain, and without frightening him by any strange sight or sound.

By degrees he learns to lead freely, to know that when the right rein is pulled he is to go to the right, and when the left rein to the left; he submits to be girthed with a surcingle or pad, and is not afraid of a loose strap, horsecloth, or stirrup flopping about. He submits to have each foot taken up, and finally becomes attached to his breaker. The longeing lessons have taught him a considerable degree of obedience.

The next stage of instruction may be compared to the lessons in drill and gymnastics, through which every military recruit has to pass. The object of military gymnastics is to give the soldier the free use of each limb, an accurate balance on each foot, and enable him to move in every direction firmly and with the utmost rapidity and certainty at a moment's notice.

In the same way the colt intended for hunting or harness has to be taught to collect himself to an even bearing on each of his four legs, and to turn on the point of his hind-legs on receiving an indication from his rider.

The first step is to put on a bit, either a plain snaffle with players, or a simple ring-bar, or a wooden bit of either Stokey's or Blackwell's pattern. On first bitting, Rarey's directions are very judicious:—

"A horse should be accustomed to a bit before you fasten the reins to the bitting-harness (dumb jockey). When you first put him on the bit, only rein his head up to that point at

* Colonel Greenwood's "Hints to a Nephew and Niece."

which he naturally holds it, let it be high or low; he will soon learn that he cannot lower his head, and that raising it a little will loosen the bit in his mouth. By degrees you can tighten the reins, until you get his head and neck as near the right position as the conformation of his neck and shoulders will allow, without making his mouth sore or irritating his temper.

"If you draw the bitting-rein tight the first time you attach it to the dumb jockey, he will bear on it, sweat, paw, and perhaps rear, slip, and fall backwards, and if he does not break his back, he will become nervous for life."

It is absolutely necessary to put all colts on the bit (with the exception of a few horses of rare formation and temper) to get them balanced on their haunches, but the operation requires great care if it is not to do more harm than good.

"Colts should never be on reins tightly buckled to a dumb jockey more than fifteen or twenty minutes at a time; a long penance destroys all the good effect. Their mouths should always be wetted before they are bitted, and they should have a drink of water when the bit is taken off or relaxed.

"Before a colt receives his first lessons from a mounted horseman he may be taught a great deal by the breaker on foot—with both snaffle and curb-bit—to turn to either side, to collect himself, champ the bit, and to back readily on slight indications from the reins."

Mr. Blackwell, of Oxford Street, London, has a most complete and ingenious collection of colt-breaking apparatus. His Dumb Jockey, with gutta-percha and whalebone horns, avoids the dangers of the old wooden horns. All the contrivances are worth the examination of a horse-breeder.

HOW TO SADDLE A COLT.

The better plan is to accustom the colt from a very early period to bear first a surcingle, then a pad, and then a dumb jockey, from which light stirrups and a skirt may by degrees be suspended, trying and accustoming him to each new thing thoroughly before another is introduced to his notice. Supposing that the colt has been led about in the longeing-rein until accustomed to all ordinary sights and sounds, has learned to obey the breaker, and has become so much accustomed to him that he will allow him, or any quiet person, to approach him on either side without starting back affrighted—that he has, in fact, learned that man is both his friend and his master—a saddle may then be placed on his back.

Commence this, like every breaking operation, by fondling, or, as Rarey has it, "gentling" the colt; then take up a saddle from which the stirrup-leathers have been detached. Either lay it down on the floor of the stable or barn for him to smell, or quietly hold it up for him to thoroughly examine. When he is quite satisfied that it will do him no harm, raise it, and rub it gently against his neck, gradually slipping it back, stopping if he shows the least signs of alarm to soothe him, until it is behind his withers, and you can softly slip it into its place; then move it gently with your hand, slip it backwards and forwards, lift it up and put it down again, until you are satisfied that he is not afraid of it. Instead of girthing the saddle in the usual manner, be satisfied at first to fasten it with a racing surcingle, which does not require to be drawn so tight as a girth, and is more easily buckled.

If he has been already driven by a man walking after him, with long reins passed through the terrets of a dumb jockey, in what is called the Yorkshire fashion, he will understand that when you pull the left rein he must go to the left, and that when you pull the right rein he must turn to the right; but if you are in a wild country with a wild horse to tame, then, if you are hurried, you may adopt Rarey's advice, always remembering that these operations should be performed in a very quiet place, and, if possible, under cover within four walls, with no other horses or noisy men to distract your pupil's attention.

"After he is saddled, take a switch in your right hand and walk him about the barn a few times with your right hand over the saddle, holding the reins in each hand, and start turning him on either hand, making him if needful run up to the bridle by a gentle tap on his hind-quarters, then stopping him and always caressing him and loosing the reins when you do stop.

"As soon as you have so 'gentled' your colt that he will stand still, and is not the least afraid when you approach him on either side, take him into some enclosed place, a large stable, barn, or riding-school. Then bring a mounting-block, to the sight of which he must have previously been perfectly accustomed, and place it just behind his shoulder. Mount the block very quietly and stand on it, stroking ('gentling') him all over. If he shows the least alarm, be quiet and do not attempt anything for some time—minutes, or hours, as the case may be. As soon as he is quite reconciled to seeing you standing over him, if you use stirrups put your foot into the near one and press on it gradually, leaning at the same time with your right hand on the pommel, the left hand holding the reins loosely, so that you bring your whole weight to bear on the saddle. Repeat this several times, until he makes no sign of resistance, until, without alarming him, you can slip your leg over his croup and take your seat.

"Many breakers prefer a well-stuffed pad with good knee and thigh rests, like a Somerset saddle, without stirrups, for the first saddling lessons; but on this plan the horse-block must be so high that the rider can pass his leg over the croup without the least exertion.

"The movable block enables you to accustom the colt to see you above him in the position he will see you, looking backwards, when mounted. By leaning over him on the block, and pressing on his back, you gradually accustom him to weight, so as not to alarm him so much by the sensation of being first mounted.

"Finally, a block of proper height enables you to step into the saddle without making a spring, an action that will alarm or irritate many broken horses, when fresh with too much corn and too little exercise."

Rarey insists "that a horse should always stand to be mounted without being held," and that "*a horse is never properly broken that has to be held when being mounted;*" that a colt is never so safe to mount when you see that assurance of confidence and absence of fear which causes him to stand without holding. But this docility cannot always be obtained.

To encourage his standing still put his head to a wall. If, however, it is necessary to hold the colt, let a steady man stand at his head fondling his nose, and at a critical moment lay hold of the cheeks of the bridle just above the bit, not of the bit or reins.

When you are mounted do not start him by touching him with your heel, or startle him in any way, but speak to him in the language you have been accustomed to use; pull one rein gently to one side, so as to make him shift his leg and move, and let him walk off gently with the reins loose at first, then gather up the reins and repeat mounted the lessons in turning right and left, stopping, and backing, which you have already practised on foot and with the driving reins.

If he shows the least inclination to stand still and be restive, slip off him quietly and proceed with the old lessons, because you must not fight him unless you are quite certain to conquer.

It is as well to repeat the operation of mounting and dismounting until he gets thoroughly accustomed to it, and will permit you to mount from the stirrup in the usual manner.

The first time you wish to ride a colt out of doors let him be led out and longed for a quarter of an hour about a mile from his stable, then mount and ride him home. In early lessons on the road never fatigue him, and if possible ride in company with a steady horse and horseman. If a colt when ridden out attempts to stand still or kick, turn him round steadily once or twice, or oftener. It is a motion that no horse can resist, and one much more effective than angry wild spurring or whipping. If he still resists, slip off him before he begins to fight, and give him the lesson for stubborn horses. These instructions assume that the colt has been gradually educated from his foalhood upwards, or that he is naturally of so sweet and sensible a temperament—like the majority of well-bred unbroken horses— that he speedily learns what is required of him. But it may happen that the horse is purchased at three or four years old from a drove, or caught wild from Welsh or Devonshire hills, or he may inherit a stubborn, if not savage, disposition; or, lastly, time may be an object to a colonist or traveller, and he may have only hours instead of days at his disposal for the breaking process; then stronger measures must be adopted.

The ordinary mode, as before stated, of subduing a high-spirited or viciously-inclined colt, and compelling him to submit to be saddled and ridden, is to longe him until he is tired out; and if that does not conquer him, whip, spur, and deny food and water, until the animal surrenders, or is pronounced irreclaimable. The majority of young horses treated gradually, patiently, and firmly, as described in the preceding pages, will accept their duties without showing any vice.

Circus-riders commence the education of their ring and trick horses by lightly fastening the reins of a snaffle-bridle, like a bearing-rein, to the ring of a surcingle, which is secured in its place by a crupper, and if needful adding a standing martingale, and a pair of flap reins. Thus *pilloried*, as it were, the horse is longed in the narrow circus-ring for hours, until, if he has any intelligence, and is not irreclaimably vicious, he obeys the lessons of his master, enforced by a severe whip, and encouraged by occasional rewards, in the shape of slices of carrot or lumps of sugar. These preliminary lessons are carried out with a degree of severity very painful for an unprofessional bystander to witness.

Instead of these violent methods Rarey introduced a plan, which, mildly applied, quickly teaches the colt that man is his master and does not mean to hurt him, and severely applied will conquer the most violent animal.

TO PUT A HORSE DOWN.

The colt that absolutely declines to be saddled or mounted, that will not without a fight allow a bridle to be put in his mouth, must not be *thrown* down, as some writers ignorantly direct, but gently and slowly put down; when down, he must be strapped up so that he cannot resist, and then by gentle progressive steps handled and mounted. I am not now treating of vicious horses, because, except on very rare occasions under very exceptional circumstances, no sensible person will have anything to do with an old vicious horse.

To Rareyfy a horse you require a soft floor of deep tan or straw and dung. A space of some thirty feet from side to side, fenced off from a riding-school, or a small shed sufficiently lofty for a horse to rear without striking his head, is the best class-room for a Rarey lesson. If the floor is paved or boarded, the litter or tan must be at least a foot deep. A

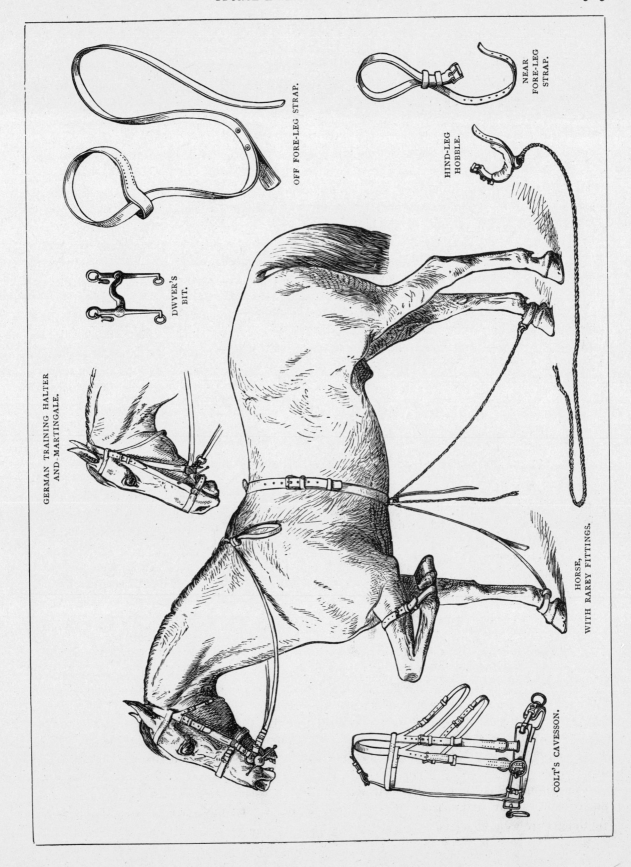

OFF FORE-LEG STRAP.

NEAR FORE-LEG STRAP.

HIND-LEG HOBBLE.

DWYER'S BIT.

GERMAN TRAINING HALTER AND MARTINGALE.

HORSE, WITH RAREY FITTINGS.

COLT'S CAVESSON.

parallelogramic shape is the best, because corners are useful in haltering a wild colt. Pillars, or any projections against which a horse might strike, are dangerous. It is better if the building is roofed, so that no living thing—no cattle, pigs, or dogs, may distract the horse's attention while under treatment; but if an enclosed building cannot be obtained, a small bullock-yard may be utilised.

The horse must have a single-reined bridle, with a plain snaffle with long horns, or wooden bit; if inclined to bite, this wooden bit must be also a gag. Make the reins so short that they will lie on the withers, by doubling them twice round the two forefingers and then knotting them. Next buckle round him a breaking surcingle, made for the purpose, with one or two large rings sewed on the belly part. This surcingle may be a plain broad strap of leather.

It is assumed that the colt has been sufficiently broken to allow you to lead him, and do anything with him except mount him.

Take strap No. 1, pass the tongue through the loop under the buckle so as to form a noose, slip it over either fore-leg—the near leg in preference—draw it close to the pastern joint, then take up the leg as if you were going to shoe him, and, passing the strap round over the fore-arm, buckle as close as you can to the arm without hurting it.

If you have confidence in yourself, work alone; if you have not, obtain a quiet and obedient assistant. When the first strap is buckled take hold of the snaffle-bridle and lead him about. It is assumed that he has already been taught to lead freely. The object of hopping him about on three legs is to teach him not to fall if he can help it. It fatigues him without irritating him, and is alone a good preparation for putting a horse in harness for the first time, as a colt not severely pressed, and with no weight on his back, can hop a mile on three legs with ease.

Strap No. 2 must now be looped round the other fore-leg, drawn tight, and passed through one of the rings on the belly of the surcingle. The best form of strap has a leather catch which prevents it from sliding back at a certain length. Put a stout glove on your right hand, the nails of which should previously be cut close. Take a firm hold of the strap, and as soon as the colt lifts his off fore-leg to hop, draw it tight and bring him down on his knees. The leather catch will hold the strap fast above the ring, and thus both fore-legs are secured. If he objects to move, "pull his head towards you with one rein, bear against his side just behind his shoulder with a steady even pressure, and in less than ten minutes he will *lie down*." Mark the words "lie down," not "be thrown down," because there is a difference between a violent operation sometimes indispensable with turbulent horses and an easy slide by which a colt can be laid down on his side, and under the irresistible control of the breaker.

As soon as he is down make the other leg quite fast; then you can handle him as you please without his being able, or even trying, to resist you. Now is the time for again "gentling" him, by softly stroking every limb—passing your hand or a soft brush over every part of his body—kindly pulling his ears, rubbing his head, breathing into his nostrils, and if he has been starved or is thirsty, unbuckling the bit for a few minutes, and rewarding him with a little green meat, a sliced carrot, or an apple. You can sit on his back or place a saddle on it after first showing it to him, and letting him smell it in the way already described.

The principle is to make the colt so fast that he cannot possibly resist. Then you can prove to him that so far from hurting him you fondle him, and show him saddle, flags, or anything else he is afraid of.

The old way of putting a horse down in order to castrate, fire, or perform any other surgical operation (which is still in use among practitioners too prejudiced to profit by Rarey's lectures), was to shackle all his four legs, and then with ropes in the hands of a number of men to violently throw him on a layer of straw, a method that frightens the animal most unnecessarily, and not unfrequently strains, sometimes breaks, his back. With a set of Rarey straps properly applied, one active man can alone put down and tie fast almost any horse without a struggle, if he chooses for the operation a fold-yard a foot deep in straw and dung. If a man has to tackle a well-bred horse full of hard food, he should be in good condition, very patient, and with that confidence in himself that cool courage gives. The great point is not to alarm the animal, or give him a chance of struggling.

If after the first lesson on lying down he shows any objection to being saddled or mounted, his leg must be strapped up again, and sometimes, but not often, he must be laid down again.

If a horse intended for harness shows a natural inclination to kick—almost all horses have a decided preference for either kicking or rearing, when they are irritated or alarmed, only the confirmed brute rears and kicks—it is a good plan, after putting him down once, to strap up one leg and harness him to a light two-wheeled vehicle, balanced like a hansom cab, so that no weight falls on his back. In this condition, his knees of course protected by well-stuffed knee-caps, he may be driven first in a school and then in a soft meadow, or along a shore of sea-sand below high-water mark. If a steady break horse, who understands every word of the driver, is harnessed to an outrigger, the lesson will be still more easy and complete.

One precaution must be adopted in using this invaluable expedient of strapping up a fore-leg. After a reasonable time it must be unstrapped, the leg first strapped being vigorously hand-rubbed to restore circulation; otherwise, a horse is likely to stumble with the benumbed limb. This plan of breaking to harness is of value where it is necessary to break thorough-bred, or nearly thorough-bred, three-year-old colts, that are not strong enough to carry more than light weight, in a place where competent light weight horsebreakers are not to be had.

TO SUBDUE A VIOLENT HORSE.

It, however, sometimes happens that you have to break, to ride, or drive a horse of full age, that either from ill-usage, or from having got the better of a timid horseman, or from natural vice, is not to be deceived into submission like a raw and placid-tempered colt. In such a case, the application of the Rarey straps in the following manner affords a better chance of success than the ordinary exhausting plans of old-fashioned colt-breakers and of circus-riders.

Such a horse, as soon as he recovers from his astonishment at being thrown on his knees, if not immediately hampered by hobbles buckled on his two hind-legs, will begin to fight, rearing and springing about with extraordinary activity. The breaker must follow him, keeping close to him behind his shoulder, steering him by the bridle. This can easily be done by an active man, even in a box not more than twenty feet long by fifteen feet wide. From time to time the horse may be forced to walk backwards by pulling at the bridle, and this will hasten his fatigue. The first struggle rarely lasts ten minutes, even with a horse in hard condition. When at length he sinks forward on his knees. covered with sweat. with heaving flanks and shaking tail, his off fore-leg, it not already secured by the catch of the strap must be made as fast as the near-leg, and a pair of hobbles with ropes buckled to the hind-legs. After allowing time enough to recover his wind, if he is a very violent or vicious animal, encourage him to get on his knees and make a second fight. It will often be more fierce than the first.

When he lies down for the second or third time, thoroughly exhausted, the moment has arrived for doing to him all that he has hitherto resisted or resented. Smooth his ears, rub his legs, scrape the sweat off him gently with a scraper, rub him down with a wisp or brush, give him a drink of water, then go over him again as if you were a shampooer at a Turkish bath. If he has been in the habit of resisting bridling, saddling, or shoeing, now is the time for going through the form of all those operations, and particularly the last, by tapping every foot with a hammer.

Then take off all the straps, repeat the shampooing process, draw his fore-legs out, and encourage him to rise. When he has risen, make much of him, mount him, and ride him about the yard or school, or harness him. If he shows, at any moment, the least inclination to resist, cry "Wo, ho!" in a firm voice, and, if needful, proceed to again strap up a leg, but never resist anything he attempts—for instance, if he attempts to rise—unless you are certain to overcome him. Let him rise and begin again.

The strapping up and laying down system is founded on the principle of inducing the violent horse to exhaust himself without hurting you, and of making him believe that it is you who, by your superior strength, have conquered, and will always be able to conquer him.

Under this "system" all the indications of the man's will are so direct that the horse must understand them. He is placed in such a position, and under such restraint, that he cannot resist anything the horsebreaker chooses to do, who caresses him when he submits, and chides him when he attempts to resist; resist strapped up he cannot, and thus, if needful, by repeated lessons persuades the animal that resistance is perfectly useless.

The most frequent occasion for the employment of the extreme discipline of Rarey's plan will be found with horses which, in consequence of some early fright or cruelty, resist being shod. In such cases farriers often inflict exquisite pain by putting a twitch on nose and ears. Even then the operation is generally performed with danger alike to the smith and the animal.

In nine cases out of ten, when a horse has by the strapping method been taught that resistance is useless, and that shoeing will not hurt it, it will in a few days submit to the smith's hands with perfect docility.

The only danger of injuring the horse Rareyfied occurs where the knees have been insufficiently protected by proper caps, and the floor of the place has been too hard; it can scarcely be too soft.

One of the curious results of the Rareyfying of strapping up and laying down is, that after being duly shampooed or mesmerised, the moment he rises he seems to have contracted a personal affection for the operator.

A remarkable example of this fact occurred to myself. To satisfy an incredulous Devonshire farmer, I undertook to Rareyfy an unbroken pony that had run wild on the moors from the day it was foaled, and which took the exertions of two mounted men and half a dozen footmen to drive into a fold-yard. "Fat, and scant of breath," I was a bad performer, but under half an hour the grass-fed filly was down, up, saddled, and ridden round a paddock by my host, a shepherd leading it. The next morning, when we came up to the gate of the field where the wild creature had been allowed to feed for the night, it came up to us and rubbed its nose against my hand! This adventure was described at the time in a paper contributed to *Household Words*.

The drawback of the Rareyfying plan, applied to a high-bred horse, if roughly and hurriedly performed, is that it is apt to destroy his spirit, and "by cowing him make him a coward."

But the same objection applies to the main-force system of the old-fashioned dare-devil colt-breaker.

"Heavy ground and plenty of work, however, will tame an elephant.

"If you are short of time and not prepared to risk your own bones, you have no business with a vicious horse.

"Restiveness out of doors in most cases arises from bad breaking. A horse seven or eight years old that is restive may possibly have been broken well in his early days, but possessing hereditary predisposition to obstinacy, may have passed into the hands of nervous people, perceived his advantage, and mastered them. Such horses require not only the utmost firmness and determination, but it is necessary in this case to have recourse to a systematic mode of *making them break themselves*. Coaxing is no earthly use. Such a horse, when full of keep, will very probably wear out the best man you can put up. To starve the horse down to submission is useless as well as cruel, because the vice will return with the corn. If, therefore, you become possessed of a thoroughly vicious one, I know of no better plan than that of *putting him in irons* in a box well padded. Put on some strong tackle, and an iron upright dumb jockey; bear him well up, and let him fight with himself until he is exhausted. Take care you are very fit yourself, and then mount him. In most cases you will find, even if you have a fight to get him into his bridle, that his punishment drill has had its effect, and that he will go up to his work. If he is still resolute, and you do not care to wear yourself out, take him back to the box, tackle him again, and give him another spell. Persevere at this until he goes true and straight. Never take the tackle off day or night, except when you ride him out, until he gives in, but let him have plenty of nourishment. In most cases, however, with a very resolute, restive one, you will find that when tackled he will refuse his food as well as his work. Do not let that induce you to remit your treatment, for, strange as it may appear, it is well known to all who have had to do with restive horses that this is only an artifice to induce you to give them their own way. When they behave themselves, let them have every luxury possible to them; but give them plenty of work, never failing, when they misbehave themselves, to send them again to 'punishment drill.'"

HOW TO BREAK COLONIAL HORSES.

In the colonies labour is dear; hence horses are roughly, hurriedly, and imperfectly broken. At the same time, well-broken horses sell for extraordinary prices in the colonies, either for use in towns or for export to India, where there is a constant demand for full-sized horses fit to be ridden by military men and ladies.

Mr. Edward Curr, an experienced colonial horseman, proposes to make use of Rarey's plan and principles in order to make a profit out of horses bred in the bush by making them docile and preventing them from becoming vicious.

"Catch the foal while sucking, put a soft band round his neck, then stop him. If he is under a fortnight old he will, in twenty minutes, allow himself to be handled, and becomes familiar when he finds you do not mean to hurt him. Rub him softly all over, wrap a cloth round him, ring a bell beside him; repeat this every day for a week, and the lesson will never be forgotten. A dozen foals may be thus treated by one man in a morning.

"At six weeks old teach him to lead with a halter. Then put him down gently with the Rarey straps, tie him when down, and flap clothes or blankets over him and on him, always caressing him until he has ceased to fear. In subsequent lessons stand astride of him, crack your stock whip over him, taking care not to touch him, fire your revolver first with caps, then with a light charge of powder, so that he may see the flash and smell the smoke without putting it so close as to deafen his ears. When you take him up, after rubbing his limbs to do away with the numbness caused by the straps, lead him about according to the directions already given. After half an hour's exercise, tie him up out of sight of his dam, leave him, then return to him every few minutes for thirty or forty minutes, then lead him back to his dam and loose him.

"On the third or fourth day the foal will lie down whenever you touch his leg—an important lesson, for a horse that will not lie down cannot travel for day after day on a journey that may last a month. All the predatory Oriental tribes, the Kirghiz, the Turcomans, the Circassians, teach their horses to lie down at a touch.

"At a year old strap up his leg, give him lessons with bells, drum, revolver, flags, &c., saddle him with a crupper and a surcingle. When he is accustomed to these, put a small courageous child on him; a black child will do best, as blacks are lighter and more precocious than white children. Let him caress the colt for a few minutes, dismount and remount on both sides. Continue this treatment every day for a week, leading the colt mounted about with a short rein, feeding him as he runs up to you, and after one week of daily lessons let the colt loose, but repeat the same lessons once in every month until he is thirty months or two years old.

"At two years old put a bit in his mouth and ride him two hours a day at a walking pace for a fortnight. You will find that at three years old he only requires riding by a competent horseman to be fit to go anywhere, and do anything a riding horse should do.

"One man would be able to prepare one hundred horses for sale on this plan, and enable the breeder to dispose of them perfectly broken, with not one buckjumper amongst them at three, four, and five years old, at from thirty to one hundred pounds a-piece. The expense for the man's wages and keep would not exceed one hundred a year.

"I tried this plan myself," says the colonist, "on two or three foals and the like number of yearlings and two-year-olds. It answered perfectly. However fat or 'flash' they might afterwards become, they were remarkably quiet to ride, none of them ever showing vice of any description."

COLONIAL AND ORIENTAL JOURNEYS.

We have no long rides or drives with the same horses in England or the Europe of railways and posting roads. But our countrymen become travellers and colonists.

"It is the pace that kills." A horse may trot and canter sixty miles in one day, or more, but he cannot go on repeating the distance at those paces day after day. On the London stones it is found that thirteen miles a day for five or six days is as much as the average omnibus horse can do and keep in condition. The jog trot—the huntsman's pace —about five miles an hour, is that at which a horse can do the greatest distances for the greatest number of consecutive days, with the least fatigue and loss of condition. The rider may be relieved by the horse occasionally walking—but *not* at the horse's best walking pace. On a long (Australian) journey, go slowly. Never remain more than two hours in the saddle without dismounting for a few minutes to ease your horse's back and legs. It is easier to save condition than to replace it.

Two miles at a trot tires as much as three at a walk, walking at top speed is as tiring as trotting. "An average colonial horse will carry his rider 100 miles in twelve or fourteen hours." To do 520 miles, Curr recommends four days' work at twenty miles a day, and one day's rest; four at fifteen miles, and two days' rest; two at twenty-five miles, and one day's rest; two at thirty miles, and two days' rest; five at thirty miles, and four days' rest; four at thirty miles, and seven days' rest—that would be twenty-one days' work and seventeen days' rest; and he states, from experience of months of overland travel, that horses that would lay down every night would finish the 520 fresh, and able to gallop.

He carries on the calculation to 1,500 miles performed with fifty-six days' work and forty-four days' rest, or at the rate of fifteen miles a day. When travelling in Syria, as so many English and American travellers do now, Mrs. Burton strongly recommends that some one of the party sees *himself* that the horses are duly fed every day, and examine the back of each horse on unsaddling. Native attendants are capable of stealing the fodder, and working animals day after day until their backs are positively festering.

TO TRAIN A SHOOTING PONY.

The shooting pony must lead and follow freely, creep up and down banks, and leap standing any reasonable fence when it has been shown to him, without requiring the urging of a whip.

He must allow himself to be loaded with dead game without resistance. He must stand still with the most perfect indifference whilst his owner fires from his back, or while a party shoots in succession or in volleys all around him. If, in addition, he will graze contentedly whenever he is left alone in a field, and allow himself to be caught without any difficulty, if he walks a steady four miles an hour and trots seven, he is, however ugly, an invaluable animal for his place.

The modes of teaching a horse to stand to be mounted, to lead, and to leap, have already been described in reference to hacks, ponies, and hunters. A pony may easily be made to stand still as long as his master is in sight; but a well-bred, well-fed pony is apt to forget his lessons. In South America gentlemen carry light shackles in their pockets, and thus restrain their horses by the fore-feet whilst making calls. Another way is to fasten a horse's head by a rein to one fore-foot. The easier and safer plan for securing a pony is

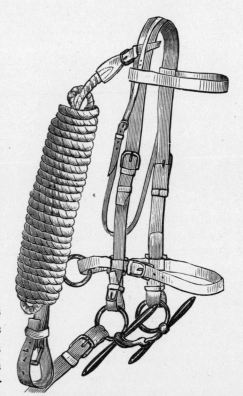

COLONIAL BRIDLE HALTER, FOR PICKETING.

to use an Australian bush-bridle, like the colonial bridle holder for picketing, but of a lighter pattern, with an iron spike for thrusting into the ground at the end of a light rope.

A horse that has never been alarmed by firearms may easily be taught to stand fire by commencing with snapping caps from a revolver when he is engaged in the stable in eating his corn, waiting and soothing between each snap, and, when well accustomed to the slight report, proceeding with gradually increasing charges, until he comes to associate gun-fire with feeding-time. After he is quite reconciled to the noise you may let him see the flash—not pointed at him—and finally fire from between his ears.

I have heard—and can fully believe—a story of a lot of horses galloping up from the meadows where they were grazing, straight into a shed on hearing the report of a gun, because they had been trained to associate their feeds of oats with the discharge of a firearm.

But where a horse that has been regularly used displays an aversion to firearms which does not yield to ordinary treatment, he must be Rareyfied, as if for an operation, and made fast. The operator must then seat himself on him, or alongside him, and give him the before-mentioned pistol lessons, caressing and feeding him between each discharge until he becomes thoroughly reconciled to the operation.

After one or two lessons, according to his temperament, he may be mounted after one leg has been strapped, and a small charge of powder fired from his back; then he may be let entirely loose in a school, and finally the same lessons may be repeated in the open air. Of course a naturally nervous pony is not fit for a shooting pony, but the experience of the army proves that any average horse can be taught to stand still and stand fire.

The *rationale* of this treatment is exemplified in the suburbs of such manufacturing cities as Manchester, where steam-engines roar at the corner of every thoroughfare, and locomotives rush along a network of railways night and day. The cattle in the fields pay no attention to the railway trains. The valuable horses ridden and driven by the wealthy manufacturers treat all these horrid sights and sounds with as much indifference as the sheep and cows "to the manner born," while a horse imported from any truly rural unrailroaded district, however naturally placid, will go half-mad at the sight of the first express train, and obstinately refuse to go down any street where steam is blowing off from a boiler.

In the preceding pages the principles and practices of the Rarey system have been sufficiently described for any horseman to understand and follow. It requires patience, it requires the habit of dealing with horses, as well as a calm, courageous temperament; but for the real work activity is more essential than strength.

Rarey's reputation has suffered from the inevitable reaction after an extraordinary season of sensation, and it is often sneered at by writers who are ignorant of or incapable of comprehending the principles of horsebreaking which he illustrated in his lectures. The best proof of his merit is the admiration which he excited amongst the finest horsemen of that or any other day, such as the late Earl of Jersey and Sir Charles Knightly.

When I visited the late Sir Tatton Sykes at Sledmere (who had passed his life amongst horses), he said "It was well worth the fee (£10 10s.) to see Mr. Rarey's manner of approaching an unbroken colt." Colonel Anstruther Thompson, who has been a Master of Fox-hounds from the time he was nineteen, a cavalry soldier, and one of the best horsemen of the day across any country, after telling me that he was always ready to buy any horse of good quality, however vicious, up to his weight and over sixteen hands, added, "Rarey taught us a great deal about horsebreaking."

VALUE OF FINISHING LESSONS.

When a colt has gone through the course of instruction described in the preceding pages he will be fit for the regular work of an ordinary riding horse, and quite ready for the hands of the hunter-breaker.

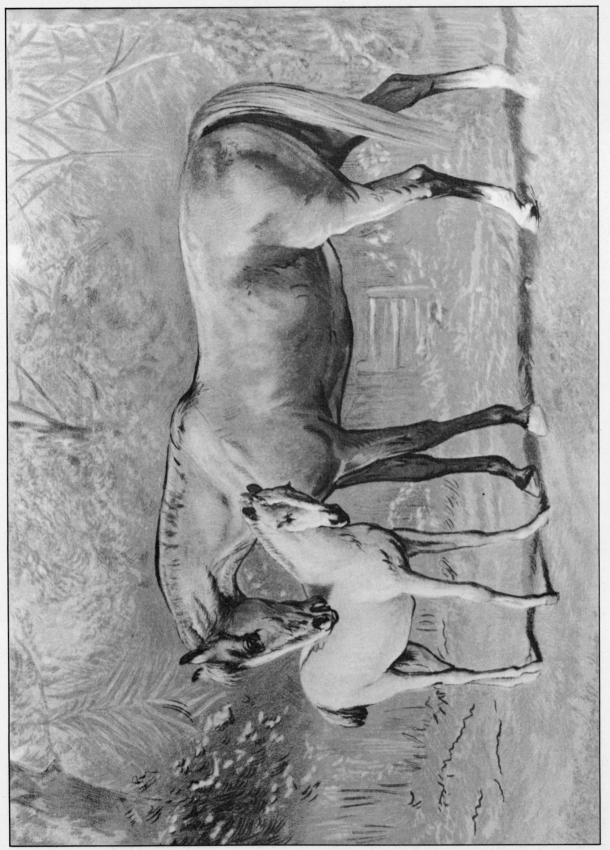

THOROUGHBRED MARE & FOAL.
FROM AN ORIGINAL PAINTING BY ALFRED CORBOULD ESQ.

EMBLEM, STEEPLECHASE MARE.

FROM A PORTRAIT SENT BY THE EARL OF CONVENTRY.

Indeed, there are many hacks and ladies' horses that have been ridden several years without being properly taught their lessons on sights and sounds. They take fright when, after a drop-leap, a hat dangles from the rider's button-hole, because they have not had a drum lesson. They obstinately refuse to allow a field-officer,

"All scarlet and plumed in his martial array,"

to approach a lady on horseback, and they become restive, or even runaways, on coming across a hissing railway train.

But if a young horse is of the stamp and quality of which the most expensive class of park hacks and ladies' horses are manufactured, he will require, in addition to the three "R's" of equine education, *finishing lessons* by a real master of the art of equitation—lessons by which originally fine action and carriage are perfected.

For this purpose, to a novice, written instructions would be worse than useless.

The severe discipline to which cavalry horses, which are parts of one vast machine, intended to move in perfect harmony, are subjected is not requisite with hacks or other riding horses, but in order that they may carry their riders pleasantly they ought, the moment they pass from the mere colt-breaker—the elementary teacher of the three equine "R's"—to be placed under some one who has the inestimable natural gift of hands cultivated by a long course of practice. At horse shows one continually sees magnificent animals passed over by judges, and rejected by purchasers, because they have neither been taught to stand or to move as they ought; sacrificed to false economy and the heavy single hand of some hard-riding clown, whose only recommendation was that he could ride anything over any country.

Appropriate bridles and bits are an important part of the machinery of refined training.

The right principles of bitting have been explained in a previous chapter, and woodcuts of the bits in ordinary use given.

For the first stage of bitting Major Dwyer recommends the use of the training halter, which have been used for some years in the central school of equitation at Vienna. The advantage of it is that, by preventing a young horse from escaping the action of a light snaffle, it renders the use of a sharp bit unnecessary. In this halter the noseband hangs below the rings of the snaffle, and is strapped in the "chin-groove" like a curb-chain, leaving sufficient play for the horse's under jaw. This arrangement affords the best means of *mouthing* young horses. (See illustration, page 563.)

One of the best curb-bits for training a young horse to the use of the double bridle is Major Dwyer's. It will be found sufficiently powerful, without being irritating, for all horses whose mouths have not already been spoiled by rough usage.

SEEGER'S AUSTRIAN MARTINGALE.

It is often necessary in training a colt to use some kind of martingale in order to get his head into the right position. The best is Seeger's running-rein.

"Seeger's running-rein consists of three distinct pieces—the chin strap, the running rein, and the martingale. The chin strap consists of a leather strap furnished at each end with a small buckle and strap, by means of which it is attached to the cheek rings of the snaffle, the entire length including the buckles being six inches. These buckles covered with leather are just wide enough to admit a strap four and one-tenth inches wide projecting over the buckle, *behind which* it is sewn on to the body of the curb. To this curb is attached by a rounded strap an ivory ring, like the ring of a common martingale. Another ring is fastened to an ordinary hunting breastplate, just in the centre of the breast at the level of the shoulders. A running rein about eight and a half feet in length is first buckled to a D ring attached to the pommel of the saddle on the near side; it is then passed through the breastplate ring, and then through the chin strap ring to the rider's right hand. A pull on this running rein will act directly on the mouthpiece, drawing it back and somewhat downwards towards the horse's

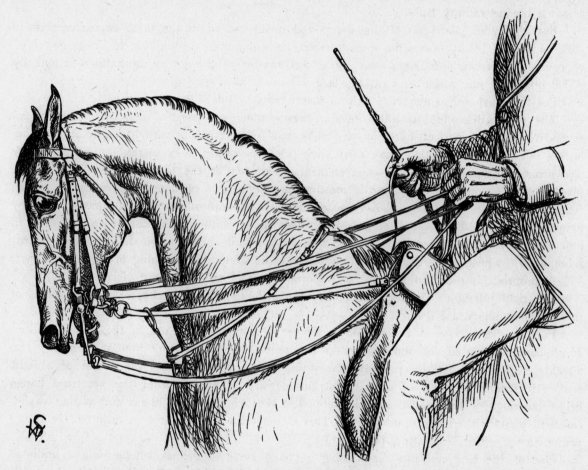

MR. G. RICE, WITH SEEGER'S RUNNING-REIN MARTINGALE ATTACHED TO A DOUBLE BRIDLE.

breast bone. Thus the rider, by taking the running rein and the right snaffle rein in his right hand, and the other snaffle rein in his left hand, can place the horse's head in any position he pleases. In handling young animals it enables one to attain our object gradually, noiselessly, with perfect certainty, without unnecessary violence. It may be used in a moment to check an attempt to bolt, and immediately relaxed, or it may be kept constantly in moderate action with a horse inclined to throw his head up too high, without interfering with his galloping. It may also enable one to dispense with the use of sharp bits."

The accompanying illustration shows this novel martingale applied to an ordinary double bridle by Mr. George Rice, of Piccadilly, who was equally pleased and astonished at its action.*

* This martingale may be obtained from Messrs. White and Coleman, saddlers, of Bishopsgate Street, as well as the Dwyer Curb. It is not a patent.

It might also be fitted to a rearing-ring bit, which might thus be used in hunting, as it has the shifting powers of the running martingale without interfering with either rein, and all the power of the standing martingale without the defect of rigidity.

TRAINING AND RIDING A STEEPLECHASER.

For the benefit of colonists and military men seeking some relaxation in regions

"Remote and savage, melancholy, slow,"

the following information has been condensed from the quoted work of a distinguished amateur steeplechaser.

In the following instructions it is presumed that the horse to be trained is full five years old.

"The object of training is to get rid of all superfluous fat and flesh, and to accustom the muscles to the greatest possible amount of exertion. If a horse is fat and fresh from grass a great deal more time will be required than if he is in ordinary hard-riding condition. The character of the animal must be studied ; some horses require scarcely any physic, and would be thrown out of, instead of into, condition by it ; others require a great deal. Some require to be sweated once a week, others will carry no muscle if sweated more than once a month. With many grooms the only idea of training is physicking and galloping a horse furiously in fair condition until he is a spiritless bag of bones.

"If the horse is stale from over-work he must be rested before being trained ; if he is in ill-health he must first be made well ; in fact, if he is not in rude health he is not fit to be trained.

"The first step is to keep your horse walking on turf or soft ground for at least four hours every day, divided into two periods of two hours each. His food should be three quarterns of moist bran, three quarterns of old oats, and about eight pounds of prime old hay. If you find his legs filling and heels tender, as you probably will at the end of a week, reduce his exercise to one hour's walking for two days, stop corn and hay, give linseed and bran mashes instead, and on the second day muzzle him at night. In the morning give him as much water as he will drink, and a mild dose of physic (see veterinary information).

"Immediately after the administration of a ball two hours' walking exercise should be given, with as much water, not too cold, as the horse will drink, and a loose bran mash, and he may be shut up and left quiet until the next morning. If by that time no symptoms of purging are apparent he should be taken for a walk in a field close to the stable, so that he may be brought in again as soon as purgation commences. If chilly an extra rug should be thrown over him, for *the action of the physic is to cause a determination of the secretions from the skin to the intestines.* Consequently, the less a horse's coat is brushed during the action of the physic the better. The purging must be continued until the excrement cease to be fœtid, and during that time bran and linseed mashes must be continued.

"After this preparation give four quarterns of oats, only six pounds of hay, and recommence walking two hours morning and evening. When you have hardened your horse's muscles by walking exercise, cleaned his skin by good grooming, and relieved his overloaded system by physic and diet, he is fit for faster work.

"The objects of quick work are twofold: to exercise and strengthen the organs of respiration, and by degrees to accustom the muscles and tendons to bear the strain of fast galloping and jumping.

"The horse should be galloped once or twice a week, according to circumstances.   He should be lightly fed on the morning of the gallop, walked about for an hour, *then stripped of his clothes*, and sent along the whole distance he will have to run in the real race at nearly his top speed, but never allowed to exhaust himself; made to do his utmost, yet keeping just inside the mark.   As soon as he is stopped slacken the girths, and lead him about until he has done blowing (which will be about ten minutes), then put on his clothes, wash out his mouth, and walk him straight back to his stable.   On removing the rugs on getting there the horse will be found to have sweated quite as much as is necessary if his skin is clean and his frame spare.   He should be rubbed perfectly dry (an operation which will take from twenty minutes to half an hour), dry clothes thrown over him, his feet and legs carefully washed and rubbed dry, and flannel bandages put on (?).   This done, the rug must again be removed, and the brush applied briskly, until every particle of dust, dirt, and scurf has been brushed out.   This will occupy an hour, after which sponging the eyes and nose and brushing the mane and tail will complete the toilet.   He may then be fed, and left alone for four or five hours, after which he must be taken for an hour's slow walking on soft ground.   If all is well, walking exercise for three days, and then another brushing gallop. But no horse should be galloped a second time until the soreness and stiffness consequent on the previous spin has subsided.   'Galloping a stiff sore horse will infallibly produce grogginess.'   Some horses will remain stiff and sore for several days after their first gallop.   There is nothing for it but patience; *time must be allowed for the vessels to relieve themselves and contract on their contents.*

"Many horses are ruined by being galloped when they are only fit to walk.   A horse in training should never be galloped until distressed.   'He should be pulled while still full of go.'   On this point, William Day's 'Racehorse in Training' may be consulted with advantage. William Day is against much physic and much galloping.

"Supposing the horse has gone through the course of practice already described in extract from Dick Christian's lecture, to accustom him to gallop safely over rough and undulating ground, in order to prepare him for steeplechasing, he may be taught to leap in the following manner :—

"When returning home 'after trotting about a water meadow with a loose rein,' have the trunk of a tree drawn across the gateway by which he has entered the field, and let him scramble over it.   The following days make him jump it into the meadows.   If he does this well, add a hurdle strapped with gorse or thorns to the tree, which will make him rear and spread himself, and prevent his running through the gorse.   After a fortnight a mile of country with fair fences may be marked out.   Let him be mounted by a resolute horseman, and let another horseman, mounted on an old clever horse, lead him at a strong pace for one round.   Take a second round alone, and a third side by side with the old horse, not racing but keeping close together.   After this four days' walking exercise.   After four weeks' going over eight or nine gorsed hurdles on alternate days, if he remains sound and shows the needful courage, he may be entered for any amateur steeplechase.

"A steeplechase horse who knows his business need not be ridden over gorsed hurdles more than once a fortnight.

"Long gallops are essential in training for a steeplechase.   The concussions from jumping at full speed are so severe that a horse will soon break down unless his joints, muscles, and organs of respiration are properly prepared.

The following rules apply equally to flat and cross-country races :—

" 1. The better the condition of your horse the more severe you should make the pace.

" 2. If you doubt your horse's gameness, jump off with the lead and keep it as long as you can.

" 3. If a horse pulls very hard, keep a steady pull, but do not haul at his mouth, which will prevent regularity of respiration, throw him out of his stride, and upset his temper.

" 4. When about seven-eighths of the distance, unless a very expert hand at timing your horse's powers, do not attempt to draw it too fine, but getting on good terms with the leading horses in the race, and laying hold of your horse's head, try and leave them, riding calmly but resolutely; above all sit quite steady; if your horse is straining every nerve, let him alone; if running sluggishly when getting into the straight run home, after the last fence, take tight hold of the reins in your left hand, give him a smart stroke with the whip, and two or three kicks with the spurs. But if you have reason to fear that he will swerve (as many bad-hearted ones do), continue to hold him between your hands, and give him some sharp kicks with the spurs.

" 5. If you find you are beaten easily, pull up; spare your horse, and avoid the cruel and unsportsmanlike practice of flogging a beaten horse all the way home."

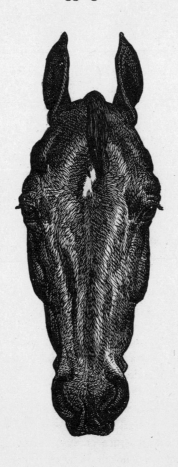

VETERINARY INFORMATION.

By GEORGE FLEMING, LL.D., F.R.C.V.S.,

Principal Veterinary Surgeon to the Army.

CHAPTER XXVII.

THE CONFORMATION OF THE HORSE.

Horse Judging—Necessity for Experience—Points Required in a Well-formed Horse—Different Shapes for Different Require-
ments—Divisions of the Horse's Exterior—The Skeleton, Muscles, and Tendons—The Bones and Cavities of the Body—
Different Regions of the Body—Head—Expression in the Horse—Differently-shaped Heads—Size or Volume of Heads—
Objectionably-shaped Heads—Nostrils and Ears—Lop-Eared Horses—Eyebrows and Eyes—Blemishes and Diseases
of the Eyes—The Lips—Setting on the Head—Neck—Mane and Forelock—Withers—Back—Loins—Croup—Haunch—
Tail—Docking—Chest—Belly—Fore Limbs—Shoulder : its Beauties, Defects, and Injuries—Arm—Elbow—Fore-arm—
Knee—Shank or Canon—Fetlock Joint—Pastern—Hoof ; Beauties and Defects of the Hoof—Hind Limb—Thigh—
Stifle—Leg—Hock : its Blemishes and Defects—Direction of the Limbs—Age—Frauds Practised.

In different chapters, allusion has already been briefly made to the conformation which horses
required for certain uses should possess ; and though the remarks were intended for guidance in selecting
such horses, yet as they were necessarily superficial and discursive, and reasons were not given for certain
shapes being better adapted for one kind of work than another, the subject of conformation may appropriately be glanced at now, and in a general manner.

Experience and observation are necessary to constitute what is designated a "good judge" of horses ;
but, nevertheless, there are men who never can acquire a good notion of outline and superficial proportions—never acquire a "good eye" for horses, try as they may, and notwithstanding unlimited experience ;
while there are other men who seem to be born judges, and who are gifted with intuitive knowledge, one
would imagine, as to the "points" which go to make up a good horse for a certain description of work.
Some men are good "all-round" judges, though these are comparatively few in number ; while others have
a good eye only for a special kind of horse, and are less confident, or less to be depended upon, when
they venture to give an opinion upon another description. Much depends upon experience gained among
certain classes of horses, and a great deal also depends upon natural aptitude in discerning good and
bad points, and in knowing when there is present that happy combination of good points which goes
to make up what may be designated a "perfect horse," or one particularly adapted to special
requirements.

A high authority, in speaking of conformation, says :—"A good horse is an animal with many good,
few indifferent, and no bad points. Any one radically bad point neutralises any number of good points. As
in a chain, any one really defective link will destroy its power of holding ; so in a horse, any one radically
bad point will render useless the aptitude and compactness of the conformation in other respects. The
greatest strength of a chain is limited by its weakest link. Similarly in a horse, his strength is limited
by his weakest point."

But this is not all. In addition to the absence of weak links, in the horse it is needed that all the
links should be of proportionate strength. Though in a chain it would not signify much if one link
were stronger or heavier than the rest ; yet in the horse, whose primary value is his power of movement,
in whom every limb or part has to be moved or carried in the process of locomotion, it is essential that

no one limb or structure should be disproportionately heavy or strong—or, in other words, cumbersome, in comparison with another. Excess of power or development in one part of a horse may not be merely useless, because the strength of the animal is limited by the weakest point; but it may be, and often is, a positive source of evil, and, if we may use the expression, of weakness. For example, a well-developed carcase, with good deep back ribs on the top of weak legs, will, by its disproportionate weight and substance, cause the under structures to fail sooner than they would otherwise do. Similarly a strong powerful fore-hand is not an advantage, if the hind-quarters are light; because the stress on the propelling agents will be unduly great, and they will, in consequence, be more liable to fail. Similarly, if the fore-legs are weak, they may suffer from excessive propulsion communicated to them by powerful hind-quarters; whilst they might perhaps have lasted for years if the propelling power had been less good. These examples, which might easily be multiplied, will probably be sufficient to illustrate our meaning. In a well-formed horse there must be no weak point; neither must there be any part disproportionately powerful to the other parts.

We cannot, however, expect to find in a horse, or indeed in any animal, our ideal of perfection. The good horse, remember, is an animal "with many good, few indifferent, and no bad points."

Minor deficiencies are often lessened, though never quite compensated for, by other points of conformation. For instance, a horse may have short back ribs, and may, therefore, appear hollow in the flank; but if he has wide hips and strong loins, it affords some compensation for the defect. It may even happen that points in themselves somewhat objectionable may to a certain degree remedy other faults. For instance, a horse deficient in bone below the knee will be less likely to fail at that point, if also somewhat light in his carcase.

Good points in a horse are not mere matters of ideal beauty, but shapes which, on principles of mechanics, are likely to answer the required ends. For every so-called good shape a sensible reason can be given; and so, likewise, a mechanical objection can be shown to every bad shape.

But shapes which may be decidedly objectionable for one class of work are not necessarily equally objectionable for another description of work. Thus, a hollow back, which would be very objectionable in a troop horse, an animal especially required to carry a heavy weight on its back, is not equally objectionable in a draught horse. Again, good feet, which are essential in hackneys, are not equally needed in harness horses. Good feet, however, are valuable in any horse, and any defect in this organ always leads to trouble, though perhaps with care and attention the animal may continue to go sound for years under favourable circumstances.

It is nearly impossible to obtain perfection of shape, except perhaps occasionally at a very long figure. The intending purchaser should, therefore, pay especial regard to those points which are essential for the class of work for which he needs something short of the ideal standard.

Again, each class of horse—the racer, the hunter, the hackney, the cob, the draught horse, etc.—has some particular points in his best conformation which would be absolutely faulty in another class. For instance, in the dray horse we look for circularity of the ribs, breadth of chest, and fore-legs wide apart: points which would be absolutely ruinous in a race horse, whose special vocation requires a deep chest and legs closer together. In the one animal we want all that contributes to strength and weight, with aptitude to put on flesh; whilst in the other we need those shapes which are most likely to give speed combined with endurance. The respective conformations of the bull-dog and the greyhound will perhaps illustrate our meaning.*

DIVISIONS OF THE HORSE'S EXTERIOR.

The exterior of the horse is divided, for facility of description and general convenience in the everyday use of the animal, into regions, which are more or less well defined, and universally recognised by horsemen, at least. The divisions are head, neck, body, and limbs; and these again are subdivided

---

* Fitzwygram, " Horses and Stables."

into particular parts, which it is more or less necessary those who have to describe, handle, or manage horses, should know.

The HEAD is described as offering for consideration, in ordinary language:—

At the *upper part*—The ears, with the poll and forelock between them.

In front—Forehead, face, end of nose.

At the sides—Temples, eyebrows, eyelids, eyes, cheeks, nostrils, lower jaw.

Lower part—Mouth, lips, gums, teeth, tongue.

Behind—Submaxillary space (between the jaws, so called), chin.

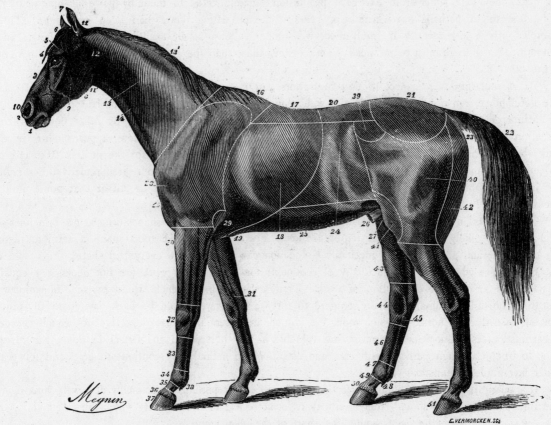

DESCRIPTION OF THE EXTERIOR, OR POINTS, OF THE HORSE.

1. Lips. 2. End of the nose. 3. Nose. 4. Forehead. 5. Hollow above the eye. 6. Forelock. 7. Ears. 8. Lower jaw. 9. Cheek. 10. Nostril. 11. Upper part of neck, or poll. 11. Neck. 12. Parotid gland. 13. Ridge of neck. 13. Mane. 14. Hollow of the neck, or jugular furrow. 15. Breast. 16. Withers. 17. Back. 18. Side, or ribs. 19. Girth. 20. Loins. 21. Croup. 22. Tail. 23. Anus and dock. 24. Flank. 25. Belly. 26. Sheath. 27. Testicles. 28. Shoulder and arm. 29. Elbow. 30. Fore-arm. 31. Ergot, or chestnut. 32. Knee. 33. Cannon, or leg bone. 34. Fetlock joint. 35. Pastern. 36. Coronet. 37. Foot. 38. Foot, or fetlock. 39. Haunch. 40. Thigh, or hind-quarter. 41. Stifle. 42. Buttock, or point of hip. 43. Leg. 44. Hock. 45. Chestnut. 46. Cannon bone. 47. Fetlock joint. 48. Fetlock. 49. Pastern. 50. Coronet. 51. Foot.

The NECK has:—

At the *upper part*—At its junction with the head, the parotid gland on each side, at the root of the ear, and immediately behind the lower jaw; along the ridge, extending from the head to the body, the mane; at the bottom, extending from the head to the chest, the throat, with a furrow on each side lodging the jugular vein, carotid artery, and nerves.

At the *sides*, immediately above the furrow, the long thick muscle that passes from the head to the arm, and pulls forward and raises this—the *levator humeri.*

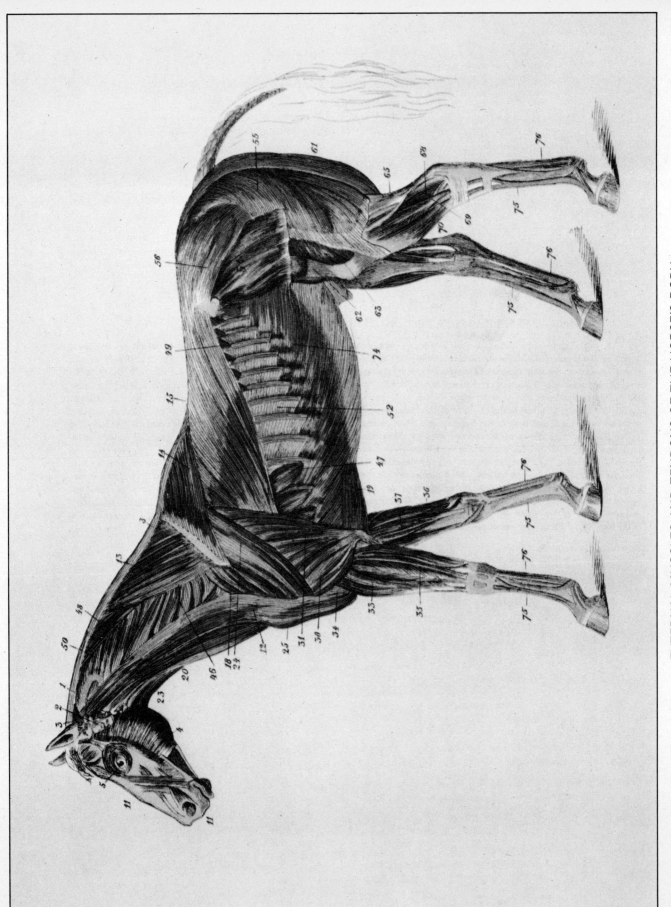

EXTERNAL MUSCLES AND TENDONS OF THE HORSE'S BODY.
(COMPLETE DESCRIPTIVE CAPTIONS ARE ON REVERSE OF PLATE.)

EXTERNAL MUSCLES AND TENDONS OF THE HORSE'S BODY.

1, 3, 3. Ligamentum nuchæ, or great elastic ligament of the head and neck. 2. Parotid gland. 4. Masseter, or masticating muscle of the jaws. 5. Orbicular or circular muscle of the eyelids. 11. Muscles of the lips and nose. 12, 25. Mastoido-humeralis, evator humeri, or elevating muscle of the arm. 13. Cervical trapezius. 14. Dorsal trapezius—the first of these pulls the shoulder upwards and forwards, the second backwards and upwards. 15. Great dorsal, or longissimus dorsi—long muscle of the back. 18, 24. Outer muscles of the shoulder-blade—antea and postea spinatus. 19. Deep pectoral muscle of the chest. 20. Sterno-maxillarias muscle, attached to the cartilage of the breast-bone and the angle of the lower jaw. 23. Subscapulo-hyoideus, attached to the shoulder-blade and bone of the tongue. 30. Short extensor muscle of the arm. 31. Large extensor muscle of the fore-arm. 33. Anterior extensor muscle of the metacarpus. 34. Short flexor muscle of the fore-arm. 35. Anterior extensor muscle of the phalanges. 36. External flexor muscle of the metacarpus. 37. Lateral extensor muscle of the phalanges. 46. Angular muscle of the shoulder-blade. 47. Serratus magnus, or great dentated muscle of the chest and shoulder-blade. 48. Elevator muscle of the shoulder. 49. Small serrated muscle. 50. Splenius muscle. 52. Intercostal muscles. 54. Fascialata muscle. 55. Long vastus, or biceps femoris muscle. 56. Middle gluteus muscle. 61. Semi-tendinosus muscle. 62. Anterior straight muscle of the thigh, or rectus femoris. 63. Vastus externus muscle. 65. Gastrocnemii muscles. 68. Deep flexor muscle of the phalanges. 69. Lateral extensor muscle of the phalanges. 70. Flexor of the metatarsus. 74. Great oblique muscle of the abdomen. 75. Extensor tendons of the foot. 76. Flexor tendons of the foot.

The BODY is divided as follows:—

At the *upper part*—the withers, back, loins, croup, and haunch or hip.

In *front*—The breast, or front of chest, and armpit.

Below—The girth, belly.

Sides—Chest, ribs, flank.

Behind—Tail, point of hip, anus, perineum; with the genital organs, according to the sex.

The LIMBS are divided into:—

Fore-legs—Shoulder-blade, arm, fore-arm, elbow, chestnut, knee, shank, back tendons, pastern, **fetlock**, ergot or corn, coronet, foot or hoof.

Hind legs—Hip-joint, thigh, **stifle**, leg, hock, chestnut, shank, back tendons, pastern, fetlock, **ergot**, coronet, foot or hoof.

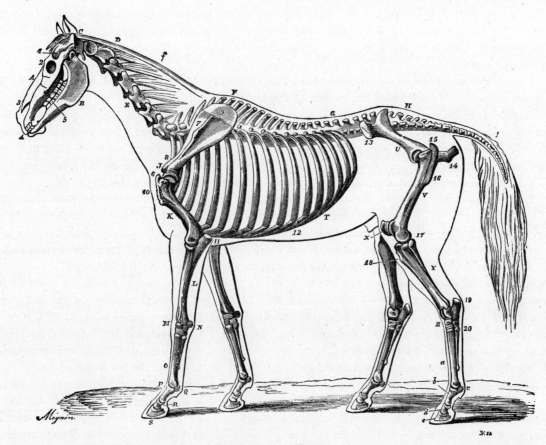

SKELETON OF A HORSE.

A. Head, or skull. B. Lower jaw. C. First bone of the neck, or atlas. D. Second bone of the neck, or axis. E. The seven neck bones, or cervical vertebræ. F. Spines of the withers. G. Bones of the back and loins (dorsal and lumbar vertebræ). H. Croup or sacrum. I. Tail bones, or coccygeal vertebræ. J. Shoulder-blade, or scapula. K. Arm bone, or humerus. L. Fore-arm bone, or radius. M. Knee, or carpal bones. N. Trapezium. O. Cannon, or metacarpal bone. P. Large pastern bone, or Os suffraginis. Q. Sesamoid bone. R. Small pastern bone, or Os Gropæ. S. Coffin bone, or Os Pedis. T. Ribs. U. Hip bones. F. Thigh bone, or femur. X. Stifle bone, or patella. Y. Tibia, or leg bone. Z. Hock bones, or tarsus. *a.* Hind cannon or large metatarsal bone. *b.* Large pastern bone. *c.* Sesamoid bone. *d.* Small pastern bone. *e.* Coffin bone. *f.* Elastic ligament of the neck. 1. Cheek bone. 2. Eye, or orbital cavity. 3. Nasal bones. 4. Incisor teeth. 5. Molar teeth. 6. Shoulder joint. 7. Point of the shoulder. 8. Hollow of the shoulder-blade. 9. Cartilage at the upper end of the shoulder-blade. 10. Tuberosity of the humerus. 11. Elbow bone. 12. Cartilages of the ribs. 13. Haunch, or anterior angle of the ilium. 14. Point of hip, or posterior angle of the ilium. 15, 16. Large and small trochanter of the femur. 17. Joint between the femur and tibia. 18 Superior tuberosity of the tibia. 19. Calcis, or point of hock. 20. Small bone of the leg, or peroneus.

THE SKELETON, MUSCLES, AND TENDONS.

The bones form the framework of the body, upon or within, or to which, the soft parts are attached, or by which important organs are protected. The muscles arising from, or inserted into them, are the organs by which the bones are moved and locomotion is effected. The shape, size, position, and arrangement of the bones are important features to be noted, either in the skeleton or in the living horse; as on these, to a large extent, depend the strength and speed, and also, to some degree, the endurance and beauty of the animal. The most powerful muscles, as well as the ligaments and tendons, are attached to the surface of bones, the points of attachment being generally roughened projections usually named "processes." The bones of the limbs, while forming support to the body, also act as levers of the most efficient and powerful kind.

As a rule, the better bred the horse is, so the denser and heavier, and therefore stronger, are the bones. The angles, formed by limb bones, are conducive to speed and elasticity in movement; the more vertically they are placed the better they afford support, though, at the same time, the more they receive concussion.

The muscles (see Plate of the External Muscles and Tendons), which are formed of tissue having the power of contraction, largely cover the surface of the body and the upper part of the limbs, though they do not extend below the knee or hock. They usually terminate in fibrous cords named tendons, which are fixed to the bones, and, through the contraction of the muscles, move these. The length and strength of muscles and tendons are in proportion, as a rule, to the length and strength of the bones; the more largely muscles and tendons are developed, and the harder or denser they are, so the more powerfully they act upon the bones, and the more vigorous and rapid are the movements of these.

The position and direction of the muscles and tendons materially depend upon the formation of the bones which compose the skeleton, and, consequently, there is the closest relationship between these and their function, so far as full and perfect movement are concerned. The bones in certain parts form, or help to form, cavities which contain organs most essential to life, and the dimensions of these cavities are largely indicative of the value or power of horses. For instance, in the head we have the bony case, the cranium, forming the cranial cavity, which contains the brain, nerves of special sense, and the commencement of the spinal cord—all most essential to the well-being of the animal, their development being dependent upon, or associated with, the volume of the cranium; and the more highly they are developed, so the more intelligent, energetic, and useful will the animal be. Between the cranium and the face are the orbital cavities, one on each side, for the reception of the eyes; and here, again, large dimensions are synonymous with large eyes—a point of beauty, intelligence, and value. It is the same with the nasal cavities.

In the trunk we have three cavities—the chest or thorax, belly or abdomen, and the pelvic cavity. The first contains the lungs, heart, and large blood-vessels, and is a large, bony kind of cage in the shape of a cone laid on its side, the apex forwards, and base behind: its outline or walls being made up, above, by the dorsal vertebræ with their spines (withers), at the sides by the ribs, below by the breast bone or sternum, and behind by that most powerful sheet of muscle which separates the chest from the abdomen—the diaphragm, or, as it is popularly named sometimes, the "midriff." Upon the dimensions and shape of this cavity depend the size of the lungs, heart, and diaphragm—organs most essential to nutrition, respiration, and circulation; its increased volume indicates strength and endurance with regard to breathing, while its form testifies whether the animal is best adapted for long-continued speed, or for the manifestation of strength at a slower pace. Besides containing the above-mentioned organs, the outside of the chest—above, or the sides, and below—affords attachment to quite a number of muscles which are mainly concerned in respiration, in attaching the fore-limbs to the body (the attachment is wholly muscular, the horse having, like many other animals, no clavicle or collar bone), which is suspended between them, or in the movements of these limbs; as well as the head and neck.

The abdominal cavity is only partially formed by the bony skeleton, the sides and floor being composed of muscles, and the roof only of bones. These are the bones of the loins or lumbar vertebræ, which, with their side prolongations or transverse processes, serve not only for the attachment of some of the abdominal muscles, but also of some of the most powerful muscles in the body—the propelling muscles of the posterior half of the trunk. The abdomen chiefly contains the digestive organs. Behind the abdomen is the pelvic cavity, the smallest of the three, and formed by very large and strong bones. Above these are the sacrum or croup bones, and those of the commencement of the tail; at the sides the hip or haunch bones, and below the pubic bones. This cavity contains part of the generative and urinary organs, and the termination of the intestinal canal; and, in addition to the muscles inside, outside it gives origin and attachment to the strongest muscles in the body—those chiefly concerned in propelling the trunk, and thus inducing progression, as well as jumping, rearing, and kicking. The largest round bones in the body— the femur or thigh bones—are fixed, one on each side, to the pelvic bones, at what is called the hip-joint, and is a most potent agent in these movements.

In movement, it has been stated that strength and speed depend not only upon the shape and arrangement of these, but also on the form and size of the muscles which act upon them. The length and thickness of a muscle influence the degree and extent of its action; for the longer it is, so the greater space will it move the bone through into which it is inserted; while the thicker it is, so the more rapidly, energetically, and continuously will it contract. Therefore, for locomotion, if we are to have speed and strength, we must have long and thick muscles, and strong, well-placed, and well-defined tendons.

We will now notice the principal points in somewhat of detail; and, in describing them, we will allude to their beauties, defects, and the blemishes from accident or disease, which damage or depreciate horses for service, or detract from their beauty.

THE HEAD.

The head is one of the most important regions of the body, as an index of breeding, intelligence, temper, and vigour; and upon its formation and size depends, to a great extent, the beauty of the horse.

In the face are portrayed the sensations of fear, ferocity, cunning, courage, pleasure, anxiety, contentment, pain and distress, apathy and indifference, which the animal experiences; and the features which, by their various and varied movements, endow the face with expression, are the ears, eyes, and eyelids, nostrils, lips, and mouth, all of which constitute a physiognomy almost as expressive, to those who have been accustomed to observe horses, as the human face itself.

The faculty of expression in the horse is in direct relation to breeding and intelligence—the latter being often in proportion to the former; but it is not always possible to determine the qualities of an animal by reference to its physiognomy alone, and it is only by familiarity and study that we can learn something of what a horse thinks or feels by watching its features. In the common breeds of horses the face is largely destitute of expression.

It is worthy of remark that, to constitute a well-formed head, it is more necessary that the different parts of it should be in harmony with each other than is required for any other part of the body, any disproportion between them destroying the effect of the whole.

In general outline, the head has been compared to that of a quadrangular pyramid; and for the purpose of describing its different portions this comparison is useful, though it is far from being exact in every instance.

The departures from this outline are somewhat numerous, and have received different designations, according to the form they present.

The head is said to be *square* when it is rectilinear in every direction, viewed from the front. There is usually a great width of forehead, of nose, and of nostrils; the ears and the eyes are wide apart, as are the branches of the lower jaw. The skin is fine. This is considered a good form of head, and is usually that in which we find much expression.

The *conical* head is that which tapers considerably towards the lower part; it is not so highly esteemed as the square head, and in many cases the animal is deficient in durability and strength. *Roman nose* and *sheep's-head* are the names given to the head when the nose is very convex. It is named "hare-shaped" when the convexity is limited to the forehead; and "round-headed" when the forehead and face are convex.

At different times different shaped heads have been in favour, and up to the end of the last century the Roman nose and round head were in favour; but now these two are looked upon with dislike, and not without reason, for they generally indicate dulness and want of energy and breeding.

Another form of head is that with a flat nose, in which, instead of being straight or slightly convex, the face is more or less concave. The rhinoceros head is that in which the concavity is limited to the lower part of the face, and the nose appears wider than usual.

A well-formed head should be in proportion to the size of the body; its length has usually been estimated as two and a half times less than the height of the body, measured from the top of the withers to the ground, or the length measured from the point of the shoulder to the point of the hip; if more than this, it is considered too long, or if less it is too short.

When it is a proper length it is gracefully carried, does not fatigue the fore-limbs, and responds to the action of the bit. When too long it is heavier, throws the centre of gravity more to the front of the body, and limits the action of the fore-limbs; while the animal is usually heavy in hand.

When the head is short it has not the same inconveniences, is more easily carried, and the centre of gravity being moved farther back from the fore-limbs, speed and action are favoured. The defects may be more or less compensated for by a longer or shorter neck, and they may not be of serious moment for certain kinds of work.

The size or volume of the head also varies. It is said to be *dry* or *clean* when all the bony prominences, muscular outlines, and subcutaneous vessels and nerves are well defined. It is an indication of breeding and a good constitution. A *coarse* head is marked by an excessive volume in all directions, but especially when the skull is too much developed; in this there is not only an excess of size, but the bony and other prominences are more or less diminished or obscured by the thickness of the skin, and the tissue beneath it. It is a sign of common breeding, and indicates a soft constitution and lymphatic temperament. An *old* head is that in which the outline of the skull is very manifest, through the wasting of the muscles; the hollows above the eyes are deepened, the eyes sunk in the orbits, the eyebrow is more prominent, the cheeks are shrunken, and the skin appears to cling closer to the bones.

The head should be small. A large head acts like a heavy weight at the end of a long lever. It has a tendency to make the horse heavy in hand, though this also much depends on its setting on, and on the obliquity or otherwise of the shoulders. It also operates unfavourably on progression, is apt to make the horse stumble, and if he does stumble, may help to overbalance him. A silly remark is sometimes made in favour of big heads, viz., that horses do not go on their heads. This is no doubt true; but a heavy weight at the end of a long lever, like the neck, is likely enough to cause a horse to come on his head.

For riding-horses, large heads are very objectionable; but for harness work, this point is not of much consequence, except as a matter of appearance. A small head is a marked sign of breeding, whilst a large head denotes an under-bred animal. A long lean head is, however, often found in well-bred horses.

The well-bred head, though usually small, is wide across the forehead, lean, unencumbered with flesh, finely chiselled, and terminates rather wide at the nostrils. The base of the skull is wide. The distance from the eye to the angle of the jaw is great. It is also wide under the jaw, or, as it is sometimes called, in the jowl or channel, in order to allow ample room for the larynx and respiratory passages. In high-bred horses we often have a prominence in the forehead, with a sinking in just above the nose.

The forehead should be wide, as not only is this an indication of intelligence and breeding, but it also shows that the air-cells or sinuses are well developed; its defects have been already pointed out. The blemishes to be looked for are the marks of trephining for disease of these sinuses. The face should be rather wide, in order to allow the passages for the air, from the nostrils to the windpipe, to be sufficiently capacious; it extends from the forehead to the nostrils.

The line of the face in a well-shaped head should be nearly straight; when concave or narrow across, it is a defect, as it diminishes the air passages. The defects or blemishes are chiefly fractures of the bones of the nose, which, by diminishing the spaces within, offer an obstacle to respiration. There are sometimes swellings on the side of the face which may lead to the suspicion of diseased teeth.

There is not much to mention with regard to the nose. It should be examined for marks of the twitch, which, if present, may indicate that the animal is vicious.

The nostrils should be covered with thin skin, and have but few long hairs. Their absolute beauty consists in their width, or rather in the extent to which they can be dilated, as the respiratory capacity is in direct proportion to their width and dilatability. The horse does not breathe by its mouth, but only through its nostrils; therefore the more capacious these are, so the larger the volume of air that can pass through them. The lungs are large in proportion to the dimensions of the nostrils. On opening the nostrils, we perceive towards the middle the lining membrane of the nose, which should be of a pink or rosy tint if the animal is at rest, but more or less red during or immediately after exercise. At the lower part, and near the junction of this membrane with the skin, is a small orifice or slit, through which the tears escape from the eye. The membrane should be of the colour or tint described, and free from ulcers or sores; the breath from the nostrils should be odourless, and there should be no discharge save that of a watery or a mucous nature. In tranquil respiration the nostrils move alike to a slight extent; as breathing is increased, their movements are more active. It is necessary to note this, because sometimes there may be paralysis of one or both nostrils, which of course prevents their dilating. Sometimes the margins of the nostrils are torn, which is more a blemish to the appearance of the animal than an absolute injury, unless the damage is great.

The ears constitute a very marked feature of the horse's head, and their proportions and position are a matter of some importance. They should be short, thin, wide at the base, and pointed, covered with fine skin, and with few hairs internally. They should not be too near each other, which happens when they are situated too high; they ought to be upright, or directed forward at an angle of about 45° to the axis of the head; they should be free in their movements, which are stimulated by the slightest sound; when they are sluggish or immovable, the suspicion is raised that the animal is more or less deaf.

"Lop-eared" horses have the ears long, thick, and drooping, and this defect very often betrays sluggishness. The ears form an excellent index to the degree of intelligence or temper of an animal, as well as of energy or weakness. Ears perpetually in movement betray a restive or nervous horse; while horses which readily throw the ears back on the neck may be looked upon as vicious or ill-natured.

With regard to blemishes, the ear is sometimes broken, and then it is deformed, thickened, and crooked; it is also sometimes torn, or amputated because of disease, or it may be cleft. Not unfrequently there is a circular mark round the root of the ear, due to the application of the twitch; this may show either that the animal is vicious, troublesome to shoe, or has been treated for some painful disease. The hairs in the interior of the ears are sometimes removed, in order to make a coarse bred horse look better bred. Lop-eared horses have had the ears made erect for purposes of sale, by bringing them together by means of a silk thread passed through them, and covered by the forelock; this makes them erect for the time being.

The eyebrow should be bold and prominent on each side of the face, and the depression behind it, in the young horse, very slight. It is often fractured in consequence of falls; but this is readily perceived by comparing both eyebrows. As age progresses the depression behind the eyebrow becomes

WELL-SHAPED HEAD OF AN ENGLISH SADDLE OR LIGHT HARNESS HORSE.

Fig. 1.—Side View.   Fig. 2.—Front View.

deepened, so that in aged animals it forms a well-marked cavity. To make the animal appear younger, dishonest horse-dealers have been known to make a small puncture in the skin covering this depression, and to blow in air, with the object of filling up this space.

The eye, being the organ of vision, has a very important part to play in the utilisation of the horse, and forms a very marked feature of the face, constituting one of its chief beauties, if not the most conspicuous feature. The absolute beauty of the eye consists in its being well away from the middle line of the head, as this coincides with a wide forehead and face; in its prominence at the side of the face; in its largeness, and perfect equality with that on the opposite side; in its dark colour and bright appearance; in its transparency; in the perfect freedom and rapidity of movement of the pupil; in the uniformly dark colour of the pupil, showing that the crystalline lens is perfectly transparent; in the moderate convexity of the front of the eye or cornea; in the completeness, the fineness, evenness, and mobility of the eyelids; in the mildness and vivacity of expression.

Small eyes, deeply set in the head, are unsightly, and show underbreeding; usually designated pig-eyes, they accompany a lymphatic temperament; they also sometimes indicate a predisposition to disease of the eye or disease already present. An eye small and little prominent, but partly concealed by a large upper eyelid, very often is a sign of sulkiness or vice. An ox-eye is characterised by being very convex in front, slow in its movements, and apparently without expression; it is often near-sighted. In old or worn-out horses, or those suffering from disease, the eye is sunk deep in the cavity. Horses which show the white of the eye around the cornea, through the eyelids being sometimes too wide apart, have an unpleasant appearance, and look as if vicious; this is seldom the case, however, and the condition is merely one of unsightliness. What is called a wall-eye, is the lighter colour of a portion or the whole of the iris around the pupil; this may be a light-blue tint, which, contrasted with the other part of the eye, gives the face a peculiar appearance. It is perfectly natural, and cannot be looked upon as anything more than an unsightly condition. When the eyes are unequal in size, that which is smallest, in all probability, has been, or is, the seat of disease. When the eye is not sufficiently convex, the animal cannot see objects near him, and is therefore far-sighted; he is liable to stumble, and to run against things in close proximity.

The diseases, defects, or blemishes of the eye which detract from the beauty or utility of the animal are very numerous, and can only be incidentally noticed. The eyelids may be torn and more or less deficient, or turned out or in—all of which conditions are damaging to the eye. The tears, instead of escaping from the orbit by the natural channel in the face, when this channel is blocked up, flow over the face, destroying the hair and leaving the skin naked. White specks or streaks on the front of the eye or cornea, caused by blows or a lash from the whip, are far from uncommon, and, if in the centre, more or less impair vision. Simple inflammation may lead to this condition, and in some cases the whole of the cornea is opaque—a condition known as *albugo*—when, of course, there is total blindness. There may also be simple inflammation of the lining membrane of the eyelids—*conjunctivitis* —which makes them swollen, and more or less obscures vision. The crystalline lens, which is behind the cornea and the pupil, may be the seat of cataract—a pearly white deposit, which varies in size from a minute speck to that of the whole of the lens. It is sometimes so small as to require the closest inspection by artificial light to discover it, and in other cases it is so conspicuous as to be seen at a distance. The humour behind the pupil and the lens may be of a greenish colour, and more or less opaque—a condition to which the name *glaucoma* has been given. Another diseased condition of the eye, named *amaurosis*, is due to paralysis of the optic nerve. The eye looks unusually dark and bright, and the pupil does not contract; blindness is the consequence. What is called *periodic* or *specific ophthalmia*, is also a serious condition which may be present, and which eventually leads to cataract. When the inflammation is active, of course there can be no doubt as to something being amiss; but when it has subsided, it is then more difficult to tell whether the eye has been so affected. The eye is usually smaller and deeper in the socket, as well as less tolerant of light, and careful examination may discover traces of disease; one marked characteristic of such an eye is to be found in the altered condition of the eyelids, the upper one being more contracted towards the inner corner, so that the space between the two lids, instead of being oval, as in health, is really triangular.

A horse blind of one eye may deceive an unobservant person, and especially when it is in the hands of an unscrupulous dealer, as the animal employs the remaining eye to the best advantage. It is not so, however, when blindness is complete in both eyes. Then it endeavours to bring its other senses more into play to compensate for the serious loss; more especially does it call upon the sense of hearing with this object: the ears are perpetually in play on the least noise. Being generally constantly directed forward, the smallest sound brings them actively into play. When made to walk or trot, this is still more observed; and the fore-limbs are carried high, the animal being also apparently afraid of stumbling, while undecided in its gait; the head is carried aloft, the nostrils dilated, as if to discover what was going on by the sense of smell; and objects brought into contact with it are sniffed with anxiety and caution.

With regard to the posterior part of the head, this is formed by the lower jaw and its branches, with a space between these latter; this space contains certain glands which can readily be felt; these glands ought to be small, not adherent to the jaw, and easily moved about. The extent of space between the branches of the jaw is greater in the well-formed head of a thorough-bred horse than in that of a common-bred horse; and the wider it is, the greater beauty does it constitute, as it leaves more room for the upper part of the windpipe (larynx), and the other parts it contains, as well as allowing the head to be drawn closer against the neck. The skin covering this space in common-bred horses is furnished with long bristly hair, which gives the head a big, clumsy appearance. Of course, any enlargement of the glands not only diminishes the beauty of this part, but is indicative of disease. Sometimes, in chronic glanders, horse-copers have the enlarged glands dissected out, in order to remove this evidence of the disease; while if there is any discharge from the nostril, this is suppressed by introducing a piece of sponge high up the cavity. Removal of the glands in this way leaves a scar at the spot where the operation has been performed, which can be felt, and seen if looked for.

With regard to the lips and the mouth, it may be noted that the former are organs of expression by no means of small importance, and have a marked influence on the physiognomy; they greatly assist in expressing suffering, pleasure, fear, terror, courage, and depression; and if not so movable and varied in their expression as those of man, yet they are none the less indicative, to the eye of the observant horseman, of the sensations the animal experiences, and especially in the well-bred animal. In the common-bred horse, however, they are not so expressive, nor are they so fine.

In health the lips should be maintained in contact, except when the mouth is opened; when they are not in contact, the cause may be due to the kind of harness the animal wears, to great debility, to under-breeding, when the lower lip is often pendulous, or to paralysis. The skin covering the lips should be thin and soft in well-bred horses, and sparingly provided with long hairs.

The lips may be torn or cut, and the angles of the mouth lacerated or indurated by improper use of the bit; this damage may lead to imperfect closure of the mouth, and consequent escape of the food or water.

With regard to the mouth, the number, position, and character of the incisor teeth are indications of age. The tongue, though it can scarcely be designated one of the points of the horse's exterior, yet deserves notice. The size of the tongue is in proportion to the capacity of the mouth. It should always be contained within the mouth during work. Some horses double the tongue over or under the bit; others project the tongue, and allow it to remain pendent beyond the mouth during work; while others, again, keep continually thrusting it out and in.

The tongue is often wounded, sometimes cut half through; in others, again, a large portion is entirely removed by accident.

VARIOUS TYPES OF BADLY-SHAPED HEADS.

Fig. 1.—A head somewhat heavy in character, the nose and lower jaw being very thick, and the head set on at too great an angle to the neck.   Fig. 2.—Front view of badly-formed head, it being nearly the same in width throughout, with the eyes placed too close together and too much in front.   Fig. 3.—Front view of a moderately good head, but with drooping or lop ears, and which, however well-shaped the head may be in other respects, give to the face a sheepish look.   Fig. 4.—A head heavy and somewhat sulky in character, with the curved profile commonly designated a Roman nose.   Both this head and Fig. 1 are deficient in the bright, intelligent look which should be seen in a well-formed and good-tempered horse.

SETTING ON OF THE HEAD.

The "setting on," or direction of the head, is of some importance, both from an æsthetical and utilitarian point of view. It may be carried in three principal directions—oblique, more or less horizontal, or vertical. A head well set on may be said to be that in which it is placed obliquely downwards and forwards, at an angle of about forty-five degrees. Not only is this direction the most favourable in a mechanical point of view, but with it the horse can best distinguish objects before him, and is, therefore, less liable to stumble or fall; it is also the position in which the bit and the reins can act most favourably on the mouth. A horse is said to be a "star-gazer" when he carries his head high and more horizontal; then the centre of gravity is raised and thrown back, and the balance is less assured. Speed, however, is accelerated in consequence of the weight being carried backwards, and respiration is easier because the larynx and windpipe are then in a straight line. This position of the head is very faulty, inasmuch as the animal cannot so well see where it is going, and the rider or driver has less purchase on the mouth, and therefore less control over the horse. The head is sometimes carried in this position, not from faulty setting on, but from undue sensibility of the mouth, or from that peculiar conformation of the neck known as "ewe-necked." Well-formed young horses are also sometimes inclined to carry the head in this position, until they get accustomed to the bit.

When the head is vertically set on, the centre of gravity is lower, and thrown towards the centre of support; so that there is more stability in equilibrium, though it is not favourable to speed. It is, therefore, objectionable in fast-paced horses, though it is not so in those for heavy draught. It is usually accompanied by a curved neck; as with the horizontal head the horse cannot see so well when the head is vertical, though it is more favourably disposed for the action of the bit. The objections to this position of the head are still further increased when the nose is carried still nearer the chest— that is, when the head is oblique downwards and backwards.

NECK.

A well-formed neck is one of the beauties of a horse. It should not be too large or thick, but be proportioned to the other parts of the body. And the harmony between it and these parts can only be ascertained by the experienced eye of the practised horseman. A thin or ewe neck is unsightly, though not so much so, perhaps, if it is not too long. In the entire horse we have the neck more largely developed than in the mare or gelding, the exaggerated crest being rather a source of beauty than otherwise. The length of the neck should be in proportion to its volume, and it should, in fact, be neither too long nor too short. When it is the proper length, the head is well carried, the movements of the shoulders are facilitated, and the neck itself moves easily and gracefully. When it is too long, the centre of gravity is carried forward to the fore-limbs, and it is, as a rule, thin and weak, and the head is carried heavily, unless the muscles are sufficiently powerful to maintain it elevated, and especially if the head is light. In fact, a long neck is not a disadvantage, but rather the contrary if the muscles are developed in proportion, and especially in race-horses; for the chief of these muscles are elevators of the shoulder-blade and arm bone, and therefore the longer and more powerful they are, so the wider and more rapid will be the movements of these bones, and particularly when the neck is rather raised.

A short thick neck is destitute of suppleness and elasticity, and is unwieldy; for fast-paced horses it is a positive defect, for the same reason that a long, well-furnished neck is an advantage. With slow-paced horses, however, such as those for draught, it is no great disadvantage; and if the muscles are powerful and the head large, it will be rather an advantage.

In shape the neck is somewhat conical, being broad laterally towards the shoulders, and gradually tapering as it reaches the head, the taper being most marked at the under part; immediately behind the head, where the wings of the first cervical vertebra are expanded, it is broad, to give attachment to the powerful muscles which move the head. The crest should be firm, and either straight or slightly convex (as in the stallion), and the large long muscle which runs from the head towards the shoulder should stand out in bold relief; while the windpipe immediately below it ought to be well defined by the groove which separates them. It may be more or less vertical, oblique, or horizontal; when inclined in a vertical direction it constitutes a beauty, and is an index of strength and breeding. The head is well carried, and the movements of the shoulder are free and extensive. This direction of the neck is the most favourable for saddle-horses, as it makes them light in hand. In the oblique neck we find that which belongs to the majority of good horses. By oblique is meant an angle of 45 degrees. A horizotnal neck is usually found in common-bred horses, and those which are not endowed with much energy; the head is carried heavily, the centre of gravity is more towards the fore-limbs, and the animal is heavy in hand.

The under line of a well-formed neck should not be directly straight, but should curve gracefully downwards towards the chest, and upwards and forwards towards the head. The movements of the neck should be in harmony with other parts of the body when these are in motion; it should be readily flexed to one side or the other, curved downwards, or easily and quickly raised.

The forelock and mane may be looked upon as appendages to the neck. The mane is, with regard to the neck, what the capital is to the column which it surmounts; it embellishes, while it conceals the hard line which forms the upper border of the neck, giving it a graceful aspect, and lending a charm to the fore part of the horse. The same may be said of the forelock, which is really the upper end of the mane. The abundance of hair varies according to breed, sex, and age. In well-bred animals and in foals it is fine, silky, and somewhat scanty; while in those which are common-bred it is thick and coarse. The mane is usually carried to one side or the other, according to fashion. The hairs are usually straight, though in some cases those of the mane are rather wavy. Not unfrequently the forelock and mane acquire extraordinary dimensions, in fine as well as in common-bred horses. In some cases the forelock reaches the nose, and the mane the knees. The mane is said to be single when it falls entirely to one side, and double when it falls to both sides. For saddle-horses the mane is usually made to incline towards the left or near side, so that the rider may seize a lock of it when mounting. For the single-harness horse it may lie on either side, but for double harness the near-side horse has it on the left, and the off-side horse on the right.

With regard to the disease or blemishes which should be looked for on the neck, at the upper part towards the ears there may be an abscess (poll-evil), or a scar, the remains of one. In the furrow immediately above the windpipe, scars resulting from bleeding may be found; and the expert examines for obliteration of the jugular vein at this part. In front of the windpipe, at its upper part and in the middle line, there will remain a vertical scar if tracheotomy has been performed; and if any of the cartilaginous rings of the windpipe have been fractured or deformed by accident, this will be perceived either by the naked eye or by passing the hand over them.

THE WITHERS.

That part named the withers is situated immediately behind the neck and mane, in front of the back, and between the two shoulder-blades. It is formed by the spines of the five or six dorsal vertebræ; its height and its thinness, or cleanness, constitute its beauty and importance. At the top it should be thin, but a little lower it gradually thickens towards the shoulder-blades. The thinness of the withers depends upon the height of the spines, upon the condition of the animal, the length and obliquity of the shoulder-blades, and the manner in which the body is suspended between the fore-limbs; but in well-formed withers the spines are the chief feature. The importance of the height of the spines is due to the large elastic ligament which arises from them and passes to the head, forming the ridge of the neck, and suspending head and neck by its great strength; also by the important muscles which are attached to these spines. The height of the withers depends upon breeding, and, to some extent, upon training.

Age and sex have their influence. In the foal it is not well defined, but only becomes gradually developed with maturity, at five or six years old; while in the mare it is not so prominent as in the gelding, though it may be the same height as in the stallion. In the coarse-bred horse it is low, thick, and heavy, as in the animal the shoulders are upright, short, and massive. In some horses the withers are so thin and high as to constitute, if not a deformity, at least a great inconvenience, especially if the animals are required for riding purposes, as they have to be fitted with specially constructed saddles. The absolute height of the withers is related, as has been stated, to the length or height of the spinous processes of the vertebræ; and a horse is said to have a high fore-hand when they are high, and low when they are less developed; and the height of the withers, again, with regard to advantages or disadvantages, is related to the height of the croup. When the withers are low, more weight is thrown on the fore-limbs, and the croup is higher; this leads to low action in front, and the head and neck are not so easily elevated, as there is not sufficient leverage for the muscles and tendons to act upon. For speed we find that a croup higher than the withers is no disadvantage, but, on the contrary, seems to be favourable. This is seen in thorough-bred horses possessing great velocity, the relative lightness of the fore-hand, and the greater length and strength of the hind-quarters, compensating for the apparent defect. Nevertheless, high withers are necessary in horses for trotting or ordinary riding, and especially for jumping; a low fore-hand is indicative of stilted action, and a tendency to "forge" and to stumble; but in horses for heavy draught, and slow-paced, they are not objectionable. In the well-bred, well-formed horse they are, or should be, always present, as accompanying them there is usually a long shoulder-blade and a deep chest.

The blemishes or diseases to be looked for in the withers are due to accidental bruising, or wounds by the saddle or harness. Scars show the existence of these at some former time, and pain or swelling, if present, is evidence that the injury is recent.

THE BACK.

The back is situated immediately behind the withers, in front of the loins, and between the ribs. It is a very important feature in the conformation of the horse, as on it is placed the weight which the animal has to carry; while it transmits to the fore-hand the impulsive efforts conveyed to it by the loins and hind-quarters. The back has, therefore, to respond to various requirements.

It may have several *directions*. It is said to be *straight* when it passes into an almost horizontal line from before to behind. This is the strongest kind of back, and is best adapted to resist weight; and provided the withers are sufficiently high, the saddle is maintained in a good situation.

A *mule*, *razor*, or *roach back*, is that in which there is more or less convexity, with thinness. Though it would appear to be stronger than the straight back, yet it is generally accompanied by flat sides and a narrow chest, and is less elastic than if the back were straight or concave; consequently, the animal is less pleasant to ride, being rough and uneasy in its paces. In addition to this, such a back is usually short, and the animal is disposed to "over-reach" and to "forge," because of the hind-limbs not having sufficient space in which to move. For saddle or light harness horses, therefore, such a back is not desirable; but for those which carry loads, or are used for slow draught, it is an advantage, because relatively stronger.

When the back is concave from before to behind, such a horse is said to be *hollow* or *saddle-backed*. Such a conformation may be congenital or acquired; whichever it is, it is the most defective, as it indicates weakness, the ligaments which maintain the vertebræ in line, sustain, in fact, the arch of the back, as well as the weight of the abdomen, being more severely taxed by this conformation than by any other; consequently, the vertebræ being so much out of the direct line cannot so well transmit the impulsion of the hind-quarters, and a portion of this impulse is lost. This loss is increased by the impulsion itself exaggerating the curve, and this exaggeration, again, is still further augmented when weight is placed upon the back. Hollow-backed horses are, therefore, unsuitable for severe work in the saddle or in harness; but for light draught or hacking they may be used; indeed, in the saddle they are often very pleasant, from the greater elasticity they possess owing to this conformation. " Horses with hollow backs have usually good crests, and one weak curve is to a certain degree compensated for by the counter curve. All backs, we may mention, though originally straight, become more or less hollow with age. This effect is due, partly to the ordinary mechanical effect of weight on a given line, and partly to wasting away of the muscles with age. In young horses, the muscles along the line of the back should stand as high as, or higher than, the spinous processes of the vertebræ of the back-bone." These muscles form a prominent ridge on each side of the spine, and a horse showing them is said to be *double-backed ;* it is most marked in heavy draught horses with wide chests, and especially those with a slightly hollow back; and also in those in which the muscular system is well developed. With age the double back disappears, and the ridge becomes thin and prominent. This is the case, also, with narrow-chested and emaciated horses.

In some cases the hollow back is more apparent than real, and is noticed in animals which are very strong and capable of drawing heavy loads. In them the concavity is due to the unnaturally short spines of the dorsal vertebræ. This accounts for so-called hollow-backed horses being frequently excellent and strong in the saddle, and not unfrequently good hunters.

Sometimes the direction of the back is oblique downwards from behind to the withers, due to the croup being higher than the withers. This direction throws the saddle forwards, as well as the centre of gravity, on the fore-hand, and is therefore defective.

The *length* of the back is in direct relation to its strength and the depth of the chest; upon it depends, to a considerable extent, the rapidity of the animal. The length may be moderate, or long or short. To be a proper length, it should be in harmony with the other parts of the body, and it is impossible to determine exactly what it should be otherwise. A *long* back implies a long and a deep chest, as it forms the upper part of that cavity; it also ensures the hind- and the fore-limbs being well apart, and this separation should be favourable to speed, as it allows a greater length in those muscles of the trunk which are most employed in progression, while it ensures sufficient space for the movements of the limbs. Nevertheless, a long back is necessarily weak, as it cannot support weight so well, and its greater flexibility, due to its length, makes it less solid in the propulsion of the body.

A short back, on the contrary, is stronger, because it transmits the propulsion more readily, and is more solid; but it is less elastic, and the chest is less capacious, because not so long. A short back also, unless the loins compensate for the shortness, does not allow the hind legs to move so freely, nor so far under the body; consequently, the animal is short in its stride, and when pushed is likely to overreach, or to forge. The length of the back must depend, in judging of the points of a horse, upon the use to which the animal is destined: where strength is required, the back should be short; but for saddle or light harness work, it should be moderately long. A long and a hollow back is defective, because weak. With race-horses, the back is usually short comparatively, this shortness being compensated for by a long pelvis and well-sloping shoulders, as well as by the width of the back and great muscular development. This width of the back is another important feature, as a narrow back is a serious defect, the sides being often flat, the chest narrow, and the muscles weak.

The back, like the withers, may show signs of injury caused by the saddle or harness.

THE LOINS.

The loins are situated behind the back, in front of the croup, and with the ribs, flanks, and haunches on each side. Their width is in direct proportion to the development of the transverse processes of the lumbar vertebræ, which constitute them, as well as the muscles covering these bony processes. The wider the loins, therefore, the stronger they will be. With regard to length, the loins should not be long; in fact, they should be as short as possible, in order to transmit the impelling power of the hind legs undiminished to the back. In direction, they should be straight, as it is only in old or worn-out horses that they become convex. In what are called "slack-backed" horses, there is a depression between the loins and the croup, which indicates weakness. Though a certain amount of rigidity is necessary, yet, through excessive work, or from disease, the loins may become completely rigid; and, in order to discover whether they are sound, experts are in the habit of passing the hand along the loins, and pressing or pinching this part, which causes the animal to slightly flinch, and bend the back. When the loins are weak, this bending is carried to an extreme degree; when disease or rigidity are present, the pinching may be resisted entirely.

Among the diseases or blemishes of the loins, there may be scars or swellings, due to injury from the saddle or harness. There may be also scars produced by the firing-iron, applied for sprains of that part.

THE CROUP.

The croup is situated behind the loins, and is terminated by the root of the tail. On each side it has the haunches, and below and behind the thighs and the hips. The length of the croup is an important characteristic in the conformation of horses, a rather long croup being always present in fast-paced animals, as the muscles mainly concerned in propulsion are situated in this region, and their length and extent of contraction will, therefore, be in proportion to the length of the croup. This length is measured from the angle of the haunch to the point of the hip, and it will be found that it is greatest in those animals which are distinguished for speed or jumping power. A short croup is an absolute defect in all horses, especially those required for speed; though this defect may be compensated for in heavy draught animals, in which it is most frequently present, by a greater width of the croup.

The width of the croup indicates an increase of power in proportion to its development, and it is most exaggerated in heavy draught animals; but in lighter and fast-paced horses great width is a defect, in consequence of the centre of gravity being thrown too much from side to side during progression, causing the animals to roll or rock when going. Nevertheless, in these horses the croup should be wide enough to allow the hind limbs to be sufficiently clear of each other, so as not to impede their movements, or to allow the lower end of the limbs to come in contact. A narrow croup is an indication of weakness, and is usually accompanied by flat sides and a narrow chest. For carriage and saddle-horses, the length should exceed the width to a slight extent; when too narrow, it is a defect, but it can scarcely be too wide in heavy draught horses, or in brood mares.

The direction of the croup in a well-formed horse (and especially of one destined for speed) is horizontal, and this is the disposition which best favours the development and the action of the propelling muscles. Observation has shown that speed is directly in proportion to their horizontality. When the croup approaches an obliquity of forty-five degrees, it is not only unsightly, but possesses marked disadvantages, in its being unfavourable to speed, and also, to some extent, to strength, while it is more or less offensive to the eye. The thigh bone is generally placed more upright, and certain muscles passing from the croup to it are much shorter than when the croup is horizontal. When, however, the thigh forms an acute angle with it, and the muscular development is good, this obliquity is not unfavourable to strength; on the contrary, it is very marked in heavy draught horses. For mixed work, requiring a certain amount of speed, a croup with a direction between horizontal and oblique is found the most useful. It may be observed that the direction of the croup is not always congenital, but is modified more or less by the work to which horses are put. With young horses, which originally had the croup more or less horizontal, when put to draw heavy loads too early, or to work on steep streets or in hilly districts, it will soon become oblique; while with those which at first had the croup oblique, when they are trained as race-horses, or used for the saddle, it gradually acquires a horizontal direction.

Whatever may be the form or direction of the croup, to be perfect it should be well covered by powerful muscles. An angular croup, in which we have a prominence at its upper part, caused by the greater development of the spine of the sacrum, is not defective, however unsightly it may be; but, on the contrary, it is an indication of strength, provided the muscles are large and well defined.

With regard to blemishes or disease, there is not much to note in this region. Wasting of the muscles should be looked for, due to prolonged inaction caused by disease.

THE HAUNCH.

The haunch is the prominence on each side of the croup, immediately above the flank and the thigh, produced by the anterior part of the pelvic bone. It gives origin and attachment to powerful muscles, and the greater its prominence, therefore, within certain limits, the more strength will it confer When too angular, however, from malformation, bad direction of the croup, or loss of condition, it is unsightly, or may even be a defect. When not sufficiently prominent, as occurs in horses which have a narrow croup, it is an indication of weakness; though in those which are very fat it is more or less concealed.

As the result of accident, either from falls, or from blows against the sides of doors, this part is liable to be fractured, partially or totally, giving rise to deformity of more or less extent—sometimes so slight as scarcely to attract attention; at other times so great as to make the side appear flattened and distorted.

THE TAIL.

The tail, which may be looked upon as an appendage to the body, is a continuation of the croup, and constitutes an ornament to the horse, as well as an organ of great utility in freeing it from the attacks of insects. Formed by a number of small bones and of muscles, as well as fine adherent skin, it is covered throughout its whole extent, except at the root and the under surface, with long hairs. In well-formed horses, the tail should be strong at the root, arising high up from the croup, the direction of which it follows; when the latter is horizontal, the tail is carried gracefully, especially during movement; but when the croup is oblique, it is what is called "badly set on," droops, and looks ungraceful. With powerful, well-formed horses, it is often carried upwards, or even curved over the back. The health and strength of a horse are, according to popular notions, indicated by the resistance which the tail offers to manual interference, or by the way in which it is carried.

To some extent, the tail affords an indication of the animal's disposition, by the manner in which it is carried. A fidgety horse usually has the tail, like the ears, always in motion; when about to kick, the tail is drawn downwards between the legs; when pleased or excited, or alarmed, it is raised; when the horse is fatigued or exhausted, it is drooping; and with some horses when galloping, it is swung about in a circular manner, or lashed from side to side. There can be no doubt, also, that, like the tail of birds, it assists in guiding the movements of the horse; as when turning rapidly round a corner or in a circle, it is carried to the inner side.

With well-bred horses the hair of the tail is fine and straight, and often grows to such a length, that it reaches the ground; coarse-bred horses may also have the hair long, but then it is usually very thick and coarse, and more or less curly; though fine curly hair may rarely be found in the tails of thorough-bred horses.

In some horses there is a tendency to shedding of the hair of the tail, which may ultimately leave it almost denuded; the horse is then said to be "rat-tailed," and a popular saying has it that a rat-tailed horse is never a bad horse. In other cases the hair falls off, leaving only a tuft at the end, like a brush; this is a "cow-tailed" or "mule-tailed" horse. The length of the dock—that is, the tail itself minus the hair—is from a foot to two feet in length, at the very longest; but a morbid taste at times appears to consider the natural dock too long to please the eye; the tail is, therefore, amputated to a variable extent, from an inch or two at the extremity, to within a few inches of the body. There can be no doubt that, in the great majority of cases, the painful operation of "docking"—as chopping off a piece of the tail is termed—is performed without any reasonable pretext, and simply to gratify a morbid taste. Nothing can be more disfiguring, or even hideous, than such a fashion when carried to such an extent as to leave a perfect horse with only a few inches of this most graceful and useful appendage, which was intended by nature not only as an adornment and defence to the animal, but also is a protection to most delicate and sensitive parts beneath.

Not only does this docking make the horse a ludicrous effigy, but it renders it for life a victim to the torments inflicted by flies and other insects. The importance of the tail in this respect has been so fully recognised by the British army authorities, that an order has been recently issued to the effect that no docked horses are to be purchased as troopers. At one time British cavalry horses were docked and "nicked" (the muscles on the under surface of the tail so divided that this could not be drawn downwards, but ever after carried rigidly upwards like a wooden stump), as well as having the ears cropped close to the head. History tells us of the disastrous effects of this mutilation, at least so far as the tail is concerned. For instance, Hartmann (*Traité des Haras*, p. 279) informs us that the English cavalry, during the last century, was several times almost rendered useless from the losses amongst the horses caused by the attacks of flies, from which they could not protect themselves; this happened in 1743 near Dettingen, and also at Fritzlar, Hochkirch, Wilhelmsthal. He also specially notes that in the Seven Years' War, which commenced in 1756, the flies caused such disorder amongst the horses of the English cavalry at Minden that the battle was nearly lost.

All lovers of horses should enter their protest against the continuance of this absurd and pernicious mutilation, which is rarely required in order to render the horse more useful, and then only in cases of disease or malformation; or it may be, in altogether exceptional instances, with a view to safety in harness. The latter, however, can only be extremely seldom, as in many countries—for example, the United States, Russia, and elsewhere, where harness horses are as largely employed as in the United Kingdom—docking is not practised.

"Nicking" the tail is equally objectionable, except in those cases in which it is badly carried, when division of the muscles may rectify malposition or deformity.

Of course, no objection can be raised to cutting the hair to any length which may be necessary, on the score of cleanliness or utility.

Diseases or blemishes of the tail are few. It is sometimes fractured or paralysed; in grey horses which have become light coloured, tumours (melanotic) are generally found on its under surface at the root. Not unfrequently, and especially soon after docking, the end of the tail is diseased and the bones carious, as the result of this operation, when amputation has to be again performed. There may be also wounds, especially from the crupper, which may be more or less serious.

THE CHEST.

The form and capacity of the chest is a very important point in conformation. It comprises the breast and sides. (*See* Plate, Longitudinal Section of the Horse.)

The *breast* is the portion of the chest which we see on looking at a horse in front, and its dimensions vary according to breed and quality. Its width depends upon the development of the muscles which cover it, and also upon the dimensions of the chest itself. It should be deep and elongated, moderately wide, and the muscles on each side large and prominent. This is the usual appearance of the breast

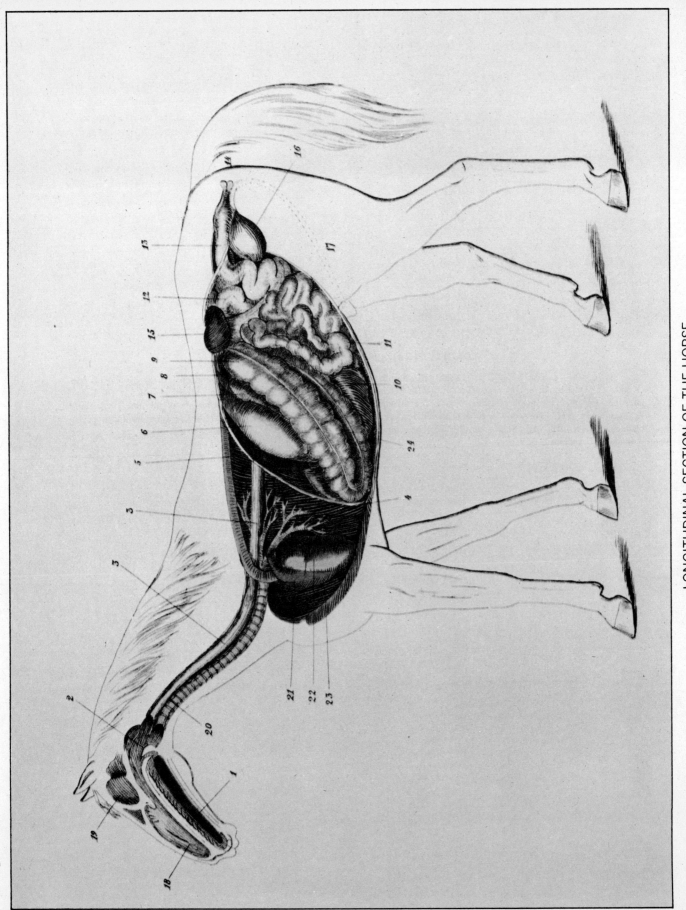

LONGITUDINAL SECTION OF THE HORSE.
(COMPLETE DESCRIPTIVE CAPTIONS ARE ON REVERSE OF PLATE.)

LONGITUDINAL SECTION OF THE HORSE.

1. Mouth.   2. Pharynx.   3, 3. Œsophagus, or gullet.   4. Diaphragm, or "midriff."   5. Spleen.   6. Stomach—left side or end.   7. Duodenum, or commencement of small intestine.   8. Upper part of liver.   9. Large intestine—colon.   10. Large intestine—cæcum.   11. Small intestine.   12. Large intestine—floating or free colon.   13. Termination of intestine, or rectum.   14. Anus.   15. Left kidney and its tube, or ureter, leading to the bladder.   16. Bladder.   17. Urethra, or canal leading from the bladder.   18. Nostril.   19. Brain.   20. Trachea, or windpipe.   21. Heart—left side.   22. Heart—right side.   23. Chest, or thorax.   24. Abdomen, or belly.

in well-formed horses, designed for speed and endurance. When wider than it is deep, it has the inconvenience of causing a rolling action in progression, and is not adapted for speed. In draught horses, and in those intended for slow and heavy work, an unusually wide chest is not objectionable, provided the muscles are large and well defined; indeed, this may be considered a good feature in the conformation of such animals. A narrow chest, however, is always objectionable, as it indicates insufficient space for the lungs, and usually weak muscles, while the fore-limbs are too near each other. Animals with such a chest, though they may perform a moderate amount of work satisfactorily, yet do not possess endurance or sustained vigour.

The sides of the chest are formed by the ribs, and it is the size, position, and direction of these which limit its capacity. At the front part, on each side, the chest is covered by the shoulder-blades, and here it is narrowest; but behind these it widens out, and attains its greatest dimensions some distance from them. A wide and deep chest indicates capacious lungs and well-developed heart, and, therefore, powerful respiration and circulation, as well as greater surface for the attachment of muscles concerned in breathing and locomotion. The depth of the chest depends upon the length of the ribs, and not upon the height of the spines of the vertebræ, which forms the withers; so that in estimating the depth this fact should be kept in view. Its width is the consequence of the curvature which the ribs form in passing from the spine downwards and forwards, to the breast bone Therefore, it is upon the ribs that the depth and width of the chest depend, while it is to the distance between the ribs, individually, that the length of the chest must also be ascribed. This length is measured from the point of the shoulder to the middle part of the last rib. The distances between the ribs, called the intercostal spaces, is therefore a point of some importance in the conformation of the chest; as when the spaces are large the chest is all the greater in length, and, taken in conjunction with a good curvature, is an index of good breathing or staying power; wide intercostal spaces are always filled up by wide and strong muscles, which pull the ribs forward, and therefore produce deep inspiration. The ribs, therefore, behind the shoulder, and proceeding backwards, should be well arched, long, project well backwards, and be placed well apart. Short, flat ribs close together, and only slightly projecting backwards, are a defect, and a horse with such a conformation must be defective in wind. Ribs well curved and projecting backwards are a sign of strength, and the nearer the last rib is to the haunch, so the better the horse is said to be "ribbed-up." As has been remarked, a chest too wide or circular, especially in front, is disadvantageous, because it produces a rolling or swaying motion when the animal is moving; but a deep chest has not this disadvantage. A horse with a deep and moderately wide chest always carries the saddle well; but if circular and shallow, the girths in many cases slip forward and chafe the skin behind the elbows, and the saddle itself has a tendency to get on the withers.

In examining the chest, it must be remembered that loss of condition occasioned by illness or idleness will diminish its dimensions, just as training or full work will increase it. Sometimes the sides of the chest exhibit traces of blistering, or the application of mustard poultices, in the treatment of inflammation. When such traces exist, the nature of the cough and the character of the breathing, as observed at the flank, should be noticed, in order to ascertain whether the organs within the chest are sound. The sides of the chest may also show one or more hard tumours or depressions in the situation of the ribs, due to fracture or displacement of these, and which may be co-existent with adhesion between the lung and the side. The lower part of the chest may show scars which have been caused by the girths, and if immediately behind the elbows, are often an indication that the saddle is badly carried.

THE BELLY.

The belly is another important feature in the conformation of the horse, as by its volume and its weight it influences progression, and in other ways affords indications of health or disease. (*See* Plate.) Its volume varies with different breeds, as well as before and after feeding, in the mare during pregnancy, and in other circumstances. In healthy, well-thriving animals it should be moderately developed, as its size corresponds with the volume of the digestive organs, and the development of these is generally related to their functional activity, particularly when the food is of good quality. A horse with a narrow belly—"tucked-up," as it is usually designated—is either insufficiently fed and nourished, or has the digestive organs imperfectly developed, and is therefore a bad thriver. Nevertheless, we often find horses undergoing severe work, and receiving very nutritious food in small bulk, with the belly very much retracted—drawn up as that of a greyhound is—and which, under ordinary circumstances, would have this part much more voluminous.

A large belly indicates a gross feeder, and is often seen in common-bred horses, which usually consume a large quantity of bulky food containing little nutriment. In young horses the belly is also usually large.

The shape of the belly is intimately allied to its volume; it should be cylindrical in well-fed well-formed animals, and its outline should continue that of the chest, passing gradually into the circle formed by the ribs and the flanks; while, inferiorly, it should form a gentle convex curve from the breast-bone to the region of the stifle. When this curve does not exist, but, instead, an almost straight line from the sternum up to the flank, it is a defect, not only to the eye, but to the animal itself; for such horses are usually bad doers, are easily fatigued, and, after severe exertion, refuse their food, or feed badly—their digestive apparatus being imperfectly developed. If, on the contrary, the curved line is too convex, falling suddenly downwards from the sternum, and rising as suddenly from the flank—"pot," or "cow-bellied"—it testifies that the animal is a gross feeder, soft, slow-paced, short-winded, and, if used for saddle, likely to carry this on the withers.

"The belly is mainly supported by the back ribs. Horses which are short in the chest, or long and loose-loined, and, at the same time, great feeders, often distend their bellies, so that they 'hang down.' Such animals are unpleasant to ride, because the saddle has a tendency to work forward on the shoulder. The same unpleasant result is produced when the sides of the chest are narrow, and the ribs just behind the saddle are unduly circular.

"There is also an opposite evil. If, from want of proper length and due convexity of the middle ribs, the circumferent measurement decreases from the fore-hand to the rear, the girths (and, with them, the saddle) will slip back; and, in the stable, the same result will happen with the roller and the clothes."

The *sheath* does not require much notice. It is well developed in entire horses, and in geldings a fair development is generally considered as an indication of robustness, and a very small sheath a sign of weakness. When the sheath is large and pendulous, owing sometimes to weakness of its suspensory ligaments, or other cause, the horse, in moving at a fast pace (as in trotting), makes an unpleasant gurgling kind of noise, which seems to be produced by the intestines, but which is, in reality, caused by the air passing into and from the sheath. This noise generally subsides after the horse has been moving for some time; but it can always be stopped by introducing a piece of sponge into the sheath for a short distance, and withdrawing it again when the horse returns to the stable

THE LIMBS.

The limbs, four in number, and divided into fore and hind, or anterior and posterior, support and move the body. The fore-limbs are closer together than the hind ones; they chiefly serve to sustain the weight, or the front part, of the body, while the posterior limbs not only sustain the weight of the hinder part of the body, but are the chief instruments in propelling it. In order to accomplish their different functions perfectly, they are not attached to the body in the same manner; for while the fore-legs are attached simply by means of powerful muscles and tendinous structures (so as to suspend the trunk between them in the manner of a C-spring, without any bony intervention), the hind-legs are attached solidly to the pelvis by means of the hip-joints, which gives them their great power in pushing the body forward. In addition to this, the fore and the hind limbs differ from each other, inasmuch as, in the former, the articular or joint angles are more open—one, indeed, being entirely dispensed with; while, in the latter, the angles are more acute and numerous, and the muscles which close or straighten these are larger and greater in number. It is to be noted, also, that in both fore and hind limbs their individual bulk and weight is at their upper extremity; the large bones, surrounded by powerful muscles, being there. At the lower extremity we find nothing but light bones, with tendons and ligaments, this arrangement being the most favourable for strength and speed.

Fore-Limbs.

The fore-limb consists of shoulder, arm, fore-arm, elbow, knee, cannon or shank, fetlock, pastern, and foot.

The *Shoulder*, in reality, is formed by the shoulder-blade, though it is very often made to include the arm as well, the two portions apparently being one. This is a very important point in the conformation of the horse, and is one to which the attention of all horsemen is usually directed, especially when speed and action are concerned. Situated on the side of the chest, at its anterior part, covering the ribs there, and a portion of the withers, the shoulder-blade is directed more or less obliquely downwards and forwards, to meet the arm-bone (humerus), with which it forms the shoulder-joint; though their conjunction does not constitute what is called the point of the shoulder, this really being the prominence formed by the head of the arm-bone. At its upper part, where it is expanded (the bone itself being triangular in shape), the shoulder-blade is surmounted by an elastic cartilage, the convex margin of which lies against the withers. In the shoulder commences the movement of the limb which is about to be raised from the ground; and this takes place by a swinging kind of motion, the lower end of the shoulder-blade being raised and advanced, while the upper end is carried backwards and downwards, the extent of the movement depending upon the length of the muscles which produce it, as well as that of the bone itself. When the limb is properly formed this movement should be extensive and free.

The first condition, therefore, is the length of the shoulder; the second, its direction; the third, the muscles which move it. The longer the shoulder, so the more extensive will be the movement of the entire limb, and especially if the former is oblique; in fact, a long shoulder-blade is nearly, if not always, an oblique one. In horses designed for speed, this obliquity is most marked, whether considered with regard to the horizon or with that of the arm-bone, with which it should form an acute angle. Any other direction of the shoulder is unfavourable for speed, though perhaps not for the exercise of strength. For race-horses, hunters, and saddle-horses, long sloping shoulders are very essential; as not only do they insure speed, and good easy action, but they also guarantee safety, whether the horse is ridden on the flat or across country. Though desirable in harness or heavy draught horses, they are not so essential. Nevertheless, a long shoulder is necessary in these (though its obliquity is not of so much moment), as it is important that the collar should have as wide bearing as possible, and this it can only obtain with a long shoulder.

A short and upright shoulder is defective for any kind of work, but more especially for speed or pleasant riding, and an animal so formed will soon fail in its fore-limbs when put to hard labour. More especially is this the case if the shoulder is not well placed on the side of the chest; if too forward, it exaggerates the evil. The muscular development of the shoulder is an important factor in its beauty and movement. The muscles should not only be well formed and prominent, but they should also be dense and clean. Excess in volume, constituting a thick, heavy shoulder, is better adapted for draught than riding purposes. Clean or dry shoulders are seen in the thoroughbred race-horse, or well-bred hunter; thick, massive, or heavy shoulders in the cart or dray horse; in the former, the upper part is fine and firm, the bulk of the muscles attaining its maximum at their junction with the arm. Loss of condition, as well as disease, will produce wasting of the shoulder muscles; while, with regard to direction, it has been observed that grazing and feeding on the ground has a tendency to make even sloping shoulders upright in the course of time.

In examining the shoulders, we look for injuries caused by the collar, and to wasting of the muscles produced by sprains.

The *Arm* is formed by the large bone, named the humerus, which forms a joint with the shoulder-blade at the point of the shoulder, and, proceeding backwards and downwards, makes another joint with the bones of the fore-arm and elbow, its direction placing it at an angle with the scapula. Like the latter, this bone should be as long as possible, in order to give attachment to the important muscles which move it and the shoulder, as well as the fore-arm. This length, however, should be in proportion to that of the shoulder, as, if too long, the horse is inclined to stumble, and go close to the ground. It has been remarked that, in the *bas-reliefs* of the Parthenon, all the horses have the arm-bone too long, the length of this in a well-formed horse—measuring from the point of the shoulder to the centre of the elbow-joint, or a trifle beyond—being about a moiety of that of the head. A short arm is even more objectionable than one too long, inasmuch as it affords less attachment for the muscles which move the fore-arm, which is then unduly elevated, without being suffi-ciently extended, producing that kind of action called "plodding," "hammering," or "pottering," in which the movement is altogether in excess of the pace.

The direction of the arm is an important consideration. For speed it should incline backwards and downwards, at an angle of from 50° to 55°; though it may be less, provided the scapula has a good slope. In harness or draught horses the angle may be from 45° to 60°. For speed, the slope of the shoulder-blade downwards and forwards, and that of the arm-bone backwards and downwards, should be in due proportion. It is very important that the direction of the humerus should be favourable, with regard to its being inclined outwards or inwards. In this respect its greater axis should be nearly parallel to the middle line of the body. If its lower end projects too much outwards, the whole limb will be twisted in the same direction, and the toe will be turned inwards; while if, on the contrary, it is directed inwards (the elbow turned in) the leg and toe will be twisted outwards.

The *Elbow*, situated behind the lower end of the arm-bone and the head of the fore-arm, constitutes the arm of a very powerful lever, which acts in keeping the limb straight and rigid while the horse is standing, and so assists in sustaining the weight of the body: while during progression its muscles tend to bring the limb into a straight position when it has been flexed. In order to fulfil its part well, the bone forming the elbow should be long and extend well backwards and upwards, and be parallel with the direction of the body. When it is short, the limb is generally weak, and there is a tendency to go over at the knees; when it is directed too much outwards, the toe is turned inwards; but if, on the contrary, it is turned inwards, the toe is then directed outwards—both of which directions are faulty, as they disturb the stability of the limb, and besides giving it a very unsightly appearance, predispose it to diseases and premature decay.

The elbow, of course, should be free from blemishes and swelling. Some horses have the bad habit of lying like a cow—that is, with the leg bent under the body, and the elbow resting on the heel of the foot; in this position, the end of the branch of the shoe immediately impinges on the point of the elbow, producing not only abrasions, but often a large swelling or tumour, which is not only very unsightly, but often requires an operation for its removal.

The *Fore-arm* extends from the arm to the knee, and is covered with muscles in front, outside, and behind, but not inside; its movements are those of flexion and extension, flexion being all the more extensive as the bone is long. The fore-arm should be long, thickly covered with muscles, and well placed. A short fore-arm implies a short stepper or galloper; while even if the arm is sufficiently long, unless the bone is large or wide laterally, in order to give good attachment to muscles, the limb will be weak. Therefore, not only should the bone be large, but its muscles should also be largely developed, especially those before and behind, towards its upper part; the muscles in front, more particularly, should stand out boldly and prominently, their tendons towards the knee being firm and clean. A thin fore-arm is a sign of weakness in other parts of the body, as well as in the limb.

In addition to its length and its strength as points of beauty, it is necessary that the fore-arm should be perfectly vertical, whether it is looked at in profile or in front; any deviation forwards or backwards being more or less a serious defect in proportion as it is exaggerated.

Inside the fore-arm is a horny mass, commonly called the "chestnut," which is very rarely absent, and which varies in size according to breed, being usually very small in well-bred horses, and very large in the commoner sorts.

The *Knee* is a very important portion of the fore-limb, situated between the fore-arm and the shank, or cannon-bone, and the two splint-bones; it is formed of these bones and two rows of smaller bones, which, between each other, constitute a number of joints, as they all move upon and against each other. Looked at in front, the knee is slightly convex from side to side, and in well-bred horses with fine thin skin, the outlines of the bones are more or less visible. In depth the knee is slightly less than its width, while it is wider at the upper than the lower part. Viewed sideways, while in front the outline is nearly straight, behind it is very angular, owing to the presence of a bone that projects considerably backwards—the trapezium.

A well-formed knee should be deep, wide, and clean, as well as straight, with the bony prominences well marked and covered by a fine skin. Its width in front, as well as its thickness, is very important, as it indicates that the bones are well developed, and have large articular surfaces; its breadth, also, from before to behind, with regard to the trapezium, is of as much importance, as it insures powerful bending of the knee, and a solid support for the whole limb. The depth of the knee is also a matter of moment, for the same reason, though perhaps it is not so necessary as the breadth.

The direction of the knee is as important as that of the fore-arm, with regard to its being vertical, in order to insure solidity; when it deviates from a vertical direction it is defective. The most common deviation is that forward—"over at the knee," as it is commonly called; this may be so slight as to be scarcely noticeable, or it may be so great as to become positively painful to witness. It may be congenital, when it is usually slight; but it is most frequently induced by overwork, and especially in horses which have been made to labour severely when too young. When it is congenital, even though the deviation forward may be somewhat great, it is less objectionable than when brought about by overwork; inasmuch as in the former the muscles, tendons, and ligaments may be in their normal condition and perfectly capable of performing their function—indeed, in some of these cases, the limbs are particularly strong and safe; while in the latter these are weak, contracted, or rigid, can only perform their duty imperfectly, and the horse is consequently unsafe. In the last case, the knee is usually shaky when the horse is standing at rest, and the knee projecting forward.

When the knee is inclined backwards, it constitutes what is known as "buck-kneed," and is undoubtedly a defect. The knee, instead of being straight in front, is more or less concave, while behind it is more prominent and angular than in a well-formed knee. It is not such a serious defect, perhaps, as the knee inclined forwards; its chief drawback, in addition to its unsightliness, is the severe strain imposed upon the ligaments at the back and sides of the knee, which in time injures them. When a horse has the knees deviated inwards (looked at in front), it is known as "calf-kneed," and bears some resemblance to what is known as "knock-knees" in man. This is defective, not only from unequal strain or bearing thrown upon certain bones and ligaments while the horse is standing at rest, but it causes the lower part of the limb to be thrown outwards in an unsightly manner in trotting.

The other deviation is that in which the knees are bent outwards, and the horse is "bowlegged." This is a very serious defect, the knees being wide apart, and the feet rather close together, so that the strain is thrown upon the outside ligaments of the joints, as well as unequally on the bones; while, from the toes being turned inwards, the fetlock and pastern-joints, as well as the feet, have the weight unfairly disposed upon them; consequently, these are soon fatigued, damaged, and prematurely worn out.

The distance of the knee from the ground is an important point in conformation, and depends on the length of the fore-arm above the knee, and the shank or cannon-bone below it. A knee well let down is that which is most to be sought for in speed and strength, and is due to the greater length of the fore-arm over that of the shank—this greater length, of course, being associated with proportionate development of the muscles of the fore-arm.

The chief blemish to be looked for in the region of the knee is that due to wounds or contusions in front, commonly known as "broken-knee," which, when present, so seriously detract from the value of a horse, as it only too often indicates faulty action or instability of the limb, and consequent stumbling or falling on the knees. "Broken-knees" are marked by the presence of a scar more or less apparent, and which may not be accompanied by any injury to the tendons, ligaments, and bones beneath, or which may, on the contrary, be so serious as to materially interfere with movement. In slight cases the hair on the outer surface of the skin may only be shaved off, producing perhaps change in the colour of the hair, which becomes white; in other cases the injury is so great that there is a large cicatrix with more or less thickening, on which the hair cannot be regenerated; while usually the hairs above and below project more or less, and render the blemish more marked. In very slight cases, when there is any doubt as to whether the knee is really broken, lifting the limb forward, bending the joint, and slightly damping the hair, will show whether it has been damaged.

The *Shank* or *Cannon* is constituted by three bones—the shank-bone, or large metacarpal bone, and the two splint or small metacarpal bones, one on each side, inner and outer; it extends from the knee to the fetlock. In front there are several tendons which go to the pastern and the foot-bone, and behind are also powerful tendons which pass to the same destinations; and, in addition, two strong ligaments, one of which, the *suspensory*, extends from the knee to the fetlock, sending branches to the bones below; and a much shorter ligament, known as the *check* ligament, which arises slightly above the suspensory ligament, and joins the deep flexor tendon of the foot, known as the back tendon.

There are no muscles worth mentioning below the knee, but only bones, tendons, and ligaments. Above, the cannon is in contact with the three lower bones of the knee, forming part of the knee-joint; the small metacarpal or splint-bones, however, do not extend to the end of the shank-bone, which alone forms a very movable joint by its union with the large pastern-bone, with the addition of the two sesamoid bones, behind at the fetlock.

The importance of the cannon-bone in movement, and in insuring stability, as well as in propulsion, is of considerable moment. Its direction should be vertical, and in proportion to the parts above it should be short and thick, its large diameter being an indication of strength and beauty; while the tendons and ligaments behind should be well separated from it, and be large and distinct. Any deviation from the vertical direction of the cannon, either forwards or backwards, outwards or inwards, is a defect more or less grave. The size of the shank is considered from before to behind, and depends upon the thickness of the bone, as well as the degree of detachment of the flexor tendons and suspensory ligament from it; the detachment of the flexor tendons again chiefly depends upon the breadth of the knee, laterally, this again depending upon the development of the trapezium, and, below, on the size and situation of the sesamoid bones behind the fetlock. So it happens that, in proportion to the development of these, we have the projection of the tendons backwards; when badly developed, the horse is said to be "tied in" below the knee. A certain amount of breadth of the shank in front is also necessary, this breadth being greater in the fore than in the hind limbs, a narrow shank being a sign of weakness; in fact, the shank should be developed in proportion to the weight of the body; when it is narrow, the knee is also narrow, the pastern bones thin and light, and the tendons slender, while the sesamoid bones at the fetlock are small and ill-formed. A light and long shank is a very serious defect. In well-bred horses the skin covering the shank is fine and soft, and lies closely to the bones and tendons, showing these and the ligaments distinct and prominent. With coarse-bred horses, on the contrary, the skin is thick and hairy, especially at the back part, where the hairs are bristly and of considerable length, even as high as the knee, completely concealing the bones and tendons, and giving this part of the leg a round appearance; at the same time, the tendons feel soft and flaccid—a condition which is not present in the well-bred horse, in which the firmness and density of the tendons is a marked characteristic. In the heavy cart-horse, thickness of skin and abundance of hair is not so objectionable as in light horses; nevertheless, fine silky hair, even though long, is an evidence of quality.

The diseases or blemishes to be looked for in the region of the shank are somewhat important. In the first place, there is the bony deposit or tumour known as "splint," which may be situated between the cannon and splint bones, either to the outside or to the inside of the leg, close to the knee or some distance from it, and the serious character of which will depend upon its proximity to the knee, or upon its interference with tendons or ligaments. Secondly, marks, contusions, or swellings, produced by striking the inside of the leg, from the knee to the fetlock, with the opposite foot— known as "cutting," or "striking." This injury is most frequently inflicted on the inside of the fetlock; less frequently, perhaps, on the inner and lower part of the knee, when it occurs in horses with high action, which usually turn their toes out, and is known as "speedy-cut." Thirdly, sprains of the tendons or of the ligaments, recognised by thickening of these, sometimes tenderness on manipulation, and more rarely shortening; this condition is most readily discovered by passing the fingers down these parts, though when the most posterior tendon is sprained it forms a projection or convexity behind the leg, which is easily perceptible. Fourthly, there are the puffy swellings, due to distension of the sheaths through which the tendons play, with the lubricating fluid which is secreted there, and vulgarly termed "wind-galls." These swellings may exist behind and near the knee, or towards the fetlock, and are an indication of injury to the tendons or their sheaths, of disease (such as rheumatism), or of severe exertion. In examining a horse as to soundness, all these things have to be looked for, and, in addition, traces of the firing-iron, or the small scar on each side of the leg, a short distance above the fetlock, immediately in front of the flexor tendons, which shows that the operation of neurotomy, or "nerving" or "unnerving," has been performed.

The *Fetlock Joint* is that part of the limb immediately between the shank and the pastern which, behind, is covered by a tuft of hair (the "foot-lock"), and has a small, horny growth, known as the ergot. In addition to the shank-bone and the large pastern-bone, there are two bones behind, one on each side, called the sesamoid bones, into which the suspensory ligament is fixed, and which are firmly bound down to the cannon and pastern bones by other ligaments, which greatly strengthen this important part of the limb. Behind these two bones, the flexor tendons play in a shallow groove, and this arrangement enables the bones to play the part of a pulley during the movement of the tendons over them.

In front of the fetlock joint, the extensor tendons of the pastern and foot also pass. This joint should be large, straight, and clean; its width, from before to behind, should be considerable, as the larger the sesamoid bones are, the greater advantage the flexor tendons will have in bending the pastern and foot, while there will be greater surface for the insertion of ligaments, and thus more strength conferred. The wider, therefore, the fetlock joint is, looked at in profile, the stronger the part will be; while, viewed in front, it should also possess a certain breadth. A small, round pastern is a defective one. The insertions of the suspensory ligament into the sesamoid bones on each side should be clearly defined, and the interspaces between this ligament, the shank, and the flexor tendons should be wide and well-marked.

The fetlock joint should be free from puffiness, scars, or thickening: in well-bred horses, it is

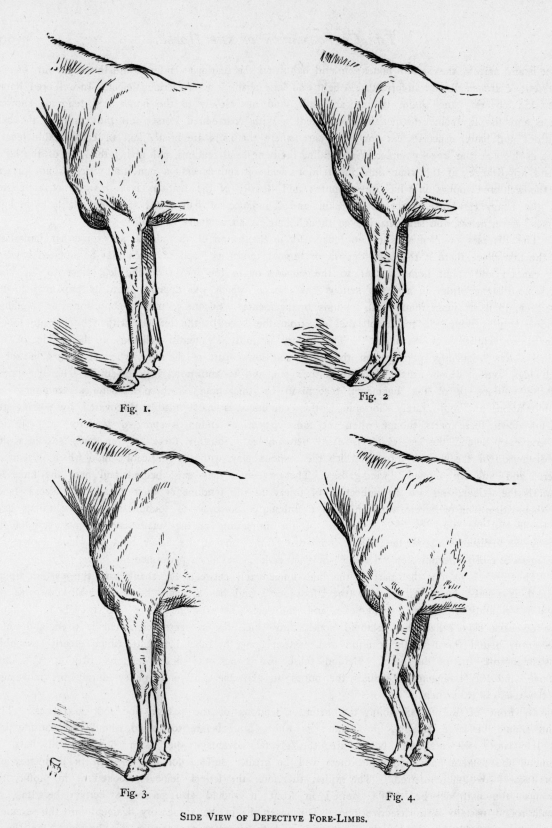

SIDE VIEW OF DEFECTIVE FORE-LIMBS.

Fig. 1. Shows a straight shoulder with a heavy chest, and legs too much under the body. Fig. 2. Similar shoulders, with weak legs, and long light pasterns. Fig. 3. Better-placed shoulder, but legs too much under the body, and pasterns too short and upright. Fig. 4. Limbs over at the knees to excess.

covered by fine skin, and the fetlock is scanty, and the hair silky, while the ergot, or horny excrescence, is small and rudimentary.   In coarse-bred horses, the skin is thick and pasty, the fetlock hairs long and coarse, and the ergot large and long.

The *Pastern* is situated between the fetlock joint and the coronet, or upper margin of the hoof; it is formed by two bones (large and small pastern-bones, or *os suffraginis* and *os coronæ*), and is, in reality, the most slender part of the limb.   The first pastern-bone is the longest and most slender, while the small pastern-bone is short and thick.   The pastern is not vertical, like the shank, but is more or less obliquely directed forward.   In front it is rounded, and behind, where it forms the hollow of the pastern, flat; certain prominences can be felt at the sides, which give insertion to the lateral ligaments.   When well formed, it is broad, thick, of a moderate length, of a certain obliquity, clean, and free from bony deposit. The breadth and thickness give an indication not only of the increased surface for ligaments and tendons, but also for space for joints.   The length of the pastern is important: when too long, it is often a sign of weakness, unless the bones, ligaments, and tendons compensate for this in their development; while, on the contrary, if they are too short, they diminish the elasticity of the limb, and lead to jar and premature wearing-out.   So that a pastern too long, or too short, must be considered defective conformation.

With regard to direction, or obliquity, this is usually related to the length of the pastern: if too long, it often approaches a horizontal direction; if too short, always a vertical position.

The horizontal obliquity is often set down at from 40° to 45°, but it will be found that this is not correct in a well-formed limb, which will show a slope of about 60°.   In very well-bred horses of light conformation, 45° will be sometimes noted; but in these the pasterns are long, and the tendons and ligaments should be proportionately strong.   Long and oblique pasterns possess the advantage of rendering

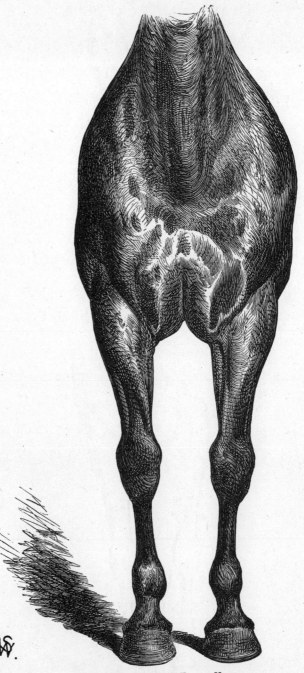

CHEST AND FORE-LIMBS: FRONT VIEW.
A well-formed harness horse.

the horse's paces more elastic and agreeable for the saddle, as well as being more graceful in appearance; while they diminish concussion during rapid movement, though they impose more strain on the tendons and ligaments.   Short and upright pasterns do not possess the latter disadvantage, and are stronger;

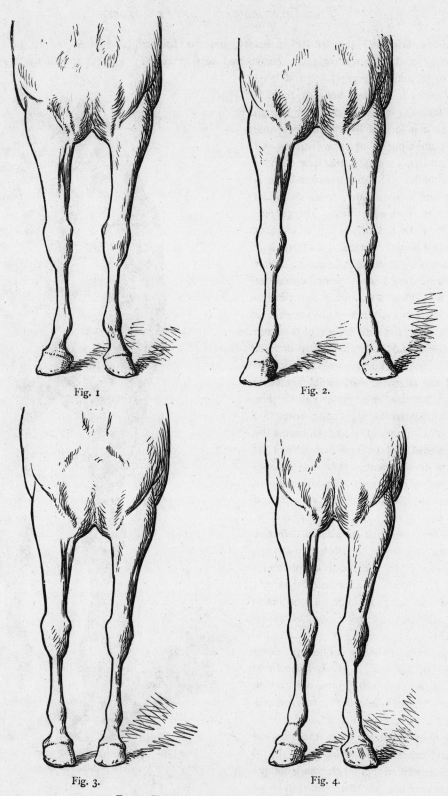

FRONT VIEW OF DEFECTIVE FORE-LIMBS.

Fig. 1. Legs too wide apart from the knees, and toes turned outwards. Fig. 2. Legs too wide apart from the chest, and toes directed outwards. Fig. 3. Legs too close from the knees downwards, and toes twisted inwards. Fig. 4. Very defective weak limbs, with calf-knees.

but they expose the limbs to shock or concussion during movement, predispose to disease of the bones and cartilages, and are very unpleasant in riding horses, though for draught horses they are not so objectionable.

With regard to blemishes or diseases, it may be observed that the pasterns become upright from severe exertion, the fetlock joint in extreme cases knuckling forward, this producing not only deformity, but unsafe instability. The most serious defect or disease is the presence of bony tumours or deposits on the pastern-bones, especially the smaller and commonly known as "ringbones." These are most frequently found in short upright pasterns, and are generally due to inflammation produced by concussion. Sometimes there are scars more or less great in the hollow of the pastern, due to ulceration of the skin, or "cracked heels," and a small cicatrix is found on each side of the pastern immediately over the flexor tendons, showing that the operation of neurotomy (lower operation) has been performed.

The *Coronet* is the name given to the prominence around the upper margin of the hoof, and extending to the heels of the frog. It is formed partly by the lower part of the small pastern-bone and the extensor tendon in front, at each side by the upper part of the lateral cartilages, which spring from the wings of the coffin or pedal bone, and behind by the deep flexor tendon, and a portion of the plantar cushion in addition—what is called the coronary cushion—an elastic body fitting into a recess on the inner side of the upper part of the hoof, completes the composition of the coronet. It is covered by somewhat long hairs, which fall over the front of the hoof. These hairs are fine and short in well-bred animals, coarse and long in the under-bred, and are generally removed in the process of trimming or clipping.

The beauty of the coronet consists in its development and its cleanness; its largeness indicating a well-formed coronary cushion and cartilages, to prevent jar and promote elasticity, as well as a large joint between the small pastern and pedal bone. In examining this part ossification of the lateral cartilages ("side-bones"), shown by loss of elasticity on pressure, is the most important defect to be looked for. Wounds and contusions may also be present, as well as the troublesome fistulous abscess known as "quittor."

The *Hoof* terminates the limb, and is the part that comes in contact with the ground while supporting weight. It is a horny box containing a portion of the small pastern-bone, the coffin or pedal bone, and the small bone behind these, over which the flexor tendon of the foot plays, known as the navicular bone—a sketch of the anatomy and structure of which will be given in the chapter on shoeing. In the meantime, we may remark that perhaps no part of the fore-limb is more deserving of study than this portion, commonly designated the foot; indeed, the importance of a sound foot has been insisted upon in the remark made by an old writer, Jeremiah Bridges, in his work on the horse's foot, "No foot, no horse."

The hoof consists of wall, sole, frog, bars, and commissures, three in number, which separate the bars from the frog, and divide the frog itself to some extent into two portions.

The size of the hoof varies to some extent in different breeds of horses, without being in any way defective. Well-bred horses, those reared in dry climates, as well as those living on rocky ground and in mountainous regions, have the hoofs smaller than those of common, coarse breed, or which are bred in low-lying or marshy countries. As a rule, the hoof ought to be in proportion to the height, weight, and conformation of the animal. A well-shaped fore-foot is nearly circular in shape on the ground surface, though sometimes it is a little longer than it is wide, but this is rare in the unshod fore-foot. Looked at in front, it appears to be narrower above than below, wider a little to the outside than the inside, and the same height on both sides.

In profile, from the coronet to the ground in front, the slope varies from 48° to 52°, the height of this part being twice that of the heel, while the coronet inclines in a straight line from the front to the heels. Seen from behind, the heels are wide and of the same height, the inner being slightly more vertical than the outer. When raised from the ground backwards, the sole is seen to be slightly concave and thick, the frog large towards the heels, hard and sound in the cleft, and giving evidence of contact with the ground ; the bars are somewhat prominent, and the commissures well spaced and clean.

With regard to colour, this varies ; but undoubtedly the best hoofs are the black or slightly grey. The front of the wall should be smooth and shining, showing its fibrous structure ; while the hairs of the coronet should cover its upper margin, and, like a thatch, protect this part against dryness and undue humidity.

A hoof too large, even though well formed, constitutes a notable defect, and generally belongs to under-bred, coarse horses ; it is most objectionable in fast-paced horses, and least in heavy draught horses. In addition to its own weight, it requires a large shoe, and this renders the action heavy and clumsy, while concussion on hard ground is severe, and there is also a tendency to strike the opposite limbs, or tread on the opposite feet ; on soft or heavy ground it is also more difficult to withdraw it.

A too small hoof, on the contrary, does not afford sufficient support, and the horn is frequently thin, dry, and brittle ; while there is a tendency to disappearance of the frog, and tenderness after long journeys.

A narrow hoof is one in which the length exceeds the width, and the toe is usually long, throwing increased strain upon the pastern and tendons. The term is usually synonymous with contracted foot.

Front hoofs of unequal size are to be looked upon with suspicion, the smaller of the two, unless its diminution is due to loss of horn through travelling without a shoe, being generally the seat of disease.

A flat hoof is one in which the sole, instead of being more or less concave, is quite flat, with low heels ; the horn is usually thin and soft, and the sole, heels, and frog liable to be bruised ; an exaggeration of this is found in the convex sole, which extends below the level of the wall, and is known as pumiced foot. It is usually due to chronic inflammation of the foot (laminitis). This is always a very serious condition.

A hoof with the heels too high, sometimes termed "buck-hoof," is also a defective shape, inasmuch as the pastern is upright also, and the frog is generally small and removed from the ground. It may be remarked, however, that the heels may be allowed to grow too high through the neglect of, or from bad shoeing, and can be remedied by lowering the heels.

Heels too low are sometimes congenital, but are perhaps more frequently rendered so by improper management of the hoof. The toe of the hoof is generally too long, and the pastern too oblique, and the weight of the body being thrown mainly on the heels, these are liable to be bruised.

We have also the hoof with the toe turned inwards, due, as already noticed, in most cases to a deviation in the limb. At times, however, it may be owing to twisting outwards of the foot itself. There is a tendency to strike the opposite limb, and the inside heel is liable to be bruised from its being brought more under the centre of gravity, while the horse's action is ungraceful as well as unsightly.

A hoof turned in at the toe is equally defective as the last, and the outside heel is the one most likely to be bruised.

A hoof higher at one side than the other is defective, inasmuch as the lower side bears more weight and strain than the higher, and that part of the foot suffers accordingly, as well as the limb above.

The other defects of the hoof, which are really diseases, or are due to these, are somewhat numerous. Contraction, manifested particularly towards the heels, is in the majority of cases caused by disease in the back part of the foot ; when this is so the frog is usually greatly diminished in size, unsound, and the sole unusually concave. In rare cases only one heel is contracted, and that generally the inner one. Suppuration of the frog, commonly termed "thrush," is due to an inflammatory condition of this part, in which we have a fetid discharge from the cleft, which is ragged and irregular, and very deep. Fissures in the hoof, known as "sand-cracks," are found in the wall situated in front of the hoof, or to one side—in the hind-foot usually in front, and in the fore-foot generally on the inside quarter, rarely on the outside. These fissures may extend from the coronet to the ground, and to the sensitive parts within, when they are termed "complete;" or they may neither be so deep nor so long, when they are "incomplete." In examining the hoof, it is well to remember that such cracks are often concealed by the dishonest vendor, who fills them up with gutta-percha, pitch, or any other likely material. What are wrongly designated "corns," but which are really bruises of the vascular parts of the foot, are found in that part of the sole which is enclosed by the angle formed between the wall and its inflexion, the bar. This contusion or bruise is most frequently observed in hoofs with low, weak heels, as well as in narrow, contracted feet; though it may also be produced in well-formed hoofs by bad or neglected shoeing. The injury is rendered evident by the presence of blood-stained horn at the part indicated; the staining may appear very trifling, and in the form of small points, the mass of the horn itself being rather yellow; or the horn may be deeply saturated with, and softened by, the blood and serum thrown out from the bruised membrane beneath. The first may be removed entirely by paring, though the latter cannot be eradicated in this way, but, on the contrary, becomes more and more evident the greater the amount of horn removed. A suppurating corn is a bruise which has run on to suppuration from the injury, the consequent inflammation being greater.

Any part of the sole may be bruised like the heel, and present the same appearances; it is usually designated bruised sole, and may be produced by treading on a sharp stone, or other hard and angular body, or from stones or hard mud getting between the ordinary shoe and the sole.

Inflammation of the foot, technically known as laminitis, gives rise, after a time, to deformity of the hoof, and especially if the inflammation assumes a chronic form. It most frequently attacks the fore-feet, and causes the horse to place more weight upon the heels than usual during progression. The heels are higher and wider than usual; the toe is long, and projects forwards and upwards, making the hoof appear as if it had fallen in towards the middle in front; and there are circles or rings of horn around the hoof, thick and narrow in the middle, shallow and wide towards the heels. The sole, instead of being concave, is more or less flat, or even convex, and there is a wide space between the wall and the margin of the sole at the toe, filled with a mass of imperfect horn, which is usually stained yellow, brown, or red, porous and soft, or dry, and easily broken into powder.

This is a serious condition of the foot, as it is beyond remedy, and the horse is always more or less lame.

What is commonly called "seedy toe" may be due to laminitis, but it is as frequently caused by contusions, and not unfrequently by driving the clip of the shoe too tight against the wall of the hoof. It consists in a separation of the wall from the sole and the parts within, the cavity often extending to near the coronet, and sometimes containing a brittle, powdery horn, to which it probably owes its name. This defect is not readily detected without removing the shoe, though, by tapping on the front of the wall with a hammer, the hollow sound produced is indicative of its presence.

"False quarter" is a defect in the hoof-wall towards the quarter, due to a defective secretion of horn caused by an injury to the coronet: it is shown by a deficiency—sometimes extensive—in the wall, in which there is not unfrequently a deep fissure from the top to the bottom.

HIND-LIMBS.

The hind-limbs, like the fore, support the weight of the body, but they have a far larger share than these in propelling it; and, for this reason, they are more solidly fixed to the trunk by means of the hip joint, the fore-limbs (as has been stated) being attached to the body by means of muscles. In the hind-limbs, we find similar parts to those in the fore ones, though some of them are differently disposed as to situation and direction: thus, the thigh is analogous to the arm, the stifle to the elbow, the leg to the fore-arm, and the hock to the knee.

The *Thigh*, properly speaking, is the part of the hind-limb extending from the hip joint to the stifle; it is composed of the largest round bone in the body (the femur), and a number of powerful muscles. The femur extends, in a diagonal manner, forward from the hip joint to the stifle, its direction being an important element in conformation; indeed, it has been said that this bone can scarcely be too oblique.

But, although great obliquity is favourable for speed, yet it must be remembered that, when it is exaggerated, it prevents the limb being carried sufficiently under the body in movement, though it is too much so when the horse is standing; while, when too vertical, it does not permit sufficient spring. The length of the thigh is important: for speed it should be long, "well let down," thick, when looked at from behind, and broad; the muscles inside the thigh should be particularly well-developed, and the thigh itself should stand well apart from its fellow on the opposite side.

The *Stifle*, which corresponds to the knee of man, is formed by the lower end of the femur, the head of the tibia, or leg-bone, and, in front, by the patella, or knee-cap. The stifle is about the same height as the elbow; it should be low, towards the belly, rather directed slightly outwards, so as not to interfere with the latter.

The *Leg*, or, as it is more commonly designated, the thigh, extends from the stifle to the hock; it is formed of two bones (tibia and fibula), with muscles behind, outside, and in front, but only the skin covering the bone inside. This part is somewhat conical or pyramidal in shape, being wide above, and tapering towards the hock; behind—passing in a straight line, downwards and backwards, to the point of the hock—is the large tendon named after Achilles, but which is, in reality, two tendons, twisted one over the other: the terminations of two muscles, the gastrocnemii. The length of this part (which ought to be designated the leg) should be equal to that of the fore-arm, and well clothed with muscles. A long, well-developed leg is always found in horses of speed. It should have a moderate degree of obliquity from the stifle backwards, this obliquity being, in a well-formed horse, from sixty-five to seventy degrees (horizontal), and that of the thigh above (inclined in the opposite direction) at an angle of about eighty degrees, while the shank below should be vertical. The muscles in front and to the side, should stand out boldly, while, behind, the tendinous cord passing to the point of the hock should be well clear of the leg.

There are not many defects or blemishes to be looked for in the thigh and the leg.

The patella has sometimes a tendency to slip off to the outside, giving rise to peculiar lameness—inability to bring the leg forward, and the toe being dragged on the ground. Rarely it happens that the attachment of one of the tendons at the point of the hock is ruptured, and the tendon slips off to the side. In some horses, there is sometimes a bony tumour as large as a pigeon's egg at the lower end of the tibia, inside the hock, due to injury. It may be found in both tibias. Rupture of the flexor tendon of the hock, in front, is sometimes noted, and causes symptoms not unlike those of fracture of the tibia.

The *Hock* is composed of six bones, disposed somewhat like the bones of the knee, in two rows. This is a very important but complex joint, the movements of which, though confined to simple flexion and extension, are of serious moment with regard to progression, it being one of the most energetic centres of propulsion in the hind-limb.

The hock should be wide, large, and clean, with the bones and tendons well defined and prominent. Its width or breadth, laterally or sideways, is a very important feature. The calcis or heel-bone, which forms the point of the hock, should be long, standing well back, while below, where the hock meets the shank, width is no less necessary; narrowness at either part is a grave defect. A small hock is a weak hock, and when narrow below it is doubly defective. The direction of the hock is to be noted; it should be parallel with the body; it is defective when the point is turned inwards (cow-hocked), and also when the point is turned outwards. When the point turns outwards, the toe of the foot is correspondingly turned inwards; when it is inclined inwards, then the toe is directed outwards, and there is a tendency to strike the opposite limb.

The *Shank*, passing from the hock downwards, should be vertical; when it inclines forwards, the hock is too much bent, and is then designated "sickle-hocked," the lower part of the limb being too much under the body. When the shank is directed obliquely backwards from the hock, the limb is placed in a false position, and is not only weakened thereby, but the weight of the body is thrown more on the fore-legs.

The diseases and blemishes of the hock are somewhat numerous, and several of them are serious. The most important of them all is formation of a bony tumour, called a "spavin," which appears on the inner face of the hock, a little to the front, and unites two or more of the bones of this joint. It is best seen when the observer stands at the horse's shoulder with his face directed towards the hock, the inner profile of which he can then readily perceive. For the purpose of detection, the same part of both hocks should be surveyed from the same point at each shoulder, so as to compare them one with the other. Sound hocks should be symmetrical in outline; even when both are spavined, the spavins are never exactly alike. The touch is also another important guide, though perhaps not so reliable as the eye. Mistakes have sometimes been made in examinations, by taking for a spavin what was really the distension of one of the capsules between the bones of the hock; but such mistakes should not occur if ordinary attention is paid, as the capsular distension is soft and elastic, while the spavin is hard and immovable. It is sometimes said that a horse has "coarse hocks" when the natural processes on the bones are largely developed; these should not be mistaken for spavin, and so far from being a defect they are the very opposite. Spavin sometimes causes lameness, often rather intense, depending upon its situation, and upon the manner in which the bones are involved.

"Curb" is a swelling at the back part of the hock, at its junction with the shank, and is best seen when the hock is looked at sideways; the back line of the hock, instead of being straight, is more or less convex. There is sometimes a bony enlargement at the head of the shank on the outside, between the splint and the cannon-bones, which is analogous to a splint in the fore-limb.

"Bog spavin" is a swelling in front of the hock, to the inner side, soft and elastic to the touch, and is due to distension of the capsule of the proper hock-joint. "Thorough-pin" is a soft swelling between the point of the hock and the leg-bone, and is due, in most cases, to strain, either of the hock-joint or of the tendons connected therewith. Sprain of the flexor tendon of the foot, as it passes over the inside of the hock close to the calcis, also gives rise to a swelling, which is readily perceived when the hock is looked at from behind. "Capped-hock" is a swelling at the point of the hock, caused by injury.

There is nothing very particular to remark with regard to the parts of the limb below the hock, as they do not differ very widely from those of the fore-limb. The horny excrescence named the "chesnut," is situated immediately below the hock, to the inner side of the limb. The shank-bone is narrower than in the fore-limb. The hoof, instead of being circular, is, on the contrary, oval, more sloping, sole more concave, and the heels wider and higher.

The direction of the limbs, *les aplombs*, as our French friends designate the position of these, is an essential point in conformation; as, however well they may be formed, if their direction is faulty it will more or less interfere with their durability, stability, or free movement.

In a well-formed horse, looking at the fore-limb sideways, a vertical line commencing in the middle, at the elbow-joint, should divide the knee, shank, and fetlock equally, and fall a little behind the heels. If the knees go forward beyond this line, the horse is "over at the knees;" if behind it, it is "buck-kneed." If the line falls too much behind the heels, the pasterns are too oblique and long; but if touching the heels, then the pasterns are too short and upright.

The fore-limbs, though straight, may be too forward, or too much under the body. Looked at in front, in a well-placed limb, a vertical line, commencing at the point of the shoulder, should pass through the middle of the knee, shank, pastern, and hoofs; while, with regard to the two limbs, it has been laid down that the space between the hoofs should be equal to the width of the hoof measured across the quarters. Through defective formation of the chest, the limbs may be too close together from their commencement—appear to be "coming out of one hole," as the saying is; while an excessive width of chest will throw them too far apart.

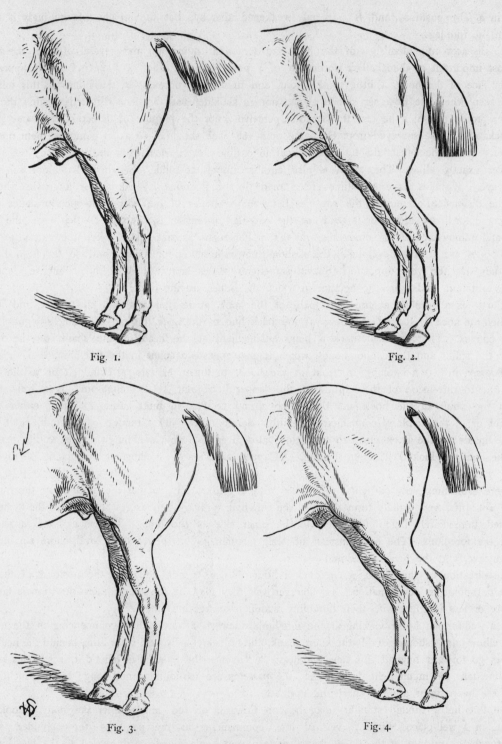

Fig. 1.

Fig. 2.

Fig. 3.

Fig. 4.

SIDE VIEW OF DEFECTIVE HIND-QUARTERS AND LIMBS.

Fig. 1. Quarter too short and round, and legs too straight and beyond the vertical.   Fig. 2. Quarter too long and drooping, and legs far behind the vertical line.   Fig. 3. Legs too much in front of the vertical line and beneath the body.   Fig. 4. A better quarter than Fig. 2, but the legs have the same defects.

With regard to the hind-limbs, looked at sideways, a vertical line from the hip-joint should pass through the middle of the leg at a point between the stifle and hock, and fall alongside the quarter of the hoof. If the limb is in front of this line, it is too much under the body; and if behind it, then the line falls in front

BACK VIEW OF HIND-QUARTERS AND LEGS.

This figure represents the hind-quarters and legs of a strong hunter or harness horse of good shape, though the legs are if anything rather close from the hocks downwards

of the hoof, and the leg is too far back. Long and oblique pasterns, and short upright ones, will alter the fall of this line. A good representation of well formed hind-quarters and legs for a powerful hunter or harness horse, as looked at sideways, will be found on page 197.

Looked at from behind, a well-shaped quarter and hind-leg should so appear that a vertical line will

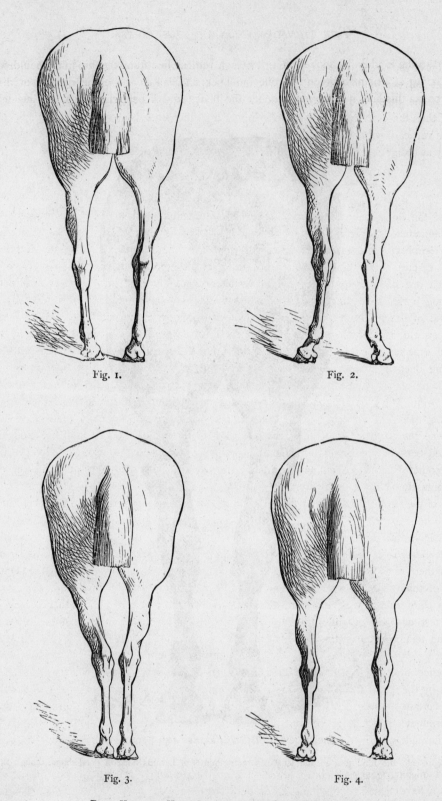

Fig. 1.   Fig. 2.

Fig. 3.   Fig. 4.

BACK VIEW OF HIND-QUARTERS AND LEGS (DEFECTIVE).

Fig. 1. Legs too wide apart, especially from the hocks, which are twisted outwards, and the toes turned in.   Fig. 2. The opposite condition, with the quarter and legs light, and the toes turned out.   Fig. 3. Legs too close together from the hocks downwards—"cow-hocked."   Fig. 4. Hind-legs too wide apart.

fall from the point of the hip, behind the point of the hock and shank, to the heels of the hoof, dividing these parts into equal halves; while between the two hind-hoofs there should be a space equal to the width of one hoof. If the limb, as a whole, passes outside this line, the horse is "too wide" behind; if only from the hocks, then these twist outwards; and if from the pastern, the horse is liable to "brush." If the limb passes inside the vertical line, and the hoofs are near each other, then the legs are too close together; if this commences only at the hocks, the horse is said to be "crooked," or "cow-hocked."

AGE.

The age of the horse may be determined, with more or less certainty, by certain signs which are manifested by the animal at different periods of its life. To the majority of experienced horsemen some of these signs are familiar, while some others require close observation and experience to detect them.

The most certain signs of age are to be noted in the teeth; but, nevertheless, there are other indications which are obvious to the eye or accessible to the touch. Thus, it does not require much experience among horses to distinguish old from very young animals; the outline of the body, the shape of the limbs and of the head, the character of the coat, forelock, mane, and tail, are sufficient for this purpose. In very old animals, there is a tendency in the hairs to become grey or white, in those with dark coats, and especially on the sides of the head, around the eyes, nostrils, etc. The hollows above the eyes become deeper, and the lower part of the head and the sides of the face are shrunken; the back and the loins often become more hollow; and the limbs show signs of wear, either in "standing over," or "knuckling over." One notable sign is to be found in the borders of the branches of the lower jaw becoming thinner, owing to the fangs of the teeth in that jaw rising up higher in their cavities. Another sign, known since the days of Aristotle, is the elasticity of the skin of the head. If the skin of the face or lips is pinched between the fingers and thumb, and pulled outwards, then suddenly let go, if it retracts quickly and becomes smooth without any wrinkles, the animal is young and in good health; but should it remain for some time ridged, it is old.

The bones of the tail have also been supposed to afford evidence of age. These bones, and especially those towards the root of the tail, have small prominent eminences, known as "processes," at their sides. Up to twelve or thirteen years of age, no important change takes place in these; but at thirteen years of age, there is felt at the root of the tail a small bony enlargement; at fourteen, it has increased; at fifteen years there is a hollow behind it, and another eminence is felt—each year subsequently adding to the growth of this, until at from seventeen to eighteen years it is fully developed, and at twenty-one years there is a third eminence of the same description. We do not know what reliance may be placed upon this tail test of age; and all the other signs mentioned are more or less uncertain, except those furnished by the teeth, which in the horse, of all the domesticated animals, affords the surest and most persistent guide.

Much practice and intelligent observation are needed to render a person expert in telling or in judging the age by the teeth, and even the most experienced are at times puzzled to give a definite opinion with regard to certain animals. Although in the horse dentition is more regular, and the growth of the teeth more determinate than in most other animals, yet there can be no doubt that precocity in development of the frame, through improved breeding or highly artificial management, may influence their growth, and render their eruption more rapid.

The period of birth must also have some effect on the development of the teeth. A foal born early in January must have a much more forward mouth than one which has been foaled, say in July or August. There are also cases in which the teeth are irregularly developed, either from natural or artificial causes—among the latter being the reprehensible and cruel practice among breeders and horse-dealers, of tearing out the foal or milk teeth, in order that the permanent teeth may appear sooner, and thus deceive the purchaser.

For ascertaining the age, all the teeth—incisors and molars—can be made available; but for the amateur, and indeed for the expert—except in cases where there is much doubt—the incisor teeth, being the most accessible, are those generally examined.

To ascertain the age, the incisor teeth are viewed on their cutting surface or *table*, and in *profile*. The lower incisors are preferred to the upper, though the latter afford good corroborative evidence. The "tush," or "tusk," also yields additional evidence to some extent, though it must be noted that these do not appear until later in life, and that they are seldom present in the mare. In examining the incisors, attention is given to the form and the details of their tables; to their direction and their length; and to the shape of the corner teeth. The size and colour of the teeth are also points to be noted. In the young animal they are smaller and whiter than in the adult or aged horse.

For convenience in studying the age, dentition may be divided into five periods or stages:— 1, The appearance of the "milk" or "foal" incisors; 2, their growth and progressive wear; 3, their removal and replacement by the permanent incisors; 4, the development of these; 5, the successive changes in the *tables* of these, due to friction or wear. The following remarks should be compared with the illustrations in the two plates.

First Period.—This demands but little notice. At birth, the foal has rarely any incisor teeth, but in about a week or eight days two appear above and below. In thirty to forty days two more appear, one on each side of the others, and until six months these are developing; from SEVEN or EIGHT to TEN MONTHS, the corner teeth appear; and at A YEAR OLD the four middle teeth in each jaw are well up in wear, but the corner ones are not yet in apposition.

Second Period.—From TWELVE to about SIXTEEN MONTHS, the corner teeth are gradually getting into wear, and the middle teeth are in contact over the whole of their tables. At TWENTY MONTHS, the lower corner teeth are in wear throughout the whole of their anterior border. At TWO YEARS, all the incisors above and below are in full wear over their tables, and it is well to remark the appearance of a mouth at this age, as mistakes have been made in confounding it with an adult mouth. In the first place, the teeth are smaller and whiter than those of the adult horse; in the next place, the spaces between them, close to the gum, are also wider, due to their narrower and well-defined neck. The corner teeth, also, are generally deficient at their posterior edge, and the front of all the teeth is level and smooth, while each tooth is destitute of the vertical depression or groove which is noticed in the adult incisor tooth.

Third Period.—This commences at about TWO YEARS AND A HALF, and finishes at FIVE YEARS. Soon after TWO YEARS the gum appears to shrink from the necks of the teeth, and becomes red along its border; and at TWO YEARS AND A HALF one or two of the central incisors will be shed in each jaw, and the permanent teeth, which have to replace them, are growing up. This gives the mouth a very characteristic appearance, there being a deficiency in contact between the two jaws at this part, when they are brought together. At about TWO YEARS AND NINE MONTHS, however, these permanent teeth are in contact by their anterior borders when the mouth is closed, though their tables are not yet in wear. During the THIRD YEAR, the tooth on each side of the middle teeth is becoming narrower at the neck, and at THREE AND A HALF YEARS is shed, being replaced by the permanent tooth; so that at this time the same appearance is noted with these teeth as with the two central the year before. At FOUR YEARS old the four middle teeth in each jaw are in contact when the mouth is closed, and the tusks (if a male) are usually through the gums. Between FOUR and FIVE YEARS the corner milk teeth are shed—usually at four and a half years—and replaced by the permanent teeth. These continue to grow until the horse is FIVE YEARS old, when their edges meet at the anterior part, though not behind. At this time the mouth is completed with permanent incisors, and the following appearance may be noted: each tooth, on its table, is an elongated oval, with a more or less deep and rather dark cavity of the same shape in its centre, surrounded by a thin white line of enamel. This constitutes the "mark," and is of a certain depth, which becomes diminished with wear. At FIVE YEARS old, the mark in the two middle teeth is becoming shallow or defaced; the corner teeth are defective

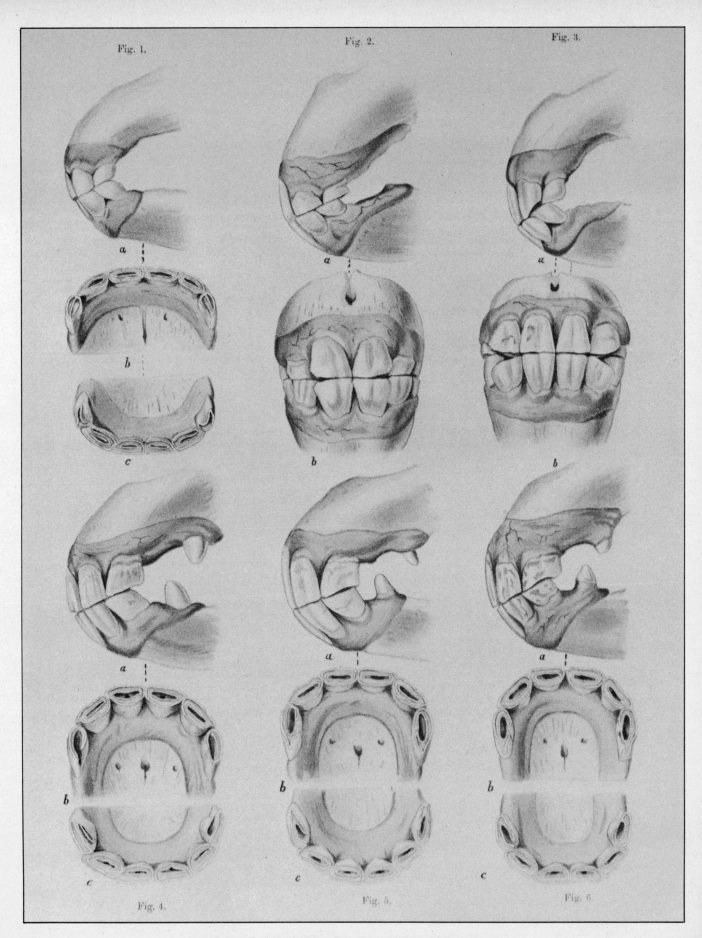

Fig. 1.   Fig. 2.   Fig. 3.

Fig. 4.   Fig. 5.   Fig. 6.

AGE, AS INDICATED BY THE TEETH (FIGS. 1–6)
(COMPLETE DESCRIPTIVE CAPTIONS ARE ON REVERSE OF PLATE.)

DESCRIPTION OF PLATE SHOWING THE AGE, AS INDICATED BY THE TEETH.

The figures on the annexed plate show the mouth in *profile*, the upper and lower incisors being in apposition and viewed in profile or sideways (*a*); and also the upper and lower jaws apart, showing the *tables* of the incisors, those in the upper jaw being above (*b*), and those of the lower jaw below (*c*):—

Fig. 1.—MOUTH OF A TWO-YEARS OLD COLT, showing, in *profile*, all the tables in contact, the general shape, narrow neck, and smooth even surface of the incisor teeth; and on their *tables* is evidence of general wear on all the surface, with the exception of the posterior border of the corner teeth.

Fig. 2.—MOUTH OF A THREE-YEARS OLD COLT, showing, in *profile*, the central permanent teeth replacing the temporary, but not yet in contact; while the temporary teeth on each side are becoming narrower in the fang, which is being absorbed, and the approaching eruption of another permanent tooth is indicated by its situation at the bottom of one of these fangs. On the *tables* of the milk teeth on each side, the result of wear is seen by the disappearance of the mark, and the levelled condition of the corner teeth.

Fig. 3.—MOUTH OF A COLT NEARLY FOUR YEARS OLD.—In this are seen, in *profile*, the corner milk teeth—small, smooth, and narrow—showing a portion of their fangs, especially the upper, which will soon be shed; and in the lower jaw the tush is appearing. The two permanent teeth in each jaw contrast in a marked manner with the temporary teeth. On the *tables* the contrast is as marked; the surface of the permanent teeth, showing the marks, is pretty generally in wear, the upper teeth being most so.

Fig. 4.—A FULL FIVE-YEARS OLD MOUTH.—In *profile*, it is seen that all the permanent teeth are now up, and in contact when the mouth is closed; the tushes are also well up. The corner teeth are not fully in wear. On the *tables* the corner teeth are undergoing wear on their anterior border; the middle teeth have their entire surface in wear, and the mark has nearly disappeared, though the central ring of enamel is still elongated transversely and very narrow, and is approaching the posterior border of the tooth. The tooth on each side of these is approaching the same condition. It will be noticed that the incisors in each jaw form a nearly regular semicircle.

Fig. 5.—A SIX-YEARS OLD MOUTH.—There is not much apparent difference between this and that of five years old. In *profile*, the tushes are seen to be more developed (though in this example they were later than usual), and the notch on the upper corner tooth—caused by wear against the lower one, and its projecting beyond it behind—is beginning to be made. On the *tables* of the lower incisors we find the best evidence. On the middle teeth the surface is becoming oval in shape; the central enamel is thicker from before to behind, and is not so long as at five years, while it is also nearer the posterior margin of the teeth. The same remarks are applicable to the tooth on each side of these. The upper corner teeth are rather "shelly" (*i.e.*, incomplete behind—a rather common occurrence) or fissured.

Fig. 6.—A SEVEN-YEARS OLD MOUTH.—In *profile*, the notch in the upper corner tooth is deeper, the lower corner tooth shorter, laterally, at its upper part, the upper and lower incisors in the closed mouth being also less vertical than at five years old. The tushes are also worn and blunted. On the *tables* the effects of wear are more evident in all the incisors; the four middle teeth in each jaw are oval, the centrals even having a tendency to a round form, the central ring of enamel is thicker, narrower, and nearer the back of the tooth. In the lower corner teeth the wearing surface is more extensive, and the central ring of enamel may be complete, though in some instances—as in the figure—it is still incomplete, especially in "shell teeth."

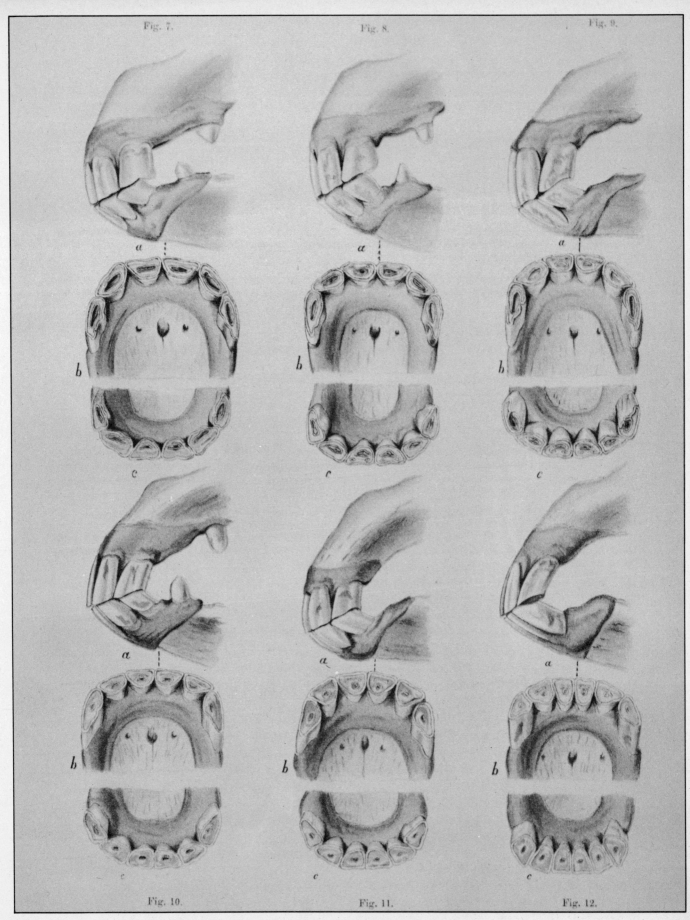

Fig. 10.   Fig. 11.   Fig. 12.

AGE, AS INDICATED BY THE TEETH (FIGS. 7–12).

(COMPLETE DESCRIPTIVE CAPTIONS ARE ON REVERSE OF PLATE.)

DESCRIPTION OF PLATE SHOWING THE AGE, AS INDICATED BY THE TEETH.

The figures on the annexed plate show the mouth in *profile*, the upper and lower incisors being in apposition and viewed in profile or sideways (*a*); and also the upper and lower jaws apart, showing the *tables* of the incisors, those in the upper jaw being above (*b*), and those of the lower jaw below (*c*) :—

Fig. 7.—AN EIGHT-YEARS OLD MOUTH.—In *profile*, when the jaws are closed, the upper and lower incisors meet more obliquely, and the tush is shorter and blunter. The *tables* of all the lower incisors are much worn, the mark or cavity has disappeared from all, the four middle teeth are oval and approaching the circular form, and the corner teeth are becoming oval. The central enamel is assuming an angular shape at the back part and is diminishing in size, and between it and the anterior border of the four middle teeth yellowish marks are appearing.

Fig. 8.—A NINE-YEARS OLD MOUTH.—In *profile*, the teeth are still more oblique, and in some instances the notch in the corner teeth has disappeared. Looking at the *tables* of the lower incisors, it is seen that those of the two middle teeth are round and their central enamel has assumed a triangular shape, and the "star"—as the newly appearing marks between this enamel and the front of the teeth is named—is nearer the middle of the table. The tooth on each side of the middle ones is becoming round, and the corner teeth are oval. The curve formed by the six teeth is much diminished, particularly in the centre.

Fig. 9.—A TEN-YEARS OLD MOUTH.—The obliquity of the teeth in the mouth is still more marked when looked at in *profile*, those in the two jaws meeting at a more acute angle; the obliquity of the corner teeth has also increased, and there is a larger interspace between them and the adjoining teeth. On the *tables* of the lower incisors, it is perceived that the two middle teeth are rounder, their central enamel smaller, more markedly triangular, and close to the posterior border of the teeth; the star is also more apparent, and nearer the middle. The adjoining teeth are round, and the corners nearly so, though the latter being shell teeth this shape is not so obvious. The curve formed by the teeth is straighter in the middle.

Fig. 10.—A TWELVE-YEARS OLD MOUTH.—The incidence of inclination of the incisor teeth, in *profile*, is still greater than at ten years, and the necks are becoming more exposed at the gums, leaving wider interspaces between them. All the lower tables are round and levelled, and in some instances traces of the central enamel may yet remain, though usually it is absent, and in its stead, in the centre, is a small yellow spot—the last evidence of the "star." The mouth is narrower and straighter in front than at eight or ten years.

Fig. 11.—A FIFTEEN-YEARS OLD MOUTH.—In *profile*, the features noted in the twelve-years old mouth are still more marked at this period. The notch is deeper in the corner upper teeth. The *tables* of the two middle incisors below are now triangular in shape, and those next them are becoming so. The mouth is narrower across and its convexity greatly decreased.

Fig 12.—A THIRTY-YEARS OLD MOUTH.—Up to this period, the changes already delineated have been progressive, and more or less recognisable; and at thirty years the incisor teeth indicate extreme old age. The upper incisors are generally wider than the lower, and therefore project beyond them on each side in the closed mouth. In *profile*, the lower incisors are very horizontal, especially the corner ones, and these rarely come into close apposition by their tables. The *tables* of the lower incisors are longer before to behind than transversely, and, having lost their triangular form, are now biangular or, rather, quadrangular. The coating of enamel which envelops the teeth is disappearing from their posterior surface. In some instances the teeth are irregular in length in one or other jaw, sometimes in both, being excessively long from defective wear; in other instances, on the contrary, they are worn down nearly to the gums. The curved line formed by the incisors at adult age has now become nearly straight, and the jaws are thin and narrow. The remains of the star are indicated by a faint yellow spot in the middle of the table of each tooth.

in their posterior border, and the cavity is deep; when the mouth is closed, it is noticed that the corner teeth do not meet exactly throughout, while all the teeth are nearly vertical in the jaws. At this time the tusks are well developed.

Fourth Period.—After five years old all the incisors are in full contact, and the age is then judged by the attrition of the tables: indicated by their longitudinal extent, and the length of the central cavity or mark, as well as the wear of the corner teeth.

At SIX YEARS old, the tables of the middle teeth are assuming a short oval shape; the posterior border of the corner tooth is in wear; the mark in the two central teeth is nearly or quite obliterated, and these teeth are usually whiter than at five years old. A marked feature at this time is noticed when the mouth is closed, and the incisor teeth are consequently in contact. This consists in the appearance of a slight notch at the upper corner incisor tooth, caused by its wear against its fellow of the lower jaw, which it overlaps slightly behind; wear not taking place throughout the whole surface, the corner of the tooth is untouched, and consequently a kind of notch is formed, which increases as age advances.

At SEVEN YEARS old, the incisor teeth all appear to be whiter than at an earlier period; the lower corner tooth is narrower across than the upper one—has made a deeper notch than the latter; the mark in the two central teeth has entirely disappeared, and the tooth at each side is in much the same condition, while the shape of the table itself is becoming a shorter oval.

At EIGHT YEARS, the mark or cavity in all the lower incisors is worn out, and the two middle teeth are becoming round in shape on their tables, while those next them are oval, and the corner teeth are approaching that shape. Instead of the mark in the middle teeth, there is a yellow transverse line, which is often not so distinct in the other teeth, and the central circle of enamel is diminishing in extent, becoming a little angular towards the back part, and approaches nearer the posterior border of the tooth. Looked at in *profile*, when the mouth is closed, it is now observed that the teeth instead of being vertical, as they were at five years old, have changed their direction, and are now rather oblique, while the notch is deeper in the upper corner teeth, and all have assumed a yellowish tinge.

Fifth Period.—This period commences when the horse is said, wrongly, to be aged, and to have lost "mark of mouth." It extends from nine years to extreme old age, and, so far as the teeth are concerned, affords indications which every year are less reliable; so that it is not always possible to state, with any degree of certainty or precision, what the age of an animal during this period may be, unless the examiner has made a profound and wide study of well-ascertained mouths at all ages.

At NINE YEARS, the two middle teeth are round on their tables, and the central enamel assumes a triangular shape; the teeth on each side of them are also becoming round, while the corner teeth are oval; the notch in the corner upper teeth sometimes disappears at this period.

At TEN YEARS, the tables of the middle teeth are still more round, the central enamel smaller and markedly triangular; and in *profile*, in the closed mouth, the incidence of the jaws is still more oblique.

At ELEVEN YEARS, the corner teeth are rounded in outline on their tables, and the central enamel is still further diminished, and nearer the posterior border of the teeth. The upper corner teeth are more oblique, and again show a notch.

At TWELVE YEARS, the tables of all the teeth are rounded, and some of them only show a trace of the central enamel; at this part, if there is no enamel showing, a yellowish spot is observed. The mouth has become narrower in front, and less convex in outline. The lower border of the jaw is also thinner; the cheeks look flattened, and the face appears to be depressed on each side. In many cases the teeth are much elongated, and when the two jaws are together the obliquity has increased.

At THIRTEEN YEARS, the central enamel is no longer seen on the tables of the lower incisors, but in the upper middle ones it is round and narrow in form. At FOURTEEN YEARS, the lower middle incisors tend to assume a triangular shape; and the curve of the whole of the teeth has nearly disappeared, while the jaw is very much narrower.

At FIFTEEN YEARS, the middle incisors are triangular, while the tooth on each side is commencing to be so.

At SIXTEEN YEARS, all the teeth offer the characteristics of the previous year in a more exaggerated form.

At SEVENTEEN YEARS, all the lower incisors are triangular in shape; the teeth look a little apart, and the obliquity of the corner teeth is still more apparent.

At EIGHTEEN YEARS, the jaw is still narrower in front, and the tables of the teeth, instead of being elongated longitudinally, as at five years old, are now elongated in the opposite direction—that is, from before to behind.

At NINETEEN YEARS, this change is still more manifest; the teeth are more horizontal, and often longer than they should be.

At and after TWENTY YEARS of age, the appearance of the mouth is somewhat variable, but, to the expert, it indicates old age. In *profile*, the jaws meet at a very acute angle, their teeth do not appear so close-set, and their tables are more flattened at their sides. Sometimes the teeth are excessively long, and very horizontal; while in other cases they are very short, or worn to nearly the level of the gums. In all cases, only a small part of their fang remains in the socket; spaces generally exist between the teeth, close to the gum; into these spaces the gum itself projects, and they often contain the remains of food.

Extreme old age, as already mentioned, is manifested in other ways: such as the temples and the eyebrows becoming grey, the mane and the tail are thinner, the head and the body usually become emaciated, and the limbs and joints give evidence of weakness.

IRREGULARITIES OF THE TEETH.

As might be expected, irregularities of the teeth of the horse are by no means uncommon. These irregularities are related to the number of the incisors, either more or less being present; to their shape; to the fusion of two of their number; to the shape or depth of the mark or cavity; to a deficiency in their length, or excess in width of one of the jaws; to excessive or defective wear; to changes produced by crib-biting; and to the employment of fraudulent measures.

With regard to these irregularities, we need only here remark that they may modify, more or less considerably, the appearances of the teeth as a guide to age, and must be taken into account by the examiner. The effect of crib-biting especially is to be noted, inasmuch as it not only damages the incisor teeth very considerably, but it is also a sign of the existence of a most objectionable vice in the animal. The incisor teeth of a crib-biting horse are characterised by the anterior border being worn away, the sharp edge having been taken off obliquely, often from the middle of the table, or even some distance down the front of the tooth. In some cases, the abnormal wear affects the lower incisors only; in other cases, the upper; and in other cases, again, both upper and lower. In some very rare instances, strange to say, the posterior border of the incisor teeth, not the anterior, is worn in crib-biting, this wear being confined to the upper or lower teeth, or both, or to one jaw posteriorly and the other anteriorly.

In some instances, again, the tables of the teeth are worn away in seizing the manger, and in some peculiar cases the sides of the teeth are involved. In extremely unfrequent cases, the front of the incisors of the lower jaw, between the gum and the tables of the teeth, has been alone worn away by pressure against the edge of the manger, while the animal has been swallowing the air. At first in crib-biting, the middle incisors are involved, but in time the lateral and corner ones also suffer.

With regard to the FRAUDULENT MEASURES employed to conceal defects or to mask the age, a few remarks may be useful. It is to be noticed, however, that in many cases much skill is required to detect these frauds.

In order to make a young animal appear older, it is by no means an uncommon custom to lance the gums, or burn them with a hot iron, so as to expedite the appearance of the teeth; but the plan most usually adopted is that of tearing out the temporary teeth, so as to allow the permanent ones to grow up more rapidly. This cruel operation, often brutally performed, causes the most acute pain, and often subsequent suffering, not unfrequently causing the animal to neglect its food, to become feverish and wasted, and even so ill as to die. In nearly all cases, it causes the animal to be very much afraid of its head being touched, or makes it even vicious for a long time afterwards.

In some instances, this extraction of the teeth commences when the animal is two years old, by tearing out the middle incisors; in other cases, it is only those on each side of the middle ones which are extirpated; and in other cases, again, only the corner ones are removed. But it is by no means uncommon for all these teeth to be extracted at successive periods.

To make a horse appear to be three years and a half old, the fraud is practised when it is three years old, and at four to four and a half years when it is desired to make him appear in his fifth year.

This fraud is detected by the laceration of the gums where the teeth have been torn out, by the undeveloped condition of the permanent teeth which are appearing, and by a careful examination and comparison of the other teeth. The general immature appearance of the animal, also, will assist in arriving at a conclusion with regard to this deception.

To make an old animal appear young, the lower class of horse-dealers resort to the practice commonly known as "bishoping;" but this fraudulent measure should only impose on the very ignorant or inattentive examiner.

When we look at the incisor teeth of a five or six year old animal, we observe that the tables have a greater diameter from side to side, or laterally, than from before to behind. We have already noticed that, as age progresses, this shape becomes modified by the assumption, successively, of an oval, then a rounded, then a triangular form, until at last the tooth is narrowed from side to side. It was also remarked that the cavity, or "mark," in the centre of the table at first occupied nearly the whole surface, and was rather deep; that it gradually diminished in size and depth; and instead of being in the middle, it approached nearer and nearer the posterior border, until at last it disappeared, leaving only a yellow spot to show where it had once been.

The fraud alluded to is usually practised on horses which, though old, are in fair condition, have good limbs, and do not show many signs of wear. They may be from eight up to fourteen or sixteen years old; but usually they are ten or twelve years old, as after that time the teeth have become too oblique, the jaws narrower transversely, the circle formed by the teeth too rectilinear, and the teeth themselves too much altered in shape on their tables, for the trick to be successful. The object is to give the mouth the appearance of that belonging to an animal six or seven years old; and a great deal of skill and clever manipulation are often displayed in the attempt.

The operation is effected by the horse's head being held fast, and the mouth kept open by a gag, so as to leave the tables of the lower incisors convenient for the hands of the operator. Then the tables of the teeth are filed down to a level surface; this being done, with a narrow gouge or graving tool, a small longitudinal cavity, resembling the natural cavity or "mark," is dug out of the corner teeth and the tooth next them. This cavity is not easily made, for the central enamel is very hard, and it must be cut through. The cavities being completed, they are darkened by some substance, usually the nitrate of silver, so as to still further give them a resemblance to the natural mark. If the tushes are very blunt and worn, as they usually are, the more "knowing bishopers" not unfrequently file them on their inner surface and towards the point, so as to make them sharp and look younger.

When the horse is about to be sold, if these "copers" have any reason to apprehend detection, they generally contrive to have the horse's mouth full of saliva, by giving him food which will increase the secretion of that fluid, and so sufficiently conceal their handiwork.

Detection of the fraud is very easy to the expert. In profile or in front, when the two jaws are together, if the tables of the teeth have been much filed down, they will not exactly meet, because the incisor teeth have been abnormally shortened, while the molar teeth have not been interfered with. In the upper jaw, the posterior projection of the corner tooth, which forms the notch, will probably have been removed by the file; but the obliquity of the teeth and their length will be noted. On separating the jaws, and looking at the tables of the teeth carefully, the marks of the file will be plainly perceived. The shape of the tables, also, should correspond with the cavities, as we have already described in treating of age; for it must be remembered that when the cavity is natural, it is surrounded by a white ring of enamel which slightly projects above the general surface; but when the cavity is artificial, no enamel surrounds it, and consequently there is no projection, as is ascertained by the eye and the touch. If the notch has been removed from the upper corner tooth, the marks of the file will also be apparent.

In this kind of fraud, as in the other, the general appearance of the animal will, in many cases, confirm detection.

CHAPTER XXVIII.

SHEOING.

In order to understand the general principles of shoeing, a glance at the different parts of the hoof is necessary. The wall is that portion which surrounds the foot, and is alone seen when this is placed on the ground. It is fibrous in structure, the fibres passing from above to below, as they grow from where the skin terminates. Externally the fibres are dense and resisting, but those nearer the interior gradually become soft and spongy. The growth of the wall is indefinite, it being the part which has to sustain wear through contact with the ground.

When the foot is lifted, the sole and the frog are seen on its lower or ground surface. The sole is usually more or less concave in a healthy foot. It is fibrous, like the wall, its fibres passing in the same direction ; but they are much softer, and their growth is definite, they breaking off in the form of flakes when they have attained a certain length. The frog is a triangular mass of somewhat soft and elastic fibrous horn, situated at the posterior part of the sole. Like that part, its fibres are also of definite growth, and flake off in large patches from time to time.

The wall sustains weight and wear on all kinds of ground ; the sole is adapted for sustaining weight, on soft ground more particularly ; while the frog has a most important use in acting as a cushion to support the powerful tendon which flexes the limb, in diminishing jar, and preventing slipping.

The unpared sole and frog of the healthy foot need no protection on any kind of soil. The flakes of loose horn on the former serve a very useful purpose in retaining moisture, and so keeping the solid horn beneath soft and elastic, while they act as so many springs when the foot is placed on projecting stones. The more the frog is exposed to wear, so the larger and sounder it grows, and the better it is for the entire foot and limb.

The fore-foot is of more importance, in the matter of shoeing, than the hind one ; inasmuch as it has to support much more weight, and is consequently more exposed to disease and injury.

The fore-foot when well formed is nearly, if not quite, circular ; the hind-foot is somewhat oval, the frog smaller, and the sole more concave.

When the hoof is shod, the wall is not exposed to wear, and, therefore, would grow to an indefinite, and, consequently, most inconvenient, length if the shoe should chance to be retained too long, and the excessive growth of horn not removed. The sole and frog, on the contrary, never cause inconvenience, as their growth is limited.

What is required in shoeing, then, in principle, is merely protection from undue wear, with the least possible interference with, or disturbance to, the functions of the foot and limb. The excess in length of the wall must be removed at frequent intervals—between a fortnight and a month—according to the activity of the growth ; but the sole and frog, if healthy, should not be disturbed. Not a grain of iron more than is absolutely necessary should be allowed as a protection ; and this question of weight of shoes is an important one, especially with horses which are compelled to travel beyond a walk. There are no muscles below the knee and hock, and those which are chiefly concerned in the movements of the limb arise high up, and act upon short levers.   An ounce weight at the shoulder or stifle, therefore, progressively

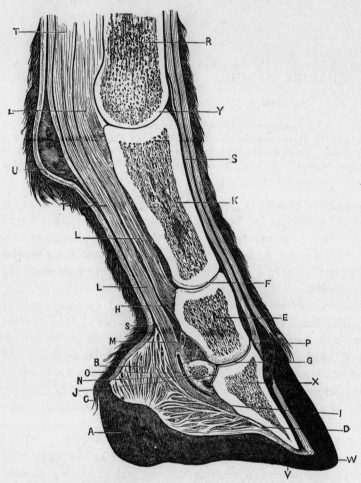

VERTICAL SECTION OF HORSE'S FOOT.

and rapidly increases, until at the foot it has become several pounds.   Therefore it is, that a shoe six or twelve ounces heavier than is absolutely necessary to protect the wall from wear, occasions a great waste of muscular power of the limb, and consequent fatigue.   If we consider the rapidity with which the weight increases from the shoulder or hip towards the foot, the number of steps a horse takes in a journey of a few hours, and that there are four feet so surcharged, we shall gain some notion of the many needless tons which the animal has been compelled to carry, and the strain thrown upon foot and limb—a strain they were never intended, and are not adapted by nature, to bear. All shoes should, then, be as light as may be compatible with the wear demanded from them.

For all horses, except, perhaps, the heaviest animals employed in drays and heavy waggons, the lower or ground face of the shoes should be concave, and the upper or foot surface plane, or nearly so.   They should be retained by the smallest number of nails possible—six or seven in the fore-shoes, and eight in the hind-shoes.   Calks should never be employed.   With the heaviest horses —the dray or waggon animals—it may be advantageous to have toe and heel calks to afford secure foothold.

The procedure in shoeing is simple in the extreme.   When the old shoe is removed from the hoof, nothing more is required than to remove the excessive growth of the wall by means of the rasp, applied to the lower margin or ground, or sole border—not

A, horny frog; B, plantar cushion, or fatty or sensitive frog, covered by secreting membrane (C) of horny frog; D, attachment of pedal or coffin bone (X); E, coronary or small pastern bone, and the joint (F) it forms with the large pastern bone, or os suffraginis (K) and the joint (G) between it and the pedal bone; H, insertion of the perforatus tendon (L L) into the small pastern bone; I, insertion of the perforans tendon (T T) into the sole of the coffin bone; J, joint between the pedal and navicular bone; K, os suffraginis or large pastern bone (L L); L, perforatus or deep flexor tendon of the foot; M, ligament attaching the perforatus tendon to the small pastern and navicular bone (N); N, navicular bone; O, capsule between the flexor tendon and navicular bone, the seat of navicular disease; P, insertion of the extensor tendon (S) of the foot into the top or pyramidal process of the pedal bone; R, large metacarpal, or cannon, or shank bone; S, extensor tendon of the foot; T, perforatus tendon; U, fetlock; V, horny sole; W, toe of hoof; X, pedal or coffin bone; Y, joint between the cannon and large pastern bone.

the front of the wall.   The amount to be removed will depend upon the growth, and of this the farrier's skill in his art should enable him to judge.   It is at the toe, or front, portion that the excess is usually found, and this should be removed until, in an ordinary hoof, when placed on the ground, the angle should be about 50° or 52°. The angle can be easily measured by the instrument shown on the next page. The sole or frog should not be touched, not even the loose flakes removed; and all the work

ought to be accomplished by means of the rasp. Paring out and hacking at these parts with the drawing-knife should be absolutely condemned, as destructive to the foot.

In reducing the wall to a proper length, care should be exercised in keeping both sides of the hoof of the same height; as, if one is left higher than the other, the foot, fetlock, and, indeed, the whole limb, will be thrown out of the perpendicular. This causes the horse to travel painfully, as it twists the joints, and in time leads to disease. *Nearly always the inside of the foot is left higher than the outside*, and this throws severe strain on the outside of the foot and fetlock. Standing in front of the horse when the foot is on the ground, one can perceive at once whether this deviation is present. In a well-formed foot and leg, a plumb-line should fall from the point of the shoulder through the middle of the knee, shank, pastern, and front of the hoof.

The wall having been reduced sufficiently, the shoe should fit *full* all round the circumference, and project slightly beyond the heels. Heat is not absolutely necessary in fitting it, or procuring accurate co-aptation between it and the hoof. The nails should take a short, thick hold of the wall, so that, if possible, the old nail holes may be obliterated when the excess of horn is removed at the succeeding shoeing. In the forefoot, the nails should be driven home more firmly at the toe than the heels, particularly the inside heel. The clinches must be laid down as smoothly as possible, and with only

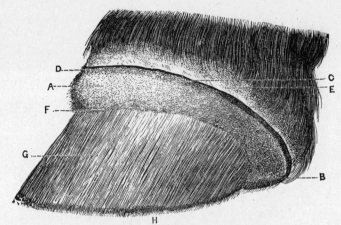

HORSE'S FOOT, WITH THE HOOF REMOVED.

A B, the coronary cushion fitting into a cavity around the inner and upper part of the hoof, and covered with velvet-like tufts of blood-vessels, which secrete the horn of the wall; C, upper border of the cushion, with a shallow groove (D) separating it from the modified skin that secretes the thin, soft, whitish horn, covering the outside of the hoof at its upper part; F, lower border of the cushion where the laminæ commence; G, sensitive, vascular, or fleshy laminæ, or leaves, which interlock with similar horny leaves inside the wall of the hoof; H, fine tufts of blood-vessels at the lower end of the vascular laminæ, which secrete the soft white horn uniting the horny sole to the wall of the hoof.

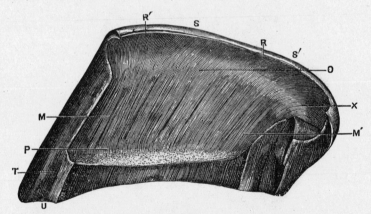

LONGITUDINAL VERTICAL SECTION OF A HOOF, SHOWING ITS INTERIOR.

M M', horny laminæ, or leaves, which interlock with the vascular and sensitive leaves on the coffin bone shown in the preceding figure; O P, upper and lower ends of the laminæ, commencing at the cavity (X) which receives the coronary cushion, and terminating at the junction of the horny wall with the sole; R R', upper border of the cavity which receives the coronary cushion; S S', border of the thin, soft, white horn that covers the upper and outer surface of the wall, and is continuous with the horny frog; T, junction between the wall and the sole; U, lower margin of the wall.

the most trifling rasping. The front of the hoof, or wall, should on no account be otherwise touched with the rasp, but ought to pass in a straight line from the top, or coronet, to the shoe. Rasping this part of the hoof is most injurious, and should not be tolerated on any consideration. It removes the dense tough fibres, which are best adapted for holding the nails that retain the shoe, and exposes the soft spongy horn beneath; this soon dries, cracks, and breaks, and does not afford sufficient support to the nails.

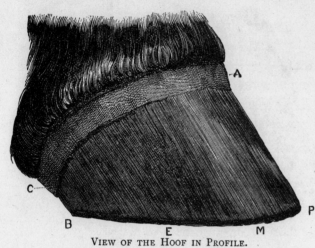

VIEW OF THE HOOF IN PROFILE.

A C, the soft thin horn covering the upper part of wall, known as the coronary frog-band; B, heel; E, quarter; M, outside toe; P, toe.

FLEMING'S INSTRUMENT FOR ASCERTAINING THE ANGLE OR SLOPE OF THE WALL.

The evils of shoeing, as too often practised, are:—

1. Paring of the sole and frog; 2. Applying shoes too heavy and of a faulty shape; 3. Employing too many or too large nails; 4. Applying shoes too small, and removing the wall of the hoofs to make the feet fit the shoes; 5. Rasping the front of the hoof.

The shoe should give the hoof a level, natural bearing on the ground. Calkings are hurtful to fast-moving horses, and may be dispensed with if the shoes have a concave ground surface, and the frog is allowed to come fully in contact with the ground; if they are resorted to, their injurious effects should be averted by employing a toe piece of the same height.

For the race horse, the narrowest iron rim is sufficient, provided it is strong enough not to twist or bend, and to permit a grip of the ground. For hunters, hacks, and harness horses, a shoe of the modified pattern described, and here figured, is well adapted. Even the ordinary Fullered hunting pattern, but without the calkin on the hind-shoe, is infinitely preferable to that usually employed for hacks and harness horses. For these no better kind of shoe can be recommended than that recently introduced for troop, artillery, and transport horses in her Majesty's service. This is, in shape, based on the requirements

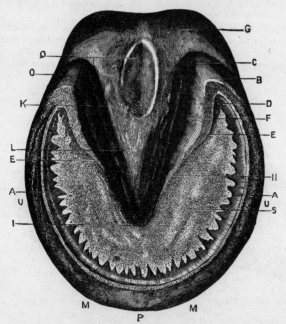

VIEW OF THE LOWER OR GROUND FACE OF THE HOOF.

A A, white line, composed of soft horn, uniting the sole to the wall; B, angle of the bars or inflexion of the wall; C, summit of the bar; D, angle of the sole or "heel;" E E, bars; F, lateral cleft or commissure; G, heel or bulb of the frog; H, termination of bar; I, point of frog; K O, a branch of frog; L, body of frog; M M, outside and inside toe; P, toe; Q, cleft or middle commissure of frog; S, sole; U U, quarters of the hoof.

pointed out, and which it meets in every particular. Since its introduction, it has admirably fulfilled all the demands of a perfect horse-shoe.

Hitherto, great difficulty has been experienced in obtaining shoes of good material, uniform shape, and easy application. But the introduction of machinery into horse-shoe manufacture promises to revolu-tionise the farrier's art. The Horse-Shoe and Nail Manufacturing Company of London,* are now producing horse-shoes which, for elegance, durability, and safety, are far superior to anything which has yet been made by hand, and at a much less cost. They are supplying shoes in large quantities, of the

SHOE WITH CONCAVE GROUND SURFACE AND CATCH   ORDINARY FULLERED SHOE.
AT EACH HEEL (FLEMING'S MODEL).

pattern we have described and recommended, to the army; and as these shoes are completely finished and ready for immediate application, the time required to shoe a horse is reduced by at least one-half —often a matter of some importance. Not only this, but the shoes can be fitted in a cold state, and put on in the stable or anywhere else without the aid of a forge; consequently, sending horses to the

FORE- AND HIND-SHOE IN USE IN THE BRITISH ARMY.
Made by Machinery, by the Horse-Shoe and Nail Manufacturing Company, London.

farrier's establishment can be dispensed with. These shoes are made of such good iron that they very rarely break; they can easily be altered in shape without heating, and are sold in all sizes.

With regard to nails, all horsemen know how important it is that these should be of the very best quality and shape. The hand-made nails are now being altogether supplanted by those made by machinery, as they—the hand-made nails—are often very inferior or uncertain in quality, and have to be hammered and pointed by the farrier before they can be driven into the hoof. This hammering and pointing requires time, and is not always effected with skill; the surface of the nail is always

* Offices, 115, Cannon Street, London, E.C.

uneven and ridged, which makes it more difficult to drive; and not unfrequently the point is too thin or unsound, which, in many cases, causes it to run into the living parts of the foot, or to break, producing serious results. The Globe Horse-Nail, which is also made by the above Company, is finished ready for immediate use, is perfectly smooth on its surface, strong at the point, and has withstood the most severe tests with regard to tenacity and durability; while, being made by machinery, it is always uniform in size and thickness, and does less harm to the hoof than the hand-made nail. These machine nails are made to fit exactly all the shoes manufactured by the Company, as well as the special shoes provided for the army horses.

PERIPLANTAR SHOEING.

Knowing that the horse's foot is admirably constructed to perform certain definite functions, and that the hoof, in ordinary conditions, is designed to act as the medium through which the most important of these are carried out, but that its circumference is liable to be broken away and worn when unduly exposed, we have only to substitute, for a certain portion of this perishable horn, an equivalent portion

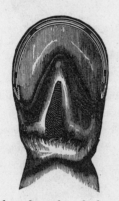   

Fig. 1. View of the under surface of a foot shod with a periplantar shoe.   Fig. 2. Side view of a shod foot.

PERIPLANTAR SHOEING.

of a more durable material, and the hoof is secured from damage by wear, while its natural functions remain unimpaired.

With this object in view, what has been designated the Periplantar, or Charlier, method of shoeing has been introduced, and with considerable success.

In this method the sole and frog, as well as the bars, are left unpared. The crust, or wall, is bevelled off at the edge by the rasp, and by means of a special knife, with a movable guide, a groove, or recess, is made along this bevelled edge to receive the shoe. Into this groove is fitted the shoe. This is a narrow, but somewhat deep, band of iron (or, as now, a mixture of iron and steel; or, better still, *Bessemer steel*). It is perforated by from four to six oval nail-holes of small size, and, if required, may be provided with a clip at the toe, though this is seldom found necessary.

Its upper inner edge is rounded by the file to prevent it pressing too much against the angle of the sole, and the ends of the branches are narrow, and bevelled off towards the ground.

The nails are very small, and have a conical head and neck. They must be of the finest quality.

It is best to fit the shoe in a hot state, as it must have a level bed, and follow exactly the outline of the wall. After it has been fitted, it is advisable to remove, by a small drawing-knife, a little of the horn from the angle of the groove in the hoof, to correspond with the rounded inner edge of the shoe. This ensures a proper amount of space between the latter and the soft horn, at the margin of the pedal bone.

In strong hoofs, the shoe is almost entirely buried in the groove; but in those which have the soles flat or convex, with low heels, or which have been partially ruined by the ordinary method of shoeing, it is not safe to imbed it so deeply, at least to commence with.

SHOEING FOR ICE AND SLIPPERY ROADS.

Provided the frog comes largely in contact with the ground, there is not usually much danger of slipping; but as it is not always possible to secure this, recourse is had to artificial means. Among these

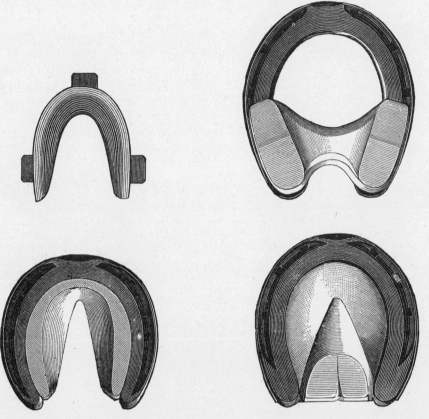

VARIOUS FORMS OF INDIARUBBER PADS, WITH STEEL SPRINGS, OR TO BE FIXED BENEATH THE SHOE BY NAILS WHEN THE SHOE IS APPLIED.

are calkins, which, as has been already mentioned, are objectionable in all but slow-paced horses; and indiarubber pads of various forms, to fit between the shoe and the hoof, and come in contact with the ground, aiding, as well, in diminishing concussion.

For ice-covered roads there are various contrivances. In ordinary "roughing," the shoes are taken off and a sharp calkin is turned up; but this requires a forge, much time, is injurious to the horse's feet, does not last long, and is expensive. "Frost nails" are sometimes employed, but these also require the farrier, last a very short time, and likewise damage the hoofs. Screw studs or pegs are more convenient, screw holes being made in the shoes when they are first put on, into which sharp or blunt pegs are screwed as occasion may require. But these sometimes break at the neck, or fall out, require to be screwed in, and the thread is liable to become rusty, while they are somewhat expensive. Another much simpler and cheaper method is the introduction of a square sharp peg into a square hole punched in each branch of the shoe, and, if necessary, at the toe—this stud and the hole having a slight taper, which permits the former to be easily inserted and removed; it should not project beyond the foot surface of

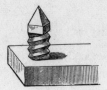

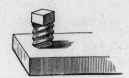

Fig. 1. Sharp pyramidal stud for travelling on ice.   Fig. 2. Blunt square stud for non-frosty weather.

SCREW STUDS FOR WINTER.

the shoe. The studs and holes may be round and tapering in the same manner. Blunt studs may be used when there is no ice, or on wooden pavements, or asphalte. When required to be used, these

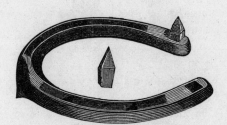

Stud with round hole in shoe.   Fleming's Stud with Square Hole.

studs are merely inserted into the holes and receive a smart blow; when it is desired to remove them, a few taps on each side, and a blow on the face of the shoe, will generally make them jump out.

This stud method of winter shoeing has been adopted for some years in her Majesty's Household Cavalry, and is in use in most of the Continental armies.[*]

---

[*] For more minute details of shoeing, see Fleming's " Horse-Shoes and Horse-Shoeing," and " Practical Horse Shoeing."

CHAPTER XXIX.

DISEASES AND THEIR TREATMENT.

Introduction—Nursing—Administering Medicines—Fomentations or Bathing—Poultices—Enemas or Clysters—Fevers—Simple Fever—Influenza—Strangles—Glanders and Farcy—Lymphangitis, Weed, or Inflamed Leg—Rheumatism—Diseases of the Air Passages—Roaring—Catarrh—Chronic Nasal Catarrh—Sore Throat—Bronchitis—Chronic Bronchitis—Congestion of the Lungs —Inflammation of the Lungs—Asthma—Broken Wind—Pleurisy—Disease of the Digestive Organs—Indigestion without En- gorgement—Indigestion with Engorgement—Colic—Flatulent Colic—Enteritis, or Inflammation of the Bowels—Diarrhœa— Constipation—Lampas—Irregular Teeth—Worms—Choking—Diseases of the Urinary Organs—Inflammation of the Kidneys —Cystitis—Retention of Urine—Incontinence of Urine—Diuresis or Excessive Staling—Diseases of the Nervous System— Tetanus or Lock-Jaw—Megrims—Epilepsy—Fainting—Apoplexy—Stringhalt—Diseases of the Eye—Simple Ophthalmia— Specific Ophthalmia—Cataract—Amaurosis—Diseases of the Skin—Surfeit—Prurigo and Eczema—Mange—Ringworm— Grease—Cracked Heels—Mud Fever—Warts.

In the following pages, the treatment of horses suffering from disease or injury is given in such a way as to assist those who, not being sufficiently skilled in veterinary medicine or surgery, may yet on occasions have to minister to these animals before a professional man arrives, or may be able, from the hints here given, to assist in carrying out the treatment he prescribes. Nothing beyond this is attempted, as it would be in the highest degree culpable and misleading to endeavour to make the amateur play the part of a veterinary surgeon by mere written instruction, and try to make him understand what to do by book, which really requires years of special and close study in a veterinary college and hospital stable. It is, in the long run, more profitable to obtain skilled advice for sick or injured horses; and what is now offered for consideration is merely a number of hints for emergencies in ordinary or special cases.

NURSING.

When a horse is sick or ill from injury, recovery is much accelerated by careful and sympathetic nursing. However indifferent a horse may be to caressing or kind attention during health, when ill he certainly appreciates these, and when in pain will often apparently endeavour to attract notice and seek relief from those with whom he is acquainted. Therefore it is that kindness and careful nursing will sometimes do more in effecting recovery than drugs and medical attendance. Fresh air and cleanliness, quiet and comfort, are always to be allowed, if possible. The stable or loose box should be warm, without being close, and free from draughts. If the weather is cold, and especially if the horse be suffering from disease of the air passages, it may be necessary to maintain the warmth by artificial means, though care should be taken that this does not render the air too dry to breathe. The surface of the body can be kept warm by rugs, and the legs by woollen bandages; yet it must be remembered that a sick horse is easily fatigued and annoyed by too much clothing, and therefore it is better to resort to artificial heating of the stable than to overload the body or impede movement by heavy clothing. If blankets must be used, should the horse have an irritable skin, it is well to place a cotton or linen sheet innermost.

For bedding, long straw should be employed as little as possible, as it hampers movement. Clean old litter, saw-dust, or moss litter, are the best. If the hoofs are strong, and the horse likely to be confined for some weeks, it affords relief to take off the shoes. Tying up should be avoided if possible, unless it is urgently required, the horse being allowed to move about or lie down as he may prefer.

With regard to food, a sick horse, if the appetite is lost, should be tempted to eat by offering him that which is enticing. It should be given frequently, and in small quantities, but not forced on him; and it often happens that food will be taken if offered from the hand, when it will not be eaten out of the manger. Whether fed out of a bucket or manger, any that is left should be thrown away and the receptacle well cleaned out after each meal. As a rule, during sickness a horse requires laxative food, in order to allay fever or inflammatory symptoms, while supporting the strength. The following list comprises the usual good laxative food employed: green grass, green wheat, green oats, green barley, lucerne, carrots, parsnips, gruel, bran-mash, linseed and bran-mash, boiled barley, linseed tea, hay tea, and linseed oil. Green grass, lucerne, and similar articles of food, should be dried before being given, if cut when in a wet state. Boiled grain should be cooked with as little water as possible, so that it may be floury and comparatively dry when ready; a little salt should be mixed with it.

One gallon of good *gruel* may be made from a pound of meal, which should be thrown into cold water, set on the fire and stirred till boiling, and afterwards permitted to simmer over a gentle fire till the water is quite thick.

To make a *bran - mash*, scald a stable bucket, throw out the water, put in three pounds of bran and one ounce of salt; add two and a half pints of boiling water; stir well up, cover over, and allow the mash to stand for fifteen or twenty minutes, until it is well cooked.

For a *bran* and *linseed - mash*, we may boil slowly, for two or three hours, one pound of linseed, so as to have about a couple of quarts of thick fluid, to which two pounds of bran and one ounce of salt may be added. The whole should be stirred up, covered over, and allowed to steam, as before described. The thicker the mash, the more readily will the horse eat it.

Linseed tea is made by boiling one pound of linseed in a couple of gallons of water, until the grains are quite soft. It may be economically made by using less water to cook the linseed, and afterwards making up the quantity of water to about a gallon and a half.

Hay tea may be prepared by filling a bucket, after scalding it, with good sweet hay, pouring in as much boiling water as the bucket will hold, covering it over, and allowing it to stand until cold, when the fluid may be strained off and given to the horse. This forms a refreshing drink.

Linseed oil, in quantities of from one quarter to half pint daily, may be mixed through the food. It keeps the bowels in a lax condition, has a good effect on the skin and air passages, and is useful as an article of diet.

When debility has to be combated, as in low fevers or other weakening diseases, strengthening and easily digested food must be administered; though some of the foods already mentioned, such as boiled grain, answer this purpose to a certain extent. Milk, eggs, bread and biscuits, malt liquor, corn, etc., are often prescribed with this object. Milk may be given skimmed or unskimmed; a little sugar may be mixed in it, and one or two gallons of it may be given daily, according to circumstances. One or two eggs may be given beaten up with a little sugar, and mixed with milk, three or four times a day, or more frequently; or they may be boiled hard and powdered, and mixed in the milk. A quart of stout, ale, or porter, may be given two or three times a day, or a half to one bottle of port wine daily. Scalded oats, with a little salt added, are very useful when convalescence is nearly completed.

With regard to *water*, as a rule a sick horse may have as much as he likes to drink, though it may be necessary in certain cases to give a limited quantity, and to have the chill taken off; but it should never be warmer than seventy-five to eighty degrees.

As for *grooming*, as little of this as possible should be allowed when a horse is very weak, and it should be limited to sponging about the mouth, nostrils, eyes, and forehead with clean water, to which a little vinegar may be added; hand-rub the legs and the ears; take off the clothing, and shake or change it once a day; and, if agreeable, rub over the body with a soft cloth.

Exercise, of course, is not required during sickness or injury, and the period at which it is allowed will depend upon circumstances. Care must be taken that it is not ordered too early, or carried too far at first.

ADMINISTERING MEDICINES.

How to give a ball.—Much care is required in administering medicines in the form of ball or bolus; and practice, as well as courage and tact, are needed in order to give it without danger to the administrator or to the animal. The ball may be held between the four fingers of the right hand, the tips of the first and fourth being brought together below the second and third, which are placed on the upper side of the ball; the right hand is thus made as small as possible, so as to admit of ready insertion into the mouth. The left hand grasps the horse's tongue, gently pulls it out, and places it on that part of the right side of the lower jaw which is bare of teeth. The right hand carries the ball along, and leaves it at the root of the tongue. The moment the right hand is withdrawn, the tongue is released. This causes the ball to be brought still further back. The operator then closes the mouth, and looks at the left side of the neck, in order that he may note the passage of the ball down the gullet. Many horses keep a ball in the mouth a considerable time before they will allow it to go down. A mouthful of water or a handful of food will generally make them swallow it readily. If this does not succeed, the horse's nostrils may be grasped by the hand, and held a few moments. A running halter should be used, so that the mouth may be quickly and securely closed.

If the operator has had but limited experience in giving balls, he should station an assistant on the near side, to aid in opening and steadying the mouth, by placing the fingers of his left hand on the lower jaw, and the thumb of the right on the upper jaw. Holding the mouth in this manner facilitates the giving of the ball, and saves the operator's right hand, to a great extent, from becoming scratched by the horse's back teeth.

A most essential precaution to observe is to have the ball moderately soft; nothing can be more dangerous than a hard one.

To give a drink or drench.—This requires as much care as giving a ball, in order to avoid choking the horse, though it is unattended with risk to the administrator. An ordinary glass or stone bottle may be used, provided there are no sharp points around the mouth, though the usual drenching horn or a tin vessel with a narrow mouth or spout are safer. When giving the drink, it is necessary to raise the horse's head, so that the nose be a little higher than the horizontal line; this may be done, if the horse is quiet, by an assistant; but if he is restless, it is necessary to keep the head elevated by a loop of cord inserted into the mouth over the upper jaw, the prong of a stable fork being passed through it, and the handle steadily held by the assistant. The drink is then to be given by a person standing on the right side (the assistant being in front or on the left side of the horse), the side of the mouth being pulled out a little, to form a sack or funnel, into which the medicine is poured a little at a time, allowing an interval now and again for the horse to swallow. If any of the fluid gets into the windpipe (which it is likely to do if the head is held too high), coughing will be set up, when the head should be instantly lowered. Neither the tongue nor the nostrils should be interfered with.

Powders may be given in a little mash or gruel, well stirred up.

Fomentations or *bathing*, are the application to the skin or feet of warm water. If a wide surface is to be fomented (as the chest, abdomen, or loins), a blanket or other large woollen cloth should be dipped in water as hot as the hand can comfortably bear it, moderately wrung out, and applied to the part, the heat and moisture being retained by covering it with a waterproof sheet or dry rug. When it has lost some of its heat, it should be removed, dipped in the hot water, and again applied. In case of acute inflammation, it may be necessary to have the water a little hotter; and, to avoid the inconvenience of removing the blanket, or the danger of chill when it is removed, the blanket may be secured around the body by skewers or twine, the hot water being poured on the outside of the blanket by any convenient vessel; of course the water should be poured on the top part, so as to allow it to run down. With regard to the feet, these may be placed in a bucket or tub (the latter should have the whole bottom resting on the ground) containing warm water; a quantity of moss litter put in the tub or bucket, so as to make a thick mass, is an excellent mode of fomenting, as it prevents splashing, and retains the heat longer.

POULTICES.

Poultices are used for allaying pain, promoting suppuration, softening horn or other tissues, and bringing on a healthy action in wounds. To be beneficial, they should be large, and always kept moist.

For applying poultices to the feet, a *poultice-shoe*, constructed as follows, may be used with advantage.

Take a circular piece of hard wood, a little longer and broader than a horse-shoe, and about one and a half inches thick. Get one surface of it rounded in a lathe, so that there may be a rise of about three-quarters of an inch in the centre, while the other surface remains flat. Round the circumference of the board have leather nailed, so as to form a convenient boot for retaining the poultice. This is similar to the boot in ordinary use, except that the part which comes on the ground is rounded. The fact of its being round will enable the horse to whose foot it is applied to ease the affected spot by throwing weight on the toe, the heel, or on either quarter, as he chooses. (Hayes.)

Poultices are usually made with bran, though this has the disadvantage of drying very quickly, to remedy which it may be mixed with linseed meal or with a little linseed oil. Boiled turnips or carrots, mashed up, make a good poultice, as does linseed meal, when mixed with boiling water, and a little olive oil added by stirring.

A charcoal poultice is sometimes used when there is a bad smell to be got rid of. It is made by adding linseed meal to boiling water, and stirring until a soft mass is produced; with this some wood-charcoal in powder is mixed, and, when ready to be applied, some more powder is sprinkled on the surface.

It may be noted that, in lieu of these materials for poultices, the material known as spongio-piline can be usefully employed. A piece of sufficient size is steeped in hot water, applied to the part, covered with a larger piece of oiled silk or waterproof stuff, and secured there. Even an ordinary sponge, steeped in hot water, and covered with any waterproof material, makes a very good poulticing medium; it is well adapted for the throat, near the head, as well as for the space between the branches of the lower jaw.

ENEMAS OR CLYSTERS.

These are given in fevers, inflammations, constipation, etc., to empty the posterior part of the bowels. They are administered by a large syringe, which can contain a quart or more of water, with a nozzle about twelve inches in length; with an ox's bladder tied to a pipe; or a large funnel with a long nozzle at a right angle; but the syringe is best. Water alone is usually employed for enemas; it should be about the temperature of the body, not less, but perhaps a degree or two more. To administer it, one of the horse's fore-feet should be held up, while the operator (having filled the instrument, and smeared the end of the nozzle with a little lard or oil) pushes the latter very gently and steadily for a few inches into the intestine, and then presses out the water. The amount injected will depend upon the size of the animal; from two to three quarts would suffice for an ordinary-sized horse.

FEVERS.

Fever is the term given to a condition of the body in which the temperature is higher than natural, this is accompanied by a quickened pulse and, generally, quickened breathing. It may be noted that the natural pulse in the horse is from thirty-five to forty-five beats in the minute, being slowest in heavy horses, quicker in those which are well bred, and quickest in small and young animals. The pulse is usually felt at the edge of the lower jaw, a little in front of its circular margin. The middle finger is the best to feel it with, and this is best done by passing it inside the border of the jaw, and pressing the artery steadily against the bone. The number of respirations in the horse is twelve to fourteen per minute. It is best observed at the flank.

There are several kinds of fever in the horse, and fever is also a frequent accompaniment of diseases, as well as of wounds or injuries. The temperature of the horse in health is about 100° F., but in fever and disease it may rise as high as 108° or 110°, while in recovery from acute fevers it may fall one or two degrees below the normal standard. The temperature of the surface of the body may vary even when fever is present (the legs or ears being cold, or cold and hot by turns), but the internal temperature may remain constant during these external fluctuations. This temperature is best ascertained by means of a clinical thermometer; though a finger passed into the mouth will afford a pretty good indication as to whether fever is present or absent.

There are several kinds of fever, some of which are due to the entrance of a particular poison into the body—specific fevers, for example; others are due to wounds or injuries; but others, again, may be due to functional derangement of certain organs—such as simple fever.

SIMPLE FEVER.

In this condition no particular organs are involved, but there is simply higher temperature, quicker breathing, more frequent pulse, dulness, dry mouth and skin, and diminished appetite. It may be due to various causes, such as fatigue, exposure to extremes of temperature, change from the open air or well-ventilated stables to those which are close, hot, foul, etc.

There are no indications that the animal is suffering pain, and the breathing, though a little quicker, does not show that the chest is involved.

Treatment.—The first thing to be done is to remove the animal to a cool, clean, airy loose box. If the limbs are cold have them well hand-rubbed, and apply flannel bandages; if the surface of the body is also cold, put on a woollen rug or two if necessary; but if, on the contrary, it is very hot and dry, benefit may be obtained by sponging it over with cold water and vinegar now and again. Should the horse appear to have headache—which is manifested by drooping head and listlessness, with, frequently, swollen eyelids, and tears running down the cheeks, and hot forehead—the application of cloths dipped in vinegar and water to the forehead and temples will afford relief. In ordinary cases little more is required than to give sloppy food and gruel to drink, in which a little nitrate of potass—one ounce to the pailful—may be dissolved; or the latter may be put in the drinking water. Green forage, if procurable, should be allowed, and if constipation is present a dose of Epsom salts (about half a pound) dissolved in water ought to be given as a drench. If much debility supervenes, two or three quarts of beer may be given in the course of the day.

INFLUENZA.

This is a fever of a specific kind known by various names, such as Pink Eye, Bilous Fever, Epizootic Catarrh, Distemper, etc., which in almost every outbreak shows somewhat different symptoms: sometimes appearing as catarrhal fever; at other times involving the lungs, liver, bowels, or brain; and in other invasions being complicated with rheumatism, or inflammation of the skin and connective tissue beneath. But in whatever form it may appear, the chief symptom is great debility. Though it sometimes is widely spread, affecting nearly all the horses of a town or country, and though its appearance in a stable or district is generally due to the introduction of horses, healthy or sick, from places in which it is prevalent, yet opinions are divided as to whether it is infectious, or due to some morbid influence in the air; nevertheless, it is best and safest to look upon it as an infectious disease, and to treat it accordingly.

It begins very suddenly, with marked fever, great dulness, and extreme weakness. Symptoms of headache are present, the limbs seem stiff and weak, the pulse is quickened, and the eyelids swollen and tearful, and if inverted they appear pink or dark red. There is disinclination to move, the legs become more or less swollen, and a short, painful cough, betraying soreness of the throat, and difficulty of swallowing, are sometimes noted. The expired air is hot, and the breathing more or less hurried; if the nostrils are dilated, and the breathing hurried and shallow, inflammation of the lungs is to be apprehended. Sometimes there is a discharge from the nostrils, as in catarrh; or this may be absent, and only a thin, yellow, transparent fluid escaping from the nostril. When the bowels are involved, the horse exhibits signs of abdominal pain, such as stamping with the hind-feet and general uneasiness. And if the liver is involved also, the lining membrane of the eyelid will be of a yellowish-red hue; while constipation or diarrhœa are almost invariably present. In the rheumatic form, the knees or hocks, or both, become swollen and extremely painful, as well as the sheath of the back tendons.

Treatment.—This is a fever which often demands all the skill of the veterinary surgeon to grapple with successfully, as in some outbreaks it is very fatal unless judiciously treated. A most important precaution to be adopted is laying the horse off work the moment illness is apparent. To prevent the spread of the disease also, a sick horse should at once be isolated from those yet healthy, and all communication between it and them, by means of persons, stable utensils, etc., should be interdicted.

The chief part in the treatment to which the amateur should attend, is careful nursing. An airy stable or loose box, at a temperature of 60° if possible, should be secured; the surface of the body ought to be kept equable by means of clothing, and the legs maintained at the normal temperature by hand-rubbing and woollen bandages. Gruel of bran or oatmeal, with a little nitre therein, or cold water with nitre, should be allowed for drink; while as for food, this may be bran-mash with a few scalded oats, or a little boiled linseed, and green forage or carrots. If the throat is sore, this may be stimulated well up towards the ears, between the branches of the lower jaw and down the neck, with white liniment; and if the cough is severe, the inhalation of steam from a bucket of boiling water, in which hay is soaked, may be ordered.

Should there be constipation, without symptoms of bowel complication, enemas should be administered, and a mild dose of Epsom salts. If great debility is present, a mild stimulant may be given, such as a quart of ale, with a little powdered ginger therein, twice or three times a day; and when recovery is taking place, scalded oats in larger quantity, with a little good hay, ought to be given until the health be fully established. When rheumatism is present, the joints and inflamed parts may be frequently rubbed with the white or turpentine liniment, to which a few drops of the tincture of aconite have been added, and kept warm. If diarrhœa is present, this should not be checked unless it decreases the debility, and the surface of the body and the legs become cold, when starch, or flour gruel, with an ounce or two of prepared chalk mixed in it, should be given to the animal to drink, or administered as a drench. If the abdominal pain is very acute, and causes distress, blankets wrung out of water as hot as the hand can bear, should be applied around the belly; and the same treatment ought to be adopted if the chest is involved.

The chief indications in the treatment of influenza are fresh air, careful nursing, and the maintenance of the strength.

STRANGLES.

This is a specific fever, contagious in its nature, peculiar to the horse species, chiefly attacking young animals, and somewhat allied to mumps in the human species, or distemper in the dog. Horses between two and six years old are those specially predisposed; and one attack—like small-pox or measles in man—generally secures immunity from a second. Of its contagiousness there can be no doubt, and that it exists only by its contagious properties there is powerful evidence to show. Horses transferred from the country to town stables are most liable to the disease, and especially if the stables are hot and crowded; but unless there is or has been a sick animal in these stables, or the horses have been brought in some way into contact with the disease, they will not have strangles.

The early symptoms are fever, dulness, loss of appetite, sometimes a cough, and discharge from the nostrils. The space between the jaws becomes filled up with a soft, diffused swelling, which increases day by day, sometimes extending behind the jaw towards the ears, involving the glands in that locality. This swelling is very tender on pressure, and in about a week or ten days an abscess forms, which, if not opened, bursts spontaneously, and a large quantity of matter escapes, when the animal experiences relief, and the fever subsides; swallowing, which was before difficult, becomes easy; and the breathing, if hitherto impeded and noisy, becomes normal; at the same time, the head, which had the nose poked out, and was held stiff and immovable, is now moved freely about. The appetite returns, the animal is bright and lively, and feeds well. This is the favourable course of strangles, and is that which is generally noted.

Among foals, or animals in poor condition, however, the disease often assumes a more serious character, and may even prove fatal. The swelling may be so great, or situated so near the top of the windpipe, as to threaten suffocation; and this may be so imminent that, to save the patient, it may be necessary to open the windpipe below the swelling, and insert a tube, through which it can breathe. Or the abscess between the jaws may not form properly, or even when it does so form, may be succeeded by one or more abscesses in other parts, as at the root of the ear, on the back, at the bottom of the neck, in the chest, or in the abdomen. Sometimes these abscesses are of considerable extent, and may appear at widely distant parts of the body. When they form internally, in the chest or the abdomen, a fatal termination is almost certain. In this irregular form of strangles—usually termed bastard, or malignant—the fever runs much higher, wasting is greater, and if the animal survives it may be a long time in recovering from the effects of the disease.

A very common sequel to strangles is the occurrence of "roaring," from implication of the nerves and muscles of the larynx—a result which is much to be dreaded, from its causing the animal to be unsound, and one which should impel horse-owners or breeders to adopt every measure possible to extinguish the disease.

Treatment.—This disease, like influenza, requires careful nursing. The animal should be put into an airy, loose box, kept comfortable, and the sanitary surroundings attended to; sloppy diet, such as bran- and linseed-mashes, boiled barley, or oatmeal gruel; the solid food given that easily masticated, such as sliced carrots, freshly cut grass, or hay steeped in boiling water, the horse being allowed to eat the hay and drink the infusion when cold. If constipation is present, this may be overcome by enemas, though these are rarely required. If the fever runs very high, or the disease assumes a malignant form, one or two drachms of quinine may be given in a little water (a few drops of sulphuric acid having been added) in drench twice or three times a day, until the fever is diminished. In order to expedite formation of the abscess, the swelling between the jaws may be frequently fomented with warm water, or a poultice, consisting of linseed-meal or bran in a bag, may be tied upon the part by means of tapes across the face and behind the ears; or a little cantharides ointment may be rubbed into the part. When the tumour is ready for opening, it begins to point—*i.e.*, a prominence forms which is soft, and the hair falls off; the matter may then be allowed to escape by making a small incision at this part, and afterwards inserting a small piece of lint or tow into the wound, so as to insure the complete evacuation of the contents.

Should the breathing become difficult and noisy, the horse should be made to inhale steam from boiling water and hay, on which two or three ounces of oil of turpentine have been poured. Abscesses forming in other parts of the body should be opened as soon as ripe. It is well not to attempt to administer drenches while the swelling exists, as swallowing is difficult, for fear of choking the animal; but when this has subsided, if there is much loss of condition, or the animal is very weak, two or three quarts of ale per day may be carefully administered. When the fever has completely subsided, and the animal is recovering, a liberal allowance of good food should be given.

In order to diminish the chances of "roaring" appearing, one or two drachms of iodide of potassium may be given in a small quantity of water, for a week or so after the appearance of the disease.

GLANDERS AND FARCY.

These two designations are applied to the same disease, according as it shows itself upon the surface of the body or in the interior; and both manifestations are not unfrequently met with in the same animal. Glanders is a specific disease of horses and other soliped animals (ass, mule, etc.), to which it is peculiar, and is accompanied by more or less fever. It is a very contagious and fatal disease, its course being rapid or acute, and chronic or slow, and it is transmissible not only from sick to healthy animals, but also to mankind. It exists solely because of its contagious properties, and cannot be developed spontaneously — *i.e.* without pre-existing contagion; though bad sanitary arrangements—such as dirty, foul stables, bad drainage and ventilation, and general uncleanliness, or over-exertion, or bad or insufficient food—are greatly in favour of its attacking horses and spreading amongst them, by weakening them. It is a most difficult disease to eradicate when it appears in large stables, and the greatest possible care is necessary to prevent its spread. It is a loathsome malady, and a real plague of horses. Healthy horses will take it by drinking from infected water-troughs, being put into stables in which glandered horses have stood, as well as by coming in contact with diseased horses, directly or indirectly, and in other ways. The infection can be retained in stables, horse-clothing, and other articles, for a very long time; and, therefore, in order to get rid of the disease, it is necessary to adopt the most energetic measures as regards cleansing and disinfection.

In some cases of glanders, the internal organs may be alone involved for some time, and when these are the lungs, the horse may be quite capable of infecting others without its condition being suspected, the symptoms then being a short hacking cough, like that of broken wind, disturbed respiration, and altered sounds in the lungs, perceived when the ear is applied to the sides and chest. Glanders, however, is, in the majority of cases, manifested by three classical signs, which are, when present at the same time, confirmatory of the presence of the disease. These signs are: the discharge from one or both nostrils of a thick glutinous matter, which adheres around the nostril, and gives it a very characteristic appearance; ulcers or sores of an unhealthy character inside the nose; and a hard, painless enlargement of the gland between the branches of the lower jaw, the enlargement feeling dense and nodular, as if it were a walnut under the skin. The discharge, ulceration, and enlarged gland are usually confined to one side of the head; in some rare cases, the ulceration may be so high up the nose as to be non-apparent; but in such cases the sticky discharge is often streaked with blood, and, if ulceration is suspected, the barb of a goose-quill passed up the nostril will generally remove any doubt, by its becoming blood-tinted. In other cases, again, there may be ulceration and enlarged gland without much, if any, discharge (dry glanders), while in other cases the discharge so much resembles that of ordinary catarrh, or chronic non-contagious inflammation of the cavities of the head, that, to remove doubt, it is essential to inoculate a donkey or a worthless horse, in order to ascertain whether it is really glanders, as, if the inoculated animal shows signs of farcy at the seat of inoculation, all doubt is dispelled. In chronic glanders, after the early fever has passed off, a horse may remain in good condition, and perform a considerable amount of work, for a long time, though he will eventually have the disease in an acute form, and die. In acute glanders a horse may succumb in a few days.

In farcy, the skin is the chief seat of the disease, and here we have, in some cases, swellings take place, sometimes on the legs, sometimes on the face, and other times the surface of the body, with small knots or lumps here and there, and swollen lines, like cords, passing from them.

These knots soon burst, leaving ulcers of a very unhealthy character, which spread and become deeper, with matter and blood discharging from them. When a limb is attacked (usually a hind one), there is generally much lameness and great pain.

In glanders and farcy, as a rule, the animals lose condition, the coat looks unthrifty, and the hairs of the mane and tail are easily pulled out.

Treatment—There is no cure known as yet for this disease, and, whenever any of the above symptoms are discovered in a horse, a veterinary surgeon should at once be sent for. Should it be pronounced glanders or farcy, the animal ought at once to be destroyed and buried, or sent to the knacker, and every precaution taken with regard to cleansing and disinfection of the stable, harness, clothing, etc.; while other horses which may have been in contact with it, or inhabiting the same stable, should be isolated from others, if possible, and closely watched for a period of at least six months.

LYMPHANGITIS, WEED, OR INFLAMED LEG.

This is an inflammation of the lymphatic vessels and glands of a limb, accompanied by much swelling, pain, and fever. It occurs suddenly, more frequently attacks a hind- than a fore-limb, and, in the great majority of cases, is caused by over-feeding and insufficient exercise. It very often appears (and especially in coarse-bred horses) after resting on Sunday, the week-day allowance of food having been given on that day. It sometimes follows from an injury to the foot. The symptoms are well marked. There is at first a shivering fit, which is followed by a hot one, quickened pulse and breathing, and high fever; coincident with this, the leg begins to swell, the glands in the groin being, perhaps, first affected, and the swelling extending downwards until it reaches the hoof. There are great soreness and lameness in the limb, and the animal suffers so much that the body is often covered with perspiration. The inflammation continues for three or four days, or longer, according to circumstances, and then subsides, generally leaving the leg thicker than before. The inflammation is very liable to recur, and each attack leaves the limb more enlarged, until it may attain a great size, especially in waggon horses.

Treatment.—A full dose of physic should immediately be given, and an enema administered; while sloppy food, or grass, ought only to be given as diet. The limb should be fomented continuously with warm water, and when this is stopped it should be well dried, and enveloped in flannel bandages.

An ounce or two of nitre may be mixed in the drinking water. The animal should be kept at rest until the inflammatory symptoms have subsided, and the body kept warmly clothed.

After the pain and swelling have considerably diminished, exercise may be allowed. Great care should be observed afterwards in feeding and working the horse, and in apportioning the food to the amount of labour undergone.

RHEUMATISM.

Rheumatism is characterised by pain and inflammation of joints or other parts, which has a tendency to shift from one part of the body to another, and is accompanied by fever, which may be more or less acute. Exposure to wet and cold, or to draughts of cold air, is generally the cause, and young animals appear to be more disposed to it than old ones. If acute, it is a serious disease, as it always leaves alterations in the parts affected, and has a tendency to involve the heart; it is also liable to recur, and subsequent attacks are generally more severe than the first.

In acute rheumatism there are all the indications of high fever, and one or more joints become swollen and very painful, the inflammation producing intense lameness. The stifle, hock, knee, and fetlock joints are those usually affected, though the sheaths of the tendons may also suffer. Sometimes the inflammation appears only in one joint, to suddenly leave it and attack another, flying about in the most erratic way.

In very severe cases, the inflammation may run on to suppuration, but this result is not very frequent. The acute is very often followed by the chronic form, in which there is less fever, and the inflammation does not so readily move about. This usually leads to permanent enlargement, with partial destruction, of the joints.

When the muscles are the seat of rheumatism, swelling is not noticeable to any extent, and the fever is not high, though there is great pain on movement or on handling the parts. The shoulders, loins, and quarters are the most frequent seat of this kind of rheumatism.

Treatment.—In acute rheumatism, warmth is of the greatest moment. Fomentations with warm water, to which poppy heads have been added, afterwards drying the skin well and enveloping the parts in flannel bandages, should be at once resorted to, and the animal warmly clothed, and kept as quiet as possible. Before the application of the bandages, after the fomentations, the inflamed part may be rubbed with aconite liniment. A mild dose of physic should be administered, and sloppy food given, with two or three ounces of the bicarbonate of soda mixed in it daily, nitre being given in the drinking water. Should the pain be very distressing, hypodermic injections of morphia may be given. When the inflammation is subsiding, the parts should be well rubbed with turpentine and ammonia liniment.

The same treatment should be adopted in the chronic form. In muscular rheumatism, nursing and warmth are the chief agencies to be relied upon to effect recovery. For local application, the liniment just mentioned may be used, with laxative food and alkaline medicines, such as the bicarbonate of soda.

DISEASES OF THE AIR PASSAGES.

ROARING.

The sound generally recognised as "roaring" is indicative of some obstruction at one part or another of the air passages, which is particularly manifest when the affected horse is put to undue exertion.

The respiratory act in the healthy horse, even when greatly accelerated by severe exertion, is devoid of harsh "whistling," or "roaring" sounds; on the contrary, respiration is performed with a certain amount of smoothness and clearness.

Lesions capable of producing the unnatural sounds may be met with in the nasal passages, in the form of abnormal growths, such as nasal tumours, enlarged bones, etc.; also diminution of the calibre of the nasal passages may arise from injuries from without, resulting from a fall or kick, and so reduce the area of the nasal cavity, which must alter the sound of the air current passing through them.

The application of surgical skill, in many of these cases, will result frequently in permanent relief or cure.

Roaring is sometimes produced by various growths at the posterior part of the mouth; various secretions in, and bulging of, the guttural pouches also serve to diminish the diameter of the windpipe by pressing upon it.

Roaring and "whistling" (for the two have the same origin) are most frequently brought about by disease of the larynx; and even in this situation, it may sometimes be of a temporary character, such as abnormal respiratory sounds during convalescence after a severe catarrhal affection with a retarded recovery, or during any inflammatory process in connection with the structures of the laryngeal regions.

In these cases, the products of the inflammatory action may become sufficiently organised to be of permanent derangement. In treating such cases, severe irritants must be applied to the skin covering the affected regions. The application of a seton to the throat is frequently productive of much benefit, unless the affection has been apparent for a considerable time.

The most common cause of roaring is atrophy, degeneration, and paralysis of important muscles of the larynx.

The disease probably arises from a diseased condition of the recurrent nerve which supplies nearly all the muscles of the larynx with motor power.

When the tone of the muscles is thus lost, they cease to have the power of opening the cartilages of the larynx; consequently the calibre of the opening is diminished, and alteration of the respiratory sounds must follow, oftener during the act of inspiration than expiration.

Distortion of the trachea from pressure, or long-continued use of the tight bearing-rein, may aid in the production of "roarers."

Of the methods of detection employed in ascertaining the existence of roaring, galloping is perhaps the best. A horse can be made to cough by pressing the larynx between the fingers. A deep, hollow cough generally accompanies the disease, and if startled whilst firmly being held by the head, a grunting sound will sometimes be emitted.

Though grunting does not necessarily denote a "roarer," it should always be looked upon with great suspicion, and the animal be put to a severe test.

A "wheezer" is a mild roarer, but a "whistler" is an intense roarer. As has been already stated, contraction of the windpipe produces roaring, and further contraction causes the higher pitched sound known as "whistling."

The fact of roaring being undoubtedly hereditary, indicates that breeding from sires or dams so affected should be discouraged.

CATARRH.

Catarrh, coryza, or common cold, is one of the most ordinary affections of the horse. It is an acute inflammation of the membrane which lines the nasal chambers, the posterior nasal structures, and upper portions of the trachea. It may or may not be accompanied with febrile symptoms, of which the chief is elevation of temperature. There is more or less sneezing, with increased redness of the lining membranes of the nose and eyelids. The nasal discharge is at first thin, but after a few days it becomes rather yellow in colour, and irregularly discharged. Tears flow freely, and the cough is at the beginning hard and dry, afterwards moist, from the secretions which are thrown out.

In addition to these symptoms, the horse appears languid and dull; the coat is staring, and shivering fits may occur. The pulse is more frequent, and respiration accelerated; in the more severe cases, the appetite is impaired, and there is thirst.

Catarrh is most common in young horses, especially when first brought into stables during the spring and autumn.

A sudden fall in the temperature is a frequent cause of common cold; though a low temperature has little influence on horses existing under favourable circumstances, such as being located in warm and thoroughly dry stables, with ample ventilation, and no draughts.

Treatment.—In mild cases of catarrh, good nursing is of more importance than medicine. The patient should be moved into a light, well-ventilated, and roomy loose box, and be allowed extra clothing and flannel bandages; moist and warm food, without much corn; and while the throat is sore, it is better not to give medicine in any form which would cause pain or difficulty in swallowing.

Two drachms of nitrate or chlorate of potash, or two drachms of each, given twice daily in the drinking water or bran-mash, will be found useful; also inhalations of steam.

If constipation be present, two ounces of sulphate of magnesia are to be given twice daily, until the desired effect is produced. Enemata of tepid water are very beneficial when the bowels are confined.

The exhibition of aloes, or any powerful purgative, may produce dangerous results. In severe cases, where throat symptoms are marked, the application of mustard or stimulating liniment, or even cantharides ointment, must be resorted to.

Mild cases generally recover after a few days' treatment; but severe cases, especially if neglected, frequently run on to laryngitis, bronchitis, and other diseases of the respiratory organs, and occasionally nasal gleet will follow.

CHRONIC NASAL CATARRH.

Chronic nasal catarrh, or nasal gleet, shows itself by an unhealthy looking discharge, either continuous or intermittent, from the nostrils; cough and fever being absent.

Treatment.—Should it be the result of a cold, local and general treatment will be necessary. Local astringents can be applied to the membranes by means of a syringe or nasal funnel.

The ordinary steam applications are very useful, when a little carbolic or sulphuric acid has been placed in the bran or hay used for steaming. Astringents may also be used in the form of powder, blown up the nostrils, such as iodine or carbolic acid, mixed with finely ground liquorice-root or starch.

When the discharge is due to disease of the membranes of the nasal chambers, the odour of the discharge is rarely fœtid; but if the sinuses of the skull be invaded with disease, or the discharge proceed from a decayed molar, it will be fœtid and highly disagreeable.

Here surgical skill alone will remedy the derangement.

All cases of nasal gleet should be looked upon with suspicion, and kept isolated until a skilled veterinary surgeon is satisfied that the discharge is not glanderous.

SORE THROAT.

Sore throat, or laryngitis, is due to inflammation of the tissue surrounding the larynx, and of the mucous membrane which lines it. It is frequently associated with a similar condition of the pharynx, when the disease is known as pharyngo-laryngitis.

During an attack of sore throat, local pain is evident. The temperature is raised, denoting a feverish condition; and difficulty in swallowing is manifest, probably more from soreness of the throat than from fever.

The horse coughs often, and particularly during swallowing; also carries his nose rather elevated, to relieve pressure of the inflamed structures by straightening the angle in the throat.

An extra quantity of saliva is present in the mouth.

In severe cases combined with œdema—œdematous laryngitis—the animal may be suffocated by pressure of the swollen membrane, the fatal result being brought about in some instances after two days' illness.

In these cases the disease may not be alone confined to the throat, but may spread along the air passages, and if life be prolonged for a few days, there is generally fœtid breath, and discharge from the nostrils. The submaxillary glands are enlarged in most cases of sore throat.

Treatment.—Cold air must be avoided during an attack; the atmosphere should be warm and moist. Febrifuges, in the form of powders, placed in the drinking water, are very useful, inasmuch as it is painful and difficult to swallow medicine in the form of bolus. Medicated steam must be inhaled by the patient, though care must be taken not to irritate the membranes and produce needless coughing. Externally, liniment, hot water, or hot oil, may be applied to the laryngeal and parotideal regions, and will generally produce exceedingly good results.

Where there is danger of suffocation, surgical interference will be necessary in the operation of tracheotomy.

The likelihood of severe laryngitis producing roaring, has been already mentioned.

BRONCHITIS.

Bronchitis is, in itself, a diseased condition of the small bronchial or air tubes. Inflammation of these tubes causes difficult breathing, and fever is generally present, especially in the earlier stage. The pulse is frequent, and a harsh cough is present.

A horse once attacked with bronchitis is more or less liable to a second attack; therefore, such animals, during convalescence, require extra care and protection from wet, cold, and draught.

The effusion and mucus present in the air tubes produce a crackling sound during respiration, heard if the ear be placed against the side of the horse's chest. If the large tubes are chiefly affected, the bubbling sound will be less heard at the anterior part of the chest; and when the small tubes are the principal seat of disease, the abnormal sound is best auscultated behind the shoulder; the sound will then more closely resemble hissing than when the larger tubes are affected.

Serious, if not fatal, results may follow from the inflammatory products being inhaled into the minute tubes and air vesicles during laboured inspiration. Sore throat is sometimes an accompaniment of bronchitis. In this, as well as most febrile diseases—though a mild attack may not be associated with fever—there are loss of appetite and general weakness.

Treatment.—Medicated steam is a valuable agent in the affection; the chest and breast should be blistered or stimulated.

The extremities must be kept warm, and if constipation is present, enemata of tepid water, and linseed oil given in a bran-mash, will relieve 'the condition; powerful purgatives must be withheld. Powders of nitrate and chlorate of potash will allay fever, if present, and also act on the kidneys.

Tonics will be required during convalescence.

CHRONIC BRONCHITIS.

Acute bronchitis occasionally terminates in chronic bronchitis, in which there is chronic cough; and when the animal is put to undue exertion, that condition recognised by some as "thick wind," will manifest itself.

This condition will vary according to the circumstances under which the animal exists.

Treatment.—Though the chronic form does not readily yield to treatment, a ball containing about half a drachm each of camphor, extract of belladonna, and digitalis, given twice a day for a week or two, may be productive of some benefit; at the same time the bowels should be kept in a relaxed condition.

The work performed by the horse should not be very heavy.

CONGESTION OF THE LUNGS.

Pulmonary congestion, or "congestion of the lungs," is due to engorgement of the small blood-vessels which ramify throughout the lung tissue.

Acute congestion of the lungs is frequently seen in over-heated and badly-ventilated stables; and is by no means rare in horses in high condition, during an exhibition under cover, where heat and over-crowding both operate in the production of the disease.

Those atmospheric influences which tend to produce bronchitis, or common cold, are capable of producing this congestion.

Horses called upon to undergo a severe day's work when unprepared, are frequent subjects of congestion when suddenly brought into warm stables.

Animals which are suffering from disturbance of the respiratory system, or which have recently recovered from an attack, are more or less prone to congestion. Some cases are very distressing to the animal attacked.

The horse breathes heavily, with head and neck extended, and stands with its limbs wide apart. The mucous membranes of the nostrils are dark and bluish in colour, showing a deficiency of oxygen in the blood; the membranes of the eyelids are similarly affected. The extremities are generally cold, and the skin is covered with patchy perspiration.

Congestion, if not interrupted by death, may pass on to inflammation; but an ample supply of fresh air will often restore the horse to a normal state, though there is some weakness or liability to recurrence, which will remain for awhile.

Treatment.—In all cases of pulmonary congestion, the circulation in the extremities must be promoted by friction. The body should be kept warm by clothing, and the animal must have an unlimited supply of fresh air, and stimulants in moderation.

If other complications arise, they must be treated accordingly.

INFLAMMATION OF THE LUNGS.

The true lung substance is liable to inflammation, and this is associated with general fever. The tissue of the lung becomes invaded with the products of the inflammation, and the disease is generally spoken of as pneumonia.

Pneumonia is prevalent during sudden alternations of temperature.

It may be the result of previous disease, such as catarrh, debility, bronchitis, and sore throat; it sometimes breaks out among horses as an epizootic disease, and is even caused by direct irritation—such as irritating fluids given as medicine gaining access to the trachea, and ultimately the lungs. Pneumonia is usually preceded by catarrh; so that cough is generally present, though not necessarily so. The temperature is raised, and the pulse increased, but not easily felt.

The mucous membranes are injected, and a slight discharge, having a rusty appearance, frequently shows itself at the nostrils.

Rigors, or shivering fits, are by no means unfrequent, and the coat has a staring appearance.

The respiratory sounds are duller than usual. Urine is scanty, and the bowels rather confined; though powerful purgatives must be withheld. Respiration is accelerated and painful, the pain not being so manifest as in some other diseases of the chest—such as pleurisy.

Treatment.—No general line of treatment, applicable to every case of inflammation of the lungs, can be laid down; since it is generally attended with different complications in different individual cases, which must be treated accordingly.

Bran and oats, moistened with hot water, should be given, also febrifuges and saline diuretics. Stimulants will be necessary, and the bowels rendered moist by linseed oil in draught and enemata. Local treatment is very beneficial; it consists in the application of heat and moisture to the side of the chest, by means of hot-water cloths, over which a little turpentine has been sprinkled. On removing the fomenting cloth, the parts should be well hand-rubbed to ensure their drying readily.

The application of soap liniment and mustard is found useful, but powerful vesicants should be avoided. During convalescence, the animal will require much nursing and care to promote a good appetite, and restore the system to its usual tone.

ASTHMA

Paroxysmal attacks of difficult breathing are sometimes seen in the horse, closely resembling that condition known as "broken wind;" but it differs from it, inasmuch as the difficult breathing makes its appearance suddenly, and the duration of the attack is uncertain.

Asthma frequently precedes "broken wind," and is due to spasm of the muscular tissue of the small air-tubes; owing to this their calibre is diminished, and exceedingly distressing symptoms, while they last, are the result. During an attack, a wheezing noise may be heard on auscultation.

The disease is often complicated with a certain amount of fever; cough is generally very troublesome, and it will be noticed that the animal uses its abdominal muscles to aid respiration. Unlike "broken wind," asthma may yield to antispasmodics and sedatives; and when breathing is very severe, a blister to the side may relieve the symptoms.

BROKEN WIND.

"Broken wind" is a disturbed condition of the respiration, mostly marked during expiration, when a double respiratory effort seems necessary, inspiration being performed with comparative ease and steadiness.

It is accompanied with a short, suppressed, and characteristic cough.

During expiration, the abdominal muscles will be seen to contract with a double effort, as if to get rid of air which the paralysed contractile tissue of the lungs is unable to do.

Post-mortem examinations of lungs taken from broken-winded horses have frequently shown—though not always—an emphysematous condition. The partitions between the air sacs being ruptured, causes union of several of them into one cavity, and here the air lodges, leading to difficulty in its expulsion.

Though broken wind is incurable, it may be greatly modified in its effects by careful feeding; innutritious food and large quantities of water, with exertion immediately after such feeding, increases the severity of the disease.

Broken wind is more commonly seen in the coarser-bred horses, probably from the effects of injudicious dieting more than the breed.

Previous disease of the lungs, especially asthma, seems to have great influence in producing this peculiar and distressing malady. Severe exertion, when there is over-distension of the stomach and intestines, will sometimes suddenly give rise to it. Broken wind is, by some authorities, said to be hereditary.

Treatment.—Modification of the disease can only be brought about by feeding and watering in such a manner as to avoid physical discomfort from distension.

The horse should be fed in small quantities and often; the food to be nutritious and easily digested; for indigestion greatly aggravates the symptoms.

Of all medicines employed in this disease, arsenic seems to be the nearest to a specific. It is best given in the form of Fowler's solution; half an ounce of the solution, given night and morning, will generally moderate the symptoms in a remarkable manner. Now and again the use of the drug should be stopped for a few days.

This method of treatment only benefits the animal during its exhibition, a relapse to the previous degree of discomfort occurring soon after its discontinuance

PLEURISY.

The fine, thin membrane which lines the inside of the chest, and covers the lungs and heart, is named the pleura, and in its natural condition its smooth, moist surface enables the lungs to move easily, during their expansion and contraction of breathing, against the ribs, while it suspends them from the upper part of the chest. This membrane is very liable to inflammation, either in connection with inflammation of the lungs or independently, the inflammation being caused by the same agencies which give rise to pneumonia. Generally only one side of the chest is affected, especially at first. When independent of the latter, the symptoms appear suddenly, and are usually ushered in with a shivering fit; then the breathing becomes quick and shallow, the nostrils being dilated, the ribs, as it were, fixed, and the abdominal muscles being chiefly brought into play in respiration. Fever is present, with a dry, short, interrupted, painful cough, with a kind of sighing grunt, emitted now and again during expiration, or when turning round. The pulse is increased in frequency, and is generally small and hard; the horse stands with his head drooping, and disinclined to move, while pressure between the ribs of the affected side will produce manifestations of great pain. In the early stage, if the ear is applied to the side, a rustling sound will be heard, as if two sheets of parchment were rubbed together; but at a later stage this disappears. Should the inflammation not subside quickly, water is effused into the cavity of the chest, from the diseased membrane, and adhesion may take place between the lungs and the side. This condition of the chest is known by the absence of sound, on applying the ear to the chest, or the production of a dull sound on striking it with the knuckles. At this period there may be some abatement of the fever, with decrease of the pain; but if there is much effusion, the breathing is still quick, though more laboured, the nostrils being widely dilated, and the animal exhibits distress. Recovery is then rather doubtful; consequently, it is very important to call in a veterinary surgeon when the earlier symptoms appear, as a cure greatly depends upon prompt treatment at the commencement.

It may be noted that, in pneumonia and pleurisy, the horse very rarely lies down; if he does so, it is a sign either that he is much recovered, or sinking from exhaustion.

Treatment.—This is much the same as that for pneumonia: a comfortable, well-ventilated stable or loose box, free from draughts; mustard applied to the sides; or, better, fomentations to the sides by steeping a blanket in hot water, wringing the superfluous moisture from it, and then placing it round the chest, with a dry blanket or waterproof sheet over it; continue this for as long as possible, and when the fomentations are discontinued, dry the sides well, then rub some soap liniment into them; clothe the body comfortably. If the legs are cold, hand-rub and wrap them in flannel bandages. Give sloppy diet, with some nitrate of potass in the water given to drink; administer enemas.

DISEASES OF THE DIGESTIVE ORGANS.

With a few rare exceptions, diseases of the digestive apparatus result from errors in dieting.

INDIGESTION WITHOUT ENGORGEMENT.

The causes are very various, such as improper food; diseased teeth, causing improper mastication; debility, both constitutional and of the organs themselves; and many other causes. There is loss or capriciousness of appetite; the animal evinces a desire to eat filth, and has a sour mouth and great thirst. He becomes hide-bound, and the coat stares; the bowels are irregular, and there is a frequent escape of flatus by the anus. The urine is commonly of a dark colour, and thick.

Treatment.—This will depend upon the cause. The diet in all cases should be changed, and given in smaller quantities at shorter intervals. It will be found advisable to give a mild aperient, such as a moderate dose of aloes, followed by small doses (two drachms) of bicarbonate of soda, combined with vegetable tonics, such as gentian.

INDIGESTION WITH ENGORGEMENT.

This is caused by the distension of the stomach, either with solids, or gases arising from fermentation of substances within the organ, generally resulting from the food being taken in too great quantity, or by its being imperfectly masticated. There is great restlessness, pawing with the fore-feet, especially the near foot; escape of flatus, distension of the abdomen, rigors, patchy sweats upon the body, and colicky pains.

Treatment.—Aloetic purgatives; if the animal is in great pain, enemas and hot fomentations to the abdomen will be found of great service. If the stomach is distended with gas, turpentine, oil, and carbonate of ammonia should be administered, care being taken to prevent the animal from throwing himself about, and thus preventing rupture of the stomach, for which there is no remedy.

COLIC.

Colic is the most common disease of the digestive organs, and is generally observed in two forms— spasmodic and flatulent. *Spasmodic colic* is a spasmodic contraction of the muscular coats of the intestines, which often runs on to inflammation. The causes are improper food or cold water, changes of diet, exhaustion from over-work associated with fasting, and many other causes, which, though trivial, yet, when combined with certain influences, are quite sufficient to produce the disease. Colicky pains are often caused by parasites contained in the intestines, and also by diseases of other organs, such as the kidneys and liver. The pain is usually sudden; the horse paws with his feet, kicks at his belly, looks round with a longing, uneasy expression at the flanks, lies down, and rolls on his back, or else lies outstretched; then, suddenly rising, he shakes himself, and is free from pain for a short time until again attacked. During the pain the breathing is hurried, the animal sighing and panting; the pulse is quickened, full or hard. There are usually frequent ineffectual efforts to urinate; and if the animal has been fed on green food, diarrhœa is usually present.

Treatment.—Colic is best treated with purgative medicine and enemas. A ball may be given which should contain from five to ten drachms of aloes, depending upon the size of the animal and its food. The enemas should be of tepid water, to which a small quantity of tincture of opium may be added with advantage. Hot fomentations to the belly, and friction, are also serviceable. In slight attacks, a draught, composed of a stimulant combined with an opiate, as nitric ether and tincture of opium, will generally afford relief. Free urination is the most favourable sign of the subsidence of colic.

Flatulent colic is sometimes primary, but more often follows an attack of the spasmodic form, and is of a more serious nature.

Its causes are usually weak digestion, but more commonly food which easily ferments, as raw potatoes, green clover, or brewers' grains. It may also be due to crib-biting or wind-sucking.

In this form the pain is more constant than in the spasmodic form; the abdomen is more or less swollen, and sounds hollow when struck; the pulse is quick and feeble; the breathing is difficult; and the animal is more careful when rolling than when suffering from spasm. The treatment is the same as that given for indigestion with engorgement.

ENTERITIS, OR INFLAMMATION OF THE BOWELS.

This is, perhaps, the most rapidly fatal inflammatory disease to which the horse is liable, killing in a very few hours. The small intestines are most involved.

The most frequent causes are exposure to cold, over-fatigue, washing with very cold water (when the animal is heated, and afterwards not properly clothed), indigestion, strangulation of intestines, and colic.

The first perceptible signs are evidence of abdominal pain, preceded by constitutional disturbance, shivering, quick breathing, general depression, dulness, and repeated evacuations of small quantities of fæces. The appetite is lost, the pulse is hard and quick; as the pain increases the animal becomes restless, paws, rolls about (though with care), and stands as if trying to balance himself. At last he falls, and dies after a few convulsive struggles.

Treatment.—Two great principles are to be attended to: arrest the pain, and stop, as much as possible, the movements of the intestines. For these purposes, opiates must be administered in large doses.

One to two ounces of tincture of opium, or two or three drachms of opium powder in water, may be administered, followed by smaller doses at intervals, or one ounce of extract of belladonna may be given. Hot fomentations should be applied for at least an hour to the abdomen; enemas of warm water may be administered very gently, but not too often, and if they increase the pain, they must be stopped at once.

Subcutaneous injections of morphia are very useful, when used locally, in some cases.

When the appetite returns, the food must be of the most easily digestible character, such as bran mashes and boiled linseed, in very moderate quantity.

Stimulants should not be given, unless tympanitis is present, when one or two doses may be tried; they may be continued if they give relief; but, if not, they should at once be discontinued.

DIARRHŒA.

This is a term usually applied to all simple purging in which the fæces are liquid. It may be an effort to discharge from the bowels anything obnoxious to them, or to the system generally.

Horses that are not well "ribbed up," and those of a nervous temperament, are particularly prone to diarrhœa ; they are difficult to keep in condition, but will sometimes do very well if kept on good food and at slow work.

The symptoms are purging, the fæces being semi-fluid, and either clay-coloured and fœtid, or light brown without offensive odour.

If it last over a lengthened period, the animal loses appetite and flesh, and sometimes dropsy of the belly may ensue.

Treatment.—A mild aperient (as linseed oil) will be found sometimes to act very well, more especially if the purging is produced by some irritant in the intestines.

The diet must in all cases be changed.

If the bowels do not regain their normal condition after the action of the aperient has subsided, it will be found necessary to use, very cautiously, some mild astringent (as prepared chalk, combined with opium) ; and, if the animal is very weak, repeated doses of nitric ether should be given.

If this treatment is found to be unsuccessful, more powerful astringents must be administered, such as catechu. Oil of turpentine and opium, beaten up with eggs, has been found to be very useful in many cases.

The animal should be allowed flour gruel to drink, and the best of food in small quantities. He should be kept as quiet as possible, and warmly clothed.

CONSTIPATION.

Various causes give rise to this condition in the horse, some of them serious or even fatal (strangulation of the bowel), while others are simple, and easily removed. When due to a torpid condition of the bowels, or to improper feeding, it may continue for a long time, and the animal may recover by suitable treatment. Symptoms of uneasiness are generally manifested now and again, and the abdomen is distended, but the pulse and respiration are little, if at all, disturbed.

Treatment.—This will depend upon the cause of the constipation, and it is generally better to get skilled advice, in order to discover this. If due, however, to improper feeding, copious enemas of tepid water should be administered and a dose (about a pint and a half) of linseed oil given by the mouth. Little, if any, food should be allowed, and that of a sloppy nature. Exercise at a slow pace is beneficial.

LAMPAS.

Lampas is a very favourite disease with the groom or farrier. It is simply a swollen condition of the roof of the mouth, caused by cold, indigestion, or appears when the teeth are growing. If the swelling is somewhat great, and the palate tender, mastication may be somewhat interfered with ; but, as a rule, this condition, in many cases, does not require notice.

Treatment.—Attention to the diet is the chief thing to be observed, this being soft and easily masticated, and, if necessary, a dose of laxative medicine should be given. The palate may be rubbed with a little salt, or alum and water.

IRREGULAR TEETH.

The back or molar teeth very often either grow irregularly, or become so through being chipped by stones in the food, or they may wear sharp at the edges : the upper molar teeth, the outer edge (that next the cheek) ; the lower molar teeth, the inner edge (that next the tongue). When the upper molar teeth are affected, rubbing the outside of the cheek against them will cause the animal to evince pain ; but the most usual sign of this condition is the inability of the animal to masticate properly, from the injury caused to the cheeks or tongue during the movements of the jaws. This imperfect mastication leads to what is termed "quidding"—ejecting pellets of semi-masticated hay ; there are also, generally, loss of condition and unthriftiness.

Treatment.—This condition will require a dental operation, after a careful examination of the mouth by an expert. The examination will also permit it to be ascertained whether the teeth are carious— a condition which may give rise to toothache, the symptoms of which are very foetid breath, hanging the head to one side, and dribbling of saliva from the mouth.

WORMS.

The most common worms found in the horse's intestines are long, round worms, white, tapering at each end, and inhabiting the stomach and small intestine, and sometimes also the large intestine. When these are present in considerable numbers, they cause derangement in health, manifested by loss of condition, harsh, rough skin, which clings to the ribs, and distended abdomen, with a morbid appetite. These symptoms give rise to suspicion of the existence of worms, and this suspicion is confirmed by their being passed now and again.

The other kind is a small thread-like worm, not much more than an inch in length, which generally infests the rectum, not far from its termination under the tail. Its presence is shown by the intense itchiness it produces, causing the horse to rub his tail and hind-quarters continually against anything with which he can come in contact; as well as little yellow streaks or patches on the skin immediately underneath the tail, which are the eggs of the worm.

Treatment.—For the larger worms, any tonic medicine—such as powdered gentian, sulphate of iron, sulphate of copper, etc.—will generally suffice to weaken or kill them, when they should be removed by a dose of physic. It has been recommended to give the horse, in his food, every day for a week, one and a half drachm of sulphate of iron and tartar emetic, and then administer a purgative; the diet meanwhile to be bran and hay.

For the smaller worms, an enema of salt and water will very often suffice; or after an ordinary enema has been given, to clear out the intestine, another enema, composed of a quart of linseed oil, in which six ounces of oil of turpentine have been mixed, should be administered. Young horses are most liable to worms, and as a preventive it is well to have a piece of rock-salt always in their manger.

CHOKING.

Choking is not very frequent in the horse. It is usually caused by a piece of carrot, turnip, or potato becoming lodged in the gullet; or by the horse greedily attempting to swallow dry food, such as bran, meal, etc. It is also sometimes caused by administering a bolus which is hard or too large. The animal is seen to be making attempts at swallowing or vomiting, looking distressed and anxious, while saliva may flow from the mouth; and if drink is offered, it either escapes from the mouth or through the nostrils. The substance causing the choking may also be felt at the upper part of the throat, or along the course of the gullet down the neck.

Treatment.—Veterinary aid should be procured as soon as possible. Until it arrives, an attempt may be made to remove the substance with the hand, or by pressing the gullet upwards outside, if the substance is solid; but if it is dry food, water or oil drenches should be administered, until the mass is softened, when it can be swallowed.

DISEASES OF THE URINARY ORGANS.

Next to affections of the digestive organs, those of the urinary apparatus may be taken as an example of an important and interesting class. The kidneys, which form the principal organs of the urinary system, are unlike many others of the body. They are not engaged in the formation or elaboration of any fluid or material which plays some important part in the building up of the body; but, on the contrary, are exclusively employed in the separation of compounds from the blood, which, if retained, would prove highly injurious. Their office is simply one of purifying, by separating the deleterious and worn-out portions of the body from the blood.

Owing to the fact that the lower animals are free from mental emotions, the cares and troubles of the world, and that they do not indulge in alcoholic drinks, the kidneys are in a great measure exempt from those diseases which so often destroy human life. However, the horse, from various causes, both extrinsic and intrinsic, occasionally suffers from kidney disease.

INFLAMMATION OF THE KIDNEYS.

Inflammation of the substance of the kidney, otherwise called nephritis, is fortunately very rare in the horse. It is said to occur from injuries, such as blows or strains, exposure to wet and cold, producing derangement of the secretion of the skin; also prolonged or severe work, and from the internal administration of irritant diuretics, which are a class of medicines that act directly on the kidneys, and, when given in large doses, over-tax them; the result is inflammation. Another cause is the application of blistering ointments, composed chiefly of cantharides, to large portions of the body at the same time; as the cantharidine, which is the active principle of the ointment, becomes absorbed, and acts as an irritant diuretic on the kidneys. Mow-burnt hay and kiln-dried oats, or other irritating food, frequently cause derangement and inflammation.

The horse is restless and uneasy, and has considerable fever, characterised by increased temperature and thirst; a hot, clammy mouth; and the mucous membranes of the nostrils and eyes injected. He often lies down cautiously, and rises up again, as if suffering from colic. At frequent intervals he stretches himself as if about to stale; but passes no urine, or only a small quantity highly coloured, and often tinged with blood. On applying pressure to the loins, the animal will evince pain by wincing, and if turned sharply around will groan. He moves very stiff, and often looks back at his loins. The pulse is hard and quick, and the bowels constipated. The urine, if examined by the aid of the microscope, will be found to contain casts of the urinary tubules, blood, and, in advanced stages, pus cells. Death generally takes place from exhaustion.

Treatment.—The chief object to be considered in the treatment of nephritis, or, indeed, in any other disease of the horse, is the comfort of the animal. He is to be placed in a well-ventilated loose box, and the body warmly clothed, and bandages put on his legs; his bed is to be made of good fresh straw. Next, we must try and give the kidneys all the rest we can, and endeavour to reduce the inflammation, and get rid of a portion at least of the urea of the blood by the bowels. This must be accomplished by purgatives. Aloes is the medicine generally used by practitioners for this purpose; but great caution should be observed in the use of it in this disease, as it contains a certain resinous substance which may excite the kidneys to increased action; indeed all resinous compounds are classed as diuretic medicines. Linseed oil, in doses of a pint, with the addition of a few drops of croton oil, will have the desired effect, without irritating the inflamed organs. The inflammation must be attacked by hot fomentations to the loins, and by the internal administration of medicines calculated to reduce the supply of blood to the diseased organs. This is best achieved by fomentations of woollen rugs or blankets wrung from warm water, and wrapped around the animal's body; and by the application of mustard and ammonia liniment over the loins. Care must be taken not to use blister or liniments in which cantharides forms the active ingredient; for, as before stated, it is liable to become absorbed, and act on the kidneys. Fleming's tincture of aconite, in doses of ten drops, every four hours, mixed in a little lukewarm gruel, might be given for some time; but if the pain is very violent, and the animal restless, and rolling about the box, two ounces of the tincture of opium will tend to allay the pain; and if relief is not obtained in an hour or so, half the above dose may be repeated. The action of the skin must be stimulated by warm clothing, and the administration of saline febrifuges, such as the solution of acetate of ammonia, in ounce doses, combined with a drachm of camphor in a little warm ale or gruel. Enemas, consisting of warm water, often do good, both in relieving the bowels and helping the purgative to act, and also as an internal fomentation to the inflamed organs. However, soap or turpentine (which are frequently used in clysters) should not be contained in the water, as they have a diuretic action on the kidneys. The animal should have lukewarm drinks—as hay- or linseed-tea, bran-mashes, and a little grass. When the inflammation is reduced, and the kidneys begin to act a little, tonic medicine—in the shape of sulphate of iron, one drachm, powdered gentian, two drachms—may be given in the corn for a few days, and care should be taken not to expose the animal to cold or wet, or over-work, too soon after leaving the sick stable.

CYSTITIS.

Cystitis, or inflammation of the bladder, is happily not often met with in the horse; indeed, nine-tenths of the cases which occur can be traced to the effect either of cantharadine blisters, or some other irritant diuretic medicine administered internally. It is frequently induced by sympathy with inflammation of the kidneys—that is, the process of inflammation extends along the canal which conveys the urine as it is formed in the kidney to the bladder, and known as the ureter.

The symptoms of inflammation of the bladder differ very little from those of nephritis. There are great restlessness, whisking of the tail, and violent straining; the animal appears to suffer much pain and distress. The urine is passed frequently, and with difficulty and pain, in small quantities. On passing the hand into the rectum, the bladder will be found empty and contracted, and hot and tender on pressure, the animal straining and wincing when the organ is pressed upon. Occasionally he looks at his flanks, and lies down and rolls as if from colic. As the disease advances, great prostration ensues. The most common cause of death is rupture of the bladder.

Treatment.—The treatment of cystitis must be conducted on the same principles as for nephritis, having for its object the reduction of the inflammation. If the pain is great, the tincture of opium may be given in gruel. The bowels require moving by salines, and warm-water clysters passed into the rectum at frequent intervals; but caution must be taken not to administer oil if the disease has been brought about by the administration internally, or absorption of a blister composed of cantharides; as by so doing, by its solvent power upon cantharadine—the active principle of cantharides blister—greater havoc is induced. Small doses of the sulphate of magnesia, or the sulphate of soda, act very well, both in relieving the intestines and at the same time reducing any attendant fever. The bladder should be evacuated as speedily as possible. A little manipulation will often cause it to contract and expel its contents; otherwise the catheter must be inserted, and the urine drawn off in that manner. The tincture of aconite may be given in ten-drop doses every four hours for a little time, allowing the animal to have linseed-tea, gruel, and milk with bicarbonate of soda dissolved in it. Diuretic medicines should be scrupulously avoided in this disease. Sometimes the neck of the bladder only is involved; the chief symptom is the retention of urine, with slight pains on attempting to stale. Often a little sedative medicine will frequently set matters right in this case.

RETENTION OF URINE.

This affection consists of an accumulation of urine within the bladder without any means of discharge. It is seen in most cases of colic, owing to the spasm extending from the intestines to the neck of the bladder; also in inflammation of the neck from the pain caused by the urine passing over the inflamed mucous lining of the orifice through which it ought to pass. A very common cause of this disease is when horses are driven or hunted for long distances without staling; the accumulated urine causes increased pressure on the walls of the bladder, which become paralysed from the strain brought upon them, and therefore are unable to contract and discharge their contents. This state is often seen in spinal disease.

Calculi, or stone in the bladder, is another cause, together with dirt and other matter accumulating and stopping up the opening of the urethra.

The animal shows great uneasiness, has slight pains resembling colic, lies down and rises frequently; the hind-legs are alternately raised, and the position shifted from side to side. The nose is often turned towards the flank. The animal makes frequent and abortive attempts to urinate, and will groan with pain, the body being covered with a clammy sweat. Examination per rectum will often show the bladder distended and full of urine. This symptom at once helps us to find out the disease.

Treatment.—The evacuation of the urine is the chief thing to be looked for in the treatment of this disease; warm-water injections and gentle manipulations of the organ will very often cause it to discharge its contents. If these means are not successful, passing the catheter must be resorted to. This instrument is a hollow, flexible tube, about five feet long for the horse, and about two and a half feet for the mare, closed at one end. It is perforated at the shut end for the egress of urine. In the mare the catheter is easily passed, but in the horse the operation requires more care and skill. The penis will usually be found retracted; the hand being well oiled, must first be passed up the sheath, and the penis must be grasped and gradually brought forward and held by an assistant. The catheter now being oiled, should be introduced and carefully pushed forward, and when the point reaches the perinæum it should be worked with continued gentle pressure, so as to guide it upwards. The animal should be well attended to for some time after recovering from an attack of retention; and a mixture of vegetable and mineral tonics, as gentian and the sulphate of iron, given every night in the corn, would help towards recovery.

INCONTINENCE OF URINE.

This is just the reverse of the condition we have been considering. It consists of an inability to retain the urine within the bladder. It is often seen in young animals, from the non-closure of the aperture at the navel communicating with a tube called the urachus, which conveyed the urine from the bladder before birth. It also occurs from paralysis of the coats of the bladder, and the sphincter at the neck of that organ. Cold and exposure will often cause this disease, bringing about local paralysis.

Treatment.—In the treatment of this malady, nerve tonics should be given, as a drachm of nux vomica combined with iron and gentian, twice daily in the food. In the form described as occurring in young animals, the opening at the navel should be secured by a ligature, or dressed with some caustic preparation, as the nitrate of silver or the sulphate of zinc or copper, which will often effect a cure.

DIURESIS OR EXCESSIVE STALING.

This disease often occurs when the animals are supplied with bad forage, as mow-burnt or mouldy hay and kiln-dried oats; it is also due to the internal administration of diuretic medicines, as the nitrate of potass, turpentine, and the gum resins, in large and too frequent doses. The very common practice of giving condition powders, for the improvement of the animal's coat, is a frequent cause of excessive staling.

Treatment.—All that is required in the way of treatment is the administration of a little laxative medicine, as linseed oil, or small doses of calomel. A little linseed-tea, in which may be dissolved a drachm or two of the iodide of potassium, afterwards the preparation of iron, will be useful in giving tone to the system, which has become deteriorated from the drain brought about by excessive staling. *Clay mixed in the water given to drink,* is also useful.

DISEASES OF THE NERVOUS SYSTEM.

LOCK-JAW OR TETANUS.

This is a very serious disease, due to a number of causes, chiefly injuries which affect the spinal cord, which, again, acts upon the muscles, producing in them a continuous condition of cramp. The muscles involved may be only those of the jaws and neck (*trismus*), or all the muscles of the body. The first symptom usually observed is a tremulous movement of the tail, which is more erect than usual; then the nose is poked out; the nostrils are dilated; there is a particuliar kind of grin on the closed lips; if the head be slightly raised, the animal startled, or made to move, the particular membrane which protects the eye on special occasions is jerked partly over it. The animal is very disinclined to move, and when it does so appears as if wooden; the flanks are tucked up, the jaws cannot be opened, and gruel or water is laboriously sucked through between the teeth. A slight noise increases the spasm of the muscles; the animal appears to be terrified.

Treatment.—This disease requires veterinary skill. The patient should be placed in a very quiet and totally dark loose box, the body clothed lightly, enemas administered gently and frequently, and plenty of oatmeal gruel, placed in a bucket, raised to about the level of the head, should be placed before him. If the disease is due to a wound or injury, this should be attended to. The greatest success in treatment appears to be due to quietude, and sustaining the strength by nutritious sloppy food.

MEGRIMS.

Megrims is a condition in which the horse shows signs of giddiness or stupor, usually manifested after being at work a short time, especially when the pace is fast, particularly in harness, when he commences to shake his head as if something had got into the ears; then he becomes unsteady in his gait, carries his head high, and, if not immediately stopped, will stagger and fall. When on the ground, he will lie perfectly still for a few minutes; then get up, look stupefied and depressed, shake himself, and gradually gain his ordinary condition. From the fact that the attack usually comes on when the horse is driven in harness, it may be due to a badly fitting bridle or collar, or a tight bearing-rein. It may also be due to over-feeding, or being put to work too soon after a hearty meal. In some cases, doubtless, it is caused by a diseased condition of the circulation of the brain. The ears, inside and outside, should be carefully examined in cases of head-shaking.

Treatment.—This, of course, must depend upon the cause, which should be removed, if possible. When it is chronic—that is, due to diseased brain—the horse should either be disposed of or destroyed, as dangerous accidents may arise from working him. If the horse falls, the throat strap should be unbuckled, the collar eased off the neck, and cold water dashed on the head.

EPILEPSY.

In this disease the horse may be seized with convulsions of the face, neck, and limbs, while standing, the attack coming on suddenly; the eyes wink and roll about, and the animal presents a painful spectacle. When he falls, the convulsions continue; there is champing of the jaws, the tongue is often badly wounded by the teeth, and sometimes a slight scream or moan is emitted.

Treatment.—There is no remedy for this nervous malady, which arises from a disordered condition of the brain and spinal cord. In the great majority of cases, the horse should be destroyed, as he is dangerous. If he falls during the attack, the head should be held down on the ground to prevent its being damaged by striking. Cold water should be dashed on the face, and the mouth washed out with it. Great attention should be paid to the diet.

FAINTING.

Fainting may be due to exhaustion after severe exertion, to a weak state of the heart, or as a result of a debilitating disease. The horse falls, and lies perfectly still and unconscious; the breathing may be slower than natural, and the pulse weak and small; or they may both be more frequent than usual, though feebler. If the tongue is withdrawn from the mouth, it will not be retracted while the animal is unconscious.

Treatment.—Sponge out the mouth with cold water, and, if possible, get the animal to swallow some. Hand-rub the legs and the ears well, removing the bridle and slackening the girths, or taking off the saddle. When the horse can swallow, administer a stimulant in the shape of one or two wine-glassfuls of whisky or brandy in a quart of water; or a quart of old ale warmed, with some powdered ginger added. When the horse rises, have the surface of the body well wisped and dried.

APOPLEXY.

This occurs most frequently when horses are exposed to the direct rays of the sun in very hot weather, but it may also be due to deranged circulation of blood in the brain, or to a diseased condition of the blood-vessels there, which leads to rupture. The horse suddenly stops, staggers for two or three paces, then falls, and becomes quite unconscious; the breathing is stertorous and laboured for a short time, and the limbs are motionless; death may rapidly take place.

Treatment.—As a rule, little can be done for a horse in this condition. If the attack is due to sunstroke, then getting the animal in the shade, and applying cold water to the head and face, as well as to the poll, is all that can be done.

STRINGHALT.

This is an irregular, convulsive jerking up of the leg, in nearly all cases the hind one, sometimes both, when the horse is going, or when turning round in the stable. It is most frequent in adult or old horses, and is caused by derangement of the nerves supplying the limb or limbs.

Treatment.—All attempts to cure this disease have hitherto resulted in failure.

DISEASES OF THE EYE.

SIMPLE OPHTHALMIA

This is merely inflammation of the membrane lining the eyelids, and covering a portion of the surface of the eye. It may be caused by injuries (as a lash from the whip), from hay seeds or dirt getting into the eye, or from cold, or as a result of influenza, etc. The eyelids are swollen and closed, tears flow down the face, the horse avoids the light, and, if the lids be gently opened, the lining membrane will be seen of a bright red colour, while the cornea will be more or less clouded, and of a bluish tint.

Treatment.—The first thing to be ascertained, is whether the inflammation is due to injury or a foreign body, or simply to cold; if the former, measures must be taken accordingly. In all cases, the eyes should be fomented with warm water, and a swab or bandage tied over them, to protect and keep out the light. After two or three days, a very weak solution of sulphate of zinc (three grains to the ounce of water) may be dropped into the eye now and again.

SPECIFIC OPHTHALMIA.

This is a much more serious condition than that last described, inasmuch as the interior of the eye is involved. It is of the nature of rheumatism, and usually attacks first one eye (which apparently recovers), then the other; in this way, both eyes may be attacked alternately several times, until cataract forms on the lens, resulting in partial or total blindness. The attack usually comes on suddenly, the symptoms being somewhat similar to those of simple inflammation, except that (when examined) the interior of the eye is seen to be altered in colour, the pupil contracted, and very often an effusion of blood or white matter in the anterior chamber; there are great pain and intolerance of light, and the horse is dull and indisposed to eat.

The symptoms last for about a week, when the inflammation begins to subside, and the eye may be clear again in the course of a few days. Recurrence of the inflammation generally takes place in about two months, and from its being supposed to be due to lunar influence, the disease was termed moon-blindness.

Treatment.—This consists in subduing the inflammation by means of purgatives, a blister, or a seton between the jaws, and rubbing in belladonna ointment around the eyelids, or dropping a solution of atropine into the eye.

CATARACT.

Cataract is a result of the last described disease, and consists of an opacity or speck on the lens occupying more or less of its surface. It may be so large as to be readily seen at a short distance from the eye, or so small as to require very close scrutiny to detect it. It is situated behind the pupil, and must not be confounded with a speck on the cornea, which is the front part of the eye.

AMAUROSIS, OR GLASS-EYE.

Sometimes a horse may be totally blind of one or both eyes without there being any signs of disease present; on the contrary, the eyes are perfectly clear, and the pupils generally widely dilated and immovable, but the horse has the gait and the expression of one which is sightless. It is due to paralysis of the nerve of vision, which may take place from various causes.

Treatment.—In the majority of cases this is hopeless, and if attempted it should only be undertaken by a skilled person.

DISEASES OF THE SKIN.

The diseases of the skin of the horse, although somewhat numerous, need not be described with any amount of detail here, and only the principal of them will be referred to.

SURFEIT.

This is a common designation for nearly every disease of the skin, and it is, therefore, difficult to limit it to any one of these. It may, however, be confined to nettle-rash (urticaria), which appears suddenly as an eruption of hard lumps of irregular size, sometimes in the form of weals in different parts of the body, accompanied by more or less itching, with sometimes falling off of the hair. They gradually disappear in the course of a few days, and their advent usually depends upon derangement of the stomach; at other times it may be due to exposure to a hot sun, cold wind, or standing in draughts after being heated, or it may arise from drinking a quantity of cold water when the animal is hot.

Treatment.—If due to indigestion, give a mild dose of physic, and allow sloppy food, mixing in it an ounce or two of bicarbonate of soda once or twice a day; linseed-mashes are good. If the eruption continues, and is likely to become obstinate, tonic medicines (as sulphate of iron or iodide of potassium) must be given in the food frequently; while a local application to the lumps (such as citrine ointment one part, vaseline two parts, or ointment of the iodide of sulphur) must be resorted to. The body should be kept warm by clothing.

PRURIGO AND ECZEMA.

These two affections, which may be considered as one, have also been included under the denomination of surfeit; and their chief manifestation is an eruption of little blisters, which, bursting, form crusts or pimples; these are intensely itchy, causing the animal to bite himself over all parts of the body—as the neck, shoulders, loins, flanks; but more especially perhaps the root of the tail, which is sometimes rubbed raw, owing to the annoyance the animal experiences. The hair either falls off, or is rubbed or bitten off, and the skin is rendered quite unsightly. The cause is difficult to ascertain in all cases; but it probably depends upon digestive derangement, and this more particularly during the summer or autumn.

Another form of the disease is the breaking out of large, irregular, isolated blotches on the skin, chiefly on the sides or quarters, which become covered with crusts.

Treatment.—This condition, in the great majority of cases, must be treated as a constitutional disease. Great attention should be paid to the diet, which should be laxative, such as boiled linseed in small quantity mixed with the oats, and green forage. An ounce or so of nitrate of potass or bicarbonate of soda may be given in the water, and in the food a drachm or two of tartar emetic daily for five or six days, will generally effect a cure. Should the itching of the skin persist, it may be necessary to give an ounce of liquor arsenicalis daily for a few days in the food instead of the tartar emetic; and the skin should be dressed with diacetate of lead, mixed in eight parts of glycerine or oil; or a dressing, composed of petroleum one part, oil four parts, may be applied after the skin has been well washed with warm water and dried. In milder cases, ordinary vinegar, diluted in twenty parts of water, will allay the itching. It is well to wear a linen sheet next the skin, under the woollen rug, as the latter often increases the irritation.

MANGE.

This is a contagious disease, due to the presence of a microscopical insect, differing but little from that which produces itch in mankind. There are three kinds of insect, each of which has its particular locality: one infests the mane and sides of the neck and the tail, and causes intense itching with scurfiness of the skin and falling off of the hair, and is most common in coarse-bred horses. Another kind inhabits the skin of the legs—more particularly below the knees and hocks—and produces the same condition of the skin as that last mentioned. The itchiness is very great, and causes the horse to rub his legs continually, and stamp his feet on the floor; it is rarely seen in any but coarse-bred, hairy-legged horses. The third kind, by far the most common, inhabits the skin on the neck, face, sides of the body, quarters, and insides of the thighs, the insect burrowing into the cuticle, and giving rise to a multitude of little hard pimples, which feel as if small seeds had been sown at the roots of the hair and had adhered to the skin. There is a little scab on each of these pimples, in which are two or three hairs, and if this is removed there appears a little red spot. The itchiness is very great, the horse rubbing and gnawing himself continually, or when the hand scratches the skin, expressing satisfaction by movements of the lips. In a short time the hair falls off, the skin becoming dry, wrinkled, and scaly, with raw spots and cracks over the body. This is the ordinary form of mange, and it is transmissible to mankind.

Treatment.—The first thing to be done is to destroy the parasite, and for this purpose the skin should be well washed with warm water and soap, by means of a brush, in order to remove the scales and allow the dressing to be more closely applied. There are numerous applications which are quite effective in destroying the insect. Paraffine oil applied once a day, and allowed to dry on the skin, is very efficacious; as is also a mixture of sulphur and common oil well rubbed into the skin, or oil of tar and sulphur, of each two ounces to a pint of common oil. McDougall's sheep dip, also Jeyes' fluid, are likewise good preparations. Two or three days after the skin has been dressed, the horse should be again washed with soap and water, and if the itching reappears he must be again dressed; but this is rarely required if every part of the body has been well treated. The blankets, harness, and everything which the animal has worn, should be thoroughly cleaned—the clothing by boiling, and the harness, etc., by oil of turpentine or paraffine; while the stall should also be thoroughly scrubbed out, and the litter destroyed. Precautions should also be taken to keep diseased horses from healthy ones.

RING-WORM.

This is a disease due to a microscopical vegetable fungus, which, commencing to grow in the hair follicles, destroys the hairs, and makes bare, circular patches of varying size, with scales or scurf upon them. There is but little itching, though the inflammation set up may cause soreness. The disease is very contagious and disfiguring, and if not treated in time may be rather intractable. Young horses are more susceptible to it than old ones. Before the bare patches appear, when the hand is passed over the skin, little rough spots can be felt, and the hair can be seen to stand erect over these.

Treatment.—If there are only isolated patches, these may be treated by rubbing in a little Stockholm tar or iodine ointment; if the disease be more diffused over the skin, then the treatment as for mange should be adopted.

GREASE.

Grease is a diseased condition of the skin of the pasterns, due to inflammation of the oil glands at this part, the secretion of which is greatly increased (hence the name), with, as it advances, cracks and ulcers, and accompanied by pain and lameness and swelling of the legs. This condition is, in nearly every case, due to bad stable management, and very rarely to digestive derangement.

Treatment.—Fomentations and poultices to subdue the inflammation, afterwards dressing with carbolised oil, will generally effect a cure in mild cases; citrine ointment, or oxide of zinc ointment, is also very useful.

CRACKED HEELS.

This may be said, in the majority of cases, to be a form of grease, though generally it may be unaccompanied by any increase of the oily secretion of the skin. The hollow of the pasterns is the part where the cracks usually occur, and the tendency of this part to become affected is greatly increased by trimming the heels, and exposing the skin to cold and damp; sometimes it may be due to derangement of the stomach. Cracked heels are much more common in cold, wet weather, and especially if the horse is working on muddy, chalky, or sandy ground; also if the legs and feet are washed with cold water, and not thoroughly dried. There are great pain and lameness, the horse going on the toes, the cracks in the skin discharging a watery fluid, and even bleeding when the horse is moving. When the pastern is handled, the horse jerks up his leg, which often becomes swollen above the fetlock. It is customary in big towns during the winter, when the roads are slippery, to melt the ice on the tracks of tramways by sprinkling salt; this, mixing with the mud, produces a very acrid compound, which is particularly active in producing cracked heels, and even sloughing of the skin.

Treatment.—In very mild cases, a little oxide of zinc ointment or carbolised oil may be rubbed into the skin once or twice a day; if the skin is broken, it should be thoroughly cleansed by washing with soap and water before applying these. Should the inflammation be rather intense, and the lameness great, after washing, a linseed-meal poultice should be applied for a day or two, when the dressing may be used. Should the cracks show a tendency to become chronic, they may be touched with nitrate of silver or pure carbolic acid, after which the ointment or carbolised oil may be applied; pledgets of tow smeared with these may be tied round the pastern. In very bad cases, the application of a high-heeled shoe will greatly expedite recovery. To prevent cracked heels, a little vaseline or lard, rubbed into the hollows of the pasterns and around the coronets, is very useful. To prevent injury from salted roads, white lead, made into a thin paste with common oil, is an excellent application when smeared around the pasterns. These parts should not be deprived of the hair, nor yet washed in cold weather, but the mud be removed with a wisp of straw when the horse returns to his stable.

MUD FEVER.

This is the same condition of the skin of the other parts of the limb as cracked heels, and is due to the same cause, or causes, the inflammation often extending to the under parts of the belly. The skin is hot and painful (it may be even swollen), and the hair on it is erect, while, when the hand is passed over it, a roughness or eruption can be felt; if not checked, the hair will fall off, sores appear on the skin, and much stiffness or lameness, with a certain amount of fever, will be present.

Treatment.—This consists in applying to the inflamed skin Goulard's extract (one part) and olive oil or glycerine (four parts), or veterinary vaseline. If fever is present, give sloppy diet and a mild dose of physic. To prevent mud fever, the body and legs should not be washed when the horse returns to the stable, the dirt being removed by scraping and rubbing with a straw wisp. If there are draughts in the stable—or, indeed, under any circumstances—it is well to apply woollen bandages as high as possible on the limbs. When quite dry, the remainder of the dirt may be removed by the brush, or by a damp sponge and a soft cloth. If the legs must be washed, then this should be done in the stable, and the skin quickly and thoroughly dried, and hand-rubbed, some vaseline being afterwards applied, and then flannel bandages. As a preventive, the legs should not be clipped.

WARTS.

These grow on different parts of the skin, and are sometimes very troublesome when they are situated where the harness rubs them; they are frequently of such a size or formation as to constitute a disfigurement. They may be removed by caustics, ligature, the knife, or the hot iron. As a rule, it is better to employ the veterinary surgeon to remove them, especially if they have a wide base, and require the knife.

CHAPTER XXX.

WOUNDS, INJURIES, AND LAMENESS, WITH HINTS FOR EMERGENCIES.

Detection of Lameness—Detection of Lameness during Movement—Peculiarities of Action Simulating Lameness—Wounds and Injuries—Wounds—Bleeding or Hæmorrhage—Dressing for Wounds—Punctured Wounds—Broken Knees—Sore Back—Injuries—Fractures—Sprains—Bruises—Speedy-Cut—Wounds from Thorns—Poll-Evil—Capped Elbow—Capped Hock—Thoroughpin—Bog Spavin—Windgalls—Burns—Diseases and Injuries of the Feet—Treads—Quittor—Sand-Crack—Wounds of the Sole and Frog—Corns—Thrush—Canker—Laminitis or Inflammation of the Feet—Seedy Toe—Navicular Disease—Pricks and Injuries in Shoeing—Side-Bones—Splints—Sore Shins—Ring-Bone—Spavin.

DETECTION OF LAMENESS.

ALTHOUGH the majority of people can tell when a horse is very lame by its unequal gait, yet it requires much experience to detect the leg upon which a horse is lame, and especially if the lameness is slight; and still more experience, with a certain amount of anatomical and physiological knowledge, to discover in many cases where the seat of lameness is.

Percivall defines lameness "as the manifestation in the act of progression, by one or more of the limbs, of pain or weakness, inability or impediment." Under this heading we may, for convenience sake, include "pointing" of the foot, any unnatural position assumed by the horse, and altered action which indicates unsoundness. Irregularity of gait is commonly supposed to constitute lameness, but we may have a lame horse going level when he is equally affected in both fore- or in both hind-legs. Although deficiency of action is its usual cause, we find that, in stringhalt, lameness is due to its excess.

In the examination of a horse for lameness, we should first endeavour to find out the affected leg, and then we should try to discover the seat of the disease in that limb. When it pains a horse, whether moving or standing still, to put the natural share of weight on any particular leg, or to bend it, or when he is unable to bend it with freedom, he is then *lame*. Hence, to detect lameness, we should endeavour to observe any tendency to favour one limb, or disinclination or inability to bend it, or any want of freedom in the gait.

Pointing.—Our first step should be, if possible, to see the animal in the stable, when he is standing quietly, and is free from all excitement. He will then, if sound, often rest one hind-leg by bending its fetlock, while he keeps both fore-legs firmly planted. He will, after a time, ease the other hind-leg, which, in its turn, will be relieved by its fellow, and so on. Although he may stand with one fore-leg slightly advanced beyond the other, still it will never, unless when diseased, be relieved of its own share of weight; for he will always stand, when on level ground, with equal bearing on both fore-legs. A fatigued horse may rest a near hind and an off fore, or an off hind and a near fore, alternately without disease. A horse lame in one fore-leg usually stands with its pastern straighter than that of the sound one.

If we find that the animal points with one foot, while maintaining a position which indicates that he prefers to stand in a constrained attitude than to put weight on it, we may reasonably suspect that limb.

As a general rule, when the disease is in the front of the foot, the animal rests his heel on the ground; when towards the heel, he points with the toes and raises the heel. The former is the case with laminitis, and generally in ring-bone; the latter in confirmed navicular disease.

In almost all cases of pointing, when the disease is not in the foot, the horse keeps the foot flexed, and the heel consequently raised.

In bad cases of lameness in the hind-leg, the animal often keeps the foot altogether off the ground.

At the commencement of navicular disease, the horse sometimes points with the heel down, but he soon commences to bring the toe only to the ground, and to "round," the fetlock joint. In other cases, the patient will stand perfectly firm, although in the great majority of cases the pastern of the lame limb is more upright than that of the sound one, as if he feared to put much weight on it.

Laminitis is often manifested by the horse frequently shifting his feet when standing.

The pointing of elbow lameness is characteristic, the fore-arm being extended, the knee in a state of flexion, and the foot perhaps on a level with, or posterior to, its fellow. In severe shoulder lameness, the pointing, if it can be called such, is backwards, the limb relaxed, knee bent, and the foot posterior to its fellow; sometimes the toe only touches the ground, and the whole limb is semi-pendulous, consequent upon the inability of the muscles to elevate and bring it forward without pain.

In laminitis, when the disease is in the fore-feet, the horse advances them so as to relieve the toes of pressure; when in the hind-feet, he draws back his fore-feet, and advances his hind with the same object.

Animals affected with navicular disease often acquire the habit of lying down a great deal in their stalls. Cases of slight lameness behind, such as those of spavin and stringhalt, are often best seen when the horse is pushed over from one side to the other, or when turned round in his stall. We may then observe that the horse shifts the weight on one hind-leg quicker than he does on the other, which we may regard as the unsound limb.

DETECTION OF LAMENESS DURING MOVEMENT.

Lameness must be very acute for the horse to show it in the walk. As a rule, the slow trot is the best pace at which to observe lameness. The animal should be led in a halter or snaffle bridle, with plenty of rein, so that the man who leads him may not interfere with the movements of his head. As soon as possible after leaving the stable, the horse should be trotted for inspection on hard ground, which should be free from stones and inequalities. The observer may stand about twenty yards in front of the horse, and on the near side. He should note, as the animal approaches, whether he "dwells" in the slightest on one fore-foot more than on the other, and whether he nods his head. If he does either, the observer may conclude that he dwells on the sound limb, and nods his head as it comes to the ground, while the other is the lame leg, which the animal naturally favours by throwing the weight on its fellow. An exception to this is when a horse is very lame on a hind-leg—the near one, for instance; he may then nod his head on the off fore coming to the ground, so that he may throw as much weight in front as possible, which he naturally does to the sound side. When a horse is very lame in front, he may chuck up his head on the lame leg coming to the ground.

A horse lame in both fore-feet, although he may not drop in his gait, will be short in action—will go, as it has been more forcibly than elegantly expressed, "like a cat on hot bricks." Each foot is carefully put to the ground, and quickly lifted up again, while at the same time there is a rolling motion of the body.

When a horse is suspected of being equally lame on both fore-feet, he should be taken on to soft ground, and there slowly trotted. If a marked amendment in the gait is then observed, one may regard the suspicion as confirmed. The time to observe him is when turning. As the chief portion of the weight of the horse's body is borne by his fore-legs, he will not, unless when very lame, dwell on one hind-foot more than the other, but will endeavour to keep the weight off the unsound limb by "hitching" up its quarter, and consequently keeping it straighter than its fellow. Hence, when the animal has passed the observer, he should take a rear view of the croup, and should mark whether one quarter rises more than the other as their respective feet come to the ground.

When the horse has trotted past about thirty yards, he should be turned, somewhat sharply, to the right-about, for instance, while the person who is examining him should note the manner in which he turns on his off hind-leg, so as to be able to compare it with the way he goes to the left-about the next time he turns. In this second trot past, the observer should try to detect if there be any difference in the action of the horse as viewed from the off side, from that which it presented when regarded from the near. If, after two or three trots past, there be still any doubt remaining, perhaps the best way to solve it is to mount the animal and trot him, alternately slowly and rapidly, for a short distance on hard ground, and give him a few moderately sharp turns.

If we suspect the existence of spavin, we may take up the foot and bend the hock, retaining it in that position for a couple of minutes; if after that the animal trots quite sound, we may consider the joint to be all right.

In obscure cases of lameness of one leg, we may suspect bone disease—such as incipient ringbone—as the cause, if the horse stands level in his stall, but trots very lame on hard ground.

Before putting the horse in, we should also try if he backs with freedom and regularity of gait.

If no lameness be noticed, we may send him back to his stable, and, as a final test, may allow him to stand for a few hours, and then, when he has thoroughly cooled down, try him again. If he passes satisfactorily through this second ordeal, we may, as a rule, regard him to be sound in limb.

Certain obscure cases of lameness can be detected only during the first few steps the animal takes on quitting his stable, for he may subsequently "work sound." Such cases of lameness are usually caused by insidious and serious disease at its early commencement. They are quite beyond the skill possessed by the ordinary amateur.

Lameness at its first commencement in the cross-country horse is often evinced by a want of the customary freedom and boldness in fencing; while in the race horse it is shown by a slight shortening of stride; by unaccustomed ability to "act" well on hard ground, by his showing an unusual preference for leading with one leg rather than the other, and by his changing his leg oftener than he was wont to do.

PECULIARITIES OF ACTION SIMULATING LAMENESS.

Some horses, from bad riding or driving, acquire a sort of *hitch* or *lift* in their trot.

There are some horses which walk down hill in so peculiar a manner, that they may be supposed to be lame. This kind of walk has been termed a three cornered walk. The animal sways from side to side most awkwardly, his hind-quarters being turned to one side or the other, going forwards *broadside on*, similar to an animal going down hill with a heavy load behind him.

If a sound horse, when trotting, has his head turned towards the man who leads him—going in a sort of "left shoulder in" fashion—he may appear to be lame on the near fore-leg, on account of stepping shorter with it than with the off fore.

Some horses, when trotting very fast, appear to go lame behind by reason of the hind-legs not being able to keep time with the fore.

I have known a horse always to "go" lame in harness, although he went quite sound in saddle; the cause being that, on a previous occasion, when working between the shafts, one of his shoulders became galled, and continuing the work for some time in this state, he acquired the habit of bearing against the collar as much as possible with the other shoulder.

Intermittent lameness is often caused by rheumatism, and may also characterise the early stage of navicular disease.

Lameness improves with exercise, except, as a rule, in cases of splints, sore shins, corns, chronic laminitis, inflammation of the coronet (villitis), and sprains.

A horse suffering from navicular disease goes up hill sounder than he goes down; the reverse is the case in laminitis.

When the animal is lame behind, the disease is generally in the hock; when in front, in the feet of cart horses, or in the suspensory ligaments of those that are used for fast work.

When a horse goes lame on a fore-leg without any perceptible cause, and wears away the toe of the shoe, we may suspect that foot of navicular disease. But if he goes on the heel, the probability is that he has either laminitis or incipient ring-bone. If the lameness be behind, and the toe becomes worn, we shall generally find that it is due to spavin.

Side-bones are almost peculiar to cart horses, sore shins to race horses, and navicular disease to cab and carriage horses. Navicular disease and occult spavin are hardly ever found in horses under seven years of age.*

WOUNDS.

Every one who keeps a horse soon finds out that this animal is liable to many wounds and injuries These occurrences will be briefly and practically treated. Every part of the body may be wounded; if the wound is clean cut, and there are no foreign matters about it, an attempt should be made to heal it by "adhesion" or the "first intention"—that is, to unite the divided edges at once. The parts should, therefore, if possible, be brought together without delay; and to do this the injury must be treated while fresh, as if not done very soon it will be useless. Sometimes the object in view—to bring the divided edges into apposition—may be accomplished by means of a bandage, smoothly, but rather firmly, applied; but more frequently it can best be done by sutures. To insert these, it is nearly always found necessary to keep the horse quiet by "twitching" to prevent injury to the operator and attendants. There is nothing cruel in twitching a horse, if it be properly and humanely done, and if pressure only be put on the imprisoned part of the upper lip when the animal shows signs of resistance. Some people have an absurd prejudice against the use of the twitch, and will in preference to employing it "cast" or throw a horse down; thereby causing much annoyance to the animal, besides losing valuable time, and running the risk of breaking his back.

SINGLE-PIN SUTURE WITH CLOSE HITCH.

Sutures may be inserted in many different ways to bring the divided edges of wounds together; but for the non-professional operator, what is called "the interrupted suture" is most convenient and efficient. This is made by passing a pin through both edges of the divided skin, half an inch deep or more, according to circumstances, and then putting a piece of twine or tow over the point and head in the form of a figure 8 "close hitch," or round and round, so drawing the edges of the skin together, and tying moderately tight; or instead of pins, a needle armed with twine, thread, or wire may be used, and passed through both edges of the skin, as above described, and the ends tied together, the superfluous pieces being then cut off. Suture wire has the advantage of not irritating the skin so much as twine or thread, and, besides, it cannot absorb irritating and acrid discharges or other matter.

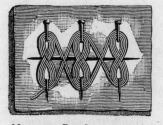

MULTIPLE-PIN SUTURE, WITH INTERWOVEN TWINE.

When the wound is too long to be closed by one pin or suture, several may be employed. If pins are used, each may be fastened separately with twine, in the manner just described, or one piece of twine may be twisted round all of them in figure-of-8 fashion, so as to make them support each other, as shown in the figure. When wounds are lacerated and torn, it is of little use—except in certain cases—to bring the divided edges together by sutures, as such lesions will not close, except by a gradual growth from the bottom and sides, called "healing by granulation." In this event, care must be taken that no cup or pouch is left for pus or matter to collect in the parts; but we must have what is called a "dependent orifice," so that all discharges can drain away as they form; otherwise they are apt to burrow amongst the tissues and under the skin, and so form deep-seated and troublesome abscesses and sinuses. Attention to this dependent orifice is a most important point in the treatment of wounds.

* Hayes. "Veterinary Notes for Horseowners."

If matter is collecting, exit *must* be given to it by puncturing at the lowest part, so that it may readily escape, and do no further harm.

We must not forget, when we are treating a wound, to examine whether any foreign body is concealed in it—such as pieces of wood, iron, thorns, or splinters, or other objects, such as we frequently find in cases occurring to hunting horses. If such foreign bodies are not extracted, of course the wound will rarely heal, and we then have much loss of time and aggravation of the original injury. We may here remark that wounds of the horse show a much greater liability to suppurate than obtains in mankind, where there is a greater tendency to heal by adhesion or the "first intention."

Over-reaches are wounds of the fore-heels, caused usually by the inner edge of the toe of the hind-shoe. For this reason the inner edge of the hind-shoe of hunters is, by a farrier who knows his business, bevelled so that no sharp surface is left. If this is not done, the shoe cuts like a knife if by any accident the hind-foot reaches the fore-heel, and a lip of horn, with the soft part to which it is attached, is cut down, forming in many cases a troublesome and annoying sore. To treat this, the detached horn should be carefully cut off, so as to leave no harbour for dirt or gravel, and the part should be well washed and dressed with tar or other medicament, and then bandaged up with tow, when a cure is generally soon effected. In treating over-reaches, it is necessary to thin the horn below the wound, so as to allow it to expand to the swelling which naturally occurs in the injured parts. If this be not done, much irritation is often caused to the patient, and the cure is retarded.

Bleeding or Hæmorrhage.—People are often at a loss to know what to do in cases of profuse bleeding. If the injured vessel is small, the bleeding will usually stop of itself; but if large, a remedy is often required. Sometimes pressure will do this, or plugging the wound with tow or soft material. An instance of arresting hæmorrhage by pinning up the cut in the skin is observed after bleeding a horse in the jugular vein running down the neck. Sometimes bleeding from a large artery may be stopped by the pressure of the finger; a *tourniquet* may be improvised until further assistance arrives. In the case of wounded arteries, ligatures are sometimes necessary, or the vessels may be twisted on themselves until their channel is obliterated.

The particular method of stopping bleeding must be determined by the circumstances of the case. Cold water will often stop bleeding from small vessels. Hæmorrhage from an artery may be known by the red colour of the blood, and by its spouting out in jets, in unison with the beat of the pulse. In hæmorrhage from a vein the blood does not jerk out, but runs in a continuous stream, and is darker in colour than that from an artery.

Dressing for Wounds.—It is now believed that there are germs of disease floating about in the atmosphere, which are apt to settle on wounds, and cause unhealthy action in them. For this reason we apply dressings; and very good ones are carbolic acid one part to forty of water, or carbolised oil, one part of the acid to twenty or thirty of olive oil. Sometimes wounds are very indolent, and in such cases sharper and more stimulating dressings are required, such as lotion of sulphate of zinc and water, or mild caustic solutions, or even painting them with nitrate of silver or butyr of antimony. Of course, this must not be overdone, or too frequently. When proud flesh forms, we should not be in too great a hurry to remove it, as it will very often disappear spontaneously; but should it not do so, no time should be lost in excising it, or destroying it by caustics. In reference to the latter, we may remember that where there is much fungus or proud flesh, time is often lost by employing caustics, when it could be at once removed by a cut with a razor or sharp knife.

Punctured Wounds.—These are of various kinds. (Some further remarks will be made on those penetrating the joints, under the heading of "Broken Knees.") When a punctured wound is deep, and does not very soon heal, but shows that it is irritated by the occurrence of swelling and pain, the external orifice must be enlarged by a cut, and kept open, so as to afford exit to any imprisoned matter. Of course, if a joint is injured, the great object is to close the wound as soon as possible therefore, in such cases no cutting is required.

Sometimes the eyelid of the horse is torn, and hangs down, being only attached at one end. This should not be cut off, but an attempt be made to preserve it. The raw edges, if it is not attended to immediately, should be made to bleed all over, by careful paring with a sharp knife or fine scissors, and the divided parts, having been carefully adjusted, should be united by pin or thread or wire sutures. An astonishing cure, without any blemish, is thus very often effected, and the patient is saved from the life-long annoyance caused by the loss of so important a protection to the visual organ as an eyelid.

The lips should also, when wounded, be treated in the same conservative manner; of course, the animal must be kept quiet by a twitch while the sutures are inserted, and afterwards he should be so fastened that he cannot rub the parts against the manger, rack, or sides of the stall or box in which he may be confined.

BROKEN KNEES.

Broken knees are of frequent occurrence, and are a very great annoyance and trouble, not only in themselves, but also because the blemish may materially lessen the horse's value when he is to be sold. They very often arise from the horse falling while trotting down hill, and most frequently when he is being ridden by a servant or groom; and for this reason some horse-owners are always in the habit of strictly forbidding the trotting of any of their riding horses down hill while they are out at exercise. If the accident is slight, and one or both knees may have been merely "grazed," and only a portion of hair removed, and, in addition, there may be a little abrasion of the skin—in such cases sponging well with warm water will often be the only remedy required. In other cases, the skin is cut through, and the tissues underneath may be exposed, and more or less wounded. Here, unless the injury is superficial, the advisability of getting the horse into a stable as soon as possible must be considered. If the knee is deeply cut, it is obvious that the patient had better not walk further than is absolutely necessary. In such a case, when the horse has reached a stable, the parts should be gently fomented, and, if need be, veterinary assistance should be sought without delay; in the meantime, care being taken to keep the injured limb as quiet as possible, and the animal free from anything disturbing or exciting. If the knee joint is opened, the case is serious, and the leg cannot be kept too still, after bandaging with a little tow and some dressing, such as carbolised oil or carbolic lotion. It may be found judicious to turn the horse round in the stall, and keep him on pillar reins, to prevent him from knocking or rubbing the injured limb against the manger; and, if he attempts to bite the wounds, a "cradle" should be placed on his neck. In very severe cases, "slinging" the patient will be found a very great advantage. In some cases, when laceration or contusion is superficial, and freed from dirt or grit, a favourable result will be obtained by spreading some Canada balsam on a piece of lint, and applying it to the part, leaving it there until it drops off.

Cases of broken knees vary so much that only general principles of treatment can be here given, and great professional experience is required to treat all but simple cases.

SORE BACK.

Sore backs may be considered under the head of wounds, and occur even in the best managed stable; but careful attention to the fitting and stuffing of saddles will—at least, for civilian purposes—almost always prevent them. Sometimes, however, they occur from the roller or surcingle pad having become too flat, thus letting it press down on the spinous processes of the vertebræ. In such cases, a large and troublesome sore is formed. Whenever, therefore, a sore is seen on the spine where the roller pad crosses it, the latter should receive attention.

As to the treatment of sore back, if there be a swelling without abrasion of the skin, it should be fomented or poulticed. If the skin is abraded, it should be fomented, and then dressed with a little oil to keep it soft. Sometimes what is called a "sit-fast" forms, this being a portion of dead leathery skin firmly fixed by the roots to the subjacent supports. It is hard, and painful when touched, and the quickest and best remedy is to cut it out with a knife and forceps, when it becomes a simple wound, often only requiring to be kept soft with vaseline or oil, to heal rapidly. Sometimes the pommel of the saddle presses on the withers, causing a fluctuating tumour, often the size of a walnut or small orange. These enlargements frequently contain serous fluid, which remains a long time, unless exit be given to it by puncturing with a knife or lancet. If the horse is ridden with one of these enlargements still pressed upon by the saddle, it increases in size, and becomes very painful; and at last an abscess forms and bursts, and we may have that very troublesome and obstinate disease, "fistulous withers," to deal with—one which taxes the greatest skill of the experienced veterinary surgeon. This shows how necessary it is not to neglect saddle galls of the withers, but to remove the cause at once, and attend to the injury.

Girth galls usually only require to be fomented and kept clean, to get rapidly well. Before the saddle is again used, it should be attended to by the saddler.

Injuries by harness should be treated in the same manner, alum and water, or salt and water, being sponged over the skin, to make it hard if it is tender. For tender skin from saddle or harness, ordinary writing ink has often been used with good effect.

FRACTURES.

This part may conveniently be begun by some practical remarks on "fractures," which are classified as *simple*, *compound*, *comminuted*, and *complicated*.

A *simple fracture* is when the bone alone is broken, without protrusion through the skin; *compound*, when the bone pierces the skin; *comminuted*, when the bone is broken into many pieces; and *complicated*, when other tissues than the bone are also injured.

Very many, in fact most, fractures, are treated under great disadvantages in the horse, as he cannot be induced to keep the injured parts still; and he will, therefore, often destroy the reparative work of months by a few moments of struggling or restlessness. One of the most common fractures is that of the *point of the hip*, which is often caused by knocking that bone against the door or gate post while going too hastily past it, or by falls or other accidents. In this fracture, the affected hip (when we view it from behind the animal) is flatter than the sound one, and, when newly done, the broken bone can be easily felt. It is, as a rule, curable, so far as the horse becoming sound goes: the fractured parts either unite, or the fragment becomes encysted, and does not cause lameness. A horse with a broken point of the hip is called "hip down." It is a fault too frequently overlooked by purchasers, and it is, of course, an unsoundness. When such a fracture has recently occurred, the horse should be kept in a stall, as quiet as possible, for six weeks or two months, when the parts have either united or the detached fragment become encysted, as above explained.

There are other fractures of the pelvis, but a description of them is only suitable for a work on veterinary surgery. So many recoveries take place from these fractures, that the patient should not be too hastily given up as hopeless. An experienced veterinary surgeon should always be consulted in such cases.

A very common and fatal fracture is that of the *tibia*, the large bone between the stifle and hock. On the inside of the limb the bone is only covered by skin, and, should it receive a severe kick in this situation, a fracture, or, at least, a chipping, is the probable consequence. For this reason, it is judicious to keep any horse which has been thus kicked from work for three weeks or a month, so as to give any partial fracture or splitting a chance of uniting. It is by no means uncommon for horses which have been kicked (as just described) to go almost sound at work for a day or two, or longer, and then the bone suddenly snaps, and there is a broken tibia. For this there is rarely any alternative but that of destroying the horse, as only under exceptional circumstances is it worth while to attempt a very improbable cure.

Sometimes the ribs are broken, and often the accident is not observed, and a spontaneous cure is effected. If the broken ends overlap, they must, if possible, be readjusted, and kept in place by a broad roller bandage round the body. If the broken ends irritate any of the tissues, they must be cut off. If after a fall a horse shows any tenderness of the sides when girthed or being ridden, the region of the ribs should be carefully examined, to ascertain if there is any fracture.

The *cannon bone* is sometimes broken, usually by a kick from another horse. Treatment is here more likely to be of service than in cases of fracture of the tibia or the radius—the bone between the elbow and the knee. If the horse is very valuable, it is sometimes advisable to attempt the cure of fracture of the cannon bone.

The bones of the head are sometimes fractured, those of the *nose* and *lower jaw* most frequently suffering. Here every means of cure should be tried before the case is pronounced hopeless, but the services of the veterinary surgeon are indispensable.

In fracture of the *scapula*, or *shoulder blade*, the toe is drawn along the ground. These fractures generally necessitate the destruction of the animal.

The *sesamoid bones*—two in number—are just behind the upper part of the fetlock joint. They are sometimes broken in a very extraordinary manner while the horse is galloping. This injury is fatal.

The *pastern bones* are frequently fractured. It is, in some cases, worth while to attempt a cure. If the fracture be lengthways, there is a greater chance of success; but if the bone be broken into a number of pieces, the horse can never again be fit for anything but very slow work on soft ground, and treatment, therefore, is rarely advisable.

The method of applying splints and bandages for fractures cannot be entered into, as each particular case demands particular treatment, adapted to its varying circumstances. To keep the animal as still and undisturbed as possible, however, is a most important part of the treatment.

SPRAINS.

Sprains may be classed as injuries, and notice of some of the most important must be taken. A very common sprain is that of the ligaments or tendons of the fore-leg.

Tendons and ligaments are formed of strong fibres; and when some of these are unduly stretched and broken, inflammation sets in, and we have heat, pain, and more or less swelling, according to the severity of the injury. If pressure be applied to the swelling, the horse shows pain, but so he will if it arises from a blow or kick; therefore, such swellings should not be too hastily called sprains; and the owner of the animal would do well to wait a day or two before coming to a decision. If the swelling arises from a blow, the pain will soon begin to disappear and the enlargement to diminish. Sometimes the swelling "pits" on pressure of the fingers, and by this symptom an experienced veterinary surgeon can almost always give a correct opinion.

There is a ligament which arises from the back of the knee, and is inserted into the flexor tendon, called the "perforans," about half way between the knee and fetlock. This ligament, named the "metacarpal," is strong, and may be said to brace up the leg, and greatly help it to bear the violent strain it is continually sustaining during rapid progression. This metacarpal ligament is often sprained, and the symptoms are a painful swelling and lameness. There is also another powerful ligament arising behind the lower part of the knee, called the "great suspensory ligament." It runs down behind the cannon bone, and just above the fetlock it bifurcates or divides into two branches, each of which is attached to the sesamoid bone on its own side, and then continues downwards and forwards until it reaches the front of the pastern, where it becomes attached to the expanded tendon of a muscle called the extensor of the foot. The suspensory ligament is liable to sprain, and the symptoms are painful swelling and lameness.

Treatment.—The treatment of these sprains varies. Of course, in all sprains it is essential to keep the affected limb as still and quiet as possible; and therefore owners of horses, who, in their impatience, take the animal out of his stable every two or three days to see how he is getting on, are acting very injudiciously. The treatment should begin by the application of cold water, by means of a loose linen bandage, frequently wetted. This bandage should be removed altogether at night, because the groom being then absent from the stable, it would soon become dry, and only irritate and heat the injured parts. It is not necessary to take the bandage off to wet it. The limb should be put into a bucketful of water, which ought then to be "slopped" on the bandage for a few seconds. If this be done frequently during the day by the groom while he is about the stable, the bandage will be kept sufficiently wet and cool. Some people prefer diligent fomentations for sprains, and there is much to be said in favour of their views. Whether fomentations or cold applications have been adopted, the swelling usually becomes gradually less inflamed, and the pain diminishes. After about a fortnight it is generally advisable, unless the inflammation still continues, to consider the propriety of applying a strong blister to the part. When this has been done, it is advisable that it be not oiled, or have any greasy or emollient substance applied to it for at least three weeks, and that the crusts should on no account be washed off, or any part of the scurf removed. More haste is worse speed here; and for the blister to have fair play, its results should not be meddled with, at the least under three weeks. Sometimes, in sprains of the flexor tendons and ligaments of the leg, a high-heeled shoe is applied to take strain and pressure off the parts. It should not be forgotten that a horse thrown out of work and exercise, for sprain and lameness, should have light diet. Bran-mashes should be given for the first few days instead of oats, and afterwards half bran-mash and half oats mixed should be allowed—of course, with the addition of hay or grass. If blistering for sprains is not successful, firing may be tried; and it often succeeds when all other remedies have failed.

The foregoing may be called the general principles of treatment for sprains, and they can be applied according to the varying circumstances of each particular case.

There are sprains of the flexor tendons and ligaments of the hind-legs, as well as those of the fore, and also sprains of tendons and muscles in different parts of the body, which it is beyond the scope of this book to describe. Allusion may, however, shortly be made to the injury called "curb," which is a sprain of a strong ligament going from the point of the hock to the lower and back part of that joint. This shows itself to the observer, when he views the hock from one side, by a swelling or convexity, and it cannot well be overlooked. It usually causes lameness when recent, but under blistering, and, in severe cases, firing, a cure is almost always effected, although some permanent swelling or thickening be left. In many cases, the addition of a high-heeled shoe, to take the strain off the parts, is, in the earlier stages, advisable.

BRUISES.

Bruises have not been mentioned before. For them the best treatment is, as a general rule, frequent fomentations for at least half an hour at a time, and this remedy is usually successful. Some mild, stimulating liniment may, after a time, be applied, to remove any obstinate remaining swelling.

The eye is sometimes injured, the part most frequently suffering being the outer transparent coat, called the cornea. Sometimes this is injured by the rider carelessly striking the horse about the head; or it may be injured by blows against trees or other objects. When the cornea has been injured, the eyelids are often nearly or quite closed. On opening them, the cornea is probably found to be abraded, and perhaps more or less of a milky whiteness. This is very apt to alarm the inexperienced owner, as it seems unlikely that so much opacity would ever clear away; yet it often will, in a very astonishing manner. Fomentations are the best treatment here, and many recommend that a wet cloth should be placed over the eye, to keep out the light. Sometimes the opacity will, to a certain extent, disappear; but at one point it obstinately remains, and looks as if it would never be removed. Nor will it unless treatment be resorted to, in the form of applying something very stimulating to the part, in the shape of nitrate of silver or other strong remedy. Of course, this should only be done after all inflammation has quite disappeared, and when all progress has ceased.

An amateur, however, cannot be recommended to employ such remedies on his own account; they should only be used by an experienced veterinary surgeon, and the effects require careful watching. Suffice it here to say that, even in long-standing cases of partial opacity of the cornea, the treatment above described is often attended by marked success.

SPEEDY-CUT.

This is an injury caused by the horse striking one of the legs with the opposite foot, the damage being inflicted on the inside of the fore-legs, at any part, from close to the knee to near the fetlock; in rare cases, as high as the upper part of the knee. It is inflicted when galloping or trotting in horses with high action, and especially if the toes are turned out. It is a dangerous habit, as it may cause the horse to fall. Sometimes young horses, or horses put to unaccustomed work, or when tired, speedy-cut, and afterwards do not. The part struck may be more or less swollen or wounded, and to such an extent as to cause lameness and the formation of an abscess.

Treatment.—Fomentations or poultices, and dressing with cooling lotions.

WOUNDS FROM THORNS.

Hunters are very liable to be injured by punctures from thorns or splinters of wood, this taking place more especially in the limbs. When they penetrate a joint or the sheath of a tendon, then they may cause serious damage, producing swelling, pain, and lameness, and even, in some cases, general disturbance of the health.

Treatment.—Fomentations and poultices, when the foreign body cannot be immediately extracted, are advisable, or a little blistering ointment may be rubbed around the wound; it is dangerous to probe or cut in searching for these bodies, which generally require patience in being got rid of when they cannot be removed immediately.

POLL-EVIL.

This is a swelling, followed by abscess, immediately on the top of the head, behind the ears, caused by blows—as on entering a low stable door, or a bruise from harness, or any other cause. There is great pain on pressure, and the horse keeps the head rigid, with the nose poked out.

Treatment.—This should be undertaken by a veterinary surgeon, but, in the meantime, fomentations should be resorted to, and the animal fed from an elevated bucket or manger. When abscess forms, it must be opened, and a counter opening made at the bottom; this requires surgical skill.

CAPPED ELBOW.

Capped elbow is a tumour, in most cases filled with a watery fluid, depending from the back part of the elbow, and caused by repeated bruises from the heels (usually the inside one) of the shoe, when the horse lies down with the limb doubled under him at the knee. It rarely produces lameness, but is a serious eyesore.

Treatment.—The shoe ought to be shortened, and, if possible, made to lie with the fore-foot away from the elbow. If the tumour is hot and painful, warm fomentations or refrigerant lotions may be applied; or a seton may be passed through it, or its contents evacuated by lancing. In some cases, where the tumour is solid, removal by the veterinary surgeon (by an operation) may be advisable.

CAPPED HOCK.

Capped hock is a similar condition to capped elbow, when it is immediately on the point of the hock. It is caused by a bruise, as in kicking, or by a blow from some hard body following on the hock. It rarely causes lameness, although it is an eyesore, and gives rise to the suspicion that the horse is vicious.

Treatment.—If recent, and the point of the hock is sore and inflamed, warm fomentations or cooling lotions may be resorted to; afterwards, if it is desired to reduce the swelling, a very mild solution of corrosive sublimate in spirits of wine may be repeatedly applied until the skin becomes scurfy, or a blister of biniodide of mercury may be rubbed in from time to time, or a small seton may be passed through it.

Another form of capped hock consists in a swelling on each side of the point of the hock, caused by distension of the sheath of the tendon passing over this part; it may be due to a sprain or injury of this tendon, and is at first usually accompanied by more or less lameness.

Treatment.—A high-heeled shoe should be applied to the foot; the animal must be kept quiet, fomentations applied to the hock, and afterwards blistering, or even firing.

THOROUGHPIN.

This is a large, soft swelling, immediately in front, and to the inside of the point of the hock, caused by sprain of the large tendon which passes down the leg to be inserted into the pedal bone, the sheath through which it passes at this part being distended by fluid.

Treatment.—Fomentations, if pain and lameness are present; a high-heeled shoe on the foot and rest; afterwards, if lameness persists, a blister.

BOG-SPAVIN.

This may be due to sprain of the hock, or it may come on gradually as the result of chronic inflammation, or of simple over-work, without any actual disease being present. It consists of a more or less large elastic swelling bulging out at the front and inner part of the hock, and which, if pressed upon, will appear above and behind the hock towards the seat of thoroughpin. It is due to distension with synovia of the proper capsule of the hock-joint. When lameness is present it indicates that inflammation is going on, and is a serious condition; but in many cases it has no perceptible influence on the action of the animal, and is merely an eyesore.

Treatment.—If due to sprain or disease of the joint, treat as for thoroughpin. When the distension in this and in thoroughpin is offensive to the eye, a truss may be applied to cause pressure, and assist in the absorption of the fluid. Such a truss may be procured from any veterinary instrument maker.

WIND-GALLS.

These are distensions of the sheaths through which tendons play, the lubricating fluid they contain naturally being in excessive quantity, and sometimes altered quality. They may be due to inflammation, when they are hot and painful, and the horse is lame; or to severe work, when there is really no active disease present.

Treatment.—If there is no pain or lameness, and the wind-galls are merely unsightly, equable pressure by means of bandages, with pledgets of tow between the folds, immediately over the wind-galls, may be tried, and the operation may be assisted by saturating them now and again with a little lead lotion. If there are inflammation and lameness, treat as for sprained tendons.

BURNS.

Horses are sometimes burned accidentally by fire, or by boiling water. The first thing to be done is to cover the parts with rag, cotton wool, or lint, soaked in olive-oil, to which a little sugar of lead has been added; or, better, oil mixed with an equal quantity of lime-water (the famous Carron-oil). If there is much pain, oil, to which a small quantity of carbolic acid has been added, will tend to allay it. The object of all dressings in these cases, is to exclude the air and allay the pain; if the latter is very acute, an ounce or two of laudanum may require to be given at intervals, until the arrival of the veterinary surgeon.

DISEASES AND INJURIES OF THE FEET.

The foot of the horse, and particularly the fore-foot, is especially liable to disease and injury. Some of the diseases are so serious, as to require the utmost skill of the veterinary surgeon; while others are so simple that, though it is always better to obtain skilled assistance, an amateur may yet be able to do something towards curing them, or at least directing a farrier or groom how to proceed in cases of emergency.

TREADS.

These are wounds at the top of the hoof in the region of the coronet, and are usually caused by the animal placing one foot on the top of the other when turning round, and especially when weak or fatigued. Of course they vary in severity—from a simple injury which does not produce lameness, to a bruise or lacerated wound which produces great pain and lameness. If not carefully attended to, especially when severe, very serious results may follow.

Treatment.—The wound should be well washed if there is any mud or dirt in it, and then dressed with a little tincture of opium or compound tincture of myrrh; or painting with collodion will form a protective covering. If the wound is lacerated and torn, all the loose parts should be detached, the foot immersed in a warm-water bath or a poultice, and in a few hours afterwards dressed with tow steeped in carbolised oil, and retained by a bandage.

QUITTOR.

This is usually the result of a tread, or other injury to the foot, followed by the formation of abscess, in most instances at the coronet, towards the quarters or heels, and causing great lameness and the manifestation of much pain on handling it. It is a very serious condition, and requires time, patience, and skill.

Treatment.—If a veterinary surgeon's assistance is not available, the shoe should be taken off and the sole pared, to discover whether the abscess is due to injury there, when an opening should be made so as to allow the matter to escape from below. The horn of the wall should be rasped away from it, so as to relieve the pressure; the foot should then be fomented with warm water for an hour or two, and a large poultice applied. When the abscess opens, the wound may require to be enlarged; but whether or not, a thin pledget of tow, steeped in crude carbolic acid, should be passed down to the very bottom of it with a probe every day, until the discharge is completely dried up.

SAND-CRACK.

Sand-crack is a split in the wall of the hoof, which may occur at any part; but usually in the front of the hind-foot and the quarter of the fore-foot, and generally the inside one. This crack may occur quite suddenly from severe exertion, aided in some cases by faulty horn secretion. It commences at the top, near the coronet, and extends downwards, penetrating to the sensitive parts within, which bleed and are bruised, causing great lameness and intense pain.

Treatment.—When much pain and lameness are present, the shoe should be removed, the horn rasped away at the crack, so as to remove the pressure, and the foot immersed in a bucket of warm water for an hour or so, and afterwards poulticed. If the lameness continues, a veterinary surgeon must be called in, and the part well exposed, so as to discover whether matter is forming. When this has been done, it may be necessary to poultice for some days until the inflammation is subdued, and if any fungus granulations appear, the horn on each side of them must be carefully pared away. The part should now be dressed with tow and Stockholm tar or carbolised oil, retained by a bandage, and when the part is hardened, the shoe may be put on, and gentle exercise allowed if there is no lameness; but before the shoe is applied, it is better to remove a portion of the lower part of the wall below the sand-crack, so as to remove it from the pressure of the shoe. In the meantime, some blistering ointment should be rubbed into the coronet; sometimes a notch is made by the hot iron at the top of the crack, and immediately below the coronet: this and the blister expediting a new growth of horn. In some cases the fissure is clamped by special clips or clasps, which are made to grasp the wall on each side. In any case it is well, if the horse is put to work, to have the part protected by tar and tow, retained by a strap or tarred twine until the sound horn has grown down.

WOUNDS OF THE SOLE AND FROG.

The sole and frog are particularly liable to wounds and bruises from broken glass, sharp stones, nails, or splinters of wood. These will cause lameness and pain in proportion to their severity, wounds of the frog being sometimes accompanied by extensive hæmorrhage, which must be checked by padding with tow, or applying a little muriate of iron. Nearly in all these cases the services of a farrier are required to examine the foot, and to pare away the horn from the punctures and wounds, so as to relieve the sensitive parts from pressure when they begin to swell. Immersion of the foot in hot water for some time, and subsequent poulticing, may be necessary. Particular care should be taken that no part of the foreign body is allowed to remain in the wound.

CORNS.

A corn is really a bruise of the lining membrane covering the bone of the foot, immediately beneath the horny sole, and may occur at any part of this; though it is most frequently observed at the inside heel, in the angle between the frog and the bar, where the sole is thinnest and the pressure is greatest. It is manifested by the blood-stained horn, which is sometimes quite soft and spongy, and increasing in this, on being pared down to the sensitive part. In other cases the stain is yellow and red; and in other cases, again, it is quite superficial, and can be removed. Certain kinds of feet are more predisposed to corns than others, those with weak heels, or very strong ones, being most liable. The kind of work has also something to do with their production, fast pace and hard roads very often causing them; but perhaps the most frequent cause is paring and rasping in shoeing, and faulty shape, or bad application of the shoe, or allowing the shoe to remain too long on. In slight cases lameness may not be present, though even apparently bad corns do not always produce lameness.

If there is pain when the horse is standing, he usually "points" the foot; and a tap with a hammer on the wall adjoining the seat of corn, will make him wince and exhibit uneasiness.

Treatment.—The prevention of corns largely depends upon a proper method of shoeing; this has already been touched upon. If there is a natural tendency to them, the horse should either be shod with periplantar shoes, with tips, or with three-quarter shoes. In all cases the frog should be allowed to come on the ground, if possible. If there is lameness, the shoe should be removed, and the seat of corn pared out to ascertain the amount of damage; and if there be matter, to allow it to escape. Afterwards foment and poultice until the pain and lameness have disappeared; then apply a shoe which will not press upon the heel, the kind of shoe depending upon the extent of the injury and the structure of the foot. The danger from a suppurating corn, is in the matter burrowing its way up to the coronet, and forming a "quittor."

THRUSH.

This is a diseased condition of the frog, accompanied by a very offensive discharge from the cleft. It may be brought about by standing in moisture, on foul litter, the absence of pressure, and undue paring of the frog, etc. It is generally an indication of bad hoof management.

Treatment.—Thrush does not often cause lameness, unless there be much disease and sensitiveness of the frog; and frequent dressings with Stockholm tar or carbolic acid, spread on tow, which should be pushed into the cleft and crevices, will, in most cases, effect a cure. If there is lameness, fomentations and poultices (charcoal poultices) will be necessary. To prevent thrush, as well as to cure it, the hoof should be kept as dry as possible, the frogs unpared by the farrier, and pressure allowed there by lowering the wall of the hoof as much as may be necessary, and applying thin shoes.

CANKER.

This is an advanced degree of "thrush," and is most frequently seen in coarse-bred draught horses. It is entirely due to bad stable or foot management, and is manifested by fungous inflammation of the sensitive membrane of the frog and sole, chiefly of the hind-feet.

Treatment.—This is a most intractable disease, and requires much skill and patience; so that a cure should not be attempted by an amateur.

LAMINITIS, OR INFLAMMATION OF THE FOOT.

Inflammation of the foot, or laminitis, is chiefly confined to the sensitive laminæ or leaves which unite the hoof wall to the parts within (see diagram on p. 621), and of these leaves those in front are most seriously affected. These leaves number five or six hundred or more, and surround the front and sides of the pedal bone, the largest and most vascular being in front, and it is these which are involved most acutely. Congestion of these leaves, especially if acute, will produce symptoms like those of inflammation. The causes are: long continued standing in one position, severe exertion, especially on hard ground, derangement of the stomach or bowels by improper food, or as the result of inflammation of these, or super-purgation; a gross condition and want of exercise, injury to the foot, inflammation of the lungs, improper shoeing, etc. The fore-feet are those most frequently involved, though the hind-feet may also suffer, and in certain cases all the feet may be inflamed.

This is a most painful disease, and causes great suffering, from the fact that the inflamed parts are confined in a rigid horny box which does not allow of any expansion for the swelling that takes place. The breathing and the pulse are much affected, and the horse shows signs of acute distress. To relieve the front part of the feet, if the fore ones are involved, the horse throws the fore-limbs forward, so as to place as much of his weight as possible on the heels, with the hind-feet well under the body for support. In this position he will remain fixed, as it were, and it is most difficult to induce him to move. Should the inflammation affect the hind-feet, these are also placed under the body; but the fore ones are thrown back, so as to relieve the latter as much as possible. When attempting to move the animal backwards, the condition of the feet is at once made apparent by the animal's unwillingness to move them, the body swaying back, but the feet remaining fixed to the ground. Attempts to lift one of the feet also cause the animal to evince great pain. In some rare cases the horse is lying down, and then there is great unwillingness to get up. The hoofs are burning hot, and tapping with a hammer or stick greatly increases the pain.

Treatment.—Laminitis is a very serious condition when acute, and may lead not only to serious deformity of the hoof, or its being shed, but even death may result. In congestion, or the less acute form of inflammation, the consequences are not so serious. In the latter it may suffice to take off the shoes, lower the wall of the foot by means of the rasp, so as to allow the sole and frog to bear as much of the weight as possible, and keep them in a tub of warm or cold water for some time, and poultice for a few days. It is a good plan to induce the horse to lie down, or even to throw him down if he will not do so voluntarily.

The floor of the stall or box should be laid with soft bedding or moss litter. Gentle exercise on soft ground should be allowed as soon as the pain subsides. The diet should be sloppy mashes or gruel, and a mild laxative, such as a pint of linseed oil, may be necessary. In an acute case, the same treatment has to be followed out, with the addition of an ounce or two of the bicarbonate of soda, two or three times a day, in the food; with scarification of the coronets with the lancet, and the administration of from ten to twenty drops of Fleming's tincture of aconite in a pint of water two or three times at intervals of four hours. Care is required in working and shoeing the horse for some time after recovery, the soles being kept unpared, and the frog being allowed to come in contact with the ground.

When the inflammation becomes chronic—a very common sequel—the horse's action is more or less altered, the heels coming to the ground in a conspicuous manner, and in the stable the animal has a tendency to rest on the heels. The feet are also generally hotter than in a healthy condition, especially after movement, and they become more or less altered in shape, the soles becoming flatter, the heels deeper, and the front of the wall losing its straight oblique line; there are also characteristic rings, narrow and deep in front, wider and flatter behind. The feet are also more sensitive when travelling on hard roads, the knees being kept more or less straight. Separation often occurs between the wall, the sole, and the laminæ, leaving a cavity containing powdery horn, and known as "seedy-toe." For this condition, treatment must be chiefly palliative; the horse should stand on tan or moss litter, and for some hours of the day in a stall laid with clay tempered with salt and water, or be allowed to run on moist meadow land.

A mild blister may be applied round the coronet now and again, and shoeing be carefully performed.

SEEDY-TOE.

We have already referred to the cause of this condition. It may also be due to injury by the clip of the shoe, by driving a nail too near to the quick, or by any other cause which will excite inflammation. Sometimes this condition may exist without any external indication until the shoe is removed, unless the hoof is tapped, when it will emit a hollow sound immediately over the separation.

Treatment.—This condition, though very objectionable, does not always cause lameness. If a cure is to be attempted, all the separated wall should be removed as far as the white solid horn, every crack or unsoundness being obliterated. A blister should then be applied round the coronet to hasten the secretion of sound horn, and tar and tow bound on the exposed surface until the wall has grown down solid and strong.

NAVICULAR DISEASE.

Navicular disease is, perhaps, the most serious malady to which the foot of the horse is liable. It is confined to the back part of the foot, where the large tendon (perforans) passes over the navicular bone, just before its insertion into the sole of the pedal bone. It is most frequent in carriage and riding horses, and is brought on by severe exertion, or fast pace on hard roads, particularly if the feet are badly shod and the frog is not allowed to reach the ground. In some cases there is supposed to be a natural predisposition to the disease. The fore-feet are, it may be said, exclusively affected.

The feet are, as a rule, contracted at the heels, and hotter than usual. In the stable, or when at rest, the horse "points" the affected foot (*i.e.* he places it forward with the heel slightly raised), as that position gives it relief; if both feet are affected, he rests first one and then the other foot. In movement, unless the disease is very advanced, he may walk sound, or nearly so; it is in trotting, and especially on hard ground, and more particularly with a rider on his back, that he manifests lameness— stepping short, and going more especially on his toes. Because of this manner of going, the shoes are most worn towards the toes. The animal stumbles badly, and goes down hill with much discomfort; after working some time, the lameness passes off to a certain extent. Tapping on the sole, on each side of the frog, will produce pain, and pressure made by the thumb deep in the hollow of the heel will also cause pain and increase the lameness.

Treatment.—Even in the earliest stage, treatment of this disease is seldom satisfactory. The wall of the hoof should be lowered as much as possible, so as to allow the frogs to rest on the ground; and, to this end, periplantar shoeing answers very well. Cold applications (such as poultices) to the feet, or compelling the animal to stand in cold water, a running stream, or in clay tempered with salt and water, may be resorted to. The stall or loose box in which he rests should be laid with peat, tan, or moss litter; and the food should be light, such as green forage, sloppy mashes, etc.

After a week or two of this treatment, a blister should be applied around the coronet, and especially in the hollow of the heel. Turning out on a damp meadow for a month or two, may produce very beneficial effects. If the lameness still persists, however, a seton may be passed through the frog; should this not effect a cure, neurotomy (dividing the nerves of sensation on each side of the leg), by depriving the foot of feeling, will enable the horse to go sound, though it does not cure the disease. In many cases, this operation is productive of much benefit, as it relieves the horse from great pain, and allows him to be utilised, sometimes for years; care, however, has to be taken by the farrier in shoeing, lest he wound the foot by the nails; and injuries to the foot must also be attended to with more than ordinary care, as the animal does not feel any pain, and therefore does not manifest lameness. It may be mentioned, however, that wounds and injuries heal as rapidly in a foot in this condition as in one which has sensation.

PRICKS AND INJURIES IN SHOEING.

In the operation of shoeing, injury is sometimes inflicted by the farrier, either through ignorance, carelessness, or pure accident. Corns have been already alluded to as often due to bad shoeing; but, in driving the nails, the sensitive part is liable to be damaged by a nail being either driven into it, or so near it, as to cause pain and lameness. When the farrier discovers that he has made this mistake, he usually withdraws the nail at the time, and, if he leaves it out altogether, no harm may ensue, provided dirt does not get into the part; if, however, the nail be left in, or grit find admission, inflammation will be set up, which may run on to suppuration, causing much suffering and lameness. The foot will be very hot, and the animal, if standing quiet, continually resting it, or moving it about uneasily, afraid to put his weight on it. It tapped with a hammer over the spot, or if the sole and wall at the part be pressed upon by pincers, great suffering will be manifested; this is usually the guide to the seat of injury.

Treatment.—Remove the shoe, pare away the sole immediately over the injury, until it is quite thin; make an opening between the sole and the wall with a small drawing knife across the track of the nail, so as to relieve pressure, and give exit to any matter which may have formed; then put the foot in a bucket of hot water for an hour or so, afterwards applying a large poultice. When the lameness has gone, have the shoe put on again, leaving out the nail at the part which had been injured, and filling up the cavity with tar and tow.

Sometimes in driving back the clip of the shoe against the hoof, this is done improperly, which results in pressing tightly against the wall, and bruising the sensitive parts within. In putting the clip against the hoof, the hammer should be applied at the base first, and then come lightly up to the point. It is the opposite procedure which usually causes damage.

The treatment consists in taking off the shoe, and fomenting the foot in hot water for some time; if need be, a poultice may be applied.

It not unfrequently happens that, with a tender-footed horse, the farrier nails on the shoe too tightly, causing a short and crippled gait, which may not disappear for some days; inflammation may even ensue. The remedy for this is to take off the shoe, and put it on more easily, or with smaller nails.

SIDE BONES.

On each wing of the pedal bone is a large elastic plate of cartilage, the upper margin of which can be distinctly felt above each side of the hoof towards the heels of the foot, and the use of which is very important, in giving springiness to the movements of this part of the limb. In some horses—and more especially those which are coarse-bred—these become rigid or ossified, either through wearing shoes with high calkins, or from concussion on hard roads, this change usually taking place in the fore-feet. With slow-paced horses, this alteration is not of so much consequence as with riding or harness horses, in which it usually causes lameness. If it causes lameness, the horse generally steps short, and throws his weight more on the front than the back part of the foot; and the condition of the cartilages may be readily detected by pressing them with the fingers immediately above the hoof, when they will be found hard and unyielding.

Treatment.—At the commencement, if inflammation is present and the alteration suspected to be taking place, fomentations and poultices should be employed, followed by blistering or firing, as a last resource, should the lameness not disappear. If this does not effect a cure, then special shoeing must be resorted to, as bar or periplantar shoes, to allow the frog to sustain weight.

SPLINTS.

A splint is a deposit of bone which may take place on the outside or inside—generally the inside— of the cannon bone, at its junction with the splint bone; in some cases there is a splint on each side of the leg. The splint may be very close to the knee or lower down; sometimes there is one in both situations on the same leg. Splints may arise without any perceptible cause, as in very young horses; by concussion on hard roads, or by blows from the opposite foot. When forming, a splint generally causes considerable lameness in trotting, and pain is manifested when pressure is applied to the part; there is also heat, and more or less swelling. When fully formed, it does not usually cause lameness, unless it interferes with the movement of the knee, or is so far back on the leg as to press upon ligaments or tendons. They are very common in all classes of horses, and the cases are rare in which they cause permanent lameness.

Treatment.—If splint be forming, and there is lameness, the horse should be rested, and a cold water bandage applied to the limb to subdue the inflammation; after which, a mild blister of biniodide of mercury should be rubbed over the place; in some cases this may be done at the very commencement. If the tumour threatens to become very large, or to involve tendons and ligaments, a veterinary surgeon should be called in, who will probably deem it necessary to pass a seton over it, or to cut down upon it to relieve the tension.

SORE SHINS.

Inflammation is liable to be set up in young horses in the cannon bone of the fore-legs (rarely the hind) from concussion, generally in galloping; the result may be deposits of bone on the lower and front part of the cannon. There is much lameness, and swellings appear above the fetlock joint, which are extremely painful on pressure.

Treatment.—Rest is, above all, necessary, with cooling applications, as cold water and lead lotion, followed by one or more blisters. When the inflammation and lameness have disappeared, exercise should be given for some time on soft ground.

RING-BONE.

This is also a deposit of bone on one or both of the pastern bones, resulting from inflammation, due to hereditary predisposition, or concussion on hard roads through fast driving. The deposits are usually confined to the front and sides of these bones, and may appear on the fore- and hind-limbs— most frequently the latter; they are readily felt by passing the fingers over the pastern bones. In the early stage of formation there are, of course, inflammation and lameness, the horse usually going on his heels; there is also pain on manipulation.

Treatment.—Cooling lotions and fomentations may be resorted to at the commencement, though the heroic treatment, which is often most successful, consists in resorting at once to blisters, or even to firing.

SPAVIN.

Spavin is allied to ring-bone and splints, in its chiefly consisting in deposition of bone on the surface of other bones, as the result of inflammation, the tumour appearing on the inner and lower part of the hock; it is best seen in viewing this part of the joint in profile, when standing at the horse's shoulder. The higher the tumour, and the nearer it is to the front, the greater is the lameness. Spavin is caused by severe strain on the hock, and also concussion on hard ground, or shoeing with high calkin shoes. Certain forms of hock are predisposed to spavin. What is called "occult" spavin is due to ulceration taking place between the bones of the hock at the seat of spavin, producing all the symptoms of spavin, but without the external sign.

When spavin commences, there is usually much lameness, which is most apparent when the horse is first taken out of the stable, and the horse goes more especially on the toe, so that the shoe at this part is most worn away; after moving for some time the lameness diminishes, and may pass off nearly altogether as the animal "gets warm." In the stable the animal generally rests the hock as much as possible; there is, of course, heat, and pain on pressure. In some cases the lameness continues as long as the animal lives, and this is especially so when the spavin has formed in adult age; if it has formed when the horse is young, the lameness may disappear, and the animal remain sound for all practical purposes.

Treatment.—As in all other lamenesses, rest—absolute if possible—is the chief factor in a cure. Blisters, setons, and firing are only accessories, but very important, nevertheless; and the utmost skill of the veterinary surgeon is required in their employment.

INDEX.

THE END.